lonely planet

England

David Else
Paul Bloomfield
Fionn Davenport
Abigail Hole
Martin Hughes

LONELY PLANET PUBLICATIONS
Melbourne • Oakland • London • Paris

KEY

National Park

Elevation

	1000m (3250ft)
	500m (1625ft)
	200m (650ft)
	100m (325ft)
	0
	Below Sea Level

DURHAM
Ancient town with stunning cathedral, overwhelming in scale, on a truly spectacular site

YORK
Historic city with one of England's most outstanding cathedrals

CAMBRIDGE
England's most beautiful university town, full of historic colleges

LAKE DISTRICT
England's highest peaks, plus scenic valleys, traditional villages and, of course, picturesque lakes

YORKSHIRE DALES
Wild hills, scenic valleys, sturdy villages; rural northern England at its finest

MANCHESTER
Vibrant city and capital of the north, with trendsetting music scene and unstoppable nightlife

NORTH SEA

IRISH SEA

NORTH CHANNEL

SOLWAY FIRTH

To IJmuiden, Bergen, Stavanger & Kristiansand

To Rotterdam & Zeebrugge

SCOTLAND

NORTHERN IRELAND

IRELAND

BELFAST
DUBLIN
Bangor
Larne

Dundee
Perth
St Andrews
Dunfermline
Edinburgh
Dalkeith
Dunbar
Motherwell
Abington
Glasgow
Selkirk
Coldstream
Berwick-upon-Tweed
Holy Island
Farne Islands
Seahouses
Alnwick
Ashington
Newcastle Airport
Newcastle-upon-Tyne
South Shields
Sunderland
Hexham
Durham
Bellingham
Hadrian's Wall
Cheviot Hills
Northumberland National Park
Gretna Green
Carlisle
Alston
Kirkby Stephen
Penrith
Keswick
Whitehaven
Workington
Scafell Pike (977m)
Lake District National Park
The Pennines
Windermere
Kendal
Morecambe
Lancaster
Barrow-in-Furness
Isle of Man
Douglas
Holyhead
Bangor
Caernarfon
Porthmadog
Wrexham
Chester
Crewe
Market Drayton
Whitchurch
Warrington
Liverpool
Hoylake
Southport
Blackpool
Preston
Wigan
Bolton
Bury
Oldham
Manchester
Manchester Airport
Stockport
Macclesfield
Stoke-on-Trent
Blackburn
Burnley
Rochdale
Halifax
Bradford
Leeds
Keighley
Skipton
Settle
Ilkley
Harrogate
York
Wakefield
Huddersfield
Sheffield
Chesterfield
Worksop
Doncaster
Derby
Nottingham
Newark-on-Trent
Grantham
Stamford
Spalding
King's Lynn
Hunstanton
The Wash
Boston
Skegness
Mablethorpe
Lincoln
Lincolnshire Wolds
Gainsborough
Scunthorpe
Grimsby
Cleethorpes
Barton-upon-Humber
Beverley
Hull
Bridlington
Scarborough
Whitby
Saltburn-by-the-Sea
Middlesbrough
Stockton-on-Tees
Darlington
Richmond
Thirsk
Pickering
North York Moors National Park
Cleveland Hills
Yorkshire Wolds
Grassington
Yorkshire Dales National Park
Forest of Bowland
Peak District National Park
Sheringham
North Walsham

Tweed
Tyne
Tees
Swale
Ure
Nidd
Wharfe
Aire
Derwent
Hull
Trent
Dove
Derwent

M9
M8
M74
M77
A9
A82
A7
A702
A1
A68
A696
A697
A69
A1
A6
A66
A65
A683
A59
A6
M6
M55
M61
M62
M6
M56
M62
M1
M18
M1
A38
A50
A6
A1
A15
M62
A19
A19
A1
A1
A5
A55
A41
A5
A470
A16
A17
A1

Contents – Text

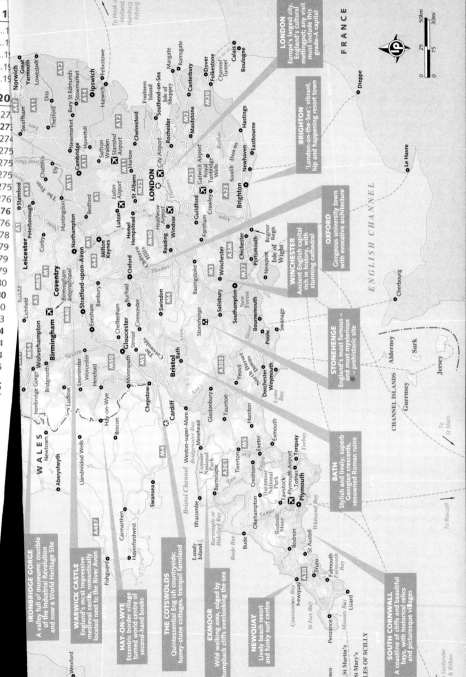

ENGLAND

LONDON
Europe's largest city, England's cultural melting pot; any visit must include this grade-A capital

BRIGHTON
'London-on-the-Sea'; vibrant, hip and happening resort town

OXFORD
Gorgeous university town with evocative architecture

WINCHESTER
Ancient English capital rich in history, with stunning cathedral

STONEHENGE
England's most famous – and most mysterious – prehistoric site

BATH
Stylish and lively; superb Georgian crescents, renowned Roman ruins

IRONBRIDGE GORGE
A valley full of museums; crucible of the Industrial Revolution and now a World Heritage Site

WARWICK CASTLE
England's most impressive medieval castle, romantically located next to the River Avon

HAY-ON-WYE
Eccentric border village turned world centre of second-hand books

THE COTSWOLDS
Quintessential English countryside; honey-stone cottages, tranquil farmland

EXMOOR
Wild walking area, edged by humpback cliffs overlooking the sea

NEWQUAY
Lively beach resort and funky surf centre

SOUTH CORNWALL
A coastline of cliffs and beautiful bays, with historical relics and picturesque villages

England
2nd edition – May 2003
First published – June 2001

Published by
Lonely Planet Publications Pty Ltd ABN 36 005 607 983
90 Maribyrnong St, Footscray, Victoria 3011, Australia

Lonely Planet Offices
Australia Locked Bag 1, Footscray, Victoria 3011
USA 150 Linden St, Oakland, CA 94607
UK 10a Spring Place, London NW5 3BH
France 1 rue du Dahomey, 75011 Paris

Photographs
Many of the images in this guide are available for licensing from
Lonely Planet Images.
w www.lonelyplanetimages.com

Front cover photograph
Stonehenge: the famous prehistoric stone circle at sunrise – Wiltshire,
England (Manfred Gottschalk)

ISBN 1 74059 342 1

text & maps © Lonely Planet Publications Pty Ltd 2003
photos © photographers as indicated 2003

Printed by The Bookmaker International Ltd
Printed in China

Contents – Text

DEVON & CORNWALL 364

THE MARCHES 416

OXFORDSHIRE, GLOUCESTERSHIRE & THE COTSWOLDS 449

THE MIDLANDS 492

NORTHEAST ENGLAND

GLOSSARY

THANKS

INDEX

MAP LEGEND

METRIC CONVERSION

Contents – Maps

YORKSHIRE

NORTHWEST ENGLAND

CUMBRIA

NORTHEAST ENGLAND

MAP INDEX

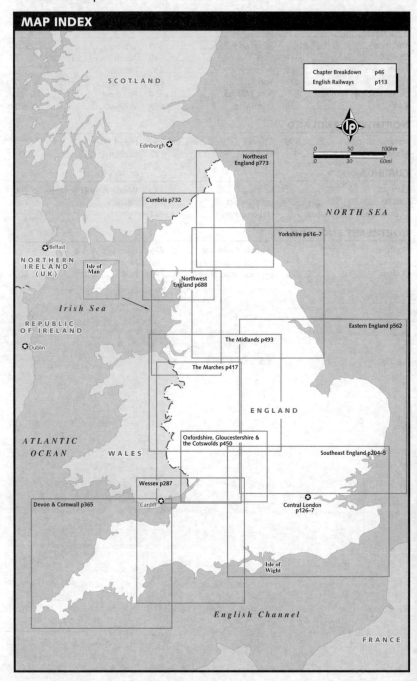

Chapter Breakdown   p46
English Railways   p113

SCOTLAND

Edinburgh

Northeast
England p773

Cumbria p732

NORTH SEA

Yorkshire p616–7

Belfast

NORTHERN
IRELAND
(UK)

Isle of
Man

Northwest
England p688

Irish Sea

REPUBLIC
OF IRELAND

Dublin

Eastern England p562

The Midlands p493

The Marches p417

ENGLAND

ATLANTIC
OCEAN

WALES

Oxfordshire, Gloucestershire &
the Cotswolds p450

Southeast England p204–5

Wessex p287

Devon & Cornwall p365

Cardiff

Central London
p126–7

Isle of
Wight

English Channel

FRANCE

The Authors

David Else

David Else was coordinating author of this book, and worked on the main front-end chapters, as well as sections on Yorkshire and the Midlands. His knowledge of England comes from a life of travel around the country; he was born in London and over the following decades slowly trekked northwards, via Wiltshire and Derbyshire (and a spell of exile in Wales), to his present base on the edge of the Peak District in northern England.

Many of David's journeys in England have been by bicycle or on foot. This passion for the outdoors started during his university years, when any chance to head for the hills was better than visiting the library. More recently, trips by train, car, motorbike and canoe have added to the experience.

David is a full-time travel writer – although still rarely seen in libraries – who divides his time between Britain and Africa. His other books for Lonely Planet include *Britain* and *Walking in Britain*. Further afield he has written or cowritten *Trekking in East Africa*, *Southern Africa*, *West Africa*, *The Gambia & Senegal*, *Zambia* and *Malawi*, and contributed to *East Africa* and *Africa on a shoestring*.

Abigail Hole

From London, Abigail worked for a literary agency and mental health charity before moving to Hong Kong in 1997. Three years in Asian publishing and a lot of eventful travels later, she came back to London and was employed as an editor for Lonely Planet for two years. In between, she fitted in as much travelling as possible, which was great and meant she could avoid having to unpack. Abigail cowrote the Lonely Planet *Britain* guide, and contributed reviews to *Out to Eat – London 2002*.

Fionn Davenport

Fionn was born and raised in Dublin – an idyllic youth interrupted only by jarring moves to Buenos Aires, Geneva and New York (thanks to his Dad's job) that left him incapable of spending more than a couple of years in any one place without uprooting and moving somewhere else. He stayed in Dublin long enough to complete a degree in French and History at Trinity College (but still took a year off somewhere in the middle) before moving to Paris and then New York. A series of odd jobs and adventures eventually landed him behind an editor's desk, and he spent three years editing other people's travel experiences for a travel guide publication. These days he splits his time between New York, Dublin and wherever the call of work and travel brings him. What is he looking for? He has no idea, but something about the perfect climate (hot, not too humid and tempered by a gentle breeze) seems to spur him on. He has written about many destinations throughout the world and has previously worked on Lonely Planet's *Spain*, *Dublin*, *Ireland*, *Sicily* and *Britain* guides, as well as a host of pan-European books.

Martin Hughes

Martin was born and bred in Dublin where, as an adult, he dithered for five years between journalism and public relations before ditching them both and hitting the road via an extended stint in London. After more than three years travelling, he eventually settled in Melbourne, Australia where he helped to set up Lonely Planet's World Food series, for which he wrote two titles. He's happily freelancing these days and returns to London annually for a cultural catch-up.

Paul Bloomfield

Paul grew up in London suburbia and, as is often the way, drifted into studies both fascinating and essentially going nowhere (zoology). Subsequently he tried his hand at those obligatory offbeat jobs people like to guffaw about over a pint (poodle parlour labourer, harassed benefits officer, bone bank technician), while occasionally nipping off to attractive-sounding destinations and quite enjoying it, really. Some more drifting led into publishing, and eventually Lonely Planet's London office. Currently he's a freelance writer, waiting to see if that will drift somewhere interesting.

FROM THE AUTHORS

David Else A big thank you goes to my wife Corinne, who assisted with much of the ground research, in Yorkshire and around England, and kept me supplied with coffee during the long nights of write-up. Together we vany castles, museums and stately homes, testing buses, ferries, cafés, B&Bs, pubs and hostels en route. Thanks also to various friends who joined us along the way; without their company on the road, their humour when things got tiring, and their sandwiches when we were up mountains, we'd never have made it.

Many thanks also go to the various specialists who gave me their thoughts and the benefit of their experience, including Jill Leheup and Andrew McColl for advice on wildlife and environmental matters, Nia and Chris Harland for input on paragliding and Charlotte Hindle for the immaculately researched Arts and Film sections, and Tom Parkinson, Tom Hall, Peter Bennett, Rod Grant and Rachel Hollis for sound feedback on the Pop & Rock section.

I also want to say a big thank you to the coauthors of this book: Abigail Hole, Fionn Davenport, Martin Hughes and Paul Bloomfield. As well as work on their own sections, they helped provide information and paragraphs for the main front-end chapters, and put up with my comments and 'suggestions for improvement' (who said interference?). My name goes down as coordinating author, but I really couldn't have done it without them.

On the other side of the fence, my thanks go also to the Lonely Planet editorial and production staff who made working on this book so effortless and enjoyable: Amanda Canning in London, and Tegan Murray, Kieran Grogan, David Kemp, Indra Kilfoyle, Hunor Csutoros, Julie Sheridan, Sarah Sloane and the great team in Melbourne.

And, finally, many thanks to the staff at the national park offices and tourist information centres around England for their professional knowledge and always helpful service.

Abigail Hole Thanks to Tom for his very patient company, and family and friends for all their help. A huge thank you to all the tourist offices, especially Berwick and Newcastle. Big cheers to David Else for his excellent advice, Amanda Canning for her steady stewardship, Rachel Suddart for her help, Tom Hall and Maltmarsh for their spectator sports expertise, Jimi Ellis for his Toon Army tips, Imogen Franks and Toni Scott for their fab Leeds and Newcastle recommendations, Mat and Sarah Bird for their hospitality (best B&B in Leeds), Kate for help in York, Sandi and Helena for putting me in touch with people, Rory and Geordie Dave for a crash course in Newcastle nightlife, Jay for making Carlisle entertaining and Kelda for sorting out all those bits of paper.

Fionn Davenport Updating such a vast swathe of territory would have been impossible without the help of a bunch of folks. First and foremost my thanks to the Brighton gang – Howard Simpson, Anna Noble and, most of all, Sorcha O'Callaghan, who sheltered, advised and guided me with expert patience and knowledge. A special acknwledgement to Sorcha, who was there for some of the long, rainy drives and made it all the more enjoyable by just being there. And yes, you did pick the best B&B.

A big thumbs up to Laura Fraser and her wonderful London apartment; having somewhere to dump my notes and my tired old bones made my life that little bit easier. Thanks also to Anto Howard, whose hard-earned and painful love of Manchester City gave me a valuable insight into that rivalry.

Finally, a huge debt of gratitude is owed to the excellent team that worked on the book – David Else, Amanda Canning, and all the other authors; without your excellent advice, help and support, none of it would have been possible. It was hard, but it was a lot of fun (except for my car being broken into). Thanks to all.

Martin Hughes Thanks to Kirsti Anderson, Penny Platts, Jim Davies, Jeremy Moorhead, Matt King, Janei Anderson, Michelle Chan, Alan Murphy, Emma Evans, Alan and Andrea Hughes, all at the London Tourist Board and the patient, friendly and helpful staff at TICs throughout the Marches.

Paul Bloomfield Thanks to the following kind souls who provided beds, sofas, floors and good company (and, more often than not, copious quantities of booze) when a night sleeping in the car seemed unavoidable: Claire Heseltine, Margaret and Roger Stevens and Lorraine, Alex Milne, Paul and Michelle Heaton, Pat Calloway, Peter Thompson, Jan and Dave Hall, and Alison and Claus Stroander.

Notable mentions to those who, generously and foolishly, divulged tips about their favourite secret spots: Elinor Thompson and Ken Gordon, Melanie Hall, Liese Perrin, Serena McCall, Martin Bloomfield, Debbie Robel, Maya Twardzicki, John King and Julia Wilkinson. Big up to Tom Robbins, electro-clash guru, for insights into the Nottingham scene. Staff in tourist offices provided heaps of information; special thanks to Fran at the Somerset Visitor Centre for help above and beyond.

Finally, apologies to anyone I've forgotten, and special mentions to my folks, who showed superhuman restraint in refraining from slaughtering a grumpy and overstressed son, and to Rex (King of the Road), who will be missed.

This Book

The 1st edition of Lonely Planet's *England* was the work of coordinating author Ryan Ver Berkmoes, who teamed up with Neal Bedford, Lou Callan, Fionn Davenport and Nick Ray. David Else was the coordinating author for this 2nd edition. He wrote many of the introductory chapters, as well as the section on Pubs, and parts of The Midlands and Yorkshire. He was joined by Paul Bloomfield, who wrote Wessex, Devon & Cornwall, and parts of The Midlands; Fionn Davenport, who wrote Eastern England, Southeast England, Oxfordshire, Gloucestershire & the Cotswolds, and Northwest England; Abigail Hole, who wrote some of the introductory chapters, as well as Northeast England, Cumbria and parts of Yorkshire; and Martin Hughes, who wrote London and The Marches.

FROM THE PUBLISHER

This 2nd edition of England was produced in Lonely Planet's Melbourne office. Editing was coordinated by Tegan Murray, with invaluable assistance from Monique Choy, Tony Davidson, Simone Egger, Hilary Ericksen, Kyla Gillzan, Rebecca Hobbs, Evan Jones, Danielle North, Kristin Odijk and Helen Yeates. Hunor Csutoros drew the maps, with help from Daniel Fennessy, Anneka Imkamp, Jolyon Philcox, Tessa Rottiers, Julie Sheridan, Sarah Sloane, Simon Tillema and Natasha Velleley. Climate Charts were in the safe hands of Csanad Csutoros.

The book was designed and laid out by David Kemp, with assistance from Pablo Gastar, Cris Gibcus and Sally Morgan. Indra Kilfoyle selected the colour images, with help from Katie Cason and Cris Gibcus. Thanks to Pepi Bluck for assistance with illustrations, and to Lonely Planet Images for the photographs. Annika Roojun designed the cover.

Commissioning Editor Amanda Canning and Project Managers Kieran Grogan and Bridget Blair streamlined the entire process.

Grateful acknowledgment is made for reproduction permission: London Underground map: London's Transport Museum © 2002.

Foreword

ABOUT LONELY PLANET GUIDEBOOKS

The story begins with a classic travel adventure: Tony and Maureen Wheeler's 1972 journey across Europe and Asia to Australia. There was no useful information about the overland trail then, so Tony and Maureen published the first Lonely Planet guidebook to meet a growing need.

From a kitchen table, Lonely Planet has grown to become the largest independent travel publisher in the world, with offices in Melbourne (Australia), Oakland (USA), London (UK) and Paris (France).

Today Lonely Planet guidebooks cover the globe. There is an ever-growing list of books and information in a variety of media. Some things haven't changed. The main aim is still to make it possible for adventurous travellers to get out there – to explore and better understand the world.

At Lonely Planet we believe travellers can make a positive contribution to the countries they visit – if they respect their host communities and spend their money wisely. Since 1986 a percentage of the income from each book has been donated to aid projects and human rights campaigns, and, more recently, to wildlife conservation.

> Although inclusion in a guidebook usually implies a recommendation we cannot list every good place. Exclusion does not necessarily imply criticism. In fact there are a number of reasons why we might exclude a place – sometimes it is simply inappropriate to encourage an influx of travellers.

UPDATES & READER FEEDBACK

Things change – prices go up, schedules change, good places go bad and bad places go bankrupt. Nothing stays the same. So, if you find things better or worse, recently opened or long-since closed, please tell us and help make the next edition even more accurate and useful.

Lonely Planet thoroughly updates each guidebook as often as possible – usually every two years, although for some destinations the gap can be longer. Between editions, up-to-date information is available in our free, monthly email bulletin *Comet* (**w** www.lonelyplanet.com/newsletters). You can also check out the *Thorn Tree* bulletin board and *Postcards* section of our website, which carry unverified, but fascinating, reports from travellers.

Tell us about it! We genuinely value your feedback. A well-travelled team at Lonely Planet reads and acknowledges every email and letter we receive and ensures that every morsel of information finds its way to the relevant authors, editors and cartographers.

Everyone who writes to us will find their name listed in the next edition of the appropriate guidebook. The very best contributions will be rewarded with a free guidebook.

We may edit, reproduce and incorporate your comments in Lonely Planet products such as guidebooks, websites and digital products, so let us know if you don't want your comments reproduced or your name acknowledged.

How to contact Lonely Planet:
Online: **e** talk2us@lonelyplanet.com.au, **w** www.lonelyplanet.com
Australia: Locked Bag 1, Footscray, Victoria 3011
UK: 10a Spring Place, London NW5 3BH
USA: 150 Linden St, Oakland, CA 94607

Introduction

For centuries, England has dominated the island of Great Britain and the state of the United Kingdom. In many ways it still does, to such an extent that the words 'England', 'Britain' and 'the UK' are frequently regarded as synonymous by foreigners, and often by the English themselves – much to the chagrin of their Scots, Welsh and Irish neighbours.

While England still dominates Britain at home, for many years England also dominated the vast political entity that was the British Empire. Although the people of Scotland and Wales made an enormous contribution to imperial endeavour, it was always really an *English* empire; almost unbelievably this small country on the edge of the Atlantic at one time ruled half the earth's population and seriously impacted on much of the rest.

For citizens of countries once part of the Empire, a visit to England may seem cliched but it's also in many ways essential – a peculiar mix of homecoming and confrontation. And for foreign visitors, as well as the English themselves, England is a country where world-renowned institutions and symbols remain cherished and intact – from the Westminster Parliament to Canterbury Cathedral, from Eton College to the universities of Oxford and Cambridge, from Wembley Stadium to Lord's Cricket Ground, from Stonehenge to Tower Bridge.

But for every famous English icon there's a wonderful array of lesser-known gems just waiting to be discovered. Perhaps the key to enjoying travel in England is appreciating its astounding variety. In the space of a few hours, or at the most a few days, you can immerse yourself in bygone eras at ancient castles, marvel at the soaring spires of majestic churches, eat in world-class restaurants or friendly local cafés, drink in traditional pubs, stroll through picture-postcard villages, hike over wild moors and mountains, shop till you drop in the finest stores, or dance all night in venues where the music takes your breath away. One thing's for sure: England is never boring. And all this in a country that takes about eight hours to drive from top to bottom.

So welcome to England. Whether you're from far-flung regions, or just exploring your own back yard, you're sure to enjoy its wonderful diversity. See the world-famous sights, get off the beaten track, and create some memories for when you return home. Then start planning your next trip back!

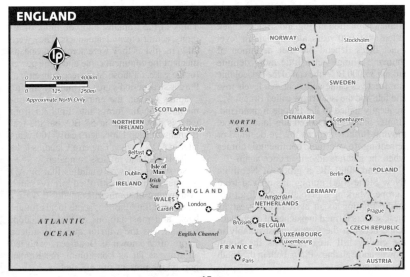

ENGLAND

Facts about England

The country of England, along with Wales and Scotland, is part of the state of Great Britain. Three countries in one might seem a strange setup, but getting a grip on this basic principle will ease your understanding of this chapter. Then of course England is also a part of the United Kingdom (UK). To work out how it all fits together, see the 'England? Britain? What's in a Name?' boxed text later in this chapter.

HISTORY

It may be on the edge of Europe, but England was never on the sidelines of history. For thousands of years, newcomers have arrived, settled and made their mark, or moved on as the next wave of incomers entered the scene. The result is a mix of cultures, landscapes and languages – a dynamic pattern that shaped the nation and continues to evolve today.

For many visitors, England's main attraction is its rich historic legacy; everything from Stonehenge and Hadrian's Wall, through the Battle of Hastings, the Tower of London, Canterbury Cathedral, hundreds of castles, and endless lines of kings and queens. History will certainly dominate your visit to England, so the bare essentials outlined here will just as certainly help you enjoy it.

England's First Arrivals

Human habitation in England stretches back at least 400,000 years, although at this level exact dates depend on your definition of 'human'. Things get a little more definite around 35,000 BC – the end of the Palaeolithic era. Ice Ages came and went, sea levels rose and fell, and the island now called Britain was frequently joined to the European mainland. Hunter-gatherers crossed the land bridge, moving further north as the ice declined or retreating to warmer continental climes when the glaciers advanced once again.

Around 4000 BC a group of Neolithic (New Stone Age) immigrants arrived from Europe. Marking a pivotal switch from nomadic hunting to an agricultural lifestyle, these settlers farmed in patches of open landscape between the forests, most notably in the chalky hill areas such as the South Downs and Salisbury Plain, both in the south of England.

Alongside the fields, they built massive burial mounds to intern their dead, but perhaps their most enduring legacies are the great stone circles of Avebury and Stonehenge, still visible today.

Tribal Times

Around 2500 BC was the dawn of the Iron Age; the forests were cleared with increasing efficiency as more land was turned to farming, laying down the patchwork pattern of fields, woods and small villages that still exists in many parts of rural lowland England today. And as the population expanded, people began to divide into specific groups or tribes.

During this period a group called the Celts migrated from Central Europe, and by around 500 BC had settled across much of Britain. Absorbing the indigenous people, they created a distinct Celtic-British culture, which divided into about 20 different tribes. These included the Cantiaci (in today's county of Kent), the Iceni (today's Norfolk) and the Brigantes (northwest England). You noticed the Latin-sounding names? That's because the tribal names used by historians today were first handed out by the next arrivals on England's shores – the Romans.

Enter the Romans

Think of the Romans, and you think of legions, centurions and aqueducts. They were all here, just as they were across Europe, as much of the continent came under the power (or the yoke, for those on the receiving end) of the classical period's greatest military empire.

Julius Caesar, the emperor everyone remembers, made forays into England from what is now France in 55 BC, but the real Roman invasion happened nearly 100 years later in AD 43, when Emperor Claudius led a well-planned and ruthless campaign.

So successful was Claudius that by AD 50 the Romans controlled pretty much everywhere in southern England. It wasn't all plain sailing though: some locals fought back, and most famous of these freedom fighters was the warrior queen Boudicca (more often known as Boadicea), who led an army as far as Londinium, the Roman port on the present site of London.

Nevertheless, opposition was essentially random and sporadic, and no real threat to the well-organised Roman forces. By around AD 80 the new province of Britannia (much of today's England and Wales) was firmly under Roman control. In reality, the stability and wealth the Romans brought was probably welcomed by the general population, tired of feuding chiefs and insecure minikingdoms.

Hadrian Draws a Line North of Britannia was the land the Romans called Caledonia (one day to become Scotland), and this proved a harder place to find a fan club. So in AD 122 the Emperor Hadrian decided rather than conquer these wild tribes (known as the Picts) he'd settle for simply keeping them at bay. Thus Hadrian's Wall was built across northern England – between today's cities of Carlisle and Newcastle – and for nearly 300 years it marked the northernmost limit of the Roman Empire.

South of the Wall, throughout the rest of England, the Romans built castles and garrisons (later called 'chesters', remembered today by town names such as Winchester and Colchester), and paved roads linking important regional centres – Ermine Street between London and York, Watling Street between London and Chester, and the Fosse Way between Exeter and Lincoln. Many of these ruler-straight roads are still followed by modern highways today.

The End of an Era Settlement by the Romans in England lasted almost four centuries – longer than European settlement in Australia or North America – and inevitably there was some intermarriage between indigenous British tribes and the Roman invaders (many of whom were actually from other parts of the empire such as today's Belgium, Spain, Syria and North Africa). The natives also adopted many aspects of the incomers' culture so that a distinct Romano-British population evolved, particularly in the towns, while indigenous Celtic culture remained intact in rural areas.

Alongside stability and wealth, in the 4th century AD the Romans introduced another cultural facet – the new religion called Christianity, which spread after it was recognised by Emperor Constantine in 313. But by this time, although Romano-British culture was still thriving, back in its

Mediterranean heartland the Empire was already in decline.

It was an untidy finale: the Romans were not driven out by the British (in fact, by this time, the Romano-British culture had become so established that there was nowhere for many of these people to go 'home' to). In the end, England was simply dumped by the rulers in Rome. Things ended not with a bang, just with a faint and drawn out whimper. But historians are neat folk, and the end of Roman power in England is generally dated at around 410.

The Emergence of England

As Roman power faded, things went downhill. The use of money dwindled and trade declined. Romano-British towns were abandoned and rural areas became no-go zones as local warlords established fiefdoms and territories. Not inappropriately, the next few centuries are known as the Dark Ages.

The vacuum didn't go unnoticed and during the 5th century once again a bunch of pesky continentals invaded. This time the main groups were Angles and Saxons – Teutonic tribes from northern Europe. They advanced across the former Roman turf, overcoming or absorbing Celts with such thoroughness that even today much of the English language is Anglo-Saxon in origin, many place names in England have Anglo-Saxon roots, and the very term 'Anglo-Saxon' has become a (much abused and factually incorrect) byword for having purely an English background.

Celtic-British culture and the Christian religion were forced to the edges of the British Isles – to Wales, Scotland and Ireland – and by the end of the 6th century the country we now call England was almost 100% Anglo-Saxon, and divided into several distinct kingdoms, including Mercia, Northumbria and Wessex.

The Angles and Saxons were 'pagans', so in AD 597 Pope Gregory of Rome sent missionaries to England to try and revive interest in Christianity. St Augustine successfully converted Angles in Kent (some good-looking ones were even taken to Rome, giving rise to Pope Gregory's famous quip about Angles looking like angels), while in northern England another missionary called St Aidan was even more successful. With faith and fervour, almost single-handedly, he converted the entire populations of Mercia and Northumbria, and in 635 founded a monastery at Lindisfarne, which can still be seen today.

The Viking Era

Just as Christianity was becoming re-established, from the late 8th and through the 9th century England was once again invaded from the European mainland. It was time for the Vikings to appear on the scene.

It's another classic historical image: blonde Scandinavians, horned helmets, big swords, raping and pillaging, square-sailed longboats and all that. School history books give the impression that the Vikings turned up, killed everyone, took everything, and left. There's some truth in that, but in reality some Vikings settled and their legacy is still evident today in northern England.

In AD 850 a wave of Vikings from Denmark conquered and occupied eastern and northeast England, making their capital at the city of Yorvik (today's York). They spread across northern and central England until, in 871, they were confronted by armies of Anglo-Saxons under the new king of Wessex, Alfred the Great. There followed a series of battles, seminal to the foundation of the nation-state of England, but they didn't all go Alfred's way; for a few months he was on the run, wading the swamps of Somerset, hiding in peasant hovels, and famously burning cakes while evading his enemies. It was the stuff of legends and by 886 Alfred had garnered his forces once again and pushed the Vikings back to the north.

Thus England was divided into two parts: in the north and east was Viking 'Danelaw' territory, while in the south and west was Anglo-Saxon England, with the old Roman road of Watling Street roughly marking the border. Alfred was hailed as the king of the English – the first time the Anglo-Saxons truly regarded themselves as a united people.

Alfred's son and successor was Edward the Elder; he eventually gained control over the Danelaw territories and consolidated the king-of-all-England idea. His son, Athelstan, took the process a stage further and was specifically crowned King of England in 927.

But it was hardly cause for major celebration: the Vikings were still entrenched in northeast England and later in the 10th century more raids from Scandinavia threat-

ened this fledgling English unity. Over the following decades, control of England see-sawed from Saxon (King Edgar, Alfred's great-grandson), to Dane (King Canute, or Knut, famous for trying to hold back the sea), and back to Saxon once again (King Edward the Confessor). As England came to the end of the 1st millennium, things could hardly have been viewed as rosy.

1066 & All That

Although a Saxon, King Edward the Confessor had been brought up in Normandy (in today's France) alongside his cousin William. When Edward died, the crown passed to Harold, his English brother-in-law.

Harold energetically threw himself into the job, determined to establish English control. Meanwhile Edward's cousin William sat brooding in Normandy. He thought *he* should have succeeded Edward to the throne of England, and while Harold kept busy, he bided his time.

For anyone who's studied British history (or for anyone who hasn't), 1066 is the most memorable of dates. In that year William sailed from France across the English Channel, with an army of 12,000 Norman soldiers, to defeat the army of Harold at the Battle of Hastings. Harold was killed (according to tradition, by an arrow in the eye), and William became king of England, earning himself the prestigious title of William the Conqueror. For more details see 'The Last Invasion of England' boxed text in the Southeast England chapter.

The conquest of England by the Normans was completed rapidly. To control the Anglo-Saxons, castles were built (many are still visible today) and by 1085–86 the Domesday Book provided a census of the country, its inhabitants and its potential.

William I was followed in 1087 by William II, and (following a mysterious assassination during a hunting trip) he was succeeded by Henry I. To a certain extent, the French-speaking Norman invaders and the English-speaking Saxon inhabitants kept to themselves: a feudal system of lords, barons, masters, servants and slaves hindered mixing. But intermarriage was not uncommon; Henry himself married a Saxon princess.

These unifying moves stood for nothing after Henry I's death. A bitter struggle for the succession followed, finally won by Henry II (the Count of Anjou) who took the throne as the first king of the House of Plantagenet.

Royal & Holy Squabbling

The fight to follow Henry I had established the enduring English habit of royal squabbling, but an equally enduring habit of bickering between royalty and the church was also under way. Things came to a head when Henry II had 'turbulent priest' Thomas Becket murdered in Canterbury Cathedral in 1170.

Perhaps the next king, Richard I (also called Richard the Lion-Heart), wanted to make amends for his forebears' unholy sentiments by fighting for Christianity against Muslim 'infidels' in what was then called the Holy Land (today's Middle East).

Unfortunately, he was too busy crusading to bother much about governing England, and after his brother King John took the reins things got even worse: Norman territories in France were lost, and the powerful landowning barons found John's erratic rule increasingly hard to swallow.

In 1215 the barons forced King John to sign a document called the Magna Carta, limiting the power of the monarch for the first time in English history. Although originally intended as a set of handy ground rules between lords and ruler, the Magna Carta effectively became a fledgling bill of human rights and eventually led to the creation of a parliament – a body to rule the country, independent of the throne.

The Plantagenets Plough On

By 1265 John had been succeeded by Henry III, who was followed in 1272 by Edward I – who turned out to be one of the most influential figures of the century. Nicknamed 'Longshanks' due to his height and stature, he was a skilled ruler and ruthless military tactician. During his 56-year reign, he further sowed the seeds of English nationalism and was unashamedly expansionist in his outlook. Shortly after taking control, he turned his eye to Wales, then to Scotland where his ruthless activities earned him another title – 'Hammer of the Scots'.

Edward I was succeeded by Edward II, but the new model lacked the military success of his forebear. Edward failed in other departments, too. His favouring of personal friends over his barons didn't do him any favours, and his rule came to a grisly end

Houses & Dynasties

Throughout this section, and throughout British history, you'll see references to 'Houses': the House of Plantagenet, the House of York, the House of Windsor and so on. In this context, 'House' simply means 'Dynasty'. But perhaps with memories of a glitzy 1970s American TV soap still strong in the minds of most English, such a term is rarely used.

when his wife, Isabella, and her lover, Roger Mortimer, had him murdered in Berkeley Castle. (For more gruesome details see the Berkeley section in the Oxfordshire, Gloucestershire & the Cotswolds chapter.)

Next in line was Edward III, but during his 50-year reign things were scarcely better. The year 1337 saw the start of the Hundred Years' War with France and things got worse in 1349 with the arrival of a plague called the Black Death, which eventually carried off 1.5 million people – more than a third of the country's population.

A change of king didn't improve things either. The young Richard II had barely taken the throne before he was confronted with the Peasants' Revolt in 1381. This attempt by the commoners to overthrow the rigid feudal system was brutally suppressed, further injuring an already deeply divided and unsettled country.

Houses of Lancaster & York

The ineffectual Richard II was ousted in 1399 by a powerful baron called Henry Bolingbroke, who seized the throne as Henry IV and became the first monarch of the House of Lancaster.

Henry IV was followed, neatly, by Henry V, who decided it was time to stir up the dormant Hundred Years' War with France. He defeated the French at the Battle of Agincourt and the patriotic tear-jerker speech ('cry God for Harry, England and St George') he was given by Shakespeare in the eponymous play later ensured him a pole position among the most famous British kings of all time.

Still keeping things neat, Henry V was followed by Henry VI. His main claim to fame was overseeing the building of great

Ruling the Roost

A glance at England's tempestuous history clearly shows that life was never dull for the folk at the top. Despite immense power and privilege, the position of monarch (or, perhaps worse, *potential* monarch) probably ranks as one of history's least safe occupations. English kings have died in battle (eg, an arrow through the eye for Harold), been beheaded (Charles I), been murdered by a wicked uncle (Edward V) or been knocked off by their queen and her lover (Edward II, for whom a particularly horrible death was concocted as 'punishment' for his homosexuality).

Below is a brief overview of the past 1200 years. As you visit the castles and battlefields of England, having this basic grasp of who ruled when should make your visit much more rewarding.

Saxons & Danes

Alfred the Great 871–99
Edward the Elder 899–924
Athelstan 924–39
Edward the Martyr 975–79
Ethelred II (the Unready)
   979–1016
Canute 1016–35
Edward the Confessor 1042–66
Harold II 1066

Normans

William I (the Conqueror)
   1066–87
William II 1087–1100
Henry I 1100–35
Stephen 1135–54

House of Plantagenet

Henry II 1154–89
Richard I (Lion-Heart) 1189–99
John 1199–1216
Henry III 1216–72
Edward I 1272–1307
Edward II 1307–27
Edward III 1327–77
Richard II 1377–99

House of Lancaster

Henry IV (Bolingbroke)
   1399–1413
Henry V 1413–22
Henry VI 1422–61 & 1470–71

House of York

Edward IV 1461–70 &
   1471–83
Edward V 1483
Richard III 1483–85

House of Tudor

Henry VII 1485–1509
Henry VIII 1509–47
Edward VI 1547–53
Mary I 1553–58
Elizabeth I 1558–1603

House of Stuart

James I 1603–25
Charles I 1625–49

Protectorate (Republic)

Oliver Cromwell 1649–58
Richard Cromwell 1658–59

Restoration

Charles II 1660–85
James II 1685–88
William III (of Orange)
   1688–1702
Mary II 1688–94
Anne 1702–14

House of Hanover

George I 1714–27
George II 1727–60
George III 1760–1820
George IV 1820–30
William IV 1830–37
Victoria 1837–1901

Houses of Saxe-Coburg & Windsor

Edward VII 1901–10
George V 1910–36
Edward VIII 1936
George VI 1936–52
Elizabeth II 1953–

places of worship (King's College Chapel in Cambridge and Eton Chapel near Windsor), interspersed with great bouts of insanity.

The War of the Roses When the Hundred Years' War finally ground to a halt in 1453, you'd have thought things would be calm for a while. But no. The English forces returned from France and threw their energies into the War of the Roses.

For more on this period, see 'The War of the Roses' boxed text in the Northwest England chapter, but briefly it went like this: Henry VI of the House of Lancaster (whose emblem was a red rose) was challenged by Richard, Duke of York (proud holder of a white-rose flag). Henry VI was weak and it was almost a walkover for Richard, but Henry's wife (Margaret of Anjou) was made of different mettle and her forces defeated the challenger. But it didn't rest there. Richard's son Edward came on the scene with an army, turned the tables and become King Edward IV – the first monarch of the House of York.

Dark Deeds in the Tower

But life was never easy for the guy at the top. Edward IV hardly had time to catch his breath before facing a challenger to his own throne. Enter scheming Richard Neville, the Earl of Warwick, who liked to be billed as 'the kingmaker'. In 1470 he teamed up with the energetic Margaret of Anjou to bring Henry VI back to the throne and shuttle Edward IV into exile. But a year later Edward IV came bouncing back to defeat and kill the earl, capture Margaret and have Henry snuffed out in the Tower of London.

Edward IV's position was now secure, but he ruled for only a decade or so before dying and being succeeded by his 12-year-old son Edward, now called Edward V. But the boy-king's rule was even shorter than his father's – only two months. In 1483 he was mysteriously murdered, along with his younger brother, and once again the Tower of London was the scene of the crime.

With the 'little princes' dispatched, this left the throne open for their dear old uncle Richard. Whether he was the princes' killer has been the subject of some debate, not least by omnipresent commentator Shakespeare, but his rule as Richard III was short-lived. Despite a famous Shakespearean sound bite ('A horse, a horse, my kingdom for a horse'), few tears were shed when he was tumbled from the throne in 1485 by Henry Tudor.

Moves Towards British Unity

There hadn't been a Henry on the throne for a while and this new incumbent, Henry VII, harked back to the days of his namesakes with a skilful reign. After the York-vs-Lancaster War of the Roses, his Tudor neutrality was important. He still had family links with the House of Lancaster, though, and managed to patch things up with the Yorks by marrying the daughter of Edward IV. He also diligently mended fences with his northern neighbours by marrying off his daughter to James IV of Scotland, thereby neatly linking the Tudor and Stewart lines.

Matrimony may have been more useful than warfare for Henry VII, but the multiple marriages of his successor, Henry VIII, were a very different story. Fathering an heir was this Henry's immediate problem and the Pope's unwillingness to cooperate with this quest by not allowing Henry to divorce and re-marry (who can forget his famous six wives?) led to a split with the Catholic Church. Parliament made Henry the head of the Protestant Church of England and he followed this up by 'dissolving' many monasteries – as much a blatant takeover of their land and wealth as another stage in the struggle between church and state. At the same time, the Acts of Union (1536–43) formally united England and Wales.

The Elizabethan Age

Henry VIII died in 1547 and was briefly succeeded by his son Edward VI, then daughter Mary I, but their reigns were short. So, unexpectedly, the third child, a daughter called Elizabeth, came to the throne.

As Elizabeth I, she inherited a nasty mess of religious strife and divided loyalties, but after an uncertain start, with great skill and increasing confidence, she turned the country round. She refused marriage, borrowed from biblical imagery and became known as the Virgin Queen – perhaps the first English monarch to deliberately create a cult image. It paid off: her 45-year reign (1558–1603) was a period of boundless English optimism epitomised by the defeat of the Spanish Armada, the expansion of trade and the global explorations of English seafarers fronted by Walter Raleigh and Francis Drake.

Meanwhile, Elizabeth's Scottish cousin Mary (the daughter of James V), now called Mary Queen of Scots, had spent her childhood in France. Aged 15, and a devout Catholic, she married the French dauphin, thereby becoming queen of France as well.

Following her husband's death, Mary returned to Scotland, still only aged 18, and ambitiously claimed the English throne on the grounds that Elizabeth I was illegitimate. But Mary's plans failed; she was forced to abdicate in favour of her son (who became James VI) and then was imprisoned in Scotland.

Mary escaped to England and – perhaps unwisely – appealed to Elizabeth for help. Not surprisingly, Mary was seen as a security risk and imprisoned once again. In an uncharacteristic display of indecision, Elizabeth held Mary prisoner for 19 years before finally signing the warrant for her execution.

United & Disunited Britain

When Elizabeth died in 1603, despite a bountiful reign, the one thing the Virgin Queen had failed to provide was an heir. So she was succeeded by her closest relative, James, the (safely Protestant) son of the murdered Mary. He became James I of England and VI of Scotland, the first English monarch of the House of Stuart (Mary's time in France had Gallicised the Stewart name). Most importantly, James united England, Wales and Scotland into one kingdom for the first time in history – at least on paper.

But James was a Protestant and attempts to smooth relations with the Catholics were set back by the anti-Catholic outcry that followed Guy Fawkes' famous Gunpowder Plot, a terrorist attempt to blow up king and parliament in 1605. (This event is still celebrated throughout Britain every 5th of November, with fireworks, bonfires and burning effigies of Guy himself.)

Alongside the rift between Catholics and Protestants, the divide between monarchy and parliament dating from Magna Carta days continued to smoulder. The power struggle got worse during the reign of the next king, Charles I, and eventually degenerated into the Civil War of 1644–49, pitching the king's royalists forces (known as the Cavaliers) against the army of Oliver Cromwell's parliamentarians (the Roundheads).

Cromwell was victorious, the king was executed (he famously wore two shirts on the day to avoid shivering and being thought cowardly) and shortly afterwards England was established as a republic. But by 1653 Cromwell was finding parliament too restricting and assumed near dictatorial powers. On his death, he was followed half-heartedly by his son, but in 1660 parliament decided to re-establish the monarchy in the person of Charles II (the exiled son of Charles I), as the republican alternatives were proving to be far worse.

The Return of the Monarchy

Charles II proved to be an able, although often ruthless, king. His period of rule, known as the Restoration, saw scientific and cultural activity eager to burst forth after the strait-laced Puritan ethics of Cromwell's time. Exploration and expansion was also on the agenda; backed by the power of the army and navy (modernised, ironically, by Cromwell in the preceding decades), colonies of traders and settlers soon stretched down the American coast, and the East India Company set up its headquarters in Bombay, laying foundations for what was to become the British Empire.

Unfortunately, the next king, James II, couldn't pick up where Charles II left off. His attempts to ease restrictive laws on Catholics ended with his defeat at the Battle of the Boyne by William III, the Protestant king of Holland, better known as William of Orange. Ironically, William was married to James' own daughter Mary (also a staunch Protestant), but it didn't seem to stop him doing the dirty on his father-in-law.

William and Mary both had equal rights to the throne and their joint accession in 1688 was known as the Glorious Revolution. Lucky they were married or there might have been another civil war.

Final Full Unity

In 1694 Mary died, leaving just William. He died a few years later and was followed by his sister-in-law Anne (the second daughter of James II). During Anne's reign, in 1707, the Act of Union was passed, bringing an end to the independent Scottish Parliament, and finally linking the countries of England, Wales and Scotland under one parliament – based in London – for the first time in history. The nation of Britain was now established as a single state, with a bigger, better and more powerful parliament, and a constitutional monarchy with clear limits on the powers of the king or queen.

In 1714 Anne died without an heir, marking the end of the Stuart line. The throne then passed to distant (but still safely Protestant) German relatives – the House of Hanover.

The Empire Expands

By the 18th century, struggles for the throne seemed a thing of the past and the Hanoverian kings increasingly relied on parliament to govern the country. As part of the process, from 1721 to 1742 a senior parliamentarian called Robert Walpole effectively became Britain's first prime minister. The British Empire – which, despite its official title, was predominantly an *English* entity – continued to grow in America, Canada and India. The first claims were made to Australia after Captain James Cook's epic voyage in 1768.

The Empire's first major reverse came when the American colonies won the War of Independence (1776–83). This setback forced England to withdraw from the world stage for a while, a gap not missed by French ruler Napoleon. He threatened to invade

England and hinder the power of the British overseas, before his ambitions were curtailed by navy hero Nelson and military hero Wellington at the famous battles of Trafalgar (1805) and Waterloo (1815).

The Industrial Age

While the Empire expanded abroad, at home Britain had become the crucible of the Industrial Revolution. Canals (first built in 1765), steam power (patented by James Watt in 1781) and steam trains (launched by George Stephenson in 1830), along with the modernisation of coal mines, transformed forever the methods of production and transport. Growth was fastest in the centre of England and the rapidly expanding towns of the Midlands became the first industrial cities.

Alongside industrial progress, medical advances led to a sharp increase in the population, but the rapid change from a rural to an urban society caused great dislocation. For the majority, poverty, deprivation and tough conditions at home and at work were the adverse side effects of Britain's economic blossoming.

Nevertheless, by the time Queen Victoria took the throne in 1837, Britain's fleets dominated the seas, linking an enormous empire, and Britain's factories dominated world trade. The rest of the 19th century was seen as Britain's Golden Age (in fact, for some people, it still is) – a period of confidence and optimism not seen since the days of the last great queen, Elizabeth I.

Victoria ruled over a proud nation at home, and a great swathe of territories abroad, from Canada and the Caribbean through much of Africa, India and Southeast Asia to Australia and New Zealand – all proudly shaded red on world atlases and trumpeted as 'the Empire where the sun never sets'. In a final move of PR genius, Queen Victoria's chief spin doctor and most effective prime minister, Benjamin Disraeli, had her crowned as Empress of India. The British people loved it, even though she'd never actually been there.

The times were optimistic, but it wasn't all about tub-thumping jingoism. Disraeli and his successor William Gladstone also introduced social reforms to address the worst excesses of the Industrial Revolution. Education became universal, trade unions were legalised and the right to vote was extended to commoners. Well, to men commoners. Women didn't get the vote for another few decades. Disraeli and Gladstone may have been enlightened gentlemen, but there *were* limits.

World Wars I & II

Queen Victoria died in 1901 and the ever-expanding Britain of her era died with her. In 1914 Britain bumbled into the Great War (only later did it became known as a *World* War), a vicious conflict of stalemate and horrendous slaughter. The conflict not only added 'trench warfare' to the dictionary, but also further deepened the huge trench that had existed between the ruling and working classes since the days of the Norman feudal system.

By the war's weary end in 1918 over a million Britons had died and there was hardly a family, street or village untouched by death, as the sobering lists of names on war memorials all over the country still show.

For the soldiers who did return from WWI, disillusionment with the way the war was waged led to a questioning of the accepted social order. A new political force – the Labour Party, to represent the working-class – upset the balance enjoyed by the Liberal Party and the Conservative Party, as the right to vote was extended to all men aged over 21 and women over 30. (It wasn't until 1928 that women were granted the same rights as men, despite the opposition of an up-and-coming politician called Winston Churchill.)

The Labour Party won for the first time in the 1923 election, albeit in coalition with the Liberals, with James Ramsay MacDonald the first Labour prime minister. A year later the Conservatives were back in power, but the rankling post–WWI 'us-and-them' mistrust, fertilised by soaring unemployment, led to the 1926 General Strike. When half a million workers marched through the streets, the government's heavy-handed response included sending in the army – setting the stage for industrial unrest that was to plague Britain for the next 50 years.

The unrest of the 1920s worsened in the '30s as the world economy slumped and the Great Depression took hold, ushering in a decade of misery and political upheaval. Even the royal family took a knock when Edward VIII abdicated in 1936 so he could marry a woman who was twice divorced and – horror of horrors – American. The ensuing scandal was good for newspaper sales and hinted at the prolonged 'trial by media' suffered by the royal family during recent times.

The throne was taken by Edward's less-than-charismatic brother George VI and Britain dithered through the rest of the '30s with a mediocre and visionless government failing to confront the country's problems.

Meanwhile on mainland Europe, the '30s saw the rise of imperial Germany under Adolf Hitler, leader of the Nazi party. Prime Minister Neville Chamberlain met Hitler in 1938 and promised Britain 'peace in our time'. But he was wrong, and on 1 September 1939 Hitler invaded Poland. Two days later Britain was once again at war with Germany.

Hitler's generals moved with astonishing speed. The German army swept west through France and pushed back British forces to the beaches of Dunkirk in June 1940. Neville Chamberlain, reviled for his appeasement policy, stood aside to let Prime Minister Winston Churchill lead a wartime coalition government. Churchill's extraordinary dedication (not to mention his radio speeches) inspired the country to resist and Hitler's invasion plans were blocked.

Japan entered the war to support Germany, and, following the bombing of Pearl Harbour in 1941, the USA was mobilised behind Britain. By 1944 Germany was in retreat. Britain and the USA had command of the skies, Russia's Red Army pushed back the Nazi forces from the east and the long-awaited D-day Normandy Landings to retake Europe took place in June 1944. In May 1945 it was all over: Hitler was dead, Germany a smoking ruin. Three months later, two atomic bombs forced the surrender of Japan and finally brought WWII to a close.

Post-war Reconstruction

In Britain, despite the victory, there was an unexpected swing on the political front. An electorate tired from the war and hungry for change tumbled Churchill and the Conservatives from power and ushered in the Labour Party, led by Clement Attlee. Rebuilding Britain was a slow process and the post-war 'baby boomers' experienced food rationing well into the 1950s, but the royal family was still going strong. In 1952 George VI was succeeded by his daughter Elizabeth II. Following the trend set by earlier queens Elizabeth I and Victoria, she has remained on the throne for a very long time (2002 was her Golden Jubilee 50th anniversary) overseeing a period of massive social and economic change.

Swinging '60s & Sad '70s

By the late 1950s, Britain's glory days were over, but recovery was still strong enough for Prime Minister Harold Macmillan to famously remind the British people that they'd 'never had it so good'. Some saw this as a boast for a confident future, others as a warning about difficult times ahead, but most probably forgot all about it because by this time the 1960s had started and grey old England was suddenly more fun and lively than it had been for generations – especially if you were over 10 and under 30. There was the music of the Beatles, the Rolling Stones, Cliff Richard and the Shadows, while cinema audiences flocked to see Michael Cain, Peter Sellers and Glenda Jackson.

Away from the glamour, British business looked strong and resilient, but the 1970s brought inflation, the oil crisis and increased international competition. It was a deathly combination that quickly revealed everything that was weak about the British economy and a lot that was rotten in British society, too, and the struggle between a disgruntled working class and an inept ruling class was brought to the boil once again. It was a decade of industrial disputes, walkouts, three-day weeks and general all-round unhappiness.

Neither Labour, under Harold Wilson and Jim Callaghan, nor the Conservatives, under Ted Heath, proved capable of controlling the strife and it wasn't until 1979, when elections returned the Conservatives led by Margaret Thatcher, that things began to turn and Britain saw the dawn of the tough new era, referred to as Thatcherism.

The Thatcher Years

Love or hate Mrs Thatcher, no-one could argue that her methods weren't dramatic. British workers were Luddites? She fired them. The trades unions were archaic? She smashed them. British industry was inefficient? She shut it down. Nationalised companies were a mistake? She sold them off – all with a sense of purpose that made Henry VIII's dissolution of the monasteries seem like a Sunday school picnic.

And just in case there was any doubt about Mrs Thatcher's patriotism, in 1982 she led Britain into war against Argentina following their invasion of the Falkland Islands – a British outpost off the coast of Argentina in the South Atlantic. This made Mrs Thatcher one of the most popular British prime ministers of all time and led to a bout of flag-waving which hadn't been seen the end of WWII, or probably since Agincourt.

By economic measures, Mrs Thatcher's policies were mostly successful, but the new harder-working, more competitive Britain was also a greatly polarised Britain. Once again a trench formed, but not between the classes; this time it was between the people who gained from the prosperous wave of Thatcherism and the many others left drowning in its wake – not only jobless, but jobless in a harsher environment. Even Thatcher fans were unhappy about the brutal style and the uncompromising methods favoured by the 'iron lady' and her team, but by 1988 she was the longest serving British prime minister of the 20th century, although repeated Conservative electoral victories were helped in no small way by the opposition Labour Party's total incompetence and destructive internal struggles.

Labour's Return

When any leader believes they're invincible, it's time to go and in 1990 Mrs Thatcher was finally dumped by the Conservatives when her introduction of the hugely unpopular flat-rate 'poll tax' reached even her own party's limits of tolerance. The electorate regarded the Labour Party with even more suspicion, however, allowing new Conservative leader John Major to unexpectedly win the 1992 election.

Another half-decade of political stalemate followed, as the Conservatives imploded and Labour was rebuilt on the sidelines. It all came to a head in 1997 when 'New' Labour swept to power with a record parliamentary majority of more than 170 seats. After nearly 18 years of Conservative rule, it really did seem that Labour's victory call ('things can only get better') was right and some people literally danced in the street when the results were announced.

Under Prime Minister Tony Blair, the government disappointed many old socialist stalwarts who expected a political swing back to the left. But Labour ministers kept a tight rein on public spending – much to the pleasure of financial institutions, although many ordinary voters, hoping for immediate improvements in the creaking health and transportation systems that the Conservatives had neglected for almost two decades, were disappointed by a lack of progress.

New Labour, New Millennium

The election in 2001 was pretty much a walkover for Tony Blair and the Labour party, while on the opposition benches the Conservatives replaced John Major with William Hague, a little-loved leader who tried to soften his staid image by wearing a baseball cap. It didn't work and he was soon followed by Ian Duncan-Smith, a more serious contender from the 'Euro-sceptic' right of the party.

Away from politicking, for most people in Britain, the main issue of 2001 involved 'foot-and-mouth', a disease contracted by farm animals, which spread through the countryside. By early 2002 the all clear was sounded, but not before Britain's tourist industry – a much bigger earner than farming in many rural areas – lost *billions* of pounds.

Another issue that raged through 2001 and 2002 (and shows no sign of disappearing) concerns the increasing number of asylum seekers coming to Britain from impoverished or war-torn parts of the world. For the often desperate people who leave everything to come here, Britain is seen as some kind of El Dorado with lots of jobs and welfare services, and many go to extraordinary lengths to cross from mainland Europe, hiding for days in trucks or transport containers, and even hanging underneath the trains that trundle through the Channel Tunnel every day – sometimes with fatal results. Of those that do make it, most asylum seekers find they are not welcomed by the British people (especially those influenced by xenophobic newspapers), nor by Britain's increasingly stringent immigration laws, which firmly differentiate between political and economic refugee status: if you're escaping a brutal government that's persecuting you, there's a chance you can stay; if you're here pretty well because you're poor, you'll probably be shipped back home pretty soon.

The year 2002 also enjoyed celebrations for the Queen's Golden Jubilee, marking 50 years on the throne. This coincided with the England football team doing rather well in the World Cup and a successful Commonwealth Games in Manchester – boosting national

England? Britain? What's in a Name?

Visitors are sometimes confused about the difference between England and Britain – and a lot of English people get it wrong, too. Just so you know, the state of Great Britain (usually shortened to Britain) is made up of three countries: England, Wales and Scotland. The United Kingdom (UK) consists of Great Britain, Northern Ireland and some semiautonomous islands such as the Isle of Man and the Channel Isles. The island of Ireland consists of Northern Ireland and the Republic of Ireland. The latter, also called Eire, is a completely separate country. The British Isles is a geographical term for the whole group of islands that make up the UK and the Republic of Ireland. Got that?

pride and patriotism to levels not seen for decades. The end result for Britain's monarchy seems to be a few more years of security, before the next inevitable round of bad press and public indifference begin again.

Perhaps cashing in on the optimism, in 2002 the Labour government finally opened the taps on public expenditure, pumping billions of pounds into health, education and transport. The Chancellor of the Exchequer, Gordon Brown (regarded by many as prime minister in waiting), took what may have been the biggest gamble of his life, and his party's, when he raised (albeit slightly) National Insurance – a form of health tax – to specifically pay for improvements in the National Health Service.

Polls show that the people of Britain are unanimous in their desire for change in the major social sectors, but after decades of mismanagement by both political sides many commentators believe that the task is just too big – redressing all these issues is like turning around an oil tanker on a duck pond. With talk already turning to the next election, due in 2007 at the latest, it remains to be seen if the voters think the promised improvements are too little too late.

GEOGRAPHY

England is the largest of the three political divisions within the island of Britain, with Scotland to the north and Wales to the west. France is just 20 miles (32km) away across the narrowest part of the English Channel (although, with the Channel Tunnel, England is no longer *totally* cut off from mainland Europe). The approximate areas of England and Britain are as follows.

England: 50,000 sq miles (130,000 sq km)
Britain: 88,500 sq miles (230,000 sq km)
UK: 95,000 sq miles (246,000 sq km)
British Isles: 123,000 sq miles (319,000 sq km)

If you want some comparisons, France is about 550,000 sq km, Texas 690,000 sq km, Australia seven million sq km and the USA over nine million sq km.

England's landscape in the south, south-central and east of the country is fairly flat or dotted with small hills, covered in a mix of farmland, towns and large cities. The eastern part of this region, East Anglia, is almost entirely flat and, at some points, only just above sea level. The Fens of Lincolnshire will be submerged when predictions about global warming and rising oceans are realised.

The southwest peninsula, known as the West Country, is a plateau with wild grass-covered moors, granite outcrops and a rugged coastline. A high rainfall and rich pastures provide good dairy farming – Devon cream is famous – while sheltered coves and beaches make it a favourite holiday destination.

In the north and north-central parts of England, there's still a mix of farmland and moors, interspersed with towns and cities, but the landscape gets noticeably more bumpy when compared to much of the south. A line of large hills called the Pennines (fondly tagged 'the backbone of England') dominates much of the landscape, running from Derbyshire to the Scottish border. Forming parts of this extensive chain are the peaty plateaus and cosy green farmland of the Peak District, the wild moors around Haworth that were immortalised by the novels of the Brontë sisters (see Arts later in this chapter for more details), the delightful valleys of the Yorkshire Dales and the remote, austere, frequently windswept but ruggedly beautiful hills of Northumberland.

In the northeast are more hills: the whale-back ridges, steep escarpments and stunning coastal cliffs of the North York Moors and the gentle rolling countryside of the Yorkshire Wolds. And in northeast England is the Lake District, a small but spectacular cluster of hills and mountains, including Scafell Pike (978m), England's highest peak, not to mention a wonderful selection of scenic valleys, some quaint but hardy villages and – of course – some of the most beautiful lakes in the country.

And where do the English live? Many live in London – the largest city in the country – and in the surrounding counties of the southeast. Outside here, the main centre of population is Birmingham, England's second-largest city, and the Midlands, an industrial heartland since the 19th century. Further north are more cities: Manchester and Sheffield rank third and fourth in size, with other main players such as Liverpool and Leeds not far behind.

CLIMATE

Meteorologists classify England's climate as 'temperate maritime' – read 'mild and damp' – but despite being fairly far north (London is on roughly the same latitudes as Moscow in Russia and Edmonton in Canada) extremes of heat and cold are moderated by warm seas – although it may not always seem very warm when you're on the beach at Blackpool!

In summer (June to August), temperatures rarely rise above 30°C and are often much lower – the average summer high in London or the West Country is around 21°C; the average low is 12°C. In northern England, averages are a touch lower. In winter (December to February), temperatures rarely fall below 0°C. Or if they do, it's not for long.

When it comes to rain, England gets its fair share of the wet stuff – although more falls in winter than in summer. There's also a general pattern of western areas getting more rain than eastern areas and, as you might expect, rainfall is greatest in the hills. For an idea of figures, parts of the Lake District can get up to 4500mm of rain a year, while parts of Essex and Kent get less than 600mm.

The main thing to remember about British weather is that it's always changeable – bad one minute, better the next, with a rainy day often followed by a sunny one. There are also wide variations over small distances: southern England might suffer floods, while the north enjoys a heat wave.

ECOLOGY & ENVIRONMENT

Some of the environmental issues facing England today are presented here. Inevitably,

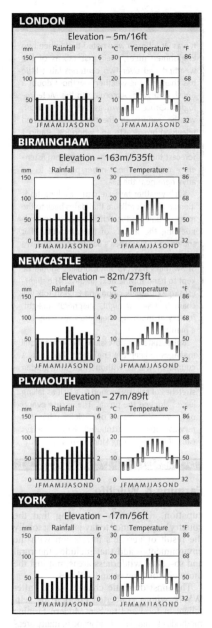

there's a pessimistic tone, although the bad news is often followed by the good. For more optimism, see also the Flora & Fauna section.

Whither the Weather?

It was Dr Johnson who noted that 'when two Englishmen meet, their first talk is of the weather' and over two centuries later, little has changed: the weather is without doubt a British obsession. According to the Meteorological Office (known as the Met Office), weather reports are the third-most-watched television broadcasts, and when BBC Radio 4 proposed dumping the late night shipping forecast there was a huge outcry from listeners – most of whom never planned to go anywhere near the sea.

Such weather fans are part of a long tradition and British folklore that dates back to the mists of time and is rich in ways of second-guessing the moods of the elements. If it snows on St Dorothea's day (6 February), we can expect no heavier snowfall. If it rains on St Swithin's day (15 July), brollies should be kept to hand for the next 40 days. The slightest tinge of a pink cloud and English folk will chant 'red sky at night, shepherd's delight, red sky at morning, shepherd's warning' like a mantra.

But despite the obsession, the weather still manages to keep the English on their toes. A couple of weeks without rain and garden hose bans are rushed in, and a few years ago stretches of railway ground to a halt as falling leaves clogged the points. The excuse everyone remembers came one winter when the railway authorities attributed blame to delays caused by the 'wrong kind of snow'.

Farming & Wildlife

With England's long history of human occupation, it's hardly surprising that the country's appearance today is almost totally the result of people's interaction with the environment – and that includes the rural and so-called wilderness areas, not just the more obvious towns and villages.

The most dramatic changes came after WWII, with a concerted effort to be self-reliant in food and timber. Modern farming methods changed the landscape in many areas from a patchwork of small fields to a scene of vast prairies, as walls were demolished, trees felled, ponds filled, wetlands drained and – most notably – hedgerows ripped out.

The hedgerows in most cases were a few metres wide, a dense network of bushes, shrubs and trees (we're not talking spindly garden borders here) that stretched across the countryside. As well as protecting fields from erosion, hedgerows supported a rich and varied range of flowers and provided shelter for numerous insects, birds and small mammals. But in the rush to improve farming yields, thousands of miles of hedgerows have been destroyed since 1950. And the destruction continues – since 1984, another 25% of hedgerows have disappeared. However, farmers are now encouraged to maintain and 'set aside' such areas as havens for birds.

Other farming methods such as irrigation, 'mono-cropping', the increased use of pesticides and a trend towards intensive rearing of cows, sheep and other stock have all had an impact on the environment as well. Rivers run dry, or fish are poisoned by runoff. Most fields consist of one type of grass, with not another plant to be seen, and these 'green deserts' support no insects, which in turn means populations of some wild bird species dropped by an incredible 30% to 70% from 1970 to 1990. So it's not just a case of old wizened peasants that recall the idyllic days of their forbears; you only have to be over about 30 in England to remember a countryside where birds such as skylarks or lapwings were visibly much more numerous.

Ironically, despite farming development, the food produced is often of dubious quality, as simple realities such as tasteless carrots or national emergencies such as the 'mad cow' disease of the late 1990s clearly show. But you can't blame the farmers – well, not all of them. They have a living to earn just like everyone else and are often encouraged to be environmentally irresponsible by misguided directives (and vast subsidies) from the government and the European Union (EU).

But all is not lost. In the face of apparently overwhelming odds, England still boasts a great biodiversity and some of the best wildlife habitats are protected to a greater or lesser extent, thanks to the creation of national parks and similar conservation zones (see the Flora & Fauna section later in this chapter for more details.) As well as national parks, some of the best protection lies within areas privately owned by conservation campaign groups, such as the Wildlife Trusts, Woodland Trust, National Trust or Royal

Society for the Protection of Birds. Many of these areas are open to the public – ideal spots for walking, bird-watching or simply enjoying the peace and beauty of the countryside.

Habitat Protection

As well as national parks, nature reserves, blue-flag beaches and all the rest, environmental protection continues to be improved as the government gradually tightens the regulations on businesses and individuals – partly in response to continent-wide rules imposed by the EU. An example of this is the Countryside Act of 2000, which (among many other things) provides better protection for several wild animal species; you're not allowed to disturb bats and their roosting spots, for example, if you happen to be repairing your roof.

Fox-Hunting

One of the most controversial issues in England today concerns fox-hunting – an ancient traditional activity in which large numbers of people on horseback, assisted by hounds, chase a fox through the countryside.

Opinion polls suggest that over two-thirds of British people see hunting as a cruel 'sport' and would support a ban. In Scotland, they've already had their way and a ban came into force in August 2002. In England and Wales, similar debates rage on. The 'pro' lobby say hunting represents the country way of life, which townies can't appreciate, and claim the hunting industry creates thousands of jobs in rural areas. Behind the urban-rural split is an even deeper emotion – good old English class divide; for many, hunting is seen as a pursuit for the upper classes, even though in reality a number of 'ordinary' folk take part as well.

Despite several government efforts through 2001 and 2002 to ban hunting with hounds, the pro-hunters are powerful and well organised, and continually manage to stave off antihunt laws. The situation is still fluid and volatile. Visitors are well advised not to join in conversations about hunting, especially in country pubs, without a very firm grasp of the facts.

Tourism

Also a major issue is Tourism – with massive ecological implications for visitors and the places they visit.

Every year, around 100 million people (foreigners and locals) go to England's national parks – mostly by car. The Peak District alone gets 20 million, making it Britain's most visited park, and the second busiest in the world (after Mount Fuji). Eight million day-trippers a year flock to the New Forest in Hampshire and it's a similar story in the Lake District.

Unfortunately, the fragile environments, local resources, country lanes, footpaths and villages in many places simply cannot cope.

However, you can't keep the visitors out. The whole idea of a national park in Britain is that it's somewhere *everyone* can enjoy. And, just as importantly, many locals depend on tourism for their livelihoods – everything from hotels and pubs to gift shops and bicycle hire. For example, in the Peak District alone visitors spend over £175 million each year and tourism supports around 2000 jobs. In Wales and Scotland particularly, where traditional industries have declined over the last few decades, tourism is a major part of the national economy.

Park authorities realise that one problem – the traffic – can be resolved by providing better public transport and, in many national parks, the (heavily subsidised) bus services are very good, and often ideal for visitors. The problem is persuading the great English public to consider using their cars just a little bit less.

FLORA & FAUNA

England is a small country, but has a surprisingly diverse range of plants and animals. OK, it's not the Serengeti – many native species are small and hidden away – but there are some undoubted gems here: woods carpeted in shimmering bluebells, sea cliffs thronging with thousands of nesting birds, or a herd of red deer in the Lake District mountains. This wildlife is part of the fabric of Britain and having a closer look may enhance your trip enormously.

Grassland & Farmland

Grassland areas include the chalky hills in southern England (notably the South Downs) and the limestone further north, such as the Peak District and Yorkshire Dales. In fields that evade large-scale farming, great profusions of wildflowers such as cowslips and primroses flower in April and May.

With flowers come insects and if the meadows are near trees, birds can drop by for a snack. The warbling song of a skylark as it flutters high over open farmland is an integral, but now threatened, sound of the English countryside.

Hedgerows and field perimeters also support wildlife that includes the robin with a red breast and cheerful song, the wren, one of Britain's smallest birds, constantly restless, whose trilling song is one of the loudest and longest, and the yellowhammer – easily recognised by its 'little-bit-of-bread-and-noooooo-cheese' song. Britain's new 'hedgerows' are motorway verges, which support many small mammals, so kestrels are often seen hovering nearby.

Another common bird is the pheasant, whose nervous habit of flying from cover at the last moment makes it ideal, to some, for shooting. Originally introduced from Russia, pheasants are now considered naturalised and are commonly seen in farmland, woodland and moorland.

Among mammals, rabbits are extremely common in farmland, while brown hares, with longer legs and ears, choose to stay in the open where they can see predators. Males who battle for territory in early spring are, of course, as 'mad as a March hare'.

Woodland
Natural deciduous woodland contains trees such as oak, ash, hazel and rowan, which encourage an enormous biodiversity, and today these species are frequently planted. The New Forest in southern England and the Forest of Dean on the Wales-England border are examples of this type of habitat. Surprisingly, the most wooded county in Britain is Surrey, despite its proximity to London. The soil is too poor for agriculture and so the trees got a stay of execution.

One of the best times to see woodlands is the spring, before the leaf canopy is fully developed, as sunlight breaks through to encourage a carpet of flowers such as bluebells – a beautiful and internationally rare species. They're full of birds, too, but you'll more often hear them than see them. Listen out for willow warblers (which have, not surprisingly, a warbling song with a descending cadence) and chiffchaffs (which, also not surprisingly, make a repetitive 'chiff chaff' noise).

On the woodland floor, hedgehogs search leaf litter for insects and earthworms. Other woodland mammals include the small white-spotted fallow deer and the even smaller roe deer. Red foxes are very widespread and have adapted well to a scavenging life in country towns, and even in city suburbs. Grey squirrels have also proved very adaptable. They were introduced from North America and have almost entirely replaced the smaller native red squirrels.

Heathland
Areas of heath are generally low lying with poor soils. Common plants are gorse and heather, and in southern England pockets of heath remain most notably in the New Forest and parts of Surrey. Legend says that it's the season for kissing when gorse blooms – luckily its vivid yellow flowers show year-round.

Birds common in heathland include small meadow pipits, which have a habit of flying up from the path ahead of you so you never quite get a good look. Stonechats are also commonly seen, typically perching on a gorse bush, with a metallic 'chak chak' call sounding like two stones banging together. After dark you may hear the distinctive chirring song of nightjars.

Moorland
Classic moorlands, covered in tough grass or swathes of heather, include Dartmoor, the northern Peak District and the Pennines. In autumn the heather plants flower in a riot of purple and one of the finest areas to see this is the North York Moors.

Moorland birds include the red grouse and the elegant curlew with its long curved bill. Golden plovers are beautifully camouflaged but their mournful cries betray their position, while lapwings are just show-offs with their spectacular aerial displays.

The most visible moorland mammal is the red deer. Herds survive on Exmoor and Dartmoor, and in the Lake District. Males grow their famous large antlers between April and July, and shed them again in February.

Freshwater Areas
Lowland streams and rivers are abundant with life. Birds include the iridescent kingfisher, which you may see perched patiently, waiting for a chance to dive, but is most often seen as a flash of bright blue disap-

pearing down the river. Little grebes are less nervous and fun to watch as they pop up from underwater foraging, while grey herons silently stalk at the waters edge and black moorhens noisily boss each other around.

Ponds and lakes are home to insects such as dragonflies, while smaller damselflies sun themselves on water plants. Birds you might see include great crested grebes, which put on a fancy bonding display in spring, with long-neck rubbing and lots of splashing.

Marshes and reed beds, such as those in the Norfolk Broads, are an ornithological paradise. Nesting birds such as reed buntings, redshanks and, very rarely, bitterns may be seen, while marsh harriers glide low overhead.

Aquatic mammals include water voles, endearing rodents that were once very common, but now have been all but wiped out by the American mink, which was introduced from abroad to stock fur farms and escaped to wreak havoc on smaller native animals. In contrast, formerly rare otters are beginning to make a comeback after suffering from polluted water, habitat destruction and persecution by anglers, but although their numbers are growing, they are mainly nocturnal and you'll need luck or a lot of patience to see one.

Coastal Areas

The dramatic cliffs around the coast of England, particularly in Cornwall or the east coast of Yorkshire, are a marvellous sight and most spectacular during early summer when they are home to hundreds of thousands of breeding sea birds. Guillemots, razorbills and kittiwakes, among others, all fight for space on impossibly crowded rock ledges and it's one of Britain's finest wildlife spectacles as the cliffs become white with their droppings and the air filled with their shrill calls.

Estuaries and mudflats are feeding grounds for numerous migrant wading birds. Handsome black-and-white oystercatchers with their long red bill are a familiar sight, and flocks of small ringed plovers may skitter along the sand, then rise in a compact bunch.

Two seal species frequent English coasts; the larger grey seal is more often seen than the misnamed common seal. Dolphins, porpoises and minke whales (as well as basking sharks) can all be seen off the western coasts – especially from about May to September when viewing conditions are better – as long as you go with someone who knows where to look!

National Parks & Protected Areas

Way back in 1810 William Wordsworth, famous poet and outdoor-lover ('I wandered lonely as a cloud'), suggested that the Lake District should be 'a sort of national property, in which every man has a right'. But it took more than a century before the Lake District became a national park and then it was a very different one from Wordsworth's vision.

Today there are eight national parks in England – Dartmoor, Exmoor, Lake District, Norfolk & Suffolk Broads, Northumberland, North York Moors, Peak District and Yorkshire Dales – enjoying the highest designation for landscape protection in Britain. Two more parks, the New Forest and the South Downs, are due to be created by 2003.

Despite this impressive total, the term 'national park' can cause some confusion. Firstly, they are not state-owned: nearly all the land is private, belonging to farmers, landowners, companies and conservation organisations, although the area is administered by a National Park Authority (NPA). Just to increase the confusion, large sections of several national parks are owned by the National Trust (NT), but this private charity has no direct link with the NPA. Secondly, these are not areas of total wilderness, as in many other countries, and in national parks you'll see roads, railways, villages and even towns.

Despite these apparent anomalies, national parks still contain vast tracts of wild mountain and moorland, rolling downs and river valleys, and other areas of quiet countryside, all ideal for long walks, cycle rides, easy rambles, sightseeing or just lounging around. To help you get the best from the parks, they all have information centres, and various recreational facilities (trails, car parks, campsites etc) are provided for visitors.

Alongside national parks, many other parts of England are protected as Areas of Outstanding Natural Beauty (AONBs), ranging from the grassy plateau of Bodmin Moor in the southwest, through the picture-postcard Cotswolds, to the wild hills of the North Pennines. These beautiful parts of England are often quieter than national parks, and just as good for activities such as cycling and walking.

As you travel around you'll also see National Nature Reserves (NNRs), where nature conservation is the main focus, although agriculture, forestry and recreation may also be involved. Look out, too, for Heritage Coasts which, as the name suggests, protect particularly scenic or environmentally important areas of coastline.

GOVERNMENT & POLITICS

The UK's system of government is a parliamentary democracy, with a hereditary monarch (currently Queen Elizabeth II) as 'titular' head of state – ie, a figurehead with no real power. The head of government is the prime minister, the leader of the ruling political party, and parliament is made up of the Monarch, the House of Lords and the House of Commons – the latter being today's supreme decision-making body. Unusually, the UK has no written constitution; instead, government is guided by a mix of parliamentary statutes, common law (precedents dating back to Anglo-Saxon customs) and simple convention that evolves over time.

The House of Commons and the House of Lords sit in the Parliament building at Westminster in London – that's the one with the famous tower of Big Ben on the side.

House of Commons

Members of Parliament (MPs) are elected to the House of Commons every five years, unless an earlier election is called. Anyone over 18 can vote, but it's not compulsory and election turnouts are generally around 65%. There was notable voter apathy in the recent election: just over half of those eligible bothered to poll. In fact, more people voted in a 2002 TV talent show called Pop Idol than they did for their government the previous year.

Voting is based on a 'first past the post' system and MPs are elected if they win a majority in their constituency. There are 659 MPs in the UK parliament – 529 for England, 40 for Wales, 72 for Scotland, 18 for Northern Ireland, although if all of them arrived at once there wouldn't be enough room in the chamber. Fortunately for the MPs, if not for their constituents, this rarely happens.

House of Lords

For centuries, the House of Lords consisted of around 900 'hereditary peers' (titles passed from one generation to the next), plus about 25 Church of England bishops and 12 Law Lords – who also act as the UK's highest court. In more recent times, 'life peer-

ages' were introduced – a way for prime ministers to hand out top jobs to loyal MPs without the bother of having to be elected. It was a system ripe for abuse, but at least when these Lords gave up the ghost their first-born child didn't swan into the vacant position.

From the late 1990s, the Labour government of Tony Blair introduced several significant reforms. Nearly all hereditary peers were relieved of their posts, leaving around 90 as an interim measure. However, the number of life peers increased, raising cries of 'Tony's cronies' and calling the whole reform process into disrepute.

The Parties

For the last 150 years a predominantly two-party system has operated. Since 1945 the Conservatives or the Labour Party has held power, with the Liberal-Democrats the largest minority party.

Traditionally, Conservatives are regarded as right-wing, free-enterprise supporters, drawing support mainly from the English countryside and comfortable sectors of suburbia, while Labour was left-wing in the social-democratic tradition, with power bases mainly in working-class urban areas.

In the 1990s Labour shed much of its socialist credo and the 'New Labour' government elected in 1997 proved to be quite centrist, adopting many market reforms long favoured by moderate Conservatives. In turn, this sometimes blurred the distinction between Labour and the 'Lib-Dems', and forced the Conservatives – in true Rocky Horror style – to take a sizable jump to the right.

ECONOMY

After WWII, most of Britain's industries – trains, coal mines, shipyards, steel mills, automobile factories – were brought under government control. But lack of investment under public ownership, the outdated work practices of managers and trade unions, and the changing nature of world trade (including the breakup of the British Empire) meant industry declined through the '60s and '70s. It was against this background that Prime Minister Thatcher waged a ruthless assault on old-style industry through the '80s. (For more details see the History section earlier in this chapter.)

The social costs of Thatcherism were enormous and questionable, but in line with a global upswing by the late 1990s the

British economy was in better shape than it had been for years. In two decades, the economic base has shifted away from heavy industry and today the majority of Britons are employed in light engineering, hi-tech and electronic fields (including computers and telecommunications), finance, retail, and the service sectors. Despite, or because of, this shift, Britain still ranks as the fourth-largest economy in world.

Unfortunately, across Britain, the number of jobs made obsolete does not equal the number of new jobs created. However, in 2000, unemployment fell below one million for the first time since the 1970s and keeps falling – although the figures are debatable, due to the numerous revisions of how they are calculated, and many jobs are part-time.

The last few decades have also seen a growth in the great economic divide between the south and the north of Britain, or even between the southeast (around London) and the rest of the country. For example, along the M4 motorway west of London there are towns with less than 1% unemployment. With hi-tech jobs on the rise, this is the nearest Britain gets to Silicon Valley. In sharp contrast, parts of the Midlands and north of England still suffer economic depression. Of course, the north-south split is oversimplified and across the country there are pockets of affluence in traditionally 'poor' areas, and zones of massive deprivation sometimes only a few blocks away from Millionaires Row.

And there's no sign this will change. Despite the cost of living in London being considerably higher than in other parts of Britain (double the price for a beer, 10 times more for a house), businesses – and people – still seem inexorably drawn to the capital.

POPULATION & PEOPLE

England has a population of 51 million (around 80% of Britain's total of 60 million) and growth has been virtually static in recent years. To these figures you can add an annual influx of about 26 million tourists.

The English are a diverse bunch, as you would expect given the variety of peoples who have made this their home over the centuries. Particularly since the Industrial Revolution, England has attracted large numbers of people from Scotland, Wales and Ireland, and in the 19th and 20th centuries there were

Vital Statistics

Throughout this book, we give population figures for cities and towns based on the 1991 national census, as figures from the 2001 census were not released until late 2002. So, some numbers may be outdated, especially for rapidly growing towns in the southeast, but overall they'll still give you the most important message: whether a place is a tiny village or a massive metropolis.

significant influxes of refugees – Russians, Poles, Jews, Vietnamese and so on.

Since the 1950s, significant numbers have come to Britain from ex-colonies, especially the Caribbean (the West Indies etc), Bangladesh, Pakistan and India, and to a lesser extent from Africa. Many immigrants arrived in Britain in the 1970s after being forced out of Uganda by Idi Amin. Most recently, refugees have come from Bosnia, Somalia, Afghanistan and eastern Turkey.

Generally speaking, in the last century or so, incomers have settled in urban areas (because that's the place to find jobs, housing and people of the same ethnic background), while in country areas of England the population remains overwhelmingly indigenous (for which, read 'white').

Finally, it's worth noting that, despite the 'waves of foreigners' scares you'll read in some more excitable newspapers, the number of people leaving Britain is often more than the number coming in.

EDUCATION

Schooling is compulsory for children aged between five and 16, with most kids 'going up' from primary to secondary school at about age 11. Many young people stay on until they're 18, either at school or college.

Education in state-run schools and colleges is free and education at university (mostly for 19 to 21 year olds) was state-funded until the 1990s, however the number of people going on to university (and the number of universities) increased to such a degree in recent decades that students now pay towards their education costs by taking out loans.

Alongside the state schools sit a relatively small number of private or independent schools (ranging from tiny homespun schemes with a couple of teachers and a dozen kids, to grand and ancient institutions such as Eton and Harrow – which are rather confusingly called 'public schools'), where loving parents cough up thousands of pounds a year to have their offspring 'properly' educated.

ARTS

Literature

Modern English literature pretty much starts with Geoffrey Chaucer's classic *The Canterbury Tales* (written around 1387), about a group of pilgrims on their way to the shrine of St Thomas Becket. For more details see the Canterbury section in the Southeast England chapter.

Two centuries later William Shakespeare emerged, best known for his plays (discussed in Theatre following) and for his many great poems. The famous lines 'Shall I compare thee to a summer's day? Thou art more lovely and more temperate' comes from *Sonnet No. 18* – in all he penned 154.

Very different to Shakespeare were the metaphysical poets of the early 17th century whose wordplay, vivid imagery and far-fetched conceits (comparisons) often landed them in trouble. In *A Valediction: Forbidding Mourning*, for instance, John Donne compares a couple of lovers with two compass points. A little later, John Milton's rich language and brilliant thought characterised his famous epic poem *Paradise Lost*, which traces the role of Satan in the downfall of Adam and Eve.

The 19th century 'golden age' of English literature ushered in the Romantic poets. John Keats, Percy Bysshe Shelley and Lord Byron all wrote with emotion, exulting the power of senses and imagination. They were also passionate about nature; perhaps the best known Romantic, William Wordsworth, set *The Prelude* in the Lake District. Another member of the Romantic set was poet, painter and engraver William Blake, particularly known for his poem beginning 'Tyger! Tyger! burning bright' from *Songs of Experience*.

The Romantic movement produced a genre called 'literary Gothic' and the best-known example is *Frankenstein* by Mary Shelley, which she originally penned in a ghost story competition with her husband Percy Bysshe Shelley. This genre was then satirised in *Northanger Abbey* by Jane Austen, one of Britain's best-known and best-loved novelists. Her favoured subjects were

the provincial middle classes – the intrigues and passions boiling away under the stilted preserve of social convention are beautifully portrayed in *Emma* and *Pride and Prejudice*.

Next came the era of Queen Victoria and the great Victorian novel often took as subject matter the social and political issues of the day: in *Oliver Twist*, Charles Dickens captures the lives of young thieves in the London slums and in *Hard Times* he paints a brutal picture of capitalists profiting from the Industrial Revolution; George Eliot (the male pseudonym of Mary Ann Evans) set her masterpiece *Middlemarch* at the time of the 1832 Great Reform Bill; and the classic *Tess of the D'Urbervilles* by Thomas Hardy deals with the decline of the peasantry. Also popular at the time were the Brontë sisters – Charlotte Brontë's *Jane Eyre* and Emily Brontë's *Wuthering Heights* are passionate love stories with dark, moody heroes.

In the 20th century, the pace of English writing increased. WWI made poetic heroes of Rupert Brooke (1887–1915) and Wilfred Owen (1893–1918). Brooke's *The Soldier* is romantic and idealistic but Owen's *Dulce et Decorum Est* is harshly cynical about the 'glory' of war.

The 1920s saw many great English authors produce books that make them famous today: EM Forster explored the hopelessness of British colonial rule with *A Passage to India*; DH Lawrence shocked the world with *Lady Chatterley's Lover*, then banned from sale as pornographic; and Virginia Woolf, a key member of the elite Bloomsbury literary group, wrote *To the Lighthouse*. (For more details, see 'The Bloomsbury Group' boxed text in the Southeast England chapter.)

The 1930s saw it all – murder, romance, satire and hobbits. 'Queen of Crime' Agatha Christie invented detective Hercule Poirot, who used his little grey cells in *Murder on the Orient Express* and *Death on the Nile*; Daphne du Maurier set the romantic suspense novel *Rebecca* (which English director Alfred Hitchcock later turned into a film) on the Cornish coast; JRR Tolkien published *The Hobbit* and followed it some 20 years later with his awesome trilogy *The Lord of the Rings*; and Evelyn Waugh poked fun at the newspaper business in his witty *Scoop*.

After WWII, a new breed of writer emerged. George Orwell (1903–50) wrote *Animal Farm* and *Nineteen Eighty-Four*, his closely observed satires on communism and fascism. The latter, which begins with the famous line 'It was a bright cold day in April, and the clocks were striking thirteen', is often compared with *Brave New World* by Aldous Huxley. The cold war inspired Graham Greene's *Our Man in Havana*, in which a secret agent studies the workings of a vacuum cleaner to inspire fictitious spying reports.

Another secret agent of the same era was James Bond, Ian Fleming's full-blooded hero. He first appeared in 1953 in *Casino Royale*, swiftly followed by *Live and Let Die*, then swashbuckled through numerous thrillers for a further 11 years. A Fleming contemporary was TH White whose *The Once and Future King* covers battles of a different time, effortlessly capturing the magical world of King Arthur and the Knights of the Round Table.

As well as the novelists, the 20th century was a great time for poets. Big names include: Philip Larkin (a famously reclusive librarian); WH Auden (*Funeral Blues* is his most popular work thanks to the film *Four Weddings and a Funeral*); and TS Eliot (an American who became a British citizen in 1927), particularly known for having his *Old Possum's Book of Practical Cats* made into Andrew Lloyd Webber's musical *Cats*. Ted Hughes also gained recognition, sometimes as much for the relationship with his wife, American poet Sylvia Plath (who gassed herself at age thirty), as for his works. Meanwhile, Brian Patten, Adrian Henri and Roger McGough came together as the Liverpool Poets, determined to make their art more relevant to daily life. Their first publication was *The Mersey Sound* in 1967 – pop poetry for the streets.

Many writers breaking new ground in the 1970s are the old hands of today's literary scene. In 1973 Martin Amis was just 24 when he wrote the *The Rachel Papers* – a witty, minutely observed story of sexual obsession in puberty. Since then Amis has published fifteen books, including *London Fields* and *The Information*, all greeted with critical acclaim and high sales. Similarly, Ian McEwan was one of Britain's angriest young novelists, earning the nickname 'Ian Macabre' for his early work such as *The Cement Garden* and *The Comfort of Strangers*. But in 1998 he cracked the establishment and became a Booker Prize winner with *Amsterdam*. Another big name whose work covers at least two decades is Salman Rushdie; his best-known works include *Midnight's Children*

and *The Satanic Verses* – the latter won the Booker prize in 1981 and the dubious award of a fatwa from Islamic scholars who thought his work heretical.

Two authors who struggled for recognition with early books then hit the jackpot in the 1990s were Sebastian Faulks, catapulted to fame by *Birdsong*, a tale of passion and the utter waste of WWI, and Louis de Bernières whose *Captain Corelli's Mandolin* became a runaway success after 1995.

Conversely, Alex Garland, a young backpacker, found immediate success with his first novel *The Beach* about a group of Western travellers in Thailand, and Zadie Smith was only 25 when her first novel *White Teeth*, set in north London, topped bestseller lists in 2000. Someone to watch is first-time novelist Hari Kunzru, who received one of the largest advances in publishing history in 2002 for *The Impressionist*. He went on to win the Betty Task Prize, following Zadie Smith's footsteps. Topping this is the reputed £3.5 million paid to Manchester United's star player David Beckham in August 2002 for his official autobiography – a huge sum for someone more used to cashing in on the skills of his right foot than his right hand!

As well as what might be termed 'serious' literature, classifications abound for numerous other genres. In the 1980s Jilly Cooper made the 'bonkbuster' her own in *Riders*, and with seven further books of froth, frolic and infidelity she is cited as the *grande dame* of 'chick-lit'. Lumped in the same bracket is Helen Fielding's late-1990s work *Bridget Jones's Diary*, about the heartache of a single, modern girl's blundering search for love. These days, the 'chick-lit' genre is overflowing, with endless young female authors cashing in on its popularity. Naturally, the guys have responded with 'lad lit', which is usually more confessional, personal and often autobiographical. It grew from Tony Parson's *Man and Boy*, which he followed with *One for My Baby* and *Man and Wife*. Nick Hornby proved a master of this genre with *Fever Pitch* (about football and relationships) and *High Fidelity* (about music and relationships); his follow-ups *About a Boy* and *How to be Good* have proved just as popular.

As we enter the 21st century, a phenomenon that looks set to continue is the children's book that can be equally enjoyed by adults. JK Rowling's *Harry Potter and the Philosopher's*

Stone and the next three bestselling sequels are ageless in their appeal, while Philip Pullman, with *His Dark Materials* trilogy, has managed to repeat this successful formula.

Theatre

England has a long, robust theatrical history. The whole country is awash with theatres, first-rate performances and world-renowned stars, and – whatever New Yorkers say – London is the world centre for theatrical arts.

The country's first theatre was built in 1576 on the northern outskirts of London and was rather unimaginatively called 'The Theatre'. More appeared south of the river, including the Rose and the Globe – famous for staging numerous plays by William Shakespeare – which can still be visited today (for details about the Globe see the London chapter). Shakespeare's brilliant plots and sharp prose have turned him into an icon, and his most famous works include *Macbeth* ('the Scottish play'), *Hamlet* and *Romeo and Juliet*. (For more on the iconic bard, see the Stratford-upon-Avon section in the Midlands chapter.) Shakespeare's rival at the time was Christopher Marlowe, best known for his play *Dr Faustus* and for his somewhat inglorious exit from the Elizabethan stage – he was stabbed to death in a pub brawl.

The theatres were closed as dens of iniquity by Oliver Cromwell's Puritans, but when Charles II returned from exile to Britain in 1660, he encouraged the use of theatrical practices he had seen on the Continent. Most significant was the use of women to play female roles. This innovation took London audiences by storm and was also opportune for one new actress, Nell Gwyn, who became Charles II's mistress. The humorous plays of that era are known as Restoration comedies – bawdy, witty, and often making fun of the upper classes and social pretensions. William Congreve's *The Way of the World* was a huge hit in 1700, full of gossipy intrigue and adultery.

In the 18th century, theatres were built in the larger English cities – the Bristol Old Vic and The Grand in Lancaster date from this time. Plays such as Oliver Goldsmith's uproarious *She Stoops to Conquer* and Richard Sheridan's *The Rivals* date from this time. The era was also dominated by great actors such as David Garrick, who gave his name to one of London's leading theatres.

The innovation of gas-lighting at London's Drury Lane and Covent Garden theatres in 1820 set the 19th-century stage for some wonderful theatre. There were the brilliant comedies of Oscar Wilde (1854–1900), including *The Importance of Being Ernest* and *An Ideal Husband*. At the same time George Bernard Shaw (1856–1950) came up with such classics as *Pygmalion* and *Major Barbara*.

Comedy continued in the early 20th century with plays by Noel Coward such as *Private Lives* and *Blithe Spirit*, and in the late 1940s JB Priestley's *An Inspector Calls* premiered and has rarely been off the English stage since.

By the 1950s the great actors Sir Laurence Olivier, Sir John Gielgud and Dame Peggy Ashcroft were at their professional peak, while John Osborne's *Look Back in Anger* launched the career of Alan Bates, with the angry and rebellious Jimmy Porter becoming a symbol of an unhappy and frustrated postwar generation. This era also marked the emergence of new playwrights with new freedoms, such as Harold Pinter, whose works include the sinister *Birthday Party*.

In the 1960s and 1970s, plays by Tom Stoppard *(Rosencrantz and Guildenstern are Dead)*, Peter Shaffer *(Amadeus)*, Michael Frayn *(Noises Off)* and Alan Ayckbourn *(The Norman Conquests)* took Britain by storm and actors such as Helen Mirren, Glenda Jackson, Dame Judi Dench and Tom Courtenay did justice to them on stage.

At this time, the young Andrew Lloyd Webber had just written his first musical. It was a failure. Undeterred, he followed it with *Joseph and the Amazing Technicolor Dreamcoat* and *Jesus Christ Superstar*, which became internationally successful. Now, Lloyd Webber's string of long-running musicals on the London stage are legendary – the most famous being *Cats* and *Starlight Express*, which both closed in 2002 after clocking up 21- and 17-year runs, respectively.

A continuing trend in London is for film stars, rock musicians or models to take a paycut and perform on the stage. In mid-2002, Madonna was getting terrible reviews in David Williamson's *Up For Grabs*, and Gwynneth Paltrow fairly good ones in David Auburn's *Proof*. They follow in the footsteps of Kathleen Turner, Jerry Hall and Nicole Kidman, who all recently trod the West End boards – sometimes naked, which is always good for getting the critics' attention.

Another London tradition is the 'long run' – the record holder is *The Mousetrap* by Agatha

Christie; the play celebrated its Golden Jubilee in 2002.

Outside theatres, there's a strong tradition in Britain of open-air performances during the summer months. Many take place in the grounds of country houses or at purpose-built places such as Regents Park Open Air Theatre in London and the spectacular cliff-edge Minack Theatre in Cornwall.

Cinema

In the early years of the 20th century, Britain's silent movies gave the Americans a run for their money and, in 1929, *Blackmail* by Alfred Hitchcock launched the British film industry into the era of sound production. Hitchcock, the 'master of suspense', went on to become one of England's best-known film directors, making films such as *The Thirty-Nine Steps* in England. He moved to the US in 1939 where he enjoyed even more success with *Rear Window* and *Vertigo*.

After a decline in film output during WWII, a recovery was led by Ealing studios with a series of eccentric and very English comedies such as *Kind Hearts and Coronets* (1949) where Alec Guinness plays eight members of the same upper-class family, and *Passport to Pimlico* where a district of London declares independence from the rest of the country. At this time, the big box-office successes were *Hamlet*, starring Laurence Olivier (the first British film to win an Oscar in the Best Picture category), Carol Reed's *The Third Man* and David Lean's *Brief Encounter*. Lean went on to make many more classic movies including *Bridge on the River Kwai, Lawrence of Arabia* and *Doctor Zhivago*.

In the 1950s, television became a force in the film market. William Hinds, whose stage name was William Hammer, turned this to his advantage and made a film version of the BBC's *The Quatermass Experiment*. This was followed by a series of scary Gothic films, which soon became known as 'Hammer Horrors'.

In 1958, the first *Carry On* film appeared and these sexist but classic comedies continued into the 1970s. James Bond arrived in 1962 with *Dr No*. Since then 20 Bond movies have been made, the latest being *Die Another Day* – some of which was shot in Norfolk, where farmland near Burnham Deepdale (see the Eastern England chapter) gamely stood in for North Korean paddy fields!

In 1963, famous English actor Peter Sellers became bumbling Inspector Clouseau in *The Pink Panther*; a world-wide hit that spawned four sequels.

By the end of the 1960s, British film production had declined again and didn't really pick up until David Puttnam's *Chariots of Fire* won four Oscars in 1981. At the same time, TV company Channel 4 started financing films for the large and small screen, one of the first being *My Beautiful Laundrette* – a story of multicultural Britain during the Thatcher era. The following year, Richard Attenborough's big-budget epic *Ghandi* carried off eight Oscars including best director and best picture.

In the 1990s there was a mini-renaissance in British film-making, ushered in by *Four Weddings and a Funeral* (1994), starring the self-deprecating and very English Hugh Grant. This movie spearheaded a genre of quirky low-budget 'Brit flicks', including Mike Leigh's *Secrets and Lies*, which won the Palme d'Or at Cannes, and *The Full Monty*, which became England's most successful film ever (see Sheffield in the Yorkshire chapter for more details).

In the late 1990s, Guy Ritchie made the London gangster movie *Lock, Stock and Two Smoking Barrels* and Ayub Khan Din was successful with *East is East*, about the clash between first- and second-generation Pakistanis in 1960s England. Most popular was *Notting Hill* where Hugh Grant fell for Julia Roberts in a travel bookshop – a film so sweet it bordered on saccharine.

In 2001 Colin Firth starred in *Bridget Jones's Diary*, about a neurotic, 30-something 'singleton', but that year's biggest hit was *Harry Potter and the Philosopher's Stone*, with an almost exclusively British cast.

Audiences in 2002 were treated to the winning combination of Judi Dench, Jim Broadbent and Kate Winslet – darlings of the British film industry – in *Iris*, a heart-wrenching dramatisation of Iris Murdoch's descent into Alzheimer's. The ever-popular Hugh Grant starred in *About a Boy* and Gurinder Chadha scored an unexpected success with *Bend it like Beckham*, about an Indian girl footballer.

In 2001 FilmFour went head-to-head with Hollywood and produced *Charlotte Gray*. It was an expensive flop which led to the company's collapse in July 2002 and left the British film industry in a state of uncertainty about its future – again!

For details on films about England, see Films in the Facts for the Visitor chapter.

Music

Pop & Rock Music Since the dawn of the swinging '60s, England has been firmly on the main stage in the world of pop and rock music. The first big exports were the Beatles, the Rolling Stones, the Who and the Kinks. They were followed in the glam years of the '70s by stardust-speckled heroes such as Marc Bolan and David Bowie – the latter is still an influential figure today.

Other bands and artists of the time included Roxy Music, Cream (featuring Eric Clapton), Genesis (initially fronted by Peter Gabriel and later by Phil Collins), Pink Floyd, Deep Purple and Led Zeppelin – all very different, but all globally renowned. Towards the end of this era, an uncategorisable four-piece called Queen emerged and went on to become one of Britain's most successful bands. Elton John is another '70s glam rocker made good; he can still be seen today – often playing at major events or royal funerals.

In the late '70s and into the '80s everything changed, as self-indulgent dinosaur bands were left floundering in the wake of punk music. It was energetic, anarchic ('here's three chords, now go form a band') and frequently tuneless, but punk was great fun and undeniably returned pop to grassroots level – at least for a while. The kings of punk were the Sex Pistols, although they only produced one album and a clutch of (mostly banned) singles. More prolific were the Clash, the Damned, the Buzzcocks, the Stranglers and the UK Subs (the latter are still touring today).

Then punk begat 'New Wave' (ie, everything else that was a bit punky), with leading exponents including the Jam and Elvis Costello, and this crossed over with the brief ska revival of the 1980s led by the Specials and tapped into by bands such as the Beat (known overseas as the English Beat) and the nutty boys of Madness. Meanwhile, a punk-and-reggae-influenced trio called the Police – fronted by bassist Sting – became one of the biggest names of the decade.

Around this time, heavy metal enjoyed an upsurge, with bands such as Black Sabbath (featuring the once-again-famous Ozzy Osbourne) and Judas Priest exporting soulful melodies and intriguing interpretations of established religion to concert halls worldwide.

The turbulent, ever-changing music scene of the '80s also saw the 'New Romantics' such as Spandau Ballet, Duran Duran, Human League and Culture Club – all frills and fringes, and a definite swing of pop's pendulum away from the rather untidy punks. Other big names of that decade included Wham! (a two-piece boy band headed by a bright young fellow called George Michael), Joy Division (who evolved into New Order), Dire Straits, UB40 and the painfully morose but curiously engaging The Smiths – once again, all very different, but all quintessentially English, and all with worldwide followings.

The '90s saw the renaissance of the indie band with the likes of Blur, Elastica, Suede, Supergrass, Ocean Colour Scene, the Verve, Pulp, Radiohead and, above all, Oasis. Heralded as the Britpop revolution, these bands reclaimed and revived the flagging guitar-based format by giving it energy and stadium appeal, and were promptly followed by a host of soundalikes. The city of Manchester was a particular hotbed, and more details are given in 'The Madchester Sound' boxed text in the Northwest England chapter. It is largely thanks to the indie bands that the guitar sound remains such a major feature of rock music, although recent exponents such as Coldplay, Starsailor and Elbow tend towards the more introspective, soulful side of the genre.

While the indie scene was being revived, dance music had exploded on the scene since the late '80s. The arrival of house music coincided with the increasing popularity of illegal 'rave' parties and sparked the birth of a whole new club culture, often associated with use of Ecstasy. The most mainstream branch stuck mainly to the beats of house, trance and techno, and has become increasingly big business in recent years, elevating DJs such as Paul Oakenfold, Carl Cox and Pete Tong to rock-star status and establishing as brand names the so-called 'superclubs' such as Gatecrasher and the Ministry of Sound. The sound of 2002 was hard house, a pounding hybrid of house and techno, but there was also a backlash towards chill-out music, popularised by the bands Groove Armada and Zero 7.

Outside the clubs, the dance scene has a reputation for more experimental and innovative music represented by artists such as Massive Attack, Leftfield, Underworld, Faithless, Fila Brazillia, the Chemical Brothers and the unavoidable Fatboy Slim.

Black music is also an important feature of the contemporary scene, comprising much of the urban 'underground'. British hip-hop remains far more low-key than its US counterpart, but artists such as Mark B & Blade, Ty and Roots Manuva have achieved national recognition. Drum'n'bass, or jungle, also has a large following; key names here are LTJ Bukem, Roni Size, Moving Shadow records and the scene's godfather, Goldie. But the surprise commercial success of the past few years, despite its reputation for violence, has been London-based UK garage; leading artists include So Solid Crew and (with a softer mainstream reputation) Craig David.

Away from the underground scene, mainstream pop music has been dominated since the late 1990s by the legacy of the now-defunct Spice Girls and Take That. It's a telling indication of the present climate that England's current biggest export is ex–Take That crooner and Sinatra wannabe Robbie Williams. More promisingly, solo songstress Dido is the latest English artist to follow in the footsteps of Dusty Springfield and achieve success with an adult audience – her debut album hogged the number 1 slot for more than 50 weeks in 2000/1.

Through 2001 and 2002, the latest step in the progress of pop is the success of TV shows such as Fame Academy, where hopefuls are discovered, briefly groomed and then, with little apparent effort, launched to instant stardom. Getting a number one hit has always been about marketing as much as music, but today you might think the charts are full of nothing but manufactured cover bands. If you scratch beneath the surface, though, you'll undoubtedly discover that real talent runs deep though the English music scene.

Classical Music & Opera The country that gave the world the Beatles, the Sex Pistols and Oasis is also fond of classical music, with 10 symphony orchestras, dozens of amateur orchestras, an active National Association of Youth Orchestras and concert halls in most major towns. In addition, from mid-July to mid-September each year The Royal Albert Hall in London hosts The Proms, one of the world's greatest music festivals.

Such enthusiasm is all the more remarkable given England's limited achievements in classical music, especially compared with Austria, Germany and Italy. The only signifi-

cant English composer before the 20th century was Henry Purcell (1659–95). Since then, there have been only a handful: Edward Elgar, famous for his *Enigma Variations*; Gustav Holtz who wrote *The Planets*; Vaughan Williams whose *London Symphony* ends with chimes from Big Ben; and Benjamin Britten, best known for his operas *Peter Grimes* and *Turn of the Screw*. More recently, English composers Sir Michael Tippett and Peter Maxwell Davies have found international fame.

Spurred on by the late-19th-century success of Gilbert and Sullivan's light operas such as *HMS Pinafore* and *The Mikado*, English National Opera has a full-time repertory company and venue in London. The Royal Opera House in Covent Garden has recently enjoyed millions of pounds worth of renovation, while Glyndebourne in Sussex is one of the world's best-known opera venues.

Visual Arts

In the 18th century, William Hogarth emancipated English art from European influences with a series of paintings and engravings satirising social abuses. The most celebrated of these is *A Rake's Progress*, displayed today at Sir John Soane's Museum, London. Hogarth helped form the Royal Academy of Arts (RA) in 1768, along with Sir Joshua Reynolds, who became its first president. The RA is still at the forefront of the British artistic establishment.

At this time, portraiture was the mainstay of art in England. Reynolds painted historical portraits in the 'grand style' such as *Lady Anstruther* (now in Tate Britain, London) and his rival, Thomas Gainsborough, informal works with sitters at ease in a landscape, such as *Mr and Mrs Andrews* (National Portrait Gallery). For more details on the rivals Reynolds and Gainsborough see the 'Celebrity Duel' boxed text in the Eastern England chapter.

Two other important artists of the 18th century were Joseph Wright, whose interest in light and science inspired *An Experiment on a Bird in the Air Pump* (1768, National Gallery), and George Stubbs, whose passion for animal anatomy, particularly horses, is evident in many works at Tate Britain.

The tradition of landscape painting started by Gainsborough was continued by John Constable who painted many scenes in Suffolk (still known as 'Constable Country' today). His most famous work is *The Haywain* (1821, National Gallery), but most are found at London's Victoria & Albert Museum.

Constable's contemporary Romantics JMW Turner and William Blake were very different. Blake used personal symbolism to express a mystical philosophy in drawings, prints and poetry, and Turner, happy using either oil or watercolour, increasingly subordinated picture details to the effects of light and colour. By the 1840s, with paintings such as *Norham Castle, Sunrise*, Turner's compositions became almost entirely abstract and were widely vilified. Both artists have rooms dedicated to their work at Tate Britain, and the Turner collection at Petworth House in West Sussex is exquisite.

In 1848 Sir John Everett Millais, William Holman Hunt and Dante Gabriel Rossetti formed the Pre-Raphaelite Brotherhood, which combined the simplicity of early Italian art with a closely observed realism. The drowned body of *Ophelia* by Millais is an excellent example of their style and can be seen in the Tate Britain Gallery in London, but one of the best collections of Pre-Raphaelite art is in the Birmingham Museum and Art Gallery.

A good friend of the Pre-Raphaelites was William Morris; he saw late-19th-century furniture and interior design as increasingly vulgar, and with Rossetti and Edward Burne-Jones founded the Arts and Crafts movement, which encouraged the revival of a decorative approach to features such as wallpaper, tapestries and windows. Many of his designs are still used today. (For more details on this movement see the Birmingham section in the Midlands chapter.)

In the 20th century, the place of English art in the international arena was ensured by Henry Moore's and Barbara Hepworth's monumental sculptures, Francis Bacon's contorted, almost surreal, paintings, and David Hockney's stylish, highly representational paintings of swimming pools and dachshunds. Much of Hockney's work can be seen at Salt's Mill Gallery in Bradford (his hometown, and described in the Yorkshire chapter), while Hepworth is forever associated with St Ives in Cornwall – for more details see the Devon & Cornwall chapter.

Paul Nash, an official war artist in WWI and WWII, and Graham Sutherland, his counterpart in WWII, followed in the Romantic and visionary tradition of Blake and Turner. Nash introduced surrealism to English painting and Ben Nicholson – who was married to Barbara Hepworth – introduced Cubism.

Howard Hodgkin and Patrick Heron then ushered in the English version of American abstract expressionism. At the same time, Manchester rent collector LS Lowry was painting his much-loved stick figures pouring out of smoky factories; a good place to see his work is in The Lowry Centre, Manchester.

In 1956 a young artist called Richard Hamilton crated a photomontage *Just what is it that makes today's homes so different, so appealing?* as a poster for the Whitechapel Art Gallery in London. It launched the pop art movement in England, which culminated with record covers such as Peter Blake's psychedelic *Sergeant Pepper's Lonely Hearts Club Band* for the Beatles.

In the 1970s and '80s, conceptual and land artists, such as Richard Long, competed for attention with performance artists, such as Gilbert and George, and the 1990s art scene was dominated by the 'Brit pack', a group of artists championed by advertising tycoon Charles Saatchi. They include Rachel Whiteread, who casts commonplace objects in resin; Damien Hirst, whose use of animals, both alive and dead, caused outrage; and Tracey Emin, short-listed for the 1999 Turner Prize with *My Bed*, a sluttish combination of mattress, soiled sheets and 'lifestyle objects'.

At the turn of the century there was an explosion in experimental film and video art seen in the work of Sam Taylor-Wood and the Wilson Twins. In 2001 Martin Creed won the Turner Prize for his installation *The Lights Going On and Off*.

Artists of today working in more traditional media include Antony Gormley, whose *Angel Of The North*, England's largest sculpture, stands beside the busy A1 highway at Gateshead near Newcastle; Mark Wallinger, whose life-size sculpture of Christ adorned Trafalgar Square's Fourth Plinth in 1999; and Julian Opie, whose work has become fashionable again – see his *Best of Blur* (2000) album cover. Young artists to watch are Fiona Banner and Keith Tyson, both short-listed for the 2002 Turner Prize.

Architecture

One of the many good reasons to visit Britain is to savour its extensive and rich architectural heritage, which stretches back more than 5000 years. Some of the earliest constructions are the Neolithic and Bronze Age communal burial mounds, or 'barrows', dating from around 3500 BC, found especially in the chalky regions of Dorset and Wiltshire in southwest England. Here you'll also find Europe's most famous historical landmark, the mysterious stone circle of Stonehenge, which dates from the same era.

Remains from Celtic and Iron Age times still survive in various parts of England. Many of these are hilltop forts or fortified villages – Maiden Castle in Dorset is one of the most impressive examples.

From around 2000 years ago, the Roman occupation of Britain left an impressive architectural legacy, including grand Fishbourne Palace in West Sussex – built around AD 75 – and several Roman baths such as the well-preserved example that gave the town of Bath its name.

When the Roman period ended around AD 400, the Saxon peoples arrived in Britain (for more details see the History section earlier in this chapter) and much of the architecture that survives from Saxon times, and the following 15 centuries, is religious. And it's not just cathedrals, minsters, abbeys and monasteries, although many are magnificent; over 12,000 parish churches in Britain have noted historical or architectural significance and are fascinating to wander around in, especially once you learn something about the various periods, styles and designs.

Having said that, although distinct architectural styles and periods in English architecture are identifiable, the categories were not always rigid – different styles often influenced each other and certain periods overlapped. Also, very few religious buildings have a uniform style; a window from one period may be cut into a wall from another and growing congregations or increased wealth often inspired extensions, towers or impressive spires – inevitably in the latest fashion, which may or may not match the style of the original church.

Some styles seen in churches also appear in castles, but while churches focused on decorative or imaginative elements, the design of castles was based largely around their military function. The benefits of living in a large utilitarian pile of stones, however, gradually vanished as times grew more peaceful and a boom in the construction of country houses

began in the 16th century. Today, one of the most distinctive features of Britain's countryside and culture is a wealth of these enormous and beautiful residences.

Alongside the stately homes, ordinary domestic architecture from the 16th and 17th centuries can also be seen in rural areas: thatched cottages or timber-beamed houses still characterise counties such as Kent, Cheshire and Gloucestershire.

Since the Industrial Revolution, though, architects have taken a different view and the guiding principle for new buildings has often been to spend as little money as possible. In the rebuilding that followed WWII, much construction has shown a lack of regard for the overall fabric of the cities, although in the last two decades, English architecture has redeemed itself and many big cities now have good numbers of contemporary buildings of which to be proud. Highlights include London's spiky MI6 building in Vauxhall and Manchester's theatrical Imperial War Museum North, opened in 2002.

Architectural Styles & Periods The following sections only skim the surface, or scratch the plasterwork, of this massive subject. However, it should be enough to guide you through the aisles and passageways of Britain's churches, castles and stately homes.

Anglo-Saxon Britain's first churches were built during the Anglo-Saxon period, from around AD 700 to 1050. They were generally small and solid with round arches and square towers, and were mostly built of wood – so few survive. Stone churches fared better and good examples are St Laurence in Bradford-on-Avon, Wiltshire; All Saints at Brixworth and All Saints at Earls Barton, both near Northampton.

Norman After 1066, the Normans built on a massive scale. Many parish churches were established or extended and England's great cathedrals of Durham, Norwich and Peterborough were constructed. These had the rounded arches and squat towers of their Saxon predecessors, but were much larger and bulkier with thicker walls.

Gothic This period spanned almost four centuries and is classified into three styles: Early English, Decorated and Perpendicular.

Early English (around 1150 to 1280) churches looked lighter and more delicate than the heavier Norman ones, with pointed arches, ribbed vaults and lancet windows (narrow, pointed windows used singly or in groups). Good examples include Salisbury Cathedral and Rievaulx Abbey in Yorkshire.

The Decorated style (1280 to 1380) was marked by ornate window tracery and other elaborate design elements. Examples include York Minster and the naves of Lichfield and Exeter Cathedrals.

The Perpendicular phase (1380 to 1550) was more ornate than anything seen before. Engineering developments meant arches could span further and windows could be much larger, so perpendicular churches are fantastically light and spacious. King's College Chapel in Cambridge and Bath Abbey's choir provide wonderful examples.

Renaissance In the early 16th century, church architecture came to a virtual standstill for a century, but this is when some of the finest Tudor and Jacobean country houses were built; Longleat in Wiltshire and Hatfield House in Hertfordshire are excellent examples.

The Renaissance style in Britain was capped by the influential architect Inigo Jones, in turn inspired by the principles of Italian architect Andrea Palladio. His formidable classical style is apparent in the Banqueting House and the Queen's House, Greenwich, both in London.

English Baroque Originating in Italy (like the Renaissance style), English Baroque was a late-17th- and early-18th-century phenomenon, characterised by sculptural, dramatic architecture using classical features such as columns, arches and pediments. The most influential Baroque architect was Sir Christopher Wren; his masterpiece was St Paul's Cathedral in London, but he was also responsible for 53 churches. His pupil Nicholas Hawksmoor and colleague Sir John Vanburgh collaborated on Castle Howard in Yorkshire, and Blenheim Palace in Oxfordshire – buildings that represent the height of English Baroque and which still draw gasps of wonder from visitors today.

The Classical Revival Lord Burlington was responsible for a return to simpler classical forms after the excesses of the Baroque. The design of his own house in London led the way, with strict adherence to rules of proportion and symmetry called Neo-Palladianism. Soon the accepted form for country houses was a central block with a columned portico and flanking wings; Holkham Hall in Norfolk is a fine example.

The same ideals were put to different use in a city context by the father-and-son team, John Wood the Elder and John Wood the Younger. Their masterpieces include the beautiful terraced crescents and squares of Bath.

The 19th Century In the early 19th Century, Sir John Soane and John Nash ushered in the Picturesque style, where unusual lighting effects from domes or skylights became fashionable. Soane's own house at Lincoln's Inn Fields in London was remodelled in this style; it has been a museum since 1813. John Nash's most famous commission was the fantastical Brighton Royal Pavilion, which introduced oriental elements to the seaside town and foreshadowed the Gothic Revival of the 1830s – London's Houses of Parliament by Augustus Pugin and Sir Charles Barry are a fine example of this style.

Arts & Crafts Movement As the 19th century came to a close, heavy-handed church 'restorations' (often a complete rebuilding) inspired the artist, designer and leader of the Arts and Crafts movement, William Morris, to found the Society for the Protection of Ancient Buildings in 1877. Morris' ideas, together with the writings of John Ruskin, led to an increased appreciation of craft skills in restorations and new buildings. (More details on this movement are given in the Birmingham section of The Midlands chapter.)

The 20th Century In the 1930s, the rise of the Nazis in Central Europe meant that many European architects fled to Britain and continued their work here. One of the most adventurous and fun émigré examples is the Penguin Pool at London Zoo by Berthold Lubetkin.

After WWII modern architecture in England moved into a purely functional phase with the need to build new housing quickly. The tough, concrete buildings in the brutalist style of the 1950s and '60s, such as the Royal National Theatre on London's South Bank by Sir Denys Lasdun, are still disliked by many today. However, balancing them was a more romantic approach to modern design such as St Catherine's College in Oxford, by Arne Jacobsen, and the Metropolitan Cathedral by Sir Frederick Gibberd, which looks like a space ship about to take off.

During the late 1970s and early '80s, architecture moved away from the bleak tower-block housing of the Modern Movement towards the more colourful, individual and surprising style of Postmodernism. In London, the greatest scope for this new architectural freedom is the long-running redevelopment of London's Docklands area – dominated by 500m-high, pyramid-topped Canary Wharf tower.

In contrast, architecture in the late 1980s and early '90s celebrated the potential of technology, usually with complex lightweight structural skeletons, such as the Lloyd's Building in London by Richard Rogers, with its brilliantly coloured service pipes on the outside, or Stansted Airport by Sir Norman Foster, a bold and bright exclamation point to any journey. Other big-name examples include Nicholas Grimshaw, whose Waterloo International train station at night resembles a glowing blue slug, and Terry Farrell, a postmodernist who's worked on several public projects, the most famous being the MI6 Building and Charing Cross train station in London, the International Centre for Life in Newcastle and The Deep in Hull.

The Millennium Years In the final years of the 20th century, and the first few of the 21st, diverse additions to London's cityscape include the new Tate Modern (a world-class gallery transformed from the old Bankside Power Station by Swiss architects Herzog & de Meuron) and several more astounding works by Richard Rogers and Norman Foster. (For more on these two colossi see 'The Norman & Richard Show' boxed text.)

Outside the capital, the Gateshead Millennium Bridge by Wilkinson Eyre opened in 2001 across the River Tyne near Newcastle; it is the world's first rotating bridge and looks like a winking eye when it lifts. A year later, Gateshead also saw the conversion of old flour mills, by the architectural firm Ellis Williams, into the Baltic Centre for Contemporary Art, firmly establishing South Tyneside as a significant artistic location.

New buildings and new designs continue to inspire, and sometimes appal, the English public. In 2002 Manchester's Imperial War Museum North by Daniel Libeskind was opened; the building represents three pieces of a globe (earth, air and water) shattered by war. Meanwhile, in southwest England, the Eden Project in Cornwall lets visitors into futuristic 'biomes' designed by Nicholas Grimshaw – a structure so dramatic that it quickly became a set for a James Bond film.

The Norman & Richard Show

Two men dominate modern English architecture: Sir Norman Foster and Lord Richard Rogers. They were partners in the 1960s and for the past 30 years have won many major architectural commissions around London and the southeast.

Foster favours clean designs with flowing lines. This is reflected in his sinuous and sensuous glass roof for the Great Court of the British Museum; try to visit on a sunny day to catch the crisscross of shadows. The same can be said for his Millennium Bridge between St Paul's and the Tate Modern, while Canary Wharf station for the Jubilee Line extension is almost organic in its flow of form.

In contrast, the work of Rogers is anything but sinuous. Rather, it is technical and intricate, and often looks like the work of a mad child. Perhaps Rogers' best-known work is the Millennium Dome, with spindly yellow towers and vast fields of curving white that always provoke a reaction. Coming soon from Rogers is a massive complex called Paddington Basin, near the train station of the same name. He is also working for Ken Livingstone, Mayor of London, on 20,000 new homes, for which his rumoured daily rate is £1,600 – half his normal tariff.

Meanwhile, Foster's new project for Mayor Ken is City Hall, opened in July 2002. From the outside it looks like a tilted glass and steel beehive; inside all the offices are glass too, so you can watch everyone at work, while at the top there's the spectacular Londoner's Lounge with panoramic views and a café. Looking to the future, Foster was one of the architects short-listed to design a building to replace the World Trade Center in New York.

SOCIETY & CONDUCT
Traditional Culture

It's difficult to generalise about a homogenous English culture – mainly because there isn't one! Not surprisingly, English culture contains characteristics from the cultures of Wales, Scotland and Ireland, and has been greatly influenced by peoples from all over the world who have immigrated here over the centuries.

Despite being hard to pin down, for many visitors a strong preconception is that the English are reserved, inhibited and stiflingly polite. While these characteristics may indeed apply in some parts of England (notably the south and southeast) and to people from the middle and upper classes, in general they simply don't. Anywhere in the country, if you visit a pub, a nightclub, a football match, a seaside resort, or go walking in the hills and parks, you'll soon come across other English characteristics – uninhibited, tolerant, exhibitionist, passionate, aggressive, sentimental, hospitable and friendly. It hits you like a breath of fresh air.

Having said all that, a major factor running through English culture and society, even in these egalitarian days, is class. People are often defined as either working class, middle class or upper class, and although the days of peasants docking their caps to the lord of the manor may be gone, some English folk still judge others according to their place of birth, their school, club, accent, family name or family wealth (and how long they've had it),

rather than according to their skills, intelligence and personality.

On a more positive note, another cultural trait that runs through English society is the obsession with hobbies and pastimes. We're not talking about obvious things such as football and cricket (although fanatical supporters number in their millions), but about birdwatchers, train spotters, bus spotters, model makers, vintage-car restorers, steam revivalists, home improvers, pigeon fanciers, royal watchers, antique hoarders, stamp collectors, coin collectors, teapot collectors, ramblers, anglers, caravanners, pet lovers, gardeners, pub-quiz fans, crossword fans, jigsaw fans… the list goes on, with many participants verging on the edge of complete obsession. It's great and Britain just wouldn't be the same without them.

Dos & Don'ts

Britain is a reasonably tolerant place, so it's hard to cause offence without meaning to. That said, it's worth being aware that most locals in large towns and cities would no sooner speak to a stranger in the street than fly to the moon. If you're obviously a tourist battling with directions, there's no problem – but try starting a general conversation at a bus stop and people will stare as if you're mad.

When you're in country areas (or places such as pubs and cafés) it's a different story; talking to strangers might well be a local pastime – but it's still wise to adopt a 'speak when you're spoken to' approach, rather than go blundering around trying to engage every charming native in joyful banter. And wherever you go, remember to take note of the surrounding atmosphere; the locals in quiet country pubs or urban cafés may take a dim view of loudmouthed outsiders – even if dominating the room with your voice is perfectly acceptable back home.

On top of this it's good to remember that differences of politics and religion exist in parts of Britain (as in many parts of the world). To this already potent brew, a dash of sport is sometimes added, notably in Liverpool where a sectarian divide runs across local football teams – Protestant Liverpool FC vs Catholic Everton FC.

Although the English may be tolerant, strong views can lie beneath the surface, and perhaps not all that far below. Whenever subjects such as religion and politics come up, as

---

Queuing for England

The English are notoriously addicted to queues ('lines' for Americans) – for buses, train tickets, or to pay at a supermarket counter. The order is sacrosanct and woe betide an impatient foreigner who gets this wrong! Few things are more calculated to spark an outburst of affronted tutting – about as publicly cross as most English get – than 'pushing in' at a queue.

The same applies to escalators and moving walkways. If you want to stand still, stand on the right, so people can walk by you on the left. There's a definite convention here and people have been hung, drawn and quartered (well, at least heavily tutted at) for getting it wrong and blocking the path of folk in a hurry.

Going to the Dogs

The famous English love for animals extends especially to pets. As an outsider you'll notice that, although striking up conversation with strangers is unusual, many English are quite happy talking to another person's dog.

This special affection for dogs means these particular animals can get away with anything. On city streets, pet dogs on leads obstruct pedestrians and crap all over the parks and pavements. In the countryside, pet dogs chase sheep, disturb wildlife and – you've guessed it – crap all over the footpaths. Of course, we can't blame the dogs, it's the owners who are at fault, but these antisocial habits are tolerated to an incredible degree by most other people.

Such is the tolerance that most dog-owners are convinced that 'Keep Dogs on Lead' signs don't apply to *their* dogs and they often let them run around in blatant disregard for the rules. They think it especially charming when their dogs approach other people. If while out walking in a park or the countryside you're terrified by the unwanted attentions of a giant muddy hound, be prepared for the usual response from the owner – 'Don't worry, he's only being friendly'.

---

a visitor, it's probably a good time for you to practise your listening skills. The same goes for football.

Dress codes How you dress in the street is up to you; few people will bat an eyelid, however outlandish or straight your gear. If you're visiting churches and cathedrals, however, it's polite (but not obligatory) to dress with at least a touch of modesty. This doesn't mean monkish habits, but bare chests or bikini tops are a bit off. And men should remove their hats. If you go into mosques or temples you may be expected to take off your shoes and cover your arms, legs and/or head.

Some classy restaurants operate strict dress codes, which usually means a jacket and tie for men and no trainers for anyone. In clubs the dress code means whatever the bouncers choose and can vary from night to night.

Treatment of Animals

The English are widely believed to love their animals more than their children: the Royal Society for the Prevention of Cruelty to Animals was established before the National Society for the Prevention of Cruelty to Children and still rakes in more donations.

Recent years have seen high-profile lobbies against factory farming and the export of live animals, and most supermarkets stock free-range eggs and meat from animals who have been allowed to roam free.

Not surprisingly, fox-hunting, the ancient sport derided by Oscar Wilde as 'the unspeakable in pursuit of the inedible', is highly controversial (see the Ecology & Environment section for more details).

RELIGION

The Church of England (or Anglican Church), a Christian religion that became independent of Rome in the 16th century at the behest of Henry VIII (see the History section earlier in this chapter), is the largest, wealthiest and most influential in the land. It's an 'established' church (the official national church), with a close link to the state; the monarch, for example, is still head of the church and appoints archbishops and bishops. Traditionally, conservative (and predominantly Conservative – in fact, the Church of England has been called 'the Tory Party at prayer'), it's only since 1994 that women have been ordained as priests. The debate has now moved on to the rights and wrongs of gay clergy.

About 10% of English people consider themselves Roman Catholic and there are also sizable groups of Methodists, Baptists and other nonconformists. Generally, attendances are down in the mainstream churches, with about a million people attending Church of England Sunday services and falling. Evangelical and charismatic churches are the only ones attracting growing congregations.

There are well over a million Muslims in Britain, together with significant numbers of Sikhs and Hindus. Other faiths include Judaism and Buddhism. Nowadays, more English non-Christians visit their places of worship than do Christians.

Facts for the Visitor

HIGHLIGHTS

Planning a trip around England can be bewildering for the first-time visitor and it's no less straightforward if you live here. The country may be small, but it boasts an astounding collection of busy cities, historic towns and quaint villages, plus a seemingly endless list of impressive castles, cathedrals and stately homes. Add to this the attractions of national parks, beaches and bays, plus the wonderfully wild moors and mountains, and the feast of delights can make your head spin. This section, we hope, will help make deciding where to go more manageable, and more fun.

Historic Cities & Towns

London Any list must with this great city; an amazing collection of vast buildings and hidden remains from every century since the Bronze Age to satisfy even the most demanding history fans

Winchester (Southeast England) Ancient English capital, rich in history, with cathedral and college

Bath (Wessex) Stylish and lively, with superb Georgian crescents and famous Roman ruins

Oxford (Oxfordshire, Gloucestershire & the Cotswolds) Gorgeous university town with evocative architecture and 'dreaming spires'

Cambridge (Eastern England) Famous university town with stunning architectural heritage

Richmond (Yorkshire) Historic outpost, with cobbled streets and marketplace, and ruined castle

CHAPTER BREAKDOWN

Whitby (Yorkshire) Atmospheric port on magnificent coastline, with Captain Cook and Dracula connections

York (Yorkshire) Proud, ancient city with medieval walls, spectacular minster and fine museums

Liverpool (Northwest England) Former great port with superb legacy of Victorian architecture

Cathedrals, Churches & Abbeys

St Paul's Cathedral (London) Masterpiece and icon of the city, with stunning views from the dome

Westminster Abbey (London) Steeped in history – the place of coronation for 1000 years, full of tombs of Britain's great and good

Canterbury Cathedral (Southeast England) Anglican mother-church, full of ghosts from the past

Salisbury Cathedral (Southeast England) Stylistic coherence and soaring elegance; a vision of beauty

Winchester Cathedral (Southeast England) The church of England's ancient capital; a range of styles in harmony

Wells Cathedral (Wessex) Medieval excellence, with rich and brilliant sculptures

King's College Chapel (Eastern England) Ecclesiastical masterpiece with brilliant acoustics

Lincoln Cathedral (Eastern England) England's Cinderella cathedral – surpassed in setting only by Durham

Rievaulx Abbey (Yorkshire) Romantic ruins in an idyllic rural valley setting

York Minster (Yorkshire) England's greatest medieval cathedral, with superb stained glass

Durham Cathedral (Northeast England) Ancient in origin, overwhelming in scale – truly spectacular

Castles

Tower of London (London) Centuries-old fortress and palace, with foundations from Roman times, and more recent walls from 1078; today home of the crown jewels

Dover Castle (Southeast England) Massive fortress from Norman period, encompassing Roman lighthouse, Saxon church and WWII tunnels

Leeds Castle (Southeast England) Extraordinarily beautiful castle in the middle of a lake (and nowhere near Leeds, Yorkshire)

Windsor Castle (Southeast England) Magnificent royal residence with restored state rooms and beautiful chapel

Belvoir Castle (The Midlands) A marvellous fantasy with a fine art collection and delightful grounds full of sculptures and peacocks

Warwick Castle (The Midlands) One of England's largest castles, with a stack of history attached

Alnwick Castle (Northeast England) Dramatic castle, now a house, still oozing medieval character

Historic Houses

Hampton Court Palace (London) Royal residence in 16th, 17th and 18th centuries, with beautiful gardens and famous maze

Brighton Royal Pavilion (Southeast England) Indian-Chinese-Gothic melange built in 1815 for a prince's exotic fantasy; still outrageous today

Blenheim Palace (Oxfordshire, Gloucestershire & the Cotswolds) The mother of all stately homes; huge 18th-century house, set in superb parkland

Haddon Hall (The Midlands) One of Britain's best medieval manor houses

Castle Howard (Yorkshire) The Blenheim of the north – same era, same architects and superb landscaped gardens

Prehistoric Remains

Avebury Stone Circle (Wessex) Big, imposing and very old; nearby Silbury Hill adds archaic aura

The Ridgeway (Wessex) Ancient track across big-sky chalklands; a walk or ride though history

Stonehenge (Wessex) Iconic symbol of ancient England; a circle of giant stone arches and pillars, still overwhelming after 5000 years

Castlerigg Stone Circle (Cumbria) Stone circle with a beautiful Lake District location

Roman Sites

Fishbourne Palace (Southeast England) England's only Roman stately home, with beautiful mosaics

Bath (Wessex) Hot water bath and sauna rooms, now topped by Georgian elegance

Chedworth Villa (Oxfordshire, Gloucestershire & the Cotswolds) Grand rural villa with well-preserved mosaic floors

Fosse Way (Oxfordshire, Gloucestershire & the Cotswolds and the Midlands) Highroad of the Empire, still followed by modern roads in parts

Hadrian's Wall (Northeast England) Monumental remains separating civilisation from the barbarians (or vice versa)

Industrial Heritage

National Motor Museum (Southeast England) The car park of history, with 250 vehicles on show, spanning the era of motor transport

Bristol Industrial Museum (Wessex) Impressive dockside setting and gems from the age of steam railways and ships, including SS *Great Britain*

Cornwall Tin Mines (Devon & Cornwall) Former mines are dotted across the countryside; the excellent Industrial Discovery Centre at Camborne helps relive the mining heyday

Ironbridge Gorge (The Marches) Ten museums in the cradle of the Industrial Revolution

Kelham Island (Yorkshire) Large and lively museum in the heart of 'Steel City', with working engines, grease and steam

Magna (Yorkshire) Former steelworks turned science adventure park; makes learning great fun

National Railway Museum (Yorkshire) Temple to the golden age of rail

Beamish Open Air Museum (Northeast England) Alive and kicking display of pre- and post-industrial working life

Museums & Galleries

British Museum (London) Superb, comprehensive coverage; archaeology to high technology

National Gallery (London) Stunning collection of five centuries of European art

National Portrait Gallery (London) Face-to-face intro to anyone who's ever been anyone in Britain – royals, aristocrats, film stars, the lot

Tate Britain (London) Stunning collection of key British artists

Tate Modern (London) Quite simply one of the world's most impressive art galleries

Victoria & Albert Museum (London) England's attic; a vast eclectic array of costumes, photography, stained glass, furniture, artistic artefacts and much, much more

HMS Victory & HMS Mary Rose, Portsmouth (Southeast England) Flagships of Admiral Horatio Nelson and King Henry VIII

Tate St Ives (Devon & Cornwall) Superb collection of St Ives School and other modern British artists in dramatic cliff-top venue

Baltic – The Centre for Contemporary Art (Northeast England) Vast cutting-edge art space in a converted riverside grainhouse

Nightlife & Entertainment

London Nightlife capital, with pulsating live music and cutting-edge club scenes

Brighton (Southeast England) 'London-on-the-Sea'; undoubtedly hip and vibrant resort town

Bristol (Wessex) A hotbed of musical innovation, with loads of clubs and venues

Birmingham (The Midlands) Big-name clubs, ground-breaking arts venues, comedy, theatre and classical music

Nottingham (The Midlands) Top clubs, old-world pubs, plus buzzing venues and theatre

Leeds (Yorkshire) Sleek bar and club land, with lots of late-night choice

Manchester (Northwest England) Vibrant northern capital, renowned for trendsetting music scene and unstoppable nightlife

Liverpool (Northeast England) Famous for Beatles connections, birthplace of several bands; with rugged cultural identity and first-rate club scene

Newcastle (Northeast England) Charismatic, to-the-hilt partying to please a range of tastes

Natural Beauty

South Downs (Southeast England) Rolling grassy hills with clear views and spectacular chalk cliffs

North Devon (Devon & Cornwall) Beautiful Exmoor overlooking the sea, edged by cliffs

South Cornwall (Devon & Cornwall) A coastline of cliffs and beautiful bays, dotted with historical relics and picturesque villages

North York Moors (Yorkshire) Heather-clad hills, quiet farmland valleys, and a dramatic coastline with fishing villages, cliffs and bird reserves

The Lake District (Cumbria) England's highest mountain peaks, plus scenic valleys and, of course, picturesque lakes

Farne Islands (Northeast England) Tiny rocky islets, with vast colonies of nesting seabirds

SUGGESTED ITINERARIES

With so many places to visit in England, you'll always be spoilt for choice. But what a choice! However long you stay, there will always be something extra you want to see. In reality, where you go will depend on your form of transport, the time at your disposal and the money in your pocket, but whatever your means, the following suggestions will be a good starting point.

With just one week, if you want to see England's major highlights – and who doesn't? – spend a few days in London, with quick trips out to Bath and Oxford (maybe including a glimpse of Wells or the Cotswolds as well).

If you've got two weeks, enjoy more time in London, then do a circuit tying in Salisbury, Stonehenge and Bath, through the Cotswolds to Oxford, then up to York, maybe with a side trip to Cambridge on your way back to London.

With a month, a pack-it-in itinerary might be as follows: London, Salisbury, Stonehenge, Avebury, Bath, Wells and maybe a loop down to Devon. Then to Oxford through the Cotswolds, with time to sample scenic villages and Stratford-upon-Avon, then to Chester and Liverpool, followed by a jaunt through the Lake District, and up to Hadrian's Wall. Then it's time to head south, through Northumberland and north Yorkshire to York, maybe with a loop out to Whitby, then down to Cambridge and East Anglia before returning to London once again.

Of course, if you don't want to rush, just leave out some of the places on the itinerary above – or take two months to do it. With two months you could expand it even further to include Cornwall, the Isles of Scilly, the Channel Isles, the Peak District or the quiet countryside of the Marches.

PLANNING
When to Go

Anyone who spends some time in England will soon sympathise with the locals' obsession with the weather. Generally, conditions are mild and the rainfall not spectacular but at any time of year the weather can be *changeable* (see the Climate section in the Facts about England chapter). Even in summer you can go for days without sun, and showers (or worse) should be expected. Conversely, there may be fantastic winter days, and some of the best weather can happen in spring or autumn. Be prepared for anything and you won't get a surprise!

Overall, the least hospitable time for visitors is from November to February – it's cold in the south, and very cold in the north, and the days are short. March and October are marginal, but if you hit a warm spell it can be a good opportunity to avoid crowds. Note, though, that in country areas, many hotels, B&Bs and tourist attractions close from October to Easter, and Tourist Information Centres (TICs) have limited opening times.

From April to September is undoubtedly the best period. It's also when most people visit. July and August are busiest, and crowds in coastal towns, national parks, and especially towns such as Oxford, Bath and York can sometimes be overbearing.

Having said all that, London is an exception. It's busy all the time, but there's such a lot to see that the weather is immaterial, so any time is good. Besides, you're almost as likely to have a damp miserable day in June as you are in January.

Maps
The best introductory map is *Britain* (covering England, Wales and Scotland), published by the British Tourist Authority (BTA) and found in BTA offices globally, or from TICs around England. The TICs also usually have regional maps covering their area.

If you're travelling by car (or even if you're not) a road atlas is very handy. The main publishers are Ordnance Survey (OS) and the Automobile Association (AA). Atlases come in a range of sizes and scales – pick the one best suited to your purpose (and eyesight). If you plan to go off main roads, you'll need a scale of about 1:200,000 (or 3 miles to 1 inch). Most cost £7 to £10, and are updated annually, which means old editions are sold off cheaply every January – look out for bargains at garages and motorway service stations.

For more detail, OS also produces maps at a scale of 1:50,000 (called *Landrangers*) which are ideal for walking and cycling. OS *Explorer* maps (1:25,000) are more detailed and even better for walking in lowland areas,

but can sometimes be hard to read in complex mountain landscapes. Your best choice here is the excellent series of specialist walking maps produced by Harvey Maps, covering mountain areas, national parks and so on.

What to Bring
Since anything you think of can be bought in England's towns and cities, it's best to pack light and pick up extras as you go.

Baggage A suitcase is fine for keeping your stuff tidy, but harder to carry through towns (so may mean more frequent use of taxis). A backpack is more convenient – and especially handy if you plan to do some hiking. A travel pack (combined backpack and shoulder bag) is the most popular baggage item. Most have shoulder straps that are comfortable even for long hikes, which zip away when not needed.

In addition to your main bag, a smaller day-pack is very useful for strolling round towns or short walks in the countryside.

Equipment For budget travellers, a tent is not essential, but will definitely save you money on accommodation in country areas. If you plan to do some hiking, a tent is handy, but again not essential, as most walking areas and trails are well served by hostels and B&Bs. A sleeping bag is required for basic hostels and camping barns. (See Accommodation later in this chapter for more details).

Whatever your budget, wet weather gear is a must – a coat or umbrella if you're doing cities, and full-on jacket and overtrousers if you're walking in the hills. And because England is such a land of contrasts, don't forget sunglasses either, plus a tube of sun block. Basic toiletries are easily purchased, even in the smallest village store.

RESPONSIBLE TOURISM
England is a crowded place even before the peak tourist season brings in more millions. Traffic congestion on roads in popular cities, coastal areas and national parks, especially in summer, is a major problem, so visitors will do residents – as well as themselves – a favour if they swap driving for public transport.

When walking in the countryside, remember that almost all land is privately owned. In mountain and moorland areas, you can often (but not always) walk where you like but in lower areas you must stick to legal footpaths and other 'rights of way'. (More details are given in the Walking section of the Activities chapter.) Dogs should always be kept under control and should not be allowed to chase sheep or wild birds.

Off-road mountain bikers are not allowed on footpaths, but can ride on bridleways (originally intended for horses) and other designated tracks. Even where it's legal, bikers should go with care, especially on downhill breaking, as ruts caused by skidding are eroded into canyons after rain.

TOURIST OFFICES

The **British Tourist Authority** (BTA; ☎ 020-8846 9000; w www.visitbritain.com; Thames Tower, Hammersmith, London W6 9EL) stocks masses of free information. Contact this office by phone or mail to get what you need.

Also in London, the **Britain Travel Centre** (no phone, walk in only; 1 Lower Regent St) is a good starting point for research.

Local Tourist Offices

Every English city and town has a TIC, usually piled high with free leaflets, and books and maps for sale, covering places to go and things to see in the local area. Most TICs have incredibly friendly staff, and they can also help with booking accommodation. Some TICs are run by national parks (these are called Visitor Centres, or similar) and often have small exhibitions about the area.

Most TICs open from 9am to 5pm Monday to Friday, and in popular tourist areas they also open on weekends, especially in summer. In honeypots such as Stratford and Bath, they open daily year round. Smaller TICs close from October to March.

Tourist Offices Abroad

The **BTA** has over 40 offices around the world, and you should contact your nearest office before you leave home – some discount travel cards are only available if you book before arrival. Travellers with special needs (disability, diet etc) should also contact their nearest BTA office. The main ones are listed here (others are on the BTA website).

Australia (☎ 02-9021 4400, fax 9021 4499, w www.visitbritain.com/au) Level 2, 15 Blue St, North Sydney, NSW 2060

Canada (☎ 905-405 1720, fax 405 1835, w www.visitbritain.com/ca) 5915 Airport Rd, Suite 120, Mississauga, Ontario L4V 1T1

France (☎ 01 44 51 56 20, fax 01 44 51 56 21, w www.amb-grandebretagne.fr) Maison de la Grande Bretagne, 19 rue des Mathurins, 75009 Paris – entrance in les rues Tronchet et Auber

Germany (☎ 01801-46 86 42, fax 069-9711 2444, w www.visitbritain.com/de) Westend-strasse 16–22, 60325 Frankfurt

Ireland (☎ 01-670 8000, fax 670 8244, w www.visitbritain.com/ie) 18–19 College Green, Dublin 2

Netherlands (☎ 020-689 0002, fax 689 0003, w www.visitbritain.com/nl) Stadhouderskade 2, 1054 ES Amsterdam

New Zealand (☎ 09-303 1446, fax 377 6965, w www.visitbritain.com/nz) 17th floor, Fay Richwhite Building, 151 Queen St, Auckland 1

USA (brochures & information ☎ 800 462 2748, 212-986 2200, fax 986 1188, w www.travel britain.org) Suite 701, 551 Fifth Ave, New York, NY 10176

VISAS & DOCUMENTS

Unlike many other European countries, the laws in England do not require people to carry identification. Nevertheless, it's usually a good idea to carry some ID.

Passport

Your most important travel document is a passport, which should remain valid for at least three months after your trip. Citizens of European countries might not need a passport to travel to England. A national identity card can be sufficient. Check with your travel agent or nearest British embassy. (Throughout this section 'embassy' also covers high commission or consulate.)

Visas

Citizens of Australia, Canada, New Zealand, South Africa and the USA are given 'leave to enter' England at their point of arrival for up to six months, but are prohibited from working. If you're a European Economic Area (EEA) national, you don't need a visa, and may live and work in England freely.

Visa regulations are always subject to change, so it's vital to check with your local British embassy before leaving home. This especially applies to Australians travelling to England, particularly those planning to study or use a Working Holiday Entry Certificate.

English immigration authorities are tough; when you enter, you may need to prove that you have funds to support yourself (complete bank statements for the last three months) and have a letter from the people you are visiting that mentions the dates of your stay (if appropriate). Having a return ticket helps. For more information check **w** www.ukvisas.gov.uk.

Visa Extensions Tourist visas can only be extended in clear emergencies (eg, an accident). Otherwise you will have to leave England (perhaps going to Ireland or France) and apply for a fresh one, although this tactic will arouse suspicion after the second or third go. To extend (or attempt to extend) your stay, contact the **Home Office Immigration & Nationality Directorate** *(☎ 0870 6067766;* **w** *www.ind.homeoffice.gov.uk; Lunar House, 40 Wellesley Rd, Croydon CR9 2BY; open 10am-4.45pm Mon-Thur, 9am-4.30pm Fri)* before your existing visa expires.

Student Visas EEA nationals can enter England to study without any formalities. Otherwise, you must be enrolled in a course of at least 15 hours per week (Monday to Friday) of daytime study at a single educational institution. Consult the British embassy in your own country for details. You may work for 20 hours per week with a student visa.

Work Permits EEA nationals don't need a permit to work in England, but everyone else does. If this is the main purpose of your visit, you must be sponsored by an English company.

If you're aged 17 to 27 and a citizen of a Commonwealth country, you may apply for a Working Holiday Entry Certificate (WHEC), which allows up to two years in the UK and work that is 'incidental' to a holiday. You're not allowed to engage in business, pursue a career (evidently serving in bars is not considered a career pursuit) or provide services as a professional athlete or entertainer. Commonwealth, and some other, nationals may also arrange au pair placements.

You must apply to the nearest British embassy; WHECs are *not* granted on arrival. Also, you can't switch from a normal visa to a WHEC, and the two-year period keeps running even if you go abroad from the UK. Applicants may not have children aged over five years, and must have sufficient funds to maintain themselves and cover a return journey.

A Certificate of Entitlement to the Right of Abode, eligible to Commonwealth citizens with a UK-born parent, allows you to live and work in England free of immigration control.

If you're a Commonwealth citizen with a grandparent born in the UK, or if the grandparent was born before 31 March 1922 in what is now the Republic of Ireland, you may qualify for a UK Ancestry Employment Certificate, which means you can work full time for up to four years in the UK.

Full-time students from the USA over 18 years old can get a six-month work permit; it costs US$200. The **British Universities North America Club** *(BUNAC; ☎ 020-7251 3472;* **w** *www.bunac.org; 16 Bowling Green Lane, London EC1R 0QH)* can also help organise permits and employment.

If you have any queries once you're in England, contact the Home Office's Immigration & Nationality Department (see the earlier Visa Extensions section).

Travel Insurance

Make sure you take out insurance that covers medical expenses, luggage and ticket theft or loss, and travel cancellation or delays. There are many policies available, but those handled by STA Travel and other student travel organisations are usually good value. Some policies offer lower and higher medical expense options; go for as much as you can afford – even if you are eligible for free treatment (see the Health section later in this chapter). It is a good idea to ensure you are covered for any sports you might do during your stay and, no matter what policy you get, always read the small print carefully.

Driving Licence & Permits

EEA driving licences are legal for 12 months from the date you last entered the UK (other licence holders should check with their embassy); you can then apply for a British licence at post offices. The International Driving Permit (IDP) is not usually needed in England.

Travel Discounts

If you're travelling on a budget, membership of the Youth Hostel Association (YHA) or Hostelling International (HI) is a must. There are hundreds of YHA hostels in England, and members are also eligible for all sorts of discounts. See the Accommodation section later for more information.

The International Student Identity Card (ISIC) is a photo-ID that costs £5 in the UK and provides cheap or free admission to museums and sights, inexpensive meals in some restaurants, and discounts on some transport.

An International Youth Travel Card (IYTC) issued by the **International Student Travel Confederation** *(ISTC; w www.istc.org)*, or a **Euro<26 Card** *(w www.euro26.org)* gives similar discounts for around the same fee as the ISIC, and anyone aged under 26 is eligible. All these cards are issued by student unions, hostelling organisations and student travel agencies.

Many attractions reduce admission costs for people aged over 60 or 65 (sometimes 55 for women), and discount cards for the over 60s are available for rail and bus travel. See the Bus Passes & Discounts and Railcards sections in the Getting Around chapter.

Photocopies

Photocopy all important documents (passport data page and visa page, credit cards, travel insurance policy, air/bus/train tickets, driving licence etc) before you travel. Leave one copy with someone at home and keep another with you, separate from the originals.

You can also store details of your travel documents in Lonely Planet's free online password-protected **Travel Vault** *(w www .ekno.lonelyplanet.com)* accessible online anywhere in the world.

EMBASSIES & CONSULATES
British Embassies & High Commissions Abroad

For details of British missions overseas, see the website of the **Foreign & Commonwealth Office** *(w www.fco.gov.uk)*.

Australia
High Commission: (☎ 02-6270 6666, w www .uk.emb.gov.au) Commonwealth Ave, Yarralumla, Canberra, ACT 2600

Canada
High Commission: (☎ 613-237 1530, w www .britainincanada.org) 80 Elgin St, Ottawa, Ontario K1P 5K7

France
Embassy: (☎ 01 44 51 31 00, w www.amb-gran debretagne.fr) 35 rue du Faubourg Saint Honoré, 750383 Paris Cedex 8

Germany
Embassy: (☎ 030-204 570, w www.britischebot schaft.de) Wilhelmstrasse 70, 10117 Berlin

Ireland
Embassy: (☎ 01-205 3822, w www.britishem bassy.ie) 29 Merrion Rd, Ballsbridge, Dublin 4

Netherlands
Embassy: (☎ 070-427 0427, w www.britain.nl) Lange Voorhout 10, 2514 ED The Hague

New Zealand
High Commission: (☎ 04-472 6049, w www .britain .org.nz) 44 Hill St, Wellington 1

USA
Embassy: (☎ 202-588 6500, w www.britainusa .com/consular/embassy) 3100 Massachusetts Ave, NW, Washington, DC 20008

Embassies & Consulates in England

Your own embassy won't be much help in emergencies if the trouble is remotely your own fault. Even as a foreigner, you are bound by the laws of England, and you won't get much sympathy if you end up in jail after committing a crime locally, even if such actions are legal in your own country.

In genuine emergencies you might get some assistance, but only if other channels have been exhausted. If you have all your money and documents stolen, your embassy might assist with getting a new passport, but a loan for onward travel is out of the question.

Some foreign missions in London include:

Australia
High Commission: (☎ 020-7379 4334, w www .australia.org.uk) Australia House, Strand WC2 4LA

Canada
High Commission: (☎ 020-7258 6600, w www .canada.org.uk) 1 Grosvenor Square W1X 0AB

France
Embassy: (☎ 020-7073 1000, w www.amba france.org.uk) 58 Knightsbridge SW1 7JT

Germany
Embassy: (☎ 020-7824 1300, w www.german -embassy.org.uk) 23 Belgrave Square SW1X 8PX

Ireland
Embassy: (☎ 020-7235 2171) 17 Grosvenor Place SW1

Netherlands
Embassy: (☎ 020-7590 3200; w www.netherlands -embassy.org.uk) 38 Hyde Park Gate SW7 5DP

New Zealand
High Commission: (☎ 020-7930 8422, w www .nzembassy.com/uk) New Zealand House, 80 Haymarket SW1 4TQ

USA
Embassy: (☎ 020-7499 9000, w www.usem bassy.org.uk) 24 Grosvenor Square W1A 1AE

CUSTOMS

Like other EU nations, the UK has a two-tier customs system: one for goods bought duty-free and one for goods bought in another EU country where taxes and duties have already been paid.

Duty Free

Duty-free sales to people going from one EU country to another were abolished in 1999. For goods bought at airports or on ferries *outside* the EU, you can import 200 cigarettes or 250g of tobacco, 2L of still wine plus 1L of spirits over 22% or another 2L of wine, 50g of perfume, 250cc of toilet water, and other duty-free goods (including beer) to the value of £136. You can still buy duty-free goods in the Channel Islands, as they are not in the EU.

Tax & Duty Paid

Although you can no longer bring in duty-free goods from another EU country, you *can* import cheaper goods from elsewhere if taxes have been paid on them (for personal use). If you want to take advantage of cheaper goods outside the UK, customs officials use the following guidelines to distinguish personal from commercial imports: 800 cigarettes, 200 cigars, 1kg of tobacco, 10L of spirits, 20L of fortified wine, 90L of wine (of which not more than 60L are sparkling) and 110L of beer – still enough to have one hell of a party.

Pets

To protect its rabies-free status, England's draconian pet policies usually require incoming animals to be quarantined for six months. The rules thawed slightly in 2000, when the Pets Travel Scheme allowed dogs and cats from certain countries (mainly European ones) to enter. Pets from farther afield may qualify if they journey along an approved route. Information is available at **w** www.defra.gov.uk.

Watch Out for the Euro

In January 2002, most countries in the European Union (of which Britain is a member) started using a single currency called the euro. In the UK, things are different: the pound remains the unit of currency as the government has decided not to adopt the euro, although it might in a year or two – when 'economic conditions are right' or when Brits come home from holiday abroad realising that the euro is not too scary, and that sentimental attachment to the pound might not be the soundest of arguments for staying out of the euro-zone. You're likely to see some acrimonious debate on the issue in the press during your visit.

MONEY

Currency

The English currency is the pound sterling (£), which is divided into 100 pence (p). Coins of 1p and 2p are copper; 5p, 10p, 20p and 50p coins are silver. The £1 coin is gold-coloured and the £2 coin is silver with a gold-coloured rim. Notes come in £5, £10, £20 and £50 denominations. The £50 notes can be difficult to change because fakes circulate; avoid them.

Exchange Rates

For current exchange rates check the website **w** www.oanda.com. Exchange rates at the time of going to print were:

country	unit		pounds
Australia	A$1	=	£0.35
Canada	C$1	=	£0.40
Euro zone	€1	=	£0.65
Japan	¥100	=	£0.52
New Zealand	NZ$1	=	£0.33
USA	US$1	=	£0.62

Exchanging Money

Changing your money is never a problem in large cities and places that see a lot of tourists, as banks, bureaux de change and travel agencies all tout for your business. Be careful using bureaus, however; they frequently levy outrageous commissions.

In smaller cities and towns you can change money at a bank, or at some post offices.

Exchange desks at international airports usually open for incoming flights, and charge less than most high-street banks (around 1.5% of the transaction value, with a £3 minimum).

Travellers Cheques Travellers cheques offer protection from theft, and can be bought in banks or travel agencies in your home country. Travellers cheques should ideally be in pounds, preferably issued by American Express (AmEx) or Thomas Cook, which are widely recognised, well represented and don't charge for cashing their own cheques.

It's important to note that travellers cheques are rarely accepted for purchases (a few large hotels may accept them, and then only in pounds), so you need to go to a bank or bureau and change them into cash.

Lost or Stolen Travellers Cheques Keep a record of travellers cheque numbers and cheques you have cashed, and keep this separate from the cheques themselves. If cheques are lost or stolen, contact the issuing office or their nearest branch. **AmEx** (☎ 0800 587 6023; open 24hr) and **Thomas Cook** (☎ 01733-318950; open 24hr) can often arrange replacements within 24 hours.

ATMs Plastic cards make the perfect companions – you can use them in many shops, and withdraw cash from ATMs, God's greatest gift to travellers since the backpack. But ATMs aren't fail-safe, and it can be a major headache if your card gets swallowed, so take a back up.

Debit cards, which withdraw money directly from your account, are widely linked internationally – ask your bank for information on which UK banks will accept your card and the fees charged. Most ATMs are also linked to the Visa and MasterCard networks and accept credit cards, but you must specifically ask your bank to set this up and request a PIN.

Credit Cards Visa, MasterCard, AmEx and Diners Club cards are widely accepted in England. Note that some businesses charge extra for credit card payment and small businesses, such as B&Bs, often only take cash or cheque.

You can get cash advances using your Visa and MasterCards at many banks, and if you have an AmEx card, depending on the type, you can cash from £500 to £1000 worth of personal cheques at AmEx offices in any seven-day period.

Lost or Stolen Cards If a card is lost or stolen you must inform the police and the issuing company as soon as possible – otherwise you may have to pay for the purchases the unspeakable thief has made with your card. Emergency numbers include: **AmEx** (☎ 0800 587 6023), **Diners Club** (☎ 01252-516261), **MasterCard** (☎ 0800 964 767) and **Visa** (☎ 0800 891 725).

International Transfers If you tell your bank back home to send you a draft, specify the *receiving* bank and the branch. The whole process will be easier if you've authorised someone back home to access your account. Money sent by telegraphic transfer should arrive within a week, and will most likely be converted into pounds – you can then take it

as is, or buy travellers cheques. The charge for this service is usually around £20.

You can also transfer money using AmEx, Thomas Cook, post office MoneyGram, or **Western Union** (☎ 0800 833833; **w** www .westernunion.com).

Other Methods If you plan to stay a while in England, you may want to open a bank account. Ideally it should come with a chequebook and a debit/ATM card. You'll need proof of a permanent UK address, and it will smooth the way if you have a reference from your bank at home, plus bank statements for the previous year. Owning credit/charge cards also helps. It's worth consulting your bank at home before you leave, as it may be affiliated with an English bank and able to help with paperwork.

Security
Keep your funds safe, and keep an eye on your wallet and bag. You could use a money belt, a pouch worn under your shirt, or something similar. Take extra care in crowded places.

Costs
Whatever your budget, compared to many other countries, England is undoubtedly an expensive place to travel – especially in London and the southeast.

In London you need £30 to £35 a day for bare survival. Dormitory accommodation costs £10 to £20 a night, a one-day public transport Travelcard (Zones 1 and 2) is around £4, while the most basic sustenance will cost £10 to £15 per day. To enjoy some of the city's culture and entertainment, add another £20 a day (though many museums and galleries across England are free).

Up a grade, hotels in London cost around £30 per person and restaurant meals around £10. Add a couple of pints (about £2.50 each) and some admission fees and you could easily blow £65 per day without being extravagant.

Out of London, costs will drop, but you'll still need at least £30 per day, and will need to budget for long-distance transport (see the Getting Around chapter for more details).

On £50 to £75 per day outside London, things get much easier. Allow around £20 per person for a B&B; £7 to £15 for dinner; £10 to £15 for lunch, snacks and drinks; and £10 to £15 for miscellaneous items and admission fees. Local train and bus fares will average around £5 to £10, while by car you'll probably spend £8 to £15 per day on petrol and parking (not including hire charges).

Tipping & Bargaining

In restaurants you're expected to leave around 10% tip, unless the service was unsatisfactory (or already added to your bill – and you don't have to pay this if the food or service was bad). The same might apply at the smarter cafés and teashops. Toilet attendants (if you see them loitering) may get tipped around 50p. Taxi drivers also expect to be tipped (about 10%), especially in London; it's less usual to tip minicab drivers.

In pubs, when ordering drinks at the bar, tips are not expected. When eating in pubs the tipping situation is fluid. If you order and pay for food at the bar, tips aren't expected. If you order at the table, and your meal is brought to you, then a tip may be appropriate – if the food and service have been good, of course!

Bargaining is almost unheard of, although occasionally encountered at markets. It's fine to ask if there are student or YHA-member discounts on items such as tickets or books.

Taxes & Refunds

Value-added tax (VAT) is a 17.5% sales tax levied on most goods and services. Non-EU and EU residents who will leave the EU within three months of making a purchase may claim back the VAT paid (EU residents must be due to stay outside the EU for more than a year).

Participating shops will advertise 'Tax-Free Shopping' in their window. The minimum-purchase amount is around £75, and you have to show ID and ask for the VAT refund form, part of which the retailer must complete.

When you leave England, you can claim your refund at the airport – but allow at least an extra hour for this. You must show your receipts, the form, and the goods to customs (VAT-free goods can't be posted or shipped home). At some airports you will receive a cash refund straight away. Alternatively you can send the form back to the shop, which will send you a UK£ cheque. To avoid bank charges, use a credit card for purchases, then refunds can be credited to your account.

POST & COMMUNICATIONS
Post

Post office hours vary, but most open from 9am to 5.30pm Monday to Friday, and main branches open 9am to noon on Saturday. Post offices in country towns may close early on Wednesday or Thursday. For more information on post offices call ☎ 0845 722 3344.

Although the queues in main post offices can be long, **Royal Mail** (☎ 0845 774 0740) delivers quite a good service. Within England, first-class mail (27p) takes one day, while 2nd-class mail (19p) takes up to three.

Airmail letters cost 27p to EU countries, 36p to other European countries and 45p or 65p to the Americas or Australasia (up to 10g or 20g). An airmail letter generally takes four to eight days to destinations outside Europe.

If you don't have a permanent address, mail can be sent to poste restante in the town where you are staying. AmEx Travel offices will also hold cardholders' mail free of charge.

Telephone

To call England from abroad, dial your country's international access code, then 44 (the UK's country code), then the area code (dropping the first 0), and the phone number.

England's famous red phone boxes survive only in conservation areas. More common these days are the glass cubicles with phones that accept coins, prepaid phonecards and/or credit cards. Minimum charge is 20p.

All phones come with reasonably clear instructions. British Telecom (BT) offers Phonecard Plus cards for £3, £5, £10 and £20 that are widely available from all sorts of retailers, including post offices and newsagents showing the green logo.

Some special phone codes worth knowing are:

free-phone (toll-free)	☎ 0500 or ☎ 0800
local-call rate	☎ 0845 or ☎ 08457
national-call rate	☎ 0870
premium rate	☎ 0891 or ☎ 09064

For premium rate numbers, costs vary, and should be specified where the number is listed. Codes for mobile phones (cellphones) usually start with ☎ 07 and can be considerably more expensive than calling a land line.

Local & National Calls & Rates Local calls are within 35 miles. Cheaper rates apply from 6pm to 8am Monday to Friday, and the cheap weekend rate applies from midnight Friday to midnight Sunday. From private phones, rates vary between telecom providers,

Mobile Phones

Around 40 million Britons now have the facility to tell their loved ones that they're 'on the train'. And the terse medium of text is a national passion – the English exchange over a billion messages a month. The mobile-phone industry boomed resonantly at the tail end of the last century, but it had to end, and a saturated market now sags.

England uses GSM 900/1800, which is compatible with the rest of Europe and Australia but not with the North American GSM 1900 or the totally different system in Japan (though some North Americans have GSM 1900/900 phones that do work here). If you have a GSM phone, check with your service provider about using it in England, and beware of calls being routed internationally (very expensive for a 'local' call).

If your handset works here, one solution is to buy one of the SIM card packages available (£10 to £30) and use a local card. However, check that this will operate in your phone – your handset may not work with a different SIM card, or may be locked by your home network. Sales staff can advise you. If you are here for a while, another solution is to buy a pay-as-you-go phone. For around £60 to £90 you get a phone with your own telephone number. As you use up your credit, you simply buy 'top-up' cards at newsagents or garages. All four main mobile phone companies in England – Orange, Vodaphone, One2one and O2 – have variations on both these schemes.

---

but from BT public phones the daytime rate is about 5p for one minute and the cheap weekend rate is 5p for five minutes.

For directory inquiries or information call ☎ 192. These calls are free from public phones but cost 40p if you call from a private phone. To get the operator call ☎ 100.

International Calls & Rates To call outside the UK dial ☎ 00, then the country code, the area code (you usually drop the initial zero) and the number. International direct dialling (IDD) calls to most countries can be made from almost all public telephones.

To make a reverse-charge (collect) call, dial ☎ 155 for the international operator. Direct dialling is cheaper. For international directory inquiries dial ☎ 153 (£1.50 per minute up to a maximum of £6 from private phones).

From England, it's cheaper to phone most overseas countries (including Europe, the USA and Canada) between 8pm and 8am Monday to Friday and at weekends; for Australia and New Zealand, it's cheapest from 2.30pm to 7.30pm and from midnight to 7am every day.

There's a wide range of local and international phonecards. Lonely Planet's **ekno Communication Card** (**w** www.ekno.lonely planet.com) is aimed at independent travellers and provides budget international calls (for local calls, you're usually better off with a local card), a range of messaging services, free email and travel information. You can

join online, or by dialling ☎ 0800 376 1704 from England. Once you've joined, to use ekno from England, dial ☎ 0800 169 8646 (or ☎ 0800 376 2366 from a payphone). Check the ekno website for joining and access numbers from other countries, updates on local access numbers and new features.

It is also possible to undercut BT international call rates by buying a phone card (usually denominated £5, £10 or £20) with a PIN that you use from any phone by dialling a special access number (you don't insert it into the machine). There are dozens of cards, usually available from newsagents. Posters with the rates of the various companies are often displayed in shop doors or windows.

Fax

Some newsagents, stationers and Internet cafés offer a fax service. Ask at a TIC or just look for the signs.

Email & Internet Access

If you're planning to use your laptop to get online, it's a good idea to get a US RJ-11 telephone connector (connectors between this and the unique English version are readily available in the UK).

Places with Internet access are common in England. Many are listed in this book, or TICs can point you in the right direction, although charges are steep – around £6 per hour. Public libraries often have free access, but only for 30-minute slots.

DIGITAL RESOURCES

Good places to begin cyber travelling include the websites listed under Tourist Offices earlier in the chapter.

Useful sites are listed throughout this book, but there's no better place to start than at **w** www.lonelyplanet.com. Here you'll find succinct summaries on travelling to most places on earth, postcards from other travellers and the Thorn Tree bulletin board, where you can ask questions before you go or dispense advice when you get back. You can also get travel news and updates on many of our most popular guidebooks, and the subwwway section links you to the most useful travel resources elsewhere on the Web. City-Sync downloads are also available for your handheld Palm OS and the *London* guide is regularly updated; try out the free demo.

Here are some useful sites on all things English.

Able to Go (**w** www.abletogo.com) provides excellent listings for visitors with mobility difficulties

Automobile Association (**w** www.theaa.com) answers your administrative vehicular questions

BBC News (**w** www.bbc.co.uk) has the latest coverage of national news and current affairs

Britain Visitor Atlas (**w** www.visitmap.com) is useful for pinpointing locations

Directory Enquiries (**w** www.192.com) will help you track down English phone numbers and addresses

Holiday Cottages (**w** www.stilwell.co.uk) opens up the self-catering and B&B scene

Hostels.com (**w** www.hostels.com) has information on worldwide dorm life, and input from hostellers

Met Office (**w** www.met-office.gov.uk) discusses the all-important weather

Tour Britain (**w** www.tour-britain.com) provides good links to local attractions

UK Guide (**w** www.uktheguide.com) offers no-nonsense, wide-ranging travel information

Whatsonwhen (**w** www.whatsonwhen.com) fills you in on current entertainment events worldwide

Which? (**w** www.which.net) is a consumer guide, with a well-respected hotel section

Yell.com (**w** www.yell.com) proffers contact details for countrywide businesses.

BOOKS

This section covers a small selection of books to help you get around England or get a deeper insight into the country's nooks and crannies. Detailed books on specific areas are listed in the relevant sections, while English works of literature are covered in the Arts section of the Facts about England chapter.

We don't list publisher details here, as bookshops and libraries search under title and author. TICs are an excellent source of specialist local titles.

Lonely Planet

If you're looking for exercise, Lonely Planet publishes *Walking in Britain* and *Cycling Britain*, which make excellent companions to this book. For wider travels, Lonely Planet's *Britain* guide will be useful, and there are also separate *Scotland* and *Wales* books.

If cities are your thing, *London* is a comprehensive guide to the capital while *London Condensed* provides essential information in a handy format, and the *London* video provides a visual complement. *Out to Eat – London* reviews more than 300 restaurants.

Those who want to come to grips with local lingoes – particularly Cockney – should get hold of the Lonely Planet *British phrasebook*.

Guidebooks

Numerous accommodation guides are available in England, but objectivity is sometimes questionable as places pay to be listed. Publications produced by national or local tourist organisations are more reliable (if not comprehensive) and widely available in TICs. The *Which?* books, produced by the Consumers' Association, are accurate and fair: no money changes hands for recommendations.

Specialist guidebooks approach the country from every conceivable angle. If you're of a bookish bent, the *Oxford Literary Guide to Great Britain and Ireland* gives details of many writers who immortalised towns, villages and countryside. Other edifying favourites are the annual *Good Beer Guide to Great Britain*, which steers you to the best English beers and the pubs that serve them, and the *Good Pub Guide*, which details thousands of fine establishments across the country. Or escape it all with *Wild Britain: A Traveller's Guide* by Douglas Botting – excellent advice on finding England's outback.

Travel

Classic travelogues from the past (arranged roughly historically) include:

A Tour Through the Whole Island of Great Britain by Daniel Defoe. An absorbing account of the writer's journey in 1724–26

English Hours by Henry James. Describes the vanished world of late 19th century society

The Road to Wigan Pier by George Orwell. A compelling record of northern working-class life in the 1930s

English Journey by JB Priestley. An insight into local life in the 1930s. Beryl Bainbridge retraced his steps in 1997 with book of the same title.

Travelogues from our own era include:

Notes from a Small Island by Bill Bryson. Entertaining and perceptive, from one of the few foreigners to really capture the spirit of England

The Kingdom by the Sea by Paul Theroux. Irritable and keenly observed; written in 1982 and now a little dated, but nonetheless very readable

Lights Out for the Territory by Iain Sinclair. An exploration of London in the 1990s – taking in a Kray gangster funeral, among other things – forms the basis for this powerful, acerbic account

Tales from Two Cities by Dervla Murphy. The veteran travel writer's view of life among England's ethnic minorities in mid-1980s' Bradford and Birmingham

Park and Ride by Miranda Sawyer. A sojourn through English suburbia in 2001

Danziger's Britain by Nick Danziger. A grim view of life among homeless, unemployed and marginalised people

History & Politics

A History of Britain by Simon Schama. Incisive and highly accessible three-volume set encompassing events from 3000 BC to AD 2000

The Isles: A History by Norman Davies. Much-acclaimed coverage of the British Isles and their restive peoples; 10,000 years in a svelte 1000 pages

Londinium by John Morris. A fascinating insight on everyday life in London under Roman rule

The Year 1000 by Robert Lacey and Danny Danzinger. A study of English life a millennium ago (it was cold and damp then too)

Medieval Women by Henrietta Leyser. Female life from AD 500 to 1500; work, marriage, sex and children – not necessarily in that order

London – The Biography by Peter Ackroyd. Absorbing and original treatment of the capital as a living organism, approaching its history through themes such as drinking and crime

Windrush – The Irresistible Rise of Multi-Racial Britain by Mike and Trevor Phillips. Traces the history of Britain's first West Indian immigrants

The Course of My Life by Edward Heath. The autobiography of this former prime minister gives an insider's view of events in 1970s

Things Can Only Get Better by John O'Farrell. Witty, self-deprecating story of 1980s and early '90s politics – the era of Thatcher and the Conservatives – from a struggling Labour viewpoint

General

Myths and Legends of the British Isles by Richard Barber. King Arthur and the Knights of the Round Table, plus lots more from the mists of time

The Queen and Di by Ingrid Seward. Just one of hundreds of books on the soap opera that is the British royal family

The Queen's Story by Marcus Kiggell. A new royal biography; more studied and serious, and far less gushing than many similar titles

A Brief History of British Kings & Queens by Mike Ashley. A concise and comprehensive rundown on the rulers, with time-lines, lists, biographies and family trees

Northern Exposure

Many movies about England concentrate on London and the south, so to correct the bias, here's a short prompt-list of some excellent movies all made in the north of the country. To search for more film locations, see **W** www.visitbritain.com/moviemap.

Brief Encounter (1945) – Wartime weepy by David Lean, set at Carnforth station, Lancashire

Kes (1969) – Touching story of a Yorkshire lad who finds his identity through the training of a kestrel

Get Carter (1971) – Michael Caine in a classic crime thriller filmed in Newcastle

Distant Voices, Still Lives (1988) – A dysfunctional working-class family being dragged up in Liverpool

Bhaji on the Beach (1993) – A group of South Asian women on a day trip to Blackpool

Brassed Off (1996) – The sad story of a brass band in Yorkshire which tries to keep going after the pit closes down; filmed in Grimethorpe, near Barnsley

The Full Monty (1997) – Sheffield-based comedy about unemployed steelworkers turned strippers

Little Voice (1998) – Delightful tale of an odd but talented singer, filmed in Scarborough, Yorkshire

East is East (1999) – Comedy of cultures as a Pakistani family come to terms with 1970s' Manchester

Billy Elliot (2000) – In the pit town of Easington, County Durham, a miner's son takes to ballet rather than boxing

Purely Belter (2000) – The story of two Geordie lads desperate for Newcastle United tickets

Buildings of England by Nikolaus Pevsner. An invaluable multivolume architectural resource

The English by Jeremy Paxman. An exploration of the English psyche by the toughest interviewer on the airwaves

Walks through Britain's History (published by AA). Wander through castles and battle sites, and 100 other locations with a link to the past

FILMS

In the Cinema section of the Facts about England chapter we give a quick run down on England's cinematic history. In this section we list a selection of films set in England, which are well worth a watch for a taste of local scenery or peculiar cultural traits.

The 2001 film *Harry Potter and the Philosopher's Stone* comprised a veritable tour of England. Goathland on the Yorkshire Moors doubles for Hogsmead, Alnwick Castle in Northumberland provides exterior shots of Hogwarts school, while the Bodleian Library in Oxford is the set for inside scenes.

England's well-preserved country houses and stately homes also provide authentic film settings. Hampton Court in London is the setting for *A Man for all Seasons* (1966), and the adaptation of Jane Austen's *Mansfield Park* (1999) was filmed at Kenwood House on London's Hampstead Heath.

Country houses also feature in Robert Altman's *Gosford Park* (2001), a study of England's equally well-preserved class system, while *Another Country* (1983) looks at the public school tradition. For a feel of an even earlier era, *Shakespeare in Love* (1998) gives a hint of Elizabethan London and is well worth a watch, and for more up-to-date London scenes there's always *Sliding Doors* (1998).

NEWSPAPERS & MAGAZINES
Newspapers

Breakfast need never be boring in England. For such a small country, there's an amazing range of daily papers.

The bottom end of the market is occupied by the easy-to-handle, easy-to-read tabloids, full of sensational celebrity 'exclusives' and simplistic political coverage. The *Sun* is a national institution with headlines based on outrageous puns and mean-spirited contents. The *Mirror* was once the 'paper of the workers', then competed head-on with the *Sun* for a while, and more recently started to rediscover its left-of-centre heritage. The *Sport* takes bad taste to the ultimate extreme, with stories of

celebs and aliens (sometimes in the same report), and pictures of seminaked women of improbable proportions.

The *Daily Mail* and *Daily Express* bill themselves as middle-market, but are really just tabloids in disguise, thunderously right-of-centre and playing to the fears of middle England with a steady diet of crime reports and thinly veiled scare stories on threatening immigrants and rampant homosexuals.

At the upper end of the market, the broadsheets are stimulating and well written: The *Daily Telegraph* is right-of-centre and easily outsells its rivals, the *Times* is conservative, thorough and influential, the *Guardian* is left-of-centre and innovative, and the *Independent* lives up to its title.

Most dailies have a Sunday stable mate (filled more with comment and analysis than hot news), and on their day of rest the English settle into armchairs to plough through the main paper and its endless supplements. There's the *Sunday Mirror*, *Sunday Express*, *Sunday Telegraph*, and the long-standing *Observer* – the seventh-day version of the *Guardian*. The *Sunday Times* alone comes in 12 different parts and must destroy a rainforest every issue.

Magazines

Walk into any newsagent and you'll see that England boasts a magazine for every possible interest – there are literally hundreds of consumer publications catering for fans of music, football, health, sex, horses, fashion, collecting, cars, sex again, cookery, and endless other pursuits and interests.

For news, European editions of *Time* and *Newsweek* are available, but the *Economist* remains the best news weekly in England or anywhere. Worth looking for is *Private Eye*, a no-frills satirical publication that retains its sharp edge, even at the risk of regular run-ins with the law.

Most cities have a listings magazine broadly along the lines of London's famously informative *Time Out*. In towns that can't muster a separate listings mag, you can find out what's happening from the local paper.

RADIO & TV
Radio

The BBC is a venerable institution, with several channels dominating radio across the country. Outsiders are amazed that public service broadcasting can produce such a range of professional, innovative, up-to-date and stimulating programmes. All this without adverts!

BBC Radio 1 (275M/1089kHz and 285M/1053kHz MW, 98.8MHz FM) is a music station, with coverage from syrupy pop to underground garage, some inane DJs, and a predominantly young audience. When you're too old for this, turn to Radio 2 (88 to 90.2MHz FM); it plays favourites from the 1960s to the 1990s, plus country, jazz and world music, and employs presenters who got too old for Radio 1 as well.

BBC Radio 3 (247M/1215kHz MW, 91.3 MHz FM) offers predominantly classical music, but also goes into roots and world music, while Radio 4 (1500M/198kHz LW, 417M/720kHz MW, 93.5MHz FM) offers a mix of news, comment, current affairs, drama and humour. Radio 5 Live (463M/693kHz MW), sometimes known as 'Radio Bloke', provides a mix of sport and talk; the latter aspect is considered low-rent, but is downright intelligent by some American talk-radio standards.

Alongside the BBC are many commercial broadcasters. Every city has at least one music station, while national commercial stations include Classic FM (100-102MHz FM), surprisingly popular and pleasantly non-highbrow; Galaxy 105 (105MHz FM), seriously dance and R&B-orientated; and Jazz FM (102.2MHz FM in London; 100.4MHz FM in northwest England).

TV

Britain turns out some of the world's best terrestrial TV, although increasing competition from cable and satellite channels means standards sometimes slip as ratings are constantly chased. Early-evening schedules are dominated by soaps, sitcoms, quiz shows and a shed-full of programmes about gardening, cookery and home improvement. Recent years have also seen a spate of fly-on-the-wall documentaries about everyday situations (airports, hotels, driving schools, even Lonely Planet's UK office), which may leave you amused but none the wiser. Whatever channel you watch, things get better after about 9pm.

There are five regular terrestrial TV channels – BBC1 and BBC2 are publicly funded and don't carry advertising; ITV and Channels 4 and 5 are commercial stations.

Of these, BBC2 and Channel 4 have the most interesting programming.

PHOTOGRAPHY & VIDEO

For information on travel photography, Lonely Planet's *Travel Photography: A Guide to Taking Better Pictures*, written by internationally renowned photographer Richard I'Anson, is designed to take on the road.

Film & Equipment

Although print film is widely available, slide film can be more elusive; if there's no specialist photographic shop around, Boots, the high-street chemist chain, is the most likely stockist. Print film (36-exposure) costs from £3.50 for ISO 100 to £5 for ISO 400.

Restrictions

Many tourist attractions either charge for taking photos or prohibit it altogether. Use of flash is frequently forbidden to protect delicate pictures and fabrics. Video cameras are often disallowed because of the inconvenience they can cause to other visitors.

Airport Security

You will have to put your camera and film through the X-ray machine at all English airports. The machines are supposed to be filmsafe, but you may feel happier if you ask for exposed films to be examined by hand.

TIME

Wherever you are in the world, time is measured in relation to Greenwich Mean Time (GMT) – and you may well visit Greenwich, and its famous line dividing the western and eastern hemispheres, while in London. Strictly speaking, GMT is used only in air and sea navigation, and is otherwise referred to as Universal Time Coordinated (UTC).

British summer time (BST) is Britain's daylight saving, meaning the whole country is one hour ahead of GMT from late March to late October.

To give you an idea, if it is noon in London, it is 4am on the same calendar day in San Francisco, 7am in New York, and 10pm in Sydney.

ELECTRICITY

The standard voltage throughout England is 230V, and equipment rated at 230V to 240V will work. Plugs have three square pins.

WEIGHTS & MEASURES

England is in an awkward transition period when it comes to weights and measures, as it has been for the last 20 years – and probably will be for 20 more.

Most people still use the old 'imperial' units of inches, feet, yards and miles. All road signs give distances in miles, although a few footpath signposts use kilometres, and on maps the heights of mountains are given in metres only.

For weight, many people use pounds (lb) and ounces (oz), even though since January 2000 goods in shops must be priced in pence per kilogram. And nobody knows their weight in pounds (like Americans) or kilograms (like the rest of the world); Brits weigh themselves in stones, an archaic unit of 14 pounds.

When it comes to volume, things are even worse: most liquids are sold in litres or half-litres, except milk and beer, which come in pints. Garages sell petrol priced in pence per litre, but measure car performance in miles per gallon. Great, isn't it?

In this book we have reflected this rather wacky and typically English system of mixed measurements. Heights are given in metres (m) and distances are mostly stated in miles, with kilometre (km) equivalents given where necessary. For conversion tables, see the inside back cover.

LAUNDRY

Most hotels offer a laundry service, but B&Bs and hostels usually don't, so you may need to seek out a laundrette. Most towns and cities have at least one, although they're rarely central – you have to trek out to the suburbs – but these fun-filled social centres are a great place to meet interesting locals. The average cost for a single load is about £3 to £5 to wash and dry. Take a pocket full of change: the washers usually take £1 coins, the dryers 50p or 20p coins, and the soap machine about 50p per cupful.

TOILETS

In cities and towns you're never far from a public toilet (or 'public convenience' as they're sometimes coyly called). Those in parks and streets are pretty grim, covered in graffiti or rendered vandalproof in stainless steel, while those at train and bus stations are slightly better, usually with facilities for disabled people. At major stations you pay 20p,

but at least they're clean. Other options include using the loo in large department stores, fast-food restaurants or crowded pubs (if it's quiet, you'll be noticed, so it's best to simply ask permission – buying a drink to use the loo kinda defeats the purpose).

Many disabled toilets can only be opened with a special key obtainable from some tourist offices or direct from an organisation called RADAR (see the Disabled Travellers section later in this chapter).

HEALTH

Travel health largely depends on predeparture preparations, day-to-day care while travelling, and how you handle any medical problem or emergency that does develop.

England is a healthy place to travel. Hygiene standards are high (despite what your nose tells you on a hot and crowded tube train) and there are no unusual diseases to worry about. Your biggest risks will be from overdoing it on any activities you engage in, be they physical, chemical or other.

Predeparture planning

Immunisations No immunisations are necessary.

Health Insurance & Medical Services EEA nationals can obtain free emergency treatment on presentation of an E111 form, validated in their home country. Reciprocal arrangements with the UK allow residents of Australia, New Zealand and several other countries to receive free emergency medical treatment and subsidised dental care through the National Health Service (NHS) at hospital emergency departments, general practitioners (GPs) and dentists.

Long-term visitors with proper documentation receive care under the NHS by registering with a GP. Check the phone book for one close to you.

Regardless of nationality, anyone will receive free emergency treatment at Accident and Emergency departments of NHS hospitals. Travel insurance, however, is advisable as it offers greater flexibility over where and how you're treated and covers expenses for an ambulance and repatriation (see the Travel Insurance section under Visas & Documents earlier in this chapter).

Chemists can advise on minor ailments such as sore throats and earache. In large cities, there's always one chemist open 24 hours; other chemists should display details.

Travel Health Guides Check out Lonely Planet's *Read This First: Europe* by Paul Harding for step-by-step advice on staying safe and healthy. From the Lonely Planet website (**w** www.lonelyplanet.com) there are links to the World Health Organization and the US Centers for Disease Control & Prevention.

Water
Tap water in England is always safe unless there's a sign to the contrary (eg, on trains). Don't drink straight from a stream or river – you never know what's upstream.

Environmental Hazards
Sunburn In summertime in England, even when there's cloud cover, it's possible to get sunburnt surprisingly quickly – especially if you're on water. Use 15+ sunscreen, wear a hat and cover up with a shirt and trousers.

Infectious Diseases
Diarrhoea Simple things like a change of water, food or climate can all cause a mild bout of diarrhoea, but a few rushed toilet trips with no other symptoms are not indicative of a major problem.

Dehydration is the main danger with diarrhoea, particularly in children or the elderly. Under all circumstances *fluid replacement* (at least equal to the volume being lost) is the most important thing to remember. Weak black tea with a little sugar, soda water, or soft drinks allowed to go flat and diluted 50% with clean water are all good. Stick to a bland diet as you recover.

HIV & AIDS Infection with the human immunodeficiency virus (HIV) may lead to acquired immune deficiency syndrome (AIDS), which is a fatal disease. Any exposure to blood, blood products or body fluids may put the individual at risk. The disease is often transmitted through sexual contact or dirty needles – acupuncture, tattooing and body piercing can be potentially as dangerous as intravenous drug use.

Sexually Transmitted Infections HIV/ AIDS and hepatitis B can be transmitted through sexual contact. Other STDs include gonorrhoea, herpes and syphilis; sores, blisters or rashes around the genitals and discharges or pain when urinating are common symptoms. In some STDs, such as wart virus or chlamydia, symptoms may be less marked or not observed at all, especially in women. While abstinence from sexual contact is the only 100% effective prevention, using condoms is also effective. The different STDs each require specific antibiotics.

Insect Bites & Stings Bee and wasp stings are usually painful rather than dangerous. Anti-itch creams and lotions will provide relief, and ice packs will reduce the pain and swelling. However, people with allergies may develop severe breathing difficulties and require urgent medical care.

WOMEN TRAVELLERS
Attitudes Towards Women
The occasional wolf-whistle and groper on the London Underground aside, women will find England fairly enlightened. There's nothing to stop women going into pubs alone – although you may feel conspicuous. Some restaurants still persist in assigning the table by the toilet to lone female diners, but fortunately such places are becoming fewer.

Safety Precautions
Solo female travellers should have few problems, although commonsense caution should be observed in big cities, especially at night. Hitching is always unwise.

The contraceptive pill is available free on prescription in England, as is the 'morning-after' pill (effective for up to 72 hours after unprotected sex; also on sale at chemists).

Organisations
Most big towns have a Well Woman Clinic that can advise on general health issues. Find its address in the local phone book or ask in the library.

If you'd like to stay with women while you're travelling it's worth joining **Women Welcome Women** (*☎/fax 01494-465441;* **w** *www.womenwelcomewomen.org.uk; 88 Easton St, High Wycombe, Bucks HP11 1LT*), an organisation that puts women travellers in touch with potential hostesses.

GAY & LESBIAN TRAVELLERS
England is a generally tolerant place for gays and lesbians. People can acknowledge their

homosexuality in a way that would have been unthinkable 20 years ago. For example, there are several openly gay MPs.

That said, pockets of hostility do exist. The government remains committed to repealing the notorious Section 28, a law forbidding 'the promotion of homosexuality in schools', but it seems very much on the back burner.

London, Manchester and Brighton have a flourishing gay and lesbian scene, and in other sizable cities you'll find a community not entirely in the closet. However, overt displays of affection are not necessarily wise away from known gay venues and districts.

The capital is covered in several guides, including Thomas Cook's *Out Around London* and Ellipsis' *Dyke London*. Gay Times published *Great Britain and Ireland* (£12.95) in 2001. For current listings try the *Pink Paper* (£1.80), *Boyz* (free) or the *Gay Times* (£2.95, w www.gaytimes.co.uk). *Diva* (£2.25, w www.divamag.co.uk/diva) is for lesbians. They're available at larger newsagents. Most gay venues have freebie mags.

Another useful source of information is the **Lesbian & Gay Switchboard** (☎ 020-7837 7324; w www.llgs.org.uk; open 24hr).

DISABLED TRAVELLERS

The 1995 Disability Discrimination Act makes it illegal to discriminate against people with disabilities in employment or the provision of services, and says 'reasonable adjustments' have to be made to improve access by 2004. These days few buildings go up that are inaccessible to wheelchair users. However, most B&Bs and guesthouses are in hard-to-adapt older buildings. This means that travellers with mobility problems may end up paying more for accommodation.

It's a similar story with public transport. Newer buses sometimes have steps that lower for easier access, as do trains, but it's always wise to check before setting out.

Organisations

If you have a physical disability, get in touch with your national support organisation. They often have libraries devoted to travel, and can put you in touch with specialist travel agents. Websites w www.abletogo.com and w www .accessibletravel.co.uk are useful travel, accommodation and listings resources, while w www.everybody.co.uk provides information on hotels and airlines. See the Railcards section of the Getting Around chapter for details on obtaining the Disabled Persons Railcard, which gives discounts on fares.

Holiday Care Service (☎ 01293-774535; w www.holidaycare.org.uk; 2nd floor, Imperial Buildings, Victoria Rd, Horley, Surrey RH6 7PZ) publishes *Accessible Britain* (£3.50) and can offer general advice.

Royal Association for Disability and Rehabilitation (RADAR; ☎ 020-7250 3222; w www.radar.org.uk; 250 City Rd, London EC1V 8AF) stocks several useful titles, including *Holidays in Britain and Ireland: A Guide for Disabled People* (£8) and supplies regional accommodation addresses online.

Tripscope (☎ 0845 7585641, 0117-939 7782; w www.tripscope.org.uk) provides advice and information on getting around.

SENIOR TRAVELLERS

Senior citizens are entitled to discounts on public transport, museum admission fees etc, provided they show proof of age. They will also sometimes require a special pass. The minimum qualifying age is generally 60 to 65 for men, and 55 to 65 for women. See the Railcards section of the Getting Around chapter for details on obtaining the Senior Railcard, which gives discounts on fares.

In your home country, a lower age may entitle you to special travel packages and discounts (on car hire, for instance) through organisations and travel agents that cater to senior travellers.

TRAVEL WITH CHILDREN

Attitudes to children in England can vary from delightfully warm to decidedly frosty. To avoid cold blasts, check your intended restaurant or hotel's stance on the matter.

Many pubs now have playgrounds, family rooms and children's meals. Some places, such as the Café Rouge chain, give out crayons and colouring sheets.

Breastfeeding in public remains controversial. An indication of the English attitude is that it's banned in the House of Commons – special rooms are provided to protect governmental modesty.

See Lonely Planet's *Travel with Children* by Cathy Lanigan for more information. It's also worth looking up w www.babygoes2 .com – packed with tips, advice and encouragement for parents on the move with babies and toddlers.

USEFUL ORGANISATIONS
Historic Organisations
Membership of National Trust (NT) and English Heritage (EH) are worth considering if you plan to visit many heritage sights, as this gets you in free or at a discounted rate.

National Trust *(NT; ☎ 0870 458 4000;* **w** *www.nationaltrust.org.uk)* is one of the largest charities in England, protecting hundreds of historic buildings and gardens, and vast tracts of land with scientific or scenic importance. Most NT buildings and gardens cost nonmembers up to £5.50 to enter. Membership is available at most major sites, costs £32.50 per year (£15 for under 26s, and £60 for a family) and provides free admission to all the NT properties in England. There are reciprocal arrangements with other heritage organisations, and you get an excellent guidebook and map.

English Heritage *(EH; ☎ 0870 333 1181;* **w** *www.english-heritage.org.uk)* is a state-funded organisation, responsible for the upkeep of numerous historic sites and buildings. Some are free, while others cost nonmembers between £1.50 and £6 to visit. Annual membership costs £31.50 per adult, £53.50 per couple (£37.50 if you're both over 60) and £58.50 per family. Membership gives free admission to all EH properties, discounts with other heritage organisations and a reliable guidebook and map.

Great British Heritage Pass This pass gives you access to almost 600 properties

Historic Property Prices
In this book, where historic properties are listed, NT before the phone number indicates National Trust, EH indicates English Heritage. Nearly all NT and EH properties charge half-price for children, so only adult admission fees are quoted.

run by the National Trust and English Heritage in England (and similar properties in Scotland and Wales), and many privately owned sites. A seven-day pass costs £32, 15 days is £45, one month is £60. It's available overseas from the BTA or from larger TICs throughout England, and can only be purchased by non-Brits (show your passport).

DANGERS & ANNOYANCES
Crime
England is a remarkably safe country considering the disparities in wealth that you'll see in many areas, but crime is certainly not unknown in London and other large urban areas, so you should take care – especially at night.

Pickpockets and bag snatchers operate in crowded public places, so make sure your bag is safe. Money and important documents are best out of sight and out of reach, rather than in a handbag or waist-bag.

[Continued on page 74]

Tracing Your Ancestors
If you're a visitor with ancestors who once lived in England, your trip could be a good chance to find out more about them. You may even discover long lost (or unknown) relatives. Here are a few guidelines to get you started.

Start your search at the **Family Records Centre** *(☎ 020-8392 5300;* **w** *www.familyrecords.gov.uk; 1 Myddelton St, London EC1R 1UW; open 9am-5pm Mon, Wed & Fri, 10am-7pm Tues, 9am-7pm Thur, 9.30am-5pm Sat).* This very helpful department, part of the Public Records Office (PRO), is used to ancestor hunters and has several publications (available by post) outlining the process. You'll need a passport or ID to see original records. Remember that documents referring to individuals are closed for 100 years to safeguard personal confidentiality.

Another good source, whatever your religion, is the online archive of the **Mormon church** *(*w *www .familysearch.org).*

For more advice, *Tracing your Ancestors in the Public Records Office* by Amanda Bevan (£15.99) is a helpful guide. The **Association of Genealogists & Researchers in Archives** *(*w *www.agra.org.uk; 29 Badgers Close, Horsham, West Sussex RH12 5RU)* lists professional record agents and researchers, available online or by post, who (for a fee) can search for ancestors or living relatives on your behalf.

CHARLOTTE HINDLE

SIMON BRACKEN

Title page: Traditional pub sign, London (Photograph by Richard l'Anson)

Top: Crystal Palace pub, Bath

Bottom: Classic English pub, London

For visitors to England traditional pubs are a quintessential feature, and for the English themselves the pub is one of the country's finest social and cultural institutions. There are more than 50,000 pubs scattered across the country, in market towns and busy city centres, in picturesque villages and remote rural backwaters. They range from vast and ornate Victorian drinking-palaces, through no-frills workers' retreats, to simple country inns with low beams and sloping flag-stoned floors polished smooth by the passage of time and a thousand spilt pints.

Wherever you find them, and whatever their form, pubs will almost certainly play a big part in your travels around England. This section covers some general history and background, and throughout this book we take great pleasure in listing many of the finer English pubs discovered by our team of authors during their many months of extensive and painstaking research. It's a tough job, but somebody's got to do it.

Pubs – A Potted History

'You can't fit a quart in a pint pot', as the old saying goes, and it is indeed hard to cover the intriguing story and numerous traditions of England's pubs in just a few pages. But we'll certainly try. So sit back, make yourself comfortable, and we'll skim through 2000 years of social history before you reach the bottom of your glass.

Early Days, Early Doors The people of the Bronze Age – the Picts, the Celts and so on – certainly enjoyed beer, as excavations of tombs and burial mounds show. However, it seems drinking was mainly done at home, and it's unlikely these ancient English folk met for an ale or two at the Chief's Arms or Druid & Firkin.

The first prototype pubs appeared in England during the days of the Roman occupation. Drinking houses called *tabernas* were built in the towns or along the famously straight Roman roads, and were places where citizens might gather or centurions could relax with some crude wine after a hard day contending with the natives. It was around this time that the first pub signs appeared too: a bunch of grapes or garland of vine leaves were hung at the door to show that wine was available within. Some *tabernas* provided games such as chess for their patrons, and landlords with a keen eye for marketing would advertise this service by painting a chequer board on the wall outside. Today, pubs called The Chequers can still be found in England – a title with 2000 years of history attached. (For more on pub signs see the boxed text 'What's in a Pub Name?' later in this section.)

When the Roman Empire came to an end, England became the land of the Saxons, and the tipples of the time were ale (a beer made from barley, and later malt and hops), and mead (a stronger drink, made from honey). Initially, almost every household brewed their own ale, and this was traditionally women's work, along with baking the bread, tending the crops, raising the animals, and having about 20 children.

But ale in the Dark Ages was not brewed for pleasure or entertainment only – there was an important practical purpose too. Water from wells or streams at the time often contained enough foul elements to make it deadly, while a beer's fermentation killed off harmful bacteria, making it in many cases the only safe form of drinking liquid available.

Beers were produced at different strengths (by accident or design), and the stronger brews were consumed by adults, while the less potent stuff was given to the kids. Thus the weaker brew was called 'small beer' – an old ale-related phrase still in use today to describe anything minor or inconsequential.

As with any home-made product, consistency was never a strong point, and over the decades and centuries some people learned how to make better ale than others. Those who were especially skilled soon found their product in demand. People came to buy ale and would stay for a drink, and the houses became popular gathering spots. Sometimes a separate room was built for the customers, and thus was born the alehouse, another early forerunner of the pub.

Once the demand was there, it seems that business was brisk, and records dating from the 7th century show that the king of Kent had to limit the number of alehouses in his realm. A few hundred years later, in the 10th century, another English king introduced a law to standardise the drinking cups used in alehouses – presumably so the punters would know how much they'd get for their hard-earned farthing each time they called by. At this time, drinking cups were very large and shared by several drinkers, with individual measures marked by a peg in the side of the cup. Drinkers were supposed to drink down to their peg, then pass the cup on. Drinking over your measure was 'taking someone down a peg or two' – yet another beer-related expression still common in today's language.

Norman Wisdom After the Saxons came the Norman conquerors (see 1066 & All That in the History section of the Facts about England chapter). With skill and ruthless efficiency, they established a new order across England in a remarkably short time. Just 20 years after the invasion, the Doomsday Book, a national census carried out in 1086, showed that most landowners in England were now Norman. More importantly they showed that most major alehouses were owned by Normans as well.

The Norman period also saw the growth of great abbeys and monasteries as centres of prayer, power and learning – each with their own lands, farms, mills, bakeries and brewing facilities to provide earthly sustenance for the hundreds of monks they contained. The monasteries became England's first large-scale breweries; outside their gates hostelries were established as places for pilgrims and other visitors to eat, drink and sleep, and these gradually developed into inns.

In the following centuries many monasteries disappeared, but the hostelries remain as inns or pubs today, often with names recalling the titles or heraldic symbols of the wealthy and powerful noble families who patronised the monastery (eg, the Norfolk Arms, the Devonshire Arms, the Fleur de Lys, the Three Cups) and sometimes with names of a more direct religious significance – the Lamb, the Angel, the Abbey, and so on.

Middle Age Spread By medieval times, the English drinker had a wide choice of establishment to frequent, and these fell into three distinct types: taverns, alehouses and inns.

The tavern had developed out of the Roman *taberna*, and in the Middle Ages this was primarily an urban establishment. The main drink sold was wine (the 'sack' so beloved by Shakespeare's Falstaff) and food was also served. Most important, the tavern was a place of enjoyment, where educated townies could relax and meet friends or acquaintances, and discuss the issues of the day. In many modern pubs

The Oldest Pub in England?

It often comes as a surprise to studious drinkers to learn that the word 'pub', although apparently steeped in history, only dates from the 19th century. But places selling beer have a much longer history, and the title 'oldest pub in England' is a hotly contested claim. One of the country's oldest pubs, with the paperwork to prove it, is Ye Olde Trip to Jerusalem in Nottingham, which was serving ale to departing Crusaders in the 12th century. (For more on this see the boxed text 'What's in a Pub Name?' later in this section.)

Other contenders sniff at this newcomer: a fine old hotel called the Eagle & Child in Stow-on-the-Wold (Gloucestershire) claims to have been selling beer since around AD 950, and Ye Olde Fighting Cocks in St Albans (Hertfordshire) apparently dates back to the 8th century.

But then back comes Ye Trip with a counter claim one of its bars is a cave hollowed out of living rock, and that's more than a million years old!

you can see pictures of old taverns: men in red coats sit on large chairs called 'settles' with high wooden backs to keep off the draft, holding big tankards and long pipes, while a couple of dogs stretch out by the fire and a buxom landlady stands nearby ready to bring more ale or no doubt a meal of boar's head and chips.

In contrast to the comfortable tavern, the typical alehouse of the time was a basic and notorious place where poor people went to get drunk and escape from their wretched hovels. There was no decoration, and furniture was usually limited to a couple of rough benches. Anyone not spending money, or not drinking fast enough, was soon asked to leave.

Inns had developed out of the monastic hostelries, and differed from taverns and alehouses in that they also offered customers a place to sleep (with or without accompanying vermin, and sometimes various other pleasures). Originally established on pilgrimage routes, they later grew up along roads used for trade, commerce and administration, usually one day's travel apart (a distance of about 20 miles), and in places where traders or officials could meet and do business – often around the market square of each town.

During the long reign of Elizabeth I, royal couriers travelled around the country carrying the queen's commands to her administrators in the shires and distant cities. They stopped off at inns, of course, and those with the best facilities were awarded a royal warrant – an early version of the Good Pub Guide window sticker – which ensured continued business, and encouraged other inns to raise their own game to compete.

In the early 17th century, Elizabeth's successor, James I of England and VI of Scotland, formalised pub standards even further. He introduced a law obliging all inns to offer accommodation, whilst forbidding taverns and alehouses to do the same, and this arcane legal difference between inns and other types of pubs remains in place today.

In the 18th century, the great turnpike roads developed across England, and inns enjoyed a boom time. As roads improved, more people travelled, and coaches with large teams of horses covered great distances between the major towns such as London, Bath and York.

Today, venerable 'coaching inns' can still be seen in the central squares of many market towns, complete with a grand archway for the coach and horses to drive straight through into the courtyard beyond. Many more old inns survive along historic roads throughout England, although the 20-mile intervals are a thing of the past, and vermin and other pleasures have a much lower profile these days too.

Gin & Orange In 1688, a new monarch came to the throne of England. This was King William of Orange, and he introduced his new English subjects to gin, the favourite drink of his native Holland. The English took to gin like ducks to water – except that this new spirit was rather more addictive than water, and in a very short time proved to be the heroin of its day, prized for its affordability and quick intoxication. Gin shops sprang up everywhere, and by the mid-18th century, huge numbers of Londoners were hooked, and gin-related deaths were so common that the population fell for the first time since the days of the Plague.

The following decades saw the development of plate glass for large mirrors, which were widely used to turn the gin shops into glittering rooms of temptation, even more enticing for the poverty-stricken slum-dwellers. Thus mere shops became 'gin palaces', but despite the grand title many were truly dens of iniquity, and worse than the ale-houses they frequently replaced. To keep the turnover high, there was no seating at all. You came, you drank, you left, you collapsed. If that happened in the wrong order, bales of hay were scattered about in shadowy corners so patrons could pass out on the premises and start drinking again upon coming to.

The epidemic was immortalised by William Hogarth's famous picture 'Gin Lane' – a sickening scene of chaos and destruction, with tumble-down buildings, dying people, desperate addicts pawning their goods, and a mother so drunk she drops her baby off the top of a staircase.

Porter & Stout are Good for You! While gin palaces catered for the poor and desperate, by the end of the 18th century another, more respectable, type of drinking establishment began appearing in the cities. These were known as porter houses, and marked another step in the development of the pub, becoming increasingly similar to the type of establishment we'd recognise today. They took their name from porter, a robust form of ale, which in turn took its name from its main customers – labourers and market porters – who favoured its nutritious qualities. In many cases, people literally drank their supper, and it was probably better than some of the food available at the time.

In about the same period, another drink called 'stout' appeared. As the name implies, it was a heavier, darker, stronger version of porter and also favoured for its nutritious and calorific values. (Contrary to popular thought, stout was originally an English drink. It was only in WWI that rationing meant English brewers couldn't produce this strong dark drink, and the industry switched to lighter ales. Ireland, without such restrictions, continued to brew stout and Guinness cleverly exploited this gap in the market, and remains the best-known brewer of stout to this day.)

Despite the existence of respectable porter houses, gin consumption was still having a debilitating effect on many. In the early 19th century, the British government legislated against gin by increasing import and sales taxes. Farmers at the time were encouraged to stop growing corn (the main ingredient for gin) and switch to barley (used for beer) instead.

GIN LANE

With beer back on the rise, William Hogarth would have certainly approved. Contrasting sharply with 'Gin Lane', he produced another picture called 'Beer Street' in which a group of happy, healthy Londoners are gainfully employed or reading books while quaffing merrily from their tankards. The only person out of a job in this picture is the pawnbroker.

Firing Up a Thirst The 19th century saw the height of the Industrial Revolution. Coal mines, shipyards and railways were developed, and factories were built across many parts of England. At the same time, demand for beer increased as workers, engaged in hard, hot labour, emerged from mills and mines with tremendous thirsts. Breweries capitalised on this demand by establishing houses specifically for selling beer to the public, and the 'public house', or 'pub' for short, made its first official appearance.

Initially, the pubs of this period were based on the alehouses of previous centuries, rather than on taverns or inns, and were extremely basic. Furniture was minimal, as were the manners of the clientele, and sawdust covered the bare boards to soak up various spillages – real 'spit-and-sawdust' establishments. Many pubs were tiled with curved (rather than angular) corners so landlords could simply swill out the room with buckets of water when their customers finally went home. In the really serious drinking-holes it was not uncommon for bars to

Top right: William Hogarth's *Gin Lane*, a salutary warning against the perils of the potent brew (reproduced by permission of the Founders' Library, University of Wales, Lampeter).

BEER STREET.

have a trough along their front so that male patrons could drink and urinate without moving – which lends a whole new meaning to yet another quaint old English expression: 'a night out on the piss'.

Obviously, the efficiencies of the early pubs were not to everybody's taste and through the second half of the 19th century the breweries, keen to increase their sales, attracted a wider range of customers by building grander and more welcoming pubs. Typically these were divided into two sections: the public bar was more basic, and designed for standing and drinking, while the saloon bar or lounge bar was more comfortable, often with seating, carpets and decorations – and higher prices. The lounge would also be the place for women – as long as they were with a man, of course. Unaccompanied women still had to wait another century or so before they could enjoy a drink in a pub without their morals being questioned.

While pubs were improving, the developments of the Industrial Revolution also affected their main commodity. The use of coal and gas was now widespread, and industrialisation meant beer could be produced on a vast scale to standardised qualities. In pre-industrial days, beer had been brewed over wood fires, which rarely yielded consistent temperatures so that one day's batch would be dark brown while another day's batch would be pale. On top of that, old-style beer generally had a smoky taste, whereas the beer of the 19th century had

Top left: Hogarth's *Beer Street*, celebrating the benefits of beer for one and all (reproduced by permission of the Founders' Library, University of Wales, Lampeter)

What's in a Pub Name?

As you travel around England, you can't help but notice the splendid selection of pub names, often illustrated with attractive signboards. In days gone by, these signs were vital because most of the general ale-swilling populace couldn't read, and might otherwise confuse the King's Head with the Queen's Arms. In our more literate times, pub signs are still a feature of the landscape, and remain as much a part of English tradition and history as medieval churches or stately homes.

The vine leaves hung by tavern-owners in Roman times to show that wine was sold developed through the centuries, so that any clump of leaves or clipping of shrubbery on display outside a tavern became a sign that drinks were available within. To save replacing drooping foliage, alehouses took to painting permanent signs – and this gave us pub names such as the Holly Bush, the Thorn Bush, or even the Old Bull and Bush.

Many pub names have connections to royalty, including the most popular name in the country, the Red Lion, with almost 900 pubs in Britain, and over 500 pubs in England, bearing this title. It dates from the early 17th century, when King James VI of Scotland became King James I of England, and, lest the populace forget his origin, he ordered that the lion, his heraldic symbol, be displayed in public places.

The second-most popular pub name is The Crown, which has more obvious royal connections, while the third-most popular, the Royal Oak, recalls the days of the Civil War when King Charles I escaped pursuers by hiding in a tree (look hard at most Royal Oak pub signs and you'll see his face peeping out from between the leaves). These pubs would have been named after the Restoration, when Charles II regained the throne. During the Civil War, some landlords had to think quick, and changed their pub names according to which army passed by. Thus, if the royalists were in town, the pub would be the Crown or the King's Head. If it was Oliver Cromwell's army passing by, the sign would be swiftly switched and the pub given a neutral name such as the Bell or the Nag's Head – and some stand-in titles have remained in place to the present day.

The King's Arms is another popular pub name with obvious royal connections, as is the Queen's Head, the Prince of Wales, and so on. Less obvious is the White Hart – a deer – the heraldic symbol of Richard II, who in 1393 decreed that every pub should display a sign. Landlords were eager to please the king, especially as the decree rounded off by stating that anyone failing in this duty 'shall forfeit his ale', and many chose the White Hart as a sign of allegiance and an insurance policy against stock loss.

The symbol of the king pops up again in signs for pubs called the Five Alls. This shows the king who rules over all, the parson who prays for all, the lawyer who pleads for all, the soldier who fights for all, and John Bull (ie, John Citizen) who pays for all.

Another common pub name is the Rose and Crown. Again, the regal links are obvious, but look carefully at the colour of the rose painted on those signs, especially if you're in the north of England. West of the Pennine Hills it should be the red rose of the House of Lancaster; east of the Pennines it's the white rose depicting the House of York. Woe betide any pub sign that is sporting the wrong colour!

While some pub names crop up in their hundreds, others are far from common, or downright unique, although many still have links to history. Nottingham's most famous pub, Ye Olde Trip to Jerusalem, commemorates knights and soldiers departing for crusades in the Holy Land in the 12th century. Pub names such as the George, or the George and Dragon, may date from the same era – England's patron saint was actually Greek, and his dragon probably a crocodile, as the story brought back from the east by returning crusaders. Move on several centuries and pub names such as the Spitfire, the Lancaster or the Churchill recall the days of WWII.

For a more local perspective, the Nobody Inn at Doddiscombsleigh, near Exeter in Devon, is said to recall a mix-up over a coffin, the Hit or Miss near Chippenham in Wiltshire recalls a close-run game of village cricket, while the Quiet Woman near Buxton in Derbyshire, with a sign of a headless female, is a reminder of more chauvinistic times.

a flavour that would not be unfamiliar to drinkers of some 'real ale' today.

The Industrial Revolution also led to a change in the temperature of beer. Although it was typically served at a tepid 65°F (18°C) until well into the 20th century, advances in refrigeration coupled with popular demand meant that the average temperature started to fall. This is a pattern that has continued into our own time: the beer in your glass has moved from room temperature to cellar temperature, and in many pubs it continues to fall – presumably to hold its own against the icy lagers that are now popular with many of today's drinkers.

Brave New World Pubs continued to grow in popularity and sheer numbers, but at the turn of the century they faced a major threat as the emergence of music halls and then cinemas meant that people went elsewhere for evening entertainment. By the 1920s, pubs were forced to compete against the newfangled attraction of the radio, and by the 1950s television was another draw, tempting people to stay at home instead of drinking at their local.

Landlords and breweries responded in numerous ways, and the 1960s and 1970s were a period of major modernisation in pubs across the country. Some pubs installed their own TVs, others brought in billiard or snooker tables, and later American pool tables – the height of cool in 1970s England. Other pleasures from across the pond included jukeboxes and pinball games or one-armed bandits and fruit machines.

Of even greater significance than these added attractions were the changes to the structure of the pub itself. As the new gear came in, the old was cast out, and the demand for all things 'modern' meant beautiful 100-year-old interiors in city pubs or much older beams, walls and stonework in rural inns were torn out to make way for vast bars, vinyl seats, Formica tables, chrome piping, dropped ceilings and industrial nylon carpets which soaked up spilt beer and became sticky overnight. For traditional pubs which had stood unchanged for decades, or even centuries, these were grim times.

The Pub Today

Back with the Old In our own time, pubs continue to evolve. In recent years many pubs have been turned into fake Irish bars and Australian watering-holes (O'Neill's, Walkabout Inns etc) or rebranded as chain outlets with infantile names (Slug & Lettuce, Floozy & Firkin etc, etc), while others mirror whatever their conglomerate owners deem the flavour of the moment. But elsewhere the changes have been positive, especially since the end of the 1990s. Today, quality is the key. Customers are more demanding, and – just as in centuries past – many pubs have had to raise their game in order to survive.

Once again, pub decor has enjoyed a major revamp, with a move towards simple interiors or retro styles, and things have turned full circle as many formerly modernised pubs are reinstating a 'traditional' ambience – which often means a rural look. This rustic makeover is fine in the genuine country areas, and it beats 1970s chrome and plastic any day, but it does sometimes look a bit odd in city pubs which never previously encountered anything like the scythe-and-dried-wheat arrangements that decorate the walls today.

Overall, however, good pubs are better than they've ever been, with a range of wine and food unthinkable only 10 or 15 years ago, and surroundings a long way removed from those accursed sticky carpets.

The Good, the Bad & the Ugly What makes a good pub? It's often hard to pin down. Good atmosphere and ambience are key requisites, but of course these can mean different things to different people. The best pubs follow a simple formula – they welcome people of all types, are relaxing and comfortable, offer friendly service and pleasant surroundings, serve good beers, wines and food, and are congenial places to pass a few hours, either alone or in the company of friends – and this is the type of pub that we have often sought out and recommended in this book.

But nothing beats the fun of doing your own research, so here are a few things to look for as you hunt for a good pub:

- A choice of beers from good local or regional brewers. Classic names to look out for include: Adnams (eastern England), Aarkells (south, southwest), Black Sheep (north), Fullers (southeast), Greene King (eastern, central, south), Hardys & Hansons (central), Hook Norton (south, midlands), Jennings (northwest), Marstons (south, central, north), St Austel (west), Shepherd Neam (southeast), Timothy Taylor (north), Wadworth (west), Youngs (southeast)
- Hand-pulled pumps to serve the beer. This means real ale, and a willingness on the part of the landlord or manager to put extra effort into serving it, which often translates into extra effort spent on food, atmosphere, cleanliness and so on
- A chalkboard showing 'guest beers' (beers from a small brewery which may not be local, or available for a short period), again showing willingness on the part of the landlord or manager to put in extra effort and provide a choice for customers
- Newspapers and magazines on the tables, showing that patrons are encouraged to sit around and relax
- A good menu of snacks and meals.

And what makes a bad pub? Here are a few warning signs: a limited choice of mass-produced beers, toxic air, comatose patrons, rude staff, noisy fruit machines, blaring TVs, insipid piped music, signs for wet T-shirt contests or karaoke evenings, overflowing ashtrays, overflowing toilets, general dirt and filth, and – you've guessed it – a sticky carpet.

Other signs which may set off warning bells include:

- 'pub carvery' (for which read: cold bits of overcooked beef and wilting veg served here)
- 'curry club' (for which read: two pints of cheap lager and a reheated plate of dubious meat and vague spices for only £6.95 served here)
- 'family friendly pub' (for which read: bouncy castle in the bar and kids everywhere)
- 'your friendly local' (no-one will talk to you, especially if you sit in their seat)
- 'all day sport on large TV' (no-one talks at all).

[Continued from page 64]

In London and other big cities, when travelling by tube or tram (especially at night) choose a carriage containing lots of other people. It's also best to avoid some deserted suburban tube stations at night; a bus or taxi can be a safer choice.

In large hotels, don't leave valuables lying around; put them in your bag, or use the room safe if there is one. There's no harm doing the same at B&Bs in cities, although in rural areas there's much less risk. In hostels with shared accommodation, keep your stuff packed away and carry valuables with you. Many hostels provide lockers, but you usually need your own padlock.

If you're driving, never leave valuables in a car, and remove luggage when parking overnight. The same applies even in seemingly safe rural locations. While you're out walking in the countryside, someone may well be walking off with your belongings. Where possible, look for secure parking areas near TICs.

Racism
Many parts of England are not without racial problems, which can turn into violence in some urban areas, but elsewhere general tolerance prevails, and visitors holidaying in England are very unlikely to have problems associated with their skin colour. Having said that, racism can still lurk close to the surface: it's not unusual to hear people openly discuss other races in quite unpleasant terms – and this can be in smart country pubs as much as rough city bars.

Beggars
There are beggars on the streets of most cities in England, and there are arguments for and against giving handouts – it's up to you – but remember to keep your wallet out of sight as you're handing over the coins. The *Big Issue* is a weekly magazine (£1) sold by homeless people who benefit directly from sales.

Touts & Cabs
Touts promoting backpackers hostels lurk at train stations such as London's Earl's Court and Victoria. Treat their 'free lift' claims with scepticism as you could end up in a pricey place miles from anywhere.

Also in large cities, beware of unlicensed minicabs unless you know exactly where you're going. A common ruse is to drive round in circles, then charge an enormous fare. Use a metered taxi, or phone a reputable minicab company and get a quote for the ride.

Drunkenness
In cities and towns, the sight of bleary-eyed lads ordering four pints of beer 15 minutes before closing time may be a sign of trouble to come; England's archaic pub laws mean groups of liquored-up 'lager louts' are all tossed onto the streets shortly after 11pm. The answer is a liberalisation of the rules, although it may do nothing for the splattered evidence of too much ale followed by an extra large vindaloo which decorates the pavements of many cities every Sunday morning. When in cities, keep a low profile around closing time, give drunken yobs a wide berth – and watch where you step.

Midges
Not a danger, but very annoying if you're camping between June and August, are the tiny biting insects called midges which take to the air on windless evenings, especially in northern England. If you're staying in hostels or B&Bs, it's no problem. Ways to counter the attack include light-coloured clothing and midge repellents (available in pharmacies and outdoor stores – brands with natural ingredients include Moziguard and Swamp Gel).

EMERGENCIES
England's national emergency number is ☎ 999. Use it for police, fire, ambulance, mountain rescue or coastguard.

LEGAL MATTERS
Drugs
Illegal drugs are widely available, especially in clubs. All the usual dangers apply and there have been numerous high-profile deaths associated with ecstasy. The government reclassified cannabis in 2002: possession remains a criminal offence, but the punishment for carrying a small amount is usually a warning. Dealers face far stiffer penalties, as do people caught with any other drugs.

Driving Offences
Drink-driving is a serious offence. For more information, and details of speed limits and parking rules, see Car & Motorcycle in the Getting Around chapter.

Fines

On trains (including the London Underground) and buses, people without a valid ticket for their journey may be fined on the spot: £5 on buses, £10 on trains.

Fines were introduced in some areas in 2002, allowing police to levy charges ranging from £40 to £80 for offences relating to anti-social behaviour. These fines work like parking tickets – offenders are given a fixed amount of time to pay.

Legal Ages

The age of consent in England is 16 (gay and straight), and you can get married at 16 (with permission from parents or guardians), but you'll have to wait two years for the toast – you must be over 18 to buy alcohol. Over-16s may buy cigarettes, so you can have a celebratory smoke instead.

You usually have to be 18 to enter a pub or bar, although the rules are different if you have a meal (or if the pub has a 'children's licence'). Some establishments are for over-21s only, so you're unlikely to see highchairs.

BUSINESS HOURS

Offices generally operate from 9am to 5pm, Monday to Friday. High-street shops may be open longer (to 6pm), most are open Saturday from 9am to 5pm, and many also on Sunday, perhaps from 11am to 4pm. In London and large cities there are 24-hour convenience stores. In suburban areas and small towns, some shops close for lunch (normally 1pm to 2pm), and shops in country towns may close on either Tuesday, Wednesday or Thursday afternoon.

Large museums and places of interest are usually open every day. Some smaller places open at the weekend, but close on Monday and/or Tuesday.

PUBLIC HOLIDAYS

In England and Wales, most businesses and banks close on official public holidays (hence the quaint term 'bank holiday'). These are:

New Year's Day	1 January
Good Friday	March/April
Easter Monday	March/April
May Day	1st Monday in May
Spring Bank Holiday	last Monday in May
Summer Bank Holiday	last Monday in August
Christmas Day	25 December
Boxing Day	26 December

If a public holiday falls on a weekend, the nearest Monday is usually taken instead.

On public holidays, some small museums and places of interest close, but larger attractions specifically gear up and have their busiest times, although nearly everything closes on Christmas Day and Boxing Day. Generally speaking, if a place closes on Sunday, it'll probably be shut on bank holidays as well.

SPECIAL EVENTS

Countless events are held around the country all year. Even small towns and villages have annual fairs or fetes, and many re-enact traditional customs and ceremonies, some dating back hundreds of years.

January

New Year Celebrations Get drunk and kiss strangers as the bells chime midnight in city centres nationwide. The biggest crowds are in London's Trafalgar Square.

February

Jorvik Viking Festival (York) Mock invaders, battles and longship races; mid-February

March

University Boat Race (River Thames, London) Traditional rowing contest between Oxford and Cambridge; late March

Cheltenham Festival Premier event to kick off the National Hunt (jumping) horse-race calendar; mid-March

Crufts Dog Show (Birmingham) Highlight of the canine year; mid-March

April

Grand National (Aintree, Liverpool) The most famous horse race of them all, with notoriously high jumps; first Saturday in April

May

FA Cup Final (Cardiff) Gripping end to venerable football tournament; traditionally held at Wembley (London) but in Cardiff (Wales) until 2005 at least; early May

Chelsea Flower Show (London) A blooming marvellous riot of colour; late May

Glyndebourne (near Lewes, Sussex) World-class opera in country-house grounds; runs until August

Brighton Festival Lively and innovative three-week feast of the arts

Bath International Festival Two more weeks of arts, in case Brighton wasn't enough

June

Beating Retreat (Whitehall, London) Military bands march in strict tempo; early June

Derby Week (Epsom, Surrey) Horse racing and people watching; early June

Trooping the Colour (Whitehall, London) Queen's birthday parade with spectacular pageantry; mid-June

Royal Ascot (Berkshire) More horses and more people, plus outrageous hats; mid-June

Lawn Tennis Championships (Wimbledon, London) Two weeks of rapid-fire returns; late June

Mardi Gras (London) Loud and proud, one of Europe's largest gay and lesbian festivals; late June

Glastonbury Festival (Pilton, Somerset) Huge, open-air, musical hippy happening; late June

Royal Regatta (Henley-on-Thames, Oxfordshire) Premier rowing and social event; late June

July

Hampton Court Palace International Flower Show (London) The name says it all; early July

Cowes Week (Isle of Wight) Yachting spectacular; late July

International Aerospace Exhibition and Flying Display (Farnborough, Surrey) World's largest aeroplane show; late July

York Early Music Festival Churches host countless medieval concerts; late July

August

Notting Hill Carnival (London) A spectacular multicultural feast, Caribbean style; late August

Reading Festival (Berkshire) Three-day open-air rock, pop and dance extravaganza; late August

Leeds Festival (Yorkshire) The Reading of the North, and just as good; late August

October

Horse of the Year Show (Birmingham) Top show-jumping event in Britain held at the National Exhibition Centre (NEC)

November

Guy Fawkes Day Bonfires and fireworks around the country; 5 November

December

New Year Celebrations That's another year gone! Get ready for midnight – see January.

COURSES

Whether you want to study astronomy or upholstery, somewhere in England there's going to be a course. Local libraries are often a good starting point for finding information. **Floodlight** (w www.floodlight.co.uk; £3.75 to £6.50) is the guide to all London-based courses; it's available from newsagents.

Language

Every year thousands of people come to England to study English, and there are tuition centres all around the country. The problem is identifying the reputable ones, which is where the **British Council** (☎ 0161 957 7755; w www.britishcouncil.org; 10 Spring Gardens, London SW1) comes in. This organisation produces a free list of accredited colleges, and offers general advice to overseas students on educational opportunities (as many normal colleges now offer courses specifically aimed at students from abroad).

The British Council has 229 offices in 111 countries around the world that can provide the same information. You can also get information from the BTA (see the Tourist Offices section).

WORK

If you'll accept long hours, low pay and menial tasks, you'll almost certainly find work in England. But if you want to save money, it's difficult to find a job that pays well enough – unless you've got desirable skills. Like millions before you, you'll probably want to start your search in London, although work opportunities do exist elsewhere.

Traditionally, unskilled visitors have worked in pubs and restaurants, or as nannies (as these jobs often provide live-in accommodation). However, you'll be lucky to get £180 per week. Before you accept a job, make sure you're clear about the terms and conditions. The minimum wage was set at £4.20 per hour (£3.60 for those aged 18 to 21) in 2002, but if you're working unofficially no-one's obliged to pay you even that.

Accountants, health professionals, journalists, computer programmers, lawyers, teachers and clerical workers with computer experience stand a better chance of finding well-paid work. Don't forget copies of your qualifications, references (which will probably be checked) and a CV (résumé).

Teachers stand a good chance in London. Contact the individual borough councils, which have separate education departments, although some schools recruit directly.

To work as a trained nurse you have to register with the United Kingdom Central Council for Nursing, which can take up to three months. The initial application fee is £117 (for non-EU overseas-trained nurses) and once the application has been accepted, a fee of £93 (£60 for EU citizens) is required. The registration is then renewable every three years for a fee of £60. Contact the **Nursing & Midwifery Council** (☎ 020-7333 9333; **e** *new reg@nmc.uk.org;* **w** *www.nmc-uk.org).* If you are not registered you can still work as an auxiliary nurse.

The free *TNT Magazine* (**w** *www.tntmag .co.uk)* is a good starting point for jobs and agencies aimed at travellers. For au pair and nanny work buy the quaintly titled *The Lady*. Also check the London *Evening Standard*, national newspapers and the temping agencies scattered throughout cities. For details on all aspects of short-term work consult the excellent *Work Your Way Around the World* by Susan Griffith.

If you have artistic talents, you could try busking. As every Peruvian pipe-player knows, this is common in London, although it's banned in the Underground (£25 fine) – not that you'd notice. The tube now plans to license approved buskers to play in certain stations. Westminster Council licenses pitches in Covent Garden and Leicester Square, for which, in theory, performers are vetted. To perform in these competitive areas you have to turn up early and join a rota organised by the performers themselves.

A good option if you're prepared to work in exchange for accommodation, rather than money, is a scheme run by the nonprofit **Anchor Trust** (☎ 08457 758595; **w** *www .anchor.org.uk),* where volunteers (including overseas visitors) live with and care for older people in the London area. Training and supervision are provided, and you must commit for three months or more.

Tax

As an official employee, you'll find income tax and National Insurance automatically deducted from your weekly pay-packet. However, the deductions will be calculated on the assumption that you're working for the entire financial year (which runs from 6 April to 5 April). If you don't work as long as that, you may be eligible for a refund. Contact the Inland Revenue or use one of the agencies that advertise in *TNT Magazine* (but check their fee or percentage charge first).

ACCOMMODATION

The accommodation you'll use in England can be as varied as the places you visit, and – whatever your budget – finding a place to sleep every night is likely to be your main expense. But the list of choices (from basic bunkhouses to smart hotels, tiny cottages to grand castles) is all part of the attraction.

Camping

The opportunities for camping are numerous – which is particularly handy if you're on a tight budget, or simply enjoy fresh air and the great outdoors.

In rural areas, camping grounds (called campsites in England) range from farmers' fields with a tap and a basic toilet costing £1 to £2 per night, to smarter affairs with hot showers and many other facilities, charging £5 or more.

Many cities and towns have campsites outside the centre, which can be awkward if you don't have wheels. Facilities are usually good though, and rates are about £5 per person.

Throughout this book, we've generally given the per-adult price charged by campsites. Children are about half price, and cars cost another pound or two. A few places charge per 'unit' – usually two people, one tent and one car.

Camping Barns

A camping barn is a converted farm building, providing simple shelter for walkers and visitors to country areas. They have sleeping platforms and a cooking area, and basic toilets outside. You need to have everything you'd need to camp except the tent. To sleep in a barn costs £2 to £4 per person per night.

Bunkhouses

The next grade up from a camping barn is a bunkhouse, also handy for walkers, cyclists, or anyone on a budget in the countryside. They usually have heating and cooking stoves, and may supply utensils. Sleeping platforms may have mattresses, but you'll need a sleeping bag. Other facilities may include showers and a drying room. Most charge around £5 to £7.50 per night, although some top-end places charge around £10.

Hostels

There are two types of hostel in England: those run by the Youth Hostels Association (YHA) and independent hostels. To give an idea of facilities, many hostels are awarded stars (from one star to three star) by local tourism authorities.

Hostel Charges

Note: Throughout this book we list adult prices for staying at YHA hostels. Under-18s pay about 75% of adult rates.

There are hostels in rural areas, towns and cities, and they're aimed at all types of travellers – whether you're a hardy long-distance walker or touring by car – and you don't have to be young or single to use them.

YHA Hostels Despite the old-fashioned image, YHA hostels are nowhere near as austere as they used to be, and always provide a good, clean, efficiently run option for budget travellers. Some are purpose built, but many are in converted cottages, farms and country houses, usually with between two and 20 bedrooms (divided into male and female rooms), each with four to 10 beds. Other facilities include showers, drying room, lounge, and an equipped self-catering kitchen. Many hostels also have twin rooms, some with private bathroom, and there are a lot more bathrooms to go round these days as well. The days of boarding school–style dormitories and queues for a cold shower are long gone.

Charges for YHA hostels vary. Small, simple places in country areas cost £8 to £10. Larger hostels with more facilities in towns or national parks cost £13 to £18. London has several excellent YHA hostels, with many facilities and a lively cosmopolitan atmosphere, charging £20 to £25. To stay, you have to be a YHA member, which costs £13 per year (£6.50 for under-18s). You can join in advance, or at your first hostel. Members get a handbook, with contact details and opening times of all 230 hostels in England and Wales, and discounts on things like coach travel, outdoor equipment, attractions, guidebooks and maps. The YHA is affiliated with Hostelling International (HI), so if you're a member of your own national HI-linked hostelling association, you get the same deal as local members.

Meals (optional) cost about £3.50 for breakfasts and packed lunches, and around £5 for three-course dinners – often large and very good value.

Hostels tend to have very complicated opening periods, especially in rural areas out of tourist season, so it's always best to check these before turning up. Opening times differ too: smaller hostels may close from 10am to 5pm, but busier places open all day. City hostels open 24 hours. Reservations are usually possible, and you can often pay in advance by credit card. To join or for more details contact **YHA** (within UK ☎ 0870 870 8808, from overseas ☎ 01629-592700, fax 01629-592627; w www.yha.org.uk; Trevelyan House, Dimple Rd, Matlock DE4 3YH). For reservations you can phone individual hostels direct, or use the YHA's **central reservations service** (☎ 0870 241 2314, from overseas ☎ 01629-592700) or book online.

Independent Hostels Also known as private hostels or backpackers hostels, England has a large – and constantly growing – selection of independent hostels. In rural areas, some are little more than simple bunkhouses (charging around £5), some are very good bunkhouses (around £9), and some are almost up to B&B standard, charging £12 or more. You don't need to be a member of any hostel organisation to stay.

Independent/backpackers hostels in cities are aimed at young budget travellers from around the world. These are often very lively indeed, with a range of rooms (doubles or dorms), bar, café, internet and laundry facilities and so on. Prices are £10 to £15 for a dorm bed, or £20 to £30 for a bed in a private room. (Some hostels in London have been described as 'backpacker ghettos', very crowded and with few facilities, so you may want to choose carefully here.)

For more information, the annual *Independent Hostel Guide* by Sam Dalley covers 300 places in England and beyond, and is the best listing available. It costs £4.95 and it's available at hostels or direct from **The Backpackers Press** (☎ 01629-580427; e sam@backpackerspress.com; Speedwell House, Upperwood, Matlock Bath DE4 3PE).

Also worth looking out for is *Backpax*, a free quarterly minimagazine covering independent hostels nationwide, with plenty of info on activities and organised trips. For details check out w www.backpaxmag.com.

University Accommodation

Many universities offer student accommodation to visitors during the July and August holidays. You usually get a functional single bedroom, sometimes with a private bathroom, and self-catering flats are also available. Prices range from £10 to £30 per person.

B&Bs & Guesthouses

The B&B (for 'bed & breakfast') is a great British institution. Basically, you get a room in somebody's house, and small B&Bs may only have one guest room, so you'll really feel like part of the family. Larger B&Bs may have four or five rooms, and more facilities. 'Guesthouse' is sometimes just another name for a B&B, although they may tend towards a small hotel, with prices to match.

In country areas, your B&B might be in a village or isolated farm; in cities it's usually a suburban house. Price differences are usually reflected in the facilities: at the bottom end (£12 to £14 per person) you get a simple bedroom and share the bathroom. Smarter B&Bs charge about £15 to £20, and have extras like a TV or 'hospitality tray' (kettle, cup, tea and coffee), and a private bathroom – either down the hall, or 'en suite'. B&Bs in cities charge about £25 to £30 per person, although often get cheaper further out in the suburbs.

It's important to note that B&B prices are usually quoted per person, but may be based on two people sharing a room. Single rooms are rare, and lone travellers need to plan ahead a little in order to find one. Even then, for a single room you may pay 20% to 50% on top of the 'usual' per person price. Some B&Bs simply won't take single people (unless you pay the full double-room price).

Some other points to note include:

- The use of the terminology: you stay *at* a B&B, but hotels and inns *do* B&B

- In cities, some B&Bs are set up for long-term residents or people on welfare; these places don't normally take passing tourists
- Most B&Bs cater for walkers and cyclists, but some don't, so check this if you may be turning up with dirty boots or wet gear
- Many B&Bs are nonsmoking establishments, or only allow smoking in the lounge
- Bookings are always preferred, and are essential for busy places during popular periods
- If you're on a flexible itinerary you can simply turn up and take a chance; places with spare rooms hang a 'Vacancies' sign outside
- If a B&B is full, owners can usually recommend another place nearby, or they may guide you to a private house taking occasional guests which you'd never find in tourist listings
- Many B&Bs raise their rates in busy times (usually summer or if there's a festival in town) and lower them at other times, so be prepared for prices which are slightly different from those indicated in this book
- Some places give cheaper rates for stays of more than one night, and require a minimum stay of two nights over the weekend
- Most B&Bs serve enormous breakfasts (see the boxed text 'The Full English' later in this chapter), and many country B&Bs offer packed lunches (around £3) and evening meals (around £10), which is handy if it's 3 miles to the nearest village
- If you're in a hurry, on a diet, or just not hungry, a few B&Bs will give you a discount for not having breakfast (a saving of £5 is possible), but most hosts will find this a pretty unusual request. Bed-only rates are more common at ferry ports

Pubs & Inns

As well as selling drinks, many pubs and inns offer B&B, particularly in country areas. The difference between an inn and a pub is technical, but just to confuse things some pubs are

Something Different for the Weekend?

England has a huge and varied choice of hotels and B&Bs, but if you thirst for the truly unusual, contact the **Landmark Trust** (☎ 01628-825925; **w** www.landmarktrust.co.uk; Shottesbrooke, Maidenhead, Berkshire SL6 3SW). This architectural charity restores and rents historic buildings; your options include medieval houses, castles, Napoleonic forts and 18th-century follies.

Another option is **Distinctly Different** (**w** www.distinctlydifferent.co.uk), a fascinating list of places to stay that are unusual, bizarre or even vaguely risqué. Can't sleep at night? How about booking into a former funeral parlour? Need to spice up your romance? Then go for the former brothel or the 'proudly phallic' lighthouse. Feeling brave? We have just the haunted inn for you, sir.

Back safely down to earth with the final option: the **National Trust** (see Useful Organisations earlier in this chapter) produces a very handy *Bed & Breakfast* leaflet detailing over 80 places to stay. Most are NT-owned working farms, and some are on estates of stately homes owned or run by the Trust.

Totting up the Stars & Diamonds

Most accommodation in England is registered with a tourist board, and hotels are awarded stars (ie, one star to five stars) according to their standards, which they put on a plaque on the door. B&Bs and guesthouses are awarded diamonds.

Note that stars are based more on facilities and standards, rather than the character of the building or the attitude of the staff. Many places with one or two stars are owner-managed, and guests are made especially welcome. Conversely, some five-star places may have loads of facilities, but can feel a bit impersonal. Diamonds attempt to take this into account – a B&B with few facilities but great service can still earn a high diamond rating.

It's also worth noting that all establishments have to pay to be listed by tourist boards, and many small B&Bs don't register, even though the service they offer is absolutely fine. Accommodation lists provided by Tourist Information Centres help you find places that meet set standards, but if you use these lists as your only source you might miss out on a real gem.

called hotels. (For more information, see the Pubs special section.) Whatever, staying in a pub can be good fun – you're automatically at the centre of the community – although accommodation varies enormously, from stylish suites to threadbare rooms aimed at (and last used by) 1950s commercial salesmen. Conditions are usually reflected in the price:

Making Reservations

Most Tourist Information Centres can book accommodation, usually charging a 10% fee, which is *usually* subtracted from the price of the B&B or hotel. Most TICs also have a Book-A-Bed-Ahead (BABA) scheme that arranges accommodation for the next two nights anywhere in England. This costs around £3 plus the 10% deposit.

When booking accommodation in advance, whether a hostel, hotel or B&B, check where it actually *is*. In country areas, postal addresses include the nearest town, but this may be 20 miles away – quite important if you're walking or cycling! For walkers, if a B&B *is* some distance from your route, some owners will pick you up for a small charge.

If you book over the phone, larger B&Bs and YHA hostels take a deposit on a credit card. Independent hostels and small B&Bs often do not require money in advance. This can be very handy, but owners sometimes hold beds for people who never turn up, while turning away others who arrive on spec. If you book ahead and your plans then change, please phone and let them know.

around £15 per person at the bottom end, up to £25 to £30 at the top end. A major advantage for solo tourists is that pubs are more likely to have single rooms.

If a pub does B&B, it normally does meals – served in the bar, or in a smarter restaurant. Breakfast is often also served in the bar next morning, and not always enhanced by the smell of stale beer and ashtrays.

Hotels

The term 'hotel' is used to describe simple pubs with a few rooms or huge country houses with fancy facilities, acres of grounds, grand staircases and the requisite row of stag-heads on the wall. Charges vary as much as quality and atmosphere, with singles/doubles costing from £30/40 to more than £100/150. Whatever your budget, some hotels are excellent value while others overcharge.

Purpose-built chain hotels along motorways and in city centres depend on business trade, and so offer competitive weekend rates to attract tourists; they also often have a flat room-rate (with twin beds and private bathroom), making them relative bargains for couples or small families.

Self-Catering

If you want to slow down, renting a place for a week or two can be ideal. In holiday areas you can find neat town apartments, quaint old houses or converted farm buildings (usually called 'cottages'), all with bedrooms, bathroom, lounge and equipped kitchen.

At busy times (especially July and August), you'll need to book ahead, and cottages for four people cost around £200 to

£300 per week. At quieter times, £150 to £180 is more usual. You may also be able to rent a place for a weekend.

Most TICs produce lists of self-catering cottages, and countrywide agencies include **Hoseasons Country Cottages** (☎ *01502-501515, fax 584962;* **w** *www.hoseasons.co.uk; Sunway House, Lowestoft NR32 2LW).* Alternatively, get a copy of *Stilwell's Independent Holiday Cottages,* a comprehensive directory produced annually. Stilwell's is not an agency; you phone the cottage owners and book direct. The directory is available free from **Stilwell's Publishing** (☎ *01271 336028;* **w** *www.stilwell.co.uk).* The website is also a very handy source of information.

FOOD

England once boasted a cuisine so undesirable that there's still no English equivalent for *bon appétit.* These days, though, it's easy to find decent food – and for even the poorest of visitors healthy eating (or just tasty eating) definitely won't break the bank.

To a large extent, food in England has changed thanks to outside influences. For decades, cities and towns have boasted Chinese and Indian restaurants (although some curry houses are actually Pakistani or Bangladeshi-run), and in more recent times food from Thailand and other countries east of Suez has become available too. Closer to home, pastas, pizzas and other Mediterranean dishes are commonplace in speciality French or Italian restaurants, but also in everyday pubs and cafés. A more recent trend is tapas – the little plates of goodies you get in Spanish bars. Of course, tapas have been around for ages in London, but the fad has slowly moved north, and now you find them everywhere. Many Italian restaurants have transmogrified into Italian-Spanish, and quite a few add Mexican dishes to the repertoire too.

The overall effect of these influences has been the introduction to English restaurants of revolutionary ingredients (like crisp fresh vegetables) and new techniques (like steaming, or tossing stuff in olive oil). We've also seen the creation of what some restaurants call 'modern British cuisine', which often just means 'Pretty good food, not like the old British'. Even humble 'bangers and mash' can rise to new heights when handmade thyme-flavoured sausages are paired with a mix of lightly chopped fennel and new potatoes.

And finally – it's official – vegetarianism is no longer weird. Many restaurants have at least a token vegetarian dish (although it's often restricted to lasagne); it's common for menus at better places to offer several choices. Of course, in curry and pizza places there are always several options, although vegans will find the going tough, except at dedicated veggie-vegan restaurants.

Most restaurants – at least mid-range and upwards – provide no-smoking areas but you may not always have that luxury and smokers at the next table won't hesitate in sparking up even if you're halfway through your main. If you're an ardent non-smoker, make sure to say so when you book which, by the way, isn't essential but is always advisable, especially at the weekend.

Takeaways

Every town and city has its complement of takeaway restaurants. Some are genuine takeaways – at others you can 'eat in'. To escape homogenised chains like McDonald's and Pizza Hut, every town has at least one local curry house and a fish-and-chip shop. Although there are some top-notch 'chippies' about, the best you can say about most is they provide piles of stodge for reasonable prices. Perhaps that's why curries have overtaken fish and chips as England's most popular takeaway.

One of the best developments in high-street cuisine has been the emergence of takeaways specialising in fresh food – although this tends to be more of a southern phenomenon. Chains such as Pret-a-Manger sell wonderful sandwiches and salads made from fresh ingredients in innovative combinations.

Cafés & Teashops

The traditional English café is nothing like its continental European namesake. For a start, the usual café accent is often omitted, and it's pronounced 'caffy', or shortened to 'caff'. Most are simple places serving filling food at reasonable prices; meals like meat pie or omelette with chips cost around £3. Sandwiches, cakes and other snacks are £1 to £2.

Some cafés verge on hideous – definitely earning their 'greasy spoon' handle – while others are neat and tidy, with a friendly atmosphere. Like B&Bs, good cafés are a wonderful institution and always worth a stop.

In towns, cafés are aimed at workers, and may not always open at weekends, but on

The Full English

As you travel around England, you'll often come across the breakfast phenomenon known as the 'Full English' – bacon, sausages, egg, tomatoes, mushrooms, baked beans and fried bread. In B&Bs it's preceded by cereals, served with tea or coffee, and followed by toast, butter and marmalade. In northern England (if you're really lucky) you might be served with black pudding – a mixture of meat, blood and fat, served in slices.

If you don't feel like eating half a farmyard it's quite OK to ask for just the egg and tomatoes. Some B&Bs and hotels offer other alternatives such as kippers or a 'Continental Breakfast' – which completely omits the cooked stuff and may add something really exotic like croissants or fresh fruit.

weekdays they always open for lunch, for dinner until about 7pm, and maybe in the morning for breakfast. In country areas, cafés cater for tourists, walkers, cyclists and so on, and in summer they're open every day.

Smarter cafés in country areas and well-to-do towns are called teashops. As well as drinks, they also serve cakes, snacks and light meals, usually at slightly higher prices than cafés, but then you might be paying for extras like tablecloths, twee decor and service.

In most cities and towns you can now find American-style coffee shops and Euro-style cafés and café-bars, serving a range of decent lattes and espressos, as well as meals or snacks in sweet and savoury flavours. Chains in cities everywhere include Starbucks, while places like Café Rouge try to replicate casual French brasseries, with good meals around £10 to £15, and menus heavy with salads, omelettes, steaks and *frites*. Some of these new-style cafés even have outside chairs and tables, sidewalk-style – rather brave considering the narrow pavements and inclement weather much of England enjoys.

Pubs

Perhaps surprisingly, in recent years pubs in England have become a good-value option when you're looking for something to eat – whether a toasted sandwich or a top-class three-course meal. Details are given in the Pubs special section.

Restaurants

There are many good and excellent restaurants in England, with seafood, various meats, roasts and many other dishes very well prepared. London has scores of restaurants that could hold their own in major cities worldwide, while places in Bath, Leeds and Manchester can give the capital a fair run for its money (actually, often for rather less money).

Just to give you an idea, as prices vary considerably across the country, a main course in a straightforward restaurant would be around £7 to £10, rising to £10 to £15 at places with good-quality menus. Beyond this category are the real high-class establishments, where excellent food, service and surroundings are reflected in similarly high prices; to eat a fine full meal might cost £30, £50 or more.

England has a few BYO restaurants (where you can 'bring your own' bottles of wine), but it's not that common, and some places have a 'corkage' charge of about £2.

Regional Cuisine

For every greasy spoon and unimaginative pasta joint, there's a pub or restaurant serving up tasty local specialities. Well, perhaps not for *every* basic joint, but the number of places serving good meals of home-grown and home-produced ingredients is increasing all the time.

For years, the stereotypical English dinner has been roast beef and Yorkshire pudding (that's why the French call the English 'rosbif'). Beef consumption took a bit of a knock in 2000 and 2001 following 'mad-cow' scares and the foot-and-mouth outbreak, but good-quality roasts from well-reared cattle now grace menus everywhere.

Yorkshire pudding is simply roast batter, but when well-cooked it's very tasty, and accompanies many meals in England, although in Yorkshire itself the pudding is traditionally eaten *before* the main meal, usually with gravy. In olden days it was a simple stomach-filler, but even today in northern England you can buy a big bowl-shaped Yorkshire pudding, filled with meat stew, beans, mixed vegetables or – in these multicultural days – curry.

Also in northern England, another local speciality to look out for is Cumberland sausage – a tasty mix of good meat and herbs so large it has to be curved in a spiral to fit on your plate. Bring sausage and Yorkshire pud together and you have another famous English speciality – toad in the hole.

Fish and chips are available from takeaways, but in the north of England particularly fish-and-chip shops (often called 'fisheries') also offer inside dining. A traditional fish supper involves fish, chips, peas, bread and butter, and tea.

Near the coasts, seafood is always a local speciality. Yorkshire's coastal towns are famous for servings of cod, while restaurants in Cornwall regularly conjure up prawns, crab, lobster, oysters, mussels and scallops, although a lot of the best stuff is exported. Other local specialities include Norfolk crab, Northumberland kippers, and eels in London – traditionally served with mashed potato.

A southwest England speciality you can now buy everywhere – especially in pubs – is the ploughman's lunch. Originally just a lump of cheese and a lump of bread, which hearty yokels carried into the fields in days of yore wrapped in a red spotted handkerchief, over the years this lunch has been prettified to include butter, salad, pickled onion and dressings – even a selection of cheeses. You might also find other variations – farmer's lunch (bread and chicken), stockman's lunch (bread and cold meats), fisherman's lunch (you guessed it, with fish), Frenchman's lunch (brie and baguette), and so on.

Another favourite originally from the Westcountry are Cornish pasties – a mix of cooked vegetables wrapped in pastry – now available everywhere, and often including meat varieties. They were originally invented in the days before cling-wrap so tin miners could carry their food underground and leave it on a ledge ready for lunchtime. So pasties weren't mixed up, they were traditionally marked with owners' initials – always at one end of the pasty, so the miner could eat half and safely leave the other half to snack on later, without it mistakenly disappearing into the mouth of a workmate.

DRINKS
Pubs & Bars
The difference between pubs and bars is sometimes vague, but generally speaking bars are more modern, smarter, larger and louder than pubs, with a predominantly younger crowd. And the drinks are more expensive too. Generally, pubs are open all day from 11am to 11pm, although some shut in the afternoon. Bars may keep the same opening hours as pubs, or they may be classed as

---

Restaurant Hours

Most restaurants in England are open for lunch and dinner, usually on every day of the week, although some may close on Sunday evening, or all day Monday. Throughout this book, many restaurants are listed and reviewed, but opening times and days are given only if they differ markedly from this usual pattern.

---

clubs and get to keep the doors open, and the drinks flowing, much longer.

A feature of many bar developers is their preference to take over interesting city-centre buildings. As just one example, the city Sheffield has bars in a former bank, a former fire station and a former office of the National Union of Mineworkers. One finance company even based a TV ad campaign around so many banks becoming trendy wine bars.

Pubs – and the drinks they serve – are covered in more detail in the Pubs special section.

Takeaway Drinks
If you want drinks to take away (or 'carry out'), some pubs sell beer in cans or bottles,

---

The Regional Meal Divide

Depending where you go, the term 'dinner' can be used differently, and may cause confusion. In the south of England, and at any restaurant, it's a cooked evening meal. But in northern England, 'dinner' is the meal eaten at midday. Thus, factory workers in the south have a lunch break, while those in the north have a dinner break. So if somebody refers to 'after dinner', check if this means afternoon or sometime in the evening.

The term 'tea' also has different meanings. As well as being the English national drink, in the south it's usually a light meal (eg, small cakes and cucumber sandwiches) eaten at the end of the afternoon. But in the north of England, where 'dinner' is eaten at midday, 'tea' is the cooked evening meal.

The great mystery, however, is where the border lies. Some put it between Birmingham and Derby, but if anybody finds out exactly where 'tea' becomes 'dinner', and 'dinner' becomes 'lunch', please let us know.

but it's more usual (and cheaper) to go to a neighbourhood shop or 'off-licence'. Opening hours vary, but most off-licences keep pub hours. You can also buy beer and wine in supermarkets; most have very impressive selections, at very good prices.

ENTERTAINMENT

In English cities you need never be short of entertainment, with a wonderful choice of concert halls, theatres, cinemas and nightclubs to fill your evenings. The world-class venues are mainly in London but most cities have at least one good theatre and an art cinema to supplement the multiplex. Choice is much more restricted if you're staying in the countryside – but then you're in the wrong place for bright lights anyway.

However you budget your time and money, make sure that you see some English theatre. It easily lives up to its reputation as the best in the world. And it's not all in London's West End – although there can be some fine shows there. Small, impressive theatre companies can be found all over England, and over the summer period (June to September) some of the best troupes go on the road and perform in towns throughout the country.

Summer is also the best time to catch outdoor productions. Many stately homes put on open-air plays (*Macbeth* at dusk is magic). The best-known event is Glyndebourne – a programme of world-class opera in the spectacular setting of a country-house grounds – which runs from May through August (for more details see 'The Sussex Fitzcarraldo' boxed text in the Southeast England chapter).

Summertime inspires towns and cities across the country to run performing arts festivals – everything from village events over a weekend, up to the massive Bath International Festival, via specialist events like Buxton Opera Festival or Whitby Folk Festival. Don't forget, too, the loud and colourful pop and rock extravaganzas such as Glastonbury and Reading, or the lively and colourful Womad world music gathering.

For live rock, pop, folk or roots music on a smaller scale, bands continue to emerge from all over the country. Once again, London has the largest choice, but you can hear great music (and some really dire stuff) in pubs and clubs everywhere.

For clubbing, the major cities have the best choices. Perhaps it's because the pubs close so

early, but England has an excellent range of clubs, with DJs and theme nights that bring in eager punters from miles around. Of course, London is right up there, but Bristol, Nottingham, Manchester, Sheffield, Leeds and Liverpool all have large and ecstatic club scenes.

Whatever your taste when it comes to entertainment, the best way to find out who's who and what's hot is to scan the local listing mags, or simply ask around. Enjoy!

SPECTATOR SPORTS

The English have been responsible for inventing or codifying many of the world's most popular spectator sports: cricket, tennis, football (soccer) and rugby. To this list add billiards and snooker, lawn bowls, boxing, darts, hockey, squash and table tennis. Trouble is, having invented these games, the English aren't always so good at playing them – as Aussie cricket and rugby fans will delight in telling you.

England also hosts premier events for a number of sports, including Test Cricket, Badminton Horse Trials, Wimbledon tennis, the Derby and the Grand National horse races, and the Henley rowing regatta.

All year round, London hosts major sporting events. If you want to see live action, consult *Time Out* for fixtures, times, venues and ticket prices. See also Spectator Sports in the London chapter.

Football (Soccer)

The English football league is acknowledged as being one of the world's most entertaining. It's big business, and the money associated with TV deals has contributed much to the balance of power in the sport today. The Premiership – an elite league for the country's top 20 clubs – ensures that most players earn more than £15,000 a week (with top ones raking in £100,000 – before sponsorship deals), while satellite channel Sky not only helps keep the players in Gucci, but also beams them around the world, maintaining the game's profile and creating international stars.

Unfortunately, outside the Premiership, few of the less successful clubs have benefited from these multimillion pound deals. The collapse in 2002 of ITV Digital, which owned the rights to games in Divisions 1, 2 and 3, was a crushing blow for many smaller fry.

The domestic football season lasts from August to May. Tickets for Premiership games cost from £20 to £50 and are difficult to get hold of, but it's worth trying (see the regional chapters for details). Those for lower division games are cheaper and much easier to obtain.

In the 1980s, English football was associated with violence. This problem has been considerably addressed, and the image largely shed. Every now and then hooliganism raises its bony head, but it's generally rare, and most grounds are good for a family day out.

Cricket

The rules and terminology of cricket can easily escape those not brought up in the tradition, but application can reveal the inner tension and excitement of what appears to be at first sight the world's most boring game.

Created in the 16th century, possibly on Hambledon Down in Hampshire, the game consists of head-to-head confrontations within the framework of an 11-a-side team-game which, at times, aspires to sporting ballet.

In the 19th century, English imperialists taught the Empire how to play, and now those nations are regularly victorious in various one-day games, county games and five-day Test Matches (which sometimes finish without an overall winner!) played on seminal grounds such as Lords and The Oval in London, Old Trafford in Manchester, Edgbaston in Birmingham and Headingley in Leeds.

Tickets cost £25 to £100 and tend to go fast. County championship matches usually charge a much more manageable £12 per adult and kids get in for half-price.

Rugby

Rugby (aka rugby football or 'rugger') takes its name from Rugby school in Warwickshire where the game is supposed to have originated when William Ellis picked up the ball and ran off with it during a football match in 1823. Today, it's an old adage that football is a gentlemen's game played by hooligans while rugby is the other way around.

The rugby union code turned professional in 1995 (since then the number of injuries have doubled – apparently because protective equipment tempts the wide men to take more risks). An alternative code of the game, rugby league, is played predominantly in the north of England, in which the team has 13 rather than 15 players, and rules and tactics differ slightly.

Leicester, Bath and Gloucester are among the better union clubs. Fans will find London rewarding, with a host of good-quality teams (including the London Irish, Wasps and Saracens). Twickenham is the impressive national stadium and headquarters for the English game (call ☎ 020-8831 6666 for tickets).

Rugby league is a summer sport; the Super League final is held at Old Trafford in September. Teams to watch include the Wigan Warriors, Bradford Bulls and Leeds Rhinos.

Tickets for normal fixtures are easy to obtain at reasonable prices (around £15 to £40

The Sweet FA Cup

The Football Association held its first interclub tournament in 1871, inspired by the knockout competitions played in England's public schools. Fifteen clubs took part, playing for a nice piece of silverware called the FA Cup – then worth about £20.

Nowadays, around 600 clubs compete for this legendary and priceless trophy. The preliminary rounds begin in August, and the world-famous Cup Final has been staged at Wembley Stadium for decades, although its current venue is Cardiff's Millennium Stadium.

Monster-club Manchester United has won the most FA Cup Finals, with 10 victories. But with the English affection for the underdog, one of the Cup's great attractions is that outsiders are in with a chance. Notorious giant-killers include Wrexham, then ranked 24th in the Division 3, taking out reigning champions Arsenal in the third round in 1992.

However, in recent years the Cup's lustre has dimmed. English clubs were banned from Europe from 1985 to 1990 and when they returned to the fold European football dominated their imagination. Certain clubs started to rest key players during domestic games, and Manchester United didn't even take part in 1999/2000 due to fixture clashes.

Now, as competitions have multiplied, the FA Cup has become one among many. The Premier League (competing for the highest place in the country) and Champion's League (against European teams) have a higher profile, bigger kudos, and – simply – more money to play with.

for club matches, much more for international games; ☎ 0990-582582 for details). Even if you're not a rugby zealot, it's worth catching a game for the atmosphere and singing in the terraces.

Tennis

The grassy drama of **Wimbledon** (☎ 020-89462244; **w** www.wimbledon.org) ensures the onset of English tennis fever for the last week of June and first week in July. The All England Tennis tournament, held in London's SW19, is the daddy of the grand slam events, and the only one played on grass. There's something quintessentially English about the combination of grass courts, and strawberries and cream. Less quintessential are the winners. The last times the trophies decked a local mantelpiece were 1936 (Fred Perry) and 1977 (Virginia Wade).

Tickets are sold through a public random ballot. Send a stamped addressed envelope to: All English Lawn Tennis & Croquet Club, PO Box 98, London, SW18 5AE (from overseas send an International Reply Coupon), between August and December, and you may get lucky. If so, you will hear in March and be asked for payment. About 6000 tickets are sold on the day (not the last four days) – queuing from around 7am should get you into the ground, though not a seat in Centre Court.

The week-long **Stella Artois Grass Court Championship** (☎ 020-7413 1444 for tickets) takes place at the Queen's Club in leafy Kensington, just before Wimbledon, and attracts the world's leading male players.

Golf

Although games that involve hitting a ball with a stick have been played in Europe since Roman times, it was the Scottish version that caught on. Apparently dating from the 15th century, golf was popularised by the Scottish monarchy and gained popularity in London after James VI of Scotland became James I of England – and played on London's Blackheath in 1608. Naturally, the Royal Blackheath golf club claims to be the world's oldest, taking the date of its founding from this royal teeing off.

See the Activities chapter for information about playing golf in England.

Horse Racing

Even the Queen turns up for **Royal Ascot** (bookings ☎ 01344-622211), which lasts a week in late June. The cheapest tickets cost £3, but for the Royal Enclosure you must be well dressed and expect to cough up around £70. Booking is essential.

The Derby is run at **Epsom** (☎ 01372-726311) the first Saturday in June. It's traditionally popular with the masses so, unlike Ascot, you won't see a tuxedo in the place.

Run in early April, the Grand National steeplechase at Aintree is probably the best known of all England's famous horse races.

SHOPPING

There's ample scope for shopaholics in England. The country has its fair share of internationally cloned chain-laden malls, but there are countless individual shops, and all over the country are outdoor markets specialising in clutter, flowers and food. London has some of the world's greatest department stores, including Liberty's, Selfridges, Harvey Nicks (also in Leeds), Harrods and the delectably prim Fortnum & Mason.

Souvenirs

A kitsch convention is taking place at a venue near you. Anywhere tourists gather, shops gather too – selling the things tourists need. Pick up a beautifully crafted miniature London bus, regal key ring, or Wordsworth-inspired tea towel (dishtowel). Covetable stuff can also be bought from museum and gallery shops; this is the place for good quality posters, specialist books or reproductions of collection pieces.

Books & Comics

Book shopping in England offers excellent choice and value. In London, genre bookstores throng Charing Cross Road. Comic bookstores, such as Forbidden Planet, fill the thought-bubble gap. Stanfords has the world's largest stock of map and travel books. You can pick up fine antiquarian tomes in York, and Barter Bookshop in Alnwick (Northumberland) is one of England's largest second-hand outlets, and certainly the only one warmed by coal fires.

Clothes & Textiles

In most cities local designers sell sartorial breaths of fresh air. Try Notting Hill, Spitalfields, Brick Lane and Camden in London, the Corn Exchange in Leeds, Brighton's North Lanes and Leicester's Silver Arcade.

Agent Provocateur in London sells expensive and thought-provoking underwear.

England is also good for vintage finds and the dedicated follower can combine these with international designer swank, available in all the major cities. Chains worth a loiter include Jigsaw, French Connection, Marks & Spencer, Whistles and Accessorize. Topshop, with its mother ship at Oxford Circus (London), is good for fashion ephemera.

Records
Everybody wants to be a DJ and vinylphiles can train spot till they drop in most cities. Good bets are Brighton, Manchester, Leeds, Bristol, Sheffield, and of course London (at legendary Rough Trade, Black Market Records, and so on), where independent stores can fulfil your every aural desire.

Food & Drink
Some items worth tucking into include: clotted cream or scrumpy cider from Devon and Cornwall; Cadbury chocolate – you can savour where it's made at Cadbury World in Birmingham; and chutney, pickles, pre-serves, honey, Marmite and real ale from anywhere. You could also source a few big English cheeses, such as Stilton, Cheddar, Wensleydale and Double Gloucester.

Antiques & Collectibles
One person's junk is another's treasure, and so it's always worth a rummage around England's many markets, antique and junk shops. There's a thriving trade in collectibles countrywide, from Christie's – the historic auction house – to car boot sales – where people gather to sell junk out of their... you've guessed it (look out for local signs and flyers, usually at the weekend).

China, Porcelain & Ceramics
Seemingly prosaic Stoke-on-Trent is the place to head for fine porcelain produced by world-renowned Wedgwood and Royal Doulton. Any ornate ceramic requirements may also be met by the Queen's other favourite manufacturers Royal Worcester or Royal Crown Derby. Choice china is available from the factory shops, and sometimes seconds are sold at bargain prices.

Activities

As you travel around England, pursuing a favourite outdoor activity is an ideal way to escape the beaten track and get beyond the inevitable veneer of major tourism sites. Fresh air is also good for your body and soul, of course, and becoming actively involved in the country's way of life is much more rewarding than staring at it through a camera lens or car window.

Some tourists find England an expensive place to visit, but the most popular and most accessible activities – walking and cycling – are well within reach of the tightest budget and open up some of the most beautiful and fascinating corners of the country. Whatever your cost limitations, a walk or ride through the English countryside will almost certainly be a highlight of your trip. Although modern developments have negative impact in some areas, much of the countryside appears frozen in time and will readily live up to your picture-postcard expectations.

In addition to walking and cycling and the other outdoor pursuits listed here, almost every sport and hobby known to humankind has an obsessive following in England, and most devotees are pleased to meet others who share their interest – especially from overseas. See Society & Conduct in the Facts about England chapter for examples of hobbies that the English get fanatical about.

Behind the enthusiasts, most activities have national associations that can give visitors invaluable information. The websites of these organisations make a useful place to start, although when surfing for details, it's important to note that alongside the official websites, most sports and activities have a host of commercial sites too, as well as unofficial webzines and chatrooms. Not that it's a problem – just be aware exactly where you're getting the information from, and how unbiased and reliable it might be.

If you're coming to England from overseas, many organisations have international affiliations, so check with local clubs before you leave home. There are over 40 overseas offices of the British Tourist Authority (see Tourist Offices in the Facts for the Visitor chapter) with brochures and websites covering most activities; these provide an excellent starting point for further research.

Walking

Perhaps because England is such a crowded place, open spaces are highly valued, and every weekend millions of English people get their boots on and take to the countryside. You could do a lot worse than join them!

The infrastructure for walkers in England is excellent. Every village and town is surrounded by a web of footpaths, and most patches of countryside are also covered in a network of paths and tracks. The options are limitless too. You can walk from place to place in true backpacking style, or base yourself in one interesting spot for a week or so, and go out on day walks to explore the surrounding countryside.

INFORMATION

Numerous walks are described throughout this book and the start of each chapter gives an overview of walking opportunities in that region. For more information and inspiration on any area, your first stop should always be a Tourist Information Centre (TIC). These have racks of free leaflets on local walks, and also sell booklets (for a nominal fee) and more detailed books and maps (around £5) describing everything from half-hour strolls to week-long expeditions. In rural areas, guidebooks and maps are also available in local newsagents, bookshops and outdoor-equipment shops.

The website of the **British Tourist Authority** (W *www.visitbritain.com*) has a very good walking section, with details on routes, maps, guidebooks, tours and the annual walking festivals promoted by several towns around the country.

What to take

The English countryside can look deceptively gentle but, especially in the hills or open moors, the weather can turn nasty very quickly at any time of the year. If you're walking in upland areas, it's vital to be well equipped. You should carry (and know how to use) good maps and a compass, and if you're really going off the beaten track, leave details of your route with someone. Wear sturdy shoes or boots, carry warm and waterproof clothing (even in summer) and make sure you've got some drink, food and high-energy stuff like chocolate, plus a whistle and torch in case of emergency.

Guidebooks & Maps

The shelves in bookshops and TICs groan beneath the weight of a vast number of guidebooks, maps and leaflets that cover walking routes and areas throughout England. We list some general books here, and describe specific titles in the individual chapters throughout this book.

For comprehensive coverage of a selection of walking routes and areas, we recommend Lonely Planet's *Walking in Britain*, which also covers places to stay and eat along several long-distance walks and in popular walking areas, plus detailed information on what to take and what to see along the way.

For detailed coverage of individual routes and areas there are hundreds of specialist walking guides. Aurum Press publishes a good series – the books include detailed track notes and sections from Ordnance Survey (OS) 1:25,000 maps. For more information see Maps in the Facts for the Visitor chapter.

Useful Organisations

The country's leading walking body is the **Ramblers' Association** *(RA;* ☎ *020-7339 8500;* w *www.ramblers.org.uk)*. The website has numerous links and information on many walks, and RA's *Yearbook* (£4.99) is invaluable – it outlines many routes and walking areas, and has a handy list of walker-friendly B&Bs and hostels all over Britain.

Access

A major part of walking in England is the 'right of way' – a path or track allowing you to cross private land. This is important because nearly all land (even inside national parks) is privately owned, but if there's a right of way, you can follow it through fields, woods, even farmhouse yards, as long as you keep to the correct route and do no damage.

The right of way network has existed for centuries (some paths literally for millennia), so the concept of a single recent 'trail' slicing through the wilderness, as found in Australia or the USA, simply doesn't exist here. Even long-distance routes are just one way of linking many shorter paths.

The two main types of right of way are footpaths and bridleways (the latter can also be used by horse riders and mountain bikers). You may also see byways, which due to a quirk of history are open to *all* traffic so don't be surprised if you're disturbed by off-road driving fans.

Rights of way are marked on maps and often signposted where they intersect with roads or other paths. Others, however, are completely unmarked on the ground, so a good map can be essential. In some mountain and moorland areas walkers can move freely beyond the rights of way and this is clearly advertised. For instance, the National Trust (NT) is one of the largest landowners in England and many of its properties are freely open to the public.

But that's enough legal stuff. You're keen to get started!

WHERE TO WALK

Here's a quick rundown of a range of good walking areas, covering everything from gentle farmland to high mountains. For more details, see the Information sections of the relevant regional chapters, which list regional tourism boards, websites and so on.

Lake District

If anywhere is the heart and soul of walking in England, it's the Lake District (see the Cumbria chapter), a wonderful area of high mountains, deep valleys and, of course, beautiful lakes. The choice of walking routes here is literally endless. There are hundreds of high walks, peak walks, ridge walks, valley walks and (naturally) lake walks. Good places to base yourself include Ambleside, Keswick and Patterdale. Long-distance paths in the Lake District include the Cumbria Way and the Coast to Coast Walk.

Yorkshire Dales

The Yorkshire Dales (see the Yorkshire chapter) is an area of valleys and hills, roughly in the centre of northern England. Some of the so-called hills are fairly mountainous, but most are lower, smoother and less foreboding, making the Dales ideal for walkers; it's one of the most popular walking areas in England. Good bases for walks include Grassington, Malham or Horton in Ribblesdale; farther north the valleys of Wensleydale and Swaledale have more options. Long-distance paths here include the Dales Way and the Coast to Coast Walk.

North York Moors

The North York Moors (see the Yorkshire chapter) is an area of wild and empty rolling hill country cut by dales that shelter woods, fields and small villages, plus the occasional ruined abbey or castle. On the western and northern sides, the Moors are buttressed by steep hills and escarpments, while on the southern side the gradients are more gradual. On the eastern side is the coast of the North Sea, with high cliffs, quiet bays and not too many caravan parks. Long-distance paths here include the Cleveland Way and the Coast to Coast Walk.

Northumberland

For walkers, Northumberland (see the Northeast England chapter) has two main attractions: the starkly beautiful hills and valleys of Northumberland National Park (containing Hadrian's Wall, one of England's most famous ancient monuments); and the Northumberland Coast, the eastern side of the county.

In the heart of the national park, good bases include Wooler, Rothbury and Bellingham. For walks following the most accessible and most interesting parts of Hadrian's Wall, good bases include the towns of Hexham and Haltwhistle, and the tiny settlement of Once Brewed.

On the coast, good bases include Alnmouth, and one of the finest walks is between Bamburgh and Dunstanburgh – two of the area's most spectacular castles.

The Cotswolds

This classic English countryside (see the Oxfordshire, Gloucestershire & the Cotswolds chapter) is excellent for shorter walks, with gentle paths leading through neat fields and mature woodland, past clear rivers flowing down grassy valleys, along narrow hedge-lined lanes, past pretty villages with houses, churches, cottages and farms all built with the famously honey-coloured Cotswold stone. Walking here is simply a delight.

The western edge of the Cotswolds is marked by a steep escarpment, and the area's best-known long-distance route, the Cotswold Way, follows this for much of its length. East of the escarpment, the Cotswolds slope off more gently and in this area the marvellously named trio of Moreton-in-Marsh, Stow-on-the-Wold and Bourton-on-the-Water make ideal bases for walking.

Wiltshire

In the heart of southern England (see the Wessex chapter), this rural county offers surprisingly varied walking. From near the famous stone circle of Avebury, the Ridgeway runs across the North Wessex Downs past mysterious ancient monuments, while in the southwest, the West Wiltshire Downs are famous for giant white horses carved in the chalky hillsides. A great series of walks called Wiltshire's White Horse Trail winds through the area, and good bases include Devizes, Avebury, Marlborough or Westbury.

Isle of Wight

A few miles off the Hampshire coast, the Isle of Wight (see the Southeast England chapter) is an excellent place if you're new to walking in England, or simply not looking for high peaks and wilderness. The local authorities have put a lot of effort into footpaths and trails; most are linear and can be done in a day and you can always get back to your starting point using the island's bus service.

Chiltern Hills

Covered in a mix of woods and farmland, the Chilterns (see the Southeast England chapter) are the nearest 'proper' hills to London and the area is very popular with walkers, especially at weekends. Good bases to explore the central Chilterns include Princes Risborough and Wendover, while the towns of Tring and Berkhamsted are ideal for the northern area. The eastern section of the Ridgeway runs through the heart of the Chilterns; it's a good starting point for day walks.

New Forest

Visitors to England love this name, as the area (see the Southeast England chapter) is more than 1000 years old (William the Conqueror christened it) and there aren't *that* many trees – it's mainly conifer plantation and great open areas of gorse and heathland. But apart from these minor details, it's a wonderful place for easy strolls, and the towns of Lyndhurst or Brockenhurst make good bases.

Dartmoor

Dartmoor (see the Devon & Cornwall chapter) is a huge and spectacular expanse of moorland – the emptiest, highest and wildest area in southern England. The rounded hills are dotted with piles of granite rocks called 'tors' – looking for all the world like abstract sculptures – and are also covered by many ancient remains, including prehistoric burial mounds, and the largest concentration of Bronze Age hut circles in England. Good places to base yourself for day walks include Buckfastleigh on the south side of Dartmoor, or Sticklepath on the north side. For something more challenging, a long-distance route called the Two Moors Way crosses the whole Southwestern Peninsula via the national parks of Dartmoor and Exmoor.

Exmoor

On the north Devon coast, Exmoor (see the Wessex chapter) is a wild area of grassy heather-covered hills, cut by deep valleys and edged by spectacularly high cliffs, great beaches, quiet villages and busy seaside resorts. The opportunities for walking are immense and good bases for walking include Exford and Simonsbath, while on the coast you can head for Lynton and Lynmouth. The South West Coast Path runs through the area, from the start in Minehead, which also makes a good base for shorter walks.

LONG-DISTANCE WALKS

There are hundreds of long-distance walks in England; the shortest are about 40 miles (65km), taking two or three days to complete, while the longest are several hundred miles,

Walking Highlights

Still undecided? Here's our list of favourite routes and walking areas.

Best Coast Walk
The rollercoaster cliffs of Devon and Cornwall are hard to beat. This is the place for secluded beaches, traditional fishing villages, wildflowers, birds, seals and fantastic views. For a wilder edge try Northumberland.

Best High Walks
Dartmoor and the North Pennines have high areas of moorland, while the Lake District provides wonderful airy walking among proper mountains that are not to be taken lightly.

Best Long-Distance Walk
The Pennine Way and the Cleveland Way are classics, but the Coast to Coast has it all: transecting northern England, it takes you through a wonderful variety of landscapes, from coast to high mountain, to wild dale and tranquil farmland. It can be busy, but don't let that stop you.

Best Typical English Countryside
For country cottages and classic English farmland, you can't beat the Cotswolds. The Yorkshire Dales is also good, with a slightly more rugged atmosphere.

Best Weekend Walk
There are many to chose from, but consider the North Norfolk Coast, the Limestone Way in the Peak District, or the Coniston to Keswick section of the Cumbria Way in the Lake District.

Best River Walk
The Thames Path is a long-distance classic, with a lot of variation, from countryside to city centre. A shorter option is the Dales Way, which follows the beautiful River Wharfe for a few days.

Best Bird Walk
The Northumberland coast is a must for ornithologists, with a side trip to the nearby Farne Islands, home to thousands of seabirds. The Norfolk coast also has several excellent bird reserves.

Best Ancient Culture Walk
Dartmoor has a wealth of standing stones, burial mounds and Bronze Age settlements. Another option is to walk the Ridgeway from England's largest stone circle, past Neolithic long barrows and mysterious figures carved in chalk hillsides.

and take many weeks. The most popular distance is between about 80 miles (135km; five days) and 200 miles (335km; two weeks). If you like the idea of a linear trip, but don't want to lug a heavy pack, many major routes are served by baggage-carrying services.

Some of the finest routes through the most scenic areas are officially designated national trails, which have better signposting and maintenance than other routes, making them ideal for beginners or visitors. There are around 10 national trails in England, with several more planned. Many other long routes have no signs at all, so it's best to carry a map and guidebook.

Long-distance routes don't have to be a major challenge. You can easily keep the daily distances down, and you're rarely far from villages with hotels, hostels, pubs and cafés. You don't have to do the whole thing either – many long routes make a perfect focus for shorter walks: you can follow the main trail one way and take a bus back to your start-point, or loop back on other footpaths in the area.

Some long-distance walks, particularly in coastal areas, the Lake District or the Yorkshire Dales, can be crowded in the June to August holiday period. Book ahead for accommodation, and avoid starting on a weekend to make finding beds easier.

For specific information on long-distance trails in England see **w** www.countryside .gov.uk/nationaltrails or **w** www.national trail.co.uk.

Cycling

Travelling by bicycle is an excellent way to explore back-road England. Once you escape from the busy main highways, there's a vast network of quiet country lanes leading through fields and peaceful villages. These are ideal for touring on a road bike or mountain bike, and off-road riders can go farther into the wilds on the many tracks and bridleways that cross England's farmlands, forests and high moorland areas.

Depending on your energy and enthusiasm, the opportunities are endless: amble round flat lanes and tracks taking it easy and stopping for cream teas or pub lunches, or thrash all day through hilly areas, revelling in steep ascents and swooping downhill sections. You can cycle from place to place either camping or staying in B&Bs (many are specifically 'cyclist friendly'), or you can stay in one place for a few days and go out on rides in different directions.

INFORMATION

Numerous cycle routes are described or suggested throughout this book, and the start of each chapter gives an overview of opportunities in that region. Wherever you go though, your first stop should be a TIC; these helpful offices stock an ever-increasing range of leaflets (free or for a nominal charge) on suggested on- and off-road cycling routes, as well as more detailed maps and guidebooks. They can also tell you where to hire bikes, find repair shops and so on.

If you're a regular cyclist you might want to bring your own bike or consider buying one when you arrive (to sell when you leave). Another option is to hire a bike for a few days or longer – most tourist areas have at least one rental outlet although the majority have mountain bikes rather than road bikes.

Guidebooks & Maps

For a good overview of the whole country, your best bet is Lonely Planet's *Cycling Britain*, covering a selection of top routes, with information on places to stay and eat, and a section on bicycle maintenance.

Another book for good nationwide coverage is the *Official Guide to the National Cycle Network* (£10.99), published by Sustrans (see Useful Organisations), describing 30 one-day rides throughout Britain. Sustrans also publishes a vast range of maps and guidebooks covering specific local routes – everything from easy potters to cross-country epics.

All touring routes mentioned in the introductory Activities sections of each chapter (the Thames Valley Cycle Route, the West Country Way, the White Rose Cycle Route, the Sea to Sea and so on) have their own excellent maps and guides (each about £6), which are invaluable for any trip. Smaller guides cost around £3.

If you're not following specific routes on the National Cycle Network, the best maps for cycle touring are OS 1:50,000 *Landrangers*. For off-roading you may need more detail so the OS 1:25,000 maps are ideal. For more details see Maps in the Facts for the Visitor chapter.

Sustrans & the National Cycle Network

Anyone riding a bike through England today will almost certainly come across the National Cycle Network, a web of roads and paths that spreads across Britain, measuring over 6500 miles (over 10,000km) in 2002, and on target for 10,000 miles (over 16,000km) by 2005 – with half of that distance on traffic-free routes. Strands of the network pass through the heart of busy cities, while others follow some of the most remote roads in the country. For all cyclists it's an absolute boon, whether you're a long-distance tourist or simply riding to work.

The whole scheme is the brainchild of Sustrans (the name is derived from 'sustainable transport') a non-profit campaign group barely taken seriously way back in 1978 when the idea for the network was first announced. But the growth in the popularity of cycling, coupled with near-terminal car congestion in some areas, has earned the scheme lots of attention – not to mention a £40 million wedge of government funding. The eventual goal is to have the network pass within 2 miles (3km) of the homes of half the British population.

Most of the network keeps to quiet lanes, and many traffic-free sections make use of old roads and former railways, as well as purpose-built cycle paths. Where the network follows city streets, cyclists normally have their own lane, separate from motor traffic.

Several great touring routes have been designed to make use of the most scenic sections of the National Cycle Network, all with dedicated maps and guides. Other features include clear signposting and a great selection of sculptures and other outdoor works of art to admire along the way. In fact, the network is also the country's largest outdoor sculpture gallery. The whole scheme is a resounding success, and a credit to the visionaries who persevered against inertia all those year ago.

When to Cycle

The best seasons for cycling are pretty much the same as those for walking (see the Walking section earlier). Cyclists should beware of midges, prevalent in Scotland and northern England during summer, as getting these blighters in your eyes can be painful and dangerous; you'll never be so glad you bought those sexy shades to keep them out.

Useful Organisations

The country's leading recreational cycling and campaigning body is the **Cyclists' Touring Club** *(CTC;* ☎ *0870 873 0060;* **w** *www .ctc.org.uk)*. This organisation provides comprehensive information (free of charge to members) about cycling in England and overseas, lists of suggested routes (on- and off-road), local cycling contacts and clubs, recommended cyclist-friendly accommodation, organised cycling holidays, a cycle-hire directory and a mail-order service for maps and cycling books.

Anyone planning a cycle tour in England should also contact **Sustrans** *(*☎ *0117-929 0888;* **w** *www.sustrans.org.uk)*, the originators of the National Cycle Network (see the boxed text 'Sustrans & the National Cycle Network') and get a copy of its mail-order catalogue. It includes a huge range of dedicated

maps and guidebooks, as well as general information, cycling tips and useful contacts.

Transporting your Bicycle

Air If you're bringing your bike to England, most airlines will carry a bike free of charge, as long as the bike and panniers don't exceed the per-passenger weight allowance (usually 20kg). If it's over this limit, hefty excess-baggage charges kick in. Some airlines make a flat charge of around US$50 to take a bike on board. Your own national cycling association can advise on cycle-friendly airlines and on the minimum dismantling usually required.

Train Bikes can be taken on most train journeys for a cost of about £3 but space limitations and a ridiculously complicated series of advance booking regulations often makes this difficult, especially on long-distance journeys, although with persistence and patience you can usually get where you need to be. Start with **National Rail Enquiries** *(*☎ *08457 484950;* **w** *www.nationalrail.co.uk)*. For more details see the main Getting Around chapter.

Generally, on local train services and shorter trips in rural areas there's much less trouble and bikes can be taken free of charge on a first-come first-served basis. But even then there may be space limits, so be careful if you're in a group of six or more.

A final warning: when railways are being repaired, cancelled trains are replaced by buses – and they won't take bikes.

Roads Rules & Access

Bikes aren't allowed on motorways, but you can cycle on all other public roads (remember: keep to the left!), although main roads (A-roads) tend to be busy and should be avoided. Many B-roads (the next grade down – for details see the Getting Around chapter) suffer heavy motor traffic too, so the best places for cycling are the small C-roads and unclassified roads ('lanes') covering rural England, especially in lowland areas, meandering through quiet countryside and linking small, picturesque villages. Lanes are clearly shown on OS maps, and the signposting from village to village is usually good.

Cycling is not allowed on footpaths, but mountain bikers can ride on any unmade road, track or bridleway (named because they were originally for horses) that is a public right of way. For more details on rights of way see the Walking section earlier. For mountain biking it's often worth seeking out forestry areas – among the vast plantations, signposted tracks of varying difficulty have been opened up for bikes.

Wherever you go, it's worth noting that the surface conditions of tracks and bridleways vary considerably: on some you can zip along nicely, but others may be very rough and slow going. For touring on the road, the condition of most country lanes is very good, although you should always watch out for the occasional pothole, or the debris left behind by farmers trimming thorn hedges.

WHERE TO CYCLE

While you can cycle anywhere in England, some areas are better than others. This section gives a brief overview. With a map and a sense of adventure, the rest is up to you!

Southeast England

This corner of England – essentially the region around London – has more traffic than other parts of the country, but with careful planning you can find quiet roads and tracks and forget how close you are to the capital.

Northwest of London, the Chiltern Hills offer scenic cycling through woods, fields and cosy villages and there are several good mountain bike routes too. Southeast of London are the long rolling hills and ridges of the North and South Downs. The North Downs area has more woods and villages, while the South Downs is sheep-farming country with a more open aspect – both are good for touring and mountain biking.

In London itself, traffic is very heavy but even here you can find quieter routes and car-free paths. Contact the **London Cycling Campaign** (☎ 020-7928 7220; **w** www.lcc.org.uk) for maps and information.

Southwest England

In the eastern part of this region, the counties of Somerset, Dorset and Wiltshire are largely rural areas with gentle rolling hills (plus a few steep valleys to keep you on your toes) and a beautiful network of quiet lanes linking scenic villages. In many areas the motor traffic is very light, making this area one of the best in the whole of England for leisurely cycle touring. East of Dorset is Hampshire, another fine cycling area; the ancient woodland and open heath of the New Forest is especially good for on- and off-road pedalling.

In the western part of this region, the counties of Cornwall and Devon are beautiful, and enjoy the best of the English climate, but the landscape is more rugged, which can make for a challenging day in the saddle. Along the coastline, especially in the north, small roads drop steeply to beaches and pretty fishing villages nestling in coves. The south coast goes more for seaside towns and roads can be busy.

Inland, the high landscapes of Dartmoor, Exmoor and Bodmin Moor offer fine cycle touring and mountain biking on sunny days, but can be austere when rain or wind whips in off the Atlantic.

Central England

The Cotswolds area of Gloucestershire and Oxfordshire is a particularly attractive place to cycle, with quiet lanes and tracks through woodland, farmland and quaint villages full of honey-coloured cottages. From the Cotswold Edge on the western side of the hills you get fantastic views over the Severn Valley, but you wouldn't want to go up and down this escarpment too often!

Farther north, the landscape is swamped by busy roads serving Birmingham and the surrounding industrial cities, so you'll need some careful route-planning here. To the west, the Marches region (the counties of Shropshire, Herefordshire and Worcestershire), where England borders Wales, is another rural delight, with good quiet lanes and some off-road options in the hills.

The Midlands

North of Birmingham and the surrounding cities you reach Derbyshire, much of which is covered by the Peak District, a very popular cycling area. The White Peak is rolling limestone landscape covered by farms and villages and a network of lanes and tracks, some quite steep in places. There's also an excellent set of cycle routes that cut through the landscape along disused railways – dramatic and effortless at the same time. The Dark Peak marks the southern tip of the Pennines where the cycling is more challenging. There are steep hills and a smaller choice of quiet lanes and tracks here, although the fine scenery more than rewards your efforts.

Eastern England

This is a great area for easy-going cycling; the counties of Norfolk, Suffolk and parts of Lincolnshire are generally low-lying and flat, with small areas of gently undulating hills, particularly in Suffolk, and a network of quiet lanes. In Norfolk, the farmland is dissected by rivers, canals and lakes ('broads') and the whole area has many picturesque villages.

Northern England

This region offers superb cycle touring and mountain-biking, much of it strenuous, especially high up in the Pennines where you're exposed to the elements. It's no accident that many of England's top racing cyclists come from this area – these hills make an excellent training ground.

There are some exhilarating on- and off-road rides in the North York Moors, with great descents down the western escarpment. The eastern side has good rides down to the coast too, but the roads around seaside resorts such as Whitby and Scarborough can be busy.

The Yorkshire Dales is God's own country (say Yorkshire folk), with the valleys offering great cycling plus plenty of villages for rest and refreshment. To get from one valley to the next, though, can mean a tough push over the moors, but the scenery is superb, and well worth the effort. As in many popular areas,

car traffic can be a problem; it's worth avoiding this area on summer weekends.

The county of Cumbria contains the Lake District and England's highest mountains, offering frequently challenging touring and mountain biking in truly magnificent scenery. Once again, the area is best explored by cyclists outside July and August when tourist traffic congests the limited network of roads. At any time of year the little-visited Cumbria coast or the lower areas to the north and south of the main mountains are worth exploring.

In the north of England, Northumberland has quiet roads and plenty of historical interest. Some sections of the coastline are attractive and not as busy as seaside zones farther south, and inland, the Cheviot Hills and Kielder Forest offer quiet lanes and tracks.

Rock Climbing & Mountaineering

One of the many outdoor activities pioneered in England over a century ago is rock climbing, and today it's a rapidly growing and internationally recognised sport. There are numerous indoor climbing competitions in various venues, but this section concentrates on the outdoor noncompetitive side.

INFORMATION

In England, the difference between rock climbing and mountaineering is hazy and there's a lot of overlap, but generally speaking rock climbing is about shorter routes, whereas mountaineering tends to be longer routes, on bigger mountains, and may be done in winter snow and ice conditions as well as at warmer times of year.

If you're a climber from overseas, you'll notice that British grades are different from those in the USA and continental Europe (although the hardest British climbs are sometimes given 'French grades'). In Britain, climbs get an overall grade (including Difficult, Severe, Hard Very Severe and 10 levels of Extreme) and a technical grade (5a, 5b, 5c, 6a, 6b etc) for the hardest section, or 'crux', of each pitch. If you're not used to British grades, it's well worth getting hold of a conversion table – there's a good one at w www .absolutemotions.com/rock_climbing/climb ing_grades.htm.

Useful Organisations

The main organisation for all climbing and mountaineering is the **British Mountaineering Council** (BMC; ☎ 0870 010 4878; **w** www .thebmc.co.uk). From its website you can find out about indoor climbing walls, access rules (don't forget, all mountains and rock outcrops are privately owned, even if the public can go there at any time), competitions and so on.

WHERE TO CLIMB

England's main centre for long routes is the Lake District; there are some fine short routes here as well. Another popular climbing area is the Peak District, where climbers come from miles around to test out the world-famous gritstone 'edges' of Stanage and Froggat. There's also high-quality limestone in the Peak District and Yorkshire Dales. In southern England, Cheddar Gorge and the tors (rocky outcrops) of Dartmoor have good climbing. England also offers the exhilaration of sea-cliff climbing, most notably around the Lands End area in Cornwall. Nothing makes you concentrate on finding your next hold more than waves crashing 30m below!

Swimming & Surfing

For foreigners, England is not renowned as a place to go for a beach holiday (there's no Bondi or Malibu) and there are good reasons for this, not least the climate and the water temperature. But England has some truly magnificent stretches of coastline and some wonderful long flat sandy beaches.

From June to August some beaches get busy – don't forget, the English have been taking seaside holidays since the 18th century. In fact, they basically invented the whole idea of sea bathing and there's a fascinating, almost bizarre tradition underlying the whole scene today, with seaside resorts providing an intriguing view of English society. These vary from staid retirement enclaves (eg, Eastbourne) or fun family centres (Hastings) to vibrant cultural hot-spots (Brighton). And then there's Blackpool – part beach, part themepark, part tacky dive. One thing remains common to them all, however: swimming is only part of the reason for being there. A lot of the fun happens on shore while fully clothed.

INFORMATION

If you've come from the other side of the world, you'll be delighted to learn that summer water temperatures in England are roughly equivalent to winter temperatures in southern Australia (approximately 13°C). In winter, English sea temperatures are about 6°C colder – but that still gives a temperature range not unlike northern California's.

Thanks to the Gulf Stream bringing warm water from the tropics, you can take dips in the ocean all day in the summer without getting too cold. But if you're into surfing, and want to be in the water for any decent length of time, then a 3mm wetsuit is a definite must. Winter requires a 5mm suit plus boots, hood and gloves. The most unusual aspect of surfing in England is the huge tidal range, which means there's often a completely different set of breaks at low and high tides.

Useful Organisations

The main national organisation is the **British Surfing Association** (BSA; ☎ 01736-360250; **w** www.britsurf.co.uk). Its website has news on approved instruction centres, courses, competitions and so on. Another excellent surfing site is **w** www.britsurf.org, with comprehensive links and surf reports from all around Britain. There is accommodation information, lively chat rooms, classified ads and much more. Also worth checking is **w** www.coldswell.com for weather reports. **Surfers Against Sewage** (**w** www.sas.org.uk) is an active campaign group – and the name says it all. Although the situation is improving, many English municipalities still discharge a fair amount of crap into the sea.

Guidebooks

You can't go wrong with *Surf UK* by Wayne Alderson (published by Fernhurst); it's the most comprehensive guide, covering almost 400 breaks.

WHERE TO SWIM & SURF

There are beaches suitable for swimming all around England, but it's worth looking for those that have been awarded 'blue flags', a sign the local town authority is taking sand and sea cleanliness as a serious matter.

Good beaches for surfing, with the best chance of sun and the genuine possibility of luring you into the water, are in Cornwall and Devon. The entire western coast here is

Hiking, Lake District National Park

Cyclists passing York Minster, York

Horse riding in Hyde Park, London

North York Moors National Park, Yorkshire

Peak District National Park, Midlands

Brighton Beach, Brighton

Along an Oxfordshire canal

exposed to the Atlantic and there is a string of surf spots from Land's End to Ilfracombe. The shallow continental shelf, however, means the waves rarely get over 2.5m. Spring and autumn are the best times. Newquay in Cornwall is the capital of the English surf scene and home to the main surfing contests. There's a plethora of surf shops and all the trappings, from Kombis to bleached hair. The boards and wetsuits sold are good quality and competitively priced in international terms.

Elsewhere in England, the east coast of Yorkshire has a small surf scene, notably on the beaches around Scarborough. This area has a more relaxed, less pretentious atmosphere than the scene 'down south'. There are waves and a fairly hardcore surf scene north of Yorkshire, including Cleveland, Teeside, Newcastle and Northumberland.

Hang Gliding & Paragliding

There's a relatively small but thriving hang gliding and paragliding scene in England with a good selection of varied flying sites. Before doing anything, contact the **British Hang Gliding & Paragliding Association** (BHPA; ☎ 0870 870 6490; w www.bhpa.co.uk) for details on clubs and training schools. If you've got your own gear, it's also essential to check local rules and regulations regarding access – launching or landing in the wrong place can cause big problems.

Regions for good flying include the Peak District, the Yorkshire Dales and the Lake District. A ridge called the Long Mynd, near Shrewsbury, is particularly renowned for fine conditions.

Golf

Golf may be 'a good walk spoilt' but combining your travels in England with a few rounds on some scenic courses would be a fine way to see the country.

Golf courses in England fall into two main categories: private club courses and public courses. Some of the more exclusive private clubs only admit members or golfers who have a handicap certificate from their own club, but most welcome visitors. Public golf

courses are usually run by a town or city council and are open to anyone.

INFORMATION

Most golf courses are open year round, but it's usual for clubs to give members priority in booking tee-off times. It should be easier to book a tee-off time on a public course, but weekends on all courses are usually busy. You should also check whether there's a dress code, and whether the course has golf clubs for hire if you don't have your own.

A round of golf on a public course will cost around £10 (cheaper on weekdays, more at weekends). Private courses are more expensive, with fees ranging from £10 up to £50 or more for championship courses (but averaging more like £35 to £40). Many clubs offer a daily or weekly ticket, and it's always worth asking about these. If you're staying in hotels at the smarter end of the range, many have arrangements with nearby courses, which can get you reduced fees or guaranteed tee-off times. If you need to hire, a set of golf clubs costs £5 to £10 per round.

Useful Organisations

A very good starting-point for golfers from overseas is the **Golf Club of Great Britain** (GCGB; ☎ 020-8390 3113; w www.golfclub gb.co.uk) and the closely related **International Golfers Club** (IGC). These friendly membership organisations can advise on where to play, and arrange regular meets and tournaments. The IGC also administers the International Handicap Scheme.

The **English Golf Union** (☎ 01526-354500; w www.englishgolfunion.org) is the governing body and can, among other things, provide a list of affiliated clubs.

Sailing

England is traditionally a sea-going nation, with a long heritage of boats and boating, and today sailing is an increasingly popular pastime – covering everything from tiny dinghies to ocean-going yachts.

INFORMATION

Your first port of call for any sailing matter should undoubtedly be the **Royal Yachting Association** (RYA; ☎ 023-8062 7400; w www .rya.org.uk). This organisation can provide all the details you need about places to sail and training centres where you can learn the ropes, improve your skills or simply charter a boat for pleasure.

This august body is not restricted to boats with sails – the RYA covers jet-skis, motor-cruiser boats and other personal craft, and also administers a series of qualifications and certificates (such as 'yacht master'), which are internationally recognised.

RYA publications include the invaluable *RYA Sailing Centres*, an annual booklet listing every RYA-recognised place in the country, as well as manuals on navigation, racing and so on. To pinpoint these sailing centres and get more information on the courses they offer and the boats they charter out go to the RYA website and follow the links to 'training' and 'teaching establishments'.

WHERE TO SAIL

Places to sail in England include coastal locations, of course, but also many inland lakes; some are natural but many are former quarries and gravel pits now filled with water and are excellent spots for learning or racing.

Sea-sailing areas with a good choice of sailing centres include the Norfolk and Suffolk coasts, the Solent (between Southampton and the Isle of Wight), the coast of Southeast England (places such as Brighton, Eastbourne and Dover), the south coasts of Devon and Cornwall, and the Channel Islands.

Fishing

Angling, as a sport and pastime, was well established in England by medieval times. A *Treatyse of Fysshnge With an Angle*, published in 1496, described fishing flies that are still in use today, and the 17th century is regarded as a major stepping stone for fishing enthusiasts, as equipment was improved and Izaak Walton wrote his classic manual, *The Compleat Angler*.

Today fishing in England (as anywhere) is divided into several distinct categories: river, coast, sea, coarse, game, fly and so on. Dry-fly fishing – using a lure to imitate a small insect on the surface in order to deceive and catch trout – is considered the highest form of the sport. If you've come from overseas, be prepared for widely differing English and American angling vocabularies.

INFORMATION

Wherever you are, the best place to cast around for information is a local TIC. The staff can direct you to local clubs or to places that may offer fishing opportunities just for a day or two, such as stocked reservoirs that allow public access and smart hotels or country clubs with their own private lakes or stretches of river.

Fishing is enormously popular in England, but also highly regulated. Many prime stretches of river are privately owned with highly exclusive fishing. There's a place on the idyllically trout-filled River Itchen in Hampshire where it's rumoured even Prince Charles had to join the waiting list.

Even on stretches of river that can be freely fished, everyone needs a licence – these are administered by the **Environment Agency** (☎ 08701 662 662; ⓦ *www.environ ment-agency.gov.uk*). The easiest places to get a licence are post offices or from the Environment Agency's website.

A licence for one year (valid from 1 April to 31 March) for non-migratory trout and coarse fishing costs £20 for an adult (£5 for juniors, free for under-12s). Eight days costs £6.50 (no concessions) and one day is £2.50. Prices for salmon and sea trout are roughly triple these figures.

There is a statutory close season (15 March to 15 June) when coarse fishing is banned on all rivers and streams – different rules apply on canals, lakes, ponds and reservoirs. The actual dates for close seasons vary according to the region and need to be checked in advance – once again, the Environment Agency can advise.

If you're interested in fishing from a boat or a beach rather than a river bank, the website of the **National Federation of Sea Anglers** (ⓦ *www.nfsa.org.uk*) is a good place to start looking for information.

Horse Riding & Pony Trekking

There's a theory that humans are genetically programmed to absorb the world at a pace of 3 miles per hour (5km/h). It's all to do with our nomadic ancestors, apparently. Add the extra height from sitting in a saddle and the view improves even more. It all makes seeing the country from the back of a horse or pony a highly recommended way to go.

INFORMATION

Across England, there are riding schools and centres catering to all levels of proficiency, from expert to total beginner, and many of these are in national parks and other rural, hill and moorland areas that lend themselves to riding. Generally, pony trekking is aimed more at novice riders, with most outings at walking speed with the occasional trot. If you're more experienced in equestrian matters there are numerous riding schools with horses to hire.

To find a place to ride, local TICs have details and many pony trekking centres advertise in the free national park newspapers. Pony trekking is a popular holiday activity, and a half-day should cost around £10 to £15 per person (hard hats are included); a full day is £20 to £30. Serious horse riders might pay higher rates for superior mounts.

Useful Organisations

For more information, the **British Horse Society** (☎ *01926-707700;* **w** *www.bhs.org.uk*) has a useful website, and publishes *Where to Ride*, which lists riding centres throughout the UK. Also available are detailed lists on specific areas (eg, the Cotswolds) and guides on short and long-distance riding routes – ideal if you're in the mood for adventure (and happen to have your own horse).

WHERE TO RIDE

Areas where riding can easily be arranged include Dartmoor, Exmoor, the New Forest, South Downs, North York Moors, South and North Pennines, Yorkshire Dales, Cheviot Hills, Brecon Beacons, Cambrian Mountains of mid Wales, and the Galloway Hills in Scotland. Established long-distance horse-riding routes include the South Downs Way in Southeast England and the TransPennine Trail in northern England; both are also open for walkers and cyclists. An exiting new project called the Pennine Bridleway is under development (and already open in places) linking Matlock in Derbyshire to Kirkby Stephen in Cumbria – a distance of 206 miles (332km). It should be fully open by 2004, and a farther 141-mile (227km) extension to Byrness (Northumberland) is planned.

Canal & Waterway Travel

England's inland waterways consist of natural rivers and lakes plus a surprisingly extensive network of canals that were built in the early years of the Industrial Revolution and were the country's main form of transport until they died with the coming of the railways in the 19th century. Today however, canals are alive once again and the key part of a booming leisure-boating industry being hailed as the 'New Canal Age'. Canals are being restored and re-opened at the same rate that they were being built in their 1790s heyday.

All over the waterway network, boats are easily hired from numerous operators (for a few hours, a day, a week, or longer – no special skills are needed) and exploring England this way can be fascinating. For a family or a group, it's also a fun and surprisingly economical combination of transport and accommodation.

There's at least 2000 miles (3300km) of navigable canals and rivers in Britain, so there is plenty to explore. Many canals are just over 4m wide and fit snugly into the landscape as they follow the contours around hillsides, or work they way uphill by a series of locks. While travelling these waterways it's easy to forget that the world of busy roads and motorways even exists. Canals lead through an England of idyllic villages, pretty countryside and convenient and colourful waterside pubs. More surprisingly, they can also show a very different side of some cities; Birmingham from its canals is nothing like Birmingham from the ring road.

INFORMATION

There are two main sorts of boat for hire: narrowboats, which are, not surprisingly, long narrow boats about 10m to 20m in length and no more than 2m wide, specially designed for narrow canals; and cabin cruisers, which are generally wider (or at least not as long) and used on rivers, lakes, lochs and other open stretches of water.

A boat trip can vary from lazy relaxation to surprisingly hard work. When you're chugging down a wide river, it's the easiest transport imaginable. On the other hand, on a steep section of canal it can be a combination of aerobics (keys to be wound, paddles to be raised), weight lifting (heavy lock-gates to be pushed open) and jogging (someone has to run ahead to prepare the lock before the boat arrives). Canal travel is great if you have children – there's plenty to keep them occupied, and they're often nicely exhausted by the end of the day.

Guidebooks & Maps

Most canals have their own guidebooks listing places to moor up, buy food or stop for a pint along the way. These are free or cost a

---

Defying Gravity

England's canal system is a wonderful example of the power and vision of the Industrial Revolution's great engineers. No obstacle stood in their way, as they threw flights of locks up steep hillsides or flung amazing aqueducts across wide valleys. They built to last as well – the lock equipment that you 'work' as you travel along the canals today is often well over a century old.

Some astounding examples of canal engineering include the 2-mile Blisworth Tunnel near Stoke Bruerne (Northamptonshire), the graceful aqueducts near Bath on the Kennet & Avon Canal.

For particularly long inclines, locks were sometimes arranged in 'flights', where the top gate of one lock was also the bottom gate of the next. The best example is just outside Devizes, also on the Kennet & Avon Canal.

But locks, however skilfully they were built, slowed boats down and ingenious attempts were made to design alternatives. The inclined plane at Foxton near Market Harborough in Leicestershire moved boats 23 vertical metres – the equivalent of a flight of 10 locks – all in one go. But England's masterpiece of canal engineering is the Anderton Boat Lift near Northwich in Cheshire. Known as the 'cathedral of the canals', it's a massive machine of tanks, pylons and hydraulic rams by which boats (and the water they floated in) were lifted 15m skywards and simply floated out again on the new upper level. Built in 1875, it's the world's first (and today Britain's only) boat lift and really is a stunning spectacle. If this is the kind of thing that gets you excited, visit W www.andertonboatlift.co.uk.

---

few pounds and can be ordered through the **Inland Waterways Association** (☎ 01923-711114; W www.waterways.org.uk) or the **British Waterways Board** (☎ 01923-201120, ☎ 226422; W www.britishwaterways.co.uk). The websites of both these organisations are packed with information. The Inland Waterways Association has an on-line shop where you can order *The Inland Waterways Guide* (£3.50), an introductory booklet covering routes, rules and hire companies. The British Waterways Board publishes *The Waterways Code for Boaters,* a free, handy booklet packed with useful information and advice. It also has a complete list of boat-hire and hotel-boat companies.

Also well worth looking out for are the marvellous series of full-colour map-guides published by GeoProjects, including *Kennet & Avon Canal, The Thames, The Grand Union* and *The Oxford Canal.*

Rules & Regulations

No particular expertise is needed to operate a boat on inland waterways and you don't need a licence. The main regulations involve keeping the speed below 4mph, giving way to other craft and only mooring at permitted spots. The rest is mainly common sense. When you pick up your hire boat you're normally given a quick once-over of the controls, a rundown on lock operation and etiquette, a full list of waterway rules, followed by a brief foray out onto the river or canal. Then you're on your way. Proceed with caution at first; you'll soon find yourself cruising nicely and working the locks like a veteran.

Boat Rental & Tours

There are hundreds of firms renting boats in England. If you just want to potter around for a day, a small cruiser costs about £10 per hour or £50 per day.

For longer trips (usually a week – although three- or five-day periods are sometimes available) you can hire a cabin cruiser or narrowboat. Modern cruisers are well equipped with bunks or beds, kitchen and dining areas, fridge, cooker, flush toilet, shower and other mod cons. Most narrowboats have the same facilities, and some older boats have been very nicely restored. Boats usually come so well equipped that all you need to worry about is food supplies. There are plenty of shopping opportunities along the waterways, while careful planning can see you moored at a riverside pub or restaurant for most meals, if you really want to take it easy. (The Leeds & Liverpool Canal, one of the longest in the country, allegedly has an average of one pub every 1½ miles!)

Boats can accommodate from two or three people up to 10 or 12. Costs vary with the size of boat, the standard of equipment and the time of year. At the height of the summer season, a boat for four is around £500 to £1000 per week. Larger boats work out cheaper per person, which means canal travel can cost as little as £125 per person for a week's transport and accommodation – a terrific travel bargain.

Although there are independent boat operators scattered all over the country, centralised booking agencies handle bookings for many of the individual companies. One of the biggest is **Hoseasons Holidays** (☎ *01502-501010, fax 514298;* w *www.hoseasons.co.uk).*

WHERE TO GO

For cabin-cruising, one of the most popular regions is the Broads area of Norfolk and Suffolk – a fabulous system of rivers, lakes and wide canals. Farther north, the Fens of Cambridgeshire and Lincolnshire are quieter and also highly rated.

For narrowboating, England's canal network includes the Kennet & Avon Canal between Bath and Reading in southern England, which connects to the Thames. The main concentration is in central and northern England and includes the Oxford Canal; the Grand Union Canal, the big daddy of them all, linking London and Birmingham (which, incidentally, has its own waterway network and more miles of canal than Venice); and the Leeds & Liverpool canal system, which takes in Wigan Pier and the famous Anderton Boat Lift (see the boxed text 'Defying Gravity').

The main rivers for cruising are the Thames, which is navigable for over 130 miles (210km), the Severn and the Ouse. The upper reaches of the larger rivers often link in with the canal network, so they're open to both cabin cruisers and narrowboats.

For more information have a look at the canal and river cruising section in the website of **Britain Afloat** (w *www.britain-afloat.com).*

Getting There & Away

London is a transport hub for the world and airline competition means that you should be able to find transport to England at good prices from just about anywhere.

Most people come by air, and the emergence of several discount airlines has increased competition on flights to/from Europe and Ireland – routes that were once characterised by their ridiculously high fares. If you're on a budget, bus travel to/from Europe and Ireland is usually the cheapest option, but it can be bone-crunching and exhausting, and the savings are not huge compared to cheap airfares.

The Channel Tunnel has provided stiff competition for the multitude of ferries to/from Europe and there are frequent fare wars. Ferries have increased the speed of their services between England and Europe. The Eurostar train between London and Paris and Brussels has frequent special offers and is comfortable and convenient.

Getting to England from Scotland and Wales is easy. The bus and train systems are fully integrated and in most cases you'll have no idea when you've actually crossed the border.

AIR
Airports & Airlines

London's Heathrow and Gatwick are the two main airports for transcontinental flights, though some also zip direct to Manchester and Birmingham.

All the major, and many minor, English airports are served by numerous continental European and Irish flights.

Most of the world's major airlines serve London at least. The following are telephone numbers for reservations; they can be used throughout England. Note that most are not freephone (toll free).

Aer Lingus	☎ 08459 737 747
Aeroflot	☎ 020-7355 2233
Air Canada	☎ 0870 524 7226
Air France	☎ 0845 0845 111
Air New Zealand	☎ 020-8741 2299
Alitalia	☎ 0870 544 8259
American Airlines	☎ 08457 789 789
British Airways	☎ 0870 773 3377
British Midland	☎ 0870 607 0555
Cathay Pacific Airways	☎ 08457 581 581

Continental Airlines	☎ 01293-776464
Delta Air Lines	☎ 0800 414767
El Al Israel Airlines	☎ 020-7957 4100
Emirates Airlines	☎ 0870 243 2222
Iberia	☎ 0845 601 2854
KLM-Royal Dutch Airlines	☎ 08705 074 074
Lufthansa	☎ 08457 737 747
Olympic Airways	☎ 0870 606 0460
Qantas Airways	☎ 08457 747 767
Scandinavian Airlines (SAS)	☎ 08456 072 772
Singapore Airlines	☎ 0870 608 8886
South African Airways	☎ 0870 747 1111
Thai Airways International	☎ 0870 6060911
United Airlines	☎ 08458 444 777
Virgin Atlantic	☎ 01293-616161

There are also now several discount no-frills airlines serving European destinations. To check their fares you'll have to visit their websites (which often have extra discounts for tickets bought online) or call them direct.

Buzz (☎ 0870 240 7070, **w** www.buzzaway.com), an offshoot of KLM, flies to London Stansted.
easyJet (☎ 0870 600 0000, **w** www.easyjet.com) flies to London Luton and Liverpool.
Go (☎ 0870 607 6543, **w** www.go-fly.com), owned by easyJet, flies to London Stansted.
Ryanair (☎ 08701 569 569, **w** www.ryanair.com) flies to numerous English airports from Ireland, and to London Stansted from elsewhere in Europe. However, check the distance and

transportation links as Ryanair sometimes uses out-of-the-way airfields.

Virgin Express (☎ 020-7744 0004, **w** www.virgin -express.com) flies to London Stansted, Gatwick and Heathrow.

Buying Tickets

With a bit of research you can often get yourself a good deal. Start early as the cheapest tickets often must be bought well in advance and popular flights can sell out.

Full-time students and those under 26 years (30 in some countries) have access to better deals than other travellers. You have to show a document proving your date of birth or a valid International Student Identity Card (ISIC) when buying your ticket.

Buying direct from an airline is usually expensive, and the cheapest deals going are those bought from travel agents and specialist discount agencies.

However, an exception is the no-frills carriers, who sell direct to travellers. Unlike the full-service airlines, they often make one-way tickets available at around half the return fare, meaning that it is easy to put together an open-jaw ticket (when you fly to one place but leave from another).

The other exception is booking on the Internet. Many airlines, full-service and no-frills, offer discounts to Web surfers. They may sell seats by auction or simply cut prices to reflect the reduced cost of electronic selling.

It's quick and easy to compare prices on the Internet. There's also an increasing number of exclusively online agents such as **w** www.travelocity.co.uk and **w** www.deck chair.com. Online ticket sales work well if you are doing a straightforward trip on specified dates. But for more complex trips there's no substitute for a travel agent who knows about special deals and so on.

The cheapest flights are often sold by obscure agencies. Most are honest, but exercise caution. Credit-card payment offers some protection, as most card issuers provide refunds if you can prove you've been cheated. Agents who only accept cash should hand you the tickets straight away. Tickets sold by a bonded agent, such as one covered by the Air Travel Organiser's Licence (ATOL) scheme in the UK, are safe bets.

Many travellers change their routes halfway through their trips, so think carefully before you buy a ticket which is not easily refunded or costs a lot to alter.

Travellers with Special Needs

With advance warning, airlines can often make special arrangements for travellers, such as wheelchair assistance at airports. The website **w** www.everybody.co.uk has a directory listing the facilities for the disabled offered by various airlines.

Children under two years travel for 10% of the standard fare (or free on some airlines) as long as they don't occupy a seat. They don't receive a baggage allowance. 'Sky-cots', baby food and nappies should be provided by the airline if requested in advance. Children aged between two and 12 can usually occupy a seat for half to two-thirds of the full fare, and do get a baggage allowance.

England's ferocious quarantine laws have recently changed, so depending on where you're coming from your guide dog or hearing dog might not have to go through six months quarantine (see Pets in the Facts for the Visitor chapter).

Departure Tax

Domestic flights and those to other EU destinations carry a £10 departure tax. For flights to non-EU countries you pay £20. This is usually included in the ticket price.

Scotland

British Airways, British Midland and various no-frills services fly to Scottish centres. Fares can cost from £30 to £200. Taking into account transport to the airport and check-in, the train can be just as quick and is usually cheaper.

Reaching London from smaller Scottish airports, or flying between Glasgow and Edinburgh and England's regional airports, tends to be expensive.

Ireland

You can often get a discount ticket between Ireland and England for as little as €80. As well as the main Dublin to London route, regional services link smaller airports in both countries.

Continental Europe

There are frequent deals on routes to/from mainland Europe, so shop around. Discounted return tickets range from €80 to

€320 on major airlines. No-frills carriers fly the most competitive routes (€80 to €240).

Many European travel agencies have ties with **STA Travel** (**W** *www.statravel.com*). These are good places to start looking, and will also alter STA-issued tickets (usually for a €25 fee). Outlets in major cities include: **Voyages Wasteels** in Paris (☎ 08 03 88 70 04 in France; **W** *www.wasteels.fr*); **STA Travel** in Berlin (☎ 030-2859 8264); **Passaggi** in Rome (☎ 06-488 1678); and **ISYTS** in Athens (☎ 21 0322 1267). A good German online agency is at **W** *www.justtravel.de*.

Supplying discount tickets to all travellers, France's student network includes **OTU Voyages** (☎ 01 44 41 38 50; **W** *www.otu.fr*) with countrywide offices, and **Acceuil des Jeunes en France** (☎ 01 42 77 87 80). Good general Parisian travel agencies include **Nouvelles Frontières** (☎ 08 25 00 08 25; **W** *www.nouvelles-frontieres.fr*) and **Voyageurs du Monde** (☎ 01 42 86 16 00).

In Belgium, **WATS Reizen** (☎ 03-233 70 20) is a well-known agency. In Switzerland, **SSR Voyages** (☎ 01-297 11 11; **W** *www.ssr.ch*) specialises in student, youth and budget fares. There are branches in most major Swiss cities.

The Netherlands official student agency is **Mytravel Reiswinkel** (☎ 020-692 77 88). **Malibu Travel** (☎ 020-638 22 71) is also recommended, and a good online agent is at **W** *www.airfair.nl*.

The USA

There is a continuous price war on the world's busiest transcontinental market. Consequently, fares have remained the same for about 10 years. Prices from the east coast to London range from US$300 to US$600. From the west coast fares are about US$100 higher.

STA Travel (☎ 800 781 4040; **W** *www.statravel.com*), America's largest student travel organisation, has offices in most major cities. Call for details of your local office or visit its website. As fares are so low, it may also be worth contacting airlines direct.

Canada

Canada enjoys the same kind of discounts as the USA, though fares tend to be about 10% higher. The *Globe & Mail*, the *Toronto Star*, the *Montreal Gazette* and the *Vancouver Sun* often advertise cheap deals.

Travel CUTS (☎ 866 246 9762; **W** *www.travelcuts.com*) is Canada's national student travel agency and has offices in all major cities.

Australia

Many airlines compete on Europe–Australia routes, and there is a wide range of prices. Round-the-world (RTW) tickets are often real bargains and can sometimes work out cheaper than a straightforward return ticket.

Flights generally go via Southeast Asia, involving stopovers at Kuala Lumpur, Bangkok, Hong Kong or Singapore. If there's a long stopover, transit accommodation is sometimes included. If it's not, it may be worth considering a pricier ticket. The cheapest flights may be on carriers, such as Emirates Airlines, that make two stops on the way to/from England.

Expect to pay anywhere from A$1800 to A$3000. Some travel agencies, particularly smaller ones, advertise cheap fares in the weekend press, such as the *Age* in Melbourne and the *Sydney Morning Herald*. **STA Travel** (☎ 03-8417 6911; **W** *www.statravel.com.au*) has offices in all major cities and at many universities. Call ☎ 1300 733 035 Australia-wide for the location of your nearest branch. **Flight Centre** (☎ 133 133 Australia-wide; **W** *www.flightcentre.com.au*) has offices throughout Australia.

New Zealand

RTW and Circle Pacific fares for travel to/from New Zealand tend to be the best value. Depending on the airline, you may fly across Asia, with possible stopovers in India, Bangkok or Singapore, or across the USA, with possible stopovers in Los Angeles, Honolulu or one of the Pacific Islands.

Prices match those from Australia, but the trip is even longer; about two 12-hour flights minimum.

The *New Zealand Herald* travel section carries fare ads. **Flight Centre** (☎ 09-309 6171; **W** *www.flightcentre.co.nz*) has many branches, as does **STA Travel** (☎ 09-309 0458; **W** *www.sta.travel.co.nz*).

Asia

If you're heading for England via Asia, then Bangkok, Singapore and Hong Kong are still the discount ticket emporiums, but most Asian countries offer competitive deals.

Bangkok has some excellent travel agencies, and some suspect ones. **STA Travel** (☎ *02 236 0262*) is a good place to start. The budget-traveller honeypot, Khao San Rd in Bangkok, has various agencies, but ask the advice of other travellers before splashing your cash.

In Singapore, **STA Travel** (☎ *6737 7188*) offers competitive fares to England. Singapore, like Bangkok, has hundreds of travel agencies, so you can shop around before you buy. **Chinatown Point shopping centre** *(New Bridge Rd)* has a good selection.

In Hong Kong, a good way to check on a travel agency is to look it up in the phone book: dodgy operators don't usually stay around long enough to get listed. Try the **Hong Kong Student Travel Bureau** (☎ *2730 3269*) or **Phoenix Services** (☎ *2722 7378*).

India Delhi is discount central, though you can buy cheap tickets in Mumbai (formerly Bombay) and Calcutta too.

In Delhi, travel agencies are clustered around Connaught Place. As always, be careful before handing over your cash. If you use one of these discount agents, double-check your booking with the airline. **STIC Travels** (☎ *011-332 4789*) is an agent for STA Travel.

In Mumbai, **STIC Travels** (☎ *022-218 2831*) and **Transway International** (☎ *022-262 6066*) are both recommended. Most of Mumbai's international airline offices are in or around Nariman Point.

LAND
Bus
See the boxed text 'Long-Distance Bus & Coach Fares from London' below for details of the bus network that spans England, Wales and Scotland.

You can get to England from mainland Europe via bus and ferry, and although buses may be slower and less comfortable than trains, they are cheaper, especially if you are aged 13 to 25 or over 60, or take advantage of the frequent special offers. (Long-distance buses are usually called coaches in England.)

Eurolines (☎ *0870 514 3219*; W *www .eurolines.com)*, an association of companies forming an international bus network, connects an enormous number of European destinations. Its website has links to all the national operators.

You can book Eurolines tickets through National Express offices, including Victoria Coach Station in London, at many travel agencies or on the website of **National Express** (W *www.gobycoach.com)*.

Eurolines offices and affiliates can be found in **Amsterdam** (☎ *020-560 87 88)*, **Barcelona** (☎ *93 490 4000)*, **Frankfurt** (☎ *069-79 0350)*, **Brussels** (☎ *02-274 1350)* and **Madrid** (☎ *91 506 3360)*.

Some sample single/return adult fares and journey times are: Amsterdam €51/76 (10 to 12 hours); Barcelona €124/191 (24 to 26 hours); Dublin €32/59 (12 hours).

Long-Distance Bus & Coach Fares from London

Standard National Express returns are listed here, but if you book ahead cheaper fares are available on many routes (although savings are not as dramatic as for train fares).

On some journeys you will have to change coaches/buses one or more times.

destination	road miles from London	best time (hrs)	return fare (£)
Wales			
Cardiff	155	3¼	26
Aberystwyth	211	6¾	31
Scotland			
Edinburgh	375	9	37
Glasgow	397	9	37
Dundee	434	10½	44
Perth	450	9¾	44
Aberdeen	503	12	50
Inverness	536	12½	50

Cheaper promotional fares are available if you book in advance.

From May to August, fares rise by about 5% to 10%, and you should book ahead. Note that with some destinations, you may pay the same fare and save a large chunk of lifetime by getting a discount fare with a no-frills airline.

Train

See the boxed text 'Rail Fares from London' for information on getting to England from Scotland and Wales on Britain's integrated rail network.

The Channel Tunnel has made travel between England and continental Europe faster, more pleasant and less tiring, with two different services: Eurostar (or Le Shuttle) for walk-on passengers, and Eurotunnel for people with vehicles (see Car & Motorcycle later for details about bringing these into England). A new high-speed rail link is being built on the English side, which will run from St Pancras to Fawkham in Kent. It'll be complete in 2007 and slice 30 minutes off the journey.

Eurostar The high-speed rail service **Eurostar** (in the UK ☎ 08705 186 186, in France ☎ 08 92 35 35 39; ⓦ www.eurostar .com) travels between London Waterloo and Paris (three hours, 16 daily) via Ashford (UK) and Calais and Lille (France). It also runs to/from Brussels (two hours and 40 minutes, 11 daily).

You can buy tickets from travel agencies, major train stations or direct from Eurostar. The normal single/return fare from Paris and Brussels is an eye-widening €270/475, but the APEX return fare (must be booked 14 days in advance) costs around €126. There are also reductions for children and those aged 12 to 25. Bicycles are only allowed on the Eurostar if you have a bike bag.

Eurostar connects with European trains in Brussels, Lille and Paris. For inquiries about European trains contact **Rail Europe & French Travel Service** (☎ 08705 848 848), or check on the Internet – for example, **Deutsche Bahn** (ⓦ www.bahn.de) or **Rail Europe** (ⓦ www.raileurope.com).

Eurotunnel With the **Eurotunnel** (☎ 0870 535 3535; ⓦ www.eurotunnel.com) service, you drive onto a shuttle train at one end and drive off at the other. These trains (Folkestone to Calais) depart up to four times hourly each way from 6am to 10pm, and hourly between 10pm and 6am. Loading and unloading is one hour; the shuttle itself takes 35 minutes.

You can either book in advance or pay by cash or credit card at a toll booth. A car and its passengers costs around €410 return (day return €195), but there are lots of promotional fares.

Motorway networks connect with the clearly signposted Eurotunnel terminals.

Train & Ferry Connections Various trains link with cross-channel ferries. For information, telephone individual ferry companies (see the boxed text later) or try

Rail Fares from London

Journey times given are the best times possible and may involve one or more connections.

destination	rail mileage from London	best time (hrs)	return fare (£)
Wales			
Cardiff	151	2-3	41.90
Aberystwyth	237	4¾	46.10
Scotland			
Edinburgh	393	4½	82.80
Glasgow	402	5½	82.80
Dundee	452	6	86
Perth	450	6	86
Aberdeen	524	7	95
Inverness	568	8	96

National Rail Enquiries (☎ 08457 484950, outside the UK ☎ 1332-387601).

A cheap way to buy tickets between Belgium and London is via the Internet travel agency **Taxistop-Airstop** (**w** www.taxi stop.be), which offers bargain 'last-minute' rail and ferry tickets (to be booked at least two weeks before travel). An Ostende–London return costs €50.

Fares to/from London depend on your starting point. Here are some sample routes (see Sea later for ferry details) with train links at both ends, and standard return fares (once again, special deals are usually available):

Netherlands: Amsterdam–Hook of Holland–
  Harwich–London €126
Belgium: Brussels–Ostende–Dover–London €104
France: Paris–Calais–Dover–London €110
Ireland: Dublin–Dun–Laoghaire–Holyhead–
  London €134

Car & Motorcycle

Drivers of EU-registered vehicles will find bringing a car into England fairly straightforward. The car must have registration papers and a nationality plate, and the driver must have insurance.

Although the International Insurance Certificate (Green Card) is no longer required, it remains excellent proof that you are covered.

SEA

There are fleets of marine operators and routes between England and mainland Europe; this section just introduces the main options. Competition from Eurotunnel and low-fare airlines has led to mergers of once competing ferry lines, but prices are still low and there are constant discounted fares.

The same company often has a host of different prices for the same route, depending upon the time of day or year, ticket type or vehicle size. Returns are often much cheaper than two singles; on some routes a standard five-day return is the same as a single. There are cheap day-return tickets, but they're strictly policed.

To get the best deals, plan ahead and consult ferry company sales staff. The sample fares given in the table are standard high-season return fares for a single foot passenger/car and one or more passengers (sometimes the price includes up to four). The quotes include an economy berth on the longer trips (more deluxe accommodation is usually available too). You will often be able to beat these fares through special offers. See the boxed text 'Ferry Companies' for contact information.

France

The shortest sea link between England and mainland Europe is from Dover to Calais, and many companies ply this route (see the table 'Ferry Connections to England').

Ferry Companies

Europe to England

Brittany Ferries	☎ 0870 901 2400	**w** www.brittany-ferries.co.uk
DFDS Seaways	☎ 0870 533 3000	**w** www.dfdsseaways.co.uk
Fjord Line	☎ 0191-296 1313	**w** www.fjordline.no
Hoverspeed	☎ 0870 240 8070	**w** www.hoverspeed.co.uk
P&O European Ferries	☎ 0870 242 4999	**w** www.poferries.com
P&O North Sea Ferries	☎ 0870 129 6002	**w** www.ponsf.com
P&O Scottish Ferries	☎ 01224-572615	**w** www.poscottishferries.co.uk
P&O Stena Line	☎ 0870 600 0600	**w** www.posl.com
Smyril Line	☎ 01595-690845	**w** www.smyril-line.fo
Stena Line	☎ 08705 707070	**w** www.stenaline.com
Superfast Ferries	☎ 0870 234 2222	**w** www.superfast.com

Ireland to England

Irish Ferries	☎ 08705 171717	**w** www.irishferries.ie
P&O Irish Sea	☎ 08702 424777	**w** www.poirishsea.com
Sea Containers Ferries	☎ 01624-661661	**w** www.steam-packet.com
Stena Line	☎ 08705 707070	**w** www.stenaline.com
Swansea Cork Ferries	☎ 01792-456116	**w** www.swansea-cork.ie

Ferry Connections to England

France

crossing	operator	duration (hrs)	frequency	price €
Calais–Dover	P&O Stena	1¼	hourly	83/421
Calais–Dover	Hoverspeed	¾	hourly	76/293
Dieppe–Newhaven	Hoverspeed	2½	3 daily Apr–Oct	76/110–351
Cherbourg/Le Havre–Portsmouth	P&O European	5–6 day/7–8 night	3–4 daily	93/454
Cherbourg–Poole				
(ferry)	Brittany	4¼	2 daily (June–Sept only)	138/539
(fast ferry)	Brittany	2¼	1 daily (June–Sept only)	158/728
Plymouth–Roscoff	Brittany	6 day/7 night	1–3 daily (Mar–mid Nov)	187/772
St Malo–Portsmouth	Brittany	11	at least one daily	119/460
Caen–Portsmouth	Brittany	6 day/7¾ night	3 daily	150/440

Spain

crossing	operator	duration (hrs)	frequency	price €
Santander–Plymouth	Brittany	24	twice weekly	247/781
Bilbao–Portsmouth	P&O European	35	twice weekly	290/926

Scandinavia

crossing	operator	duration (hrs)	frequency	price
Norway				
Bergen–Newcastle	Fjord	27	2–3 weekly	2645/8655Nkr
Kristiansand–Newcastle	DFDS Seaways	17	twice weekly	2272/3835Nkr
Stavanger–Newcastle	Fjord	20	2–3 weekly	2645/8655Nkr
Sweden				
Gothenberg–Newcastle	DFDS Seaway	24	twice weekly	3892/5815Skr
Denmark				
Esbjerg–Harwich	DFDS Seaways	22	2–3 weekly	2272/3835Dkr

Belgium, the Netherlands & Germany

crossing	operator	duration (hrs)	frequency	price €
Belgium				
Ostende–Dover	Hoverspeed	2	2 daily	76.50/269–365
Zeebrugge–Hull	P&O North Sea	13	daily	151/344
Zeebrugge–Rosyth	Superfast	17½	daily	207/435
Germany				
Cuxhaven–Harwich	DFDS Seaways	17	3 weekly	269/445
Netherlands				
Hook of Holland–Harwich	Stena Line	3¾	2 daily	83/440
Rotterdam–Hull	P&O North Sea	11	daily	151/344
Ijmuiden–Newcastle	DFDS Seaways	15	daily	166/341

Ireland

crossing	operator	duration (hrs)	frequency	price €
Cork–Swansea	Swansea Cork	10	1–2 daily (Apr–Dec)	108/470–507
Dublin–Liverpool	Sea Containers	4	daily	96/561
Belfast–Heysham	Sea Containers	4	1 daily (Apr–Sept)	67/355

Dover is the most convenient port for those who plan onward travel (in England) by bus or train.

Spain
There are two crossings to England from Santander and Bilbao in the north of Spain.

Scandinavia
Until you see the ferry possibilities, it's easy to forget how close Scandinavia and England are, and why the Vikings found English villages so convenient to pillage.

In southern England, Harwich is the major port linking England to Denmark and northern Germany. In northern England the main ports are Hull and Newcastle.

Belgium, the Netherlands & Germany
There are direct links with Germany, but many people prefer to drive to/from the Dutch ferry ports.

Ireland
England to Ireland services are profuse, with lots of special deals, return fares and other money savers worth investigating. From October to April fares are significantly lower.

Getting Around

England's public transport is variable and expensive, compared to many other European countries, and for such a small and relatively wealthy country there are surprising failures in the system. Underinvestment and neglect, long-term car bias in transport policy, and ill-judged decisions, such as the privatisation of British Rail, have left a tangled conundrum that taints politicians and leaves passengers waiting on platforms.

Having said all that, breakdowns in the rail and bus networks tend to afflict commuters rather than visitors; there are good coach and train services between towns and cities, although in some rural areas the services can be patchy, and a car can often be handy for reaching out-of-the-way spots.

As long as you have time, with a mix of local buses, the odd taxi, walking and occasionally hiring a bike, you can get almost anywhere. You'll certainly see more of the countryside than you might slogging up and down the grey motorways, and do so in the serene knowledge that you're doing less environmental damage.

To give a quick overview, if you're on a tight budget, long-distance buses and coaches are nearly always the cheapest way to get around. Unfortunately, they're also the slowest (sometimes by a considerable margin). Trains cost more but with discount tickets they can be competitive; they're also quicker, less tiring, and often take you through beautiful countryside.

Public Transport Information (w *www.pti.org.uk*) is a very useful site with helpful links and phone numbers that will help you plan your journey.

AIR
Domestic Air Services

British Airways (BA), British Midland, easyJet, Go and Ryanair are the major domestic players (see the Getting There & Away chapter for contact details). BA and British Midland serve most regional centres, and fares range from around £60 to £200. Ryanair links London Stansted and Newquay (from £38, one hour), and Go flies from London to Newcastle (£30 to £100, one hour). There are discounts for under-25s, but special fares booked in advance are usually your cheapest option.

BUS & COACH

Road transport in England is mainly privately run. **National Express** (☎ 08705 808080; w *www.gobycoach.com*) runs the largest national network – and comes under the Eurolines umbrella.

In England, long-distance express buses are usually called coaches, and in towns there are separate bus and coach stations. Where coaches and buses run on the same route, coaches are more expensive (though quicker) than buses. There are many smaller regional operators across the country, several forming

---

Return Fares

On buses, coaches and trains in England, ticket types and prices vary considerably, with passengers frequently faced with a bewildering array of options. More details are given later in this chapter but it's important to note that throughout this book the prices quoted are **standard returns** (unless otherwise specified). These are the fares you might pay on a bus or train if you buy your ticket on the day you travel but outside peak times (which are usually when people go to work, so from about 7am to 9.30am and 4pm to 6pm on weekdays).

If you're coming back the same day, ask about **day returns** as these are often cheaper than standard returns, and sometimes only a little more expensive than a single. Single fares are usually around 70% of the return price, but can be 50% or even 99%.

On coaches and trains you'll save a lot if you book your ticket at least a few weeks ahead (subject to availability), and even three days in advance can get you a discount.

If you're making several journeys, it's often worth getting a day-pass (with names like Day Rover, Wayfarer or Explorer), which will be cheaper than buying several singles or a return. Sometimes it's cheaper to get a day-pass than pay for one long journey. Different variations are available covering buses and/or trains. You will find recommendations of useful day-tickets in the regional chapters, and it's always worth asking ticket clerks or bus drivers about this.

part of the Stagecoach or First networks. There's also a web of local bus companies, and the important ones are highlighted in each chapter.

For information on buses all over the country, call the helpful national **Traveline** (☎ 0870 608 2608; w www.traveline.org.uk; open 8am-8pm daily). You will get transferred automatically to the department of the region you're phoning from, so if you need advice about another region you'll have to be put through.

Local Buses
Away from cities, bus timetables often seem strangely random and complex – this is because they are designed to serve schools and industry, and there may be few midday and weekend services. The best thing to do is to phone Traveline or double-check at a Tourist Information Centre (TIC) before planning your day's activities around a bus that you later find out only runs on Thursday after the full moon.

Bus Passes & Discounts
If you are going to linger in one area, you should find out what regional passes are available (often they can be bought on the bus). Worthwhile passes are highlighted in the regional chapters.

Some of the passes mentioned in the Train section later in this chapter include certain bus services.

Discount Card National Express agents sell £9 discount coach cards that get 20% to 30% off standard adult fares. The cards are available to full-time students as well as people aged between 16 and 25, and 50 or over. A passport photo and proof of age (such as a passport) or student status (such as an ISIC) are required.

Tourist Trail Pass Anyone in England can buy this pass, which is available from National Express agents. It allows unlimited bus travel for a number of days within a certain period of time. The costs (adult/

Fares from London

Standard National Express returns are listed here, but if you book ahead cheaper fares are available on many routes (although savings are not as dramatic as for train fares).

On some journeys you will have to change coaches/buses one or more times.

destination	road mileage from London	best time (hrs)	return (£)
Brighton	51	2	14
Cambridge	54	2	14
Canterbury	56	2	14.50
Oxford	57	1¾	11
Dover	71	2½	17
Salisbury	83	3	18.50
Stratford	92	3	18
Bath	106	3	21
Birmingham	110	2½	17
Bristol	115	2½	19.50
Lincoln	131	4¼	26
Shrewsbury	150	4¼	19.50
Exeter	172	4½	32.50
Manchester	184	4¾	28
York	188	5	29
Liverpool	193	5	28
Scarborough	215	7	36
Durham	255	6	36
Carlisle	299	6¾	36

child & discount-card holders) of the various passes are:

2 days in 3	£49/39
5 days in 30	£85/69
8 days in 30	£135/99
15 days in 30	£190/145
15 days in 60	£205/160

Backpackers Buses

The excellent **Stray Backpacker Travel Network** (☎ 020-7373 7737; **w** www.stray travel.com) runs hop-on, hop-off buses on a regular circuit between London, Bath, Manchester, Haworth, the Lake District, Glasgow, Stirling, Edinburgh, York, Stratford-upon-Avon, Oxford and London, calling at hostels.

1 day	£34
3 days in 2 months	£109
4 days in 2 months	£129
6 days in 4 months	£159

Tickets are available from branches of STA Travel; searches can be made at **Yell.com** (**w** www.yell.com) for the nearest branch.

Postbus

Postbuses provide a good service to remoter areas and can be useful for walkers. For information and timetables contact **Royal Mail** (☎ 0845 774 0740; **w** www.postbus.royalmail .com). Most don't carry bicycles.

Tour Buses

Several companies have regular buses circulating on a fixed route in tourist towns, and your one-day ticket allows you as many stops as you like. Useful local tour companies are mentioned throughout this book.

TRAIN

Despite the damage wrought by long-term underinvestment, England still has an adequate rail service – that is, if you're travelling as a tourist rather than trying to get to work on a weekday morning – and trains can be a rewarding and relaxing way to get around. There are several beautiful lines running through sparsely populated country, and on the main routes fast trains travel at speeds of up to 125mph whisking you, for example, from London to Manchester in 2½ hours.

Despite the wonderful scenery and impressive timetables, some English trains are old (and show it). High-profile rail disasters in 2000 and 2002 were both caused by damaged rails, and the resulting speed restrictions and emergency repairs to tracks caused horrendous delays (although these tragic occurrences should not cloud the fact that rail is by far the safest means of transport). Rail administration is part of the problem. A single company called Railtrack was established to maintain tracks and stations, while numerous private operators run the trains. In 2002 the increasingly calamitous Railtrack was sold to a nonprofit company called Network Rail, and by the end of that year at least the mammoth task of improving the railway network was being addressed.

The different train operators can set their own fares, so on some routes passengers can choose to buy a cheaper ticket with a company offering a less direct service, or pay more for a faster service. Don't automatically go for the fastest route: the slower, less direct service is sometimes a more beautiful journey. The competition also means that companies often have special offers.

The main railcards (see Railcards later) are accepted by all operators. Train stations sell tickets to all destinations, and authorised travel agents sell some options.

Information

The individual operators publish free timetables, but frustratingly they only cover their own services. **National Rail Enquiries** (☎ 08457 484950, outside the UK ☎ 44 1332-387601; **w** www.nationalrail.co.uk) is a helpful, centralised service providing timetable and fare information.

The *Thomas Cook European Timetable* (£9.50) and the *OAG Rail Guide* (£7.50) list all the most important services yet manage to be reasonably svelte. Both can be found at larger newsstands in train stations.

Classes

There are two classes of rail travel: 1st and standard (often called 2nd class). First class costs at least 30% to 50% more than standard and, except on very crowded trains, is not really worth it. However, at weekends some operators will upgrade many standard-class tickets for a bargain £8.

On overnight trains (between London and Exeter, and Plymouth and Penzance) there are 1st-class or standard sleeping cabins.

There's a variety of fares (advance reservation essential), and at times they can work out to be better value than a night in a hotel.

Train Passes

There are more local and regional passes than you can imagine, and many are mentioned throughout this book. If you will be spending any amount of time in one place, it is always worth checking to see if there is a local rail pass, many of which include bus travel.

Unfortunately, English passes are not valid abroad, and Eurail passes are not accepted in England. Holders of BritRail, Eurail and Euro passes can get discounted fares on Eurostar trains (eg, London to Paris or Brussels for £79), subject to availability. Children's passes are usually half the adult cost or less.

The popular BritRail passes are *not available in England* and must be bought in your country of origin. A variant includes Ireland for not much more. Most large travel agencies will have details. Adult standard fares are quoted here.

BritRail Classic There are several flavours of BritRail Classic passes, all of which are for consecutive days of travel. Costs are as follows: four days US$185; eight days US$265; 15 days US$399; 22 days US$499; and 1 month US$599. Anyone getting their money's worth out of the last pass should qualify for some sort of award for heroism.

BritRail Flexipass These passes are usually preferable as you don't have to get on a train every day to get full value. They are good for a certain number of days within a 60-day period. A pass costs US$349 for four days of travel, US$509 for eight days and US$769 for 15 days.

BritRail Pass 'n Drive This combines a BritRail Flexipass with the use of an Avis

Train Operating Companies

Anglia	☎ 0845 650 4090	w www.angliarailways.com
Arriva Trains Northern	☎ 0870 602 3322	w www.arrivatrainsnorthern.co.uk
c2c	☎ 0845 601 4873	w www.c2c-online.co.uk
Central Trains	☎ 0121-654 1200	w www.centraltrains.co.uk
Centro	☎ 0121-200 2700	w www.centro.org.uk
Chiltern Railways	☎ 01296-332113	w www.chilternrailways.co.uk
Connex	☎ 08706 03 04 05	w www.connex.co.uk
First Great Eastern	☎ 0845 950 5000	w www.ger.co.uk
First Great Western	☎ 08457 000 125	w www.firstgreatwestern.co.uk
First North Western	☎ 0845 600 1159	w www.firstnorthwestern.co.uk
Gatwick Express	☎ 0870 530 1530	w www.gatwickexpress.co.uk
Great North Eastern Rail	☎ 08457 225 225	w www.gner.co.uk
Heathrow Express	☎ 0845 600 1515	w www.heathrowexpress.co.uk
Hull Trains	☎ 01482-606388	w www.hulltrains.co.uk
Island Line	☎ 01983-812591	w www.island-line.co.uk
Midland Mainline	☎ 08457 125 678	w www.midlandmainline.com
ScotRail	☎ 08457 55 00 33	w www.scotrail.co.uk
Silverlink Trains	☎ 0845 601 4868	w www.silverlink-trains.co.uk
South Central Trains	☎ 0870 830 6000	w www.southcentraltrains.co.uk
South West Trains	☎ 023-8021 3600	w www.southwesttrains.co.uk
Stansted Express	☎ 0870 530 1530	w www.stanstedexpress.com)
Thameslink	☎ 0845 330 6333	w www.thameslink.co.uk
Thames Trains	☎ 0118-9083678	w www.thamestrains.co.uk
Valley Lines	☎ 029-2044 9944	w www.valleylines.co.uk
Virgin	☎ 08457 222 333	w www.virgintrains.co.uk
Wales & Borders Trains	☎ 0870 900 2320	w www.walesandborderstrains.co.uk
Wessex Trains	☎ 0870 900 2320	w www.wessextrains.co.uk
West Anglia	☎ 0870 850 8822	w www.wagn.co.uk

rental car. The package is available in various combinations: a three-day Flexipass plus two days car rental in one month costs US$289 for one person, or US$141 for each additional person in one car. You can customise this pass in countless ways.

Eurostar Plus BritRail Pass This combines a three-day BritRail Flexipass with a single/return Eurostar ticket. An adult standard single costs US$279 and a return US$349.

All Line Rail Rovers These passes (£325/495 for seven/14 days) allow unlimited travel anywhere on the national rail network, and can be purchased in England.

Railcards

You can get discounts of up to 33% on most fares (except certain heavily discounted tickets) with various railcards, valid for one year and mostly available from major stations.

Young Person's Railcard (**W** www.youngpersons-railcard.co.uk) Costs £18 and gives you 33% off most tickets and some ferry services; you must be aged between 16 and 25, or a mature full-time UK student. You need proof of age or student status (if necessary) and a passport-size photo.

Senior Railcard (**W** www.railcard.co.uk) Available to anyone over 60, this card also costs £18 and gives a 33% discount. Proof of age required.

Family Railcard (**W** www.family-railcard.co.uk) Costs £20 and allows discounts of 33/60% per adult/child for up to four adults and four children travelling together, providing a card-holder is a member of the party. Just a couple of journeys can pay for the cost of the rail card.

Disabled Person's Railcard (**☎** 0191-2690303, textphone **☎** 2690304, **W** www.disabledpersons-railcard.co.uk) Costs £14 and gives a 33% discount to a disabled person and one companion. Pick up an application form from a station or download it from the website and then send it to the Disabled Persons Railcard Office, PO Box 1YT, Newcastle-upon-Tyne, NE99 1YT. It can take up to three weeks to process this card.

Network Card (**W**.www.railcard.co.uk/network/network.htm) If you're planning to do a lot of rail travel in the south of England, a Network card may be worth considering. This is valid for London and the entire southeast, from Dover to Weymouth, Cambridge to Oxford. It costs £20. Discounts of 33% apply to up to four adults travelling together providing a card-holder is a member of the party. Children pay a flat fare of £1. Travel is permitted only after 10am from Monday to Friday and at any time at the weekend. A couple of journeys can pay for the card.

Tickets

The various operators all have their own special offer schemes. National Rail Enquiries and ticket offices will advise you on the cheapest ticket available. Just like airlines, bargain fares have advance-purchase and minimum-stay requirements, as well as limited seating. Many are nonrefundable, so if you miss your train, you're stuck.

Children under five travel free; those aged between five and 15 pay half-price for most tickets (except for certain heavily discounted tickets). When travelling with children it is almost always worth buying a Family Railcard.

The following are the main fare types. The varying prices of a York–London ticket are given, where applicable (not every type of fare is offered on this route – it's unusual for the full gamut to be offered for a journey), to show the kind of saving you might make if you book a restricted ticket in advance.

Open Single/Return ticket Has no restrictions and is expensive, but is valid for a month. You can usually stop several times along the way, staying as long as your ticket is valid. (York–London single/return £65/130)

Day Return ticket Valid any time on the day specified and relatively expensive; this ticket is usually available on short journeys.

Cheap Day Return ticket Also only available on short journeys and valid on the specified day, but has time restrictions (such as no travel before 9.30am). Often about the same price as a single, this is a great day-trip deal.

Saver This ticket has some limited restrictions, but doesn't have to be bought in advance. The name Saver could be thought a bit of a misnomer. (York–London single/return £62.60/63.60)

SuperSaver Is cheaper but only allows travel at off-peak times, on off-peak days (usually Sunday to Thursday). Bank holidays and Christmas are considered to be peak times.

SuperAdvance May be bought up to 6pm on the day before travel, but in reality must be booked ahead as will sell out quite quickly (limited numbers available for select journeys). Valid for one month, but you must fix your return journey date. (York–London single/return £48/49)

Apex Must be bought at least seven days in advance. Again, valid for one month and requires a fixed return date. Limited numbers are available for select journeys, so book well ahead in order to get this fare. (York–London single/return £36/37)

Rail Fares from London

For ease of comparison, destinations are listed in the same order as the bus fares from London, but note that there are great variations in the train versus road mileage. Journey times given are the best times possible and may involve one or more connections.

destination	rail mileage from London	best time (hrs)	return (£)
Brighton	51	¾	20.10
Cambridge	56	1	20
Canterbury	62	2	18.30
Oxford	64	¾	18.40
Dover	77	1¾-2¼	21.90
Salisbury	84	1¼	28.70
Stratford	121	2	23.20
Bath	107	1½-2	39.30
Birmingham	110	1½	20-33.40
Bristol	118	1½-2	41.10
Lincoln	137	1¾	43.50
Shrewsbury	156	3	41.30
Exeter	174	2½	43.40-53.80
Manchester	184	2½-3	49.40
York	188	2	63.20
Liverpool	194	3	49.40
Scarborough	230	3	70
Durham	254	2½	79
Carlisle	299	4	70-81.50

Buying Tickets You can buy tickets at ticket offices or travel agents, both of which should tell you the best ticket price available.

Alternatively, you can phone the **National Rail Enquiries** (☎ 08457 484950, from outside the UK ☎ 1332-387601), who will advise you on the most economical trains and tickets. It will give you a number for the appropriate operator, which you will have to phone to make a credit-card booking for your journey. You can arrange to have the ticket posted to you, or pick it up at the originating station on the day of travel. But be sure to get to the station with time to spare, as queues can be long.

You can also check out fare deals and book tickets for any operators' trains at **w** www .thetrainline.com. Again, you may pick up your ticket from the originating station, or have it posted to you (UK only).

CAR & MOTORCYCLE

Travelling by private car or motorcycle enables you to get to remote places, and to travel quickly, independently and flexibly. However, in cities you'll need superhuman skills to negotiate one-way systems and heaving traffic, not to mention deep pockets to pay for parking.

In 2002 rail fares were raised specifically to reduce overcrowding on trains – it seems extraordinary that the same logic doesn't generally get applied to clogged roads, but it is indicative of the power of the British motor lobby. Tolls are being mooted. In 2003 a congestion charge was introduced in London (it's best to avoid bringing a car into the capital, as traffic is heavy and parking fines heavier), and other cities may follow suit. However, tolls are uncommon, and if there is more than one of you travelling, car travel will work out considerably cheaper than public transport.

There are five grades of road. Motorways and main A-roads are triple or dual carriageways and deliver you quickly from one end of the country to another, but you miss the most interesting countryside. Be careful if you use them in foggy or wet conditions. Lesser A-roads, B-roads and minor roads are much more scenic and fun. Fenced by hedgerows, these roads wind through the countryside from village to village. You can't travel fast, but you won't care.

Rural driving can be an adventure; in some areas roads have only one lane. At passing places (it's illegal to park in these places), a vehicle stops to allow oncoming cars through, or to allow someone from behind to overtake. Some of the highest roads may be snowbound in winter, and even when the snow clears, ice can linger to make driving conditions treacherous, especially on windy, narrow mountain roads. In remote areas petrol stations are few and far between and sometimes closed on Sunday.

At around 75p per litre (unleaded; equivalent to about US$4.50 for a US gallon), petrol is expensive by American or Australian standards, and diesel is only a few pence cheaper. Note also that fuel prices rise the further you get away from regional centres.

Road Rules

Anyone using the roads should read the *Highway Code* (available online at w www .roads.dft.gov.uk/roadsafety, or often stocked by TICs). A foreign driving licence is valid in England for up to 12 months from the time of your last entry into the country. If you plan to bring a car from Europe make sure you're insured.

Some important rules are: drive on the left(!); front seat belts are compulsory and if belts are fitted in the back they must be worn; the speed limit is 30mph (48km/h) in built-up areas, 60mph (96km/h) on single carriageways, and 70mph (112km/h) on dual or triple carriageways; give way to your right at junctions and roundabouts.

Drinking and driving is taken very seriously. You're allowed to have a blood-alcohol level of 80mg/100mL and campaigners want it reduced to 50mg/100mL.

Parking

England is small, and there's a constant battle against traffic in some areas. In London, traffic wardens and wheel-clampers operate with stealthy efficiency and if your vehicle is towed away it'll cost you over £100 to get it back. Most cities operate 'Park and Ride' systems – you park your car in a large satellite car park and then ride to the centre on the regular buses provided.

Cities often have 'short-stay' and 'long-stay' car parks. Prices will often be the same for two or three hours, but over that long-stay car parks are cheaper (though maybe slightly less convenient).

Yellow lines (single or double) along the edge of the road indicates there are parking restrictions. Find the nearby sign that spells out when you can and can't park. In some cities there are also red lines, which mean no stopping at all.

Rental

Compared to many countries (especially the USA) rates are expensive in England; arranging a package deal prior to arrival may be more economical. The big international rental companies charge from around £140 to £160 per week for a small car. Easyrentacar operates internationally and is often the cheapest option, as the daily rate varies according to demand.

The main companies include:

Avis (☎ 0870 606 0100, w www.avis.co.uk)
Budget (☎ 0541 565656, w www.budgetcar.com)
Easyrentacar (☎ 0906 3333333, w www.easycar .com)
Europcar (☎ 0870 607 5000, w www.europcar .co.uk)
Hertz (☎ 0870 844 8844, w www.hertz.co.uk)
National Car Rental (☎ 0870 400 4502, w www .nationalcar.com)
Thrifty Car Rental (☎ 01494-751600, w www .thrifty.co.uk)

Purchase

If you're planning to tour around England you may want to buy a vehicle. It's possible to get something reasonable for around £1000. Pick up a copy of *Loot* (w www.loot.com; five times weekly in London, less often elsewhere) or *Autotrader* (w www.autotrader.com; every Thursday) for adverts.

All cars require:

- a Ministry of Transport (MOT) safety certificate (valid for one year);
- third-party insurance – shop around but expect to pay at least £300;
- a registration form signed by both the buyer and seller;
- a 'tax disc' proving you've paid your Vehicle Excise Duty (VED) of £88/160 for six months/one year (£57.75/105 for engines under 1100cc). Brand-new cars are taxed according to their emissions. Tax discs are sold at post offices; you need a valid MOT certificate, registration document and proof of insurance.

ROAD DISTANCES (MILES)

1 mile = 1.61km

	Birmingham	Bristol	Cambridge	Cardiff, Wales	Carlisle	Dover	Edinburgh, Scotland	Exeter	Glasgow, Scotland	Lincoln	Liverpool	London	Oxford	Penzance	Sheffield	York
Birmingham	---															
Bristol	85	---														
Cambridge	95	146	---													
Cardiff, Wales	100	45	190	---												
Carlisle	199	282	257	300	---											
Dover	178	187	130	240	400	---										
Edinburgh, Scotland	295	375	338	390	98	450	---									
Exeter	164	84	251	111	355	244	454	---								
Glasgow, Scotland	295	375	370	390	97	470	44	453	---							
Lincoln	85	170	90	200	182	200	260	260	280	---						
Liverpool	95	165	170	170	126	278	219	258	220	120	---					
London	110	115	54	155	313	71	375	200	397	131	193	---				
Oxford	66	75	83	110	271	130	360	154	360	127	160	57	---			
Penzance	270	190	360	230	465	350	560	110	560	365	363	280	263	---		
Sheffield	76	183	122	201	159	247	236	256	256	47	79	168	141	366	---	
York	135	215	150	245	117	266	195	299	220	75	100	188	185	405	58	---

You're strongly advised to buy a vehicle with a valid MOT certificate and tax disc; both remain with the car through a change of ownership. Third-party insurance goes with the driver rather than the car, so you'll still have to arrange this. You can get more information at post offices.

Camper Van These are popular for touring Europe, particularly for shoestring travellers. Adverts in *TNT Magazine* can be a useful way to form a group to buy or rent a van.

Both *Autotrader* and *Loot* carry adverts for vans. Private sellers congregate daily at the long-running Van Market, in Market Rd N7 (off Caledonian Rd) in London. Some second-hand dealers offer a 'buy-back' scheme for when you return, but buying and reselling privately is preferable to avoid paying for the dealer's profits. You will need to spend a minimum of £1000 to £2000 for something reliable enough to get you around.

Motorcycling

England, especially the north, is made for motorcycle touring, with stunning scenery and good-quality winding roads. Just make sure your wet-weather gear is up to scratch. Crash helmets are compulsory.

The **Auto-Cycle Union** (☎ 01788-566400; w *www.acu.org.uk*) publishes a very useful booklet, the *Motorcycling GB Handbook*, also available online.

Motoring Organisations

The two largest motoring organisations in England, both offering 24-hour breakdown assistance, are the **Automobile Association** (AA; ☎ 0800 444999; w *www.theaa.com*) and the **Royal Automobile Club** (RAC; ☎ 0800 550550; w *www.rac.co.uk*). One year's membership starts at £40 for the AA and £34 for the RAC, and both can also extend their cover to include continental Europe. Check with your local motoring organisation – it may have a reciprocal arrangement.

HITCHING

Hitching is not as common as it used to be in England. It's never entirely safe, and we don't recommend it. Travellers who hitch should understand that they're taking a small but potentially serious risk. Hitching is safer in pairs, and you should let someone know where you're planning to go. Note that it's against the law to hitch on motorways; you must use approach roads or service stations.

BOAT

Refer to the various regional chapters for local services.

LOCAL TRANSPORT

English cities usually have good public transport, although buses are often run by a confusing number of separate companies – a legacy of the former Conservative government's penchant for privatisation. For more details see the Bus & Coach section earlier in this chapter. In large cities, TICs usually provide a useful, comprehensive map of bus routes. Fortunately London managed to retain overall control of its partially privatised system, and it's reasonably decipherable.

Taxis

See the London chapter for information on the famous London black cabs and their minicab rivals. Outside London and other big cities, taxis are usually reasonably priced. In rural areas you can expect to pay around £1.60 per mile, with a minimum charge of £2.30. A taxi over a short distance will compare well with a local bus, especially if you are sharing the cost. More importantly, when it's Sunday and you find that the next bus due to visit the charming town you've hiked to is on Monday, a taxi can get you to a transport hub for a reasonable price. If you call **National Cabline** (☎ 0800 123444) from a landline phone, the service will pinpoint your location and transfer your call to an approved local company.

ORGANISED TOURS

If your time is limited, you prefer to travel in a group, or want to do a specific activity, there are some excellent tours available. The British Tourist Authority (BTA) can supply information. Local special-interest tours are listed throughout this book, and you can also enquire at TICs.

Acorn Activities (☎ 0870 740 5055, **w** www .acornactivities.co.uk) Provides tours with themes from cycling to jewellery making

British Trust for Conservation Volunteers (☎ 01491-821600, **w** www.btcv.org) Recruits volunteers for environmental projects and offers UK and international conservation holidays

Contiki (☎ 020-82906777, **w** www.contiki.com) Has rugged adventure trips aimed at 18- to 35-year-old market, lasting 12 days

Contours (☎ 01768-867539, **w** www.contours .co.uk) Offers walking tours along many long-distance paths, such as the West Highland Way, or Cumbria Way, both guided and self-guided (when accommodation and routes are arranged, but you travel independently)

Country Lanes (☎ 01425-655022, **w** www .countrylanes.co.uk) A large bicycle-touring company that runs guided and self-guided cycling tours throughout England

Drifters (☎ 020-7262 1292, **w** www.driftersclub .com) Aimed at people in their 20s, runs day trips from London starting from £17, and trips lasting up to two weeks around Britain

Pathways (☎ 01229-889400, **w** www.pathway suk.co.uk) Guides Lake District walking holidays of varying difficulty

Peak National Park Centre (☎ 01433-620373, **w** www.peakdistrict.org) Has Peak District one- to three-day tours for wildlife enthusiasts, nature painters and walkers

Saddleback Trails (☎ 017684-86432) Small company arranging horse-riding holidays (mainly four-day) in and around the upper Eden Valley in the northern Lake District

YHA (☎ 0870 241 2314, **w** www.yha.org.uk) Offers all sorts of family trips – including paint-ball weekends to work out all those issues – as well as caving, climbing, horse riding, biking, kayaking and countless others

London

☎ 020 • pop 12 million

The mammoth metropolis of London is one of the truly great capitals of the world: at once exhilarating, irrepressible, intimidating, and brimming with spectacle and possibilities. It can be different things to different people but always in abundance. In fact, it's the quantity of its qualities that make London such an essential destination for anyone who's ever packed a bag.

Not only is it home to magnificent historical architecture and familiar landmarks such as Big Ben, the Tower of London, Westminster Abbey and St Paul's Cathedral, it's a cornucopia of cultural wealth, boasting some of the world's best museums and art galleries (treasures which, since 2002, are largely ours for free). But as much as it's the crucible of an ancient and fascinating history, London is also one of the most dynamic hubs on earth, propping up the vanguard in music, visual arts, fashion, film and sometimes even food.

It is propelled by the energy, vitality and aspirations of a population made up of more than three dozen different ethnic groups and is the frame for a tapestry of different cultures, unparalleled in complexity and colour. It is home to between seven and 12 million inhabitants (depending on where you stop counting), and some 30 million of us tramp through its rain-sodden streets each year. And while it receives incomers with usually open arms – today's Londoner is more likely to wear a turban than a bowler hat – it still manages to retain its unique personality beneath the cosmopolitan veneer and amid the onslaught of globalisation.

After dark, when London isn't huddled around bantering at the pub, it fizzes with boundless creative energy expressed in a bristling music scene, unparalleled club culture and mainstream arts to match anywhere on the planet. Your opportunities for being entertained are limited only by your spending and staying power.

London is not a place one can ever 'do'; it's evolving too quickly even for residents to fully grasp, never mind the casual tourist. As London cabbies are wont to say, 'If you tire of London, you tire of life'. (Have they ever considered that maybe we're just tired of London cabbies?)

Highlights

- Scanning the capital from the London Eye
- Marvelling at the art and architecture of the Tate Modern
- Shopping around Covent Garden and the Portobello Road market
- Passing time at extraordinary Greenwich
- Being dazzled at the British Museum, again and again
- Finding refuge and sinking pints in a traditional pub
- Stepping back in history at the Tower of London

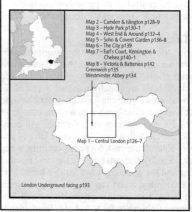

Map 2 – Camden & Islington p128–9
Map 3 – Hyde Park p130–1
Map 4 – West End & Around p132–4
Map 5 – Soho & Covent Garden p136–8
Map 6 – The City p139
Map 7 – Earl's Court, Kensington & Chelsea p140–1
Map 8 – Victoria & Battersea p142
Greenwich p135
Westminster Abbey p134

Map 1 – Central London p126–7

London Underground facing p193

HISTORY

Celts first established themselves around a ford across the River Thames which, at the time, was twice as wide as it is today and probably served as a barrier between competing tribes. But it was the Romans who developed the square mile now known as the City of London (which lies within the 659 sq miles of today's Greater London city – note the small 'c'). They built a crossing, near today's London Bridge, which became the hub of their road system. The colony was sacked by a rival tribe in the 1st century AD but later rebuilt. By the end of the 3rd century AD 'Londinium' was almost as multicultural as it is today with 30,000 people of various ethnic groups (albeit all Roman citizens, of course) and temples dedicated to a large number of cults. Parts of London like Aldgate and Ludgate get their names from the gates of the original city walls built by the Romans. Londinium weakened in the following centuries as internal strife and relentless barbarian attacks took their toll. The Romans abandoned Britain altogether in the 5th century and, while the conurbation survived, it was no more than a sparsely populated backwater.

The Saxons moved in, establishing farmsteads and villages, and their 'Lundenwic' prospered, becoming a large, well-organised town divided into 20 different wards. As the Saxon city grew in importance, it attracted the attention of the Vikings from Denmark who launched many invasions and razed the city in the 9th century. The Saxons held on until, finally beaten down in 1016, they were forced to accept the Danish leader Canute (Cnut) as King of England. During this time, London replaced Winchester as capital of England. In 1042 the throne reverted to the Saxon Edward the Confessor whose main contribution to the city was the building of Westminster Abbey, consecrated a week before he died in 1065.

A dispute over his successor led to what's known as the Norman Conquest (Normans broadly being Vikings with shorter beards). When William the Conqueror won the watershed Battle of Hastings the following year, he and his forces marched into London – by then the richest and largest city in the kingdom – where he was crowned king. He raised the White Tower (the core of the Tower of London), negotiated taxes with the merchants, and affirmed the City's independence and right to self-government.

The throne passed through various houses in the millennium or so since (the House of Windsor has been in the hot seat since 1910) but royal power has been concentrated in London since the 12th century.

Politics in London during the Middle Ages, from the 12th century to the late 15th century, was largely taken up by a three-way power struggle between the monarchy, the church and City guilds.

The greatest threat to the burgeoning city was that of disease caused by unsanitary living conditions and impure drinking water. In 1348 rats on ships from Europe brought the bubonic plague and, over the next year, more than a third of London's population of 100,000 was wiped out by the Black Death.

There followed especially hard times for the working man and violence became a way of life. In 1381, miscalculating or just disregarding the mood of the nation, the king tried to impose a poll tax on everyone in the realm. Tens of thousands of peasants marched on London to make their feelings known. Several ministers were murdered and many buildings were razed before the so-called Peasants' Revolt ran its course. The ringleaders were executed although there was no more mention of poll tax (until Margaret Thatcher, not heeding the lessons of history, shot herself in the foot by trying to introduce it in the 1980s).

Despite these setbacks, London was consolidated as the seat of law and government in the kingdom during the 14th century. Once the jostling for power settled and an uneasy compromise was reached, the city expanded rapidly under the House of Tudor, particularly during the reign of Elizabeth I (1558–1603), the daughter of King Henry VIII and Anne Boleyn. The first recorded map of London was published in 1558, while John Stow produced the first comprehensive history of the capital in 1598.

The bubonic plague returned in the form of the 'Great Plague' in 1665 and 100,000 Londoners were wiped out by the time the winter cold arrested the epidemic. Just as the population considered a sigh of relief, another disaster struck.

London had for centuries been prone to fire but the mother of all blazes, the Great Fire of 1666, virtually razed the place, destroying most of its medieval, Tudor and Jacobean architecture. One plus was that it created a blank canvas upon which master architect Christopher Wren could build his magnificent churches. By way of commemorating the inferno – and symbolising the restoration and resurgence of subsequent years – the so-called Monument was erected (see The Monument section later in this chapter).

London's growth continued unabated and by 1700 it was Europe's largest city with 600,000 people. An influx of foreign workers brought expansion to the east and south, while those who could afford it headed to the more salubrious environs of the north and west. London today is still, more or less, divided along these lines.

Georgian London saw a great surge in creativity in architecture, music and art: Dr

Johnson produced the first English-language dictionary; Handel wrote *Water Music* (1717) and *The Messiah* (1742) while living here; Gainsborough and Reynolds made a splash with their painting; while Georgian architects created imposing symmetrical architecture and breathing space for the metropolis.

At the same time the gaps between the city's haves and have-nots became more marked and lawlessness was rife. Even King George II was robbed as he strolled through the gardens of Kensington Palace.

In 1837 the 18-year-old Victoria ascended to the throne. During her long reign (1837–1901), London became the fulcrum of the expanding British Empire, which covered a quarter of the earth's surface. New docks were built to meet the demands of booming trade, railway lines fanned out from London, the Great Exhibition of 1851 showcased London to the world, and the world's first underground railway opened between Paddington and Farringdon Rd in 1863. Propelled by this, and the Industrial Revolution, London's population mushroomed from 2.7 million in 1851 to 6.6 million by the end of Victoria's reign.

Road transport was revolutionised in the early 20th century when the first motor buses were introduced to the streets of London and quickly replacing the horse-drawn versions that had trotted their trade since 1829.

Although London suffered relatively minor damage during WWI, it was devastated by the Luftwaffe in WWII when huge swathes of the centre and East End were totally flattened and much of Georgian and Victorian London was reduced to rubble. After the war, ugly housing and low-cost developments were thrown up on the bomb sites. The Docklands declined to a state of dereliction, until rediscovered by developers in the 1980s.

Immigrants from around the world flocked to postwar London, changing the city's character forever. Notting Hill and Brixton became Caribbean in tone, Bengalis and Indians replaced the Jewish community in the East End, and the Jews, in turn, moved to Golders Green. Finsbury saw an influx of Cypriots while Chinese settled in Soho and the Irish took over parts of Kilburn and shared Camden with the Greeks.

The latest major disaster to beset the capital arrived in the form of the great smog on 6 December 1952, when a lethal combination of fog, smoke and pollution descended on the city and killed some 4000 people. These types of dense smogs became known as 'peasoupers'.

Prosperity gradually returned, and the creative energy that had been bottled up in the postwar years was suddenly unleashed. London became the capital of cool in fashion and music, and Carnaby St became synonymous with the 'swinging '60s'. Two seminal events were the Beatles recording at Abbey Road and the Rolling Stones performing for free in front of half a million people in Hyde Park.

The party didn't last long, however, and London returned to the doldrums in the harsh economic climate of the 1970s. Recovery began – for the business community at least – under the iron fist of Margaret Thatcher, who was elected Britain's first woman prime minister in 1979. Her monetarist policy and determination to crush socialism sent unemployment skyrocketing and her term was marked by unrest. Rioting in Trafalgar Square, in response to her proposed introduction of a poll tax, helped to finally see her off.

London got its first true mayor in 2000 when feisty 'Red' Ken Livingstone swept to victory on the promise that he would lock horns with the central government when it came to doing what was best for London. His big plan has been to improve public transport and reduce traffic congestion although, at the time of writing, Londoners were still complaining about both.

ORIENTATION

The city's main geographical feature is the murky Thames, a river that was sufficiently deep (for anchorage) and narrow (for bridging) to attract the Romans here in the first place. It divides the city roughly into north and south.

London is divided into 33 diverse boroughs, which are all run by local councils with significant autonomy. The 'square mile' of the City of London – the capital's financial district – is counted as a separate borough and is referred to simply as 'the City' (look for the capital 'C'). The M25 ring road encompasses the 607 sq miles that is broadly regarded as Greater London.

Despite all the flak it receives, London's Underground system ('the tube') makes this enormous city relatively accessible. The underground map – now a London icon – is easy to use although geographically misleading. Most important sights, theatres, restaurants and even affordable places to stay lie within a reasonably compact rectangle formed by the tube's Circle Line (colour-coded yellow), which encircles central London just north of the river.

In this chapter, the nearest tube or train station has been given for each address; Map 1 shows the location of tube stations and the areas covered by the detailed district maps.

Londoners commonly refer to areas by their postcode. The letters correspond to compass directions from the centre of London, approximately St Paul's Cathedral. EC means East Central, W means West and so on. The numbering system after the letters is less helpful: 1 is the centre of the zone but after that it goes in alphabetical order of the postal-district names, which are not always in common use.

Districts and postal codes are often given on street signs, vital when names are duplicated (there are 47 Station Rds), or cross through a number of districts. Streets run into each other and change name but, even more confusing, street numbers sometimes appear to follow no logic at all.

Most of London's airports lie some distance from the centre, but transport is relatively simple and efficient although not cheap. See the Getting Around section later in this chapter for details.

INFORMATION

If you want more specific coverage on the city of London, try Lonely Planet's comprehensive *London* or the more choosy, pocket-sized *London Condensed*.

Time Out London magazine (issued every Tuesday, £2.20) is the listings bible and a good place to take the city's pulse. The right-wing *Evening Standard* (35p) is the only dedicated London daily and has a decent listing supplement, *Hot Tickets*, on Thursday.

There's a glut of free mags available around tube stations. *TNT Magazine*, *Southern Cross* and *SA Times* are the most useful to travellers, with entertainment listings, travel sections and classified sections along with Australasian and South African news and sports results.

Loot (£1.30), issued five times weekly, is the main classified paper and the best place to look for flats and house-share ads.

Tourist Offices

Britain Visitor Centre The Britain Visitor Centre *(Map 5; w www.visitbritain.com; 1 Regent St SW1; ⊖ Piccadilly Circus; open daily 9am-6.30pm Mon-Fri year round, 10am-4pm Sat & Sun Oct-late Jun, 9am-5pm Sat, 10am-4pm Sun late Jun–Sept)* is a comprehensive information and booking centre with a map and guidebook shop, accommodation desk, entertainment and transport ticket desks, a bureau de change, international telephones and computer terminals for accessing tourist information on the Internet. It handles walk-in inquirers only but there's lots of good information on its website. You can also get the lowdown on the rest of the British Isles here.

Tourist Information Centres As well as providing information, London's main **Tourist Information Centre** *(TIC; Map 8; Victoria train station; ⊖ Victoria; open 8am-8pm Mon-Sat, 8am-6pm Sun Apr-Oct, 8am-7pm Mon-Sat, 8am-6pm Sun Nov-Mar)* handles accommodation bookings. It too can get positively mobbed in the peak season.

There are also TICs at: the arrivals hall at **Waterloo International Terminal** *(Map 4; ⊖ Waterloo; open 8.30am-10.30pm daily)*, **Liverpool Street station** *(Map 6; ⊖ Liverpool St; open 8am-6pm daily)*, Heathrow terminals 1, 2 and 3 (open 8am to 6pm); and Gatwick, Stansted, Luton and London City airports. You'll find information desks at Paddington train station and Victoria coach station.

Written inquiries should be sent to the **London Tourist Board & Convention Bureau** *(fax 7932 0222; w www.londontown.com; Glen House, Stag Place, London SW1E 5LT)*. While in Britain, you can also make use of the **London Line** *(☎ 09068 663344)* where you'll get the lowdown on events and attractions (calls cost 60p per minute).

Money

Banks and ATMs abound across central London and most are linked to the international money systems such as Cirrus and Maestro. If you're carrying cash (besides asking for trouble), you won't have a problem changing it over because banks, bureaux de change and travel agents are tripping over themselves to get your business. If you use bureaux de change, make sure to check commission rates *and* exchange rates; some can be extortionate.

There are 24-hour bureaus in Heathrow Terminals 1, 3 and 4 (the one in Terminal 2 opens 6am to 11pm), in Gatwick's South and North Terminals and at Stansted. The airport bureaus are good value; they charge less than most high-street banks – usually about 1.5% of the transaction value, with a £3 minimum.

American Express *(AmEx; Map 5; ☎ 7930 4411; 6 Haymarket SW1; ⊖ Piccadilly Circus; currency exchange open 9am-6pm Mon-Sat, 10am-5pm Sun)* has branches all around town.

Thomas Cook *(Map 4; ☎ 7853 6400; 30 St James's St SW1; ⊖ Green Park; open 9am-5.30pm Mon, Tues, Thur & Fri, 10am-5.30pm Wed, 9am-4pm Sat)* also has branches around London. Both have outlets at Victoria station.

Discounts Since 2002 many of London's main museums and galleries have dropped their admission fees. If you're on an exhaustive tour you might consider investing in the **London Pass** *(☎ 0870 242 9988; W www.londonpass.com; 1/2/3/6 days adult £30/52/68/107, child £19/32/43/56)*, which allows you to skip the queues and swan straight into some 60 museums, galleries, historical buildings and leisure facilities. It also gives you unlimited travel on the tube and loads of useful extras like free Internet access. You can buy a version without transport; either way you'll get more punch for your pound.

Post & Communications

Poste Restante Unless the sender has specified otherwise, poste restante mail sent to London ends up at the **Trafalgar Square post office** *(Map 5; 24-28 William IV St, London WC2N 4DL; ⊖ Charing Cross; open 8am-8pm Mon-Fri, 9am-8pm Sat)*. Mail will be held for four weeks; ID is required.

Telephone See the Telephone section in the Facts for the Visitor chapter for details on beating British Telecom's (BT) high rates on international calls using special cards such as Lonely Planet's eKno card.

CallShop *(Map 7; ☎ 7390 4549; 181a Earl's Court Rd SW5; ⊖ Earl's Court • 189 Edgware Rd; ⊖ Edgware Road; open 9am-12am)*, a private company, has cheaper international calls than BT. You can also send and receive faxes.

Email & Internet Access The no-frills airline easyJet has several Internet cafés around London under the name **easyInternetcafé** *(Map 5; ☎ 7930 4094; 7 The Strand EC2; ⊖ Charing Cross; open 24hr • Map 8; ☎ 7233 8456; 9-13 Wilton Rd; ⊖ Victoria; open 24hr • Map 4; ☎ 7491 8986; 358 Oxford St W1; ⊖ Bond St; open 24hr • Map 3; ☎ 7938 1841; 160-166 Kensington High St W8; ⊖ High Street Kensington; open 7.30am-11.30pm daily)*. Charges can vary: £1 buys you from 40 minutes to six hours of access.

Travel Agencies

If you're earning sterling or stronger, London is a centre for cheap travel. It has countless travel agencies although not all of them are of stellar reputation. Refer to the Sunday papers (especially the *Sunday Times*), *TNT Magazine* and *Time Out* for listings of cheap flights.

STA Travel *(Map 7; European inquiries ☎ 7361 6161, worldwide inquiries ☎ 7361 6262, tours, accommodation, car hire or insurance ☎ 7361 6160; W www.statravel.co.uk; 86 Old Brompton Rd SW7; ⊖ South Kensington (Map 2; 117 Euston Rd NW1; ⊖ Euston)* is long-standing and reliable.

Trailfinders *(Map 3; long-haul travel ☎ 7938 3939, 1st- & business-class flights ☎ 7938 3444; W www.trailfinders.com; 194 Kensington High St W8; ⊖ High Street Kensington; open 9am-5pm Mon-Wed & Fri, 9am-6pm Thur, 10am-5.15pm Sat)* has a visa and passport service (☎ 7938 3848), immunisation centre (☎ 7938 3999), foreign exchange (☎ 7938 3836) and information centre (☎ 7938 3303).

Bookshops

See Books under Shopping later for bookshops in London that have extensive ranges of useful travel books and maps.

Laundry

Many hostels and some hotels have self-service washing machines and dryers, and nearly every main street has a laundrette. The average cost to wash and dry a single load is £3. Your lodging will be able to guide you to the nearest laundrette but, if you're stuck, you can get your whites whiter at **Bobo's Bubbles** *(Map 7; 111 Earl's Court Rd SW5; ⊖ Earl's Court)*, **Red & White Laundrette** *(Map 4; 78 Marchmont St WC1; ⊖ Regent's Park)* or **Forco** *(Map 2; 60 Parkway NW1; ⊖ Camden Town)*.

Left Luggage

There are left-luggage facilities at all of the airports (see Getting There & Away later in this chapter), train stations and at Victoria coach station. Storage costs between £3 and £6 a day, depending on the bulk.

Medical Services

To find a local doctor or hospital, consult the local telephone directory or call ☎ 100 (toll free). The following hospitals have 24-hour accident and emergency departments:

Charing Cross Hospital (Map 1; ☎ 8383 0000) Fulham Palace Rd W6; ⊖ Hammersmith
Guy's Hospital (Map 6; ☎ 7955 5000) St Thomas St SE1; ⊖ London Bridge

In the event of a dental crisis, phone the **Dental Emergency Care Service** (☎ 7955 2186) weekdays between 8.45am and 3.30pm or call into **Eastman Dental Hospital** *(Map 2; ☎ 7915 1000; 256 Gray's Inn Rd WC1; ⊖ King's Cross St Pancras)*.

The travel agency **Trailfinders** (see Travel Agencies earlier) has a clinic with a full range of travel vaccines.

Dangers & Annoyances

Crime Considering its size and the disparities in wealth, London is remarkably safe and the closest you'll probably come to robbery is the daylight variety in tourist areas. That said, you can't let your guard down, particularly in heavily touristed areas.

Take particular care at night. When travelling by tube, choose a carriage with other people in it and avoid deserted suburban stations. Solo women travellers should avoid unlicensed minicabs at night. The drivers are often unreliable and occasionally dangerous.

Terrorism London remains the occasional target of terrorists with a point to make, although the situation has calmed down considerably since the Northern Ireland peace process began. Even before September 11, there was a much higher sense of security here than in other world capitals, and the public and authorities are well drilled in precautionary measures. *Never* leave your bag unattended – you may trigger a security alert and have your bag seized by authorities. If you see an unattended package, alert the authorities but do *not* touch it.

Touts & Scams Wherever tourists congregate, you're always going to get a few scal-

lies trying to part them and their money, although London's not nearly as bad as many other capitals. Scams come and go. ATM distraction was popular at the time of researching this book. When your cash is about to be delivered, con artist No 1 alerts you to a £20 dropped at your feet while con artist No 2 swipes the notes the ATM has just produced.

Hotel and hostel touts descend on backpackers at popular tube and main-line stations – don't accept lifts from them unless you know exactly where you are going. In general, if an offer appears too good to be true, then it probably is.

Some Soho strip clubs and hostess bars are dodgy and you should be especially wary of those that tout for business on the street.

CENTRAL LONDON
Trafalgar Square (Map 5)

In many ways this is the focal point of London – certainly visitors' London – where many great rallies and marches have taken place, the new year is ushered in by tens of thousands of revellers and where city folk congregate to celebrate anything from a football victory over Germany to the ousting of the Tories. It was once famous for the flocks of pigeons that would dive-bomb anyone with a morsel of food on their person but numbers have dwindled considerably since Mayor Ken Livingstone banned the feeding of the pesky blighters.

The square was designed by John Nash in the early 19th century on the site of the King's Mews, and is flanked by the National Gallery, the National Portrait Gallery and the eye-catching church of St Martin-in-the-Fields. The 43.5m-high **Nelson's Column** – upon which the admiral surveys his fleet of ships to the southwest – was completed in 1843 and commemorates Admiral Nelson's victory over Napoleon off Cape Trafalgar in Spain in 1805.

Three of the square's four plinths are occupied by such worthies as King George IV on horseback, but one, which was originally intended for a statue of William IV, remained vacant for more than 150 years before local contemporary artists were invited to use it as a showcase for their works. Reactions to the pieces have been mixed and there's still debate over how it should be used; a wax model

[Continued on page 143]

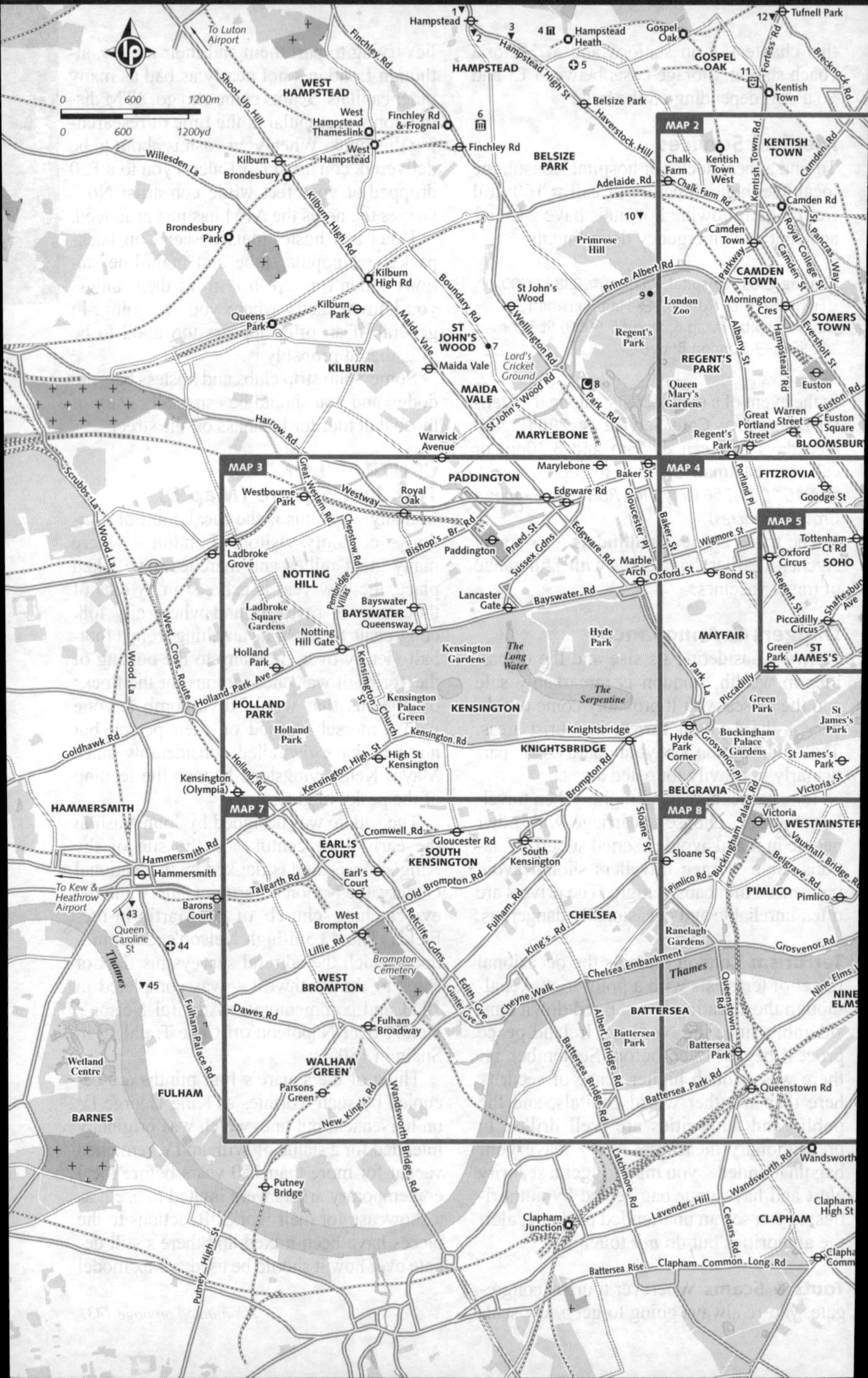

MAP 1

LP

To Luton Airport

Shoot Up Hill

0 600 1200m
0 600 1200yd

WEST HAMPSTEAD

Finchley Rd

1 Hampstead
2
3
4 Hampstead Heath
5 Hampstead High St
Gospel Oak
12 Tufnell Park

HAMPSTEAD

GOSPEL OAK
11
Kentish Town

West Hampstead Thameslink
Finchley Rd & Frognal
Finchley Rd
West Hampstead
Kilburn
Brondesbury

Belsize Park
Haverstock Hill

6
BELSIZE PARK

MAP 2

KENTISH TOWN

Chalk Farm
Kentish Town West

Camden Rd

Willesden La

Brondesbury Park

Kilburn High Rd
Boundary Rd
Maida Vale

Kilburn High Rd
Queens Park
Kilburn Park

KILBURN

ST JOHN'S WOOD
7
Maida Vale

St John's Wood
Wellington Rd
Prince Albert Rd

Adelaide Rd
Chalk Farm Rd

10

Primrose Hill

Camden Town
Mornington Cres

CAMDEN TOWN

SOMERS TOWN

Camden Town
Camden Rd
Royal College St
St Pancras Way
Kentish Town Rd
Camden Town Rd

9 London Zoo

Regent's Park

REGENT'S PARK

Queen Mary's Gardens

Albany St
Hampstead Rd
Crowndale Rd

Euston

Great Portland Street
Warren Street
Euston Square
Euston

MAIDA VALE

MARYLEBONE

Warwick Avenue

Harrow Rd

Scrubs La
Wood La

Maida Vale
St John's Wood Rd
Park Rd
8

Regent's Park

BLOOMSBURY

MAP 3

Marylebone
Baker St
Edgware Rd

PADDINGTON

MAP 4

FITZROVIA
Goodge St

Westbourne Park
Royal Oak

Westway
Great Western Rd
Chepstow Rd

Bishop's Br Rd
Praed St
Paddington
Sussex Gdns
Gloucester Rd

MAP 5

Tottenham Ct Rd
Oxford Circus
SOHO

Ladbroke Grove

NOTTING HILL

Ladbroke Square Gardens
Pembridge Villas

Bayswater
BAYSWATER
Queensway

Notting Hill Gate
Holland Park

Lancaster Gate
Bayswater Rd

Edgware Rd
Marble Arch
Oxford St
Bond St

Wigmore St
Baker St

Regent St
Shaftesbury Ave

Piccadilly Circus

MAYFAIR

ST JAMES'S

Green Park

Holland Park Ave
Holland Park

HOLLAND PARK

Holland Park

Kensington Palace Green

Kensington Gardens

The Long Water

Hyde Park

The Serpentine

KENSINGTON

Kensington Church St
Kensington Rd
Kensington High St

KNIGHTSBRIDGE

Knightsbridge

Hyde Park Corner

Brompton Rd

Piccadilly

Green Park

Buckingham Palace Gardens

St James's Park

St James's Park

Kensington (Olympia)

Goldhawk Rd

Wood La
West Cross Route

MAP 7

EARL'S COURT

Cromwell Rd
Gloucester Rd
SOUTH KENSINGTON
South Kensington

Grosvenor Pl

BELGRAVIA

MAP 8

Victoria
WESTMINSTER

HAMMERSMITH

Hammersmith Rd
Hammersmith

Talgarth Rd
Earl's Court

West Brompton

Old Brompton Rd
Fulham Rd

Sloane St

Sloane Sq

Belgrave Rd
Vauxhall Bridge Rd

PIMLICO
Pimlico

Victoria

To Kew & Heathrow Airport

Queen Caroline St

Barons Court
43
44

Lillie Rd

WEST BROMPTON

Brompton Cemetery

Redcliffe Gdns
Edith Grove
Earl's Ct
Game Rd

King's Rd

CHELSEA

Cheyne Walk

Chelsea Embankment

Ranelagh Gardens

Thames

Pimlico Rd
Buckingham Palace Rd

Grosvenor Rd

NINE ELMS

45

Dawes Rd

Fulham Broadway

Albert Bridge Rd

BATTERSEA

Battersea Park

Battersea Park

Queenstown Rd

Wetland Centre

WALHAM GREEN

Parsons Green

New King's Rd

Fulham Palace Rd

Wandsworth Bridge Rd

Battersea Bridge Rd

Queenstown Rd

Queenstown Rd

BARNES

FULHAM

Putney Bridge

Putney High St

Bridge Rd

Thames

Wandsworth Rd

Lavender Hill

Clapham Junction

Battersea Rise
Clapham Common Long Rd

Wandsworth

Clapham High St

CLAPHAM

Clapham Common

Cedars Rd

MAP 1

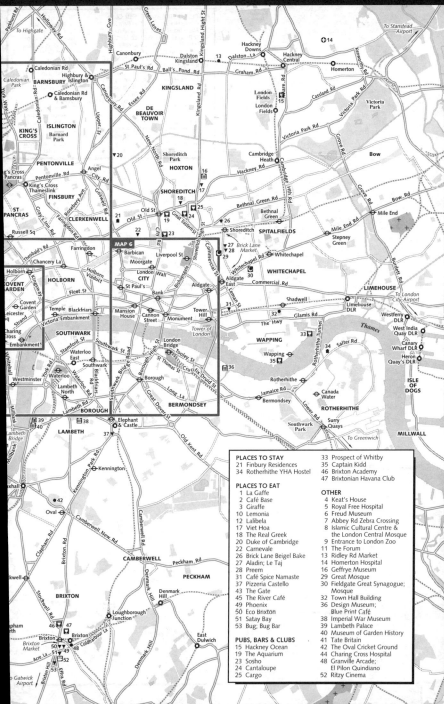

PLACES TO STAY
21 Finbury Residences
34 Rotherhithe YHA Hostel

PLACES TO EAT
1 La Gaffe
2 Café Base
3 Giraffe
10 Lemonia
12 Lalibela
17 Viet Hoa
18 The Real Greek
20 Duke of Cambridge
22 Carnevale
26 Brick Lane Beigel Bake
27 Aladin; Le Taj
28 Preem
31 Café Spice Namaste
37 Pizzeria Castello
43 The Gate
45 The River Café
49 Phoenix
50 Eco Brixton
51 Satay Bay
53 Bug; Bug Bar

PUBS, BARS & CLUBS
15 Hackney Ocean
19 The Aquarium
24 Sosho
24 Cantaloupe
25 Cargo

33 Prospect of Whitby
35 Captain Kidd
46 Brixton Academy
47 Brixtonian Havana Club

OTHER
4 Keat's House
5 Royal Free Hospital
6 Freud Museum
7 Abbey Rd Zebra Crossing
8 Islamic Cultural Centre & the London Central Mosque
9 Entrance to London Zoo
11 The Forum
13 Ridley Rd Market
14 Homerton Hospital
16 Geffrye Museum
29 Great Mosque
30 Fieldgate Great Synagogue; Mosque
32 Town Hall Building
36 Design Museum; Blue Print Café
38 Imperial War Museum
39 Lambeth Palace
40 Museum of Garden History
41 Tate Britain
42 The Oval Cricket Ground
44 Charing Cross Hospital
48 Granville Arcade; El Pilon Quindiano
52 Ritzy Cinema

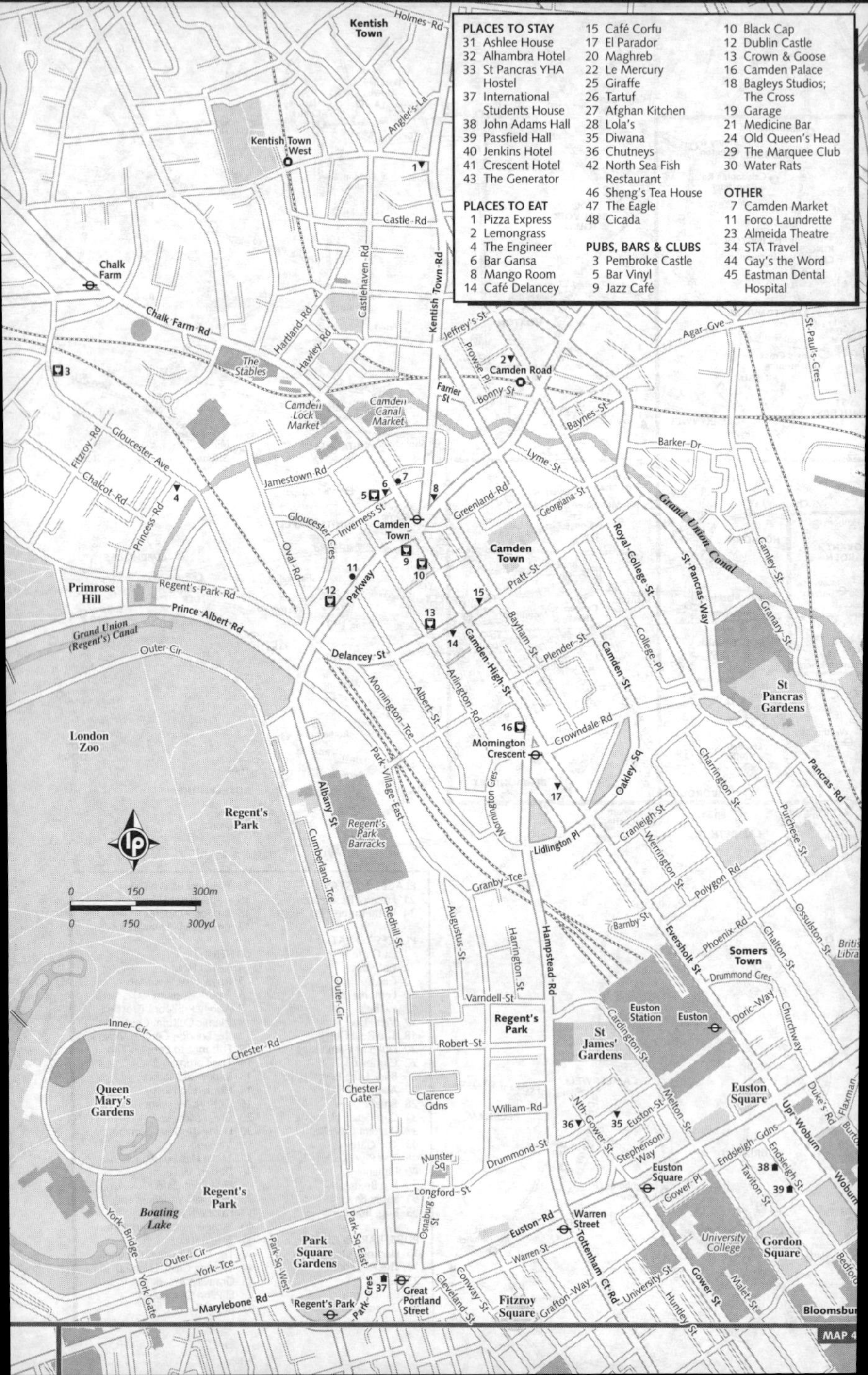

MAP 2

Kentish Town

Holmes-Rd

Angler's-La

Kentish Town West

Castle-Rd

Chalk Farm

Chalk Farm Rd

Hartland-Rd

Hawley-Rd

Castlehaven-Rd

Kentish Town-Rd

Jeffrey's-St

Prowse-St

Farrier-St

Bonny-St

Camden Road

Baynes-St

Lyme-St

Barker-Dr

PLACES TO STAY
31 Ashlee House
32 Alhambra Hotel
33 St Pancras YHA Hostel
37 International Students House
38 John Adams Hall
39 Passfield Hall
40 Jenkins Hotel
41 Crescent Hotel
43 The Generator

PLACES TO EAT
1 Pizza Express
2 Lemongrass
4 The Engineer
6 Bar Gansa
8 Mango Room
14 Café Delancey

15 Café Corfu
17 El Parador
20 Maghreb
22 Le Mercury
25 Giraffe
26 Tartuf
27 Afghan Kitchen
28 Lola's
35 Diwana
36 Chutneys
42 North Sea Fish Restaurant
46 Sheng's Tea House
47 The Eagle
48 Cicada

PUBS, BARS & CLUBS
3 Pembroke Castle
5 Bar Vinyl
9 Jazz Café

10 Black Cap
12 Dublin Castle
13 Crown & Goose
16 Camden Palace
18 Bagleys Studios; The Cross
19 Garage
21 Medicine Bar
24 Old Queen's Head
29 The Marquee Club
30 Water Rats

OTHER
7 Camden Market
11 Forco Laundrette
23 Almeida Theatre
34 STA Travel
44 Gay's the Word
45 Eastman Dental Hospital

The Stables

Camden Lock Market

Camden Canal Market

Fitzroy-Rd

Gloucester-Ave

Chalcot-Rd

Princess-Rd

Jamestown-Rd

Gloucester-Rd

Inverness-St

Oval-Rd

Camden Town

Greenland-Rd

Georgiana-St

Grand Union Canal

Camden Town

Camden-St

Camden-Rd-Rd

St Pancras Way

Camley-St

Granary-St

Primrose Hill

Regent's-Park-Rd

Prince-Albert-Rd

Parkway

Pratt-St

Royal College-St

College-Pl

St Pancras Gardens

London Zoo

Regent's Park

Grand Union (Regent's) Canal

Outer-Cir

Delancey-St

Mornington-Tce

Albert-Rd

Arlington-Rd

Camden High-St

Bayham-St

Plender-St

Camden-St

Pancras-Rd

Albany-St

Park Village East

Regent's Park Barracks

Mornington Crescent

Crowndale-Rd

Oakley-Sq

Churlton-St

Churnton-St

Cranleigh-St

Werrington-St

Polygon-Rd

Lidlington-Pl

Granby-Tce

Cumberland-Tce

Chester-Rd

Redhill-St

Augustus-St

Hampstead-Rd

Barnby-St

Phoenix-Rd

Eversholt-St

Chalton-St

Ossulston-St

Somers Town

Drummond-Cres

British Library

Queen Mary's Gardens

Inner-Cir

Chester-Gate

Clarence-Gdns

Munster-Sq

Varndell-St

Robert-St

William-Rd

Euston Station

Euston

Doric-Way

Drummond-St

Euston Square

Euston Square

Melton-St

Carnarvon-St

Stephenson Way

Gower-Pl

Euston-Rd

Upr-Woburn-Pl

Duke's-Rd

Endsleigh-Gdns

Taviton-St

Gordon Square

Boating Lake

Regent's Park

Longford-St

Osnaburg-St

Park-Sq-East

Chester Gate

Warren Street

Warren-St

Tottenham Ct-Rd

University College

Gower-St

Mabel-St

York-Bridge

York-Tce

Marylebone-Rd

Regent's Park

Park-Sq Gardens

Park-Cres

Great Portland Street

Conway-St

Grafton-Way

University-St

Fitzroy Square

Bloomsbury

St James' Gardens

Regent's Park

0   150   300m
0   150   300yd

MAP 4

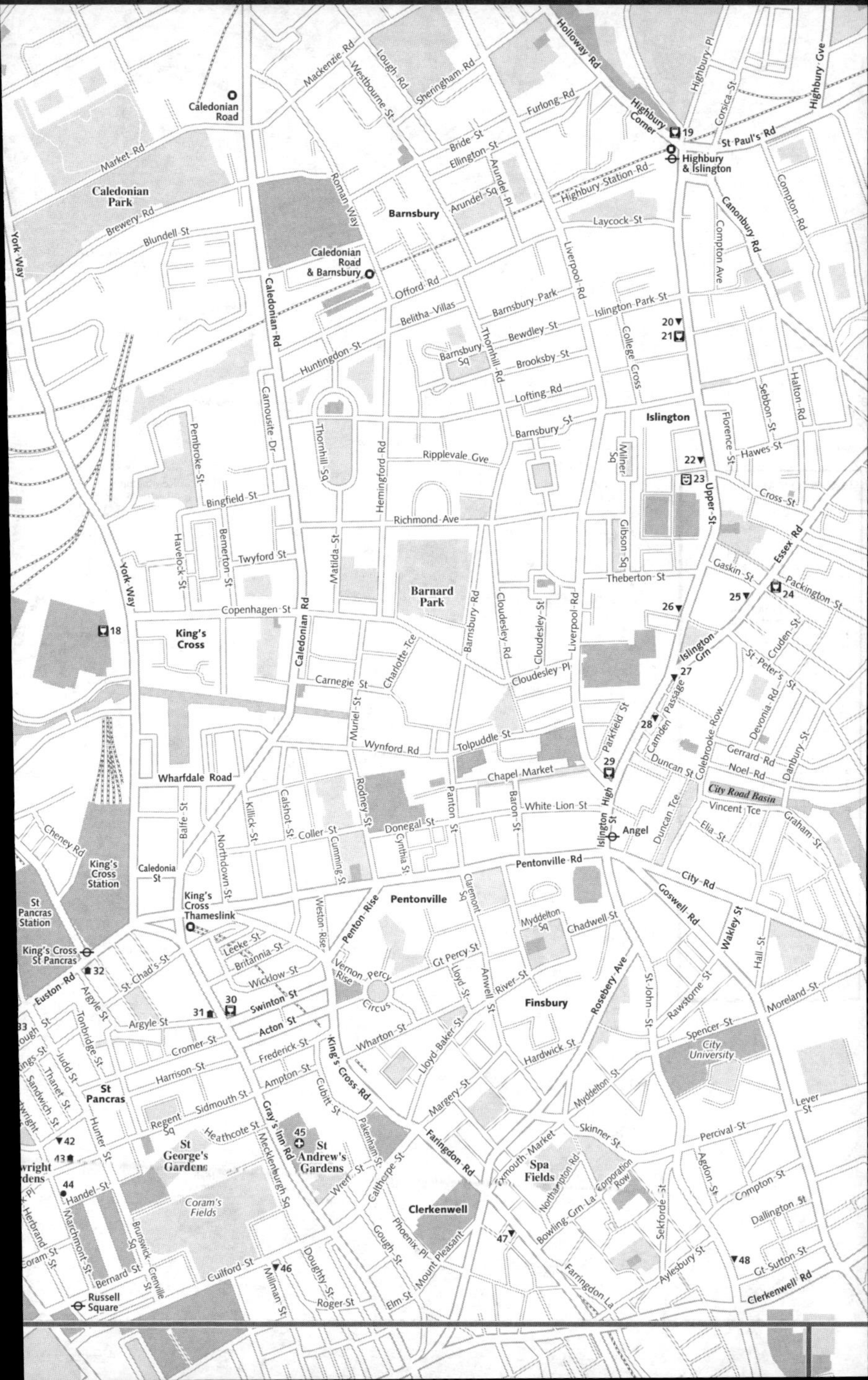

MAP 2

Holloway Rd
Highbury Pl
Conicla St
Highbury Gve

Mackenzie Rd
Westbourne St
Sheringham Rd
Furlong Rd
Highbury Corner
19
St Paul's Rd

Market Rd
Lough Rd
Bride St
Ellington St
Arundel Sq Pl
Highbury Station Rd
Highbury & Islington
Compton St

Caledonian Road

Caledonian Park
Brewery Rd
Roman Way
Arundel Sq
Barnsbury
Laycock St
Canonbury Rd
Compton Ave

Blundell St
Belitha Villas
Caledonian Road & Barnsbury
Offord Rd
Liverpool Rd
Islington Park St
20
21

York Way
Pembroke St
Carnoustie Dr
Huntingdon St
Barnsbury Sq
Barnsbury Park
Bewdley St
Islington Park St
College Cross
Selbon St
Halton Rd

Thornhill Sq
Thornhill Rd
Brooksby St
Lofting Rd
Barnsbury St
Islington
Florence St
Hawes St

Bingfield St
Hemingford Rd
Ripplevale Gve
Milner Sq
22
23
Upper St
Cross St

Havelock St
Bernerton St
Twyford St
Matilda St
Richmond Ave
Barnard Park
Gibson Sq
Theberton St
Gaskin St
25
24
Essex Rd
Packington St

18
King's Cross
Copenhagen St
Caledonian Rd
Charlotte Tce
Barnsbury Rd
Cloudesley Rd
Cloudesley St
Liverpool Rd
26
Islington Grn
St Peter's St
Cruden St
Devonia Rd

Carnegie St
Muriel St
Cloudesley Pl
27
Camden Passage
28
Colebrooke Row
Gerrard Rd
Noel Rd
Danbury St

Wharfdale Road
Rodney St
Wynford Rd
Tolpuddle St
Chapel Market
29
Duncan Tce
City Road Basin
Vincent Tce
Graham St

Killick St
Calshot St
Coller St
Cummings St
Donegal St
Cynthia St
White Lion St
Baron St
Islington High St
Angel
Duncan Tce
Elia St
City Rd

Cheney Rd
Balfe St
Northdown St
Weston Rise
Penton Rise
Claremont
Pentonville Rd
Goswell Rd
Wakley St
Hall St

King's Cross Station
Caledonia St
King's Cross Thameslink
Leeke St
Britannia St
Wicklow St
Vernon Rise
Percy Circus
Gt Percy St
Lloyd St
Pentonville
Myddelton Sq
Chadwell St
River St
Finsbury
St John St
Rawstorne St
Moreland St

St Pancras Station
King's Cross St Pancras
32
St Chad's St
Argyle St
31
30
Swinton St
Acton St
Wharton St
Lloyd Baker St
Rosebery Ave
Spencer St
City University
Lever St

Euston Rd
Tonbridge St
Cromer St
Frederick St
Ampton St
Margery St
Hardwick St
Myddelton Sq
Percival St
Compton St

St Pancras
Judd St
Thanet St
Sandwich St
Harrison St
Sidmouth St
Gray's Inn Rd
Cubitt St
King's Cross Rd

42
43
44
Handel St
Regent Sq
Heathcote St
St George's Gardens
45
St Andrew's Gardens
Mecklenburgh Sq
Gray's Inn Rd
Calthorpe St
Faringdon Rd
Yarmouth Market
Skinner St
Northampton Rd
Corporation Row
Dallington St
48
Gt Sutton St

wright Gardens
Herbrand St
Coram St
Bernard St
Russell Square
Coram's Fields
Brunswick Sq
Guilford St
46
Doughty St
Roger St
Millman St
Gough St
Phoenix Pl
Elm St
Mount Pleasant
Clerkenwell
47
Bowling Grn La
Farringdon La
Sekforde St
Aylesbury St
Clerkenwell Rd

Spa Fields

MAP 3

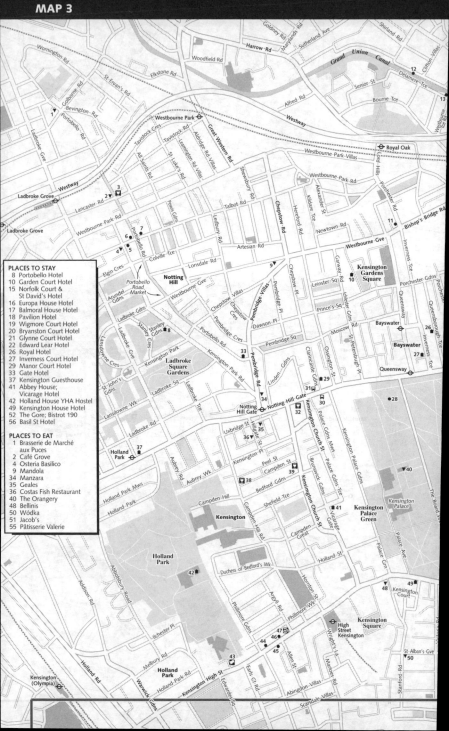

PLACES TO STAY
8 Portobello Hotel
10 Garden Court Hotel
15 Norfolk Court &
   St David's Hotel
16 Europa House Hotel
17 Balmoral House Hotel
18 Pavilion Hotel
19 Wigmore Court Hotel
20 Bryanston Court Hotel
21 Glynne Court Hotel
22 Edward Lear Hotel
26 Royal Hotel
27 Inverness Court Hotel
29 Manor Court Hotel
33 Gate Hotel
37 Kensington Guesthouse
41 Abbey House;
   Vicarage Hotel
42 Holland House YHA Hostel
49 Kensington House Hotel
52 The Gore; Bistrot 190
56 Basil St Hotel

PLACES TO EAT
1 Brasserie de Marché
   aux Puces
2 Café Grove
4 Osteria Basilico
9 Mandola
34 Manzara
35 Geales
36 Costas Fish Restaurant
40 The Orangery
48 Bellinis
50 Wódka
51 Jacob's
55 Pâtisserie Valerie

MAP 3

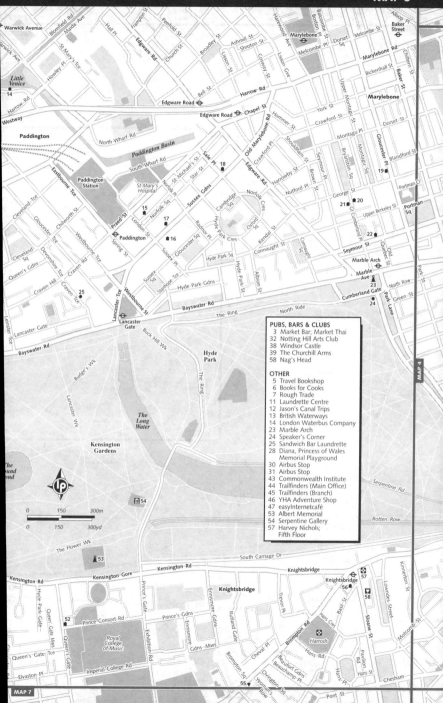

PUBS, BARS & CLUBS
3 Market Bar; Market Thai
32 Notting Hill Arts Club
38 Windsor Castle
39 The Churchill Arms
58 Nag's Head

OTHER
5 Travel Bookshop
6 Books for Cooks
7 Rough Trade
11 Laundrette Centre
12 Jason's Canal Trips
13 British Waterways
14 London Waterbus Company
23 Marble Arch
24 Speaker's Corner
25 Sandwich Bar Laundrette
28 Diana, Princess of Wales
     Memorial Playground
30 Airbus Stop
31 Airbus Stop
43 Commonwealth Institute
44 Trailfinders (Main Office)
45 Trailfinders (Branch)
46 YHA Adventure Shop
47 easyInternetcafé
53 Albert Memorial
54 Serpentine Gallery
57 Harvey Nichols;
     Fifth Floor

MAP 7

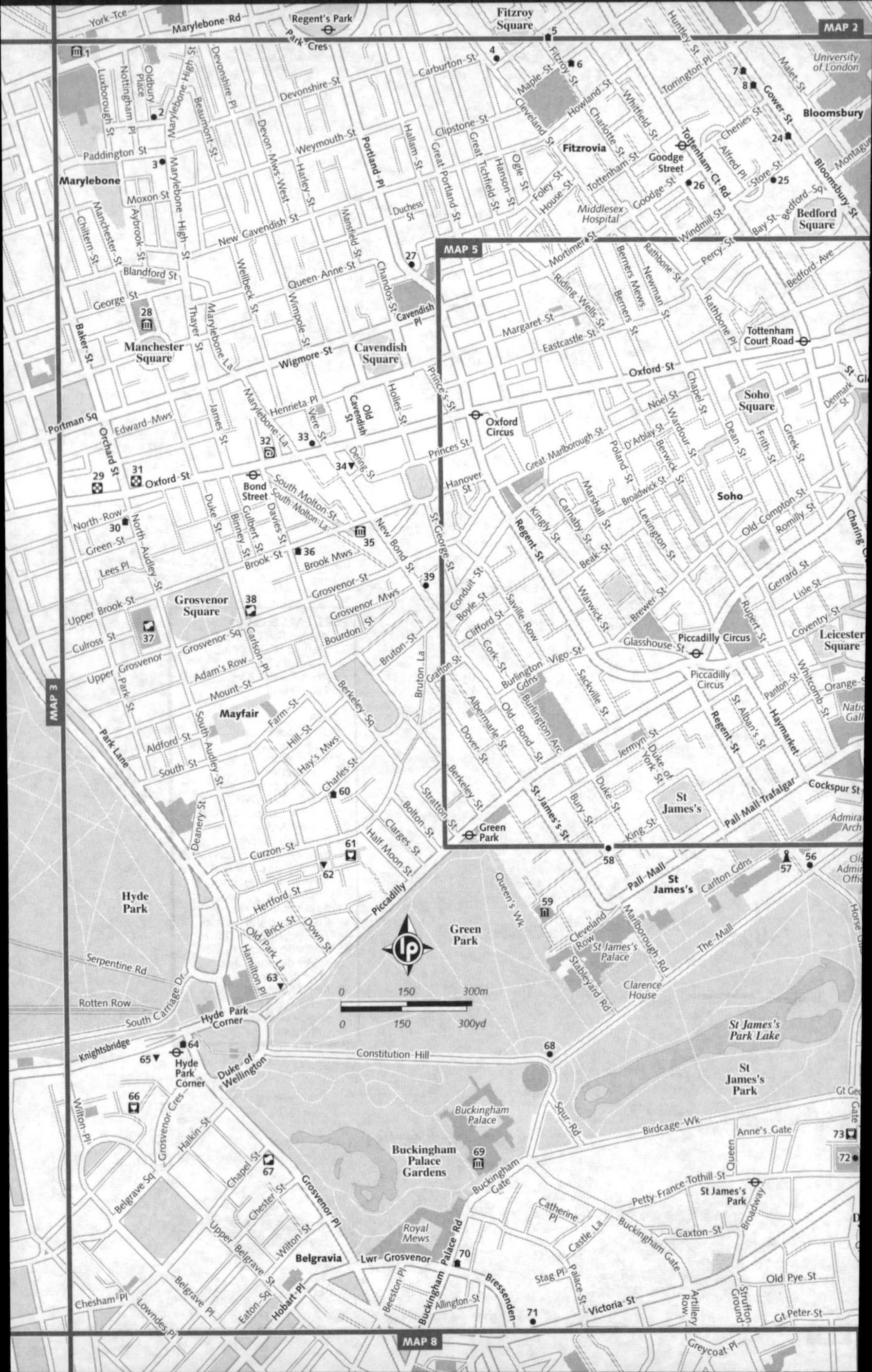

MAP 4

York-Tce
Marylebone-Rd
Regent's Park
Park-Cres
Fitzroy Square
MAP 2

Marylebone
Fitzrovia
Goodge Street
Bloomsbury
Bedford Square

MAP 5

Manchester Square
Cavendish Square
Tottenham Court Road
Soho Square

Portman Sq
Oxford St
Bond Street
Oxford Circus
Soho

Grosvenor Square
Piccadilly Circus
Leicester Square
Piccadilly Circus

Mayfair
St James's
Pall Mall
Trafalgar

Hyde Park
Green Park
St James's
Pall Mall

Serpentine Rd
Rotten Row
South Carriage Dr
Hyde Park Corner
Duke of Wellington
Knightsbridge
Hyde Park Corner

Green Park
St James's Park Lake
St James's Park

Constitution Hill
Buckingham Palace
Clarence House
St James's Palace

Buckingham Palace Gardens
Birdcage-Wk
St James's Park

Royal Mews
Belgravia
Lwr Grosvenor
Victoria St

MAP 8

0   150   300m
0   150   300yd

MAP 4

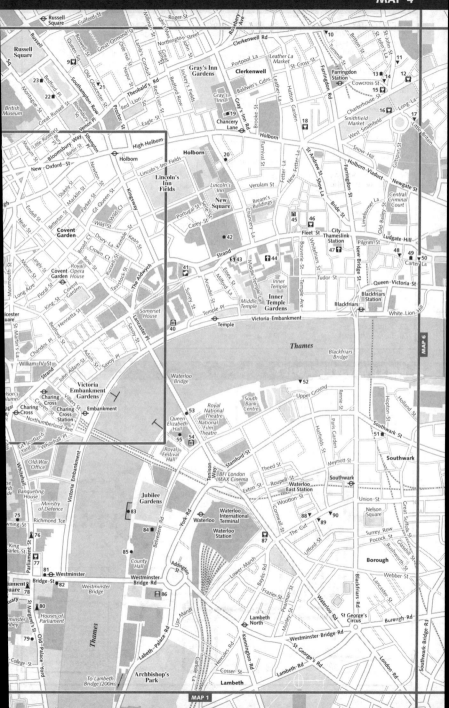

MAP 4

PLACES TO STAY
5 Indian Student YMCA
6 Carr-Saunders Hall
7 Hotel Cavendish; Arran House Hotel
8 Jesmond Hotel; Ridgemount Hotel
13 The Rookery
22 Haddon Hall
23 St Margaret's Hotel
24 Academy Hotel
30 Goldsmid House
36 Claridges
49 City of London YHA Hostel
51 Holiday Inn Express Southwark
60 Chesterfield
64 The Lanesborough
70 Rubens at the Palace
84 County Hall Travel Inn Capital

PLACES TO EAT
10 Gaudi
11 St John
14 The Greenery
17 Club Gascon
21 Mille Pini
34 Rasa W1
48 Da Vinci
50 Dim Sum
52 Oxo Tower Restaurant & Brasserie
62 Sheperd Café Bar
63 Hard Rock Café
65 Pizza on the Park

88 Konditor & Cook
89 Mesón Don Felipe
90 Tas

PUBS, BARS & CLUBS
9 The Queen's Larder
12 Fox & Anchor
15 Fabric
16 Cock Tavern
18 Ye Olde Mitre
46 Ye Olde Cheshire Cheese
61 Ye Grapes
66 Grenadier
73 Westminster Arms
77 The Red Lion
87 The Fire Station

OTHER
1 Madam Tussaud's; London Planetarium
2 Childminders
3 Daunt Books
4 Red & White Laundrette
19 Inns of Court
20 London Silver Vaults
25 STA Travel
26 STA Travel
27 Broadcasting House
28 Wallace Collection
29 Marks & Spencer
31 Selfridges
32 easyInternetcafé
33 Thomas Cook Branch
35 Handel House Museum
37 US Embassy

38 Canadian High Commision
39 Sotheby's
40 Gilbert Collection
41 Australian High Commission
42 Royal Courts of Justice
43 Lloyds Bank
44 Temple Church
45 Dr Johnson's House
47 St Bride's Church
53 Riverside Walk Market
54 Hayward Gallery
55 Purcell Room
56 Institute for Contemporary Arts; ICA Café
57 Duke of York Column
58 Christies
59 Spencer House
67 Irish Embassy
68 Buckingham Palace Ticket Office (Summer Only)
69 Queens Gallery
71 American Express; Thomas Cook
72 Westminster Central Hall
74 Cabinet War Rooms
75 No 10 Downing St
76 Cenotaph
78 Winston Churchill Statue
79 Jewel Tower
80 Cromwell Statue
81 New Parliament Building
82 Big Ben
83 BA London Eye
85 London Aquarium
86 Florence Nightingale Museum

WESTMINSTER ABBEY

1 Innocent Victims Memorial
2 Statues of 20th-Century Martyrs
3 Churchill Memorial
4 Tomb of the Unknown Warrior
5 Screen; Scientists' Corner
6 Musicians' Aisle
7 Quire
8 The Lantern
9 Statesmen's Aisle
10 Disraeli Monument
11 Gladstone's Tomb
12 Robert Peel Monument
13 High Altar
14 Crewe Chapel

15 Edward I's Tomb
16 Chapel of St Edward the Confessor
17 Henry III's Tomb
18 Eleanor of Castile's Tomb
19 Coronation Chair
20 Queen Elizabeth Chapel

21 Henry VII's Tomb
22 Cromwell Plaque
23 Royal Air Force Chapel
24 Mary Queen of Scots' Tomb
25 Cloister Entrance
26 Handel Memorial
27 Poets' Corner
28 Shakespeare Memorial
29 St Faith Chapel Entrance
30 Chapter House
31 Pyx Chamber
32 Undercroft Museum

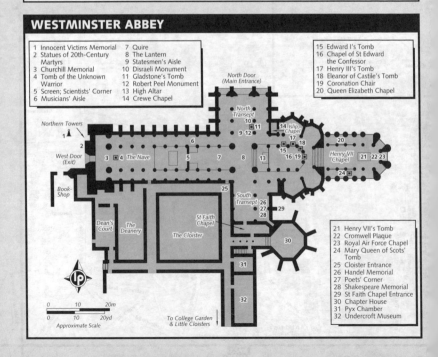

Northern Towers

West Door (Exit)

Book-Shop

Dean's Court

The Deanery

The Cloister

St Faith Chapel

The Nave

North Door (Main Entrance)

North Transept

Islip Chapel

Henry VII Chapel

South Transept

Chapter House

To College Garden & Little Cloisters

0   10   20m
0   10   20yd
Approximate Scale

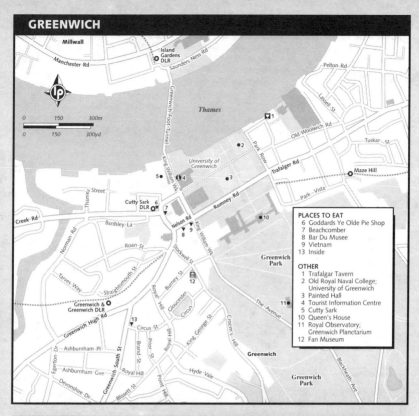

GREENWICH

Millwall

Manchester Rd

Island Gardens DLR

Saunders Ness Rd

Thames

Pelton Rd

Lassell St

Old Woolwich Rd

Tuskar St

Park Row

Trafalgar Rd

Maze Hill

University of Greenwich

Romney Rd

Park Vista

Thames Street

Cutty Sark DLR

Nelson Rd

King William Wk

Creek Rd

Bardsley La

Roan St

Greenwich Park

Norman Rd

Tarves Way

Straightsmouth St

Stockwell St

Burney St

Greenwich & Greenwich DLR

Greenwich High Rd

Royal Hill

Gloucester Circus

King George St

Croom's Hill

The Avenue

Circus St

Prior St

Ashburnham Pl

Brand St

Greenwich South St

Royal Hill

Hyde Vale

Greenwich

Ashburnham Gve

Point Hill

Devonshire Dr

Blissett St

Greenwich Park

Blackheath Ave

PLACES TO EAT
6 Goddards Ye Olde Pie Shop
7 Beachcomber
8 Bar Du Musee
9 Vietnam
13 Inside

OTHER
1 Trafalgar Tavern
2 Old Royal Naval College; University of Greenwich
3 Painted Hall
4 Tourist Information Centre
5 Cutty Sark
10 Queen's House
11 Royal Observatory; Greenwich Planctarium
12 Fan Museum

0   150   300m
0   150   300yd

Crested Gates, Westminster, London

NICK RAY

MAP 5

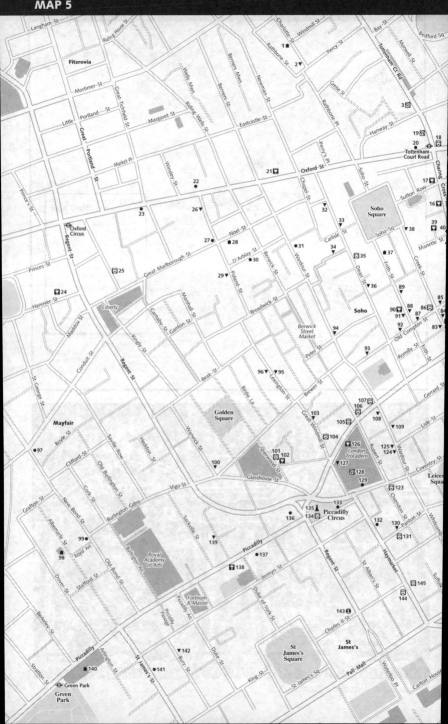

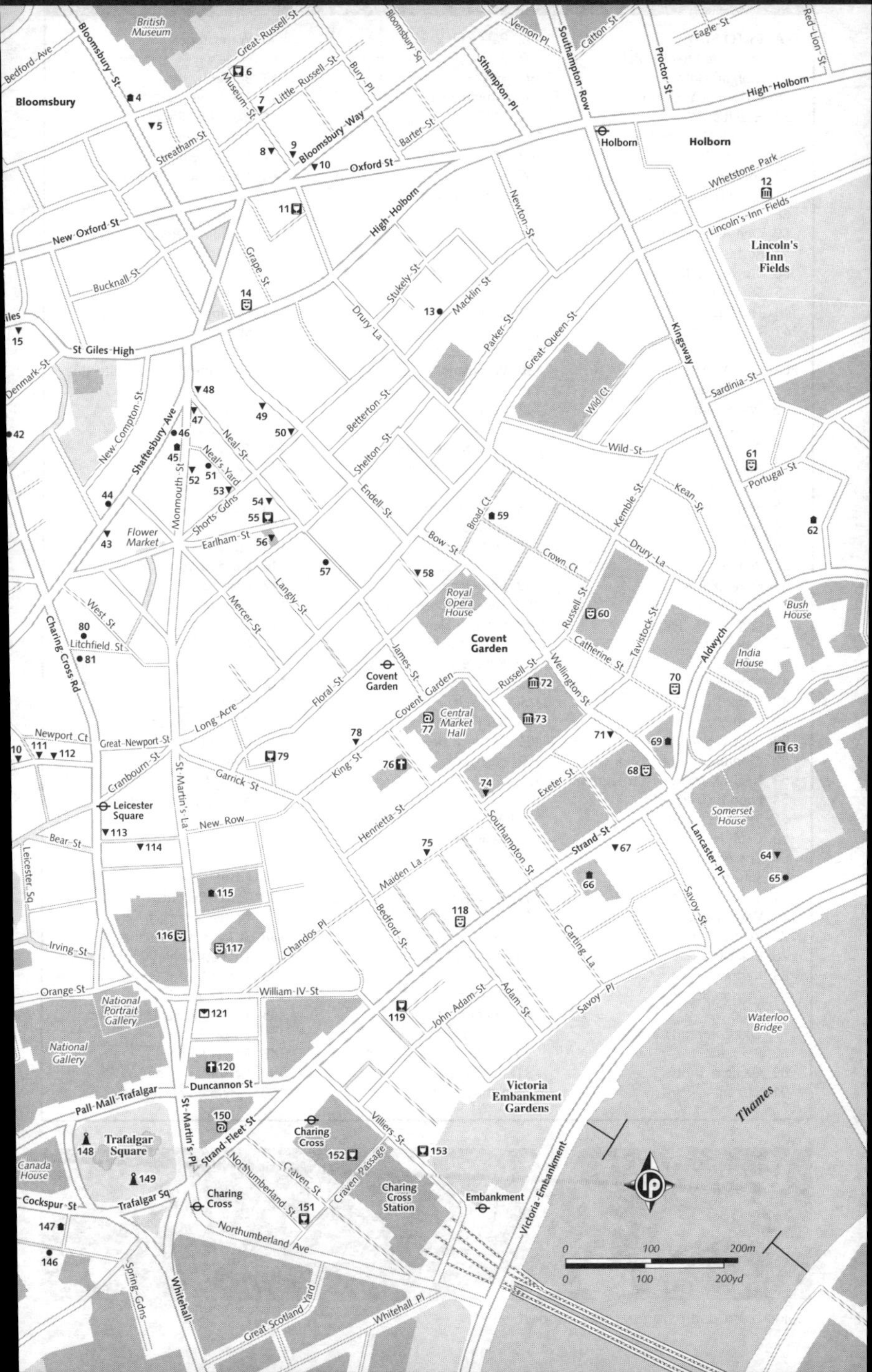

MAP 5

British Museum

Bloomsbury

Bedford Ave
Bloomsbury St
Great Russell St
Bloomsbury
Vernon Pl
Southampton Row
Catton St
Eagle St
Red Lion St
Proctor St
High Holborn

▼4
6
Museum St
7
Little Russell St
Bury St
Barter St
Shampton Pl
Whetstone Park
12
Lincoln's Inn Fields

Streatham St
8 ▼ 9
Bloomsbury Way
Oxford St
▼10

New Oxford St
11
High Holborn
Newton St
Lincoln's Inn Fields

Bucknall St
Grape St
Stukely St
Macklin St
Parker St
Great Queen St
Kingsway
Sardinia St

St Giles High
14
13 •
Drury La
Wild Ct
Wild St

iles
15

Denmark St
42 •

▼48
Shaftesbury Ave
47
New Compton St
Neal St
49
50 ▼
Betterton St
Shelton St
61
Portugal St

46
45
Neal's Yard
51
52
53
54
55
56
Shorts Gdns
Earlham St
Endell St
Bond Ct
59
Crown Ct
Kemble St
Kean St
Drury La
62

44
Flower Market
43
57
Langly St
▼58
Bow St
Russell St
60
Tavistock St
Bush House

West St
Mercer St
Royal Opera House
Catherine St
Wellington St
Aldwych
India House

80
Litchfield St
81
Floral St
James St
Covent Garden
Covent Garden
70
72
73

Newport Ct
Great Newport St
Long Acre
Covent Garden
Central Market Hall
71 ▼
69
68
63

10 111 112
Cranbourn St
St Martin's La
Garrick St
King St
78
77
74
Exeter St
Somerset House

Leicester Square
New Row
76
Henrietta St
Strand St
64 ▼
65 •

Bear St
113
114
Maiden La
75
Southampton St
67
66
Lancaster Pl
Savoy St

Leicester Sq
115
116
117
Chandos Pl
Bedford St
118
Carting La
Savoy Pl

Irving St

Orange St
National Portrait Gallery
121
William IV St
119
John Adam St
Adam St

National Gallery
120
Duncannon St
Waterloo Bridge

Pall Mall Trafalgar
148
Trafalgar Square
St Martin's Pl
Strand Fleet St
150
Charing Cross
Villiers St
Victoria Embankment Gardens
Thames

Canada House
149
Trafalgar Sq
Charing Cross
Northumberland St
Craven St
152
Craven Passage
153
Embankment

Cockspur St
147
146
Whitehall
Northumberland Ave
Charing Cross Station
Victoria Embankment

Spring Gdns
Great Scotland Yard
Whitehall Pl

0   100   200m
0   100   200yd

MAP 5

PLACES TO STAY

1 Charlotte Street Hotel
4 Morgan Hotel
28 Oxford St YHA Hostel
37 Hazlitt's
45 Covent Garden Hotel
59 Fielding Hotel
62 London School of Economics & Political Science
66 The Savoy
69 One Aldwych; Axis Restaurant & Bar
98 Brown's Hotel
115 St Martins Lane
140 The Ritz
147 The Trafalgar

PLACES TO EAT

2 Rasa Sumudra
5 Wagamama
7 Ruskins Café
8 Coffee Gallery
9 Abeno
10 Mandeer
15 First Out
26 Soba
29 Yo! Sushi
32 Red Veg
33 Pizza Express
34 Soho Thai
36 Quo Vadis
38 Gay Hussar
43 Mela
47 Mon Plaisir
48 Franx Snack Bar
49 Mode
50 Rock & Sole Plaice
52 Monmouth Coffee House
53 Neal's Yard Bakery & Tearoom
54 Food for Thought
56 Belgo Centraal
58 Café des Amis du Vin
64 The Admiralty
67 Simpson's-in-the-Strand
71 Orso
74 Wagamama
75 Rules
78 Calabash
83 Kettners
84 Maison Bertaux
85 Pollo
87 Old Compton Café
88 Bar Italia
89 Garlic & Shots
91 Saigon

92 Pâtisserie Valerie
93 Balans
94 Spiga
95 Wagamama
96 Mildred's
100 Country Life
103 Melati
108 Wong Kei
109 Gerrad's Corner
110 Fung Shing
111 Tokyo Diner
112 Zipangu
113 Gaby's
114 J Sheekey
124 Chuen Cheng Ku
125 1997
127 Rainforest Café
130 Woodlands
139 The Gaucho Grill
142 Quaglio's

PUBS, BARS & CLUBS

6 Museum Tavern
11 The End
16 Velvet Room
17 Astoria
21 100 Club
24 Hanover Grand
39 Borderline
55 Freedom Brewing Company
79 Lamb & Flag
82 Coach & Horses
90 Ronnie Scott's
102 Scruffy Murphy's
119 Retro Bar
126 Bar Rumba
151 Sherlock Holmes
152 Heaven
153 Gordon's Wine Bar

OTHER

3 easyInternetcafé
12 Sir John Soane's Museum
13 Bikepark
14 Shaftesbury
18 Dominion
19 easyInternetcafé
20 Virgin Megastore
22 HMV
23 Borders
25 London Palladium
27 Harold Moores Records
30 Black Market Records
31 Itchy Feet
35 Soho Theatre

40 Waterstone's
41 Foyle's
42 Borders
44 STA Travel
46 Ray's Jazz Shop
51 Rough Trade
57 The Tea House
60 Theatre Royal Drury Lane
61 Peacock Theatre
63 Courtauld Gallery
65 Hermitage Rooms
68 Lyceum
70 Strand
72 Theatre Museum
73 London Transport Museum
76 St Paul's Church
77 Internet Exchange
80 Zwemmer Art & Architecture
81 Zwemmer Books
86 Prince Edward
97 Burberry
99 Tiffany & Co
101 Piccadilly
104 Lyric
105 Apollo
106 Gielgud
107 Queen's
116 Duke of York
117 Coliseum
118 Adelphi
120 St Martin-in-the-Fields; Cafe in the Crypt
121 Trafalgar Square Post Office
122 Leicester Square Half-Price Ticket Booth
123 Prince of Wales
128 Internet Exchange
129 HMV
131 Comedy
132 American Express (Main Office)
133 Virgin Megastore
134 Criterion
135 Eros Statue
136 Tower Records
137 Waterstones
138 St James's Piccadilly
141 Thomas Cook (Main Office)
143 Britain Visitor Centre
144 Her Majesty's
145 Theatre Royal Haymarket
146 British Council
148 Empty Plinth
149 Nelson's Column
150 easyInternetcafé

Coldstream guards on parade, London

NEIL SETCHFIELD

MAP 6

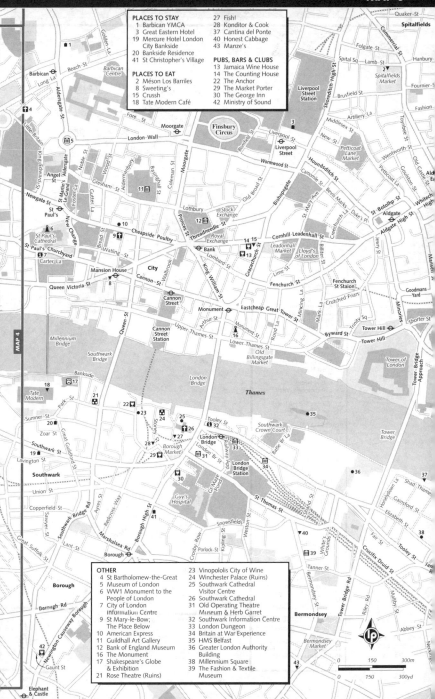

PLACES TO STAY
1 Barbican YMCA
3 Great Eastern Hotel
19 Mercure Hotel London City Bankside
20 Bankside Residence
41 St Christopher's Village

PLACES TO EAT
2 Méson Los Barriles
8 Sweeting's
15 Crussh
18 Tate Modern Café
27 Fish!
28 Konditor & Cook
37 Cantina del Ponte
40 Honest Cabbage
43 Manze's

PUBS, BARS & CLUBS
13 Jamaica Wine House
14 The Counting House
22 The Anchor
29 The Market Porter
30 The George Inn
42 Ministry of Sound

OTHER
4 St Bartholomew-the-Great
5 Museum of London
6 WW1 Monument to the People of London
7 City of London Information Centre
9 St Mary-le-Bow; The Place Below
10 American Express
11 Guildhall Art Gallery
12 Bank of England Museum
16 The Monument
17 Shakespeare's Globe & Exhibition
21 Rose Theatre (Ruins)
23 Vinopololis City of Wine
24 Winchester Palace (Ruins)
25 Southwark Cathedral Visitor Centre
26 Southwark Cathedral
31 Old Operating Theatre Museum & Herb Garret
32 Southwark Information Centre
33 London Dungeon
34 Britain at War Experience
35 HMS Belfast
36 Greater London Authority Building
38 Millennium Square
39 The Fashion & Textile Museum

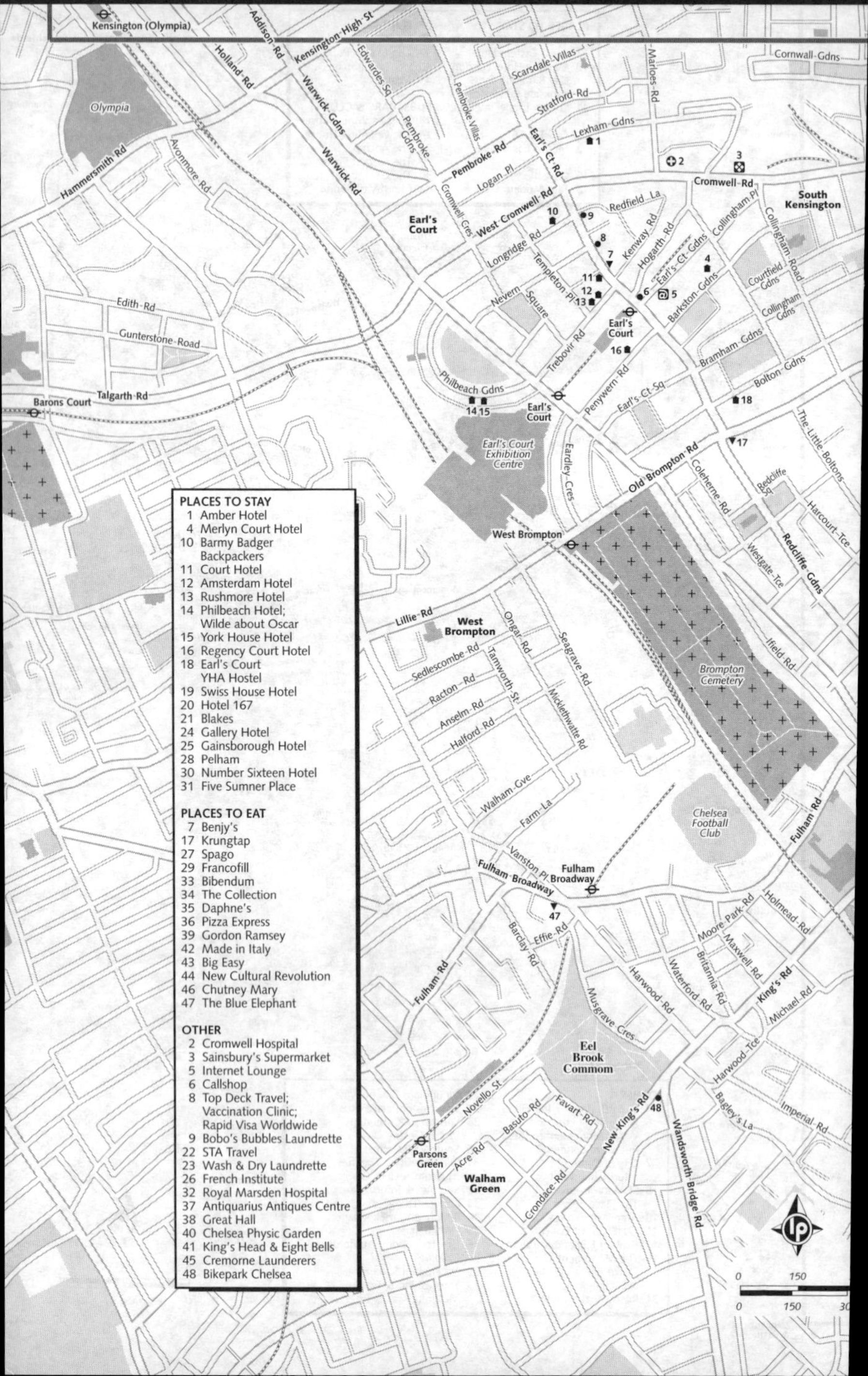

MAP 7

Kensington (Olympia)

Olympia

Kensington High St

Addison Rd

Holland Rd

Warwick Gdns

Kensington High St

Edwardes Sq

Scarsdale Villas

Stratford Rd

Cornwall Gdns

Pembroke Gdns

Pembroke Rd

Pembroke Villas

Logan Pl

Lexham Gdns

■ 1

✪ 2

3
✪

Cromwell Rd

South Kensington

West Cromwell Rd

Cromwell Cres

Longridge Rd

10 ■

● 9

Redfield La

Kenway Rd

Collingham Pl

Collingham Road

Earl's Court

Nevern Square

Templeton Pl

Hogarth Rd

8 ●
7 ●

Earl's Ct Gdns

Barkston Gdns

4 ■

Courtfield Gdns

Collingham Gdns

11 ■
12 ■
13 ■

6 ●
■ 5

Earl's Court

Bramham Gdns

16 ■

Bolton Gdns

■ 18

Hammersmith Rd

Avonmore Rd

Warwick Rd

Earl's Court Rd

Edith Rd

Gunterstone Road

Talgarth Rd

Barons Court

Philbeach Gdns

14 15

Earl's Court

Earl's Ct Sq

Trebovir Rd

Nevern Rd

Penywern Rd

Eardley Cres

▼ 17

The Little Boltons

Redcliffe Sq

Harcourt Tce

Redcliffe Gdns

Wetherby Tce

Hereford Tce

Earl's Court Exhibition Centre

Old Brompton Rd

Coleherne Rd

West Brompton

Ifield Rd

Hfield Rd

Fulham Rd

Lillie Rd

West Brompton

Sedlescombe Rd

Lillie Rd

Ongar Rd

Tamworth St

Seagrave Rd

McDonwall Rd

Anselm Rd

Racton Rd

Halford Rd

Brompton Cemetery

Walham Gve

Farm La

Chelsea Football Club

PLACES TO STAY
1   Amber Hotel
4   Merlyn Court Hotel
10 Barmy Badger
    Backpackers
11 Court Hotel
12 Amsterdam Hotel
13 Rushmore Hotel
14 Philbeach Hotel;
    Wilde about Oscar
15 York House Hotel
16 Regency Court Hotel
18 Earl's Court
    YHA Hostel
19 Swiss House Hotel
20 Hotel 167
21 Blakes
24 Gallery Hotel
25 Gainsborough Hotel
28 Pelham
30 Number Sixteen Hotel
31 Five Sumner Place

PLACES TO EAT
7   Benjy's
17 Krungtap
27 Spago
29 Francofill
33 Bibendum
34 The Collection
35 Daphne's
36 Pizza Express
39 Gordon Ramsey
42 Made in Italy
43 Big Easy
44 New Cultural Revolution
46 Chutney Mary
47 The Blue Elephant

OTHER
2   Cromwell Hospital
3   Sainsbury's Supermarket
5   Internet Lounge
6   Callshop
8   Top Deck Travel;
    Vaccination Clinic;
    Rapid Visa Worldwide
9   Bobo's Bubbles Laundrette
22 STA Travel
23 Wash & Dry Laundrette
26 French Institute
32 Royal Marsden Hospital
37 Antiquarius Antiques Centre
38 Great Hall
40 Chelsea Physic Garden
41 King's Head & Eight Bells
45 Cremorne Launderers
48 Bikepark Chelsea

Chelsea

Fulham Broadway

Vanston Pl

Fulham Broadway

Fulham Rd

▼ 47

Effie Rd

Barclay Rd

Moore Park Rd

Maxwell Rd

Britannia Rd

Waterford Rd

Holmead Rd

King's Rd

Michael Rd

Musgrave Cres

Harwood Rd

Harwood Tce

Eel Brook Common

Novello St

Favart Rd

New King's Rd

Wandsworth Bridge Rd

Bagley's La

Imperial Rd

Parsons Green

Acre La

Basuto Rd

Cronddace Rd

48 ●

Walham Green

0   150
0   150   30

LP

MAP 7

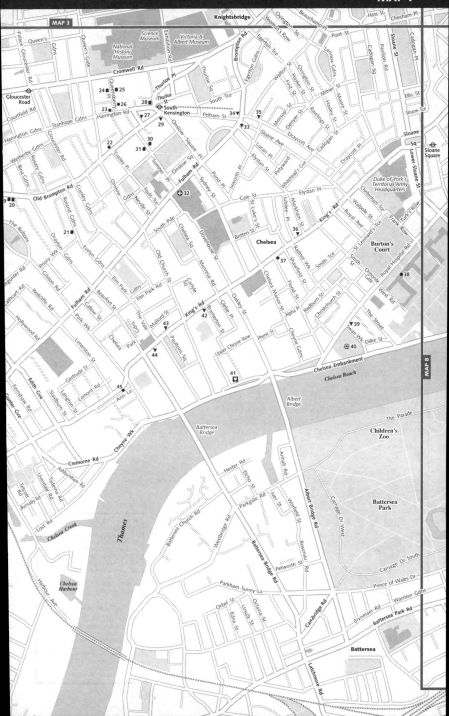

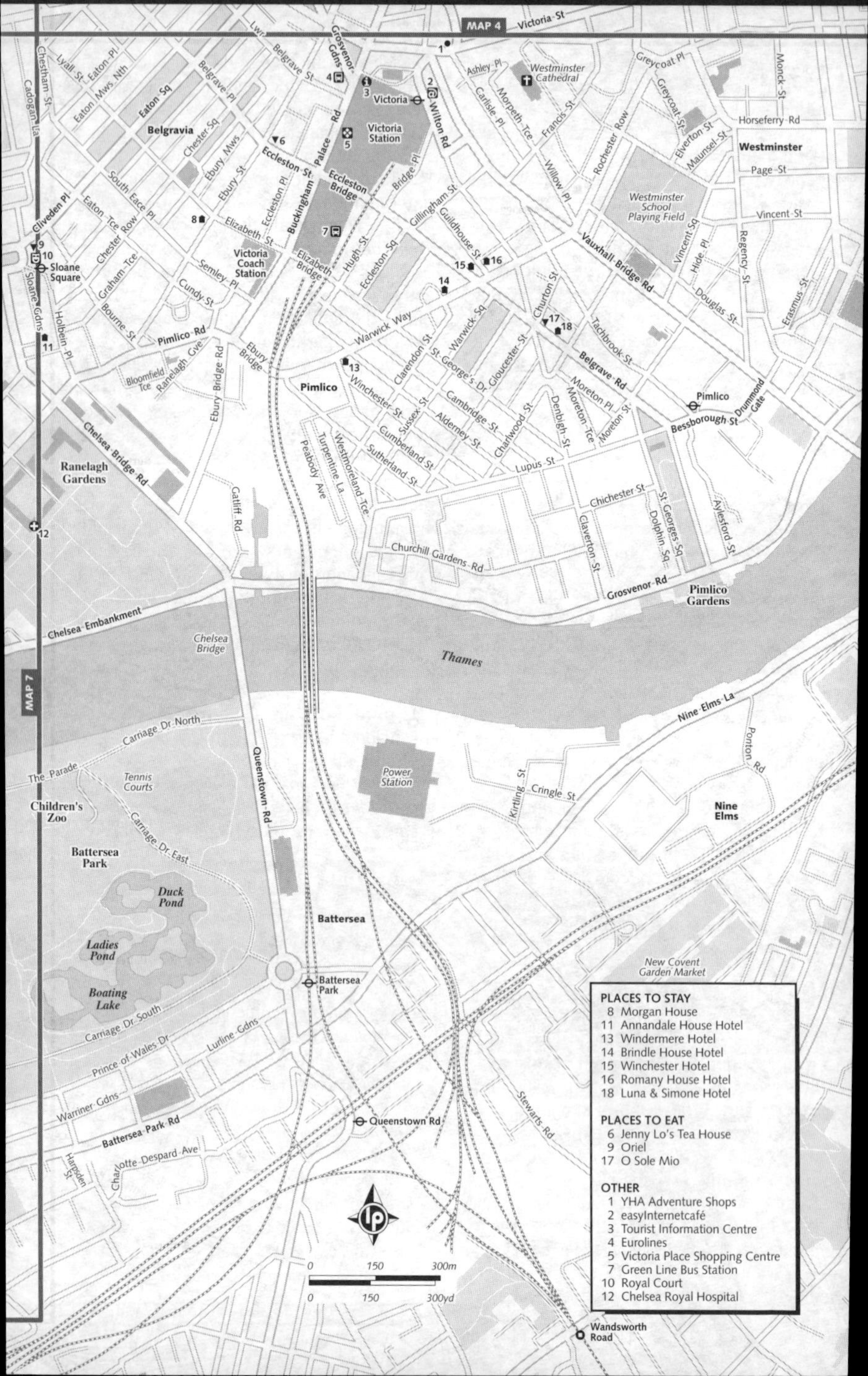

MAP 8

MAP 4 Victoria St

Victoria St

Belgravia

Eaton Sq

Chester Sq

Belgrave St

Grosvenor Gdns

Ebury Mews

Elizabeth St

Eccleston St

Eccleston Pl

Chesham St
Lyall St
Eaton Pl
Eaton Mews Nth
South Esk St
Eaton Tce Row
Chester Tce
Graham Tce
Bourne St
Cundy St
Semley Pl

Belgrave Pl

Ebury St

Buckingham Palace Rd

Eccleston Bridge

Elizabeth Bridge

Bridge Pl

Hugh St

Eccleston St

Victoria

Wilton Rd

Victoria Station

Ashley Pl

Morpeth Tce

Carlisle Pl

Francis St

Westminster Cathedral

Greycoat Pl

Greycoat St

Monck St

Horseferry Rd

Westminster

Page St

Vincent St

Rochester Row

Willow Pl

Gillingham St

Guildhouse St

Warwick Way

Clarendon St

Vauxhall Bridge Rd

Westminster School Playing Field

Hide Pl

Regency St

Erasmus St

Douglas St

Elverton St

Maunsel St

Cadogan Lane

Cliveden Pl

Eaton Tce

Holbein Pl

Sloane Square

Sloane Gdns

Pimlico Rd

Bloomfield Tce

Ranelagh Gve

Ebury Bridge Rd

Ebury Bridge

Cutliff Rd

Turpentine La

Peabody Ave

Westmoreland Tce

Sutherland St

Cumberland St

Alderney St

Cambridge St

St George's Dv

Gloucester St

Moreton Pl

Moreton Tce

Denbigh St

Clarendon St

Winchester St

Sussex St

Pimlico

Tachbrook St

Belgrave Rd

Charlwood St

Moreton St

Lupus St

Bessborough St

Drummond Gate

Pimlico Gardens

Chichester St

Claverton St

St George's Sq

St Dolphin's Sq

Aylesford St

Nyesford St

Chelsea Bridge Rd

Ranelagh Gardens

Churchill Gardens Rd

Grosvenor Rd

Chelsea Embankment

Chelsea Bridge

Chelsea Bridge

Thames

Nine Elms La

Ponton Rd

Kirtling St

Cringle St

Nine Elms

Power Station

Carriage Dr North

Queenstown Rd

Battersea

Tennis Courts

Children's Zoo

Battersea Park

Carriage Dr East

Duck Pond

Ladies Pond

Boating Lake

Carriage Dr South

Lurline Gdns

Prince of Wales Dr

Warriner Gdns

Battersea Park Rd

Charlotte Despard Ave

Battersea Park

Queenstown Rd

Stewarts Rd

New Covent Garden Market

Wandsworth Road

MAP 7

0   150   300m
0   150   300yd

PLACES TO STAY
8 Morgan House
11 Annandale House Hotel
13 Windermere Hotel
14 Brindle House Hotel
15 Winchester Hotel
16 Romany House Hotel
18 Luna & Simone Hotel

PLACES TO EAT
6 Jenny Lo's Tea House
9 Oriel
17 O Sole Mio

OTHER
1 YHA Adventure Shops
2 easyInternetcafé
3 Tourist Information Centre
4 Eurolines
5 Victoria Place Shopping Centre
7 Green Line Bus Station
10 Royal Court
12 Chelsea Royal Hospital

[Continued from page 125]

of England football captain, David Beckham, was cheekily erected there during the last World Cup. There is also talk of erecting a statue to Nelson Mandela, one of the world's greatest statesmen who made a monumental contribution to human rights with his struggle against apartheid in South Africa.

The traffic whizzing past has traditionally made it difficult to appreciate Trafalgar Square but that's being changed in a bold and imaginative scheme being pushed by the mayor. Traffic has been banished from the northern flank in front of the National Gallery, and a new pedestrian plaza will be in place some time in 2003. It's an exciting new development that will help this grand square to realise its full potential as a public space. There are also plans to expand a programme of cultural events – begun in recent summers – to showcase the city's multiculturalism.

National Gallery (Map 5) One of the world's largest and finest art galleries, the National Gallery (☎ 7747 2885; w www.na tionalgallery.org.uk; Trafalgar Square WC2; ⊖ Charing Cross; admission free, temporary exhibition prices vary; open 10am-6pm Thur-Tues, 10am-9pm Wed) admits almost 5 million people each year to view its astonishing collection of European paintings.

The paintings are hung in a continuous time-line; by starting in the Sainsbury Wing (added in 1991) and progressing eastwards you can take in a collection of pictures painted between the mid-13th and 20th centuries in chronological order. The Sainsbury Wing contains the real oldies (1260–1510) while you can catch the Renaissance (1510–1600) in the West Wing in the museum's main building. Rubens, Rembrandt and Murillo are in the North Wing (1600–1700); if you're after Gainsborough, Constable, Turner, Hogarth and the impressionists visit the East Wing (1700–1900). For a larger collection of paintings by British artists you should visit the Tate Britain (see the Westminster & Pimlico section later in this chapter) or the Tate Modern (see Southwark later).

The highlights listed in the boxed text show the cream of the gallery's exhibits but if you want to know a lot more borrow an audioguide (contribution suggested) from the central hall and simply punch in the number

of each painting that grabs your interest. The gallery also provides activity sheets for kids. Free one-hour guided tours, which introduce you to a manageable half-dozen paintings at a time, leave at 11.30am and 2.30pm on weekdays and at 2pm and 3.30pm on Saturday (additional tour at 6.30pm on Wednesday). A **Micro Gallery** (open 10am-5.30pm Thur-Tues, 10am-8.30pm Wed), located on the 1st floor of the Sainsbury Wing, has interactive screens providing a visual encyclopedia of the collection, which enables you to explore any particular areas of interest or design your own tour and print out a plan.

A new pedestrian plaza being built in front of the gallery (see the Trafalgar Square section earlier) will enhance the elegant 19th-century William Wilkins facade of the building and create a splendid new vista. It may also highlight the statue of George Washington, the man who denied England its colonies in the new world, which stands rather incongruously in this the centre of the erstwhile British Empire. Perhaps spurred on by the goings-on outside its door, the National Gallery is planning to open up more exhibition space over the coming years.

National Portrait Gallery (Map 5) As much about history as about art, the National Portrait Gallery (☎ 7306 0055; w www.npg .org.uk; St Martin's Place WC2; ⊖ Charing Cross; admission free; open 10am-6pm Sat-Wed, 10am-9pm Thur-Fri) provides a great

---

National Gallery Highlights

The Arnolfini Portrait – van Eyck
Rokeby Venus – Velázquez
The Wilton Diptych
Bathers – Cézanne
Venus and Mars – Botticelli
The Virgin of the Rocks – da Vinci
The Virgin and Child with St Anne and St John the Baptist – da Vinci
The Battle of San Romano – Uccello
The Ambassadors – Holbein the Younger
Equestrian Portrait of Charles I – Van Dyck
Le Chapeau de Paille – Rubens
The Hay Wain – Constable
Sunflowers – Van Gogh
The Water-Lily Pond – Monet
The Fighting Temeraire – Turner

opportunity to put faces to the famous and infamous names of Britain's past. There is an imaginative calendar of temporary exhibitions, which helps the gallery overcome what used to be a rather staid atmosphere.

The gallery, founded in 1856, houses a primary collection of some 10,000 works from all sorts of different media – from water colours to electronic art – spread out over five floors. The pictures are displayed roughly in chronological order, starting with the early Tudors on the top floor and descending to the late 20th century. The portraits of Elizabeth I in all her finery from 1575 and Byron in romantic oriental garb (1813) by Thomas Phillips are as wonderful as the more recent works including Elizabeth II as seen by Andy Warhol and Prince Charles posing under a banana tree.

If you think the portrait of cravat-wearing James Scott, Duke of Monmouth, is unusual, consider this: shortly after the protestant duke was beheaded by the Catholic James II in 1685, some bright spark remembered that there was no official portrait of the royal. The royal surgeon was summoned to stitch the duke's head back on and he was propped up in front of the painter who had 24 hours to capture his subject before it 'went off'.

Since the 1990s the gallery has seen a major revamp with expansions to exhibition spaces and the creation of a café and shop in the basement, while escalators in the new Ondaatje Wing can whisk you up to the **Portrait Restaurant** on the top floor and a splendid view.

St Martin-in-the-Fields (Map 5) There's been a church on this site since the 13th century, although this influential masterpiece by James Gibbs (1682–1754), the 'royal parish church' of St Martin-in-the-Fields *(☎ 7930 0089; Trafalgar Square WC2; ⊖ Charing Cross; open 8am-6.30pm daily)*, was only completed in 1726. Its ornate Italian plasterwork is best appreciated during lunch time when free concerts help set the mood. There's an adjoining craft market and in the crypt you'll find a **brass-rubbing centre** *(☎ 7930 9306; open 10am-6pm Mon-Sat, noon-6pm Sun)*, bookshop and a popular café (see Trafalgar Square under Places to Eat later in this chapter).

Westminster & Pimlico

While the City of London (known simply as 'the City') has always concerned itself with the business of making money, Westminster is the centre of political power and most of its places of interest are linked with the monarchy, parliament or the Church of England.

Pimlico, to the south and southwest, contains some wonderful early-19th-century houses and is like a paler version of Belgravia. What Belgravia doesn't have, however, is the incomparable Tate Britain.

Whitehall & Walking Tour (Map 4)

Lined with government buildings, statues, monuments and other historical sights, Whitehall SW1 *(⊖ Charing Cross or Westminster)*, and its extension Parliament St, is the wide avenue that links Trafalgar Square with Parliament Square. The best way to take it all in is with the following short walk.

Start your walk at the southern end of Trafalgar Square as it leads into Whitehall, once the administrative heart of the British Empire and still the focal point for British government. As you walk south you'll see **Admiralty Arch** (1910) and the **Old Admiralty** on the right.

Further along on the left is the **Ministry of Defence**, on the far side of which you'll find the **Banqueting House** *(☎ 7930 4179; ⓦ www .hrp.org.uk/webcode/banquet_home.asp; adult/ child £4/2.50; open 10am-5pm Mon-Sat)*, the only surviving part of the Tudor Whitehall Palace, which once stretched most of the way along Whitehall but burned down in 1698. Designed by Inigo Jones in 1622, this was England's first purely Renaissance building and looked like no other building in the country at the time. The highlight is the ceiling of the 1st-floor ceremonial hall, which features nine panels painted by Rubens in 1634. A bust outside commemorates 30 January 1649 when Charles I, accused of treason by Cromwell, was executed on a scaffold built against a 1st-floor window here. There's a video account of the house's history.

On the other side of Whitehall is **Horse Guards Parade** *(11am Mon-Sat, 10am Sun)*, where the mounted troopers of the Household Cavalry are changed in a ceremony you'll find more accessible than the one outside Buckingham Palace.

The next intersection south of Horse Guards Parade brings you to **Downing St**, the traditional site of the British prime minister's official residence since 1732 when George II presented No 10 to Robert Walpole. Tony Blair and his family actually now live in the larger apartments at No 11. During Margaret Thatcher's time in office gates were erected and the street closed off to the public for fear of IRA terrorist attacks.

Whitehall becomes Parliament Street and, on your left, you'll see the **Cenotaph** (Greek for 'empty tomb'), a memorial to Commonwealth citizens killed in the two world wars.

On your right is the **Foreign & Commonwealth Office** (FCO; 1872) restored by Sir George Gilbert Scott and Matthew Digby Wyatt. If you're interested in how Britain projects itself through global diplomacy, there's a **visitor centre** (☎ 7270 1500; admission free; open 10am-4.30pm Mon-Fri) with audio and visual exhibitions as well as an information technology centre.

A right turn down King Charles St will bring you to the **Cabinet War Rooms** (Map 4; ☎ 7930 6961; W www.iwm.org.uk/cabinet; adult/child £5.80/free; open 9.30am-6pm daily May-Sept, 10am-6pm daily Oct-April), the bunkers in which the British government took refuge during the hairier moments of WWII. So-called Secret Rooms, including Churchill's private dining room and kitchen as well as education facilities, are due to open by summer 2003 and will triple the size of the rooms on display. A Churchill museum is slated to open in 2005.

Whitehall ends at **Parliament Square**, watched over by statues of past prime ministers. Left along Bridge St is the ultramodern **New Parliament Building**. You're now in place to explore the sights below.

Westminster Abbey (Map 4) One of the most visited churches in Christendom, Westminster Abbey (☎ 7222 5152; W www.west minster-abbey.org; Dean's Yard SW1; ✚ Westminster; adult/child £6/3; open 9am-4.45pm Mon-Fri, 9am-2.45pm Sat, services Sun) has played a pivotal role in the history of both England and the Anglican Church. With the exception of Edward V and Edward VIII, every sovereign has been crowned here since William the Conqueror in 1066. All the monarchs from Henry III (died 1272) to George II (1760) were also buried here, but since the death of George III in 1820 they have been laid to rest in St George's Chapel in Windsor.

The abbey, though a mixture of various architectural styles, is the finest example of Early English Gothic (1180–1280) still standing. The original church was built by the 11th-century King (later Saint) Edward the Confessor, who is buried in the chapel behind the main altar, the most sacred spot of the abbey. Henry III (reigned 1216–72) began work on the new building but didn't complete it; the French Gothic nave was finished in 1388. Henry VII's huge and magnificent chapel was added in 1519.

Unlike St Paul's, Westminster Abbey has never been a cathedral but is a 'royal peculiar', administered directly by the crown. Inside is chock-a-block with small chapels, elaborate tombs of monarchy, and monuments to various luminaries from down the ages.

Just past the barrier through the north door is what's known as **Statesmen's Aisle** where politicians and eminent public figures are commemorated mostly by enormous marble statues. At the eastern end of the sanctuary, opposite the entrance to the Henry VII Chapel, is the rather ordinary-looking **Coronation Chair**, upon which almost every monarch is said to have been crowned since the late 13th century. The current chair only dates from the 13th century so must have replaced an earlier one. Below it used to sit the Stone of Scone (pronounced skoon), the Scottish coronation stone that Edward I pilfered in 1297. Amid much fanfare and nationalistic back-slapping the stone was returned north of the border in 1996 although the Scots are required to loan it out for future coronations.

The **Henry VII Chapel** itself is an outstanding example of late perpendicular architecture (a variation of English Gothic) with spectacular circular vaulting on the ceiling. Beyond the chapel's altar is the **Royal Air Force (RAF) Chapel** with a stained-glass window commemorating the force's finest hour, the Battle of Britain. A plaque next to it marks the spot where Oliver Cromwell's body lay for two years until the Restoration, when it was disinterred, hanged and beheaded.

East down a passageway off the Cloister, English Heritage runs the octagonal **Chapter House** (admission with/without abbey ticket £1/2.50; open daily 9.30am-5pm Apr-Sep, 10am-5pm Oct, 10am-4pm Nov-Mar), which has one of Europe's best-preserved medieval tile floors and traces of religious murals. The adjacent **Pyx Chamber** (☎ 020 7222 5897; closed until further notice) is one of the few relics of the original abbey and contains the abbey's treasures and liturgical objects.

Westminster Abbey Museum (☎ 020 7222 5897; closed until further notice) exhibits the death masks of generations of royalty as well as armour and stained glass.

To reach the 900-year-old **College Garden** (open 10am-6pm Tues-Thur Apr-Sept, 10am-4pm Tues-Thur Oct-Mar), the oldest in England, enter Dean's Yard and the **Little Cloisters** (admission free; open 8am-6pm daily) off Great College St. There are free lunch-time concerts in the College Garden from 12.30pm to 2pm on Thursday in July and August.

There are 1½-hour **guided tours** (☎ 7222 7110; £3; Mon-Sat) leaving several times during the day and limited **audio tours** (£2). One of the best ways to visit the abbey is to attend a service (evensong 5pm weekdays, 3pm at weekends). Sunday Eucharist is at 11am.

There is an extraordinary amount to see here but, unless you enjoy the company of tour groups, come either very early or very late; last entry is one hour before closing.

Houses of Parliament (Map 4) Comprising the House of Commons and the House of Lords, the Houses of Parliament (☎ 7219 4272; Parliament Square SW1; ⊖ Westminster) are in the Palace of Westminster. Sir Charles Barry and Augustus Pugin built it in 1840 when neogothic style was all the rage and a thorough cleaning has revealed the soft golden brilliance of the original structure. The most famous feature *outside* the palace is the Clock Tower, commonly known as **Big Ben** (although the name actually refers to the 13-tonne bell hung within the tower and named after Benjamin Hall, commissioner of works when the tower was completed in 1858). Big Ben has rung in every new year since 1924. **Victoria Tower**, completed in 1860, is at the opposite end of the building. For the best view of the complex, pitch yourself on the eastern side of Lambeth Bridge.

Originally built in 1099, **Westminster Hall** (Storeys Gate) is the oldest surviving part of the Palace of Westminster, the seat of the English monarchy from the 11th to the early 16th century. Added between 1394 and 1401, the roof is the earliest-known example of a hammer-beam roof and has been described as 'the greatest surviving achievement of medieval English carpentry'. The hall doubled as a courthouse until the 19th century and the trials of William Wallace (1305), Thomas More (1535), Guy Fawkes (1606) and

Charles I (1649) all took place here. It has also been used to lay in state monarchs and notables such as Winston Churchill.

The **House of Commons** is where Members of Parliament (MPs) meet to propose and discuss new legislation, and to grill the prime minister and other ministers. Although the Commons is a national assembly of 659 MPs, the chamber has seating for only 437 of them. Government members sit to the right of the speaker and opposition members to the left.

If you'd like to observe the House in action, apply to your embassy or high commission in London for a permit to the **Strangers' Gallery** (admission free; entrance via St Stephen's Entrance) or be prepared to queue for at least an hour (evening sessions are usually quieter). Either way, expect stringent security checks. The house normally sits from 2.30pm to 10.30pm Monday to Wednesday, 11.30am to 7.30pm Thursday and 9.30am to 3pm Friday, but you should call ☎ 7219 4272 to make sure.

Parliamentary recesses (holidays) last for three months over the summer and another few weeks over Easter and Christmas. There are 75-minute **guided tours** (☎ 0870 9063773) for £7/3.50 per adult/child of most of the principal rooms in August and September.

Jewel Tower (Map 4) Once part of the Palace of Westminster, the moated Jewel Tower (☎ 7222 2219; Abingdon St SW1; admission £1.60; open 10am-6pm daily Apr-Sept, 10am-5pm daily Oct, 10am-4pm daily Nov-Mar), opposite the Houses of Parliament and beside Westminster Abbey, was built in 1365 to store Edward III's gold and jewels. Run by English Heritage (EH), it now houses exhibitions exploring the history and procedures of parliament, and is a useful stopoff before attending a House of Commons debate.

Westminster Cathedral (Map 8) Completed in 1903, Westminster Cathedral (☎ 7798 9064; Victoria St SW1; ⊖ Victoria; admission free, donation suggested; open 7am-7pm daily) is the headquarters of the Roman Catholic Church in Britain and the only good example of neo-Byzantine architecture in London. Its distinctive candy-striped red-brick and white-stone tower features prominently on the west London skyline.

The interior is part splendid marble and mosaic and part bare brick; funds dried up and the cathedral was never completed. It features the highly regarded stone carvings of the 14 Stations of the Cross (1918) by Eric Gill. For £2 you can take a lift up to the 83m (273ft) Campanile Bell tower for splendid panoramic views of London, or take an **audioguide** for £2.50.

Tate Britain (Map 1) *The* place to see, appreciate and interpret British art from the 16th century to the present, Tate Britain *(☎ 7887 8008; w www.tate.org.uk; Millbank SW1; ⊖ Pimlico; admission free, temporary exhibitions vary; open 10am-5.50pm daily)* was recently spruced up, expanded and rearranged in broadly chronological order. It features works by notables such as William Blake, the Hogarths, Gainsborough, Whistler, Spencer and many more. Adjoining the main building is the quirky **Clore Gallery**, where the bulk of JMW Turner's paintings can be found.

There are free one-hour guided tours, a general tour at 11.30am weekdays, one on Turner and his contemporaries at 2.30pm and 3.30pm weekdays, and a Tate Highlights tour at 3pm Saturday. There are also children's activities throughout the week. The immensely popular **Tate Restaurant** *(☎ 7887 8825; open noon-3pm Mon-Sat & noon-4pm Sun; mains £9-17.50)*, with an impressive Rex Whistler mural, is open for lunch only.

St James's & Mayfair (Map 4)

There are some 150 historically noteworthy buildings within the 36 hectares that make up St James's, an atmospheric – and unusually well-preserved – blend of establishment clubs, historic shops and elegant buildings.

Mayfair – the area bordered by Oxford St, Piccadilly, Park Lane and Regent St – is characterised by broad Georgian avenues and inhabited by the seriously well-to-do (as anyone who's ever played the British version of Monopoly will know). At its heart is **Grosvenor Square**, dominated by the ugly US embassy and a memorial to Franklin D Roosevelt. Shepherd's Market, bordering the southeastern corner of Hyde Park, was once a popular red-light district but is now a tiny enclave of pubs and restaurants and is regarded as the village centre of Mayfair.

Institute for Contemporary Arts (Map 4)
Renowned for being at the cutting edge is the Institute for Contemporary Arts *(ICA; ☎ 7930 3647; w www.ica.org.uk; The Mall SW1;* ⊖ *Charing Cross; admission varies; open noon-7.30pm daily)*. In any given week you might see art-house films, dance, photography, art, theatre, music, lectures, multimedia works or book readings. The complex includes a bookshop, gallery, cinema, bar, theatre and café (see ICA Café in the Places to Eat section).

St James's Park & St James's Palace (Map 4)
The neatest and most royal of London's royal parks, St James's Park *(The Mall SW1;* ⊖ *St James's Park or Charing Cross)* also has the best vistas, including Westminster, Buckingham Palace, St James's Palace, Carlton Terrace and Horse Guards Parade. The flowerbeds are spectacular in summer but it's the lake and waterfowl – including a pod of narky pelicans – that make a stroll or a lounge in St James's Park so special.

The striking Tudor gatehouse of St James's Palace, the only surviving part of a building initiated by the palace-mad Henry VIII in 1530, is best approached from St James's St to the north of the park. It is the residence of Prince Charles and his sons – for whom he recently built their own nightclub here – although they've been thinking of shifting next door to **Clarence House** (1828), former residence of the Queen Mother.

Spencer House (Map 4)
The ancestral home of Princess Diana's family, Spencer House *(☎ 7499 8620; w www.spencer house.co.uk; 27 St James's Place SW1;* ⊖ *Green Park; adult/child £6/5; open 10.30am-5.45pm Sun Feb-July & Sept-Dec)* was built in the Palladian style between 1756 and 1766. Although the Spencers moved out in 1927 and the house became offices, a recent £18m restoration project has returned it to its former glory. Visits through the house are by guided tour only. The restored gardens are planned to be reopened in the summer of 2003 and will cost £3.50 (no concessions); telephone or check the website for opening times.

Buckingham Palace (Map 4)
The official residence of Queen Elizabeth II, Buckingham Palace *(☎ 7830 4832, credit-card bookings ☎ 7321 2233;* ⊖ *St James's Park or Victoria; adult/child £11.50/6; open 9.30am-4.30pm daily early Aug-late Sep)* is at the end of The Mall, where St James's Park and Green Park meet at a large roundabout topped by the 25m-high **Queen Victoria Memorial**.

LONDON

Buckingham Palace was built in 1803 for the Duke of Buckingham and has been the royal family's London home since 1837 when St James's Palace was judged too old-fashioned and unimpressive. Nineteen lavishly furnished staterooms, used by the royals to meet and greet, are open to visitors during part of the summer when HRH takes her holidays in Scotland. The tour includes **Queen Victoria's Picture Gallery** (a full 76.5m long, with works by Rembrandt, Van Dyck, Canaletto, Poussin and Vermeer) and the **Throne Room**, with his-and-hers pink chairs initialled 'ER' and 'P' sitting smugly under what looks like a theatre arch. The Queen has also swung open the gates to part of her backyard although many people still find the visit overpriced and distinctly underwhelming.

Changing of the Guard London's quintessential tourist attraction takes place when the old guard (Foot Guards of the Household Regiment) comes off duty to be replaced by the new guard on the forecourt of Buckingham Palace. If you're dedicated to pomp – and arrive early to get a good vantage point by the rails – you can gape at the soldiers' bright-red uniforms and bearskin hats as they shout and march in one of the world's most famous displays of pageantry. Otherwise, you'll see little more than the backs of heads. The ceremony (☎ 0839-123411) takes place at 11.30am daily from April until the end of July and on alternate days for the rest of the year, weather permitting.

Queen's Gallery The Queen's Gallery (*Map 4; admission £6.50/3; open 10am-5.30pm daily*) is a permanent space housing changing displays from the extensive Royal Collection of art and treasures, shaped by the tastes of monarchs through the centuries. The Queen has kindly offered to take care of the collection on behalf of the nation.

It was originally designed by Nash as a conservatory, converted into a chapel on Victoria's command in 1843 and blown to smithereens by the Luftwaffe in 1940 before being reopened as a gallery in 1962. The exhibition space was greatly expanded in a £20m renovation project and reopened for the Queen's Golden Jubilee in 2002.

Royal Mews The Royal Mews (*Map 4; Buckingham Palace Rd SW1; ⊖ Victoria; adult/child £5/2.50; open 11am-4pm Apr-Oct)* used to house falcons but is now a working stable looking after the royals' immaculately groomed horses along with the opulent vehicles the monarchy uses for getting from A to B. Highlights include the stunning gold coach of 1762, which has been used for every coronation since that of George III, and the Glass Coach of 1910, used for royal weddings. The Mews is closed in June during the four-day racing carnival of Royal Ascot, when the royals head to the races for a flutter.

Handel House Museum (Map 4) The house where George Frideric Handel lived and wrote some of his greatest works, including *Messiah*, opened as a museum (☎ 7495 1685; ⓦ www.handelhouse.org; 25 Brook St W1K; ⊖ Bond Street; adult/child £4.50/2; open 10am-6pm Tues-Wed & Fri-Sat, 10am-8pm Thur, noon-6pm Sun) in late 2001. This 18th-century Mayfair building has been restored to how it would have looked when the composer lived here – for 36 years until his death in 1759 – and visitors can wander through the rooms, see personal belongings and hear recitals of his music. Handel was reputedly a keen art collector and the museum has borrowed artworks from the Queen and other British museums to recreate the mood.

Green Park (Map 4) Green Park is less manicured than the adjoining St James's Park, and has trees and open space, sunshine and shade. It was once a duelling ground and served as a vegetable garden during WWII.

The West End
No two Londoners ever agree on the exact borders of the West End (more a cultural term than a geographical one) but let's just say it takes in Piccadilly Circus and Trafalgar Square to the south, Oxford St and Tottenham Court Rd to the north, Regent St to the west and Covent Garden and the Strand to the east. A heady mixture of consumerism and culture, the West End is where outstanding museums, galleries, historic buildings and entertainment venues rub shoulders with tacky tourist traps.

Piccadilly Circus (Map 5) Piccadilly Circus is home to the popular landmark the **Eros statue** and was named after the stiff collars ('picadils') that were the sartorial staple of a 17th-century tailor who lived nearby. It is a ridiculously busy hub characterised by gaudy neon advertising hoarding (billboards), choking fumes and reliable Tower Records.

London Trocadero Basically just a huge indoor amusement arcade, the Trocadero *(Map 5; ☎ 09068-881100; W www.londontrocadero .com; open 10am-midnight Sun-Thur, 10am-1am Fri & Sat)* has six levels of hi-tech, high-cost fun for youngsters, and cinemas, US-themed restaurants and bars for anyone else with nothing better to do. Each ride costs from £3 but you can get discounts on multiple tickets.

Piccadilly (Map 5) Running west from Piccadilly Circus, Piccadilly is home to **St James's Piccadilly** *(☎ 7734 4511; W www.st -james-piccadilly.org; 197 Piccadilly W1J)*, a church designed by Sir Christopher Wren, along with the quintessential British icons of the Ritz Hotel and Fortnum & Mason's department store (see the Places to Stay – Deluxe and Shopping sections later for details).

Royal Academy of Arts Britain's first art school, the Royal Academy of Arts *(Map 5; ☎ 7300 8000; W www.royalacademy.org.uk; Burlington House, Piccadilly W1; ◉ Green Park; admission varies; open 10am-6pm Sat-Thur, 10am-10pm Fri)* used to play second fiddle to the Hayward Gallery but has created a storm in recent years with perfectly pitched shows ranging from the art of the Aztecs to its popular Summer Exhibitions showcasing the work of contemporary British artists.

Burlington Arcade Flanking Burlington House – home of the Royal Academy of Arts – you'll find the curious Burlington Arcade *(Map 5; 51 Piccadilly W1; ◉ Green Park)*, built in 1819 and evocative of a bygone era. Today it is a shopping precinct for the very wealthy and is most famous for the Burlington Berties, uniformed guards who patrol the area keeping an eye out for punishable offences such as running, chewing gum or whatever else might lower the arcade's tone. Never mind that the arcade once served as a brothel.

Regent St (Map 5) Regent St was originally designed by John Nash to separate refined Mayfair from the teeming, working-class Soho. Distinguished by elegant shop fronts, it's where you'll find Hamley's, Lon-

don's premier toy and game store, and the upmarket department store Liberty (see Shopping later in this chapter).

The BBC Experience North of Oxford Circus is **Broadcasting House** *(Map 4; Portland Place W1)*, from which the BBC began broadcasting in 1932. The basement houses the BBC Experience *(☎ 0870 603 0304; adult/child £7.95/5.95; open 10am-5.30pm Tues-Sun, 11am-5.30pm Mon)*, where you can get an insight into the media of radio and television or just watch clips from popular BBC creations. Aficionados should make a beeline for the shop that sells a huge number of videos, CDs, tapes and books relating to the BBC's prolific output.

Oxford St (Maps 4 & 5) Oxford St is the zenith of High Street shopping, a must or a miss depending on your retail persuasion and eye for style (see Shopping later in this chapter). West towards Marble Arch, you'll find many famous department stores including the incomparable Selfridges.

Soho (Map 5) East of Regent St and south of Oxford St, with Shaftesbury Ave and Charing Cross Rd to the south and the east, is Soho, one of the liveliest corners of London and the place to come for fun and games after dark. A decade ago it was known mostly for strip clubs and peepshows. The sleaze is still there, of course, but these days it blends with some of London's trendiest clubs, bars and restaurants. West of Soho proper, is **Carnaby St**, the epicentre of London's 'swinging '60s'. It descended into tourist tack but has lately regained much of its cred.

Leicester Square (Map 5) Pedestrianised Leicester (pronounced les-ter) Square is usually heaving with tourists – and inevitably buskers – but it essentially feels like somewhere you pass through on the way elsewhere. It has been smartened up in recent years and has four huge cinemas, various nightclubs, pubs and restaurants.

Chinatown (Map 5) Immediately north are Lisle and Gerrard Sts – the heart of Chinatown – full of verve and unfairly hip Japanese youngsters. Street signs are bilingual and the streets themselves are lined with Asian restaurants (see Places to Eat later). If you're in town in late January or early February, don't miss the sparkles and crackles of Chinese New Year.

Covent Garden (Map 5) This elegant piazza (⊖ Covent Garden), London's first planned square, is a tourist mecca where chain restaurants, souvenir shops, balconied bars and street entertainers vie for the punters' pound. It positively heaves in summer, especially weekends, yet seems unfettered by the fickleness of fashion and is still one of the few parts of London where pedestrians rule.

In the 1630s Inigo Jones converted the former vegetable field into a graceful square that at first housed the fruit and vegetable market immortalised in the film *My Fair Lady*. The area eventually slumped and became home to brothels and coffee houses but the market was shifted in the 1980s and Covent Garden was transformed into one of the city's grooviest hubs.

Beyond the piazza are lively streets of clothes shops and bars, restaurants and designer gift shops. Throughout the ages, Covent Garden has remained a prestigious precinct for theatre and opera, and was recently crowned by the dazzlingly redeveloped Royal Opera House (see Opera & Dance in the Entertainment section later in this chapter).

To the north, Floral St is where swanky designers have their outlets.

London Transport Museum Tucked into the corner of Covent Garden between the Jubilee Hall and Tutton's restaurant, the London Transport Museum *(Map 5; ☎ 7836 8557; w www.ltmuseum.co.uk; Covent Garden Piazza WC2; ⊖ Covent Garden; adult/child £5.95/free; open 10am-6pm Sat-Thur, 11am-6pm Fri)* is an unexpected delight exploring how London made the transition from streets choked with horse-drawn carriages to streets choked with horse-powered cars. It conserves and explains London's transport heritage and is full of interactive and hands-on displays from old buses to tube simulators.

St Paul's Church Known as the 'actors' church' because of its long association with theatre and thespians, St Paul's *(Map 5; ☎ 7836 5221; Bedford St WC2; open 9am-4.30pm Mon-Fri & 9am-12.30pm Sun)* was designed by Inigo Jones as part of the com-

mission for Covent Garden in the 17th century. It is little more than a stone rectangle with a pitched roof – 'the most handsomest barn in England' reckoned Jones – and the interior walls are lined with memorials to actors such as Charlie Chaplin and Vivien Leigh. The first recorded Punch and Judy show took place under the church's portico in 1662.

Theatre Museum This museum *(Map 5; ☎ 7836 7891; Russell St WC2; ⊖ Covent Garden; admission free; open 10am-6pm Tues-Sun)* is a branch of the Victoria & Albert Museum. It displays costumes, artefacts and curiosities relating to the history of British theatre, and is also a wonderful distraction for the kiddies, for whom there are regular programmes and activities.

The Strand (Maps 4 & 5) Described by Benjamin Disraeli in the 19th century as Europe's finest street, this 'beach' of the Thames – which was built to connect Westminster (the seat of political power) and the City (the commercial centre) – has since lost much of its lustre. The Strand still boasts a few classy hotels and theatres but today is as well known for the homeless who sleep in its doorways.

Somerset House The splendid Palladian masterpiece of Somerset House *(Map 4; w www.somerset-house.org.uk; Strand WC2; ⊖ Temple)* was designed by William Chambers in 1775 and contains three fabulous galleries: the Courtauld Gallery, the Gilbert Collection and the Hermitage Rooms. Its expansive central courtyard – a car park for civil servants only a few years ago – was returned to its former glory in a millennial make-over and is now one of the most elegant spaces in London, with dancing water fountains, outside tables and all the panache of Paree. It hosts a summer programme of open-air events from music to theatre. Out the back there's a wonderful terrace and café overlooking the Thames while the Admiralty restaurant is a little bit special (see Places to Eat later).

Housed in the North Wing (or Strand Block), the **Courtauld Gallery** *(☎ 7848 2526; adult/child £5/free, free 10am-2pm Mon; open 10am-6pm daily)* displays some of the Courtauld Institute's marvellous collection of paintings in grand surroundings. There's a wealth of 14th- to 20th-century works including a roomful of Rubens and Impressionist and post-Impressionist works by Van Gogh, Renoir and Toulouse-Lautrec.

One of London's newest museums, the **Gilbert Collection** (☎ 7240 5782; adult/child £5/free, free after 4.30pm; open 10am-6pm daily) includes such treasures as European silverware, gold snuffboxes and Italian mosaics bequeathed to the nation by London-born American businessman Arthur Gilbert.

Sharing space with the Gilbert Collection, the **Hermitage Rooms** (☎ 7845 4630; w www.hermitagerooms.co.uk; adult/child £6/free; open 10am-6pm daily) displays diverse and rotating exhibitions from St Petersburg's renowned (and underfunded) State Hermitage Museum, to which goes a slice of your admission fee.

Royal Courts of Justice Designed in 1874, the gargantuan melange of Gothic spires, pinnacles and burnished Portland stone of the Royal Courts of Justice (Map 4; ☎ 7936 6000; 460 The Strand; ⊖ Temple; open 9am-4.30pm Mon-Fri) is where civil cases are heard. It's usually pretty dry stuff – the more colourful criminal cases are heard at the Old Bailey – but citizens and tourists are welcome to watch justice being served. Expect airport security.

Bloomsbury

Largely nonresidential Bloomsbury – bounded by Tottenham Court Rd, High Holborn, Euston Rd and Gray's Inn Rd – is a genteel blend of the University of London, beautiful Georgian squares, the British Museum and literary history. **Russell Square** (Map 4), its very heart, was laid out in 1800 and is London's largest square. It was smartened up recently and given a 10m-tall fountain.

Between the world wars these pleasant streets were colonised by a group of artists and intellectuals known collectively as the Bloomsbury Group, which included the novelists Virginia Woolf and EM Forster, and the economist John Maynard Keynes (see 'The Bloomsbury Group' boxed text in the Southeast England chapter). Many of the scribes lived in **Gordon Square** (Map 2) while up until fairly recently publishing houses were based in **Bedford Square** (Map 4), the last original Georgian square in Bloomsbury.

British Museum (Map 4) London's most visited attraction – with more than six million punters each year – the British Museum (☎ 7636 1555; w www.thebritishmuseum.ac.uk; Great Russell St WC1; ⊖ Tottenham Court Road or Russell Square; admission free; open 10am-5pm Mon-Sat, noon-6pm Sun) is the largest in the country and one of the oldest and finest in the world. It was started in 1749 in the form of a 'cabinet of curiosities' belonging to Dr Hans Sloane (one of the royal physicians) which he later bequeathed to the country and has been augmented over the years partly through the plundering of the empire (see the boxed text 'Britain & Greece Squabble Over Marbles' later).

The museum's inner courtyard, hidden from the public for almost a century and a half, was covered with a spectacular glass and steel roof designed by Norman Foster and opened to the public as the **Great Court** in late 2000. The stunning design opens up the labyrinth that is the British Museum and makes its mind-bogglingly vast collection just a tad more accessible. Even so, you'd need at least a couple of visits to take it in, which isn't a problem any more because admission is free (to most of the permanent collection anyway).

The back entrance at Montague Place is usually quieter than the porticoed main one off Great Russell St. Don't try and see too much or you'll end up savouring nothing. Relax, take a few deep breaths, peruse the written guides available, consider from the choice of nine 50-minute **'eye opener' tours** (free; 11am-3pm Mon-Sat, 1pm-4pm Sun) and decide which part of the collection you want to focus on. Other tours include the 1½-hour **highlights tour** (adult/child £8/5; 10.30am, 1pm & 3pm Mon-Sat) and a range of **audio-guides** (£3.50).

To help whet your appetite, the following are some highlights that you should definitely try and catch. The **Rosetta Stone** (Room 4), discovered in 1799, is written in two forms of ancient Egyptian and was the key to deciphering Egyptian hieroglyphics, which had stymied scholars up to that time. The **Parthenon Marbles** (Room 18, better known as the Elgin Marbles) once adorned the walls of the Parthenon on the Acropolis in Athens. They are thought to show the great procession to the temple that took place during the Panathenaic Festival, on the birthday of Athena, one of the grandest events in the Greek world. The stunning **Oxus Treasure** (Room 52) is a collection of 7th- to 4th-century BC pieces of Persian gold, which is believed to have originated from the ancient Persian capital of Persepolis and was rescued from bandits. The **Sutton Hoo Ship Burial** (Room 41) is an Anglo-Saxon ship burial site dating from AD 620, excavated in Suffolk in 1939. The **Lindow Man** (Room 50) is an Iron Age unfortunate who appears to have been smacked on the head with an axe and then garrotted. His remains were preserved in a peat bog until 1984 when a peat-cutting machine sliced him in half.

In the centre of the Great Court – and heart of the museum – is the **Reading Room**, which was formerly the British Library and where George Bernard Shaw and Mahatma Gandhi studied, and Karl Marx wrote *The Communist Manifesto*. The northern end of the courtyard's lower level houses the new **Sainsbury African Galleries**. A restored **King's Library**, which will specialise in the evolution of museums, is due to open in 2003 as will the new **Wellcome Gallery of Ethnography**.

Despite the kudos, all's not well at the cash-strapped museum. Cost-cutting measures such as wholesale job losses and reduced opening hours at various galleries have led to industrial strife, which forced the temporary closure – albeit only for one day – of the museum in 2002. Administrators are considering extending admission fees to some of the lesser-known exhibitions to help the museum stay afloat.

Holborn & Clerkenwell (Maps 4 & 5)

Holborn (pronounced hoe-bun) is the smallest of London's former metropolitan boroughs and takes its name from a tributary of the former River Fleet. Its distinctive features are the wonderful Sir John Soane's Museum and the atmospheric Inns of Court, built here to symbolise the law's role as mediator in the traditional power struggle between Westminster and the City.

Northeast of Holborn is the little pocket of Clerkenwell, for most of the 19th and 20th centuries a dilapidated working-class area of no interest to anyone but its inhabitants. In the 1980s property developers realised the value of such central, tourist-free real estate and Clerkenwell has since been transformed into a glaringly trendy corner of the capital replete with new pubs, restaurants and clubs.

Sir John Soane's Museum (Map 5)

Considered by many as their favourite 'small' sight in London, Sir John Soane's Museum (☎ 7405 2107; w www.soane.org; 13 Lincoln's Inn Fields WC2; ❸ Holborn; admission free, tour 2.30pm Sat £3; open 10am-5pm Tues-Sat & 6pm-9pm 1st Tues of month) is partly a beautiful, bewitching house and partly a small museum representing the taste of celebrated architect and collector extraordinaire Sir John Soane (1753–1837). In his

Britain & Greece Squabble Over Marbles

Wonderful though it is, the British Museum can sometimes feel like one vast repository for stolen booty. Much of what's on display wasn't just 'picked up' along the way by Victorian travellers and explorers, but stolen, or purchased under dubious circumstances.

Restive foreign governments occasionally pop their heads over the parapet to demand the return of their property. The British Museum says 'no' and the problem goes away until the next time. Not the Greeks, however. They have been kicking up a stink demanding the return of the so-called Parthenon Marbles, the ancient marble sculptures that once adorned the Parthenon. The British Museum, and successive British governments, steadfastly refuse to hand over the priceless works that were removed from the Parthenon and shipped to England by the British ambassador to the Ottoman Empire, the Earl of Elgin, in 1806. (When Elgin blew all his dough, he sold the marbles to the government.) All along, the British Museum has sniffed that the marbles were better off under its protective care. This arrogance proved tragicomic when it emerged in 1999 that earlier in the 20th century the museum had 'cleaned' the marbles using chisels and wire brushes, thereby destroying the finishing applied by the ancient Greeks.

The Greek government has upped the anti in recent years and has begun work on a €86m museum in Athens designed specifically to exhibit the marbles as they were originally displayed in the 5th century BC. With all the media attention that will surround the Olympics in Athens in 2004, the Greeks hope to embarrass the British into returning the marbles. Only time will tell who blinks first.

work and life, Soane drew on ideas he picked up while on an 18th-century Grand Tour of Italy. He married into money, which he then poured into building this house and one next door, which the museum plans to expand into over the coming years.

The house is largely as it was when Sir John was taken out in a box and is part of the attraction of the museum. It has a glass dome that brings light right down to the basement, a lantern room filled with statuary, rooms within rooms and a picture gallery where each painting folds away when pressed and reveals another one behind. Among his eclectic acquisitions are an Egyptian sarcophagus, ancient vases and works of arts, and the original *Rake's Progress*, William Hogarth's set of cartoon caricatures of late-18th-century London lowlife.

The tour is well worth catching should you be in the neighbourhood on Saturday afternoon; tickets are sold at the museum from 2pm.

Inns of Court (Map 4) Clustered around Holborn to the south of Fleet St are the Inns of Court whose alleys, atmosphere and open spaces provide an urban oasis. All London barristers work from within one of the four Inns, and a roll call of former members would include the likes of Oliver Cromwell and Charles Dickens to Mahatma Gandhi and Margaret Thatcher. It would take a lifetime working here to grasp the intricacies of the arcane protocols of the Inns – they're similar to the Freemasons, and both are 13th-century creations – and it's best to just soak up the dreamy atmosphere, relax, and thank your lucky stars you're not one of the bewigged and deadly serious barristers scurrying around you.

Lincoln's Inn (☎ 7405 1393; *Lincoln's Inn Fields WC2; ⊖ Holborn; grounds open 9am-6pm Mon-Fri; chapel open 12.30pm-2.30pm Mon-Fri)*, largely intact with several original 15th-century buildings, is the most attractive of the bunch with a chapel and pretty landscaped gardens. **Gray's Inn** (☎ 7458 7800; *Gray's Inn Rd WC1; ⊖ Chancery Lane; grounds open 10am-4pm Mon-Fri; chapel open 10am-6pm Mon-Fri)* is not as interesting and was largely rebuilt after the Luftwaffe levelled it. **Middle Temple** (☎ 7427 4800; *Middle Temple Lane EC4; ⊖ Temple; grounds open 10am-11.30am & 3pm-4pm Mon-Fri)* and **Inner Temple** (☎ 7797 8250; *King's Bench Walk EC4; ⊖ Temple; grounds open 10am-4pm Mon-Fri)*,

the former being the best preserved, are both part of the Temple complex between Fleet St and Victoria Embankment (see also Temple Church in The City section following).

The City (Maps 4 & 6)

The City of London, the commercial heart of the capital, is 'the square mile' on the northern bank of the Thames where the Romans first built their walled community two millennia ago. Its boundaries have changed little down the ages, and you can always tell you're within them because the Corporation of London's coat of arms appears on the street signs.

Less than 10,000 people actually live in the City but some 300,000 descend on it each weekday, where they generate almost three-quarters of Britain's entire GDP before nicking back off to wherever it is they live.

Flattened a couple of times – by the Great Fire of 1666 and the Luftwaffe of WWII – the City has become a model of architectural savvy and houses the impressive headquarters of many of Britain's and the world's largest financial institutions. St Paul's Cathedral and the Tower of London are also here and a quiet weekend stroll offers a unique opportunity to explore the architectural richness of the area, including the many atmospheric alleyways snaking between the modern office towers.

Fleet St (Map 4) Twentieth-century London's 'Street of Shame', Fleet St (*⊖ Blackfriars*) was synonymous with the UK's scurrilous tabloids until the mid-1980s when the press barons embraced computer technology, ditched a load of staff and largely relocated to the Docklands. It was here in 1850 that Reuters news agency, the last media outlet to stick with Fleet St, began its service with a loft of carrier pigeons.

Here you'll find **St Bride's**, one of the best of Christopher Wren's churches, designed in 1671 and his tallest after St Paul's. With its 69m-high spire and octagonal arcades it is reputed to have been the inspiration for the traditional tiered wedding cake. The church was bombed during WWII and the interior is modern and not very interesting apart from a touching chapel honouring journalists who lost their lives in the course of their work.

Dr Johnson's House (☎ 7353 3745; ⊠ www .drjh.dircon.co.uk; *17 Gough Square EC4; ⊖ Chancery Lane; adult/concession £4/3; open 11am-5.30pm Mon-Sat May-Sep, 11am-5pm* *rest of yr*) is where Samuel Johnson and his assistants compiled the first English dictionary between 1748 and 1759. The well-preserved Georgian house is full of prints and portraits of friends and intimates, including Johnson's Jamaican servant to whom he bequeathed the house in his will.

Temple Church (Map 4) Just off Fleet St is Temple Church (*☎ 7353 1736; Inner Temple, King's Bench Walk EC4; ⊖ Temple; open 10am-4pm Wed-Sat*), which – after Westminster Abbey and St Paul's Cathedral – is possibly London's most interesting and architecturally important church. Duck under the archway beyond No 17 and you'll be in the Inner Temple, one of the Inns of Court. Temple Church was originally planned and built by the secretive Knights Templar between 1161 and 1185. They modelled it on the Church of the Holy Sepulchre in Jerusalem and the core of the building is the only round church left in London. The knights were eventually suppressed and their lands leased to the lawyers who set up the Inns of Court. Thirteenth-century stone effigies of some of them still adorn the floors of the circular nave.

The most interesting external feature is the Norman western door with its elaborate porch. It is set into a dip that shows how far the ground level has risen over the centuries.

St Bartholomew-the-Great (Map 6) The oldest parish church in London, St Bartholomew-the-Great (*☎ 7606 5171; West Smithfield EC1; ⊖ Barbican; open 8.30am-5pm Mon-Fri, 10.30am-1.30pm Sat, 8am-8pm Sun*) is a tabernacle's throw from the Barbican and worth an unhurried visit. Although Henry VIII tore down its nave during his monastic purge, the original Norman arches and details lend this holy space an ancient calm; approaching from nearby Smithfield Market through the restored 13th-century archway is like walking back in time.

Central Criminal Court (Old Bailey) (Map 4) Many of Britain's most notorious criminals – and a few Irishmen who were in the wrong place at the wrong time – have been convicted at the Central Criminal Court, better known as the Old Bailey after the street on which it stands. Look up at the great copper dome and you'll see the figure of justice holding a sword and scales in her hands;

oddly she is *not* blindfolded, which has sparked many a sarcastic comment from those being brought in here.

You can visit the court's **public gallery** (*☎ 7248 3277; Newgate St; open 10.30am-1pm & 2pm-4pm Mon-Fri*).

St Paul's Cathedral (Map 6) Dominating the City with a dome second in size only St Peter's in Rome, St Paul's Cathedral (*☎ 7236 4128; w www.stpauls.co.uk; ⊖ St Paul's; adult/child £6/3; open 8.30am-4pm Mon-Sat*) was built between 1675 and 1710 by Sir Christopher Wren, on the site of four previous cathedrals, the first of which dated from AD 604. It was one of 50 commissions given to Wren to rebuild London after the Great Fire of 1666. Plans for alterations had already been made but the blaze provided him with a blank canvas. Several plans were spurned before the authorities finally gave the green light – followed by much controversy – to the current design.

The dome is renowned for dodging the bombs during the Blitz of WWII; photographs in the southern choir aisle show how it miraculously survived the surrounding devastation and became an icon of the resilience shown in the capital at the time. Outside the cathedral, to the north, is a **monument to the people of London**, a simple and elegant memorial to the 32,000 Londoners who weren't so lucky.

Inside, some 30m above the main paved area, is the first of three domes (actually a dome, inside a cone, inside a dome) supported by eight huge columns. The walkway around its base is called the **Whispering Gallery**, because if you talk close to the wall your words are carried to the opposite side 32m away.

The Whispering Gallery, **Stone Gallery** and the **Golden Gallery** can be reached by a staircase on the western side of the recently scrubbed-up southern transept. It is 530 lung-busting steps to the very top, the Golden Gallery, and an unforgettable view of London. But even if that's too much, you can still get terrific city vistas from the lower galleries.

In the northern transept chapel, you can admire Holman Hunt's celebrated painting *The Light of the World*, depicting Christ knocking on an overgrown door that, symbolically, can only be opened from the inside.

The **Crypt** has memorials to up to 300 military demigods, including Wellington, Kitchener and Nelson, whose body lies below the dome in a black sarcophagus. But the most poignant memorial of all is to Sir Christopher Wren himself. It is a simple slab bearing his name and an inscription in Latin, which translates as: 'If you seek his memorial, look about you'. Nice touch.

Audio tours lasting 45 minutes are available for £3. **Guided tours** *(adult/child £2.50/1)* lasting 90 minutes leave the tour desk at 11am, 11.30am, 1.30pm and 2pm. There are organ concerts at St Paul's at 5pm most Sundays. Evensong takes place at 5pm most weekdays and at 3.15pm on Sunday.

Guildhall (Map 6) The Guildhall *(☎ 7606 3030; Basinghall St EC2; ✪ Bank; admission free; open 10am-5pm Mon-Sat, 10am-4pm Sun May-Sept; 10am-5pm Mon-Sun Oct-Apr)* sits exactly in the centre of the square mile and has been the seat of the City's local government for eight centuries. The present building dates from the early 15th century.

Visitors can see the **Great Hall** where the mayor is still elected, a vast empty space with ecclesiastical-style monuments and the shields and banners of London's 12 principal livery companies, which emerged from the guilds of the Middle Ages.

Beneath the Great Hall is London's largest **medieval crypt** *(☎ 7606 3030, ext 1463; visited by free guided tour only)*, which has 19 stained-glass windows showing the livery companies' coats of arms.

The **Guildhall Art Gallery** *(adult/child £2.50/1)*, which was closed from WWII to 1999, holds more than 4000 artworks primarily of historical import. Only 250 or so are displayed at any one time. Up until July 2002 it housed a marble sculpture of Margaret Thatcher, which was being housed here until it could take up its rightful position in the House of Commons whenever the baroness died. One irate visitor couldn't wait for nature to take its course and, grabbing one of the poles supporting the keep-out ropes, he used it to knock the Iron Lady's block off.

Barbican (Map 6) Tucked into a corner of the City of London where a watchtower (or 'barbican') once stood, the Barbican *(☎ 7638 4141; Silk St EC2; ✪ Barbican or Moorgate)* is a prime example of a local council making a pig's ear of development.

The plan was to create an ultramodern complex for offices, residences and the arts

on a vast bombsite provided by WWII. The result – which was only completed in the early 1980s, by which time the ultramodern plans should have been museum pieces – is a forbidding series of wind tunnels and gloomy high-rise apartments, with an enormous cultural centre hidden somewhere in the middle.

The Barbican Centre is the home of the Royal Shakespeare Company (RSC), the London Symphony Orchestra and the London Classical Orchestra. It also houses the **Museum of London** and the wonderful **Barbican Art Gallery** *(☎ 7588 9023; adult/child £4.50/ 2.50; open 10am-6pm Mon-Sat, noon-6pm Sun)* on Level 3, with some of the best photographic exhibits in London. The programmes are generally first-rate but it's a hassle finding the complex in the first place, never mind reaching the right spot at the right time.

Museum of London (Map 6) Despite its unprepossessing setting amid the concrete walkways of the Barbican (look for gate 7), the Museum of London *(☎ 7600 3699, recorded message ☎ 7600 0807; w www.mu seumoflondon.org.uk; London Wall EC2; ✪ Barbican; admission free; open 10am-5.50pm Mon-Sat, noon-5.50pm Sun)* is one of the city's finest, and is expanding its exhibitions depicting the city's evolution from the Ice Age to the Internet. A new permanent gallery opened at the end of 2001, World City, which explores the social and industrial changes in London life. The museum's latest acquisition is a 2000-year-old stone plaque, discovered in late 2002, and engraved with the Latin word 'Londiniensium'. The word is believed to refer to the 'people of Londinium' and the remarkably well-preserved plaque is the earliest-known physical proof of the capital's original Roman name.

Tower of London (Map 6) Despite the heaving crowds and all the marketing claptrap, the Tower of London *(☎ 7680 9004; w www.hrp.org.uk; Tower Hill EC3; ✪ Tower Hill; adult/child £11.50/7.50; open 9am-6pm Mon-Sat, 10am-6pm Sun Apr-Oct; 9am-5pm Mon-Sat, 10am-5pm Sun Nov-Mar)* is one of the most essential sights in London and a window into a gruesome and fascinating history. It is also one of the city's three World Heritage Sites (the others are Westminster Abbey and its surrounding buildings, and Maritime Greenwich). Well over two million people visit each year and, even in winter, you should arrive early to commandeer enough space to savour the experience.

To help get your bearings, take the hugely entertaining and free **guided tour** with any of the Tudor-garbed Beefeaters. These gentlemen, all retired servicemen, are officially known as Yeoman Warders but were enviously nicknamed Beefeaters because in the 17th century they were given rations of beef, a very rare commodity at the time. Hour-long tours leave every 30 minutes from the Middle Tower between 9am and 3pm Monday to Saturday and from 10am Sunday.

In 1078 William the Conqueror laid the first stone of the White Tower to replace the timber-and-earth castle he'd already built here. By 1285 two walls with towers and a moat were built around it and the medieval defences have barely been altered since.

In the early Middle Ages, the tower was used as a royal residence as well as a treasury, a mint, an arsenal and a prison. Its role as a prison became increasingly important after Henry VIII moved to Whitehall Palace in 1529 and started dishing out his preferred brand of punishment.

The most striking building in the tower is the huge **White Tower**, in the centre of the courtyard, with its solid Romanesque architecture and four turrets. It got its name after it was whitewashed during Henry III's reign and now houses a collection from the Royal Armouries. On the 2nd floor is the **Chapel of St John the Evangelist**, which dates from 1080 and is therefore the oldest church in London.

What appears quite a peaceful, picturesque corner to the west of the White Tower is in fact one of its most tragic. On the small green in front of the church stood the **scaffold**, set up during Henry VIII's reign, where seven people were beheaded, among them Anne Boleyn and her cousin Catherine Howard (his second and fifth wives).

Facing the White Tower to the north is the **Waterloo Barracks**, which now contains the Crown Jewels: orbs, sceptres and the centrepiece, the Imperial State Crown, set with 2868 diamonds, sapphires, emeralds, rubies and pearls. On a busy day, you'll be whisked past and hardly have time to blink.

On the far side of the White Tower from here is the **Bloody Tower**, one of the best-known parts of the complex. This is where the 12-year-old Edward V and his little brother were held 'for their own safety' and later murdered, probably by their uncle, the future Richard III. Sir Walter Raleigh did a 13-year stretch here, when he wrote his *History of the World*, a copy of which is on display.

Don't leave the tower without visiting the patch of green between the Wakefield and White Towers where the Great Hall once stood. Here you'll find the latest in the tower's long line of famous ravens, which legend says could cause the White Tower to collapse should they leave. Their wings have been clipped just in case they get any ideas.

Tower Bridge (Map 6) When it was built in 1894, London was still a thriving port and Tower Bridge was designed to rise and allow ships to pass through. It is raised electronically these days although you can still see the steam engines that were originally used for the job. As you would expect, there are excellent views from the bridge's walkways.

For the **Tower Bridge Experience** *(Map 6; ☎ 7378 1928; w www.towerbridge.org.uk; ⊖ Tower Hill; adult/child £5/3; open 10am-6.30pm daily Apr-Oct, 9.30am-6pm daily Nov-Mar)*, a lift takes you up from the modern visitors' facility in the northern tower where the story of its building is recounted with videos and animatronics.

Bank of England Museum (Map 6) Guardian of the country's financial system, the Bank of England was established in 1694 when the government needed to raise some cash to support a war with France. It was moved here in 1734 and largely renovated by Sir John Soane. The museum *(☎ 7601 5545; w www.bankofengland.co.uk; Bartholomew Lane EC2; ⊖ Bank; admission free; open 10am-5pm Mon-Fri)* traces the history of the bank and bank notes and uses various interactive technology – including an interactive video that lets you try your hand at dealing in foreign exchange – to bring this rather dry subject to life.

The Monument (Map 6) Designed by Christopher Wren to commemorate the Great Fire of 1666, the Monument *(☎ 7626 2717; Monument St; ⊖ Monument; adult/child £1.50/50; open 10am-5.40pm daily)* is 60.6m high, the exact distance from its base to the bakery on Pudding Lane east where the blaze began. If you're up to it, 311 tight steps lead to a balcony beneath the gilded bronze urn at the top and a splendid view.

South of the Thames

As recently as a decade ago, the southern part of central London was the city's forgotten underside – run-down, neglected and offering little for foreign visitors once they'd visited the South Bank arts venues. Over recent years, however, all that has changed and even north Londoners are venturing 'sarf' of the river for play and stimulation.

Bermondsey (Maps 1 & 6) Although parts of Bermondsey still look a little dejected, there are pockets of refurbishment and revitalisation, as exemplified by the Design Museum and the brand new Zandra Rhodes Fashion & Textile Museum.

Design Museum The gleaming white Design Museum (Map 1; ☎ 7403 6933; 28 Shad Thames SE1; ♦ Tower Hill; w www.designmuseum.org; adult/child £6/4; open 11.30am-6pm Mon-Fri, 10.30am-6pm Sat & Sun) is a must for anyone interested in the evolution of design and all its applications. The 1st floor is dedicated to innovation from around the world while the 2nd floor concentrates on the practicalities of design and how it can make the difference between success and failure for items intended for the mass market. There is also a new gallery devoted specifically to contemporary design. Check the listings for details on the museum's busy and diverse schedule of temporary exhibitions.

The Fashion & Textile Museum Due to open in 2003, kooky British designer Zandra Rhodes' Fashion & Textile Museum (Map 6; ☎ 7403 0222; w www.ftmlondon.org; 83 Bermondsey St SE1; ♦ London Bridge) promises to showcase the best of vintage and modern, local and international, fashion and textile design (as well as thousands of her own pieces, of course). The garish orange and pink exterior indicates a bright future.

Southwark (Maps 4 & 6) During the Middle Ages, when London Bridge provided the only crossing over the Thames, Southwark (pronounced **suth**-erk) was an important thoroughfare. The borough is in a transition period, retaining at least some of its working-class gritty edge while a slew of

sights and attractions – such as the magnificent Tate Modern Gallery – open up along the Thames in Bankside.

HMS Belfast Launched in 1938, the HMS Belfast (Map 6; ☎ 7407 6328; w www.iwm.org.uk; Morgan's Lane, Tooley St SE1; ♦ London Bridge; adult/child £5.80/free; open 10am-6pm daily Mar-Oct, 10am-5pm Nov-Feb) is a large, light cruiser built with 16 six-inch guns. It saw much action during WWII and played a leading role in the Normandy Landings. That won't mean much to little boys but they'll love it all the same.

London Dungeon Under the arches of London Bridge station, the overpriced London Dungeon (Map 6; ☎ 7403 7221; w www.thedungeons.com; 28-34 Tooley St SE1; ♦ London Bridge; adult/child £10.95/6.95; open 10am-6.30pm daily Apr-June & Sept, 10am-9pm daily July & Aug) is long on gore and short on substance. The reconstruction of the French guillotine in action is gruesome but doesn't hold a candle to the section dealing with Victorian serial killer Jack the Ripper. Kids, of course, love it. Beware of touts selling fake tickets.

The Britain at War Experience Designed to educate future generations about the hardships endured, and spirit exemplified, during WWII, the Britain at War Experience (Map 6; ☎ 7403 3171; w www.britainatwar.co.uk; 64-66 Tooley St SE1; adult/child £6.50/3.50; open 10am-5.30pm daily Apr-Sept, 10am-4.30pm daily Oct-Mar) is crammed with fascinating memorabilia from a bombarded London.

Old Operating Theatre Museum & Herb Garret One of London's most genuinely gruesome attractions is the Old Operating Theatre Museum (Map 6; ☎ 7955 4791; w www.thegarret.org.uk; 9a St Thomas St SE1; ♦ London Bridge; adult/child £3.75/2.25; open 10.30-5pm daily). Visitors can gather around an original wooden operating table in the roof space – high enough for natural light, isolated enough for soundproofing – where unanaesthetised women were opened up and operated on, largely for medical experiments. A box of sawdust was placed beneath the table to catch the blood and guts. 'Nuff said.

There's also an apothecary where medicinal herbs were once stored; it now houses a medical museum hung with bunches of herbs.

Southwark Cathedral There was already a church on this site in 1086, but it was rebuilt in 1106 and then again in the 13th century. By the 1830s it had fallen into decay and much of what you see today is actually Victorian – the nave was rebuilt in 1897 – although the central tower dates from 1520 and the choir from the 13th century. In 1905 the old church became Southwark Cathedral *(Map 6; ☎ 7367 6722; Montague Close SE1; ⊖ London Bridge; admission by donation; open 8am-6pm daily)*, with its own bishop. It's been scrubbed up in recent years and has a new visitors centre.

Inside are monuments and details galore and it's worth picking up one of the small guides. Along the southern aisle of the nave, stop and look at the green alabaster **monument to William Shakespeare**, whose great works were originally written for the Bankside playhouses. Catch Evensong at 5.30pm on Tuesday and Friday, 4pm on Saturday and 3pm on Sunday.

Vinopolis – City of Wine In a hectare of Victorian railway vaults in Bankside, Vinopolis *(Map 6; ☎ 0870 444 477; w www.vinop olis.co.uk; 1 Bank End, Park St SE1; ⊖ London Bridge; adult/child £11.50/5; open 10am-5.30pm Mon-Fri, 10am-8pm Sat & Sun)* cashes in on Londoners' infatuation with things red, white and rosé. The hi-tech exhibits introduce visitors to the history of winemaking and there are tastings – more like sips – of five wines as you tour. If you come from a wine-growing country you won't get much out of this: save your cash for the off-license. Last entry is two hours before closing.

Shakespeare's Globe & Exhibition The Globe Theatre *(Map 6; ☎ 7401 9919; w www .shakespeares-globe.org; 21 New Globe Walk SE1; ⊖ London Bridge; adult/child £8/5.50; open 10am-5pm daily)* consists of the reconstructed Globe Theatre and, beneath it, an exhibition focusing on Elizabethan London and the struggle by American actor and director Sam Wanamaker to get the theatre rebuilt.

The original Globe (known as the 'Wooden O' after its circular shape and roofless centre) was erected in 1599, burned down in 1613 and immediately rebuilt. Puritans, who regarded theatres as dreadful dens of iniquity, eventually closed it down in 1642. The new Globe opened in 1997 and is meant to replicate the original, right down to the thatched roof and

lack of seats for the 500 'groundlings', who stand to watch performances.

A visit to the exhibition also includes a guided tour of the Globe Theatre itself although, in summer, there are usually matinee performances and tours take place in the morning only.

Tate Modern The vast Bankside Power Station – designed by Giles Gilbert Scott after WWII but stunningly remodelled for the new millennium by Swiss architect duo Herzog & De Meuron – is home to the wonderful Tate Modern *(Map 6; information ☎ 7887 8000; w www.tate.org.uk; Queen's Walk SE1; ⊖ Blackfriars or London Bridge; admission free; open 10am-6pm Sun-Thur, 10am-10pm Fri & Sat)*, the largest modern art gallery in the world and a must-see for anyone with even a passing interest in contemporary art.

Enter through the vast and dramatic Turbine Hall and lick your lips. The collection is spread over five floors and encompasses art in all its forms from the beginning of the 20th century. The works are displayed thematically rather than chronologically and some of the early-20th-century stuff gets a little lost compared to the bolder contemporary works. Although the displays change regularly, you're certain to clap eyes on pieces by Monet, Picasso, Dali, Pollock, Warhol and Rothko as well as various members of Britain's new brat pack (including Damien Hirst and Tracey Emin). Anyone who thinks modern art is crap should check out the canned faeces of controversial Italian artist Piero Manzoni for confirmation.

However, it's with its temporary exhibitions (for which there are always admission fees) that the Tate really shines. Shows on Andy Warhol and Matisse/Picasso in 2001 and 2002 were unrivalled. Another attraction is the view from the top-floor restaurant and café. The £1 audioguides are worthwhile for their descriptions of some of the works.

Millennium Bridge The Queen first opened London's so-called Millennium Bridge *(Map 6; w www.arup.com/millenniumbridge)* in June 2000 with all the pomp and ceremony befitting the first new crossing to span the Thames in more than a century. But as crowds flocked to watch, the bridge began to wobble so badly that the unsuspecting thrill-seekers had to clutch the rails and each other to keep from toppling over. It was unceremoniously closed three days later. After much hand-wringing, finger-pointing and additional millions the 'wobbly bridge' reopened some two years later. Despite its awkward arrival, the 320m-long bridge is a stunning addition to central London and provides a boon for travellers who can now walk directly from St Paul's Cathedral on the north side of the river to the Tate Modern gallery on the south, avoiding all the traffic and noise along the way. Esteemed – and ubiquitous – architect Norman Foster designed the 'blade of light', which looks spectacular when illuminated at night. (For more information see the boxed text 'The Norman & Richard Show' in the Facts about England chapter.)

The South Bank (Map 4) Twentieth-century planners weren't too kind to the area south of Waterloo Bridge. Although presenting the South Bank with a wealth – and a labyrinth – of cultural and arts venues like the Royal National Theatre and the National Film Theatre (see the Entertainment section), the architecture in which they were housed was indescribably ugly. They've been making amends of late; the South Bank is now home to the cherished London Eye, the Jubilee Gardens are being extended northwards and the area is booming like nowhere else in central London. The latest Norman Foster landmark, a futuristic glass egg designed to house the Greater London Authority (GLA) Headquarters, was unveiled here in mid-2002. Mayor Ken Livingstone, the principal tenant, originally labelled it a 'glass testicle' but has since revised his opinion.

Ad mogul Charles Saatchi plans to open a major new **contemporary art gallery** between the Tates in 2003. It will feature the controversial works of the 1990s Britart scene, which brought the likes of Damien Hirst and Tracey Emin to prominence. To give you an idea of Saatchi's taste: in mid-2002 national newspapers reported that *Self*, a £1m sculpture of artist Marc Quinn's head made with nine pints of his own blood, was thawed in a gory domestic meltdown when builders renovating the Saatchi home accidentally unplugged the fridge upon which it was mounted.

Hayward Gallery One of London's most important spaces for contemporary art, Hayward Gallery *(Map 4; ☎ 7928 3144; w www.hay-ward-gallery.org.uk; Belvedere Rd SE1; ⊖ Waterloo; admission prices vary)* is housed in an austere 1968 building that is loved and derided by Londoners in equal measure. Whichever camp you fall into, you'll agree that it makes an excellent hanging space for the blockbuster exhibitions held here.

The London Eye Right on the Thames, the British Airways London Eye *(Map 4; ☎ 0870 500 0600; w www.ba-londoneye.com; ⊖ Waterloo; adult/child £10.50/5; open 9am-10pm daily Apr-Oct, 10am-6pm Nov-Mar)* is the world's largest sightseeing wheel (for all sorts of technical reasons it can't be called a Ferris wheel) and certainly the most cherished of all London's millennium projects.

It is a thrilling experience to be in one of the 32 enclosed glass gondolas, enjoying views of some 25 miles (on rare clear days) across the capital. The 135m-tall wheel takes 30 minutes to rotate completely and it's best experienced at dusk.

Such is the wheel's popularity that, even though the opening hours keep extending, if you turn up without a ticket you might not get a ride; phone ahead or book online. To rock up and ride, you either have to arrive before opening to nab one of the few same-day tickets or run the gauntlet of the touts.

London Aquarium One of the largest in Europe, the London Aquarium *(Map 4; ☎ 7967 8000; w www.londonaquarium.co.uk; County Hall, Westminster Bridge Rd SE1; ⊖ Westminster or Waterloo; adult/child £8.75/5.25; open 10am-6pm daily)* has three levels of fish organised by geographical origin, none of which you'll see during school holidays when the place is stuffed to the gills with kiddies.

Lambeth (Maps 1 & 4) Lambeth is the district just south of Westminster Bridge, home to a few interesting museums and Lambeth Palace, the official residence to successive archbishops of Canterbury since the 12th century. You may have heard of it through the old music-hall song 'Doing the Lambeth Walk', which older generations will break into at the slightest encouragement. The Lambeth Walk is best described as a jaunting strut.

Imperial War Museum Housed in a striking building, the Imperial War Museum *(Map 1; ☎ 7416 5000; w www.iwm.org.uk; Lambeth*

LONDON

Rd SE1; ⊖ Lambeth North; admission free; open 10am-6pm daily) dates from 1815 and is capped by a copper dome.

Although there's plenty of military hardware on show, the main thrust of the sober exhibitions these days is the social cost of war, a point driven home by the disturbing **Holocaust Exhibition**. Opened in 2000, the exhibition uses artefacts and the recollections of survivors to tell the story of the Nazis and their deeds. Other exhibits cover topics such as the Blitz, the WWI Trench Experience and the work of the British secret services; there are also many temporary exhibitions.

Florence Nightingale Museum Attached to St Thomas's Hospital and celebrating the achievements of social campaigner and the world's most famous nurse is the Florence Nightingale Museum (*Map 4;* ☎ *7620 0374;* ⓦ *www.florence-nightingale.co.uk; 2 Lambeth Palace Rd SE1;* ⊖ *Westminster or Waterloo; adult/child £4.80/3.80; open 10am-5pm Mon-Fri, 11.30am-4.30pm Sat & Sun, last admission 1 hr before close)*, which recounts the story of 'the lady with the lamp' who led a team of nurses tending to the injured during the Crimean War. Upon returning to London she established a training school for nurses at this hospital in 1859. The small and thoughtful museum contains displays of personal mementos and other belongings.

Chelsea, South Kensington & Earl's Court

Much of west London could be classed as uptown; the residents of Kensington and Chelsea have the highest incomes of any London borough (shops and restaurants will presume you do too) and the area, like the Chelsea football team, is continental chic through and through. Thanks to the 1851 Great Exhibition, South Kensington is first and foremost museum land, boasting the Natural History, Science and Victoria & Albert Museums all on one road.

Further west, Earl's Court is lively and cosmopolitan, although less prosperous. It's particularly popular with travelling antipodeans and was once known as Kangaroo Valley.

Victoria & Albert (V&A) Museum (Map 7) A vast, rambling and wonderful museum of decorative art and design, the Victoria & Albert Museum (☎ *7942 2000;* ⓦ *www.vam .ac.uk; Cromwell Rd SW7;* ⊖ *South Kensington; admission free; open 10am-5.45pm Thur-Tues, 6.30pm-9.30pm Wed)* is part of Prince Albert's legacy to Londoners in the wake of the successful Great Exhibition of 1851.

It's a bit like the nation's attic, comprising four million objects collected over the years from Britain and around the globe. Spread over nearly 150 galleries, it houses the world's greatest collection of decorative arts including ancient Chinese ceramics, modernist architectural drawings, Korean bronze and Japanese swords, samples from William Morris' 19th-century Arts and Crafts movement, cartoons by Raphael, spellbinding Asian and Islamic art, Rodin sculptures, Elizabethan gowns and dresses straight from this year's Paris fashion shows, ancient jewellery, a 1930s' wireless set, an all-wooden Frank Lloyd Wright study, and a pair of Doc Martens. Yes, you'll need to plan. And that's without even considering the wonderful temporary exhibitions (prices vary) put on here.

Grab a free guide, choose a section and make a beeline for it. Alternatively, take one of the free introductory hour-long **guided tours**, available between 10.30am and 4.30pm.

Natural History Museum (Map 7) Kids – and most adults – will lose their minds at the Natural History Museum (☎ *7938 9123;*

Crystal Palace & the Great Exhibition

In 1851 Queen Victoria's consort, the German-born Prince Albert, organised a huge celebration of global technology in Hyde Park. The so-called Great Exhibition was held in a 7.5-hectare revolutionary iron-and-glass hothouse, a 'Crystal Palace' designed by gardener and architect Joseph Paxton. So successful was the exhibition – more than 2 million people flocked to see its more than 100,000 exhibits – that Albert arranged for the profits to be ploughed into building two permanent exhibitions, which today house the Science Museum and the Victoria & Albert Museum. The Crystal Palace itself was moved to Sydenham, where it burned down in 1936.

Craft stall, Covent Garden

Book market, South Bank

Tattoo studio, Camden

Notting Hill Carnival

Portobello Road Market

NEIL SETCHFIELD

Royal Opera House, Covent Garden

ELLIOT DANIEL

NEIL SETCHFIELD

The London Eye, South Bank

Canary Wharf, Docklands

COLIN DAVID SHAW

View of St Paul's Cathedral from the River Thames

W www.nhm.ac.uk; Cromwell Rd SW7; ⊖ South Kensington; admission free; open 10am-5.50pm Mon-Sat, 11am-5.50pm Sun), where the main collections are divided between adjoining Life and Earth Galleries. Where once the former was full of dusty glass cases of butterflies and stick insects, there are now wonderful interactive displays on themes such as Human Biology and Creepy Crawlies. Plus there's the crowd-pulling exhibition on mammals and dinosaurs, which includes animatronic movers and shakers such as the 4m-high Tyrannosaurus Rex.

The **Earth Galleries** are equally impressive. Enter from Exhibition Rd and you'll find yourself facing an escalator that slithers up and into a hollowed-out globe where two main exhibits – Earthquake and the Restless Surface – explain how wind, water, ice, gravity and life itself impact on the earth.

A new **Darwin Centre** – Phase I of which opened in late 2002 – showcases some 22 million zoological exhibits; it also serves as an education centre. Phase II of the centre, some years off, will focus on botanical and entomological exhibits.

Science Museum (Map 7) With seven floors of interactive and educational exhibits, the Science Museum (☎ 7942 4455; W www .sciencemuseum.org.uk; Exhibition Rd SW7; ⊖ South Kensington; admission free; open 10am-6pm daily) allows you to explore everything from the history of the Industrial Revolution to the exploration of space. There is something for all ages from vintage cars, old trains and antique aeroplanes to labour-saving devices for the home, a wind tunnel and flight simulator. The even more hi-tech extension, the **Wellcome Wing**, focuses on contemporary science and makes presentations on recent breakthroughs. There's also a 450-seat **IMAX cinema** (which will come in handy should someone make a decent film for this format).

Chelsea Physic Garden (Map 7) Established in 1673 to provide a means for students to study medicinal plants and healing, the Chelsea Physic Garden (☎ 7352 5646; W www.chelseaphysicgarden.co.uk; 66 Royal Hospital Rd SW3; ⊖ Sloane Square; adult/child £4/2; open noon-5pm Wed, 2pm-6pm Sun 7 Apr-26 Oct) is one of the oldest botanical gardens in Europe and contains many rare trees and plants. Opening hours are lim-ited because the grounds are still used for research and education; tours can be organised by appointment. Check out the website for special events during the year such as the Chelsea Flower Show in May and Snowdrop Days on the first two Sundays in February.

Royal Hospital Chelsea (Map 8) Designed by Christopher Wren, the Royal Hospital Chelsea (☎ 7881 5204; Royal Hospital Rd SW3; ⊖ Sloane Square; admission free; open 10am-noon & 2pm-4pm Mon-Sat, 2pm-4pm Sun) is a superb structure that was built in 1692 to provide shelter for ex-servicemen, which it has done since the reign of Charles II. Today it houses hundreds of war veterans known as Chelsea Pensioners, who are fondly regarded as a national treasure. As you wander around the grounds or inspect the elegant chapel you may see them in their winter blue coats or summer reds. The Chelsea Flower Show takes place in the hospital grounds in May.

Knightsbridge & Kensington

These are among London's poshest precincts and of particular interest to shoppers with lots of disposable funds. Knightsbridge is where you'll find some of London's best-known department stores, including Harrods and Harvey Nichols, while Kensington High St has a lively mix of chains and boutiques.

Kensington Palace (Map 3) Dating from 1605, Kensington Palace (☎ 7937 9561; W www.hrp.org.uk; Kensington Gardens W8; ⊖ High Street Kensington; adult/child £10/6.50; open 10am-5pm daily) was the birthplace of Queen Victoria in 1819 but is best known today as the last home of Princess Diana.

Hour-long tours take you around the surprisingly small **Staterooms**. A collection of Princess Di's dresses recently went on permanent display along with frocks and ceremonial gowns from HRH and her predecessors. There's an **audio tour**, included in the entry fee, if you want to explore on your own.

Kensington Gardens (Map 3) These royal gardens (open from dawn until dusk) are part of Kensington Palace but blend in almost seamlessly to Hyde Park. There's a splendid, contemporary art space, the **Serpentine Gallery** (☎ 7402 6075; W www.serpentinegallery.org; ⊖ Knightsbridge or Lancaster Gate; admission free; open 10am-6pm daily), beautifully located south of the lake. The **Sunken Garden**, near the palace, is at its prettiest in summer while tea in **The Orangery** is a pricey treat.

On the southern edge of the gardens, opposite the Royal Albert Hall, is the **Albert Memorial** (⊖ *South Kensington or Gloucester Road),* as over-the-top as the subject, Queen Victoria's German husband Albert (1819–61), was purportedly humble. The memorial was designed by George Gilbert Scott in 1872 but unveiled again in 1998 after an eight-year restoration project.

On the far side of the gardens is **Diana, Princess of Wales Memorial Playground,** an elaborate amusement park your kids will love.

Notting Hill

The status of the Notting Hill Carnival (in late August) reflects the multicultural appeal of this part of West London, into which West Indian immigrants moved in the 1950s. After decades of exploitation and strife, the community took off in the 1980s and the area is now a thriving, vibrant corner of central London. It's a lovely place to visit, although there are a lot more tourists since *that* eponymous and saccharine film. Portobello Road is the de facto centre (as opposed to Notting Hill Gate).

Bayswater, to the east, was neglected for centuries but is now mainly a fairly well-to-do residential area with Queensway as its main thoroughfare.

Hyde Park (Map 3)

At 145 hectares, Hyde Park *(Map 3; open 5.30am-midnight daily)* is central London's largest open space. Henry VIII expropriated it from the Church in 1536, when it became a hunting ground and later a venue for duels, executions and horse racing. The 1851 Great Exhibition was held here and during WWII it became an enormous potato field. These days, it serves as an occasional concert venue and a full-time green space for fun and frolics. There's boating on the Serpentine for the physically energetic or, near Marble Arch, there's **Speakers' Corner** for oratorical acrobats. These days, it's largely nutters and religious fanatics who maintain the tradition begun in 1872 as a response to rioting.

A plaque on the traffic island at Marble Arch indicates the spot where the infamous Tyburn Tree, a three-legged gallows, once stood. It is estimated that up to 50,000 people were executed here between 1300 and 1783, many having been dragged from the Tower of London.

A more soothing memorial – a fountain honouring Princess Diana – was at the time of writing planned to be in place beside the Serpentine by September 2003.

Marble Arch (Map 3) London's grandest bedsit – with a one-room flat inside – Marble Arch (⊖ *Marble Arch)* was designed by John Nash in 1827 as the entrance to Buckingham Palace. However, it was too small and unimposing for the job so was moved here in 1851.

Marylebone & Regent's Park

Increasingly hip Marylebone is home to several attractions from London's primo tourist trap Madame Tussaud's (the city's most popular sight) to the artistic treasure trove that is the Wallace Collection (relatively unknown). It leads to the haven that is Regent's Park.

Wallace Collection (Map 4) Arguably London's finest small gallery, the Wallace Collection (☎ *7935 0687;* w *www.the-wallace -collection.org.uk; Hertford House, Manchester Square W1;* ⊖ *Bond St; admission free; open 10am-5pm Mon-Sat, 2pm-5pm Sun)* comprises a wealth of 17th- and 18th-century European artefacts and art including works by Rubens, Titian, Rembrandt and Gainsborough, all housed in a splendid and sumptuously restored Italianate mansion.

Free guided tours take place daily; phone for the exact times.

Madame Tussaud's (Map 3) Unbelievably, Madame Tussaud's (☎ *0870 400 3000;* w *www.madame-tussauds.com; Marylebone Rd NW1;* ⊖ *Baker Street; adult/child including Planetarium £16.95/12.50; open 10am-5.30pm Mon-Fri, 9.30am-5.30pm Sat & Sun),* the outrageously overpriced and rigidly uninteresting collection of waxworks, lures in some 2.7 million visitors a year and is London's most popular paying attraction. To avoid the long queues (particularly in summer) arrive early in the morning or late in the afternoon, reserve your ticket or visit any of London's more worthy sights.

London Planetarium (Map 3) Attached to Madame Tussaud's (and included in the admission charge), the London Planetarium (w *www.madame-tussauds.com; adult/child*

£2.45/1.50; open 10am-5.30pm Mon-Fri, 9.30am-5.30pm Sat & Sun) presents a 15-minute star show projected onto the dome ceiling. It has galactic bits and bobs in the foyer to keep the kids occupied while you wait for the next screening.

Regent's Park (Map 2) A former royal hunting ground, Regent's Park (✜ Baker Street or Regent's Park) was designed by John Nash early in the 19th century, although what was actually laid out is only a fraction of the celebrated architect's grand plan. Nevertheless, it's a lovely space in the middle of the city – at once lively and serene, cosmopolitan and local – with football pitches, tennis courts and a boating lake. **Queen Mary's Gardens**, towards the south of the park, are the prettiest part of the gardens with spectacular roses in summer when the open-air theatre hosts performances of Shakespeare (call ✆ 7486 7905).

The **Islamic Cultural Centre and the London Central Mosque** (Map 1; ✆ 7724 3363; w www.islamiccultralcentre.co.uk; 146 Park Rd NW8; ✜ Wellington Road or Baker Street) is on the western fringe of the park and the zoo is to the north.

London Zoo (Map 2) Established in 1828 and one of the world's oldest, London Zoo (✆ 7722 3333; w www.londonzoo.co.uk; Regent's Park NW1; ✜ Camden Town; adult/child £11/8; open 10am-5.30pm daily Mar-Oct, 10am-4pm daily Nov-Feb) got into hot water because its historical buildings weren't conducive to animal comforts. In response, the zoo has embarked on a 10-year, £21-million project focusing on conservation, education and breeding programmes. All the same, you'll find this zoo as thrilling or upsetting as any other. Feeding times, reptile handling and the petting zoo are always popular.

NORTH LONDON

The northern reaches of central London stretch in a broad arc from St John's Wood in the west to Islington in the east. Camden Market and Hampstead Heath are among North London's most popular attractions, while Islington has good pubs and eateries and Upper St, in particular, is well worth a wander.

Euston & King's Cross

These aren't especially inviting areas and will be most familiar to users of the tube and any-

one taking a train to the north of England. If you're due to pass through King's Cross St Pancras, rise to the surface and check out St Pancras station, the pinnacle of the Victorian Gothic revival architecture.

British Library (Map 2) As the country's most expensive building – it opened in 1998 after 15 years of construction and £500 million in cost – it's only natural that the British Library (✆ 7412 7000; w www.bl.uk; 96 Euston Rd NW1; ✜ King's Cross St Pancras; admission free; open 9.30am-6pm Mon & Wed-Fri, 9.30am-8pm Tues, 9.30am-5pm Sat, 11am-5pm Sun) should come in for some stick. Most of it has been hurled at architect Colin St John Wilson's redbrick construction described by Prince Charles as a 'secret police building'.

Most of the complex is devoted to storage and scholarly research, but there are some public displays including the **John Ritblat Gallery**, a vast collection of rare and historical books spanning almost three millennia and every continent. It includes the Magna Carta (1215), Shakespeare's First Folio (1623) and original manuscripts from many of Britain's greatest authors. There's also a stamp collection and a hands-on exhibition relating to book production. For fans of facts, the library counts 186 miles of shelving and will have some 12 million volumes when it reaches its full capacity.

St John's Wood

Posh St John's Wood is where you'll find Lords, the address of world cricket. It will also be of interest to Beatles fans as 3 Abbey Rd is where the fab four recorded most of their albums, including *Abbey Road* (1969) itself, with its cover shot taken on the zebra crossing outside (Map 1).

Lord's Cricket Ground (Map 1) The next best thing to watching a test at Lord's Cricket Ground (✆ 7432 1033; w www.lords.org; St John's Wood Rd NW8; ✜ St John's Wood; adult/child £6.50/4.50; tours 10am, noon & 2pm daily Apr-Sept, noon & 2pm daily Oct-Mar when there's no play), dominated by a striking media centre resembling a clock radio, is the absorbingly anecdotal 90-minute tour of the ground and facilities. It takes in the famous Long Room, where members watch the games surrounded by portraits of cricket's

Dick Whittington

London's current mayor, Ken Livingstone, may be popular but it's unlikely he'll ever earn the respect and affection Londoners have for the 15th-century Lord Mayor Dick Whittington.

Legend has it that Dick, with his faithful feline in tow, was quitting town when he heard the bells of St Mary-le-Bow ringing out the message, 'Turn again, Whittington, thrice mayor of London'. Never one to ignore the advice of a talking bell, Dick returned to the city where he found fame and fortune as *four*-time mayor. A 19th-century plaque on Highgate Hill – near the hospital that bears his name – marks the spot where his fortunes turned.

great and good, and a museum featuring evocative memorabilia that will appeal to fans old and new.

Camden (Map 2)

Camden's popularity has grown out of all proportion in recent years, largely propelled by **Camden Market** (see the boxed text 'To Market, To Market' later), now London's most popular 'unticketed' tourist attraction with an estimated 10 million visitors a year. This was a working-class Irish and Greek enclave just two decades ago but has been largely gentrified since. Although there are really no outstanding pubs or restaurants, it's the Camden vibe that fans swear by. But if it hasn't already happened, Camden is at risk of choking on its own popularity.

Hampstead & Highgate

These quaint and well-heeled villages, perched on hills above central London, are home to an inordinate number of celebrities and intelligentsia. The villages are largely as they were laid out in the 18th century and boast close proximity to the vast Hampstead Heath, where it's as easy to forget you're in a big city as it is to get completely lost.

Hampstead Heath With its rolling woodlands and meadows, Hampstead Heath (✆ Hampstead, Gospel Oak or Hampstead Heath station) is a million miles away – well approximately four – from the city of London. A walk up Parliament Hill affords one of the most spectacular views of the city.

Kenwood House (☎ 8348 1286; Hampstead Lane NW3; ✆ Archway or Golders Green; admission free, tour adult/child £3.50/1.75; open 10am-6pm daily Apr-Sept, 10am-5pm Mar & Oct, 10am-4pm Nov-Feb) is a magnificent neoclassical mansion on the northern side of the heath. It has a wonderful collection of European art, including works by Gainsborough, Reynolds, Turner, Vermeer and Van Dyck, and there are weekend concerts by the lake in summer. There's also a pub-restaurant called the Brew House & Garden Café that opens for refreshments, snacks and light meals daily. From the station catch bus No 210.

The Heath also has several swimming ponds – for the strong and hardy – with separate ponds for single-sex and mixed bathing. Once you've worked up a thirst, that's *after* your swim, there are a couple of good pubs in the vicinity (see Pubs in the Entertainment section later).

Highgate Cemetery Most famous as the final resting place of Karl Marx and other notable mortals, Highgate Cemetery (☎ 8340 1834; Swain's Lane N6; ✆ Highgate; admission £1; eastern section open 10am-5pm Mon-Fri, 11am-5pm Sat & Sun Apr-Oct; 10am-4pm Mon-Fri, 11am-4pm Sat & Sun rest of yr) is set in 20 wonderfully wild and atmospheric hectares with absurdly over-decorated Victorian graves and sombre tombs.

The cemetery is divided into two parts. You can visit Marx on the maintained east side on your own but to visit the fantastically moody western section of this Victorian Valhalla you'll have to take a *tour* (adult/child £3/1; noon Mon-Fri, on the hour 11am-4pm Sat & Sun Apr-Oct; on the hour 11am-3pm Sat & Sun Nov-Mar).

Keats House (Map 1) The golden boy of the Romantic poets lived in this elegant Regency house (☎ 7435 2062; w www.keats house.org.uk; Wentworth Place, Keats Grove NW3; ✆ Hampstead) from 1818 to 1820 – until doctors advised him to move to sunnier climes – and penned some of his most famous works here. He wrote *Ode to a Nightingale* under a tree in the secluded garden although, unfortunately, the original tree has long since been replaced. Among the personal mementos are love letters and old manuscripts. Keats House was closed for maintenance at the time of research so call for details.

Freud Museum (Map 1) After fleeing Nazi-occupied Vienna in 1938, Sigmund Freud came to this house where he lived the last 18 months of his life. His daughter – a renowned child psychologist – lived in the house until she died in 1986, after which, and according to her wishes, it became the Freud Museum (☎ 7435 2002; w www.freud.org .uk; 20 Maresfield Gardens NW3; adult/child £4/2; open 12pm-5pm Wed-Sun). Along with Freud's original couch, the house is crammed with an extensive collection of books and artefacts, and commentary is provided with extracts from his writings. There's also footage of the pre-eminent doctor and his family, and a photograph showing how meticulously Freud tried to recreate his Viennese home in the unfamiliar surroundings of London.

EAST LONDON

The eastern reaches of central London are taken up by the East End – the London of old Hollywood films and Christmas pantomimes – and the sprawl of the Docklands, where the brand new sits alongside the old and decaying.

East End

The East End districts of Shoreditch, Hoxton, Spitalfields and Whitechapel may lie within walking distance of the City, but the change of pace and style is extraordinary. Traditionally this was working-class London, settled by immigrants, including Irish, French Huguenots, Bangladeshis and Jews, all of whom have left their mark. Run-down and neglected in the early 1980s, the East End is now looking up and pockets of it, like Hoxton, are being taken over by nouveau trendy. There are no major attractions to drag you into the East End but it's a good place to immerse yourself in modern, multicultural London.

Geffrye Museum (Map 1) These beautiful 18th-century almshouses were originally built to house the elderly poor, with funds bequeathed by Robert Geffrye, former Lord Mayor of London who made a mint on the slave trade. Today they house the Geffrye Museum (☎ 7739 9893; w www.geffrye-museum.org.uk; 136 Kingsland Rd E2; ⊖ Old Street then bus No 243; admission free; open 10am-5pm Tues-Sat, noon-5pm Sun), a delightfully engaging peek at British domestic interiors from Elizabethan times to the present day. There's a lovely walled herb garden, a design centre, shop and restaurant.

Docklands

The Port of London was once the world's greatest port, the hub of the British Empire

A Dickie Bird About Cockney

Cockneys are generally regarded as the cheeky, chappy, salt-of-the-earth, working-class East Enders born within earshot of the church bells of St Mary-le-Bow. Cockney rhyming slang was possibly developed by rogues here in the 19th century as a code to evade the attention of the newly formed police force.

The term is also sometimes, mistakenly, used to describe people speaking what is called Estuary English, in which 't's and 'h's are regularly discarded. The true cockney language replaces common nouns and verbs with rhyming phrases, whereby wife becomes 'trouble and strife' and so on. With familiarity, the actual rhyming word in some phrases gets dropped so the wife simply becomes trouble, 'loaf' (of bread) is used instead of the word head, 'china' (plate) means mate, 'on the dog' (and bone) is on the phone, while 'syrup' (of fig) is a wig.

You'll still hear conversations peppered with cockney phrases, although the slang has evolved considerably, often ridiculously, since its East End origins. You wouldn't Adam and Eve the number of new versions and sometimes even the locals don't have a Danny La Rue what's being said – and that's no word of a porky pie.

The cockney monarchs are the Pearly Kings and Queens, the sparkly spectacles who wear tens of thousands of studded buttons sewn into their clothes. A 19th-century barrow boy by the name of Henry Croft, keen to raise money for the poor, began sewing pearly buttons into his garments to attract attention. Others soon followed pearly suit and a tradition was born. Today's pearlies – often descendants of the originals – work for charities and gather at St Martin-in-the-Fields Church in Trafalgar Square in early October for their annual festival (w www.pearlies.co.uk) to sing songs, speak in slang, slap their thighs and pose for photographs.

and its enormous global trade. By the 19th century it was hard-pressed to cope with the quantity of cargo flowing through. It was pummelled by the Luftwaffe in WWII but managed to recover by the 1950s only to come unstuck when it couldn't adapt to changing technologies. From the 1960s strikes were rife, docks were closed, workers were laid off and most of the dockland area was left derelict.

Its topsy-turvy fortunes continued into the early 1980s when a rejuvenation programme was launched. New development was encouraged and the Docklands Light Railway (DLR) was built to link the area with the rest of London. But, within a decade, recession hit and the Docklands' bubble burst again – the flagship development of Canary Wharf was left towering forlornly over vacant buildings.

But its luck has turned again. The Docklands' Achilles heel, transportation, has been largely solved through expansion of the DLR and the building of the Jubilee Line tube extension. (Norman Foster's Jubilee Line Underground station is impressive.) Tenants are moving in, more buildings are going up and the area presents stark contrasts between the very old and the very new.

The new **Museum in Docklands** (☎ 7001 9800; w www.museumindocklands.org.uk; Hertsmere Rd, West India Quay E17; adult/ child £5/3; open 10am-6pm daily), housed in a heritage-listed warehouse, uses artefacts and multimedia displays to chart the history of the Docklands from Roman trading to its renewal in the twilight of the 20th century. It's a fascinating look through the Docklands window into Britain's fascinating past.

SOUTH LONDON

Glamorous Greenwich is the main attraction south of London's centre but you will also have fun exploring Brixton's colourful market or visiting the excellent Horniman Museum in Forest Hill.

Greenwich

Quaint and village-like, Greenwich (pronounced gren-itch) is a delightful place with a refreshing sense of space, splendid architecture and strong connections with the sea, science, sovereigns and time, which have earned it a place on Unesco's list of World Heritage Sites. A visit is a highlight of any trip to London and you should allow a day to do

it justice. All the great architects of the Enlightenment made their mark here, largely due to royal patronage, and there's an extraordinary cluster of classical buildings to explore.

The **TIC** (☎ 0870 608 2000, fax 8853 4607; 2 Cutty Sark Gardens SE10; DLR Cutty Sark; open 10am-5pm daily) has all the information you need on the area and sells the **Greenwich Passport ticket** (adult/child £12/2.50) covering admission to the Cutty Sark, National Maritime Museum and Royal Observatory.

Cutty Sark A famous Greenwich landmark, the Cutty Sark clipper (☎ 8858 3445; w www .cuttysark.org.uk; King William Walk; adult/ child £3.90/2.90; open 10am-5pm daily), at the top of King William Walk beside Greenwich Pier, was the fastest ship in the world when it was launched in 1869. It is the only surviving clipper, a kind that dominated the mid-19th-century trade in tea and wool.

Today you can stroll on its decks, admire the beautiful and ongoing restoration and descend into the hold to inspect maritime prints, paintings and the world's largest collection of ship figureheads.

Old Royal Naval College Walk south along King William Walk and you'll see the Old Royal Naval College (☎ 8858 2154; w www.greenwichfoundation.org.uk), Wren's magnificent example of monumental classical architecture (he planned it however, other illustrious architects later completed his grand design). Since the Royal Navy baled out in 1998, the buildings have largely been taken over by the University of Greenwich but you can still view the **chapel** and the fabulous **Painted Hall** (adult/child £5/free; open 10am-5pm Mon-Sat, 12.30pm-5pm Sun), which took artist Sir James Thornhill 19 years of hard graft to complete. It was here, in January 1806, that Admiral Nelson's body lay in state after the battle of Trafalgar until he was taken upriver by funeral barge for burial at St Paul's Cathedral.

National Maritime Museum Farther south along King William Walk, you'll come to the National Maritime Museum (☎ 8312 6565; w www.nmm.ac.uk; Romney Rd SE10; admission free; open 10am-5pm daily), a light and airy space housing a massive collection of marine paraphernalia arranged, in no particular order, to recount

LONDON

Britain's seafaring history. Exhibits range from interactive displays focusing on various marine themes to old-fashioned humdingers like Nelson's tunic complete with a hole from the bullet that killed him.

Queen's House Attached to the National Maritime Museum on its eastern side, the Palladian Queen's House (☎ 8858 4422; admission free; open 10am-5pm daily) was recently restored to something like Inigo Jones intended when he designed this place in 1616. It is a stunning exhibition venue, focusing on illustrious seafarers and historic Greenwich.

Royal Observatory In 1675 Charles II had the Royal Observatory (☎ 8858 4422; w www .rog.nmm.ac.uk; admission free; open 10am-5pm daily) built on a hill in the middle of Greenwich Park, intending that astronomy be used to establish longitude at sea.

The preserved rooms are intriguing and you can see the actual timepieces described in Dava Sobel's *Longitude*, the bestselling book about the fascinating quest to measure longitude.

In 1884 the Royal Observatory's contribution in solving the longitude riddle was acknowledged when an international conference designated Greenwich as the prime meridian of the world, and Greenwich Mean Time (GMT) became the universal measurement of standard time.

The globe here is divided between east and west and, by placing one foot either side of the meridian line, you can straddle the two hemispheres.

If you arrive just before lunch time, you will see a bright red ball climb the observatory's northeastern turret at 12.58pm and drop at 1pm; as it has every day since 1833, when it was introduced to allow the ships on the Thames to set their clocks. If you arrive just *after* lunch time, you can console yourself with superb views across London.

Fan Museum Apart from things nautical, Greenwich is also where you'll find the engaging Fan Museum (☎ 8305 1441; w www.fan-museum.org; 12 Croom's Hill SE10; DLR Greenwich; adult/child £3.50/2.50; open 11am-5pm Tues-Sat, noon-5pm Sun), housed in an 18th-century Georgian house and one of only two of its kind in the world. Only a fraction of the hand-held folding fans, collected from around the world and dating back to the 17th century, are on display at any one time, although there's always enough to stoke your enthusiasm and you'll find yourself eagerly exploring the history.

Getting There & Away Greenwich is now most easily reached on the DLR; Cutty Sark is the station closest to the TIC and most of the sights. There are fast, cheap trains from Charing Cross to Greenwich station (preferably Maze Hill) about every 15 minutes.

Alternatively, to get yourself in the mood, come by boat. **Thames River Services** (☎ 7930 4097; w www.westminsterpier.co.uk; adult/ child return £7.50/4) departs hourly from Westminster Pier (Map 4) and Greenwich, and the trip takes approximately 50 minutes.

Around Greenwich
Millennium Dome What was supposed to be the centrepiece of Britain's millennium celebrations – but turned into one of the biggest cultural disasters in the country's history – garnered almost as many newspaper column inches as punters when it opened. Of the relatively few people who visited the mix of exhibits, interactive technology and live shows under the world's biggest roof, most considered it 'enjoyable' at most. Not good enough for a project that cost close to £1 billion to erect. It gobbled up millions more as the government held on waiting for a white knight to save its white elephant. Help eventually came from a multinational consortium, which took out a 999-year lease on the Dome in 2002. Plans are to transform it into a 20,000-seater sports and music venue, surrounded by shops, offices, bars and parkland by 2005.

Eltham Palace A curious and compelling hybrid, Eltham Palace (☎ 8294 2548; Court Rd SE9; Rail Eltham; admission grounds only £3.60, grounds & house £6.20; open 10am-6pm Wed-Fri & Sun Apr-Sep, 10am-5pm Wed-Fri & Sun Oct, 10am-4pm Wed-Fri & Sun Nov-Mar) is a magnificent country home that was built by Stephen Courtauld (of the Courtauld Institute) in the Art Deco style of the 1930s. It also incorporates some features from the Tudor royal palace that was first built here in 1305 and abandoned in the 16th century. Run by English Heritage, the meticulously restored Art Deco interior incorporates the former Great Hall of the Palace (which was the second largest in the country) along with stunning features such as the enormous circular carpet with geometric shapes in the domed entrance hall.

Brixton (Map 1)

West Indian immigrants flocked to Brixton after WWII and infused the ramshackle area with Caribbean flavour. A generation or so later, economic decline, Margaret Thatcher and hostility between the police and black residents (who accounted for less than a third of the local population at the time) sparked several serious riots, which earned Brixton infamy around the world. The mood is decidedly upbeat these days, and the streets are full of vitality and verve. Despite gradual gentrification, Brixton retains its edge, and the partying is hardcore. The Caribbean charisma lingers as you'll hear from the boom boxes and see in the colourful market (see Shopping later in this chapter).

Forest Hill

Horniman Museum If you dig African art and sculpture – or haven't found what you're looking for elsewhere – get down to the Horniman Museum (☎ 8699 1872; **w** www .horniman.ac.uk; 100 London Rd SE23; ⊖ Forest Hill; admission free; open 10.30am-5.30pm Mon-Sat, 2pm-5.30pm Sun), an extraordinary little place, comprising the original collection of Frederick John Horniman, the son of a wealthy tea merchant. The main ethnographic hall in this specially built 1901 Art Nouveau building is given over to African Worlds, the first permanent gallery of African, Afro-Caribbean and Brazilian art and culture in Britain.

The Music Room houses a superb collection of instruments, another is devoted to nomadic life, while the small Living Waters Aquarium magnifies the life of a river as it heads towards the sea.

Turn left out of Forest Hill station along Devonshire Rd and then right along London Rd, and you'll see the Horniman on your right.

WEST LONDON
Kew Gardens

From 1759 botanists started rummaging around the world's gardens looking for specimens they could plant in the three-hectare plot known as the Royal Botanic Gardens at Kew (☎ 8332 5000, recorded message ☎ 8940 1171;

w www.rbgkew.org.uk; Kew Rd, Kew; ⊖ Kew Gardens; adult/child £5/2.50; open 9.30am-6.30pm Mon-Fri, 9.30am-7.30pm Sat & Sun). They never stopped collecting and now the gardens, which have bloomed to 120 hectares, provide the most comprehensive botanical collection on earth as well as a delightful pleasure garden for the people of London.

Anytime is a good time to visit these beautiful grounds although they are at their most picturesque in spring and summer, when weekends are normally chock-a-block. First-time visitors should board the **Kew Explorer** (adult/child £2.50/1.50), a hop-on hop-off road train that leaves from Victoria Gate – where you will enter from if you get the tube – and takes you around the gardens' main sights.

Its wonderful plants and trees aside – including the world's largest collection of orchids – Kew has all sorts of charms within its borders. Highlights include: the enormous **Palm House**, a hothouse of metal and curved sheets of glass that houses all sorts of exotic tropical greenery; the stunning **Princess of Wales Conservatory** housing plants in 10 different computer-controlled climatic zones – everything from a desert to a cloud forest; the redbrick 17th-century **Kew Palace** (closed for extensive renovations until 2004 at the earliest); the **Temperate House**, the world's largest ornamental glasshouse and home to its biggest indoor plant, the 18m Chilean Wine Palm; the **Marianne North Gallery**, full of the spirited 19th-century traveller's horticultural art; and the celebrated **Great Pagoda** designed by William Chambers in 1761. **The Orangery** near Hampton Court Palace has a restaurant, café and shop.

The gardens are easily reached by tube but, during summer, you might prefer to cadge a lift on a riverboat from the **Westminster Passenger Services Association** (☎ 7930 2062; **w** www.wpsa.co.uk; 1½ hrs; adult/child return £15/7.50), which runs boats several times daily departing from Westminster Pier from April to September.

Hampton Court Palace

Built by Cardinal Thomas Wolsey in 1514 but coaxed out of him by Henry VIII just before the chancellor fell from favour, Hampton Court (☎ 8781 9500; **w** www.hrp.org.uk; Hampton Court station; adult/child £10.50/7; open 9.30am-6pm Tues-Sun, 10.15am-6pm Mon mid-Mar–Oct; 9.30am-4.30pm Tues-Sun,

10.15am-4.30pm Mon Nov–mid-Mar) is the largest and grandest Tudor structure in England. It was already one of the most sophisticated palaces in Europe when, in the 17th century, King William and Queen Mary looked up the Yellow Pages and called in one 'Christopher Wren, architect' to build an extension. The result is a beautiful blend of Tudor and 'restrained baroque' architecture.

Steeped in history, the palace makes for an enthralling visit and you should set aside the best part of a day to savour it. At the ticket office by the main Trophy Gate, pick up a leaflet listing schedules for the themed guided tours led by historians bedecked in period clobber.

If you're in a rush, or have an aversion to guided tours, highlights include: **Henry VIII's State Apartments**, including the Great Hall with its spectacular hammer-beamed roof; the **Tudor Kitchens**, manned by 'servants'; and the **Renaissance Picture Gallery**. Try and spend some time in the superb gardens, which include a 300-year-old **maze**, a 17th-century **tennis court** and the **Great Vine** planted in 1768 and still producing grapes. It's purported to be the world's oldest vine although the wine growers of Slovenia's Maribor would have a thing or two to say about that.

Hampton Court Palace is 13 miles (21km) southwest from the centre of London and is easily reached by train from Waterloo via Hampton Court station. Alternatively, you can take the 3½-hour journey by riverboat (see Kew Gardens earlier).

Richmond Park
London's wildest park, Richmond Park spans more than 1000 hectares and is home to all sorts of wildlife, most notably herds of red and fallow deer. It's a terrific place for bird-watching, rambling and cycling.

To get there from the Richmond tube station, turn left along George St, left at the fork up Richmond Hill until you come to the main entrance of Richmond Gate.

Ham House
Sometimes referred to as a miniature Hampton Court, Ham House *(☎ 8940 1950; Ham, Richmond; ➔ Richmond, then bus No 371; admission gardens £2, house & gardens £6; house open 1pm-5pm Mon-Wed, Sat & Sun Apr-Oct, gardens open 11am-6pm Mon-Wed, Sat & Sun Apr-Oct)* was built in the 17th century. Now run by National Trust, it is best known for its lavish interiors including the Great Staircase, considered a magnificent example of Stuart woodworking. The grounds slope down to the Thames and the gardens are on their way to being restored to their original splendour.

Syon House
The London home of the Duke of Northumberland's family for more than four centuries, Syon House *(☎ 8560 0881; w www.syon park.co.uk; Syon Park, Brentford; rail Syon Lane; adult/child £6.95/5.95; open 11am-5pm Wed, Thur & Sun mid-March–Oct)* is a superb example of an English stately home. Henry VIII's coffin stopped here en route to Windsor in 1547; somehow the coffin burst open in the night and the house dogs were found gnawing at his remains. The house was remodelled in the 18th century and features a Robert Adam interior, oak panelling and many paintings from the likes of Gainsborough and Reynolds. The gardens, which face Kew Gardens across the river, were landscaped by Lancelot 'Capability' Brown.

ORGANISED TOURS
If you're short on time and big on company, the **Original London Sightseeing Tour** *(☎ 8877 1722)*, the **Big Bus Company** *(☎ 7233 9533)* and **London Pride Sightseeing** *(☎ 7520 2050)* offer tours of the main sights on hop-on hop-off double-decker buses. They're all expensive (£12.50 to £14 for adults, £5.50 to £7.50 for children) for the day and probably only worth getting if you're in town for a short stopover and want to strike some sights off your list (in which case you might want to check out the London Pass in Discounts earlier).

Convenient starting points are in Trafalgar Square in front of the National Gallery; in front of the Trocadero on Coventry St between Leicester Square and Piccadilly Circus; and in Wilton Gardens opposite Victoria station.

London Pride Sightseeing includes Docklands and Greenwich in one of its tours, while the Original London Sightseeing Tour has an express tour for those with limited time.

River trips are always recommended; see the Greenwich and Kew sections as well as Getting Around later in this chapter.

PLACES TO STAY
Wherever you stay in London, the cost of accommodation is going to put a serious dent in your travel funds, so you should weigh up

your options very carefully and decide whether centrality, comfort or affordability is paramount. At the lower end of the market, demand can outstrip supply so it's worth booking at least a couple of nights' lodgings before you arrive, particularly in July and August. If you're travelling solo, bear in mind that single rooms are scarce and most places are reluctant to let a double room – even during quiet periods – without adding a hefty surcharge or even charging the full rate.

Booking Offices
It's possible to make same-day accommodation bookings for free at most of the TICs. The **telephone bookings hotline** (☎ 7604 2890; open 8.30am-6pm Mon-Fri) charges £5 per booking. The **British Hotel Reservation Centre** (☎ 0800 282888; open 24hr) is on the main concourse of Victoria train station and doesn't charge for bookings.

The Youth Hostels Association (YHA) operates its own **central reservations service** (☎ 0870 870 8808; e lonres@yha.org.uk) provided you can give them at least two weeks' notice. Otherwise, they can provide information on availability but you'll have to book with the hostels directly.

If you want to stay in a B&B, bookings for a minimum of three days can be made free through **London Homestead Services** (☎ 8949 4455, fax 8549 5492; w www.lhslondon.com; Coombe Wood Rd, Kingston-upon-Thames KT2 7JY), which charges either 5% of the total or £5 per person.

London Bed & Breakfast Agency Ltd (☎ 7586 2768, fax 7586 6567; e stay@londonbb.com; 71 Fellows Rd, London NW3 3JY) specialises in central London stopovers with a minimum of two nights' stay and charges a £5 administration charge.

Places to Stay – Budget
Camping Camping is obviously not an option in central London although there are a few places within striking distance.

Abbey Wood Caravan Park (☎ 8311 7708, fax 8311 6007; Federation Rd SE2; Abbey Wood station; 2-person tent/caravan pitches £5/8 plus caravan club members/nonmembers per night £3/4.50; open year round), south of the river and east of Greenwich, has 360 pitches. Electricity costs £1.50.

Lee Valley Leisure Centre (☎ 8345 6666, fax 8804 4975; w www.leevalleypark.com;

Pickett's Lock Lane, Meridian Way N9; Edmonton Green Station, then bus W8; tent sites adult/child £5.35/2.25, electricity £2.30; open year round) is to the northeast and has more than 200 pitches for tents and caravans.

YHA/HI Hostels Central London's seven YHA hostels can get very crowded in summer, which is testament to their reliability and value. All of them take advance credit-card bookings by phone and will hold some beds for those who show up on the day (arrive early and be prepared to queue). They all offer 24-hour access, and most have facilities for self-catering and relatively cheap meals (eg, £3.50 for a large packed lunch, £4.70 for a three-course evening meal).

City of London (Map 4; ☎ 0870 5764, fax 0870 5765; e city@yha.org.uk; 36 Carter Lane EC4; ⊖ St Paul's; dorm beds £24) is an excellent facility (193 beds) that stands in the shadow of St Paul's Cathedral. Rooms have mainly two, three or four beds though there are a dozen rooms with five to eight beds. There's a licensed cafeteria but no kitchen. Although right in the centre of London, it's pretty quiet around here outside business hours.

Earl's Court (Map 7; ☎ 0870 770 5804, fax 0870 770 5805; e earlscourt@yha.org.uk; 38 Bolton Gardens SW5; ⊖ Earl's Court; dorm beds £19), with 159 beds, is a Victorian town house in a shabby, though lively, part of town. Rooms are mainly 10-bed dorms with communal showers. There's a café, a kitchen for self-catering and a small garden courtyard for summer barbecues. This is a good base for exploring Kensington's museums.

Hampstead Heath (☎ 0870 770 5846, fax 0870 770 5847; e hampstead@yha.org.uk; 4 Wellgarth Rd NW11; ⊖ Golders Green; dorm beds £20.40), with 200 beds, is perfect if you want easy access to the centre of London but value fresh air at the same time. There's a well-kept garden, the dormitories are comfortable and each room has a washbasin. There's a licensed café and a kitchen.

Holland House (Map 3; ☎ 0870 770 5866, fax 0870 770 5867; e hollandhouse@yha.org .uk; Holland Walk W8; ⊖ High Street Kensington; dorm beds £21), with 201 beds, is built into the Jacobean wing of Holland House and overlooks Holland Park. It's large, very busy and rather institutional, but the position can't be beaten. There's a café and kitchen, and breakfast is included.

Oxford St (Map 5; ☎ 0870 770 5984, fax 0870 770 5985; **e** oxfordst@yha.org.uk; 14 Noel St W1; ⊖ Oxford Circus; beds in 3- or 4-bed dorms £22, twin rooms per person £22), the most central of the hostels, is basic, clean and welcoming. There's a large kitchen but no meals are served apart from a packed breakfast. Most of the 75 beds are twins.

Rotherhithe (Map 1; ☎ 0870 770 6010, fax 0870 770 6011; **e** rotherhithe@yha.org.uk; 20 Salter Rd SE16; ⊖ Rotherhithe; dorm beds £23.50), YHA's flagship London hostel, is right by the River Thames and the perfect choice for anyone keen on spending time in historical Greenwich who doesn't mind being a little isolated. There are 320 rooms, most of which have four or six beds, though there are also 22 doubles (four of them adapted for disabled visitors); all have an en suite. There's a bar and restaurant, as well as kitchen facilities and a laundry. Rates include breakfast.

St Pancras (Map 2; ☎ 0870 770 6044, fax 0870 770 6045; **e** stpancras@yha.org.uk; 79-81 Euston Rd NW1; ⊖ King's Cross St Pancras; dorm beds £23.50, twin/premium rooms per person £25/26.50) is a central place with 152 beds. The area itself isn't great, but the hostel is modern, with kitchen, restaurant, lockers, cycle shed and lounge, and it's in the hub of London's transport links.

Independent Hostels London's independent hostels tend to be more relaxed and cheaper than the YHA ones though standards can be pretty low; some places are downright grotty.

Most hostels have at least three or four bunk beds jammed into each small room, a kitchen and some kind of lounge. Some have budget restaurants and a bar attached. Be careful with your possessions and deposit your valuables in the office safe, safe-deposit box or secure locker if provided. If you find a hostel with dorm beds for less than say £12, check that you have access to the fire escapes.

Ashlee House (Map 2; ☎ 7833 9400, fax 7833 9677; **w** www.ashleehouse.co.uk; 261-265 Gray's Inn Rd WC1; ⊖ King's Cross St Pancras; dorm beds low/high season from £13/15, singles £34/36, twins per room £44/48) is friendly and well maintained, on three floors close to King's Cross station.

Barmy Badger Backpackers (Map 7; ☎ /fax 7370 5213; **e** barmy_badger.b@virgin.net; 17 Longridge Rd SW5; ⊖ Earl's Court; dorm beds from £14, twins with/without facilities £34/32)

is a basic dormitory with dorm beds, and rates include breakfast. There's a big kitchen and safe-deposit boxes.

The Generator (Map 2; ☎ 7388 7666, fax 7388 7644; **w** www.the-generator.co.uk; Compton Place, 37 Tavistock Place WC1; ⊖ Russell Square; beds in 7- or 8-bed dorm £15-20, in 3- to 6-bed dorm £19-22, singles £38, twins £45-48) is one of the liveliest budget options in central London and the futuristic decor looks like an updated set from Terry Gilliam's film Brazil. Along with 207 rooms (830 beds), it has flirtatious staff and a bar that stays open until 2am – but the two don't go together. There's also a pool, Internet access, safe-deposit boxes and a large eating area but no kitchen. All prices include breakfast.

International Students House (Map 2; ☎ 7631 8300, fax 7631 8315; **w** www.ish.org .uk; 229 Great Portland St W1; ⊖ Great Portland Street; beds in 8-bed dorm £10, singles with washbasin £30, singles/doubles with bath £30/47), a Marylebone hostel, feels more like a university hall of residence. The single and double rooms are ordinary but clean, and there are excellent facilities and a friendly, relaxed atmosphere. It's open year round. The cheapskates in the dorms don't get breakfast included but private occupants do.

St Christopher's Village (Map 6; ☎ 7407 1856, fax 7403 7715; **w** www.st-christophers .co.uk; 163 Borough High St SE1; ⊖ Borough; dorm beds from £14) is the flagship of a chain of hostels that has gained a reputation in recent years for being cheap and reliable, fun and relaxed. The empire is expanding and it now has hostels at Camden, Shepherd's Bush, Greenwich, and three along this street in Southbank. The facilities at this bustling place, which has 164 beds, include a sauna, solarium and hot tub. The same people own the Belushi's chain of boisterous bars, and you can get a Beds & Bars Privilege Card that entitles you to discounts at all of their venues.

Student Accommodation If you don't want to bunk and can't afford a hotel room of your own, consider contacting university halls of residence, which often let rooms to nonstudents during the holidays, usually from the end of June to mid-September and sometimes over the Easter break. They're a bit more expensive than the hostels, but at least you're assured of a private box, although you'll probably still have to share facilities.

University catering is usually reasonable and includes bars, self-service cafés, take-away places and restaurants. Full-board, half-board, B&B and self-catering options are usually available.

The **London School of Economics and Political Science** (Map 5; ☎ 7955 7370; Room B508, Page Building, Houghton St, London WC2A 2AE) lets half a dozen of its halls in summer and sometimes during the Easter break. These include the following: **Carr-Saunders Hall** (Map 4; ☎ 7323 9712, fax 7580 4718; 18-24 Fitzroy St W1; ✪ Warren Street; singles/doubles £27/46), well located, recently refurbished and rates include breakfast; **Bankside Residence** (Map 6; ☎ 7633 9877; 24 Sumner St SE1; ✪ Southwark or Blackfriars; beds in 4-bed dorm £20-35, quads £80), in an enviable location near the Globe Theatre and Tate Modern; and **Passfield Hall** (Map 2; ☎ 7387 3584, fax 7387 0419; 1-7 Endsleigh Place WC1; ✪ Euston; singles/twins/triples £25/46/60), comprising 10 late-Georgian houses in the heart of Bloomsbury.

Other halls of residence that are let outside term-time include: **Goldsmid House** (Map 4; ☎ 7493 8911, fax 7491 0586; 36 North Row W1; ✪ Marble Arch; singles/twins £16/24; available mid-June–mid-Sept), centrally located with 10 singles and 120 twins; **John Adams Hall** (Map 2; ☎ 7387 4086, fax 7383 0164; e jah@ioe.ac.uk; 15-23 Endsleigh St WC1; ✪ Euston Square; singles/doubles from £24/42; open Easter, July-Sept), quite a grand residence in a row of Georgian houses; and **Finsbury Residences** (Map 1; ☎ 7040 8811; 15 Bastwick St EC1; ✪ Barbican or Old Street; singles/twins/doubles all year except Christmas £32/50/60, cheaper rooms per person 24 June-22 Sept singles/twins £21/18), two modern halls belonging to the City University. There are no cooking facilities at this residence.

YMCAs There are 29 YMCAs (accommodating men and women) in the London and wider London area. **YMCA England** (☎ 8520 5599; w www.ymca.org.uk; 640 Forest Rd E17) can supply you with a list of all its hostels but not whether there's room at the inns or not. YMCAs are popular and you may have to book well in advance to get a room.

Barbican YMCA (Map 6; ☎ 7628 0697, fax 7638 2420; w www.barbicanymca.com; 2 Fann St EC2; ✪ Barbican; singles/doubles per night £26/44, per week £165/270), just a hop

and skip from the Barbican Centre, has more than 200 rooms and normally accommodates long-term stayers. Room rates include breakfast and evening meals.

Indian Student YMCA (Map 4; ☎ 7387 0411, fax 7383 4735; w www.indianymca.org; 41 Fitzroy Square W1; ✪ Warren Street; singles/doubles £33/46, en-suite doubles £52) is a characteristic slice of Indian life right down to the excellent – and lukewarm – food and baffling bureaucracy. Room rates include breakfast and evening meals.

B&Bs, Guesthouses & Hotels Brace yourself: anything below £35/55 for a single/double with shared facilities and below £45/65 with private bathroom is considered 'budget' in London. What's more, these prices can jump by 25% or more between July and September, when it is strongly recommended that you book ahead or be left with the dregs. According to demand, prices following can vary quite a bit so don't take them as gospel. On the flip side, at quiet times, it's always worth sniffing around for special offers. You'll quickly tire of the stodgy cooked breakfasts so consider negotiating a rate sans the calories. Bear in mind that the managers at most budget B&Bs recoil at the sight of credit cards.

Pimlico & Victoria (Map 8) Victoria isn't the most attractive part of town although you'll be close to the action and the budget accommodation is generally better value than in Earl's Court. Pimlico is more residential and is convenient for Tate Britain at Millbank.

Luna & Simone Hotel (☎ 7834 5897, fax 7828 2474; w www.lunasimonehotel.com; 47/49 Belgrave Rd SW1; ✪ Victoria; standard singles/doubles from £35/50; en-suite doubles from £60) is a central, spotlessly clean and comfortable place, the best among many on this street. A full English breakfast is included and there are free storage facilities if you want to leave bags while travelling. If all of London's budget hotels were like this, we would all be happy campers. Or, not.

Brindle House Hotel (☎ 7828 0057, fax 7931 8805; w www.brindlehousehotel.co.uk; 1 Warwick Place North SW1; ✪ Victoria; standard singles/doubles £35/48, en-suite singles/doubles/triples/quads £45/60/75/89) is in a renovated old building in a quiet street; the rooms are small but clean.

Romany House Hotel (☎ 7834 5553, fax 7834 0495; 35 Longmore St SW1; ⊖ Victoria; standard singles/doubles from £30/40) is partly built into a 15th-century cottage that boasts tales of highwaymen. You'll share a bathroom but breakfasts are good.

Bloomsbury Bloomsbury is very convenient, especially for the West End and the British Museum. There are lots of places on Gower and North Gower Sts.

Hotel Cavendish (Map 4; ☎ 7636 9079, fax 7580 3609; w www.hotelcavendish.com; 75 Gower St WC1; ⊖ Goodge Street; singles/ doubles from £38/48) is a clean and pleasant family-run place, where rates include breakfast. If the Cavendish is full, you'll be referred to its sister hotel **Jesmond Hotel**, nearby, where rates and standards are similar.

Morgan Hotel (Map 5; ☎ 7636 3735, fax 7636 3045; 24 & 40 Bloomsbury St WC1; ⊖ Tottenham Court Road; singles/doubles £60/88) is a homely, slightly shabby, family-run establishment with 20 small, pleasant rooms and big apartment-style suites in a nearby annexe.

King's Cross & St Pancras The only reason to stay in this area is its convenience to tube and mainline train stations.

Alhambra Hotel (Map 2; ☎ 7837 9575, fax 7916 2476; w www.alhambrahotel.com; 17-19 Argyle St WC1; ⊖ King's Cross St Pancras; standard singles/doubles/triples £32/45/65, en-suite singles/doubles/triples/quads £43/50/ 72/90) is the best budget option around these parts. It has 55 simple and spotlessly clean rooms and a warm welcome.

Southwark (Map 4) The former home of the Greater London Council, County Hall is now home to one of the many chain hotels cropping up south of the river.

County Hall Travel Inn Capital (☎ 7902 1600, fax 7902 1619; w www.travelinn.co.uk; Belvedere Rd SE1; ⊖ Waterloo; rooms for up to 2 adults & 2 children £69.95) is one of those one-price, one-room deals. It's fairly bare bones but the rooms are large and reasonable.

Earl's Court (Map 7) Earl's Court is not really within walking distance of many places of interest but the tube station is a busy interchange, so getting around is easy and it's got a holiday atmosphere with lots of transients.

Regency Court Hotel (☎ 7244 6615; e regencycourt@hotmail.com; 14 Penywern Rd SW5; ⊖ Earl's Court; dorm beds from £18, singles £35-45, doubles £50-60, triples £65-75) has undergone a much-needed renovation and its 15 bright rooms all have en-suite facilities.

York House Hotel (☎ 7373 7519, fax 7370 4641; 27-28 Philbeach Gardens SW5; ⊖ Earl's Court; standard singles/doubles/triples/quads £34/54/64/78, en-suite singles/doubles/triples/ quads £47/73/86/95) is good value for what and where it is – on a quiet crescent. The service is courteous and the welcome warm.

Merlyn Court Hotel (☎ 7370 1640, fax 7370 4986; 2 Barkston Gardens SW5; ⊖ Earl's Court; standard singles/doubles/triples/quads £35/55/65/70, en-suite singles/doubles/triples/ quads £45/70/75/80) is an unpretentious place with a polite and social atmosphere and a lovely location close to the tube. Chance your arm negotiating in the off-peak.

Holland Park (Map 3) Holland Park is a quiet, leafy district that is convenient for Notting Hill.

Kensington Guesthouse (☎ 7229 9233, fax 7221 1077; w www.hotellondon.co.uk; 72 Holland Park Avenue W11; ⊖ Holland Park; standard twin £60, en-suite twin/triples/quads £75/85/95) gets the thumbs up from several readers. All rooms have cooking facilities.

Bayswater & Paddington (Map 3) Bayswater is an extremely convenient location though some of the streets immediately to the west of Queensway, which has a decent selection of restaurants, are pretty grim. Scruffy Paddington has lots of cheap hotels and it's a good transit location.

Royal Hotel (☎ 7229 7225; 43 Queensborough Terrace; ⊖ Bayswater; standard singles/ doubles/triples £36/45/52, triples/quads with shared facilities £40/48) is halfway between a backpackers and a guesthouse. If you're staying for a week and paying in advance, you'll get a night free.

Garden Court Hotel (☎ 7229 2553, fax 7727 2749; w www.gardencourthotel.co.uk; 30-31 Kensington Gardens Square W2; ⊖ Bayswater; standard singles/doubles £39/ 58, en-suite singles/doubles £58/88) is one of London's best budget options although it barely squeezes into this category. It is cobbled from two 19th-century town houses and overlooks an attractive Victorian square. The same friendly family has run it for aeons and all of its 34 rooms have a phone and TV.

Norfolk Court & St David's Hotel (☎ 7723 4963, fax 7402 9061; **w** www.stdavidshotels .com; 16-20 Norfolk Square W2; ⊖ Paddington; standard singles/doubles/triples £39/59/ 70, en-suite singles/doubles/triples £49/69/ 80) is right in the centre of the action. They really cram the beds in here, leaving hardly enough room to swing the proverbial moggy but the rooms are clean, the breakfasts generous and the staff friendly.

Balmoral House Hotel (☎ 7723 7445, fax 7402 0118; 156 & 157 Sussex Gardens W2; ⊖ Paddington; standard singles £35, en-suite singles/doubles £45/65) is immaculate and comfortable although they've gone totally over the top with the room decor (not for light sleepers). There are two properties directly opposite one another on a street lined with small hotels and, unfortunately, lots of traffic.

Europa House Hotel (☎ 7723 7343, fax 7224 9331; **w** www.europahousehotel.com; 151 Sussex Gardens; ⊖ Paddington; en-suite singles/doubles £35/52) is another excellent choice, where you're always assured a warm welcome (something not as common as you'd think at small London hotels). All rooms have TV and phone.

Marylebone (Map 3) Increasingly hip and groovy Marylebone is central and characterised by graceful Georgian squares and bustling high streets.

Glynne Court Hotel (☎ 7723 4613, fax 7724 2071; 41 Great Cumberland Place W1; ⊖ Marble Arch; singles/doubles from £50/60) is fairly typical for this price range and location. It has 15 rooms, all with TV and phone.

Places to Stay – Mid-Range

Pimlico & Victoria (Map 8) Comfortable, clean and convivial, the **Winchester Hotel** (☎ 7828 2972, fax 7828 5191; **w** www.win chester-hotel.net; 17 Belgrave Rd SW1; ⊖ Victoria; doubles from £85) is good value for the area. Rooms are en suite and have TVs.

Morgan House (☎ 7730 2384, fax 7730 8842; **w** www.morganhouse.co.uk; 120 Ebury St SW1; ⊖ Victoria; standard singles/doubles £42/62, en-suite singles/doubles £68/80) is owned by the same people who run the nearby Woodville House but the rooms are brighter and more cosy here. There are also many more places to stay on this street.

Windermere Hotel (☎ 7834 5163, fax 7630 8831; **w** www.windermere-hotel.co.uk; 142-144 Warwick Way SW1; ⊖ Victoria; standard singles £69, en-suite singles/doubles £84/89) has 22 small and distinctive rooms in a sparkling white mid-Victorian town house. It also has a small restaurant.

Covent Garden (Map 5) Nothing could be more central than Covent Garden, although if you're not contributing to the late-night racket it could come between you and your zzz.

Fielding Hotel (☎ 7836 8305, fax 7497 0064; **w** www.the-fielding-hotel.co.uk; 4 Broad Court, Bow St WC2; ⊖ Covent Garden; singles/doubles from £76/100), on a pedestrianised street a block away from the Royal Opera House, is clean, well run and remarkably good value for the locale. All rooms have private bathroom, TV and phone.

Bloomsbury Tucked away in leafy Cartwright Gardens (Map 2) to the north of Russell Square and within walking distance of the West End, you'll find some of London's best-value hotels. The lodgings on Gower St (Map 4) are also pretty good value if you're sensitive to traffic noise.

Jenkins Hotel (Map 2; ☎ 7387 2067, fax 7383 3139; **w** www.jenkinshotel.demon.co.uk; 45 Cartwright Gardens WC1; ⊖ Russell Square; standard singles £52, en-suite singles/ doubles £72/85) is a smoke-free zone and has pretty rooms with washbasin, TV, phone and fridge. The rooms are small but the welcome is huge. All prices include breakfast, which you are welcome to work off on the tennis courts across the road.

Crescent Hotel (Map 2; ☎ 7387 1515, fax 7383 2054; **w** www.crescenthoteloflondon .com, 49-50 Cartwright Gardens WC1; ⊖ Russell Square; standard singles from £45, en-suite singles/doubles/triples/quads from £72/87/ 97/106) is a friendly, family-owned operation, maintained at a very high standard.

Arran House Hotel (Map 4; ☎ 7636 2186, fax 7436 5328; 77-79 Gower St WC1; ⊖ Goodge Street; standard singles/doubles/triples £45/ 57/75, en-suite singles/doubles/triples £55/ 80/98) is a welcoming place with laundry facilities and a lovely garden. Prices include breakfast. The front rooms are soundproofed and all have TV and phone.

Ridgemount Hotel (Map 4; ☎ 7636 1141, fax 7636 2558; **w** www.ridgemounthotel.co.uk;

65-67 Gower St WC1; ⊖ Goodge Street; standard singles/doubles £33/50, en-suite singles/doubles from £45/65), an old-fashioned place, offers a warmth and consideration you don't come across very often in the city. Rates include breakfast and there's a laundry.

Haddon Hall (Map 4; ☎ 7636 2474, fax 7580 4527; W www.haddonhallhotel.demon.co.uk; 39 Bedford Place WC1; ⊖ Russell Square or Holborn; standard singles/doubles £50/66, en-suite singles/doubles £66/90) is hushed and well maintained.

St Margaret's Hotel (Map 4; ☎ 7636 4277, fax 7323 3066; W www.stmargaretshotel.co.uk; 26 Bedford Place WC1; ⊖ Russell Square or Holborn; standard singles/doubles £51.50/63, en-suite doubles £98) is an exceedingly friendly Italian family-run hotel in a classic Georgian town house. It's not as good as 'classic Georgian' suggests although the rooms are clean, spacious and well furnished.

Southwark Spurred on by gentrification south of the Thames as well as by Tate Modern, a few chain hotels have appeared.

Holiday Inn Express Southwark (Map 4; ☎ 7401 2525, fax 7401 3322; W www.sixcontinentalhotels.com/h/d/Ex/hd/londsw; 103-109 Southwark St SE1; ⊖ Southwark; rooms £95) is perfect if you want to be anonymous for the length of your stay – rooms are functional.

Mercure Hotel London City Bankside (Map 6; ☎ 7902 0808, fax 7902 0810; W www.mercure.com; 75-79 Southwark St SE1; ⊖ Southwark; singles/doubles £140/160), an outpost of the French mid-range hotel chain, has comfortable, modern rooms that will appeal to business travellers (and sexy French accents that might appeal to everyone else). Ask about special packages for rooms; breakfast is a non-negotiable £12.

Earl's Court (Map 7) Positioned in a lovely spot, **Amsterdam Hotel** (☎ 7370 2814, fax 7244 7608; W www.amsterdam-hotel.com; 7 Trebovir Rd SW5; ⊖ Earl's Court; en-suite singles/doubles from £78/88) has a plant-filled foyer and wicker furniture. Rooms – including family versions and suites – are lovely and large. There's free Internet access and coffee, and you get the run of a soothing garden patio.

Rushmore Hotel (☎ 7370 3839, fax 7370 0274; W www.rushmore.activehotels.com; 11 Trebovir Road SW5; ⊖ Earl's Court; en-suite singles/doubles from £61/82) has oodles of personality and provides good value for this category (and could charge more). Individually decorated rooms are comfy and large.

Philbeach Hotel (☎ 7373 1244, fax 7244 0149; W www.philbeachhotel.freeserve.co.uk; 30-31 Philbeach Gardens; ⊖ Earl's Court; standard singles/doubles from £55/70; en-suite singles/doubles £65/90), in a pleasant, quiet side street, is London's largest pink hotel, popular with both gays and lesbians. **Wilde about Oscar** is a lovely conservatory bar and restaurant in the hotel premises.

Chelsea & South Kensington (Map 7)
Classy Chelsea and 'South Ken' offer easy access to the museums and some of London's most fashionable shopping.

Annandale House Hotel (☎ 7730 5051, fax 7730 2727; W www.annandale-hotel.co.uk; Sloane Gardens SW1; ⊖ Sloane Square; standard singles/doubles £60/95, en-suite singles/doubles £70/120) is a discreet, traditional hotel just south of Sloane Square and a good choice for light sleepers.

Hotel 167 (☎ 7373 0672, fax 7373 3360; W www.hotel167.com; 167 Old Brompton Rd SW5; ⊖ Gloucester Road; en-suite singles/doubles from £72/90) is a small, stylish hotel with great decor and a cheery atmosphere.

Swiss House Hotel (☎ 7373 2769, fax 7373 4983; W www.swiss-hh.demon.co.uk; 171 Old Brompton Rd SW5; ⊖ Gloucester Road; standard singles £51, en-suite singles/doubles from £71/89), clean and welcoming, has something of a country feel about it. It's good value, rooms are large and there's one single with shower and detached (but private) loo for £51.

Five Sumner Place (☎ 7584 7586, fax 7823 9962; W www.sumnerplace.com; 5 Sumner Place SW7; ⊖ South Kensington; singles/doubles from £85/130), on a quiet leafy road just off Old Brompton Rd, is restful, refined and elegant. It has 13 well-equipped rooms (any room with a drinks cabinet is 'well-equipped') and there's an attractive conservatory and courtyard garden.

Gainsborough Hotel (☎ 7957 0000, fax 7957 0001; W www.eeh.co.uk; 7-11 Queensberry Place SW7; singles/doubles from £67/120) is an outstanding hotel that combines Victorian grace, country manor charm and modern luxury. The same people own the equally elegant **Gallery Hotel** (☎ 7915 0000, fax 7915 4400; W www.eeh.co.uk; 8-10 Queensberry Place SW7; doubles £130).

Amber Hotel (☎ 7373 8666, fax 7835 1194; 101 Lexham Gardens W8; ❸ Earl's Court; singles/doubles £45/90) is good value for its location, halfway between Kensington and Earl's Court. Rates include breakfast.

Kensington (Map 3) These hotels are well placed for Kensington Gardens, Notting Hill and Kensington High St.

Vicarage Hotel (☎ 7229 4030, fax 7792 5989; W www.londonvicaragehotel.com; 10 Vicarage Gate W8; ❸ High Street Kensington; standard singles/doubles £46/76, en-suite doubles £100), pleasant and well kept, has good showers and large rooms in an impressive Victorian house. Rooms are spread over five floors but, heavy packers beware, there's no lift.

Abbey House (☎ 7727 2594, fax 7727 1873; W www.abbeyhousekensington.com; 11 Vicarage Gate W8; ❸ High Street Kensington; standard singles/doubles/triples/quads £45/74/85/100), in an original Victorian house, is outstandingly good value for the money. The floral motif may be a little overdone but the rooms are cosy and the standards are high. Rates include English breakfast.

Bayswater, Paddington & Notting Hill (Map 3) Bayswater is residential and convenient for busy Queensway. Though central, Paddington is a bit scruffy. Notting Hill is relatively expensive but has lots of good bars and restaurants.

Pavilion Hotel (☎ 7262 0905, fax 7262 1324; W www.msi.com.mt/pavilion; 34-36 Sussex Gardens W2; ❸ Paddington; singles/doubles from £60/100) has 'Fashion, Glam & Rock 'n' Roll' as its motto so if you like to cap off your holiday by throwing a TV out the window, this could be for you. There are 30 individually themed rooms (Moorish, 1970s, all-red) although it's not for B-list.

Inverness Court Hotel (☎ 7229 1444, fax 7706 4240; W www.cghotels.com; Inverness Terrace W2; ❸ Queensway; singles/doubles £84/108) is an impressive property that was commissioned by Edward VII for his 'confidante' (ie, bit on the side), the actress Lillie Langtry, and comes complete with a private theatre, now the cocktail bar. The panelled walls, stained glass and huge open fires of the public areas give it a Gothic feel but most of the 183 rooms – some of which overlook Hyde Park – are modern and pretty ordinary although the atmosphere is pleasantly kooky.

Gate Hotel (☎ 7221 0707, fax 7221 9128; 6 Portobello Rd W11; ❸ Notting Hill Gate; singles/doubles from £45/65) is an old town house with classic frilly English decor, lovely floral window boxes and snug rooms.

Marylebone (Map 3) These three are all within walking distance of Hyde Park (and staggering distance from the West End nightlife).

Edward Lear Hotel (☎ 7402 5401, fax 7706 3766; W www.edlear.com; 28-30 Seymour St W1; ❸ Marble Arch; standard singles/doubles from £48/68, en-suite singles/doubles from £75/93) was once the home of the famous Victorian painter and limerick writer. The rooms in this small, comfortable place have satellite TV and there's also free Internet access in the lounge.

Bryanston Court Hotel (☎ 7262 3141, fax 7262 7248; W www.bryanstonhotel.com; 56-60 Great Cumberland Place W1; ❸ Marble Arch; singles/doubles £95/120) has the atmosphere of an exclusive club, with leather armchairs, sepia-toned lighting and a formal feel.

Wigmore Court Hotel (☎ 7935 0928, fax 7487 4254; W www.wigmore-court-hotel.co.uk; 23 Gloucester Place W1; ❸ Marble Arch; standard singles/doubles £48/70, en-suite singles/doubles £58/95) has over-the-top decor (pink, pink, pink) but is well organised and guests have access to a kitchen and self-service laundry. On the down side, there's no lift and the reception is understaffed.

Hampstead A lovely place to stay is the **Hampstead Village Guesthouse** (☎ 7439 8679, fax 7794 0254; W www.hampsteadguest house.com; 2 Kemplay Road NW3; ❸ Hampstead; standard singles/doubles £54/72, en-suite singles/doubles £66/84), with rustic and antique decor and furnishing, comfy beds and a delightful back garden in which you can enjoy a cooked breakfast (if you pay the extra £7). There's also a studio flat, which can accommodate up to five people.

Places to Stay – Top End
With a couple of exceptions, you won't get a double in this section for less than £150.

Bloomsbury (Map 4) Pretty and polished, cool and restrained, the **Academy Hotel** (☎ 7631 4115, fax 6636 3442, W www.etontown house.com; 17-25 Gower St WC1; ❸ Goodge

Street; doubles from £136) is convenient for the British Museum. Though the street is noisy, double glazing protects light sleepers.

Victoria (Map 4) Rubens at the Palace (Map 4; ☎ 7834 6600, fax 7233 6037; e reservations@rubens.redcarnationhotels.com; 39 Buckingham Palace Rd SW1; ⊖ Victoria; singles/doubles from £135/150) is as close you'll get to shacking up with the Queen. It overlooks the walls of the Royal Mews and Buckingham Palace and is very popular with groups.

Mayfair (Map 4) Located in one of London's most exclusive neighbourhoods, the **Chesterfield** (☎ 7491 2622, fax 7491 4793; w www.redcarnationhotels.com; 35 Charles St W1; ⊖ Green Park; singles/doubles from £132/150) has 111 rooms and is just a block west of Berkeley Square. The Chesterfield also has some fine outlets, particularly the Conservatory restaurant and the Library bar.

The West End & Covent Garden (Map 5)
Staying in such central locations doesn't come cheap.

Hazlitt's (☎ 7434 1771, fax 7439 1524; w www.hazlittshotel.com; 6 Frith St W1; ⊖ Tottenham Court Road; singles/doubles from £175/195), the former abode of author William Hazlitt, is a charming Georgian house and one of central London's finest hotels. There are 23 individually decorated rooms, each brimming with character.

St Martins Lane (☎ 7300 5500, 0800 634 5500; w www.ianschragerhotels.com; 45 St Martin's Lane; ⊖ Leicester Square; rooms from £195) is a joint effort between international hotelier Ian Schrager and French designer Philippe Starck, and is so cool that you would hardly notice it was there. The rooms have floor-to-ceiling windows affording sweeping views of the West End, the public rooms are bustling meeting points and everything – and everyone – is beautiful. This prolific duo are also responsible for the similarly priced 'urban spa' of **Sanderson** (☎ 7300 1400; w www.ianschragerhotels.com; 50 Berner St W1).

Fitzrovia (Map 5) This one-time bohemian enclave is off the tourist map, yet within easy walking distance of Soho and lots of good restaurants.

Charlotte Street Hotel (☎ 7806 2000, fax 7806 2002; w www.firmdale.com; 15 Char-lotte St W1; ⊖ Goodge Street; singles/doubles from £185/210), a favourite with visiting media types (ie, those in the know), is where Laura Ashley goes postmodern and comes up smelling of roses. The bar buzzes by night while Oscar restaurant is a delightful spot any time of day, but particularly for afternoon tea.

Clerkenwell (Map 4) This area is not blessed with a wealth of quality accommodation; however, there is a notable exception.

The Rookery (☎ 7336 0931, fax 7336 0932; w www.rookeryhotel.com; Peter's Lane, Cow-cross St EC1; ⊖ Farringdon; singles/doubles from £190/225) occupies a row of once derelict 18th-century Georgian houses and provides a discreet and luxurious hideaway in fashionable Clerkenwell. Rooms, named after 19th-century local 'characters', are attractively fitted with period furniture including a museum-piece collection of Victorian baths, showers and toilets.

South Kensington (Map 7) South Kensington presents London at its elegant best.

Number Sixteen Hotel (☎ 7589 5232, fax 7584 8615; w www.numbersixteenhotel.co.uk; 16 Sumner Place SW7; ⊖ South Kensington; singles/doubles from £100/175) is a gorgeous spot, with bright and muted rooms, embroidered bedspreads, relaxing guest lounges and a tree-filled garden and conservatory.

Blakes (☎ 7370 6701, fax 7373 0442; w www.blakeshotels.com; 33 Roland Gardens SW7; ⊖ Gloucester Road; singles/doubles £130/260) is a sophisticated stalwart from the 1970s and London's original boutique hotel. It occupies five Victorian houses knocked into one and rooms are decked out with four-poster beds, sumptuous fabrics, rich colour schemes and antique treasures.

Kensington & Knightsbridge (Map 3)
A veritable palace, **The Gore** (☎ 7584 6601, fax 7589 8127; w www.gorehotel.com; 189 Queen's Gate SW7; ⊖ High Street Kensington or Gloucester Road; singles/doubles from £152/200) features lots of polished mahogany, Turkish carpets, antique-style bathrooms, aspidistras, thousands of portraits and prints and a great bar. The attached **Bistrot 190** is a fine place for brunch.

Basil St Hotel (☎ 7581 3311, fax 7581 3693; w www.thebasil.com; Basil St SW3; ⊖ Knights-bridge; singles/doubles from £138/198) is a lovely antique-stuffed hideaway in the heart of Knightsbridge, perfectly placed for carrying heavy bags back from Harrods, Harvey Nicks or Sloane St.

Kensington House Hotel (☎ 7937 2345, fax 7368 6700; w www.kenhouse.com; 15-16 Prince of Wales Terrace W8; ⊖ High Street Kensington; singles/doubles £145/170), graceful on the outside, is cool and modern inside.

Pelham (Map 7; ☎ 7589 8288, fax 7584 8444; w www.firmdale.com; ⊖ South Kensington; 15 Cromwell Place SW7; singles/doubles from £180/212), the choice of the fashion industry, is close to Harvey Nichols, and has huge wardrobes, classic decor and baths big enough for two.

Bayswater & Notting Hill (Map 3) You'll get more luxury for your lolly in these areas than you would to the south and east of town.

Portobello Hotel (☎ 7727 2777, fax 7792 9641; w www.portobello-hotel.co.uk; 22 Stanley Gardens W11; ⊖ Notting Hill Gate; singles/doubles £140/185), a favourite with rock stars from the Sex Pistols to George Michael, is one of the most attractive hotels in London. Rooms are coolly plush and loosely colonial, and the location is terrific.

East End (Map 6) This area's top option is a classic Victorian railway hotel.

Great Eastern Hotel (☎ 7618 5010, fax 7618 5011; w www.great-eastern-hotel.co.uk; Liverpool St EC2; ⊖ Liverpool Street; singles/doubles from £195/225), a major addition to the East End, is the place for proximity to the City for contemporary style enthusiasts. It's on the site of what was the Bethlehem Royal Hospital from the 13th to the 17th century, which is where the English language got the word 'bedlam' (meaning madhouse). Anyone who's attended 'room parties' at the hotel will know that a version of the tradition still exists.

Places to Stay – Deluxe

Some of central London's hotels are so luxurious and well established that they are tourist attractions in their own right. However, even those relying on their old world splendour are set up to accommodate business travellers. Double rooms here are from £250, although they seem to think it's a measure of their appeal the harder it is to get the frigging room rates.

Claridges (Map 4; ☎ 7629 8860, fax 7499 2210; w www.savoy-group.co.uk/claridges; Brook St W1; ⊖ Bond Street; singles/doubles £315/370) is one of the greatest of London's five-star hotels, a leftover from a bygone era and the place to sip martinis whether you're a paying guest or not. Many of the Art Deco features of the public areas and suites were designed in the late 1920s and some of the 1930s furniture once graced the staterooms of the lost SS Normandie. Celebrated chef Gordon Ramsay recently took over the kitchen.

The Ritz (Map 5; ☎ 7493 8181, fax 7493 2687; w www.theritzhotel.co.uk; 150 Piccadilly W1; ⊖ Green Park; singles/doubles/suites from £357/405/910) is London's most celebrated hotel. After lending its name to the English lexicon, you might expect this most ritzy of establishments to rest on its laurels, don some slippers and fade out. Not so. While it's still the royal family's home away from home, such is the Ritz's unyielding cred that even the new generation of cultural elite are taking to it. The rooms are expectedly opulent while the restaurant is decked out like a rococo boudoir.

The Savoy (Map 5; ☎ 7836 4343, fax 7240 6040; w www.savoy-group.co.uk; Strand WC2; ⊖ Charing Cross; singles/doubles from £290/340) stands on the site of the old Savoy Palace, burned down during the Peasants' Revolt of 1381. Some have been so taken with its palatial grandeur that they've taken up permanent residence. Many rooms have spectacular views of the Thames – Monet was so impressed that he painted it from his room.

Brown's Hotel (Map 5; ☎ 7493 6020, fax 7493 9381; w www.brownshotel.com; 30 Albemarle St W1; ⊖ Green Park; singles/doubles from £320/370) is a stunning hotel that opened in 1837 and was the first in London to have a lift, telephone and electric lighting. Service is tip top and the atmosphere quintessentially English.

Covent Garden Hotel (Map 5; ☎ 7806 1000, fax 7806 1100; w www.firmdale.com; 10 Monmouth St WC2; ⊖ Covent Garden; singles/doubles £230/275) combines gorgeous fabrics and a theatrical theme to stake out its individuality among the deluxe boutiques (although it's really the location you pay for).

The Trafalgar (Map 5; ☎ 7870 2900, fax 7870 2911; w www.thetrafalgar.hilton.com; 2 Spring Gardens SW1; ⊖ Charing Cross; doubles from £340) made something of a splash when it opened as the Hilton's first 'lifestyle' hotel in 2001. The young, hip and fashionable have been lapping up its tasteful minimalism and the views of the square from some of the rooms are spectacular.

The Lanesborough *(Map 4; ☎ 7259 5599, fax 7259 5606; w www.lanesborough.com; Hyde Park Corner; ⊖ Hyde Park Corner; rooms from £310)* is where visiting divas doze and Regency opulence meets state-of-the-art technology. The Royal Suite, the most expensive digs in town, comes with a chauffeured Bentley and costs £5350 although you could probably get a couple of quid off if you haggle.

One Aldwych *(Map 5; ☎ 7300 1000, fax 7300 1001; 1 Aldwych WC2; w www.onealdwych.com; ⊖ Covent Garden; singles/doubles/suites from £350/370/570)* is luxurious and trendy, with (mostly) spacious rooms and lots of modern art. The highly regarded **Axis Restaurant & Bar** is the place to be seen and hosts food and live jazz evening on Tuesday and Wednesday.

Airport Hotels

If you have an early flight out of Heathrow, you might want to stay at one of the anonymous hotels that ring its periphery. The extortionate **Hotel Hoppa shuttle bus** *(☎ 01293 507099; adult/child £3/free)* links the airport's terminals and bus, tube and rail stations with the hotels; see the Getting There & Away section later in this chapter for details.

Hotel Ibis Heathrow Rd *(☎ 8759 4888, fax 8564 7894; 112/114 Bath Rd, Hayes UB3 5AL; rooms weekend/weekday £45/65)* has clean and serviceable rooms, and the restaurant is relatively cheap. This could be a utilitarian hotel anywhere in the world, which can be a bit disconcerting when your alarm goes off.

Novotel Heathrow Airport *(☎ 01895-431431, fax 431221; Cherry Lane, West Drayton UB7 9HB; singles/doubles £90/110)* offers more anonymous corporate comfort. It's near the M4 and M25. The large atrium boasts a pool.

Serviced Apartments

Several agencies can help track something down. **Holiday Serviced Apartments** *(☎ 7373 4477, fax 7373 4282; e reservations@holidayapartments.co.uk; 273 Old Brompton Rd SW5; ⊖ Gloucester Road)* and **Aston's Budget & Designer Studios** *(☎ 7590 6000, fax 7590 6060; w www.astons-apartments.com; 39 Rosary Gardens SW7; ⊖ Gloucester Road)* has three Victorian town houses on the same street, which provide for 54 units ranging in

price from £60 to £160 a night (5% and 10% discounts for week-long and month-long stays respectively).

Long Stays

If you're here for an extended stay, finding a share house or flat will offer the best value. Most landlords demand a security deposit (normally one month's rent) plus a month's rent in advance.

Rents vary dramatically according to location – you can get a feel for the market from *Loot* classifieds newspaper. Rooms, flats and flat-shares are also advertised in *TNT*, *Time Out* and the *Evening Standard* among others.

If you prefer to use an agency, make sure that it doesn't charge fees to tenants. The **Jenny Jones Agency** *(☎ 7493 4381; 40 South Molton St W1; ⊖ Bond Street)* charges the landlord.

PLACES TO EAT

To borrow a well-worn cliche, food and dining out have become the new rock and roll in London over recent years. There has been an astonishing growth in the number of restaurants here and you can hardly open a menu without banging into some celebrity chef or restaurateur. Look hard enough and you'll find some 70 different cuisines, a reflection of London's vibrant multiculturalism. It's no hyperbole to say that the city is a world culinary capital; its top restaurants compare favourably with the best anywhere and the city has exported talented chefs to the four corners of the globe.

But, unfortunately, this status doesn't equate to value for money. You generally have to dig deep to get a decent feed although, even then, choosing a restaurant can still be a hit-and-miss affair. You could as easily drop £30 on a 'modern European' meal that tastes like it came from a can or spend a fiver on an Indian dish that will make your palate spin and your heart sing. Regrettably, if you come from a foodie culture, you're more likely to experience the former.

In this section, we've tried to steer you towards the restaurants and cafés that are distinguished by their location and value for money, and have unique features, original settings and, of course, good food. Our list ranges from convenient breakfast cafés to scintillating world-beaters worthy of a big splurge – the reviews are all relative to the food scene in general.

Opening hours vary – many restaurants in Soho close Sunday, those in the City for the whole weekend – and we've tried to note where places stray from the standard 'open daily for lunch and dinner' but it's always safest to call and check. 'Gastropubs' are all the rage in the capital these days and you'll find that many of the pubs listed in the Entertainment section serve food.

Vegetarianism has long been integral to London dining – largely because of the health scares with British meat – and, in addition to a host of dedicated meat-free joints, most restaurants offer vegetarian options.

Trafalgar Square (Map 5)

There aren't many good places on London's main square although the new pedestrian plaza – slated for completion some time in 2003 – is set to have a new café and there are a couple of cafés within striking distance.

The National Gallery's **Crivelli's Garden** (☎ 7747 2869; Trafalgar Square WC2; ⊖ Charing Cross; mains £9-13; afternoon tea £3.40) is a decent, busy Italian restaurant with views of the square; there's also a self-serve café.

Café in the Crypt (☎ 7839 4342; St Martin-in-the-Fields, Duncannon St WC2; ⊖ Charing Cross; mains £5-7, 'quick meals' from £3.95; open 10am-8pm Mon-Sat, 10am-6pm Sun) is an atmospheric crypt in which to rest weary bones and enjoy good food from soups to casseroles. Lunch time is frantic.

Westminster & Pimlico

Given the dearth of restaurants in Westminster, you can expect to bump into a few MPs in Pimlico, which is much more well endowed.

Jenny Lo's Tea House (Map 8; ☎ 7259 0399; 14 Eccleston St SW1; ⊖ Victoria; mains £4.50-7) is a simple and friendly Asian place offering good fried noodles and other wok-based specials.

O Sole Mio (Map 8; ☎ 7976 6887; 39 Churton St SW1; ⊖ Victoria; mains £5-8) is a reliable frills-free Italian restaurant with pizzas and pastas.

ICA Café (Map 4; ☎ 7930 8619; ICA, The Mall SW1; ⊖ Charing Cross; mains £5-9), in the Institute for Contemporary Arts, is a bohemian magnet with a 1am licence, good cocktails and diner-style food that hits the mark more often than not. Standards are more casual at lunch time and you can tack on an additional £1.50 for day membership of the ICA.

St James's & Mayfair (Map 4)

Shepherd Market is popular with locals and is lined with a variety of fine restaurants.

Shepherd Café Bar (☎ 7495 5509; 7 Shepherd Market W1; ⊖ Green Park; mains around £4) is a friendly Italian joint with outdoor tables. It's long on pasta, short on ceremony.

Hard Rock Café (☎ 7629 0382; 150 Old Park Lane W1; ⊖ Hyde Park Corner; mains from £8-15), the original, has been here since 1971 and is largely a Londoner-free zone (because tourists are the only ones with the time to queue). Tried, tested and huge burgers are the staple, impressive rock memorabilia the decor.

Rasa W1 (☎ 7629 1346; 6 Dering St W1; ⊖ Bond Street; dishes around £10), a South Indian vegetarian restaurant, has great food.

Quaglino's (Map 5; ☎ 7930 6767; 16 Bury St SW1; ⊖ Green Park; entrees £4.50-6.50, mains £11-16.50) is a huge, dim basement that was once a pioneer of London's foodie scene. Newer, more fashionable establishments have largely eclipsed this leading light but it's still a wonderful choice for all things crustacean.

The West End: Piccadilly, Soho & Chinatown (Map 5)

Soho is London's gastronomic heart with a choice of numerous restaurants and cuisines. The liveliest streets tend to be Greek, Frith, Old Compton and Dean Sts. Gerrard and Lisle Sts are chock-a-block with Chinese eateries of every description.

Chinese The choice in Chinatown can be a bit overwhelming. If you're in a dithering pack, take control and lead your friends to any of the following and then order Cantonese dim sum where you can select numerous small dishes.

Wong Kei (☎ 7437 3071; 41-43 Wardour St W1; ⊖ Leicester Square; mains £4.50-7.50, set menus from £6) is legendary for its rude waiters although they're really not that bad (or good, depending on what you're after). The Cantonese food is a little stodgy but as good value as you'll find on a (plastic) plate.

Fung Shing (☎ 7437 1539; 15 Lisle St WC2; ⊖ Leicester Square; mains £6-10) is a stalwart with a relaxed café-style front dining room and a more formal chandeliered one out back. Don't be put off by the lack of Chinese diners.

Chuen Cheng Ku (☎ 7437 1398; 17 Wardour St W1; ⊖ Leicester Square; dim sum £2, mains £6-12) is ideal for the uninitiated as all the dishes – dumplings, noodles, prawns etc – are trundled around on trolleys (so you can point then cross your fingers).

Sheng's Tea House *(Map 2; ☎ 7405 3697; 68 Millman St; ✆ Holborn; mains £7-9)* offers the best welcome on the strip and the lightly spiced food is always fresh and wholesome.

Gerrard's Corner *(☎ 7437 0984; 30 Wardour St WC2; ✆ Leicester Square; meals £6-10)* is reliable for quality and value.

1997 *(☎ 7734 2868; 19 Wardour St W1; ✆ Leicester Square; mains around £7)*, named after the year Hong Kong was reclaimed by China, does a perky Peking duck beneath pictures of distinguished communists and, er, Princess Diana.

Japanese & Southeast Asian Asian food in the West End is by no means restricted to Chinese and there are lots of other cuisines to tickle your fancy.

Zipangu *(☎ 7437 5042; 8 Little Newport St WC2; ✆ Leicester Square; set menus £10-14)* isn't much to look at but it's got three storeys of outstandingly tasty, constantly fresh and exceedingly good food and graceful service.

Tokyo Diner *(☎ 7287 8777; 2 Newport Place WC2; ✆ Leicester Square; mains around £8-10)* is good for a quick and hassle-free bowl of noodles or plate of sushi to launch you into the night, or a set bento box on the run.

Soba *(☎ 7734 6400; 38 Poland St W1; ✆ Oxford Circus; noodles £5)* is always our first choice for an easy (and cheap) bowl of Japanese noodles.

Yo! Sushi *(☎ 7287 0443; 52-53 Poland St W1; ✆ Oxford Circus; sushi £2-4, meals around £10)* is one of London's livelier sushi joints, where diners sit around the bar and dishes come to them on a 60m-long conveyor belt. Drinks, on the other hand, arrive on a robotic trolley. Children under 151cm tall eat for free on Sunday at the County Hall branch.

Wagamama *(☎ 7292 0990; 10A Lexington St W1; ✆ Leicester Square; mains £5-8)*, or any of its dozen or so central London branches, is the place to throw back a bowl of Japanese noodles while sitting at long communal tables and listening to anything but your own thoughts (which you won't be able to hear).

Melati *(☎ 7437 2745; 21 Great Windmill St W1; ✆ Piccadilly Circus; mains £6-8.50)*, in the heart of Soho and a local institution, does a lip-smacking laksa among its splendid Indo-Malay staples.

Saigon *(☎ 7437 7109; 45 Frith St W1; ✆ Leicester Square; mains around £11)* is required dining for anyone on a gastronomic tour of Asia, via Chinatown. While London isn't particularly well endowed with Vietnamese eateries, this one manages to satisfy body and soul with authentic tastes and furnishings.

Soho Thai *(☎ 7287 2000; 27 St Anne's Court W1; ✆ Tottenham Court Road; mains £4.50-9)* is down a quiet alleyway but the delightful aroma coming from its kitchen will help you find it. The food is as rich and diverse as the culture it represents.

Italian A popular cheapie, **Pollo** *(☎ 7734 5917; 20 Old Compton St W1; ✆ Leicester Square; mains £4-8)* draws a regular, relaxed crowd with its pastas, risottos and pizzas.

Spiga *(☎ 7734 3444; 84-86 Wardour St W1; ✆ Tottenham Court Road; mains £9-14)* is the place to come when you want modern Italian food – feisty pizzas are just the start – in sleek and casual surroundings, and don't want to pay the world for it.

Kettners *(☎ 7734 6112; 29 Romilly St W1; ✆ Leicester Square; mains £9-16)* is a gem, serving mouth-watering pizzas and burgers in a cultured atmosphere of gently fading grandeur with a piano tinkling softly in the background.

Pizza Express *(☎ 7439 8722; 10 Dean St W1; ✆ Tottenham Court Road; pizzas £5-8)* is much loved by Londoners and has about 50 branches dotted around town, all serving reliable, undistinguished pizzas in a family-friendly environment. This branch, however, has jazz accompaniment downstairs.

On the High Teas

Going out for 'afternoon tea' is something dear to the heart of many English people, for whom a trip to the centre of London wouldn't be complete without a visit to one of its atmospheric tearooms. A traditional tea set comes with a selection of delicate sandwiches (cucumber or smoked salmon), freshly baked scones with cream and jam, and a selection of assorted sweet nibbles all washed down with lashings of tea. It will cost you about £25 per person but the best places to indulge are **Brown's Hotel**, **Claridges** and the venerable department store **Fortnum & Mason**.

Vegetarian Small and popular, **Mildred's** (☎ 7494 1634; 45 Lexington St W1; ✆ Piccadilly Circus; mains £5-7) is packed most lunch times. Don't be shy about sharing a table or you'll miss out on excellent, inexpensive and hugely portioned wholesome veggie fare from stir-fries to beanburgers. It also has a licence.

Red Veg (☎ 7437 3109; 95 Dean St W1; ✆ Tottenham Court Road; snacks £3) has corny communist decor but does a very solid line in vegetarian fast food from oriental noodles to falafel.

Country Life (☎ 7434 2922; 3-4 Warwick St W1; ✆ Piccadilly Circus; mains £10-12) is a terrific vegan restaurant where the atmosphere is a little virtuous but the flavours of the wholesome food are undeniably good.

Other Innumerable other cuisines are also represented in the West End.

Franx Snack Bar (☎ 7836 7989; 192 Shaftesbury Ave WC2; ✆ Tottenham Court Road; meals £3) is as authentic a London 'caff' as you'll find in these parts; expect eggs, bacon and other artery-clogging one-plate specials.

Gaby's (☎ 7836 4233; 30 Charing Cross Rd WC2; ✆ Leicester Square; snacks £3.50-8), beside Wyndham's Theatre, is a Middle Eastern snack bar that's been here forever. Queues for falafel and couscous move quickly.

Garlic & Shots (☎ 7734 9505; 14 Frith St W1; ✆ Leicester Square; mains £9-13) is a novelty place popular with Goths and people with red hair. It's dedicated to the odorous bulb and getting hammered on flavoured vodka shots. All of the dishes are infused with garlic – even the cheesecake!

Rasa Samudra (☎ 7637 0222; 5 Charlotte St W1; ✆ Goodge Street; mains £9-12), just north of Oxford St, is one of many restaurants on this street but its tantalising South Indian vegetarian cuisine and Keralan seafood sets it apart.

Mon Plaisir (☎ 7836 7243; 21 Monmouth St WC2; ✆ Covent Garden; mains £14-17) is the oldest French restaurant in London and produces outstanding versions of the original cuisine in a Parisian-style brasserie.

Woodlands (☎ 7839 7258; 37 Panton St SW1; ✆ Leicester Square; thalis £7-9) is an Indian chain that in India is only so-so but here…wow. Superb thalis (all you can eat mixed plates) are a highlight as is anything from the South Indian menu.

J Sheekey (☎ 7240 2565; 28-32 St Martin's Court WC2; ✆ Leicester Square; mains £10-25),

a jewel of the local scene, is incredibly smart and has four discreet rooms in which to savour the riches of the sea.

The Gaucho Grill (☎ 7734 4040; 19 Swallow St W1; ✆ Piccadilly Circus; mains £9-35) is the most central of a respected Argentinian chain and serves huge slabs of meat.

Rainforest Café (☎ 7434 3111; 20 Shaftesbury Ave W1; ✆ Piccadilly Circus; mains £9-15) – the first of this chain to open outside the US – is a green, exotic and at times chaotic version of the Hard Rock Café, with live birds and animatronic wild beasts roaring and hooting, waterfalls cascading and thunder crashing among fake banyan trees. The menu comprises US standards with tropical touches and the kids will love it.

Quo Vadis (☎ 7437 9585; 26-29 Dean St W1; ✆ Leicester Square; mains £11-30) occupies a building that Karl Marx once called home. When the restaurant first opened, it was famous for featuring the controversial works of one of its founders, contemporary artist Damien Hurst, although he has since taken his art and moved on. These days the restaurant is best known for providing excellent European fare and impeccable service in cool surroundings.

Gay Hussar (☎ 7437 0973; 2 Greek St W1; ✆ Tottenham Court Road; mains £12.50-18.50) is an old-style Hungarian eatery and Soho institution that's hardly changed in half a century. The menu is rich, authentic and meaty, and the portions are colossal.

Cafés Soho's cafés are great for whiling away the hours inside or, weather permitting, on underused street furniture.

Maison Bertaux (☎ 7437 6007; 28 Greek St W1; ✆ Tottenham Court Road) has exquisite confections, unhurried service, a French bohemian vibe and 130 years of history.

Bar Italia (☎ 7437 4520; 22 Frith St W1; ✆ Leicester Square) is a great favourite with slumming celebrities lapping up the reviving juices and hunky paninis amid cool 1950s decor. It's always packed and buzzing but you can normally get a seat – after 1am.

Pâtisserie Valerie (☎ 7437 3466; 44 Old Compton St W1; ✆ Tottenham Court Road or Leicester Square) is a sweet Soho institution with delicious, delicate pastries, stylish sandwiches and strictly no phones le mobile.

Monmouth Coffee House (☎ 7836 5272; 27 Monmouth St WC2; ✆ Covent Garden) brews beans sourced from all over the coffee-growing world. It's essentially a shop but has a few seats upon which you can slowly savour the magnificent blends.

Covent Garden & the Strand (Map 5)

Right beside Soho and technically part of the West End, Covent Garden (⊖ *Covent Garden*) is also densely packed with places to eat.

Rock & Sole Plaice (☎ *7836 3785; 47 Endell St WC2; fish & chips £8-13*) is a classic, central chippy with restaurant, outdoor tables and takeaway. It's a model for modern British cuisine (ie, traditional foods, even mushy peas, cooked the right way).

Food for Thought (☎ *7836 0239; 31 Neal St WC2; dishes under £5*) is a vegetarian joint that's big on sociability and flavour and small on price and space. Food ranges from soups to traditional Indian thalis (mixed plates).

Calabash (☎ *7836 1973; 38 King St WC2; mains £5-8*) is a simple and relaxed eatery in the Africa Centre that pulls in flavours from all over the continent. There's a descriptive menu to guide the uninitiated on a gastronomic tour from *egusi* (Nigerian meat stew) to *yassi* (Senegalese chicken).

Belgo Centraal (☎ *7813 2233; 50 Earlham St WC2; set lunches/dinners £5/13.95*) is a gimmicky Belgian restaurant good for *moules et frites* (mussels and chips) and, of course, beer.

Café des Amis du Vin (☎ *7379 3444; 11-14 Hanover Place WC2; mains £10-17*), down an alley, is a handy pre-theatre option for solid French brasserie fare.

Orso (☎ *7240 5269; 27 Wellington St WC2; mains £13-16*) is a refined and polished Italian eatery especially popular with journalists (perhaps attracted by the Bloody Mary provided in the set lunch). The food is outstanding, the waiters unreasonably handsome.

Simpson's-in-the-Strand (☎ *7836 9112; 100 Strand WC2; mains around £15*) is where to head for traditional English roasts – it's been dishing up hot meats in a fine panelled dining room since 1848.

Neale's Yard Bakery & Tearoom (☎ *7836 5199; 6 Neal's Yard WC2; snacks £2.50-4.50; open for lunch only*) is a sensational vegetarian café – relaxed upstairs, hectic below – with terrific filled rolls, burgers and soups. There is a cluster of veggie places nearby.

Mode (☎ *7240 8085; 57 Endell St WC2; focaccias £2-5; closed Sun*) is a laid-back and funky Italian escape from the tourist throngs of Covent Garden.

Mela (☎ *7836 8635; 152-156 Shaftesbury Avenue WC2; ⊖ Leicester Square; mains £6-13*) is perfect if you like Indian food but are getting bored with the same old staples. Its innovative twists hit more than they miss.

The Admiralty (☎ *7845 4646; Somerset House, Strand WC2; ⊖ Embankment; set lunches £25*), the flagship restaurant of the restored Somerset House, has a traditional interior and modern French food. There's a lovely terrace outside overlooking the Thames. The degustation menus – one of which is vegetarian – are sublime.

Rules (☎ *7836 5314; 35 Maiden Lane; mains £18-24*), established in 1798, is London's oldest restaurant and specialises in classic game cookery, serving some 18,000 birds a year. Despite the history, it's not a museum piece and its sustained vitality attracts locals as well as the tourist masses.

Bloomsbury

If you're visiting the British Museum it's worth knowing that Museum St (Map 5) is lined with cafés and simple lunch places offering better value than the museum café itself.

Abeno (*Map 5;* ☎ *7405 3211; 47 Museum St WC1; ⊖ Tottenham Court Road; mains £5-25*) is a splendidly sumptuous restaurant specialising in the Japanese fast food staple of *okonomi-yaki* (savoury pancakes).

Ruskins Café (*Map 5;* ☎ *7405 1450; 41 Museum St WC1; ⊖ Tottenham Court Road; light meals around £3*) does no-fuss soup and filled jacket potatoes.

North Sea Fish Restaurant (*Map 2;* ☎ *7387 5892; 7-8 Leigh St WC1; ⊖ Russell Square; mains £8-17*) cooks fresh fish and potatoes: a simple ambition, realised with aplomb.

Coffee Gallery (*Map 5;* ☎ *7436 0455; 23 Museum St WC1; ⊖ Tottenham Court Road; many mains under £7*) is a tremendously popular place that serves pasta dishes and mains such as grilled sardines and salad in a bright, cheerful room with modern decor.

Mille Pini (*Map 4;* ☎ *7242 2434; 33 Boswell St WC1; ⊖ Russell Square or Holborn; 2-course lunches/dinners around £6/10*) is a genuinely old-fashioned Italian joint – when you eventually leave the table, you'll waddle.

Mandeer (*Map 5;* ☎ *7405 3211; 8 Bloomsbury Way WC1; ⊖ Holborn; meals around £6; closed Sun*) is a terrific vegetarian restaurant that follows the Indian holistic philosophy of Ayurveda, which – in relation to food – focuses on the combination and balancing of ingredients to promote taste and health.

Holborn & Clerkenwell

Holborn has only a few restaurants and nightspots to tempt you after dark. Clerkenwell, on the other hand, has truly arrived and you'll have more difficulty getting out. The following places are mostly accessible from Farringdon tube station.

The Greenery (Map 4; ☎ 7490 4870; 5 Cowcross St EC1; light meals £2-7) is a salt-of-the-earth veggie café, surviving for the moment amid the gentrification of Clerkenwell.

St John (Map 4; ☎ 7251 0848; 26 St John St EC1), next to Smithfield Market, offers an intrepid romp through Ye Olde English staples such as pigs trotters, smoked eel and an awful lot of offal.

Gaudí (Map 4; ☎ 7608 3220; 63 Clerkenwell Rd EC1; mains £16-18) takes its cue from the Catalan architect's designs to provide a backdrop for a classy restaurant specialising in modern Spanish cuisine.

Cicada (Map 2; ☎ 7608 1550; 132-136 St John St EC1; mains £7-12) is a lovely, modern restaurant that mingles Asian tastes and flavours with great success.

Club Gascon (Map 4; ☎ 7253 5853; 57 West Smithfield EC1; mains from £30), right next to glorious St Bartholomew's-the-Great (of *Four Weddings and a Funeral* fame), serves superb food from southwest France, including dozens of tasting dishes.

The Eagle (Map 2; ☎ 7837 1353; 159 Farringdon Rd EC1; mains £5-12.50) is a small, vivacious gastropub with a seasonal and creative menu that doesn't try to be too clever despite its trendy appeal.

The City

The City can be an irritating place to try and find a decent, affordable restaurant that stays open after office hours. The following recommendations are the pick of the crop.

Dim Sum (Map 4; ☎ 7236 1114; 5-6 Deans Court EC4; ⊖ St Paul's; mains £4-7; open Mon-Fri), a budget traveller's delight and convenient for St Paul's and the City of London YHA hostel, serves Peking and Sichuan dishes and has an all-you-can-eat buffet (minimum four people) available in the evening from Monday to Friday.

Da Vinci (Map 4; ☎ 7236 3938; 42-44 Carter Lane EC4; ⊖ St Paul's or Blackfriars; mains £5-14) is a rare bird indeed: an affordable neighbourhood Italian place in the City. A 'cheap lunch' costs £5.

Sweeting's (Map 6; ☎ 7248 3062; 39 Queen Victoria St EC4; ⊖ Mansion House; mains £9-20) is an old-fashioned place, with a mosaic floor and waiters in white aprons standing behind narrow counters serving up a cavalcade of fresh and seasonal seafood.

The Place Below (Map 6; ☎ 7329 0789; St Mary-le-Bow Church, Cheapside EC2; ⊖ St Paul's or Mansion House; light meals £6-8; open lunch only, closed weekend), a vegetarian café in a church crypt, is free of pinstripes and serves decent salads, pastas and quiches.

Crussh (Map 6; ☎ 7626 2175; 48 Cornhill EC3; ⊖ Bank) is the perfect place to pep up with a range of juices and light, healthy snacks.

Café Spice Namaste (Map 1; ☎ 7488 9242; 16 Prescot St E1; ⊖ Tower Hill; mains £8-15), perhaps the best Indian restaurant in town, serves dishes that reflect the rich, complex cuisine of India (not just kormas and baltis).

Bermondsey

This area's culinary highlights include Terence Conran's gastronomic palaces at Shad Thames (tube Bermondsey or Tower Hill).

Blue Print Café (Map 1; ☎ 7378 7031; Design Museum, Butlers Wharf, Shad Thames SE1; ⊖ Tower Hill; starters £5-6.50, mains £11-16.50), the flagship Conran restaurant, offers modern European cooking. There are spectacular views of the river from here and the Design Museum is next door.

Cantina del Ponte (Map 6; ☎ 7403 5403; Butlers Wharf, 36c Shad Thames SE1; ⊖ Tower Hill; mains £9-16) has middling Mediterranean food but a fabulous riverside setting.

Honest Cabbage (Map 6; ☎ 7234 0080; 99 Bermondsey St SE1; ⊖ London Bridge; mains £7-14), a sophisticated snug not far from the Bermondsey flea market, has terrific, innovative dishes with a modern British bent. It usually gets a big turnip (tch!) so you might want to make a reservation for dinner.

Southwark (Map 6)

The number of options in this part of town should increase, thanks in no small part to Tate Modern.

Manze's (☎ 7407 2985; 87 Tower Bridge Rd SE1; ⊖ London Bridge; pie & mash £2.50) is

London's oldest pie shop and has been doling out the working-class staples of jellied eels and pie and mash for over a century.

Konditor & Cook (☎ 7620 2700; 10 Stoney St SE1; ⊖ London Bridge; most dishes under £3), the original location of arguably the best bakery in London, serves excellent hot and cold lunches. There's not much space but everything is yours to take away.

Tate Modern Café (☎ 7401 5020; Bankside SE1; ⊖ Southwark; meals £5-12; open 10.15am-5.30pm daily, dinner Fri & Sat) is actually two cafés. The main one, a restaurant on level 2, has a stunning industrial interior as you might expect. The other, a perpetually packed café on level 7, has equally impressive views out over London, which the food, inevitably, doesn't quite match.

Fish! (☎ 7836 3236; Cathedral St SE1; ⊖ London Bridge; mains £9-18), situated in an all-glass Victorian pavilion overlooking Borough Market and Southwark Cathedral, is part of a fast-breeding chain serving fresher-than-fresh fish and seafood prepared simply: steamed or grilled. Noisy!

Waterloo & Lambeth (Map 4)
This part of south London is not immediately attractive as a place for eating out, although the cafés and restaurants in the Royal Festival Hall, the Royal National Theatre and the National Film Theatre are popular places to meet and the food is reasonable.

Konditor & Cook (☎ 7620 2700; 66 The Cut SE1; ⊖ Waterloo; snacks under £3; open 8.30am-11pm when there's a show, to 9pm at other times) is a café branch of the famous Southwark bakery at the Young Vic Theatre.

Mesón Don Felipe (☎ 7928 3237; 53 The Cut SE1; ⊖ Waterloo; tapas £2.50-5) is tops for tapas and authentic Spanish atmosphere, helped along by classical Spanish guitar in the evenings. There are about half a dozen vegetarian options, more than you get in Spain.

Tas (☎ 7928 1444; 33 The Cut SE1; ⊖ Southwark; mains £5-15) is an outstanding Turkish place with plush surroundings, fab kebabs and an unusually large range of light – it's all relative – vegetarian fare.

Oxo Tower Restaurant & Brasserie (☎ 7803 3888; Barge House St SE1; ⊖ Waterloo; mains around £17) offers good grub – a bit Mediterranean, a bit French, some Pacific Rim – with splendid views. This price guide is for the slightly cheaper brasserie.

Pizzeria Castello (Map 1; ☎ 7703 2556; 20 Walworth Rd SE1; ⊖ Elephant & Castle; pizzas £5-10) is where you'll end up if you ask a south Londoner for the best pizzeria in town, although it's not worth a long detour.

Chelsea, South Kensington & Earl's Court (Map 7)
These three areas boast an incredible array of eateries to suit all budgets, ranging from Michelin-starred indulgence to reliable caffs.

There is such a concentration of French people in South Kensington that it's sometimes referred to as 'Little France'. You'll find a lot of French-operated businesses, particularly along Bute St, just southwest of South Kensington tube station.

Francofill (☎ 7584 0087; 1 Old Brompton Rd SW7; meals around £10), around the corner from Bute St, is a delightful café-restaurant.

Benjy's (☎ 7373 0245; 157 Earl's Court Rd SW5; ⊖ Earl's Court; breakfasts around £4, lunches £5) is a bustling café with cheap and filling nosh available until 10pm.

Krungtap (☎ 7259 2314; 227 Old Brompton Rd SW10; ⊖ Earl's Court; mains around £6) – the Thai name for Bangkok – is a busy, friendly café open until midnight. There's weekend karaoke to either join in or avoid.

Oriel (Map 8; ☎ 7730 2804; 50-51 Sloane Square SW1; ⊖ Sloane Square; light meals £6-8.50, mains £9-14), with its comfy wicker chairs, mirrors, and tables overlooking Sloane Square, makes a great place to meet before going shopping in King's Rd or Sloane St.

The Collection (☎ 7225 1212; 264 Brompton Rd SW3; ⊖ South Kensington; mains £11-19) has a wonderful location in a converted gallery, with the main restaurant on a balcony overlooking the bar – perfect for people-watching – although it's more relaxed downstairs. The bar buzzes at weekends.

Spago (☎ 7225 2407; 6 Glendower Place SW7; ⊖ South Kensington; mains £6-10) has good, inexpensive pizzas and pastas, and is handy for the South Kensington museums.

New Cultural Revolution (☎ 7352 9281; 305 King's Rd SW3; ⊖ Sloane Square; mains around £6) is a trendy, good-value dumpling and noodle bar.

Made in Italy (☎ 7352 1880; 249 King's Rd SW3; ⊖ Sloane Square; mains £6-15), family-run and convivial with the best pizzas for miles, is as close as you'll get to southern Italy without packing a bag.

Daphne's (☎ 7589 4257; 112 Draycott Ave SW3; ⊖ South Kensington; mains £13-25) is popular with the fashionable Chelsea set and a good spot to watch and be watched. The Mediterranean-style food is divertingly good.

Bibendum (☎ 7581 5817; 81 Fulham Rd SW3; ⊖ South Kensington; full meals with wine around £60), a Conran establishment, is in one of London's finest settings for a restaurant, the Art Nouveau Michelin House (1911). The popular **Bibendum Oyster Bar** (half-dozen oysters £3.60-10.20) is on the ground floor, where you really feel at the heart of the architectural finery. Upstairs is lighter and brighter.

Big Easy (☎ 7352 4071; 332-334 King's Road SW5; ⊖ Sloane Square; mains £5-15) is an American-style restaurant full of stars, stripes and terrific barbecue-style tucker.

Jacob's (Map 3; ☎ 7581 9292; 20 Gloucester Road SW7; ⊖ Gloucester Road; meals around £10) serves inexpensive Armenian food and is a revelation.

Gordon Ramsay (☎ 7352 4441; 68-69 Royal Hospital Road SW3; ⊖ Sloane Square; set lunches/dinners £35/65) is one of Britain's finest restaurants, the only one in the capital with three Michelin stars and the creation of celebrity chef Mr Ramsay himself. The food is, of course, blissful and perfect for a luxurious treat. The only quibble is that you don't get time to linger. Bookings are made in specific eat-it-and-beat-it time slots and, if you've seen the chef on television, you won't argue for fear that he might come rushing out of the kitchen brandishing a meat cleaver.

Kensington & Knightsbridge

Many of the establishments in these posh 'villages' of west and southwest London cater for a very well-heeled clientele but, even if you're on a budget, you'll be able to find something to suit off the high streets.

Pizza on the Park (Map 4; ☎ 7235 5273; 11 Knightsbridge SW5; ⊖ Hyde Park Corner; pizzas £9-10) is as popular for its nightly jazz (from 9.15pm, admission around £16) in the basement as for its pizza. There's also a spacious restaurant upstairs and, if you're lucky, a few tables overlooking Hyde Park. Breakfast is available all day and afternoon tea, well, in the afternoon.

Bellini's (Map 3; ☎ 7937 5520; 47 Kensington Court W8; ⊖ High Street Kensington; 2/3-course lunches £7.50/9) is a stylish Italian

restaurant, with a few pavement tables and views of a flower-bedecked alley.

Fifth Floor (Map 3; ☎ 7235 5250; Harvey Nichols, 109-125 Knightsbridge SW1; ⊖ Knightsbridge; mains £17-25), upstairs from the unfailingly fashionable Harvey Nichols, is the perfect place to drop after you've shopped. It's a lovely, light and airy restaurant and the modern European food is always top-notch. There's also a less expensive café.

Wódka (Map 3; ☎ 7937 6513; 12 St Alban's Grove W8; ⊖ High Street Kensington; mains £11-14) is an authentic Polish joint providing Kraków-chic on a quiet residential strip not far from Kensington High St. Specialities include blinis (filled pancakes), fishcakes and eye-popping vodkas.

Notting Hill & Bayswater (Map 3)

Notting Hill teems with good places to eat, from cheap takeaways to atmospheric pubs (see Entertainment later) and restaurants worthy of the fine-dining tag.

Market Thai (☎ 7460 8320; 240 Portobello Rd; ⊖ Ladbroke Grove; mains £5-8), gentle and hospitable, offers fresh and delicious Thai cuisine one floor above a pub and way beyond the market crowds. Specials are good value.

Geales (☎ 7727 7528; 2 Farmer St W8; ⊖ Notting Hill Gate; fish & chips £10), a popular fish restaurant, is more expensive than your average chipper (prices vary according to weight and season) but worth every penny.

Café Grove (☎ 7243 1094; 253a Portobello Rd; ⊖ Ladbroke Grove; breakfast £5-7) is a Polish place where you can get gigantic and imaginative breakfasts, as well as cheap and cheerful vegetarian food. The large balcony overlooking the market is great for watching all the action on a weekend morning.

Mandola (☎ 7229 4734; 139-141 Westbourne Grove W2; ⊖ Bayswater; mains £5-7) is a jolly good Sudanese joint offering staples such as tamia (a version of falafel).

Osteria Basilico (☎ 7727 9372; 29 Kensington Park Rd W11; ⊖ Notting Hill Gate or Ladbroke Grove; mains £10-15), a friendly neighbourhood Italian place, combines rustic charm, west London chic and satisfying food.

Manzara (☎ 7727 3062; 24 Pembridge Rd W11; ⊖ Notting Hill Gate; mains around £10) is a simple place offering cheap but fresh and well-prepared Turkish food.

Brasserie de Marché aux Puces (☎ 8968 5828; 349 Portobello Rd; ⊖ Ladbroke Grove;

mains £9-13), on a quiet stretch of street north of the Portobello Rd market, has French classics at good prices, and tables outside should the sun shine.

Costas Fish Restaurant (☎ 7727 4310; 18 Hillgate St; ⊖ Notting Hill Gate; mains £4-7) puts a Cypriot spin on the traditional chippy.

Euston (Map 2)

Drummond St (tube Euston Square or Euston) has a number of interesting South Indian vegetarian restaurants.

Diwana (☎ 7387 5556; 121 Drummond St; mains £3-6.50) was the first of its kind – and is still the best according to many – on the street and specialises in Bombay-style *bel poori* (a sweet and sour, soft and crunchy 'party mix' snack) and *dosas* (filled pancakes). There's an all-you-can-eat lunch-time buffet for £5.45.

Chutneys (☎ 7388 0604; 124 Drummond St), nearby, does a cheaper, and better, lunch buffet for £5.25 (available all day Sunday).

Camden (Map 2)

Camden High St is lined with good places to eat, although to watch the Sunday daytrippers gorging themselves on takeaway sausages and chips you'd hardly believe it.

Café Delancey (☎ 7387 1985; 3 Delancey St NW1; ⊖ Camden Town; mains £7-15), the granddaddy of French-style brasseries in London, offers the chance to get a decent cup of coffee with a snack or full meal in relaxed, European-style surroundings complete with newspapers. The bickering staff and Charles Aznavour soundtrack are suitably Parisian.

El Parador (☎ 7387 2789; 245 Eversholt St NW1; ⊖ Mornington Crescent; tapas £4-5.50) is a quiet Spanish place where the selection of tasty tapas – including mucho vegetarian tidbits – is taken from all over Spain.

Bar Gansa (☎ 7267 8909; 2 Inverness St NW1; ⊖ Camden Town; tapas £2.50-4) is more like a traditional Spanish tapas joint: smoky, loud, cramped and run by Spanish staff. It's a focal point of the Camden scene and has a late licence.

Lemongrass (☎ 7284 1116; 243 Royal College St; ⊖ Camden Town; mains £5-7), the best Thai in Camden, has fresh and tasty authentic food (with Cambodian twists thrown in), bright and calming decor and chirpy staff.

The Engineer (☎ 7722 0950; 65 Gloucester Ave NW1; ⊖ Chalk Farm; mains £10-15) is

one of London's original gastropubs serving up consistently good international cuisine to hip north Londoners. There's a good selection of wines and beers, and a splendid garden.

Café Corfu (☎ 7269 8088; 7-9 Pratt St NW1; ⊖ Camden Town; mains £8-12) is among the best of a host of Greek restaurants around here. Decor is quirkily varied, the food feels light but fills and there's more than retsina to slake your thirst.

Lemonia (Map 1; ☎ 7586 7454; 89 Regent's Park Rd NW1; ⊖ Chalk Farm; mains £8.50-13.50, 2-course set lunches £6.75) is a warmly eccentric, and very popular, Greek establishment that provides good value, full-bodied flavours and an unhurried atmosphere.

Lalibela (Map 1; ☎ 7284 0600; 137 Fortess Rd NW5; ⊖ Tufnell Park; mains £7-15) is not far from Kentish Town and a wonderful foray into Ethiopian cuisine. It's as relaxed as dining out can get, with low stools and cushions providing support. The menu won't be too taxing either with just four mains (spicy/mild vegetarian or meat) to choose from.

Mango Room (☎ 7482 5065; 10-12 Kentish Town Rd NW1; ⊖ Camden Town; mains £9-12) is a funky, rough diamond of a place dishing up a cavalcade of different Caribbean specials. Service is quick and friendly, and you're expected to be the same.

Islington (Map 2)

Islington is a veritable Aladdin's cave for diners, with more than 60 cafés and restaurants between Angel and Highbury Corner. Most of the action is on Upper St, perfect for a gastronomic wander.

The Duke of Cambridge (Map 1; ☎ 7359 3066; 30 St Peter's St N1; ⊖ Angel; mains £10-17), London's first 'organic gastropub', has good, solid food in welcoming surroundings.

Afghan Kitchen (☎ 7359 8019; 35 Islington Green N1; ⊖ Angel; mains around £5; closed Sun & Mon) is small, laid-back and perpetually hip. It serves simple and tasty Afghan fare – half vegetarian, half with meat – and the prices are charitable.

Tartuf (☎ 7288 0954; 88 Upper St N1; ⊖ Angel; all-you-can-eat £10.80) is a fun and casual place where classic Alsatian *tartes flambeés* star. The wafer-thin crusts – French pizzas, if we must – come with a variety of toppings and cost about £6.

Lola's (☎ 7359 1932; The Mall, 359 Upper St N1; ⊖ Angel; mains £12-16) is an award-winning restaurant celebrated for its lovely decor, seasonal modern European menu and popular Sunday jazz brunch.

Maghreb (☎ 7226 2305; 189 Upper St N1; ⊕ Angel or Highbury & Islington; mains £7-12), if you're in the mood for Moroccan, is one of the highlights of Upper St. The menu features all the Moroccan classics – tagines, couscous, bastilla – served with panache in beautiful surroundings reminiscent of a *souq*.

Le Mercury (☎ 7354 4088; 140a Upper St N1; ⊕ Highbury & Islington; mains £5.95, specials £7-12) is a cosy Gallic haunt ideal for an inexpensive and romantic tête-à-tête. Sunday lunch by the open fire upstairs is a treat although you'll have to book.

Hampstead (Map 1)
Hampstead, London's most authentic village, has loads of good (and expensive) restaurants within walking distance of the tube station.

Café Base (☎ 7431 3241; 70-71 Hampstead High St NW3; evening mains £9-15), by day, is a bright and clean café with creative ciabatta sandwiches. Service, prices and clientele get more sophisticated after sundown when the menu is broadly, and reliably, French.

La Gaffe (☎ 7794 7526; 107 Heath St NW3; ⊕ Hamstead; mains £11-18) is a cosy, family-run Italian restaurant in an 18th-century cottage that has been one of the benefits of living in Hampstead since the 1960s. It's worth coming for the coffee alone.

Giraffe (☎ 7435 0343; 46 Rosslyn Hill NW3; ⊕ Hamstead; mains £7-11) is a delightful comfy and casual café, well worth a visit if you're checking out the village or the heath. Expect a global gamut from curries to burgers.

East End
From the hit-and-miss Indian and Bangladeshi restaurants of Brick Lane to the trendy eateries of Hoxton and Shoreditch, the East End has finally made it onto London's culinary map. Spitalfields Market (Map 6) has a rich palette of eateries ranging from casual and fun to stylish and urbane.

Brick Lane Beigel Bake (Map 1; ☎ 7729 0616; 159 Brick Lane E2; ⊕ Shoreditch; most bagels less than £1; open 24hr), a relic of London's Jewish East End, is more of a delicatessen than a café and sells the cheapest bagels anywhere in London. You only get what you pay for but they're a good snack on a bellyful of booze.

Mesón Los Barriles (Map 6; ☎ 7375 3136; 8a Lamb St E1; ⊕ Liverpool Street; tapas around £3-4), a Spanish bar and restaurant in Spitalfields Market, has a wide selection of fish and seafood tapas and mains.

The Real Greek (Map 1; ☎ 7739 8212; 15 Hoxton Market N1; ⊕ Old Street; meze £9, mains £14-17; closed Sun) is in Hoxton Market, London's trendy area du jour. This popular restaurant, in an old pub, specialises in innovative Greek cuisine and if you think it looks familiar, you're thinking of the fight scene in the film *Bridget Jones's Diary*.

Viet Hoa (Map 1; ☎ 7729 8293; 70-72 Kingsland Rd E2; bus No 67 or 149; mains £2.50-7), a simple, canteen-style eatery with checked tablecloths and mellow background music, serves excellent and authentic Vietnamese dishes and is always full.

Le Taj (Map 1; ☎ 7247 4210; 134 Brick Lane E1; ⊕ Liverpool Street or Shoreditch; mains £4-8), a modestly dressed Bengali favourite, is one of the better restaurants on this strip. Other Indian/Bangladeshi places to try include **Preem** (☎ 7247 0397; 120 Brick Lane E1; ⊕ Aldgate East; mains £4-10) and **Aladin** (Map 1; ☎ 7247 8210; 132 Brick Lane; ⊕ Liverpool Street or Shoreditch; mains £4-8).

Carnevale (Map 1; ☎ 7250 3452; 135 Whitecross St EC1; ⊕ Barbican; mains £8-9.75) is a tiny vegetarian place that packs a mighty punch of Mediterranean flavours and provides a fiesta for the visiting palate.

Greenwich
Beautiful Greenwich has a medley of old-style eateries and trendy new restaurants from which to choose. The Cutty Sark DLR station is convenient for all of the following. See also the Entertainment section for pub grub. Greenwich Church St has a few decent and inexpensive cafés.

Goddards Ye Olde Pie Shop (☎ 8293 9312; 45 Greenwich Church St SE10; meals under £3.50; open Tues-Sun lunch only) is truly a step back into the past: a real London caff with wooden benches and things such as steak and kidney pie with liquor and mash, and shepherd's pie with beans and a rich brown gravy.

Bar Du Musee (☎ 8858 4710; 17 Nelson Rd SE10; mains £9-14), more café than bar, is a relaxed French place with a good wine selection by the glass, *très bon* steaks and good fish dishes.

Vietnam (☎ 8858 0871; 18 King William Walk SE10; mains around £4) has inexpensive lunch plates such as spring rolls with rice.

Beachcomber (☎ 8853 0055; 34 Greenwich Church St SE10; mains £9-25) is an old stalwart festooned with flower baskets and potted plants. It specialises in decent seafood dishes and is a wonderful place to spend a sunny afternoon (or weekend morning for breakfast).

Inside (☎ 8265 5060; 19 Greenwich South St SE10; mains £10-15) flies the flag for fine modern European dining in Greenwich – superlative dishes within aubergine and cool-white walls.

Brixton (Map 1)

If you're coming for the market (tube Brixton), don't restrict yourself to the eateries in the covered market itself. The surrounding streets (eg, Atlantic Rd and Coldharbour Lane) have a number of worthy places.

The Phoenix (☎ 7733 4430; 441 Coldharbour Lane SW9; ⊖ Brixton; mains £3-5), just beyond the covered market, is a classic London caff with a warm cockney welcome. Daily roasts complement all the old favourites including bangers and mash, pies of every persuasion and chips, chips, chips.

Eco Brixton (☎ 7738 3021; 4 Market Row SW9; mains £6-11; open Tues-Sun) has broadly Italian and specifically tasty fare in a bustling, buzzy atmosphere.

El Pilon Quindiano (☎ 7326 4316; Granville Arcade, Coldharbour Lane SW9; set lunches £6) is an authentic Colombian café specialising in delicacies such as arepa (small maize pancakes with various fillings), yucca and empañadas (filled turnover with a pastry crust).

Satay Bar (☎ 7326 5001; 447-450 Coldharbour Lane SW9; mains £6-12), one of our favourite Asian eateries, serves very authentic Indonesian food in a colourful, funky bar.

Bug (☎ 7738 3366; St Matthew's Peace Garden, Brixton Hill SW2; mains £8-13), in the crypt of St Matthew's Methodist Church, is one of the best (largely vegetarian) restaurants in London. The mood is bright and the menu global.

Fulham

Fulham Rd is a good place for a meal and a night out.

The Gate (Map 1; ☎ 8748 6932; 51 Queen Caroline St W6; ⊖ Hammersmith; mains £8-12) alone is enough reason to include a Fulham section here. This is one of London's best restaurants: taste, service and presentation are paramount but never get in the way of fun and friendliness. And it just happens to be vegetarian.

The Blue Elephant (Map 7; ☎ 7385 6595; 4-6 Fulham Broadway SW6; ⊖ Fulham Broadway; mains £10-20), a Fulham institution, serves up-market (and pricey) Thai food in jungle-like surroundings.

The River Café (Map 1; ☎ 7386 4200; Thames Wharf, Rainville Rd W6; ⊖ Hammersmith; mains from £20-30) is a see-and-be-seen Italian eatery that owes its fame as much to the cookbooks it has spawned as to the food actually served here, which is based on the very best ingredients cooked simply.

Chutney Mary (Map 7; ☎ 7351 3113; 535 King's Rd SW10; ⊖ Fulham Broadway; mains £14.50-24) is not the kind of Indian you visit on your way home from the pub. For food this good – a gastronomic tour of India – you need your sobriety intact.

Kew

Newens Maids of Honour (☎ 8940 2752; 288 Kew Rd; ⊖ Kew Gardens; set teas £5.45; open Tues-Sun) is an old-fashioned tearoom that wouldn't seem out of place in a Cotswolds village. It owes its fame to a special dessert, 'maid of honour', which was supposedly concocted by Henry VIII's second wife, the ill-fated Anne Boleyn. It is made with puff pastry, lemon, almonds and curd cheese, and a visit to the gardens isn't complete without a sample. You'll find it a short distance north of Victoria Gate, the main entrance to Kew Gardens.

The Glasshouse (☎ 8940 6777; 14 Station Parade W9; ⊖ Kew Gardens; set lunches/dinners £17.50/30), virtually next door to the tube station, specialises in modern British cuisine and is a fabulous way to round off a visit to the gardens. The menus are set although the choice is large and the flavours will be etched on your palate all the way home.

Richmond

Chez Lindsay (☎ 8948 7473; 11 Hill Rise; ⊖ Richmond; 3-course set dinners £15) is a gregarious neighbourhood French restaurant specialising in sweet and savoury crepes chased with cider, as done in Brittany, the birthplace of these flat, filled pancakes.

ENTERTAINMENT
Pubs & Bars

The pub is the social focus of London life and sampling a range of them is one of the pleasures of any visit. From ancient atmospheric taverns to slick DJ bars, London has a lot to offer the discerning tippler no matter how hard the themed and chain bars try to take over. This list features many of our favourite boozers but there's no substitute for individual research – your tolerance is the only limit. For locations at a glance, see the nearest tube stations for those pubs listed here.

Lamb & Flag (Map 5; 33 Rose St WC2; Covent Garden) is a popular historic pub and everyone's Covent Garden 'find' so is always jammed. It was built in 1623 and was formerly called 'the Bucket of Blood'.

The Queen's Larder (Map 4; 1 Queen Square WC1; Russell Square), in a lovely square southeast of Russell Square, is so called because Queen Charlotte, wife of 'Mad King' George III, rented part of the pub's cellar to store special foods for her afflicted hubbie who was getting treatment nearby. There are benches outside for fair weather fans and there's a good dining room upstairs.

Museum Tavern (Map 5; 49 Great Russell St WC1; Tottenham Court Road) is where Karl Marx used to retire for a sup after a hard day in the British Museum Reading Room. If it was good enough for him…

Sherlock Holmes (Map 5; 10 Northumberland St WC2; Charing Cross) is where Sir Arthur Conan Doyle reputedly wrote many of his most famous stories. It's a classic English pub with a museum of Holmes memorabilia so you can guess how many tourists it gets.

Freedom Brewing Company (Map 5; 41 Earlham St WC2; Covent Garden) is London's primo microbrewery although it might be a little expensive for the casual drinker.

Gordon's Wine Bar (Map 5; 47 Villiers St WC2; Embankment) is an atmospheric wine bar in ancient vaults beneath the street.

Bar Vinyl (Map 2; 6 Inverness St NW1; Camden Town), with loud music and groovy clientele, is an earful of the Camden scene.

Ye Grapes (Map 4; 16 Shepherd Market W1; Green Park) is a decent, if unremarkable, boozer that combines good beer, period decor, a friendly crowd and good views of life on Shepherd Market.

Scruffy Murphy's (Map 5; 15 Denman St W1; Piccadilly Circus) is the most authentic of the Irish bars in Soho, short on ceremony and tall on tales.

Coach & Horses (Map 5; 29 Greek St W1; Leicester Square) is a splendidly seedy Soho institution, made famous by writer and newspaper columnist Jeffrey Bernard who, more or less, drank himself to death here.

The Churchill Arms (Map 3; 119 Kensington Church St W8; Notting Hill Gate) is a lovely traditional tavern stuffed with Winston memorabilia and bric-a-brac. There's an excellent Thai restaurant upstairs (mains around £7) and a pleasant conservatory out back.

Windsor Castle (Map 3; 114 Campden Hill Rd W11; Notting Hill Gate) is a memorable pub with oak partitions separating the original bars. The panels have tiny doors so big drinkers will have trouble getting past the front bar. It also has one of the loveliest walled gardens (with heaters in winter) of any pub in London.

Market Bar (Map 3; 240a Portobello Rd W11; Ladbroke Grove) is convenient for the market and has an interesting, eclectic decor and entertaining crowd.

Westminster Arms (Map 4; 9 Storey's Gate SW1; Westminster) is a pleasant, atmospheric place just around the corner from Big Ben so it gets its fair share of politicians. It's great for a swift half pint after a tour of Westminster Abbey (think of the convenience).

The Red Lion (Map 4; 48 Parliament St SW1; Westminster) is a classic late 19th-century pub with polished mahogany and etched glassware, where the TV shows parliamentary broadcasts just in case it kicks off in the house and the MPs have to rush back.

Nag's Head (Map 3; 53 Kinnerton St SW1; Knightsbridge), in a serene mews not far from bustling Knightsbridge, is a terrific early-19th-century drinking den with eccentric decor, a sunken bar and no mobile phones.

Grenadier (Map 4; 18 Wilton Row SW1; Hyde Park Corner), also down a quiet and rather exclusive mews, is pretty as a picture from the outside and welcoming within (despite the sabres and bayonets on the walls).

King's Head & Eight Bells (Map 7; 50 Cheyne Walk SW3; Sloane Square) is an attractive corner pub pleasantly hung with flower baskets in summer. It was a favourite of the painter Whistler and the writer Carlyle.

Brixtonian Havana Club (Map 1; 11 Beehive Place SW9; Brixton) is as laid-back as a bar with hundreds of different kinds of rum can be.

George Inn *(Map 6; Talbot Yard, 77 Borough High St SE1; ⊖ London Bridge or Borough)*, tucked away in a cobbled courtyard not far from the Thames, is London's last surviving galleried coaching inn and dates from 1676. Charles Dickens used to frequent the Middle Bar.

The Anchor *(Map 6; 34 Park St SE1; ⊖ London Bridge)*, an 18th-century boozer just east of the Globe Theatre, has a terrace offering superb views over the Thames. Dr Johnson is said to have written some his dictionary here.

The Fire Station *(Map 4; 150 Waterloo Rd SE1; ⊖ Waterloo)* is a very popular gastropub.

The Market Porter *(Map 6; 9 Stoney St SE1; ⊖ London Bridge)*, across the road from Borough Market, has a good range of beers and a diverse crowd.

Trafalgar Tavern *(Park Row SE10; DLR Cutty Sark)* is a Regency-style pub that was built in 1837 and stands above the site of the old Placentia Palace where Henry VIII was born.

Captain Kidd *(Map 1; 108 Wapping High St E1; ⊖ Wapping)* is a great little pub on the Thames and has large windows, a fine beer garden and a mock scaffold recalling the hanging of the eponymous pirate in 1701.

Prospect of Whitby *(Map 1; 57 Wapping Wall E1; ⊖ Wapping)* dates from 1520 – last remodelled in the 18th century – and is one of London's oldest boozers. It's firmly on the tourist trail but there's a terrace overlooking the Thames, a decent restaurant upstairs and open fires in winter.

Ye Olde Mitre *(Map 4; 1 Ely Court EC1; ⊖ Chancery Lane)* is an 18th-century treasure hidden down an alley and just finding it makes you feel like claiming it as your local.

Cock Tavern *(Map 4; East Poultry Ave EC1; ⊖ Farringdon)* is a legendary pub where you can top up between 6.30am and 10.30am when it feeds and waters the workers from Smithfield Market.

Fox & Anchor *(Map 4; 115 Charterhouse St EC1; ⊖ Farringdon or Barbican)*, in a side street off Smithfield, is a late-Victorian treasure full of interesting nooks and crannies; it has an early licence to accommodate the market porters and does gargantuan brekkies.

Cantaloupe *(Map 1; 35-43 Charlotte Rd EC2; ⊖ Old Street or Shoreditch)* was one of the pioneers of the Shoreditch warehouse conversion scene and is still popular. The bar is bright and breezy and the restaurant reliable (mains £8-15).

Sosho *(Map 1; 2 Tabernacle St EC2; ⊖ Moorgate)* is sexy, glamorous and off limits if you're not feeling either of the above; although the cocktails could soon get you in the mood.

Jamaica Wine House *(Map 6; 12 St Michael's Alley EC3; ⊖ Bank)* stands on the spot of London's first coffee house and is actually a traditional Victorian pub, not a wine bar.

Ye Olde Cheshire Cheese *(Map 4; Wine Office Court EC4; ⊖ Blackfriars)*, rebuilt six years after the Great Fire and popular with Dr Johnson, Thackeray, Dickens and the visiting Mark Twain, is touristy but always atmospheric and enjoyable for a pub meal (mains around £7).

Crown & Goose *(Map 2; 100 Arlington Rd NW1; ⊖ Camden Town)* is a newish pub with a young crowd and decent, no-nonsense food.

Medicine Bar *(Map 2; 181 Upper St N1; ⊖ Highbury & Islington)* is coolly unpretentious, plays good music from funk to disco and stays open until 2am at the weekend. This place is members-only at weekends; it also has a sister bar in Shoreditch.

Old Queen's Head *(Map 2; 44 Essex Rd N1; ⊖ Angel)* is loud, popular and packed to the rafters most nights.

Pembroke Castle *(Map 2; 150 Gloucester Ave NW1; ⊖ Chalk Farm)* is a light, airy retro place where you can feel just as comfortable supping wine as ale.

Old Bull & Bush *(North End Way NW3; ⊖ Hampstead)* has origins dating back to Charles I. One of London's most celebrated pubs, it was immortalised in the old music hall song *Down by the Old Bull and Bush*.

Spaniard's Inn *(Spaniard's Road NW3; ⊖ Hampstead, then bus No 210)* is a gregarious and historic pub associated with Dick Turpin and more savoury characters like Shelley and Dickens.

Clubs

Propelled by an insatiable appetite for lights, loud music and hedonism – and perhaps in response to the lame pub licensing hours – London is a clubber's capital that's been propping up the vanguard of dance since the term 'recreational party drugs' was coined. From low-key DJ bars to warehouses and 'superclubs', the city has an astonishing range of venues offering everything from sexy R&B to thumping garage. Even within each club, the variety can be enormous. Some venues have several different rooms while others change the tempo according to the night.

During the week, you can expect to pay between £3 to £6 for admission to most clubs while you can triple that on Friday and Saturday. Check *Time Out* for party nights and prices.

Bagley's Studios *(Map 2; ☎ 7278 2777; King's Cross Freight Depot, York Way N1; ⊖ King's Cross St Pancras)* is a huge, converted warehouse with five dance floors, four bars and an outside area in the summer. It's a safe bet for house and garage.

The End *(Map 5; ☎ 7419 9199; 16a West Central St WC1; ⊖ Holborn)* has industrial decor, a big sound and is the best venue around the West End for serious clubbers who like their music hard.

Fabric *(Map 4; ☎ 7490 0444; 77a Charterhouse St EC1; ⊖ Farringdon)* is the latest feather in Clerkenwell's well-plumed cap and boasts three dance floors in a converted meat cold-store. Residences have included Sasha and Groove Armada. Expect to queue.

The Cross *(Map 2; ☎ 7837 0828; Goods Way Depot, York Way N1; ⊖ King's Cross St Pancras)* is a little out of the way but has hugely popular weekend parties that will keep you pumpin' until 5am.

Camden Palace *(Map 2; ☎ 7387 0428; 1a Camden High St NW1; ⊖ Mornington Crescent)* is a multilevel monster of sound and light, filled with young, sweaty boppers and good for a night of clubbing with a small 'c'.

Ministry of Sound *(Map 6; ☎ 7378 6528; 103 Gaunt St SE1; ⊖ Elephant & Castle)* is London's most famous club and continues to pack in a diverse crew with big local and international names. Open until 8am.

Velvet Room *(Map 5; ☎ 7439 4655; 143 Charing Cross Rd WC2; ⊖ Tottenham Court Road)* is an intimate and stylish West End club for which you will have to dress to impress.

Bug Bar *(Map 1; ☎ 7738 3184; The Crypt, St Matthew Peace Garden, Brixton Hill SW2; ⊖ Brixton)* is a great little club, where the nights are varied, the vibe laid-back and lively, and the toilets unisex.

Hanover Grand *(Map 5; ☎ 7499 7977; 6 Hanover St W1; ⊖ Oxford Circus)* has a balconied dance floor perpetually full of beautiful clubbers. Friday night sees the unbelievably popular school disco complete with school uniforms, slow sets and snogging in the toilets.

Cargo *(Map 1; ☎ 7739 3440; 83 Rivington St EC2; ⊖ Old Street)* is a hugely popular new club with local and international DJs and a courtyard where you can simultaneously enjoy big sounds and the great outdoors.

Bar Rumba *(Map 5; 7287 2715; 36 Shaftesbury Ave W1; ⊖ Piccadilly Circus)*, along a Soho backstreet, is a small club with a big reputation. There's a different style each night – from Latin and jazz to deep house and garage – but every one's a winner.

Gay & Lesbian London

London's gay scene has exploded in recent years and there are gay – and to a lesser extent lesbian – venues all over the city. To help you crack the capital, pick up the free *Pink Paper* (very serious and politically correct) or *Boyz* (more geared towards entertainment) available from most gay cafés, bars and clubs. The four-page gay section of *Time Out* is another excellent source of information. The **Lesbian & Gay Switchboard** *(☎ 7837 7324)* answers calls 24 hours.

In the 'gay village' of Soho (tube Tottenham Court Road or Piccadilly Circus) – particularly along Old Compton St – bars and cafés are thick on the ground. Unless otherwise indicated, all the establishments in this section can be found on Map 5.

Old Compton Café *(☎ 7439 3309; 34 Old Compton St; open 24hr)* is a friendly, often frantic place with cheap snacks while **Balans** *(☎ 7437 5212; 60 Old Compton St)* is a popular, moderately priced continental-style café.

First Out *(☎ 7240 8042; 52 St Giles High St WC2)*, near Tottenham Court Road tube station, is a long-established, friendly, mixed lesbian-gay café that serves vegetarian food and has rotating exhibitions.

Astoria *(☎ 7434 9592; 157-165 Charing Cross Rd WC2)*, near First Out, is a dark, sweaty and atmospheric club with a gay night. There are good views of the stage and a huge dance floor.

Retro Bar *(☎ 7321 2811; 2 George Court WC2)*, tucked away down a small lane off the Strand, is a friendly bar with a host of theme nights in the upstairs bar during the week.

Black Cap *(Map 2; ☎ 7428 2721; 171 Camden High St NW1; ⊖ Camden Town)* is a late-night bar famous for its drag shows.

Heaven *(☎ 7930 2020; The Arches, Villiers St WC2; ⊖ Charing Cross)* is a long-standing favourite club with three rooms; some nights are mixed but it positively fizzes with party boys on Saturday night.

PAUL BEINSSEN

Outside the Royal Festival Hall

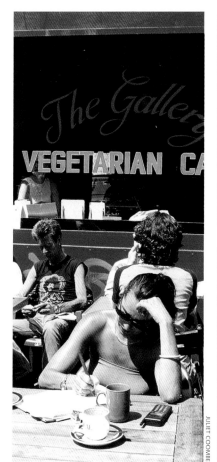

JULIET COOMBE

Portobello Road café

NEIL SETCHFIELD

Club scene in Camden

ANGUS OSBORN

Sunbathing in Hyde Park

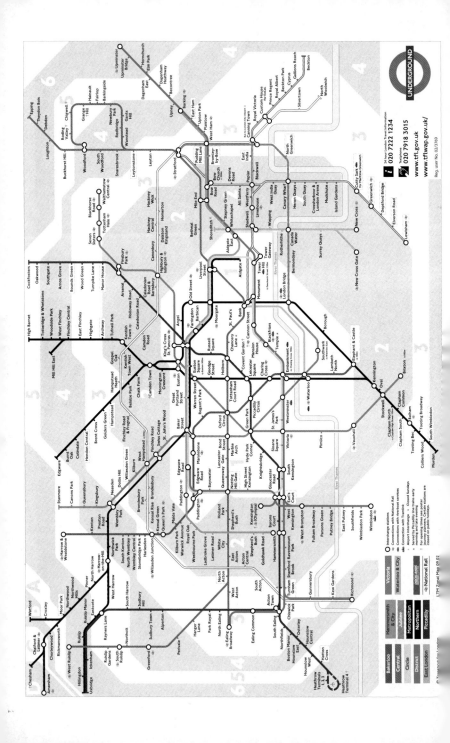

Live Music

London's live music scene is one of its principal attractions; any night of the week you can catch bands and performances that would be the envy of the rest of the world, or take a punt on seeing the hotly tipped in a small venue before they go on to megastardom. This list merely scratches the surface – check the press to see what's on.

Rock & Pop Brixton Academy *(Map 1; ☎ 7771 2000; 211 Stockwell Rd SW9; ⊖ Brixton)* is an enormous, user-friendly place with a sloping floor that allows you to see the band no matter how far back you are.

Garage *(Map 2; ☎ 7607 1818; 20-22 Highbury Corner N5; ⊖ Highbury & Islington)* is a good, medium-sized venue that hosts local and visiting bands on their way up, although it's ridiculously hot and sweaty in summer.

Borderline *(Map 5; ☎ 7734 2095; Orange Yard W1; ⊖ Tottenham Court Road)*, a small, relaxed venue, hosts bands on the verges of the mainstream. It's also your best bet to see big-name acts performing under pseudonyms.

The Forum *(Map 1; ☎ 7344 0044; 9-17 Highgate Road NW5; ⊖ Kentish Town)*, a grand old theatre, is one of London's best large venues.

The Marquee Club *(Map 2; ☎ 7494 1449; ☒ www.themarquee.com; 16 Parkfield St N1; ⊖ Angel)* is the latest incarnation of one of London's most famous venues where the Rolling Stones played their first gigs and every major act from Hendrix to Bowie and U2 have previously strut their stuff. The new 1200-seater venue is a good size and a welcome, independent boost to the local scene.

Hackney Ocean *(☎ 8986 5336; 270 Mare St E8; ⊖ Bethnal Green)* is London's newest mega venue and has sensational acoustics. It hosts the usual headliners but also does a strong line in world music, reflecting the multiculturalism of Hackney.

If you want to check out new bands, the following venues are worth a visit.

Dublin Castle *(Map 2; ☎ 7485 1773; 94 Parkway NW1; ⊖ Camden Town)* is a pub where many successful bands cut their indie teeth.

Water Rats *(Map 2; ☎ 7837 7269; 328 Gray's Inn Rd WC1; ⊖ King's Cross St Pancras)* has lost its edge a little these days but is still a nostalgic favourite. Bob Dylan made his British debut in this atmospheric boozer.

Notting Hill Arts Club *(Map 3; ☎ 7460 4459; 19 Notting Hill Gate W11; ⊖ Notting Hill Gate)* is a relaxed and funky venue that hosts different nights, often for free.

Jazz London's jazz scene is diverse and spread throughout the city. Many venues put on occasional jazz nights although the following three are the most reliable.

Jazz Café *(Map 2; ☎ 7344 0044; 5 Parkway NW1; ⊖ Camden Town)* is a rather swanky restaurant venue. While you don't have to eat, it's better to book a table when the big names are in town.

100 Club *(Map 5; ☎ 7636 0933; 100 Oxford St W1; ⊖ Oxford Circus)* is a legendary London venue that once showcased the Stones and was at the centre of the punk revolution. It now divides its time between jazz, rock and swing.

Ronnie Scott's *(Map 5; ☎ 7439 0747; 47 Frith St W1; ⊖ Leicester Square; admission Mon-Thur £15, Fri & Sat £25)* will be a familiar name to jazz aficionados and is the best club in London. It's expensive but the food, atmosphere and acts are always spot-on.

Classical Music London is one of Europe's capitals of classical music and has several symphony orchestras, a raft of smaller ensembles, brilliant venues and reasonable prices (anywhere between £5 and £50).

South Bank Centre *(Map 4; ☎ 7960 4242; South Bank; ⊖ Embankment)* has three premier venues in the **Royal Festival Hall** and the smaller **Queen Elizabeth Hall** and **Purcell Room**, which host classical, opera, jazz and choral music. There's a range of pricey cafés and restaurants, and free recitals in the foyer.

The Barbican Centre *(Map 6; ☎ 7638 8891; Silk St EC2; ⊖ Barbican)* may be aesthetically challenged but its acoustics are sound and it is home to the London Symphony Orchestra, which plays some 80 concerts here every year.

Cinema

Glitzy British film premieres take place in Leicester Square, usually at the awesome near-2000-seater Odeon. Blockbusters apart, London is a great place to catch a range of flicks that might not even make it to a cinema near you at home. This is one category where *Time Out* is indispensable.

The National Film Theatre *(Map 4; ☎ 7928 3232; South Bank Centre; ⊖ Waterloo)* is a film-lover's dream and screens some 2000 flicks a year, ranging from vintage classics to foreign art-house.

BFI London IMAX Cinema (*Map 4; ☎ 7902 1234; Tenison Way SE1; ⊖ Waterloo*) is a stunning structure housing Europe's largest IMAX screen.

Theatre

London is a world capital for theatre and there's a lot more than mammoth musicals to tempt you into the West End. Incidentally, the downturn in world travel over recent years dealt a bit of a hammering to the musicals and the final curtain came down on Andrew Lloyd Webber's *Cats* in 2002 after a run of exactly 21 years.

The term 'West End' – like Broadway – generally refers to the big-money productions like the musicals, but also includes heavyweights such as: the **Royal Court** (*Map 7; ☎ 7565 5000; Sloane Square SW1; ⊖ Sloane Square*), the patron of new British writing; the **Royal National Theatre** (*Map 4; ☎ 7452 3000; South Bank; ⊖ Waterloo*), which has three auditoriums and showcases classics and contemporary plays from some of the world's best companies; and the **Royal Shakespeare Company** (*☎ 7638 8891; Barbican Centre EC2; ⊖ Barbican*), which hosts productions of the Bard's classics as well as stuff he might have been interested in.

On performance days you can buy half-price tickets for West End productions (cash only) from the **Leicester Square Half-Price Ticket Booth** (*Map 5; ⊖ Leicester Square; open noon-6.30pm daily*), on the south side of Leicester Square. The booth is the one with the clock tower – beware of imitations that may rip you off. It charges £2 commission for each ticket.

Off West End – where you'll generally find the most original works – includes venues like the **Almeida** (*Map 2; Almeida St N1*), **Battersea Arts Centre** (*Map 1; Lavender Hill SW1*) and the **Young Vic** (*Map 4; 66 The Cut, Waterloo Rd SE1*). The next rung down is known as the fringe and these shows can take place anywhere there's a stage (and can be very good).

For a comprehensive look at what's being staged where, consult *Time Out*, pick up a copy of the free pamphlet *The Official London Theatre Guide* or visit **w** www.official londontheatre.co.uk.

Opera & Dance

Following a £213-million redevelopment, the magnificent and gleaming **Royal Opera House** (*Map 5; ☎ 7304 4000; **w** www.royal opera.org; Covent Garden WC2; ⊖ Covent Garden*) has welcomed home the peripatetic Royal Opera and Royal Ballet.

The home of the English National Opera, the **Coliseum** (*Map 5; ☎ 7632 8300; St Martin's Lane WC1; ⊖ Leicester Square*) presents opera in English.

Spectator Sports

Football Tickets for Premier League football matches are ridiculously hard to come by for casual fans these days and London's top-flight clubs play in full stadiums most weeks. If you really want to see a match, you're better off dropping a division and going to see Crystal Palace or Wimbledon, who both play at **Selhurst Park** (*☎ 8771 8841*) in South London.

But if you want to try your luck, the telephone numbers for the premiership clubs are:

Arsenal	☎ 7704 4040
Chelsea	☎ 7386 7799
Tottenham Hotspur	☎ 0870 112222
West Ham United	☎ 8548 2700
Fulham	☎ 7893 8383
Charlton	☎ 8333 4010

Rugby The shrine of English rugby union is **Twickenham** (*☎ 8892 2000; Rugby Rd, Twickenham; ⊖ Hounslow East, then bus No 281 or Twickenham station; tickets around £30*) but, as with football, tickets for internationals are next to impossible to get unless you have contacts. The ground also boasts a **Museum of Rugby** (*adult/child including stadium tour £6/4; open 10am-5pm Tues-Sat, 2pm-5pm Sun*).

Cricket Although the game was invented here, the England team hasn't done too well on the international stage over recent years. However, the game of gentlemen continues to flourish. Test matches take place at two venerable grounds: **Lord's** (*Map 1; ☎ 7289 1300; St John's Wood Rd NW8; ⊖ St John's Wood*) and **The Oval** (*Map 1; ☎ 7582 6660; Kennington Oval SE11; ⊖ Oval*). Tickets are expensive (from £15 to £50) but, if you're a fan, you'll know it's worth it.

SHOPPING

Many people come to London just to shop: from world-famous department stores to quirky backstreet retail revelations, if you can't find it here, it probably doesn't exist.

Bear in mind that many stores – including Virgin, Miss Selfridge and around 40 others on Oxford St alone – now accept euros. Watch out for the blue and yellow 'euros welcome here' stickers.

If you're looking for something 'British', eschew the Union Jack–emblazoned kitsch of the tourist thoroughfares and fill your bags with things the Brits themselves appreciate: Burberry accessories, Duffer layers, Tiffany sparkles and Ben Sherman shirts are just starting points. Your tailor-made suit will fit more sharply when you know it's from Saville Row and everything tastes better in Royal Doulton glass and china. And everything seems more prestigious when it's in a Harrods bag.

Fashion

If there's a label worth having, you'll find it in central London. Shopping options are well scattered although some streets are renowned for their specialities. Oxford St is the place for High Street fashion, the chains of Regent St crank it up a notch while Covent Garden has a cluster of urban and street labels. Kensington High St has a nice mix of chains and boutiques while you should hotfoot it to Neal St in Covent Garden if you're looking for

To Market, to Market

London has more than 350 markets selling everything from antiques and curios to flowers and fish. Some, such as Camden and Portobello Rd, are well known to tourists while others exist just for the locals, and have everything from dinner to underwear for sale in the stalls.

The following is a highly selective list of the more noteworthy markets (note that they only operate certain days).

Bermondsey Market (Map 6; ☎ 7351 5353; Bermondsey Square SE1; ⊖ Borough; 5am-1pm Fri) is the place to come if you're after old opera glasses, bowling balls, hatpins, costume jewellery, porcelain or other curios. The main market is outdoors on the square although adjacent warehouses shelter the more vulnerable furnishings and bric-a-brac.

Borough Market (Map 6; cnr Borough High & Stoney Sts SE1; ⊖ London Bridge; 9am-6pm Fri, 9am-4pm Sat) is a farmer's market sometimes called London's Larder, and has been here in some form since the 13th century. It's a superb – and moody – food market, where you'll find everything from organic falafel to a boar's head.

Brick Lane Market (Map 1; Brick Lane E1; ⊖ Shoreditch or Aldgate East; 8.30am-1pm Sat) is an East End pearl, a sprawling bazaar featuring everything from fruit and veggies to paintings and bric-a-brac.

Brixton Market (Map 1; Electric Ave & Granville Arcade; ⊖ Brixton; 8am-5.30pm Mon-Sat, 8am-1pm only Wed) is a cosmopolitan treat that mixes everything from the Body Shop and reggae to slick Muslim preachers, South American butcher shops and exotic fruits. On Electric Ave and in the covered Granville Arcade you can buy wigs, unusual foods and spices, and homeopathic root cures.

Camden Market (Map 2; Camden High St NW1; ⊖ Camden Town; 9am-5pm Thur-Sun) is now one of London's most popular tourist attractions and stopped being cutting-edge several thousand cheap leather jackets ago. It started out in the mid-1970s as a collection of attractive craft stalls by Camden Lock but now extends most of the way from Camden Town tube station to Chalk Farm tube station. You'll find a bit of everything but a lot of tourist-oriented tack. It's positively mobbed at the weekend.

Petticoat Lane Market (Map 6; Middlesex St E1; ⊖ Aldgate, Aldgate East or Liverpool Street; 8am-2pm Sun) is a cherished East End institution overflowing with cheap consumer durables of little interest to tourists (although you'll see a hell of a lot of them).

Portobello Rd Market (Map 3; Portobello Rd W10; ⊖ Notting Hill Gate, Ladbroke Grove or Westbourne Park), one of London's most famous (and crowded) street markets, has taken over from Camden in the hip stakes. New and vintage clothes are its main attraction although you'll also find lots of antiques, handmade jewellery, paintings and ethnic stuff.

Spitalfields Market (Map 6; Commercial St E1; ⊖ Liverpool Street; 9.30am-5.30pm Sun, organic market 9.30am-5pm Fri), in a Victorian warehouse, has a great mix of arts and crafts, clothes, books, food and joie de vivre. It is also the site of a long-running battle between developers who want to tear down part of the market and local residents who want it left alone.

LONDON

shoes. Mayfair's South Molton St is the strip for local and international urban chic while Bond St is the fat end of the high-fashion wedge. Knightsbridge draws the hordes with quintessentially English department stores.

Carnaby St, which will be forever remembered as the centre of '60s fashion, has a few good new shops and stalls among the tourist tack. The twee shops and stalls inside the old market building at Covent Garden (Map 5) in the centre tend to be pricey and tourist-oriented, but the streets running off it – particularly around Neal's Yard – are crammed with groovy street labels and alternative boutiques.

Department Stores It's hard to resist the lure of London's famous department stores, even if you don't intend to spree. Their cafés are generally good places to catch your breath.

Harrods *(Map 3; ☎ 7730 1234; 87 Brompton Rd SW1; ✆ Knightsbridge)* is like a theme park for fans of the British establishment. It is always crowded with slow tourists and there are more rules than at an army boot camp but even the toilets will make you swoon.

Harvey Nichols *(Map 3; ☎ 7235 5000; 109-125 Knightsbridge SW1; ✆ Knightsbridge)* is London's temple of high fashion and is where you'll find all of the names that matter in local and international *haute couture*. There's a great food hall on the fifth floor, an extravagant perfume department and jewellery worth a short prison sentence.

Fortnum & Mason *(Map 5; ☎ 7734 8040; 181 Piccadilly W1; ✆ Piccadilly Circus)* is the byword for quality and service from a bygone era. It is steeped in almost 300 years of tradition and is especially noted for its old-world ground-floor food hall where Britain's elite come for their cornflakes and bananas. It is also renowned for its outstanding range of teas and establishment fashion.

Selfridges *(Map 4; ☎ 7629 1234; 400 Oxford St W1; ✆ Bond Street)* is the funkiest and most vital of London's one-stop shops where fashion runs the gamut from street to formal, the food hall is unparalleled and the cosmetics hall is the largest in Europe. It's what Harrods was before it became a self-parody.

Liberty *(Map 5; ☎ 7734 1234; 214-220 Regent St W1; ✆ Oxford Circus)* is an irresistible blend of contemporary styles in an old-fashioned atmosphere. It has a huge and recently refurbished cosmetics department – along with a new lingerie section on the 1st floor – and you can't leave London without some 'Liberty Florals'(printed fabrics).

Antiques

Curios, baubles and period pieces abound along Camden Passage, Bermondsey market, the Saturday market at Portobello and along Islington's Upper St from Angel towards Highbury Corner.

Antiquarius Antiques Centre *(Map 7; ☎ 7969 1500; 131 King's Rd SW3; ✆ Sloane Square)* is packed with 120 stalls and dealers selling everything from top hats and corkscrews to old luggage and jewellery.

London Silver Vaults *(Map 4; ☎ 7242 3844; 53-63 Chancery Lane WC2; ✆ Chancery Lane)* has 72 subterranean shops forming the world's largest collection of silver under one roof.

Books

If you read the book or saw the film *84 Charing Cross Road*, **Charing Cross Rd** *(Map 5; ✆ Tottenham Court Road or Leicester Square)* will need no introduction. It's still the best place to head for reading material old and new. The big chains, like Waterstone's and Borders, have branches all over London with the flagship stores in Piccadilly and Oxford St respectively. **Riverside Walk Market** *(Map 4; South Bank; ✆ Waterloo; open 10am-5pm Sat & Sun, fewer stalls Mon-Fri)*, under the arches of Waterloo Bridge, is one of the best patches for cheap second-hand tomes.

Foyle's *(Map 5; ☎ 7437 5660; 113-119 Charing Cross Rd WC2)* is the biggest – and most confusing – bookshop in London but often stocks titles you may not find elsewhere.

Daunt Books *(Map 4; ☎ 7224 2295; 83 Marylebone High St W1; ✆ Baker Street)* has a huge range of specialist travel titles – and general material – in a beautiful, old sky-lit shop.

Zwemmer Art & Architecture *(Map 5; ☎ 7379 7886; 24 Litchfield St WC2; ✆ Charing Cross • ☎ 7240 4157; 80 Charing Cross Rd; ✆ Leicester Square)* stocks all kinds of art books while its Charing Cross Road branch specialises in cinema and photography.

Books for Cooks *(Map 3; ☎ 7221 1992; 4 Blenheim Crescent W11; ✆ Ladbroke Grove)* is brimming with kitchen potential, and also has a small café.

Gay's the Word *(Map 2; ☎ 7278 7654; 66 Marchmont St WC1; ✆ Russell Square)* stocks guides and literature for, by and about gay men and women.

Travel Gear

YHA Adventure Shop *(Map 5; ☎ 7836 8541; 14 Southampton St WC2; ⊖ Covent Garden)* is an excellent place to stock up on all sorts of camping and walking gear.

With a well-established store in Bath, **Itchy Feet** *(Map 5; 162 Wardour St W1; ⊖ Oxford Circus)* has recently opened up shop in London. There's a wide selection of guidebooks, maps and clothing for various travel needs.

Music

If it's been recorded, you can buy it in London. For the biggest general collections of CDs and tapes take on the West End giants of **Tower Records** *(Map 5; ☎ 7439 2500; 1 Piccadilly Circus W1; ⊖ Piccadilly Circus; open until midnight Mon-Sat)*, **HMV** *(Map 5; ☎ 7631 3423; 150 Oxford St W1; ⊖ Oxford Circus; open until 8pm Mon-Fri)* and **Virgin Megastore** *(Map 5; ☎ 7631 1234; 14-30 Oxford St W1; ⊖ Tottenham Court Road; open until 9pm Mon-Sat)*. For personality, visit the following.

Rough Trade *(Map 5; ☎ 7240 0105; 16 Neales Yard WC2; ⊖ Covent Garden • ☎ 7229 8541; 130 Talbot Rd W11; ⊖ Ladbroke Grove)*, in the basement of Slam City Skates, is the most central outlet of this famous store that was at the forefront of the punk explosion in the 1970s. This – and its original store in Notting Hill – is the best place to come for underground specials, vintage rarities and pretty much anything of an indie or alternative bent.

Ray's Jazz Shop *(Map 5; ☎ 7240 3969; 180 Shaftesbury Ave WC2; ⊖ Tottenham Court Road)* is where aficionados will find those elusive back catalogues from their favourite jazz and blues artists.

Harold Moores Records *(Map 5; ☎ 7437 1576; 2 Great Marlborough St W1; ⊖ Oxford Circus)* has a brilliant range of classical.

Black Market Records *(Map 5; ☎ 7437 0478; 25 D'Arblay St W1; ⊖ Oxford Circus)* is your best bet for dance, and if they haven't got what you're after, they'll know who will.

GETTING THERE & AWAY

London is the major gateway to Britain, so further transport information can be found in the main Getting There & Away and Getting Around chapters.

Airports

Heathrow Fifteen miles west of central London, Heathrow (LHR) is the world's busiest commercial airport, has four terminals, and handles upwards of 63 million passengers a year. The tube and Heathrow Express each have two stations serving Heathrow: one each for Terminals 1, 2, and 3, and one each for Terminal 4. Make certain you know which terminal your flight is departing from as airlines and flights can shift around the airport.

Heathrow can appear chaotic and crowded, and you should allow yourself plenty of time to get lost in the labyrinth of overpriced shops, bars and restaurants. Each terminal has competitive currency-exchange facilities, information counters and accommodation desks.

There are several large international hotels – none particularly cheap or noteworthy – at or near Heathrow should you be leaving or arriving at a peculiarly early or late hour. To reach them you must take the distinctive blue **Heathrow Hotel Hoppa bus** *(☎ 01293-507099; adult/child £3/free)* – a service that is free at most other airports. The buses run between 6am and 11pm, with a service every 10 minutes at peak times, and every 15 minutes otherwise, for the first three terminals. Services from Terminal 4 run every 30 minutes.

There are left-luggage facilities at **Terminal 1** *(☎ 8745 5301)*, **Terminal 2** *(☎ 8745 4599)*, **Terminal 3** *(☎ 8759 3344)* and **Terminal 4** *(☎ 8745 7460)*. They open from 6am to 11pm. The charge is £3.50 for up to six hours, or £4 per day. All can forward baggage.

For general inquiries and flight information phone ☎ 0870 000 0123. There is no booking fee at the London Underground **Hotel Reservation Service** *(☎ 8564 8808)*, which can help book rooms near the airport although the service on the arrivals floor charges £5.

Gatwick Much smaller than Heathrow, Gatwick *(LGW; ☎ 0870 000 2468; w www.baa.co.uk/gatwick)* is, in many ways, easier and more pleasant to use. The northern and southern terminals are linked by an efficient monorail service; check which terminal you will use. There are all the predictable shops, and several eating and drinking areas.

There are left-luggage offices at the **North Terminal** *(☎ 01293-502013; open 6am-10pm daily)* and the **South Terminal** *(☎ 01293-502014; open 24hr)*. Each charges £4 per piece, per day.

For British Airways information, phone ☎ 0870 000 0123. For airport and all other flight information phone ☎ 01293-535353.

Stansted Some 35 miles northeast of central London, **Stansted** *(STN; ☎ 0870 000 0303; w www.baa.co.uk/stansted)*, London's third international gateway, handles many of the discount airlines such as Buzz, Go and Ryanair. Sir Norman Foster designed the futuristic terminal building.

Luton The other major airport for the discount airlines, **Luton** *(LTN; general inquiries, hotel reservations, transport options and car park information ☎ 01582 405100)* is 35 miles north of the city. It is the home of easyJet discount airline.

London City Six miles east of central London, **London City** *(LCY; ☎ 7646 0000; w www.londoncityairport.com)* is in the Docklands. Largely seen as a businessperson's airport and underutilised until recently, London City now has flights to 20 continental European destinations as well as eight in the British Isles.

Airline Offices See the Getting There & Away chapter for airline telephone numbers for flight, booking and office information.

Bus
Most long-distance express coaches leave London from **Victoria Coach Station** *(Map 8; ☎ 7730 3466; 164 Buckingham Palace Rd SW1)*, a lovely 1930s-style building (tube Victoria, then about a 10-minute walk). The arrivals terminal is in a separate building across Elizabeth St from the main coach station.

Train
London has 10 main-line terminals, all linked by the tube and each serving a different geographical area of the UK:

Charing Cross (Map 5) Southeast England
Euston (Map 2) Northern and northwest England, Scotland
King's Cross (Map 2) North London, Hertfordshire, Cambridgeshire, northern and northeast England, Scotland
Liverpool Street (Map 6) East and northeast London, Stansted airport, East Anglia
London Bridge (Map 6) Southeast England
Marylebone (Map 3) Northwest London, the Chilterns
Paddington (Map 3) South Wales, western and southwest England, southern Midlands, Heathrow airport

St Pancras (Map 2) East Midlands, southern Yorkshire
Victoria (Map 8) Southern and southeast England, Gatwick airport, Channel ferry ports
Waterloo (Map 4) Southwest London, southern and southwest England

Most stations now have left-luggage facilities (around £4) and lockers, toilets (a 20p coin) with showers (around £3), newsstands and bookshops, and a range of eating and drinking outlets. Victoria and Liverpool Street stations have shopping centres attached.

Car
See the Getting Around chapter for reservation numbers of the main car rental firms, all of which have airport and various city locations.

GETTING AROUND
Transport for London *(TfL; w www.transport forlondon.gov.uk/tfl)* is a new organisation under the control of London's mayor, which aims to integrate the entire London transport network. Its website is very handy for information on all modes of transport in the capital.

To/From the Airports
Heathrow The airport is accessible by bus, the Underground (between 5am and 11pm) and main-line train. Of course, there's always the taxi option but that might become even less attractive if London mayor Ken Livingstone gets his way and slaps a £5 levy on cars entering Heathrow Airport (see the Car & Motorcycle section later).

The fastest way to and from central London is on the **Heathrow Express** *(☎ 0845 600 1515; w www.heathrowexpress.co.uk; adult/child single £13/6, return £25/11.50)*, an ultramodern train that whisks passengers to and from Paddington station in just 15 minutes. You can purchase tickets on board (£2 extra), online or from self-service machines (cash and credit cards accepted) at both terminals. Trains leave every 15 minutes from around 5am to approx 11.30pm. Many airlines have advance check-in desks at Paddington.

The Underground station for Terminals 1, 2 and 3 is directly linked to those terminals; there's a separate station for Terminal 4. Check which terminal your flight uses when you reconfirm. Trains leave every five to 10 minutes and the journey takes about one hour to Piccadilly station (adult/child £3.60/1.50).

The **Airbus A2** (*☎ 08705 808080; single/ return £8/12*) links King's Cross station and Heathrow some 30 times between 4am and 8pm daily, making more than 20 stops along the way. The entire trip takes 1¾ hours.

Heathrow and Gatwick airports are linked by various bus services. **Speedlink** (*☎ 0870 574 7777; w www.speedlink.co.uk; single tickets only £17*) has offices in the arrival areas of Heathrow Terminals 1, 3 and 4, and both Gatwick terminals. Buses leave about every 30 minutes and the journey takes 70 minutes.

A minicab to and from central London will cost from around £25, a metered black cab closer to £40.

Gatwick The **Gatwick Express train** (*☎ 0870 530 1530; w www.gatwickexpress.co.uk; adult return £21*) runs nonstop between Victoria train station and the South Terminal every 15 to 30 minutes from 4.30am to 12.30am, and takes 30 minutes. Gatwick's North and South Terminals are linked by monorail; check which terminal your flight uses. Some airlines have check-in desks at Victoria. The normal train service from Victoria costs £8.20 and takes only a little longer.

See the previous Heathrow section for details on buses linking the two airports.

Stansted The airport is served by the **Stansted Express** (*☎ 0870 530 1530; w www.stanstedexpress.com; adult return £23*) from Liverpool Street station and takes 45 minutes. The trains depart every 15 minutes from 8am to 4pm, and every 30 minutes up until 11pm.

The **Airbus A6** (*☎ 0807 574 7777; single/ return £8/12*) links with Victoria coach station some 40 times daily around the clock and the journey takes 1½ hours.

Luton The **Thameslink** (*☎ 0845 748 4950; w www.thameslink.co.uk; single adult/child £9.50/4.75*) runs trains from King's Cross and other central London stations to Luton Airport Parkway station, from where a shuttle bus will get you to the airport within eight minutes. Trains depart every five to 15 minutes from 7am to 10pm, and the journey takes 35 minutes.

London City The blue **airport shuttle bus** (*☎ 7646 0088; w www.londoncityairport.com/ shuttlebus; single/return £6/12*) connects the airport with Liverpool Street train station via Canary Wharf (£3/6) between 6.50am (11am on Sunday) and 9.20pm (1.10pm on Saturday) daily. The first bus leaves Liverpool Street station (bus stop A) at 6.30am (10.30am on Sunday); the last departs at 9.08pm weekdays (12.40pm on Saturday and 8.50pm on Sunday). Services are every 10 minutes and the journey takes 25 minutes from Liverpool Street and eight minutes from Canary Wharf.

A black taxi costs about £15 to or from central London.

London Underground

The London Underground, or 'tube', first opened in 1863 when it was essentially a roofed-in trench. Sometimes it feels like not a whole lot has changed: on bad days, it can be slow and unreliable, and breakdowns are increasingly common on the ageing system. Sometimes entire sections are closed and commuters had to endure wave after wave of one-day strikes throughout 2002 as the battle over its proposed privatisation raged on. But worst of all, it's terribly expensive; significantly more than its distant cousins in Paris, New York and Hong Kong, and not nearly as user-friendly.

Still, it's normally the quickest and easiest way of getting around London and will probably be your best friend for the duration of your stay. On its good days – and when you're not relying on it during peak hours – it's fast and frequent and manages to shrink London down to an almost manageable size.

It extends as far afield as Amersham in Buckinghamshire to the northwest, Epping in Essex to the northeast, Heathrow airport in the southwest and, via the DLR, Beckton to the southeast. An estimated 2.5 million tube journeys are made every day.

Information Underground travel information centres sell tickets and provide free maps. There are centres at all four Heathrow terminals, and at Victoria, Piccadilly Circus, Oxford Circus, St James's Park, Liverpool Street, Euston and King's Cross tube and main-line train stations.

Network Greater London is served by 12 tube lines, along with the independent (though linked) DLR and an interconnected railway network (see the DLR & Train section later). The first tube train is at around 5.30am Monday to Saturday and around 7am on Sunday; the last train leaves between

11.30pm and 12.30am depending on the day, the station and the line.

Remember that any train heading from left to right on the map is designated as eastbound, any train heading from top to bottom is southbound. If your two stations are not on the same line, you need to note the nearest station where the two lines intersect, where you must change trains.

The biggest change to the Underground in recent years was the completion of the 10-mile Jubilee Line extension in 1999, from Westminster to Stratford via Canary Wharf. Different architects designed all the 11 new Jubilee Line stations and many are ultramodern works of art in themselves.

If you're caught on the Underground without a valid ticket (and that includes crossing into a zone that your ticket doesn't cover) you're liable for an on-the-spot £10 fine. If you do get nabbed, do us all a favour: shut up and pay up. The inspectors – and your fellow passengers – hear the same stories every day of the year.

Fares The London Underground divides London into six concentric zones. The basic fare for adult/child for Zone 1 is £1.60/60p, for Zones 1 & 2 £1.90/80p, for three zones £2.20/1, for four zones £2.70/1.20, for five zones £3.30/1.40 and for all six zones (including Heathrow) £3.60/1.50. But if you're travelling through a couple of zones or several times in one day, consider a travel pass or some other discounted fare.

Travel Passes & Discount Fares A one-day travelcard is the cheapest way of getting about in London and can be used after 9.30am Monday to Friday and all day at the weekend on all forms of transport in London: the tube, suburban trains, the DLR and buses (although *not* night buses).

Most visitors will find that a Zones 1 & 2 card (£4.10) will be sufficient. A card to cover all six zones costs £5. A One Day Travelcard for those aged five to 15 costs £2 regardless of how many zones it covers, but those aged 14 and 15 need a Child Rate Photocard to travel on this fare. You can buy Travelcards several days ahead but not on buses.

If you plan to start moving before 9.30am on a weekday, you can buy a Zones 1 & 2 LT Card for £5.30/2.60, valid on the tube, the DLR and buses (but *not* suburban trains) for one day with no time restrictions.

Weekly Travelcards are also available but require an identification card with a passport-sized photo. A Zone 1 card for adult/child costs £16.20/6.70 and a Zones 1 & 2 card £19.30/7.90. These allow you to travel at any time of day *and* on night buses.

At £6.10 for Zones 1 & 2, Weekend Travelcards valid on Saturday and Sunday are 25% cheaper than two separate one-day cards. Family Travelcards are also available for one or two adults and up to four children aged under 16 (who need not be related to them); they start at £2.70 per adult and 80p per child for Zones 1 & 2.

If you will be making a lot of journeys within Zone 1 *only*, you can buy a carnet of 10 tickets for adult/child £11.50/5, a saving of £4.50.

Bus

If you're not in much of a hurry, travelling round London by double-decker bus is a more enjoyable way to explore London and get a feel for its districts and size. The Central London bus map, available free from most travel information centres and at many tube stations, is an essential planning tool. For short journeys in London, it's often more efficient to take a bus than to struggle with the tube for a couple of stops.

The Tube – Fun Facts to Know & Tell

The tube is the world's oldest (1863), most extensive (253 miles of track) and busiest (785 million journeys a year) underground transport system in the world. With breakdowns every 16 minutes on average, it is also the most unreliable, and for the journey between Covent Garden and Leicester Square (£1.60 for 250m), the per-kilometre price makes taking the tube more expensive than flying Concorde.

The London Underground map, used by millions of people every day, is so familiar that it's often used as a symbol for the city itself. It was created in 1931 by Henry Beck, an engineering draughtsman, who received five guineas (£5.50) for his efforts.

Wheelchair Access The Stationlink buses (☎ 7941 4600) have a driver-operated ramp for wheelchair access, and follow a similar route to the Underground Circle Line, joining up all the main-line stations. People with mobility problems and those with heavy luggage may find this easier to use than the tube, although it only operates once an hour. From Paddington there are services clockwise (the SL1) from 8.15am to 7.15pm, and anticlockwise (the SL2) from 8.40am to 6.40pm.

Night Routes Trafalgar Square is the focus of two-thirds of the night buses (prefixed with the letter 'N') that wheel into action when the tube stops rattling. They run from about midnight to 7am but services can be infrequent. They stop on request so you should clearly signal the driver with an outstretched arm.

Fares It's fairly easy to come to grips with London's bus fares. As far as fares are concerned, there are two zones: the first is the same as Zone 1 on the tube, the second covers the rest of London. Travel within Zone 1 or in both zones costs £1; travel outside Zone 1 only costs 70p. Children pay 40p no matter where they ride. Night buses cost £1.50. Travelcards and other tube passes are good on buses.

In 2002 London Buses started introducing ticket machines at busy stops (and, whatever the circumstances, sullen drivers would force passengers to go back to the machines rather than just sell them tickets on board). Presumably, these machines will become more common but where there is none, you can still buy your ticket on the bus.

DLR & Train
The independent, driverless Docklands Light Railway (DLR) links the City at Bank and Tower Gateway with Canary Wharf, Greenwich and Stratford. It provides good views of development at this end of town. The fares operate in the same way as those on the tube.

Several rail companies also operate suburban rail services in and around London. These are especially important south of the river where there are few tube lines. Once again, fares operate in the same way as those on the tube.

Car & Motorcycle
Bringing a car into London is the perfect way to ruin a good holiday. The roads are horribly clogged, the average speed in the centre is

---

Useful Routes

The following are two examples of scenic bus routes where the ride can be an attraction in itself. The buses run in both directions.

No 24
Beginning at South End Green near Hampstead Heath, it travels through Camden and along Gower St to Tottenham Court Rd. From there it goes down Charing Cross Rd, past Leicester Square to Trafalgar Square, then along Whitehall, past the Palace of Westminster, Westminster Abbey and Westminster Cathedral. It reaches Victoria station and then carries on to Pimlico, which is handy for Tate Britain.

No 8
From Bow in east London, it goes along Bethnal Green Rd and passes the markets at Spitalfields and Petticoat Lane, Liverpool Street station, the City, the Guildhall and the Old Bailey. It then crosses Holborn and enters Oxford St, travelling past Oxford Circus, Bond St, Selfridges and the flagship Marks & Spencer store at Marble Arch before terminating at Victoria.

---

less that 10mph, drivers can be very aggressive and parking space is at a premium.

And if you're still not convinced, consider that mayor Ken Livingstone recently introduced a £5 congestion tax on every private vehicle entering central London between 7am and 6.30pm Monday to Friday. Passes can be bought in advance by post, phone, online, or in shops and garages and up to 10pm on the day of travel (without incurring an additional charge). Vehicles entering the 8-sq-mile toll zone are monitored by video and their registration numbers checked for compliance – anyone who hasn't paid will be slapped with an £80 fine.

Taxi
London's famous **black cabs** (☎ 7272 0272; w www.londonblackcabs.co.uk) are as much a feature of London as its famous red double-decker buses, although these days they come in a variety of colours (and advertising motifs). They are an excellent, if expensive, way of getting around town and the cabbies know the ins and outs of London streets like the backs of their metaphoricals (see the boxed

Some Have the Knowledge – Others Haven't a Clue

Once you've been around the block a few times with a hackney cab driver – during which the car's broken down, he's consulted the A to Z twice and telephoned base for directions – you'll begin to appreciate the more expensive black cabs. To get an all-London license, 'cabbies' must pass a rigorous test which requires them to memorise up to 25,000 streets within a 6-mile radius of Charing Cross and know all the points of interest from hotels to churches. It's a feat that can sometimes take years to achieve and ensures, according to the Public Carriage Office, that only the most committed join the noble trade.

text 'Some Have the Knowledge – Others Haven't a Clue'). A cab is available for hire when the yellow sign is lit. Fares are metered and a 10% tip is expected. They can carry five people. If you leave something behind in a cab – millions do every year – call the Public Carriage Office on ☎ 7230 1631.

Minicabs (or 'hackney cabs') can carry four people and are cheap, freelance competitors to the official black cabs. Anyone with a car can work as a minicab driver and, although they can supposedly only be hired by phone or at a minicab office (there's at least one on every main street), hawkers abound in busy places such as Soho. Beware: some of these guys haven't got a frigging clue how to drive, never mind how to get you to your destination. Neither do they have meters so it's essential that you get a quote before the ignition turns. Some of these cabs are driven by unsavoury characters and solo women travellers should think seriously before catching one of these cabs at night (and steer well clear of the lunatics who tout for business on the street).

Small minicab companies are based in particular areas. Ask a local for the name of a reputable company or phone one of the large **24-hour operations** (☎ 7272 2612, 8340 2450, 8567 1111). Women can phone **Lady Cabs** (☎ 7254 3501). Gays and lesbians can choose **Freedom Cars** (☎ 7734 1313).

Bicycle

Cycling around London is one way of cutting transport costs but it can be a grim business, with heavy traffic and fumes detracting from the pleasure of getting a little exercise. It's advisable to wear a helmet and increasingly Londoners wear face-masks to filter out pollution.

Bikepark (Map 5; ☎ 7430 0083; 11 Macklin St WC2; ⊖ Holborn) rents out bikes and has bicycle parking. The minimum charge is £10

for the first day, £5 for the second day and £3 for subsequent days.

Boat

There is a myriad of boat services on the Thames, with more being announced all the time. Travelling by boat allows you to avoid the traffic while enjoying great views.

From Westminster Pier (Map 4), **City Cruises** (☎ 7930 9033; w www.citycruises.com) operates a service to/from the Tower of London. The adult fare is £5.20/6.30 single/return and the child fare £2.60/3.15. The journeys take 30 minutes and operate every 20 minutes or so from 9.40am until an hour before dusk April to October. There is also a service to Greenwich Pier approximately every 40 minutes through the day which costs £6.30/7.80. A River Red Rover Day Ticket costs £8/4 (adult/child) and allows you to hop on and off.

Westminster Passenger Services Association (☎ 7930 2062; w www.wpsa.co.uk) is the only company that operates a schedule service upriver from Westminster. It takes in Kew Gardens and Hampton Park (see Kew Gardens earlier in this chapter for prices).

Canal Trips

London has 40 miles of inner-city canals, mostly constructed in the early 19th century to transport goods from the industrial midlands to the Port of London. After years of neglect, they are being given a new lease of life as a resource for boaters, walkers, anglers and cyclists. Consult **British Waterways** (Map 3; ☎ 7286 6101; w www.british-waterways.co.uk; Toll House, Delamere Terrace W2; ⊖ Warwick Avenue) about activities on the canals.

If you're interested in getting on the water, contact **The London Waterbus Company** (☎ 7482 2660), which runs trips between Camden Lock and Little Venice, or **Jason's Canal Trips** (☎ 7286 3428; w www.jasons.co.uk) at Little Venice.

Southeast England

England's most populated – and most popular – corner is more than just London's ever-widening hinterland. Beyond the M25 (a contender for the world's largest circular traffic jam), in the counties of Berkshire, Surrey, Kent, East and West Sussex, Hampshire, Buckinghamshire, Hertfordshire and Essex, you will find the kind of space and tranquility that has made the whole region the most sought-after place to live in England.

A rich repository of English history, the country's wealthiest corner has gone to great lengths to preserve those unshakeable, traditional images of old and glorious England. Amid the rolling hills and manicured farmland that stretches right to the edge of the spectacular coastlines, you will find picturesque villages with welcoming pubs and elegant, historical towns that proudly proclaim their Tudor or Victorian heritage. Newly cobbled, pedestrianised streets and restored shop fronts are but the most glaring examples of a concerted effort to echo a time when Britannia ruled the waves and its citizens slept in the certain knowledge that they were the envy of the world. Contemporary realities may indicate otherwise, but it hasn't deterred the region's inhabitants from striding confidently backwards into the future.

Yet while some visitors may find the region bursting with faux and genuine quaintness, behind the cute facade there's a sophisticated dynamism that belies its 'old-style' appearance. Here you will find a highly developed and elaborate tourist infrastructure created to capitalise on the enormous numbers of visitors. Inside sloping, half-timbered Tudor buildings you may find an Internet café with high-speed connections, a trendy Asian fusion restaurant or an expensive, ultra-sleek hotel.

HISTORY

With the French coast only a measly 20 miles (32km) away at its nearest point, the southeast was early English's hot spot, and one of the important stages for events thereafter. The first boatload of Romans landed on the Kent Coast in 55 BC, while St Augustine came ashore armed only with the Good Word a few miles further up the coast in AD 597.

The town of Hastings in East Sussex will forever be associated with the arrival of the

Highlights

- Visiting the fairy-tale Leeds Castle in Kent
- Walking on the white cliffs of Dover on a clear day
- Marvelling at Brighton's Royal Pavilion: folly at its most fantastic
- Nightclubbing on Brighton Beach in summer
- Taking the excellent tour of HMS *Victory* in Portsmouth
- Exploring Canterbury Cathedral in all its wonderful glory
- Surprising yourself with the impossible beauty of Rye
- Taking a guided walk around the battlefield of 1066 at Battle in East Sussex

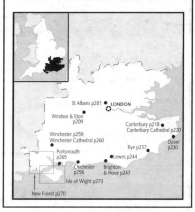

St Albans p281 • LONDON
Windsor & Eton p209
Canterbury p218 •
Canterbury Cathedral p220
Winchester p259
Winchester Cathedral p260
Rye p237
Dover p230
Portsmouth p265
• Lewes p244
Chichester p256
Brighton & Hove p247
Isle of Wight p273
New Forest p270

Normans in 1066, while the castles and fortifications they built throughout the region proved to be a successful bulwark against anyone ever repeating their feat of successfully invading the island. Those same castles may no longer feature in the Defence Ministry's list of key defensive structures, but they remain the favourites of British royalty, who regularly visit them to unwind from the cut-and-thrust world of monarchical privilege.

The British Empire may have been governed from London, but it was won and maintained from Portsmouth, the traditional home of the British Navy from 1194 to the present day. Both Portsmouth and the region's

SOUTHEAST ENGLAND

203

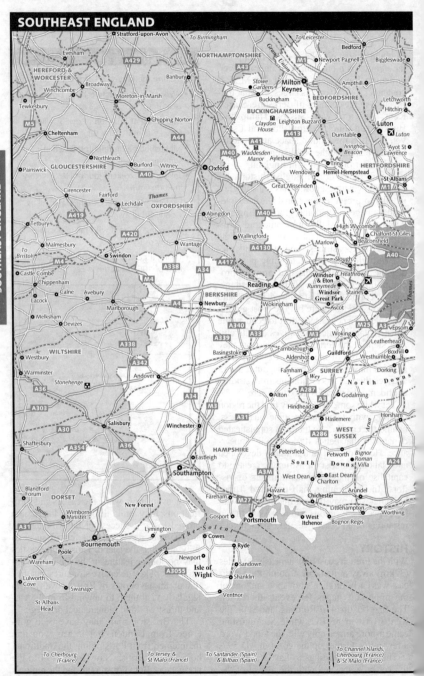

SOUTHEAST ENGLAND

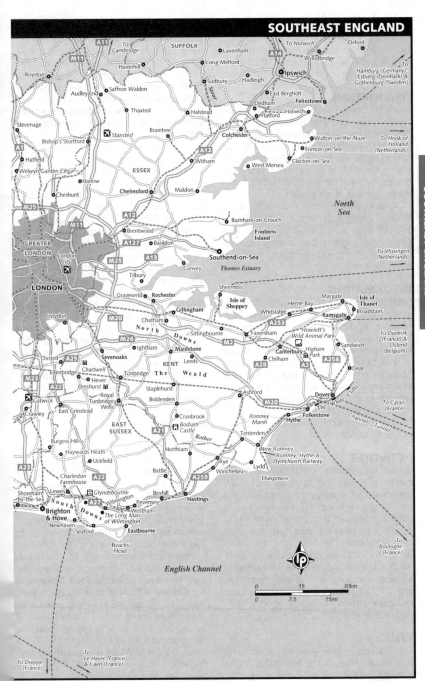

other great port, Southampton, were heavily bombed during WWII, but it didn't stop the British from eventually winning the war, with no small part played by the Allied Command base deep in the white cliffs of Dover.

ORIENTATION

South of London two lines of hills, called 'downs', run east–west through the region. The North Downs curve across the Kent farmland to Dover and the famous white cliffs. The South Downs run from near Portsmouth and end spectacularly at Beachy Head, near Eastbourne. Between the two lie the orchards and market gardens of the Weald.

Northwest of London is the comfortable wooded countryside of the Chiltern Hills, and east from here, the rolling woodland of Essex gives way to flatter countryside, with motorways the prominent feature until you reach the coast.

INFORMATION

Southeast England is a heavily visited region, with plenty of tourist information centres (TICs) offering brochures, maps and booking services. Accommodation of all kinds is plentiful, though you're best advised to book in advance to beat the tourist rush. There are youth hostels in most of the larger towns and cities and the many universities rent out rooms during summer. Banks, post offices and Internet cafés abound, so you'll have no problems communicating with home or getting cash to spend.

ACTIVITIES

Southeast England may be the most crowded corner of Britain, but there are still many opportunities for enjoying the great outdoors on foot or two wheels. This section gives a quick rundown of the options. More information is given in the main Activities chapter near the start of this book, and suggestions for shorter walks and rides are given throughout this chapter. Regional tourism websites all contain walking and cycling information, and TICs all stock leaflets (free) plus maps and guides (usually £1 to £5) covering walking, cycling and other activities.

Walking

The southeast region is well endowed with long-distance national trails, which all make a great focus for walking, even if it's just for a few hours, a day or a weekend. These include the **South Downs Way**, an exhilarating 100-mile (160km) roller-coaster walk across wide open grasslands between Winchester, the ancient capital of England, and Eastbourne, a resort on the south coast. Fit walkers can easily cover it in a week.

In contrast, the **North Downs Way** skirts the southern edge of London's commuter belt yet remains surprisingly rural in places, with leafy woods, nature reserves, farmland, orchards, vineyards, and grassy hills with great views, ending with a grand finale across the famous white cliffs of Dover. The total length is 157 miles (253km), walkable in 12 days, but the two best sections are the far western end from Farnham to Dorking, and the far eastern end from Ashford to Dover. Each section takes two days to cover, and both make ideal weekend excursions from London.

Also easily reached from London, the **Thames Path** follows Britain's best-known river from its source in the Cotswolds through the heart of southern-central England, all the way to London. The trail's total distance is 173 miles (279km), and takes about two weeks to walk, but it divides very neatly into two roughly equal sections at the town of Goring. The western section is more rural, while the eastern section winds through the Chiltern Hills, passing famous and historical towns such as Henley-on-Thames and Windsor, before becoming a major artery through the capital itself.

Yet another long-distance trail in this region is **The Ridgeway**. This starts near Avebury Stone Circle (covered in the Wessex chapter) and runs for 90 miles (145km) along the chalky ridge of the North Wessex Downs and through the woody Chiltern Hills to end at Ivinghoe Beacon near Aylesbury. The whole route can be done in a week, although as with all the long-distance trails covering just a short section is perfectly feasible.

Perhaps not surprisingly, the areas traversed by the long-distance routes are also ideal for shorter walks; the **South Downs** and the **Chiltern Hills** both have extensive footpath networks and are especially popular, as are the **New Forest** and the **Surrey Hills**, and semi-urban areas such as **Epping Forest** on the northeast edge of London. Off the south coast, the **Isle of Wight** is especially walker-friendly, with a good network of paths and some fine stretches of coastline.

Cycling

Seeking out quiet roads for cycle touring can take persistence in southeast England, but some good routes definitely exist here. For starters, there's the **Garden of England Cycle Route**, part of the National Cycle Network (see the main Activities chapter for details), which runs from London to Dover and continues to Hastings – a total of around 170 miles (274km), although shorter options are possible, and you can just follow the route for a day or two if you prefer. Or you can make the whole thing a great circuit by returning from Hastings to London on the 150-mile (242km) **Downs & Weald Cycle Route**.

At just under 100 miles (160km), another popular southeast option is the **Thames Valley Cycle Route**, which escapes from London by following the river upstream (with several traffic-free sections) via Reading and the Chiltern Hills to end at Oxford.

But even if you can't escape the city, London offers cyclists several opportunities. Guidebooks include the *Cycling without Traffic* series, and *The London Cycle Guide* by Nicky Crowther.

For off-road cycling, a great favourite is the **South Downs Way** National Trail; this 100-mile (160km) switchback classic is also for walkers (see the details under Walking, earlier), but mountain bikes can legally ride it end to end. Hard nuts do it in two days. Four would be more enjoyable.

Other great off-road areas in the region include **Epping Forest** on the northeast edge of London. The **North Downs** has lanes which are good for touring, and some good tracks for off-road riding. The **Chiltern Hills** also have a good selection of quiet country lanes and bridleways, including the dedicated mountain-bike venue of Aston Woods at Wendover, while the **New Forest** has a wonderfully vast network of tracks, ideal for gentle or beginner mountain biking, and also offers a week of organised cycling tours every July.

GETTING AROUND

All the places mentioned in this chapter are quite easy to reach by train or bus, and could be visited in a day trip from London. The National Traveline (☎ 0870 608 2608) provides information on all public transport throughout the region.

Bus

Several companies operate fast, regular services from London. Explorer tickets (£5.50/4 per adult/child) give a day's unlimited travel on most buses throughout the region; buy them at bus stations or on your first bus. Country Rover tickets (£5/2.50) cover the same counties and are valid after 9am Monday to Friday and all day at weekends. Diamond Rover tickets (£7/5) can also be used on most **Arriva** (☎ 01279-426349) buses in Buckinghamshire, Hertfordshire and Essex. Tickets allowing one week's unlimited travel on **Stagecoach Coastline** (☎ 01903-237661) and Sussex Bus Services cost £12.50 each.

Train

The yearly Network SouthEast Card costs £20 and gives you a 33% discount off the normal fares. It is recommended for extensive rail travel, though you can only travel after 10am on weekdays (any time at weekends). Accompanying children up to the age of 15 travel for £1. A BritRail SouthEast Pass allows unlimited rail travel for three or four days out of seven, or eight days out of 15, but they must be purchased outside the UK. See the introductory Getting Around chapter for more information. For general rail information call ☎ 08457 484950.

Travelling by public transport in the counties north of London (Essex, Hertfordshire and Buckinghamshire) is not so simple as the towns of interest are not necessarily linked by rail to London or to each other.

Berkshire

If England's conservative 'old money' has a preferred postal district, then it is undoubtedly posh and prosperous Berkshire. Sir Winston Churchill, defender of the might and glory of empire, was born here, while the top toff of the lot, the Queen, regularly stops in to spend time at her favourite castle. But aside from the splendour of Blenheim Palace and the impressive fortress at Windsor, the county is full of exquisitely maintained villages and fabulous countryside populated by quietly proud traditionalists whose mores and lifestyles reflect conservative England's obsession with buffing Albion's faded chalice to a sparkling shine.

WINDSOR & ETON

☎ 01753 • pop 31,000

To most visitors, Berkshire is all about Windsor and the adjacent college town of Eton, separated only by a narrow footbridge across the River Thames. And rightly so, too, as Windsor Castle is a must-see attraction, while the country's most famous public school is not only architecturally elegant but it offers up tangible evidence of England's nearly intractable class system, a key to understanding the English and their ways.

Orientation

The town of Windsor sits beside the River Thames, literally dwarfed by Windsor Castle. Skirting the castle are Thames St and High St, but the town's main drag is pedestrianised Peascod St. The village of Eton is on the far side of a small pedestrian bridge spanning the Thames.

Information

The **Tourist Information Centre** (*TIC; ☎ 743 900, fax 743904;* e *windsor.tic@rbwm.gov .uk; 24 High St; open 10am-6pm daily Apr-Nov, 9.30am-4.30pm Mon-Sat, 10am-4.30pm Sun Dec-Mar*) has all the information on the town and the surrounding area and offers a B&B booking service (£5).

Both the TIC and post office have **bureaux de change**. There are plenty of **ATMs** along High and Thames Sts.

The **post office** (*open 9.30am-5.30pm Mon-Sat*) is in Peascod St. You can use the Internet at **Tower Express** (*Peascod St*), the music shop. Online time costs £1 for 15 minutes. **Round Dot** (*☎ 830620; 5 Church St*) has much faster ISDN lines, and charges £2 for 20 minutes.

The **Eton Bridge Book Store** (*77 High St; open 9.30am-5.30pm Mon-Sat*) is an excellent choice, with all the latest titles. There are also a number of second-hand bookstores – with a mix of academic tomes and classic works of fiction – along Peascod St in Windsor.

Just off St Mark's Rd, **Laundro Coin** (*56 St Leonard's Rd; open 8am-8pm daily*) will take care of all your washing needs.

There are public toilets near the entrance to the castle.

Windsor Castle

Standing on chalk bluffs overlooking the Thames, Windsor Castle (*☎ 831118; adult/ child/over-60 £11.50/6/9.50; open 9.45am-5.15pm Mar-Oct, 9.45am-4.15pm Nov-Feb*) is the largest and oldest occupied fortress in the world. In fact, there has been a royal residence here since the 9th century, but the existing structure owes its beginnings to William the Conqueror, who ordered the construction of a wooden motte and bailey fort in 1070. In 1165, Henry II replaced the wooden stockade with a stone round tower and built the outer walls to the north, east and south. Successive monarchs tinkered, enlarged and altered the castle up to the 19th century, resulting in the gargantuan affair visible today, which occupies five hectares.

In 1992, a fire destroyed or damaged more than 100 rooms in the castle, but an extraordinary restoration was completed within five years and today there is little to indicate that the fire ever started.

From March to October the last admission is at 4pm and, weather and other events permitting, the changing of the guard takes place at 11am daily except Sunday. The State Apartments are closed when the royal family is in residence, traditionally during April and June. It is thought that the Queen has a particular fondness for Windsor, as it was where she spent much of her childhood, and she returns whenever she can. The Union Jack flying over the castle doesn't mean the Queen's at home; instead look for the Royal Standard flying from the Round Tower.

St George's Chapel and the Albert Memorial Chapel close on Sunday. Guided tours of the State Apartments take about 45 minutes and leave at various times during the day; ask at the ticket office.

St George's Chapel One of Britain's finest examples of Gothic architecture, this chapel was designed for the Order of the Garter and was commenced by Edward IV in 1475. It was built in two stages: the choir and the aisles were completed by 1483, but the stone vaulting was not finished until 1528. The nave is one of the best examples of perpendicular architecture in England, with beautiful fan vaulting arching out from the pillars. Henry VIII built the **wooden oriel window** for Catherine of Aragon. The **garter stalls** dating back to 1478–85 are the chapel's equivalent of choir stalls. The banner, helm and crest above each stall indicate the current occupant. Plates carry the names

WINDSOR & ETON

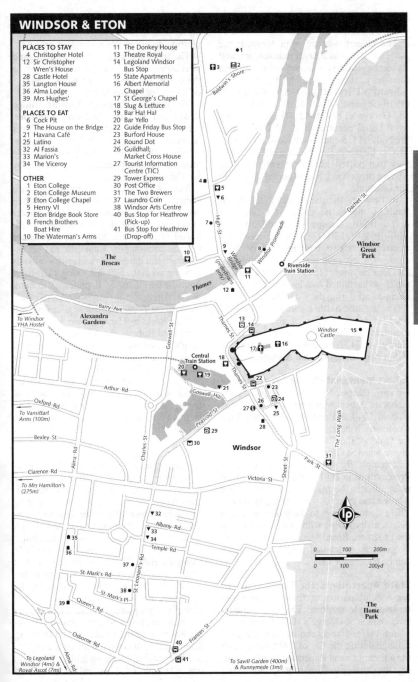

PLACES TO STAY
4 Christopher Hotel
12 Sir Christopher Wren's House
28 Castle Hotel
35 Langton House
36 Alma Lodge
39 Mrs Hughes'

PLACES TO EAT
6 Cock Pit
9 The House on the Bridge
21 Havana Café
25 Latino
32 Al Fassia
33 Marion's
34 The Viceroy

OTHER
1 Eton College
2 Eton College Museum
3 Eton College Chapel
5 Henry VI
7 Eton Bridge Book Store
8 French Brothers Boat Hire
10 The Waterman's Arms
11 The Donkey House
13 Theatre Royal
14 Legoland Windsor Bus Stop
15 State Apartments
16 Albert Memorial Chapel
17 St George's Chapel
18 Slug & Lettuce
19 Bar Ha! Ha!
20 Bar Yello
22 Guide Friday Bus Stop
23 Burford House
24 Round Dot
26 Guildhall; Market Cross House
27 Tourist Information Centre (TIC)
29 Tower Express
30 Post Office
31 The Two Brewers
37 Laundro Coin
38 Windsor Arts Centre
40 Bus Stop for Heathrow (Pick-up)
41 Bus Stop for Heathrow (Drop-off)

SOUTHEAST ENGLAND

of knights who occupied the stalls right back to the 14th century.

The chapel – along with Westminster Abbey – serves as a **royal mausoleum**, and its tombs read like a history of the British monarchy. Here you'll find the tombs of Edward VI (ruled 1461–83), George V (1910–36) and Queen Mary (1867–1953) and George VI (1936–52). The most recent royal burial occurred in April 2002, when the body of George VI's widow, the Queen Mother Elizabeth Bowes-Lyon (1900–2002), was transported here in a splendid and sombre procession. She is buried alongside her husband.

In between the garter stalls, the **Royal Vault** is the burial place of George III (1760–1820), George IV (1820–30) and William IV (1830–37). Another **vault** between the stalls contains Henry VIII (1509–47), his favourite wife (the third of six) Jane Seymour (1509–37), and Charles I (1625–49), reunited with his head after it was chopped off during the Civil War.

The gigantic **battle sword** of Edward III, founder of the Order of the Garter, is mounted on the wall near the tombs of Henry VI (1422–61 and 1470) and Edward VII (1901–10) and Queen Alexandra.

Albert Memorial Chapel After leaving St George's Chapel, don't miss the fantastically elaborate Albert Memorial Chapel. It was built in 1240 and dedicated to Edward the Confessor. It became the original chapel of the Order of the Garter in 1350, falling into disuse when St George's Chapel was built. It was completely restored after the death of Prince Albert in 1861. A major feature of the restoration is the magnificent vaulted roof whose mosaic pieces were crafted in Venice. There's a monument to the prince, although he's actually buried with Queen Victoria in the Frogmore Royal Mausoleum in the castle grounds. A detailed guide to the chapel can be bought for £1.50.

State Apartments The State Apartments are a combination of formal rooms and museum-style exhibits. The most impressive room is St George's Hall, which is still used for state dinners and incurred the most damage during the fire of 1992, along with the adjacent Grand Reception Room. To repair the damage to these rooms, 350 mature oak trees were felled, provoking protest and horror among conservationists. A small exhibition describes the restoration process.

The main entrance is through the **Grand Vestibule**, where you'll also come across the **Grand Staircase** and a fairly impressive collection of armour and weaponry.

You then move through the **Ante Throne Room** and into the **Waterloo Chamber**, named in commemoration of the victory over Napoleon and still used for formal banquets. Adorning the walls are the portraits of the men who beat the French in 1815, painted by Sir Thomas Lawrence.

Next is the **King's Drawing Room**, once named the Rubens Room after the three paintings hanging there. If the Dutch master didn't provide enough eye candy for the bed-bound monarch, the **King's Bed Chamber** features paintings by Canaletto and Gainsborough. But the castle's real artistic trove is to be found in the adjoining **King's Dressing Room**, where Charles II preferred to bunk down. Alongside Sir Anthony Van Dyck's magnificent *Triple Portrait of Charles I* you will see works by Hans Holbein, Rembrandt, Peter Paul Rubens and Albrecht Dürer. The **King's Closet** was used by Charles II as a study and contains works by Canaletto, Sir Joshua Reynolds and William Hogarth.

Next is the **Queen's Drawing Room**, which also has paintings by Holbein and Van Dyck, and the **King's Dining Room**. Here there's a fine ceiling painting by Verrio – one of only three to survive – and woodcarvings by Grinling Gibbons. The **Queen's Ballroom** has a remarkable collection of Van Dyck paintings, including one of Charles I's children, while the Queen's Audience Chamber boasts another ceiling by Verrio. More Gobelins tapestries and another Verrio ceiling adorn the **Queen's Presence Chamber**. The **Queen's Guard Chamber** is decorated with armoury, weapons and a bust of Churchill.

From here you move into the splendid **St George's Hall**. The hammerbeam roof is painted with the arms of the Knights of the Garter. The **Lantern Lobby** stands on the site where the fire started and is used to display silver gilt plate. A corridor leads to the magnificent plush-and-gold **Crimson Drawing Room**, with the smaller **Green Drawing Room** visible through a door on the right.

After passing through a hallway lined on one side with a fine collection of English porcelain, you come to the French-style **Grand Reception Room**. The ceiling caved in during the 1992 fire, but has now been replaced and leads through to the **Garter Throne Room**, used for investing new Knights of the Garter.

The State Apartment circuit eventually winds up back in the Waterloo Chamber. Note that some of the smaller rooms are not always open to the public at busy times – an excellent reason for visiting out of season!

Queen Mary's Dolls' House Designed by Sir Edwin Lutyens, the dolls' house was built in 1923 on a 1:12 scale with the aim of raising money for children's charities. There are occasional special exhibitions here, such as displays of the Queen's childhood toys.

Windsor Great Park Stretching behind Windsor Castle almost all the way to Ascot, Windsor Great Park covers about 40 sq miles (104 sq km). There is a lake, walking tracks, a bridleway and gardens. The **Savill Garden** (☎ 860222; open 10am-6pm daily Mar-Oct, 10am-4pm daily Nov-Feb) is particularly lovely.

The **Long Walk** is a 3-mile (4.8km) walk along a tree-lined path from King George IV Gate to the Copper Horse statue (of George III) on Snow Hill, the highest point of the park. There are some great views of the castle along here. Locals have informed us that the Queen occasionally drives herself down the Long Walk, accompanied only by a bodyguard. The walk is signposted from the town centre.

Around Town
Windsor's fine **Guildhall** (High St) was built between 1687 and 1689, the construction completed under the supervision of Sir Christopher Wren. The council insisted that central columns were required to support the 1st floor even though Wren thought them unnecessary. The few centimetres of clear air proved him right.

The visibly leaning **Market Cross House** of 1768 is right next to the Guildhall. Charles II kept Nell Gwyn, his favourite mistress, in **Burford House** on Church St.

Eton College
Cross the Thames by the pedestrian Windsor Bridge to arrive at another enduring symbol of England's class system: Eton College (☎ 671177; adult/child £3/2; open 2pm-4.30pm during term, 10.30am-4.30pm Apr-Sept), the largest and most famous public (meaning very private) school in England. It was founded by Henry VI in 1440–41 with a view toward educating 70 highly qualified boys awarded a scholarship from a fund endowed by the king. Every year since then, 70 King's Scholars have been chosen based on the results of a highly competitive exam for boys aged 12 to 14, and they are housed in separate quarters from the rest of the 1000 or so other students, known as Oppidans.

While the King's Scholars are chosen exclusively on the basis of exam results, Oppidans usually come from Britain's wealthiest and most aristocratic families, the only ones who can afford the £15,000-per-annum fees. Eton prides itself on educating the cream of the crop (rich and thick, scoff its detractors), and counts no fewer than 18 prime ministers among its alumni, as well as a few royals, including Prince William.

The college has one-hour guided tours at 2.15pm and 3.15pm, which cost £4/3 per adult/child.

Legoland Windsor
Windsor's other great attraction – at least for the four to 12s – is the elaborate mix of model masterpieces and pink-knuckle rides at **Legoland** (bookings ☎ 0990 040404; adult/child £22.95/19.95; open 10am-5pm daily mid-Mar–mid-July, Sept & Oct, 10am-7pm daily mid-July–Aug), and you're unlikely to avoid a visit if you're pestered enough. The idea is family fun, but you'll have to dig deep to entertain everyone. Child admission is for children aged three to 15. If you pre-book it costs a whole £1 less per ticket.

Buses run from Thames St to Legoland between 10am and 5.15pm.

Organised Tours
Guide Friday's open-top double-decker bus tours of the town cost £6.50/2.50 per adult/child. They run from the TIC virtually every half-hour daily between March and September. From Easter to October, **French Brothers** (☎ 851900; Clewer Court Rd) runs 35-minute riverboat trips along the Thames. They depart every half-hour from 11am to 5pm from outside the Riverside station. Tickets cost £4.20/2.10 per adult/child.

SOUTHEAST ENGLAND

Places to Stay

Windsor has a good selection of quality hotels and B&Bs (bed and breakfast hotels). The cheaper B&Bs can be found in the area south of Clarence Rd, between Alma and St Leonard's Rds.

The **Windsor YHA Hostel** (☎ 0870 770 6096, fax 832100; e yhawindsor@compu serve.com; Edgworth House, Mill Lane; beds £11.25) is a mile west of the Riverside train station in a large house with its own garden. Facilities at the hostel include Internet access and a bike rental shop (£6 per day). Catch bus No 50A/B from outside Barclays Bank on Thames St, or follow Arthur Rd or Barry Ave (along the riverbank) from the centre.

An extremely comfortable place to stay is **Mrs Hamilton's** (☎ 865775; 22 York Ave; B&B single/double £35/60), with large, bright rooms and very friendly service.

Mrs Hughes' (☎ 866036; 62 Queens Rd; single with kitchenette £40, double £55, family room per adult/child £30/15) has a family room that sleeps six and, all rooms have fridges and en-suite bathrooms.

Alma Lodge (☎ 854550, fax 855620; 58 Alma Rd; doubles £65) has beautifully decorated double rooms. Singles are negotiable but you may be out of luck in high season.

Langton House (☎ 858299; 46 Alma Rd; singles/doubles £60/70) is the pick of Windsor's B&Bs. Its four en-suite rooms are superb, and its friendly owners are always on hand to answer questions about the town and fill you in with local knowledge.

Castle Hotel (☎ 851011, fax 830244; 10 High St; singles/doubles £175/285) is popular with well-to-do American tourists. The front-facing rooms are the best spot in town from which to view the changing of the guard.

Sir Christopher Wren's House (☎ 861 354, fax 442490; Thames St; singles/doubles £170/175) is a magnificent house built by the famous architect in 1676, and now one of the fanciest hotels in town. It combines an old-world look with up-to-date, comfortable amenities.

Christopher Hotel (☎ 852359, fax 830 914; 110 High St; singles/doubles £135/175), across the river in Eton, dates from 1511. Be sure to ask for a room in the older, more luxurious building rather than in the newer motel-style annexe.

Places to Eat

There is no shortage of places to eat in town, but many are overpriced and a little bland. Following are the best of the lot.

Latino (☎ 857711; 3 Church Lane; mains £7-11) is a cosy and friendly Greek/continental restaurant with live music on Friday and Saturday nights.

The Viceroy (☎ 858005; 49-51 St Leonard's Rd; mains £6.95-11.95) is probably the best Indian restaurant in town.

Marion's (☎ 470079; 45 St Leonard's Rd; mains £8-10) serves well-prepared dishes of mixed Italian and French cuisine. It is also a popular spot for people to meet before going to the pub.

Al Fassia (☎ 855370; 27 St Leonard's Rd; mains £8.50-10.50) is an excellent Moroccan restaurant considered to be as good as – if not better – than the top Moroccan eateries in London.

Havana Café (☎ 832960; 3 Goswell Hill; mains £10-12) is under the railway arches, but don't let its slightly off-putting location deter you: this is a really good Cuban restaurant that also serves excellent cocktails.

Along Eton High St, places to eat jostle shoulders with antique shops.

Cock Pit (☎ 860944; 47-49 High St, Eton; mains from £10), a rickety place, dates back to 1420 and serves good, simple Italian food. The fireplaces and exposed beams give it a cosy atmosphere.

The House on the Bridge (☎ 790197; 67 High St, Eton; 3-course set menu £32.95) is an elegant and pricey restaurant, overlooking the river and the castle. The food is modern French and Spanish.

Entertainment

Windsor and Eton are simply packed with pubs, although most of them cater to the tourist trade. The following have a more local appeal.

The Vansittart Arms (☎ 865988; 105 Vansittart Rd) is definitely our favourite pub in town. It's a regular, no-nonsense locals' watering hole.

The Donkey House (☎ 620003; 10 Thames St) is one of the only riverside pubs in Windsor, and a terrific place to have a drink on a warm summer's evening.

The Two Brewers (☎ 855426; 34 Park St) is at the top of the Long Walk and a great spot to have a drink.

Bar Ha! Ha! (☎ 770111; Unit 40, Royal Windsor Station) is a modern chain pub that is a big hit with Windsor's younger crowd.

Slug & Lettuce (☎ 864405; 3-4 Thames St) is another chain pub, directly opposite the castle, that attracts trendies in their carefully manicured droves.

Bar Yello (☎ 622667; Goswell Hill) is the funkiest place in town, with DJs at weekends.

The Waterman's Arms (☎ 861001; Brocas St, Eton) is a typical olde Englishe pub with ubiquitous, characteristic charm. It is popular with rowers.

Henry VI (☎ 866051; 37 High St, Eton) has an outdoor terrace and live music in the evenings from Thursday to Sunday.

The **Windsor Arts Centre** (☎ 859336; cnr St Leonard's & St Mark's Rds) contains a bar, theatre and live music venue.

The **Theatre Royal** (☎ 853888; Thames St) is the town's main theatre.

Royal Ascot

Anyone with an elementary knowledge of horse racing will have heard of Royal Ascot, a four-day festival that takes place at the Ascot racecourse in the middle of June. Aside from the Derby at Epsom, this is *the* main event of the flat racing calendar, attracting royals and commoners alike. Book tickets well in advance. In 2002, tickets for the Grandstand and Paddock were £49 per day.

If you're not around for Royal Ascot, the racecourse hosts about 20 other meetings throughout the year, where tickets are considerably cheaper (around £18). The flat season runs from May 1 to mid-October, while National Hunt races (over fences) take place during other months.

Call ☎ 01344-876876 for information, or check their website at **w** www.ascot.co.uk.

Ascot is at the southeastern end of Windsor Great Park, about 7 miles (11.3km) south of Windsor along the A332. The best way of getting here is by train. From Windsor (£5, 25 minutes), they run every 15 minutes but you'll have to change at Staines.

Getting There & Away

Windsor is 21 miles (33.8km) west of central London and only about 15 minutes by car from Heathrow airport.

Bus Greenline bus Nos 700 (express service) and 702 depart for Windsor and Legoland from London Victoria coach station hourly (eight Monday to Saturday, six on Sunday; £7.40; 1¼ hours, or 65 minutes express).

Bus Nos 192 (Monday to Saturday), 190 and 191 (Sunday) connect Windsor with Heathrow airport. For further details phone ☎ 524144.

Train There are two Windsor and Eton train stations – Central station on Thames St, opposite Windsor Castle, and Riverside station near the bridge to Eton.

From London Waterloo, trains run to Riverside station every half-hour (hourly on Sunday). Services from London Paddington to Central station require a change at Slough, five minutes from Windsor, but take about the same time (£5.90, 50 minutes).

AROUND WINDSOR & ETON
Runnymede

In June 1215 King John met his barons and bishops in a large field 3 miles (4.8km) southeast of Windsor, and over the next few days they hammered out an agreement on a basic charter of rights guaranteeing the liberties of the king's subjects and restricting the monarch's absolute power. The document they signed, of course, was the Magna Carta, the world's first constitution. It formed the basis for statutes and charters throughout the world's democracies. Both the national and state constitutions of the United States, drawn up more 500 years later, paraphrase directly from this document.

Runnymede – from the Anglo-Saxon words *ruinige* (take council) and *moed* (meadow) – was chosen because it was the largest piece of open land between the king's residence at Windsor and the bishop's palace at Staines. Today the field remains pretty much as it was, except now it features two lodges (1930) designed by Sir Edward Lutyens. In the woods behind the field are two **memorials**, the first to the Magna Carta designed by Sir Edward Maufe (1957). The second is to John F Kennedy, and was built by Geoffrey Jellicoe in 1965 on an acre of land granted in perpetuity to the US government following Kennedy's assassination in 1963.

The **Magna Carta Tea Rooms** (☎ 01784-477110; Gate Lodge, Windsor Rd) is in one of Lutyens' lodges, and does a pretty good cream tea (tea and scones with clotted cream and jam) in the afternoons.

Bus No 43 stops near here on the Windsor to Slough route. The best way to get here, however, is by boat along the Thames: **French Brothers** (☎ 851900) operates a Runnymede to Windsor service on Wednesday and Friday to Sunday, April to September only. You can catch the returning boat from Windsor Promenade at 4pm, it arrives at Runnymede Boathouse at 5.30pm. The fare is £4.70/5.20 single/return. Unfortunately, you'll have to get the bus back into Windsor.

Reading
☎ 0118 • pop 142,900

This prosperous industrial town, only 12 miles (19km) southwest of Windsor but a world away in atmosphere, straddles the Thames on the Berkshire-Oxfordshire border. Once an important guarding post for London, there is now little to see in the town itself apart from the **abbey ruins**. What puts Reading on the map, however, is its flourishing arts scene, which culminates in the excellent **Reading Festival** (☎ 020-8963 0940; **w** www.readingfestival.com), a three-day extravaganza during the third week in August that features top acts in pop, rock and dance music. Tickets cost about £40 per day.

The Festival is preceded (at the end of July) by the **World of Music, Arts & Dance Festival** (WOMAD; ☎ 9390930; **w** www .womad.org), founded by Peter Gabriel in 1982. Tickets cost from £16 to £40 per day.

There are trains every 15 minutes from London Waterloo or Paddington stations to Reading (£10.60, 25 minutes).

Surrey

Often derided as nothing more than a concrete extension of London, Surrey is a firm favourite with the city's professional classes, who've moved here in ever-increasing numbers (hence the derision). But busy suburban trains and long queues on the motorway in and out of the capital are a small price to pay for living in a county that has some wonderful corners, all a short hop from the city.

FARNHAM
☎ 01252 • pop 38,000

Surrey's most attractive market town may seem a bit conservative at first, a tranquil haven for well-to-do commuters to spend their weekends manicuring hands and lawns, but Farnham's obvious affluence coexists comfortably with a thriving arts community.

It has four galleries, a crafts centre and an award-winning museum, and the town has done plenty to promote local arts and crafts, many of which are visible throughout the town. To top it off, Farnham is also home to the Surrey Institute of Art & Design.

Farnham's most famous son was Formula One racer Mike Hawthorn (1929–59), who was born in Yorkshire but lived most of his life in the area. He won the Formula One title in 1958, whereupon he immediately retired. He was killed in a car crash at the Guildford by-pass on January 22, 1959.

Orientation & Information

Farnham is easily explored on foot. The most interesting part of Farnham is its historical centre, where East, West, South and Castle Sts meet.

The Borough (the eastern end of West St) is the town's main shopping street. The train station is at the southern end of South St (Station Hill).

The friendly **TIC** (☎ 715109, fax 725083; **e** itourist@waverley.gov.uk; South St; open 9.30am-5.15pm Mon-Thur, 9.30am-4.45pm Fri, 9am-noon Sat) has the free *Farnham Heritage Trail*. You can use the Internet and check email for free across the hall in the public library.

You'll find an **ATM** on The Borough, near the corner of Castle St. The **main post office** and a **bureau de change** are on West St, which is the continuation of The Borough. There are public toilets in the car park on The Hard which runs off West St, near the main post office.

Guided walks (☎ 712014; adult/child £2/50p) run at 3pm on the first Sunday of every month between April and October. Meet at the entrance of the Wagon Yard Car Park at the southern end of Downing St. They last approximately 1½ hours.

Farnham Castle

Run by English Heritage (EH), Farnham Castle (☎ 713393; adult £1.50; open 2pm-4pm Wed) consists of a castle keep and a residential palace house. The **palace house** was built in the 13th century for the bishops of Winchester as a stopover on London journeys; from 1926 to the 1950s it was taken over by the bishops of Guildford. The house has been changed and altered on a massive scale over the centuries, with most of the changes undertaken by Bishop Morley in the 1660s. It is now a Centre for International Briefing, holding courses for people going to live abroad, and can only be visited by guided tour.

The **castle keep** *(adult/child £2/1; open 10am-6pm daily Apr-Oct)* has fallen into serious disrepair since its construction in 1138 by Henri de Blois, the grandson of William the Conqueror, but there are still some terrific views from the top (accessible by rickety stone steps). The castle and keep can be reached by steps at the end of Castle St.

Museum of Farnham

This excellent museum *(☎ 715094; 38 West St; admission free; open 10am-5pm Tues-Sat)* is located in the splendid Willmer House, a Grade I Georgian townhouse built in 1718. Since it opened in 1962, the museum has won a number of awards, including the European Museum of the Year Award.

The museum's permanent exhibits include a timeline of Farnham from prehistory through Saxon and Norman times to the present day. Next to it is an extraordinary **doll's house**, built in the 1780s for the Manwaring children who lived next door at No 39. Lucky kids. The **Art & Architecture Room** features exhibits on the town's architectural heritage, particularly the work of artist William Herbert Allen (1863–1943) and architect Harold Falkner (1875–1963). Also on display are examples of the famous **Farnham Greenware**, sculpted in nearby Wrecclesham until the end of WWII. The pieces here are fine examples of the Arts and Crafts movement that was all the rage between the wars.

The **Countryside Room** features Farnham as seen through the eyes of its most famous writers, William Cobbett (1762–1835) – the farmer turned radical social commentator who was the first person to publish parliamentary debates (now done by Hansard) – and George Stuart (1863–1927).

Perhaps the most precious exhibit on display is a nightcap that once belonged to Charles I. He stayed in Vernon House (now the library) on his way to trial in the Tower of London in 1648, and gave the cap to the innkeeper as a souvenir, oblivious to the fact that within a year he would lose the thing that his nightcap kept warm.

Other Things to See & Do

Locals claim that Castle St is one of England's finest thoroughfares, and it certainly is beautiful. Among the Georgian frontages you'll find the **alms-houses**, recognisable by their blue doors. They were built in 1619 by Andrew Windsor 'for the habitation and relief of eight poor honest old impotent persons'. Atop the Town Hall Buildings (site of the TIC), at the corner of Castle St and The Borough, is a **weather-vane** that is an exact replica of Sir Francis Drake's *The Golden Hind*. It was designed by Harold Falkner and Guy Maxwell Aylwin in 1931.

Take a stroll around the cobbled Middle, Lower and Upper Church Lanes where you'll see a string of 15th- and 16th-century **timber-framed houses**. Their original facades are hidden behind 18th-century brickwork.

If you walk along Castle St, past Farnham Castle for about half a mile, you will come to **Farnham Park**, a one-time bishops' deer park spread over 128 hectares. Today it is a nice place to go for a stroll, and also includes a golf course, cricket pitch, football ground and children's playground.

Places to Stay

Most of Farnham's cheaper B&Bs are a 10- to 15-minute walk from the centre.

Mrs Burland's *(☎ 723047; 15 Vicarage Lane; rooms per person 1st/subsequent nights £18/16)* is great value but it's 1½ miles (2.4km) from the centre. If you can manage the distance then you are in for a treat. Large, comfortable en-suite rooms have views over the valley. There are a few short walks around the country lanes in this area – just ask Mrs Burland.

Sandiway *(☎ 710721; 24 Shortheath Rd; rooms per person £25)* is about the same distance as Mrs Burland's from town (around a 15-minute walk) and has very comfortable and clean rooms.

The Bishop's Table *(☎ 710222, fax 733494; e welcome@bishopstable.com; 27 West St; singles/doubles £90/110)* is a beautiful old Georgian hotel right in the town centre.

Places to Eat

Downing St is home to a number of excellent eateries.

The Stirling Sandwich Shop *(☎ 711602; 49a Downing St; sandwiches £1.50-2.90)* makes scrumptious sandwiches and has such a loyal clientele that at lunch times the queue stretches the length of Downing St.

The Nelson Arms (☎ 716078; 50 Castle St; meals around £5) is an old timber-framed pub with an open fireplace. It escaped a brick makeover but was stuccoed instead.

The Banaras (☎ 734081; 40 Downing St; mains around £8) is an Indian restaurant with a very good reputation locally.

The Traditional Plaice (☎ 718009; 50 Downing St; mains around £8) is a fish and chip shop with a restaurant out the back. It serves filling if unadventurous dishes.

Café Rouge (☎ 733688; 4-5 Town Buildings, The Borough; mains around £8) is part of the popular chain, but we recommend it because it is one of the most popular eateries in town. It's always crammed, and the food is usually excellent.

Getting There & Away

Stagecoach (☎ 01256-464501) bus No 64 runs between Winchester and Guildford via Farnham (twice hourly). It takes 70 minutes from Winchester (£4.50) and 30 minutes from Guildford (£2.90). The Stagecoach stop is on The Borough. National Express has a service from London Victoria (£4.80, 1¼ hours). They drop off at South St and pick up from The Borough.

The train station is at the end of South St, on the other side of the A31 from the old town centre. Half-hourly services run from London Waterloo (£9.40, 50 minutes) and Guildford (£3.70, 22 minutes).

AROUND FARNHAM
Waverley Abbey

The inspiration for Sir Walter Scott's eponymous novel, the Waverley Abbey ruins sit almost forlornly on the banks of the River Wey about 2 miles (3.2km) southeast of Farnham.

This was the first Cistercian abbey built in England (construction began in 1128) and, like Beaulieu Abbey in the New Forest (see later in this chapter), was based on a parent abbey at Citeaux in France.

The Cistercians were an austere order who placed a strong emphasis on humility and rigid discipline. They believed in the salutary effects of manual labour, and spent much of their time carrying out odd jobs for the local community and tilling the land. Naturally, the locals loved them, as they were a source of unquestioning labour.

It all ended in 1536 when Henry VIII dissolved the monasteries. Waverley's buildings were torched and ransacked, leaving us the ruins visible today. What is left (and there's not that much) is in excellent condition, and it is still worth making the effort, if only to wander about the beautiful landscape.

Across the Wey is the impressive **Waverley Abbey House** (closed to the public), built in 1783 using bricks from the demolished abbey. In the 19th century, it was owned by Florence Nightingale's brother-in-law, and the famous nurse was a regular visitor. Fittingly, the house was used as a military hospital in WWI. Since 1973, it has been the headquarters of the Crusade for World Revival (CWR), a Christian charity.

The abbey and house are off the B3001.

Hindhead

The tiny hamlet of Hindhead, 8 miles (12.9km) south of Farnham off the A287, lies in the middle of the largest area of open heath in Surrey. During the 19th century, this was considered one of the most beautiful parts of the southeast, and a number of prominent Victorians bought up property in the area, including Sir Arthur Conan Doyle (1859–1930), creator of Sherlock Holmes. One of the three founders of the National Trust, Sir Robert Hunter, lived in nearby Haslemere, and today much of the area is administered by the foundation.

The most beautiful part of the area is to the northeast, where you'll find a natural depression known as the **Devil's Punchbowl**. Its ominous name comes from local legends that told of all kinds of satanic rituals and other forms of black magic, but these were actually a smoke-and-mirrors act concocted by thieves and highwaymen that preyed upon the coaches that passed through here on their way between London and Portsmouth. Today, there are a number of excellent trails and bridle-paths that make for a most enjoyable walk. To get the best view of the surrounding area, we suggest that you make for Gibbet Hill (280m), once an execution ground. It is well signposted.

Hindhead YHA Hostel (☎/fax 01428-604285; Devil's Punchbowl, Thursley; dorm beds £7.75), a beautifully restored cottage on the northern edge of the Punchbowl, about a mile from Hindhead, is run by the National Trust (NT). You'll have to do without a shower here, as there are only wash basins. It's a little out of the way, and you'll have to walk about half a mile to get here from the nearest bus stop (the car park is also half a mile away), but it's a wonderful spot far from the madding crowds.

Undershaw Hotel (☎ *01428-604039; singles/doubles £30/50*) is the former home of Sir Arthur himself. The rooms are comfortable and well-appointed.

Bus Nos 60, 71 and 92 from Farnham run almost hourly (£2.30; 20 minutes).

Box Hill

This hill on the North Downs, 20 miles (32.2km) west of Farnham along the North Downs Way, was famous as a beauty spot long before Jane Austen's Emma came here for her disastrous picnic. For everyone else it's an excellent place for a long walk, with 20-mile views from the top of the hill. Great stretches of sloping grassland are interspersed with heavily wooded areas. This is also a good area to come for mountain biking, as there are a number of bridleways.

On top of the hill is a **visitor information centre** (☎ *01306-885502; open 10am-6pm daily Easter-Sept, 11am-5pm Mon-Sat Oct-Easter*) where you'll find trail maps, as well as a kiosk. Behind them are the remains of a fort and arsenal, built in 1899 as one of 13 immobilisation centres in case of attack by the French.

There are hourly trains between London Victoria and Boxhill & Westhumble station (£6.60, 45 minutes).

Kent

Close to London, Kent's popularity as a holiday destination began with the construction of the railway in the 19th century, which carried the first hordes of urban holidaymakers to the pretty seaside resorts. Inevitably, the beauty of the coastline has been somewhat scarred by mass tourism, but there are still a number of gorgeous little towns worth checking out.

Inland, beautiful Canterbury and its marvellous cathedral is the main crowd-pleaser, but the surrounding countryside is equally attractive. Probably the most distinctive feature of the fertile, rolling hills of inland Kent are the white, cone-shaped roofs of oast houses (see the following boxed text 'Oast Houses').

The trails along the North and South Downs attract walkers from all over the world (see the Activities section at the start of this chapter). Between the North and South Downs lies an area known as the Weald, much of it designated an Area of Outstanding Natural Beauty (AONB).

For general information about the county, contact the new **Kent Tourism Alliance** (☎ *01622-696165, fax 01622-691418;* **e** *tourism@kent.gov.uk; Invicta House, Maidstone, Kent ME14 1XX*).

CANTERBURY
☎ 01227 • pop 38,670

Canterbury should make the Top Ten of any English must-visit list, and for good reasons. For one, it has one of the most beautiful cathedrals you'll find anywhere in Europe. Surrounding it is a gorgeous medieval centre that has retained much of its original character, which is a minor miracle considering the numbers of visitors that descend upon the city throughout the year to explore the best of England's past.

Oast Houses

Oast houses were basically giant, housed kilns for drying hops, a key ingredient in the brewing of beer, introduced to the region in the early 15th century.

An oast house is made up of four rooms: the kiln (oven), the drying room (located above the kiln), the cooling room, and the storage room where hops was pressed and baled, ready to go to the local inn brewery. The cone-shaped roof was necessary to create a draught for the fire. The bits sticking out from the top of the cone are cowls. They could be moved to regulate the airflow to the fire.

Many oast houses have been converted into homes, and are increasingly sought after as prime real estate. Oast House B&Bs are becoming more and more common throughout the county; check with the various tourist information centres for information on local possibilities or call the **Kent Tourism Alliance** (☎ *01622-696165*), who will locate a B&B in your area.

History

And what a past Canterbury has too. From AD 200, there was a Roman town called Durovernum Cantiacorum here, which later became the capital of the Saxon kingdom of Kent. When St Augustine arrived in England in 597 to carry the Christian message to the pagan hordes, he chose Canterbury as his *cathedra*, or primary see, and set about building an abbey on the outskirts of town. Following the martyrdom of Thomas Becket (see the boxed text 'Keep Your Enemies Close…'), Canterbury became northern Europe's most important centre of pilgrimage, which in turn led to Geoffrey Chaucer's *The Canterbury Tales*, one of the most outstanding poetic works in English literature.

Blasphemous murders and rampant tourism aside, Canterbury remains the primary see for the Church of England, also known as the Anglican Church.

Orientation

The old town of Canterbury is enclosed by a medieval city wall and a modern ring road. Cars are banned from the Old Town, so you'll get to do most of your exploring on foot.

Information

The **TIC** (☎ 378100, fax 459840; **e** canterburyinformation@canterbury.gov.uk; 34 St Margaret's St; open 9.30am-5.30pm Thur-Tues, 9.30am-4pm Wed) is near the cathedral. There's a bureau de change at Lloyd's

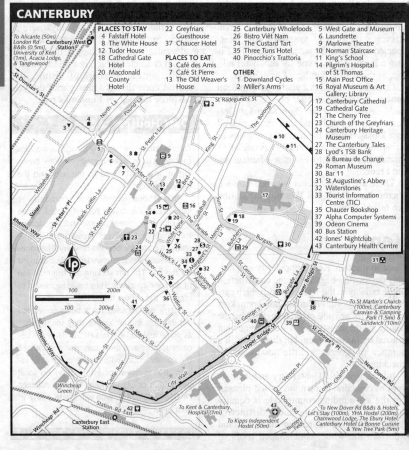

CANTERBURY

PLACES TO STAY	22	Greyfriars
4	Falstaff Hotel		Guesthouse
8	The White House	37	Chaucer Hotel
12	Tudor House		
18	Cathedral Gate		**PLACES TO EAT**
	Hotel	3	Café des Amis
20	Macdonald	7	Café St Pierre
	County	13	The Old Weaver's
	Hotel		House

25	Canterbury Wholefoods
26	Bistro Việt Nam
34	The Custard Tart
35	Three Tuns Hotel
40	Pinocchio's Trattoria

| **OTHER** |
| 1 | Downland Cycles |
| 2 | Miller's Arms |

5	West Gate and Museum
6	Laundrette
9	Marlowe Theatre
10	Norman Staircase
11	King's School
14	Pilgrim's Hospital of St Thomas
15	Main Post Office
16	Royal Museum & Art Gallery; Library
17	Canterbury Cathedral
19	Cathedral Gate
21	The Cherry Tree
23	Church of the Greyfriars
24	Canterbury Heritage Museum
27	The Canterbury Tales
28	Lyod's TSB Bank & Bureau de Change
29	Roman Museum
30	Bar 11
31	St Augustine's Abbey
32	Waterstones
33	Tourist Information Centre (TIC)
35	Chaucer Bookshop
37	Alpha Computer Systems
39	Odeon Cinema
40	Bus Station
42	Jones' Nightclub
43	Canterbury Health Centre

TSB *(28 St Margaret's St).* You'll find all the other major banks and **ATMs** on High St, near the corner of St Margaret's St.

There is a **post office** *(cnr St Peter's & Stour Sts; open 9.30am-5.30pm Mon-Sat)* for snail mail, or check your email at **Alpha Computer Systems** *(☎ 472555; 10-11 Burgate Lane; open 9.30am-6pm Mon-Sat).* Internet access costs £4.50 for an hour.

The **Chaucer Bookshop** *(Beer Cart Lane)* is a cluttered, chaotic used-book shop that also sells histories of Canterbury and rarities of the book world. If you want more organisation, there's also a **Waterstones** *(20 St Margaret's St).*

The local **laundrette** *(36 St Peter's St)* charges £6 per regular load.

You'll find public toilets inside the cathedral grounds.

For general medical consultations try the **Canterbury Health Centre** *(☎ 452444; 26 Old Dover Rd).* In the case of an emergency go to **Kent & Canterbury Hospital** *(☎ 766877; Etherbert Rd),* about a mile south of the centre.

Canterbury Cathedral

The Church of England could not have a more splendid and imposing mother church. This extraordinary complex *(☎ 762862; adult/child £3.50/2.50; open 9am-7pm Mon-Sat, 12.30pm-2.30pm & 4.30pm-5.30pm Sun Easter-Sept; 9am-5pm Mon-Sat, 12.30pm-2.30pm & 4.30pm-5.30pm Sun Oct-Easter)* is undoubtedly worth the half day you'll need to visit. The sheer wealth of detail, treasure and stories associated with the cathedral can be overwhelming, so we strongly recommend that you join a tour. They take place at 10.30am, noon and 2pm for £4, or you can take a self-guided audio tour for £3.50 (30 minutes).

The first church built here was badly damaged by fire in 1067. A replacement cathedral was begun in 1070, but only fragments of this remain today, as a second fire in 1174 destroyed most of the eastern half of the building. Thankfully, the magnificent crypt beneath the choir survived.

Following the martyrdom of Thomas Becket (see the boxed text 'Keep Your Enemies Close...'), the cathedral's fortunes increased dramatically. Pilgrims began appearing in droves, and a new cathedral, created by William of Sens, was constructed to

reflect the town's growing importance. It is the first major Gothic construction in England, built in a style now known as Early English. Most of the cathedral east of Bell Harry tower dates from this period. In 1988 Unesco declared the cathedral a World Heritage Site – along with St Augustine's Abbey and St Martin's Church (see later in this section).

The main entrance is through the **south-west porchern** (1), which was built in 1415 to commemorate the English victory at Agincourt. From the centre of the nave there are impressive views east down the length of the church, with its ascending levels, and west to the **window** (2) with glass dating from the 12th century.

From beneath **Bell Harry** (3), with its beautiful fan vault, more glass that somehow survived the Puritans is visible. A 15th-century screen, featuring six kings, separates the nave from the choir.

The spot where Becket was murdered is in the northwest transept, but the original **Altar of Sword's Point** (4) – the final destination of millions of pilgrims over the last 1000 years – was replaced by a modern version of the same in 1982, when Pope John Paul II came here. The adjoining **Lady Chapel** (5) has beautiful perpendicular fan vaulting. Descend a flight of steps into the Romanesque crypt, the main survivor of the Norman cathedral.

The **Chapel of Our Lady** at the western end of the crypt has some of the finest Romanesque carving in England. St Thomas was entombed in the Early English eastern end (6) until 1220. It was here that Henry came to pray for forgiveness, and is reputed to be the site of a number of miracles. The **Chapel of St Gabriel** (7) features 12th-century paintings, and the **Black Prince's Chantry** (8) is a beautiful perpendicular chapel, donated by the prince in 1363 and now used by Huguenots (French Protestants). The chapel is named after Edward (1330–76), heir to the throne and father of Richard II. At 16, he commanded the English armies at the Battle of Crécy, but didn't outlive his father, Edward III, and so never became king. His sobriquet was given to

him by the French on account of the black armour he wore in battle.

Exit the crypt to the southwestern transept. The **Chapel of St Michael** (9) includes a wealth of tombs, including that of Archbishop Stephen Langton, one of the chief architects of the Magna Carta. The superb 12th-century **choir** (10) rises in stages to the **High Altar** (11) and **Trinity Chapel**. The screen around the choir stalls was erected in 1305 and evensong has been sung in this inspiring space every day for 800 years. **St Augustine's Chair** (12), dating from the 13th century, is used to enthrone archbishops.

The stained glass in Trinity Chapel is mostly from the 13th century and celebrates the life and miracles of St Thomas. **St Thomas' shrine** (13) no longer exists, but it

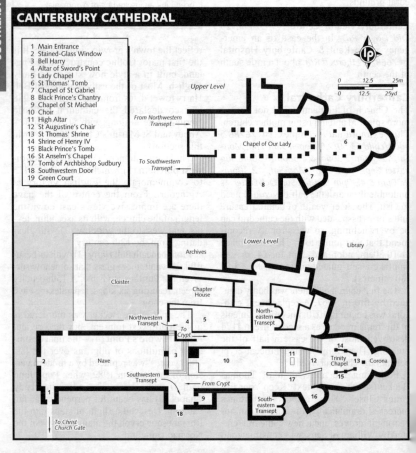

CANTERBURY CATHEDRAL

1   Main Entrance
2   Stained-Glass Window
3   Bell Harry
4   Altar of Sword's Point
5   Lady Chapel
6   St Thomas' Tomb
7   Chapel of St Gabriel
8   Black Prince's Chantry
9   Chapel of St Michael
10 Choir
11 High Altar
12 St Augustine's Chair
13 St Thomas' Shrine
14 Shrine of Henry IV
15 Black Prince's Tomb
16 St Anselm's Chapel
17 Tomb of Archbishop Sudbury
18 Southwestern Door
19 Green Court

Keep Your Enemies Close...

In 1162 King Henry II did what every good monarch should do. He appointed his good mate Thomas Becket to the highest clerical office in the land in the hope that a friendly archbishop could force the increasingly vocal religious lobby to toe the royal line. But Henry didn't count on Thomas taking his job as seriously as he did, and by 1170, Henry had become exasperated with his former favourite's penchant for disagreeing with virtually everything the king said or did. He sulked and raged for a while, then late in the year 'suggested' to four of his knights that Thomas was a little too much to bear. The dirty deed was done on December 29. Becket's martyrdom – and canonisation in double-quick time (1173) – catapulted the cathedral to the top spot in northern Europe's top 10 pilgrimage sites. Mindful of the growing opprobrium at his role in Becket's murder, Henry arrived here in 1174 for a dramatic *mea culpa*, and after allowing himself to be whipped and scolded was granted absolution.

is still possible to see the alabaster **shrine of Henry IV** (14), buried with his wife Queen Joan of Navarre, and the **Black Prince's tomb** (15) with its famous effigy, along with the prince's shield, gauntlets and sword.

Opposite **St Anselm's Chapel** (16) is the **tomb of Archbishop Sudbury** (17) who, as Chancellor of the Exchequer, was held responsible for a hated poll tax – he was beheaded by a mob during the Peasants' Revolt of 1381. His body was buried with a ball of lead; his head is in a Suffolk church.

Leave the cathedral by the **southwestern door** (18) and turn left towards the city wall. **Queningate** is a small door through the wall which, according to tradition, Queen Bertha used on her way to the Church of St Martin before the arrival of Augustine.

Go round the eastern end of the cathedral and turn right into **Green Court** (19), which is surrounded on the eastern (right) side by the Deanery and the northern side (straight ahead) by the early-14th-century Brewhouse and Bakehouse, which now house part of the very exclusive King's School. In the northwestern corner (far left) is the famous **Norman Staircase** (1151).

The Canterbury Tales

The Canterbury Tales (☎ 479227; St Margaret's St; adult/child £6.50/5; open 9am-5.30pm daily Apr-Oct, 10am-4pm daily Nov-Mar) provides an entertaining introduction to Chaucer's classic story. The general concept, however, is strange: jerky, hydraulic puppets seem an inefficient way to recreate history. Perhaps the promoters feel they need something in three dimensions to justify the ticket prices. The centre is usually crammed with school children.

Museums

The **Royal Museum & Art Gallery** (☎ 452747; High St; admission free; open 10am-5pm Mon-Sat) has military memorabilia and works by local artists.

The city's three other museums can all be visited with one passport ticket costing £5/3 per adult/child. Individual admission costs are given below.

The West Gate and Museum (☎ 452747; St Peter's St; adult/child £1/65p; open 11am-12.30pm & 1.30pm-3.30pm Mon-Sat) dates from the 14th century and is the only remaining city gate. It's now a small museum featuring arms and armour. Kids – and some adults – might enjoy trying on the replica armour.

Once the Poor Priests' Hospital, **The Canterbury Heritage Museum** (☎ 452747; Stour St; adult/child £2.60/1.65; open 10.30am-5pm Mon-Sat, 1.30pm-5pm Sun June-Oct, 10.30am-5pm Mon-Sat Nov-May) is in a converted 12th- and 13th-century building. The museum provides good, although rather dry, coverage of the city's history and its local characters. Last admission is at 4pm.

An excellent place to visit, the **Roman Museum** (☎ 785575; Butchery Lane; adult/child £2.60/1.65; open 10am-5pm Mon-Sat, 1.30pm-5pm Sun June-Oct, 10am-5pm Mon-Sat Nov-May) is one of the few museums of this kind where you are allowed to actually touch stuff. And not only can you handle original artefacts uncovered in the remains of a Roman town house lying below the museum, you can also walk around a reconstructed kitchen (smelling the odours) and check out the extensive remains of a mosaic floor.

The Canterbury Tales

If English literature has a father figure, then it is certainly Geoffrey Chaucer (1342/3–1400) who, along with Dante, Boccaccio and Petrarch, defined the literature of his age. Chaucer was the first English writer to introduce characters – rather than 'types' – into fiction, and he did so to greatest effect in his most popular work, *The Canterbury Tales*.

Written between 1387 and his death, the *Tales* is an unfinished series of 24 stories supposedly told by a party of pilgrims on their journey from London to the shrine of Thomas Becket at Canterbury and back. Chaucer successfully created the illusion that the pilgrims, not Chaucer (though he appears in the tales as himself), are telling the stories, which allowed him unprecedented freedom as an author to explore the rich fictive possibilities of a number of genres.

In *The Man of Law's Tale* and *The Prioress' Tale* he examines the genre of pious legend. He pokes fun at chivalric romance in *The Knight's Tale* and animal fables in *The Priest's Tale*, and writes an ironic version of popular romance in the *Tale of Sir Thopas*, told by his own character.

The sheer scale of Chaucer's achievement – he successfully incorporates all popular genres into one thoroughly original masterpiece – remains a high point of European literature, but it was also the first time that English came to match Latin (the language of the Church) and French (spoken by the Norman court) as a language of high literature. *The Canterbury Tales*, summed up by Dryden as 'God's Plenty', remains one of the pillars of the literary canon, even if contemporary modern readers would probably enjoy a modern transliteration more than the original old English version.

St Augustine's Abbey

Henry VIII acted with thoroughness when St Augustine's Abbey (☎ 767345; adult £3; open 10am-6pm Apr-Sept, 10am-5pm Oct, 10am-4pm Nov-Mar) was demolished in 1538 – only its foundations remain. A small museum run by English Heritage (EH) houses original artefacts dug up in and around the abbey. Admission includes an audio tour.

St Martin's Church

England's oldest parish church (☎ 459482; North Holmes Rd; admission free; open 9am-5pm daily except during services), about 300m east of St Augustine's Abbey, is where Queen Bertha (wife of the Saxon King Ethelbert) welcomed Augustine upon his arrival. The original Saxon church has somewhat disappeared under a thorough medieval refurbishment, but it's worth a quick visit if only to tell your mates back home that you stood in the oldest church in the country.

Pilgrim's Hospital of St Thomas

Founded in 1180, the Pilgrim's Hospital (☎ 471688; St Peter's St; adult/child £1.50/1; open 10am-5pm Mon-Sat) is well worth a visit. Originally built as a hospice for pilgrims to Becket's shrine in the cathedral, it is still used today to house elderly folk. You will see here a Norman undercroft, a refectory hall and, on the upper level, the Pilgrims'

Chapel. The building was extensively restored in the 16th century and again in the 20th century but the 13th-century roof of the chapel is original.

Church of the Greyfriars

The Franciscans (called the Grey Friars due to the colour of their cassocks) built their first English monastery on a tiny tributary of the River Stour in 1267. The small upstairs chapel (admission free; open 2pm-4pm Mon-Sat mid-May–Sept) is well worth a visit, while the Eucharist is celebrated here every Wednesday at 12.30pm.

Weavers' Houses

Just off St Peter's St, along the River Stour, are a number of Tudor-style houses dating from around 1500. Most of them are inhabited and not open to the public, but if you want to know what they are like inside, stop for a bite at The Old Weaver's House (see Places to Eat later in the chapter).

Organised Tours

There are guided walks from the TIC at 2pm daily from April to October and also at 11.30am Monday to Saturday in July and August. The walks take 1½ hours and explore the cathedral and museum precincts, King's School and the town's medieval centre. They cost £3.75/2.75 per adult/child.

Popular ghost tours of the Old Town depart from the TIC at 6.30pm every Friday, Saturday and Sunday from April to August. For bookings call ☎ 454888.

From April to October, you can also take a **rowing-boat tour** *(☎ 07790-534744)* from behind The Old Weaver's House. Tours cost £5 per person.

Special Events

For two weeks in the middle of October, the **Canterbury Festival** features arts, music and theatre from around the world. Contact the TIC for a detailed programme of events.

Places to Stay

We recommend that you book in advance, and note that prices often double in July and August.

Camping Just under 2 miles from the centre, off the A277, **Canterbury Caravan & Camping Park** *(☎ 463216; Bekesbourne Lane; camping for 2 people & tent from £9.50)* is comfortable and well stocked.

Yew Tree Park *(☎ 700306; Stone St, Petham; camping per tent & 1/2 adults £5/8; open Apr-Oct)* is 5 miles (8km) south of Canterbury off the B2068; take New Dover Rd out of the centre and turn right just after the YHA hostel. A bus from Canterbury to Petham village (a half-mile walk to the camp site) leaves hourly.

Hostels A marvellous, family-run place is **Kipp's Independent Hostel** *(☎ 786121;* e *info@kipps-hostel.com; 40 Nunnery Fields; dorm beds from £11)*, with clean facilities, Internet access and even a small tuck shop.

The **YHA Hostel** *(☎ 0870 770 5744, fax 470 5752; 54 New Dover Rd; dorm beds £11.25, singles/twins £18/32; open Feb–late Dec)* is in a fine Victorian Gothic house 1¼ miles southeast of the centre. There is a bureau de change, Internet access and a small garden.

Let's Stay *(☎ 463628; 26 New Dover Rd; dorm beds £11.50)* is more homely than the YHA hostel. Beds are in four-bed dorms and a cooked breakfast is included. Men and women are usually accommodated separately; couples and families may be accommodated but you'll need to call ahead to check on availability.

The University of Kent *(☎ 828000;* e *hospitality-enquiry@ukc.ac.uk; Tanglewood; B&B*

singles/doubles from £19.50/49.50; open Apr & July-Sept) has fine, comfortable lodgings 20 minutes' walk northwest of the centre.

B&Bs A quaint (and slightly eccentric) 450-year-old building, **Tudor House** *(☎ 765650; 6 Best Lane; singles/doubles £22/50)* is central and very good value. There are canoes and boats which guests can hire for £11 per day.

Greyfriars Guesthouse *(☎ 456255;* e *christine@greyfriars-house.co.uk; 6 Stour St; singles/doubles with en suite from £25/45)* was once the dormitory for the Church of the Greyfriars, but has now been restored to provide excellent accommodation right in the heart of the city.

The White House *(☎ 761836; 6 St Peter's Lane; singles/doubles from £35/70)* is a gorgeous Regency townhouse with spacious, comfortable rooms and service that is second to none. You won't find class like this any cheaper.

Alicante *(☎/fax 766277; 4 Roper Rd; singles/doubles from £28/42)* is a lovely B&B about a minute's walk from Canterbury West station. The rooms are larger than most you'll find in town, and clean to boot.

There's a string of decent B&Bs along New Dover Rd, all five or 10 minutes' walk to the centre.

Charnwood Lodge *(☎/fax 451712;* e *charnwood.bb@btinternal.com; 64 New Dover Rd; singles/doubles from £25/30)*, with a sign out front just saying 'B&B', is the best value in town and we can highly recommend it. You get a clean self-contained flat that can sleep up to three people.

The London Rd B&Bs are 10 minutes' walk from the centre.

Acacia Lodge and **Tanglewood** *(☎ 769955; 39 London Rd; singles/doubles from £30/38)* are actually the same place. Rooms are cute, cottage-style and very tidy.

Hotels A wonderful Tudor building close to the West Gate, **Falstaff Hotel** *(☎ 462138, fax 463525; 8-10 St Dunstan's St; singles/doubles from £51/86)* has exquisitely appointed rooms, some with four-poster beds.

Chaucer Hotel *(☎ 464427, fax 450397; 63 Ivy Lane; singles/doubles from £60/90)* is a Georgian house that has been substantially altered to create a comfortable, top-class hotel, but it retains elements of the original building.

Cathedral Gate Hotel (☎ 464381, fax 462800; e cgate@cgate.demon.co.uk; 36 Burgate; singles/doubles £23.50/45, with en suite £61.50/95.50), next to the cathedral gate, is a one-time pilgrim's hostel. Not much has changed here, including the sloping floors, thin walls and seriously low doorways. The rooms are very comfortable, however, and the views of the cathedral are magnificent.

Macdonald County Hotel (☎ 766266; 30 High St; singles/doubles £90/145) is the best hotel in town, with elegant rooms decorated in a Tudor, Georgian or Colonial theme. Breakfast is not included.

A few cheaper hotels can be found on New Dover Rd.

The Ebury Hotel (☎ 768433, fax 459187; e info@ebury-hotel.co.uk; 65-67 New Dover Rd; singles/doubles from £50/70) has the feel of an upmarket B&B minus the familiarity or warmth. The hotel does have an indoor heated pool though!

Canterbury Hotel (☎ 450551, fax 780145; e canterbury.hotel@btInternet.com; 71 New Dover Rd; singles/doubles/triples £55/75/95) has a jovial atmosphere and helpful staff but the rooms are not quite as good as those at the Ebury. The La Bonne Cuisine restaurant here is excellent (see Places to Eat).

Places to Eat

There's a good range of eateries in Canterbury. Bookings are recommended for the pricier spots, especially at weekends.

The Old Weaver's House (☎ 464660; 1 St Peter's St; mains £8-13) is a historic, early 16th-century building with a large terrace overlooking the Stour. With everything from salads to curries, the menu is varied but unexciting, but this place is recommended more for its ambience.

Bistro Viêt Nam (☎ 760022; The Old Linen Store, White Horse Lane) is simply fabulous. The modern Southeast Asian menu features a range of well-presented dishes including a superb Vietnamese tapas menu with dishes costing from £3.95 to £4.50.

Pinocchio's Trattoria (☎ 457538; 64 Castle St; pasta dishes from £5.35, pizzas £4.70-7.30) is a cheerful spot with a superb Italian wine selection and a terrace out the back.

Café des Amis (☎ 464390; 93-95 St Dunstan's St; mains £8-13) is, despite the name, actually a Mexican restaurant, and it is very, very popular. The fare is typical but excellent.

Three Tuns Hotel (☎ 456391; 24 Watling St; meals from around £5), standing on a Roman theatre site, serves good-value pub meals. The hotel itself dates from the 16th century.

La Bonne Cuisine (☎ 450551; Canterbury Hotel, 71 New Dover Rd; starters £8-9.50, mains £12-18) is a superb French restaurant with outstanding service. The atmosphere is a little stiff, but what else would you expect from an upmarket French restaurant?

The Custard Tart (☎ 785178; 35a St Margaret's St) is extremely popular and serves delicious baguettes from £2.30 and cream teas for £2.95. The downstairs takeaway counter is excellent value with sausage rolls for £1 and sandwiches for £1.30. Get in before the 1pm lunch rush.

Café St Pierre (☎ 456791; 41 St Peter's St; breakfast around £3) is our favourite coffee spot for the perfect morning pick-me-up.

Canterbury Wholefoods (☎ 464623; 1-2 Jewry Lane; lunch £5) is a wholefood shop and café that serves excellent fruit smoothies (£1.75) and a range of healthy sandwiches.

Entertainment

Canterbury is a big student town, so there are plenty of nightlife options.

Two free magazines, *What, Where & When* and *The Sticks*, have details of what's on in Canterbury. They're both available from the TIC.

Pubs There are dozens of pubs and bars throughout the city. Take your pick, but we recommend the following.

Miller's Arms (*Mill Lane*) is a beautiful waterside pub that has become a favourite student hangout.

Bar 11 (*11 Burgate*) is probably the coolest bar in town, a modern drinking hole that attracts the well-dressed weekenders.

The Cherry Tree (*White Horse Lane*) is a no-nonsense, old-style pub that can get really full at weekends.

Clubs With something for (virtually) everyone across three separate floors, **Jones' Nightclub** (☎ 462520; 15 Station Rd East) is the busiest spot in town. The Works is most popular with the serious clubbers, mostly young people who sweat to hard, commercial house. The Bizz caters to a slightly older crowd and features salsa dancing on Monday nights. The Baa Bar is a horrible sports bar (complete with giant TV screens and loud, conversation-killing music) but it's the only spot in town to get a drink after midnight from Monday to Saturday.

Theatre The **Marlowe Theatre** (☎ /8//8/; e boxoffice@canterbury.gov.uk; The Friars) puts on a variety of plays, dances, concerts and musicals year round.

Gulbenkian Theatre (☎ 769075; University of Canterbury), on the university campus, puts on a varied selection of contemporary plays, modern dance shows and music gigs.

Cinemas Showing the latest mainstream movies is **Odeon Cinema** (☎ 453577; cnr Upper Bridge St & St George's Place).

Cinema 3 (☎ 769075; University of Canterbury) is part of the same complex as the Gulbenkian Theatre and usually shows offbeat, arty films and old classics.

Getting There & Away
Canterbury is 58 miles (93km) from London and 15 miles (24km) from Margate and Dover.

Bus The bus station is just within the city walls at the eastern end of High St.

National Express buses to Canterbury leave every hour from London Victoria (£9.50, 1 hour 50 minutes). Buses also run between Canterbury and Dover every hour (£3.50, 35 minutes).

Bus No 100 from Canterbury runs to Margate (£2.80, 40 minutes), Broadstairs (£3.50,

1¼ hours) and Ramsgate (£3.70, 1½ hours), while Bus No 200 does the route in reverse.

Train There are two train stations: Canterbury East (for the YHA hostel), accessible from London Victoria; and Canterbury West, accessible from London's Charing Cross and Waterloo stations. Trains run every half-hour between London and Canterbury (£15.90, 1½ hours) and from Canterbury East to Dover Priory (£4.40, 30 minutes).

Getting Around
Cars are not permitted to enter the centre of town. There are car parks at various points along and just within the ring road. For a taxi, try **Laser Taxis** (☎ 464422) or **Cabwise** (☎ 712929).

Downland Cycles (☎ 479643) is based at Canterbury West station is. Mountain bikes cost £12 per day or £60 per week with a £25 deposit.

AROUND CANTERBURY
Howlett's Wild Animal Park
The world's largest collection of Lowland gorillas can be observed at this 28-hectare park (☎ 01227-721410; Bekesbourne; adult/child £10.50/8.50; open 10am-dusk daily). However, rather than simply keep them in captivity, the park funds a project in Zaire to reintroduce these magnificent animals back to the wild. You'll also see elephants, monkeys, wolves, small wild cats and tigers, though in the last decade two keepers have been mauled to death by escaped tigers.

The Real Chitty Chitty Bang Bang

Polish nobleman and racing car enthusiast Count Louis Vorrow Zborowski (1895–1923) would have faded into history as just another crackpot aristocrat who loved driving at high speeds were it not for Ian Fleming. In 1964, the creator of James Bond wrote a children's story whose inspiration was a super-racer built by Zborowski in 1921 – for the petrol heads, it was a pre-1914, 75-horsepower Mercedes with a six-litre Mayback aero engine similar to the ones used in the German Zeppelins. Zborowski named his creation Chitty Chitty Bang Bang, and the rest is children's movie history. In 1968, Ken Hughes made the classic film, based on Roald Dahl's adapted screenplay, starring Dick Van Dyke as Caractacus Potts. Christmas television in England just wouldn't be the same without it.

Zborowski built the car at **Higham Park** (☎ 01227-830830; adult/child £3/2 for garden, £2/1 for house tour only; open 11am-6pm Sun-Thur Apr-Oct), a magnificent Palladian mansion about 3 miles (5km) south of Canterbury off the A2. The neoclassical building is one of the best examples of the Georgian style to be found in the southeast, but the real draw here are the Italianate gardens, largely designed by master gardener Harold Peto around the turn of the 20th century.

From Canterbury, Bus Nos 16 and 17 to Folkestone stop nearby (£1, 10 minutes).

The park is 4 miles (6.5km) east of Canterbury. By car, take the A257 and turn right at the sign for Bekesbourne, then follow the signs to the Animal Park. From the main bus station you can catch Stagecoach bus Nos 111/211 or 611-14 to Littlebourne, from where it's an eight-minute walk to the park.

Chilham

Five miles (8km) southwest of Canterbury on the A252, Chilham is one of the best examples of a medieval village you'll see anywhere on your travels through England. Built in true feudal fashion around the small square at the front of a castle, the village consists of a 13th-century Norman church (added to in the 15th century) and a collection of Tudor and Jacobean timber-framed houses.

Chilham lies on the North Downs Way (see the Activities section at the start of this chapter) and would make a pleasant day's walk from Canterbury. Alternatively you can catch bus No 400 from Canterbury (£1.70, 15 minutes).

WHITSTABLE
☎ 01227 • pop 2300

This overgrown fishing village overlooking Whitstable Bay is nicknamed the 'Pearl of Kent' and is famous for its seafood – particularly oysters – and its relatively unspoilt charm. Weather-boarded cottages line the lanes off High St, which have odd names like Squeeze Gut Alley and Skinner's Alley, recalling Whitstable's main pastime.

To the east of town are the cliff-top lawns of Tankerton Slopes, lined with multi-coloured beach huts and perfect views of The Street, which is actually a narrow shingle ridge stretching half a mile out to sea (but only visible at low tide).

The **TIC** (☎ 275482; 7 Oxford St; open 10am-5pm Mon-Sat July & Aug; 10am-4pm Mon-Sat Sept-June) runs a free accommodation booking service.

Things to See & Do

Whitstable isn't really a museum or church kind of place. People come here to soak up the atmosphere, swim (in good weather) and generally just hang around.

If you need to see something, however, the **Whitstable Museum & Gallery** (☎ 276998; 8 Oxford St; admission free; open 10am-4pm Mon-Sat year round; 1pm-4pm Sun July &

Aug) has pretty good exhibits on Whitstable's fishing industry, with a special emphasis on oysters.

In recent years, Whitstable has developed a vibrant artistic scene, and there are plenty of **art galleries** that you can wander into for a look. Most of the best ones line Harbour St, on the seafront.

Since 2001, the third week in July has hosted the **Whitstable Oyster Festival**, an arts and music extravaganza where you can wash down oysters with pints of Guinness or glasses of Champagne. The programme of events is varied and interesting, featuring everything from how-to demonstrations of various crafts to jazz bands and classical quartets. The whole town lends a hand and it's the highlight of the summer. For info on upcoming events, contact the TIC.

Places to Stay

As Whitstable is popular with tourists from all over southeast England, there are plenty of B&Bs.

The Windmill (☎ 265963; Miller's Court; singles/doubles £30/50) is *actually* a large windmill, complete with working sails. The rooms are quite nice; try to get one at the top of the mill as they have panoramic views over town.

Wavecrest B&B (☎ 770155; e wavecrest bandb@aol.com; 2 Seaway Cottages; singles/doubles from £45/55) is a marvellously bohemian place right on the beach. All beds have linen bedclothes.

Hotel Continental (☎ 280280, fax 280257; 29 Beach Walk; doubles from £55) is an art deco building on the seafront with elegantly appointed double rooms.

Places to Eat

As Whitstable is a fishing town, you had better like seafood. Oysters are the real treat, but all restaurants serve up a varied seafood menu.

Royal Native Oyster Stores (☎ 276856; The Horsebridge; mains around £8) has a terrific seafood platter for £13.

Pearson's Crab & Oyster House (☎ 272 005; The Horsebridge) is the most atmospheric of the restaurants we found in Whitstable. The seafood platter is £15.95.

Wheeler's Oyster Bar (☎ 273311; 8 High St) serves up half a dozen delicious oysters for £3.50.

Getting There & Away

Stagecoach Bus No 25A serves Whitstable (£1.90, 40 minutes) on its Canterbury to Seasalter route.

AROUND WHITSTABLE
Herne Bay

About 6 miles (9.7km) east of Whitstable is the less-than-charming town of Herne Bay, once a popular seaside resort but now little more than a motley collection of tacky amusements and greasy-spoon restaurants. The only reason to visit is to take a ride on the **Wildlife** (☎ 01227-366712), a small boat that makes trips to an offshore sandbank that is packed with seals. Guide and captain Mike Turner is a local wildlife specialist, and his excellent tours also include visits to bird sanctuaries. Trips last about 4½ hours and cost about £12.

Two miles (3.2km) east of Herne Bay is **Reculver Country Park** (☎ 01227-740676; admission free; open daily), where you can enjoy a pleasant stroll that will lead you to the remains of a Roman fort built in AD 280 and the 7th-century Saxon Church of St Mary, which collapsed in 1809 due to coastal erosion. The following year, the government bought the site and rebuilt the twin Reculver Towers, which had been added to the church in the 12th century. The adjacent **information centre** (open 11am-5pm Tues-Sun Apr-Aug, 11am-5pm Wed-Sun Sept, 11am-3pm Sun Oct-Mar) has excellent displays on the area's ecological significance as well as on the fort and church.

There are buses every 30 minutes from Whitstable to Herne Bay (£1.30, 15 minutes). Local buses also go from Herne Bay train station to Reculver Park, but the 2-mile (3.2km) walk is a great way to stretch your legs and see a bit of the coastline.

ISLE OF THANET

Bounded by low-lying chalky cliffs, this peninsula used to be an island, separated from the mainland by the Watsun Channel. The Romans landed here a couple of times during the first century AD, around the same time as the channel began silting up. It was here that Augustine landed in AD 597, met King Ethelred and kicked off his Conversion of Pagan England Tour. Your reason for coming, however, is to visit a couple of pretty seaside towns.

Margate

☎ 01843 • pop 38,535

Because of its proximity to London and its nice sandy beach, Margate was one of the first seaside resorts to be developed in England. It remains very popular, but most of the Victorian glamour – when the well-to-do perambulated the length of the pier under their parasols before taking afternoon tea on the large terraces that line the esplanade – has disappeared.

Yet there is enough evidence of its one-time elegance to make a visit worthwhile. Even the incredibly noisy **Dreamland** (open 11am-10pm daily May-Oct), a typical seafront amusement arcade, is fronted by a beautiful 1930s doorway and features a wooden rollercoaster from the 1860s.

The **TIC** (☎ 220241, fax 230099; 12-13 The Parade; open 9am-5pm Mon-Fri, 9am-4pm Sat & Sun) will tell you all you need to know about the town.

Margate's most famous attraction is the **Shell Grotto** (Grotto Hill; adult/child £2/1; open 10am-5pm Mon-Fri, 10am-4pm Sat & Sun), discovered in 1835 and lined with elaborate shell mosaics.

The Margate **caves** (Northdown Rd; adult/child £2/1; open 10am-5pm daily May-Sept) are the town's other big draw, but there's really nothing to do here, and you're better off just strolling around the Old Town with its antique shops and cafés.

Places to Stay & Eat On the water's edge by the beach the **YHA Hostel** (☎ 0870 770 5956, fax 221616; e margate@yha.org.uk; The Beachcomber, 3-4 Royal Esplanade; dorm beds £12.00; open mid-Apr–Oct) is a well-kept and tidy place. You must book at least 48 hours in advance.

Malvern Private Hotel (☎ 290192; Eastern Esplanade, Cliftonville; rooms per person £22-27), with large, comfortable rooms, is a little run down, but the service is friendly.

Newbys Wine Bar (☎ 292888; Market Place; mains around £8) is the place to try for local seafood. Snacks cost around £4.

Getting There & Away National Express bus No 22 runs from London Victoria to Margate and on to Broadstairs and Ramsgate (£9.50/15 one-way/return or £11 day return, 2¼ hours, five daily). Stagecoach East Kent has a service from Canterbury to Margate and on to Broadstairs and Ramsgate. Trains run hourly from London Victoria or Charing Cross (£21.70, two hours).

Broadstairs
☎ 01843 • pop 23,691

When Margate became too popular, 19th-century holidaymakers brought their buckets and spades to nearby Broadstairs, which had grown up thanks to a lucrative business in smuggling and shipbuilding. It has preserved itself better than its busier neighbour – and has a nicer beach. The most famous fan of the place was Charles Dickens, who holidayed here regularly, and you'll be reminded of this virtually everywhere. Frankly, the Dickens connection is a little overplayed, and the town is pretty enough to warrant a visit without needing constant reminders of one Victorian writer's affections for the place.

The TIC (☎ 862242, fax 865650; 6b High St; open 9am-5pm Mon-Fri year round, 9.30am-5pm Sat Mar-Sept) has all the information you'll need, including details of the annual, week-long **Dickens Festival** in June which culminates in a ball in Victorian dress.

Dickens wrote parts of *Bleak House* and *David Copperfield* in the cliff-top house above the pier between 1837 and 1859. Now a museum, the appositely named **Bleak House** (☎ 862224; adult/child £3.25/2; open 10am-6pm daily Mar-June & Sept-Nov, to 9pm July & Aug) has three rooms arranged pretty much as they were when Dickens rented it. They're quite interesting, but what makes this place worth visiting are the displays on local shipwrecks and a terrific room devoted to local smuggling, Broadstairs *other* claim to fame. Interestingly, after Dickens died, nearly 2500 unlabelled bottles of wine were discovered in his cellar, which suggests that the writer bought them from smugglers rather than from licensed wine merchants.

The **Dickens House Museum** (☎ 862853; 2 Victoria Parade; adult/child £1.50/80p; open 2pm-5pm daily Apr-Oct) wasn't actually his house but the home of Mary Pearson Strong, on whom he based Betsey Trotwood. Dickensiana on display includes personal possessions and letters.

There are a few nice places to stay in Broadstairs, most of them only a stone's throw away from the beach.

Places to Stay & Eat The staff at the **YHA Hostel** (☎ 0870 770 5730, fax 604121; e broadstairs@yha.org.uk; Thistle Lodge, 3 Osborne Rd; singles/doubles £6.90/10) is are helpful. From the station, turn right under the railway and continue for 30m to a crossroads with traffic lights, then turn left into The Broadway.

Royal Albion Hotel (☎ 868071, fax 861509; e enquiries@albionbroadstairs.co.uk; 6-12 Albion St; singles/doubles from £69/99, 1-/2-room suites £140/240) is the town's top spot, but you'll have to make do with slightly small rooms, albeit elegantly appointed, if you're not prepared to shell out for one of the two Dickens suites. Sea-facing rooms are £10 more expensive than others.

Daisy's Café Bar (☎ 602454; 92 High St; mains around £5) is a good vegetarian spot.

Marchesi Brothers (☎ 862481; 18 Albion St; mains from £10), part of the Royal Albion Hotel, is the fanciest eatery in town, a swish Italian restaurant with excellent dishes.

Getting There & Away Stagecoach bus Nos 100, 101, 200 and 201 all run hourly from Broadstairs to Margate, Ramsgate, Sandwich, Deal and Dover. Bus Nos 100 and 200 also go to Canterbury. A bus guide to the area is available from the TIC.

Trains run from London Victoria, London Bridge or Charing Cross to Broadstairs (£21.50, 2½ hours, hourly), but you may have to change trains at Ramsgate.

SANDWICH
☎ 01304 • pop 6000

Once an important port for ships travelling between England and the continent, Sandwich is perhaps the most complete medieval town in all of southern England. The imposing walls, built to protect the town against Danish raids in the 11th century, have largely disappeared, but the raised earthworks still remain, which make for a pleasant walk around the now sleepy town, which has retained its original, twisting street plan and peg-tiled rooftops. The port silted up during the 17th century but is now the location of Royal St George, perhaps the finest golf links in England and a regular host of the British Open Championship.

The **TIC** (☎/fax 613565; New St; open 11am-3pm daily May-Sept) has a good information pack detailing seven walks near the area. Guided tours of the town can be arranged by contacting **Frank Andrews** *(☎ 01304-611925, evenings only).*

Apart from admiring the marvellous half-timbered houses on **Strand St**, there's very little to do in the town, and the only museum of note is in the **Guildhall** *(☎ 617197; adult/child £1/50p),* which has fairly dramatic and detailed exhibits on the town's rich history and a choice selection of Roman artefacts.

Elsewhere, a number of buildings have Dutch or Flemish influences (note the stepped gables in some buildings), the legacy of Protestant Flemish refugees who settled in the town in the 16th century. The impressive **Barbican** is a tollgate dating from this period.

The **Church of St Clement** has one of the finest surviving Norman towers in England. **St Peter's Church** *(King St)* is the earliest of Sandwich's churches though its tower was rebuilt in 1661.

Accommodation options are few and far between.

King's Arms Hotel *(☎ 617330; rooms from £55)* is a gorgeous old inn built in 1580, and apart from those all-important concessions to modern-day amenity like comfortable beds, TVs, phones and en suites, the place is pretty much as it was built.

Getting There & Away
Bus Nos 111 and 211 connect Sandwich to Dover (£3.80, 45 minutes, hourly), Deal and Canterbury. Bus No 93 runs between Sandwich and Dover, and No 94 runs from Ramsgate to Dover via Sandwich.

Trains run half-hourly from Dover Priory (£6, 25 minutes) or from London Charing Cross to Deal, from where a bus takes you to Sandwich (£21.50, two hours).

AROUND SANDWICH
Standing amid the ruins of **Richborough Castle** *(EH; ☎ 612013; adult £2.80; open 10am-6pm daily Apr-Sept, 10am-5pm daily Oct, 10am-4pm Wed-Sun Mar & Nov, 10am-4pm Sat & Sun Dec-Feb),* 4 miles (6km) north of Sandwich, you'll have to really use your imagination to recreate the imposing Roman fort built in AD 275. The visible walls and defensive ditches offer some kind of clue, but the panorama has been seriously marred by the construction of the large, Pfizer pharmaceutical plant on Pegwell Bay below. You'll be thrilled to know, however, that this is the spot from which the successful Roman invasion of Britain was launched in AD 43. Some of the relics found here are on display in Sandwich's Guildhall Museum (see Sandwich section, earlier).

The Stour River Bus to Richborough, which runs from the northern side of the toll bridge in Sandwich, operates erratically. Phone ☎ 820171 for details.

The nearby town of **Deal** was the place where Julius Caesar and his armies landed in 55 BC. It's a peaceful town with a great stretch of beach and an unusual circular castle – another link in Henry VIII's chain of defence on the south coast. Also here is **Walmer Castle**, the official residence of the warden of the Cinque Ports (see the boxed text).

Cinque Ports

Due to their proximity to Europe, the coastal towns of southeast England were the frontline against Viking raids and invasions during Anglo-Saxon times. In the absence of a professional army and navy, these towns were frequently called upon to defend themselves, and the kingdom, at land and sea.

In 1278, King Edward I formalised this already ancient arrangement by legally defining the Confederation of Cinque (pronounced sink, meaning five) Ports. The five head ports – Sandwich, Dover, Hythe, Romney (now New Romney) and Hastings – were granted numerous privileges in exchange for providing the king with ships. The number of Cinque Ports gradually expanded to include about 30 coastal towns and villages.

By the end of the 15th century most of the Cinque Ports' harbours had become largely unusable thanks to the shifting coastline, and a professional navy was based at Portsmouth.

Although their real importance and power have evaporated, the pomp and ceremony remains. The Lord Warden of the Cinque Ports is a prestigious post now given to faithful servants of the crown. The most recent warden was the Queen Mother, while previous incumbents included the Duke of Wellington, Sir Winston Churchill and Sir Robert Menzies, former prime minister of Australia.

DOVER

☎ 01304 • pop 37,826

If you're arriving in Britain by boat from continental Europe, chances are you'll land at Dover, a most English port. Apart from the odd bilingual sign aimed at French visitors and their euro, you'll never get the sense that this is the closest point in Britain to the rest of Europe: Calais is a paltry 20 miles (32km) away, across the English Channel.

Strategically, Dover has been important since Roman times, while the Saxons (who called it Dubrae) used it as a fortified port in their chain of defences along the shore. The Normans, needless to say, built a castle immediately upon their arrival.

It is the castle, added to and changed over the centuries, that today is Dover's biggest tourist attraction, along with the spectacular white cliffs to the east of the port. The town itself has some charming elements, most notably the Victorian seafront, but there's little else to distract you from moving on.

Orientation

Dover Castle dominates the town from a high promontory to the east of town, above the white cliffs. The town itself runs back from the sea along a valley formed by the unimpressive River Dour. Ferry departures are from the Eastern Docks (accessible by bus) southeast of the castle, but the Hoverport is below the Western Heights. Dover Priory train station is a short walk to the west of the town centre. The bus station is closer to the centre of things on Pencester Rd.

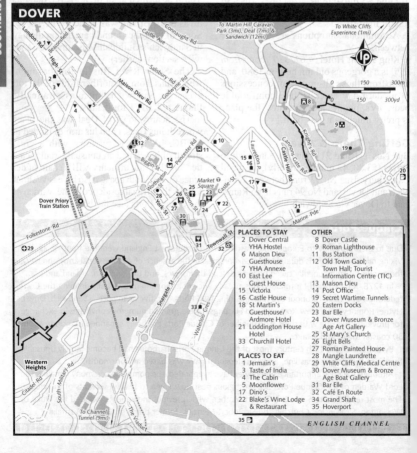

DOVER

To Martin Hill Caravan Park (3mi), Deal (7mi) & Sandwich (12mi)

To White Cliffs Experience (1mi)

Dover Priory Train Station

Western Heights

To Channel Tunnel (9mi)

ENGLISH CHANNEL

PLACES TO STAY
2 Dover Central YHA Hostel
6 Maison Dieu Guesthouse
7 YHA Annexe
10 East Lee Guest House
15 Victoria
16 Castle House
18 St Martin's Guesthouse/ Ardmore Hotel
21 Loddington House Hotel
33 Churchill Hotel

PLACES TO EAT
1 Jermain's
3 Taste of India
4 The Cabin
5 Moonflower
17 Dino's
22 Blake's Wine Lodge & Restaurant

OTHER
8 Dover Castle
9 Roman Lighthouse
11 Bus Station
12 Old Town Gaol; Town Hall; Tourist Information Centre (TIC)
13 Maison Dieu
14 Post Office
19 Secret Wartime Tunnels
20 Eastern Docks
23 Bar Elle
24 Dover Museum & Bronze Age Art Gallery
25 St Mary's Church
26 Eight Bells
27 Roman Painted House
28 Mangle Laundrette
29 White Cliffs Medical Centre
30 Dover Museum & Bronze Age Boat Gallery
31 Bar Elle
32 Café En Route
34 Grand Shaft
35 Hoverport

Information

The **TIC** (☎ 205108, fax 245409; e tic@ doveruk.com; The Old Town Gaol, Biggin St; open 9am-6pm daily) has an accommodation and ferry-booking service (both free). All the major **banks** and **ATMs** are located on Market Square.

There's a **post office** (open 9.30am-5.30pm Mon-Sat) on Pencester Rd. **Café En-Route** (☎ 206633; 8 Bench St; open 9am-5pm Mon-Sat, noon-5pm Sun) has Internet access for £5 per hour.

The **Mangle laundrette** (Worthington St; open 8am-8pm daily) will do laundry for around £3 a load.

There are toilets in Pencester Gardens near the Stagecoach East Kent office.

White Cliffs Medical Centre (☎ 201705; 143 Folkestone Rd) is five minutes' walk from the centre of Dover. The nearest hospital with an accident and emergency department is in Folkestone, 8 miles (13km) west of Dover.

Dover Castle

The virtually impregnable Dover Castle (EH; ☎ 211067; adult/child £7.50/3.80; open 10am-4pm daily Nov-Mar, 10am-6pm daily Apr-Sept) is one of the most impressive in Britain, a mighty fortress commanding a superb view of the English Channel and the town below. On the vast grounds there is a restored **Saxon church** and, interestingly, the remains of a **Roman lighthouse**, which dates from AD 50 and is possibly the oldest standing building in Britain.

Henry II's mighty **keep** was built between 1181 and 1188, its walls are seven metres thick in places. It withstood a prolonged siege by Prince Louis of France (later Louis VII) in 1216 when, along with Windsor Castle, it was the only fortification in southern England not to fall into French hands. Had it fallen, we can only speculate as to how different European history might have been.

Although the keep itself, with its various audiovisual displays and exhibits, is mightily impressive, it's the series of **secret wartime tunnels** under the castle that are the most interesting attraction here. The first tunnel was dug during the Napoleonic Wars to act as an overflow barracks for soldiers, but in 1938 Vice-Admiral Bertram Ramsey was called out of retirement to oversee the renovation and expansion of the tunnel network. With the outbreak of war a year later,

Ramsey moved his command post into the tunnels, and it was from here in May 1940 that he engineered the virtually miraculous evacuation of over 300,000 British, French and Belgian troops from Dunkirk, where they were cornered by two German armies. The highly entertaining 50-minute tour is included in the general admission price.

Bus No 90 runs from Dover Priory station to the castle.

Dover Museum & Bronze Age Boat Gallery

The Dover Museum (☎ 201066; Market Square; adult/child £1.75/95p) is one of the best around and definitely shouldn't be missed. The ground floor covers Dover's prehistoric past, the first floor hosts a series of rotating exhibitions, while the second covers the history of the town from 1066 to the present day.

Also on the second floor is the new, award-winning **Bronze Age Boat Gallery**, which features a 3600-year-old boat discovered off the Dover Coast in 1992. It is the world's oldest known seagoing vessel and measures a pretty impressive 9.5m by 2.4m.

Other Things to See & Do

Next door to the TIC is the **Maison Dieu** (admission free; open 10am-6pm daily) which was built as a hospice for pilgrims and wounded soldiers in 1203. It now contains a collection of arms, armour, portraits of England's kings and dignitaries, and a magnificent stained-glass window depicting events in England's history.

The **Roman Painted House** (☎ 203279; New St; adult/child £2/80p; open 10am-5pm Tues-Sun Apr-Sept) is the finest Roman house on show in Britain. It was built around AD 200 as a *mansio*, or official hotel, for travellers crossing the channel – Britain's first B&B? The house was largely destroyed by Roman troops in AD 270, but thankfully they inadvertently preserved over 400 sq ft (37 sq metres) of painted plaster, the most extensive wall painting found north of the Alps.

Beginning at Snargate St, the **Grand Shaft** (admission £1; open 2pm-5pm Tues-Sun July & Aug) is a 43m triple staircase which was cut into the white cliffs as a short cut to town for troops stationed on the Western Heights during the Napoleonic Wars. According to popular tradition, one staircase was for officers

SOUTHEAST ENGLAND

and their ladies, the second for the non-commissioned officers and their wives, and the third for soldiers and their women!

Organised Tours

Guide Friday (☎ 01273-540893) runs hourly hop-on, hop-off tours of Dover and the surrounding area between 10am and 4pm daily. Tours cost £7/2.50 per adult/child, and tickets can be bought at the Market Square stop, the TIC or on board the bus.

Places to Stay

Camping & Hostels Three miles (4.8km) northeast of Dover, off the A258, the **Martin Mill Caravan Park** (☎ 852658; Hawthorn Farm; camping per 1/2 people & tent £6.50/8, with car £8/10; open Mar-Nov) is a pretty good spot.

The **Dover Central YHA Hostel** (☎ 0870 770 5798, fax 202236; 306 London Rd; beds per adult £11.50) is in a restored Georgian building. It also has a very convenient **annexe** (Godwyne Rd; beds per adult/under-18 £11.50/8).

B&Bs & Hotels Most B&Bs are along Castle St and Maison Dieu Rd, but there are others along Folkestone Rd.

St Martin's Guesthouse/Ardmore Hotel (☎ 205938, fax 208229; e res@stmartinsgh .co.uk; 17 Castle Hill Rd; singles/doubles £24/48) is highly recommended. The landlady is helpful and friendly and rooms are spotless and cosy. The two guesthouses are basically one, and rooms are similar in both.

Castle House (☎ 201656, fax 210197; e dimechr@aol.com; 10 Castle Hill Rd; singles/ doubles £30/50) is another good choice, with comfortable, en-suite rooms and a terrific breakfast.

Maison Dieu Guesthouse (☎ 204033, fax 242816; e lawrie@brguest.co.uk; 89 Maison Dieu Rd; doubles £56), a well-appointed and elegant house, has large, comfortable rooms.

East Lee Guest House (☎ 210176, fax 206705; e eastlee@eclipse.co.uk; 108 Maison Dieu Rd; singles/doubles £26/52) is a large Victorian townhouse with individually furnished, luxurious bedrooms.

Victoria (☎/fax 205140; e wham101496@ aol.com; 1 Laureston Place; rooms per person £28) is a highly attractive Victorian home with large and comfortable rooms – and plenty of stairs.

If you want a sea view, be prepared to pay for it. Most of the accommodation on the water isn't worth the money, but there are two exceptions.

Loddington House Hotel (☎/fax 201947; e sscupper@aol.com; 14 East Cliff, Marine Parade; singles/doubles £45/60) is more of an upmarket B&B, and features the kind of personalised attention missing from most mid-range hotels.

Churchill Hotel (☎ 203633, fax 216320; e enquiries@churchill-hotel.com; Waterloo Cres; B&B per person £68), popular with business travellers, is the poshest hotel in town.

Places to Eat

Dover is not really going to tickle anyone's taste buds; most eateries are of the grease-disguised-as-food variety, but there are a few places where you can get a decent meal and one that is truly outstanding.

Moonflower (☎ 212198; 32 High St; closed Sun; mains around £5.80) is the best of Dover's Chinese restaurants. The Kung Po chicken is very tasty.

Taste of India (☎ 240122; 332 London Rd; mains £6) is the best Indian restaurant in town, although the competition is hardly staggering.

Dino's (☎ 204678; 58 Castle Hill Rd; mains around £8) is a good Italian restaurant that is popular with locals.

Jermain's (☎ 205956; Beaconsfield Rd), a clean, efficient eatery near the YHA Hostel, has good-value traditional fare, such as roast beef for £5.50 and pudding for £1.

Blake's Wine Lodge & Restaurant (☎ 202 194; 52 Castle St; mains £9-13) is a fancy English restaurant with – as the name suggests – a good selection of wines.

The Cabin (☎ 206118; 91 High St) is the best restaurant in town and a real treat for gourmets of English cuisine (believe us, it does exist!). Everything is made to order, and the constantly changing menu encourages diners to try some typically British dishes that have sadly been pushed aside by nouvelle cuisine. Anyone for sherried lamb's kidneys (£3.65) followed by haunch of wild boar in a red wine sauce (£11.90)?

Entertainment

Dover offers little in terms of nightlife, but we can recommend a couple of decent bars for a post-prandial nightcap.

Eight Bells *(16 Cannon St)* is a popular watering hole with locals; it's nothing fancy, just a decent pub to have a drink.

Bar Elle *(18-19 Market Square)* is new and hyper-trendy. Dover's young followers of fashion can be seen here most nights sipping alco-pops and nodding their heads to the pounding beats laid on by the DJs.

Getting There & Away
Dover is 75 miles (120km) from London and 15 miles (24km) from Canterbury.

Bus Dover's **bus station** *(☎ 240024; Pencester Rd)* is in the heart of town. Stagecoach East Kent has a Canterbury to Dover service (£2.90, 40 minutes). National Express coaches leave hourly from London Victoria (£9.50/17 one-way/return, two hours 50 minutes).

There's an hourly bus to Brighton but you'll need to change at Eastbourne. The £5.50 Explorer ticket is the best value on this route. Bus No 711 will take you to Hastings (£4.50). Bus Nos 111 and 211 go hourly to Canterbury (£2.10, 40 minutes) via Sandwich and Deal, weekdays only.

Train There are over 40 trains daily from London Victoria and Charing Cross stations to Dover Priory via Ashford and Sevenoaks (£19.80, 1¾ hours).

Channel Tunnel The Channel Tunnel begins its descent into the English Channel 9 miles (14.5km) west of Dover, just off the M20 between London and Dover. The nearest station foot passengers can board the **Eurostar train** *(☎ 01233-617575)* is at Ashford. From Dover, it's easier if you have a car: take junction 11A for the Channel Tunnel (it's very well-signposted). To cross the channel via the Eurotunnel costs £164.50 for a standard car plus up to four passengers. Call ☎ 08705-353535 for information.

Boat Ferries depart from the Eastern Docks (which are accessible by bus; see Getting Around later) below the castle. **P&O Stena** *(☎ 0870 600 0600)* ferries leave for Calais every 30 minutes (one-way/return £26/52, car and two passengers £139/264, 1¼ hours). Seafrance ferries leave every 1½ hours (£17/34, 1¼ hours). The Hoverport is below the Western Heights; a one-way/return ticket

on the hourly Hoverspeed to Ostende costs £24/48.

Call ☎ 401575 for information on day trips to France and special offers.

Getting Around
The ferry companies run complimentary buses between the docks and the train station as they're a long walk apart. On local buses a trip from one side of town to the other costs about £1.70.

Central Taxis *(☎ 240441)* and **Heritage** *(☎ 204420)* both have 24-hour services. You could also try **Star Taxis** *(☎ 228822)*. A one-way trip to Deal costs about £8.90; to Sandwich it's about £13.

AROUND DOVER
The White Cliffs
The world-famous white cliffs extend for 10 miles (16km) on either side of Dover, but it is the 6-mile (10km) stretch east of town – properly known as the Langdon Cliffs – that has captivated visitors for centuries.

The chalk here is about 250m deep, and when you consider that it was created by the accumulated debris of lime-scaled plankton and other microscopic life forms gathering at the bottom of the ocean at a rate of 0.015mm *a year*, it is a work in progress that has lasted for more than 16.5 million years. Much has happened since then, of course, including the disappearance of the massive ocean that covered this part of the world. The cliffs themselves date only from about half a million years ago, when the melting waters from the giant icecap that covered all of northern Europe forced a channel through the landmass that was then France and England, creating at once the English Channel and the cliffs.

You can appreciate their majesty – and get in some decent exercise – by walking along the path that snakes its way for 2 miles (3.2km) along the top. It's a pretty bracing walk so be sure to wear appropriate footwear. On the eastern side is the **South Foreland Lighthouse** *(adult/child £2/1; open 11am-5.30pm daily July & Aug, 11am-5.30pm Thur-Sun Mar-June, Sept & Oct)*, built in 1843. It was from here, on 24 December 1898, that Guglielmo Marconi made the world's first shore-to-ship and international radio transmission, with a call to a ship navigating the Channel and another to Wimereux in France.

Just next to the lighthouse is the stunningly located **East Cottage** (☎ 01225-791199), which can be rented as a holiday home. Rates range from £290 in January to £623 in July and August. Call for details.

The Langdon Cliffs are managed by the National Trust, who have recently opened a **visitor centre** (☎ 01304-202756; admission free; open 9am-6pm daily) on the western side of this section. There isn't much to see other than a couple of wall displays and the ubiquitous coffee shop and souvenir stands.

The cliffs are at the end of Upper Rd, 2 miles (3.2km) east of Dover along Castle Hill Rd and the A258 road to Deal. Bus Nos 111 and 211 from Dover stop near the main entrance. Guide Friday include the cliffs as part of their hop on, hop off town tours (see Organised Tours in the Dover section, earlier). First departure is from Market Square in Dover at 10am; last departure from the car park at the cliffs is at 4.40pm.

If you fancy seeing them from the sea, **White Cliffs Boat Tours** (☎ 01303-271388; w www.whitecliffsboattours.co.uk) run water tours aboard the 70-seater *Southern Queen*. Trips run hourly, every day from March to September, from De Bradelei Wharf at the Eastern Docks. The tickets cost £5/3 per adult/child.

Hythe

Once a Cinque Port, Hythe is a low-key seaside resort with an attractive Old Town. In the crypt of **St Leonard's Church** is a ghoulish attraction – 8000 thigh bones and 2000 skulls, some arranged on shelves like pots of jam in a supermarket.

Hythe is 18 miles (29km) west of Dover. Bus No 558 runs from Canterbury to Hythe roughly every two hours from Monday to Saturday (£2.10; 1 hour) bus No 711 passes through Hythe hourly (every two hours on Sunday) en route between Eastbourne and Dover.

Romney Marsh

The 40-sq-mile (104 sq km) flat plain that is Romney Marsh was once submerged beneath the Channel, but the lowering of the water table during Middle Ages, as well as subsequent reclamations, added new territory to the island. However, the fact that the marsh was rife with malaria ensured that it remained a largely uninhabited and desolate spot. The risk of tropical disease has long abated, and the marsh is now the location of the world's smallest gauge public railway, the **Romney, Hythe & Dymchurch Railway** (☎ 01797-362353), opened in 1927. It runs 13½ miles (22km) from Hythe to Dungeness lighthouse, between Easter and September (weekends only in March and October). The adult/child fare between Hythe and Dungeness is £9.40/4.70.

The **Romney Marsh Countryside Project** (☎ 01304-241806) arranges guided walks and bicycle rides around the area. Pick up a pamphlet from the Royal Society for the Protection of Birds (RSPB) Nature Reserve visitor centre in Dungeness (see following).

Dungeness

On the western edge of Romney Marsh is a low shingle spit dominated by a nuclear power station and a lighthouse. Despite the apocalyptic bleakness, the area is home to the largest seabird colony in the southeast. You can visit the **Royal Society for the Protection of Birds (RSPB) Nature Reserve visitor centre** (☎ 01797-320588; Dungeness Rd; open 9am-sunset daily).

On either side of the RSPB centre you will find a number of old fishermen's cottages that have been bought up or rented by a variety of eccentric characters and artists. One of these is **Prospect Cottage** (55-60 Dungeness Rd), where avant-garde filmmaker, writer, artist and gay rights activist Derek Jarman (1942–94) lived in the years up to his death from AIDS. Although the house is in private hands and cannot be visited, such is the appeal of Jarman's extraordinary talent that fans and visitors alike make the trek just to stand outside and marvel at the beautiful shingle garden he created and adorned with a variety of plantings and sculptures. The cottage's south wall bears John Donne's poem *The Sunne Rising* in large letters.

THE KENT WEALD

Western Kent encompasses a large part of the Weald, a once heavily forested area that stretches into East Sussex. Its name is a corruption of the German word for forest, *wald*, although the trees have given way to rolling hills and small, prosperous towns that rank among England's most prestigious addresses. It's also home to three extraordinary castles and two much-visited manor houses.

Sevenoaks

☎ 01732 • pop 18,000 • elevation 164m

It used to be a charming Kent village 25 miles (40km) from London, but the capital's ever-extending suburban tentacles have all but swallowed up this town; even the trees that gave Sevenoaks its name have gone, knocked over in a freak storm in 1987. Concrete charm notwithstanding, there is a reason to visit, and you won't be disappointed.

At the southern end of High St, **Knole House** (NT; ☎ 450608; adult £5; open 11am-4pm Wed-Sun Mar-Oct) is one of the most important treasure houses in England. The estate has existed since the 12th century, but in 1456 the Archbishop of Canterbury, Thomas Bouchier, bought the whole property for £266 and set about rebuilding the lot to make it 'fit for the Princes of the Church'. The result is impressive indeed, and is curiously designed to match the calendar, so there are seven courtyards, 52 staircases and 365 rooms. You can also visit the **garden** (admission free; open 1st Wed of month May-Sept).

Four more archbishops of Canterbury resided here before Henry VIII took it from the church, spent a ton of money on its enlargement and then ignored it. In 1566 Elizabeth I made a gift of the house to her cousin Thomas Sackville, and his descendants have lived here ever since.

The house features fine plasterwork ceilings, a magnificently carved wooden screen in the main hall, and a series of extraordinary painted walls, along the staircases and in the oddly named Cartoon Gallery. The really eye-catching feature, however, is the great chimney and overmantel in the ballroom, once Archbishop Bouchier's living room. The elaborately carved marble and alabaster structure reaches from floor to ceiling and is considered one of the finest works of Renaissance sculpture in England.

Although ransacked by Parliamentarians during the Civil War, the house was restocked by William III's Lord Chamberlain, the Earl of Dorset, with a fabulous collection of 17th-century furniture and artworks that have no equal in any of England's country houses.

Virginia Woolf was a close friend of the Sackville family (particularly Vita Sackville-West), and her novel *Orlando* is loosely based on the history of the house and its inhabitants (see the boxed text 'The Bloomsbury Group', later).

The house is about 1½ miles (2.4km) from Sevenoaks train station and less than 1 mile (1.2km) from the bus station.

There are no direct bus services from London to Sevenoaks so you're better off catching the train. From nearby Tonbridge however, bus No 402 runs to Sevenoaks (£1.40, 30 minutes).

Sevenoaks station is on London Rd. Trains leave three times an hour from London Charing Cross (£6.90, 35 minutes) and continue to Tunbridge Wells (£5.10, 20 minutes) and Hastings (£13.70, one hour 10 minutes).

Chartwell

Six miles (10km) east of Sevenoaks is Chartwell (NT; ☎ 01732-868381; Westerham; adult £5.80, garden and studio only £2.90; open 11am-5pm Tues-Sun July & Aug, 11am-5pm Wed-Sun Apr-June & Sept), Sir Winston Churchill's home from 1924 until his death in 1965. Architecturally unremarkable, this much-altered Tudor house is nevertheless a fascinating place, as well as being one of the most visited of all NT-owned properties.

The rooms and gardens are pretty much as Winnie left them, full of pictures, books, personal mementos and plenty of maps. Churchill was also an artist of considerable talent, and the interesting collection of sketches and watercolours in the garden studio display a softer side of the cigar-chomping bombast of popular perception.

The Chartwell Explorer bus runs six times a day between Sevenoaks train/bus stations and Chartwell on the weekend and bank holidays from mid-May to mid-September, and Wednesday to Friday during July and August. The trip takes 30 minutes and the ticket (adult/child £3.50/2) includes a pot of tea at Chartwell. A combined ticket, including return rail travel from London to Sevenoaks, bus transfer to Chartwell and entry costs £15/7.50; enquire at Charing Cross train station.

Hever Castle

Idyllic Hever Castle (☎ 01732-861702; adult/child £8.20/4.50, gardens only £6.50/4.30; open noon-5pm daily Apr-Oct, noon-4pm Mar & Nov) near Edenbridge, a few miles west of Tonbridge, was the childhood home of Anne Boleyn, mistress to Henry VIII and then his doomed queen. Walking through the main gate into the courtyard of

SOUTHEAST ENGLAND

Hever is like stepping onto the set of a period film. Hollywood, eat your heart out!

The moated castle dates from 1270, with the Tudor house added in 1505 by the Bullen (Boleyn) family, who bought the castle in 1462. Although the castle was home to two queens – Anne Boleyn and, later, Anne of Cleves – it fell into disrepair until 1903, when it was bought by the American multimillionaire William Waldorf Astor, who poured obscene amounts of money into a massive refurbishment. The exterior is unchanged from Tudor times, but the interior now has superb Edwardian carved wooden panelling.

The lower level of the gatehouse is home to a horrifying collection of torture and execution instruments. Our particular favourite is the flesh gouger!

The castle is surrounded by a garden, again the creation of the Astors, that incorporates a number of different styles, including a formal Italian garden with classical sculptures.

From London Victoria trains go to Hever (change at Hurst Green), a mile's walk from the castle (£7.30, 52 minutes). Alternatively, you could take the train to Edenbridge, from where it's a 4-mile (6.4km) taxi ride. A nice idea is to hire a bicycle in Edenbridge and ride to Hever. From Edenbridge High St the route to Hever is signposted.

Penshurst

The attractive village of Penshurst, 10 miles (16km) east of Edenbridge on the B2176, is lined with timber-framed Tudor houses and features a gorgeous church with four spires.

What draws people here, though, is the wonderful medieval manor house that is **Penshurst Place** *(☎ 870307; adult/child £6.50/4.50; open noon-5.30pm Sun-Fri, noon-4pm Sat Apr-Oct)*, the home of Philip Sidney, Viscount de L'Isle, whose family have owned the property since 1522. At its heart is the magnificent **Baron's Hall** where a number of English monarchs, including Henry VIII, enjoyed lavish feasts and spectacles beneath the stunning 18m-high chestnut roof.

With the exception of the state dining room, the other rooms in the castle were added in the early 15th century, with further modifications continuing into the 19th century. Furniture and decor from all over Europe date from the 16th to the 18th centuries. An information page at the entrance to each room will tell you about the main features.

Surrounding the house are the splendid 4.5-hectare walled **gardens** *(open 10.30am-6pm daily Apr-Oct)*, which were originally designed in 1346 and have remained virtually unchanged since Elizabethan times. The remainder of the grounds are wonderful for a bit of walking. Taking in parkland and riverside, the walks vary from 2 to 4 miles (3.2km to 6.4km) in length and usually take one to two hours. The ticket office has details.

From Edenbridge, bus Nos 231, 232 and 233 stop in Penshurst (£2.40; 25 minutes; hourly) on their way to Tunbridge Wells.

Ightham Mote

A small, moated medieval manor, Ightham (pronounced eye-tam) is a remarkable place, if only because of the haphazard way in which the building has developed over the centuries. Although parts date from around 1340, the building today is an architectural jigsaw puzzle, and you need a detailed guide to unravel which bit belongs to which century. Despite all of this, the building's scale, materials (wood, stone, clay) and the frame of water create a harmonious whole.

Ightham Mote *(NT; ☎ 01732-811145; adult £5; open 11am-5.30pm Wed-Fri, Sun & Mon Apr-Oct)* is 6 miles (10km) east of Sevenoaks off the A25, and 2½ miles (4km) south of the village of Ightham off the A227. There are six daily buses from Sevenoaks to Ivy Hatch, one mile (1.6km) from the manor.

Leeds Castle

Just to the east of Maidstone, Leeds Castle *(☎ 01622-765400; adult/child Mar-Oct £11/7.50, Nov-Feb £9.50/6; open 10am-5pm daily Mar-Oct, 10am-3pm daily Nov-Feb)* is one of the most famous and most visited castles in the world. It stands on two small islands in a lake surrounded by a huge estate that contains woodlands, an aviary and a really weird grotto that can only be entered once you've successfully negotiated your way through a hedge maze.

The building dates from the 9th century. Henry VIII transformed it from a fortress into a palace, and it was privately owned until 1974 when Lady Billie, the castle's last owner, died. Paintings, furniture and other decor in the castle date from the last eight centuries.

A private trust now manages the property and, as part of a requirement that the castle serve as more than just a tourist attraction, some of the rooms are used for conferences and other events. This creates a problem for the visitor in that some of the rooms are closed to the public quite regularly. If you want to be sure you can see all the rooms and get your money's worth, ring ahead. Another problem is the sheer number of people to be negotiated – at weekends it's the families, during the week it's the school groups.

National Express runs one direct bus daily from London Victoria coach station, leaving at 9am and returning at 3.45pm (1¼ hours). It must be pre-booked and the price combines admission and travel (£16/10 per adult/child). **Greenline** (☎ 020-8668 7261) buses have the same deal (£16.50/10.50, 9.35am from London Victoria, return 4pm).

East Sussex

Dominated by the lovely countryside of the South Downs, East Sussex is one of the most popular southeastern destinations, and a favourite weekend spot for Londoners looking to unwind and relax. There's some-

thing for everyone here, from the exquisite beauty of Rye to the historically important Battle, where William the Conqueror first engaged the Saxons in 1066. Farther down the coast, remarkable Brighton is without doubt one of the coolest cities in England, with the best nightlife south of London. Nearby, Lewes is often ignored by visitors, but the town oozes charm and elegance.

RYE
☎ 01797 • pop 5400

Rye is almost impossibly beautiful. Once a Cinque Port, this desperately picturesque medieval town looks like it has been preserved in historical formaldehyde. Not even the most talented Hollywood set designers could have come up with a better representation of Ye Olde Englishe Village: the half-timbered Tudor buildings, winding cobbled streets, abundant flowerpots and strong literary associations should be enough to temper even the most hard-bitten cynic's weariness of the made-for-tourism look.

Inevitably, such beauty *has* made it a tourist magnet, but thankfully most wander about the town in almost muted appreciation,

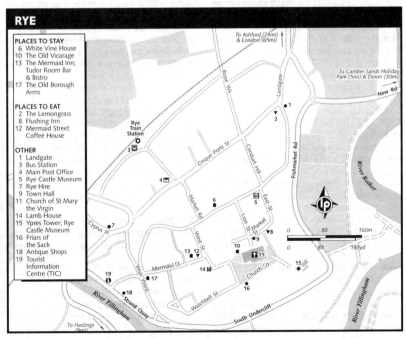

RYE

PLACES TO STAY
6 White Vine House
10 The Old Vicarage
13 The Mermaid Inn;
   Tudor Room Bar
   & Bistro
17 The Old Borough
   Arms

PLACES TO EAT
2 The Lemongrass
8 Flushing Inn
12 Mermaid Street
   Coffee House

OTHER
1 Landgate
3 Bus Station
4 Main Post Office
5 Rye Castle Museum
7 Rye Hire
9 Town Hall
11 Church of St Mary
   the Virgin
14 Lamb House
15 Ypres Tower; Rye
   Castle Museum
16 Friars of
   the Sack
18 Antique Shops
19 Tourist
   Information
   Centre (TIC)

To Ashford (24mi)
& London (65mi)

To Camber Sands Holiday
Park (5mi) & Dover (30mi)

New Rd

Rope Wk

Landgate

River Rother

Rye
Train
Station

Cinque Ports St

Conduit Hill

Fishmarket Rd

Market Rd

East St

Cyprus Pl

West St

Lion St

Market

Mermaid St

West Ward

Church Sq

River Tillingham

Strand Quay

Watchbell St

South Undercliff

River Tillingham

To Hastings
(9mi)

0   80   160m
0   80   160yd

lest their gasps of surprise disturb the air of genuine tranquillity and perfection that pervades the place. If you do visit – and you absolutely should – avoid summer weekends.

Orientation & Information

Rye is easily covered on foot. There is a **TIC** (☎ 226696, fax 223460; e *ryetic@rother.gov .uk; Strand Quay; open 9am-5.30pm daily Mar-Oct, 10am-4pm daily Nov-Feb)*. *Rye Town Walk* gives a detailed history of the town's buildings and costs £1. There's also an audio tour costing £2.50/1.50 per adult/child. For guided walks around town phone ☎ 01424-882343 or ☎ 01424-882466.

The town celebrates its medieval heritage with a two-day festival each August, and in September there is the two-week **Festival of Music and the Arts**.

Things to See & Do

You can start your tour of the town at the TIC's **Rye Town Model Sound & Light Show** *(adult/child £2.50/1.50; open daily)* which gives a half-hour theatrical introduction to the town's history.

Around the corner from the TIC, in Strand Quay, are a number of **antique shops** selling all kinds of wonderful junk. From here walk up cobbled **Mermaid St**, one of the most famous streets in England, with timber-framed houses dating from the 15th century.

Turn right at the T-junction for the Georgian **Lamb House** *(NT; ☎ 224982; West St; adult £2.60; open 2pm-6pm Tues-Sat Apr-Oct)*, mostly dating from 1722. It was the home of American writer Henry James from 1898 to 1916, he wrote *The Wings of the Dove* here.

Continue around the dogleg until you come out at Church Square. This gorgeous square is surrounded by a variety of attractive houses, including the **Friars of the Sack** on the southern side at No 40. Now a private residence, it was once part of a 13th-century Augustinian friary. The **Church of St Mary the Virgin** incorporates a mixture of ecclesiastical styles. The turret clock is the oldest in England (1561) and still works with its original pendulum mechanism. There are great views from the **church tower** *(adult/child £2/1)*.

Turn right at the eastern corner of the square for **Ypres Tower** *(adult/child £1.90/1, with museum £2.90/1.50)*, pronounced

wipers, part of a 13th-century fort. It now houses one part of the **Rye Castle Museum** *(☎ 226728)*. The main museum *(3 East St; adult/child with Ypres Tower £2.90/1.50; open 10am-5pm Thur-Mon Apr-Oct, 10am-4pm Sat & Sun Nov-Mar)* is on East St.

At the northeastern edge of the village is **Landgate**. Built in 1329 to fortify the town, it's the only remaining gate out of four.

Places to Stay

Accommodation is plentiful and of a very high standard.

Camber Sands Holiday Park *(☎ 225555, fax 225756; New Lydd Rd, Camber; pitch £20, late July–Aug £25; open Mar-Oct)*, 5½ miles (9km) east of Rye, runs alongside a marvellously remote and rugged stretch of beach.

The Mermaid Inn *(☎ 223065, fax 225069; Mermaid St; B&B per person from £75)* is a marvellously atmospheric hostelry that has been around since 1420, and comes complete with a resident ghost.

The Old Vicarage *(☎ 222119, fax 227 466; e oldvicarageye@tesco.net; 66 Church Square; doubles from £56)*, next to St Mary's Church, is a salmon-coloured former vicarage with a lovely garden. The rooms are exquisitely appointed.

White Vine House *(☎ 224748, fax 223599; e irene@whitevinehouse.freeserve.co.uk; 24 High St; doubles from £80, 5-bed family room £130)* is our favourite place in town. This sumptuous Tudor house, built in 1560, has been converted into a stunning hotel with superb service and superbly appointed rooms.

The Old Borough Arms *(☎/fax 222128; e info@oldborougharms.co.uk; The Strand; doubles £50-90)*, a 300-year-old former smuggler's inn, has recently been converted into a truly lovely guesthouse, with neo-rustic rooms complete with four-poster beds. The café is excellent. It serves great sandwiches for £2.50 and cream teas for £2.95.

Places to Eat

The Lemongrass *(☎ 222327; 1 Tower St; curries £7)* is the only Thai restaurant in town, and a pretty good one at that.

Flushing Inn *(☎ 223292; 4 Market St; mains £8.80-13.50)* has a '1066 Maritime Menu' – mostly seafood – and local wines.

Tudor Room Bar & Bistro *(☎ 223065; Mermaid St)*, at the Mermaid Inn, is a tiny, low-ceilinged, half-timbered pub with an outdoor terrace. Baguettes cost around £5.50 or you can have something more substantial, such as baked local fish pie with smoked cheese for £7.95.

Mermaid Street Coffee House (☎ 224858; cnr Mermaid & West Sts) is the place to try a smorgasbord of coffee and snacks. Cake and coffee costs £3.

Getting There & Away
Bus No 711 runs hourly between Dover and Brighton via Rye (£3.80, 50 minutes), while Nos 344 and 345 link Rye with Hastings twice hourly (not at weekends).

From London Charing Cross, trains run hourly, Monday to Saturday – with five on Sunday – to Rye (£17.90; 1½ hours) via Ashford. The service continues to Hastings (£3.30, 1¼ hours).

Getting Around
You can rent bikes from £9 per day (with a £25 deposit) from **Rye Hire** (☎ 223033; Cyprus Place). A cycling map of East Sussex is available from the TIC.

HASTINGS
☎ 01424 • pop 80,820

Once an important Cinque Port, Hastings is a curious place these days. Sure, it has its tacky seafront, complete with questionable attractions, but it is still a small but vibrant fishing port and, in recent years, it has attracted a substantial artistic community whose presence is noted by the renaming of a section of town as Bohemia.

The **TIC** (☎ 781111, fax 781186; e hic@ hastings.gov.uk; Queen's Square, Priory Meadow; open 8.30am-6.15pm Mon-Fri, 10am-5pm Sat, 10am-4.30pm Sun) is beside the town hall. There's another branch on the foreshore near the Stade. There is a **post office** on Cambridge Rd.

The **Hastings Museum & Art Gallery** (☎ 781155; Bohemia Rd; admission free; open 10am-5pm Mon-Sat, 2pm-5pm Sun) is a surprisingly interesting place, with a good mix of modern art and historical exhibits.

The surviving fragmentary remains of **Hastings Castle** (☎ 781112; adult/child £3/2) date from after the battle. The **1066 Experience** (adult/child £3.20/2.10; open 11am-5pm daily Easter-Sept, 11am-4pm daily Oct-Easter) is an audiovisual show on the events of that year. You can get to the castle

Walking in Norman Footsteps

The 1066 Country Walk links Rye to Pevensey, passes through 31 miles (50km) of East Sussex's countryside and joins the South Downs Way (see the Activities section at the start of this chapter). From Rye it's 3 miles (4.8km) to the village of Winchelsea, which is almost as attractive as Rye yet without the tourists. The path is an excellent way to reach Battle, which is 15 miles (24km) away. There are also links to Hastings, about 15 miles (24km) from Rye. Another good walk from Rye is to Camber Castle, which is 1½ miles (2.4km) away.

A leaflet showing the route of the 1066 Country Walk and listing places to stay along the way is available free from TICs in Rye, Battle, Hastings and Pevensey.

via the **West Hill Lift** cliff railway (£1/50p per adult/child).

West of the castle (and also accessible via the West Hill Lift) is the **Smugglers' Adventure** (☎ 434229; St Clement Caves, West Hill; adult/child £5.50/3.50; open 10am-5pm daily), a series of caves that were once populated by pirates and their loot. It's good fun, and kids love it.

The **Stade**, at the eastern end of town, is a hive of fishing activity.

Places to Stay & Eat
The cheapest B&Bs can be found along Cambridge Gardens.

Apollo Guest House (☎ 444394; 25 Cambridge Gardens; rooms per person June-Aug £22, Sept-May £18) is only a short walk from the waterfront and is recommended.

Senlac (☎ 430080; e senlac@1066-country .com; 47 Cambridge Gardens; rooms per person with/without en suite £20/18) also gets a big tick for friendly service and comfort.

Jenny Lind Hotel (☎ 421392; 69 High St; singles/doubles £35/50), in the Old Town, has large, comfortable rooms.

The Cinnamon Tree (☎ 437075; 69 High St; mains around £7), above the Jenny Lind, has excellent curries, and plenty of choice for vegetarians.

Gannets (☎ 439678; 45 High St; open breakfast & lunch; mains around £6) offers pretty standard fare (roasts, sandwiches etc) but the portions are good and tasty.

The Blessing of the Sea

One of the more curious traditions in this part of the world is Rogationtide, which takes place before the beginning of the fishing season. From the Latin word *rogatio*, meaning intercession, this rite began in AD 467 with the blessing of the harvest at Ascension. In Hastings the harvest is of a fishy kind, and every year the local fishing community wades knee-deep into the sea alongside the clergy who bless the nets and the mackerel in the hope that there's plenty more where they came from.

Getting There & Away

Bus No 711 runs from Dover to Brighton via Hastings (£4.80, hourly, nine on Sunday). There are regular trains to/from London Charing Cross (£26.30, 1¼ hours) via Battle and to/from Ashford via Rye. Every 15 minutes, trains head west around the Sussex coast from Hastings to Portsmouth (£20.70, 2½ hours) via Brighton (£12.40, 1¼ hours).

AROUND HASTINGS
Burwash

The quiet village of Burwash, 14 miles (22.5km) northwest of Hastings, has a lovely Norman church tower and some elegant redbrick homes along a tree-lined street. During the 18th and 19th centuries, the village was a smuggler's haven, and one of the tombs in the churchyard has a skull and crossbones.

About half a mile south of town along the A259 is **Bateman's** *(NT; ☎ 01435-882302; admission £5.20; open 11am-5pm Sat-Wed Mar-Sept)*, the home of Rudyard Kipling from 1902 until his death in 1936. Inside this beautiful Jacobean home built in 1634, everything is pretty much just as the writer would have left it, down to the blotting paper on the desk of his cluttered study. The furnishings reflect Kipling's love of the East, and there are plenty of oriental rugs and Indian artefacts.

A small path leads down to the River Dudwell, where the writer converted a watermill to generate electricity. These days, the mill grinds corn every Saturday at 2pm. Also on display is the last of Kipling's Rolls Royces.

BATTLE
☎ 01424 • pop 5732

It is ironic that the English should celebrate so proudly the victory of a French duke over a local king, but William of Normandy's defeat of King Harold in 1066 stands as one of the highlights of British history.

The lovely town grew up around the abbey that William, flush with the thrill of victory, ordered built to commemorate his success.

Orientation & Information

The train station is a short walk from High St, and is well signposted. There is a **TIC** *(☎ 773721, fax 773436; 88 High St; open 10am-4pm daily Oct-Apr, 10am-6pm daily May-Sept)*. The **post office**, **banks** and **ATMs** are also on High St.

Battlefield & Battle Abbey

Battle Abbey *(EH; ☎ 773792; adult £4.50; open 10am-6pm daily Apr-Oct, 10am-4pm daily Nov-Mar)* is a pretty interesting place, but more for its unique location. Built smack in the middle of the actual battlefield, your visit should be steeped in historical significance. The guided walk – courtesy of a free audio unit – gives blow-by-blow descriptions of the battle.

Construction of the abbey began in 1070. It was occupied by Benedictines until the Dissolution of the Monasteries in 1536. Only the foundations of the church can now be seen and the altar's position is marked by a plaque, but quite a few monastic buildings survive and the scene is very painterly.

Bodiam Castle

If the traditional castle of childhood imagination – four towers, crenellated walls, a drawbridge and a moat – has an archetype, then Bodiam *(NT; ☎ 01580-830436; adult £3.90; open 10am-5pm daily Feb-Oct, 10am-4pm Sat & Sun Nov-Jan)* is surely it.

After the French captured the Channel ports in 1372, Sir Edward Dalyngrigge built the castle in 1385 to guard the lower reaches of the River Rother from further French attack. In its day it was a top-notch military fortress. From the outside, the castle looks pretty much untouched, but once you step inside the solid walls it's a different story.

Following the Civil War, Parliamentarian forces deliberately ruined it and it fell into such disrepair that photographs from the

1890s show ivy-clad ruins and vegetables planted in the courtyard. In 1917 Lord Curzon, former Viceroy of India, bought it and initiated a substantial programme of renovation; though the exterior has been restored to its impressive origins, the interior is still little more than a collection of ruins. It's possible to climb to the top of the battlements for some excellent views of the surrounding countryside, and the small **museum** *(admission free)* has a collection of iron tools and pottery dating from the 15th to 18th century.

Bus No 326 from Hastings and bus No 19 from Battle both stop at the gate three times a day; twice at the weekend. Bus No 349 goes from Hastings to Bodiam five times a day, Monday to Saturday. The **Kent and East Sussex steam railway** *(☎ 01580 765155)* runs from Tenterden in Kent through 10½ miles (17km) of beautiful countryside to the village of Bodiam from where a bus takes you to the castle. It costs £8 and operates daily during July and August and at the weekend and school holidays the rest of the year.

Places to Stay & Eat
Clematis Cottage *(☎ 774261; 3 High St; singles/ doubles £40/50, with en suite £45/55)* is a wonderfully romantic spot opposite the abbey entrance.

Abbey View *(☎/fax 775513; Caldbec Hill, Mount St; rooms per person May-Oct £35, Nov-Apr £30)* is five minutes' walk from High St. It has clean, tidy rooms with lovely views over the surrounding countryside.

Pilgrim's Rest *(☎ 772314; 1 High St; meals around £5.50)* is a home-style restaurant opposite the abbey with hearty English meals.

Getting There & Away
National Express bus Nos 023 and 024 from London to Hastings pass through Battle twice daily (£9.25, 2¼ hours), and Eastbourne Buses No 22 service runs from Eastbourne to Battle on weekdays (three daily). From Battle you can reach Pevensey (45 minutes) and Bodiam (20 minutes) on the irregular No 19 service. Local Rider bus No 4/5 runs hourly to Hastings.

Trains run to and from London Charing Cross every half-hour (£15.90, 1½ hours), via Hastings (£2.30, 20 minutes).

EASTBOURNE
☎ 01323 • pop 81,395

Slightly eccentric Eastbourne has long been the favourite south coast resort for octogenarians, which makes the town less tacky and more genteel than other seaside spots. However, there is very little to do here other than pray for a sunny day, as most of the action takes place down the coast in Brighton.

The town centre is just north of the pier, while the few interesting old buildings and handful of antique shops that make up the Old Town lie about a mile northwest of the new town centre. To the west the stunning chalk cliffs steer the way to Beachy Head, a 3-mile (4.8km) walk away.

The **TIC** *(☎ 411400, fax 649574; **e** east bournetic@btclick.com; Cornfield Rd; open*

SOUTHEAST ENGLAND

The Last Invasion of England

The Battle of Hastings in 1066 was a fairly dramatic event. Harold's army arrived on the scene on October 14th and created a three-ring defence consisting of archers, then cavalry, with his massed infantry at the rear. William marched north from Hastings and took up a position about 400m south of Harold and his troops. He tried repeatedly to break the English cordon, but Harold's men held fast. William's knights then feigned retreat, drawing some of Harold's troops after them. It was a fatal mistake. Seeing the gap in the English wall, William ordered his remaining troops to charge through, and the battle was as good as won. Among the English casualties was King Harold who, according to events depicted in the Bayeux Tapestry, was hit in or near the eye by an arrow. While he tried to pull the arrow from his head he was struck down by Norman knights. At the news of his death the last of the English resistance collapsed.

In their wonderfully irreverent *1066 And All That*, published in 1930, WC Sellar and RJ Yeatman suggest that 'the Norman conquest was a Good Thing, as from this time onward England stopped being conquered and thus was able to become a top nation...' When you consider that England hasn't been successfully invaded since, it's hard to disagree.

9.30am-5.30pm Mon-Sat, 10am-1pm Sun, Apr-Sept) has a number of helpful leaflets and runs an accommodation booking service (£3).

Things to See & Do
Eastbourne's **pier** has the usual selection of arcades, trinket shops, bars, one terrible disco and lots of bird droppings. It's a nice place to watch the sun set over the water though.

The **Eastbourne Heritage Centre** *(☎ 411 189; 2 Carlisle Rd; adult/child £1/50p; open 2pm-5pm daily May-Sept & bank holidays)*, west of the centre, explores the development of the town from 1800 to the present day. There's a special exhibit devoted to the work of Donald McGill, the pioneer of the 'naughty postcard'!

The **Wish Tower Puppet Museum** *(☎ 417776; King Edward's Parade; adult/child £1.80/1.25; open 11am-5pm daily Easter-Sept, 11am-5pm Sat & Sun Oct)* has a collection of traditional puppets from all over the world, including Punch and Judy.

The **Museum of Shops** *(☎ 737143; 20 Cornfield Terrace; adult/child £3/2.50; open 10am-5.30pm daily)* is devoted to nostalgic, how-we-lived memorabilia – antiques, books, toys, you name it. It's perfect for Eastbourne's favourite clientele.

Places to Stay
Lindau Lodge *(☎ 640792; 71 Royal Parade; B&B per person £18-22)*, five minutes' walk west of the centre along the seafront, is the best choice of places around here. A three-course evening meal costs £10.

Devonshire Park Hotel *(☎ 728144, fax 419734; e info@devonshire-park-hotel.co.uk; Carlisle Rd; rooms per person £28-50)*, a large Victorian building with its own private garden about 200m from the Wish Tower, has wonderfully elegant and sophisticated rooms.

Alexandra Hotel *(☎ 720131, fax 417769; e alexandrahotel@mistral.co.uk; King Edward's Parade; rooms per person £25-32)* is directly opposite the Wish Tower. It's a stunning Victorian building with large, en-suite rooms.

The Grand Hotel *(☎ 412345, fax 412233; e reservations@grandeastbourne.com; rooms per person £82.50)* is Eastbourne's fanciest hotel, thanks to a recent refurbishment. The bedrooms are stunning and the hotel has its own swimming pool.

Places to Eat
Oartons Restaurant *(☎ 731053; 4 Bolton Rd; 2-/3-course set menu £14.95/16.95; closed Tues lunch)* is an upmarket French restaurant with an imaginative menu.

The Lamb *(☎ 720545; cnr High St & Ocklynge Rd)*, in the Old Town, is a half-timbered pub with traditional bar meals, such as a ploughman's lunch for £4.95, or more modern meals for around £8.

Getting There & Away
National Express runs two buses daily to Eastbourne from London Victoria (£9.50; 2¾ hours) and one daily to Brighton (£3.50, 50 minutes). The slower No 712 runs every 15 minutes (30 minutes on Sunday) to Brighton (£3.20; 1¼ hours). Bus No 711 runs hourly (every two hours on Sunday) from Dover to Eastbourne (£5.20; two hours, 40 minutes).

Trains from London Victoria leave every half-hour for Eastbourne (£17.50; 1½ hours), and there are half-hourly trains (£9 return; 20 minutes) between Eastbourne and Brighton.

AROUND EASTBOURNE
Pevensey Castle
The ruins of William the Conqueror's first stronghold, Pevensey Castle *(adult/child £3.20/1.50; open 10am-6pm Wed-Sun Apr-Oct, 11am-4pm Wed-Sun Nov-Mar)*, lie 5 miles (8km) east of Eastbourne, off the A259. They sit within a Roman defensive wall and on the site of a Roman fort which was built between AD 280 and 340.

The Mint House *(adult/child £1/50p)*, just across the road from the castle, dates from 1342 and is absolutely bursting with one of the biggest and weirdest collections of antiques and bits and pieces you may ever see. The atmosphere is decidedly nutty.

Regular train services between London and Hastings via Eastbourne stop at Westham, half a mile from Pevensey. Eastbourne Buses No 18 stops at Westham and Nos 7 and 19 stop at Pevensey.

Beachy Head
The chalk cliffs at Beachy Head are at the southern end of the South Downs. The sheer, 175m-high coastal cliffs are awe-inspiring enough in themselves, but when they're chalk white and backed by emerald green turf they're breathtaking. There are also spectacular views of the South Downs.

There's a **countryside centre** (☎ 01323-737273; open 10am-5.30pm daily late Mar–Sept) with interactive displays on the area and a restaurant. If you're coming by car, Beachy Head is off the B2103, from the A259 between Eastbourne and Newhaven. There is a regular bus (No 3) from Eastbourne during summer.

The Long Man of Wilmington

If you're travelling along the A27 between Eastbourne and Lewes, be sure to look southwards out the window, just east of the town of Wilmington, to see this amazing sight. No-one really knows how this 70m-high man got here. The original markings in the grass have been replaced by white concrete blocks to preserve the image.

There is a turn-off for the Long Man at the town of Wilmington from where you can get a better view. Wilmington is 7 miles (11.3km) west of Eastbourne. If you're walking this section of the South Downs you will pass him and get a close-up view.

Charleston Farmhouse

Five miles (8km) west of Eastbourne, Charleston Farmhouse (☎ 01323-811265; off A27; adult/child £6/4.50; open 2pm-6pm Wed-Sun Apr-Oct & Bank Holidays) was the

SOUTHEAST ENGLAND

The Bloomsbury Group

They may have been little more than a coterie of aesthetically-minded, upper-middle-class snobs, but the Bloomsbury Group – so-called because they met regularly in the Bloomsbury district of London – happened to include some of the most brilliant and influential minds of pre-war English society.

At their heart were Thoby, Adrian, Vanessa and Virginia Stephen, who lived at 46 Gordon Square in London. In 1907 Thoby began bringing home a select few of his Cambridge buddies (most of them members of the semisecret Apostles Society) for Thursday night 'discussions', while sister Vanessa began organising a Friday Club for painters. Their themes were aesthetics and the search for good, beauty and truth; they were heavily influenced by GE Moore's *Principia Ethica* (1903) and later by AN Whitehead's and Bertrand Russell's *Principia Mathematica* (1910–13).

Edwardian England was awash with similar clubs and groups, but the Bloomsbury crowd shocked polite London society with their almost total disregard for social conventions. They were flagrantly Dionysian in their pursuits, particularly of the sexual kind: not only were most of them bisexual, but the thought of two unmarried and outspoken sisters (Vanessa and Virginia) leading the charge was just a little too much to bear for their more conservative peers.

Yet they would have been dismissed as a bunch of partner-swappers with too much free time on their hands were it not for their undoubted brilliance and prodigious creative output. Biographer Lytton Strachey (1880–1932) drew nationwide attention to the set in 1918 when he published *Eminent Victorians*, an irreverent biography written in an iconoclastic style that 'excludes everything that is redundant and nothing that is significant'. Meanwhile, Vanessa and her husband, art critic Clive Bell, were deeply involved in Roger Fry's Omega Workshop, which sought to emulate William Morris' Arts & Crafts Movement by encouraging artists to decorate everyday functional objects like furniture, drapes and china. Other members included John Maynard Keynes, who later became the most important economic theorist of his day, while Aldous Huxley and Bertrand Russell were loosely associated with the group.

Yet it is Vanessa's younger sister Virginia who is best remembered for her Bloomsbury links. Insecure yet deeply intelligent and witty, she married Leonard Woolf in 1913 and in 1917 they set up Hogarth Press in their basement, publishing Sigmund Freud in English (the first to do so), TS Eliot's *The Wasteland* (1922) and works by Maxim Gorky and Katherine Mansfield. They also published Virginia's own work – with cover art exclusively by sister Vanessa.

The Bloomsbury Group's unabashed espousal of a loose moral code, however, took its toll. Their sexual and marital liberalism provoked deep jealousies and hurts, and by the mid-1930s the group had all but disbanded. Many of them sought refuge in the Sussex countryside where they pursued still eccentric but more mainstream lives. For Virginia, however, this was not to be: plagued by depression for most of her life, these bouts got progressively worse and on 28 March 1941 she committed suicide by drowning in the River Ouse.

country retreat of the Bloomsbury Group (see the boxed text) and a superb example of the rich intellectual and aesthetic life that they came to represent.

In 1916 Virginia Woolf's sister, painter Vanessa Bell, moved here with her lover Duncan Grant and they set about painting and decorating the place in a style that owed much to the influence of Italian fresco painting and the Post-Impressionists. Every wall, door and piece of furniture was decorated thus, and in 1939 Vanessa's husband Clive brought his collection of exquisite furniture here, and the walls featured paintings by Picasso, Derain, Delacroix and others.

This intellectual and artistic hive survived well into the 1960s by which time the group had more or less dissolved itself or simply blended into the London scene. Thankfully, the house has survived almost intact, and is well worth a stop. There's also a handsome garden and interesting outbuildings, including a medieval dovecote.

Visits are by guided tour only except on Sunday. The nearest train station is at Berwick, on the Brighton to Eastbourne line, a 2-mile (3km) walk from the farmhouse.

LEWES
☎ 01273 • pop 16,000

This old town occupying a spur above the River Ouse may seem a little staid and old-fashioned, but it is fast emerging as one of the most desirable places to live on the south coast, as well as one of the most expensive.

Surrounding William de Warenne's ruined castle, built shortly after the Norman invasion of 1066, Lewes today is mostly Georgian in appearance, but the medieval street plan – basically a bunch of narrow, winding streets called *twittens* off the main High St – gives it a really intimate feel.

The town's past is pretty turbulent, culminating in the burning of 17 Protestants in 1556 at the height of Mary Tudor's Catholic revival. Lewes has not forgotten, and every 5 November tens of thousands of people gather for the famous fireworks display, and an effigy of the Pope is burnt in memory of the Protestant martyrs. Locals dress in medieval garb and bonfires are lit throughout the area. It all sounds a little ominous, but there's absolutely no sectarian fervour and in recent years it's become one of the most enjoyable nights on the southeastern calendar.

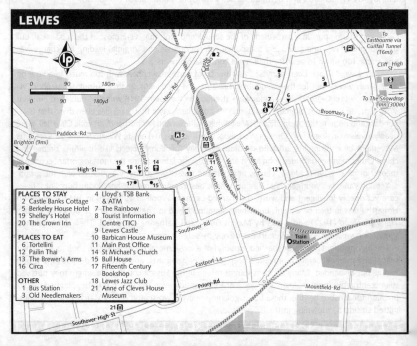

LEWES

PLACES TO STAY
2 Castle Banks Cottage
5 Berkeley House Hotel
19 Shelley's Hotel
20 The Crown Inn

PLACES TO EAT
6 Tortellini
12 Pailin Thai
13 The Brewer's Arms
16 Circa

OTHER
1 Bus Station
3 Old Needlemakers
4 Lloyd's TSB Bank & ATM
7 The Rainbow
8 Tourist Information Centre (TIC)
9 Lewes Castle
10 Barbican House Museum
11 Main Post Office
14 St Michael's Church
15 Bull House
17 Fifteenth Century Bookshop
18 Lewes Jazz Club
21 Anne of Cleves House Museum

Orientation & Information

The town occupies a particularly steep ridge between the river and the castle ruins, with High St climbing the spine and the *twittens* running off it.

The **TIC** (☎ 483448, fax 484003; 187 High St; open 9am-5pm Mon-Fri, 10am-5pm Sat year round; 10am-2pm Sun Apr-Sept) has a free *Town Guide*, which includes a descriptive walking tour.

The **main post office** (High St) is near the corner of Watergate Lane, and there's a **Lloyds TSB ATM** (Cliff High St) at the eastern end of the centre. There's an interesting collection of craft shops in the **Old Needlemakers** (West St), while the simply fabulous **Fifteenth Century Bookshop** (☎ 474160; 99 High St) is the place to go for second-hand books and new editions. There are public toilets on Market Lane.

Lewes Castle & Museum

Although little more than a set of impressive ruins, William de Warenne's castle (☎ 486 290; adult/child £4.20/2.80; open 10am-5.30pm Mon-Sat, 11am-5.30pm Sun Apr-Sept, to dusk Oct-Mar) still affords some excellent views over the town and water meadows of the surrounding countryside. The adjacent **Barbican House Museum** has a worthwhile collection of prehistoric, Roman, Saxon and medieval objects, as well as an excellent 20-minute audiovisual introduction to the town and its history. During the summer months the castle grounds host a variety of concerts; check with the TIC for details.

Anne of Cleves House Museum

When Henry VIII divorced Anne of Cleves in 1541 (because she hadn't borne him a male heir), the settlement included this handsome timber-framed house (☎ 474610; 52 Southover High St; adult/child £2.80/1.40; open 10am-5pm Mon-Sat, noon-5pm Sun Mar-Oct, 10am-5pm Tues-Sat Nov-Feb), although the one-time queen never actually moved in.

Today the house is an excellent folk museum, with a fascinating collection of all kinds of items, from toys to a witch's effigy complete with pins. Also here is a marble tabletop that supposedly had magical qualities – it allegedly prevented Thomas Becket's murderers from eating off it.

St Michael's Church

This church (High St), just west of the castle, is a striking building due to its mishmash of architectural styles. The flint tower is from the 12th century and the arcade was built in the 14th century. The facade is Georgian and built of knapped flint and the stained glass is Victorian.

Places to Stay

Not many tourists land in Lewes, so there isn't a big choice of accommodation.

Castle Banks Cottage (☎/fax 476291; 4 Castle Banks; rooms per person from £22.50) is a small, period cottage with comfortable rooms and a lovely, easy-going atmosphere.

Berkeley House Hotel (☎ 476057, fax 479575; 2 Albion St; singles/doubles from £42.50/55) is bright and airy, with five tastefully appointed rooms.

The Crown Inn (☎ 480670, fax 480679; 191 High St; singles/doubles with en suite £50/65) is a historic 17th-century inn with comfortable, elegant rooms. We highly recommend it.

Shelley's Hotel (☎ 472361, fax 483152; High St; singles/doubles from £105/145) was originally built in the 1520s, but was converted to a manor house in the 1590s. It is the poshest place in town, full of antiques and an old-world atmosphere.

Places to Eat

The Brewer's Arms (☎ 479475; 91 High St; pub grub around £5.50) is the place to go for a traditional pub meal, which you should wash down with a pint of the local brew, Harvey's.

Tortellini (☎ 487766; 197 High St; mains from £6.50) is a cut above your average Italian restaurant, with a range of traditional dishes that are extremely well-prepared.

Pailin Thai (☎ 473906; 20 Station St; mains around £7) is the place to go if you fancy some excellent Thai cuisine.

Circa (☎ 471777; 145 High St; mains from £9) is our top spot in town. The menu is wonderfully imaginative, featuring a range of continental dishes and some Asian fusion delights that will make any meal a memorable one.

Entertainment

Lewes Jazz Club (☎ 473568; 139 High St) is a great spot for good jazz. The music here is way above your average; the players are

The Sussex Fitzcarraldo

In 1934 John Christie, a science teacher at Eton, inherited a large Tudor mansion outside Lewes. But he and his opera-singer wife had bigger ambitions, which involved building a 1200-seat opera house...in the middle of nowhere. Their magnificent folly, reminiscent of Werner Herzog's 1982 film *Fitzcarraldo*, which tells the incredible story of a man who defies logic and all the odds to build an opera house in the middle of the Amazon, was the original Glyndebourne Theatre. Sixty years to the day (May 28th) after the first premiere *(The Marriage of Figaro)*, a new, award-winning theatre was inaugurated with the same opera.

Glyndebourne (☎ 01273-812321; W *www.glyndebourne.com*) is now one of England's best places to enjoy the lyric arts, with a season that runs from late May to the end of August. Tickets can be very difficult to obtain and range in price from £27 to £140. Standing-only tickets cost £12, but you need to be on the mailing list to buy them. And then there's the dress code: strictly black tie and evening dress. For all information, call the box office on ☎ 01273-813813. In October the company goes on a nationwide tour.

Glyndebourne is 4 miles (6.5km) east of Lewes off the B2192. Coaches can be arranged for pick up at Lewes station (☎ 01273-815000). See the earlier Lewes section for train services from London. By car, the trip from the capital takes about 2½ hours.

usually terrific and the atmosphere is hard to beat. It runs every Thursday and tickets cost £6-7.

The Snowdrop Inn *(South St)* is a hippy haven decorated in vibrant purple. As well as some interesting organic beers, they serve a good selection of ales in a wonderfully relaxed atmosphere.

The Rainbow *(179 High St)* is a trendy spot with good DJs imported from nearby Brighton. The roof terrace has great views of the town.

Getting There & Away

Lewes is 50 miles (80km) south of London, 9 miles (14km) northeast of Brighton and 16 miles (26km) northwest of Eastbourne.

Bus The bus station is north of the town centre off Eastgate St. Stagecoach South bus No 28 runs from Brighton to Lewes (£3, 35 minutes, hourly). The No 729 runs hourly between Brighton and Royal Tunbridge Wells via Lewes.

Train Lewes is well served by rail, being on the main line between London Victoria and Eastbourne and on the coastal link between Eastbourne and Brighton. Trains leave every 15 minutes from Brighton (£3, 15 minutes), three times an hour from Eastbourne (£5, 20 minutes) and every half-hour from London Victoria (£15.70, 55 minutes).

BRIGHTON & HOVE

☎ 01273 • pop 188,000

Of all of England's seaside resorts, Brighton is the artist among the artisans. Not only is it the country's most popular coastal resort, but one of its best cities, full stop. The artist formerly known as Brighton Town, mind you, is now the City of Brighton & Hove, although it's a distinction that is lost on most Brightonians, who only hear its new name on train announcements.

Brighton's appeal is unique, at least in England. Ever since the Prince Regent came to party at the beginning of the 19th century, the town has been known for its wonderful eccentricity and its never-ending pursuit of what makes life fun. Whatever you're into, there's a spot for you here. Whether you're an urban jetsetter who likes the fast lane but can't quite afford those London prices, or an organic-farm-supporting crusty with painterly ambitions, Brighton will satisfy your needs. The locals take it all in stride, and we strongly suspect that the local shopkeeper is quietly proud of his strange and exotic city as he proffers change to the transvestite in six-inch heels and blue eye shadow.

And indeed there is so much of which to be proud. Beside the Royal Pavilion, a showpiece museum that ranks among the best in England, Brighton has the best cafés and restaurants south of the M25; its pubs and bars are plentiful and full of character;

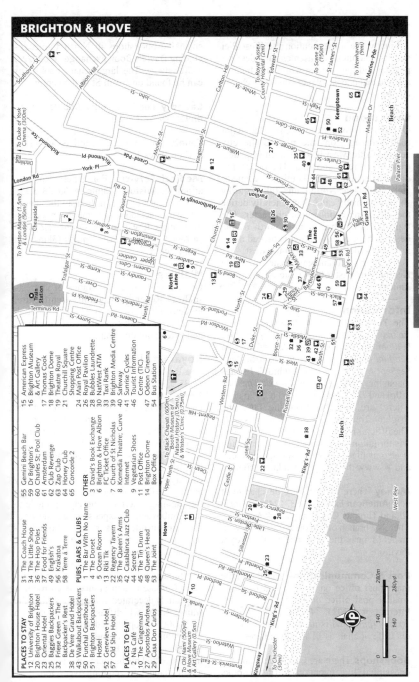

BRIGHTON & HOVE

SOUTHEAST ENGLAND

PLACES TO STAY
12 University of Brighton
20 Brighton House Hotel
23 Oriental Hotel
25 Baggies Backpackers
32 Friese Green – The Backpacker's Rest
38 De Vere Grand Hotel
43 Walkabout Backpackers
50 Funchal Guesthouse
51 Brighton Backpackers Hostel
52 Genevieve Hotel
57 Old Ship Hotel

PLACES TO EAT
2 Nia Café
10 The Gingerman
27 Apostolos Andreas
29 Casa Don Carlos
31 The Coach House
34 The Little Shop
36 The Hop Poles
37 Food for Friends
49 English's
56 Krakatoa
58 Terre à Terre

PUBS, BARS & CLUBS
1 The Bar With No Name
4 The Dorset
5 Ocean Rooms
13 Riki Tik
22 Regency Tavern
35 The Queen's Arms
42 Casablanca Jazz Club
44 Secrets
45 The Tin Drum
48 Queen's Head
53 The Joint
55 Gemini Beach Bar
59 Dr Brighton's
60 Charles St; Pool Club
61 Amsterdam
62 Club Revenge
63 Zap Club
64 Honey Club
65 Concorde 2

OTHER
3 David's Book Exchange
6 Brighton & Hove Albion FC Ticket Office
7 Church of St Nicholas
8 Komedia Theatre; Curve Internet
9 Vegetarian Shoes
11 Post Office
14 Brighton Dome Box Office
15 American Express
16 Brighton Museum & Art Gallery
17 Thomas Cook
18 Brighton Dome
19 Theatre Royal
21 Churchill Square Shopping Centre
24 Main Post Office
26 Royal Pavilion
28 Bubbles Laundrette
30 NatWest ATM
33 Taxi Rank
39 Brighton Media Centre
40 Safeway
41 Sunrise Cycles
46 Tourist Information Centre (TIC)
47 Odeon Cinema
54 Bus Station

and the nightlife is – relative to its size – easily a match for London or Manchester.

Finally, we must mention the West Pier and its ubiquitous amusement arcades: it's popular and fun (at least with kids), but rest assured that one tacky pier does not a cheesy city make.

Orientation

Old Steine (pronounced steen) is the major road running from the pier to the city centre. To the west is the warren of pedestrian-only streets known as The Lanes, full of good restaurants and boutiques. Immediately north is the North Laine, full of quirky shops and lovely cafés that generally define the city's more bohemian character. The train station is half a mile north of the beach. The tiny bus station is tucked away in Poole Valley. Hove lies to the west.

Brighton's vibrant gay scene thrives in Kemptown, east of Old Steine along St James' St.

Information

The **TIC** (☎ 292599; **e** tourism@brighton .co.uk; 10 Bartholomew Square; open 9am-5.30pm Mon-Fri, 10am-5pm Sat, 10am-4pm Sun June-Aug, 9am-5pm Mon-Fri, 10am-5pm Sat Sept-May). Copies of Brighton's listings magazines, The Brighton Latest, The List (50p) and The Source (free at TIC, 99p elsewhere) are available from the TIC. The Brighton Town Centre Map-Guide costs £1. The official Brighton website is at **w** www .visitbrighton.co.uk, but good information is also available at **w** www.brighton.co.uk and **w** www.thisisbrightonandhove.co.uk.

Money There are bureaux de change at both **American Express** (☎ 321242; 82 North St) and **Thomas Cook** (☎ 328154; North St). There's a branch of **NatWest** (Castle St) with an ATM near the entrance to the Royal Pavilion.

Post & Communications You'll find the **main post office** on Ship St and there's a smaller **post office** on Western Rd. **Curve Internet** (☎ 603031; 44-47 Gardner St; open 10am-11pm daily) is upstairs in the Komedia Cafe; it charges £1 for 20 minutes.

Bookshops There are CDs, a café and the occasional live event at **Borders Books**

(☎ 731122; Churchill Square Shopping Centre). There are a number of second-hand and specialist bookshops in North Laine, including **David's Book Exchange** (☎ 690223; 3 Sydney St). The larger chain bookshops can be found on North St in the centre.

Laundry For laundry try **Bubbles Laundrette** (75 Preston St).

Toilets You'll find public toilets behind the TIC on Black Lion St.

Medical Services For general consultations try **Wiston's Clinic** (☎ 506263; 138 Dyke Rd), just under a mile from the centre. There's an accident and emergency department at the **Royal Sussex County Hospital** (☎ 696955; Eastern Rd), 2 miles (3km) east of the centre.

Walking Tours

Guided tours covering a range of interests such as Regency Brighton, architecture, gardens and so on, can be booked through the TIC. The walks usually cost around £4 and take about one hour.

Royal Pavilion

The Royal Pavilion (☎ 290900; adult/child £5.35/3.30; open 10am-6pm daily June-Sept, 10am-5pm daily Oct-May) is an absolute must and a highlight of any trip to southern England. This extraordinarily lavish fantasy is one of the most sumptuously hedonistic buildings you'll see anywhere in England and is a fitting symbol of Brighton's 'un-English' decadence. Unlike so many of the country's grand but slightly dreary stately homes, the Pavilion does not disappoint, and the stunning exterior is merely a prelude to the flamboyant, no-expense-spared decor of the rooms inside. This is one hell of a holiday cottage (see the boxed text 'The Prince, the Palace & the Piss-Up').

While the exterior is a mix of Moorish and Indian styles, the interior is predominantly Chinese in appearance. Each room is exquisitely decorated, none more so than the **Music Room**, which has a ceiling made up of 26,000 scallop-shaped shells and is lit by nine lotus-shaped chandeliers. Also worth lingering in is the **Banqueting Hall**, where the prince and his hangers-on dined beneath a 30ft chandelier weighing over a ton.

The Prince, the Palace & the Piss-Up

The young Prince George (1762–1830), eldest son of George III, was not your typical wayward kid. By the age of 17 he was drinking with abandon and enjoying the pleasures of women. But he was the king's heir, and daddy was none too impressed. The elder George's displeasure turned to contempt when his son began hanging out with his dissolute uncle the Duke of Cumberland, who was enjoying himself royally by the sea in Brighton.

George loved the town so much that in 1787 he commissioned Henry Holland (1745–1806) to design a neoclassical villa where he could party to his heart's content. The elegant result, known as the Marine Pavilion, was George's personal pleasure palace. In the years he waited to accede to the throne (when his father was declared officially insane in 1810 he was sworn in as Prince Regent), George spent the bulk of his time organising extravagant piss-ups for himself, his mistresses and his aristocratic mates, which included the day's most notorious dandy and arbiter of fashion, Beau Brummell.

Ever conscious of what was trendy and what was not, George decided in 1815 to convert the Marine Pavilion so as to reflect the current fascination with all things Eastern. He engaged the services of John Nash (1752–1835), who laboured for eight years to create a Mogul Indian-style palace, complete with the most lavish Chinese interior imaginable.

George finally had a palace suited to his outlandish tastes, and to boot he was now the king. He continued to throw parties, but the boundless energy of his youth was fast disappearing, and he last visited Brighton in 1827. Three years later, he died of respiratory problems.

His brother and successor, William IV (1765–1837), also used the pavilion as a royal residence, as did William's niece Victoria (1819–1901) when she became queen in 1837. But the conservative queen didn't quite take to the place in the manner of her uncles and in 1850 she sold it to the town, but not before stripping it of every piece of furniture – 143 wagons were needed to transport the contents. Thankfully, many of the original items were later returned by the queen and successive monarchs, and today the house has been almost fully restored to its former elegance.

A free visitors' guide is available which takes you through the place, room by room, but we strongly recommend that you take one of the guided tours (£1.25), which take place at 11.30am and 2.30pm daily.

Brighton Museum & Art Gallery

The Brighton Museum & Art Gallery (☎ 290 900; Church St; admission free; open 10am-7pm Tues, 10am-5pm Wed-Sat, 2pm-5pm Sun) reopened in May 2002 after undergoing a £10-million redevelopment. Aside from its good collection of 20th-century art and design (including a Salvador Dali sofa in the shape of Mae West's lips), there's a fascinating exhibit on world art, including a genuine Hindu shrine created in collaboration with the local Gujerati community. Also worth checking out is the Images of Brighton exhibit, featuring a collection of interesting and revealing oral histories of the city.

Palace Pier

With the Royal Pavilion, this pier (admission free; open daily) is Brighton's most distinctive landmark and the epitome of seaside tackiness. It's got the usual selection of fairground rides (including the Helter Skelter made famous by the Beatles' song), dingy amusement arcades and food stalls, where you can buy a stick of the famous Brighton Rock. It's cheesy, but because it's the only part of Brighton to bear any resemblance to a typical British seaside resort, it's terrific fun.

On the far side of the beach is the much more beautiful **West Pier**, which sadly has been left to deteriorate for so long that part of it collapsed into the sea late in 2002; at the time of writing there were promises of a £30-million renovation scheme to restore it to its former Victorian splendour.

Preston Manor

Filled to the brim with paintings, ornaments and antiques, Preston Manor (☎ 290900; London Rd; adult/child £3.50/2.25; open 10am-5pm Tues-Sat, 2pm-5pm Sun, 1pm-5pm Mon) is a typical Edwardian upper-class home, 2½ miles (4km) north of the centre. It was originally built around 1600 but was rebuilt in 1738, which is why the exterior is so understated. The guided tour takes in about 20 rooms, but it is the section 'below stairs', comprising of the kitchen and servants' quarters, that is particularly interesting. You can get there on bus No 5 or 5A from the centre or take a local train to Preston Park station, only 200m from the house.

Booth Museum of Natural History
This museum (☎ 292777; 194 Dyke Rd; admission free; open 10am-5pm Mon-Wed, Fri & Sat, 2pm-5pm Sun) is a Victorian 'dead zoo' with more than half a million specimens. The bird room is particularly creepy, especially if you've seen the Hitchcock movie. The museum is about half a mile north of the train station.

Hove Museum & Art Gallery
You may be surprised to know that Hove is the birthplace of British cinema, with the first short film shot in 1898. You can see it, plus plenty of other early efforts, at this stunning Victorian villa (☎ 290200; 19 New Church Rd) built in the 1870s. You can also check out the wonderful children's room, which lights up with fairy lights when you enter. The exhibits include old zoetropes, a magic lantern and a small cupboard with a periscope inside. Unfortunately, the museum was closed for renovation at the time of writing but should have reopened by the time you read this.

Organised Tours
Guide Friday (☎ 746205) open-top buses stop on either side of the Palace Pier and take you around the main sights of Brighton. You can hop on and off as much as you like. Tickets are available from the driver and cost £6.70/2.70 per adult/child.

Special Events
The three-week-long Brighton Festival (☎ 292961; w www.brighton-festival.org.uk) is the largest arts festival in Britain after Edinburgh. Held in May, it features a packed and varied programme of theatre, dance and music that draws performers from all over the world. The free programme is available months in advance from the TIC; there's bound to be something to attract you. As you might expect, much of the city turns out in support, and there are plenty of sideshows running alongside the main events.

Places to Stay
There's plenty of choice for accommodation in Brighton to suit all budgets. You should book ahead for weekends in summer and during the Brighton Festival in May.

Hostels Brighton's independent hostels are a genuinely relaxed bunch, although some might say a little too much so. What they lack in tidiness, however, they make up for in atmosphere.

Baggies Backpackers (☎ 733740; 33 Oriental Place; beds/doubles £11/30) is the best hostel in town. Close to the seafront, it has good facilities but what wins our vote is its general cleanliness and easygoing atmosphere. There's a £5 room-key deposit.

Brighton Backpackers Hostel (☎ 777717, fax 887778; e stay@brightonbackpackers .com; 75-76 Middle St; beds per night/week £11/65, in seafront annexe £17 per night only) is a friendly, albeit shabby, place that does its best to cultivate a lackadaisical atmosphere. The colourful murals were painted by travellers.

Friese Green – The Backpacker's Rest (☎ 747551; 20 Middle St; dorm beds per night/week £12/60) is another untidy place, but friendly and fun all the same.

Walkabout Backpackers (☎ 770232; 79-81 West St; beds/doubles £12/14) should be your last resort if all others are booked up. The dorms are ordinary and bland, and the atmosphere is not nearly as pleasant as the others.

University of Brighton (☎ 643167, fax 642610; Grand Parade; flats per person per week from £70; open July-Sept) has flats for two to eight people available in various locations.

B&Bs & Hotels The biggest cluster of cheap B&Bs is east of Palace Pier. Cross the Old Steine roundabout and walk up St James St.

Funchal Guesthouse (☎/fax 603975; 17 Madeira Place; rooms per person £18-30) has cosy, clean rooms that are serviced daily. In the summer months, the rates go up to £30 per night.

Genevieve Hotel (☎ 681653; e genevieve hotel@aol.com; 18 Madeira Place; rooms per person £25-45), next door to Funchal, has recently been refurbished and has clean, comfortable rooms. The rate includes a continental breakfast.

Oriental Hotel (☎ 205050, fax 821096; e info@orientalhotel.co.uk; 9 Oriental Place; doubles Mon-Fri £55, Sat & Sun £90) is a real breath of fresh air among B&Bs. Decorated with bright colours, home-made furniture and cool decor, it's very funky.

Old Ship Hotel (☎ 329001, fax 820718; e oldship@paramount-hotels.co.uk; Kings Rd; singles/doubles from £70/80) is the ultimate doyen of Brighton's hotels, just refurbished in an ultra-cool, modern style.

Brighton House Hotel (☎ 323282; e enquiries@brightonhousehotel.co.uk; 52 Regency Square; singles £35-85, doubles £50-105) is a luxurious Regency hotel with immaculate rooms.

De Vere Grand Hotel (☎ 224300, fax 224321; e reservations@grandbrighton.co.uk; King's Rd; rooms from £100) made headlines in 1983 when the IRA tried to kill Margaret Thatcher and her cabinet here by exploding a huge bomb. The hotel has been restored to its former splendour and remains the top spot in town.

Places to Eat
Brighton has the best dining options on the south coast. Wander around The Lanes and North Laine or walk along Preston St, which runs back from the seafront near West Pier, and you'll uncover a wide selection of cafés, diners and restaurants of every hue and taste.

The Little Shop (☎ 325594; 48a Market St, The Lanes) has apparently won awards for its sandwiches. They *are* delicious, and very chunky, and cost from £2.25.

Apostolos Andreas (☎ 687935; George St; mains around £3) is a Greek coffee house with English-style food. It's extremely popular with students because it's such good value.

Casa Don Carlos (☎ 327177, 303274; 5 Union St, The Lanes; mains around £5) is a popular (hence crowded) Spanish tapas house and restaurant.

Food For Friends (☎ 202310; 17a Prince Albert St; mains around £4.50) is not quite as good or as well known as Terre á Terre (see later), but it serves solid vegetarian cuisine for about half the price.

The Hop Poles (☎ /10444; 13 Middle St; mains from £5.50) is the place to go for weekend brunch, although you'll probably have to wait for a table. It's a terrific spot serving large portions of chicken, meat and vegetarian dishes.

Krakatoa (☎ 719009; 7 Poole Valley; mains around £8) is a wonderful Asian fusion restaurant where you sit on cushions and select dishes from a menu of Indonesian, Thai and Japanese specialities.

English's (☎ 327980; 29-31 East Street; mains from £10) is a superb seafood restaurant in a group of what were once fishermen's cottages. The decor is Edwardian red velvet and the menu is mouthwateringly good.

Terre á Terre (☎ 729051; 71 East St; starters from £5, mains from £10) was voted the best vegetarian restaurant in Britain by the Vegetarian Society, and we can't disagree: even die-hard meat fiends will find the imaginative and delicious cuisine here hard to resist.

Nia Café (☎ 671371; 87-88 Trafalgar St; mains around £6) is our choice for best café in town. Hang out over a mug of cappuccino, or try one of the delicious ciabatta sandwiches; this is the place to linger a while.

The Coach House (☎ 719000; 59a Middle St; mains around £7), a relaxed café-bar, has a student atmosphere and live-music Fridays.

The Gingerman (☎ 326688; 21a Norfolk Square, Hove; mains around £12) is Brighton's best French restaurant, where many classic dishes are given a thoroughly creative once-over.

Oki Nami (☎ 773777; 208 New Church Rd, Hove; mains around £12) is one of the city's best Japanese restaurants, a small intimate spot that really knows how to serve raw fish.

The Black Chapati (☎ 699011; 12 Circus Parade, New England Rd; mains from £14) offers a great mix of traditional Indian and Asian fusion dishes. In a country that has made Indian cuisine its very own, you'll be hard pushed to find a better version of it than this excellent restaurant.

The De Vere Grand (☎ 224300; King's Rd; afternoon tea £12.50) is *the* place to go for that most English of afternoon activities. Ask for a table in the conservatory and discover the delights of cucumber sandwiches washed town with pots of tea. Afternoon tea is served from 3pm to 6pm daily.

There's a **Safeway supermarket** (St James' St) in Brighton.

Entertainment
Brighton has the best choice of entertainment on the south coast, with a great selection of bars and pubs, as well as a choice of clubs you won't find anywhere else outside

of London or Manchester. As with anywhere with a vibrant nightlife, pubs and clubs are constantly changing, so keep an eye out for *The Brighton Latest*, *The List* or *The Source* for what's hot and what's not.

Below is a small but choice selection of spots to check out.

Pubs & Bars The epitome of a Brighton bar, **The Bar With No Name** (☎ 601419; 58 Southover St) is a traditional pub that's popular with local artists, clubbers and those simply looking for a good pint and a chat.

The Tin Drum (☎ 777575; 43 St James' St) has an Eastern European theme – plenty of flavoured vodkas at £2.30 a shot. It gets pretty full on weekend nights, but it's a nice and relaxing spot for Sunday brunch.

Riki Tik (☎ 683844; 18a Bond St) is almost painfully cool; a favourite pre-club spot for young clubbers who kick off their night over cocktails and loud music.

Gemini Beach Bar (☎ 327888; 127 King's Rd Arches) is the perfect beach bar. On a nice summer's day, there's nowhere better to sit and watch the weird and wonderful parade down the promenade.

The Dorset (☎ 605423; 28 North Rd), in the heart of North Laine, is a laid-back spot that has DJs on weekend nights.

Clubs If Britain's top DJs aren't spending their summers playing to the crowds in Ibiza or Aya Napia, you'll most likely find them in Brighton. All clubs open until at least 2am, some as late as 5am. Door charges range from £4 to £12.

Honey Club (☎ 07000-446639; 214 Kings Rd Arches; admission Mon-Thur £4, Sat £12) plays 1970s and 80s disco classics on Monday and Thursday. It also has guest DJs on Saturday.

Concorde 2 (☎ 320724; Marine Parade, Kemptown; admission £10-11) is jam-packed every second Friday from June to September for Fatboy Slim's Big Beat Boutique. Other nights, though, are just as popular, with a choice of club sounds, from R'n'B to house.

The Joint (☎ 321692; 37 East St; admission Mon-Fri £3, Sat & Sun £4-5; open 10pm-2am Thur-Sat year round, plus additional nights June-Sept) is one of the coolest dives in town, with something for everyone, from EZ-listening to Nu Jazz beats. The dress-up theme nights are particularly good.

Ocean Rooms (☎ 699069; 1 Morley St; admission £1-10) is sumptuously decorated in red: red sofas, red drapes and red cushioned walls. It's a firm favourite with the late 20s–early 30s crowd, who come here at weekends for the excellent soul, funk and disco.

Zap Club (☎ 202407; King's Rd Arches; admission £3-9) is a slightly cheesy club that hosts glam 80s nights (Club Tropicana) and party house (Pussycat). It's a well-worked formula with phenomenal appeal, judging from the queues outside at weekends.

Casablanca Jazz Club (3 Middle St; admission £6; open 9am-2am Tues-Sat) hosts punters mainly aged 25 to 35. There's no live music but a DJ plays a range of stuff.

Theatre & Cinema There are a number of theatres in Brighton. Next to the Royal Pavilion, the Art Deco **Brighton Dome** (☎ 709709; e tickets@brighton-dome.org.uk; 29 New Rd), once the stables and exercise yard of King George IV, is the largest theatre complex in Brighton. The box office is on New Rd.

Other major theatres are **Theatre Royal** (☎ 328488; New Rd), which hosts plays, musicals and operas, and **Komedia Theatre** (☎ 647101; Gardner St, North Laine), which is home to comedy and cabaret as well as fringe theatre.

The multiscreen **Odeon Cinema** (☎ 207 977; cnr King's Rd & West St) shows mainstream films. The **Duke of York** (☎ 602 503; Preston Circus), about a mile north of North Rd, generally runs a programme of art-house films and old classics.

Spectator Sports
The **Seagulls** (Brighton & Hove Albion FC; ☎ 778855; Withdean Stadium, Tongdean Lane), although not in top flight at the time of writing, are probably your best chance of seeing good, competitive football in the area. In 2002 Norman Cook (aka Fatboy Slim) bought up 11% of the club, which benefits from the passionate support of its fans. It's relatively easy to obtain tickets: contact the **ticket office** (☎ 776992; 5 Queen's Rd). The season runs from mid-August to late May.

Shopping
The Lanes is Brighton's most popular shopping district, a confusing maze of small streets and tiny alleyways that are chock-a-block with shops and boutiques selling

Gay & Lesbian Brighton

Perhaps it's Brighton's long-time association with the theatre, but for over 100 years the city has been a gay haven. Gay icons Noel Coward and Ivor Novello were regular visitors, but in those days the scene was furtive and separate. From the 1960s onward, the scene really began to open up, especially in the Kemptown area and around Old Steine. Today, with over 25,000 gay men and 10–15,000 lesbians living in the city, it is the most vibrant queer community in the country outside London.

Kemptown (aka Camptown), on and off St James' St, is where it's all at. In recent years the old Brunswick Town area of Hove has emerged as a quieter alternative to the traditionally cruisy (and sometimes seedy) Kemptown, but the community here has responded by branching out from the usual pubs that served as nightly pick-up joints. Now you will find a rank of gay-owned businesses, from cafés and hotels to bookshops as well as the more obvious bars, clubs and saunas.

For up-to-date information on what's going on in Gay Brighton, check out the websites at **W** www.gay.brighton.co.uk or **W** www.tourism.brighton.co.uk.

For dining...
St James' St has plenty of cafés and restaurants to suit your every taste.

Scene 22 *(129 St James' St; mains around £5)* is not just a good café, but it's where you should go to get the latest word on everything going on in town, make hotel bookings, collect tickets for shows and leave messages on the bulletin board. Oh, and the back section sells all kinds of interesting toys...

For drinking...
Brighton's gay pubs are generally raucous, no-holds-barred kind of places, but in the last few years a number of cooler, more reserved bars have opened their doors.

The Regency Tavern *(32 Russell Square)* is a Brighton classic: plain on the outside but pure Regency on the inside, down to the striped green wallpaper. It's camp and brilliant.

Dr Brighton's *(16 King's Rd)* is ultra-cool, predominantly male but very welcoming of lesbians. It's a popular pre-club spot, as most of the King's Rd clubs are a short walk away.

Amsterdam *(11-12 Marine Parade)* is a newer, European-style bar on the seafront that attracts a mixed crowd.

Charles St *(8-9 Marine Parade)*, a couple of doors down, is trendier still, but fun nonetheless, though you may feel slightly out of place without designer clothing.

The Queen's Head *(10 Steine St)*, at the end of an alley just off Old Steine, is popular with an older gay crowd and is famous for its Freddy Mercury pub-sign.

The Queen's Arms *(7 George St)* has our favourite sign in town: 'A friendly welcome greets you in the Queen's Arms'. With such double-entendres on the cards, there are plenty of distractions from the nightly cabaret and karaoke acts.

For dancing...
Bars and pubs may be fun, but the real action takes place on and off the dance floor.

Club Revenge *(☎ 606064; 32-43 Old Steine; closed Sun)* is the biggest gay club on the South coast, a haven for the bodies beautiful and party hedonists who sweat it out on the huge dance floor.

Pool Club *(8-9 Marine Parade)* is upstairs from Charles St. Cool, sophisticated and trendy, it still gets down and dirty when it's full.

Secrets *(☎ 609672; 5 Steine St)* attracts a young crowd, who come for the trashy handbag music – watch the dance floor whoop and holler at the sound of Jimi Somerville's version of *I Feel Love*.

The King's Rd Arches clubs (see the main text) are also gay-friendly, and some of the nights attract a predominantly gay and lesbian crowd. The most popular of these is Friday night at the Zap Club.

SOUTHEAST ENGLAND

everything from 17th-century rifles to the latest foot fashions. There's less of a touristy, upmarket feel in **North Laine** – a series of streets northwest of The Lanes, including Bond, Gardner, Kensington and Sydney Sts – which abound with second-hand clothes shops, record and CD stalls, bong sellers and local craft outlets. Check out the **flea market** *(Upper Gardner St)* on Saturday mornings.

Getting There & Away
Brighton is 53 miles (85km) from London and bus and train services are fast and frequent.

Bus National Express has an office at the bus station and tickets can also be bought at the TIC. Coaches leave hourly from London Victoria to Brighton (£8 or £6 after 9.30am).

Stagecoach East Kent (☎ 01227-472082) bus No 711 runs between Brighton and Dover via Hastings and Rye. **Stagecoach Coastline** (☎ 01903-237661) buses operate along the south coast from Brighton to Portsmouth and Southampton. Tickets for Stagecoach buses can be purchased from the drivers.

Airlinks (☎ 020-8844 0824) is a daily coach service to/from all London airports.

Train There are twice-hourly services to Brighton from London Victoria and King's Cross stations (£15.60, 50 minutes). For £1.50 on top of the rail fare you can have unlimited travel on **Brighton & Hove** buses for the day. There are hourly services to Portsmouth (£13.90, one hour 20 minutes) and frequent services to Eastbourne, Hastings, Canterbury and Dover.

Getting Around
Brighton is large and spread out though you'll be able to cover all the sights mentioned in this section on foot if you enjoy walking.

The local bus company is **Brighton & Hove** (☎ 886200). A day ticket costs £2.70 from the driver.

Parking in Brighton can be a nightmare. To park in any street space you will need a voucher. They can be purchased from garages and various shops around town and cost about £1 per 30 minutes but prices do vary.

If you need a cab, **Brighton Streamline Taxis** (☎ 747474), **Yellow Cab Company**

(☎ 884488) or **Radio Cars** (☎ 414141) are all worth a try. There is a taxi rank on the junction of East and Market Sts.

You can hire a bike from **Sunrise Cycles** (☎ 748881) by West Pier. Rates start at £11 per day. There are cycle routes along the seafront and throughout the city centre, but traffic is very unpredictable so be careful. For more information on cycling in and around Brighton call the Walking and Cycling Office of Brighton and Hove City Council ☎ 292475.

West Sussex

Everything is just that little bit quieter in West Sussex. Far from the madding crowds of the eastern coastal resorts, the area is dominated by the rolling hills of the South Downs. Handsome Chichester makes a good base for exploring the county, which also includes some excellent Roman ruins.

ARUNDEL
☎ 01903 • pop 4000
Arundel is one of West Sussex's prettiest towns, sitting comfortable atop a hill beneath the 700-year-old castle that is the seat of the dukes of Norfolk. Despite its medieval appearance and long history, most of the town dates from Victorian times.

Orientation & Information
The **TIC** (☎ 882268, fax 882419; 61 High St; open 9am-5pm Mon-Fri, 10am-5pm Sat & Sun Easter-Oct, 10am-3pm daily Nov-Easter) is where you can pick up *A Walk Around Arundel* (40p), although everything to see in the town is pretty well signposted.

Things to See
Arundel Castle (☎ 882173; adult/child £8.50/5.50; open noon-5pm Sun-Fri Apr-Oct) was originally built in the 11th century, but it was thoroughly ruined during the Civil War. Most of what you see today is the result of enthusiastic reconstruction by the eighth, 11th and 15th dukes. The building's highlight is the library, which has paintings by Gainsborough and Holbein among others. Traditionally, touring cricket teams kick off their visit to England with a match against the Duke of Norfolk's XI on the ground directly beneath the castle.

The 4-hectare **Waterfowl Park** *(☎ 883355; Mill Rd; adult/child £5.50/3.50; open 9am-5.30pm daily Apr-Sept, 9.30am-4pm Oct-Mar)*, a mile east from the centre, is a nice place to visit for those keen on bird-watching.

The town's other architectural landmark is the 19th-century **cathedral** *(☎ 882297; open 9am-dusk daily)*, built in the French Gothic style by Henry, the 15th duke. Inside are the remains of the fourth duke's son, St Philip Howard, a Catholic martyr who made the grievous error of being caught praying for a Spanish victory against the English in 1588. He died in the Tower of London and was canonised in 1970.

Next door to the TIC is **The Museum & Heritage Centre** *(adult/child £1/50p)* with a small exhibition on local history.

Places to Stay & Eat

Dukes of Arundel *(☎ 883847, fax 889601; 65 High St; singles/doubles from £30/50)* is simply marvellous. It is an elegant, beautifully furnished B&B with a welcoming atmosphere and top-notch service.

Byass House *(☎ 882129, fax 901596; 59 Maltravers St; singles/doubles £30/55)*, a nice Victorian place, has big, comfortable rooms.

The Swan Hotel *(☎ 882314, fax 883759; 27-29 High St; singles/doubles from £60/75)* may look like a 19th-century hotel, but the rooms are all thoroughly modern.

The Norfolk Arms *(☎ 882101, fax 884275; High St; singles/doubles £70/110)*, built in 1800 by the 10th duke, is a handsome coaching inn with some exquisite touches and beautifully appointed rooms.

St Mary's Gate Inn *(☎ 883145; London Rd; rooms from £39; mains from £10)* is a lovely country-style inn next door to the cathedral. Rooms are a little small, but pleasant nonetheless. The real treat here is the excellent restaurant. We recommend the baked escalope of sea bass (£12.95).

Tudor Rose *(☎ 883813; 49 High St; mains around £5)* is a popular tearoom with the usual selection of sandwiches and hot dishes.

Belinda's *(☎ 882977; 13 Tarrant St; mains around £6)* is another traditional tearoom with a full lunch menu.

Getting There & Away

Rail is the best way of getting to/from Arundel; it's 55 miles (88.5km) from London (£17.20, 1½ hours), 20 miles (32km) from Brighton (£7.20, 50 minutes) and 11 miles (18km) from Chichester (£4.20, 20 minutes).

AROUND ARUNDEL
Bignor Roman Villa

In 1811, farmer George Tupper was doing a little ploughing when he struck a large stone. After digging around a bit, Tupper realised that he had discovered something quite out of the ordinary.

Much excavation later, it was realised that the plough had struck the remains of a Roman villa *(☎ 869259; adult/child £3.65/1.55; open 10am-6pm daily June-Sept, 10am-5pm daily May & Oct, 10am-5pm Tues-Sun Mar-Apr)* built around AD 190. Unfortunately, only the mosaic floors and hypocaust (the Roman version of duct heating) remain, but the mosaics are simply fantastic, particularly the one that shows Ganymede being transported from Mount Ida by an eagle. New findings are still being made; the most recent was the complete skeleton of a child dating from the 4th century.

Bignor is 6 miles (10km) north of Arundel off the A29, but it's a devil of a place to get to unless you have your own car. A terribly slow bus (£2.40, one hour) from Chichester stops 300m from the entrance, but it only runs twice daily.

CHICHESTER
☎ 01243 • pop 28,000

Chichester is an attractive Georgian market town on the flat meadows between the South Downs and the sea. Founded as a port garrison by the Romans shortly after their invasion in AD 43, it later became an important Norman settlement and today is the administrative capital of West Sussex.

Besides the cruciform street plan that converges on Market Cross and the foundations of the enormous villa at Fishbourne, little else remains of its Roman origins. Its Norman heritage has fared a little better in the form of its elegant cathedral, even if the once-imposing castle has long disappeared.

These days, Chichester is celebrated for its theatre and arts festival, which it hosts in early July.

Orientation & Information

The compact centre is easy to get around on foot. It is surrounded by walls, around which is a ring road.

SOUTHEAST ENGLAND

There is a **TIC** (☎ 775888, fax 539449; e chitic@chichester.gov.uk; 29a South St; open 9.15am-5.15pm Mon-Sat year round, 10am-4pm Sun Apr-Sept) and a **post office** (cnr Chapel & West Sts) in town.

There are a few public toilets in the centre – next to the Church of the Greyfriars in Priory Park, off West St near the corner of Tower St and on Friary Lane.

Chichester Cathedral

The elegant cathedral (☎ 782595; adult/child admission by donation of £3/1.50; open 7.15am-7pm June-Aug, 7.15am-6.30pm Sept-May) is one of the few Romanesque churches not to have undergone a major re-structuring. It was begun in 1075, burnt down and rebuilt in the 13th century, and only cosmetically altered since then. The only major changes were the construction of the free-standing church tower in the 15th century and the addition of a 19th-century spire. Inside is a marvellous stained glass window by Marc Chagall. The building's story is best revealed by an expert: guided tours operate at 11am and 2.15pm Monday to Saturday, Easter to October.

The cathedral has a fine choir, which sings daily at evensong (5.30pm Monday to Saturday, 3.30pm Sunday).

Pallant House Gallery

Of the many fine Georgian houses in town, Pallant House (☎ 774557; 9 North Pallant; adult/child £4/free; open 10am-5pm Tues-Sat, 12.30pm-5pm Sun) is outstanding. It was

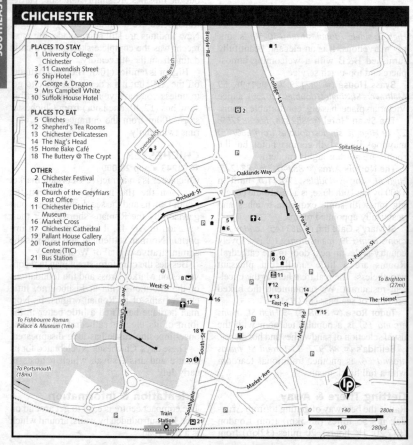

CHICHESTER

PLACES TO STAY
1 University College Chichester
3 11 Cavendish Street
6 Ship Hotel
7 George & Dragon
9 Mrs Campbell White
10 Suffolk House Hotel

PLACES TO EAT
5 Clinches
12 Shepherd's Tea Rooms
13 Chichester Delicatessen
14 The Nag's Head
15 Home Bake Café
18 The Buttery @ The Crypt

OTHER
2 Chichester Festival Theatre
4 Church of the Greyfriars
8 Post Office
11 Chichester District Museum
16 Market Cross
17 Chichester Cathedral
19 Pallant House Gallery
20 Tourist Information Centre (TIC)
21 Bus Station

Broyle Rd
Little Breach
College La
Cavendish St
Spitafield La
Oaklands Way
Orchard St
New Park Rd
St Pancras St
West St
To Brighton (27mi)
The Hornet
East St
Ave De Charters
To Fishbourne Roman Palace & Museum (1mi)
South St
Market Rd
To Portsmouth (18mi)
Market Ave
Southgate
Train Station
0   140   280m
0   140   280yd

SOUTHEAST ENGLAND

built by a wealthy wine merchant who spared no expense. It has since been carefully restored and now houses an excellent collection of 20th-century, mainly British, art in the form of paintings, furniture, sculpture and porcelain. Among them are works by Picasso, Moore, Sutherland and Cézanne. There are also a lot of works by a German artist named Feibusch who escaped the Nazis in Germany in 1933. He died in London in 1998 and left the contents of his studio to Pallant House.

Church of the Greyfriars
The Franciscans established a church (☎ 784 683; admission free; open noon-4pm Sat June-Sept) here in 1269 on the old site of the castle – now Priory Park – in the northeastern corner of the town. The simple but quite beautiful building that remains was their choir and now overlooks the local cricket pitch. After dissolution in 1536 the building became the guildhall and later a court of law, where William Blake was tried for sedition in 1804. Visits outside opening hours can be made by arrangement.

Chichester District Museum
At this museum (☎ 784683; 29 Little London; admission free; open 10am-5.30pm Tues-Sat) we learn of the history and the people of West Sussex, and the small collection of displays include a stocks used to punish local miscreants.

Special Events
Chichester Festival Theatre (☎ 781312; e box-office@cft.org.uk), built in 1962, is a striking modern building in parkland to the north of the ring road. Sir Laurence Olivier was the theatre's first director and other famous names to have played here include Ingrid Bergman, Sir John Gielgud, Maggie Smith and Sir Anthony Hopkins. It is now at the centre of an important arts festival, the **Chichester Festivities** (☎ 780192; e info@ chifest.org.uk), held every July. For details, check out the website at w www.cft.org.uk.

Places to Stay
University College Chichester (☎ 816070; College Lane; rooms per person with/without en suite £32/24; open July-Sept) has 218 single rooms for rent during the summer months. Like most student accommodation,

they're clean, comfortable and relatively basic.

11 Cavendish St (☎ 527387; rooms per person £19) has one double and one single, both with en suite and pretty comfortable.

Mrs Campbell White (☎ 788405; 5a Little London; room per person from £25.50) has a lovely townhouse with one well-appointed room.

The George & Dragon (☎ 775525; 51 North St; singles/doubles £55/75) is a new B&B in a converted barn at the back of the eponymous pub. The 10 rooms are thoroughly modern and quite luxurious.

Ship Hotel (☎/fax 778000; North St; singles/doubles from £74/114) is an historic 18th-century townhouse with elegant rooms.

Suffolk House Hotel (☎ 778899, fax 787282; e admin@suffolkhshotel.co.uk; 3 East Row; singles/doubles from £65/95) is a Georgian house in the heart of Chichester with a range of exquisitely decorated rooms.

Places to Eat
The most atmospheric spots in town are the tearooms, where you can get sandwiches and a limited selection of hot dishes in lovely surroundings. Otherwise, there's the usual choice of pubs and standard restaurants.

Shepherd's Tea Rooms (☎ 774761; 35 Little London) is a wonderful spot serving a range of sandwiches and rarebits with home-made white milk bread. It is a three-time winner of Chichester's 'Top Tea Place of the Year' award.

Clinches (☎ 789915; 4 Guildhall St; mains £4-8) is a lovely tearoom with great buns and coffee, as well as more solid dishes such as Welsh rarebits.

The Buttery @ The Crypt (☎ 537033; 12a South St; sandwiches £3.75, cakes £1.75) is another good spot, located in the old 12th-century crypt that was once part of the Guildhall. The staff are all turned out in 1930s-style uniforms.

Chichester Delicatessen (☎ 781990; 1 Sadler's Walk, 44 East St; sandwiches around £4) is one of the best sandwich shops in southern England, selling homemade bread topped with delicious fillings. If you want to eat and run, this is the place to do it.

Getting There & Away
Chichester is 60 miles (97km) from London and 18 miles (29km) from Portsmouth.

SOUTHEAST ENGLAND

Bus Chichester is served by bus No 700 which runs 11 times daily (six times on Sunday) between Brighton (£3.75, 2½ hours) and Portsmouth (£2.85, 1¼ hours). National Express has a rather protracted daily service from London Victoria (£11/£14.50 one-way/return, three hours).

Train Chichester can be reached easily from London Victoria (£17.70, 1¾ hours, hourly) via Gatwick airport and Arundel. It's also on the coast line between Brighton (£8.20, 45 minutes) and Portsmouth (£5.10, 25 minutes). Trains run every half-hour.

AROUND CHICHESTER

South of town is the gorgeous **Chichester Harbour**, an Area of Outstanding Natural Beauty (AONB). A wide, sandy beach west of the harbour offers the only real distraction, but it's a top spot for a stroll and some fresh air. At West Itchenor, 1½-hour harbour cruises are run by **Chichester Harbour Water Tours** (☎ 786418; adult/child £5/2.50), complete with resfreshments. To get here, follow the signposted towpath from Chichester.

Fishbourne Roman Palace & Museum

Fishbourne Palace (☎ 01243-785859; Salthill Rd; adult/child £4.70/2.50; open 10am-5pm daily Mar-July & Sept-Oct, 10am-6pm Aug, 10am-4pm Nov-Dec 15, 10am-4pm Sat & Sun Dec 16-Feb) is the largest known Roman residence in Britain. For decades, locals had been uncovering period artefacts in the area and were bemused as to their origin. Then, in 1960, a labourer's shovel hit upon the mother lode and excavations began in earnest.

It is thought that the house was built around AD 75 for Cogidubnus, a Romanised local king. The boy done good, because what was built for him was simply spectacular in size and luxury. Its bathing facilities were so luxurious that you'd have to check into the best hotel in the country to find something similar. Although all that survives are foundations and some extraordinary mosaic floors (look out for the marvellous 'Cupid on a Dolphin') and hypocausts, the ruins still convey a vision of 'modern' style and comfort.

The pavilion that shelters the site is an ugly creation, but there are some excellent reconstructions and the garden has been replanted as it would have been in the 1st century.

The palace is 1½ miles (2.4km) west of Chichester, just off the A259. Bus Nos 11 and 700 leave hourly from Monday to Saturday (No 56 on Sunday) from outside Chichester Cathedral and stop at the bottom of Salthill Rd (five minutes' walk away). The museum is 10 minutes' walk from Fishbourne train station, on the line between Chichester and Portsmouth.

Petworth

Twelve miles (19km) northeast of Chichester is the pleasant village of Petworth. On the outskirts is **Petworth House** (NT; ☎ 01798-342207; adult £7; open 11am-5.30pm Sat-Wed Apr-Oct), a stately home built in 1688. The architecture is impressive (especially the western front), but the art collection is extraordinary. JMW Turner was a regular visitor and the house is still home to the largest collection (20) of his paintings outside the Tate Gallery. There are also many paintings by Van Dyck, Reynolds, Gainsborough, Titian and Blake.

Petworth is, however, most famous for **Petworth Park** (adult/child £1.50/free; open 8am-sunset daily), which is regarded as the supreme achievement of Lancelot (Capability) Brown's natural landscape theory. It's also home to herds of deer.

Last admission is at 5pm. The car park and Pleasure Ground (part of the landscaped grounds which feature a number of classical follies) open noon to 6pm.

Petworth is 6 miles (10km) from the train station at Pulborough. There's a limited bus service (No 1/1A) from the station to Petworth Square (Monday to Saturday).

Hampshire

Largely rural Hampshire may have the traditional image of a gentle countryside dotted with pretty villages, but that doesn't tell the whole story. Aside from the magnificent cathedral city of Winchester, which you should absolutely visit, anyone with an interest in maritime history will relish a trip to Portsmouth, the long-time home of the once-powerful Royal Navy. The largest city in the county, Southampton, may not hold your interest for too long, but it is just a short hop from the New Forest, which is covered in a separate section later.

The county is well served by bus. The *Public Transport Map of Hampshire* is very useful and stocked by TICs. For information on all public transport in the county phone ☎ 01962-846992.

WINCHESTER
☎ 01962 • pop 96,000

If you're visiting Hampshire, Winchester should be at the top of your list. This beautiful cathedral city, nestled in a valley of the River Itchen, has a rich history that is evident throughout, nowhere more so than in the magnificent church that dominates the centre.

History

The Romans built the town of Venta Bulgarum, later giving way to a Saxon settlement, but Winchester really took off in AD 670 when the powerful West Saxon bishops moved their episcopal see here from Dorchester. Thereafter, Winchester was the most important town in the powerful kingdom of Wessex. King Alfred the Great (r. 871–99) made it his capital, and it remained so under Canute (r. 1016–35) and the Danish kings. After the Norman invasion of 1066, William the Conqueror arrived here to claim the throne of England, and in 1086 he commissioned local monks to write the all-important *Domesday Book* (pronounced doomsday), an administrative survey of the whole country that ranks as the most important clerical accomplishment of the Middle Ages. Winchester thrived until the 12th century, when a fire gutted most of the city,

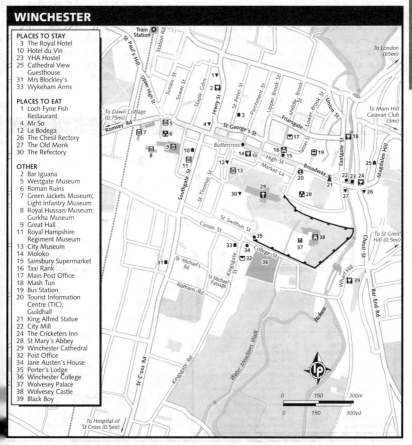

WINCHESTER

PLACES TO STAY
3 The Royal Hotel
10 Hotel du Vin
23 YHA Hostel
25 Cathedral View Guesthouse
31 Mrs Blockley's
33 Wykeham Arms

PLACES TO EAT
1 Loch Fyne Fish Restaurant
4 Mr So
12 La Bodega
26 The Chesil Rectory
27 The Old Monk
30 The Refectory

OTHER
2 Bar Iguana
5 Westgate Museum
6 Roman Ruins
7 Green Jackets Museum; Light Infantry Museum
8 Royal Hussars Museum; Gurkha Museum
9 Great Hall
11 Royal Hampshire Regiment Museum
13 City Museum
14 Moloko
15 Sainsbury Supermarket
16 Taxi Rank
17 Main Post Office
18 Mash Tun
19 Bus Station
20 Tourist Information Centre (TIC); Guildhall
21 King Alfred Statue
22 City Mill
24 The Cricketers Inn
28 St Mary's Abbey
29 Winchester Cathedral
32 Post Office
34 Jane Austen's House
35 Porter's Lodge
36 Winchester College
37 Wolvesey Palace
38 Wolvesey Castle
39 Black Boy

after which it was superseded in importance by London. A long slump lasted until the 18th century, when the town was largely re-built and found new life as a prosperous market town.

Orientation

The city centre is compact and easily managed on foot. Partly pedestrianised High St and Buttercross run from west to east through the town, and most of the sights are on or just off them. The bus and coach station is smack in the middle of town opposite the Guildhall and TIC, while the train station is five minutes' walk northwest. Jewry St borders the western side of the centre and was once part of the city's Jewish quarter – today it is where you'll find a chunk of the town's nightlife.

Information

The TIC (☎ 840500, fax 850348; W www.winchester.gov.uk; open 9.30am-5.30pm Mon-Sat, 11am-4pm Sun May-Sept; 10am-5pm Mon-Sat Oct-Apr) is in the Guildhall on Broadway.

There is a **post office** (open 9.30am-6pm Mon-Sat) on Middle Brook St and a smaller one on Kingsgate St, near the college. There are plenty of **banks** and ATMs on High St, and there are public toilets in the park off Broadway.

Winchester Cathedral

Winchester's main attraction is one of the world's great buildings, a magnificent testament to English architecture over 900 years and one of the finest examples of the Gothic Perpendicular style to be found anywhere.

The present-day cathedral (☎ 853137; admission by donation of £3.50; open 7.30am-6.30pm daily) is just south of the town's original minster church built by King Cenwalh in 643. In 1070 the first Norman bishop, Walkelin, decided to replace the old church (even then the largest in the country) with a new one built in the Romanesque style. The new cathedral, completed in 1093, featured a nave that was 164m long and was 14m wider than the current building. On August 15th of that year, the monks officially blessed the new cathedral by depositing the remains of St Swithin (bishop of Winchester from 852 to 862) in a new, purpose-built chapel.

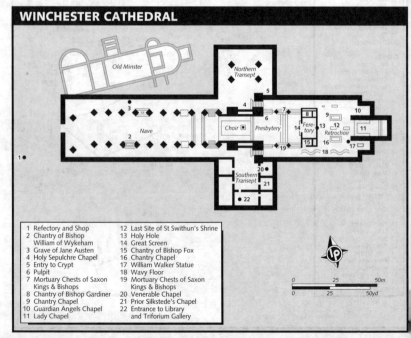

WINCHESTER CATHEDRAL

Old Minster

Northern Transept

5

Nave

3

2

4

6

7

Choir   Presbytery

8

9

10

14 Fere-tory

13 12

Retrochoir

11

15

16

17

19

18

1

Southern Transept

20

21

22

1 Refectory and Shop
2 Chantry of Bishop
   William of Wykeham
3 Grave of Jane Austen
4 Holy Sepulchre Chapel
5 Entry to Crypt
6 Pulpit
7 Mortuary Chests of Saxon
   Kings & Bishops
8 Chantry of Bishop Gardiner
9 Chantry Chapel
10 Guardian Angels Chapel
11 Lady Chapel

12 Last Site of St Swithun's Shrine
13 Holy Hole
14 Great Screen
15 Chantry of Bishop Fox
16 Chantry Chapel
17 William Walker Statue
18 Wavy Floor
19 Mortuary Chests of Saxon
   Kings & Bishops
20 Venerable Chapel
21 Prior Silkstede's Chapel
22 Entrance to Library
   and Triforium Gallery

0   25   50m

0   25   50yd

Soggy ground and poor workmanship did not augur well for the church, and the collapse of the central tower in 1107 was just one of several problems the authorities had to deal with. Major restructuring began around 1200 and continued until the mid-15th century; the nave was transformed from a Norman Romanesque to an English Gothic style between 1350 and 1450, thanks in large part to the efforts of William of Wykeham (1366–1404), who was also responsible for Winchester College and New College, Oxford.

Near the entrance in the northern aisle is the **grave of Jane Austen**, who died a stone's throw from the cathedral in 1817. The transepts are the most original parts of the cathedral. Note the early Norman rounded arches and painted wooden ceiling.

Crypt tours normally commence from the northern transept but are often suspended if the crypt is flooded. You can get access to the first part of the crypt where the wonderful sculpture by Anthony Gormley – of Angel of the North fame – called Sound 2 is on display.

At the end of the presbytery is the magnificent **Great Screen**, built around 1470. During the Reformation the figures in the screen were removed and broken up. The current figures are 1890 replacements, which is how Queen Victoria has managed to sneak in among the Saxon royalty (2nd level, 3rd row from right of minor figures). **Mortuary chests**, high up under the arches on both sides of the presbytery, contain the bones of Saxon royalty (including King Canute) and bishops.

The retrochoir has a number of **chantry chapels** – small chapels each devoted to one person. Note the unusual skeletal effigies of Bishop Gardiner and, on the other side of the cathedral, Bishop Fox (the godfather of Henry VIII). They wanted their images to be preserved like this to remind onlookers of their own human mortality and frailty.

The southern transept **library** and **Triforium Gallery** (adult/child £1/50p) house a display of cathedral treasures including damaged figures from the Great Screen and the illuminated 12th-century Winchester Bible. Opening hours are somewhat variable.

Tours of Winchester Cathedral are run by enthusiastic local volunteers at 10am and 3pm daily, except Sunday. Sunday services take place at 8am, 10am and 11.15am and

Evensong is at 3.30pm. Evensong is at 5.30pm, Monday to Saturday. There are tower tours at 2.15pm on Wednesday, and 11.30am and 2.15pm on Saturday. These tours cost £2. Crypt tours begin at 10.30am and 2.30pm daily, except Sunday. Photography is permitted inside.

City Mill
The City Mill (NT; ☎ 870057; adult £2; open 10am-5pm Sat & Sun Mar, 11am-5pm Wed-Sun Apr-Oct), on the riverbank, was built in 1743 and once ground grain for the local bakers, although there was also a mill on this site in medieval times. The building is shared by the YHA hostel and when the doors shut the Mill House doubles as hostel dining room.

Museums
The **City Museum** (☎ 863064; The Square; admission free; open 10am-5pm Mon-Fri, 10am-1pm Sat, 2pm-5pm Sat & Sun Apr-Sept; 10am-5pm Tues-Fri, 10am-1pm Sat, 2pm-5pm Sat & Sun Oct-Mar) has interesting displays on Roman ruins, a collection of Winchester shop fronts and the story of Saxon and Norman Winchester.

Westgate Museum (☎ 869864; High St; admission free; open 10am-5pm Mon-Fri, noon-5pm Sun Apr-Oct, 10am-4pm Tues-Sat, noon-4pm Sun Feb-Mar) is in the old medieval gateway, at one time a debtors' prison. The displays include a macabre set of gibbeting irons, last used to display the body of an executed criminal in 1777. You can also see graffiti carved into the walls by prisoners.

The **Great Hall** (☎ 845610; admission free; open 10am-5pm daily Apr-Sept; 10am-5pm Mon-Fri, 10am-4pm Sat & Sun Oct-Mar) was the only part of Winchester Castle that Oliver Cromwell did not destroy. The castle was begun by William the Conqueror in 1067 and was added to and fortified by many successive kings of England. It was the site of a number of dramatic moments in English history, including the trial of Sir Walter Raleigh in 1603. It was last used as a court from 1938 to 1978.

The Great Hall long claimed to house King Arthur's Round Table, but don't get too excited: it's a 600-year-old fake. The wonderful steel gates were made in 1981 to commemorate the wedding of Charles and Diana. Part of the Roman wall, built around

SOUTHEAST ENGLAND

AD 200, can be seen in an enclosure near the entrance to the Great Hall.

There are also a number of military museums open to the public: the **Green Jackets Museum** (☎ 828549; adult/child £2/1; open 10am-1pm & 2pm-5pm Mon-Sat, noon-4pm Sun), the **Light Infantry Museum** (☎ 828550; admission free; open 10am-4pm Tues-Sat, noon-4pm Sun), the **Royal Hampshire Regiment Museum** (☎ 863658; admission free; open 11am-3.30pm Mon-Fri), the **Royal Hussars Museum** (☎ 828541; admission free; open 10am-12.45pm & 1.15pm-4pm Tues-Fri, noon-4pm Sat & Sun) and the **Gurkha Museum** (☎ 828536; adult/child £1.50/free; open 10am-5pm Mon-Sat, noon-4pm Sun).

Wolvesey Castle & Palace

Wolvesey Castle (EH; ☎ 854766; admission £1.50; open 10am-6pm daily Apr-Nov) owes its name to a Saxon king's demand for an annual payment of 300 wolves' heads, or so the story goes. Work began on the castle in 1107, and was completed over half a century later by Henry de Blois, grandson of William the Conqueror. In the medieval era it was the residence of the bishop of Winchester. Queen Mary I and Philip of Spain had their wedding breakfast here. It was largely demolished in the 1680s and today the bishop lives in the adjacent Wolvesey Palace.

Winchester College

The first of Britain's exclusive public schools, Winchester College (☎ 621217; College St; chapel & cloisters open 10am-1pm & 2pm-5pm Mon-Sat, 2pm-5pm Sun) was founded in 1382 by Bishop Wykeham to educate 70 poor scholars for a career in the church. Students are still known as Wykehamists, but modern-day graduates are more likely to head a major financial institution than a parish church. One-hour guided tours leave at 10.45am, noon, 2.15pm and 3.30pm Monday to Saturday (2.15pm and 3.30pm on Sunday), April to September. Tours cost £2.50/2 per adult/child. They start from the Porter's Lodge, College St; there's no need to book.

Nearby is **Jane Austen's house** (College St). Well, it's referred to as her house, but it's just the place where she spent the last six weeks of her life.

Hospital of St Cross

Henry du Blois was a busy man, but he found time in his hectic schedule to found this hospital (☎ 851375; adult/child £2/50p; open 9.30am-5pm Mon-Sat Apr-Oct, 10.30am-3.30pm Mon-Sat Nov-Mar) in 1132. Rather than simply treat the ill or house the poor, Henry's idea was that the hospital would also provide sustenance and a bed for pilgrims and crusaders before they set off to foreign lands to convert and kill the heathens. The hospital is the oldest charitable institution in the country and is still home to 25 brothers who continue to provide alms. Within the complex you can see the church, the brethren hall, the kitchen and the master's garden. Take the one-mile Water Meadows Walk to get here. The admission entitles you to the Wayfarer's Dole, a crust of bread and horn of ale (although the horn of ale is now little more than a tiny cup of sherry).

St Mary's Abbey

A couple of ruins and a few relics mightn't seem that appealing, but this nunnery was the country's main university during the reign of King Alfred. Although eclipsed by Oxford and Cambridge in the Middle Ages, St Mary's continued in its educating role until Henry VIII dissolved it in 1536. You can see what's left of it in an enclosure off High St.

Walking

From the Wolvesey Castle entrance, the **Water Meadows Walk** goes for a mile to the St Cross Hospital. The **Riverside Walk** runs from the castle along the bank of the River Itchen to High St. The walk up to **St Giles' Hill** is rewarded by great views over the city. It's at the top of East Hill, half a mile from the castle, and is signposted.

There are also 1½-hour **guided walks** of the town conducted throughout the year (£3, under-16 free); they run twice daily at 11.30am and 2.30pm, Monday to Saturday (11.30 only on Sunday) from May to September. The rest of the year they run on Saturday only.

If you prefer you can take the **Phantasm Ghostwalk** (☎ 07990-876217), which leaves from outside the cathedral at sunset each day and lasts for one hour. You'll need to book ahead.

Places to Stay

B&Bs in Winchester tend not to hang signs out the front. The TIC, however, has a complete list.

Camping & Hostels The **Morn Hill Caravan Club** (☎ 869877; Morn Hill; tent sites £3 plus per person £4.50) is a fairly well-equipped campground 3 miles (4.8km) east of the city centre off the A31.

The **YHA Hostel** (☎ 0870 770 6092, fax 855524; City Mill, 1 Water Lane; beds per adult £9.50) is one of the first YHA hostels in England, located in the beautiful 18th-century water mill on the other side of the river from the mill entrance.

B&Bs & Hotels A charming Victorian house, **Mrs Blockley's** (☎ 852073; 54 St Cross Rd; singles/doubles £25/45) has friendly service and well-appointed rooms. It's only a short walk from the cathedral.

Dawn Cottage (☎ 869956; 99 Romsey Rd; singles/doubles £40/50) is a real find; a truly elegant B&B with beautiful rooms only a mile west of the city centre.

Cathedral View Guesthouse (☎ 863802; 9a Magdalen Hill; singles/doubles £35/50, with en suite £50/65) is a friendly, comfortable place with good rooms and a sunny breakfast-room conservatory.

Wykeham Arms (☎ 853834, fax 854411; 75 Kingsgate St; singles/doubles from £50/95), near the college, is a traditional hostelry with great rooms and a terrific atmosphere.

The Royal Hotel (☎ 840840, fax 841582; St Peter St; singles/doubles £110/120) is right in the heart of the city, down a quiet side street. The interiors are lovely and there's an attractive garden. They also have special weekend deals outside summer for two nights including dinner, bed and breakfast: singles/doubles cost £99/107 per night.

Hotel du Vin (☎ 841414, fax 842458; e admin@winchester.hotelduvin.co.uk; Southgate St; rooms £99-155) is the top spot in town these days, a modern, luxurious hotel where each room has a minibar, VCR and CD player.

Places to Eat

Loch Fyne Fish Restaurant (☎ 853566; 18 Jewry St; mains £7-12), in a Tudor-style house dating from 1509, is the best fish restaurant in town. The lobster platter is divine (£34.95).

The Chesil Rectory (☎ 851555, 1 Chesil St; 3-course set lunch £22, 4-course set dinner £40), in Winchester's oldest house (1450), has earned a reputation as perhaps the town's best restaurant. The menu offers a mix of traditional British and French cuisine.

Wykeham Arms (☎ 853834; 75 Kingsgate St; dishes £9-13) looks very olde Englishe with school desks as tables and tankards hanging from the ceiling. This is an excellent place to eat (and drink), with a cheaper bar menu; no food is served on Sunday.

La Bodega (☎ 864004; 9 Great Minster St; mains £7-14) is, despite the name, an Italian restaurant, serving excellent homemade pastas and a wide selection of meat dishes.

Mr So (☎ 861234; 3 Jewry St; mains £6-8) is Winchester's best Chinese restaurant. Its menu offers Cantonese and Szechwan specialities, as well as Peking Duck.

The Old Monk (☎ 855111; 1 High St; mains around £5) has an outside seating area overlooking the river. The bar food is excellent.

The Refectory (sandwiches £1.70, cream tea £3.45), near the entrance to the cathedral, is a good spot for a quick bite or afternoon tea.

Entertainment

On the other side of the river from **The Wykeham Arms**, the **Black Boy** (1 Wharf Hill) has the atmosphere of an art-house pub. Bookshelves line the wall and there is an outdoor terrace. A Sunday roast here costs £5.

Bar Iguana (18 Jewry St) is one of the trendiest pubs in town; on weekends there are DJs that spin a pretty good mix of funk, both old and new.

Mash Tun (60 Eastgate St) is strictly for the young bohemian set, which makes this one of the nicest places in town to chill out and enjoy a drink.

Moloko (31b The Square) is new, hyper-trendy and very modern. It is popular with Winchester's more fashion-conscious crowd.

The Cricketers Inn (5 Bridge St) is dedicated to the game and is adorned with plenty of cricket memorabilia. After all, you're in Hampshire, where cricket is king!

Getting There & Away

Winchester is 65 miles (105km) from London and 15 miles (24km) from Southampton.

Bus Bus No 32 leaves nine times daily from London Victoria via Heathrow (£10.50, two hours), and there are less frequent services to/from Oxford.

Bus No 47 runs from Southampton to Winchester (£2.20/3.50 one-way/return, 30 minutes). **Stagecoach Hampshire** (☎ 01256-464501) has a good network of services linking Salisbury, Southampton, Portsmouth and Brighton. Explorer tickets (£5.70/4.10 per adult/child) are good on most Wilts & Dorset buses, which serve the region farther to the west, including the New Forest.

Train There are fast links with London Waterloo, the Midlands and south coast. Trains leave about every 15 minutes from London (£20.50, 1 hour), Southampton (£4.90, 20 minutes) and Portsmouth (£8.20, 1 hour).

Getting Around

Your feet are the best form of transport. There's plenty of day parking within five minutes' walk of the centre or you can use the Park and Ride service which costs £1.50.

If you want a taxi try the rank outside Sainsbury's on Middle Brook St or phone **Wintax Taxis** (☎ 854838 or 866208) or **Wessex Cars** (☎ 853000).

PORTSMOUTH
☎ 023 • pop 190,000

Portsmouth is the traditional home of the Royal Navy, whose ships once exported the empire to the far-flung corners of the world. The city's main attractions are the historic ships and museums in the Naval Heritage Area, but it is still a busy naval base and the sleek, grey killing machines of recent times sit ominously close by.

Portsmouth's strategic importance resulted in the city being heavily bombed during WWII, and much of the modern city beyond The Point and The Hard is a product of myopic and uninspired post-war development. The adjoining suburb of Southsea may not be beautiful to look at but it is a bustling and vibrant spot with some excellent bars.

Orientation

Your first stop in town should be the quay known as The Hard, which is where you'll find the TIC, the entrance to the Naval Heritage Area, the Portsmouth Harbour train station and the passenger ferry terminal for the Isle of Wight. About a mile east along the water is Old Portsmouth and The Point, a cluster of sea-worn, atmospheric buildings around the old harbour, called the Camber.

Southsea, where the beaches are, as well as most of the accommodation and restaurants, is about 2 miles (3.2km) south of Portsmouth Harbour.

The rest of the city has a number of interesting museums, but most of your sightseeing and activities are likely to be concentrated along the water's edge.

Information

The **TIC** (☎ 9282 6722, fax 9282 2693; **e** tic@portsmouthcc.gov.uk; The Hard; open 9.30am-5.45pm daily June-Aug) provides guided tours and an accommodation service. There is another, next to the Blue Reef Aquarium in Southsea (☎ 9283 2464, fax 9282 7519; Clarence Esplanade; open May-Sept).

There's one **post office** (42 Broad St) in Old Portsmouth and another **post office** (Palmerston Rd) in Southsea. Both are open 9am to 5.30pm Monday to Saturday. There are **ATMs** on Osbourne Rd, Southsea, as well as a **laundrette**.

Internet access is available at **Southsea Backpackers Lodge** (4 Clarence Rd Southsea) for £2.50 per half-hour. You don't have to be a guest to use it.

Flagship Portsmouth (Naval Heritage Area)

The Naval Heritage Area (☎ 9286 1512; admission per ship around £6, adult/child 3 for 2 ticket £13.75/11, passport ticket £18/14.50, season ticket £25/21; open 10am-5.30pm daily Apr-Oct, 10am-5pm daily Nov-Mar) is the city's main (some say only) draw, and it's a humdinger. Three classic ships and a handful of excellent museums form the core of England's tribute to the historical might of the Royal Navy, on the edge of the country's most important naval port. Even the most devoted landlubber should find this a good day out.

And it is indeed a full day out. There are individual admission costs for each ship or you can buy a three-for-two ticket that includes any three attractions for the price of two. It is valid for seven days. If you want to see more than a couple of attractions, we recommend the passport ticket, which covers single admissions to all of the ships and museums and is valid for one year. The

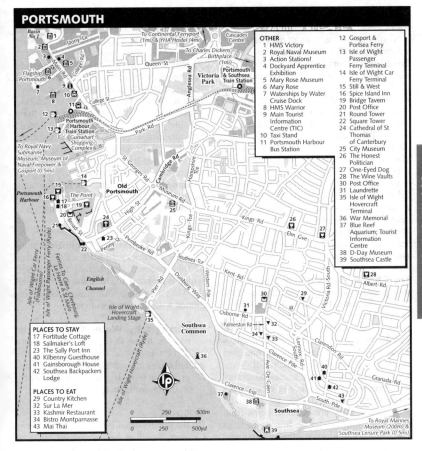

PORTSMOUTH

OTHER
1 HMS Victory
2 Royal Naval Museum
3 Action Stations!
4 Dockyard Apprentice Exhibition
5 Mary Rose Museum
6 Mary Rose
7 Waterships by Water Cruise Dock
8 HMS Warrior
9 Main Tourist Information Centre (TIC)
10 Taxi Stand
11 Portsmouth Harbour Bus Station
12 Gosport & Portsea Ferry
13 Isle of Wight Passenger Ferry Terminal
14 Isle of Wight Car Ferry Terminal
15 Still & West
16 Spice Island Inn
19 Bridge Tavern
20 Post Office
21 Round Tower
22 Square Tower
24 Cathedral of St Thomas of Canterbury
25 City Museum
26 The Honest Politician
27 One-Eyed Dog
28 The Wine Vaults
30 Post Office
31 Laundrette
35 Isle of Wight Hovercraft Terminal
36 War Memorial
37 Blue Reef Aquarium; Tourist Information Centre
38 D-Day Museum
39 Southsea Castle

PLACES TO STAY
17 Fortitude Cottage
18 Sailmaker's Loft
23 The Sally Port Inn
40 Kilbenny Guesthouse
41 Gainsborough House
42 Southsea Backpackers Lodge

PLACES TO EAT
29 Country Kitchen
32 Sur La Mer
33 Kashmir Restaurant
34 Bistro Montparnasse
43 Mai Thai

SOUTHEAST ENGLAND

season ticket offers unlimited entry to all the attractions for two years...and a subscription to the *Semaphore* newsletter.

The Ships The main attraction is **HMS Victory** (*adult/child £7/5*), Lord Nelson's flagship at the Battle of Trafalgar in 1805. This remarkable ship carried up to 900 crew and had a top speed of 10mph (16km/h) when she led the British fleet at Trafalgar, which resulted in victory against the French but cost Nelson his life. The ship limped into harbour and out of active duty in 1922, where it was fully refurbished and converted into a museum, although incredibly it remains in commission and as such is subject to military regulations, which basically means no photography.

Which is a shame, because the pre-timed, 40-minute tours of the ship are one of the best you'll find anywhere. Conducted at breakneck speed but with liberal doses of great humour, the tours are as close as you'll get to a step back in time. None of the gory details are left out, and you will undoubtedly come away happy that it wasn't you or any of your loved ones that had to serve in what can best be described as miserable conditions. Astounding facts about life at sea will stay in your mind forever, such as the crew's liquor ration of eight pints of beer and two pints of wine per day!

Also on board is a chalkboard on which are scribbled Nelson's famous words to his fleet before going into battle, although his original version read 'England *confides* that every man will do his duty', which somehow doesn't flow as well as 'England *expects...*'

Nearby are the remains of the **Mary Rose** *(adult/child £6.75/4.75)*. Built in 1509 under the orders of Henry VIII, the 700-tonne ship sank in shallow water off Portsmouth in 1545. There was much speculation about why she sank. At the time it was put down to 'human folly and bad luck'. The ship and her time-capsule contents were raised to the surface in 1982, after 437 years under water. Finds from the ship are displayed in the Mary Rose Museum (see that section later).

Dating from 1860, and at the cutting edge of the technology of the time, **HMS Warrior** *(adult/child £6.75/4.75)* was a transition ship, as wood was forsaken for iron and sail for steam. The four decks of the ship illustrate life in the navy in the Victorian era. It's not nearly as impressive as the others though. You are free to wander around at your leisure.

Royal Naval Museum Housed in five separate galleries, this huge museum *(adult/child £3.75/2)* has an extensive collection of ship models, dioramas of naval battles, and exhibits on the history of the Royal Navy, medals and paintings. Audiovisual displays recreate the Battle of Trafalgar and one even lets you take command of a battleship – see if you can cure the scurvy and avoid mutiny and execution. One gallery is entirely devoted to Lord Nelson and, among many other things, there are personal items from his private ship quarters – life at sea must have been pretty tough for the officers, who had their own wine coolers!

Mary Rose Museum In 1965 a massive salvage operation resulted in the raising of the *Mary Rose*, and you discover all there is to know about the ship and its recovery at this fascinating museum *(adult/child £6.75/4.75)* through exhibits, audiovisuals and great sound effects. It also recounts the failed salvage attempt made in the late 16th century by two hopeful Venetians. A 15-minute film about the raising of the *Mary Rose* is shown every half-hour. The ticket also covers admission to the ship itself (see The Ships section, earlier).

Action Stations! Opened in 2001, this interactive experience *(adult/child £6.75/5)* is not quite a museum but a showcase for the

modern navy. 'See It! Be It!' screams the tagline, and from the start we had the sensation that this was a poorly disguised recruitment drive. You begin by watching a 25-minute, PG-rated film called 'Command Approved', which tells the story of a daring rescue of British citizens kidnapped by evil African pirates. The body count is high, and it cost £3 million to make; the only thing missing was an appearance by Arnold Schwarzenegger or Steven Segal. Naturally, kids love it. In other sections you can experience what life is like aboard a Type 23 frigate, take command (thanks to the joys of multimedia) of a Merlin helicopter and, through a series of interactive tests, find out whether you have what it takes to make it in the navy. Apparently we don't.

Dockyard Apprentice Exhibition Shipbuilding and dockyard work are the themes of this museum *(adult/child £2.50/1.50)*, which is probably the least interesting of all the yard's exhibits. Admission is not included with the passport ticket.

Waterships by Water Cruises To be able to see all the ships, old and new, from a different angle you can take a 40-minute guided cruise around the harbour for £3.50/2 per adult/child. If you have a passport ticket the cruise is included.

Gosport

On the other side of Portsmouth Harbour is Gosport, which is easily reached by ferry from The Hard (see Getting Around later). Not surprisingly, the naval theme is continued here.

Royal Navy Submarine Museum This museum *(☎ 9252 9217; adult/child £3.75/2.50, with Royal Marines Museum £5/3; open 10am-5.30pm Apr-Oct, 10am-4.30pm Nov-Mar)* is the only place in Britain where you can climb aboard a submarine, in this case the HMS *Alliance*. It may be a massive and impressive bit of naval engineering, but conditions were awfully cramped for the sailors.

Museum of Naval Firepower If munitions and ordnance (and their effects) are of interest, then this new museum *(☎ 9250 5600; Priddy's Hard; adult/child £5/3; open 10am-5.30pm daily Apr-Oct, 10am-4.30pm* daily Nov-Mar), or more particularly its main exhibit (the appropriately named *Explosion!*), will tell, and show, you everything you need to know. The entire experience is a showcase for graphic designers and computer animators to display their skills in recreating the horror and fear of being under attack, and they do so quite convincingly.

Other Things to See & Do

One of the more pleasant spots in town is **The Point**, along the cobbled streets of Old Portsmouth, which has a few atmospheric old pubs that, on a sunny day, are ideal spots to sit and watch the ferries and navy ships go in and out of the harbour.

Nearby is the **Cathedral of St Thomas of Canterbury**, although only fragments of the original 12th-century church remain. The nave and tower were rebuilt around 1690 and more additions were made in 1703 and between 1938 and 1939. Immediately south of Old Portsmouth is the **Round Tower**, originally built by Henry V, a stretch of old fort walls and the **Square Tower** of 1494.

At the Southsea end of the waterfront there's a cluster of attractions on Clarence Esplanade. The **Blue Reef Aquarium** (☎ 9287 5222; adult/child £5.95/3.95; open 9.30am-5pm daily Mar-Oct, 10am-3pm daily Nov-Feb) is more interesting than most other sea life centres in that the attractions – including a huge walk-through aquarium filled with coloured corals and plenty of different fish – have a much more hands-on feel. The open-top tanks allow visitors to really see what goes on underwater, while the various sea habitats, from the Mediterranean to the Bay of Mexico, are extremely well presented.

Portsmouth was a major departure point for the Allied D-Day forces in 1944 and the **D-Day Museum** (☎ 9282 7261; Clarence Esplanade; adult/child £5/3; open 10am-5.30pm daily Apr-Sept, 10am-5pm daily Oct-Mar) recounts the story of the Normandy landing with the 83m-long Overlord Embroidery (inspired by the Bayeux Tapestry) and other exhibits.

Southsea Castle (☎ 9282 7261; adult/child £2.50/1.80; open 10am-5.30pm daily Apr-Sept, 10am-5pm daily Oct-Mar) was built by Henry VIII to protect the town against French invasion. It was altered in the early 19th century to accommodate more guns and soldiers, and a tunnel under the moat. It's

said that Henry VIII watched the *Mary Rose* sink from the castle.

The **Royal Marines Museum** (☎ 9281 9385; Barracks Rd; adult/child with Royal Navy Submarine Museum £5/3) tells the story of the Navy's elite force, while an assault course outside puts the kids through the paces.

City Museum (☎ 9282 7261; Museum Rd; admission free; open 10am-5.30pm daily) tells the history of Portsmouth through audiovisual displays, reconstructions of various rooms in typical houses from the 17th century to the 1950s, and other exhibits.

Charles Dickens' Birthplace (☎ 9282 7261; 393 Old Commercial Rd; adult/child £2.50/1.50; open 10am-5.30pm Apr-Sept, 10am-5pm Oct) is furnished in a style appropriate to 1812, the year of Dickens' birth, but the only genuine piece of Dickens' furniture is the couch on which he died in 1870!

Places to Stay

Although most of the cheaper B&Bs are in Southsea, the best ones are near The Point in Old Portsmouth. Rooms fill up quickly so you'll need to book in advance.

Camping & Hostels On the eastern end of Southsea esplanade the **Southsea Leisure Park** (9273 5070; Melville Rd, Southsea; tent sites £8) is a good campsite. Take bus No 15 from the Harbour train station.

With clean and spacious dorms, the **YHA Hostel** (☎ 0870 770 6002, fax 9221 4177; Old Wymering Lane, Cosham; beds per adult £10.25) is in a handsome Tudor mansion. The only problem is location; it's about 4 miles (6.5km) north of town. Local bus Nos 5 and 41 operate to Cosham from Southsea Parade Pier via Commercial Rd in Portsmouth while Stagecoach bus No 38 goes there from The Hard every hour.

Southsea Backpackers Lodge (☎/fax 9283 2495; 4 Florence Rd, Southsea; dorm beds/ doubles £10/25) is more convenient than the YHA Hostel. The friendly owners have made the place homely and comfortable.

B&Bs A tasteful place, **Sailmaker's Loft** (☎ 9282 3045, fax 9229 5961; 5 Bath Square; rooms per person with/without en suite £23/21) is highly recommended. The place is run by a retired merchant seaman who can tell you a lot about Portsmouth.

SOUTHEAST ENGLAND

Fortitude Cottage (☎ 9282 3748; 51 Broad St; en-suite rooms per person £23), around the corner from the Sailmaker's Loft, is on the small side, but the rooms are clean and very comfortable.

The Sally Port Inn (☎ 9282 1860, fax 9282 1293; High St; singles/doubles from £37/55) is a well-run, 16th-century place with sloping floors. There are no en-suite facilities but doubles have showers in the room.

Gainsborough House (☎ 9282 2322; 9 Malvern Rd, Southsea; rooms per person £17) is excellent value, with pretty comfortable rooms, but you'll have to share a bathroom.

Kilbenny Guesthouse (☎ 9286 1347; 2 Malvern Rd, Southsea; singles/doubles £17/34) is another tidy spot, with good-size rooms.

Places to Eat

Southsea offers the best dining options in town, but even then they're not particularly memorable.

Country Kitchen (☎ 9281 1425; 59a Marmion Rd; open 9am-6pm Mon-Sat; mains around £5) is a wholefood restaurant with a good selection of veggie dishes. Nothing fancy, but tasty nonetheless.

Sur La Mer (☎ 9287 6678; 69 Palmerston Rd; 2-/3-course dinner £5.95/6.95) is a French bistro that is popular with locals.

Bistro Montparnasse (☎ 9281 6754; 103 Palmerstown Rd; mains over £8) is a decent French bistro that specialises in seafood.

Mai Thai (☎ 9273 2322; 27a Burgoyne Rd; 4-course meal £11) is a good Thai restaurant just off South Parade.

Entertainment

A few pubs on The Point are good for a summer evening drink, but the real action is to be found on and around Albert Rd in Southsea.

Still & West (2 Bath Square), **Spice Island Inn** (65 Broad St) and the **Bridge Tavern** (54 East St), all on The Point, have the look of an old seadog's local. Consequently, they're very popular.

The Honest Politician (47 Elm Grove) is a wonderfully mellow bar that is perfect for an afternoon's drink over the newspaper.

The Wine Vaults (43-47 Albert Rd) is another great bar that is very popular with the local intelligentsia.

One-Eyed Dog (177-85 Elm Grove) is the students' favourite hangout, and the place to hear loud, raucous music.

Getting There & Away

Portsmouth is 75 miles (121km) southwest of London.

Bus There are National Express buses every couple of hours from London (£11, 2¼ hours), some via Heathrow airport (£9.50, 2½ hours). There's also a daily service between Brighton and Portsmouth (£7.25).

Stagecoach Coastline bus No 700 also runs between Brighton and Portsmouth (£3.50) and on to Southampton via Chichester (every 30 minutes Monday to Saturday, hourly on Sunday). No 69 runs to Winchester (every two hours on Sunday).

Train There are trains every 20 minutes or so from London Victoria and Waterloo stations (£20.10, 1½ hours). There are hourly services to Brighton (£13.90, one hour 20 minutes), and to Winchester (£8.20, one hour). There are also trains to Chichester (£5.20, 25 minutes, three hourly).

For the ships at Flagship Portsmouth get off at the final stop, Portsmouth Harbour.

Boat There are a number of ways of getting to the Isle of Wight from Portsmouth. For information see Isle of Wight later in the chapter.

Condor Ferries (☎ 0105-761555) runs a car-and-passenger service from Portsmouth to Jersey and Guernsey (6½ hours) and costs from £55 one way. **P&O Ferries** (☎ 0870 242 4999) sails twice a week to Bilbao in Spain and daily to Cherbourg (five to six hours, two hours longer at night) and Le Havre in France. **Brittany Ferries** (☎ 0870 901 2400; w www.brittanyferries.co.uk) has overnight services to St Malo, Caen (six hours) and Cherbourg in France. For more information, check the website. The continental Ferryport is north of Flagship Portsmouth.

Getting Around

Local bus No 6 operates between the Portsmouth Harbour bus station, right beside the train station, and South Parade Pier in Southsea. Bus Nos 17 or 6 will take you from the station to Old Portsmouth.

Ferries shuttle back and forth between The Hard and Gosport (£1.60 return, bicycles travel free) every few minutes Monday to Saturday (every 15 minutes on Sunday). For a taxi try **MPS Taxis** (☎ 8261

1111) in Southsea. There's also a taxi stand near the TIC in Flagship Portsmouth.

SOUTHAMPTON
☎ 023 • pop 216,031

Frankly, there isn't much to see or do in Southampton, but it wasn't always the case. Its strategic location on the Solent – an 8-mile (13km) inlet into which flow the Itchen and Test Rivers – made it one of England's most important medieval trading centres, doing roaring business with France and other continental countries. Even when trade declined, Southampton turned its efforts to large-scale shipbuilding, and made a good job of it too; the *Queen Mary* was built here, as was the *Titanic*, though the latter didn't fare so well once it was out on the open sea. The city also ran a profitable sideline in aircraft manufacturing, but during WWII its industries were the targets of a concerted bombing effort: over two nights alone, more than 30,000 bombs rained down on factories and virtually everything else as well.

Therein lies Southampton's biggest problem. Apart from the impressive city walls, there is little left of the town's medieval past, and the modern city is hardly beautiful. Still, there are a few things to pique your interest while waiting for the Isle of Wight ferry, including a couple of museums and a large-scale waterfront shopping and entertainment complex, from where you may also catch a glimpse of the huge ocean liners that still dock here, including the *QEII*.

The **TIC** *(☎ 8083 3333; 9 Civic Centre Rd; open 8.30am-5.30pm Mon, Tues & Thur-Sat, 10am-5.30pm Wed)* offers free guided walks of the old town that take place on Sunday and bank holidays at 10.30am; and at 10.30am and 2.30pm daily, late June to mid-September. Meet at the Bargate on High St.

Things to See & Do
Directly opposite the TIC is the massive Civic Centre, which houses the excellent **Southampton Art Gallery** *(☎ 8083 2277; Commercial Rd; admission free; open 10am-5pm Tues-Sat, 1pm-4pm Sun)*. The permanent collection features the best of 20th-century British art, including work by Sir Stanley Spencer, Matthew Smith and Philip Wilson Steer.

The tragic life of the Titanic, as well as the history of Southampton's port since 1838,

is told in detail at the **Maritime Museum** *(☎ 8063 5904; Wool House, Town Quay; admission free; open 10am-5pm Tues-Fri, 10am-4pm Sat, 2pm-5pm Sun)*. The building was used as a prison, and as an aircraft factory.

Of Southampton's medieval heritage, the timbered **Medieval Merchant's House** *(EH; ☎ 8022 1503; French St; adult £2.30; open 10am-6pm daily Apr-Sept, 10am-5pm daily Oct-Mar)* is a faithfully restored property dating from 1290. The **Tudor House** *(☎ 8063 5904; Bugle St; closed for restoration)* is another good example.

Getting There & Away
Air The ultra-modern **Southampton International Airport** *(☎ 8062 0021)* has flights to Brussels, Paris, Zurich, Amsterdam, Dublin and major holiday resorts in Spain. There are four trains hourly between the airport and the main train station (£2, 7 minutes).

Bus National Express coaches run to Southampton from London and Heathrow hourly (£11, 2½ hours). Bus No 700 runs between Portsmouth and Southampton. Bus Nos X34 and X35 run from Southampton to Lyndhurst (£3, 1½ hours) in the New Forest and on to Bournemouth (£4.90, two hours) every hour during the week and every two hours on Sunday. Bus Nos 47 and 29 run between Southampton and Winchester (£2.40, 40 minutes) every 30 minutes with reduced services on Sunday. Wilts & Dorset bus No 56/56A goes to all the main towns in the New Forest hourly (every two hours on Sunday). Explorer tickets are valid on these routes.

Train From London's Waterloo there are twice-hourly train services to Southampton Central (£24.70, one hour 20 minutes). Trains from Portsmouth run three times an hour (£9.10, 50 minutes). Trains for Bournemouth (£9.70, 30 minutes) and Winchester (£5.20, 17 minutes) leave about every 15 minutes.

Boat Ferries run by **Red Funnel** *(☎ 8033 4010)* go to the Isle of Wight and there is a ferry service to Hythe in the New Forest (see Getting There & Away in the New Forest section). **Channel Hoppers** *(☎ 01481-728460,* e *info@channelhoppers.com)* has a ferry service between Southampton and the Channel Islands and France.

New Forest

With national park status just around the corner, the New Forest is a remarkable 150-sq-mile (388 sq km) swathe of woodland and heathland that is the largest area of relatively natural vegetation in England. But what makes the New Forest really special is that it's not wrapped in cotton wool and preserved just for the admiring visitor (although 7 million of them do visit annually); it's a lived-in area with a very prosperous and bustling community that has managed to preserve several traditions dating back 1000 years (for more details see the boxed text 'Verderers, Agisters & Ponies' later in this section).

It is possible to explore the New Forest by car, but this wildlife-filled landscape is definitely best appreciated when you get off the roads and onto the numerous cycling and walking tracks. The New Forest is a popular destination for campers, but make sure you pitch your tent in a proper campsite; the TIC in Lyndhurst has a brochure with all the details.

Activities

Cycling The New Forest is a great place to cycle and there are several rental shops. You will need to pay a deposit (usually £20) and provide one or two forms of identification. **AA Bike Hire** (☎ 8028 3349; Fern Glen, Gosport Lane) is in Lyndhurst, and charges £10 per day. The **New Forest Cycle Experience** (☎ 01590-624204; 2-4 Brookley Rd, Brockenhurst) charges £11. **Forest Leisure Cycling** (☎ 01590-611029; National Motor Museum, Beaulieu) rents bikes from £10 a day from December to mid-February. You can pick up cycle route maps from TICs and bicycle shops.

Horse Riding This is a great way to explore the New Forest but we're not talking about saddling up one of the wild ponies here. There are a couple of trail riding set-ups where you can arrange a pleasant one- or two-hour ride. Sandy Balls (honestly!) is at **Godshill** (☎ 01425-654114) in Fordingbridge, and the **Burley-Villa School of Riding** (☎ 01425-610278) is off the B3058, just south of New Milton. Both these places welcome beginners.

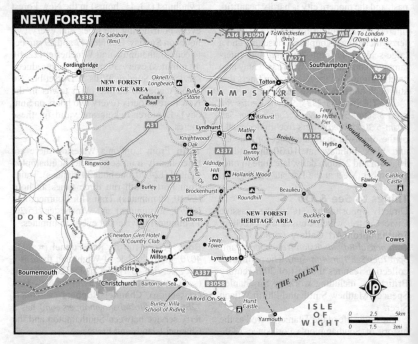

Verderers, Agisters & Ponies

The New Forest is the only area of England to remain relatively untouched since Norman times, thanks in large part to its unsuitability as agricultural land. If the presence of so much unfenced territory is remarkable enough, what is truly fascinating about the New Forest is that it still retains a code of law first handed down during the reign of William the Conqueror.

Although the presence of wild ponies was recorded by King Canute's Forest Law of 1016, William officially declared the whole area a royal hunting preserve in 1079, thereby protecting it from any form of development. The crown still owns 100 sq miles (260 sq km) of the New Forest, though it is the Forestry Commission that has been responsible for its maintenance since 1924.

The remaining 50 sq miles (130 sq km) are owned by verderers, or commoners, who in the pre-automobile age reared the ponies as work horses. Today they are either reared as riding ponies or are left to graze the land at will. The verderers' status is protected by the Commoners' Charter, first laid down in 1077, which guaranteed them six basic rights, the most important of which is the 'common', or right, to pasture. Every year, the 300-odd verderers that still exercise their rights gather to elect five agisters, who are responsible for the daily management of the 3000 ponies, 1800 cattle and smaller numbers of donkeys, pigs and sheep in the New Forest, including ensuring that each pony bears the brand of the verderer who owns it.

Although historical tensions between the verderers and the crown have largely subsided, grievances still exist, mostly to do with the payments the verderers make to the crown for grazing rights. These are dealt with by the Verderers' Court, which meets six times a year in the Verderers' Hall in Lyndhurst. Set up during Norman times, this is Britain's oldest running judicial court.

Outsiders are more than welcome to wander freely throughout the forest, but they are strongly requested not to feed or touch the ponies. These are wild animals, and feeding them will attract them onto the roads; furthermore they have been known to have a nasty bite. To protect the ponies, as well as cyclists and walkers, there is a 40mph (65km/h) speed limit on unfenced roads. If you come across an injured pony phone Lyndhurst Police on ☎ 023-8028 2813 and state the location and, if possible, the registration number of any vehicle involved in an accident. You should try to stay with the animal (but don't touch it) to protect it from further injury.

Getting There & Around
Southampton and Bournemouth bracket the New Forest and there are regular bus services from both. Wilts & Dorset bus Nos 56 and 56a run twice hourly from Southampton to Lyndhurst (£2.70/4.50 one-way/return) daily except Sunday.

Lyndhurst has no train station, and the nearest stop is Brockenhurst, 8 miles (13km) south. Trains run every half-hour from London Waterloo station via Brockenhurst (£25.60, 1½ hours) to Bournemouth, Poole and Weymouth.

White Horse Ferries (☎ 8084 0722) operates a service from Southampton to Hythe, 13 miles (21km) southwest of Lyndhurst, every half-hour (£3.90 return, 12 minutes).

Busabout tickets offer unlimited travel on main bus lines for seven days and cost £21/12 per adult/child. The Solent Blue line X1 service goes through New Forest taking the Bournemouth–Burley–Lyndhurst–Southampton route.

LYNDHURST
☎ 023 • pop 3141
Although the New Forest is dotted with small towns and villages, we recommend that you make the pretty town of Lyndhurst your base, as it has the best selection of accommodation, a number of good restaurants and essential services such as banks, a post office and pharmacies. It is a fairly wealthy town, perhaps best exemplified by the Ferrari dealership at the eastern end of High St. Just in case you were wondering, a Ferrari 360 with red leather seats will set you back a cool £97,995.

The **Lyndhurst TIC** (☎ 8028 2269, w www.thenewforest.co.uk; Main Car Park, High St; open 10am-5pm daily) sells a wide variety of information on the New Forest including cycling maps (£2 to £3.50), a map showing walking tracks (£1.50), a more comprehensive Collins map (£5.99), and a free camping and caravanning guide. It also sells the Ordnance Survey (OS) map (No 22, £5.95) which covers the area in greatest detail.

Places to Stay & Eat

South View (☎ 8028 2224; Gosport Lane; rooms per person £25), with its friendly atmosphere and lovely dog, is highly recommended.

The Fox & Hounds (☎ 8028 2098; 22 High St, Lyndhurst; doubles £60; mains from £6) is a 400-year-old coaching inn. It's a nice place for a beer and a game of pool too. The pub grub is typical, but good.

Ormonde House Hotel (☎ 8028 2806, fax 8028 2004, e info@ormondehouse.co.uk; Southampton Rd; doubles £60) has beautifully appointed rooms with all the trimmings, including whirlpool baths! It is about 450m east of town.

Le Poussin at Parkhill (☎ 8028 2944, fax 8028 3268; e sales@lepoussinatparkhill .co.uk; Beaulieu Rd; B&B per person from £65; 2-course lunch £15, 4-course dinner from £35) is one of Hampshire's finest hotels, with sumptuous rooms overlooking its own private park. The hotel is also home to an award-winning restaurant.

Mad Hatter Tea Rooms (☎ 8028 2341; 10 High St; mains £4-6) is a beautiful café where you can get a delicious Ploughman's lunch for £4.10 and rarebits for around £3.75.

The Traditional Tea House (☎ 8028 2566; 26 High St; mains around £6) is not particularly traditional, but it's a bright, airy café.

Imperial China (☎ 8028 3186; 18 High St; mains from £6.50) is a surprisingly good Chinese restaurant, specialising in Szechwan spicy cuisine, but you can also get pretty good Peking Duck.

AROUND LYNDHURST
Beaulieu & National Motor Museum

The New Forest's most impressive and most-visited (non-natural) attraction, Beaulieu (☎ 01590-612345; adult/child £10/7; open 10am-6pm daily May-Sept, 10am-5pm daily Oct-Apr), pronounced bewley, was once the site of England's most important Cistercian monastery, founded in 1204 by order of King John as an act of contrition after he ordered that a group of monks be trampled to death. The 3200-hectare abbey was dissolved following Henry VIII's monastic land-grab of 1536 and sold to the ancestors of the Montague family in 1538.

The estate's been transformed into a fascinating tourist complex with Lord Montague's **National Motor Museum** the biggest attraction. There are 250 vehicles on show, including buses, cars and motorcycles spanning the whole history of motor transport. As well as classics, you can run your hands along a £650,000 McLaren F1 and the jet-powered *Bluebird*, which broke the land-speed record (403mph, or 649km/h) in 1964. There's also a ride-through display giving you the lowdown on car history. Rev-heads will love it, but you don't need to be one to enjoy it.

The **Palace House** (open 11am-6pm daily Easter-Sept, 11am-5pm daily Oct-Easter) was once the abbey gatehouse and is an odd combination of 14th-century Gothic and 19th-century Scottish Baronial architecture, as converted by Baron Montague in the 1860s. Unlike other manor homes you might visit, this place really feels like a home and therefore exudes a certain warmth.

The **abbey** has an excellent exhibit on everyday life in the monastery, and a plaque in the courtyard tells us that the European Resistance Movement used the abbey as a training camp during WWII.

Stagecoach Hampshire bus No 66/X66 runs to Beaulieu from Winchester via Lyndhurst. You can also get here from Southampton by taking a ferry to Hythe and catching bus Nos 112 or X9. Solent Blue Line buses also run here from various towns in New Forest.

Trains from London Waterloo run to Brockenhurst (see Getting There & Around, earlier), from where it's a short taxi ride.

BUCKLER'S HARD
☎ 01590

This secluded hamlet of historic 18th-century cottages is one of the most beautiful destinations in the New Forest. It was the brainchild of John, the second Duke of Montague, who in 1722 wanted to build a port to finance an expedition to the West Indies. Despite a number of attractive incentives (99 year lease at a nominal rent and three loads of timber to build a house), only six houses were built by 1740 and his expedition never got off the ground.

But then came war with France, and a number of Nelson's warships were built in the port, whose sheltered location and gravel hard made it the perfect spot to build in secrecy and in a hurry. By the middle of the 19th century the shipbuilding industry had died out, but in 1894 the Gosport Steam Launch Company began organising day trips here from Southampton, and a tourist destination was born.

Today, the whole place is a well-run heritage centre (☎ 614645; adult/child £4.50/3; open 10.30am-5pm daily Easter-Nov, 11am-4pm daily Dec-Easter). You can wander around to your heart's content, but be sure to stop by the **Maritime Museum** and its excellent exhibits on the history of great ships. Also here is a labourer's cottage from the late 18th century, immaculately preserved for tourist curiosity.

The Master Builders House Hotel (☎ 616253, fax 616297; singles/doubles from £120/215) was exactly that before it was converted into a fine hotel with 25 luxuriously appointed rooms. Also on the premises is a fine restaurant (mains from £10) and the Yachtsman's Bar, which serves delicious pub grub for around £8 a dish.

Buckler's Hard is 2 miles (3.2km) downstream from Beaulieu along the river. You can walk the towpath alongside it, or rent a bike in Beaulieu (see Cycling, earlier in this section) and cycle.

NEW MILTON

This pretty little village on the southern outskirts of the New Forest is where you'll find **Chewton Glen Hotel & Country Club** (☎ 01425-275341, fax 01425-272310; e reservations@chewtonglen.com; rooms £250-720), one of the best resort hotels in the world. We simply couldn't not include it! The service is unsurpassed, and every comfort is provided for. It is a mile north of New Milton.

Isle of Wight

☎ 01983 • pop 125,466

If you're looking for a quiet, contemplative holiday in the midst of some truly outstanding scenery, the Isle of Wight is hard to beat. Over a third of the island is an Area of Outstanding Natural Beauty (AONB) and there are 25 miles (40km) of clean and unspoilt beaches. Another big plus is the weather, which is more clement here than anywhere else in Britain…and it's all just a couple of miles from the Hampshire shore! Although most visitors are day trippers, there's enough here to warrant staying at least a couple of

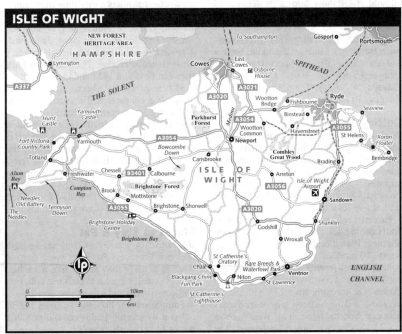

ISLE OF WIGHT

days, particularly if you set about exploring the lovely coastal towns.

For good online information, check out the website at **w** www.islandbreaks.co.uk.

Activities
Walking There are 500 miles (800km) of well-marked walking paths and bridleways, which make the island one of the best spots in Britain to indulge in the country's favourite pastime. They are so serious about their walking here that there is an annual **Walking Festival** (☎ *813818*), which takes place over two weeks in May. Over 15,000 people from around the globe participated in the 2002 event, clocking up over 65,000 miles (100,000km) – it was like walking around the world…twice.

Cycling The island is also a cyclist's paradise. There is a 62-mile (100km) cycleway, and in 2002 a **Cycling Festival** was inaugurated; check with the TICs for details. Enthusiasts should also check out the *Cyclist's Guide to the Isle of Wight* (£3.50) by Ron Crick and the two-volume *Cycling Wight* by John Goodwin and Ian Williams (£3 each), all sold at **Offshore Sports** (☎ *866269; 19 Orchard Leigh Rd, Shanklin •* ☎ *290514; Cowes •* ☎ *401515; Sandown*).

Bike rentals are available in Cowes, Freshwater Bay, Ryde, Sandown, Shanklin, Ventnor and Yarmouth. Offshore Sports (see earlier) charges £5 for five hours, £10 for a day. **Wavells** (☎ *760219; The Square, Yarmouth*) charges £10 for a day.

Getting There & Away
Wightlink (☎ *0990 827744;* **w** *www.wight link.co.uk*) operates a passenger ferry from The Hard in Portsmouth to Ryde pier (15 minutes) and a car-and-passenger ferry (35 minutes) to Fishbourne. They run about every half-hour (£7.40 day return). Car fares start at £49 for a day return.

Hovertravel (☎ *023-9281 1000*) hovercrafts zoom back and forth between Southsea (near Portsmouth) and Ryde (£8.60 day return, 10 minutes).

Red Funnel (☎ *023-8033 4010*) operates car ferries between Southampton and East Cowes (£8.70 return, from £51 with car, 55 minutes) and high-speed passenger ferries between Southampton and West Cowes (£8/9.80 one-way/return, 10 minutes). The

Wightlink car ferry between Lymington (in the New Forest) and Yarmouth costs £7.50 for passengers and £49.50 for cars. The trip takes 30 minutes and ferries run every half-hour. Children travel for half price on all these services.

Getting Around
Bus & Train Southern Vectis (☎ *827005; 32 High St, Cowes*) operates a comprehensive bus service around the island. Buses circumnavigate the island hourly, and run between the towns on the eastern side of the island about every 30 minutes. Trains run twice hourly from Ryde to Shanklin and the Isle of Wight Steam Railway branches off from this line at Havenstreet and goes to Wootton.

Rover Tickets give you unlimited use of buses and trains for £6.50 for a day, £10.50 for two days and £27 for a week.

COWES
Located at the northern tip of the island, Cowes is a hilly, Georgian harbour town. This is a major yachting centre and the late-July/early-August **Cowes Week** is an important international yachting event. Naturally, the town has a **maritime museum**.

Since its appearance in the film *Mrs Brown*, **Osborne House** (*EH;* ☎ *200022; adult £7.50; open 10am-5pm daily mid-Mar–Oct*) has become English Heritage's most visited attraction. The house was built between 1845 and 1851 and Queen Victoria died here in 1901. Osborne House has an antipodean connection: The Australian state of Victoria's Government House, near Melbourne's Botanic Gardens, is a copy, built in 1872. The house is in East Cowes, which is separated from the rest of the town by the River Medina, and linked by a chain ferry. Outside the standard opening hours, it opens from 10am to 2.30pm Sunday, Monday, Wednesday and Thursday for guided tours only (£5.50/3.50 per adult/child).

Places to Stay & Eat
Doghouse (☎ *293677;* **e** *timindoghouse@ beeb.net; Crossways Rd, East Cowes; singles/ doubles £25/35*) may sound like a kennel, but it's actually a great guesthouse with two gorgeous rooms and impeccable service.

Fountain (☎ *292397; High St; mains around £6*) is a wonderful, traditional old pub that serves filling meals as well as a good pint.

RYDE

Most visitors to the island land at Ryde, and then move on very quickly. It has a handful of elegant Victorian buildings, but it's the least pretty of the island's towns.

There is a **TIC** (☎ 562905, fax 567610; Western Esplanade). At **St Cecilia's Abbey** (Appley Rise) you can hear Gregorian chants by Benedictine nuns during Mass at 9.15am daily (at 10am Sunday).

Seahaven Hotel (☎ 563069, fax 563570; St Thomas St; singles/doubles £28/50) is a comfortable Victorian house with great views of the sea – provided you ask for a room at the front.

AROUND RYDE
Binstead
The main reason for stopping in this quiet little village is to visit the ruins of **Quarr Abbey**, built in 1132 and one of the island's oldest Christian relics. It was dissolved in 1536 and comprehensively plundered thereafter, leaving us a set of stunted-but-evocative ruins. Just to the west is another **abbey** (open daily 9am-9pm), built in 1908 for the Benedictines. You can hear vespers daily at 5pm. Binstead is 2½ miles (4km) southwest of Ryde.

Brading
What is believed to be the island's oldest standing house is in the middle of this pretty village about 4 miles (6.4km) south of Ryde. Unfortunately, it now houses the **Isle of Wight Wax Museum** (☎ 407823; adult/child £5.25/2.50; open 10am-10pm daily mid-May–Sept, 10am-5pm daily Oct–mid-May), which is pretty much what you thought it would be, including the not-so-scary Chamber of Horrors.

Just south of the village are the remains of a **Roman villa** (☎ 406223; adult/child £3/1.75; open 9.30am-5pm daily Apr-Oct), which are worth visiting for the exquisitely preserved mosaics. The villa's owners were – apparently – notoriously bacchanalian in their pursuit of pleasure, which perhaps explains the mosaic of a man with a cockerel's head.

Bembridge
The quiet town of Bembridge, about 3 miles (4.8km) southeast of Ryde, is a nice spot to chill out. If you're looking for something to do you should pop your head into the pretty interesting **Shipwreck Centre & Maritime Museum** (☎ 872223; adult/child £2.70/1.50; open 9.30am-5pm daily Apr-Oct), basically a collection of nautical bits and bobs salvaged from the sea by the museum's diver owner. The village's **Heritage Centre** (☎ 873100; adult/child 50/25p; open 10am-4pm Mon-Fri, 10am-noon Sat Mar-Oct) is stacked with maritime curios and old photographs.

Xoron Floatel (☎ 874596; Embankment Rd; en-suite rooms per person £24) is an actual houseboat that is very clean and surprisingly roomy.

Bus Nos 1 and 2 go from Ryde every 30 minutes. A scenic 5-mile (8km) coastal walk leads from Bembridge to Sandown.

VENTNOR

Of the island's larger towns, Ventnor is easily the most pleasant, probably because it's chilled out and doesn't seem to notice whether visitors are around or not.

One mile south of the town, off the A3055, is the **Rare Breeds & Waterfowl Park** (☎ 852582; adult/child/under-5 £4/2.50/free; open 10am-5.30pm daily late Mar–late Oct) which is home to a large array of rare and not so rare farm animals, including llamas, African cattle and Falabella miniature horses. Bus Nos 7, 7A and 31 will get you there from Ryde or Ventnor.

Ventnor Guided Walks (☎ 856647) organises a mixed bag of walks, including ghost walks, rock pool rambles and explorations of smugglers' caves. They run on Tuesday and Thursday from June to September and cost £3/1 per adult/child.

The Spy Glass Inn (☎ 855338; The Esplanade; 2-person flats £60) in Ventnor, situated above the beach with great views of the town, is highly recommended. Accommodation is in self-contained flats above the hotel (no kids, no dogs). The atmosphere in the pub downstairs is charged and friendly, and there's live music most nights.

AROUND VENTNOR
The south coast of the Isle of Wight, from Ventnor west to Alum Bay, is the quietest stretch of the island circuit. The southernmost point of the island is marked by **St Catherine's Lighthouse** which was built between 1837 and 1840. Looking like a stone rocket ship, **St Catherine's Oratory** is a lighthouse dating from 1314 and marks the highest point on the island. A couple of miles farther west

from here is the **Blackgang Chine Fun Park**
(☎ 730330; adult/child £6.25/5.50; open
10am-5.30pm daily Sept-June, 10am-10pm
daily July & Aug) which opened in 1843 as a
landscaped garden but slowly evolved into a
theme park. It is worth stopping at if you
have a couple of kids in tow.

WEST WIGHT
Henry VIII's last great fortress was **Yarmouth
Castle** (EH; ☎ 760678; adult £2.30; open
10am-6pm daily Apr-Oct). Its facade, which is
all that's left of it now, dates from 1547.

One mile (1.6km) west of Yarmouth off the
A3054 is **Fort Victoria Country Park** (adult/
child per area £1.50/80p) which is home to an
aquarium, a marine museum, a planetarium
and the Sunken History Exhibition. Only the
Exhibition warrants the admission fee.

The **Needles**, at the western tip of the island, are three towering rocks which rise out
of the sea to form the postcard symbol of the
island. At one time there was another rock, a
37m-high spire which really was needle-like,
but it collapsed into the sea in 1764.

The road and bus service to this end of the
island ends at **Alum Bay**, where there are a
few unappealing souvenir shops and a
theme park (☎ 458 0022; admission free;
open 10am-dusk daily Apr-Nov), with a range
of attractions including kiddie rides, crazy
golf, a motion simulator, boat rides and a
chairlift down to the beach. Our favourite is
the sweet factory, where you can watch how
those teeth-rotters are actually made.

A walking path leads a mile from Alum
Bay to the **Needles Old Battery** (☎ 754772;
adult/child £2.70/1.60; open 10.30am-5pm
Sun-Thur Apr-June, Sept & Oct, 10.30am-5pm
daily July & Aug), a fort established in 1862
and used as an observation post during
WWII. There's a 60m tunnel leading down
through the cliff to a searchlight lookout.
Buses run between Alum Bay and the battery
hourly (every half-hour in peak season).

Places to Stay
Brighstone Holiday Centre (☎/fax 740244;
tents/caravans £5/10, B&B £18, 2-person
cabins per week from £126), which is on the
A3055, 6 miles (10km) east of Freshwater,
is the most scenic place to stay. This caravan park and B&B, perched high on the
cliffs overlooking the island's most stunning stretch of coastline, is also close to

walking trails. There are self-catering cabins and B&B (continental breakfast).

Totland Bay Youth Hostel (☎ 0870 770
6070, fax 756443; Hirst Hill, Totland; beds
per adult £11.25) is a marvellous Victorian
house overlooking the water.

Essex

Poor old Essex. Not only does it have to endure the ignominy of being the butt of bad,
tasteless jokes about its inhabitants (see the
boxed text 'The Essex Girl & Boy', following), but its tourist profile can't quite get
beyond Southend-on-Sea, a tacky seaside
resort that is one of the country's most
popular. Which is a shame, because here
you'll find Britain's oldest town, a number
of exquisite medieval villages and some
stunning countryside that inspired the
painter Constable. What's more, Essex is
cheaper than most of the surrounding counties, which will come as a relief to budget-
minded travellers who have seen their
purses and wallets get progressively lighter
on their way through the southeast.

SOUTHEND-ON-SEA
☎ 01702 • pop 172,300
Essex's largest town and most popular seaside resort, Southend is typically brash and
full of the amusement arcades and sleazy
nightspots that are ubiquitous in so many of
England's fun-by-the-sea towns. Less than 50
miles (80km) from London, Southend has
been a traditionally popular destination since
the turn of the 19th century, when the Prince
Regent brought his wife Princess Caroline
here to enjoy healthier climes, while he disappeared off to Brighton to indulge himself.

Orientation & Information
The town is spread out along 7 miles
(11.3km) of coastline. The **TIC** (☎ 215120,
fax 431449; e marketing@southend.gov.uk;
19 High St; open 9am-5pm daily Sept-July,
9.30am-5pm Mon-Sat, 11am-4pm Sun Aug) is
in the centre of town, where you'll also find
banks and most of the shops.

Things to See & Do
Southend's main claim to fame is its 1.3-mile
(2km) long **pier** (open 8am-10pm daily Apr-
Oct, 8am-5pm Mon-Fri, 8am-7pm Sat & Sun

SOUTHEAST ENGLAND

The Essex Girl & Boy

She's a bottle blonde, loves Bacardi Breezers and has a wardrobe better suited to Ibiza in July than Colchester in January. His hair has enough styling gel to make him a fire risk, he wears jack-up trousers that show off his white socks and screeches around a flat urban wasteland in an XR3i with fluffy dice dangling from the rear-view mirror. They complement each other perfectly: her sexual morals are more a guide than a rule, and he thinks the cheesy chat-up is an undervalued art form (or he would if he knew what art was).

Who are they? They're Essex Girl and Boy, England's most enduring local stereotype. And it's getting more entrenched. Since WWII, Essex's inhabitants have been the butt of jokes questioning their intelligence, but in the last 10 years or so the stereotype has evolved so much that the 'typical' Essex Boy and Girl have been defined right down to their fingernails.

You won't need us to tell you that it's just a stupid myth, and that Essex is no different to most other counties, but still the jokes pour forth. Sadly, it does the county no favours, and the image is now so deep-rooted that it's in danger of scaring off potential new business and affecting the county's economy.

Nov-Mar) which is supposedly the longest in the world. There are a couple of restaurants and a bar at the end of the pier, which you can reach on the **Pier Railway** (adult/child £2/1) or on foot. Underneath the pier is a small **museum** (admission 50p; open 11am-5pm Sat-Wed May-Oct) with a collection that includes 19th-century pier train carriages and antique slot machines.

If you have kids, the **Sealife Adventure** (☎ 601834; Eastern Esplanade; adult/child £4.95/3.60; open 10am-7pm daily), about half a mile east of the pier, has the usual aquatic suspects behind glass, including a couple of sharks. The same company also runs **Adventure Island** (☎ 468023; Western Esplanade; open 11am-11pm daily Apr-Oct, 11am-dusk daily Nov-Mar), which is a pretty good amusement park near the pier. There are plenty of rides, all individually priced.

Places to Stay & Eat
Southend has dozens of B&Bs covering the entire area of the town. In recent years the town has taken on the task of housing many Eastern European refugees. What this means for the visitor is that a large number of guesthouses and a few seafront hotels are now boarding houses.

Lee Villas (☎ 317214; 1-2 Hartington Place; B&B per person £17.50) is the best choice of the cheap B&Bs around. It is just off Hartington St, about 230m east of the pier.

Regency Hotel (☎ 340747; 18 Royal Terrace; singles/doubles from £25/40, en-suite triple £60), a very central place, sits on the hill

above the pier. It's run by an expat New Yorker with a passion for naval history. This friendly place has basic but large rooms.

Southend's proximity to London has helped raise the culinary standards and there are a surprising number of really good restaurants.

Singapore Sling (☎ 431313; 12 Clifftown Parade; mains around £7), just off the seafront to the west of the pier, is a modern-looking restaurant and bar serving Chinese, Japanese, Malaysian and Thai food. Prices vary depending upon the cuisine.

Fisherman's Wharf (☎ 346773; Western Esplanade), on the seafront by the pier, claims to have the best fish and chips in town, and they're not wrong. Huge fillets of juicy, delicate fish, chips, salad and a variety of condiments will cost you about £7. There's an extensive seafood menu and it's licensed.

Getting There & Away
From London, **Greenline** (☎ 020-8668 7261) bus No 721 runs half-hourly from Bulleid Way, opposite Victoria coach station to York Rd bus station in Southend (£5 return, two hours 40 minutes).

There are several trains each hour from either London Liverpool St to Southend Victoria station or from London Fenchurch St to Southend Central station (£10, 55 minutes).

Getting Around
Distances are quite large in Southend and it's difficult to cover everything on foot. Local bus companies are **Arriva** (☎ 442444) and

First Thamesway (☎ 01245-262828) which are both based at the bus station on York Rd. The Southend Day Rover ticket gives you unlimited travel in and around Southend on First Thamesway or **First Eastern National Buses** (☎ 01245-256159) for £2.95/1.90 per adult/child.

If you need a taxi try **Southend Taxis** (☎ 334455) or **ARC Taxis** (☎ 611611).

COLCHESTER
☎ 01206 • pop 142,000

Charming Colchester is Essex's most attractive large town, as well as its most interesting. It has claims to be England's oldest city, with a recorded settlement dating back to the 5th century BC, but it really established itself when the Romans made it their capital (Camulodunum) after their landing in AD 43. Today, the town's main feature is the impressive Norman castle built by William the Conqueror. Colchester suffered horribly during the Civil War; in 1648, a Parliamentarian army led by Lord Fairfax laid a brutal siege to the town lasting three months, during which time the locals were reduced to eating anything with a heartbeat.

All you'll need is half a day to explore the sights.

Orientation & Information
There are two train stations, but most services stop at North station, about half a mile north of the town centre. The **bus/coach station** (☎ 282645) is in the centre of town, near the TIC and the castle.

The **TIC** (☎ 282920, fax 282924; 1 Queen St; open 9.30am-6pm Mon-Sat, 10am-5pm Sun Apr-Oct; 10am-5pm Sun-Fri, 9.30am-6pm Sat Nov-Mar) is opposite the castle. There are guided walking tours (adult/child £3/1.50) of the town at 11am daily, June to September, but times may vary so phone first. You can also take an open-top bus tour from mid-July to September for £5.75/3.50 (get tickets at the TIC).

There are a couple of **post offices** (North Hill • Longe Wyre St) in town. Banks and ATMs can be found on Culver St West.

Things to See & Do
Historical **Colchester Castle** (☎ 282939; adult/child £4/2.70; open 10am-5pm Mon-Sat, 1pm-5pm Sun) was built by William I on the foundations of a Roman fort. Construc-

tion began in 1076 and was completed in 1125. It boasts the largest castle keep in Europe – bigger than the Tower of London keep. During the 14th century it was used mainly as a prison. The museum contains Roman mosaics and statues. Last admission is at 4.30pm. For another £1.50/1 per adult/child you can take a guided tour of the Roman vaults, the Norman chapel on the roof of the castle and the top of the castle walls.

In Tymperleys – a magnificent, restored, 15th-century building – is the **Clock Museum** (☎ 282943; admission free; open 10am-5pm Mon-Sat, 11am-5pm Sun May-Sept), with one of the largest collections of clocks in Britain. It's also interesting to walk around the **Dutch Quarter**, just north of High St, which was established in the 16th century by Protestant refugee weavers from Holland.

Opposite the castle, the **Natural History Museum** (☎ 282931; High St; open 10am-5pm Mon-Sat, 11am-5pm Sun) has exhibits devoted to the local area.

About 5 miles (8km) northeast of town is **Colchester Zoo** (☎ 331292; Maldon Rd, Stanway; adult/child £9.50/6.25; open 9.30am-6pm daily Easter-June, Sept & Oct, 9.30am-6.30pm daily July & Aug, 9.30am-dusk daily Nov-Easter), one of the best zoos in Europe, with a huge selection of animals. It's very modern and extremely well organised (even though to our eyes half the animals still look sad).

Eastern National bus Nos 74 and 75 to Tiptree stop by the zoo, departing every half-hour from the bus station.

Places to Stay
Colchester doesn't have a great number of B&Bs, though there are plenty of small hotels with reasonable prices.

Colchester Camping (☎ 545551, fax 710443; Cymberline Way, Lexden; camping per person & tent £7.50) is 30 minutes' walk from the city centre, or you can catch bus No 5 from the bus station (twice hourly).

The Old Manse (☎ 545154, fax 545153; 15 Roman Rd; singles/doubles £30/44), a few minutes' walk from the centre, is a wonderful Victorian home with comfortable rooms. It's in a quiet square beside Castle Park and part of the Roman wall is at the bottom of the garden.

Scheregate Hotel (☎ 573037, fax 541561; 36 Osborne St; singles/doubles £25/35, with *en suite £35/45)* offers adequate rooms right in the town centre.

Peveril Hotel *(☎/fax 574001; 51 North Hill; singles/doubles from £27/40)*, conveniently located on the road to the train station, has 17 rooms, mostly without en suite.

Rose & Crown Hotel *(☎ 866677, fax 866616; East St; singles/doubles from £59/69)* is probably the best place to stay. There are 30 rooms – all doubles have an en suite.

Places to Eat

The Lemon Tree *(☎ 767337; 48 St John's St; mains around £6.50)* is very good value and offers an enticing menu of mostly French cuisine.

Forresters Arms *(☎ 542646; Castle Rd)*, off Roman Rd, is a nice old pub in a quiet part of town behind the castle. It has seating outside in the warmer months.

Picasso's *(☎ 561080; 2 St John's St; mains around £4)*, a colourful and casual café, must offer the best value in town; sandwiches cost from £1.70 and burgers from £1.40. There are also hot main meals.

Getting There & Away

Colchester is 62 miles (100km) from London. There are daily National Express buses from London (£8/9 one-way/return) and rail services every 15 minutes or so from London Liverpool St (£16.90, 45 minutes).

AROUND COLCHESTER
Dedham Vale

'I love every stile and stump and lane...these scenes made me a painter'
                                        John Constable

If Dedham Vale in the Stour Valley, near the border with Suffolk, looks strangely familiar it's because you've probably already seen the romantic, bucolic images on the canvases of early-19th-century painter John Constable. Constable County, as it's known, centres on the villages of Dedham, East Bergholt (in Suffolk, where the painter was born) and Flatford. The area is best explored in your own car but there are bus and train services.

Flatford Mill (not the original) was once owned by Constable's father but is now owned by the National Trust and used as a Field Studies Centre. You can even take an art course here (call ☎ 01206-298283 for

information). **Bridge Cottage** *(NT; ☎ 01206-298260; tours £2; open 10am-5.30pm daily Apr-Sept; 10am-5.30pm Tues, Thur & Sat Mar; 10am-5.30pm Sat & Sun Oct-Feb)*, less than a mile (1.2km) from East Bergholt, features in some Constable landscapes and now houses a display about the famous painter. Guided tours operate three times daily, May to September. **Willy Lott's House**, of *Haywain* fame, is nearby. Willy was a neighbour and friend of Constable's.

Several bus companies operate services from Colchester to East Bergholt. It's better to come by train (get off at Manningtree), as you get a nice 1¾-mile (2.8km) walk along footpaths through Constable country. If you are in Manningtree, make a quick diversion and walk up the hill to the town of Mistly for a wonderful view over the estuary of the River Stour. The TIC in Colchester sells cycling maps of Dedham Vale.

HARWICH
☎ 01255 • pop 15,374

Although the old harbour is mildly interesting, the only reason to come here is to catch a ferry to Holland with **Stena Line** *(☎ 0870 570 7070)* or to Hamburg (Germany) or Esbjerg (Denmark) with **Scandinavian Seaways** *(☎ 0870 533 3000)*. There are direct train services to Harwich from London Liverpool St (£18, 1¼ hours).

SAFFRON WALDEN
☎ 01799 • pop 14,300

The curiously titled Saffron Walden gets its name from the saffron crocus cultivated in the surrounding fields, an activity that helped make this beautiful medieval town a bustling market centre from the 15th to the first half of the 20th century. There is a small-but-interesting museum and streets that are packed with antique shops.

The **TIC** *(☎ 01799-510444, fax 510445; 1 Market Place)* sells a useful town trail leaflet. You can use the Internet (£1.50 for 15 minutes) at **AS1** *(☎ 528045; Lime Tree Court)* in the centre.

The **museum** *(☎ 510333; adult/child £1.25/70p; open 10am-5pm Mon-Sat, 2pm-5pm Sun)* has a wealth of material and is well worth a visit. It includes a very interesting exhibit on local history and has an odd collection of objects from all over the world, including a mummy from Thebes. The ruins of

Walden Castle Keep, built around 1125, are next to the museum.

The Church of **St Mary the Virgin**, off Museum St, dates mainly from 1450–1525, when the town was at the height of its prosperity. It's one of the largest in the county and has some very impressive Gothic arches, decorative wooden ceilings and a 60m spire which was added in 1832. On the eastern side of the town is an ancient earthen **maze**; a path circles for almost a mile, taking you to the centre if you follow the right route.

Places to Stay & Eat
Most of the B&Bs are in tiny houses and have only one or two rooms, but there aren't too many tourists and you shouldn't have any problems finding somewhere to stay.

YHA Hostel (☎ 0870 770 6014; cnr Myddylton Place & Bridge St; beds per adult £9.50) is in the best-preserved 15th-century building in town.

Both **The Sun Inn** and the **Queen Elizabeth Inn** (☎ 520065, 5214894; 23 Fairycroft Rd; singles/doubles £22/40) are recommended for their old-world appeal and – thankfully – modern-day comforts. Rooms can be noisy on Friday and Saturday nights, but only until 11pm.

Archway Guesthouse (☎ 501500; 11 Church St; singles/doubles £35/55) is an odd place, with an unusual mix of decor and a huge collection of 'stuff'. The rooms are lovely.

Dorringtons (☎ 522093; 9 Cross St), a bakery, is the place to try for delicious, fresh pastries and sandwiches. Sandwiches cost from 80p to £1.50.

There are some lovely old pubs around town including the 16th-century **Eight Bells** (☎ 522790; 18 Bridge St), about three minutes' walk from the centre.

Getting There & Away
Stagecoach Cambus (☎ 01223-423554) bus No 102 runs hourly between Cambridge and Saffron Walden. **Biss Brothers'** (☎ 681 155) commuter bus No 38 leaves London Victoria coach station at 5pm each weekday, and returns from Saffron Walden at 6.55am (£7.60, two hours).

The nearest train station is Audley End, 2½ miles (4km) to the west. Trains leave from London Liverpool St every 20 minutes (£14.90, 1 hour).

AROUND SAFFRON WALDEN
Audley End House
Built in the early 17th century, this Jacobean mansion (EH; ☎ 01799-522399; adult £6.95; open noon-4pm Wed-Sun Apr-Sept) was used as a royal palace by Charles II, and was described by James I as 'too large for a king'. The 30 rooms on display house a fine collection of painting, silverware and furniture. It's set in a magnificent landscaped **park** (open 11am-6pm Wed-Sun), the handiwork of Capability Brown.

One mile west of Saffron Walden on the B1383, Audley End House has last admission at 5pm. Audley End train station is 1¼ miles (2km) from the house. **Stagecoach Cambus** (☎ 01223-423554) bus No 102 from Cambridge to Saffron Walden stops here.

Hertfordshire

Amid the ever-widening commuter belt surrounding London, the tiny county of Hertfordshire has somehow managed not to lose all of its open farmland to the suburban developer's bulldozer, which lends the area a charming pastoral quality. But it's not all daisies and buttermilk here, because Hertfordshire is also home to stunning St Albans, a predominantly Georgian town that dates back to Roman times, and Hatfield House, one of Britain's most important stately homes and the county's top attraction.

ST ALBANS
☎ 01727 • pop 120,700
St Albans is a beautiful cathedral city only 25 minutes by train from London, which ensures that it's one of the most popular day trips from the capital. And for good reason. Founded by the Romans as Verularium after their invasion of AD 43, it was renamed in the 3rd century after a Roman soldier, Alban, who had made the mortal error of sheltering a Christian priest in 209. His Samaritan instincts cost him his head, but he was England's first Christian martyr and the town soon became a major centre for pilgrimage.

Visitors with more earthly concerns will find St Albans worth a stop for its magnificent cathedral, outstanding Roman museum and the town's aesthetically pleasing mix of Tudor and Georgian architecture.

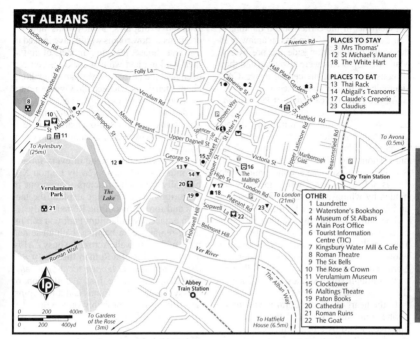

ST ALBANS

PLACES TO STAY
3 Mrs Thomas'
12 St Michael's Manor
18 The White Hart

PLACES TO EAT
13 Thai Rack
14 Abigail's Tearooms
17 Claude's Creperie
23 Claudius

OTHER
1 Laundrette
2 Waterstone's Bookshop
4 Museum of St Albans
5 Main Post Office
6 Tourist Information
   Centre (TIC)
7 Kingsbury Water Mill & Cafe
8 Roman Theatre
9 The Six Bells
10 The Rose & Crown
11 Verulamium Museum
15 Clocktower
16 Maltings Theatre
19 Paton Books
20 Cathedral
21 Roman Ruins
22 The Goat

SOUTHEAST ENGLAND

Orientation

St Peter's St, 10 minutes' walk west of the train station, is the focus of the town. St Peter's St becomes Chequer St and then Holywell Hill as it heads southwards. The marketplace is at the other end of St Peter's St, near the TIC. The cathedral lies to the west, off High St, with the ruins of Verulamium even farther to the west on St Michael's St. The Alban Way is a 6.5-mile (10.5km) path running from St Albans to Hatfield where you can visit the Jacobean Hatfield House (see Hatfield House later).

Information

The **TIC** (☎ 864511, fax 863533; **e** tic@ stalbans.gov.uk; Market Place; open 9.30am-5.30pm Mon-Sat Easter-June & mid-Sept–Oct; 9.30am-5.30pm Mon-Sat, 10.30am-4.30pm Sun July–mid-Sept; 10am-4pm Mon-Sat Nov-Easter) is in the grand town hall. It sells the useful Discover St Albans town trail (£1). The Official Visitors Guide is free and features a detailed town walk that covers all the sights. There are free guided walks of the town at 11.15am and 3pm on Sunday, Easter to September – meet at the **Clocktower** (High

St). On Wednesday and Saturday mornings the central marketplace really comes alive.

All the major banks and ATMs are on St Peter's St, near the TIC. The main **post office** (St Peter's St; open 9.30am-5pm Mon-Sat) is also in the town centre. You can check email for free in the **library** (☎ 737333; Malting Shopping Centre).

Apart from **Waterstone's** (10 Catherine St), we recommend **Paton Books** (34 Holywell Hill), a marvellous bookshop full of new titles and dusty old ones (including those hard-to-find ones) housed in an elegant 17th-century building.

There's a **laundrette** (13 Catherine St) off St Peter's St.

There are public toilets next to the Maltings Theatre, off Chequer St in the centre, and some more at the Verulamium Museum off St Michael's St.

St Albans Cathedral

In the 8th century, King Offa of Mercia had founded a Benedictine abbey on the site of Alban's martyrdom, but the actual church you see today dates from 1077, when the first Norman abbot, Paul, ordered the construction of a new one, albeit incorporating elements of the earlier Saxon building – you can see remnants of a Saxon archway in the southern aisle alongside the presbytery. Many Roman bricks were also used and they sit conspicuously in the central tower. Considerable restoration took place in 1877.

As you enter the cathedral (☎ 860780; admission by £3 donation; open 8.30am-5.45pm daily) you will notice the **murals** that decorate the Norman columns. They were painted by monks in the 13th century. One mural depicts Thomas Becket (southern side of the two pillars closest to the entrance) and above him is St Christopher. These paintings were hidden by whitewash after the Reformation and were not rediscovered until 1862.

The painted wooden panels of the choir ceiling date from the 15th century. The **Tower ceiling** is decorated with the red and white roses of the houses of Lancaster and York. The altar screen is mainly 16th century although some statues were added in the 19th century.

In the heart of the cathedral is **St Alban's shrine**, immediately behind the presbytery and overlooked by a beautifully carved oak **Watching Chamber**, dating from 1400. This is where monks would stand guard to ensure pilgrims didn't pilfer relics. As you leave the shrine, turn to your left to see a marble slab embedded with marine fossils which was once an ancient altarpiece.

There are guided tours at 11.30am and 2.30pm. In the southern aisle you can watch an audiovisual account of the cathedral's history. There are screenings from 10.30am to 4pm Monday to Saturday (with the last showing at 3.30pm Saturday) and 2pm to 5pm on Sunday. Screenings cost £1.50/1 per adult/child.

Verulamium Museum & Roman Ruins

Nowhere in England can you learn more about everyday life under the Romans than at this excellent museum (☎ 819339; St Michael's St; adult/child £3.30/2; open 10am-5.30pm Mon-Sat, 2pm-5.30pm Sun). The most impressive displays are in the **Mosaic Room**, where five outstanding floors uncovered between 1930 and 1955 are laid out. The most visually impressive is the Shell Mosaic, but the Lion and Sea God mosaics are also stunning.

The rest of the museum has plenty of interactive displays, audiovisuals and re-creations of how rooms would have looked in a Roman house, including models of craftsmen working and women cooking. You can even hear the citizens of Verulamium talking about their lives. Tickets allow you a return visit on the same day. You can take a free guided walk of the 'city' of Verulamium – essentially the grassed-over area where it once stood – from the museum at 3pm every Sunday.

On the second weekend of every month, the museum is 'taken over' by Legion XII, basically a bunch of actors togged out in centurions' uniforms who explain the tactics and formations of the Roman army.

In adjacent **Verulamium Park** you can inspect remains of a basilica, bathhouse and parts of the city wall. Across the busy A4174 are the remains of a **Roman theatre** (☎ 835 035; adult/child £2/1; open 10am-5pm daily) which appear to be just a collection of grassy ditches and mounds and a few ruins. The admission is probably only worth it if you're seriously keen on the Romans.

Museum of St Albans

The museum (☎ 819340; Hatfield Rd; admission free; open 10am-5pm Mon-Sat, 2pm-5pm Sun) begins with an exhibition of tools used between 1700 and 1950 by English tradesmen – coopers, wheelwrights, blacksmiths, lumberjacks and cabinet makers. It gives a rundown of the city's market and trade history and has good displays of Victorian memorabilia.

Other Things to See & Do

The medieval **clocktower** (High St; open 10.30am-5pm Sat, Sun & bank holidays Easter-Oct) was built between 1403 and 1412. It's the only medieval belfry in England and the original bell (called 'Gabriel') is still there. You can climb the 93 steps to the top for great views over the town.

The **Kingsbury Water Mill** (St Michael's St; adult/child £1.50/1; open 11am-5pm Tues-Sat, noon-6pm Sun Dec-Feb; 11am-6pm Tues-Sat, noon-6pm Sun Mar-Nov) was used for milling grain until 1936. It dates back to Saxon times but the current mill buildings are actually Elizabethan with a Georgian facade. There's a small museum here and a good coffee shop with home-cooking and outdoor seating.

With about 30,000 specimens, the **Gardens of the Rose** (☎ 850461; adult/child £4.50/free; open 9am-5pm Mon-Sat mid-June–mid-Oct), 3 miles (4.8km) southwest of St Albans, contain the world's largest rose collection.

Places to Stay

The following are all within five minutes' walk of the centre.

Mrs Thomas' (☎ 858939; 8 Hall Place Gardens; singles/doubles £28/42), highly recommended by us, has lovely, spacious rooms with garden views.

Avona (☎ 842216, fax 0956-857353; 478 Hatfield Rd; singles/doubles £24/45, doubles with en suite £55) is good value.

The White Hart (☎ 853624, fax 840237; 25 Holywell Hill; en-suite singles/doubles £54/70), an old half-timbered hotel with exposed beams and creaky floors, is just a couple of minutes' walk from the centre. Breakfast is £5 extra.

St Michael's Manor (☎ 864444, fax 848909; e smmanor@globalnet.co.uk; Fishpool St; singles £120-185, doubles £155-310) is St Albans' swankiest hotel, with well-appointed, comfortable rooms and lovely gardens. Weekend deals including dinner and champagne are available.

Places to Eat & Drink

St Albans has no shortage of places to eat, and they all offer pretty good grub.

Claudius (☎ 850527; 116 London Rd; meals around £6.50), a fun Italian restaurant, is covered from floor to roof with the owner's football memorabilia collection. Be sure to ask him to show you a card trick. Meals are simple and delicious.

Claude's Creperie (☎ 846424; 15 Holywell Hill; mains £6-9.50), with its rustic interior, has a huge menu combining French and Italian regional cooking.

Thai Rack (☎ 850055; 13 George St; 3-course lunch £10, à la carte mains around £6.95) has a peaceful, leafy interior.

Abigail's Tearooms (☎ 856939; 7 High St), with its lacy curtains, cream teas and elderly clientele, is in the Village Arcade.

The Goat (☎ 833934; 37 Sopwell Lane), just a few minutes' walk from the town centre, is a nice old pub in a Tudor-style building. It has live jazz from 12.30pm to 3pm on Sunday.

St Albans Beer Festival

They don't mess about with beer in England, and just to prove it, the South Hertfordshire branch of CAMRA (Campaign for Real Ale) puts on a four-day festival at the tail end of every September to celebrate the sanctity of good beer and its key role in the national culture. Close to 5000 people converge on the Civic Centre in St Peter's St to sample and talk about the 200 or so 'real' ales and ciders on display. (For more information on real ales see the Pubs special section.) Some of the beers are brewed locally just for the occasion, but most of them are available throughout the country. There's food available and, on Friday and Saturday evenings, there's music to keep everyone entertained. Depending on the day you go, tickets range from £1 to £5. For more information contact local TICs.

The Rose & Crown (☎ 851903; 10 St Michael's St) and, a little farther along, **The Six Bells** (☎ 856945; 16-18 St Michael's St) are both popular and cosy pubs with exposed beams, low ceilings and open fireplaces. Both offer traditional pub grub as well as more modern fare.

Getting There & Away

Rail is the most direct way to get to St Albans, although if you are coming from Heathrow you can catch Greenline bus No 724 which leaves hourly (£4.70, one hour). St Albans station is on Stanhope Rd, a 10-minute walk east of St Peter's St. Thameslink trains depart every 15 minutes from London King's Cross to St Albans station (£10.20, 23 minutes).

AROUND ST ALBANS
Hatfield House

England's most magnificent Jacobean mansion, Hatfield House (☎ 01707-262823; adult/child Sat-Thur £7/3.50, adult & child Fri £10.50, park only £2/1; open noon-4pm daily, gardens 11am-4pm daily Easter-Sept) is a red-brick and stone mansion, built between 1607 and 1611 for Robert Cecil, first earl of Salisbury and secretary of state to both Elizabeth I and James I. It was modelled on an earlier Tudor palace, built around 1497, where Elizabeth I spent much of her childhood. Only one wing of the

SOUTHEAST ENGLAND

royal palace survives and it can be seen in the gardens.

Inside, the house is extremely grand with a wonderful marble hall and famous portraits of Elizabeth and numerous English kings. The oak grand staircase is decorated with carved figures, including one of John Tradescant, the 17th-century botanist responsible for the gardens.

Five-course Elizabethan banquets, complete with minstrels and court jesters, are held in the great hall at 7.45pm on Tuesday (£32.50 per head), Friday (£35) and Saturday (£38). Book on ☎ 01707-262055.

The house can only be visited by guided tour, which depart as soon as a large enough group gathers. Hatfield House is 21 miles (34km) from London and 8 miles (13km) from St Albans. It's opposite Hatfield train station, and there are numerous trains from London King's Cross station (£7 day return, 25 minutes). **Greenline** (☎ 020-8668 7261) bus No 797 runs from London to Hatfield hourly and Greenline bus No 724 runs between St Albans and Hatfield every hour.

Shaw's Corner

This Victorian villa (NT; ☎ 01438-820307; Ayot St Lawrence; adult £3.60; open 1pm-5pm Wed-Sat & bank holiday Mon Apr-Oct) is where the playwright George Bernard Shaw died in 1950. It has been preserved much as he left it. In the garden is the revolving summerhouse (revolving to catch the sun) where he wrote several works including Pygmalion, the play on which the film My Fair Lady was based.

Bus No 304 from St Albans drops you at Gustardwood, 1¼ miles (2km) from Ayot St Lawrence.

Buckinghamshire

If it wasn't for the large collection of wonderful houses and stately homes – most of them now run by the National Trust – Buckinghamshire could easily be dismissed as uneventful commuter country. Yet the county's pleasant mix of urban and rural landscapes has attracted more than its fair share of well-known names, including the Rothschilds, who built a number of beautiful houses around Aylesbury. Buckinghamshire was also a favourite with the more poetic types:

John Milton lived in Chalfont St Giles, Robert Frost spent time in Beaconsfield and TS Eliot and Percy Bysshe Shelley both lived in Marlow, 100 years apart.

Stretching across the south of Buckinghamshire, the Chilterns are a range of chalky hills famous for their beech woods. The countryside is particularly attractive in autumn, and there are forest walks and mountain-bike trails in the Chilterns (see the boxed text 'Wendover Woods', later), plus footpaths along the Grand Union Canal which cuts across the county's northeastern edge on its way from London to Birmingham.

AYLESBURY
☎ 01296 • pop 52,000 • elevation 112m

Affluent Aylesbury has been the county town since 1725. Yet apart from being a transport hub with half-hourly trains to/from London Marylebone (£12.20, 54 minutes), it has very little to offer the visitor. The **TIC** (☎/fax 330559; 8 Bourbon St; open 9.30am-5pm daily Easter-Oct, 10am-4.30pm Nov-Easter) can provide general information on Buckinghamshire.

AROUND AYLESBURY
Waddesdon Manor

Baron Ferdinand de Rothschild needed a manor to house his art collection, Sévres porcelain and French furniture, so in 1870 he hired a French architect to build him a chateau-style house (NT; ☎ 01296-653211; adult £7; open 11am-4pm Thur-Sun Apr-June, Sept & Oct, 11am-4pm Wed-Sun July & Aug), which was completed in 1889. The baron used it for parties, but today your reason for visiting is to admire the astonishing collection of French bric-a-brac, from gold boxes to buttons. If these don't tickle your fancy, then the selection of paintings by Gainsborough, Reynolds and a number of 17th-century Dutch masters should do the trick. Downstairs, the family's extensive wine cellar is on show, but it's strictly look-don't-taste.

The **gardens** (adult £3; open 10am-5pm Wed-Sun Mar–mid-Dec) are also worth exploring, beginning with the Rococo-revival **aviary** and its breeds of exotic birds.

Admission to the grounds is by timed ticket. You can book in advance but must pay a £3 booking fee.

The chateau is 6 miles (10km) northwest of Aylesbury. From Aylesbury bus station,

Wendover Woods

About a mile northeast of the town of Wendover (off the B4009) are the **Wendover Woods** (☎ 01296-625825 for the forest ranger), 325 hectares of beechwood and conifer forest lining the northern edge of the Chiltern Hills. There are a number of walks you can do, ranging from the half-mile walk to the top of Coombe Hill, the highest point in the Chilterns at 260m, to the 2-mile (3.2km) firecrest trail. There are cycling routes and bridleways but if you don't want to be too active you can just come to this peaceful spot for a picnic.

The **TIC** (☎ 01296-696759, fax 622460; High St; open 10am-4pm daily) in the clocktower, Wendover, has information on the Chilterns, the Ridgeway path (see the Activities section at the start of this chapter) and the Wendover Woods. You can also pick up a walking map from the information stand at the woods themselves.

There are half-hourly train services to Wendover from London Marylebone (£11, 45 minutes). Aylesbury bus No 54 goes to Wendover every half-hour (15 minutes).

take Aylesbury bus Nos 16 or 17. The trip takes 15 minutes.

Claydon House

The decoration of Claydon's *(NT; ☎ 01296-755561; adult £4.40; open 1pm-5pm Sat-Wed Apr-Oct)* grand rooms is said to be England's finest example of the light, decorative rococo style that developed from the more ponderous baroque in early-18th-century France. Florence Nightingale lived here for several years and a museum houses mementos of her Crimean stay. Some scenes from the 1995 film *Emma* with Gwyneth Paltrow were filmed here.

Claydon House is 13 miles (21km) north-west of Aylesbury; buses drop you in Middle Claydon, 2 miles (3.2km) from the house.

BUCKINGHAM

The one-time county town (until Henry VIII gave the honour to Aylesbury in the mid-16th century) has been largely overrun by suburban commuters, but it remains a relatively quiet kind of place with a pleasant main street, Market Hill.

About 3 miles west of town is Stowe, the sort of private school so exclusive that its driveway is half-a-mile long. The extraordinary Georgian **gardens** *(NT; ☎ 01280-822850; adult £4.80; open 10am-5.30pm Wed-Sun Apr-Oct, Tues-Sun July & Aug)* on the school grounds cover 400 hectares and were worked on by the greatest British landscape gardeners, including Charles Bridgeman, William Kent and Capability Brown.

The gardens are best known for their 32 temples, created in the 18th century by the wealthy owner Sir Richard Temple (no kidding), whose family motto was *Templa Quam Delecta* (How Delightful are your Temples). There are also arches, lakes and a Palladian bridge among other buildings.

Last admission is at 4pm. There are no buses that go past the gardens. It's a £7 taxi ride from Buckingham.

Buckingham is served by hourly buses from Aylesbury (45 minutes, £2.10).

Wessex

The name won't mean a lot to you unless you've read any novels by Thomas Hardy, Dorset's most famous son, who set most of his stories in fictional Wessex. But the real Wessex was far from fictional; founded in the 6th century by the Saxon Cerdic, in the 9th century Wessex *was* England – the only sizable part of the Anglo-Saxon lands not overrun by the Danes. King Alfred (849–99, a great leader but a poor cake maker – see History in the Facts about England chapter) was its leader and, effectively, the first king of England. At its peak Wessex stretched west to Cornwall and east to Kent and Essex, but its heartland was modern-day Somerset, Dorset and Wiltshire.

Even further back in time, clues to the past glories of this region litter the landscape. The mysterious Stone Age monuments of Avebury and Stonehenge continue to enchant and intrigue visitors; Europe's most substantial Iron Age fort, Maiden Castle, can be found just outside Dorchester; and Romans left their marks at Bath and Dorchester, with more fragments scattered around. The great religious building programmes of the past millennium-and-a-half bestowed magnificent, now-ruined, charming or simply awe-inspiring cathedrals, minsters and abbeys, notably on Glastonbury, Shaftesbury, Wells Malmesbury and, above all, Salisbury. Stately homes at Wilton, Montacute and Longleat bear witness to the wealth of 16th- and 17th-century nobility, and the glorious construction continued into the 18th century in Bath's golden crescents and squares.

But if it's history that draws the crowds – stalking Bath's streets, marvelling at monumental edifices or snapping quaint medieval villages such as Lacock or Corfe Castle – there are plenty more reasons to stick around. Bristol's nightlife is largely unsung by those from outside the region, but it's up there with the best, and the city boasts plenty of fine restaurants to kick-start the evenings. Tired of looking at buildings? Seek out Wiltshire's crop circles and chalk figures, explore caves in Somerset or sift the pebbles for fossils in Dorset. And at the end of the day you can bed down in a medieval gatehouse, a converted windmill, a riverside boathouse or Bath's most regal crescent.

Highlights

- Exploring regal, Regency Bath
- Getting in touch with the ancestors at Avebury and Stonehenge
- Having it large on a wasted weekend in Bristol
- Walking the wilds of Exmoor
- Snapping stately Salisbury's cathedral and historic centre
- Exploring timeless villages like Corfe Castle, Lacock and Castle Combe

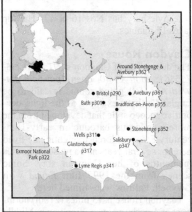

ORIENTATION & INFORMATION

The three counties of Wessex are roughly the same size; Dorset has the south coast, Somerset the north, and Wiltshire sits inland of them, wedged between Salisbury Plain and the southern edge of the Cotswolds. Bristol, in the central north of the region, is the main transport and industrial hub, and the only big city. With the exception of the Dorset and western Somerset cliffs and Exmoor National Park, the landscape is gently undulating.

In each city and town (and many villages) there are tourist information centres (TICs); most will book accommodation free of charge or with a small deposit, and all have plenty of leaflets, maps and information.

The **South West Tourist Board** covers a huge area from Gloucester and Dorset down to the Isles of Scilly. Its general website w www.visitsouthwestengland.com has tasters and snippets such as weather trends, plus links to localised sites. The other South West Tourism website **w** www.westcountrynow.com has more-specific accommodation information for Somerset.

ACTIVITIES

As such a large and contrasting area, Wessex has numerous options for outdoor activity. This section provides a few ideas, and more information is given in the main Activities chapter of this book, while suggestions for shorter walks and rides are given throughout this chapter. Regional tourism websites all contain walking and cycling information, and TICs all stock leaflets (free) plus maps and guides (usually £1 to £5) covering walking, cycling and other activities.

Walking

If you're a mile-eater, look no farther than the **South West Coast Path**; at over 600 miles (960km), this is Britain's longest national trail, and part of it strides through counties covered in this chapter (the rest is in the Devon & Cornwall chapter). The South West Coast Path starts at Minehead in Somerset, then loops round the Southwest Peninsula following the coasts of Devon and Cornwall, to come into Dorset at Lyme Regis and finish at Poole. Only the hardiest hikers do it all at once, but following a smaller section for just a week or so is very popular, eg, Minehead to Lynton, along the coast of Exmoor, or between Lyme Regis and Weymouth.

At the opposite end of the region, in northeast Wiltshire, the **Ridgeway** national trail

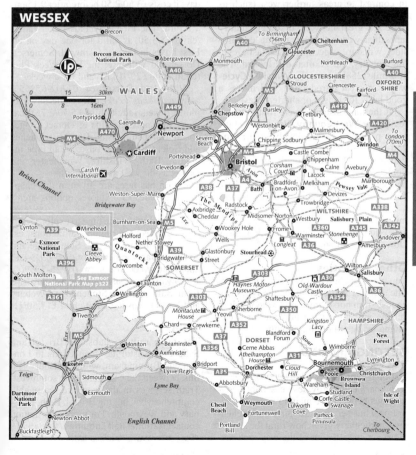

starts near Avebury Stone Circle and winds through the chalk hills of the North Wessex Downs to meet the River Thames at Goring. This 44-mile (71km) section makes an excellent three-day route. If you're still feeling strong, the Ridgeway national trail continues for another 41 miles (66km; and another three days) through the Chiltern Hills (described in the Southeast England chapter).

As with all long routes, you can use the South West Coast Path or the Ridgeway as a focus for short walks of just a few hours or one day. Stretches that are ideal for short or long walks include **Exmoor**, the **Mendip Hills** and the **Quantock Hills** in Somerset.

Cycling

The Wessex region is ideal cycling country. In contrast to areas farther west (such as Dartmoor), the hills are not too steep and there's a great network of quiet country lanes that weave through rolling countryside. Wiltshire especially is fantastic cycling country, but is often overlooked. The 160-mile (258km) circular **Wiltshire Cycleway** is a great introduction, and makes a good basis for longer or shorter rides.

Of the long-distance cycle routes in this region, the **West Country Way** is one of the most popular – a fabulously contrasting 250-mile (400km) jaunt from Bristol to Padstow in Devon, through the heart of Somerset via Glastonbury and Taunton. Of course, you can follow it for just a few days; from Bristol to Glastonbury, for example.

For off-road riding, good areas with a mix of country lanes, old unsurfaced routes and bridleways include the North Wessex Downs and Exmoor.

Other Activities

You won't get bored in Wessex. Apart from fine walking and cycling, active types can choose from horse riding on Exmoor, windsurfing and kitesurfing at Poole or scuba diving in the sea off Weymouth.

GETTING AROUND
Bus

National Express (☎ 08705 808080; w www .gobycoach.com) provides reasonable connections between the main towns.

Local bus services are fairly comprehensive, particularly given how rural the area is. However, in really out-of-the-way spots ser-

vices can be extremely sparse – some routes are served only once or twice a week – so plan carefully and be prepared to wait; in the wilds of Exmoor and rural Wiltshire, particularly, it pays to have your own wheels.

Route maps and timetables are available online for some (but not yet all) operators – websites are provided where relevant. Some local and county councils also produce comprehensive timetables covering all operators, some of which may be online.

The **First** group of companies (w www .firstgroup.com) is the largest service-provider in the region. You can buy normal one-way and return tickets; however, there are three other options. If you're travelling direct, the Corridor ticket allows unlimited travel on any single route (A to B) for one day; it costs £3.50/2.50 before/after 9.15am, and almost always works out cheaper than a return. The First Day Plus ticket (adult /child £5/3.50) is valid for one day on all First buses in Devon, Cornwall, Somerset, Dorset and Wiltshire; the First Week Plus (adult/child £20/10) is valid for a week.

Wilts and Dorset (☎ 01202-673555; w www.wdbus.co.uk) offers one-day Explorer tickets (adult/child £5.50/2.75) that cover transport on Wilts & Dorset, Stagecoach Hampshire Bus, Damory Coaches and Solent Blue Line buses in an area including Bath, Wiltshire, Winchester and Dorset as far west as Weymouth.

Return bus fares are given in this chapter when cheaper Explorer options aren't available.

For those with little time to explore, various tours visit the region's attractions, especially Wiltshire's finest: Stonehenge and Avebury. **Danwood Tours** (☎ 07977 929486) and **Mad Max Tours** (☎ 01225-325900; w www.madmaxtours.com) run one-day trips from Bath, visiting Stonehenge, Avebury and Lacock, costing adult/child £17.50/11.

Train

The main railway hubs are Bristol and Salisbury; Bristol has connections to London and Birmingham, while Salisbury is a link between the capital and the southwest. Train services in the west are reasonably comprehensive, linking Bristol, Bath, Salisbury and Weymouth. For more information contact **National Rail Enquiries** (☎ 0845 748 4950; w www.railtrack.co.uk).

The Freedom of the SouthWest Rover pass allows eight days' unlimited travel over 15 days in an area west of a line drawn through (and including) Salisbury, Bath, Bristol and Weymouth (£71.50 June to September, £61 October to May); there's a 34% discount for children and railcard holders.

Car

There are plenty of car hire companies in the region; rates start at around £30 per day, though single-day rentals can be much more. **UK Car Hire** (w www.uk-carhire.net) has pick-up locations in Bath, Bournemouth, Bristol, Salisbury, Swindon and Yeovil, and offers some good deals.

Bristol

☎ 0117 • pop 408,000

In size and vivacity, Bristol is unmatched in southwest England. With a range of excellent museums, galleries and modern attractions, there's plenty to do during the day, but it's the buzz after sundown that really kicks. Bristol is an artistic incubator that's spawned musical trendsetters such as Massive Attack, Portishead, Tricky, Nellee Hooper, Roni Size and Kosheen, and animated heroes Wallace and Grommit (assisted by plasticine maestro Nick Parks). There are plenty of bars, clubs, cinemas and restaurants in which to fuel that midnight oil-burning.

Bristol came to prominence as a port, despite its distance (6 miles, 10km) from the Severn estuary, and developed a range of manufacturing industries, making it a target for WWII bombing which devastated the centre. Typically, much reconstruction was unfortunate, to say the least; however, pockets of magnificent architecture remained, docks and warehouses have been rescued from ruin and some excellent new developments are brightening up the centre. Clifton, the graceful Georgian area to the west of the centre, has crescents, eateries and charm to rival Bath.

Bristol is an important transport hub, with connections north to the Cotswolds and the Midlands, southwest to Devon and Cornwall, and east to Bath (an easy day trip). South Wales is linked to Bristol across the Severn Bridge and the unimaginatively named Second Severn Crossing. Whether you approach by road or rail, the best is yet to come; don't be daunted by your first glimpses of Bristol.

History

The earliest known settlement was a Saxon village at the confluence of the Rivers Frome and Avon. A medieval bridge, lined with houses, became the focal point of Brigstow (which later became Bristol), and the city developed around what is now Bristol Bridge, largely funded by trading cloth and wine with France, Holland, Portugal and Spain. The centre of town was then around Wine, High, Broad and Corn Sts.

Several religious houses were established on high ground above the marshes, commemorated in the name of Temple Meads station. The importance of choosing high ground is shown by looking at Bristol's own leaning tower, attached to ruined Temple Church off Victoria St.

William Canynges, a wealthy merchant, paid for the original church on the site of St Mary Redcliffe and it was from Bristol that celebrated 'local hero' John Cabot (actually a Genoese sailor called Giovanni Caboto) sailed to discover Newfoundland in 1497. Soon Bristol's wealth was dependent on the triangular trade in slaves, cocoa, sugar, tobacco and manufactured goods with Africa and the New World.

By the 18th century the city was suffering from competition, from Liverpool in particular, and the Avon Gorge made it hard for large ships to reach the city-centre docks. By the 1870s, when new docks were opened at Avonmouth and Portishead, Britain's economic focus had shifted northwards. Bristol has since successfully turned its hand to the aerospace industry, communications and design.

Orientation

The city centre, to the north of the river and the Floating Harbour (actually a stretch of river controlled by a lock, hence being permanently full), is easy to get around on foot but very hilly. The central area around the markets and Corn Exchange, especially along Broad St, still retains some appealing architecture, mostly trade-linked; outside the exchange are four 17th-century bronze 'nails', pillars on which merchants' payments were

WESSEX

BRISTOL

BRISTOL

	PLACES TO STAY		PUBS, BARS & CLUBS	29	Clifton Suspension Bridge
7	St Michael's Guest House	5	The Junction		Visitor Centre
9	Oakfield Hotel	6	Lakota	30	Camera Obscura
10	Tyndalls Park Hotel	19	Smiles Brewery Tap	33	QEH Theatre
11	Washington Hotel	25	Baroque	35	Cabot Tower
12	Channings Hotel	26	The Park	36	Georgian House
18	Hotel du Vin	28	Coronation Tap	37	St George's
27	Victoria Square Hotel	39	Elbow Room	42	Red Lodge
31	Avon Gorge Hotel	40	Queen's Shilling	45	Colston Hall
34	Berkeley Square Hotel	41	Level	50	Corn Exchange
52	Bristol Backpackers	43	Bristol Academy	51	Trailfinders
62	Brigstow Hotel	44	Ether	53	Taxi Rank
66	Marriot Royal Hotel	47	Arc	54	Buses for Clifton Village;
75	Premier Lodge	48	Bierkeller		City Sightseeing
77	City Inn	55	Creation	57	BristolLife.co.uk
85	Bristol YHA Hostel	56	Tantric Jazz	61	St Nicholas Church
92	Baltic Wharf Caravan	60	Old Fish Market	64	Hippodrome
	Club Site	71	The Old Duke	65	Lord Mayor's Chapel
		72	Llandoger Trow	67	Bristol Cathedral
	PLACES TO EAT	73	Bed	68	Bristol Ferry Boat Co;
3	Thai Classic; Quartier Vert	81	Thekla		Bristol Packet Boat Trips
4	Touareg			69	Watershed
8	Deason's		OTHER	70	Old Vic
23	Rocatillos	1	Bristol Zoo Gardens	76	Temple Church
32	Fishers	2	Alma Laundrette	78	British Empire & Commonwealth
38	Vincenzo's	13	Royal West of England		Museum; Bristol Old Station
46	Pellegrino's City Fried Fish		Academy	79	St Mary Redcliffe Church
	& Chipped Potato House	14	Bristol Royal Infirmary	83	Industrial Museum
49	St Nicholas Market	15	Bus Station	84	Arnolfini Arts Centre
58	Mr Wolf; Bar-I	16	Galleries Shopping Centre	86	Wildwalk @tBristol; IMAX
59	Double Dutch	17	New Room	87	Tourist Information Centre
63	The Glassboat	20	Post Office	88	Explore @tBristol
74	Aqua	21	City Museum & Art Gallery	89	Maritime Heritage Centre
80	riverstation; severnshed	22	Internet Exchange	90	The Matthew
82	Mud Dock	24	STA Travel	91	SS Great Britain

WESSEX

made – hence the expression 'paid on the nail'. The genteel suburb of Clifton lies to the northwest, accessible by bus from the centre. Bristol's main shopping centre is in and around the undercover Galleries shopping mall in Broadmead, but there are more interesting one-offs, especially in Clifton and around Park St and Queens Rd.

The suburb of St Paul's, just northeast of the centre, remains a run-down, occasionally tense part of town with a heavy drug scene, best not visited alone at night.

The main train station is Bristol Temple Meads, a mile southeast of the centre and linked to it by regular buses. Some trains use Bristol Parkway, 5 miles (8km) to the north, just off the M4 and accessible from the centre by bus and train. A taxi is about £8.

The **bus station** (Marlborough St), to the northeast of the city centre, serves National Express coaches, and Badgerline buses to surrounding towns and villages.

Information

Tourist Office Bristol's **TIC** (☎ 926 0767, fax 915 7340; **w** www.visitbristol.co.uk; The Annexe, Wildscreen Walk, Harbourside; open 10am-6pm daily Mar-Oct, 10am-5pm Mon-Sat, 11am-4pm Sun Nov-Feb) stocks booklets describing the Bristol Heritage Trail (£3) and the Slave Trade Trail (£1.60), as well as mini-leaflets on literary and maritime walks and the David Haslam Bristol Visitors Map (£1.25).

Scattered around the city are **i-plus points**, free touch-screen kiosks providing tourist information.

Email & Internet Access There are several Internet options. **Internet Exchange** (☎ 929 8026; 23-25 Queens Rd; open at least 9am-7pm Mon-Sat, 11am-6pm Sun) is handy for Park St and charges £1 per 15 minutes.

BristolLife.co.uk (☎ 945 9926; 27-29 Baldwin St; open 10am-10pm Mon-Thur, 10am-

9pm Fri, 10.30am-9pm Sun) charges £4 per hour, less in the early morning, evening and on Sunday.

Travel Agencies There are branches of **STA Travel** (☎ 0870 167 6777; 43 Queen's Rd; open 9.30am-5.30pm Mon-Thur, 10am-5.30pm Fri, 11am-5pm Sat) and **Trailfinders** (☎ 929 9000; 48 Corn St; 9am-6pm Mon-Wed, Fri & Sat, 9am-7pm Thur, 10am-6pm Sun).

Laundry The handiest laundrette is **Alma Laundrette** (☎ 973 4121; 78 Alma Road; open 7am-9pm daily), just off Whiteladies Rd in Clifton.

Newspapers & Magazines The listings magazine *Venue* gives comprehensive details of what's on in Bristol (see Entertainment for details). You can get more news and information, including theatre, cinema and restaurant guides, in the *Bristol Evening Post*, or see its online version at **w** www .thisisbristol.com.

@tBristol

Next to the TIC in Millennium Square is an award-winning complex of attractions designed to illuminate and entertain, promoted together as @tBristol (☎ 0845 345 1235; **w** www.at-bristol.org.uk; Harbourside; open 10am-6pm daily).

Explore-@tBristol (adult/child £7.50/4.95) is Bristol's impressive, interactive science museum, with four themed zones covering brainpower, the history of technology, global communication and the Curiosity Zone – basically fascinating bits and pieces about the planet that aren't covered in the other three sections, including weather phenomena and the science of sound.

Wildwalk-@tBristol (adult/child £6.50/4.50) is similar but with the emphasis on the natural world, spanning the breadth of biology from DNA to dinosaurs, with a healthy dollop of enviro-info thrown in.

IMAX (adult/child £6.50/4.50) is another 3D, monster-screen cinema; the eye-popping films tend to relate to the other @tBristol attractions.

You can save money by purchasing combined tickets: adult/child £12/8.20 for Explore and Wildwalk or Explore and IMAX, £11/7.75 for Wildwalk and IMAX, and £16.50/11.45 for all three.

Look out for **Cary Grant** (born Archibald Leach in Bristol in 1904), unveiled in December 2001, among the many statues in Millennium Square.

Museums

The city's municipal museums (**w** www.bris tol-city.gov.uk/museums) are free and, unless otherwise stated, open 10am to 5pm, Saturday to Wednesday, April to October.

The **City Museum & Art Gallery** (☎ 922 3571; Queen's Rd; open daily year round) is an impressive edifice housing some interesting local ceramics and archaeological relics; other highpoints include collections of British (Millais, Leighton, Reynolds, Hepworth) and French (Pisarro, Renoir) painting, and good touring exhibitions.

More gritty is the **Industrial Museum** (☎ 925 1470; Princes Wharf, Wapping Rd; open 10am-5pm Sat-Wed Apr-Oct, 10am-5pm Sat & Sun Nov-Mar), illustrating the city's maritime, rail and aeronautical heritage; look out for the fine collection of model trains and the mock-up of Concorde's cockpit (the supersonic airliner was developed in Bristol). There are also examples of Bristol-built cars, buses and bikes. The steam-driven **Bristol Harbour Railway** (single/return £1/60p) runs along the wharf from outside the museum to SS *Great Britain*; the service operates several times on fortnightly weekends from March to October.

The **Georgian House** (☎ 921 1362; 7 Great George St) was built by 18th-century sugar merchant John Pinney and is immaculately presented, complete with period fixtures and fittings; the breakfast room (laid for the meal) and kitchen are particularly interesting. Overall it's broadly comparable with No 1 Royal Crescent in Bath – but smaller, free, and a lot less busy. It was here that Wordsworth and Coleridge had their first meeting with poet laureate Robert Southey, a Bristol lad himself.

The Elizabethan **Red Lodge** (☎ 921 1360; Park Row) was built in 1590 but much remodelled in 1730; it's now furnished in keeping with both periods. It houses fine 17th-century French engravings and boasts an attractive Tudor walled garden, but the highlight is the splendid Oak Room, with superb carved panels, doorframes and fireplace.

In the northern suburb of Henbury lies **Blaise Castle House Museum** (☎ 950 6789;

Henbury Rd); itself a late-18th-century house, the attractions of the social history museum inside include an array of vintage toys, costume displays and general Victoriana, such as a reconstructed school room. The Picture Room houses wonderful paintings from the City Museum's Victorian collection. On a hill stands a mock castle, in grounds laid out by Humphrey Repton. Across the road is **Blaise Hamlet**, a cluster of thatched cottages designed for estate servants in 1811 by John Nash; with its neatly kept green and flower-filled gardens, it's everyone's fantasy of a 'medieval' English village. Bus No 43 (45 minutes, every 15 minutes) passes the castle from Colston Ave; Bus No 1 (20 minutes, every 10 minutes) from St Augustine's Parade doesn't stop quite as close, but is quicker and more frequent.

British Empire & Commonwealth Museum

This new museum *(☎ 925 9480;* **w** *www.em piremuseum.co.uk; Clock Tower Yard; adult/ child £4.95/2.95; open 10am-5pm daily)*, opened in September 2002 in Brunel's marvellous old train station at Temple Meads, tells the story of 500 years of British exploration, trade and (somewhat dubiously) conquest, in a series of permanent displays and special exhibitions featuring artefacts, paintings, sound recordings, costumes and photographs.

Royal West of England Academy

Housed in a remarkable Grade II–listed building, the RWA *(☎ 973 5129;* **w** *www.rwa .org.uk; Queens Rd; adult/child £2.50/free; open 10am-5.30pm Mon-Sat, 2pm-5pm Sun)* opens its doors for contemporary exhibitions by its academicians and of selections from its collection, which includes key works from the St Ives school.

SS Great Britain

Bristol was home to the Victorian engineering genius Isambard Kingdom Brunel (1806–59), known for, among many other things, the Clifton Suspension Bridge. In 1843 Brunel designed the mighty ocean-going SS *Great Britain (☎ 929 1843;* **w** *www .ss-great-britain.com)*, the first large iron ship to be driven by a screw propeller (see the boxed text 'Kingdom, the (Steam) Power & the Glory'). For 43 years the ship served as a cargo vessel and a liner, carrying passengers as far as Australia before being damaged in 1886 near the Falkland Islands. The owners were not willing to have the ship repaired and sold it for storage; the ship remained in the Falklands for decades, forgotten and rusted, before it was towed to Bristol in 1970. Since then it has been undergoing restoration in the dry dock where it was originally built. You can see the huge propeller, and get a good idea of what the ship will look like once restoration is complete (planned for 2005).

WESSEX

Kingdom, the (Steam) Power & the Glory

Isambard Kingdom Brunel was born in Portsea in 1806 and at a tender age became one of Britain's most influential engineers. By 1826 he was appointed resident engineer on the Thames Tunnel, working with his father. When the river breached the tunnel in 1827 and again in 1828, Brunel made a number of descents in a diving bell and was seriously injured while rescuing workers; he saved several lives. While recovering, he entered a competition to design a bridge over the Avon at Clifton; although his original design was rejected (on the advice of Thomas Telford), his later suspension bridge was chosen as the best option, though not completed until after his death in 1864.

Brunel's subsequent achievements were numerous and lauded: he built more than 1000 miles of railway lines; designed the first great transatlantic steamship, the *Great Western*; and constructed the first iron-hulled, screw-propeller vessel, *Great Britain*, which can be visited in Bristol.

By any standards a workaholic (his honeymoon lasted only three days, taking in the opening of the Liverpool–Manchester Railway!), Brunel had a lighter side, too; while entertaining children with conjuring tricks, a coin became lodged in his throat, nearly killing him.

His last, immense project was the construction of the *Great Eastern*, at the time the world's largest passenger vessel. Plagued with management and funding problems, Brunel finally secured the ship's launch in 1858 – a PR disaster: chains snapped on capstans and men were killed. His health was damaged by these events and a subsequent seizure, he died shortly after, in 1859.

Moored nearby is a replica of John Cabot's ship *Matthew*, which undertook the journey from Bristol to Newfoundland in 1497.

Entrance is via the informative **Maritime Heritage Centre** (☎ 927 9856; *Great Western Dockyard, Gas Ferry Rd; adult/child £6.75/3.75; open 10am-5.30pm daily Apr-Oct, 10am-4.30pm Nov-Mar*), which celebrates Bristol's shipbuilding past through models, pictures and an audiovisual presentation.

Clifton & the Suspension Bridge

The genteel suburb of Clifton is often compared with Bath; it too boasts some splendid Georgian architecture, including Cornwallis and Royal York Crescents, but the day-to-day life of its residents, including a healthy student population, isn't dominated by tourism. The area effectively stretches from the bar-and-hotel enclave of Whiteladies Rd to Clifton Village and the river; the farther west you go, the posher the houses.

The much-photographed 75m-high **Clifton Suspension Bridge**, designed by Brunel, spans a dramatic stretch of the Avon Gorge and is both elegant and intriguing, with elements seemingly inspired by ancient Egyptian structures. Work on the bridge began in 1836 but wasn't completed until 1864, after Brunel's death. The bridge is an inevitable magnet for stunt artists and, more poignantly, suicides. A famous story relates how Sarah Ann Hedley jumped from the bridge in 1885 after a lovers' tiff. Her voluminous petticoats parachuted her safely to earth and she lived to be 85.

To get a feel for the magnitude of the achievement, visit the small **Clifton Suspension Bridge Visitor Centre** (☎ 974 4664; w *www.clifton-suspension-bridge.org.uk; Bridge House, Sion Place; adult/child £1.90/1.30; open 10am-5pm daily Apr-Oct, 11am-4pm Mon-Fri, 11am-5pm Sat & Sun Nov-Mar*), featuring displays on the history of bridges at Clifton and the competition that led to the building of Brunel's structure.

On Durdham Downs, overlooking the bridge, a rather tatty observatory houses a fascinating **camera obscura** (☎ 974 1242; *adult/child £1/50p; open from 12.30pm Mon-Fri, 10.30am Sat & Sun*), which offers some incredible views of the suspension bridge – and an illuminating insight into what folks did for entertainment in the days before television. Opening hours vary depending on the weather. Access to nearby **Ghyston Cave** (*aka Giant's Cave; adult/child £1/50p*) is through the observatory. The cave itself isn't up to much, but has a viewing platform in the side of the gorge to get that extra-special photo of the bridge.

Nearby is **Bristol Zoo Gardens** (☎ 973 8951; w *www.bristolzoo.org.uk; Clifton; adult/child £8.60/5; open 9am-5.30pm summer, 9am-4.30pm winter*), a facility that aims to promote conservation as well as entertain. Attractions include a group of West African gorillas, part of an ongoing conservation project in Cameroon, as well as underwater walkways for viewing seals and penguins. There's also a Brazilian rainforest section where you can get up close and personal with agouti, capybara and golden lion tamarins.

Bus Nos 8 and 9 (10 minutes, 8 hourly) run every 15 minutes to Clifton and the zoo from St Augustine's Parade; add another 10 minutes from Temple Meads. Alternatively, if you're keen for a stiff walk, you can cut from Park St through Brandon Hill Park, pausing to climb **Cabot Tower** (*open 8am-dusk daily*), built in 1897 to commemorate John Cabot's voyage and offering panoramic views of the city.

Bristol Cathedral

Originally founded as the church of an Augustinian monastery in 1140, this church (☎ 926 4879; *College Green; open 8am-6pm daily*) gained cathedral status in 1542. A remarkably fine Norman chapter house and gate remain, the attractive Lady Chapels house entertaining carvings and heraldic glass, and there's a 14th-century choir with fascinating misericords, but much of the nave and the west towers were designed by George Street in 1868. The south transept shelters a rare Saxon carving of the 'Harrowing of Hell', discovered under the chapter-house floor after a 19th-century fire.

St Mary Redcliffe

Described as 'the fairest, goodliest and most famous parish church in England' by Queen Elizabeth I in 1574, St Mary Redcliffe (☎ 929 1487; *Redcliffe Way; open 8.30am-5pm Mon-Sat*) is a stunning piece of perpendicular architecture with a soaring 89m-high spire and a grand hexagonal porch that easily outdoes the cathedral in splendour. Check out the wonderful vaulted ceiling with its fine gilt bosses, then step outside the south porch into the graveyard to spot the resting place of the favourite church cat, sent to his maker in 1927.

Lord Mayor's Chapel

Once the chapel of St Mark's Hospital, the Lord Mayor's Chapel (☎ 929 4350; Park St; open 10am-noon & 1pm-4pm Tues-Sun) is a medieval gem squeezed in between shops opposite the cathedral and packed with 16th-century stained-glass windows, medieval monuments and ancient tiles. The church-loving poet John Betjeman dubbed it 'for its size one of the very best churches in England…'

New Room (John Wesley's Chapel)

Tucked away among the shops in the Broadmead shopping precinct, the New Room (☎ 926 4740; 36 The Horsefair; admission free; open 10am-4pm Mon-Sat) was the world's first Methodist chapel when it opened in 1739. John Wesley, whose equestrian statue stands in the courtyard, preached from its double-decker pulpit. Upstairs, visit the old living quarters, with rooms for John and Charles Wesley and Francis Asbury.

Organised Tours

The **Bristol Corps of Guides** (☎ 962 8275; e annemitchell@blueyonder.co.uk) organises a variety of themed walking tours between April and September, including harbourside walks (11am Sunday) and 'Trails of the Unexpected' (7.30pm Thursday), looking at the more offbeat aspects of Bristol. Tours, which cost £3 and last 90 minutes, depart from the TIC.

From Easter to September, **City Sightseeing** (☎ 926 0767) runs hop-on, hop-off open-top bus tours visiting 19 points in Bristol, including all the major attractions. Tickets (£7/6) can be bought on board the bus or from the TIC. Buses leave St Augustine's Parade, outside the Hippodrome, hourly (every 30 minutes July to September).

Bristol Packet Boat Trips (☎ 926 8157; w www.bristolpacket.co.uk) is one of a number of companies running boat trips (with commentary) around the historic harbour. Cruises cost adult/child £3.80/2.50, last about 45 minutes and depart from the harbour next to the Watershed several times

daily, from March to October. Ask about other cruises.

For a different perspective altogether on the city, take a ride with **Bristol Balloons** (☎ 963 7858, fax 963 9555; w www.bristol -balloons.co.uk). Flights, which usually take off from Ashton Court, last about an hour and cost £135 per person.

Special Events

St Paul's Carnival (☎ 944 4176), a smaller version of London's Notting Hill Carnival, livens up the first Saturday of each July. There's a Harbour Festival (☎ 922 3148) in July, and not-to-be-missed hot-air balloon (☎ 953 5884) and kite (☎ 977 2002) festivals in Ashton Court, across Clifton Suspension Bridge, in August and September. Find information about all events on the TIC website at w www.visitbristol.co.uk.

Places to Stay

The TIC provides the free *Visitors Guide*, listing plenty of accommodation options and including a handy map.

Camping & Hostels The **Baltic Wharf Caravan Club Site** (☎ 926 8030; Cumberland Rd; pitches per tent/person £2/3.75-4.75) is 1½ miles (2.5km) southwest of the centre, just southwest of SS *Great Britain*. Bookings aren't taken, so arrive early at the weekend as there are just three tent pitches. The Baltic Wharf Loop Bus (No 500, 10 minutes, every 30 minutes Monday to Saturday) runs from Temple Meads and St Augustine's Parade, but the nicest way to get here is on the ferry (see Getting Around).

Accommodation in Bristol tends to be pricey, though there are two large, well-appointed hostels.

Bristol YHA Hostel (☎ 0870 770 5726, fax 927 3789; e bristol@yha.org.uk; Hayman House, 14 Narrow Quay; dorm beds £12.75, twin rooms from £26) is a 92-bed converted warehouse across the harbour from the happening Waterfront nightlife area and close to all attractions.

Bristol Backpackers (☎ 925 7900; e info@ bristolbackpackers.co.uk; 17 St Stephen's St; dorm beds £13) is an excellent place in the old city. Rates include free tea and coffee, and there's cheap Internet access, a bar and discounts on many attractions. This eco-friendly hostel is a lively, secure and central choice.

WESSEX

B&Bs & Hotels Finding sensibly priced, central B&Bs is quite a task. There are several places off Whiteladies Rd in Clifton, especially on St Paul's Rd; most masquerade as hotels and charge accordingly.

Oakfield Hotel (☎ 973 5556, fax 974 4141; 52-54 Oakfield Rd; singles/doubles from £30/40) is a large, rather tired-looking B&B but it's clean, well located and about as reasonably priced as you'll find in this neck of the woods.

St Michael's Guest House (☎/fax 907 7820; 145 St Michael's Hill; singles/doubles £30/40) is a simple, spick-and-span B&B over a decent café near the university. Bathrooms are shared, but it's friendly, central and good value.

Tyndalls Park Hotel (☎ 973 5407, fax 923 7965; e email@tyndallsparkhotel.co.uk; 4 Tyndalls Park Rd; B&B en-suite singles/doubles Mon-Thur £48/58, Fri-Sun £40/50) is an elegant Victorian house, one of the best places in the Whiteladies Rd enclave.

Channings Hotel (☎ 973 3970, fax 973 6394; 20 Pembroke Rd; B&B en-suite singles/doubles Sun-Thur £50/60, Fri & Sat £45/55) is a grand, ivy-clad pub which also serves decent bar food (mains £4 to £9). It's handy for both Clifton Village and Whiteladies Rd nightlife.

Washington Hotel (☎ 973 3980, fax 973 4740; e washington@cliftonhotels.co.uk; St Paul's Rd; B&B en-suite singles/doubles Mon-Thur £53/67, Fri-Sun £39/52) is the simplest and most reasonable of the row on St Paul's Rd. It has a few singles with shared bathrooms that go for £35, or £30 at the weekend.

The university offers B&B in its **Hawthorns** and **Royal Fort Gatehouse** buildings (☎ 954 5900, fax 923 7188; e client -services-office@bris.ac.uk; Woodland Rd, Clifton; singles/doubles £49.35/63.45) year round; most rooms have an en suite.

As a chain hotel, **Premier Lodge** (☎ 0870 700 1342, fax 0870 700 1343; w www.pre mierlodge.com; Kings St; en-suite doubles £49.95) may not be original or exciting, but it's good value and smack in the middle of town, part of the old Llandoger Trow pub.

Victoria Square Hotel (☎/fax 973 9058; e victoriasquare@btopenworld.com; Victoria Square; B&B en-suite singles/doubles Mon-Thur £60/80, Fri-Sun £48/58) is a gracious Victorian building on a quiet square in Clifton Village.

Upmarket **Avon Gorge Hotel** (☎ 973 8955, fax 923 8125; e info@avongorge-hotel-bris tol.com; Sion Hill, Clifton; doubles Mon-Thur £112/122, doubles Fri-Sun £85) is certainly a classy place, but the main attraction is the terrace overlooking the suspension bridge.

City Inn (☎ 925 1001, fax 907 4116; e bristol@cityinn.com; Temple Way; doubles Mon-Thur £89, Fri-Sun £65) tries hard to be a designer hotel instead of a standard business-traveller haunt, with CD players and trendy decor; irrespective, it's good value at weekends, and its **City Café** restaurant serves fine modern British cuisine.

Berkeley Square Hotel (☎ 925 4000, fax 925 2970; e berkeley@cliftonhotels.com; 15 Berkeley Square; singles/doubles Mon-Thur from £96/117, Fri-Sun from £54/85), a stylish three-star place, has a sleek wine-bar-cum-diner on one of the centre's classier squares.

It's of note that **Hotel du Vin** (☎ 925 5577, fax 925 1199; e info@bristol.hotelduvin.com; The Sugar House, Narrow Lewins Mead; twins or doubles from £115) is a converted warehouse complex. But the main point is that it's trés, trés chic, cheri. The **bistro** is well regarded, and there's an amazing humidor.

Brigstow Hotel (☎ 929 1030, fax 929 2030; e brigstow@fullers.co.uk; Welsh Back; rooms Mon-Thur from £130, B&B doubles Fri-Sun from £85) is another designer joint, modern and hi-tech (plasma-screen TV in the bathrooms) but also extremely comfortable and in a great spot by King St and Bristol Bridge.

The marble-floored lobby of the **Marriott Royal Hotel** (☎ 925 5100, fax 925 1515; e bristol.royal@marriotthotels.co.uk; College Green; rooms £145, B&B singles/doubles from £69/99) introduces the grandest place in town. Decor is 'sumptuous' – read floral – and it's got all the trimmings (swimming pool, two classy restaurants, cocktail bar).

Places to Eat

For cheap, quick grub head to **St Nicholas Market** (open Mon-Sat), behind St Nicholas St, where classics such as bangers and beans, jacket spuds and toasties are all less than £3, or pick up tasty olive bread and cheese for a picnic.

Pellegrino's City Fried Fish & Chipped Potato House (☎ 927 s3580; 17 Christmas Steps; cod & chips £2.85; closed Sun) has the longest name but smallest premises of any eatery in town; it's a shonky, oak-beamed 1590 house doling out fine fish and chips.

Rocatillos *(☎ 929 7207; 1 Queen's Row; mains £4.50-6; open 8am-5pm Mon-Thur, 8am-8.30pm Fri & Sat, 10am-5pm Sun)* is a cool café-diner, perfect for hangover-cure breakfasts (£3.50 to £6), burgers and Tex-Mex staples.

Mr Wolf *(☎ 927 3221; 33 St Stephen's St; takeaway/eat-in noodles £3/4; closed Sun)* is a find: a chilled noodle bar with colourful decor, great (and cheap) chow, beer and late opening (to 2am Friday and Saturday).

Double Dutch *(☎ 929 0433; 45-47 Baldwin St; pancakes £2.70-6.50)* is unique, a simple vault restaurant with simple ideas – fabulous pancakes, sweet or savoury, plus other classic Dutch dishes such as garlic sausage and waffles.

Vincenzo's *(☎ 926 0908; 71a Park St; mains £5.30-11)*, a stalwart on the scene, has remained aloof from pretensions, serving up authentic Italian fare on its roof terrace.

Popular spots for relaxed snacks include the café-bars in the **Watershed** *(☎ 927 5101; 1 Canon's Rd; mains £5-6)* and the **Arnolfini** *(☎ 927 9330; 16 Narrow Quay; sandwiches & wedges £3.75-5)*, trendy arts complexes on St Augustine's Reach overlooking the waterfront; both offer quick, tasty meals and pleasant spots for a tipple at night.

Mud Dock *(☎ 934 9734; 40 The Grove; mains £5-7)*, over the eponymous bike shop, serves ciabatta and meze in a converted warehouse with a balcony terrace overlooking the wharf. By night the drinks get stronger, the tunes get phatter and the hipsters chatter.

riverstation *(☎ 914 4434; The Grove; mains £10-15)*, in a postmodern building, also has water views and a good deli; both cuisine and interior are sleek and chic in the Conran mould. Set lunch (2/3 courses £11.50/13.75) is good value, as is the café hour deal (main plus drink £8; available from 6pm to 7.15pm, Sunday to Friday).

severnshed *(☎ 925 1212; The Grove; lunch £5.50-10, dinner mains £9-15)*, next door, is a light, bright converted boatshed; you'll find meze and salad by day, stiff drinks, jazz, fish and fusion cuisine after sundown.

Waterfront **Aqua** *(☎ 915 6060; Welsh Back; mains £8-17)* is ice-cool, a magnet for the beautiful and the business-minded: expect modern British cuisine and fish, though many come for sipping not supper.

The Glassboat *(☎ 929 0704; Welsh Back; mains £12-19; closed Sun)* is the spot for romance, a beautifully converted barge on Welsh Back with world cuisine and lunch deals (mains £6).

Over in classy Clifton Village, relaxed, upmarket dining is the norm. **Fishers** *(☎ 974 7044; 35 Princess Victoria St; mains £9-16.50; closed lunch Sun & dinner Mon)* plies its punters with superbly cooked fish, plus seafood platters for gourmands (£19.50 to £36).

Among the bars on Whiteladies Rd are several interesting options.

Thai Classic *(☎ 973 8930; 87 Whiteladies Rd; 2-course lunch £6, mains £5-9)* has a balanced menu of Thai and Malaysian food.

Next door, **Quartier Vert** *(☎ 973 4482; 85 Whiteladies Rd; mains £10.50-18.50)* is an impeccable modern restaurant; excellent fish and meat dishes have a French bias.

Touareg *(☎ 904 4488; 77 Whiteladies Rd; mains £15)* looks, smells and tastes like a souk – tagine, couscous and lamb dominate. Meze at lunch or early evening (2/3 courses for £10/13); open 6pm to 8pm Sunday to Friday) is a good introduction.

Deason's *(☎ 973 6230; 43 Whiteladies Rd; mains £13-23; closed lunch Sat & dinner Sun)* is the epitome of modern British dining, arguably the best restaurant in Bristol – bring someone you want to impress.

Old Possums Wine Bar *(☎ 973 2828; 2B Chandos Rd; mains £4-5)* is a chilled little place with funky tunes and good fajitas, lasagne and fisherman's pie. Chandos Rd boasts several other fine eateries, too. To get there, turn right off Whiteladies Rd past the main bar drag onto Ashgrove Rd, follow the road round and take the first left onto Hampton Park, which becomes Chandos Rd.

Entertainment

The fortnightly listings magazine *Venue* *(w www.venue.co.uk; £1.90)* gives the lowdown on what's on in Bristol and Bath – basically it's *Time Out* for the two cities, with details of theatre, music, exhibitions, bars, clubs and anything else in the entertainment field. There are a number of freebie mags: *Synergy* is the best for bars, clubs and gigs, while *Folie* is more upmarket and style-oriented; both appear monthly.

Pubs & Bars Like most cities, Bristol is becoming blessed (or cursed) by chains and trendy café-bars. Fortunately, there are still a few honest pubs to enjoy here, and liberal licensing laws mean that there are several hotspots for night owls.

Llandoger Trow *(☎ 926 0783; King St)* has been around since 1664 – as attested to by the flag-stoned floor – and may have provided the inspiration for the Admiral Benbow in *Treasure Island*. It may also have been where Daniel Defoe met Alexander Selkirk, the real-life Robinson Crusoe who inspired the book. Part of the same building is **Bed**, a youthful café-bar aiming for retro-chic (lots of beige velvet) and with good pizzas (£4.50 to £7.25).

The **Old Fish Market** *(☎ 921 1515; 61 Baldwin St)* has excellent draught ales and a wonderful mural depicting the fish market. For the peckish, there's a renowned range of pies (£6 to £7).

A must for ale fans is a visit to the **Smiles Brewery Tap** *(☎ 921 3668; Colston Yard, Colston St)*, a snug little boozer at the front of Bristol's finest brewery – sauce from source to stomach in seconds. Two-hour group tours *(☎ 01275-375894; w www.smiles.co.uk; admission £9.50; tours at 7pm Monday to Thursday)* of the brewery include beer tastings and buffet food.

Coronation Tap *(☎ 973 9617; Sion Place)*, up near the suspension bridge, will appeal to cider-lovers. It usually has five varieties of the adult apple juice available.

In the same area, **White Lion Inn** *(☎ 973 8955; Prince's Buildings, Sion Hill)* pretends to be a brasserie-bar, but the terrace with bridge views is its real *raison d'etre*.

Of the hip café-bars and pre-club drinking holes, the best are **The Park** *(☎ 940 6101; 37 Triangle West)* for bohemian feel and good oriental food; **Ether** *(☎ 922 6464; 2 Trenchard St)* for retro styling and cocktails; **Baroque** *(☎ 929 9322; 2 Byron Place)* for airy, attitude-free ambience; and **Bar-I** *(☎ 930 0951; 29 St Stephen's St)* for the inside track on the best club nights – coaches to the big venues are laid on from here. These places all have licences till 2am at the weekend, and DJs spin funky house, hip-hop and chilled beats.

Arc *(☎ 922 6456; 27 Broad St)* is a dark, slightly kitschy little disco bar-club with a small dance floor and unique styling.

The Junction *(51-52 Stokes Croft)* has DJs nightly and is a good spot to investigate the post-bar options.

Elbow Room *(☎ 930 0242; 64 Park St)* is one of a small chain of bar-club-pool-halls; there's usually a cover charge at the weekend, and plenty of tables to practise hustling.

Queen's Shilling *(aka Q/-; ☎ 926 4342; 9 Frogmore St)* is arguably the city's most popular gay bar, with DJs and late licences.

Clubs Trendy nightspots come and go with alarming frequency. Two hot areas are the Harbourside development (Canon's Rd), past the Watershed, and Stokes Croft running north from the bus station; bear in mind that the latter is a rather insalubrious area to wander after dark. Admission charges of £5 or over are the norm, depending on the night. Other bar-and-club ghettos include Baldwin St (brash) and Welsh Back (sleek and chic).

Lakota *(☎ 942 6208; 6 Upper York St)*, just off Stokes Croft, is a long-time Bristol favourite dishing up house with acid inclinations.

At **Thekla** *(☎ 929 3301; The Grove)*, a trawler moored next to riverstation, house and drum'n'bass dominate the main floor, with chill-out upstairs.

Funk, disco, breaks and tribal house power **Level** *(☎ 902 2001; 24 Park Row)* in a cool space designed to resemble a '70s airport lounge.

Bristol Academy *(☎ 0870 711 2000; Frogmore St)* is a big venue pulling appropriately sized names – Nitin Sawhney, Gilles Peterson and Scratch Perverts have taken to the decks of late, and live gigs have included Ian Brown, Suede and Sonic Youth.

Creation *(☎ 922 7177; 13-21 Baldwin St)* is the daddy of Bristol's clubs, popularity guaranteed by the ever-expanding Slinky franchise.

Live Music The **Old Duke** *(☎ 927 7137; 45 King St)*, a relaxed, chatty pub with a vibrant feel, hosts regular jazz and blues sessions.

Tantric Jazz *(☎ 940 2304; 39 St Nicholas St)* has live jazz every night of the week and is a welcome escape from the soulless chain bars in the Corn St area. This cool café-bar opens to 1am most nights.

Bierkeller *(☎ 926 8514; w www.bristol bierkeller.co.uk; All Saints St)* is a legendary place that has played host to plenty of rock stars; it still hosts some hot newcomers and older legends. Bigger names play the **Bristol Academy** (see the previous Clubs section).

Theatre, Cinema & Concerts The Hippodrome (☎ 0870 607 7500; St Augustine's Parade) largely hosts musicals with a smattering of opera, ballet and concerts.

The **Old Vic** (☎ 987 7877; w www.bristol-old-vic.co.uk; King St) sticks with classic and contemporary drama, with occasional comedy and dance.

Colston Hall (☎ 922 3686; Colston St) stages an eclectic mix of opera, comedy, world music and pop.

QEH Theatre (☎ 925 0551; w www.qehtheatre.com; Jacob's Wells Rd) is even more unpredictable – drama, dance, comedy, exhibitions and jazz are all here.

St George's (☎ 923 0359; w www.stgeorgesbristol.co.uk; Great George St) is an incredible old converted church that hosts regular classical, jazz and world-music concerts.

Arnolfini Arts Centre (☎ 929 9191; w www.arnolfini.demon.co.uk; 16 Narrow Quay) stages performance art and contemporary dance, as well as housing an exhibition space and one of the city's art-house cinemas.

Watershed (☎ 927 5100; w www.watershed.co.uk; 1 Canon's Rd), nearby, is another cinema with a steady diet of foreign and left-of-centre films.

Getting There & Away

Bristol is 115 miles (185km) from London, 75 miles (121km) from Exeter and 50 miles (81km) from Cardiff.

Air Eight miles (13km) southwest of town, off the A38 you'll find **Bristol International Airport** (☎ 0870 121 2747; w www.bristolairport.co.uk). Most flights are holiday charters to Mediterranean resorts, but **British Airways** (☎ 0845 773 3377), **Go** (☎ 0870 607 6543), **KLM** (☎ 0870 575 0900) and **Ryanair** (☎ 0541 569569) also fly to domestic and mainland European destinations.

Bus The bus company **Flightlink** (☎ 0870 575 7747) has a bus No 200 which runs at least every two hours to Heathrow Airport (single/return £26.50/28, two hours) and Gatwick Airport (£30/33.50, 3½ hours).

National Express coaches go to London Victoria Coach Station (economy return £19.50, 2½ hours, at least hourly), Cardiff (£8.75, 1¼ hours, six daily), Birmingham (£18, two hours, six daily), Exeter (£14, two hours, five daily), Plymouth (£24.50, 2½ hours, four daily) and Penzance (£36, 6½ hours, two daily). There are also daily buses to Barnstaple (£18.50, three hours), Nottingham (£24.50, 4½ hours), Oxford (£17, three hours) and Stratford-upon-Avon (£17.50, 2½ hours).

Local buses also operate out of Marlborough St bus station. Bus Nos X39, 339 and 332 run to Bath (return £3.90, 50 minutes) several times an hour. No 376/976 goes to Wells (one hour, hourly), and No 673 runs to Cheddar (£3.75, 1½ hours, roughly hourly). You'll need to change in Wells or Bath for most destinations in Somerset and Wiltshire.

Train Bristol is an important rail hub, with regular connections to London Paddington (SuperAdvance return £27, 1¾ hours, half-hourly). Most trains (except those to the south) serve both the Temple Meads and Parkway stations.

Only 20 minutes away, Bath makes an easy day trip (single £4.60, 15 minutes, at least every 15 minutes). There are frequent links to Cardiff (saver return £11.80, 45 minutes, hourly), Exeter St Davids (saver return £22.40, one hour, hourly), Oxford (saver return £25.60, 1½ hours, hourly) and Birmingham (saver return £32, 1½ hours, hourly).

Getting Around

To/from the Airport The **Bristol International Flyer** runs buses to the airport from Marlborough St bus station and Temple Meads train station (single/return £4/6, 30 minutes, half-hourly from 5am to 11pm). A taxi to the airport costs around £15.

Bus Tickets cost around £1 (eg, city centre to Clifton single/return 90p/£1.30). First-Day tickets (adult/child £3/2.15 before 9am Monday to Friday, £2.50/2.15 all other times) are valid on all buses for one day in the Greater Bristol area. A Night Bus Pass costs £1.50. Note that most bus numbers are prefaced by 50- outside peak hours; hence, bus No 8 becomes No 508.

Bus Nos 8 and 9 (10 minutes) run every 15 minutes to Clifton from St Augustine's Parade; add another 10 minutes from Temple Meads. The Baltic Wharf Loop Bus (No 500; 10 minutes, half-hourly Monday to

WESSEX

Saturday) runs from Temple Meads and St Augustine's Parade.

Taxi The taxi rank on St Augustine's Parade is central but not a good place to hang around late at night. There are plenty of companies; try **Bristol Hackney Cabs** (☎ 908 0008).

Car & Motorcycle As with most major cities, the one-way systems seem designed to confuse, and parking can be a problem. Park-and-Ride services (☎ 922 2910; return £2.50, every 10 minutes Monday to Saturday) operate at Portway, Bath Rd, Tollgate and Long Ashton; they're well signed on routes into the city.

Bicycle Hilly as Bristol is, masochists might want to hire bikes at **Blackboy Hill Cycles** (☎/fax 973 1420; 180 Whiteladies Rd; £8/day; open 9am-5.30pm Mon-Sat). To get you in the mood, the shop is at the top of a hefty climb.

Boat The nicest way to get around is to use **Bristol Ferry Boat Co** (☎ 927 3416; w www .bristolferryboat.co.uk) boats that ply the Floating Harbour every 20 minutes (weekends only in winter), from April to September, stopping at the SS *Great Britain*, Hotwells, Baltic Wharf, the centre (by Watershed), Bristol Bridge, Castle Park and Temple Meads. A short hop is £1.20/80p, or pay £5/2.50 for a day's unlimited travel.

Bath

☎ 01225 • pop 85,200 • elevation 133m
How is it Bath only has four letters and one syllable? Even the brashest of northerners will insert an R and a couple of extra As – Baaaaarth. That's because it's oh-so-grand, darling; everyone knows it, and the grandeur attracts tourists like flies around manure. For much of the past 2000 years the city's fortune has revolved around its hot springs and the visitors that the water has attracted. The wealth begat building and the glorious Georgian architecture that has won Bath Unesco World Heritage Site status.

Like Florence, Bath is an architectural gem. It too has a shop-lined, much-photographed bridge (Pulteney Bridge, designed by Robert Adam and built in 1774).

Like Florence, it can also seem entirely populated by tourists with camcorders instead of faces. Of course, the city wouldn't have retained its wealth without tourism, and it's a gorgeous town, busy or not. When sunlight brightens the honey-coloured stone, and buskers and strollers fill the streets and line the river, only the most churlish would deny its charm. Head up some of the steep hills and you can even find pockets of Georgiana that only the residents seem to appreciate. Once you've finished eyeballing past glories, today's Bath also has restaurants and bars to compete with the best.

Inevitably, Bath also has its share of residents for whom affluence is somebody else's success story. For all the glitzy shops, you'll still see beggars on the streets.

The big news is that at long last the city has a spa again; the old Hot and Cross Baths have been restored and incorporated into a brand-new spa complex designed by Nicholas Grimshaw (the architect behind the Eurostar Terminal at Waterloo) and opened in 2002.

History

Prehistoric (possibly Celtic) peoples probably knew about the hot springs, and legend has it that King Bladud, a Trojan refugee and father of King Lear, founded the town some 2800 years ago; supposedly cured of leprosy by a bath in the muddy swamps, the founding prince is commemorated by a statue at the Cross Bath. The Romans established the town of Aquae Sulis (named after the Celtic goddess Sul) in AD 44 and it was already a spa, with an extensive baths complex and a temple to the goddess Sulis-Minerva, by the reign of Agricola (AD 78–84).

Long after the Romans had departed, the Anglo-Saxons arrived in 577, finding merely ruins where the town had been. The site was believed to be holy and in 944 a monastery was founded on the site of the present abbey. Throughout the Middle Ages Bath was an ecclesiastical centre and a wool-trading town (there are still traces of the medieval town wall in Upper Borough Walls). Although some visitors did come to take the waters, it wasn't until the arrival of postal guru and baths fan Ralph Allen in the early 18th century that spa-sipping led to Bath's rebirth.

BATH

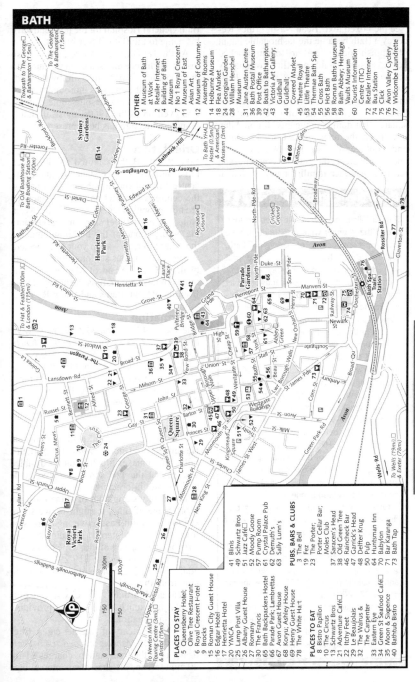

OTHER
1 Museum of Bath at Work
2 Retailer Internet
4 Building of Bath Museum
7 No 1 Royal Crescent
11 Museum of East Asian Art
12 Museum of Costume; Assembly Rooms
14 Holburne Museum
18 Flea Market
24 Georgian Garden
28 William Herschel Museum
31 Jane Austen Centre
36 Bath Postal Museum
39 Post Office
42 Boats to Bathampton
43 Victoria Art Gallery; Guildhall
44 Guildhall; Covered Market
45 Theatre Royal
53 Little Theatre
54 Thermae Bath Spa
55 Cross Bath
56 Hot Bath
58 Roman Baths Museum
59 Bath Abbey; Heritage Vaults Museum
60 Tourist Information Centre (TIC)
72 Retailer Internet
74 Bus Station
75 Click
76 Avon Valley Cyclery
77 Widcombe Laundrette

PLACES TO STAY
5 Queensberry Hotel;
  Olive Tree Restaurant
6 Royal Crescent Hotel
9 Brocks
15 Roman City Guest House
16 Edgar Hotel
17 Henrietta Hotel
20 YMCA
25 Lamp Post Villa
26 Albany Guest House
27 Romany
30 The Francis
65 Bath Backpackers Hostel
66 Parade Park; Lambrettas
67 Avon Guest House
68 Koryu; Ashley House
69 Henry Guest House
78 The White Hart

PLACES TO EAT
8 Bistro Papillon
10 The Circus
13 Schwartz Bros
21 Adventure Café
22 Itchy Feet
29 Le Beaujolais
32 The Walrus & The Carpenter
33 Eastern Eye
34 Green St Seafood Café
35 Moon & Sixpence
40 Bathtub Bistro
41 Blinis
49 Schwartz Bros
51 Jazz Café
52 Moody Goose
57 Pump Room
61 Crystal Palace Pub
62 Demuth's
63 Sally Lunn's

PUBS, BARS & CLUBS
3 The Bell
19 Fez
23 The Porter;
   Porter Cellar Bar;
   Moles Club
37 Saracen's Head
38 Old Green Tree
46 Raincheck Bar
47 Garrick's Head
48 Delfter Krug
50 Pulp
64 Huntsman Inn
70 Babylon
71 Bar Karanga
73 Bath Tap

Thanks to Allen and Richard 'Beau' Nash (see the boxed text 'Beau Nash: Prince Regency') Bath became the fashionable haunt of English society, and aristocrats flocked here to gossip, gamble and flirt. Fortunately the money of the wealthy was (at least partly) spent with taste, as demonstrated by the building drive leading to Bath's famous Palladian terraced housing, circles and squares that dominate the city. Ralph Allen developed the quarries at Coombe Down and employed the two John Woods (father and son) to create the glorious crescents and terraces. Another familiar name is that of Doctor William Oliver, who established the Bath General Hospital for the poor and gave his name to the Bath Oliver biscuit.

As the 18th century wore on, Beau Nash lost his influence and sea bathing started to draw visitors away from Bath; by the mid-19th century the city was thoroughly out of fashion. Fortunately, despite some demolition even up to the 1960s, most of Bath's grand architecture has been preserved.

Orientation

Like Rome, Bath is famed for its seven hills, and a walk any distance from the city centre will test your climbing legs. Luckily, the centre is compact and most attractions are nestled within a bend in the River Avon. Note that most street signs are carved into the golden stone of the buildings, making them hard to read – keep your eyes peeled!

The train and bus stations are both south of the TIC at the end of Manvers St. The most obvious landmark is the abbey, across from the Roman Baths and Pump Room.

Information

The **TIC** (☎ 477101, fax 477787; **w** www.vis itbath.co.uk; Abbey Chambers, Abbey Churchyard; open 9.30am-6pm Mon-Sat, 10am-4pm Sun May-Sept; 9.30am-5pm Mon-Sat, 10am-4pm Sun Oct-Apr) can help book accommodation and has a range of leaflets, including the free Jane Austen Bath Walk and the Bath Visitor, an annual free newspaper-style publication featuring ideas for places to visit and eat. The most useful map is the David Haslam Bath Visitors' Map (£1.25). Bath's hilly terrain makes life difficult for disabled visitors but the TIC supplies a free guide with helpful information.

If you're visiting a lot of attractions in a short space of time, it might be worth investing in a **Bath Pass**, covering admission to most places of interest, including some in Bristol and farther afield. One/two/three/seven-day passes cost £19/29/39/59 per adult, £14/22/25/35 per child, and are available from the TIC.

Scattered around the city are **i-plus points**, free touch-screen kiosks providing tourist information.

There are plenty of Internet cafés. **Click** (☎ 481008; 13 Manvers St; open 10am-10pm daily), near the train station, charges £1 for 20 minutes, and also has cheap international

---

Beau Nash: Prince Regency

If Ralph Allen, John Wood the Elder and John Wood the Younger were responsible for the physical construction of Georgian Bath, Richard 'Beau' Nash was the force that shaped high society in its heyday. A contradictory character, Nash was a dandy, gambler and womaniser, yet also purportedly charming, friendly, witty, influential and (at least to some degree) philanthropic.

Born in Wales in 1674, Richard Nash was an Oxford scholar and ex-soldier who had achieved little before coming to prominence in 1705 when appointed Master of Ceremonies in Bath. By revitalising spa culture and providing entertainment for the rich, Nash effectively created a prestigious social milieu over which he would rule, imposing strict regulations on behaviour and dress, for almost 50 years. His decrees governed the length and format of balls, road repairs, the wearing (or not) of various garments, smoking (not permitted in public rooms) and carrying of swords (also banned).

Quite how he wielded such power is something of a mystery; strictly speaking he wasn't a public leader or employee, deriving his income from a proportion of gambling-house profits. In any case, by the 1750s his influence was waning, the elite began to ignore him and he died in poverty in 1761 at the ripe old age of 87. Whether such a man could have such an impact on a city today is open to question, but there's no doubt that Bath as we know it, in style and substance, wouldn't be what it is without his legacy.

calls and good coffee. **Retailer Internet** (☎ 443181; 12 Manvers St; open 9am-9pm Mon-Sat, 3pm-9pm Sun), nearby, charges £1 for 20 minutes and has a second branch (☎ 445999; 128 Walcot St; open 10.30am-7.30pm Mon-Sat) where the charge is £1.50 for 30 minutes.

STA Travel (☎ 464263; Students' Union, Claverton Down; open 9.30am-5pm Mon, Tues, Thur & Fri, 10am-5pm Wed) is at the university.

Itchy Feet (☎ 337987, fax 337986; 4 Bartlett St; open 9.30am-5.30pm Mon-Sat, 11am-5pm Sun) is a well-stocked travel shop, with wide selections of guidebooks, maps and clothing.

Widcombe Laundrette (22 Claverton Buildings; open 8am-9pm daily) is the most central.

Baths

The bath-and-temple complex built by the Romans over one of Bath's three natural hot springs from the 1st century AD were left to decay after the Romans departed and, apart from a few leprous souls who came looking for a cure in the Middle Ages, it wasn't until the end of the 17th century that the numbers of those coming to 'take the cure' in Bath began to rise again. In 1702 the visit of Queen Anne set the seal on the trend, and a few years later Ralph Allen started his town expansion programme.

The **Roman Baths Museum** (☎ 477784; w www.romanbaths.co.uk; Abbey Church Yard; adult/child £8/4.60, including Museum of Costume £10.50/5.90; open 9am-5pm daily Mar-June, Sept & Oct, 9am-9pm daily Jul & Aug, 9.30am-4.30pm daily Nov-Feb) is one of England's most popular attractions and can be congested in summer – ideally, visit early on a midweek morning. Allow an hour to fully appreciate it.

Head along a raised walkway to the **Great Bath**, complete with Roman paving and lead base and surrounded by 19th-century arcading. A series of excavated passages and chambers beneath street level lead off in several directions and let you inspect the remains of other smaller baths and hypocaust (heating) systems, while an audio guide explains the details. One of the most picturesque corners of the complex is the 12th-century **King's Bath**, built around the original sacred spring; through a win-

dow there are views of the pool, complete with niches for bathers and rings for them to hold on to; 1.5 million litres of hot water still pour into the pool every day. You can see the ruins of the **Temple of Sulis Minerva** under the Pump Room, and recent excavations of the **East Baths** give an insight into its 4th-century form.

The museum outlines the history of the baths and displays excavation finds, including the fine gorgon head discovered on the site of the temple of Sul, the gilt-bronze head from the cult statue and superb mosaics.

As an addendum, head outside to Bath St and note the convenient arcading constructed so bathers could walk between the town's three sets of baths without getting wet. At the end of Bath St stands the **Cross Bath** where Mary of Modena, wife of James II, erected a cross in gratitude for her pregnancy in 1688. Opposite is the **Hot Bath**, the third bath built over Bath's hot springs. These two historic sites have been restored and, together with the Hetling Pump Room, are now part of **Thermae Bath Spa** (☎ 477051, fax 477052; w www.thermaebathspa.com; Hot Bath St; admission £17; open 9am-10pm daily), a privately run and superbly designed complex where you can relax in the thermal waters of the rooftop spa pool or opt for a number of special treatments.

Bath Abbey

Edgar, the first king of united England, was crowned in a church in Abbey Courtyard in 973, but the present abbey (☎ 422462; requested donation £2; open 9am-6pm Mon-Sat Easter-Oct, 9am-4.30pm Nov-Easter, afternoons only Sun), more glass than stone, was built between 1499 and 1616, making it the last great medieval church raised in England. The nave's wonderful fan vaulting was erected in the 19th century.

The most striking feature of the abbey's exterior is the west facade, where angels climb up and (head first!) down stone ladders, commemorating a dream of the founder, Bishop Oliver King. The abbey boasts 640 wall monuments, the second-largest collection after Westminster Abbey; among those buried here are the Reverend Thomas Malthus, the Victorian philosopher famous for his views on population control; Sir Isaac Pitman, who devised the Pitman method of shorthand; and Beau Nash, who is

WESSEX

buried at the eastern end of the south aisle – look for the memorial tablet, mentioning his notable social graces. Also worth a look are the choir stalls, carved with mythical beasts.

On the abbey's southern side, steps lead down to a vault in which the small **Heritage Vaults Museum** *(adult/child £2/1; open 10am-4pm Mon-Sat)* describes the abbey's history and its links with the baths and fashionable Georgian society, and contains fine stone bosses, robes and other artefacts.

Royal Crescent & The Circus

The crowning glory of Georgian Bath is Royal Crescent, designed by John Wood the Younger (1728–82) and built between 1767 and 1771. Its majestic sweep overlooks a private lawn and Royal Victoria Park, from which Royal Avenue leads to Queen Square, designed by John Wood the Elder (1704–54); the northern side of Queen Square, where seven houses form one cohesive unit, is especially attractive.

Superbly restored to the minutest detail of its 1770 magnificence, the grand Palladian town house **No 1 Royal Crescent** *(☎ 428126; adult/child £4/3.50; open 10.30am-5pm Tues-Sun Mar-Oct, 10.30am-4pm Tues-Sun Nov)* is well worth visiting to see how people lived during Bath's glory days; staff are dressed in period costume to complete the effect.

A walk along Brock St leads to The **Circus**, a magnificent circle of 30 houses designed by John Wood the Elder. Plaques on the houses commemorate famous residents such as Thomas Gainsborough, Clive of India and David Livingstone. To the south is the **Georgian Garden**, where you can see what a garden in Bath would have looked like during the town's 18th-century heyday, with gravel taking the place of grass to protect women's long dresses from staining.

Assembly Rooms & Museum of Costume

In the 18th century, fashionable Bath visitors gathered to play cards, dance and listen to music in the Assembly Rooms in Bennett St. You can wander round the rooms free, taking in the grand decor and engravings, but most people head for the basement Museum of Costume *(☎ 477789; adult/child £5/3.50, including Roman Baths Museum £10.50/5.90; open 10am-5pm daily)*, displaying costumes worn from the 16th to late 20th centuries, in-

cluding alarming crinolines that would have forced women to approach doorways side on. There's an audio guide to talk you through the fickle vagaries of fashion.

Jane Austen Centre

Jane Austen inspires interest bordering on obsession; for devotees, a visit to this centre *(☎ 443000; W www.janeaustin.co.uk; 40 Gay St; adult/child £3.95/2.45; open 10am-5.30pm Mon-Sat, 10.30am-5.30pm Sun)*, dedicated to one of Bath's most eminent residents, is a must. Displays include period costume, contemporary prints of the city and exhibits relating to the author's personal life, family and homes. It's a mecca for fans and insightful for the rest of us.

Of interest is a plaque at No 4 Sydney Place, opposite the Holburne Museum, commemorating the author who lived here for three (not particularly happy) years. She wrote *Persuasion* and *Northanger Abbey* here; both vividly describe fashionable life in the city around 1800.

Holburne Museum

The fine 18th-century Holburne Museum *(☎ 466669; Great Pulteney St; adult/child £3.50/1.50; open 10am-5pm Tues-Sat mid-Feb–Nov)* was originally designed as the Sydney Hotel. It now houses the booty of Sir William Holburne, a 19th-century Bath resident who brought together an outstanding collection of porcelain, antiques, and paintings by great 18th-century artists such as Gainsborough and Stubbs as well as landscapes by Turner and Guardi.

Museum of Bath at Work

Tucked away off Julian Rd, this museum *(☎ 318348; W www.bath-at-work.org.uk; Camden Works; adult/child £3.50/2.50; open 10am-5pm daily Apr-Oct, Sat & Sun Nov-Mar)* is Bath's industrial heritage centre, housed in what was originally an 18th-century 'real' tennis court. Most of the fittings belonged to Jonathan Burdett Bowler's 19th-century mineral-water bottling plant and brass foundry, and there are exhibits on the local stone industry, cabinet making and the Horstmann Car Company.

Building of Bath Museum

Housed in the 18th-century chapel of the Countess of Huntingdon in the Paragon, this museum (☎ *333895; The Vineyards; adult/child £4/1.50; open 10.30am-5pm Tues-Sun mid-Feb–June & Sept-Nov; daily July & Aug)* details how Bath's Georgian splendour came into being, a more interesting story than you might imagine. There are architectural designs, explanations of materials and techniques, and an insight into decorative styles of Bath's heyday.

William Herschel Museum

William Herschel arrived in Bath as an organist but was to become most noteworthy for his achievements in the field of astronomy. In 1781 he discovered the planet Uranus from the garden of his home, now housing this museum (☎ *311342; 19 New King St; adult/child £3.50/2; open 2pm-5pm daily Mar-Oct, Sat & Sun Nov-Feb)*. Inside is a re-creation of how the house might have looked during the city's heyday in the 18th century, including a display of contemporary musical instruments.

Victoria Art Gallery

This municipal gallery (☎ *477233; Pulteney Bridge; admission free; open 10am-5.30pm Tues-Fri, 10am-5pm Sat, 2pm-5pm Sun)* has changing exhibitions of mostly modern art, and permanent collections of fine ceramics, Flemish masters and English paintings by artists who lived and worked in the area, including Gainsborough, Turner and Sickert.

Museum of East Asian Art

This museum (☎ *464640; e museum@east-asian-art.freeserve.co.uk; 12 Bennett St; adult/child £3.50/1.50; open 10am-5pm Tues-Sat, noon-5pm Sun)* contains more than 500 jade, bamboo, porcelain and bronze objects from Cambodia, Korea and Thailand, and substantial Chinese and Japanese carvings, ceramics and lacquer ware. Visiting exhibitions from major establishments such as the British Museum complete the picture.

Bath Postal Museum

Housed in the building where the Penny Black stamp was first used in 1840, this intriguing museum (☎ *460333; w www.bath postalmuseum.org; 8 Broad St; adult/child £2.90/1.50; open 11am-5pm Mon-Sat)* describes the history of organised mail delivery, from 6th century BC Persia through Roman and medieval post to the present.

There's a reconstruction of a 1930s post office and displays on Ralph Allen, the man whose quarries fed Bath's construction but who was also a great postal reformer.

Guildhall

Completed in 1779 by Thomas Baldwin, the Guildhall (☎ *477724; High St; admission free; open 9am-5pm Mon-Fri)* has several grand chambers designed for civic functions. Many are still used daily and can't often be visited, but the substantial Banqueting Room is usually open and worth a look. The grand space is lit by vast chandeliers and its walls lined with portraits of Bath luminaries such as William Pitt, William Pulteney, Ralph Allen and King George III.

Special Events

The annual **Bath Literature Festival** *(w www .bathlitfest.org.uk)* takes place in early March; in 2002 its contributors included Jeanette Winterson and Jacqueline Wilson.

From mid-May to early June the **Bath International Music Festival** *(w www.bath musicfest.org.uk)* is in full swing with events in all the town's venues, including the abbey. This festival focuses on classical music and opera, although there are also world music and jazz weekends. Popular events are booked up well in advance.

Running concurrently is the **Bath Fringe Festival** *(w www.bathfringe.co.uk)*, the biggest fringe festival in England, second only to Edinburgh in Britain, involving a blend of comedy, drama, performance art and world music. The festival ends with a bang on **Walcot Nation Day** *(w www.walcotstreet.com; early June)* when Walcot St is closed to traffic but open to all sorts of carnivalesque chaos.

BITE (Bath International Taste Extravaganza) is the city's food festival, featuring specialist markets, restaurant deals and events. In 2002 Jonathan Dimbleby hosted a special culinary *Any Questions*. Dates for the 2003 festival were still to be finalised at the time of writing.

Bookings for all are handled by the **Bath Festivals Box Office** *(☎ 463362, fax 310377; w www.bathfestivals.org.uk; 2 Church Green, Abbey Green; open 9.30am-5.30pm Mon-Sat)*.

Organised Tours

Free 1½-hour **walking tours** *(☎ 477411)* leave from outside the Pump Room at

WESSEX

10.30am and 2pm Sunday to Friday (also 10.30am and 7pm Saturday and 7pm Tuesday and Friday from May to September).

Bizarre Bath Comedy Walks (☎ 335124) offers an irreverent look at the city that definitely makes a change from the average tour – guides proudly declare their lack of cultural and historical knowledge, but are nonetheless hilarious. They leave nightly outside the Huntsman Inn in North Parade Passage at 8pm and cost £5/4.50 per adult/child.

Tours of **Jane Austen's Bath** (☎ 443000) leave from KC Change Visitor Information Centre in Abbey Church Yard at 1.30pm daily June to September, Saturday and Sunday October to May, last 1½ hours and cost £3.50/2.50.

Two-hour **ghost walks** (☎ 463618; **w** www .ghostwalksofbath.co.uk) depart from the Nash Bar in the haunted Garrick's Head pub, off Sawclose, at 8pm Monday to Saturday, April to October (Friday only November to March). Walks cost £5/4.

City Sightseeing (☎ 330444) runs open-top, hop-on, hop-off bus tours from 9am to 5pm daily, March to November (Saturday and Sunday only December to February). The buses start at Grand Parade on High St, and pass Bath bus station. Tickets cost £8/4 per adult/child.

The **Classic Citytour** (☎ 0772 559686) runs a similar route but is slightly cheaper at £6.50/2 per adult/child.

Cleopatra Boat Trips (☎ 480541) run hourly every day from the river just south of Pulteney Bridge, behind Bath Rugby Ground. Hour-long cruises with commentary cost £4.95/2.95 per adult/child.

Places to Stay

Finding somewhere to stay during busy periods can be tough. The TIC will book rooms for a £5 booking fee plus a deposit of 10% of the first night's accommodation. It also sells a brochure, *Bath & Beyond* (£1), with comprehensive listings.

Camping & Hostels The **Newton Mill Touring Centre** (☎ 333909, fax 461556; **e** newtonmill@hotmail.com; Newton Rd; tent & 2 people from £9.95; open year round) is about 3 miles (5km) west of Bath, at Newton St Loe. To reach it, take the B3310 off the A4; bus No 5 (15 minutes, every 10 minutes) runs from the bus station.

Out towards the University, **Bath YHA Hostel** (☎ 0870 770 5688, fax 482947; **e** bath@yha.org.uk; Bathwick Hill; dorm beds £11.25) is a stiff uphill half-mile walk from the city centre, or a short hop on bus No 18 (every 10 minutes) from the bus station. There are compensatory views and the Italianate building is magnificent.

Bath Backpackers Hostel (☎ 446787, fax 331319; **e** bath@hostels.co.uk; 13 Pierrepont St; dorm beds £12), a colourfully decorated, central spot, just around the corner from the abbey and TIC. Dorm rooms have up to 12 beds, there's the usual lounge, cooking facilities and Internet access, plus the party 'dungeon' – that should give you some idea of what to expect. You can book beds at the affiliated hostels in Stratford and Oxford here.

YMCA (☎ 325900, fax 462065; **e** reserva tions@ymcabath.co.uk; International House, Broad St Place; B&B dorm beds £12, singles/ doubles £18/32), also central, takes men and women, and offers reduced rates for stays of a week or more. It has a great health suite and a cheap restaurant. Approaching from the south along Walcot St, look out for an archway and steps on the left about 180m past the post office.

The White Hart (☎ 313985; **e** sue@white hartinn.freeserve.co.uk; Widcombe; dorm beds £12.50, singles/doubles £20/50) is a friendly, clean converted pub just across the river south of the train station. It has a licensed café-bar and a pleasant courtyard area for chilling. There's usually a curfew – security is good. The doubles have an en suite.

B&Bs & Hotels Bath is a popular place to spend the weekend and is one of the few English towns where prices tend to rise rather than fall on Friday and Saturday. The main areas for B&Bs are along Upper Bristol Rd (Crescent Gardens) to the west, around Pulteney Rd in the east and along Wells Rd to the south, although the last is a busy road and suffers from traffic noise.

Henry Guest House (☎ 424052; **e** Cox@ TheHenryBath.freeserve.co.uk; 6 Henry St; rooms per person £22) is as central as you'll get. Don't be put off by the exterior – it's much more promising inside, and the owners are friendly. The eight rooms all share bathrooms.

Romany (☎ 424193; 9 Charlotte St; doubles £38) is an old-school guesthouse with large, basic rooms and shared bathrooms; the price reflects the fact that breakfast isn't provided.

Central B&Bs in the guise of 'hotels' tend to be overpriced and nothing special – along South Parade you're looking at close to £100, although late deals are often available. Just around the corner, The **Parade Park** (☎ 463384, fax 442322; e info@paradepark .co.uk; 8-10 North Parade; singles/doubles £35/50, en-suite singles/doubles from £50/60) is a 1740s town house with many original features and offers good value for this neck of the woods. The popular bar **Lambrettas** (☎ 464650) is downstairs, with Italian posters and motor scooter but British beer and clientele.

There are a few good options along or near Great Pulteney St. **Henrietta Hotel** (☎ 447779, fax 444150; 32 Henrietta St; B&B singles £35-50, doubles £45-90) and **Edgar Hotel** (☎ 420619, fax 466961; e edgar -hotel@pgen.net; 64 Great Pulteney St; B&B singles £45-50, doubles £60-90) are both elegant Georgian town houses owned by the same family. The Henrietta has more period charm, but rooms in both have an en suite, and are very comfortable and well priced for the location. Prices vary depending on room size, day and season.

Moving east, there are numerous B&Bs on and around Pulteney Rd and Pulteney Gardens, and a few around Sydney Gardens. **Koryu** (☎/fax 337642; e japanesekoryu@ aol.com; 7 Pulteney Gardens; B&B singles/ doubles from £28/48), owned by an Anglo-Japanese couple, is an excellent place, bright, friendly and modern. Most rooms have an en suite or private facilities.

The rooms at **Ashley House** (☎ 425027; 8 Pulteney Gardens; B&B singles/doubles £27.50/52) are comfortable and fresh; most have an en suite. Low-season discounts are available for longer stays.

Avon Guest House (☎/fax 313009; 1 Pulteney Gardens; en-suite doubles from £50) is another decent B&B in this handy location.

Roman City Guest House (☎ 463668; e romancityguesthse@amserve.net; 18 Raby Place; en-suite doubles £50-60) is a Grade I–listed town house with various original features and abbey views. The friendly owners have installed a huge home cinema for rainy days in the large lounge.

Old Boathouse (☎ 466407; Forester Rd; en-suite doubles £55-65, 4-person cottage £100) is a delightful converted Edwardian boating station in an idyllic location beside the river, just north of Sydney Gardens. Some rooms have river-view balconies.

West of the centre, the section of Upper Bristol Rd called Crescent Gardens is rife with B&Bs.

Lamp Post Villa (☎ 331221, fax 426783; 3 Crescent Gardens; singles £30-35, doubles £40-55) is clean and reasonable value.

Albany Guest House (☎ 313339; e the _albany@lineone.net; 24 Crescent Gardens; rooms £36-40, single occupancy £30-40, en-suite doubles £46-50) is one of the nicest places here; it also has private parking, unusual for Bath's B&Bs.

Brocks (☎ 338374, fax 334245; e marion@ brocksguesthouse.co.uk; 32 Brock St; doubles £65-78) is a beautiful town house in a fabulous position between Royal Crescent and The Circus; decor is sympathetic and all rooms have an en suite. A find.

Unsurprisingly, Bath has some classy hotels.

Abbey Hotel (☎ 461603, fax 447758; e ahres@compasshotels.co.uk; North Parade; B&B singles/doubles from £80/95) is a 1740 construction by John Wood the Elder with three-star standards, including an award-winning restaurant.

The Francis (☎ 0870 400 8223, fax 319715; e francis@heritage-hotels.co.uk; Queen Square; B&B singles/doubles Mon-Thur £133/136, Fri-Sun £78/156) takes up most of the southern side of this elegant square; character is still Georgian, though service is 21st century.

Queensberry Hotel (☎ 447928, fax 446065; e enquiries@bathqueensberry.com; Russell St; singles/doubles from £90/120) is another marvellous Georgian building but has more chic styling and a superb restaurant, the Olive Tree (see Places to Eat).

Set in extensive grounds, **Bath Spa Hotel** (☎ 444424, fax 476825; w www.bathspahotel .com; Sydney Rd; singles/doubles from £125/180) just exudes exclusivity. This five-star property has elegant rooms and just about every extra.

Royal Crescent Hotel (☎ 823333, fax 339401; e reservations@royalcrescent.co.uk; 16 Royal Crescent; rooms from £230, master suite £800), Bath's top place to stay, is on the grandest of grand crescents. There's a garden behind the hotel and an excellent restaurant; pampering comes extra in the Bath House spa with its relaxation pool and numerous treatments. Decorated with period furnishings, rooms are sometimes available at special rates (two nights B&B and one dinner £295); phone for details.

Places to Eat

Self-caterers head for the covered **Guildhall Market** next to the Guildhall, where you'll also find crepes and other takeaway food. The major supermarket chains are all represented in the city.

For hit-and-run hamburger heaven, find a branch of **Schwartz Bros** (☎ 461726; 4 Sawclose • ☎ 463613; 102 Walcot St; burgers £2.50-4; open noon-midnight daily), local boys-done-good with award-winning burgers and fries; there are plenty of vegetarian options.

At **Adventure Café** (☎ 462038; 5 Princes Buildings; sandwiches £4-5; open 9am-5pm Mon-Sat, 11am-4pm Sun) a young crowd munches breakfast or gourmet sandwiches while people-watching from the full-length windows overlooking George St.

Jazz Café (☎ 329002; 1 Kingsmead Square; mains £4-7; open 8am-10pm daily) is a lively, vibey place with a selection of world favourites (goulash, curry) and wine to back up traditional greasy spoon fare.

Art-strewn, hip **Demuth's** (☎ 446059; 2 North Parade Passage; mains £5.50-6.50) serves vegetarian and vegan Thai curries, wraps and tapas to die for.

In 1680, in a house dating from around 1482, a Huguenot refugee founded the eponymous **Sally Lunn's** (☎ 461634; 4 North Parade Passage; dinner £6.68-9.48; open 10am-10pm Mon-Sat, 11am-10pm Sun), baking brioche for Bath residents. Still going strong, it also offers a selection of very traditional English meals. In the basement is the tiny **Sally Lunn's Kitchen Museum** (admission 30p; open 10am-6pm Mon-Sat, 11am-6pm Sun), with excavations revealing artefacts from Roman times and a mock-up of the 17th-century kitchen.

Crystal Palace (☎ 482666; 10-11 Abbey Green; mains £6-8) is an attractive pub with comfy sofas, a beer garden and excellent food, especially fish and seafood dishes.

Beau Bhaji? **Eastern Eye** (☎ 422323; 8a Quiet St; mains £5.50-15) puts the Regency into rogan josh in this amazing Georgian in-

terior; the food's special too – so says Keith Floyd (um, and Donny Osmond).

The Walrus & the Carpenter (☎ 314864; 28 Barton St; mains £7-10) is a local institution, funky and informal, with home-made global cuisine and plenty of vegetarian options.

Bathtub Bistro (☎ 460593; 2 Grove St; dinner mains £7.50-12; closed lunch Mon), a tardis-like eatery by Pulteney Weir, dishes up good world food, vegetarian gems and specials such as wild boar steak.

Moon & Sixpence (☎ 460962; 6a Broad St; 2-course lunch £7.50, mains £9.50-14.50), tucked away in a courtyard, is a classy but relaxed diner serving fusion food in a stylish, understated space.

Le Beaujolais (☎ 423417; 5 Chapel Row; 2-course lunch £8.50, mains £12-16; closed Sun) draws in-the-know locals with quality regional French cuisine.

Bistro Papillon (☎ 463799; 2 Margaret's Buildings; 2-course lunch £7.50, mains £11-13.50; open lunch & dinner Tues-Sat) is no less French but brighter and more modern; it's also handily near the Crescent.

Nearby **The Circus** (☎ 318918; 34 Brock St; mains £11.50-18) is sleek, as befits the residents of this swanky neighbourhood, and produces fine modern-British cuisine with an emphasis on seafood…talking of which, **Green Street Seafood Café** (aka Fishworks; ☎ 448707; 6 Green St; mains £9-20; open 8am-11pm Tues-Sat, 11am-3pm Sun) is a fishmonger-cum-restaurant serving the freshest of fish in simple, classic dishes.

The Olive Tree (☎ 447928; Russell St; 2/3-course lunch £13.50/15.50, 3-course dinner £26), beneath the Queensberry Hotel, is chic and sleek, with good modern British cuisine; it's one of the finest restaurants in town.

Moody Goose (☎ 466688; 7a Kingsmead Square; 3-course dinner £25; closed Sun) is similarly stylish and takes the fine-dining route, with trendy dishes such as galette of turbot and pan-fried calf's liver.

Despite his two Michelin stars, chef Martin Blunos' **Blinis** (☎ 422510; 16 Argyle St; 2/3-course lunch £14.50/20, 5/7-course dinner £44.50/55; closed Sun dinner & Mon) is surprisingly unaffected; there's also a quality deli at this pleasant spot overlooking the weir.

In the elegant, 18th-century **Pump Room** (☎ 444477; Abbey Church Yard; 2/3-course lunch £10.95/12.95, cream tea from £6.75; open 9.30am-5.30pm), adjoining the Roman

Baths, one sips tea and heaps scones with jam and cream while being serenaded by a palm court trio, a tradition from Georgian times. A fountain from the King's Bath dispenses tepid spa water, and there's a statue of Beau Nash. Dinner is sometimes served during July and August; call for details.

Entertainment

Venue magazine (£1.90) has comprehensive listings with details of theatre, music, gigs – the works, basically – for Bristol and Bath.

Pubs, Bars & Clubs Bath has lots of atmospheric pubs and, thanks largely to a healthy student population, some reasonable clubs.

Parts of **The Bell** (☎ 460426; 103 Walcot St) date from the 15th century; plenty of real ales and regular live roots and jazz make this a mellow place for a pint.

The **Saracen's Head** (☎ 426518; 42 Broad St), the city's oldest pub, may have housed Dickens while he was a reporter in Bath. Now its low-ceilinged bar offers a good place for cosy drinking.

The **Hat & Feather** (☎ 425672; 14 London St) is a popular alternative pub (check out the papier-mache octopus) with regular DJs playing dub, ska, funk and hip-hop.

What the **Old Green Tree** (12 Green St) lacks in size (it's tiny), it makes up for with great beer and cosy ambience.

The **George** (☎ 425079; Mill La) is a charming waterside pub; follow the canal 1½ miles (2.5km) northeast to Bathampton village.

Bright, lively **Bath Tap** (☎ 404344; 19-20 St James Parade) is the most popular bar among Bath's gay community.

The **Porter** (☎ 404445; w www.theporter .co.uk; 2 Miles' Bldgs, George St) is a hip pub-bar; downstairs, the **Porter Cellar Bar** stages free, live music and comedy, while adjacent **Moles** (14 George St) is the best alternative club and live-music venue in town. The likes of Oasis, Radiohead, The Smiths and The Cure have played here.

Raincheck Bar (☎ 444770; 34 Monmouth St) and **Pulp** (☎ 466411; 38 Monmouth St) are both hip café-bars with streetside tables and good cocktails; the former has a rather noir, Francophile feel, the latter retro-cool.

Bar Karanga (☎ 446546; 8-10 Manvers St) is a more glamorous bar attracting attention;

it's the pre-club venue for **Babylon** (☎ 0870 444 8666; Kingston Rd), the similarly glitzy dance spot behind.

Fez (☎ 444162; 7a Bladud Buildings, The Paragon) is a souk-bar with a dance floor and DJs, but the laid-back vibe and plethora of games makes it a perfect spot for mellow (and late – to 2am) drinking.

Delfter Krug (☎ 443352; Sawclose) is the current darling, a trendy bar-club with Bridget-Riley-esque art, '60s-throwback decor and plenty of attitude. Chill out downstairs or get down above with funky house, hip-hop and r'n'b. There's a small cover charge at the weekend.

Theatre & Cinema The **Theatre Royal** (☎ 448844; w www.theatreroyal.org.uk; Sawclose) is a sumptuous venue that features drama, opera, comedy and world music in its eclectic programme.

Little Theatre (☎ 466822; St Michael's Place) is Bath's art-house cinema, screening mostly fringe and foreign-language films.

Classical Music At Bath Abbey (☎ 422462) there's a regular programme of lunch-time recitals; the price depends on who is appearing.

Shopping

The Saturday and Sunday morning **flea market** (Walcot St), selling antiques and clothes, is popular with bargain hunters. The covered **Guildhall Market** (High St) has excellent second-hand bookstalls.

Getting There & Away

Bath is 106 miles (171km) from London, 19 miles (31km) from Wells and only 12 miles (19km) from Bristol.

Bus National Express buses run to London (economy return £21, 3½ hours, 10 daily) via Heathrow, and daily to Bournemouth (£16, 2¾ hours), Manchester (£31, 6¼ hours) and Oxford (£14, two hours).

Bus Nos X39, 339 and 332 run to Bristol (single/return £3.10/3.90, 50 minutes) several times an hour. Other useful services include Nos X5 and X6 to Bradford-on-Avon (30 minutes, half-hourly), Nos X71 and X72 to Devizes (one hour, hourly), No 267 to Frome (50 minutes, hourly) and Nos 173/773 to Wells (1¼ hours, hourly).

WESSEX

Map-timetables for individual routes are available from the **bus station office** (☎ 464446; Manvers St; open 8am-5.30pm Mon-Sat).

Train There are numerous trains from London Paddington (saver return £39.50, 1½ hours, half-hourly), and also several each hour to Bristol (single £4.60, 20 minutes). There are occasional direct trains to Exeter St Davids (saver return £23, 1½ hours), Cardiff (£16.10, 1¼ hours, half-hourly) and Oxford (£22.50, 1¼ hours) but many require a change at Bristol. Trains run to Weymouth (£17.70, two hours) via Bradford-on-Avon (single £2.70, 15 minutes), Frome (single £5.90, 40 minutes) and Dorchester West (saver return £16.50, 1¾ hours) every two hours. Hourly services head to Portsmouth (£27.40, two hours) via Salisbury (£14.10, 50 minutes).

Getting Around

Bus No 18 runs from the bus station, High St and Great Pulteney St up Bathwick Hill past the YHA to the university every 10 minutes. Bus No 4 runs every 20 minutes to Bathampton from the same places. A First Day Pass for unlimited bus travel in the city costs £3/2.

Car Bath has a bad traffic problem and parking space is hard to find. In the city centre, try to find a meter and pray – clamping is big business in Bath and release fees are hefty. Most hotels and B&Bs offer free permits for on-street parking if they don't have private parking. Alternatively, park-and-ride services (☎ 464446; return £1.40, 10 minutes to centre; every 10 to 15 minutes 7.15am to 7.30pm, daily) operate at Lansdown to the north, Newbridge to the west and Odd Down to the south.

Bicycle Bikes can be hired from **Avon Valley Cyclery** (☎ 461880; w www.bikeshop .uk.com; open 9am-5.30pm Mon, Tues, Fri & Sat, 10am-5.30pm Wed, 9am-8pm Thur), behind the train station, for £9/14 per half/full day. Cyclists can use the 12-mile Bristol and Bath Railway Path that follows a disused railway line.

Boat Various companies run half-hourly passenger boats from Pulteney Bridge to Bathampton; the round trip takes 50 min-

utes and tickets cost £4.50/2 per adult/child. Alternatively, you can hire canoes, punts or rowing boats to propel yourself along the Avon from £5 per hour (£1.50 for additional hours); try **Bath Boating Station** (☎ 466407; Forester Rd; open 10am-6pm daily May-Aug, 11am-6pm Apr & Sept, 2pm-6pm Mar & Oct), which also runs Bathampton cruises.

AROUND BATH
Prior Park

This beautiful 18th-century landscaped park (☎ 833422; admission £4; Ralph Allen Drive; open 11am-5.30pm Wed-Mon Feb-Nov, Fri-Sun Dec & Jan), 1 mile (1.6km) south of the centre, is owned by the National Trust (NT). The gardens, with spectacular views of Bath, were created for Ralph Allen by Lancelot 'Capability' Brown. There's no parking, so it's accessible only by bus No 2 or 4 (every 10 minutes), or on foot. There's a £1 refund if you show your bus ticket.

American Museum

Claverton Manor (☎ 460503; w www.americanmuseum.org; admission museum £6/3.50, grounds, Folk Art & New Galleries only £3.50/2.50; house open 2pm-5pm Tues-Sun, grounds open 1pm-6pm Tues-Fri, noon-6pm Sat & Sun Easter-Oct), 3 miles (5km) southeast of Bath, is an 1820s mansion housing recreated 17th- to 19th-century American home interiors, a collection of quilts and other American memorabilia. There's also a Folk Art Gallery and changing, related exhibitions.

Bus No 18 (every 10 minutes) from the bus station drops you on The Avenue, half a mile short of the entrance.

Somerset

Long the butt of jokes about slow-speaking, cider-swilling yokels, 'Zomerzet' is a largely agricultural county known mainly for Cheddar cheese; perhaps this is fortunate – away from the tourist magnets of Bath (see the preceding entry), Cheddar and Glastonbury, the picturesque villages, beautiful countryside and historic sites are relatively peaceful.

Somerset is good walking and cycling country. The Mendip Hills are cut by gorges where caves were inhabited from prehistoric times. The Quantocks to the west are less cultivated, while to the far west of the county, the wilder Exmoor National Park (see later in this chapter) spans the border with Devon.

Orientation & Information

Somerset nestles around the crook in the elbow of the Bristol Channel; the Mendip Hills follow a line below Bristol, just north of Wells and Cheddar, while the Quantocks sit just east of Exmoor. Most places of interest are in the northern part; however, that doesn't mean that you won't find enchanting spots farther south, and Montacute House, near the Dorset border, is a treat.

Bath or Wells make good bases to the east of Somerset, as do Lynton and Lynmouth to the west.

Most towns have TICs, which stock numerous free newspapers, magazines and brochures, on (more or less) local happenings. An excellent source of more general information is the **Somerset Visitor Centre** (☎ 01934-750833, fax 750755; e somersetvisi torcentre@somerset.gov.uk; Sedgemoor Services M5 South, Axbridge, Somerset BS26 2UF), which can provide walking and cycling leaflets, tourist brochures for all parts of the county and nuggets of local information that you won't find elsewhere. The **Somerset County Council** website at w www.somerset .gov.uk/tourism has searchable accommodation listings.

Getting Around

Bus services in Somerset are roughly split between **First Badgerline** (☎ 0117-955 8211; w www.firstbadgerline.co.uk) north of Bridgwater and including Bath and Bristol, and **First Southern National** (☎ 01823-366100; w www.firstsouthernnational.co.uk) to the south, with other local operators chipping in.

Somerset bus services are coordinated by **ATMOS** (☎ 01823-251151; w www.somerset .gov.uk), which produces five area-specific timetables (West Somerset, Sedgemoor, Taunton, Mendip and South Somerset) in coordination with the county council, available at bus stations and some TICs.

WELLS

☎ 01749 • pop 9800

Wells has unfair advantages. As well as its own considerable charm, it's also within touching distance of the Mendips, Cheddar, Glastonbury and Bath, 22 miles (35km) to the northeast; unsurprisingly, it's very popular.

Taking its name from three springs that emerged near the medieval Bishop's Palace, Wells is England's smallest cathedral city. It retains a wealth of medieval buildings and an attractive city centre; the cathedral itself is one of England's finest, with a marvellous cathedral close, Bishop's Palace and other associated buildings.

Information

The **TIC** (☎ 672552, fax 670869; e wellstic@ ukonline.co.uk; Market Place; open 9.30am-5.30pm daily Apr-Oct, 10am-4pm Nov-Mar) is in the Town Hall.

There are lots of interesting walking and cycling routes nearby. The TIC has details, including the handy *Wells City Trail* leaflet (30p). Markets are held in the picturesque Market Place on Wednesday and Saturday.

Wells Laundrette (☎ 01458-830409; 39 St Cuthbert St; open 8am-8pm daily) is opposite St Cuthbert's Church.

Wells Cathedral

The Cathedral Church of St Andrew (☎ 674483; Chain Gate, Cathedral Green; requested donation £4.50/1.50; open 7am-7pm

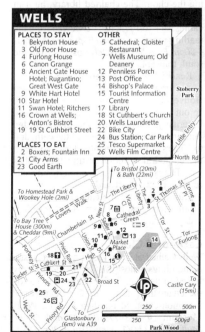

WELLS

PLACES TO STAY	OTHER
1 Bekynton House	5 Cathedral; Cloister
3 Old Poor House	Restaurant
4 Furlong House	7 Wells Museum; Old
6 Canon Grange	Deanery
8 Ancient Gate House	12 Penniless Porch
Hotel; Rugantino;	13 Post Office
Great West Gate	14 Bishop's Palace
9 White Hart Hotel	15 Tourist Information
10 Star Hotel	Centre
11 Swan Hotel; Ritchers	17 Library
16 Crown at Wells;	18 St Cuthbert's Church
Anton's Bistrot	20 Wells Laundrette
19 19 St Cuthbert Street	22 Bike City
	24 Bus Station; Car Park
PLACES TO EAT	25 Tesco Supermarket
2 Boxers; Fountain Inn	26 Wells Film Centre
21 City Arms	
23 Good Earth	

daily Sept-June, 7am-8.30pm July & Aug) was built in stages between 1180 and 1508 and incorporates several Gothic styles. Its most famous asset is the wonderful **west front**, an immense sculpture gallery with over 300 figures, built between 1230 and 1250 and restored to its original splendour in 1986. Apart from the figure of Christ, installed in 1985 in the uppermost niche, all the figures are original.

Inside, the most striking feature is the pair of **scissor arches**, separating the nave from the choir, a brilliant solution to the problem posed by the subsidence of the central tower; they were added in the mid-14th century, shortly after the tower's completion. High up in the north transept is a wonderful **mechanical clock** dating from 1392 – the second-oldest surviving in England after the one in Salisbury Cathedral. The clock shows the position of the planets and the phases of the moon, and there's an entertaining cabaret act performed above it on the hour by jousting knights on horseback.

Other highlights are the elegant **Lady Chapel** (1326) at the eastern end and the seven **effigies** of Anglo-Saxon bishops ringing the choir. The **chained library**, built in 1425 and housing books and manuscripts dating back to 1472, can be viewed from the **reading room** (admission 50p; open 2.30pm-4.30pm Fri & Sat Apr-Oct) upstairs from the south transept.

Reached by worn steps leading off the north transept is the glorious **Chapter House** (1306), the ceiling ribs of which sprout like a palm from a central column. Externally, look out for the **Chain Bridge** built from the northern side of the cathedral to Vicars' Close to enable clerics to reach the cathedral without getting their robes wet. The **cloisters** on the southern side surround a pretty courtyard.

Guided tours of the cathedral (at 10am, 11am, 1pm, 2pm and 3pm Monday to Saturday) are free.

Cathedral Close

Wells Cathedral is the focal point of a cluster of buildings whose history is inextricably linked to its own. Facing the west front, on the left are the 15th-century **Old Deanery** and a salmon-coloured building housing **Wells Museum** (☎ 673477; 8 Cathedral Green; adult/child £2.50/1; open 10am-5.30pm daily Easter-June, Sept & Oct, 10am-8pm daily July & Aug, 11am-4pm Wed-Mon Nov-Easter), with exhibits about caving and geology in the Mendips, local life, cathedral architecture and the infamous Witch of Wookey Hole.

Farther along on the left, **Vicars' Close** is a cobbled street of uniform houses dating back to the 14th century with a chapel at the end; members of the cathedral choir still live here. It is thought to be the oldest complete medieval street in Europe. Passing under the Chain Bridge, inspect the outside of the Lady Chapel and a lovely medieval house called **The Rib**, before emerging at a main road called The Liberty. In the Middle Ages this marked the boundary of the cathedral precincts within which a refugee could take sanctuary.

Penniless Porch, a corner gate leading onto Market Square and built by Bishop Bekynton around 1450, is so-called because beggars asked for alms here.

Bishop's Palace

Beyond the cathedral is the moated 13th-century Bishop's Palace (☎ 678691; adult/child £3/1; open 10.30am-5pm Tues-Fri & bank holidays, 1pm-5pm Sun Apr-July, Sept & Oct, 10.30am-5pm daily Aug), purportedly the oldest inhabited building in England, with fine Italian Gothic state rooms, imposing Great Hall and beautiful gardens. The springs that give the town its name bubble and babble here, feeding the moat.

After a decade when no swans knew the trick, a new generation of birds has now learned to ring a bell outside one of the windows when they want a feed. If you want to feed them, brown bread is better than white.

St Cuthbert's Church

For obvious reasons, stately **St Cuthbert's Church** (St Cuthbert St; open to dusk daily), is somewhat eclipsed by the cathedral, but it's worth dropping by to admire its splendid 15th-century perpendicular tower and brilliantly coloured nave roof. Look out for the boss of a sow suckling five piglets in the south porch.

Places to Stay

The nearest campsite is at Wookey Hole (see that section later in this chapter). There are several B&Bs but advance booking is advised, especially for festival weekends and November's Carnival (check with the TIC for more information).

19 St Cuthbert St *(☎ 673166; singles/ doubles £22/37)* is a small, pleasant B&B overlooking St Cuthbert's Church. Bathrooms are shared.

Bay Tree House *(☎ 677933; e stay@bay tree-house.co.uk; 85 Portway; singles £25-30, doubles £42-45)* is a bright, friendly, family run B&B. All rooms have an en suite or private bathroom. It's a 10-minute walk from the centre, but an excellent choice.

Old Poor House *(☎ 675052; e bookings@ wells-poorhouse.co.uk; 7a St Andrew St; B&B per person with/without en suite £25/22)* is an attractive 14th-century cottage tucked away in a courtyard. Decor is sympathetic and the garden has cathedral views.

Furlong House *(☎ 674064; e johnhoward wells@cs.com; Lorne Place, St Thomas St; B&B singles/doubles from £35/46)* is a charming Grade II–listed Georgian house with three substantial rooms, all with private bathroom. There's also a pretty walled garden.

Bekynton House *(☎ 672222; e reserva tions@bekynton.freeserve.co.uk; 7 St Thomas St; singles £32-38, doubles £46-56)* is an upmarket B&B with a genteel feel; all rooms have an en suite or private shower.

Canon Grange *(☎ 671800; e canongrange@ email.com; Cathedral Green; doubles & twins £45-54)* is a 15th-century house with uninterrupted views of the cathedral's west front; the flagstoned hallway adds to the atmosphere, and excellent vegetarian breakfasts are available.

There are some hotels near the cathedral; they're all old (mostly 15th century) but offer rooms with different styles and en suites.

The **Crown at Wells** *(☎ 673457, fax 679792; e reception@crownatwells.co.uk; Market Place; B&B singles/doubles from £45/60)* is an attractive old inn. In 1685 William Penn preached from an upper window.

Ancient Gate House Hotel *(☎ 672029, fax 673019; e info@ancientgatehouse.co.uk; singles/doubles £60/75)* is actually part of the Great West Gate (aka Brown's Gate) of Cathedral Close; st one spiral stairs and little passages add to the atmosphere.

White Hart Hotel *(☎ 672056, fax 671074; e info@whitehart-wells.co.uk; Sadler St; singles/doubles £63/82.50)* opposite is an old coaching inn, owned by the same people but with more-modern rooms.

Swan Hotel *(☎ 836300, fax 836301; e swan@bhere.co.uk; Sadler St; singles/ doubles £75/89)*, with plenty of wood panelling, is aimed more at the business market. The same company owns the **Star Hotel** *(18 High St)*, with the same contact details and prices; these don't include breakfast.

Places to Eat

Cloister Restaurant *(soup £2.60, jacket potatoes £3.60; open 10am-5pm Mon-Sat, 12.30pm-5pm Sun)* is the most atmospheric place to eat. Here you can munch within the cathedral's vaulted cloisters.

Good Earth *(☎ 678600; 4 Priory Rd; lunch £2-4; open 9am-5pm Mon-Sat)* is an excellent vegetarian café with tasty soups, pizza, quiche and salad. There's also a good deli.

City Arms *(☎ 673916; 69 High St; sandwiches £2.25-3.25, mains £5-11; dinner daily, lunch Sat & Sun)* cooks up good fish, steak, risotto and vegetarian options, washed down with real ale. Part of the pub was a jail in Tudor times.

Boxers *(☎ 672317; 1 St Thomas St; mains £7.50-14)*, upstairs in the Fountain Inn, turns out fine salmon, pheasant and vegetarian dishes; it's the local favourite, with good reason.

The hotels all have restaurants. **Anton's Bistrot** *(mains £8.50-14)* in the Crown at Wells has sea bass and duck, while **Rugantino** *(mains £6-16)* at the Ancient Gate House has a short menu of quality Italian regional dishes – definitely no pizza.

Ritchers *(☎ 679085; 5 Sadler St; 2/3- course meals £18.50/21)* is a smart little restaurant knocking up the city's finest modern British cuisine.

Entertainment

A year-round programme of lunch-time recitals and evening concerts provides the opportunity to hear the historic cathedral choir in full voice. For details of cathedral choir recitals phone ☎ 674483; for other bookings call ☎ 672773.

Wells Film Centre *(☎ 673195; w www .wellsfilmcentre.co.uk; £4/3)* is a little three-screen cinema next to the old Regal cinema, screening the latest films.

Getting There & Around

National Express run to London daily (economy return £23, four hours); it's easier to get an hourly local bus to Bristol (Nos 376 and 976; one hour) and Bath (Nos 173 and 773; 1¼ hours), then a connecting service. No 163 runs hourly to Glastonbury (15 minutes) and Street (25 minutes). Bus Nos 161/162 go from Frome (one hour) roughly hourly. Coming from the coast, bus Nos 126 and 826 travel hourly (every two hours on Sunday) from Cheddar (20 minutes).

There's no train station in Wells; the nearest is 15 miles (24km) away at Castle Cary.

There are a surprising number of car parks in Wells, but there are also many one-way streets and dead ends. It's best to make your way around by foot.

Bike City (☎ 671711; 31 Broad St; open 9am-5.30pm Mon-Sat) charges £9 per day for bike hire.

WOOKEY HOLE

On the southern edge of the Mendips, the River Axe has carved out a whole series of caves known collectively as Wookey Hole (☎ 01749-672243; w www.wookey.co.uk; adult/child £8/5; open 10am-5pm daily Apr-Oct, 10.30am-4.30pm Nov-Mar). The caves

contain a spectacular lake and some fascinating stalagmites (one of which gave rise to the legend of the Witch of Wookey Hole), and various Iron Age finds are displayed in the small museum, but essentially the caves are now run as a 'family attraction', with an ancient handmade-paper mill, an Edwardian fairground, a maze of mirrors and an arcade of vintage amusement machines.

Homestead Park (☎ 01749-673022; e homesteadpark@onetel.net.uk; camping per tent £3-4, per adult £2.50-3.50; open Easter-Sept) is a good campsite just steps from the caves. Note that children under 14 are not accepted.

Wookey Hole is just 2 miles (3km) north of Wells. Bus No 171 runs hourly from Wells (single/return £1.40/1.80, 10 minutes). A 3-mile walk to Wookey Hole is signposted from New St in Wells. Note that the village of Wookey is not the same as Wookey Hole, being west of Wells.

CHEDDAR GORGE
☎ 01934

The Mendips' most dramatic scenery can be found along its southern side where Cheddar Gorge cuts a mile-long swathe through the landscape, exposing great sections of 138m-high grey stone cliff. A signposted 3-mile (5km) round walk follows the cliffs along the most dramatic parts of the gorge.

The attractions of the gorge, more or less natural, are now part of **Cheddar Caves & Gorge** (☎ 742343; w www.cheddarcaves .co.uk; Explorer Ticket £8.90/5.90; open 10am-4.30pm daily, to 5pm summer school holidays), a 'family' day out – meaning tea-rooms, fish-and-chip and gift shops, and big crowds in summer. Visit out of season to better enjoy the natural features, although many of the eateries are closed weekdays in winter.

The stalactite- and stalagmite-filled Cox's and Gough's caves are indisputably very impressive; in the latter was discovered a 40,000-year-old skeleton (imaginatively named Cheddar Man). Add-on features include an open-top bus tour (Easter to September only), lookout tower and Crystal Quest theme cave fun for kids.

There's a **TIC** (☎ 744071, fax 744614; e cheddar.tic@sedgemoor.gov.uk; open 10am-5pm daily Easter-Sept, 10.30am-4.30pm Oct, 11am-4pm Sun Nov-Easter) in the gorge.

The Bee's Knees Cheese

The country's most famous cheese only began to become widely known when people started visiting Cheddar Gorge and taking home some of the local cheese, although Cheddar was just one of many Somerset villages that produced this type.

Over the years Cheddar has become a generic name for any pale yellow, medium-hard cheese; some is mass-produced and bland, but mature, traditionally made farmhouse Cheddar can be crumbly, tangy and delicious.

If you are interested in the process of making genuine Cheddar Cheese, visit the **Cheddar Gorge Cheese Company** (☎ 01934-742810; w www.cheddargorgecheeseco.co .uk; open daily). You can watch the cheese-maker at work and there are regular explanations of the process (usually every half-hour). It's part of the **Rural Village** (adult/child £1.50/1; open 10am-6pm daily May-Sept, 10am-4pm Apr & Oct), just off the B3135, that also includes demonstrations of lace-making, pottery, fudge-making and spinning.

Cheddar village, southwest of the gorge, has an elegant church and an ancient market cross but is otherwise disappointing. A mile (1.6km) southwest of the caves on a road off The Hayes is the Cheddar YHA Hostel (☎ 0870 770 5760, fax 744724; e cheddar@yha.org.uk; Hillfield; dorm beds £11.25), on the western side of the village.

Bus Nos 126 and 826 run between Wells (single/return £2.80/3.80, 25 minutes), 9 miles (14km) away, and Weston-Super-Mare (50 minutes) via Cheddar, hourly Monday to Saturday and every two hours on Sunday.

AXBRIDGE
☎ 01934
Axbridge is a small village with an attractive square ringed by medieval buildings; it's a pleasant detour from Cheddar.

One corner of the central square is dominated by the striking half-timbered King John's Hunting Lodge (NT; ☎ 732012; The Square; admission free; open 1pm-4pm daily Easter-Sept), a Tudor merchant's house now housing the Axbridge and District Museum; exhibits include a Roman skeleton and the old town stocks.

Another corner is occupied by the striking perpendicular Church of St John the Baptist, with 14th-century elements and a remarkable 17th-century nave ceiling.

Places to Stay & Eat
A 17th-century inn with low beams, The Lamb Inn (☎ 732253, fax 733821; e lamb inn@axbridge.org.uk; The Square; en-suite twins/doubles £40/50; mains £5-10) has good beer and decent pub grub (not Sunday evening).

The Oak House Hotel (☎ 732444, fax 733122; The Square; singles/doubles from £35/50; mains £7-12) looks newer but in fact has 12th-century fireplaces and an ancient well; crooked passages lead to well-appointed bedrooms. The likes of sea bass and tarte tatin grace the restaurant menu.

Another tempting option for food is the 15th-century Almshouse Bistro (☎ 732493; The Square; mains £9-16), dishes such as rainbow trout and guinea fowl are complemented by a fine wine list.

Getting There & Away
Axbridge is 1½ miles (2.5km) west of Cheddar; you can easily walk or cycle from Cheddar. Bus Nos 126 and 826 run to Cheddar (10 minutes) and on to Wells (30 minutes) hourly, every two hours Sunday.

MENDIP HILLS
The Mendips are a ridge of limestone hills stretching from the coast near Weston-Super-Mare to Frome in eastern Somerset. These are not lofty peaks – their highest point is Black Down (326m) to the northwest – but because they rise sharply, there are panoramic views towards Exmoor and across northwest Wiltshire.

Historically, the area has seen its share of action, and Neolithic earthworks, Bronze Age barrows and Iron Age forts can be found. More recently, lead mining was an important source of income around Charterhouse and Priddy, from Roman times to the 19th century, and coal mining played its part. Remains of mines dot the area around Radstock and Midsomer Norton to the east. Quarrying for stone is an important (and controversial) industry to this day. Pubs that loom up out of the middle of nowhere are survivors from a time when mining brought plenty of thirsty drinkers, and the landscape is dotted with gently pretty villages.

Until the Middle Ages, large tracts of land lay beneath swampy meadows, and the remaining wetlands provide an important habitat for wildlife and flora. The marshland hid relics too, including the Lake Village excavated at the turn of the 20th century (see the Glastonbury section).

Mendip villages are home to some delightful timbered houses, and several have fine perpendicular church towers. Especially impressive is that at Chewton Mendip (off the A37 between Bristol and Wells), where there's an attractive medieval churchyard cross. Farther west, the village of Priddy, the highest in the Mendips, has a massive sheep fair on the green that locals flock to from around the region.

The village of Compton Martin has a Norman church with a 15th-century tower. A mile to the east, West Harptree is prettier, with two 17th-century former manor houses. Near East Harptree are the remains of Norman Richmont Castle, captured from supporters of Matilda by those of King Stephen in 12th-century skirmishing.

Local TICs in the surrounding towns stock leaflets with information on walking and cycling opportunities in the area, including village trails that take in points of interest.

The A371 skirts the southern side of the Mendip Hills, and any of the towns along it – Axbridge, Cheddar, Wells or Frome – would make good touring bases, though Wells has the best range of facilities.

Getting There & Away

Don't expect buses to be very frequent off the major roads. Bus Nos 126 and 826 run between Wells, Cheddar and Axbridge (hourly, every two hours on Sunday). Nos 161 and 162 link Wells with Frome (one hour; hourly, every two hours on Sunday), while No 173 runs from Bath to Radstock (30 minutes), Midsomer Norton (40 minutes) and Wells (1¼ hours, hourly, four on Sunday).

The Mendip Hills are squeezed in between the A38 Bristol to Burnham-on-Sea and the A37 Bristol to Wells roads.

FROME
☎ 01373 • pop 23,200

Frome (pronounced froom) was an important Saxon ecclesiastical centre, then made good again via the cloth industry; today it's essentially a pretty shopping town, with attractive old buildings and narrow alleys leading up the hills from the River Frome. Its location to the east of the Mendips makes it a clear alternative to the towns of the west.

The helpful TIC (☎ 467271, fax 451 733; e frome.tic@ukonline.co.uk; The Round Tower, 2 Bridge St; open 10am-5pm Mon-Sat Easter-Oct, 10am-4.30pm Nov-Mar) can advise on accommodation and sells the Frome Town Trail walking tour leaflet (30p).

Frome Museum (1 North Parade; admission free; open 11am-2pm Tues-Sat) has a reasonable local heritage collection, with the emphasis on industry. Cheap St is home to Tudor houses, while Catherine Hill is a tumbling road of arts and antiques shops.

Frome Festival (box office ☎ 455420; w www.fromefestival.co.uk), held over 10 days in early July, boasts a varied range of events featuring classical, world and contemporary music, drama, poetry, art and food in various venues around town, and there's a street carnival and other alfresco affairs.

The Sun Inn (☎ 471913; 6 Catherine St; ensuite singles/doubles £30/50) is a lively pub offering B&B in attractive, bright rooms.

National Express coaches run daily to London (economy return £22, four hours) from Market Place. Bus Nos 161 and 162 run to Wells (one hour; hourly, every two hours on Sunday), while Nos 267 and 767 head to Bath (one hour, hourly, four on Sunday). Trains run every two hours to Bath (single £5.90, 40 minutes), Bristol (saver return £13.10, one hour) and Weymouth (£14.30, 1¼ hours).

GLASTONBURY
☎ 01458 • pop 7800

Little more than an extended village, Glastonbury is a strangely appealing place. Its important links with early Christian growth seem at odds with the pagan New Age culture that tends to envelop it, but somehow mythology and religion mingle to produce an aroma of peaceful energy. Or maybe that's the incense sticks.

According to various legends, Glastonbury played host to the young Jesus and his great-uncle Joseph of Arimathea, who may or may not have later returned with the chalice from the Last Supper. Glastonbury was also reputedly the burial place of King Arthur and Queen Guinevere, the nearby tor (hill) being the Isle of Avalon or, alternatively, a gateway to the underworld. Truth or fancy, with its mix of messiahs, massages and meat-free meals, this is the place to head for spiritual enlightenment of one kind or another.

Orientation & Information

The main bus stop is next to the town hall in Magdalene St, within sight of the market cross and the abbey ruins.

Glastonbury's TIC (☎ 832954, fax 832949; e glastonbury.tic@ukonline.co.uk; The Tribunal, 9 High St; open 10am-5pm Sun-Thur, 10am-5.30pm Fri & Sat Apr-Sept, 10am-4pm Sun-Thur, 10am-4.30pm Fri & Sat Oct-Mar) stocks free maps and accommodation lists, and sells leaflets describing local walks and the Glastonbury Town Trail (30p).

There is Internet access at Café Galatea (see Places to Eat).

Glastonbury Abbey

If you visit only one ruined abbey founded by Jesus' brother-in-law and once graced with the bones of a mythical warrior-king, make it this one; it's a peaceful place to clear your head of the omnipresent mysticism and learn a bit about ancient monasteries.

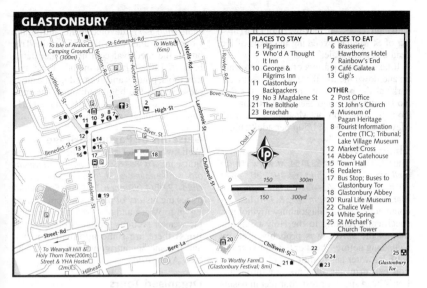

GLASTONBURY

PLACES TO STAY
1 Pilgrims
5 Who'd A Thought
   It Inn
10 George &
   Pilgrims Inn
11 Glastonbury
   Backpackers
19 No 3 Magdalene St
21 The Bolthole
23 Berachah

PLACES TO EAT
6 Brasserie;
   Hawthorns Hotel
7 Rainbow's End
9 Café Galatea
13 Gigi's

OTHER
2 Post Office
3 St John's Church
4 Museum of
   Pagan Heritage
8 Tourist Information
   Centre (TIC); Tribunal;
   Lake Village Museum
12 Market Cross
14 Abbey Gatehouse
15 Town Hall
16 Pedalers
17 Bus Stop; Buses to
   Glastonbury Tor
18 Glastonbury Abbey
20 Rural Life Museum
22 Chalice Well
24 White Spring
25 St Michael's
   Church Tower

Legend has it the first church was founded by Joseph of Arimathea in the 1st century, but the earliest evidence is from the 7th century when King Ine gave a charter to a monastery. The first abbey church reached the height of its importance in the 10th century.

In 1184 the church was destroyed by fire; reconstruction began in the reign of Henry II. In 1191 monks claimed to have had visions confirming hints in old manuscripts that the 6th-century warrior-king Arthur and his wife Guinevere were buried in the grounds. Excavations to the south of the old church uncovered a tomb, said to be theirs, and a lead cross recording that fact, which has since disappeared. The couple was reinterred in front of the high altar of the new church in 1278 and the tomb survived until 1539 when Henry VIII dissolved the monasteries.

The last abbot was hanged, drawn and quartered on the tor. After that, the abbey complex gradually collapsed, its component parts scavenged to provide building materials. It wasn't until the 19th century that Romanticism brought renewed interest in King Arthur and the sites associated with him.

The ruins you see at Glastonbury today are mainly of the church built after the 1184 fire. They include the **St Mary's** or **Lady Chapel**, built, unusually, at the western end of the church, with an elaborately carved doorway; some nave walls; parts of the crossing arches, which may have been scissor-shaped like those in Wells Cathedral; some **medieval tiles**; and remains of the choir. The site of the supposed **tomb of Arthur and Guinevere** is marked in the grass. A little to the side of the main site, don't miss the flagstone-floored **Abbot's Kitchen** (c.1340) with its soaring chimney; later use as a Quaker meeting house allowed it to survive intact.

An award-winning **museum** explores the site's history and contains a model showing what the abbey would have looked like in its heyday. Behind it, and easy to overlook, are tiny **St Patrick's Chapel** and a **thorn tree** supposedly grown from the original that sprouted on Wearyall Hill (southwest of town off Street Rd) when Joseph of Arimathea stuck his staff into the ground. It flowers in spring and at Christmas.

Entrance to the abbey is through the **Abbey Gatehouse** (☎ 832267; w www.glas tonburyabbey.com; Magdalene St; adult/child £3.50/1.50; site open 9.30am-6pm or dusk daily Mar-May & Sept-Nov, 9am-5.30pm June-Aug, 10am-dusk Dec-Feb).

Glastonbury Tor

Tor is a Celtic word used to describe a hill shaped like a triangular wedge. On the 160m-high summit of Glastonbury Tor stands a tower, all that remains of the medieval church of St Michael, a saint frequently associated with high places. On the tower front is a carving of St Michael weighing the souls of the dead in a giant scale.

It takes three-quarters of an hour to walk up and down the tor; there are short-stay car parks at the bottom of both paths. Tor Bus No 196 runs there and back every 30 minutes from the bus stop on Magdalene St from May to September (£1/50p per adult/child).

Chalice Well

The Chalice Well (☎ 831154; W www.chalice well.org.uk; adult/child £2.30/1.20; open 10am-5pm daily Apr-Oct, 11am-5pm Feb, Mar & Nov, 11am-4pm Dec & Jan) has become entwined in Glastonbury mythology, specifically relating to the Holy Grail, although the spring was probably used by Celts long before Christ or the 800-year-old well. Its water has traditions of healing and you can drink as it pours out through a lion's-head spout, or rest your feet in basins surrounded by flowers. Mysticism aside, the gardens and meadows are beautiful, peaceful spots to relax or picnic.

The Chalice Well is also known as the Red or Blood Spring; its sister White Spring surfaces across Wellhouse Lane. Spigots from both springs empty into the street, where New Age types queue up to fill containers.

Rural Life Museum

This interesting museum (☎ 831197; Abbey Farm, Chilkwell St; adult/child £2.50/1; open 10am-5pm Tues-Fri, 2pm-6pm Sat & Sun Easter-Oct, 10am-3pm Tues-Sat Nov-Easter) displays artefacts associated with farming, cider-making, cheese-making and other aspects of Somerset country life. A key exhibition follows the life of a Victorian farm worker through birth, school and marriage; don't miss the three-seater toilet, with holes for Mum, Dad and Junior. The late-14th-century tithe barn has fine carvings on the gables and porch, and an impressive timber roof; it now houses a collection of vintage agricultural machinery.

Lake Village Museum

Between 1888 and 1907, amateur archaeologist Arthur Bulleid excavated a prehistoric village that flourished near Glastonbury when the surrounding lowlands had not yet been drained. A small museum

(EH; same contact details & hours as TIC; adult/child £2/1) devoted to his intriguing work is upstairs from the TIC in the Tribunal, the medieval courthouse that dates back to 1400. Artefacts include bone and iron tools, pottery and even a dugout canoe, preserved in the bog conditions. The museum is owned by English Heritage (EH) and admission is free for members.

Museum of Pagan Heritage

Well, what better place to have it? This 'museum' (☎ 831666; W www.themuseum ofpaganheritage.org; St John's Square; adult/child £2.95/1.95; open 10.30am-5pm daily) traces the history of paganism from ancient Egypt to Wicca and modern cults. Ignoring the weaker sections (posters from Dracula films) there are some informative items, and it's another intriguing insight into the New Age world.

Organised Tours

Many companies offer tours of Glastonbury costing £40 to £50 per carload and lasting three hours. The TIC has listings; try Merlin Tours (☎ 01963-240613).

Glastonbury Festival

This three-day summer extravaganza (bookings ☎ 0115-912 9129; W www.glastonbury festivals.co.uk) is essentially now a massive music festival featuring top bands – 2002 giggers included Garbage, Air, Coldplay and, um, Rolf Harris – with a huge alternative carnival going on around it, involving world music, theatre, circus acts, natural healing and so on, although it's not quite the patchouli-scented hippy-fest of old. It takes place at Worthy Farm, Pilton, 8 miles (13km) east of Glastonbury. Admission is by advance ticket only (about £100 for the whole festival).

Places to Stay

There are several campsites in and around Glastonbury.

Isle of Avalon (☎/fax 833618; Godney Rd; camping per tent/person from £6/2), a pleasant site with good facilities, is half a mile northwest of the centre, off the B3151 (Meare Rd).

Bright and lively Glastonbury Backpackers (☎ 833353, fax 835988; e glastonbury@ backpackers-online.com; 4 Market Place;

dorm beds £10, doubles with/without en suite £30/26), in the old Crown Hotel, has a popular bar with live bands, a courtyard area and a funky café, which serves noodles, salads and burritos (£5 to £6.50).

The nearest YHA hostel is in nearby Street (see Around Glastonbury).

Many Glastonbury B&Bs offer aromatherapy, muesli breakfasts, vegetarian meals and so on. The TIC has a complete list.

The Bolthole (☎ 832800; 32 Chilkwell St; doubles from £37) is a comfortable modern bungalow near the springs. Bathrooms are shared.

Central **Pilgrims** (☎ 834722; w www.pilgrimsbb.co.uk; 12-13 Norbins Rd; en-suite singles/doubles from £30/50) is a small, mellow B&B in a pleasant Victorian terraced house; holistic treatments are available.

Berachah (☎ 834214, fax 835417; Wellhouse Lane; rooms per person £25) is a modern, New-Agey place near the tor. The fridge is packed with vegetarian goodies for a DIY breakfast.

Who'd A Thought It Inn ☎ 834460, fax 831039; e enquiries@whodathoughtit.co.uk; 17 Northload St; B&B singles/doubles £40/58) is a cheerful pub with comfortable rooms with en suites, real ales and above-average grub (mains £6.50 to £13).

George & Pilgrims Inn (☎ 831146, fax 832252; 1 High St; singles/doubles £50/65) is an imposing Gothic building from 1475 with dark wooden beams and light snacks (£5 to £7).

The grand Georgian hallway of **No 3 Magdalene St** (☎ 832129, fax 834227; e info@ numberthree.co.uk; en-suite rooms from £65-85) leads to luxurious, substantial rooms; some have abbey views, and three are in an annex in the garden.

Places to Eat

Glastonbury is perfect for vegetarians, one of the few places in England where nut roasts are more common than pot roasts. Glastonbury Backpackers, Who'd A Thought It Inn and George & Pilgrims all serve good munchies.

Café Galatea (☎ 834284; 5a High St; mains £7.50; open 11am-4pm Mon, 11am-9pm Wed-Sun) does global snacks, lunches and dinners such as enchiladas, cannelloni and stir-fries. It's also a sculpture gallery and cybercafé (£3/5 for half-/one hour).

Legendary **Rainbow's End** (☎ 833896; 17a High St; mains £3-5.50; open 10am-4pm daily) has won awards for its delicious (and substantial) vegetarian dishes and huge chunks of chocolate cake.

If you fancy linguini over lentils, try **Gigi's** (☎ 834612; 2 Magdalene St; mains £5-15; open 6pm-11pm Tues-Sun & noon-2.30pm Sat & Sun) for good pizza, pasta and meaty mains.

The Brasserie (☎ 831255; Hawthorns Hotel, 8-12 Northload St; mains £5.50-12; closed Mon lunch) is a smart spot cooking up cuisine based largely around fresh fish and (horror!) meat, with some token vegetarian pasta options.

Getting There & Away

There's one daily National Express service to London (economy return £23, 4¼ hours) and two to Bath (£8.25, one hour).

There's one bus daily to Bristol (No 327, 1½ hours) and two to Bath (Nos 327 and 403, one hour) but it's easier to get connections in Wells, 6 miles (10km) and 15 minutes away; of the many buses, Nos 163, 377 and 977 are most frequent (at least half-hourly). Bus Nos 29 and 929 go to Taunton (one hour) every two hours.

There is no train station at Glastonbury.

AROUND GLASTONBURY
Street
☎ 01458 • pop 10,500

Street took its name from an ancient causeway that ran across the River Brue to Glastonbury. These days it is notable mainly for **Clarks Village**, a discount centre that sells branded clothes as well as Clarks shoes. Clarks, the shoemaker, began business in Street in 1825, and the quirky little **Shoe Museum** (☎ 842169; Clarks Factory, 40 High St; admission free; open 10am-4.45pm Mon-Fri, 10am-5pm Sat, 11am-5pm Sun) displays footwear through the ages, from Roman times and from around the globe.

Street YHA Hostel (☎ 0870 770 6056, fax 442738; The Chalet, Ivythorn Hill; dorm beds £9.50) is a simple chalet about 2 miles (3km) south of the centre. Hourly bus No 376 from Glastonbury (15 minutes) stops at Marshalls Elm, from where the hostel is a 500m walk.

QUANTOCK HILLS
Their name originating from the Celtic word meaning rim, the Quantocks are a ridge of

red sandstone hills, 12 miles (19km) long, not much more than 3 miles (5km) wide, running down to the sea at Quantoxhead in western Somerset.

The Quantocks don't tower (385m high at most) and, like close neighbour Exmoor, they can be wild in places – bleak, even. The winding lanes and wooded dells make this enjoyable walking country.

Some of the most attractive country is owned by the National Trust, including the Beacon and Bicknoller Hills, which offer views of the Bristol Channel and Exmoor to the northwest. In 1861 red deer were introduced to these hills from Exmoor and there's a local tradition of stag hunting.

The Quantock Hills have been designated an Area of Outstanding Natural Beauty (AONB) – not quite a national park, but protected and managed by legislation and rangers. The **AONB Service** (☎ *01278-733642; fax 732763;* **w** *www.quantockhills .com; Castle St, Nether Stowey*) is in the library at Nether Stowey, and provides literature as well as organising guided walks.

The Quantock Greenway comprises two loop walking routes of around 20 miles (31km) each, circling the north and south Quantocks. The AONB Service also provides colour card-maps and leaflets describing shorter circular walks.

Bridgwater or Taunton, to the east and south, respectively, make reasonable bases for exploring the Quantocks, but it's more atmospheric to stay in one of the villages.

Nether Stowey & Holford
Poet Samuel Taylor Coleridge wrote *The Rime of the Ancient Mariner* while living in **Coleridge Cottage** (NT; ☎ *01278-732662; admission £3; open 2pm-5pm Tues-Thur & Sun Apr-Sept*) in **Nether Stowey** from 1797 to 1800. Some of the rooms have been restored to their original bright colours. Nether Stowey itself is an attractive village, with the remains of an 11th-century castle topping a nearby hill.

Coleridge's friend William Wordsworth, and Wordsworth's sister Dorothy, also spent 1797 at nearby Alfoxden House in **Holford**, a pretty village near a wooded valley. *Lyrical Ballads* (1798) was the joint product of Coleridge's and Wordsworth's stays.

Set in a wooded area 1½ miles (2.4km) west of Holford is the **Quantock Hills YHA**

Hostel (☎ *0870 770 6006, fax 01278-741224; Sevenacres; dorm beds £9.50*); it's often booked out so call ahead. Bus No 15 from Bridgwater gets you to Holford or Kilve (50 minutes, six daily), and No 23 from Taunton (one hour, five daily) will drop you at Kilve; in either case it's then a 1½ mile walk.

The Manse (☎ *01278-732917; Lime St; en-suite doubles £40; open Easter-Sept*) is a well-furnished B&B in an early-19th-century house opposite Coleridge Cottage.

Crowcombe
One of the prettiest Quantock villages, Crowcombe still has cottages made of stone and cob (a mixture of mud and straw), many with thatched roofs. The ancient Church of the Holy Ghost has wonderful carved 16th-century bench ends with surprisingly pagan themes (the Green Man is common), and part of its spire still stands in the churchyard where it fell when lightning struck in 1725. The 16th-century Church House opposite has mullioned windows and a Tudor door.

There aren't many accommodation or eating options in Crowcombe – Nether Stowey has more facilities.

Quantock Orchard Caravan Park (☎ *01984-618618;* **w** *www.flaxpool.freeserve .co.uk; Flaxpool; camping per tent & car low/high season £7.95/12.95*) is an excellent campsite with superb facilities, including a heated swimming pool; it's off the A358, just southeast of Crowcombe.

A large country house, the **Crowcombe YHA Hostel** (☎ *0870 770 5782, fax 01984-667249; Heathfield; dorm beds £9.50; open Mon-Sat Easter-June, daily July & Aug*) is 2 miles (3km) southeast of the village and half a mile from Crowcombe station on the West Somerset Railway. It's a 7-mile (11km) hike over the Quantocks from the hostel in Holford (see Nether Stowey & Holford).

Getting There & Away
The Quantocks' lanes and villages are best enjoyed by avoiding day-tripper crowded weekends. Coming by car, the M5 linking Bristol and Exeter skirts the eastern edge of the Quantocks. The A358 runs along the western side of the hills, linking Taunton to Williton in the north.

Hourly trains from Bristol call at Bridgwater (saver return £11.50, 40 minutes) and

Taunton (£15, 45 minutes); from there, you really need your own wheels as buses are limited. Half-hourly bus No 28 runs along the southern edge from Taunton to Minehead but only stops at Crowcombe (30 minutes) once daily; No 302 runs between Crowcombe and Taunton on Tuesday and three times on Saturday. Neither bus runs on Sunday. Bus No 23 runs between Taunton and Nether Stowey (30 minutes, daily Monday to Friday), and Nos 15 and 915 run between Bridgwater and Nether Stowey eight times daily.

TAUNTON
☎ 01823 • pop 35,000

Taunton is the administrative capital for Somerset, and a transport hub for central Somerset as well as a gateway to the Quantocks; however, it's basically a small shopping town, with not much to keep you. The most famous landmark is the **Church of St Mary Magdalene** *(open 10am-4pm Mon-Fri, 10am-1pm Sat)*, with its 50m-high tower carved from the red rock of the nearby Quantocks and first erected in the 15th century.

The **TIC** *(☎ 336344; e tautic@somerset .gov.uk; Paul St; open 9.30am-5.30pm Mon-Fri, 9.30am-5pm Sat)* is in the library.

Somerset County & Military Museum *(☎ 320201; Castle Green; adult/child £2.50/1; open 10am-5pm Tues-Sat Apr-Oct, 10am-3pm Tues-Sat Nov-Mar)*, displaying prehistoric and Roman artefacts, fossils and collections of silver, ceramics and toys, is housed in **Taunton Castle**, sections of which date from the 12th century. The Great Hall was where Judge Jeffreys held one of his bloodiest assizes in 1685 (see 'The Bloody Assizes' boxed text later in this chapter).

If the need arises, B&Bs are concentrated along Wellington Rd and Staplegrove. Try **Beaufort Lodge** *(☎ 326420; 18 Wellington Rd; singles/doubles from £30/50)*, a pleasant Victorian house near the centre.

There are plenty of cafés and takeaways around High St and East St. **La Bonne Vie** *(☎ 274748; 33a High St; mains £6.75-13.50; closed Sun)* mixes global flavours, with plenty of Tex-Mex and oriental dishes.

National Express coaches run to London (economy return £18.50, four hours, six daily), Bristol (£6.50, 1½ hours, four daily), Bridgwater (£3.75, 30 minutes, seven daily) and Exeter (£6, 45 minutes, four daily).

Hourly bus Nos 28 (Monday to Saturday) and 28A (Sunday) cross the Quantocks to Minehead (1¼ hours). Bus Nos 29 (Monday to Saturday) and 929 (Sunday) run to Glastonbury (50 minutes) and Wells (one hour) every two hours.

Trains run to London (saver return £49.10, two hours, every two hours), Exeter (£11.90, 30 minutes, half-hourly) and Plymouth (£21.80, 1½ hours, half-hourly).

AROUND TAUNTON
Montacute

The ancient village of Montacute, named after the pointed hill originally called Mons Acutus, is home to one of England's finest Elizabethan mansions **Montacute House** *(NT; ☎/fax 01935-823289; e montacute@ ntrust.org.uk; house admission £6.20/3, garden only Apr-Oct £3.40/1.50, Nov-Mar £2/1; house open 11am-5pm Wed-Mon Apr-Oct, garden also open 11.30am-4pm Nov-Mar)*. Montacute House boasts remarkable interior plasterwork, fine chimneypieces and carved parapets. Built in the 1590s for Sir Edward Phelips, a Speaker of the House of Commons, its state rooms display Tudor and Jacobean portraits on loan from London's National Portrait Gallery. Formal gardens and a landscaped park surround the house.

Montacute is 22 miles (35km) southeast of Taunton and 4 miles (6.4km) west of Yeovil. Bus No 681 from Yeovil (20 minutes, hourly Monday to Saturday) to South Petherton passes close by.

Haynes Motor Museum

This 300-strong car collection *(☎ 01963-440804; w www.haynesmotormuseum.co.uk; Sparkford; adult/child £6/3.50; open 10am-4.30pm daily Nov-Feb, 9.30am-5.30pm daily Mar-Oct, to 6.30pm in summer school holidays)* includes a fabulous array of the outstanding, the old and the merely odd – see Aston Martins and Ferraris rub shoulders with Austins and, well, the Sinclair C5. And yes, it's *that* Haynes, of the ubiquitous repair manuals that you'll find in charity shops throughout the country. The museum is on the A359 off the A303 near Yeovil.

Cleeve Abbey

Tucked away in Washford between Minehead and the Quantocks is this remarkable medieval abbey *(☎ 01984-640377; adult/child*

WESSEX

£2.80/1.40; open 10am-6pm daily Apr-Sept, 10am-5pm Oct, 10am-1pm & 2pm-4pm Nov-Mar), established by Cistercian monks in 1198 and named *Vallis Florida* (Valley of Flowers). It's relatively well preserved, with fascinating 13th-century floor tiles and wall paintings. Though not spectacular or grand, it paints a vivid picture of the lifestyle of medieval monks.

Washford is 5 miles (8km) east of Minehead on the A39. Bus Nos 28 (half-hourly Monday to Saturday) and 928 (every two hours on Sunday) run from Minehead (15 minutes) and Taunton (45 minutes).

West Somerset Railway

For those who enjoy extended train trips through pretty countryside, trains on Britain's longest privately run railway *(24-hr talking timetable ☎ 01643-707650, other information ☎ 01643-704996; ⊛ www.west-somerset-rail way.co.uk)* steam between Bishops Lydeard and Minehead, 20 miles (32km) away (see the Exmoor section). There are stops along the line at Crowcombe, Doniford Beach, Stogumber, Williton, Watchet, Washford, Blue Anchor and Dunster.

Trains run between four and eight times daily from mid-March to October, otherwise occasional days only. Tickets from Bishops Lydeard to Minehead cost single/return £6.50/9.80, and the journey takes 1¼ hours.

Bus Nos 28 and 28A run from Taunton (15 minutes, half-hourly Monday to Saturday); No 928 runs every 1½ hours on Sunday.

Exmoor National Park

Stretching from western Somerset into North Devon, Exmoor is a small national park (265 square miles; 687 sq km) with heather-clad moorlands, idyllic villages and breathtakingly beautiful coastal scenery: humpbacked headlands give superb views across the Bristol Channel, and rocky cliffs (the highest in England, rising to 366m) seem about to tumble into the sea.

Inland, the landscape is gentler and less rugged than Dartmoor, making it excellent walking territory, though anyone who's been caught in a storm here will know it can still be pretty inhospitable. The high plateau rises steeply behind the coast up to Dunkery Beacon (519m), cut by fast-flowing streams; the hidden valleys and dells inspired RD Blackmore's tale of feuding and romance, *Lorna Doone* (Doone Valley is a popular walking destination in the park). On the southern side the two main rivers, the Exe and Barle, wind their way along wooded valleys.

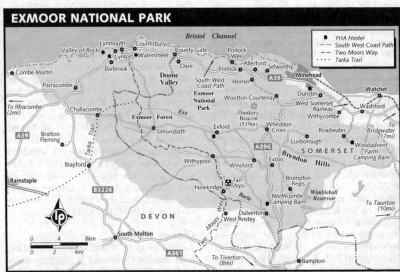

Horned sheep, Exmoor ponies (descended from ancient hill stock) and England's largest herd of wild red deer still roam the moors – the symbol of the park is the antlered head of a stag.

There are several particularly attractive villages: Lynton and Lynmouth, joined by a water-operated railway; Porlock, on the edge of the moor in a beautiful valley; Dunster, dominated by its partly medieval castle; and Selworthy, with traditional thatched cottages.

Arguably the most dramatic section of the South West Coast Path runs from Minehead, just outside the northeastern boundary of the park, to Padstow in Cornwall.

Orientation

From west to east the park is only about 21 miles (34km) and north to south just 12 miles (19km). It's accessible from the west through Barnstaple, from the southwest through South Molton, from the south via Tiverton, from the southeast through Taunton, and from the east through Minehead.

Within the park boundaries, the main centres are Dulverton on the southern edge; Exford in the centre; Dunster in the east; and Porlock, Lynton and Lynmouth on the coast.

There are over 600 miles (966km) of public footpaths and bridleways, most of them waymarked.

Information

You can get information in the TICs at Barnstaple, Ilfracombe, Lynton and Minehead, but for the best maps, books and advice, contact one of the five National Park Authority (NPA) visitor centres in and around the park: **Combe Martin** (☎ 01271-883319; Seacot, Cross St), **County Gate** (☎ 01598-741321; A39 Countisbury), **Dunster** (☎ 01643-821835; Dunster Steep), **Lynmouth** (☎ 01598-752509; The Esplanade) and the main **Dulverton Visitor Centre** (☎ 01398-323841; e dulvertonvc@exmoor-national park.gov.uk; 7-9 Fore St). They're open 10am to 5pm daily from Easter to October, with limited opening hours the rest of the year; Dulverton tends to have longer hours.

The administrative offices of **Exmoor NPA** (☎ 01398-323665, fax 323150; e info@ex moor-nationalpark.gov.uk; Exmoor House) are also in Dulverton.

The *Exmoor Visitor* is a free annual newspaper listing useful addresses, accommodation and a programme of guided walks and bike rides from the villages offered by the NPA and local organisations.

The visitor centres and TICs stock a wide range of walking guides and Ordnance Survey maps; the best for general use is Ordnance Survey Explorer OL9 *Exmoor* 1:25,000 (£12.99).

There are three comprehensive websites covering Exmoor. The NPA site is at w www .exmoor-nationalpark.gov.uk. The Exmoor Tourist Association site (w www.exmoor tourism.org) lists accommodation and details activities and w www.whatsonexmoor.com is similar but run by Exmoor residents.

Most of the villages on Exmoor are tiny so ATMs are few and far between – get cash in Dulverton, Lynton or Minehead, or bring plenty.

Activities

Walking Although a large percentage of Exmoor is privately owned, there are numerous waymarked paths. The best-known routes are the Somerset and North Devon Coast Path (part of the South West Coast Path) and the Exmoor section of the Two Moors Way, which starts in Lynmouth and follows the River Barle through Withypool and on to Dartmoor.

Part of the 180-mile (290km) Tarka Trail (based on the countryside that inspired Henry Williamson's *Tarka the Otter*) is in the park. Join it in Combe Martin and walk to Lynton/Lynmouth, then inland to Brayford and Barnstaple.

Exmoor's main walking centres are Lynton, Porlock, County Gate, Oare, Horner, Exford, Simonsbath, Withypool and Dulverton. The *Exmoor & West Somerset Public Transport Guide*, free from TICs, also includes detailed route descriptions of a dozen walks that are accessible by public transport.

Walks led by the NPA or other organisations go virtually daily in the summer, but run throughout the year; they cost £3/5 under/over four hours. Details are in *Exmoor Visitor*, or pick up the *Guided Walks & Events* leaflet from NPA centres, which also stock a variety of leaflets (75p) describing walks in specific areas, as well as guidebooks and maps to the main trails.

Cycling Cyclists are not allowed on public footpaths or the open moor, and horse

WESSEX

riders and walkers have priority on public bridleways and roads used as public paths. The visitor centres can advise on regulations.

Official areas for cyclists include a coastal route, along the old Barnstaple railway line, parts of the Tarka Trail, the Brendon Hills and Crown Estate woodland. The West Country Way runs through Exmoor from Padstow to Bristol.

NPA offices sell leaflets (75p) describing routes through areas where cycling is permitted.

Pony Trekking & Horse Riding Exmoor is popular riding country and stables scattered around the park offer ponies and horses for riders of all abilities for trips of a few hours to a full day; *Exmoor Visitor* has contact information for many. Charges start at about £10 per hour. Wet weather gear is recommended – it can turn cold and wet very quickly.

Try **West Anstey Farm** (☎ 01398-341354; *Dulverton*), **Doone Valley Riding Stables** (☎ 01598-741278; *Cloud Farm, Oare, Lynton*), or **Burrowhayes Farm** (☎ 01643-862 463; w www.burrowhayes.co.uk; *West Luccombe, Porlock*).

Moorland Safaris Several companies offer 4WD safari trips, some tracking wild red deer, costing around £15 for three hours. **Barle Valley Safaris** (☎ 01643-851386; e barlevalley@hotmail.com) trips depart from Dulverton or Minehead, while **Exmoor Safari** (☎ 01643-831229) runs from Exford.

Fishing For river fishing you will need a permit, usually obtainable from the main shop or village post office, or landowners, and you may also require a rod licence from the **Environment Agency** (☎ 01392-444000); *Exmoor Visitor* has contact details. Sea fishing is possible from harbour walls, and boats can be hired in the larger coastal villages.

Places to Stay & Eat

There are YHA Hostels in Minehead and Ilfracombe (outside the park), and Lynton and Exford in the park. Camping is allowed with the landowner's permission; local shops will usually know who owns the surrounding land. Along the coast, there are regular camping grounds with all the usual facilities.

There are also camping barns (bring your own sleeping bag) at Woodadvent Farm in the east of the park near Roadwater (£3.75) and Northcombe, a mile from Dulverton (£4.50). For bookings call ☎ 01200-420102.

There's no shortage of B&Bs and hotels in this holiday area. There are plenty of places to eat in Exmoor – old country pubs with low beams to hit your head on and log fires in the winter, little shops serving cream teas, and more upmarket restaurants.

For those who are thinking of staying for a week or more, hiring a cottage might be fun. The **Exmoor Holiday Group** (☎ 01398-323722; w www.exmoor-holidays.co.uk) is the specialist in this area.

Exmoor Visitor has accommodation listings, as do the *Exmoor Coast & Country* brochure from TICs and the websites mentioned earlier.

Getting There & Around

It's easiest to get around with your own transport, on foot or horseback, because bus services are limited, and virtually nonexistent in the west of the park. On the other hand, the narrow streets of Exmoor villages quickly clog up in peak season and parking can be tricky.

Bus National Express runs from London to Barnstaple (economy return £34, 5½ hours, four daily) and Ilfracombe (£34, six hours, twice daily), and from Bristol to Barnstaple (£18.50, three hours, daily).

You could also do part of this journey on the privately run West Somerset Railway (see Somerset earlier in this chapter).

The *Exmoor & West Somerset Public Transport Guide*, free from TICs, is invaluable, with a route map and timetables.

From Ilfracombe, bus No 300 runs to Minehead (two hours) via Lynton (one hour) and Porlock (1¼ hours) three times daily.

From Minehead, No 285 (No 400 Saturday and Sunday) follows a circuit visiting Dunster (10 minutes), Exford (1¼ hours) and Porlock (1½ hours), three times daily (£2/1 per day). No 38 is more direct, running to Porlock (20 minutes, seven daily Monday to Saturday) and Porlock Weir (25 minutes) via Selworthy. Nos 28 and 39 run to Dunster (15 minutes, every 20 minutes Monday to Saturday), while No 928 runs on Sunday (every two hours).

From Tiverton, No 398 runs to Minehead (1¾ hours) via Dulverton (30 minutes) and Dunster (1½ hours) six times daily Monday to Saturday, occasionally diverting to Exford.

From Barnstaple, No 307 goes to Dulverton (1¼ hours, every two hours Monday to Saturday) and on to Taunton (1¼ hours from Dulverton), while Nos 309 and 310 run to Lynton (one hour; hourly).

Train From London Paddington, InterCity services stop at Taunton (saver return £49.10, two hours, every two hours), Tiverton Parkway (SuperAdvance return £34, 2½ hours, hourly) and Exeter (saver return £54.10, 2½ hours, at least hourly). From Exeter, the scenic Tarka Line runs to Barnstaple (£13.80, 1¼ hours, every two hours Monday to Saturday, four on Sunday).

Bicycle Several places around the park hire mountain bikes. Try **Tarka Trail** (☎ 01271-324202; Train Station, Barnstaple) which offers tourers/mountain bikes for £6/8 per day; **Fremington Quay** (☎ 01271-372586; w www.fremingtonquaycafe.co.uk) just west of Barnstaple, with bikes at £9.50 per day or **Lance Nicholson** (☎ 01398-323409; 9 High St) in Dulverton who charges £6/10 per half/full day.

DULVERTON
☎ 01398 • pop 1300 • elevation 151m
Heading from the south, the local 'capital' is your first stop at the edge of the moor and home to the main NPA centre. Though a sleepy place, it's the largest settlement before the coast.

The **National Park Visitor Centre** (☎ 01398-323841; e dulvertonvc@exmoor-nationalpark.gov.uk; 7-9 Fore St; open 10am-5pm Easter-Oct) is in the library.

Walks
The four-hour circular walk along the river from Dulverton to Tarr Steps – an ancient stone clapper bridge across the River Barle, purportedly built by the devil for sunbathing – is recommended. Add another three or four hours to the walk by continuing from Tarr Steps up Winsford Hill for distant views over Devon.

By Tarr Steps, **Tarr Farm** (☎ 01643-851507; ploughman's lunch £6.50, mains £10-15; closed Tues & Sun evenings) is a 16th-century riverside inn with cream teas, a popular restaurant and fantastic ice cream.

Places to Stay & Eat
Northcombe Camping Barn (☎ 01200-420102; beds £4.50) is a converted watermill about 1 mile (1.6km) from Dulverton.

Town Mills (☎ 323124; w www.townmills dulverton.co.uk; singles £30-45, doubles £48-55) is a charming Georgian mill house offering breakfast in your room and log fires. The driveway is just off the High St; it's the only really central B&B.

Highercombe Farm (☎/fax 323616; e abi gail@highercombe.demon.co.uk; doubles with en suite from £39) is an excellent farmhouse B&B on the edge of the moor, 3 miles (5km) north of Dulverton at the end of a no-through road. There's also a self-catering annexe sleeping six. Be aware that there's another B&B called Highercombe nearby.

The Lion Hotel (☎ 323444, fax 323980; 2 Bank Square; en-suite singles/doubles £32/59; mains £5.50-10), the village's pleasant central pub, offers comfortable B&B and local trout and salmon dishes.

The cuisine at **Archiamma** (☎ 323397; 26 High St; lunch £6-7.50, dinner mains £9.50-13; closed Tues lunch, Sun & Mon) is strong on local produce and Exmoor beef and fish. There's also an attractive vine-decked garden for summer days at this cosy, smart bistro.

EXFORD
☎ 01643 • elevation 300m
The most picturesque inland village, Exford is a photogenic hamlet straddling the River Exe. With varied accommodation options, it's a good base for walks, especially to Dunkery Beacon, the highest point on Exmoor, 4 miles (6.5km) northeast.

Places to Stay & Eat
Westermill Farm (☎ 831238, fax 831660; e holidays@westermill-exmoor.co.uk; camping per adult/child £4/1, cottages per week Sept-May/Jun-Aug from £150/325; camping Apr-Oct) is a peaceful riverside spot just outside Exford, off the Porlock road; there are also six cottages to rent.

Exford YHA Hostel (☎ 0870 770 5828, fax 831650; Exe Mead; dorm beds £11.25; open daily July & Aug, Mon-Sat Feb-June, Sept & Oct) is a central Victorian house by the River Exe, literally steps from the pub.

WESSEX

Exmoor Lodge (☎ 831694; Chapel St; B&B per person with/without en suite £20/18) is a central and friendly; vegetarian breakfasts are available.

The White Horse Inn (☎ 831229, fax 831246; e user@exmoorwhitehorse.demon .co.uk; B&B per person from £55) is a substantial 16th-century inn offering B&B in comfortable rooms with en suites. There's bar food (sandwiches £3 to £5) during the day and local specialities (venison, crab, trout; £11.50 to £14) for dinner.

Getting There & Away
Over the moor, it's a 7-mile (11km) walk to Exford from Porlock, 10 miles (16km) from Minehead YHA Hostel, 12 miles (19km) from Dunster and 15 miles (24km) from Lynton.

See the earlier Exmoor Getting There & Around section for bus details.

SIMONSBATH
Another little oasis in the middle of the park, Simonsbath is a tiny settlement with good walks along the Barle towards Withypool, Tarr Steps and Hawkridge.

The Exmoor Forest Hotel (☎ 01643-831341, fax 831130; B&B per person with/ without en suite from £30/25) is a substantial old inn – it used to be a temperance hotel, but there's no problem getting beer these days.

LYNTON & LYNMOUTH
☎ 01598 • pop 2000
Lynmouth is a picture-postcard smugglers' harbour where the steeply wooded gorge of the West Lyn River meets the sea, while Lynton offers a range of guesthouses and eateries; an incredible water-operated cliff railway links the villages so it's easy to commute between them. There's good walking along the spectacular coast and in the northern part of the park.

The **TIC** (☎ 0845 660 3232, fax 752755; e info@lyntourism.co.uk; Lynton Town Hall, Lee Rd; open 9.30am-5pm daily Apr-Oct, 10am-4pm Nov-Mar) provides the Lynton & Lynmouth Scene, a free newspaper with accommodation, eating and activities listings.

Down by Lynmouth harbour is a **National Park Visitor Centre** (☎ 752509; The Esplanade; open 10am-5pm daily Easter-Oct).

Things to See
In 1952 storms caused the East and West Lyn rivers to flood, destroying 98 houses and claiming the lives of 34 people. The disaster is recorded at the **Lyn & Exmoor Museum** (☎ 752317; St Vincent's Cottage, Market St, Lynton; adult/child £1/20p; open 10am-12.30pm & 2pm-5pm Mon-Fri & 2pm-5pm Sun late Mar-late Oct), along with varied collections of tools, paintings, general local curios and, well, anything that fits, really.

The **Cliff Railway** (☎ 753486; w www .cliffrailwaylynton.co.uk; adult/child one way £1/50p; open 8.45am-7pm daily Easter-Nov) is a simple piece of environmentally friendly Victorian engineering, still timelessly charming. Two cars linked by a steel cable descend or ascend the slope according to the amount of water in their tanks. It's the best way to get between the two villages and the views across to the Exmoor cliffs are incredible as you descend.

From the Lynmouth crossroads follow signs 200m to **Glen Lyn Gorge** (☎ 753207; adult/child £3/1.50; open Easter-Oct); there are pleasant riverside walks and a small **exhibition centre** housing a collection of steam engines and exhibits on hydroelectric power.

Walking
Lynton TIC and the NPA visitor centre have information about the many local walks. The South West Coast Path and the Tarka Trail pass through the villages, and the Two Moors Way, linking Exmoor with Dartmoor, starts in Lynmouth.

The **Valley of the Rocks**, which is believed to be where the River Lyn originally flowed, was described by the poet Robert Southey as 'rock reeling upon rock, stone piled upon stone, a huge terrifying reeling mass'. It's just over a mile west of Lynton; the short walk along the coastal footpath is rewarded with fantastic views. East of Lynmouth, the lighthouse at **Foreland Point** is another good focus for a walk.

The hike to the confluence of two rivers at **Watersmeet**, 2 miles (3km) along the river from Lynmouth, is also popular; if you're exhausted, you can take a Land Rover back to Lynmouth (☎ 0786 643 4979; £2).

Places to Stay & Eat
Sunny Lyn Holiday Park (☎ 753384; e info@ caravandevon.co.uk; Lynbridge; camping per

person mid-Mar–Oct £3.50-5.25) is a good campsite just inland from Lynton. It also has a variety of caravans, cabins and apartments to rent.

Lynton YHA Hostel (☎ 0870 770 5942, *fax 753305; Lynbridge; dorm beds £10.25; open Mon-Sat Easter-June, daily July & Aug, Tues-Sat Sept & Oct)*, a Victorian house in the gorge, is a steep 500m walk south of town.

Near the YHA, **Pine Lodge** (☎ 753230; *Lynway; B&B per person from £20)* is a welcoming B&B with modern rooms, mostly with en suites.

St Vincent House Hotel (☎ 752244, *fax 753971; Castle Hill; B&B en-suite doubles £46)* is a Grade II-listed Regency house, with an attractive garden.

The Rising Sun (☎ 753223, *fax 753480; e risingsunlynmouth@easynet.co.uk; Harbourside; B&B per person from £49, Shelley's Cottage per person from £78; sandwiches £5, 3-course dinner £29.50)* is a 14th-century thatched smugglers' inn beside Lynmouth harbour. It's an atmospheric place to eat, though it's somewhat pricey.

Mad Hatters Bistro (☎ 753614; *The Old Bank House, Church Steps; mains £4.75-10.75; open 5pm-9.30pm Mon-Sat)*, in Lynton, is a relaxed, cosy eatery with tasty fish and vegetarian dishes as well as venison and local, free-range duck.

The old hunting lodge at Watersmeet houses an **NT teashop** (☎ 753348; *open 10.30am-5.30pm Apr-Sept, 10.30am-4.30pm Oct)* in a shady spot by the rivers.

Getting There & Away

Driving between Lynton and Porlock, note that Countisbury Hill and Porlock Hill are notoriously steep; there are two alternative toll roads (£2) avoiding Porlock Hill, both scenic and less drastic.

For bus information, see the earlier Getting There & Around in the Exmoor National Park section.

PORLOCK

☎ 01643 • pop 1500

Strangely, nobody here knows the identity of the infamous resident who made Coleridge forget most of *Kubla Khan*; nevertheless, the thatched cottages of this peaceful village make it a charming stopover. The lovely harbour of Porlock Weir is 2 miles (3km) farther west.

The picturesque NT-owned village of **Selworthy** is 2½ miles (4km) east of Porlock. Its cream-painted cob-and-thatch cottages make this a popular movie location; Thomas Hardy's *The Return of the Native* was filmed here.

Porlock's helpful **visitor centre** (☎ 863 150, *fax 863014; e porlockci@somerset .gov.uk; West End, High St; open 10am-1pm & 2pm-5pm Mon-Sat, 10am-1pm Sun Apr-Oct; 10.15am-1pm Mon-Fri, 10am-2pm Sat Nov-Mar)* has a small exhibition on Exmoor and Porlock life.

The tiny **Dovery Manor Museum** (*High St; admission free; open 10am-1pm & 2pm-5pm Mon-Fri, 10am-noon & 2.30pm-4.30pm Sat, May-Oct)* is housed in a lovely 15th-century building, and exhibits artefacts and interesting photos of the village.

Places to Stay & Eat

Sparkhayes Farm Camping Site (☎ 862470; *Sparkhayes Lane; adult/child £4.50/1.50)*, in the centre of Porlock, is a pleasant spot with sea views.

There are plenty of B&Bs and hotels along or near High St.

Myrtle Cottage (☎/fax 862978; *High St; en-suite singles/doubles £25/45)* is a cosy, thatched 16th-century B&B.

Homely **Lorna Doone Hotel** (☎ 862404; *High St; B&B en-suite singles/doubles from £30/45; dinner mains £6.25-13)* has a good restaurant with Thai specialities and plenty of vegetarian options.

The Ship Inn (☎ 862507, *fax 863224; High St; en-suite B&B per person from £25; mains £4-9)* is a wonderful 13th-century thatched hostelry mentioned in *Lorna Doone*, with roaring fires and well-kept local ales. There's excellent pub food, with local mussels a speciality.

Piggy in the Middle (☎ 862647; *2 High St; mains £9-12; open evenings daily)* specialises in local seafood and game, with global flavours (gumbo, Thai monkfish).

DUNSTER

☎ 01643 • pop 800 • elevation 115m

Southeast of Minehead, only just inside the park, Dunster is easy to access, enhancing its popularity; it's extremely charming – just be aware that you won't be the only one here. The main attraction is the castle but there's also a 16th-century stone dovecote, an old packhorse bridge and the 17th-century octagonal Yarn Market, a relic of a time when the people of Dunster made their living from weaving rather than tourism. **St George's Church** dates mostly from the 15th century and boasts a wonderfully carved fan-vaulted rood screen. The **water-mill** (☎ 821759; Mill Lane; admission £2.20; open 10.30am-5pm daily) is a working 18th-century mill, with a pleasant tea room.

The **National Park Visitor Centre** (☎ 821835; Dunster Steep; open 10am-5pm daily Easter-Oct) is in the main car park.

Dunster Castle

Heavily restored to the Victorian ideal of how castles should look – turrets, crenulations and all – Dunster Castle (NT; ☎ 821314; admission castle £6.20, garden & park only £3; open 11am-5pm Sat-Wed Easter-Sept, 11am-4pm Oct) dates back to Norman times, although only the 13th-century gateway of the original structure survives, containing displays on the castle's history. Inside are Tudor furnishings and portraits of the Luttrell family, including a bizarre 16th-century portrait of Sir John skinny-dipping, and there are stunning views to the coast.

The surrounding garden and park are open most of the year.

Places to Stay & Eat

Minehead YHA Hostel (☎ 0870 770 5968, fax 703016; dorm beds £10.25; open Mon-Sat Easter-June, daily July & Aug) is actually at Alcombe Combe, a secluded spot 2 miles (3km) south of Minehead and walking distance from Dunster. Bus Nos 28, 39 and 928 stop at Alcombe, ¾ mile (1km) north.

The Stag's Head (☎ 821229; 10 West St; B&B per person with/without en suite from £20/18; mains £3-5.50) is the oldest pub in Dunster (parts date back to 1300), with cosy rooms. There's good, cheap chow as well as fine ales and a beer garden.

Cobbles (☎ 821305; 14-16 Church St; B&B per person £22.50-25) is a delightful 400-year-old cottage with low ceilings and winding staircases. All rooms have private bathrooms.

The Old Priory (☎ 821540; Priory Green; en-suite B&B per person £30-35) is an amazing 12th-century house with a huge stone fireplace and uneven floors, in walled gardens opposite the dovecote.

Yarn Market Hotel (☎ 821425, fax 821475; e yarnmarket.hotel@virgin.net; High St; B&B en-suite singles/doubles from £35/60) is a small, friendly hotel; its restaurant hosts gourmet food evenings (three courses £18).

The Luttrell Arms (☎ 0870 400 8110, fax 821567; 32-36 High St; e luttrellarms@heritage-hotels.co.uk; B&B singles/doubles from £65/100) was a medieval guesthouse for the abbots of Cleeve; now it's the best hotel in Dunster, replete with 15th-century ambience and modern cuisine; more-modest fare (baguettes £4 to £6) is available in the Secret Garden.

The Restaurant in the High Street (☎ 821304; 3 High St; lunch £4.50-6.50, dinner mains £8-11.50) produces arguably the best food in the village, using local game and seafood; there's no arguing with the sinful desserts such as brandy-snap baskets with Belgian chocolate ice cream.

Getting There & Away

See the earlier Exmoor Getting There & Around section for bus details. You can get here by steam train on the West Somerset Railway (see the Somerset section).

MINEHEAD
☎ 01643 • pop 9200

Somerset's largest (and brashest) seaside resort is just outside the park's eastern border; unless you're here during the medieval May Day ceremonies (a hobbyhorse performs a fertility dance through the streets), there's no reason to hang around. It is, though, a transport hub so you may pass through.

The **TIC** (☎ 702624, fax 707166; e mine headtic@visit.org.uk; 17 Friday St; open 9.30am-5pm Mon-Sat Apr-Oct & 10am-1pm Sun July & Aug, 10am-4pm Mon-Sat Nov-Mar) has accommodation information.

For bus details, see the earlier Exmoor National Park Getting There & Around section. Minehead is the northern terminus for the West Somerset Railway (see the Somerset section).

Dorset

Dorset mingles an understated natural beauty with a sort of ruddy cheeked, terribly British seaside vivacity. The Dorset that usually springs to mind – Bournemouth pier, eating ice cream on Weymouth beach, fossils on the Unesco-listed coast and literary connections at Lyme Regis – is there, but the low-key nature of its less-upfront attractions means it's not usually overrun by crowds.

The Dorset Coast Path, part of the longer 613-mile South West Coast Path, runs for most of the length of the coast.

Inland is Dorchester, the heart of Thomas Hardy's fictional Wessex and once the author's home. Dorset also boasts famous earthworks (Maiden Castle), picturesque castle-villages (Corfe Castle), stately homes (Kingston Lacy), a string of Lawrence of Arabia connections, some fine churches (Christchurch Priory, Wimborne Minster and Sherborne Abbey) and one of England's best-known chalk-hill figures, the Cerne Giant.

Orientation & Information

Dorset sits on the south coast, roughly 45 miles (72km) wide, from Lyme Regis on the western (Devon) border to Christchurch abutting Hampshire, with county town Dorchester midway between. The sweep of Chesil Beach runs past Weymouth into the Portland peninsula, the southern tip of Dorset. Sherborne and Shaftesbury lie near the northern borders with Somerset and Wiltshire, respectively.

Dorchester is the most central base for exploring the best of Dorset, but Lyme Regis or Weymouth will suit those who prefer the coast.

In addition to TICs in towns and villages, there are useful district- and county-wide sources of information. The Dorset County Council website [w] www.dorset-cc.gov.uk has listings of TICs and brochure order forms. West Dorset District Council's website [w] www.westdorset.com contains a wealth of information about that part of the county and [w] www.visiteastdorset.com performs the same function for the east.

Getting Around

One of the reasons for Dorset's backwater status is that few major transport routes cross it. There are two railway lines, though trains on both are slow. Trains from London and Southampton run to Bournemouth and Poole; some continue on to Dorchester South and Weymouth. The other line runs from Bristol and Bath through Dorchester West to Weymouth.

A series of transport maps and bus timetables for services from all operators is available from TICs and bus stations, or contact **Dorset County Council** (☎ 01305-225165; [e] i.long@dorset-cc.gov.uk) for copies. For specific timetable inquiries, you'll be directed to **Traveline** (☎ 0870 608 2608).

The main operator in east and central Dorset is **Wilts and Dorset** (☎ 01202-673555; [w] www.wdbus.co.uk). For western Dorset and on to Devon and southern Somerset, **First Southern National** (☎ 01305-783645; [w] www.firstsouthernnational.co.uk) is the main operator.

BOURNEMOUTH
☎ 01202 • pop 155,500

Bournemouth, founded in 1810, has lived most of its 200-year existence as a beach resort, and seems determined to keep it that way. This popular seaside town is strangely schizophrenic: traditional guesthouses, walks on the seafront and variety shows on one hand, beery stag nights and full-on clubbing on the other, and it's also two-sided in the way that, away from the beach and the Winter Gardens, you could be in any shopping town in England, without knowing you're a short hop from the sea. The good news for surfers is that an artificial reef to improve wave consistency and size was due (at time of research) for completion in 2003.

And if you have other activities in mind, in a survey by a well-known condom manufacturer, Bournemouth beach was voted most popular place in Britain for open-air sex.

Orientation & Information

Bournemouth is a sprawling town that spreads along the coast towards Poole to the west and Christchurch to the east. The pier marks the central seafront area and northeast from there is the town centre and train station.

Bournemouth's **TIC** (☎ 0906-802 0234, fax 451743; [w] www.bournemouth.co.uk; Westover Rd; open 9.30am-5.30pm Mon-Sat year round, plus 10.30am-5pm Sun May-Sept) is beside the Winter Gardens. Note that telephone calls to the TIC are charged at 60p a minute so it may be cheaper to check out the website.

There are several Internet cafés; try **Cyber Place** (☎ 290099; 25 St Peter's Rd & 132 Charminster Rd; open 9.30am-midnight daily) which charges £2 per hour.

WESSEX

Things to See & Do

Bournemouth is noted for its beautiful *chines* (sharp-sided valleys running down to the sea).

The excellent **Russell-Cotes Art Gallery & Museum** (☎ 451800; **w** www.russell-cotes .bournemouth.gov.uk; Russell-Cotes Rd; admission free; open 10am-5pm Tues-Sun), an interesting mix of Italianate villa and Scottish baronial pile, looks out to sea near Bournemouth Pier. It hosts changing exhibitions as well as Victorian paintings by the likes of Rossetti, and an exquisite Japanese collection.

Compton Acres (☎ 700110; **w** www.comp tonacres.co.uk; adult/child £5.95/3.25; open 10am-6pm daily Mar-Oct) is a cluster of 12 gardens designed in global styles (Roman, Egyptian, Indian, Japanese) in a sheltered chine at Canford Cliffs. Between them, bus Nos 147, 150 and 151 run half-hourly from the centre (20 minutes).

Right next to Bournemouth Pier is the **Oceanarium** (☎ 311933; **w** www.oceanarium .co.uk; adult/child £5.85/3.85; open 10am-6pm daily), an aquarium with themed areas housing sea and river life from the Amazon, the Great Barrier Reef and other areas.

Vistarama (☎ 399939; **w** www.vistarama .co.uk; adult/child £9.95/5.50) is a tethered balloon offering an uplifting experience: views from 500ft (150m) above the town.

Free guided walks depart from the TIC at 10.30am Monday to Friday and 2.30pm on Sunday from June to September. **Guide Friday** (☎ 01789-294466) operates an open-top bus tour leaving every 30 minutes from opposite Bournemouth Pier and running to Westcliff and Boscombe. Buses operate from 10am until 4.30pm daily, May to September, and cost £6/2 per adult/child.

Places to Stay

Bournemouth has hundreds of options, many clustered around Priory Rd in the West Cliff area and most offering similar standards, give or take satellite TV and levels of chintz. The TIC makes free bookings (accommodation line only ☎ 451700). During summer weekends accommodation fills up fast so book ahead. There are plenty of campsites in the area, but nothing in town itself.

Bournemouth Backpackers (☎ 299491; **e** info@bournemouthbackpackers.co.uk; 3 Frances Rd; dorm beds £9-16, doubles & twins £25-42) is a clean, friendly hostel near the bus and train stations. It's small and has limited reception hours – make sure you call ahead.

Redlands Hotel (☎ 553714; **e** enquiries@ redlandshotel.co.uk; 79 St Michael's Rd; B&B per person from £22) is a reasonable, if standard, guesthouse; most rooms have an en suite.

Ventura Hotel (☎ 761265, fax 757673; **e** enquiries@venturahotel.co.uk; 1 Herbert Rd; en-suite singles/doubles from £33/46) is a relatively classy B&B in pleasant Alum Chine, west of the centre.

For a touch of history, check out **Langtry Manor** (☎ 553887, fax 290115; Derby Rd, East Cliff; B&B per person from £55), given to actress Lillie Langtry by her lover, the future King Edward VII. Nowadays it endeavours to create an air of romance with four-posters and Jacuzzis.

Places to Eat

Head away from the fish-and-chip shops and up Old Christchurch Rd and Charminster Rd for more interesting places to eat.

Retro (☎ 315865; 79-81 Charminster Rd; mains £6-9) is a bright, lively Lebanese joint with a huge range of meze and grilled meats.

Sal E Pepe (☎ 291019; 41-43 Charminster Rd; pasta & pizza £6.50-8, mains £11-16) is a smart Italian restaurant with fresh fish and steak.

Helvetia (☎ 555447; 61 Charminster Rd; mains £9-15) specialises in Swiss food such as fondues and schnitzels; the downstairs Keller Bar stays open to 1am for cheaper snacks and German *biers*.

Bistro Bon Ami (☎ 553353; 199 Old Christchurch Rd; mains £7-15; open noon-2.30pm & 7pm-10.30pm Tues-Fri, 7pm-10.30pm Sat) is the local favourite, an unpretentious French place with regular vegetarian and BYO evenings.

Entertainment

Finding a pub (as opposed to a chain boozer or café-bar) in the centre is nigh impossible. Long queues are the norm for most clubs at the weekend, plus bouncers that can't understand anything but shiny trousers. Wander along Firvale Rd, St Peter's Rd or Old Christchurch Rd for action.

Green Room (☎ 295825; 6 Lansdowne Rd), just north of the college, is a mellow little bar with chilled tunes, tapas and plenty of lethal cocktails.

Hip café-bar **Heat** (☎ 503888; 36 Holdenhurst Rd) is the warm-up joint for **The Old Fire Station** behind – yes, it's a converted fire station, but the temperature is kept high with house, r'n'b, disco and funk.

Opera House (☎ 399922; 570 Christchurch Rd), an incredible converted theatre, is Bournemouth's answer to the superclub; the omnipresent *Slinky* franchise has sunk its teeth in here, too.

Getting There & Away

National Express runs from London (economy return £20.50, 2½ hours, hourly) and Oxford (£18.50, three hours, three daily). Bus X3 runs hourly from Salisbury (1¼ hours) and on to Poole (20 minutes), while the X33 heads from Southampton (one hour, 10 daily Monday to Saturday). There's a multitude of buses between Bournemouth and Poole (15 minutes).

Trains run every half-hour from London Waterloo (saver return £41.90, two hours); half of these continue on to Poole (single £2.40, 15 minutes), Dorchester South (single £7.40, 45 minutes) and Weymouth (single £9.20, one hour). Other destinations require a change at Southampton or Weymouth.

POOLE

☎ 01202 • pop 138,500

The medieval port of Poole is now a container dock and yachting centre; the Sandbanks peninsula at the edge of the harbour is becoming a centre for watersports and upmarket eateries. Poole is also one of the most popular places in the southwest to arrange fishing trips.

The **TIC** (☎ 253253, fax 262627; **w** www .pooletourism.com; 4 High St; open 10am-5pm Mon-Sat, noon-5pm Sunday, to 3pm Sat & Sun Nov-Mar) is just back from the quay.

Things to See & Do

Poole Old Town has attractive 18th-century buildings, including a wonderful **Customs House**.

The well-presented **Waterfront Museum** (☎ 262600; admission free; open 10am-5pm Mon-Sat, noon-5pm Sun Apr-Oct, 10am-3pm Mon-Sat, noon-3pm Sun Nov-Mar), behind the TIC, recounts the town's history, with a reconstructed Victorian High St and displays of paintings, pottery, archaeology and artefacts from the fishing trade.

Scaplen's Court Museum, next to the TIC, is a medieval merchant's house used as a venue for educational activities but is open to the public in August, with local interest exhibitions (call the TIC for details). There's an interesting herb and physic garden at the rear.

Deep-sea fishing and **mackerel fishing** are popular in Poole; half-day trips start at around £15. **Poole Sea Angling Centre** (☎ 676597; behind 5 High St) is opposite the TIC, while **Sea Fishing** (☎ 679666; The Quay) is at the fisherman's dock.

Out at Sandbanks, **windsurfing** lessons start at £69 per day, with hire from £10 per hour. **Poole Harbour Boardsailing** (☎ 700503; **w** www.pooleharbour.co.uk; 284 Sandbanks Rd) also offers one/two-day **kitesurfing** courses for £95/165. **Cool Cats** (☎ 701100; **w** www.coolcatswatersports.com) hires kayaks (£10 per hour) and bikes (£10 to £19 per day) as well as offering windsurfing and catamaran sailing lessons (from £149 for two days).

Brownsea Island

This NT nature reserve (☎ 707744) at the mouth of Poole Harbour is an island of heath and woodland, home to native red squirrels and varied birdlife. From April to October **Brownsea Island Ferries** (☎ 01929-462383; **w** www.brownseaislandferries.com) sail from Poole Quay (return adult/child £5/3) and Sandbanks (return £3/2) several times daily; the NT landing fee is £3.50/1.50 per adult/child. Occasional **bird-watching cruises** (adult/child £6/3.50) around the harbour are run in conjunction with the Royal Society for the Protection of Birds.

Places to Stay & Eat

There's plenty of accommodation in Poole but if heady nightlife's your thing, stay in Bournemouth.

The Antelope Inn (☎ 672029, fax 678286; Old High St; singles/doubles from £42/54; mains £6-11) is an attractive old coaching inn by the harbour offering B&B and decent pub grub.

Sandbanks Hotel (☎ 707377, fax 708885; **e** reservations@sandbankshotel.co.uk; Banks Rd, Sandbanks; B&B per room £68-98) is a fashionable beachside hotel with good facilities (pool, sauna, gym) and stylish **Sands Brasserie** (☎ 709884; mains £10-18), offering excellent seafood and panoramic views.

Jazz Café (☎ 670851; Poole Quay; sandwiches £3.50-5.50, mains £5.50-11), a bright-and-breezy café bar with great snacks, has live jazz on Friday and Sunday.

Cool, relaxed **Storm** (☎ 674970; 16 High St; mains £8-15) serves fresh fish with fine-dining tendencies.

Getting There & Away

Countless buses, including Nos X3, X33, 101,102, 103, 104 and 105, cover the 20-minute trip to Bournemouth; you shouldn't have to wait more than a few minutes. National Express shuttle No 35 runs hourly to Bournemouth and on to London (economy return £20.50, three hours).

Train connections are as for Bournemouth, 13 minutes closer to London Waterloo (saver return £43.30).

A ferry (☎ 01929-450203) shuttles across from Sandbanks to Studland for £2.20 per single every 20 minutes. This is a short cut from Poole to Swanage, Wareham and the west Dorset coast, but summer queues can be horrendous.

CHRISTCHURCH
☎ 01202 • pop 36,400
A small town that makes a pleasant day trip from Bournemouth, Christchurch is about 5 miles (8km) to the east.

The **TIC** (☎ 471780, fax 476816; e enquiries@christchurchtourism.info; 23 High St; open 9.30am-5pm Mon-Fri, 9.30am-4.30pm Sat) closes 30 minutes later in July and August.

Magnificent **Christchurch Priory** (☎ 485 804; requested donation £1; open 9.30am-5pm daily) stands between the Rivers Avon and Stour. The Norman nave had a new choir added to it in the 15th century, when the tower was also built. Among the wonderful misericords in the choir, look for a carving of Richard III and another of a fox 'friar' preaching to a flock of geese. In summer you can climb the tower for views and learn about priory life in **St Michael's Loft Museum** (requested donation 50p).

Near the priory is the **Red House Museum & Gardens** (☎ 482860; Quay Rd; adult/child £1.50/80p; open 10am-5pm Tues-Sat, 2pm-5pm Sun), a workhouse now accommodating a local history museum.

Bus Nos 105, 121, 122, 213 and 124 run to Bournemouth (return £2.40, 30 minutes, four hourly).

WIMBORNE
☎ 01202 • pop 15,300
The attractive small town of Wimborne is centred around its interesting old minster. The **TIC** (☎ 886116, fax 841025; e wimbornetic@eastdorset.gov.uk; 29 High St; open 9.30am-5.30pm Mon-Sat Apr-Sept, 9.30am-4.30pm Oct-Mar) is near the minster.

Next to the TIC is the 16th-century **Priest's House Museum** (☎ 882533; 23-27 High St; adult/child £2.50/1; open 10am-4pm Mon-Sat Apr-Oct & 2pm-5pm Sun July & Aug), an interesting local-history museum with a reconstructed Victorian kitchen, Georgian parlour and village school room, as well as local history and archaeology displays.

Wimborne Model Town (☎ 881924; w www.wimborne-modeltown.com; adult/child £3/2; open 10am-5pm daily Easter-Sept) is an oddity, a 1:10 scale model of the town as it was in the 1950s.

Wimborne Minster

Founded around 1050, the minster (☎ 884753 parish office; open 9.30am-5.30pm daily) was considerably enlarged in Decorated style in the 14th century and became the parish church in 1537 when Henry VIII dissolved the monasteries. Aside from the impressive 15th-century perpendicular tower, highlights include the remarkable 14th-century astronomical clock, a Saxon chest hewn from a single tree and tessellated Roman mosaic tiles that can be seen in the nave. The nave columns, the piers of the central tower and the north and south transepts are the main Norman survivors. Traces of 13th- to 15th-century painted murals can be seen in a Norman altar recess in the north transept.

In Holy Trinity Chapel is the tomb of Ettricke, the 'man in the wall'. A local eccentric (but obviously one with some influence), he refused to be buried in the church or in the village and was interred in the church wall. Confidently expecting to die in 1693, Ettricke also had his memorial prematurely engraved. When he survived his prediction by 10 years, the year 1693 was rechiselled to 1703.

Be sure you're standing outside the porch on the quarter-hour to see the quarterjack chime; this military figure was originally a monk until the dictates of the Reformation necessitated a change in costume.

Above the choir vestry is a **chained library** *(open 10.30am-12.30pm & 2pm-4pm Mon-Thur, 10.30am-12.30pm Fri & Sat Easter-Oct)* established in 1686 and containing books and manuscripts from well before then.

Kingston Lacy

Kingston Lacy *(NT; ☎ 01202-880413; admission house £6.50/3, grounds only £3/1.50; house open noon-5.30pm Wed-Sun Easter-Oct, grounds open 11am-6pm daily Easter-Oct)*, 2 miles (3km) west of Wimborne, is a fine 17th-century house; the last occupant lived in the house until 1981 without selling a thing, so the house is dense with furniture and art, much of it collected by William Bankes, who was responsible for major renovations in the 1830s. The extensive 18th-century landscaped gardens and estate encompass the Iron Age hill-fort of **Badbury Rings**.

Getting There & Away

Bus Nos 132 and 133 run between Bournemouth (45 minutes) and Poole (40 minutes) via Wimborne every half-hour Monday to Saturday (every two hours on Sunday). Bus Nos 182 and 183 run to Bournemouth and, more frequently, to Shaftesbury (1¼ hours, hourly, Monday to Saturday).

SOUTHEAST DORSET

The southeastern corner of Dorset – the Purbeck peninsula – is crowded with pretty thatched villages and crumbling ruins. The Dorset Coast Path, part of the South West Coast Path, runs through some wonderful scenery. There are plenty of campsites around and B&Bs in almost every village.

Wareham

☎ 01929 • pop 2500

The small town of Wareham forms a neat square, bounded by the River Frome on its southern side and by a remarkably intact Saxon wall on the other three sides.

Purbeck TIC *(☎ 552740, fax 554491; e purbecktic@compuserve.com; Holy Trinity Church, South St; open 9.30am-1pm & 1.45pm-5pm Mon-Sat, 10am-1pm & 1.45pm-*4pm Sun Apr-Sept; 10am-3pm Mon-Sat Oct-Mar)* stocks an excellent guide and walking-tour map (free).

There's a bijou **Wareham Museum** *(☎ 553448; East St; admission free; open 10am-4pm daily Easter-Oct)* where a Lawrence of Arabia collection supplements the usual local items with relics of early settlers from the Iron Age and Roman occupation.

The sturdy **earth banks** around the town were built after a Viking attack in 876.

Standing on the wall beside North St is tiny but delightful Saxon **St Martin's Church**, which dates from about 1020. Although the porch and bell tower are later additions, and larger windows have been added over the centuries, the basic structure is unchanged. Inside there's a 12th-century fresco on the northern wall and a marble effigy of Lawrence of Arabia.

Black Bear Hotel *(☎ 553339, fax 552846; 14 South St; en-suite B&B singles/doubles from £30/45; mains £4-11)*, dating from 1770, is a substantial inn fronted by a life-size figure of a bear. It serves fine bar food and good ales.

Old Granary *(☎ 552010, fax 552482; The Quay; doubles or twins from £60; mains £6.50-15)* is a picturesque B&B by the river. Its restaurant has good standards such as baguettes (£3) and more sophisticated fare like herbed trout.

Bus Nos 142, !43 and 144 run between Poole (35 minutes) and Wareham hourly (every two hours on Sunday).

Around Wareham

Bovington Camp Tank Museum At the Tank Museum *(☎ 01929-405096; w www.tankmuseum.co.uk; adult/child £7.50/5; open 10am-5pm daily)*, 6 miles (10km) from Wareham, an audio guide leads you around the collection of more than 300 armoured vehicles, from the earliest WWI prototypes to WWII tanks from both sides, and on to examples from Cold War days. From more recent times there's also a collection of Iraqi tanks from the Gulf War. Lawrence of Arabia was stationed here in 1922 and there's a small museum in the shop.

Clouds Hill The tiny, austere former home of TE Lawrence *(NT; ☎ 01929-405616; admission £2.80; open noon-5pm Thur-Sun Apr-Oct)* is still much as he left it after his death

WESSEX

in 1935. Lawrence was an enigmatic figure renowned for his heroic achievements in WWI and his immense book *Seven Pillars of Wisdom*; his life was immortalised in David Lean's epic film *Lawrence of Arabia*. In addition to Clouds Hill, St Martin's Church in Wareham and Bovington Camp, there are other local links. He died at Bovington Military Hospital six days after a motorcycle accident, which took place between the camp and Clouds Hill. His grave is in the cemetery of St Nicholas Church, Moreton.

Monkey World Established in 1987 to provide a sanctuary for abused beach chimpanzees from Spain, most of the animals at Monkey World (☎ 0800 456 600; w www .monkeyworld.org; Longthorns; adult/child £6.25/5.25; open 10am-5pm Sept-June, 10am-6pm July & Aug) have been rescued from exploitation, whether as pets or in laboratories. The chimpanzees here form the largest group outside of Africa, and there are also orang-utans, lemurs and macaques. Last admission is one hour before closing.

Getting There & Away The Tank Museum, Monkey World and Clouds Hill are all just off the A352 about 5 miles (8km) west of Wareham. Bus Nos 101, 102, 103 and 104 run between Wareham (15 minutes) or Wool (five minutes) and Dorchester (return £2.40, one hour, hourly Monday to Saturday), but stop at Monkey World only from June to September. Clouds Hill is a 1-mile walk from the nearest stop.

Corfe Castle

The magnificent ruins of Corfe Castle (NT; ☎ 01929-481294; admission £4.30; open 10am-5pm daily Mar, 10am-6pm daily Apr-Oct, 10am-4pm daily Nov-Feb) tower above its gorgeous stone village of the same name, offering wonderful views of the countryside. Even by English standards, the 1000-year-old castle had a dramatic history, with royal poisonings, treacherous stabbings and Civil War sieges, being reduced to the present picturesque ruin after the second such assault in 1646. Elements of early Norman brickwork are still evident, but it's the fractured grandeur of the scene that draws the crowds.

The **Castle View Visitor Centre** at the bottom of the hill houses an exhibition on local stone and the castle's construction.

The village has several pubs and B&Bs, and there are campsites nearby.

Reputedly the most photographed pub in Britain, parts of **The Greyhound** (☎ 01929-480205; The Square; doubles £60; mains £9-16) date from 1580. It has a pleasant garden overlooking the castle, and provides comfortable B&B and upmarket pub food as well as baguettes (£5).

Bus Nos 142, 143 and 144 run hourly from Poole (50 minutes) through Wareham (15 minutes) to Swanage (20 minutes) via Corfe Castle.

The Blue Pool

Designated a Site of Special Scientific Interest (SSSI), the water of the Blue Pool (☎ 01929-551408; w www.bluepooluk.com; Furzebrook; adult/child £3.20/1.60; open from 9.30am Mar-Nov) has a chameleon-like tendency to change colour; the grounds are home to rare wildlife including green sand lizards and Dartford warblers. This popular local beauty spot is signposted from the A351; hourly bus Nos 142, 143 and 144 from Wareham (10 minutes) stop nearby.

Lulworth Cove & the Coast
☎ 01929

The coastline between Swanage and Weymouth is remarkable for its geology and geomorphology: Durdle Door is a natural arch formed by folding rock, while Lulworth Cove, a mile to the east, is almost perfectly circular, enclosed by towering cliffs. Science aside, the area offers fine cliff-top walks with spectacular views, and excellent beaches around Durdle Door.

Stumpy **Lulworth Castle** (☎ 400352; w www.lulworth.com; adult/child £5.50/3.50; open 10.30am-6pm daily Apr-Oct, 10.30am-4pm daily Nov-Mar) is in the village of East Lulworth, about 3 miles (5km) inland. The castle is 'modern' compared with many in England, built as a hunting lodge in 1608; it contains exhibits about its history.

There are a number of places to stay at Lulworth Cove, and more just back from the coast in West Lulworth.

Durdle Door Holiday Park (☎ 400200, fax 400260; e durdle@lulworth.com; tent sites £10-16; open Mar-Oct) has a prime location on the fields above the cliffs.

Lulworth Cove YHA Hostel (☎ 0870 770 5940, fax 400640; School Lane, West

Lulworth; dorm beds £10.25; open Mar-Oct) is a small, simple place.

Lulworth Beach Hotel *(☎ 400404, fax 400159; Lulworth Cove; B&B singles/doubles from £40/70)* is just steps from the beach and has two restaurants.

Lulworth Cove is a good spot to indulge in local (calorie-heavy) ice cream – and they mean *ice cream* – with such delicate flavours as raspberry pavlova and ginger.

Bus No 103 runs from Dorchester (return £1.80, 40 minutes, five daily Monday to Saturday) to Lulworth Cove. Other buses run to Wareham and Weymouth, but only a few times weekly, even in summer.

DORCHESTER
☎ 01305 • pop 15,000

Though best-known as the home of novelist Thomas Hardy, the menu at Dorset's slow-paced administrative centre is surprisingly varied, with some seemingly incongruous museums (Tutankhamun? Dinosaurs?) as well as the steady diet of Hardy connections.

Orientation & Information

Most of Dorchester's action takes place along South St, which runs north into pedestrianised Cornhill and then emerges in High St, divided into east and west parts at St Peter's church. A **statue** of Hardy watches the traffic from a seat by the West Gate roundabout.

The **TIC** *(☎ 267992, fax 266079;* e *dorchester.tic@westdorset-dc.gov.uk; Unit 11, Antelope Walk; open 9am-5pm Mon-Sat, 10am-3pm Sun May-Sept; 9am-4pm Mon-Sat Oct-Apr)* is just off Trinity St. It sells the guide *All About Dorchester* (£1), with interesting walks around town, as well as other free maps and leaflets. There's lots of Hardy literature, including a set of leaflets tracing the scenes of individual novels (50p each).

Museums

The Hardy memorabilia at **Dorset County Museum** *(☎ 262735; High West St; adult/child £3.50/1.70; open 10am-5pm daily May-Oct, Mon-Sat Nov-Apr)*, featuring the novelist's study, is only part of a wide-ranging collection including relics from the archaeological excavations at Maiden Castle, fossil finds from Lyme Regis and artefacts from the Roman town house.

The **Tutankhamun Exhibit** *(☎ 269571; High West St; adult/child £5.50/3.95; open*

9.30am-5.30pm daily) may seem out of place in Dorset but it's nevertheless an intriguing place to visit. The discovery of the tomb and its contents have been recreated in montages complete with sounds and smells.

The **Keep Military Museum** *(☎ 264066;* w *www.keepmilitarymuseum.org; Bridport Rd; adult/child £3/2; open 9.30am-5pm Mon-Sat year round & 10am-4pm Sun July & Aug)*, beyond the Bridport Rd roundabout, traces Dorset and Devon military valour overseas with a range of displays, costumes, guns and tableaux.

The small **Dinosaur Museum** *(☎ 269880;* w *www.dinosaur-museum.org.uk; Icen Way; adult/child £5.50/3.95; open 9.30am-5.30pm daily)* features fossils, reconstructed beasts and interactive displays.

The foundations of a 1st-century **Roman town house** are behind the town hall on Northernhay. The layout of the house is clearly visible and the remains of the main building, housed within a glass structure, boast remarkable mosaic floors. Just across the road is the pretty **Hangman's Cottage**, another reminder of Judge Jeffrey's pleasant interlude in the area.

Hardy Trail

Designed by Thomas Hardy, **Max Gate** *(NT;* ☎ *262538; Alington Ave; adult/child £2.30/1.20; open 2pm-5pm Mon, Wed & Sun Apr-Sept)* was his home from 1885 until his death in 1928; it contains pieces of his furniture,

WESSEX

but otherwise there's not exactly a wealth of memorabilia. It was here that he wrote several of his most famous works including *Tess of the D'Urbervilles* and *Jude the Obscure*. It's a mile east of the town centre on the A352.

Similarly, the small cob-and-thatch **cottage** (NT; ☎ 01305-262366; admission £2.80; open 11am-5pm Sun-Thur Apr-Oct) where Hardy was born is furnished in appropriately simple style, but unremarkable. It's at Higher Bockhampton, about 3 miles (5km) northeast of Dorchester and reached by a 10-minute walk from the car park.

Places to Stay & Eat

Hillfort View (☎ 268476, fax 269233; 10 Hillfort Close; B&B singles/doubles £22/40), 1 mile (1.6km) southwest of the centre, has views of Maiden Castle.

Good-value **Sunrise Guest House** (☎ 262425; 34 London Rd; en-suite doubles £40) is a comfortable, family run B&B just east of High St.

The **Old Ship Inn** (☎ 264455; 16 High West St; en-suite B&B £30/50; mains £3.25-4), the oldest pub in town, is a cosy place to stay, eat or make merry.

Westwood House Hotel (☎ 268018, fax 250282; 29 High West St; singles £45-55, doubles £65-75) is an excellent B&B in a Georgian town house; some of its stylish rooms have spa baths.

Casterbridge Hotel (☎ 264043, fax 260 884; e reception@casterbridgehotel.co.uk; 49 High East St; en-suite singles £45-60, doubles £75-95) is an upmarket Georgian guesthouse with fine breakfasts and a secluded courtyard.

Wessex Royale Hotel (☎ 262660, fax 251941; e info@wessex-royale-hotel.com; 32 High West St; singles/doubles £59/79) is another imposing 18th-century building, sympathetically furnished and decorated.

Judge Jeffreys' Lodgings (☎ 264369; 6 High West St; cream tea £4, mains £8-15; open 10am-5pm Mon-Sat, dinner Fri & Sat only) is a half-timbered Tudor building that hosted the infamous judge during the Bloody Assizes (see the boxed text earlier). It's an atmospheric place for a snack or dinner.

Sala Thai (☎ 260088; 5 High East St; mains £4.50-10; open 6-11pm Mon-Sat) is a quality Thai restaurant with a range of standards and not-too-chichi decor.

The Mock Turtle (☎ 264011; 34 High West St; mains £7.50-14; open noon-2.30pm Tues-Fri & 6.30pm-9.30pm Mon-Sat) is arguably the best restaurant in town, a smart but friendly spot dishing up solid English fare, with plenty of fish and game.

Getting There & Around

Dorchester is 128 miles (205km) from London. National Express coaches run daily from London (economy return £26, four hours). Bus No 31 runs from Weymouth (return £1.90, 25 minutes) and on to Lyme Regis (1¼ hours) hourly (every two hours on Sunday); No 10 also serves Weymouth every 20 minutes (every two hours on Sunday). Bus No 184 goes from Weymouth to Salisbury (1¾ hours, six daily Monday to Saturday, three on Sunday) via Dorchester.

There are two train stations, Dorchester South and Dorchester West, both southwest of the town centre. Trains run hourly from Weymouth (single £2.60, 10 minutes) to London Waterloo (saver return £48, 2½ hours) via Dorchester South, Bournemouth (single £7.40, 45 minutes) and Southampton (saver return £21.70, 1½ hours). Dorchester West has connections with Bath (£10.30, 1¾ hours) and Bristol (two hours).

Dorchester Cycles (☎ 268787; 31 Great Western Rd), rents bikes for £10 per day.

AROUND DORCHESTER
Maiden Castle

The massive earthwork ramparts of Maiden Castle, Europe's largest and finest Iron Age hill fort, stretch for 3 miles and enclose nearly 20 hectares. The site has been inhabited since Neolithic times but the first fort was built here around 800 BC. It was then abandoned, and rebuilt around 500 BC. The earth walls were later extended and enlarged in 250 and 150 BC. Despite the addition of more defences, the Romans still captured it in AD 43, finally abandoning it in the 4th century. The sheer size of the walls and ditches and the area they enclose is stunning, and there are wonderful views. Dorset County Museum displays finds from the site. It's 1½ miles southwest of Dorchester.

Athelhampton House

Haunted Athelhampton House (☎ 01305-848363; w www.athelhampton.co.uk; house adult/child £6.25/free, gardens only £4.50/

free; house open 11am-5pm Mon, 10am-5pm Tues-Thur, 10am-4pm Fri,10.30am-5pm Sun, Mar-Oct; 10.30am-dusk Sun Nov-Feb) was built in 1485 in the days when Tudor was a new dynasty, but the house has lasted a little longer, as have the ghosts – a cooper, a grey lady and an ape! The Great Hall and State Bedroom will impress, although the most popular feature is the gardens. There are Hardy connections here, too – the author's father, a builder, worked on restoration, and Hardy himself visited regularly.

Bus No 187 runs to Dorchester (15 minutes) and Poole (one hour) four times daily Monday to Saturday.

Cerne Abbas & the Cerne Giant

Delightful Cerne Abbas, with its fine 16th-century houses, is about more than just a chalk man with a huge weapon. The much rebuilt abbey house is now a private residence, although the ruins behind the house can be explored when the gate is open (adult/child £1/20p). The Abbot's Porch (1509) was once the entrance to the whole complex. Visit the 14th-century **St Mary's Church** to see rare medieval frescoes and impish gargoyles.

Just north of the village is the **Cerne Giant**, one of Britain's best-known chalk figures. The giant stands 55m tall, wields a 37m-long club and is estimated to be anything between a few hundred and a couple of thousand years old. One thing is obvious – this old man has no need of Viagra! The poor fellow only regained his manhood last century after the prudish Victorians allowed grass to grow over his vital parts.

Cerne Abbas is a peaceful, atmospheric place to stay. The ironically named **New Inn** *(☎ 01300-341274, fax 341457; 14 Long St; ensuite singles/doubles £30/55; mains £6.50-11)*, a 16th-century oak-and-beam coaching inn, offers comfortable B&B and dishes such as cottage pie and stuffed trout. There's good pub food at the thatched **Royal Oak** *(☎ 01300-341797; Long St; mains £8-11)*, serving the likes of game pie and poached salmon.

Dorchester, 8 miles (13km) to the south, is reached on bus No 216 (20 minutes, six times daily Monday to Saturday).

WEYMOUTH

☎ 01305 • pop 46,000

Although Weymouth was a busy port in medieval times, it was George III's experi-mental dip in Weymouth waters in 1789 that kick-started the resort's growth. The legacy of that late-18th-century development is the Esplanade, a gracious Georgian waterfront terrace now full of hotels and B&Bs. Today Weymouth is an example of the archetypal English seaside resort. A summer walk along The Esplanade reveals deck chairs for hire, donkey rides and Punch and Judy shows. Look for the brightly painted Jubilee Memorial Clock (1888) and the vivid statue of George III, patron saint of Weymouth tourism. With plenty of accommodation and its location in the centre of Dorset's coast, it's a handy base for exploring the county.

The less-brash Old Harbour inlet is lined with attractive old buildings used as shops, restaurants and pubs, and packed with fishing trawlers and fancy yachts from around the world.

Orientation & Information

Central Weymouth, between the beach and the Inner Harbour, is only a few blocks wide. The Esplanade is the main walk along the beach, but each block of the road has a different secondary name. St Mary St is the pedestrianised shopping centre but Hope Square, on the far (southwest) side of the pretty Old Harbour, is more inviting.

The **TIC** *(☎ 785747, fax 788092; e tourism@weymouth.gov.uk; The Esplanade; open 9.30am-5pm daily Apr-Sept, 10am-4pm Oct-Mar)* is opposite the statue of King George III.

Brewer's Quay

Brewer's Quay has a shopping centre and plentiful attractions, including the excellent **Timewalk** *(☎ 777622; Hope Square; adult/child £4.25/3; open 10am-5.30pm daily Sept-June, 10am-9pm summer school holidays)*, a series of historic tableaux depicting the town's early history as a trading port, the disaster of the Black Death plague years, the drama of the Spanish Armada and Weymouth's development as a resort.

Also in Brewer's Quay is the fascinating **Weymouth Museum** *(admission free; open 10am-5pm daily)*, uncovering the town's maritime heritage with displays on smuggling, paddle steamers and shipwrecks.

Deep Sea Adventure

This attraction *(☎ 760690; 9 Custom House Quay; adult/child £3.75/2.75; open 9.30am-*

7pm daily Sept-June, 9.30am-8pm daily July & Aug), in an old grain store, traces the history of diving, with exhibits on local shipwrecks and the *Titanic*. Don't be put off by the 'family fun' tag and gift-shop entrance. Last entry is 1½ hours before closing time.

Sea Life
A largely outdoor branch of the aquarium chain, Sea Life (☎ 761070; w *www.sealife .co.uk; Lodmoor Country Park; adult/child £7.95/5.25; open 10am-5pm daily*) is one of the more extensive and enjoyable of its ilk, featuring seal and otter sanctuaries, a penguin enclosure and a shark nursery. Tickets are cheaper (£6.50/4.25) from the TIC.

Tudor House
When this house (☎ 812341; 3 Trinity St; *adult/child £1.50/50p; open 11am-3.45pm Tues-Fri June-Sept, 2pm-4pm 1st Sun of the month Oct-May*) was built, around 1600, the waterfront would have lapped at the front door. It's furnished in Tudor style, and admission includes a guided tour delving into everyday life in those days.

Nothe Fort
Perched on the end of the promontory, 19th-century Nothe Fort (☎ 766626; *adult/child £3.50/free; open 10.30am-5.30pm daily May-Sept, 2.30pm-4.30pm only Sun Oct-Apr*) houses a museum concentrating on life in the fort for soldiers over the years. It's a substantial affair, with extensive collections of weapons and fine views of the harbour and coast.

Activities
There are excellent wreck and drift dives near Weymouth. Old Harbour Dive Centre (☎ 760888; w *www.oldharbourdivecentre .co.uk; 11 Nothe Parade*) organises trips to the best sites from £35 per day, plus £40 to hire equipment.

For windsurfing lessons (from £69 per day) and hire (£40 per day), contact Windtek (☎ 787900; w *www.windtek.co.uk; 109 Portland Rd*).

Places to Stay
The TIC makes accommodation bookings free of charge, or will make inquiries for £1.

There are plenty of campsites back near Chesil Beach and Weymouth Bay. Water-side Holiday Park (☎ 883103, fax 832830; w *www.watersideholidays.co.uk; Bowleaze Cove; tent & 2 people from £11; open Mar-Oct*) is a five-star place 1½ miles (2km) east of the centre.

Weymouth has an awesome number of guesthouses and hotels, stretching along and back from the Esplanade and around Lennox St. Most B&Bs are pretty standard in character and quality.

The Pebbles (☎ 784331, fax 784695; *18 Kirtleton Ave; en-suite rooms per person from £22*) is a friendly little B&B in a quiet area.

The Chatsworth (☎ 785012, fax 766342; e *dave@thechatsworth.co.uk; 14 The Esplanade; en-suite B&B per person £35*) is a smart guesthouse with views of the Old Harbour and the bay.

Overlooking the beach, imposing Hotel Prince Regent (☎ 771313, fax 778100; e *hprwey@aol.com; 139 The Esplanade; B&B en-suite singles £45-55, doubles £50-75*) has been hosting holiday visitors since 1855.

Hotel Rex (☎ 760400, fax 760500; e *rex@ kingshotels.co.uk; 29 The Esplanade; B&B en-suite singles/doubles from £48/72*) was the Duke of Clarence's summer residence; these days it's a comfortable mid-range hotel.

Places to Eat
Café 21 (☎ 767848; *21 East St; mains £4.50*) is a funky little vegetarian place with healthy, tasty food and low prices. It's open for dinner only occasionally.

Statue House (☎ 830456; *Statue House, The Esplanade; tapas £2-4.50, mains £5.50-7.50*) is a bright tapas bar with panini and wraps at lunch.

On the southern side of the Old Harbour are two excellent restaurants, Perry's (☎ 785799; *4 Trinity Rd; mains £10.50-22.50; closed lunch Sat & Mon*) and Mallams (☎ 776757; *5 Trinity Rd; 2 courses £20; closed lunch & Sun*), both making imaginative use of local seafood. Perry's tends towards the traditional, while cuisine and decor at Mallams is more modern.

Isobar (☎ 750666; *19 Trinity Rd; mains £11-14.50; open noon-11pm daily*), a lush, baroque bar-restaurant, offers world-tinged seafood, duck and steak. With welcoming velvet sofas it's also a tempting spot to loll for the evening with a long drink.

Red Lion (☎ 786940; *Hope St; mains £3-4*) has a nautical theme – boats and fishing nets on the ceiling – and its tables on the square are ideal for sipping the excellent local beers and munching good pub grub.

Bar on the Corner (36 St Thomas St) is a sleek, modern café-bar with electro-dance tunes and good cocktails (£5).

Getting There & Away

Bus National Express coaches run daily to London (economy return £26, four hours); the stop is by the TIC. Bus Nos 10, 31 and 184 between them serve Dorchester (return £1.90, 30 minutes) at least every 20 minutes; No 31 goes on to Lyme Regis (1¾ hours, hourly), as does bus X53 (four daily Monday to Saturday), which continues to Exeter (three hours). Bus No 184 runs to Salisbury (1¾ hours, six daily Monday to Saturday, three on Sunday).

Train Trains run hourly to London (saver return £50.80, 2¾ hours) via Dorchester South (single £2.60, 12 minutes), Bournemouth (single £9.20, one hour) and Southampton (saver return £23.40, 1½ hours), and every two hours to Dorchester West, Bath (saver return £17.70, two hours) and Bristol (saver return £19.50, 2¼ hours).

Boat High-speed catamaran car-ferries operated by **Condor** (☎ 0845 345 2000 or 761551; w www.condorferries.co.uk) whizz across to St Malo, France (4½ hours) and the Channel Islands. Day trips start at £30 return.

AROUND WEYMOUTH
Portland

South of Weymouth, Portland is essentially an island joined to the mainland by the long sweep of Chesil Beach; it's popular with bird-watchers, climbers, windsurfers and divers, as well as those interested in geology and archaeology, and the local council has produced an extensive set of leaflets covering these and other aspects. It's renowned as the source of the eponymous hard limestone, quarried here for centuries.

There are superb views from the **light house** (☎ 01305-820495; open 11am-5pm daily Apr-Sept), which houses the summer-only **TIC** (☎ 01305-861233), at the end of **Portland Bill**. It costs £2/1 to climb the 41m-high tower. An earlier, smaller lighthouse now acts as a bird observatory.

Sturdy **Portland Castle** (EH; ☎ 820539; adult/child £3.50/2.70; open 10am-6pm daily Apr-Sept, 10am-5pm daily Oct, 10am-4pm Fri-Sun Nov-Mar) is one of the finest examples of the defensive castles constructed during Henry VIII's castle-building spree, spurred by fear of an attack from France. **White Motor Boats** (☎ 01305-813246; £5/2.50 return) sail to Portland Castle from Weymouth's Old Harbour three times daily.

Portland Museum (☎ 01305-821804; 217 Wakeham St; adult/child £2.10/free; open 10.30am-5pm Fri-Tues Easter-Oct) has varied displays on local history, smuggling and literary connections, as well as some huge ammonites (fossils).

Bus No 1 runs to Portland from Weymouth every 10 minutes, while No 501 goes every 30 minutes.

Chesil Beach

Photogenic Chesil Beach, a long curving pebble-bank stretching along the coast for 10 miles (16km) from Portland to Abbotsbury, has been voted one of the most beautiful spots in England. The bank encloses the slightly stagnant waters of the Fleet Lagoon, a haven for water birds including the famed Abbotsbury swans.

The stones vary from pebble size at Abbotsbury in the west to around 15cm in diameter at Portland in the east; local fishermen can supposedly tell their position along the bank by gauging the size of the stones. In places the stone bank reaches 15m high. Although winter storms can wash right over the top, it has never broken up. The bank is accessible at the Portland end and from just west of Abbotsbury.

Chesil Beach Centre (☎ 01305-760579; Ferrybridge; admission free; open 11am-6pm daily Apr-Sept, 11am-4pm daily Oct-Mar) provides information, and organises talks and guided walks.

Abbotsbury
☎ 01305

As the name suggests, this pretty coastal village was the site of a medieval abbey; a few fragments remain. With three popular attractions and some pleasant places to stay, it's a restful place for a halt.

Things to See The huge, 83m-long tithe barn, at one time a communal storage site

WESSEX

for farm produce, now houses **Smuggler's Barn** (☎ 871817; adult/child £4.50/3.50; open 10am-6pm daily Feb-Oct, 10am-4pm Sat & Sun Nov-Jan), a children's farm and play area with a smidgen of smuggling lore.

On the coast, and offering fine views of the Fleet Lagoon, is **Abbotsbury Swannery** (☎ 871858; New Barn Rd; adult/child £5.50/ 3.50; open 10am-6pm daily mid-Mar–Oct). Swans have been nesting here for 600 years and the colony can number up to 600, plus cygnets. The walk through the swannery and reed beds will tell you all you ever wanted to know about swans. Come in May for the nests, or in late May and June for the cygnets.

The swannery was founded by the monks of Abbotsbury's Benedictine monastery, which was destroyed in 1541. Traces of the monastery remain by the tithe barn. The energetic can walk up to 14th-century **St Catherine's Chapel** for superb views of the swannery, the village and Chesil Beach.

Abbotsbury Subtropical Gardens (☎ 871387; adult/child £5.50/3.50; open 10am-6pm daily Mar-Oct, 10am-4pm Nov-Feb) were laid out in 1765 as a kitchen garden, but today are lush with camellias, hydrangeas and rhododendrons. Last admission is one hour before closing.

Joint tickets to Smuggler's Barn and either the Swannery or the Subtropical Gardens cost £9/6.50; see the website **w** www .abbotsbury-tourism.com.

Places to Stay & Eat Abbotsbury has several comfortable B&Bs and places to eat.

Right in among the abbey ruins, parts of **Abbey House** (☎ 871330, fax 871088; **w** www.theabbeyhouse.co.uk; en-suite B&B per person from £30) date back to the 15th century; it's an attractive place with charming gardens.

Ilchester Arms (☎ 871243, fax 871225; **e** enqs@ilchesterarms.co.uk; 9 Market St; B&B en-suite singles/doubles £55/65; mains £9-15) is a large old inn serving steak and fish; a ciabatta chip butty is £2.20.

Getting There & Away Abbotsbury is 9 miles (14km) northwest of Weymouth on the B3157. Bus No X53 runs between Exeter (2½ hours) and Weymouth (30 minutes) via Lyme Regis (one hour) four times daily Monday to Saturday.

LYME REGIS
☎ 01297 • pop 3900

Somehow, charming Lyme Regis, nestled between steep cliffs, pulls off the feat of being a bucket-and-spade seaside resort while retaining a graceful, tasteful air. It's easy to see why visitors crowd here on summer weekends, but for the most part it's still a peaceful, delightful spot. Dorset ends here – Devon begins just beyond the harbour wall known as the Cobb, which throws a protective arm around the harbour; it's a famous literary spot featured prominently in Jane Austen's novel *Persuasion*, and *The French Lieutenant's Woman* by John Fowles.

The town's other claim to fame is prehistoric. The limestone cliffs on either side of town are some of Britain's richest sources of fossils, and some of the first dinosaur skeletons in the world were discovered here.

In 1685 the Duke of Monmouth landed on Monmouth Beach, west of the town, to start his abortive rebellion against James II (see the boxed text 'The Bloody Assizes' earlier in the chapter).

Orientation & Information

The A3052 drops precipitously into Lyme Regis from one side and climbs equally steeply out on the other. From Bridge St, where the A3052 meets the coast, Marine Parade runs west to the harbour. From Cobb Gate towards East Cliff runs **Gun Cliff Walk**. The superstructure ingeniously conceals the town's sewage system.

Lyme Regis' **TIC** (☎ 442138, fax 444668; **e** lymeregis.tic@westdorset-dc.gov.uk; Guild-hall Cottage, Church St; open 10am-5pm Mon-Sat, 10am-4pm Sun) is situated where Church St becomes Bridge St.

Museums

The excellent **Lyme Regis Philpot Museum** (☎ 443370; **w** www.lymeregismuseum.co.uk; Bridge St; adult/child £1.60/60p; open 10am-5pm Mon-Sat, 11am-5pm Sun Apr-Oct, Sat & Sun only Nov-Mar) is a quirky building with displays of paintings and other artefacts relating to local history and literary connections. It contains a good fossil collection, and displays on the life and finds of Mary Anning, world-famous Lyme Regis palaeontologist.

If your own fossil-hunting happens to be unsuccessful, head to **Dinosaurland** (☎ 443 541; **w** www.dinosaurland.co.uk; Coombe St;

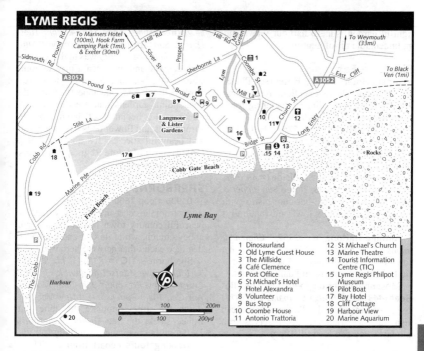

LYME REGIS

To Mariners Hotel (100m), Hook Farm Camping Park (1mi), & Exeter (30mi)

Sidmouth Rd

To Weymouth (33mi)

To Black Ven (1mi)

Pound St

Stile La

Cobb Rd

Langmoor & Lister Gardens

Cobb Gate Beach

Front Beach

Marine Pde

Lyme Bay

Harbour

The Cobb

Rocks

| 0 | 100 | 200m |
| 0 | 100 | 200yd |

1 Dinosaurland
2 Old Lyme Guest House
3 The Millside
4 Café Clemence
5 Post Office
6 St Michael's Hotel
7 Hotel Alexandra
8 Volunteer
9 Bus Stop
10 Coombe House
11 Antonio Trattoria
12 St Michael's Church
13 Marine Theatre
14 Tourist Information Centre (TIC)
15 Lyme Regis Philpot Museum
16 Pilot Boat
17 Bay Hotel
18 Cliff Cottage
19 Harbour View
20 Marine Aquarium

adult/child £3.50/2.50; open 10am-5pm daily), where you'll see extensive fossil displays and reconstructed dinosaurs – and you can pick up an ammonite in the shop.

The Cobb

The Cobb is a 183m-long stone jetty-cum-breakwater, first constructed in the 13th century. The pleasantly low-tech **Marine Aquarium** *(☎ 444230; adult/child £2/1.50p; open 10am-5pm Apr-Oct, extended hrs peak season)* has tanks housing local underwater life – find out what a furry sea mouse is here.

Places to Stay

Hook Farm Camping Park *(☎ 442801; Gore Lane; tent & 2 people £8-11.50)* is in Uplyme, about 1 mile (1.6km) north of Lyme Regis. Follow Uplyme Rd (towards Exeter), turn left at the Talbot Arms onto Gore Lane and continue 200m.

Harbour View *(☎ 443910; Cobb Rd; rooms per person £16.50)* is a small, homely place popular with cyclists and watersports enthusiasts. Rates don't include breakfast.

Coombe House *(☎/fax 443849; 41 Coombe St; en-suite B&B per person from £19)* is a

cosy stone house with a relaxed atmosphere – breakfast in bed is the norm.

Cliff Cottage *(☎ 443334; Cobb Rd; doubles with/without en suite £43/39)* is a pleasant B&B with a tea garden boasting magnificent views down to the Cobb.

Old Lyme Guest House *(☎ 442929; e oldlyme.guesthouse@virgin.net; 29 Coombe St; en-suite B&B per person from £25)* was the post office back in the early 19th century; now it's an award-winning B&B.

St Michael's Hotel *(☎ 442503; Pound St; en-suite singles/doubles from £35/50)* is a charming, salmon-pink Georgian B&B with substantial rooms and fantastic sea views.

Mariners Hotel *(☎ 442753, fax 442431; e mariners@ukgateway.net; Silver St; en-suite B&B per person from £40)*, dating from the 17th-century, is a smart place full of history and nautical atmosphere.

The excellent **Bay Hotel** *(☎ 442059; Marine Parade; B&B en-suite singles/doubles £55/90)* has a sensational location just steps from the sea.

Built in 1735, **Hotel Alexandra** *(☎ 442010, fax 443229; e enquiries@hotelalexandra.co.uk; Pound St; en-suite singles/doubles £50/88)* is one of the town's finest hotels, with a delightful garden, superb harbour views and an undeniable air of gentility.

Places to Eat

Mariners Hotel and **Bay Hotel** (see Places to Stay) both have excellent restaurants where three-course dinners featuring fresh local fish dishes cost £19.50.

Café Clemence (☎ 445757; Mill Lane; mains £8-11), in the old mill complex, is a snug little bistro with a quiet courtyard and modern Mediterranean cuisine.

A few feet away, **The Millside** (☎ 445999; Mill Lane; mains £6-13; closed Sun dinner & Mon) is another wine-bar-cum-bistro with treats such as guinea fowl and (naturally) fresh fish.

Antonio Trattoria (☎ 442352; 7 Church St; mains £7-10; open 7pm-10pm Mon-Sat), in a low-ceilinged old house, cooks up authentic Italian pasta, steak and daily specials.

Most of the pubs do good food. **The Pilot Boat** (443157; 1 Bridge St; mains £4.75-11) is a sea-front pub with a huge menu of fresh fish and vegetarian specials. It serves grub all day – you can feed till 10pm.

Entertainment

The Volunteer (☎ 442214; 31 Broad St) has the feel of a smugglers' haunt, a bustling local with a popular restaurant, and fine guest beers and ciders. Before you over-indulge, remember the long, steep hills all around!

Marine Theatre (☎ 442394; Church St) hosts a surprisingly eclectic mix of bands and plays by local or touring companies.

Getting There & Away

Lyme Regis is a convenient midway point between Dorchester or Weymouth and Exeter; they all have much better connections. Bus No 31 runs to Dorchester (1¼ hours) and Weymouth (1¾ hours) hourly (every two hours on Sunday). Bus X53 goes west to Exeter (1¾ hours, five daily Monday to Saturday) and east to Weymouth (1½ hours, four daily Monday to Saturday).

AROUND LYME REGIS
Forde Abbey

Originally a Cistercian monastery constructed in the 12th century, Forde Abbey (☎ 01460-221290; w www.fordeabbey.co.uk; admission to abbey £6.50/free, gardens £4.75/free; abbey open 1pm-4.30pm Tues-Thur & Sun Apr-Oct, gardens open 10am-4.30pm daily year round) was updated in the 17th century and has been a private home since 1649, boasting magnificent plaster-work ceilings and fine tapestries. It's the outstanding gardens that are the main attraction: 12 hectares of lawns, ponds, shrubberies and flower beds with many rare and beautiful species. It's about 10 miles (16km) north of Lyme Regis; public transport is a nonstarter.

SHERBORNE
☎ 01935 • pop 7600
Away from the coast and the Hardy trail, this peaceful country town boasts a wonderful abbey church, while its Old and New Castles face each other across Sherborne Lake.

Sherborne's **TIC** (☎ 815341, fax 817210; e tourism@westdorset-dc.gov.uk; 3 Tilton Court, Digby Rd; open 9am-5pm Mon-Sat Apr-Oct, 10am-3pm Mon-Sat Nov-Mar), just down the street opposite the abbey entrance, stocks the free All About Sherborne leaflet with a map and town trail.

Walking tours depart from the TIC at 11am on Friday, May to September, cost £2.50 and last 1½ hours.

Sherborne Museum (☎ 812252; Church Lane; adult/child £1/free; open 10.30am-4.30pm Tues-Sat, 2.30pm-4.30pm Sun Apr-Oct) features local history and prehistory, a scale model of the Old Castle and an excellent antique dolls' house.

Sherborne Abbey

The Abbey Church of St Mary the Virgin (☎ 815191, 812452; suggested donation £2; open 8.30am-6pm late Mar–late Oct, 8.30am-4pm Nov–mid-Mar) was established early in the 8th century, and became a Benedictine abbey in 998. After further expansion and decoration, the townsfolk clubbed together and bought it as their parish church after the Dissolution.

The abbey is entered via a Norman porch built in 1180. The Norman door immediately on the left was the cause of riots in 1437; when the monks attempted to narrow the doorway between the abbey and connected All Hallows Church, a battle broke out between the monks and the angry townspeople, and a flaming arrow set the roof alight. The remains of All Hallows are to the west of the Saxon wall; a Saxon doorway from 1050 survives. The superb fan vault above the choir dates from the early 15th century and is the oldest ceiling of this type and size in the country; decorated with bosses, it lends the abbey a remarkably organic feel. The similar vault over the nave is from later in the century. Solid Saxon-Norman piers support the abbey's soaring central tower. The monks' choir stalls feature interesting misericords and also date from the mid-15th century.

On the edge of the abbey close are the cloistered 1437 **St Johns' Almshouses** (admission £1; open 2pm-4pm Tues & Thur-Sat May-Sept), containing a medieval chapel.

Old Castle

East of the town centre stand the ruins of the Old Castle (EH; ☎ 812730; admission £1.80; open 10am-6pm daily Apr-Sept, 10am-5pm daily Oct, 10am-4pm Wed-Sun Nov-Mar), originally constructed from 1107 by Roger, bishop of Salisbury. Sir Walter Raleigh acquired it (with the help of Elizabeth I) in the late 16th century, and spent large sums of money modernising the castle before deciding it wasn't worth the effort and moving across the River Yeo to start work on his new castle. Cromwell destroyed the castle after a 16-day siege in 1645, and the ruined remains make an evocative spot for a picnic.

Sherborne Castle

Sir Walter Raleigh commenced building his New Castle (☎ 813182; w www.sherbornecastle.com; house admission £5.75/free, gardens only £3/free; open 11am-4.30pm Tues-Thur & Sun, 2.30pm-4.30pm Sat Easter-Sept) – really a splendid manor house – in 1594 but by 1608 he was back in prison, this time at the hands of James I, who eventually sold it to Sir John Digby, the Earl of Bristol, in 1617. It's been the Digby family residence ever since, and contains fine collections of art, furniture and porcelain, as well as grounds landscaped by Capability Brown.

Places to Stay & Eat

Just south of the abbey is **Britannia Inn** (☎ 813300; Westbury; B&B per person with/without en suite from £25/22), a 300-year-old pub with plain, tidy rooms.

Clatcombe Grange (☎ 814355; Bristol Rd; en-suite B&B per person from £26) is a charming, peaceful converted barn a little north of the centre.

Antelope Hotel (☎ 812077, fax 816473; Greenhill; singles £30-60, doubles £50-80) is an attractive 18th-century coaching inn with a respected Italian restaurant, **San Marino** (mains £5.50-11.50).

The Old Vicarage (☎ 01963-251117, fax 251515; e theoldvicarage@milborneport.free serve.co.uk; Sherborne Rd; B&B en-suite singles £42-59, doubles £56-100), in Milborne Port, 3 miles (5km) east of Sherborne on the A30, is an imposing Victorian Gothic building with plush decor, extensive grounds and excellent cuisine (Friday and Saturday only). Rates vary depending on the room, day and season.

Cross Keys Hotel (☎ 812492; 88 Cheap St; en-suite singles/doubles £30/50; mains £6-7), right by the abbey, has a large pub-food menu and a few comfortable rooms.

Tucked away behind the TIC off Digby Rd, the **Digby Tap** (☎ 813148; Cooks Lane; mains £3.50-5.50) offers a wide range of ales and good-sized portions of traditional pub fare.

The Green (☎ 813821; 3 The Green; mains £15; closed Sun & Mon) is a smart little bistro with tempting fish and duck dishes.

Getting There & Away

Nearby Yeovil is a handy transport hub. Bus No 57 runs hourly from Yeovil (30 minutes, Monday to Saturday), as does quicker No 58 (12 minutes, Monday to Saturday), which sometimes continues on to Shaftesbury (1½ hours); No 958 runs to Yeovil six times on Sunday. No 216 runs to Dorchester (one hour; six daily Monday to Saturday) via Cerne Abbas (30 minutes).

Trains run from Exeter (single £11.60, 1¼ hours) to London (saver return £43.30, 2¼ hours) via Salisbury (single £8.10, 40 minutes) roughly hourly.

SHAFTESBURY & AROUND
☎ 01747

This slow-paced country town invites a stop to see the charming Gold Hill and the remains of the ancient abbey.

The **TIC** (☎ 853514; 8 Bell St; open 10am-5pm daily Apr-Oct, Mon-Sat Nov & Dec, 10am-1pm Mon-Wed, 10am-5pm Thur-Sat Jan-Mar) is by the Bleke St car park.

Things to See

Situated on a 240m-high ridge with fine views of the surrounding countryside, **Shaftesbury Abbey** (☎ 852910; Park Walk; adult/child £1.50/60p; open 10am-5pm daily Apr-Oct) was founded in 888 by Alfred the Great and was at one time England's richest nunnery; Henry VIII's gentle attentions finished it off in 1539. Today, you can wander around the foundations with a well-devised audio guide, and visit the museum, which displays carved stones, decorated floor tiles and other relics, and tells the abbey's history. St Edward was said to have been buried here, and King Canute died at the abbey in 1035.

The small **Shaftesbury Museum** (☎ 852157; Sun & Moon Cottage, Gold Hill; adult/child £1/free; open 10.30am-4.30pm daily Apr-Oct) is worth visiting to see the Shaftesbury Hoard of coins, some dating from 871, including many Saxon pieces.

The picturesquely steep cobbled street **Gold Hill** tumbles down the ridge from beside the abbey ruins, offering great views of the surrounding plains; its photogenic qualities have been exploited by postcard-makers and advertising companies alike.

Old Wardour Castle

This unique six-sided castle (EH; ☎ 01747-870487; adult/child £2.50/1.30; open 10am-6pm daily Apr-Sept, 10am-5pm daily Oct, 10am-4pm Wed-Sun Nov-Mar) was built around 1393 and suffered severe damage during the Civil War, leaving the magnificent remains you see today. Audio guides lead you up, down and around the ruins; there are fantastic views from the upper levels, and it's an ideal spot for a picnic (or a film, as the producers of Robin Hood Prince of Thieves decided). Although it's actually in Wiltshire, Old Wardour is more easily reached from Dorset; bus No 26 runs from Shaftesbury (four daily Monday to Friday), 4 miles west.

Places to Stay & Eat

Shaftesbury has several B&Bs and hotels; alternatively, it's an easy day trip from Salisbury.

The Retreat (☎/fax 850372; e at.retreat@virgin.net; 47 Bell St; en-suite B&B per person from £25) is a substantial, attractive Georgian House in the town centre.

Terra Firma (☎ 858883; Mustons Lane; mains £6.50-12) is a deli and restaurant in a beautifully converted church; imaginative meals combining organic fish, meat and vegetables are served during the day and occasional evenings – call to check.

The **Ship Inn** (☎ 853219; Bleke St; mains £6-8.25) is a lovely old stone pub by the central car park, renowned for pie and mash as well as good ales.

Getting There & Away

Bus Nos 182 and 183 run to Blandford (40 minutes, eight daily Monday to Saturday);

White Lines

The rolling fields of Wessex are a green cloak over a chalk substructure, and the practice of cutting pictures into the hillsides has a long history. The technique is simple: mark out your picture and cut away the green grass and topsoil to reveal the white chalk below. The picture will need periodic maintenance, but not much – some of the chalk figures may date back to prehistoric times, though the history of the oldest figures is uncertain. Although Wiltshire has more chalk figures than any other county, the best are probably the 55m-tall Cerne Abbas Giant (with his even more notable 12m penis) in Dorset and the 110m-long Uffington White Horse in Oxfordshire (which really requires a helicopter or hot-air balloon for proper inspection).

Horses were particularly popular subjects for chalk figures in the 18th century and noteworthy ones can be seen in Wiltshire at Cherhill near Calne, Alton Barnes and Hackpen, and at Osmington near Weymouth in Dorset.

In more recent times, during WWI a series of regimental badges were cut into a hillside outside Fovant in Wiltshire. A New Zealand WWI regiment left a gigantic kiwi on a hillside at Bulford, near Amesbury in Wiltshire.

Get a copy of Kate Bergamar's Discovering Hill Figures (Shire Publications) for the complete lowdown on England's chalky personalities, or pick up the excellent Wiltshire's White Horse Trail booklet (£6) at TICs, which details a range of long and short walks, tying in with views and visits to the county's eight chalk horses.

some go on to Bournemouth (two hours) though most require a change. Bus Nos 26/27 run from Salisbury (1¼ hours, approximately four daily Monday to Saturday).

Wiltshire

The name has an earthy sort of air to it; appropriately so – Wiltshire is very much a rural county, particularly south of the M4, boasting wonderful rolling chalk downs. Many of its attractions are not recent: Britain's most important prehistoric sites at Stonehenge and Avebury, the fine cathedral at Salisbury and a number of the stateliest of stately homes at Wilton, Stourhead and Longleat. It's perfect country for random roaming (or even taking a weekend out), with sleepy villages such as Lacock and Castle Combe cocooned in countryside peace.

Orientation & Information

Wiltshire is a landlocked county, roughly oval in shape; the A338 between Swindon and Salisbury to the south essentially marks its eastern edge, with Bath and the Mendips just beyond its western boundary. Attractions are scattered around the county, although there are very few settlements on Salisbury Plain, stretching north and west of the county town.

In addition to town and district TICs, there's general county-wide information, including searchable accommodation listings, on **w** www.visitwiltshire.co.uk. There's a special line (☎ 0906 302 0322; 50p per minute) for ordering brochures and books.

Activities

Some walking and cycling ideas are suggested in the Activities section at the start of this chapter. For a historical slant, **Foot Trails** (☎ 01747-861851; **w** www.foottrails.co .uk; 2 Underdown Mead, White Road, Mere) leads various walks around Stonehenge, Salisbury, Old Wardour Castle and Old Sarum.

Two-wheeled travellers in Wiltshire can find the *Wiltshire Cycleway* leaflet in TICs; it details the route and it's various options, and lists cycle shops and rental outlets. *Off-Road Cycling in Wiltshire* (£6) is a waterproof guide with maps for mountain-bikers.

For transport of another type, the 87-mile-long (140km) **Kennet & Avon Canal**, which

runs all the way from Bristol to Reading, was reopened in 1990 after standing derelict for 40 years. Built by the brilliant engineer John Rennie between 1794 and 1810, it's now used by leisure-boaters and has some fine stretches of towpath for walking and cycling. The stretch from Bath to Bradford-on-Avon is accessible and scenic, with notable aqueducts, and the flight of 29 locks just outside Devizes is an engineering marvel. You can hire narrowboats at various points; weekly rates start at around £600 for four people in winter, rising to £1300 for a 10-berth boat in August. Try **Sally Boats** (☎ 01225-864923, fax 865264; **w** www.sally boats.ltd.uk) in Bradford-on-Avon.

Getting Around

To obtain bus timetables, call the **Wiltshire Bus Line** (☎ 0845 709 0899).

Wilts & Dorset Buses (☎ 01722-336855; **w** www.wdbus.co.uk) covers most destinations; timetables are available online. The Explorer ticket (adult/child £5.50/2.75) is valid on most buses (not First Badgerline) throughout Wiltshire for one day; this would be useful if, for example, you wanted to visit Old Sarum, Stonehenge and Avebury from Salisbury.

Services in the far west of the county are provided by **First Badgerline** (☎ 01934-620122; **w** www.firstbadgerline.co.uk); again, timetables are on the website.

The Wiltshire Day Rover (£6/4.25) is valid with most operators in the county, and can be bought from bus drivers. Call the Wiltshire Bus Line for details.

Rail lines run from London to Salisbury and beyond to Exeter and Plymouth, branching off north to Bradford-on-Avon, Bath and Bristol; unless you're going to Salisbury or Bradford, train travel isn't really useful within the county.

Various tours visit Wiltshire's attractions, especially Stonehenge and Avebury. **Danwood Tours** (☎ 07977 929486) and **Mad Max Tours** (☎ 01225-325900; **w** www.mad maxtours.com) run one-day trips from Bath, visiting Stonehenge, Avebury and Lacock, costing £17.50/11.

SALISBURY
☎ 01722 • pop 39,300
Salisbury boasts a stunning cathedral, many fine museums and numerous medieval and

Tudor buildings, and there's no doubting its gracious charms. Equally, it's still very much a busy, lively town; markets have been held in the centre twice weekly for over 600 years and the jumble of stalls still draws a cheery crowd. The town's architecture mixes every style since the Middle Ages and includes some beautiful, half-timbered, black-and-white buildings.

Salisbury makes a good base for visiting attractions throughout Wiltshire and for excursions to the coast.

Orientation & Information

Salisbury's compact town centre revolves around Market Square, which is dominated by its impressive guildhall. The train station is a 10-minute walk to the west, while the bus station is just 100 yards north up Endless St.

Directly behind the guildhall is the **TIC** (☎ 334956, fax 422059; e visitorinfo@salisbury.gov.uk; Fish Row; open 9.30am-5pm Mon-Sat Oct-May, 9.30am-6pm Mon-Sat June-Sept & 10.30am-4.30pm Sun May-Sept). It sells Seeing Salisbury (80p), a useful pamphlet that outlines walks around the town and across the water meadows for classic views of the cathedral.

The **I-Cafe** (☎ 320050; 30 Milford St; open 10am-8pm Mon-Sat, noon-8pm Sun) is a colourful little cybercafé charging £2 for 30 minutes. **Starlight InterNetGate** (☎ 349359; 1 Endless St; open 9.30am-8pm Mon-Sat, 9.30am-4.30pm Sun) is upstairs on the corner of Market Square where Internet access costs £1 for 15 minutes.

Wishing Well Laundrette (☎ 421874; 28 Chipper Lane; open 7.30am-8.30pm daily) is a central option.

Salisbury Cathedral

The Cathedral Church of the Blessed Virgin Mary (☎ 555100; w www.salisburycathedral.org.uk; requested donation £3.50/2; open 7.15am-6.15pm daily Sept–mid-June, 7.15am-8.15pm Mon-Sat mid-June–Aug, 7.15am-6.15pm Sun year round) is one of the most beautiful and cohesive in Britain, an inspiration to the artist John Constable who painted it from across the water meadows. It was built in uniform Early English (or early pointed) Gothic, a style characterised by the first pointed arches and flying buttresses and a feeling of austerity. The uniformity is a result of the speed with which the cathedral

was built (between 1220 and 1258) and that it has not subsequently undergone major rebuilding. The sole exception is the magnificent spire, at 123m the highest in Britain, an afterthought added between 1285 and 1315.

Salisbury cathedral had its origins 2 miles (3km) farther north with a Norman cathedral at Old Sarum (see Old Sarum later in this chapter). In 1217 Bishop Poore petitioned the pope for permission to move the cathedral to a better location; his request was granted and in 1220 a new cathedral was constructed on the plains, conveniently close to three rivers.

Construction started at the eastern end: **Trinity Chapel** was completed by 1225, the main part of the church by 1258 and the whole thing by 1266. The cloisters were added at about the same time and a few years later it was decided to add the magnificent tower and spire. Because this had not featured in the original plans, the four central piers of the building were expected to carry an unexpected extra 6400 tons. Some fast thinking was required to enable them to do this.

The highly decorative West Front is graced by scores of statues, including David, Moses and some more obscure names such as St Alphege. The cathedral is entered via the cloister passage and the **southwest door**. The 70m-long nave, with its beautiful Purbeck marble piers, was 'tidied up' by James Wyatt between 1789 and 1792; among other things he lined up the tombs in the nave neatly. At the southwestern end of the nave is the **grave slab of Bishop Joscelyn** (1141–84), at one time thought to be the tomb of Bishop Roger, who completed the final cathedral at Old Sarum where he was bishop from 1107 to 1139. A **model** in the south aisle shows the cathedral's construction.

The **Shrine of St Osmund** was installed in 1226, a year after Trinity Chapel was completed. St Osmund had completed the original cathedral at Old Sarum in 1092 and was canonised in 1457. His actual grave remains in the Trinity Chapel. The **Tomb of William Longespée** was the first new tomb in the cathedral, following his death in 1226. A son of Henry II and half-brother of King John, he was present at the signing of the Magna Carta and also laid one of the cathedral's foundation stones.

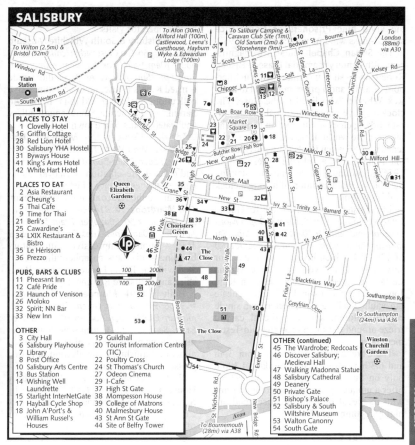

SALISBURY

To Wilton (2.5mi) &
Bristol (52mi)

To Afon (30mi),
Milford Hall (100m),
Castlewood, Leena's
Guesthouse, Hayburn
Wyke & Edwardian
Lodge (100m)

To Salisbury Camping &
Caravan Club Site (1mi),
Old Sarum (2mi) &
Stonehenge (9mi)

To
London
(88mi)
via A30

PLACES TO STAY
1 Clovelly Hotel
16 Griffin Cottage
28 Red Lion Hotel
30 Salisbury YHA Hostel
41 King's Arms Hotel
42 White Hart Hotel

PLACES TO EAT
2 Asia Restaurant
4 Cheung's
5 Thai Cafe
9 Time for Thai
21 Berli's
25 Cawardine's
34 LXIX Restaurant &
     Bistro
35 Le Hérisson
36 Prezzo

PUBS, BARS & CLUBS
11 Pheasant Inn
12 Café Pride
23 Haunch of Venison
26 Moloko
32 Spirit; NN Bar
33 New Inn

OTHER
3 City Hall
6 Salisbury Playhouse
7 Library
8 Post Office
10 Salisbury Arts Centre
13 Bus Station
14 Wishing Well
     Laundrette
15 Starlight InterNetGate
17 Hayball Cycle Shop
18 John A'Port's &
     William Russel's
     Houses
19 Guildhall
20 Tourist Information Centre
     (TIC)
22 Poultry Cross
24 St Thomas's Church
27 Odeon Cinema
29 I-Cafe
37 High St Gate
38 Mompesson House
39 College of Matrons
40 Malmesbury House
43 St Ann St Gate
44 Site of Belfry Tower

OTHER (continued)
45 The Wardrobe; Redcoats
46 Discover Salisbury;
     Medieval Hall
47 Walking Madonna Statue
48 Salisbury Cathedral
49 Deanery
50 Private Gate
51 Bishop's Palace
52 Salisbury & South
     Wiltshire Museum
53 Walton Canonry
54 South Gate

WESSEX

The soaring spire is the cathedral's most impressive feature. In 1668 Sir Christopher Wren, creator of St Paul's in London, surveyed the cathedral and calculated that the spire was leaning sideways by 75cm. In 1737 a **brass plate** was inserted in the floor of the nave, directly under the centre of the spire, and the lean was recorded. It had not shifted at all since Wren's measurement, nor had it moved any farther when rerecorded in 1951 and 1970.

Other parts of the cathedral clearly show the strain, however. The tower and spire are supported by four **piers**, each nearly 2m square, but the additional weight has bent these massive stone columns. If you look up from the bottom, the curve is quite visible, particularly on the eastern piers. Flying but-

tresses were later added to the outside of the building to support the four corners of the original tower. More buttresses were added internally and the openings to the eastern transepts were reinforced with **scissor arches** as in Wells Cathedral. Reinforcement work on the notoriously 'wonky spire' continues to this day.

Not everything in the cathedral requires peering upwards. The **tomb of Sir Richard Mompesson**, who died in 1627, and his wife Catherine, is a brilliantly colourful work. The grandiose **tomb of Edward Seymour** (1539–1621) and **Lady Catherine Grey**, sister of Lady Jane Grey (Queen of England for nine days in 1553), is at the eastern end of the ambulatory. The first part of the cathedral to be built, **Trinity Chapel**, at the eastern end, has fine Purbeck marble pillars; the vivid blue **Prisoners of Conscience** stained-glass window was installed in 1980.

The **Sudan Chapel** contains a magnificent 14th-century **memorial brass** to Bishop Robert Wyvil showing him praying in Sherborne Castle, and a **prism memorial** to artist Rex Whistler who lived in the close. The **clock** displayed in the north aisle is the oldest working clock in England and one of the oldest in the world. It was certainly in existence in 1386 when funds were provided for maintenance of a 'clocke'. Restored in 1956, it continues to operate, maintaining the 600-year-old tradition of having a clock in this position.

The cloisters lead to the beautiful Gothic **Chapter House** (*open 9.30am-5.30pm Mon-Sat Sept–mid-June, 9.30am-7.45pm Mon-Sat mid-June–Aug, noon-5.30pm Sun year round*) of 1263–84, which houses one of the four surviving original versions of the **Magna Carta**, the agreement made between King John and his barons in 1215. The delicate fan-vaulted ceiling is supported by a single central column, and a medieval carved frieze around the room recounts Old Testament tales.

There are tower tours at 11am, 2pm, 3pm and 6.30pm Monday to Saturday (4.30pm only on Sunday), which cost £3/2. These offer a unique opportunity to come to grips with medieval building practices and are highly recommended.

Cathedral Close

Salisbury Cathedral has England's largest, and arguably most beautiful, cathedral close. Many of the buildings were built at the same time as the cathedral although it owes most of its present appearance to Wyatt's late-18th-century clean-up. The Close was actually walled in, physically separating it from the town, in 1333, using the old cathedral at Old Sarum as a source of building material. To this day it remains an elite enclave, with the gates in the wall still locked every night (residents have their own keys).

Wyatt also cleared the close grounds of gravestones and demolished the late-13th-century external belfry, by then in ruins. Striding across the close lawns on the western side of the cathedral is Elizabeth Frink's **Walking Madonna** (1981); other pieces of modern sculpture are dotted around.

The close has several museums and houses open for visits.

The **Salisbury & South Wiltshire Museum** (*☎ 332151; 65 The Close; adult/child £3.50/1; open 10am-5pm Mon-Sat year round, also 2pm-5pm Sun July & Aug*), in the Grade I–listed King's House, houses an impressive collection, including exhibits from Old Sarum, an interactive Stonehenge Gallery and watercolours of the town by Turner.

In the 13th-century **Medieval Hall** (*☎ 412472; West Walk, The Close; adult/child £1.50/1; open 11am-5pm daily*), a 40-minute audiovisual presentation, *Discover Salisbury*, describes the city's history.

Home to the **Redcoats** military museum, **The Wardrobe** (*☎ 414536; 58 The Close; adult/child £2.50/50p; open 10am-5pm daily Apr-Oct, 10am-5pm Tues-Sat Nov, Feb & Mar*) – another impressive 13th-century building – displays paraphernalia associated with the Royal Gloucestershire, Berkshire and Wiltshire Regiment.

Built in 1701, **Mompesson House** (*NT; ☎ 335659; Choristers Green, The Close; admission £3.90; open noon-5.30pm Sat-Wed Easter-Sept*) is a fine Queen Anne house with magnificent plasterwork ceilings, exceptional period furnishings, a collection of period glasses and a peaceful walled garden.

With a facade by Wren, **Malmesbury House** (*☎ 327027, fax 334414; The Close*), by St Ann's Gate, was originally a 13th-century canonry and later the residence of the earls of Malmesbury, visited by notables including Charles II and Handel. It can be visited on pre-booked group tours only (£5).

From High St, the close is entered by the narrow High St Gate. Just inside is the **College of Matrons**, founded in 1682 for widows and unmarried daughters of clergymen. South of the cathedral is the **Bishop's Palace**, now the Cathedral School, parts of which date back to 1220. The **Deanery** on Bishop's Walk mainly dates from the 13th century.

Izaak Walton, patron saint of fishermen, lived for a time in the **Walton Canonry**, and no doubt dropped a line in the nearby Avon.

St Thomas's Church

Overshadowed as it is by the cathedral, were it elsewhere splendid St Thomas's Church would attract the attention it deserves. Originally built for cathedral workmen in 1219 and named, unusually, for St

Thomas à Becket (the archbishop murdered in Canterbury Cathedral), the light, airy edifice seen today dates mainly from the 15th century. It's renowned for the superb 'doom', or judgement-day painting, which spreads up and over the chancel arch. Painted around 1470, it was whitewashed over during the Reformation and uncovered again in 1881. In the centre, Christ sits in judgement astride a rainbow with scenes of heaven on the left and hell on the right; hell is supervised by a hairy devil whose foot pokes out onto the chancel arch. On the hell side look out for a bishop and two kings, naked except for their mitre and crowns, and for a miser with his moneybags and a female alehouse owner, the only person allowed to hang on to her clothes.

Market Square

Markets were first held here in 1219, and since 1361 have been held every Tuesday and Saturday. The market once spread much farther than the present car-park area and street names like Oatmeal Row, Fish Row or Silver St indicate their medieval specialities. The square is dominated by the late-18th-century guildhall.

Facing the guildhall are two **medieval houses**: John A'Port's of 1425 and William Russel's of 1306. Russel's looks newer because of a false front, but inside its age is revealed. The present shop owners, Watson's of Salisbury, are used to sightseers and produce a leaflet about what is probably the town's oldest house.

Immediately behind Market Square look out for Fish Row, with some fine old houses, and for the 15th-century **Poultry Cross**.

Organised Tours

Salisbury City Guides (☎ 518658; w www.salisburycityguides.co.uk) lead excellent 1½-hour walking tours (adult/child £2.50/1), departing the TIC at 11am daily from April to October, Saturday and Sunday November to March, and at 8pm Monday to Thursday, May to September. At 8pm on Friday (May to September) there's a ghost walk (£3/1.50).

Special Events

Salisbury Festival (☎ 320333; w www.salisburyfestival.co.uk) is a prestigious, wide-ranging arts event encompassing classical, world and pop music, theatre, literature, art

and puppetry, running over three weeks from late May to early June.

Places to Stay

Camping & Hostels The **Salisbury Camping & Caravanning Club Site** (☎ 320713; *Hudson's Field, Castle Rd; camping per tent/person £4.50/£3.90-5.50)* is a well-equipped site 1 mile (1.6km) north of Salisbury on the road to Old Sarum (A345).

Just east of the ring road, **Salisbury YHA Hostel** (☎ 0870 770 6018, fax 330446; e *salisbury@yha.org.uk; Milford Hill; dorm beds £11.25)* is a listed building in large gardens, a short walk along Milford St from the centre of Salisbury.

Matt & Tiggy's (☎ 327443; *dorm beds £10)* is a friendly, hostel-like operation with dorm beds in central houses; call to confirm availability. They can arrange cheap breakfasts, Internet access and bike hire. Note that the café of the same name on Salt Lane is not connected.

B&Bs & Hotels Castle Rd, the A345 continuation of Castle St north from Salisbury, has a wide choice of B&Bs between the ring road and Old Sarum.

Castlewood (☎ 324809, fax 421494; 45 *Castle Rd; B&B singles £20-26, doubles £40-46)* is a large Edwardian house; most rooms have an en suite.

Leena's Guesthouse (☎/fax 335419; 50 *Castle Rd; en-suite singles £24-39, doubles £39-50)* is a pleasant, family run B&B.

Hayburn Wyke (☎/fax 412627; w www.hayburnwykeguesthouse.co.uk; 72 Castle Rd; *singles/doubles from £30/40)* wins stars for friendly management. En-suite rooms are a little more expensive.

Edwardian Lodge (☎ 413329, fax 503105; e *richardwhite@edlodge.freeserve.co.uk; 59 Castle Rd; en-suite singles £30-37.50, doubles £45-55)* is up a notch on the swish B&B scale.

Byways House (☎ 328364, fax 322146; e *byways@bed-breakfast-salisbury.co.uk; 31 Fowlers Rd; singles/doubles from £30/50)* is a good option on several counts: it's central, pleasantly decorated, large and friendly, some rooms are accessible to wheelchair users, and there are cathedral views and decent vegetarian breakfasts.

Clovelly Hotel (☎ 322055, fax 327677; e *clovelly.hotel@virgin.net; 17-19 Mill Rd; en-suite singles/doubles from £45/65)* is a sizable, decent B&B in a handy but otherwise unattractive area; it's virtually opposite the train station.

Griffin Cottage (☎ 328259, fax 416928; e mark@brandonasoc.demon.co.uk; 10 St Edmunds Church St; doubles from £40) is another recommended B&B, a largely 17th-century cottage with a log fire and home-baked bread.

Opposite St Ann's Gate, **King's Arms Hotel** (☎ 327629, fax 414246; 9-11 St John St; B&B en-suite singles/doubles from £55/ 80) is all beams and sloped ceilings, with plenty of history (and good pub food).

Red Lion Hotel (☎ 323334, fax 325756; e reception@the-redlion.co.uk; Milford St; singles/doubles from £87.50/108.50), originally constructed around 1220 to house cathedral draughtsmen, has a charming courtyard and many period features. It's much nicer than the facade suggests.

Milford Hall (☎ 417411, fax 419444; e milfordhallhotel@cs.com; 206 Castle St; en-suite singles/doubles from £95/100) is a blend of Georgian grandeur and modern comfort. Weekend B&B rates are around 50% lower.

The 17th-century **White Hart Hotel** (☎ 0870 400 8125, fax 412761; e sales.white hartsalisbury@heritage-hotels.co.uk; 1 St John St; singles/doubles £95/125) is the centre's stylish option, concealed behind a grand portico near the cathedral close. Good leisure deals are available at the weekend.

Places to Eat

Cawardine's (☎ 320619; 3 Bridge St; baguettes £2.50-3.50) is a cheery café popular for veggie breakfasts (£2.95), lunches and teas.

On the market square, **Berli's** (☎ 328923; 14 Ox Row; mains £8; open 10.30am-3pm Tues-Sat & 7pm-late Fri & Sat) is a fine vegetarian restaurant with global dishes and lighter lunch-time snacks.

There are two funky little Thai places. **Time for Thai** (☎ 339339; 66 Castle St; mains £6-7.50; closed Sun) has a short but sweet-and-sour menu of Thai staples. **Thai Cafe** (☎ 414778; 58 Fisherton St; mains £4.50-8; closed Sun) bolsters its evening menu with cheap lunches (noodle soup £3.25).

Fisherton St has another couple of decent Asian restaurants.

Cheung's (☎ 327375; 60 Fisherton St; mains £3.20-7) is the locals' favourite for Chinese cuisine, while **Asia Restaurant** (☎ 327628; 90 Fisherton St; mains £4.25-11) sorts the Madras-munchers from the boys with its good Indian food.

Prezzo (☎ 341333; 52-54 High St; mains £5-8) is a sleek Italian that stands out from the pizza-pasta norm with some interesting specialities.

Le Hérisson (☎ 333471; 90-92 Crane St; mains £5.50-9; open 9.30am-5.30pm Mon-Sat) is a thriving deli and restaurant with ambitious Mediterranean cuisine and a pleasant conservatory dining area.

The terrace at **Afon** (☎ 552366; Millstream Approach; lunch mains £4-9, 2/3-course dinner £15/18), a modern riverside brasserie-bar, is ideal for those warm summer suppers.

LXIX (☎ 340000; 67-69 New St; 3 courses from £25; closed Sun) is Salisbury's – and possible Wiltshire's – hottest restaurant, serving trendy modern British cuisine in sleek surroundings. The bistro next door is more relaxed (and cheaper).

Entertainment

Pubs & Bars With panelled walls and oak beams, the **Haunch of Venison** (☎ 322024; 1-5 Minster St) is an atmospheric old pub (earliest records date from 1320). There's an interesting range of pub food – venison, naturally – and more than 100 malt whiskies on offer. Finish your meal *before* asking to see the 200-year-old mummified hand of the card player.

Pheasant Inn (☎ 327069; Salt Lane) and **New Inn** (☎ 326662; 41 New St) vie for the title of shonkiest, lowest-ceilinged, most-distressed-beams pub in town; the Pheasant pulls a younger crowd, while the New Inn is more mellow and has good beers.

Café Pride (☎ 321678; 2-4 Salt Lane; noon-midnight daily) is a vibrant gay bar with cabaret and dance nights. The food's pretty good, too.

Trendy **Moloko** (☎ 507050; 5 Bridge St; open to 1am Fri & Sat) is passionate red, with DJs that drop dance tunes at the weekend.

Spirit (☎ 338387; 46 Catherine St) is a hip bar-club with DJs, cocktails and deep house; it acts as pre-club for **NN Bar** (☎ 338387; 48 Catherine St) next door, playing a mix of sounds and with regular theme nights.

Enzo's (☎ 782618; w www.enzos.org; Highpost) is the largest club in the area, hosting some big names in breaks and drum'n'bass. It's about 4 miles (6km) towards Amesbury; free minibuses are laid on for special nights.

Theatre & Cinema Set in a converted church, the **Salisbury Arts Centre** (☎ 321744; *Bedwin St)* often hosts interesting live entertainment including high-quality contemporary music and performances. It also houses the good **Footlights Café** lunch spot.

Salisbury Playhouse (☎ 320333; **w** www .salisburyplayhouse.com; *Malthouse Lane)* puts on highbrow drama and new plays, while **City Hall** (☎ 327676; **w** www.cityhallsalis bury.co.uk; *Malthouse Lane)*, next door, hosts the likes of Bill Wyman and Danny La Rue.

Odeon Cinema (☎ 0870 505 0007; *New Canal)* must be one of the few cinemas in the world with a medieval foyer.

Getting There & Away
Salisbury is 88 miles (142km) west of London, 52 miles (84km) east of Bristol and 24 miles (39km) from Southampton.

There are excellent walking and cycling routes to and from Salisbury; the TIC stocks the useful *Cycling Around Salisbury & Wiltshire* (free). The Clarendon Way is a 26-mile (42km) walking route to Winchester.

Bus Three National Express coaches run daily from London via Heathrow to Salisbury (economy return £18.50, three hours). There are daily services to Bath (£9.25, 1½ hours) and Bristol (£9.25, two hours).

Local bus X4 runs hourly via Wilton (10 minutes) to Warminster, where there are immediate connections on buses X5 and X6 to Bath (£4.20, two hours) via Bradford-on-Avon (1½ hours). Bus X3 runs to Bournemouth (1¼ hours) and Poole (1½ hours) hourly, every two hours on Sunday.

Train Two main lines serve Salisbury. Trains run half-hourly from London Waterloo (saver return £34.40, 1½ hours) and hourly on to Exeter (£31.90, 1¼ hours). The other line runs from Portsmouth (£14.80, 1¼ hours, hourly) or Brighton (£25.40, 2¼ hours, six daily) via Southampton (single £6.10, 30 minutes, half-hourly) and on to Bradford-on-Avon (saver return £13.30, 45 minutes, hourly), Bath (£14.10, one hour, every 30 minutes) and Bristol (£17.10, 1¼ hours, half-hourly).

Getting Around
The ride to Stonehenge along the Woodford Valley is popular. Bikes can be hired from **Hayball Cycle Shop** (☎ 411378; *26-30 Winchester St; open 9am-5.30pm Mon-Sat)* for £10 per day.

AROUND SALISBURY
Old Sarum
Once an Iron Age hillfort, Old Sarum (☎ 01722-335398; *admission £2; open 10am-6pm daily Apr-Sept, 10am-5pm Oct, 10am-4pm Nov-Mar)* is unique in being essentially a Norman ghost town. What lies inside the impressive 22-hectare earthworks is the legacy of William the Conqueror, ruins of the Norman ramparts and the old cathedral foundations, with fine views of Salisbury.

In 1092 Bishop Osmund completed the first 53m-long cathedral, extended and rebuilt in 1130; abandoned with the shift to Salisbury, it was finally demolished in 1331 to provide building material for the walls of the cathedral close. What's tangible is a sense of a thriving community that one day simply upped sticks and moved. To flesh out the bare bones of these images, examine the scale model of 12th-century Old Sarum in Salisbury Cathedral cloisters.

There are free guided tours at 2.30pm on Monday, Wednesday and Friday in July and August, and medieval tournaments, open-air plays and mock battles are also held here: call ☎ 0870 333 1181 for information.

Old Sarum is 2 miles (3km) north of Salisbury; between them, bus Nos 3, 5, 6, 8 and 9 run at least hourly (10 minutes, every 15 minutes Monday to Saturday).

Wilton House
Originally the site of a Benedictine monastery, in 1542 Henry VIII gave Wilton (☎ 01722-746720; **w** www.wiltonhouse.co.uk; *house admission £9.25/5, gardens only £4/3; open 10.30am-5.30pm, last admission 4.30pm, daily Apr-Oct)* to William Herbert, who became the Earl of Pembroke in 1551; the 17th earl is the current incumbent. After a fire destroyed most of the house in 1647 it was redesigned by Inigo Jones and completed when the fifth earl took over; it's now one of the finest stately homes in the country, with marvellous art and furniture collections. An extensive redesign of the gardens in 1632, introducing delightful

WESSEX

water features, formed the basis of the wonderful grounds.

A visit to Wilton House and its 8 hectares of grounds starts with a video, followed by a tour of the kitchen and laundry. The hall has a statue of Shakespeare, who dedicated the first folio edition of his plays to the third earl. Inigo Jones was responsible for the Single and Double Cube Rooms, with their magnificent painted ceilings, elaborate plaster work and paintings by Van Dyck. You'll also spot the famous Pembroke Palace dolls' house (1907) and works by Rembrandt, Brueghel and Reynolds. The idyllic grounds are a mix of formal gardens and parkland.

Wilton House is 2½ miles (4km) west of Salisbury on the A30; bus Nos 60, 60A and 61 run from New Canal in Salisbury (10 minutes, every 15 minutes).

STONEHENGE

Stonehenge *(EH/NT; ☎ 01980-624715; admission £4.40; open 9.30am-6pm daily mid-Mar–May & Sept–mid-Oct, 9am-7pm June-Aug, 9.30am-4pm mid-Oct–mid-Mar)* consists of a ring of enormous stones (some of which were brought from Wales), built in stages starting 5000 years ago; mystical, magical, maddening – reactions vary, but it remains Europe's most famous prehistoric site and one of England's most popular attractions.

The Site

Stonehenge was built and rebuilt over a 1500-year period. Construction started

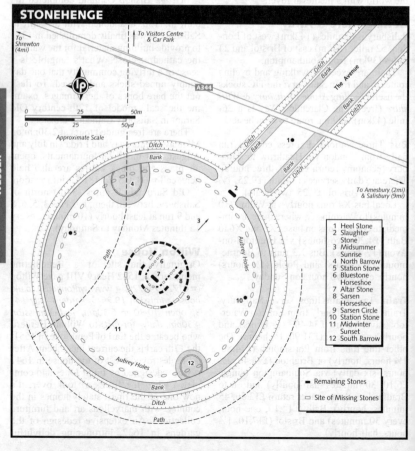

STONEHENGE

To Shrewton (4mi)

To Visitors Centre & Car Park

A344

The Avenue

Ditch
Bank
Ditch

0   25   50m
0   25   50yd

Approximate Scale

Ditch
Bank

To Amesbury (2mi) & Salisbury (9mi)

Ditch
Bank

1 ●

2

3

4

● 5

Path

6

7   8

9

10 ● ●

Aubrey Holes

11

Aubrey Holes

12

Bank

Ditch

Path

1 Heel Stone
2 Slaughter Stone
3 Midsummer Sunrise
4 North Barrow
5 Station Stone
6 Bluestone Horseshoe
7 Altar Stone
8 Sarsen Horseshoe
9 Sarsen Circle
10 Station Stone
11 Midwinter Sunset
12 South Barrow

■ Remaining Stones
□ Site of Missing Stones

WESSEX

Main meals

★ Stir Fried vegetables - £4.95 V N
   on a bed of noodles with chicken - £5.95 N
★ Shell on prawns, tomato, garlic, basil & chilli butter - £4.50
★ Caesar Salad - romaine lettuce, anchovies, garlic croutons & a parmesan
   dressing - £3.75 (with chicken) £6.25
★ lime, chilli & coriander fillet of chicken - £6.95
★ Roast red & yellow peppered mushroom sauce - £6.00 V
   on a bed of penne pasta drizzled with cream
★ Vegetarian Sausages - with dauphinoise potatoes & baked tomato - £5.25 V
★ Toulouse Sausages - with dauphinoise potatoes & baked tomato - £6.15
★ 8oz Rump Steak - with a rocket & black pepper crust, served with fries & mushrooms - £7.50
★ Westcorn ford cheese plate - 2 cheeses, fresh bread & gherkins
   & olives - £4.75

Ices
   Mystery ice cream - vanilla ice cream with meringue heart coated with praline &
   served with raspberry coulis - £3.15
   Seabreeze sundae - cranberry ice cream & hot grapefruit Sorbet - £3.50
   Vanilla & rich chocolate ice cream - with chocolate sauce - £3.50

Check chalkboards for daily specials

V - vegetarian   N - nuts

Alfresco dining, Brighton

An oast house, Kent

The white cliffs of Dover

The Royal Pavilion, Brighton

Lacock Abbey, Wiltshire

The King's Spring, Bath

Window boxes and facades, Salisbury, Wiltshire

The Battle for Stonehenge

Despite its World Heritage Site status, the 20th century wasn't kind to Stonehenge, which is hemmed in by the busy A303 to the south and the A344 to the north. Instead of being encouraged to let their imaginations rip, visitors have to put up with being funnelled through a tunnel under the A344 and then staring at the stones from behind a barbed-wire barricade with a constant backdrop of roaring traffic.

For a relatively small site, Stonehenge has always received a daunting number of visitors – over 700,000 per year at the last count. To make matters worse, in the 1980s latter-day Druids and New Age travellers began to descend on Stonehenge en masse for the summer solstice, often lingering for weeks afterwards. Archaeologists claimed that they would damage not just the stone circle, but the lesser monuments in the surrounding fields as well. The ensuing police clampdown on solstice visits turned into an annual stand-off. The barbed wire is one legacy of clashes; the 1994 Criminal Justice and Public Order Act, aimed at making it harder for convoys to assemble, is another. On the upside, solstice gatherings have returned over the past few years, with relatively positive results, thanks partly to the efforts of organisations such as the Stonehenge Peace Process (W www.green leaf.demon.co.uk/stones.htm), encouraging visitors to act respectfully and peacefully.

In 1993 Stonehenge's presentation was described by a House of Commons committee as 'a national disgrace'. Since then, a 'Master Plan' has been devised to alleviate the problems of traffic and poor facilities. The intention is that the A344 will be closed, the A303 road will run through a tunnel near the site, and a visitor centre will be built at Countess East (2.5 miles east of Stonehenge), with transit to within walking distance of the site. Hopefully this plan, due for completion by 2006, will restore the portentous ambience of the site; in the meantime, be prepared for crowds and road noise.

around 3000 BC when the outer circular bank and ditch were constructed. An inner circle of granite stones, known as bluestones from their original colouring, was erected 1000 years later. The stones weighed up to 4 tons each and were brought from the Preseli Mountains in South Wales, nearly 250 miles (403km) away.

Around 1500 BC, the huge stones that make Stonehenge instantly recognisable were dragged to the site, erected in a circle and topped by equally massive lintels to make the sarsen (the type of sandstone) trilithons (the formation of vertical and horizontal stones). The sarsens were cut from an extremely hard rock found on the Marlborough Downs about 20 miles (32km) from the site. It's estimated that dragging one of these 50-ton stones across the countryside to Stonehenge would require about 600 people.

Also around this time, the bluestones from 500 years earlier were rearranged as an inner horseshoe. In the centre of this horseshoe went the altar stone, a name given for no scientific reason in the 18th century. Around the bluestone horseshoe was a sarsen horseshoe of five trilithons.

Three of these trilithons are intact, the other two have just a single upright. Then came the major circle of 30 massive vertical stones, of which 17 uprights and six lintels remain.

Farther out was another circle delineated by the 58 Aubrey Holes, named after John Aubrey who discovered them in the 1600s. In the same circle are the South Barrow and North Barrow, each originally topped by a stone. Between them are two other stones, though not quite on the east-west axis. Outside the Aubrey Holes circle was the bank and then the ditch.

The inner horseshoes are aligned along the sun's axis on rising in midsummer and setting in midwinter. From the midsummer axis, approximately NNE, the Avenue leads out from Stonehenge and today is almost immediately cut by the A344. The gap cut in the bank by the Avenue is marked by the Slaughter Stone, another 18th-century name tag. Beyond the ditch in the Avenue, the Heel Stone stands on one side, and recent excavations have revealed that another Heel Stone stood on the other. Despite the site's sun-influenced alignment, little is really known about Stonehenge's purpose.

WESSEX

Admission includes an audio tour. Once in, you are kept at some distance from the stones. The most atmospheric way to see the stones is with an hour-long **private view** (£10/5) outside the standard opening hours. This must be arranged with **English Heritage** (☎ 01980-626267) well in advance.

Getting There & Away

Stonehenge is 2 miles (3km) west of Amesbury on the junction of the A303 and A344/A360. It's 9 miles (14km) from Salisbury (the nearest train station). Buses leave Salisbury bus station for Stonehenge (40 minutes), picking up at the train station, from 10am up to nine times a day in summer.

Guide Friday (☎ 01789-294466) operates two-hour tours to Stonehenge from Salisbury, departing three times daily April to October and costing £15/7.50, including entry to the site; this is one way to avoid the queues in peak season.

There are various minibus day tours to Stonehenge and other Wiltshire attractions, costing around £18 per person. **AS Tours** (☎ 01980-862931; e astours@globalnet.co.uk) run from Salisbury, while **Danwood Tours** (☎ 07977 929486) depart from Bath. Alternatively, **Foot Trails** (☎ 01747-861851; w www .foottrails.co.uk) leads a 6-mile (9.7km) walk from Amesbury on Saturday and Sunday during summer; the cost (£20) includes an organic picnic lunch.

AROUND STONEHENGE

The collection of prehistoric sites surrounding Stonehenge adds to the mystery of the area; fortunately, most are less busy than Stonehenge itself. Only the sites within the NT boundaries are open to the public; others are on private property. The *Stonehenge Estate Archaeological Walks* leaflet details walks around these sites.

Just north of Amesbury and 3 miles (5km) east of Stonehenge is **Woodhenge**, where concrete posts mark the site of a concentric wooden structure that predates Stonehenge.

North of Stonehenge and running approximately east-west is the **Cursus**, an elongated embanked oval, once thought to have been a Roman hippodrome; in fact it is far older, although its purpose is unknown. The **Lesser Cursus** looks like the end of a similar elongated oval. Other prehistoric sites around Stonehenge include a

number of burial mounds, like the **New King Barrows**, and **Vespasian's Camp**, an Iron Age hillfort.

STOURHEAD

Inspired by classical images of Italy, the estate of Stourhead (NT; ☎ 01747-841152; Stourton; admission house only £4.90/2.70, garden only £4.90/2.70 Mar-Oct or £3.80/1.85 Nov-Feb, combined house & garden admission £8.70/4.10; house open noon-5.30pm Sat-Wed Apr-Oct, garden open 9am-7pm or sunset daily year round) is landscape gardening at its finest. Although the Palladian house itself has some fine Chippendale furniture, for most visitors it's the sideshow to the main act: the magnificent gardens.

Wealthy banker Henry Hoare built the house between 1721 and 1725, while his son, Henry Hoare II, created the garden in the valley beside the house. Subsequent Hoares enlarged and enriched the house: traveller and county historian Sir Richard Colt Hoare added wings between 1790 and 1804, and the house was rebuilt after a fire in 1902. Landscapes by Claude and Gaspard Poussin betray the inspiration for the Stourhead gardens.

A 2-mile (3km) circuit takes you around a garden and a lake created by Henry Hoare II out of a series of medieval fish ponds. From the house, the walk leads by an **ice house**, where winter ice would be stored for summer use. At the **Temple of Flora** it continues around the lake edge, through a **grotto** and past a **Gothic cottage** to the **Pantheon**. There's a climb up to the **Temple of Apollo**, copied from a temple at Baalbek in Lebanon, which has fine views down the length of the lake. From the temple, you descend to the 15th-century **Bristol Cross**, acquired from the city of Bristol in 1765, past **St Peter's Church** and the **Spread Eagle Inn** back to the starting point. From near the Pantheon, a 3½-mile (5.5km) side trip can be made to **King Alfred's Tower** (adult/child £1.65/85p), a 50m-high folly overlooking Wiltshire, Somerset and Dorset.

Stourhead is off the B3092, 8 miles south of Frome in Somerset; public transport is virtually nonexistent.

LONGLEAT

Longleat (☎ 01985-844400; w www.longleat .co.uk; admission to house £9/6, grounds £3/2, *safari park £9/6, all-inclusive Passport £15/11; house open 10am-5.30pm Easter-Sept, guided tours only 11am-3.30pm mid-Mar–Dec, safari park 10am-4pm Mon-Fri, 10am-5pm Sat & Sun mid-Mar–Oct, other attractions 11am-5.30pm mid-Mar–Nov)* is the English stately home turned circus act. Following Henry VIII's monastic land grab, Sir John Thynne picked up the priory ruins and Longleat's 360 hectares for the princely sum of £53 in 1541. Having acquired the 13th-century Augustinian priory, he turned 16th-century architecture on its head to produce a house that looked out onto its magnificent park rather than in towards its courtyards. Although its external appearance hasn't changed since, there have been many internal alterations, notably during the Victorian era when some more baroque decor was introduced. The rooms are sumptuously furnished and boast magnificent tapestries and ornate ceilings; there are seven libraries with 40,000 books. Capability Brown landscaped the surrounding park between 1757 and 1762, planting woods and creating the Half Mile Pond.

After WWII, taxation started to nibble away at the English nobility's fortunes, just as maintenance costs skyrocketed and servants became scarce and expensive. The sixth Marquess of Bath responded by pioneering the stately home business at Longleat, opening a safari park and other, less-serious attractions in the grounds. These days Longleat boasts mazes, a narrow-gauge railway, a Dr Who exhibit, a Postman Pat village, a pets' corner, a butterfly garden and a safari park with lions, as well as the magnificent old house. The eccentric seventh Marquess has added a series of murals, 'insights into my psyche', in his private apartments; tours of the apartments and murals occasionally happen upon the Marquess.

It's hard to escape the 'family fun' (read: commercial) aspect of the place: each of the 13 attractions has an admission charge, although if you intend to visit more than one the Passport ticket is better value. However, if you can look past the franchising and gift shops, the house and grounds are themselves spectacular.

Longleat is off the A362 between Frome and Warminster, about 3 miles (5km) from both. In summer a daily Lion Link bus operated by **Wiltshire & Dorset Buses** (*☎ 0845 709 0899*) leaves Warminster station at

11.10am for the safari park's entrance gate, a 2½-mile (4km) walk from Longleat House through marvellous grounds, returning at 5.15pm.

BRADFORD-ON-AVON
☎ 01225 • pop 8800

Honey-coloured stone houses and mills tumble down the hillside towards the river crossing from which the town took its name (Bradford is a corruption of 'broad ford'). It's not just superficially attractive; there are some fine old churches, a huge tithe barn and the Kennet and Avon Canal to hold your interest. There's a pleasant 1½-mile (2.4km) walk or cycle ride along the canal to neighbouring Avoncliff, with its impressive Victorian aqueduct.

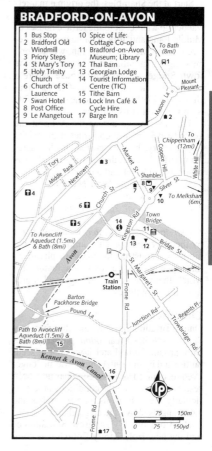

The **TIC** (☎ 865797, fax 868722; e tic@
bradfordonavon2000.fsnet.co.uk; The Greenhouse, Westbury Gardens; open 10am-5pm
daily Apr-Dec, 10am-4pm daily Jan-Mar) sells
numerous leaflets (20p) on attractions and
themed walks.

At **Cottage Co-op** (see Places to Eat),
Internet access costs £1 for 15 minutes.

Things to See & Do

A few Saxon buildings bear testament to
earlier history but it was the growth of the
weaving industry in the 17th and 18th centuries that brought wealth to Bradford; the
magnificent factories and imposing houses
were the showpieces of the town's clothing
entrepreneurs. It's a town for nosing around
and admiring your surroundings.

Start at the **Shambles**, the original marketplace, check out adjacent **Coppice Hill** and
wander up Market St to the terrace houses of
Middle Rank and **Tory**, a name probably derived from the Anglo-Saxon word 'tor',
meaning a high hill. Across the river, by the
Town Bridge, is **Westbury House**, where a
riot against the introduction of factory machinery in 1791 led to three deaths; the TIC
is now housed in its gardens.

The first bridge across the Avon at the
Town Bridge site was constructed around the
12th century, but the current bridge dates
from 1610. The small room jutting out was
originally a chapel and then a lock-up.

The **Bradford-on-Avon Museum** (☎ 863
280; Bridge St; open 10.30am-12.30pm &
2pm-4pm Wed-Sat, 2pm-4pm Sun Easter-Oct,
2pm-4pm Sun & Wed-Fri, 10.30am-12.30pm
& 2pm-4pm Sat Nov-Easter) is in the library
by the river and contains, among other exhibits, a reconstructed Victorian pharmacy
that operated in the town – a feature for
which there's a vogue among local museums in the southwest.

Churches

One of Britain's finest Saxon churches, tiny
St Laurence (open year round) probably dates
from around 1001. Later it was put to secular use and by the 19th century was no longer
even recognised as a church. It has now been
restored to its original condition; note particularly the lofty walls, narrow arches and
stone angels above the chancel arch.

Bradford quickly outgrew St Laurence
and the new **Holy Trinity Church** was completed in 1150. The original church is virtually submerged beneath 14th-century extensions and 15th- and 19th-century rebuilding.

Higher up the hill, **St Mary's Tory** was
built as a hermitage chapel about 1480. Used
as a cloth factory in the 18th century, it has
now been restored.

Tithe Barn

A pleasant short walk along the river bank
leads from the town centre to the barn (EH;
admission free; open 10.30am-4pm daily),
used to store tithes (taxes in kind) in the
Middle Ages. The imposing 51m-long structure was built in 1341 with 100 tons of stone
tiles to roof it.

Places to Stay

There are some excellent accommodation
options in Bradford.

Barge Inn (☎ 863403; 17 Frome Rd; B&B
singles/doubles £25/40, en-suite doubles £50)
is a pleasant pub by the canal, with simple
but comfortable rooms.

Georgian Lodge (☎ 862268, fax 862218;
e georgianlodge.hotel@btinternet.com; 25
Bridge St; en-suite singles £30-50, doubles
£75-95) is a large Georgian house by the
bridge, with smart rooms arranged around a
courtyard and an excellent restaurant.

The **Swan Hotel** (☎ 868686, fax 868681;
w www.comeoninn.co.uk; 1 Church St; en-
suite singles/doubles from £55/80), dating
from the 16th century, has been tastefully
refurbished, but retains its period character.

Originally six weavers' cottages, **Priory
Steps** (☎ 862230, fax 866248; e priorys
teps@clara.co.uk; Newtown, en-suite singles/
doubles from £62/74) offers luxurious B&B;
the views from its hillside garden are
wonderful.

Bradford Old Windmill (☎ 866842, fax
866648; e lp@bradfordoldwindmill.co.uk;
Masons Lane; en-suite doubles £69-109) is a
sensational place, a converted old windmill
overlooking the town. Each room is unique
(one has a waterbed) and vegetarian and
world-themed dinners are available.

Places to Eat

Spice of Life (☎ 864351; 33 Silver St; sandwiches £2; open 9am-5.30pm Mon-Sat) is a
health-food deli and café tucked away near
the bridge. **Cottage Co-op** (☎ 867444; mains
£3.95; open 10am-5.30pm Mon-Sat), a tiny

17th-century cottage with the same address, serves vegetarian and organic goodies and fabulous cakes.

Lock Inn Café (*☎ 868068; 48 Frome Rd; lunch mains £3-5, dinner mains £6-9*) is a delightful canal-side spot, famous for its monster Boatman's Breakfast (£4.55) and huge menu of home-made dishes.

Thai Barn (*☎ 866433; 24 Bridge St; mains £6-8.50; open lunch Wed-Sun, dinner Tues-Sun*) is an award-winning place with an authentic Siamese feel and a varied menu.

Le Mangetout (*☎ 863111; Silver St; 2-course lunch £10, mains £13.50-17; open 10am-late daily*) is a bright brasserie-bar that serves modern British cuisine in a relaxed conservatory area.

Getting There & Away
Bath is only 8 miles (13km) away, making a day trip an easy option. Bus Nos X5 and X6 run from Bath (return £4.40, 30 minutes, half-hourly, every two hours on Sunday), continuing to Warminster for an easy connection with bus X4 to Salisbury (1¾ hours, hourly).

Trains go roughly hourly from Bath (single £2.70, 15 minutes).

Getting Around
Bicycles can be hired for £12 a day from the **Lock Inn** (*☎ 868068;* w *www.thelockinn .co.uk; 48 Frome Rd*), which has information on towpath cycling. You can also paddle in the canal with a canoe (£10 for two hours).

NORTHWEST WILTSHIRE
The region at the edge of the Southern Cotswolds has some fabulous little villages and a number of historically interesting destinations. Unfortunately there are gaping holes in bus coverage, so either use your own wheels or be prepared for long waits. Trains from London Paddington to Bath stop at Chippenham, the area's largest town and transport hub, which is otherwise uninspiring.

Malmesbury
☎ 01666 • pop 4400
Approaching Malmesbury through its sprawling suburbs gives you little inkling of the joys of this attractive hilltop town, with its superb semi-ruined abbey church and late-15th-century market cross.

The town's **TIC** (*☎ 823748, fax 826166;* e *malmesburyip@northwilts.gov.uk; Market Lane; open 9am-4.50pm Mon-Thur, 9am-4.20pm Fri, 10am-4pm Sat*) is in the town hall.

Malmesbury Abbey A wonderful blend of ruin and living church, this abbey (*☎ 826666 parish office; donation requested; open 10am-5pm Mon-Sat late Mar-late Oct, 10am-4pm Mon-Sat Nov–mid-Mar*) has had an eventful history. A 7th-century monastery was replaced by a Norman construction, began in the 12th century; by the 14th century a massive edifice 100m long had been built, with a tower at the western end and a tower and spire at the crossing. A 1479 storm brought the tower and spire crashing down, destroying the crossing and the eastern end of the church; in 1662 the west tower fell, destroying three of the west bays of the nave. Today's church consists of the remaining six bays – about a third of the original church – framed by ruins at either end.

The church is entered via the magnificent south porch, its doorway a Norman remnant with stone sculpture illustrating Bible stories. The huge carved Apostles on each side of the porch are some of the finest Romanesque carvings in Britain. In the north-eastern corner of the church is a medieval cenotaph (empty tomb) commemorating Athelstan, king of England from 924 to 939 and grandson of Alfred the Great.

Steps lead up to the parvise, a small room above the porch containing books, including a four-volume, illuminated-manuscript Bible of 1407. A window at the western end of the church shows Elmer the Flying Monk who, in 1010, strapped on wings and jumped from the tower; he broke both legs but, remarkably survived and is a local hero.

In the churchyard the 14th-century steeple of St Paul's, the original parish church, now serves as the belfry. Towards the southeastern corner of the churchyard is the **gravestone of Hannah Twynnoy** who died in 1703, aged 33. Her headstone reads: 'For tyger fierce, Took life away, And here she lies, In a bed of clay.' The tiger belonged to a visiting circus; Hannah was killed while serving in the White Lion pub.

Places to Stay & Eat Just half a mile south of town is **Burton Hill Camping Park** (*☎ 826880; 1/2-person pitches £5/7.50*).

Bremilham House (*☎ 822680; Bremilham Rd; singles/doubles £20/36*), off Bristol St, is a homely, friendly B&B; its unfussy rooms share bathrooms.

The 13th-century **Old Bell Inn** (☎ 822344, fax 825145; **e** info@oldbellhotel.com; Abbey Row; B&B singles/doubles from £85/110) is a striking piece of history by the abbey, more like a luxurious manor house than a hotel.

The **Whole Hog** (☎ 825845; 8 Market Cross; mains £5.50-11.50) is a cheerful wine bar serving hogburgers (£5; vegetarian version available), pasta, seafood and steaks.

The **Med** (☎ 825545; 2a Silver St; mains £8-15) is a light, modern restaurant serving light, modern cuisine: expect rocket and risotto.

Getting There & Away Bus No 31 runs to Swindon (return £2.90, 45 minutes, hourly Monday to Saturday), while No 92 heads to Chippenham (£2.45, 35 minutes, hourly Monday to Saturday). There are no buses after 6pm or on Sunday.

Castle Combe
☎ 01249

Prettiest village in England? Well, that's the claim, and it's hard to dispute: Castle Combe is as close to the English ideal as you can get. Nothing remains of the medieval castle from which its name was derived, but there's a 13th-century **market cross** and a packhorse bridge with weavers' cottages reflected in a pool, and the main street is lined with flower-covered stone cottages. Pretty, medieval **St Andrew's Church** also contains a remarkable 13th-century monument of Sir Walter de Dunstanville, lord of the manor, in chain mail Bizarrely, there's also a motor-racing track nearby; the whine of engines punctures the peace on still days.

The **Gates** (☎ 782111; Market Place; B&B en-suite doubles £55), by the market cross, is a charming 15th-century stone cottage with sympathetic decor.

Castle Inn (☎ 783030, fax 782315; en-suite B&B singles/doubles from £69.50/95; lunch £3.50-8.50, dinner mains £8.50-15) has 12th-century origins but the comfort is decidedly modern, and the excellent food is somewhere between the two.

The old-world **White Hart** (☎ 782295; sandwiches £3, mains £6-12) is the people's choice for good pub grub and beers.

Bus No 35 leaves Chippenham train station for Castle Combe (return £1.45, 30 minutes) three times daily Monday to Saturday.

Corsham Court

An Elizabethan mansion dating from 1582, Corsham Court (☎ 01249-701610; adult/child £5/2.50; open 2pm-5.30pm Tues-Sun Easter-Sept, 2pm-4.30pm Sat & Sun Oct-Easter) was enlarged and renovated in the 18th century by Capability Brown and John Nash to house a superb art collection including works by Reynolds, Caravaggio, Rubens and Van Dyck.

Corsham Court is 3 miles (5km) southwest of Chippenham.

Bowood House

This stately house (☎ 01249-812102; **w** www.bowood.org; adult/child £6.05/3.85; open 11am-5.30pm daily Apr-Oct), first built around 1725 and home to the Earls of Shelburne (now Marquess of Lansdowne) since 1754, includes a picture gallery with several old masters and a fine sculpture gallery, as well as the laboratory where Dr Joseph Priestly discovered oxygen in 1774. The gardens are an attraction in themselves, designed by Capability Brown, and include a terraced rose garden. In keeping with the trend, there's also an adventure playground and ball pools for the nippers. Bowood is 3 miles (5km) southeast of Chippenham.

Lacock
☎ 01249

It's no coincidence that Lacock is a popular set location, providing the setting for many scenes in the BBC's acclaimed production of *Pride and Prejudice* and, more recently, parts of the *Harry Potter* films. It's a gorgeous medieval village with Saxon origins; few buildings date from after 1800 – it's almost a surprise to see electric light in the windows.

The NT, which owns much of the village, produces a free *Lacock Abbey* leaflet plotting a route round the most interesting buildings.

Lacock Abbey Established as a nunnery in 1232, this abbey (NT; ☎ 730227; admission abbey, museum, cloisters & grounds £6.20/3.40, abbey, cloisters & grounds only £5/2.80; abbey open 1pm-5.30pm Wed-Mon Apr-Oct) was then sold to Sir William Sharington by Henry VIII in 1539. Sharington converted the nunnery into a home, demolished the church, tacked a tower onto the corner of the abbey building and added a brewery, while retaining the abbey cloister and other medieval features. Despite his three marriages he died childless and the house passed to the Talbot family, who bequeathed the whole village to the NT in 1944. The wonderful Gothic entrance hall is lined with many bizarre terracotta figures; spot the scapegoat with a lump of sugar on its nose, first placed there in 1919. Some of the original 13th-century structure is evident in the cloisters, and there are traces of medieval wallpaintings.

In the early 19th century, William Henry Fox Talbot (1800–77), a prolific inventor, conducted crucial experiments in the development of photography here. Inside the entrance to the abbey the **Fox Talbot Museum of Photography** (☎ 730459; admission museum, cloisters & grounds only £4/2.80; open 11am-5.30pm daily mid-Mar–Oct) details his pioneering photographic work in the 1830s, when Louis Daguerre was undertaking similar work in France. Fox Talbot's particular contribution was the photographic negative, from which further positive images could be produced – before that a photograph was a one-time, one-image process. His grave can be seen in the village cemetery.

Places to Stay & Eat Staying overnight allows you to enjoy the charm of the ancient village once the coaches have left.

Lacock Pottery (☎ 730266, fax 730 948; e simonemcdowell@lacockbedandbreakfast.com; 1 The Tanyard; en-suite singles/ doubles £39/62) is an appealing, tasteful B&B (not overplaying the 'olde' card) offering home-made bread and strawberries from the garden.

Dating partly from the 13th century, **King John's Hunting Lodge** (☎ 730313, fax 730725; 21 Church St; singles/doubles from £40/75) offers B&B in two lovely rooms with exposed beams, and has a popular tea garden.

The air at **The Sign of the Angel** (☎ 730 230, fax 730527; e angel@lacock.co.uk; 6 Church St; B&B en-suite singles/doubles £68/99; mains £10-20), dating from the 15th century, is thick with history – wood panelling and huge fireplaces abound. There's solid English food, with daily fish specials.

Built in 1361, the **George Inn** (☎ 730263; 4 West St; mains £7.50-13.50) is another atmospheric old pub; note the dogwheel in the fireplace. It's strong on fresh fish and steaks, not to mention good beer.

Getting There & Away Monday to Saturday, bus No 234 operates roughly hourly from Chippenham (20 minutes) and on to Frome (one hour).

DEVIZES
☎ 01380 • pop 13,200 • elevation 121m

With some interesting medieval buildings, and several old coaching inns in the market square, Devizes is a handy stopoff between Neolithic sites and crop circles. Interesting buildings include the **Corn Exchange**, topped by a figure of Ceres, goddess of agriculture, and the **Old Town Hall** of 1750–52. The town is home to the **Wadworth brewery**, and its popular 6X beer can be sampled in local pubs (in a pot or a pie). Shire horses are still used to deliver beer to local pubs on weekday mornings.

The **TIC** (☎ 729408, fax 730319; Cromwell House, Market Place; open 9.30am-5pm Mon-Sat) provides the free Medieval Town Trail leaflet, and houses a small visitor centre with interactive displays on the town's past.

Things to See
Between St John's St and High St, **St John's Alley** has a wonderful collection of Elizabethan houses, their upper storeys cantilevered over the street. **St John's Church** displays elements of its original Norman construction, particularly in the solid crossing tower.

The **Wiltshire Heritage Museum & Gallery** (☎ 727369; 41 Long St; adult/child £3/free, free Mon; open 10am-5pm Mon-Sat, noon-4pm Sun) has excellent prehistory sections with artefacts associated with Avebury and Stonehenge, social history displays and a sizeable art collection relating to the county.

The **Kennet & Avon Canal Museum** (☎ 729489; The Wharf; adult/child £1.50/50p; open 10am-4.30pm Easter-Sept, 10am-4pm Oct-Dec & Feb-Easter), just north of the town centre, has displays detailing the conception, construction and everyday use of the canal. The **Caen Hill** flight of 29 successive locks raises the water level 72m in 2½ miles (4km) on the western outskirts of Devizes.

Places to Stay & Eat
Asta (☎ 722546; 66 Downlands Rd; B&B singles/doubles from £17/34) is a small, family-run B&B in a modern house on the outskirts.

Black Swan Hotel (*☎ 723259, fax 729966; Market Place; B&B singles/doubles £55/77; mains £6-12*) is a 17th-century coaching inn with great local dishes such as beef and Wadworth 6X pudding (£7).

Healthy Life (*☎ 725558; 4 Little Britox; lunch £3-6; open 10am-4pm & 7.30-11pm*) is a vegetarian restaurant above a health-food shop (that sells delicious pasties). Evening meals are gourmet events costing around £25; book ahead.

Otherwise, the pubs around Market Place are your best bet for reasonably priced fare, especially on market days.

Going Round in Circles

Wiltshire is the crop-circle capital of the world. Crop circles are a curious phenomenon that encourage passion and scepticism in equal measure. More than 5000 circles have appeared throughout the world, and while they are usually associated with cereals such as barley and wheat, they have also appeared in grass and heather. They range from simple circles to highly complex fractals. Romantics claim they represent an extra-terrestrial message from alien life forms, but realists argue they are a very terrestrial message from farmers, artists or practical jokers in the countryside. The release of the Mel Gibson film *Signs* has carried the story Stateside and a further influx of US circle freaks has begun.

Scientists have studied the circles in some detail, and have found them to alter the molecular structure of the plants and the chemical composition of the soil, but the crops continue to grow. Some say they also have an effect on electrical equipment, although this can usually be explained by the presence of high-voltage power lines nearby. A decade ago, the debate gripped England with a series of documentaries on contending theories, but eventually many of the circles were attributed to local cider drinkers looking to cause some mischief.

The best areas to spot the circles are the Marlborough Downs and Pewsey Vale. Visit the Barge Inn in Honeystreet, or see the website **w** www.cropcircles.co.uk for the latest locations. Remember that many of the circles are on private land so always ask the farmer before ploughing in!

Getting There & Away

Bus Nos 33 and X33 run from Chippenham (return £2.70, 30 minutes, hourly Monday to Saturday), and No X71 runs from Bath (£4.25, one hour, hourly). Bus No 49 serves Avebury (£2.70, 25 minutes, hourly Monday to Saturday, five on Sunday), while bus No 2 runs from Salisbury (1¼ hours, eight daily Monday to Saturday).

PEWSEY VALE

Heading east along the Kennet and Avon Canal from Devizes, the Vale of Pewsey is a timeless blur of undulating hills, fields and thatched villages such as Horton and Alington. There are several white chalk horses carved into the surrounding slopes, and the area is the epicentre of crop circle action. To check out where the latest mystical designs have appeared, follow the ley-lines to the **Barge Inn** (*☎ 01672-851705; camping per person £3.50; mains £5.50-8.50*) in tiny Honeystreet, 5 miles (8km) east of Devizes. The pool room is designated Crop Circle Central, with pictures and updates on the action; even if alien visits aren't your thing, it's a gorgeous canal-side spot for camping, pub food or just a cool drink.

AVEBURY

☎ 01672 • elevation 152m

If Stonehenge is the tourists', druids' (and photographers') favourite, Avebury Stone Circle is the purists' choice. Although the stones aren't as gargantuan as Stonehenge's trilithons, the site is bigger, older and quieter than Stonehenge, its stone circle at the hub of a prehistoric complex of ceremonial sites, ancient avenues and burial chambers: Silbury Hill and West Kennet Long Barrow are close by, as is the western end of the Ridgeway national trail. Avebury itself is a pretty village where even the church walls are thatched.

Orientation & Information

The Avebury stones encircle much of the village, but don't drive into it as the car park on the A4361 is only a short stroll from the circle.

The **TIC** (*☎ 539425, fax 539494; **e** alla tic@kennet.gov.uk; Chapel Centre, Green St; open 10am-5.30pm daily Apr-Sept, 10am-4.30pm Oct-Mar*) is right in the centre of the ring.

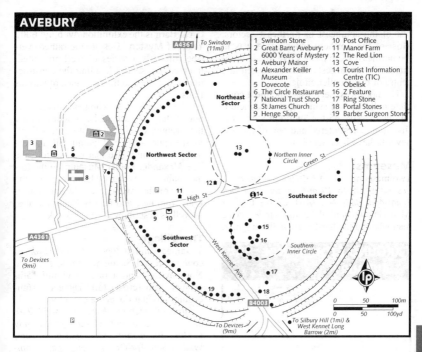

AVEBURY

1 Swindon Stone	10 Post Office
2 Great Barn; Avebury:	11 Manor Farm
6000 Years of Mystery	12 The Red Lion
3 Avebury Manor	13 Cove
4 Alexander Keiller	14 Tourist Information
Museum	Centre (TIC)
5 Dovecote	15 Obelisk
6 The Circle Restaurant	16 Z Feature
7 National Trust Shop	17 Ring Stone
8 St James Church	18 Portal Stones
9 Henge Shop	19 Barber Surgeon Stone

Stone Circle

The stone circle dates from around 2500 to 2200 BC, between the first and second phase of construction at Stonehenge. With a diameter of about 348m, it's one of the largest stone circles in Britain. The site originally consisted of an outer circle of 98 standing stones from 3m to 6m in length, many weighing up to 20 tons. These had been selected for their size and shape, but had not been worked to shape like those at Stonehenge. The stones were surrounded by another circle formed by a 5½m-high earth bank and a 6m to 9m-deep ditch. Inside were smaller stone circles to the north (27 stones) and south (29 stones).

The circles remained largely intact through the Roman period. A Saxon settlement grew up inside the circle from around 600 but in medieval times, when the church's power was strong and fear of paganism even stronger, many of the stones were deliberately buried. As the village expanded in the late 17th and early 18th centuries, the stones were broken up for building material. Fortunately, William Stukeley (1687–1765) surveyed the site around this

time so some record survives of what had existed.

In 1934 Alexander Keiller supervised the re-erection of the buried stones and the placing of markers to indicate those that had disappeared. The wealthy Keiller eventually bought Avebury in order to restore 'the outstanding archaeological disgrace of Britain'.

Modern roads into Avebury neatly dissect the circle into four sectors. Start from High St, near the Henge Shop, and walk round the circle in an anti-clockwise direction. There are 12 standing stones in the southwest sector, one of them known as the **Barber Surgeon Stone**, after the skeleton of a man found under it; the equipment buried with him suggested he was a medieval travelling barber-surgeon, killed when a stone accidentally fell on him.

The southeast sector starts with the huge **portal stones** marking the entry to the circle from West Kennet Avenue. The **southern inner circle** stood in this sector and within this circle was the **Obelisk** and a group of stones known as the **Z Feature**. Just outside this smaller circle, only the base of the **Ring Stone** remains. Few stones, standing or fallen, are to be seen around the rest of the southeast or northeast sectors. Most of the northern inner circle was in the northeast sector. The **Cove**, made up of three of the largest stones, marked the centre of this smaller circle.

The northwest sector has the most complete collection of standing stones, including the massive 65-ton **Swindon Stone**, the first stone encountered and one of the few never to have been toppled.

Museums

Two museums (*NT;* ☎ *539250; combined admission £4; open 10am-6pm daily Apr-Oct, 10am-4pm daily Nov-Mar*) tell the tale (or what's known of it) of the stone circle and the man who did the most to solve the enigmas.

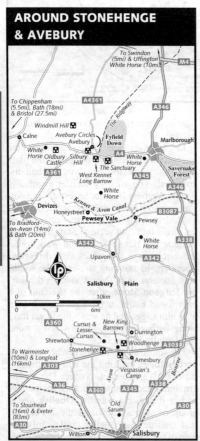

AROUND STONEHENGE & AVEBURY

Housed in the vast, 17th-century thatched Great Barn is the exhibition **Avebury: 6000 Years of Mystery**. Despite the rather over-ripe title, it's a series of well-presented, interactive displays detailing the construction of the site and the relevance of various finds.

Alexander Keiller, who made his fortune out of Dundee marmalade, bought not only the Avebury Circle but most of the village, West Kennet Avenue, Windmill Hill and virtually everything else that was up for sale. The **Alexander Keiller Museum**, in the former stables of Avebury Manor, explains the history of the Avebury Circle and houses finds from here and nearby Neolithic sites, as well as describing Keiller's work.

The Village

St James Church (*open 10am-dusk daily*) contains round Saxon windows, a carved Norman font and a rare surviving 15th-century rood (cross) loft. There's a 16th-century circular **dovecote** close by.

Graceful **Avebury Manor** (*NT;* ☎ *539250; admission to manor £3.60, garden only £2.70/1.30; manor open 2pm-5pm Tues, Wed & Sun Apr-Oct, gardens open 11am-5pm Tues, Wed, Fri-Sun*) dates back to the 16th century but has Queen Anne and Edwardian alterations; visits are by timed tour only. The garden features fine topiary and medieval walls.

Places to Stay & Eat

Manor Farm (*☎/fax 539294; singles/doubles from £40/57*) is the only real B&B in the village, a comfortable 18th-century farmhouse in the middle of the ring.

The Red Lion (*☎ 539266; singles/doubles £40/60; mains £6.50-13*) is a charming thatched pub offering B&B and some upmarket bar food (guinea fowl, garlic mussels).

The Circle Restaurant (*☎ 539514; mains £5-6*), a café beside the Great Barn, serves organic vegetarian dishes and cheaper sandwiches.

Getting There & Away

Avebury is just off the A4 between Calne and Marlborough, and can be reached easily by bus No 5, which operates a Salisbury–Marlborough–Avebury–Swindon route three times daily. Bus No 49 serves Swindon (return £3, 30 minutes) and

Devizes (£2.70, 25 minutes, hourly Monday to Saturday, five on Sunday); change at Devizes for Bath.

AROUND AVEBURY

Several excellent walks link the important sites around Avebury, starting with the stroll across the fields to Silbury Hill and West Kennet Long Barrow. The Ridgeway national trail starts near Avebury and runs westwards across Fyfield Down, where many of the sarsen stones at Avebury (and Stonehenge) were collected.

Windmill Hill

The earliest site around Avebury, Windmill Hill was a Neolithic enclosure or 'camp' dating from about 3700 BC. Ditches confirm its shape.

The Avenue & Sanctuary

The 1½-mile-long West Kennet Avenue, lined by 100 pairs of stones, connects the Sanctuary with the Avebury Circle. Today, the B4003 road follows the same route and at its southern end the A4 virtually overrides the avenue. The stone shapes along the avenue alternate between column-like stones and triangular-shaped ones; Keiller thought they might have been intended to signify male and female.

Only the site of the Sanctuary remains, although the post and stone holes indicate that there was a wooden building surrounded by a stone circle. The possible route of Beckhampton Ave, a similar 'avenue' into Avebury from the southwest, is mainly guesswork.

Silbury Hill

Rising abruptly from the surrounding fields, Silbury Hill is one of the largest artificial hills in Europe, similar in size to the smaller Egyptian pyramids. Like a truncated cone, its 40m-high summit ends in a flat top measuring 30m across. It was constructed in stages from around 2500 BC but its purpose is a mystery. Certainly no-one seems to have been buried here.

The hill has been greatly eroded by many pairs of feet, despite signs and fences asking visitors to enjoy the hill from a distance. You can view it from a car park on the A4.

West Kennet Long Barrow

Across the fields south of Silbury Hill stands West Kennet Long Barrow, England's finest burial mound, dating from around 3500 BC and measuring 104m by 23m. Its entrance is guarded by huge sarsens, massive stones like those at Stonehenge, and its roof is constructed of gigantic overlapping capstones. About 50 skeletons were found when it was excavated. The finds are displayed in the Wiltshire Heritage Museum & Gallery in Devizes.

MARLBOROUGH

☎ 01672 • pop 6400 • elevation 155m

Marlborough is a pleasant shire town with a famous public school. There's not much to the town, although its proximity to the Neolithic sites and the start of the Ridgeway national trail make it a reasonable base.

The TIC (☎/fax 513989; e mtic@kennet .gov.uk; George Lane Car Park; open 10am-5pm Mon-Sat Easter-Oct, 10am-4.30pm Nov-Easter) is just off the High St.

The High St, allegedly the widest in England, makes for an interesting stroll, particularly on market days (Wednesday and Saturday). The 17th-century **Merchant's House** (☎ 511491; 132 High St; adult/child £3/50p; open 10am-4pm Fri-Sun Apr-Sept) was built by a silk merchant, Thomas Bayly; it's being slowly restored, and is interesting as a counterpoint to the large manor houses nearby. The exclusive Marlborough College now occupies the site of the **old Norman castle**. Just to the west is a small white horse cut into the hillside by schoolboys in 1804.

Bus No 5 runs to Salisbury, Avebury and Swindon three times daily.

Devon & Cornwall

Stretching out into the Atlantic, Devon and Cornwall are worlds apart from the rest of England and, to some extent, from each other, despite the shared West Country tag; there are clear differences between agricultural Devon and proud, once-industrialised Cornwall. They do, though, both boast some of the most beautiful countryside and spectacular coastline in England, littered with the evidence of successive cultures and kingdoms. This is a land of legend, birthplace (some say) of King Arthur, and inspiration for books such as *Lorna Doone* and *Jamaica Inn*. Further back, ancient peoples left their mark here too: Grimspound on Dartmoor is the most complete Bronze Age village in Britain, while the western Cornwall landscape is littered with dolmens and standing stones.

Devon and particularly Cornwall were once England's Wild West, a remote refuge for smugglers and pirates. Cornwall even had its own language and, although the last speaker of Cornish died in the 1770s, efforts are being made to re-establish it.

So there's history in spades, but it's a smorgasbord of activities and attractions that entices visitors in droves today. Here, too, are some of England's prettiest coastal villages and towns, including Clovelly and Dartmouth in Devon, and Mousehole and St Ives in Cornwall.

Beach life? The weather in this area is milder than in the rest of Britain and there are fine stretches of sand. Gourmet dining? Padstow in Cornwall is the domain of chef Rick Stein and there are plenty of opportunities for indulging in the famous cream teas.

It's unsurprising, then, that Devon and Cornwall are, respectively, the second- and third-most popular tourist areas outside London. Come July and August, narrow roads in coastal villages are jammed with cars and accommodation is like gold dust. A visit out of season is rewarding: the surf's still there (albeit a little colder), and you'll avoid queues and traffic fumes. The wild coastline and moors have an incredible, almost violent beauty when storms rage and waves crash.

ORIENTATION & INFORMATION

Imagine this region as the leg of England – wearing jodhpurs. Devon is the thigh, Corn-

Highlights

- Soaking in the rugged beauty of the South West Coast Path
- Getting to the heart of art in St Ives
- Catching wet and wild waves in Croyde or Newquay
- Getting away from it all on the Isles of Scilly
- Rambling or riding among the moors and tors (rocky outcrops) of Dartmoor
- Getting among the hi-tech horticulture of the Eden Project
- Feasting on fabulous seafood at Padstow, Port Isaac or Penzance
- Taking in a play at the cliff-top Minack Theatre

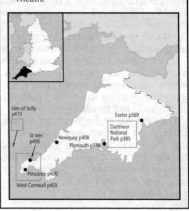

Isles of Scilly p413
Exeter p369
St Ives p405
Newquay p408
Dartmoor National Park p385
Plymouth p378
Penzance p400
West Cornwall p403

wall the calf and foot; Plymouth sits at the back of the knee, while the Isles of Scilly just avoids a kick from the toe of Land's End. With the notable exception of Dartmoor, most of the region's attractions line the coast.

The **South West Tourist Board** covers a huge area from Gloucester and Dorset down to the Isles of Scilly. Its general website (w www.visitsouthwestengland.com) has snippets such as weather trends, plus links to localised sites such as w www.cornwall -devon.com, with accommodation listed by town. The other South West Tourism website (w www.westcountrynow.com) has specific accommodation information.

DEVON & CORNWALL

DEVON & CORNWALL

English Channel

Cheddar
Axe
Wells
Cheddar
A39
Glastonbury
Yeovil
Burnham-on-Sea
Minehead
SOMERSET
Taunton
Wellington
A303
Chard
Axminster
A35
DORSET
Lyme Regis
Bridport
Chesil Beach
Lyme Bay
Honiton
Ottery St Mary
Sidmouth
Seaton
B3227
Bampton
Exmoor National Park
A396
A361
Knightshayes Court
Tiverton
Crediton
A5
Exe
Exeter
A la Ronde
Exmouth
Dawlish
Teignmouth
Powderham Castle
Newton Abbot
Compton Castle
Tor Bay
Torquay
Paignton
Brixham
Lynton
A377
South Molton
Teign
Dartmoor National Park
Totnes
Dartmouth
Kingsbridge
Barnstaple
A3072
Ilfracombe
Braunton
Croyde
Taw
Bideford
A386
Great Torrington
Holsworthy
DEVON
Okehampton
Buckfastleigh
Ivybridge
Salcombe
Westward Ho!
(Bideford Bay)
Appledore
Clovelly
Hartland Abbey
Tavistock
Buckland Abbey
Plymouth
Mount Edgcumbe
Barnstaple Bay
(Bideford Bay)
Lundy Island
Bude Bay
Bude
Stratton
A39
Launceston
Tamar
Calstock
Gunnislake
Cotehele
Saltash
Torpoint
Whitsand Bay
Bodmin Moor
Brown Willy 419m▲
Bolventor
Liskeard
Polperro
Looe
Bodinnick
Polruan
Boscastle
Tintagel
Camelford
Wadebridge
Bodmin
A30
Lostwithiel
Lanhydrock House
Par
Fowey
St Austell
Charlestown
Port Isaac
Rock
Padstow
CORNWALL
Eden Project
Mevagissey
St Austell Bay
Gorran Haven
Veryan
Roseland Peninsula
Constantine Bay
Newquay
Trerice
A3075
Truro
Heligan
St Mawes
Falmouth Bay
St Agnes Head
Redruth
A30
A39
Falmouth
Helford
Coverack
CELTIC SEA
St Ives Bay
A394
Helston
Cadgwith
The Lizard
Lizard Point
St Ives
Mount's Bay
Penzance
Land's End
St Just-in-Penwith

See Isles of Scilly Map p413

ISLES OF SCILLY
Tresco
St Martin's
Hugh Town
St Mary's
Same Scale as Main Map
To Penzance (38mi)

To Penzance (38mi)

To Isles of Scilly (28mi)
(See inset)

To Roscoff & Santander

0   15   30km
0   8   16mi

DEVON & CORNWALL

Pick up the free monthly magazine *twenty4-seven* (**w** www.twenty4-seven.co.uk) from Tourist Information Centres (TICs), bars and restaurants for listings and previews of events, bars, clubs and all that's hip in the region.

Note that, unless otherwise stated, admission prices given are for adult/child. Other concessionary rates (seniors, students, group discounts) often apply – it's always worth asking.

ACTIVITIES

With such wonderful countryside, from high moors to sandy beaches, it's no surprise that Devon and Cornwall are havens for outdoor activities. This section provides a few tempting ideas; more information is given in the main Activities chapter near the start of this book. Regional tourism websites all contain walking and cycling information, and TICs all stock leaflets (free) plus maps and guides (usually £1 to £5) covering walking, cycling and other activities.

Walking

If you're a mile-eater, look no further than the **South West Coast Path**; at over 600 miles, it's Britain's longest national trail. Only the hardiest hikers do it all in one go but following a smaller section for just a week or two is very popular – the 14-day loop around the coast of Cornwall, from Padstow to Falmouth, is reckoned to be the most scenic stretch and certainly gets the most visitors. As with all long routes, you can use the South West Coast Path as a focus for short walks of just a few hours or a day – stretches of scenic coastline are always popular strolling spots.

Other walking areas include the national park of **Dartmoor**. Larger and considerably wilder than neighbouring Exmoor (covered in the Wessex chapter), Dartmoor has some of the highest hills in southern England, with numerous opportunities for exhilarating hikes as well as gentle rambles around the edges of the moorland. Dartmoor is also crossed by several specific routes of varying lengths, including the popular Two Moors Way, which also crosses Exmoor.

Cycling

Devon and Cornwall make for spectacular cycling country, but you need to be fit for touring here. Some areas such as Dartmoor and Exmoor are surprisingly hilly in places, and the coastal routes can be very tiring as roads cross steep-sided valleys bringing streams and rivers down to the sea.

Of the long-distance cycle routes in this region, the **West Country Way** is one of the most popular – a fabulously contrasting 250-mile jaunt from Bristol to Padstow via Glastonbury, Taunton and Barnstaple. Of course, you can follow it for just a few days, or take the shorter, but just as challenging, **Devon Coast to Coast Cycle Route**, a 100-miler through the delights of Exmoor and Dartmoor.

For off-road riding, the best areas are **Dartmoor** and Exmoor, which have a good range of tracks and bridlepaths, plus some old railways that have been converted for two-wheel use. Other scenic former-railways in the area include the **Camel Trail** from Padstow (it's named after a river – not your form of transport) and the **Tarka Trail** around Barnstaple (named after a fictitious but famous otter). Bikes can be hired in most major regional centres, including Exeter, Plymouth, Penzance, Padstow and Barnstaple.

Surfing

The capital of English surfing is Newquay in west Cornwall, and surfable coast runs from Porthleven (near Helston) in Cornwall, west around Land's End and north to Ilfracombe. The most famous reef breaks are at Porthleven and Lynmouth; though good, they are inconsistent and it's very cold in winter!

Other popular spots include Sennen and Bude in Cornwall, and Croyde in north Devon. Check **Surfcall** (☎ *0906 836 0360*) for up-to-date surf conditions in the southwest; calls cost 60p per minute.

Other Activities

The many other activities available in southwest England include horse and pony riding, especially in Exmoor and Dartmoor; rock climbing on the tors (rocky outcrops) of Dartmoor or on the sea cliffs of Cornwall, which offer literally thousands of exposed and exhilarating routes; top quality scuba diving at Lundy Island and the Isles of Scilly; and windsurfing and kitesurfing off various coastal towns.

GETTING AROUND

Look out for the excellent *Car-Free Days Out* leaflet in TICs, which has comprehensive public-transport listings and advice on using trains to get to places of interest. Alternatively, visit the website at w www.car freedaysout.com for advice.

Public transport (particularly the bus network) is sketchy in rural areas; this is territory that favours those with their own transport. Most towns have car-rental outlets; Exeter is a good starting point for self-drive trips.

Bus

National Express provides reasonable connections, particularly in the east, but further west the situation becomes more tricky. Transport around Dartmoor is skimpy in summer, and virtually nonexistent at other times; the same is true for much of west Cornwall. For regional timetables, call ☎ 01392-382800 in Devon or ☎ 01872-322142 in Cornwall, or contact the **Travel-ine** *(☎ 0870 608 2608)*.

The **First** group of companies *(w www .firstgroup.com)* is the largest service provider in the region. You can buy normal single and return tickets; however, there are three other options. The Corridor ticket allows unlimited travel on any single route (A to B) for one day; the cost for an adult is £3.50 before 9.15am (or £2.50 after 9.15am). This almost always works out cheaper than a return. The First Day Plus ticket (adult/child £5/3.50) is valid for one day on all First buses in Devon, Cornwall, Somerset, Dorset and Wiltshire; the First Week Plus (adult/child £20/10) is valid for a week.

Return bus fares are given when cheaper Corridor or Day Plus options aren't available.

Train

Train services are mostly limited to the south coast. Beyond Exeter, a single line follows that coast as far as Penzance, with spurs to Barnstaple, Paignton, Gunnislake, Looe, Falmouth, St Ives and Newquay. The line from Exeter to Penzance is one of England's most scenic.

Several regional rail passes are available, including the Freedom of the SouthWest Rover pass, which allows eight days' unlimited travel over 15 days in an area west of a line drawn through (and including) Salisbury, Bath, Bristol and Weymouth

(£71.50 June to September, £61 October to May); there's a 34% discount for children and railcard holders.

Devon

With bucket-and-spade beaches, cream teas and wonderful walking, Devon is one of the most popular holiday destinations for the English. There's a noticeable difference between the north and the resorts of the south, where summer crowds continue to throng coastal towns – some tacky, many extremely charming. Away from the beaches and cream teas, however, the extraordinary beauty of the rugged north Devon coast draws walkers and nature lovers. In the centre, wild Dartmoor offers superb hiking and some key prehistoric sites, and Exmoor offers more fine rambling in the north. In the east, Exeter's marvellous cathedral and full-on nightlife win admirers. Country lanes lead to idyllic villages of thatched cottages where you can gorge on scones and clotted cream – writing tourist brochures isn't hard work here.

Orientation & Information

Devon is bounded to the east by Somerset and Dorset, the border skirting the southern edge of Exmoor and hitting the coast just west of Lyme Regis. The border to the west by Cornwall follows the River Tamar from its source near the north Devon coast to the estuary at Plymouth. Dartmoor claims much of the inland area between Plymouth and Exeter in the east.

As usual, TICs and district tourist boards provide information and brochures for towns and regions. There's a Devon-wide website (w www.devon.gov.uk/devon4all seasons/index.html) with lots of suggestions for things to do and places to stay.

Getting Around

Contact the **Devon County Public Transport Help Line** *(☎ 01392-382800)* between 9am and 5pm Monday to Friday for information and timetables. It also provides the invaluable *Devon Public Transport Map* and the useful *Discovery Guide to Dartmoor*; the website (w www.devon.gov.uk/devonbus) is also handy.

First Western National *(☎ 01271-376524; w www.firstgroup.com)* serves most of north

Devon and much of the south and east, including most Dartmoor services.

Stagecoach Devon (☎ 01392-427711; W www.stagecoachbus.com) is the other main operator in south Devon; it services mostly local runs and buses from Plymouth to Exeter or Totnes. Timetables are available to download from the website. The Explorer pass costs £6/15.75/26.65 per adult, or £5.15/8.55/14.70 per child, for 1/3/7 days of unlimited travel on the Stagecoach Devon bus network.

Devon's rail network skirts along the south coast through Exeter and Plymouth to Cornwall. There are picturesque stretches where the line hugs the seashore. Two branch lines run north: the 39-mile (63km) Tarka Line from Exeter to Barnstaple and the 15-mile (24km) Tamar Valley Line from Plymouth to Gunnislake. The Devon Rover allows three days' travel in a week (£30 mid-May to mid-September, £24 mid-September to mid-May) or eight days' travel in 15 days (£46.50 mid-May to mid-September, £39.50 mid-September to mid-May); there's a 34% discount for children and railcard holders.

Away from the main roads, Devon has good cycling country. TICs provide a free leaflet, *Making Tracks!*, which gives details of the main routes. Sustrans' West Country Way route crosses north Devon through Barnstaple and continues via Taunton to Bristol.

EXETER
☎ 01392 • pop 94,700

Perhaps because of its size and location in the east, Exeter feels less 'Devonish' than the rest of the county. The pace is somewhat quicker, and this vibrant city has the most buzzing nightlife and culture; it's also home to one of the finest medieval cathedrals in the region. Many of the older buildings were destroyed in the air raids of WWII and, outside the cathedral close, much of the city is modern and architecturally uninspiring, although its long-disused quayside is being restored into a shopping and nightlife precinct.

History

Exeter was founded by the Romans around AD 50 as the administrative capital for the Dumnonii of Devon and Cornwall, although a much earlier settlement existed on the banks of the River Exe. By the 3rd century the city, which later became an important Saxon settlement, was surrounded by a thick wall, parts of which can still be seen. Its fortifications were battered by Danish invaders and then by the Normans: in 1068 William the Conqueror took 18 days to break through the walls. He appointed a Norman *seigneur* (feudal lord) to construct a castle, the ruins of which can still be seen in Rougemont and Northernhay Gardens.

Exeter was a major trading port until a weir was built across the river, halting river traffic. It wasn't until 1563, when the first ship canal in Britain was dug to bypass the weir, that the city began to re-establish itself, making good through the wool trade.

Orientation

The old Roman walls enclosed a hill in a bend of the River Exe, and the cathedral's great square towers dominate the skyline in the centre, south of the ruined castle. In the redeveloped Quay area, around 500m south of the cathedral, are antique shops, bars, cafés and a visitor centre. There are two main train stations, Central and St David's; most long-distance trains use St David's, a mile northwest of the centre.

Information

The **TIC** (☎ 265700, fax 265260; e tic@exeter .gov.uk; Civic Centre, Paris St; open 9am-5pm Mon-Fri, 9am-1pm & 2pm-5pm Sat year round, also 10am-4pm Sun May-Sept) is opposite the bus station. The **Quay House Interpretation & Visitor Centre** (☎ 265213; The Quay; open 10am-5pm daily Easter-Oct, Sat & Sun only Nov-Easter) offers tourist information, as well as a short video (*A Celebration of Exeter*) and displays on the Quay's history.

The List is a free magazine with details of events, bars and restaurants in the Exeter area.

For Internet access visit **Hyperactive** (☎ 201544; W www.hyperactive-cafe.co.uk; 1b Central Station Crescent; open 10am-7.30pm Mon-Fri, 10am-6pm Sat, noon-6pm Sun); access costs £5 per hour. Another option is **BHTS Training** (☎ 678940; 8 Coombe St; open 8.30am-6pm Mon-Sat) where you can get online for £1.25 per half-hour.

Convenient laundrettes include **Soaps** (Isambard Parade), beside St David's train

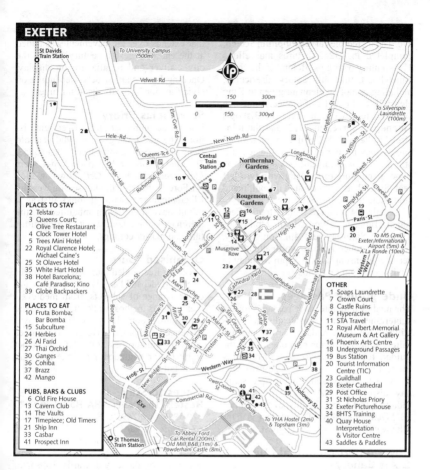

EXETER

PLACES TO STAY
2 Telstar
3 Queens Court;
  Olive Tree Restaurant
4 Clock Tower Hotel
5 Trees Mini Hotel
22 Royal Clarence Hotel;
  Michael Caine's
25 St Olaves Hotel
35 White Hart Hotel
38 Hotel Barcelona;
  Café Paradiso; Kino
39 Globe Backpackers

PLACES TO EAT
10 Fruta Bomba;
  Bar Bomba
15 Subculture
24 Herbies
26 Al Farid
27 Thai Orchid
30 Ganges
36 Cohiba
37 Brazz
42 Mango

PUBS, BARS & CLUBS
6 Old Fire House
13 Cavern Club
14 The Vaults
17 Timepiece; Old Timers
21 Ship Inn
33 Casbar
41 Prospect Inn

OTHER
1 Soaps Laundrette
7 Crown Court
8 Castle Ruins
9 Hyperactive
11 STA Travel
12 Royal Albert Memorial
  Museum & Art Gallery
16 Phoenix Arts Centre
18 Underground Passages
19 Bus Station
20 Tourist Information
  Centre (TIC)
23 Guildhall
28 Exeter Cathedral
29 Post Office
31 St Nicholas Priory
32 Exeter Picturehouse
34 BHTS Training
40 Quay House
  Interpretation
  & Visitor Centre
43 Saddles & Paddles

station, and **Silverspin** *(12 Blackboy Rd; open 8am-10pm)*, just north of the roundabout at the top of Sidwell St.

Exeter Cathedral

The magnificent Cathedral Church of St Peter *(☎ 255573; ⓦ www.exeter-cathedral.org.uk; The Close; suggested donation £3; open 7.30am-6.30pm Mon-Fri, 11.30am-5pm Sat, 8am-7.30pm Sun)* has stood largely unchanged for the last 600 years, despite some WWII bomb damage. Built within a fairly short time, it has a pleasing architectural unity and a very graceful feel: the marvellous 14th-century stained glass of the East Window, the broad West Window and the uninterrupted span of Gothic vaulting (the world's longest) create a sense of space and light.

There's been a church on this spot since 932; in 1050 the Saxon church was granted cathedral status, and between 1112 and 1133 a Norman cathedral was constructed in place of the original church. The two transept towers were built at this time – an unusual design for English cathedrals of the period. In 1270 Bishop Bronescombe instigated the remodelling of the whole building, a process that took about 90 years and resulted in a mix of Early English and Decorated Gothic styles.

You enter through the impressive Great West Front, with the largest surviving collection of 14th-century sculpture in England. The niches around the three doors are filled with statues of Christ and the Apostles surrounded by saints, angels, kings and queens.

Once inside, there's much to catch the eye. The incredible carved **Pulpitum Screen**, completed in 1325, features marvellous 17th-century paintings. Behind is the choir, which boasts fine 14th-century misericords, including one of an elephant given to King Henry III by Louis IX of France. A massive yet delicate oak canopy over the **Bishop's Throne** was carved in 1312, and the **minstrels' gallery** (1350) is decorated with 12 angels playing contemporary musical instruments. Cathedral staff will point out the famous sculpture of the **lady with two left feet**. Sir Gilbert Scott created the pulpit and side altars in 1877.

Excellent 45-minute guided tours (free) run at 11am and 2.30pm Monday to Friday, 11am on Saturday and 4pm on Sunday, April to October. It's also worth attending a service: evensong is at 5.30pm Monday to Friday and 3pm on Sunday.

Underground Passages
The medieval maintenance passages for the subterranean 14th-century lead water pipes still survive. They're dark, narrow and definitely not for claustrophobes, but the **guided tours** (☎ 665887) are surprisingly interesting. Tours run from noon to 5pm Tuesday to Friday, and 10am to 5pm Saturday, also on Monday in July and August (adult/child £3.75/2.75 July to September, £3/2 October to May). The entrance is in the alleyway beside Boots on High St.

Royal Albert Memorial Museum & Art Gallery
This multipurpose museum (☎ 665858; Queen St; admission free; open 10am-5pm Mon-Sat) tells the city's story from prehistory to the present; highlights include some decent Roman artefacts and a reconstructed town house from the late 16th century, and the huge and bizarre starfish collection is worth a peek. There are also good ethnography collections with costumes from around the globe. The gallery has a programme of changing exhibitions, emphasising local artists.

Guildhall
Parts of the Guildhall (☎ 665500; High St; admission free) date from 1160, making it the oldest municipal building in the country still in use. It was, however, mainly built in the 14th century and the impressive portico that extends over the pavement was added at the end of the 16th century. Inside, the city's silver and regalia are on display. Opening hours vary widely, depending on civic functions, so call ahead for times.

St Nicholas Priory
Built as accommodation for overnight visitors, the guest wing of the 900-year-old Benedictine St Nicholas Priory (☎ 665858; The Mint; admission 50p; open 2pm-4.30pm Mon, Wed & Sat Easter-Oct), down an alley off Fore St, became the house of a wealthy Elizabethan merchant. It looks just as it might have done when inhabited by the merchant and his family, with period furniture and plaster ceilings.

Organised Tours
Excellent free guided tours led by volunteer Exeter 'Redcoats' last 1½ to two hours and cover a range of subjects, from medieval-themed tours to ghost walks and visits to the catacomb. Tours leave from the Royal Clarence Hotel or Quay House several times a day in summer. Ask at the TIC or contact ☎ 265203 or e guidedtours@exeter.gov.uk for details.

Places to Stay
Hostels The **Exeter YHA Hostel** (☎ 0870 770 5826, fax 876939; e exeter@yha.org.uk; 47 Countess Wear Rd; dorm beds adult/child £11.25/8; open year round), in a large house overlooking the Exe, is 2 miles (3km) southeast of the city towards Topsham. From High St, catch bus K or T (10 minutes) and ask for Countess Wear post office, from where it's half a mile (750m), or take bus No 57 or 85 from the bus station to Countess Wear roundabout.

Globe Backpackers (☎ 215521, fax 215531; e caroline@globebackpackers.freeserve.co.uk; 71 Holloway St; dorm beds 1st night £11, subsequent nights £10, 7th night free), near the Quay, is a friendly, central hostel with 60 beds, Internet access and a good vibe.

University Accommodation Rooms in the university's halls of residence on the St Luke's and Streatham campuses, and in other university-owned accommodation, are available on a B&B basis during academic holidays (mid-December to early January, mid-March to mid-April and July to September). For details, contact the **Conferences Department** (☎ 211500, fax 263512; e con ferences@exeter.ac.uk). Rooms with/without en suite cost from £22.50/12.95 per person.

B&Bs & Hotels The cheapest B&Bs are on the outskirts of the city.

Old Mill (☎ 259977; Mill Lane, Alphington; per person from £13.75) is a large, pleasant old house in a quiet residential suburb about a mile (1.5km) south of the centre.

Trees Mini Hotel (☎ 259531; e treesmini hotel@aol.com; 2 Queen's Crescent; rooms per person with/without en suite from £20/18) is a decent option, a neat and tidy B&B just a short walk east from the centre.

Most B&Bs and cheaper hotels lie in the area east of St David's train station and north of Central train station. There are several on St David's Hill.

Telstar (☎/fax 272466; e reception@telstar -hotel.co.uk; 75-77 St David's Hill; singles/doubles from £20/36) is a Victorian house with a private courtyard and a happy absence of chintz.

Clock Tower Hotel (☎ 424545, fax 218445; e reservations@clocktowerhotel.co.uk; 16 New North Rd; en-suite singles/doubles from £35/49) is a handsome old town house with modern, comfortable rooms.

Queens Court (☎ 272709, fax 491390; w www.queenscourt-hotel.co.uk; 6-8 Bystock Terrace; en-suite singles/doubles from £59/64), a deluxe guesthouse, is small enough to offer a personal feel; its respected **Olive Tree** restaurant serves Mediterranean-influenced cuisine. Prices are for room only.

White Hart Hotel (☎ 279897, fax 250159; 66 South St; B&B en-suite singles/doubles Fri-Sun £49/64, Mon-Thur £61/94) is a 15th-century coaching inn, retaining the cobbled courtyard through which the coachmen drove their horses. Bedrooms are somewhat more modern and very comfortable.

St Olaves Hotel (☎ 217736, fax 413054; e info@olaves.co.uk; Mary Arches St; en-suite singles/doubles from £75/115) is an award-winning, not-quite-boutique hotel in a central Georgian town house. Its **restaurant** cooks up fine contemporary cuisine (£21/25 for 2/3 courses).

Hotel Barcelona (☎ 281000, fax 281001; e info@hotelbarcelona-uk.com; Magdalen St; singles/doubles from £75/85) is one of the hippest hotels in England. Housed in the old Eye Infirmary, each room has a unique feature (especially the former operating theatre!). The Italian-leaning marquee-cum-bistro, **Café Paradiso**, and bar, **Kino**, are also magnets for the cool and discerning. Call for details of excellent weekend deals (two nights B&B plus dinner for two people from £200).

Royal Clarence Hotel (☎ 319955, fax 439 423; Cathedral Yard; singles/doubles from £105/130) dates back to the 14th century and overlooks the cathedral; rooms aren't 'olde' or very chic but there's an air of refinement. Former guests include Lord Nelson and Tsar Nicholas I. Call central reservations (☎ 0845 300 2000) for special weekend deals.

Places to Eat

Mango (☎ 438538; The Quay; lunch £2.50-6; open 10am-6pm daily) is a funky waterside café serving wraps, salads and panini.

Subculture (☎ 491411; 21 Gandy St; ciabatta £4; open 11am-11pm daily) is a light, airy spot to munch or tipple; it's arty but comfy – jazz and sofa style.

Herbies (☎ 258473; 15 North St; mains £5.25-6.75; closed Sun & evening Mon) is an excellent, relaxed vegetarian restaurant – the locals' favourite.

Fruta Bomba (☎ 412233; 44-45 Queen St; mains £8-11) does the Latin American and Caribbean thing to some effect. **Bar Bomba** downstairs hits the after-dinner spot with cocktails and DJs.

The chefs at **Ganges** (☎ 272630; 156 Fore St; mains £5-11.50; open 6pm-11.30pm nightly) are purists – they'll do you a vindaloo but they'd prefer to tempt you with delicious regional Indian dishes.

Plenty of options are within eyeshot of the cathedral.

Thai Orchid (☎ 214215; Cathedral Yard; mains £7-9.50) is a seriously plush place serving excellent Thai cuisine.

Al Farid (☎ 494444; 3 Cathedral Yard; tapas £2.25, mains £8-13; closed Sun) plies cushion-seated customers with Moroccan tapas downstairs and more substantial Middle Eastern fare up top.

Cohiba (☎ 678445; South St; tapas £3.95, mains £7-13) offers Hispanic dishes in a sleek, brown-tinged space.

Brazz (☎ 252525; 10-12 Palace Gate; mains £5.50-15) has the brasserie market cornered;

although the look screams attitude, the modern-British cuisine (calf's liver, check) and friendly service speak louder.

Michael Caine's (☎ 310031; *Cathedral Yard; mains £12-15)*, at the Royal Clarence Hotel, has nothing to do with *that* actor. This time the MC is a chef and fine dining is in the script, peppered with jus, confit and pan-frying.

For fish, it's worth the 15-minute bus ride to Topsham (bus No 57 from the bus station or bus T from High St, at least every 20 minutes), a quaint quayside village south of the city.

The Galley (☎ 876078; e *fish@galleyre staurant.co.uk; 41 Fore St, Topsham; mains £7-9; open 7pm-9.30pm Tues-Sat, noon-1.30pm Thur-Sat)* does it better than most and with the least fuss: top-quality fresh seafood in an unpretentious environment. It also offers accommodation.

Entertainment
Pubs & Clubs In the alley between High St and the cathedral, **Ship Inn** (☎ 272040; *Martin's Lane)* is said to have been Sir Francis Drake's favourite local; it's olde but worldly, and very popular.

Prospect Inn (☎ 273152; *The Quay)* is a cosy 17th-century pub down on the redeveloped Quay. There's live jazz, and it's a great place to sit outside on a summer evening.

Old Fire House (☎ 277279; *51 New North Rd)* is a lively, chatty place, with good beer and a decent list of reasonably priced wines; there's also a courtyard area for alfresco supping.

Kino (*Magdalen St; members & guests only after 10pm)* is an urbane, cultured bar in Hotel Barcelona, with film-noir styling and live funk, blues, jazz or comedy most nights.

The Vaults (☎ 203939; *8 Gandy St)*, a friendly basement bar, is the spot to drink before heading to **Casbar** (☎ 275623; *53 Bartholomew St West)* for the hottest gay club nights on Friday and Saturday.

Cavern Club (☎ 495370; w *www.cavern club.co.uk; 83-84 Queen St)* is an excellent subterranean venue with live music or DJs each night; luminaries such as Coldplay and Groove Armada have gigged here.

Despite external appearances, **Timepiece** (☎ 493096; *Lt Castle St)* is arguably the best club in town; its Tuesday salsa night is incredibly popular. **Old Timers** (☎ 477704),

right next door, has all manner of bizarre paraphernalia hanging around, as well as decent beer and bonhomie.

Theatres & Cinemas The **Phoenix Arts Centre** (☎ 667080; w *www.exeterphoenix .org.uk; Bradninch Place, Gandy St)* is the prime venue, hosting dance, theatre, arthouse films, DJs and live music events. The café-bar's pretty hip, too.

For movies, **Exeter Picturehouse** (☎ 435 522; *Bartholomew St West)* screens a mix of mainstream and art-house flicks.

Getting There & Away
Exeter is 198 miles (317km) from London, 75 miles (121km) from Bristol, 45 miles (72km) from Plymouth and 120 miles (193km) from Land's End.

Air Scheduled services run between **Exeter International Airport** (☎ 367433; w *www .exeter-airport.co.uk)* and Dublin, the Channel Islands and the Isles of Scilly; chartered services go as far afield as the Algarve and Canada.

Bus National Express runs coaches to London (£32.50 standard return, 4½ hours, nine daily) via Heathrow airport (four hours); Bath (£18.50, three hours, daily); Bristol (£15.50, two hours, four daily); Birmingham (£37.50, four hours, four daily); and Penzance (£18.75, 4½ hours, two daily).

Express bus No X38 runs to Plymouth (1¼ hours, every 90 minutes Monday to Saturday, every two hours Sunday); Bus Nos 39 and X39 are slower (1¾ hours, at least every two hours) but stop at Buckfastleigh on the edge of Dartmoor. Bus No X46 runs to Torquay (one hour, hourly Monday to Saturday, every 90 minutes Sunday).

Train The fastest trains between London and Exeter St David's use Paddington station and take around 2½ hours (£54.10 saver return, at least hourly). Trains from London Waterloo also leave roughly hourly but take at least three hours, following a more scenic route via Salisbury (£31.90).

Exeter St David's also has hourly connections with Bristol (£22.40, one hour) and Penzance (£32.70, three hours).

The 39-mile (63km) branch line between Exeter Central and Barnstaple (£13.80, 1¼ hours, every two hours Monday to Friday, four on Sunday) is promoted as the Tarka Line, following the valleys of the Rivers Yeo and Taw and giving good views of the countryside with its characteristic, deep-sunken lanes.

Getting Around
To/From the Airport The airport is 5 miles (8km) east of the centre, off the A30. Bus No 56 runs to the airport from the bus station (20 minutes, hourly Monday to Saturday).

Bus Exeter is well served by public transport. The one-day Megarider pass (£3) gives unlimited transport on Stagecoach's Exeter buses. Bus N links St David's and Central train stations and passes near the bus station.

Car The TIC provides a list of national and local car-rental offices; try **Abbey Ford Car Rental** (☎ 254037; W www.abbeyfordcarhire .co.uk; 30 Edwin Rd).

Parking in the centre can be troublesome. Useful Park & Ride services run between Sowton and Matford via the centre (bus No PR1, at least every 10 minutes), and from Honiton Rd to the city (bus N, every 30 minutes).

Taxi There are taxi ranks outside the train stations. Alternatively, try **Capital Taxis** (☎ 433433).

Bicycles & Canoes Pick up a copy of the free *Exeter Cycle Guide & Map* from the TIC.

Saddles & Paddles (☎ 424241; W www .saddlepaddle.co.uk; 4 Kings Wharf, The Quay) rents out bikes (adult/child per day £13/10) and canoes (single kayaks per hour/day £5/15). It also organises 'paddling parties' to a nearby pub, plus canoeing weekends and cycle tours.

AROUND EXETER
Powderham Castle
Built in 1391 with later additions, Powderham (☎ 01626-890243; W www.powderham .co.uk; adult/child £6.45/2.95; open 10am-5.30pm Sun-Fri Apr-Oct) retains an air of knightly chivalry, invoked in tales told during guided tours through the state rooms. The wood-panelled great hall positively reeks of medieval feasting. The home of the 18th earl of Devon, it contains collections of French china and Stuart and Regency furniture, and features some (rather garish) rococo ceilings. Powderham is on the estuary of the River Exe in Kenton, 8 miles (13km) south of Exeter. Bus No 85A runs from Exeter (20 minutes, every 15 minutes Monday to Saturday, every 30 minutes Sunday).

A la Ronde
Jane and Mary Parminter planned to combine the magnificence of the Church of San Vitale, which they'd visited in Ravenna, with the homeliness of a country cottage to create the perfect dwelling place (☎ 01395-265514; Summer Lane, Exmouth; adult/child £3.50/1.70; open 11am-5.30pm Sun-Thur Easter-Oct). The result, completed around 1796 and owned by the National Trust (NT), is an intriguing 16-sided house whose bizarre interior decor includes a shell-encrusted room, a frieze of feathers, and sand and seaweed collages, as well as 18th-century furnishings.

It's 2 miles (3km) north of Exmouth on the A376; Stagecoach Devon bus No 57 runs close by en route to Exeter (30 minutes, at least every 30 minutes).

SOUTH DEVON COAST
Torquay & Paignton
☎ 01803 • pop 59,600
The three Torbay towns (Torquay, Paignton and Brixham) describe themselves as the English Riviera; the epithet depicts the seaside holiday mentality more than the climate. Torquay retains the stereotypical tearooms, amusement arcades and staid guesthouses of traditional beach resorts. Around the bay to the south, Paignton is effectively the 'family fun' suburb of Torquay, big on candy floss, less so on sophistication.

The **TIC** (☎ 0906-680126, fax 214885; e torbay.tic@torbay.gov.uk; Vaughan Parade; open 9.30am-6pm Mon-Sat, 10am-6pm Sun June-Sept, 9.30am-5pm Mon-Sat Oct-May) sells discounted tickets to local attractions. Calls to the TIC cost 50p per minute.

Things to See & Do Agatha Christie was born here and both **Torquay Museum** (☎ 293975; 529 Babbacombe Rd; adult/child £3/1.50; open 10am-5pm Mon-Sat, 1.30pm-5pm Sun summer, 10am-5pm Mon-Sat winter) and **Torre Abbey** (☎ *293593; Torre Abbey Meadows; adult/child £3/1.50; open 9am-6pm daily Easter-Oct, last admission 5pm*), an 18th-century house in the grounds of a ruined abbey, display Agatha mementos.

Pretty **Babbacombe Beach** is at the base of what must be one of England's steepest roads, so whether you're on a bicycle or in a car, check your brakes first! The beach is about 2 miles (3km) north of the centre; it's a delightful three-hour walk around the coast from the eastern end of the Esplanade, away from the lights and arcades.

Kitesurfing fever is taking hold here; **Torquay Wind-Surf Centre** (☎ *212411; 55 Victoria Rd*) offers a two-day course (£130) as well as kitebuggying (£65 per day) and windsurfing (£20 for two hours).

Places to Stay & Eat The travelling vibe is captured at **Torquay International Backpackers** (☎ *299924;* e *jane@torquaybackpackers.co.uk; 119 Abbey Rd; dorm beds per night/week £12/60, less in winter*); friendly owner Jane sometimes organises beach barbecues or trips onto Dartmoor, more often hops to the pub.

There are literally hundreds of B&Bs and hotels in town, with a dense cluster around the Avenue Rd–Bridge Rd ghetto.

Jesmond Dene (☎ *293062; 85 Abbey Rd; with/without en suite per person from £18/15)* is a standard old-school B&B but it's friendly, clean, cheap and central.

Kingston House (☎ *212760, fax 201425; 75 Avenue Rd; en-suite B&B per person from £20)* wins awards for service and comfort.

Palace Hotel (☎ *200200, fax 299899;* e *info@palacetorquay.co.uk; Babbacombe Rd; per person from £71)* is the class act, built for the Bishop of Exeter and boasting swimming pools and a golf course.

Mojo (☎ *294881; The Seafront, Torbay Rd; mains £6.50-10)* looks like a typically brash seaside bar but it's surprisingly mellow, with DJs Friday and Saturday, and decent fish and pasta.

Steps Bistro (☎ *201774; 1a Fleet St; mains £11-14; open nightly)*, a midget gem tucked away up (unsurprisingly) some steps from Fleet St, is worth seeking for exceptional fresh fish and seafood.

The Hole in the Wall (☎ *298020; 6 Park Lane; mains £4-10)*, allegedly the oldest pub in Torquay (15th century), offers good local beer and top-notch pub grub in a cosy, cobbled snug. There's live music most nights and it's largely a grockle-free (tourist-free) zone.

Getting There & Away The No X46 express bus service runs hourly from Exeter to Torquay and Paignton (£4.50, one hour). Bus No 120 runs from Torquay and Paignton to Kingswear for the Dartmouth ferry (£5.30 return, 45 minutes, six daily Monday to Friday).

A branch railway line runs from Exeter via Torquay (45 minutes) to Paignton (50 minutes) a few times daily. The **Paignton & Dartmouth Steam Railway** (☎ *555872;* w *www.paignton-steamrailway.co.uk*) runs from Paignton on the scenic 7-mile (11km) trip to Kingswear on the River Dart, linked by ferry (six minutes) to Dartmouth; a combined rail and ferry ticket from Paignton to Dartmouth costs £7.70/5.20 return per adult/child. You can add on a river cruise (adult/child £11.50/8) or a Round Robin boat trip to Totnes and back to Paignton by bus (adult/child £12/8.50).

Compton Castle

This minicastle (☎ *01803-875740; Marldon, Paignton; adult/child £4.10/2.90; open 10am-12.15pm & 2pm-5pm Mon, Wed & Thur Apr-Oct)* was built in phases during the 14th, 15th and 16th centuries. It's not huge but is one of the best-preserved examples of a fortified house, complete with battlements, towers and a reconstructed medieval great hall. Buses run to Marldon from Torquay (bus No 111; 30 minutes, six daily Monday to Saturday) and Paignton (bus No 7; 20 minutes, at least hourly Monday to Saturday).

Brixham

☎ 01803 • pop 15,900

In the mid-19th century Brixham was the country's busiest fishing port and it's still the place to come for a fishing expedition; with its attractive harbour, it's also the most appealing (if quiet) of the Torbay resorts.

The **TIC** (☎ *0906-680126 premium rate;* e *brixham.tic@torbay.org.uk; Old Market House, The Quay; open 9.30am-6pm Mon-Sat June-Sept, 9.30am-5pm Mon-Fri Oct-May)* is right on the harbour.

Brixham Heritage Museum (☎ *856267;* w *www.brixhamheritage.org.uk; Old Police Station, Bolton Cross; adult/child £1.50/50p;*

open 10am-5pm Mon-Fri, 10am-1pm Sat) gives a lively introduction to the town's history and its connection to the sea, as well as reconstructions of Victorian rooms and shops.

Anchored in the harbour is a replica of the **Golden Hind** (☎ 856223; adult/child £2/1.50; open 9am-5.30pm daily Mar-Sept), Drake's globe-circling ship, offering an insight into conditions aboard in his day

It costs around £20 for a half-day trip to fish for conger, ling and coalfish around the wrecks in the bay, less to fish for mackerel. To arrange a trip, contact the boats' skippers directly (kiosks line the quay) – try **Boy Richard** (☎ 529147) for mackerel or **Our Jenny** (☎ 854444) for wreck fishing. The TIC provides a list of boats, clubs and angling centres.

Maypool YHA Hostel (☎ 0870 770 5962, fax 845939; e maypool@yha.org.uk), a mile southwest of Galmpton, is an amazing old house 4 miles (6km) from Brixham, with great views over the river to Dartmouth. Stagecoach Devon bus No 12 from Brixham (10 minutes, at least every 20 minutes) stops at Churston Pottery 2 miles (3km) away.

Bus No 12 runs at least every 20 minutes along the coast from Torquay (30 minutes) to Paignton (15 minutes) and Brixham.

Dartmouth
☎ 01803 • pop 5700

Dartmouth, an appealing town with narrow streets winding down to the Dart estuary, has been an important port since Norman times. The Pilgrim Fathers sheltered here in 1620 on their way to Plymouth and D-Day landing craft sailed from this port for France in 1944. Today, the harbour is mostly filled with yachts and the historic town pulls sizable crowds.

The **TIC** (☎ 834224, fax 835631; e enquire@ dartmouth-information.fsnet.co.uk; Engine House, Mayor's Ave; open 9am-5pm Mon-Sat, 10am-4pm Sun Apr-Oct, 9am-4.30pm Mon-Sat Nov-Mar) offers free accommodation booking and houses the Newcomen Engine, an early (1712) atmospheric steam engine.

Dartmouth Castle The hands-on exhibits at Dartmouth Castle (☎ 833588; admission £3.20; open 10am-6pm daily Easter-Sept, 10am-5pm daily Oct, 10am-1pm & 2pm-4pm Wed-Sun Nov-Mar) bring its 600-year history

vividly to life. Designed so that a chain could be placed across to the companion castle on the other side of the river at Kingswear to block off the estuary, the castle boasts fantastic views of the town and river. It is run by English Heritage (EH). There's a ferry along the estuary to the castle, three-quarters of a mile (1km) outside the town, from South Embankment every 15 minutes from 10am to 4.45pm (adult/child £1.20/70p one way).

Other Things to See In the centre, the **Butterwalk** is a row of 17th-century timber-framed houses. It's where the **Dartmouth Museum** (☎ 832923; Duke St; adult/child £1.50/50p; open 11am-5pm Mon-Sat Mar-Oct, noon-3pm Mon-Sat Nov-Feb) is located, which features exhibits on local and maritime history; check out the fine collection of ships in bottles.

Places to Stay & Eat The nearest YHA hostel is about 5 miles (8km) away in Maypool; see the previous Brixham section for details.

B&Bs line Victoria Rd, running back from the river.

Captain's House (☎ 832133; e thecaptain shouse@tinyworld.co.uk; 18 Clarence St; per person from £25) is a Grade II-listed Georgian town house with pleasant en-suite rooms.

The friendly (and well-travelled) owner has swathed **Clarke's B&B** (☎ 834694; e en quiries@clarkesbanb.co.uk; 31 Victoria Rd; en-suite B&B per person from £32) with marvellous Middle- and Far-Eastern furnishings, and there's a huge home cinema for rainy days. An excellent choice.

Little Admiral Hotel (☎ 832572, fax 835815; e info@little-admiral.co.uk; 29 Victoria Rd; singles/doubles from £50/65) is on its way to being a designer joint; its maple beds are perfection and the restaurant serves classy contemporary cuisine.

The name says it all: **Café Alf Resco** (☎ 835880; Lower St; lunch around £5; open lunch Wed-Sun) offers great coffee, locally baked bread, pastries and snacks in a terraced area with a Mediterranean feel.

Strutt's Bistro (☎ 832491; 10 Fairfax Place; mains £10-14; closed Sun dinner) takes a global spin on seafood; fusion dishes such as Thai-style mussels are enticing.

Hooked (☎ 832022; 5 Higher St; 3-course lunch £19.30, 7/8-course gourmand menu

DEVON & CORNWALL

£40/45) doles out fine-dining fish dishes with a smile and style – this is the place for a treat.

Cherub Inn (☎ 832571; 13 Higher St) claims to be the oldest pub in the town, a claim borne out by the low beams and cosy feel.

Getting There & Away The best way to approach Dartmouth is by boat, either on the ferry from Kingswear (£2.50 for a car and four people, adult/child foot passenger 60/30p, six minutes) or downstream from Totnes (adult one way/return £5.50/7, child £3.50/4, 1¼ hours). **River Link** (☎ 834488; w www.riverlink.co.uk) is one operator. From Exeter, take a train to Totnes and a boat or bus No 111 (40 minutes, at least five daily) from there.

For details of the popular Paignton & Dartmouth Steam Railway, see Getting There & Away in the previous Torquay section.

Totnes
☎ 01803 • pop 6900
Medieval legend has it that Totnes was where Trojan prince Brutus founded Britain in 1170 BC. What *is* true is that Totnes became rich trading Dartmoor tin in Tudor times, and a walk up the High St reveals fine Elizabethan houses and museums; Totnes has a higher percentage of listed buildings than any other town in Britain. It's now a busy market town with a thriving arts and new-age community.

The **TIC** (☎ 863168, fax 865771; e enquire@totnesinfo.org.uk; Town Mill, Coronation Rd; open 9.30am-5pm Mon-Sat) helps with accommodation bookings.

Things to See A Tudor house dating from 1575 houses **Totnes Elizabethan Museum** (☎ 863821; 70 Fore St; adult/child £1.50/25p; open 10.30am-5pm Mon-Fri Apr-Oct). Despite the name, displays cover engineering, furniture, dolls and a reconstruction of a Victorian tea-and-coffee merchant's shop. A look at the interior is worth the price of admission.

The **Guildhall** (☎ 862147; Ramparts Walk; admission 75p; open 10am-4pm Mon-Fri Apr-Oct) was once the refectory of a Benedictine priory, constructed in 1088 and rebuilt in 1553. It contains interesting pieces, such as Oliver Cromwell's table.

The **Devonshire Collection of Period Costume** (Bogan House, High St; adult/child £1.75/75p; open 11am-5pm Mon-Fri May-Sept), in another old building (c. 1500), fea-

tures annually changing, well-presented themed selections from the extensive collection, one of the country's finest.

The motte-and-bailey remains of **Totnes Castle** (EH; ☎ 864406; admission £1.80; open 10am-6pm daily Easter-Sept, 10am-5pm daily Oct) are insubstantial but picturesque, offering good views to the Dart.

Berry Pomeroy Castle (EH; ☎ 866619; admission £2.80; open 10am-6pm daily Apr-Sept, 10am-5pm Oct) is a part-completed (and reputedly haunted) Elizabethan country house protected by 15th-century walls and a Norman gatehouse. A free audioguide leads you around the remains in the picturesque valley. Bus No 111 runs from Totnes (10 minutes, six daily), 2½ miles (4km) west.

Places to Stay & Eat The **Dartington YHA Hostel** (☎ 0870 770 5788, fax 865171; Lownard, Dartington; adult/child £9.50/6.75; open daily mid-April-Aug) is 2 miles (3km) northwest of Totnes off the A385 near Week. Bus No X80 from Plymouth to Totnes stops nearby at Shinners Bridge hourly.

Alison Fenwick (☎ 866917; e alisonfenwick@bushinternet.com; 3 Plymouth Rd; per person £16-20) offers B&B in a friendly, homely environment. Alison is a Blue Badge guide and conducts tours to Dartmoor (from £30 per car).

The **Old Forge** (☎ 862174; e enq@oldforgetotnes.com; Seymour Place; en-suite doubles from £54), 600 years old, is the most atmospheric place in town and even has its own jail.

The main drag (High St/Fore St) is lined with eateries, most offering a take on world/fusion cuisine.

Willow Vegetarian Restaurant (☎ 862605; 87 High St; mains £4-5.50; open lunch Mon-Sat, dinner Wed, Fri & Sat) offers a mix of tasty salads and global snacks.

Bistro 57 (☎ 862604; 67 Fore St; mains £6.50-9; closed Sun) casts its culinary net wide: think mesquite salmon, Thai fish cakes and risotto.

Rumours (☎ 864682; 30 Fore St; mains £8.50-14.50; open 10am-11pm Mon-Sat, 6pm-10.30pm Sun), a mellow café-bar with a daily changing menu, cooks up pasta, fish and stir-fried tofu.

Getting There & Away Totnes is 9 miles (14km) inland from Torquay and 10 miles (16km) upriver from Dartmouth.

Bus No X64 runs to Exeter (£4.70 return, one hour, eight daily Monday to Saturday, two Sunday) and bus No X80 goes to Plymouth (1¼ hours, hourly). National Express coaches also run to Exeter (£6.50 economy return, 1½ hours, twice daily) and Plymouth (£3.25, 40 minutes, daily).

Frequent trains run to Exeter (£12.30 saver return, 45 minutes, several daily) and Plymouth (£10.40, 25 minutes, hourly). The train station is half a mile from the centre.

A short walk from Totnes main-line train station, steam trains of the private **South Devon Railway** (☎ 0845 345 1420; w www .southdevonrailway.org) run to Buckfastleigh (adult/child return £6.80/4, 30 minutes, at least four daily Easter to October) on the edge of Dartmoor.

There are cruises on the river with frequent departures to Dartmouth in summer (see the previous Dartmouth section).

PLYMOUTH
☎ 01752 • pop 245,300

There's no ignoring Plymouth's lengthy maritime history, enlivened by such vivid characters as the bowls-playing Sir Francis Drake and the Pilgrim Fathers, although you'd be forgiven for not finding most of the city evocative of it. Devon's largest city has extensive modern suburbs and a bland commercial centre (resulting, as usual, from uninspired post-WWII development), but the well-preserved Barbican, the largely Tudor quarter by the harbour, is more appealing. Once you've had your fill of maritime lore, there's rum-lockers aplenty to drink with old sea dogs (or lively students).

History
Plymouth really began to expand in the 15th century with the development of larger vessels; Plymouth Sound provided a perfect anchorage for warships. Local hero Sir Francis Drake, who achieved his knighthood through an epic voyage around the world, set out from Plymouth in 1577 in the *Golden Hind*, returning three years later.

In 1588 Drake played a major part in the defeat of the Spanish Armada, the fleet sent to invade England by Philip II, who wanted to restore Catholicism to the country. Whether Drake really was playing bowls on the Hoe at the time of the Spanish attack is debatable, but the English fleet certainly did

set sail from here. Drake led the chase after the Armada up the English Channel to Calais; the English then attacked the fleet with fire ships. Many of the Spanish vessels escaped but were blown off course and wrecked off Scotland. Total losses: England nil, Spain 51.

Another famous voyage was led by Captain James Cook, who set out from the Barbican in 1768 in search of a southern continent. (For more details on Cook see the Whitby section of the Yorkshire chapter.)

The royal dockyard was established at Devonport beside the River Tamar in 1690 and there's still a large naval base here.

Orientation & Information
Plymouth has three main sections. South of the train station is the pedestrianised centre, with shopping streets and the bus station off Armada Way. South again is the guesthouse ghetto Hoe area; east of the Hoe is the Barbican, by Sutton Harbour.

The **TIC** (☎ 304849, fax 257955; e barbi cantic@plymouth.gov.uk; Island House, 9 The Barbican; open 9am-5pm Mon-Sat, 10am-4pm Sun May-Sept; 9am-5pm Mon-Fri, 10am-4pm Sat Oct-Apr) handles visitor inquiries. If you're driving from Exeter there's a **Discovery Centre** (☎ 266030, fax 266033; Crabtree; same hours as TIC) by the Sainsbury's supermarket at Marshall's Roundabout off the A38.

You can get online at **Plymouth Internet Café** (☎ 221777; 32 Frankfort Gate; open 9am-5pm Mon-Sat) for £5 per hour or £2 for 25 minutes.

Dirty clothes? Find **Hoegate Laundromat** (☎ 223031; 55 Notte St; open 8am-8pm Mon-Thur, 8am-7pm Fri-Sun) or **West Hoe Laundrette** (☎ 667373; 1 Pier St; open 9.15am-8pm Mon-Fri, 9am-6pm Sat, 10am-5pm Sun).

Plymouth Hoe
This famous promenade gives wonderful, breezy views over Plymouth Sound. In one corner there's a bowling green; the one on which Drake finished his game was probably where his **statue** now stands.

Red-and-white-striped **Smeaton's Tower** (The Hoe; adult/child £2/1; open 10am-4pm daily Apr-Oct, 10am-4pm Tues-Sat Nov-Mar) was built on the Eddystone Rocks in 1759, then rebuilt here in 1882. Not just another lighthouse, it was actually the world's first scientifically designed jointed masonry lighthouse. You can climb the 93 steps for great views and an interactive insight into the history of the Eddystone lighthouses.

The take on history in **Plymouth Dome** (☎ 603300; The Hoe; adult/child £4.50/3; open 10am-5pm daily Apr-Oct) is both hi-tech and theatrical, with excellent audio-visual shows and a Tudor street with rowdy locals (and smells!). A harbour observation deck with interactive computers and radar brings it up to the minute.

East of the Hoe is the **Royal Citadel**, built by Charles II in 1670 and still in military use. There are guided tours (☎ 0117-975 0700; EH members/nonmembers £2.75/3) of parts of the fortress, which run at 2.30pm Tuesday from May to September.

Barbican

To get an idea of what Plymouth was like before the Luftwaffe redesigned it, visit the Barbican, with its Tudor and Jacobean buildings (now galleries, craft shops and restaurants) and busy Victorian fish market.

In 1620 the Pilgrim Fathers' two ships, the *Mayflower* and the *Speedwell*, put into Plymouth. Because the second ship was badly damaged, only the *Mayflower* set sail for America on 16 September 1620. Some of the 102 passengers and crew spent their last night on English soil in Island House, now the TIC. At the **Mayflower Steps** a sign lists the passengers and marks the departure.

Plymouth Mayflower (☎ 306330; W www .plymouth-mayflower.co.uk; 3-5 The Barbican; adult/child £4/2; open 10am-6pm daily

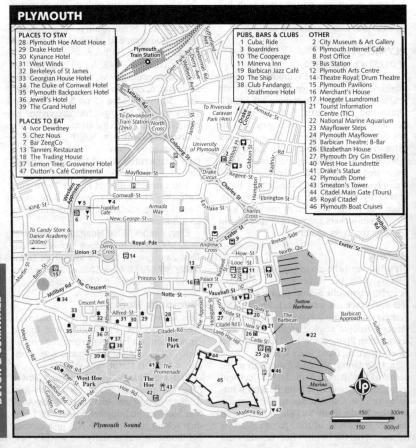

PLYMOUTH

PLACES TO STAY
28 Plymouth Hoe Moat House
29 Drake Hotel
30 Kynance Hotel
31 West Winds
32 Berkeleys of St James
33 Georgian House Hotel
34 The Duke of Cornwall Hotel
35 Plymouth Backpackers Hotel
36 Jewell's Hotel
39 The Grand Hotel

PLACES TO EAT
4 Ivor Dewdney
5 Chez Nous
7 Bar ZeegCo
13 Tanners Restaurant
18 The Trading House
37 Lemon Tree; Grosvenor Hotel
47 Dutton's Café Continental

PUBS, BARS & CLUBS
1 Cuba; Ride
3 Boardriders
10 The Cooperage
11 Minerva Inn
19 Barbican Jazz Café
20 The Ship
38 Club Fandango; Strathmore Hotel

OTHER
2 City Museum & Art Gallery
6 Plymouth Internet Café
8 Post Office
9 Bus Station
12 Plymouth Arts Centre
14 Theatre Royal; Drum Theatre
15 Plymouth Pavilions
16 Merchant's House
17 Hoegate Laundromat
21 Tourist Information Centre (TIC)
22 National Marine Aquarium
23 Mayflower Steps
24 Plymouth Mayflower
25 Barbican Theatre; B-Bar
26 Elizabethan House
27 Plymouth Dry Gin Distillery
40 West Hoe Laundrette
41 Drake's Statue
42 Plymouth Dome
43 Smeaton's Tower
44 Citadel Main Gate (Tours)
45 Royal Citadel
46 Plymouth Boat Cruises

Apr-Oct, 10am-5pm daily Nov-Mar) is another hi-tech rundown on Plymouth's nautical heritage, providing an especially detailed background to the Pilgrim Fathers' trip, with plenty of interactive gizmos and multisensory displays.

The **Elizabethan House** *(☎ 253871; 32 New St; adult/child £1/50p; open 10am-5pm Wed-Sun Apr-Oct)* is the former residence of an Elizabethan sea captain, housing 16th-century furniture.

Tours of the **Plymouth Dry Gin distillery** *(☎ 665292; w www.plymouthgin.com; 60 Southside St)*, the oldest in England and working since 1793, run between 10.30am and 5.45pm Monday to Saturday, Easter to December, plus Sunday from June to September; tickets are £2.75/2.25 per adult/child.

Other Things to See & Do
Between the Barbican and the centre is the early-17th-century **Merchant's House** *(☎ 264878; 33 St Andrews St; adult/child £1.10/60p; open 10am-1pm & 2pm-5.30pm Tues-Fri, 10am-1pm & 2pm-5pm Sat & bank holidays Apr-Oct)*, a fine Jacobean building housing a museum of social history featuring models, pictures, tools of local trades, and replicas of a Victorian schoolroom and apothecary's shop.

The **National Marine Aquarium** *(☎ 220084; The Barbican; w www.national-aquarium .co.uk; adult/child £6.75/4; open 9am-6pm daily Apr-Oct, 9am-5pm daily Nov-Mar)*, in an impressive building on Sutton Harbour, is a nonprofit venture using its sensational inhabitants to educate as well as amuse. Following a route along ramps winding through the building, visitors can examine aquatic life in a range of cleverly reproduced habitats: moorland stream, river estuary, shallow sea and deep reef.

Near the University, the **City Museum & Art Gallery** *(☎ 304774; Drake Circus; admission free; open 10am-5.30pm Mon-Fri, 10am-5pm Sat & bank holidays)* hosts touring exhibitions, plus collections of natural history, social history, porcelain and naval art. The Cottonian Collection includes some significant paintings, prints and etchings by artists such as Reynolds.

Boat Trips
Plymouth Boat Cruises *(☎ 822797; e pbc@ pbc.onyxnet.co.uk; Phoenix Wharf)* offers a number of boat trips from daily hour-long harbour cruises, including visits to the dockyards and warships (adult/child £4.50/2), to four-hour cruises up the River Tamar (adult/child £7.50/4) to Calstock, which can be combined with a rail trip on the Tamar Valley Line. Boats leave from Phoenix Wharf, along the Barbican (to the east of the citadel).

Places to Stay
Camping The well-appointed **Riverside Caravan Park** *(☎ 344122; e office@river sidecaravanpark.com; Longbridge Rd; tent sites £8)* is off Plympton Rd, 4 miles (6km) northeast of the centre. Follow signs from the Marsh Mills roundabout on the A38.

Hostels There's no YHA hostel.

Plymouth Backpackers Hotel *(☎ 225158, fax 207847; e plymback@hotmail.com; 172 Citadel Rd; dorm beds £10, singles/doubles £15/25)* is a relaxed, friendly place with a games room and laundry service (£2.50).

B&Bs & Hotels Try the northwestern corner of the Hoe around Citadel Rd for B&Bs and hotels.

West Winds *(☎ 601777, fax 662158; 99 Citadel Rd; standard singles/doubles from £18/32, with en suite from £28/35)* is one of the cheapest places and a decent-enough B&B.

Kynance Hotel *(☎ 266821, fax 254076; 107-113 Citadel Rd West; en-suite singles/ doubles from £28/42)* isn't the swishest B&B but it's big (rooms are often available when all others are full) and friendly enough.

Berkeleys of St James *(☎/fax 221654; 4 St James Place East; B&B en-suite singles/ doubles from £25/40)* is a small, quality guesthouse in a quiet side street.

Georgian House Hotel *(☎ 663237, fax 253953; e georgianhousehotel@msn.com; 51 Citadel Rd; B&B en-suite singles/doubles from £28/38)* is more of the same: spotless, family-run and a bit more personal than the bigger places.

Jewell's Hotel *(☎/fax 254760; 220 Citadel Rd; standard singles £20, en-suite doubles £40)* is an immaculate B&B, a touch smarter than the norm.

Drake Hotel *(☎ 229730; fax 255092; e reception@drakehotel.net; 1 Windsor Villas, Lockyer St; B&B standard singles £32, en-suite singles/doubles £44/56)* is bigger and more standard but the quality of service is uniformly high.

Plymouth Hoe Moat House (☎ 639988, fax 673816; Armada Way; B&B singles/ doubles £125/140) is an ugly, ugly building, but once inside it's got the mod cons (health club, swimming pool, business facilities) and it's right on the Hoe.

The Duke of Cornwall Hotel (☎ 275850, fax 275854; e duke@bhere.co.uk; Millbay Rd; B&B singles/doubles £84.50/99.50) is an impressive Victorian Gothic hotel opposite Plymouth Pavilions.

The Grand Hotel (☎ 661195, fax 600653; e info@plymouthgrand.com; Elliot St; B&B singles/doubles from £93/103) is the classic, cake-icing Victorian seafront hotel, grand in style and name. Call for details of discounted leisure rates.

Places to Eat

Dutton's Café Continental (☎ 255245; Madeira Rd; cream tea £3.75, mains £7-8.50; open 9.30am-5.30pm daily) is in an 1847 cannon room (the gun holes are now windows) with good lunch-time snacks and more substantial fish dishes.

Being next to Cornwall, pasties are ubiquitous here and **Ivor Dewdney** (99 Cornwall St; pasties £1-1.75) makes the best; some monsters take two hands to hold.

The Trading House (☎ 257345; 8 The Parade; mains £8-17) is a smart pub-cum-restaurant in the Barbican. Prop up the bar and munch tapas (£2 to £8) or take a seat and chow down on serious seafood and steaks.

Bar ZeegCo (☎ 664754; Frankfort Gate; mains £4.25-15) is bright and modern, handy for the shops and serves good Mediterranean/Middle-Eastern food.

Back at the Hoe, **Lemon Tree** (☎ 265631; 9 Elliot St; mains £13-18; open dinner Tues-Sat) offers excellent modern British cuisine in the basement of the Grosvenor Hotel.

Sleek, contemporary **Chez Nous** (☎ 266 793; 13 Frankfort Gate; 3-course dinner £33) is the city's top French restaurant, specialising in seafood. Book to be impressed.

The eponymous owner-chefs of **Tanners Restaurant** (☎ 252001; Prysten House, Finewell St; 2/3-course dinner £20/22.50; open lunch & dinner Tues-Sat) cook up the city's finest dining in Plymouth's oldest house (1498). The medieval courtyard beckons for alfresco eating in summer.

Entertainment

Pubs & Clubs A university town, Plymouth has a buzzing nightlife. The main club strip, Union St, has a reputation for trouble at kicking-out time.

The area in and around the Barbican is wall-to-wall pubs and bars. **Minerva Inn** (☎ 223047; 31 Looe St) is reputedly the oldest pub in Plymouth, home of the press gangs; it's a low-ceilinged, smoky local, with live music at the weekend. **The Ship** (☎ 667604; Quay Rd) is another popular boozer in the Barbican.

Barbican Jazz Café (☎ 672127; 11 The Parade; admission £2 Fri & Sat; open noon-2am Mon-Sat, noon-midnight Sun) is a barrelled vault with nightly jazz and a younger, livelier vibe that you might expect.

Unsurprisingly, the university area has bars galore, most open till the small hours and graced with DJs pumping chunky tunes. **Ride** (☎ 226655; 2 Sherwell Arcade) is the current cool tip, with next-door **Cuba** (☎ 201 520; 1 Sherwell Arcade) aiming more for the shooters-and-mixers crowd. **Boardriders** (☎ 229555; 45 Tavistock Place) has a surfin' theme: videos show how not to wipe out to a hip-hop and drum'n'bass soundtrack.

Vibrant **B-Bar** (☎ 242021; Castle St), in the Barbican Theatre, is hip but not hyped; there's live music, DJs and comedy, and the munchies are good.

The Cooperage (☎ 229275; w www.the cooperage.co.uk; Tin Lane, 134 Vauxhall St) is the live-music venue of choice for smaller bands.

The funkiness of **Club Fandango** (☎ 664 100; 13 Elliot St), underneath the Strathmore Hotel, is in inverse proportion to its size; it's tiny but fabulous, with a great atmosphere and comedy (Thursday, £5.50), salsa (Friday, £5) or retro club tunes (Saturday, £4), plus occasional alternative nights.

For mainstream club action, try **Candy Store** (☎ 601616; 99-101 Union St) or **Dance Academy** (☎ 220055; 121-123 Union St), which draw big-name DJs.

Theatres & Cinemas The **Theatre Royal** (☎ 267222; w www.theatreroyal.com; Royal Parade), Plymouth's big venue, has the West End musicals and dance, while its **Drum Theatre** stages the fringe plays.

Plymouth Pavilions (☎ 229922; w www .plymouthpavilions.com; Millbay Rd) hosts everything from Tom Jones to the Bolshoi Ballet.

Barbican Theatre (☎ 267131; **w** www.barbicantheatre.co.uk; Castle St) stages theatre, dance and exhibitions; its **B-Bar** also hosts jazz, comedy and cabaret.

Plymouth Arts Centre (☎ 206114; **w** www.plymouthac.org.uk; 38 Looe St) is the art-house cinema venue; there's also a good vegetarian restaurant.

Getting There & Away

Plymouth is 211 miles (340km) from London, 90 miles (145km) from Land's End and 46 miles (74km) from Exeter.

Bus Express bus No X38 runs to Exeter (1¼ hours, every 90 minutes Monday to Saturday, every two hours Sunday); bus Nos 39 and X39 are slower (1¾ hours, at least every two hours), but stop at Buckfastleigh on the edge of Dartmoor. Another useful service is bus No 86 (roughly hourly Monday to Saturday, two on Sunday), which runs to Okehampton (1¼ hours) via Tavistock (55 minutes) and Lydford (1½ hours), sometimes going on to Barnstaple (£5.50 day return, three hours).

National Express has direct connections to numerous cities, including London (£37 economy return, five hours, at least seven daily), Bristol (£29.50, three to four hours, four daily) and Birmingham (£47.50, five hours, four daily).

Train Services run to London (£41 Super-advance return, 3½ hours, hourly), Bristol (£37.30 saver return, two hours, at least hourly) and Penzance (£13.60, two hours, hourly).

The scenic line to Exeter (£14, one hour, hourly) follows the River Exe estuary, running beside the sea for part of the way. The Tamar Valley Line, through Bere Ferrers, Bere Alston and Calstock to Gunnislake, is another scenic route. In summer, it's possible to travel to Calstock by train (£3.90 single, 30 minutes, every two hours) and return by boat, or the other way round; see Boat Trips earlier in this section.

AROUND PLYMOUTH
Mount Edgcumbe

This fine, red-sandstone Tudor house (☎ 01752-822236; Cremyll, Torpoint; adult/child £4.50/2.25; open 11am-4.30pm Wed-Sun Apr-Sept), heavily reconstructed post-WWII, is actually across the water from Plymouth in Cornwall. The interior, much altered over the centuries, has 18th-century furniture, but it's the marvellous, landscaped Grade I–listed French, Italian and English formal gardens that draw visitors.

Take the Cremyll foot ferry (seven minutes, every 30 minutes) from Admiral's Hard, Stonehouse, just west of the ferry terminal.

Buckland Abbey

Originally a Cistercian monastery and incorporating elements of the 13th-century abbey church, Buckland Abbey (NT; ☎ 01822-853607; Yelverton; admission £4.70; open 10.30am-5.30pm Fri-Wed Apr-Oct, 2pm-5pm Sat & Sun Nov-Mar) was transformed into a family residence by Sir Richard Grenville and bought in 1581 by his cousin and nautical rival Sir Francis Drake. Exhibitions on its history feature Drake's Drum, said to beat by itself when Britain is in danger of being invaded. There's also a fine Elizabethan garden.

Buckland is 11 miles (18km) north of Plymouth. Take bus No 83, 84 or 86 (40 minutes, every 30 minutes) to Yelverton, then bus No 55 (10 minutes, hourly) to Buckland Abbey.

NORTH DEVON

The stretch of coastline between Exmoor and the Cornish border has it all: fine beaches, rugged cliffs and some of the top surfing spots in the country, as well as the obligatory pretty villages and fishing harbours.

Barnstaple
☎ 01271 • pop 27,700

Barnstaple is a large town and transport hub, handy for Exmoor (see the Wessex chapter), although it's more pleasant to stay in nearby villages such as Croyde.

The **TIC** (☎ 375000; **e** info@staynorthdevon.co.uk; 36 Boutport St; open 9.30am-5pm Mon-Fri, 10.30am-4pm Sat) can help with accommodation bookings.

The Tarka Trail, named after Henry Williamson's famous otter, is a popular cycling and walking route circling north Devon, running on along the river from Barnstaple to Meeth, near Hatherleigh. Bikes are available from **Tarka Trail** (☎ 324202; Train Station) from £6 per day (£8 for mountain bikes).

DEVON & CORNWALL

Two miles west of Barnstaple in a restored railway station, **Fremington Quay** (☎ 372 586; W www.fremingtonquaycafe.co.uk; open 10am-10pm daily) also rents mountain bikes (£9.50 per day); if you start from Fremington, you can drop the bike off at Okehampton (Dartmoor) or Parracombe (Exmoor). There's also a small visitor centre and a café serving delicious cakes and meals.

Barnstaple is 216 miles (346km) from London. National Express runs to London (£34 economy return, 5½ hours, four daily) and Bristol (£18.50, three hours, daily). Barnstaple is at the northwestern end of the Tarka Line railway from Exeter (£13.80, 1¼ hours, every two hours Monday to Saturday, four on Sunday) and connects with a number of bus services around the coast.

Braunton & Croyde
☎ 01271 • population 9300

Croyde Bay and the nearby beach at Saunton Sands are two of the most popular surfing spots in the country; Croyde is also a pleasant seaside village, with good campsites, B&Bs and pubs. Check the north Devon **Surfcall** (☎ 0906 800 7007) for local surfing conditions; calls cost 60p per minute.

Braunton is the centre for surf shops: the place to pick up a board, wetsuit and designer surf gear. The **TIC** (☎ 816400, fax 816947; e brauntontic@visit.org.uk; The Bakehouse Centre; open 10am-4pm Mon-Sat) provides information and also houses a small local museum. Done surfing, need more buzz? The **UK Kiteboarding Centre** (☎ 813322; W www.ukkiteboardingcentre.com; The Square; open 10am-5pm Tues-Sun) charges £99 for a day's lessons and equipment.

Croyde has numerous surf-hire shops, charging around £10 per day for board and wetsuit: try **Le Sport** (☎ 890147; Hobbs Hill; open 9am-9pm daily Apr-Sept) or, for lessons, **Surf South West** (☎ 890400; W www.surfsouthwest.com; £40/20 per day/half-day).

Campsites are plentiful but you should still book ahead. Word has it the best are **Mitchum's Campsites** (☎ 890233; e guy@croydebay.co.uk), in a couple of places; call or email for locations and prices. **Bay View Farm** (☎ 890501; W www.bayviewfarm.co.uk; tent site & 2 people £13), on the road from Braunton, is another good spot.

Chapel Farm (☎ 890429; W www.chapelfarmcroyde.co.uk; Hobbs Hill; B&B per person from £20) is a lovely old farmhouse; there's also self-catering accommodation and surfboard hire.

The Thatch (☎ 890349; e info@thethatch.com; 14 Hobbs Hill; B&B doubles with/without en suite from £60/50; mains £6-12) is legendary among surfers for its great pub atmosphere and hearty food. **Billy Budd's** (☎ 890606; Hobbs Hill) nearby is owned by the same people and offers B&B and grub at similar prices.

Croyde Manor (☎ 890350; B&B per person from £24) is a Georgian country house with four-posters and a charming feel of faded gentry.

Bus No 308 runs from Barnstaple (£2.30 day return, 40 minutes, hourly Monday to Saturday, five on Sunday).

Ilfracombe
☎ 01271 • pop 10,500

Ilfracombe is north Devon's largest seaside resort, and steep hills frame its attractive little harbour, although the best beaches are 5 miles (8km) west at Woolacombe. With Exmoor nearby, it's a more interesting spot to stay than many other resorts.

The **TIC** (☎ 863001, fax 862586; W www.ilfracombe-tourism.co.uk; The Landmark, The Seafront; open 10am-5.30pm daily June-Sept, 10am-5pm Mon-Fri, 10am-4pm Sat & Sun Oct-May) is in the striking **Landmark Theatre**.

The 11th-century **Chambercombe Manor** (☎ 862624; Chambercombe Lane; adult/child £4/2; open 10.30am-5.30pm Mon-Fri, 2pm-5.30pm Sun Easter-Oct, last tour 4.30pm) contains period furniture from Elizabethan to Victorian times, but it's the guided tours and tales of ghosts, murderous smugglers and skeletons in secret chambers that really make the place. Scooby-Doo-tastic.

Aside from building sandcastles, Ilfracombe is a centre for a range of activities. **Keypitts** (☎ 862247) offers quad biking, rally karting, paintball and more. A range of other activities (including waterskiing, diving, horse riding, climbing and surfing) costing £1 to £60 can be arranged through Ocean Backpackers (see the following Places to Stay & Eat entry).

Places to Stay & Eat The **Ilfracombe YHA Hostel** (☎ 0870 770 5878, fax 862652; e ilfracombe@yha.org.uk; 1 Hillsborough Terrace; adult/child £10.25/7, twins £23.50;

open Easter-Nov) is a steep hike above the harbour. There's Internet access and occasional music jams.

Ocean Backpackers *(☎/fax 867835;* e *in fo@oceanbackpackers.co.uk; 29 St James Place; dorm beds per night/week £10/50)* is an excellent, lively hostel opposite the bus station; the owners organise a plethora of activities. Downstairs is the **Atlantis Restaurant**, a fine eatery with world music and similarly global dishes (£4.75 to £12.65).

Greyven House *(☎ 862505; 4 St James Place; per person with/without en suite £22.50/19.50)* is a good, family-run B&B close to the harbour and the theatre.

Pier Tavern *(☎ 866225; The Quay; mains £3.50-9)* is a seafront pub with fresh seafood, a chatty crowd and live music on Sunday.

Getting There & Away National Express coaches run from London (£34 economy return, six hours) twice daily. Bus Nos 3 and 30 (£2.50 day return, 40 minutes, every half-hour Monday to Friday, hourly Sunday) run to Barnstaple. Bus No 300 heads to Lynton (one hour) and Minehead (two hours) three times daily.

Knightshayes Court

This Victorian fantasy manor *(NT; ☎ 01884-254665;* e *knightshayes@ntrust.org.uk; Bolham; admission £5.50; open 11am-5.30pm Sat-Thur Apr-Sept, 11am-4pm Sat-Thur Oct & Nov)* is remarkable largely for the evident clash in imagination and taste between the owner, Tiverton MP John Heathcoat Mallory, and original architect, William Burges. The latter was obsessed with the Middle Ages, and the stone curlicues, minstrels' gallery and richly decorated Burges room reflect his love of knightly lore; Mallory was more strait-laced and preferred simple grandeur, evident in the library and billiard room. The extensive gardens feature a delightful water-lily pool and wonderful topiary.

Bus No 398 runs from Tiverton to Bolham (10 minutes, six daily Monday to Saturday), three-quarters of a mile (1km) away.

Lundy Island

Ten miles (16km) out in the Bristol Channel, Lundy is a granite mass 3 miles (5km) long, half a mile wide and up to 122m high. There's a resident population of just 18 people, one pub, one church and no roads.

Puffin Pence

Martin Harman, owner of Lundy Island from 1925 to 1954, was a typical English eccentric. Not satisfied with owning the remote island, he was determined to make it independent from the rest of the UK, closing the post office and issuing his own stamps. Given that Lundy took its name from the old Norse word for puffin, the stamps were denominated in 'puffinage' instead of sterling.

The stamps were ignored, but in 1930 Harman carried things a step further and issued a Lundy coinage, with his own head in place of the king's and a puffin on the reverse. These, too, were denominated in 'puffins' instead of shillings and pence. Such defiance couldn't be overlooked and Harman was duly convicted of counterfeiting under the 1870 Coinage Act.

Sadly, like Lundy's coins, the once-common puffin bird is now a thoroughly endangered species; you'll be lucky to see any at all.

People come to climb the cliffs, watch the birds, plunge into the marine nature reserve (one of the top dive sites in Britain) or escape from the world in one of the holiday homes.

Interesting properties that can be rented include the lighthouse, the castle and a converted pigsty, but they need to be reserved months in advance. You can also camp for £4 to £7 per person, depending on the season. The **Lundy Shore Office** *(☎ 01271-863636;* w *www.lundyisland.co.uk)* handles ferry bookings and inquiries regarding camping and short-term B&B. The **Landmark Trust** *(☎ 01628-825925),* which manages the island on behalf of the National Trust, handles property bookings.

You can take a day trip from Ilfracombe or Bideford on the **MS Oldenburg** (adult/child day return £25/12.50, period return £40/21, two hours). There are between two and five sailings a week from these ports (sometimes departing one and returning to the other) from March to December.

You can also make day trips from Clovelly: the **Jessica Hettie** *(☎ 431042;* w *www.clovelly-charters.ukf.net; adult/child return £22.50/20, plus £3.50 landing fee)* departs Wednesday or Thursday from April to October. It's possible to dive if you bring your own kit (£262 per day for eight divers).

Appledore
☎ 01237 • pop 2200

After a brief hiatus last century, Appledore's boat-building legacy continues, although the busy shipyard is tucked back from the narrow streets and old world charm of the village. It's a restful spot to fish or just watch the sailing boats while you lick your ice cream.

The **North Devon Maritime Museum** (☎ 422064; Odun Rd; adult/child £1/30p; open 2pm-5pm daily Easter-Oct, plus 11am-1pm Mon-Fri May-Sept) tells the story of local boat-building, shipwrecks and smuggling. **Tarka Cruises** (☎ 477505) runs pleasure cruises (adult/child £6/5.50) and two-hour trips to fish for sea bass and mackerel (£8).

The **Seagate Hotel** (☎ 472589; The Quay; en-suite singles/doubles £40/60) is a friendly waterside pub offering B&B. The 18th-century **Royal George Hotel** (☎ 474335; Irsha St; mains £9.50) is renowned locally for its fresh fish dishes.

Bus Nos 2 and 16A run at least hourly to Bideford (20 minutes); bus No 2 goes on to Barnstaple (40 minutes).

Clovelly
☎ 01237

Like a kind of West-Country Brigadoon, each morning Clovelly's insanely picturesque (but cruelly steep) cobbled street, lined with the cutest cottages, becomes thronged with tourists looking to take the perfect picture of the quaint harbour. The difference is that if you stick around for the evening it's the tourists that vanish, while the village remains and peace descends.

To some extent, Clovelly has turned itself into a living gallery. During the day, it costs £3.50/2.50 per adult/child to park your car and enter via the **visitor centre** (☎ 431781), where there's a short video presentation (and the obligatory gift shops); this also includes entry to the Kingsley Museum. If you stay overnight you can let yourself in through a gate to the right of the visitors centre. From Easter to October, Land Rovers regularly ferry visitors up and down the slope (£1.60 each way) between 9.30am and 5.30pm.

At the **Kingsley Museum** (Providence House; open 9.15am-5pm daily summer, 10.30am-3.30pm daily winter) you can see Charles Kingsley's study (he wrote Westward Ho! here), then squeeze your way around the tiny old **Fisherman's Cottage** behind.

Places to Stay & Eat There are only a few independent B&Bs in the village; the visitor centre plugs the two hotels but has a list of other options.

Donkey Shoe Cottage (☎ 431601; 21 High St; per person £20) is a friendly B&B halfway up the hill; bathrooms are shared.

Just across the street, **New Inn** (☎ 431303, fax 431636; e newinn@clovelly.co.uk; High St; en-suite B&B per person from £36) is a classic old pub with comfortable, modern rooms. Bar food is hearty and traditional (ploughman's lunch £4.75-5.50), featuring fresh fish and other seafood favourites.

Red Lion Hotel (☎ 431237, fax 431044; en-suite B&B per person from £42.50; 3-course dinner £25), right by the harbour, is similar in feel, although the restaurant is a far more formal affair, serving fine cuisine with an emphasis on seafood.

Both stop serving by 9pm so don't order too late.

Getting There & Away Bus No 319 runs five times daily to Bideford (40 minutes) and Barnstaple (£2.40 day return, one hour).

Hartland Abbey

This 12th-century monastery-turned-stately-home (☎ 01237-441264; w www.hartland abbey.com; adult/child £4.50/1.50; open 2pm-5.30pm Wed, Thur & Sun May-Sept, also Tues July & Aug) was another post-Dissolution handout, given to the sergeant of Henry VIII's wine cellar in 1539. It boasts some fascinating murals, ancient documents, paintings by English Masters and Victorian photos, as well as marvellous gardens.

Hartland Abbey is 15 miles (24km) west of Bideford, off the A39 between Hartland and Hartland Quay. Bus No 319 runs five times daily (twice Sunday) from Barnstaple (1½ hours) and Bideford (£1.70 return, one hour).

Dartmoor National Park

Some 280 million years ago, large volumes of molten rock formed a granite mass stretching from the Isles of Scilly to eastern Devon, and it's at Dartmoor that the largest area (about 365 square miles; 945 sq km) has been exposed. Why the geology lesson?

Tarka Trail, Devon

Tresco Abbey Gardens, Isles of Scilly

Master thatcher at work, Devon

Round Island Lighthouse, Isles of Scilly

A windmill, the Cotswolds

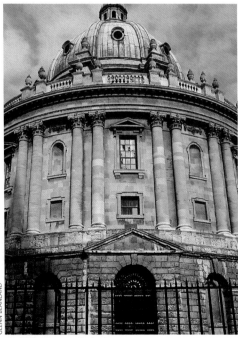

Radcliffe Camera, Oxford

The River Wye, Herefordshire

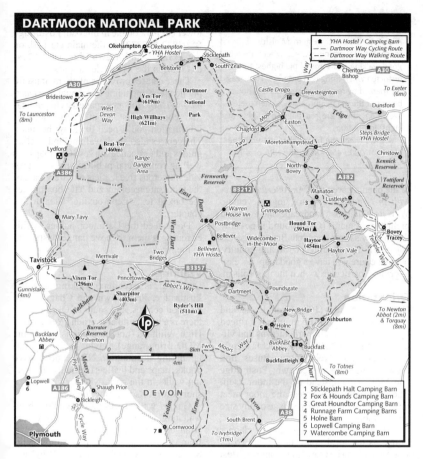

DARTMOOR NATIONAL PARK

■ YHA Hostel / Camping Barn
— Dartmoor Way Cycling Route
-- Dartmoor Way Walking Route

Okehampton ● Okehampton
YHA Hostel
Sticklepath
Belstone 1 ● South Zeal
Cheriton Bishop
To Exeter (6mi)
Bridestowe 2
West Devon Way
Yes Tor (619m)
Dartmoor
Castle Drogo
Drewsteignton
Dunsford
To Launceston (8mi)
High Willhays (621m)
National Park
Chagford
Easton
Steps Bridge YHA Hostel
Lydford
Brat Tor (460m)
Range Danger Area
Two
Moretonhampstead
Christow
Kennick Reservoir
A386
Fernworthy Reservoir
North Bovey
A382
Tottiford Reservoir
East Dart
B3212
Manaton
Lustleigh 3
Mary Tavy
Warren House Inn
Grimspound
Hound Tor (393m)
Bovey
Bovey Tracey
West Dart
Postbridge 4
Bellever
Widecombe-in-the-Moor
Haytor (454m)
Haytor Vale
Temple Way
Tavistock
Merrivale
Two Bridges
Bellever YHA Hostel
Vixen Tor (296m)
Princetown
B3357
Abbot's Way
Dartmeet
Poundsgate
Gunnislake (4mi)
Sharpitor (403m)
Ryder's Hill (511m)
New Bridge
Ashburton
To Newton Abbot (2mi) & Torquay (8mi)
Walkham
Burrator Reservoir
Yelverton
Holne 5
Buckland Abbey
Buckfast Abbey
Buckfast
Lopwell 6
A386
Shaugh Prior
Bickleigh
D E V O N
Two Moors Way
Buckfastleigh
To Totnes (8mi)
Plym Valley
Meavy
Cycle Way
Cornwood 7
Yealm
Erme
Avon
South Brent
A38
To Ivybridge (1mi)
Plymouth

1 Sticklepath Halt Camping Barn
2 Fox & Hounds Camping Barn
3 Great Houndtor Camping Barn
4 Runnage Farm Camping Barns
5 Holne Barn
6 Lopwell Camping Barn
7 Watercombe Camping Barn

0   4   8km
0   2   4mi

To illustrate why Dartmoor is so remarkably rugged: it's essentially a huge granite plateau covered by only a thin layer of peaty soil. Vegetation is sparse; purple heather and gorse cover most of the high ground, with green, marshy mire in lowland areas and a few oak woods remaining in the sheltered valleys or coombs. Sheep, cattle and semi-wild Dartmoor ponies graze the open land, interrupted by weirdly shaped *tors* – rock pillars or hills (Vixen Tor is almost 30m high) sculpted by weather erosion.

Dartmoor lies within the county of Devon and is named after the River Dart, which has its source here; the Rivers West Dart and East Dart merge at Dartmeet. The countryside towards the southeastern edge of the park is more conventionally beauti-

ful, with wooded valleys and thatched villages; the wealth generated by tin mining and stone quarrying allowed even small settlements to build impressive churches.

Most of the park is around 600m high. The highest spot is High Willhays (621m) near Okehampton. About 40% of Dartmoor is common land but 15% of the park (the northwestern section, including High Willhays and Yes Tor) is leased to the Ministry of Defence (MOD) and is closed for firing practice for part of the year.

Dartmoor encloses some of the wildest, bleakest country in England: suitable terrain for the Hound of the Baskervilles (one of Sherlock Holmes' more notorious foes). The landscape and weather (mist, rain and snow) can make this an eerie place; try not to think

Warning

Access to the northwestern Ministry of Defence (MOD) training area, where there's good walking and some of the highest tors, is restricted when firing is in progress. The areas are marked by red and white posts and notice boards at the main approaches. When there's live firing, there are red flags (red lights at night) in position.

Always check the firing schedules with the MOD (☎ 0800 458 4868), the NPA or a TIC.

of the opening scenes of *An American Werewolf in London* on a dark, foggy evening. With its wild, open landscape and scattered prehistoric remains (**Grimspound** is possibly the country's most complete Bronze Age village site), it's magnificent walking country, but make sure you have a good map: it's easy to get lost, particularly when the mist rolls in.

Orientation

Dartmoor is 6 miles (10km) from Exeter and 7 miles (11km) from Plymouth. It's ringed by a number of small market towns and villages, including Ashburton, Buckfastleigh, Tavistock and Okehampton. Buses link these towns with Princetown, Postbridge and Moretonhampstead on the moor itself. The two main roads across the moor meet near Princetown, the only village of any size on Dartmoor.

Postbridge, with its medieval clapper bridge, is the focal point for car and coach visitors, and can be crowded in summer. Most of the places to see are on the eastern side; the western part is for serious walkers.

Information

There's information about Dartmoor at the TICs in Exeter and Plymouth, and other visitor centres in and around the park at Okehampton, Tavistock, Ivybridge, Ashburton, Buckfastleigh and Bovey Tracey; check the **Dartmoor Tourist Association** website at w www.dartmoor-guide.co.uk.

The National Park Authority (NPA; w www.dartmoor-npa.gov.uk) runs the **High Moorland Visitors Centre** in Princetown, the best place to gather information (see the Princeton section later for details).

The other NPA visitor centres, generally open 10am to 5pm daily, April to October,

are at **Haytor** (☎ 01364-661520), in the lower car park on the main road; **Postbridge** (☎ 01822-880272), in the main car park on the B3212; and **Newbridge** (☎ 01364-631303), in the Riverside car park.

These centres provide a plethora of useful publications, including the annual free *Dartmoor Visitor*; this newspaper-style publication contains just about every piece of information you'll need to enjoy the moor. The centres also stock walking and cycling guides and Ordnance Survey (OS) maps. As well as commercial publications, they provide numerous free leaflets on safety, care of the moor, archaeology and letterboxing (see the boxed text 'Letterboxing' later in this chapter).

Don't feed the Dartmoor ponies as this encourages them to move dangerously near to the roads.

Walking

Dartmoor is excellent walking country. Postbridge, Princetown and Chagford are all good centres, and south of Okehampton there is a high, wild area around Yes Tor and High Willhays (note that this is within the MOD firing range). Haytor is also a popular hiking destination. NPA centres have books, maps and leaflets (some free) covering walks in the park, whether you want a short stroll or something longer.

Guided walks focusing on wildlife, birdwatching, archaeology or folklore are arranged from April to October; they start from various points in the park almost daily. Some should be booked in advance by calling the High Moorland Visitors Centre (see the Princeton section later in this chapter for contact details). Prices run from £3 for two hours to £5 for six hours (£1 for children under 14 regardless of duration); if you arrive by bus you can join the walk free of charge. Details appear in the *Dartmoor Visitor*.

Letterboxing walks (see the 'Letterboxing' boxed text later in this chapter) organised by **Dave Allen** (☎ 01822-618118, mobile 07751 315155; e info@dartmoor-letterboxing-walks.co.uk) cost £25/15 for a full/half-day, £12/8 for under-16s.

There are several waymarked walking routes on Dartmoor. The **Abbot's Way** runs along an ancient 14-mile (23km) route from Buckfast to Princetown. The **West Devon Way** is a 14-mile (23km) walk between

Tavistock and Okehampton along old tracks and through pretty villages on the western edge of Dartmoor. You can take a bus for part of this walk as the trail runs parallel to the No 187 route.

Youth hostels are conveniently placed a day's walk apart across the moor, so a five-day circuit from either Exeter or Plymouth is possible.

The **Templer Way** is an 18-mile (29km) hike from Teignmouth (on the coast east of the moor) to Haytor, following the route originally designed to transport Dartmoor granite down to the docks.

The **Two Moors Way** is a longer option, running from Ivybridge, on the southern edge of Dartmoor, 103 miles (166km) across both Dartmoor and Exmoor to Lynmouth on the north Devon Coast. The *Two Moors Way* (£4.95 not including postage) is available from the **Ramblers' Association** (☎ 020-7339 8500; W *www.ramblers.org.uk;* 2nd floor, Camelford House, 87-90 Albert Embankment, London SE1 7TW).

The **Dartmoor Way** is a 90-mile (140km) circular route round the outer edge of the national park, stretching from Buckfastleigh in the south, up through Moretonhampstead, northwest to Okehampton and south through Lydford to Tavistock. The *Dartmoor Way* pack (£7.95) includes a book and 1:25,000 scale map, and is available from TICs and NPA centres. Call ☎ 0870 241 1817 or check W www.dartmoorway.org.uk for details.

The **Tarka Trail** circles north Devon and links with Dartmoor, south of Okehampton; *The Tarka Trail: a Walkers' Guide* can be purchased for £4.95.

It's always wise to carry a map, compass and rain gear since the weather can change very quickly and not all walks are way-marked. OS OL Explorer Map No 28 (1:50,000; £6.99) is the most comprehensive map, showing the park boundaries and MOD firing-range areas.

Cycling
Cycling is only allowed on public roads, byways open to all traffic, public bridle-paths and Forestry Commission roads.

The **Plym Valley Cycle Way** follows the disused Great Western Railway between Plymouth and Yelverton, on the edge of the moor. **The Dartmoor Way** (see the previous Walking section) is also the name of a 90-

mile (140km) circular cycling route round the edge of the moor, including Okehampton, Chagford, Buckfastleigh, Princetown and Tavistock. Cyclists can also follow the **Tarka Trail**.

Pick up the leaflet *Making Tracks! Cycle Routes in Devon* from TICs. Another useful map is *Dartmoor for Off-Road Cyclists* (£10), available from the NPA. There are various short routes ranging from 3 to 30 miles in length. Devon County Council (W www .devon.gov.uk/cycling/contents.html) produces a series of book/map packs containing details; *West Devon Cycling Routes* (DP52; £3.75) includes the Tavistock and Sticklepath Routes on Dartmoor, while the *Dartmoor Way* (DP71; £7.95) contains details of the main route.

Bikes can be hired in Exeter (see Getting Around in the earlier Exeter section) and also from **Tavistock Cycles** (☎ 01822-617630; *Paddons Row, Brook St, Tavistock*), which charges £12 per day. **Dartmoor Cycle Hire** (☎ 01822-618189; *6 Atlas House, West Devon Business Park*), also in Tavistock, charges £12/6 for a full/half-day; staff will deliver bikes to a number of hotels and guesthouses in Dartmoor; call for details.

Pony Trekking & Horse Riding
There are riding stables all over the park: *Dartmoor Visitor* has details. In addition, **Lydford House Riding Stables** (☎ 01822-820321; e *relax@lydfordhouse.co.uk; Lydford House Hotel, Lydford*) charges from £13/22.50 for one/two hours (cheaper for residents).

Climbing
Popular climbing areas are at Haytor, owned by the NPA, and the Dewerstone near Shaugh Prior, owned by the NT. Groups need to book in advance. Ask at a NPA visitor centre or TIC for details.

Fishing
You can fish on certain stretches of the East and West Dart with a **Duchy of Cornwall permit** (☎ 01822-890205). Fishing is also permitted on seven reservoirs in the park; contact **South West Lakes Trust** (☎ 01837-871565). For fishing on the Rivers Tavy, Walkham, Plym, Meavy and Teign, a permit is usually needed; phone the **Environment Agency** (☎ 01925-653999) for information.

Places to Stay & Eat

If you're backpacking, the authorities and owners of unenclosed moorland don't usually object to campers who keep to a simple code: don't camp on moorland enclosed by walls or within sight of roads or houses; don't stay on one site for more than two nights; don't light fires; and leave the site as you found it. Bear in mind that there are specific, heavily used common areas which are also out of bounds; check with the NPA. With large tents, you can only camp in designated campsites. There are several camping and caravan parks around the area, many on farms.

There are YHA hostels at Postbridge (Bellever), bang in the middle of the moor, and at Steps Bridge, near Dunsford (between Moretonhampstead and Exeter), as well as at Okehampton, Exeter and Dartington.

There are six YHA camping barns ('stone tents' sleeping up to about 15 people) in the park, plus some independent barns and bunkhouses. Cooking and shower facilities and a wood burner are provided. You sleep on the floor or on a bunk bed; bring your own bedding. Charges are from £3.75 per person. For more information and centralised booking for YHA barns, phone ☎ 01200-420102, or check the YHA website (W www .yha.org.uk). The handiest barns are listed throughout this section.

The larger towns on the edge of the park (such as Okehampton and Tavistock) have plentiful B&Bs and hotels. Within the park itself, accommodation is sometimes limited, so book ahead in summer. There are also several comfortable country-house hotels.

Based upstairs from the High Moor Visitors Centre in Princetown, the **Dartmoor Tourist Association** (☎ 01822-890567; W www.discoverdartmoor .com) produces an annual *Dartmoor Guide*, with descriptions of villages and accommodation listings. There's a charge of £2.75 if you book rooms through any of the visitor centres. TICs have details of farm B&Bs.

The old pubs and inns provide a focus for local communities and are sometimes the only places you can get anything to eat in small villages.

Getting There & Around

The best starting points for the park are Exeter and Plymouth but Exeter has the better transport connections to the rest of the country. Totnes, Exeter, Newton Abbot and Plymouth have train services to London, Bristol and the Midlands. National Express has coach services between London and Exeter, Newton Abbot, Okehampton and Plymouth.

Before you start planning, get a copy of the *Discovery Guide to Dartmoor*, free from most Devon TICs and the NPA offices. It has details of bus and train links to places within and near the park, and basic coverage of some short walks.

The Dartmoor Sunday Rover ticket (adult/child £6/4, June to September) entitles you to unlimited travel on most bus routes within the area and to rail travel on the Tamar Valley Line from Plymouth to Gunnislake. Ticket holders also receive discounted admission to NT properties and other attractions. Buy your ticket from bus drivers or at Plymouth train station.

The most useful bus that actually crosses Dartmoor is No 82, the Transmoor Link, running between Exeter and Plymouth via Steps Bridge, Moretonhampstead, Warren House Inn, Postbridge, Princetown and Yelverton. It runs daily from late May to late September (three daily Monday to Saturday, five Sunday), but on Saturday and Sunday only during the rest of the year.

On Sunday in summer, Devon bus No 187 loops round from Plymouth, through Gunnislake, Tavistock, Mary Tavy and Lydford, to Okehampton; you could do part of this journey on the Tamar Valley Line or even by boat (see Plymouth earlier in this chapter).

There are four trains between Okehampton and Exeter on Sunday (£5.50 Day Rover, 40 minutes). The only other train stations near the park are at Ivybridge and South Brent on the Exeter–Plymouth line. Ivybridge (from Exeter: £12.90 saver return, 50 minutes, every two hours) is handy for the Two Moors Way.

PRINCETOWN

☎ 01822 • elevation 420m

Princetown is England's highest settlement. With its infamous jail, it's not Dartmoor's most beautiful town, but its central location and accommodation options make it a good base for walking.

The town was created in the late 18th century when a prison was built to house prisoners of war; it's now a maximum-security prison. The **Dartmoor Prison Museum** (☎ *890305; adult/child £2/1),* on the Tavistock road, gives an insight into the jail's early days, and sells crafts made by current prisoners. It's generally open 9.30am to 4.30pm Tuesday to Saturday, depending on staff availability (when warders aren't out hunting escapees?).

The **High Moorland Visitors Centre** (☎ *890414, fax 890566;* |e| *hmvc@dartmoor -npa.gov.uk; Old Duchy Hotel; open 10am- 5pm daily)* has displays on Dartmoor and an information centre that stocks a wide variety of maps and books. Donations of 20p are appreciated.

Places to Stay & Eat

Plume of Feathers Inn (☎ *890240, fax 890780; The Square; tent sites per person £3, barn bunk beds from £3.75, bunkhouse from £5.50, B&B per person £17.50),* Princetown's oldest building, is a popular pub with plenty of accommodation; book well in advance.

Railway Inn *(*☎*/fax 890232;* |e| *railway innpl20@aol.com; Two Bridges Rd; singles/ doubles £20/35)* is another pub-cum-B&B with some en-suite doubles. Both of these places are near the NPA centre; neither is spectacular, but both are friendly and dish up warming grub (fish and chips, cottage pie) for around a fiver.

Getting There & Away

Bus No 82 (the Transmoor Link) runs to Princetown from both Exeter (one hour 40 minutes) and Plymouth (50 minutes). Bus Nos 98 (six daily Monday to Saturday) and 172 (two daily Monday to Saturday, four Sunday) link Princetown with Tavistock (25 minutes).

POSTBRIDGE
☎ 01822 • elevation 393m

A tiny village in the middle of the park, Postbridge is a popular walking centre. Really just a few houses strung along the road, it's known for its granite clapper bridge across the East Dart, dating from the 13th century and made of large slabs of granite supported at each end by stone pillars.

Local legend tells of 18th-century temperance house landlady who took to serving alcohol, much to the horror of her husband, who poured it in the river. A dog that paused to quench its thirst was driven mad by the potent mixture and died. Its tormented spirit is still said to haunt Dartmoor – one version of the story that gave Conan Doyle the idea for *The Hound of the Baskervilles.*

From April to October, there's an **NPA visitor centre** *(*☎ *01822-880272)* in the car park. There's also a **post office** and **shop** in the village.

Places to Stay & Eat

Bellever YHA Hostel *(*☎ *0870 770 5692, fax 880302;* |e| *bellever@yha.org.uk; adult/child £10.25/7; open daily July & Aug, Mon-Sat Mar-June, Sept & Oct),* in former Duchy farm buildings, is a mile south of Postbridge on the western bank of the river. Bus No 98 runs from Tavistock (40 minutes, daily Monday to Saturday) and Princetown (20 minutes).

Runnage Farm (☎ *880222; beds £3.95)* has two YHA camping barns. To reach the farm, take the small road off the B3212 just before you reach Postbridge coming from the Moretonhampstead side.

East Dart Hotel (☎ *880213, fax 880313; en-suite B&B per person from £24; bar food £5-11),* run by friendly folk, is a former coaching inn 100m north of the clapper bridge. Check out the stag with the eyepatch!

Lydgate House Hotel (☎ *880209, fax 880202;* |e| *lydgatehouse@email.com; en- suite B&B per person from £35)* is a delightful place a quarter of a mile from the village centre overlooking an attractive, sheltered valley. Try the cream tea (£4.20) even if you're not staying here.

At **Warren House Inn** (☎ *880208; dinner mains £6-11)* you can warm yourself by a fire claimed to have been burning continuously since 1845. There's real ale, pub food, including home-made rabbit pie (£6.20), and more substantial dishes in the evening. It's 2 miles (3km) northeast of Postbridge, along the B3212 towards Moretonhampstead.

Getting There & Away

Bus No 82 runs through Postbridge between Plymouth (one hour) and Exeter (1½ hours). Bus No 98 runs to Tavistock daily (40 minutes).

BUCKFASTLEIGH
☎ 01364 • pop 2800

At the park's southeastern edge, Buckfastleigh is a pleasant old market town near

DEVON & CORNWALL

the valley of the upper Dart. Nearby is Buckfast Abbey, Britain's last working monastery.

For centuries Buckfastleigh made its money manufacturing woollen cloth. In the graveyard of the parish church, in a heavy tomb built by villagers to ensure he could not rise, lies Sir Richard Cabell, the most hated man in Dartmoor. When this evil landowner died in the 17th century, it's said that black phantom hounds were seen speeding across the moor to howl beside his grave.

Buckfast Abbey

Buckfast Abbey (☎ 645500; W www.buckfast .org.uk; admission free), 2 miles (3km) north of Buckfastleigh, was founded in 1016 and flourished on wool money in the Middle Ages, but was abandoned after the dissolution of the monasteries in 1539. In 1806 the ruins were levelled and a mock-Gothic mansion erected; the house was purchased in 1882 by a group of exiled French Benedictine monks. The abbey church was built between 1906 and 1938 by the monks, and an impressive, modern, stained-glass figure of Christ dominates the eastern chapel.

The abbey is a popular tourist attraction, and the successful shop sells only products of monasteries and convents, including the famous Buckfast Tonic Wine – you never knew monks were so busy.

Places to Stay & Eat

Holne Barn (☎ 631544; barn bunk beds from £3.50) is about 3 miles (5km) northwest of Buckfastleigh.

Furzeleigh Mill Hotel (☎/fax 643476; e enquiries@furzeleigh.co.uk; Old Ashburton Rd, Dartbridge; singles/doubles from £35.50/ 56) is a 16th-century country hotel on the road to Ashburton. Solid pub fare runs from £8 to £14.

Abbey Inn (☎ 642343; e enquiries@abbey -inn.co.uk; 30 Buckfast Rd, Buckfast; B&B en-suite singles/doubles £35/60) is in a shady spot by the river, just 500m from the abbey. There's a good menu featuring fresh fish and vegetarian options (£7 to £16), with cheaper bar snacks.

Getting There & Away

Bus No 39/X39 runs between Plymouth (45 minutes) and Exeter (1¼ hours) via Buckfastleigh (eight daily Monday to Saturday, six Sunday).

Steam trains of the private **South Devon Railway** (☎ 0845 345 1420; W www.south devonrailway.org) run to Totnes (adult/child return £6.80/4, 30 minutes, at least four daily Easter to October).

WIDECOMBE-IN-THE-MOOR
☎ 01364 • elevation 337m

With its village green, quaint cottages and fine 14th-century granite church known as the Cathedral in the Moor, Widecombe is one of the most comely settlements; Uncle Tom Cobbleigh and all still flock here, and not just on the second Tuesday of September when the fair, commemorated in the folk song Widdicombe Fair, takes place.

There's a **Visitor Information Point** at Sexton's Cottage, adjacent to the Church House. Built in 1537 as a brewhouse, the Church House is now the village hall.

Cockingford Farm Campsite (☎ 621258; tent sites per person £2.50), 1½ miles (2.5km) south of Widecombe, is open mid-March to mid-November.

Dartmoor Expedition Centre (☎ 621249; e earle@clara.co.uk; Rowden; tent sites per person £3, bunkhouse per person £7.50, twins or doubles £18) is about 1½ miles (2.5km) outside Widecombe. There are two private rooms as well as the bunkhouses, and a range of activities is organised.

Great Houndtor (☎ 01647-221202; bunk barn beds £3.75) is a YHA camping barn off the A382 near Manaton, between Widecombe and Moretonhampstead.

Friendly **Little Meadow** (☎ 621236; per person £18.50) offers B&B in a comfortable cottage. Bathrooms are shared.

MORETONHAMPSTEAD
☎ 01647 • elevation 169m

The market town of Moretonhampstead is pleasant enough, with its unusual two-storey almshouses, but is mainly of interest as an accommodation centre and gateway to the eastern moor.

Just inside the park's northeastern border, 4½ miles (7km) east of Moretonhampstead along the B3212, is **Steps Bridge YHA Hostel** (☎ 0870 770 6048, fax 252948; adult/child £7.20/4.95; open daily Apr-Sept). Bus Nos 82 and 359 run to Moretonhampstead (15 minutes) and Exeter (40 minutes).

Family-run, eco-friendly **Sparrowhawk Backpackers** (☎ 440318; e darran@mclane

*.freeserve.co.uk; Belgrave House, 45 Ford St;
dorm beds adult/child £10/5, family room
£30)* has a well-converted barn dorm and a
pleasant courtyard area for summer chilling.

Cookshayes *(☎ 440374;* e *cookshayes@
eurobell.co.uk; 33 Court St; with/without en
suite from £22/19)* is a quality B&B; there's
a four-poster if you're feeling medieval.

Bus No 82 runs to Princetown (40 minutes), Plymouth (1½ hours) and Exeter (50
minutes). Bus No 359 also goes to Exeter
(six daily Monday to Saturday).

CHAGFORD
☎ 01647 • elevation 148m

Sitting peacefully above the River Teign,
Chagford has an interesting pepper-pot market house on its square and is a handy base
for the northeastern moor. In the 14th century
it was a Stannary town, where locally mined
tin was weighed and checked, and taxes paid.

Three Crowns Hotel *(☎ 433444, fax
433117;* e *threecrowns@msn.com; High St;
B&B per person from £35)*, a pretty inn dating from the 13th century, is opposite the
church. Dinner (mains £12.50 to £16) features duck, fish and local lamb.

22 Mill St *(☎ 432244; en-suite doubles
£50; 2/3-course dinner £19.50/25.50)* is the
place for fine-dining fanatics: accommodation is only available to those who are indulging in the quality modern cuisine,
heavy on game and fish.

Bus No 173 goes to Moretonhampstead
(15 minutes) and Exeter (one hour) five
times daily, Monday to Saturday. Bus No
179 provides a daily service to Okehampton
(£2 return, 40 minutes).

CASTLE DROGO
This medieval-looking granite fortification
(NT; ☎ *01647-433306; admission £5.70;
open 11am-5.30pm Sat-Thur Apr-Oct)* was
designed by Sir Edwin Lutyens and constructed between 1910 and 1930 for self-
made millionaire Julius Drewe. Clearly, if
you're going to build a castle, it should be
comfortable and elegant! Almost more impressive than the stylish interior are the expansive Dartmoor views.

Castle Drogo is 2 miles (3km) northeast
of Chagford. Bus No 173 goes to Moretonhampstead (30 minutes) and Exeter (50 minutes) five times daily, Monday to Saturday.

Letterboxing

If you see a walker furtively slip an old Tupperware box into a tree stump or under a rock, you may
be witnessing someone in the act of letterboxing. This wacky pastime has more than 10,000 addicts
and involves a never-ending treasure hunt for several thousand 'letterboxes' hidden all over Dartmoor.

In 1844 the railway line reached Exeter, and Dartmoor started to receive visitors, for whom this
was a chance to imagine themselves as great explorers. One guide for these intrepid Victorian gen-
tlefolk was James Perrott of Chagford. In 1854 he had the idea of getting them to leave their calling cards in a glass jar at Cranmere Pool, the most remote part of the moor accessible at that time.
It was not until 1938 that the second 'box' was established, and the idea really took off after WWII.
Originally, people left their card with a stamped addressed envelope in a box and if someone else
found it they would send it back.

There are now about 4000 boxes, each with a visitors' book for you to sign and a stamp and ink
pad (if they haven't been stolen) to stamp your record book. Although it's technically illegal to leave
a 'letterbox' (because in effect you're leaving rubbish on the moor), as long as the boxes are un-
obtrusive, most landowners tolerate them. Now there are even German, French, Belgian and American boxes, not to mention 'mobile boxes', odd characters who wander the moors waiting for a
fellow letterboxer to approach them with the words 'Are you a travelling stamp?'!

Once you've collected 100 stamps, you can apply to join the '100 Club', whereupon you'll be
sent a clue book with map references for other boxes. Contact **Godfrey Swinscow** *(☎ 015488-
21325; Cross Farm, Diptford, Totnes, Devon TQ9 7NU)* for more information.

Inevitably, as more people go letterboxing, problems (other than general nerdiness) arise. A code
of conduct now prohibits letterboxers from disturbing rocks, vegetation or archaeological sites. Even
so, there have been mutterings about the disturbance caused to nesting golden plovers and ring ouzels.

OKEHAMPTON

☎ 01837 • pop 4800 • elevation 311m

Off the A30 just north of the national park, busy little Okehampton has accommodation and is a good base for walks in the northern part of the moor. This region is within the MOD's firing area; phone to check it's open. The part of the park to the south of Belstone, outside the MOD zone, is also good.

The TIC (☎ 53020, fax 55225; e oketic@ visit.org.uk; Museum Courtyard, 3 West St; open 10am-5pm Mon-Sat Easter-Oct, plus Sun May-Sept, 10am-5pm Mon, Fri & Sat Nov-Easter) can help book accommodation.

Things to See & Do

A Norman motte and ruined keep is all that remains of Devon's largest castle (EH; ☎ 52844; adult/child £2.50/1.30; open 10am-6pm daily Apr-Sept, 10am-5pm Oct); a free audioguide fills in the missing parts, and it's a fine picnic spot.

The Museum of Dartmoor Life (☎ 52295; West St; adult/child £2/1; open 10am-5pm Mon-Sat Easter-Oct, plus Sun June-Sept, 10am-4pm Mon-Fri Nov-Easter) has exhibits on the history and prehistory of the moor, and interesting displays on the life and work of its inhabitants.

It's a pleasant three- to four-hour walk along the Tarka Trail from Okehampton to Sticklepath, where the Finch Foundry (NT; ☎ 840046; admission £3; open 11am-5.30pm Wed-Mon Apr-Oct) has three working water wheels. Ask at the TIC for information on this hike. Bus Nos X9 and X10 link Sticklepath with Okehampton (10 minutes).

Places to Stay & Eat

Yertiz Caravan & Camping Park (☎ 52281; e yertiz@dial.pipex.com; Exeter Rd; 1 person/2 people & tent £4/7) is three-quarters of a mile (1km) east of Okehampton on the B3260.

Sticklepath Halt (☎ 840359; bunk barn beds £3.75) is a YHA camping barn, formerly a bakery, in the centre of Sticklepath village.

Okehampton YHA Hostel (☎ 0870 770 5978, fax 53965; e okehampton@yha.org.uk; Klondyke Rd; dorm beds adult/child £11.25/8, camping £5.70/4) is a funky converted goods shed at the train station. It's also an activity centre with its own climbing wall.

Meadowlea (☎ 53200; 65 Station Rd; en-suite doubles from £42) is a comfortable, central B&B.

Fountain Hotel (☎ 53900; Fore St; en-suite singles/doubles £45/60) is a delightful 15th-century coaching inn with good pub grub (steak and kidney pudding £6); its smarter Riverside Restaurant serves duck and mussels (around £10).

Getting There & Away

National Express coaches run from Exeter (£4.40 economy return, one hour, hourly) and London (£34.50, five hours, daily).

Bus No X9 runs to Bude (one hour), while No X10 goes to Boscastle (45 minutes); both also run to Exeter (one hour). Buses are roughly hourly Monday to Saturday; on Sunday No X9 runs four times each way. Bus No 86 runs to Plymouth (1¾ hours, hourly Monday to Saturday) and Barnstaple (1½ hours, every two hours Monday to Saturday); there are only two each way on Sunday.

Four trains run from Exeter Central to Okehampton on Sunday (£5.50 Day Rover, 45 minutes). More interesting is the steam Dartmoor Railway (☎ 55637) that runs south to Meldon Viaduct in the park (adult/child return £7/5, 10 minutes, five daily Monday to Saturday, nine Sunday May to October). Note that the service doesn't run daily except during August: phone for details.

LYDFORD

☎ 01822 • elevation 309m

A secluded village on the western edge of the moor, there's evidence of both Celtic and Saxon settlements and the remains of a square Norman castle keep (EH; admission free; open any reasonable time), which later acted as the Stannary courthouse and jail. Courts trying recalcitrant tin workers were particularly harsh; it was said that perpetrators would be hanged in the morning and tried in the afternoon.

Lydford is best known for the 1½-mile (2.5km) Lydford Gorge (NT; ☎ 820320; admission £3.70; open 10am-5.30pm daily Apr-Sept, 10am-4pm Oct, 10.30am-3pm Nov-Mar). An attractive but strenuous riverside walk leads to the 28m-high White Lady waterfall and past a series of bubbling whirlpools, including the Devil's Cauldron.

There's a riding stable (☎ 820321) in the grounds of the Lydford House Hotel (see Places to Stay & Eat following), which charges £13/22.50 for one/two hours for nonresidents.

A 5-mile (8km) walk leads to one of Dartmoor's best-known monuments, the **Widgery Cross** on Brat Tor, erected for Queen Victoria's golden jubilee in 1887. The scenery along the way is classic Dartmoor, rugged and windswept.

Places to Stay & Eat

Lydford Camping & Caravanning Club Site (☎ 820275; per person from £3.40; open late Mar-Oct) is in the village; turn off at the war memorial.

Fox & Hounds (☎ 820206; Bridestowe; bunk barn beds £3.75) has a camping barn 2 miles (3km) north of Lydford. There are no cooking facilities, but the pub serves food.

The 16th-century **Castle Inn** (☎ 820241, fax 820454; e castleinnlyd@aol.com; en-suite B&B singles/doubles £25/79), beside the castle, is a good place to stay, an atmospheric place for a pint and an excellent place to eat, offering great fish dishes and real ale.

Lydford House Hotel (☎ 820347, fax 820442; e relax@lydfordhouse.co.uk; en-suite B&B singles/doubles from £37.50/73), on the edge of the village, is a Victorian stone house built for Dartmoor artist William Widgery. A good three-course meal (think game pie) costs £16.50.

Getting There & Away

Bus No 86 runs to Tavistock (30 minutes), Okehampton (20 minutes), Barnstaple (1½ hours) and Plymouth (1½ hours), at least every two hours Monday to Saturday (only twice Sunday). Bus Nos 118 and 187 go to Tavistock (25 minutes) and Okehampton (30 minutes) six times a day on Sunday in the summer; No 118 is usually a vintage 1960s double-decker with conductor.

TAVISTOCK

☎ 01822 • pop 10,200 • elevation 123m

A pleasant western gateway to the park, Tavistock's copper-based wealth peaked in the late 19th century. Much earlier (and before Henry VIII intervened), Tavistock Abbey controlled huge areas of Devon and Cornwall; only slight ruins remain. A wander through the **Pannier Market** (☎ 611003; Bedford Square; 9am-4pm Tues-Sat) behind the town hall, first held in 1105, can be rewarding.

The **TIC** (☎ 612938, fax 618389; e tavistocktic@visit.org.uk; Bedford Square; open 9.30am-5pm Mon-Sat Easter-Oct, 9.30am-4.30pm Mon, Tues, Fri & Sat Nov-Easter) has some Dartmoor information and maps but mainly deals with town inquiries.

Bikes can be rented from **Tavistock Cycles** (☎ 617630; Paddons Row, Brook St) for £12 per day.

Bus No 86 runs to Barnstaple (two hours) and Plymouth (one hour) roughly hourly Monday to Saturday, twice on Sunday. First Bus Nos 83, 84 and 86 run to Plymouth around three times an hour.

Cornwall

Metaphorically and literally out on a limb stretching west into the Atlantic, there's not just one but three Cornwalls. The coastal land you'll see on the cover of holiday brochures – broad white beaches, subtropical gardens and fine surf – is the one that attracts visitors in droves and keeps resorts like Newquay and Bude packed each summer.

Then there's historic Kernow, a Celtic homeland with legends of piskies (fairies), mermaids, oddly named saints and the lore of King Arthur. Stone Age peoples from 4500 BC gave way to Bronze Age settlements, and menhirs and burial grounds can still be seen scattered around the landscape. Celtic dominance held strong for thousands of years; the Romans largely left Cornwall alone and prevented invasion from other parts of the country. It's only in the past two or three centuries that mainland culture has blended in, with the Cornish language fading away 200 years ago.

Finally, there's the industrial land that thrived on tin mining until the mines became too deep and expensive and the industry died; Cornwall's flag is that of St Piran, patron saint of miners. Cornish people travelled and settled abroad to find mining work, and even today there's a severe unemployment problem, especially in winter when seasonal tourist work evaporates.

You'll certainly appreciate walking the rugged cliffs, sunbathing on beaches and visiting quaint fishing villages, and it's still possible to sidestep the crowds. You may not be regaled with Celtic legends by jovial Cornish publicans but you can catch a glimpse of the county's prehistoric legacy and its mining heritage, which are well worth seeking out.

When Did Cornish Die?

A Celtic language akin to Welsh, Cornish was used west of the Tamar until the 19th century. Written evidence indicates that it was still widely spoken at the time of the Reformation but suppressed after a Cornish uprising against the English in 1548. By the 17th century only a few people living in the peninsula's remote western reaches still claimed it as their mother tongue.

Towards the end of the 18th century linguistic scholars foresaw the death of Cornish and scoured the peninsula for people who still spoke it. One such scholar, Daines Barrington, visited Mousehole in 1768 and recorded an elderly woman called Dolly Pentreath abusing him in Cornish for presuming she couldn't speak her own language.

Dolly died in 1769 and has gone down in history as the last native speaker of Cornish. However, Barrington knew of other people who continued to speak it into the 1790s, and an 1891 tombstone in Zennor commemorates one John Davey as 'the last to possess any traditional considerable knowledge of the Cornish language'.

Recently efforts have been made to revive the language, including a film, *Bitter Sweet* (2002), spoken entirely in Cornish. Unfortunately there are now three conflicting varieties of 'Cornish' (Unified, Phonemic and Traditional), so reintroduction could prove tricky. You can find out more on **w** www.clas.demon.co.uk.

Orientation & Information

The long boot of the southwest's leg, Cornwall is a little over 50 miles (80km) wide at its broadest, near the Devon border, and it's only 77 miles (123km) from Penzance to Plymouth, just across the Tamar from Cornwall: you're never far from the coast and the main attractions.

In addition to town TICs, tourism is coordinated by districts, most of which publish handy brochures with accommodation listings, and have good websites.

There are several websites that are particularly useful. The **Cornwall Tourist Board** website (**w** www.cornwalltouristboard.co.uk) isn't visually exciting (it's really aimed at the travel trade) but has handy accommodation listings and excellent links. **The Guide** (**w** www.cata.co.uk) lists details of virtually all the places to visit, helpfully divided into categories such as industrial heritage and maritime attractions. **Cornwall Online** (**w** www.cornwall-online.co.uk) is another good planning resource.

Getting Around

For information about buses, there's an efficient **helpline** (☎ 01872-322142). The main bus operator is **First Western National** (☎ 01209-719988).

If you're taking the train, phone **rail information** (☎ 0845 748 4950). The main route from London ends in Penzance but there are branch lines to St Ives, Falmouth, Newquay and Looe. The Cornish Rover allows three days' travel in a week (£25.50 mid-May to mid-September, £18 mid-September to mid-May) or eight days' travel in 15 days (£40.50 mid-May to mid-September, £33 mid-September to mid-May); there's a 34% discount for children and railcard holders.

TICs stock the county council's annual *Public Transport Timetable* (with a map; free), listing all the air, bus, rail and ferry options in Cornwall.

Various tour companies operate trips to Cornwall. **Road Trip** (☎ 0845 200 6791; **w** www.roadtrip.co.uk) runs the 2½-day Cornwall Connection bus tour for £109, including transport, accommodation and some meals, and visits Exeter, Newquay, Land's End, St Ives and most of the key attractions.

SOUTHEAST CORNWALL

With its mild climate, traditional fishing villages and gently rolling landscape, southeast Cornwall is a more mellow, agricultural area than the wilder central and northern parts, although the coastal villages get packed in summer. Naturally verdant and with wonderful flowers in spring, the area is home to several stunning gardens and many plants that thrive nowhere else in England grow here. TICs stock the free *Gardens of Cornwall* map and guide with full details.

The district has its own website at **w** www.southeastcornwall.co.uk.

Gardens of Southeast Cornwall

It seems flippant to use the word 'garden' to describe the **Eden Project** (☎ 01726-811911;

w *www.edenproject.com; Bodelva; adult/child £9.80/4; open 10am-6pm daily Apr-Oct, 10am-4.30pm Nov-Mar).* Set in a disused china-clay pit, its two huge (10m high) geodesic domes are vast, space-age greenhouses containing two biomes: the Humid Topics biome is effectively an indoor rainforest, while the Warm Temperate biome is based on environments like South Africa and California, with citrus fruit and cork trees. The third biome consists of terraced plant beds outside the domes, with more familiar species. It's impressive and immensely popular: crowds (and queues) can be large, so avoid peak times if possible.

Eden is about 3 miles (5km) northeast of St Austell. Bus No T9 connects with trains at St Austell (adult/child day return £4.15/ 2.10, or combined Eden admission and return fare £12.50/5.75, hourly).

Another renowned attraction is **Heligan** *(☎ 01726-845100; adult/child £6/3; open 10am-6pm daily summer, 10am-5pm daily winter),* 4 miles (6km) south of St Austell. Often known as the Lost Gardens, they were abandoned by the start of the 20th century and lay neglected for many years before an ambitious restoration cultivated impressive jungles, pleasure gardens and glasshouses.

At the head of the Fal estuary, **Trelissick Garden** *(NT; ☎ 01872-862090; Feock; admission £4.50; open 10.30am-5.30pm or dusk Mon-Sat, 12.30pm-5.30pm Sun mid-Feb–Oct)* has panoramic views and superb rhododendrons, hydrangeas and tree ferns. It's 4 miles (6km) south of Truro.

Cotehele

One of Britain's finest Tudor manor houses, Cotehele *(NT; ☎ 01579-351346; St Dominick; admission £6.40, garden & mill only £3.60; open 11am-5pm Sat-Thur Apr-Oct)* was built between 1485 and 1627 and was the Edgcumbe family home for centuries. The hall is particularly impressive, and many rooms are hung with fine tapestries; because of their fragility, there's no electric lighting. Outside are lovely terraced gardens.

Cotehele Quay is part of the National Maritime Museum and has a small museum with displays on local boat-building and river trade. The *Shamrock*, the last surviving River Tamar barge, is moored nearby.

Cotehele Mill is a 15-minute walk away and can be seen in operation.

Cotehele is 7 miles (11km) southwest of Tavistock on the western bank of the Tamar. You can get to Calstock, 1 mile from Cotehele, from Tavistock on bus No 79.

East & West Looe

☎ 01503 • pop 5000

The twin villages of Looe are linked by a seven-arched Victorian bridge. England's second-largest fishing port, Looe is still very much a working community as well as attracting beachgoers and shark-fishers – on summer weekends it's *very* busy.

East Looe is the main part of the town, with narrow streets and little cottages; the wide, sandy beach is to the east. There are boat trips from the quay to tiny Looe Island, a nature reserve, and to Fowey and Polperro.

The **TIC** *(☎ 262072, fax 265426; Fore St; open 10am-5pm Mon-Sat, 2pm-5pm Sun Apr-Sept, 10am-2pm Mon-Fri Oct-Mar)* is in the Guildhall.

The **South East Cornwall Discovery Centre** *(☎ 262777; Mill Pool, West Looe; admission free; open 10am-5pm Sun-Fri Jul & Aug, 10am-4pm Mon-Fri, 11am-3pm Sun Mar-Jun & Sept-Dec)* houses the **Oceana** exhibition, an impressive interactive insight into the Cornish coastline.

Monkey Sanctuary *(☎ 262532; **w** www .monkeysanctuary.org; St Martins; adult/child £4/2; open 11am-4.30pm Sun-Thur Easter-Sept)* is home to a colony of unfeasibly cute woolly monkeys, rescued from various uncomfortable cages.

An excellent 5-mile (8km) walk (part of the South West Coast Path) links Looe to nearby Polperro via beaches, cliffs and the old smuggling village of Talland. You should allow around two hours; buses connect the villages every day in summer.

If you fancy catching Jaws, contact **MarineCo** *(☎ 265444; Buller Quay, East Looe)* for details of shark-fishing trips (from £28 per person, depending on the boat).

Trains travel the scenic Looe Valley Line from Liskeard (£2.60 Cheap Day return, 30 minutes, eight daily Monday to Saturday), on the main London–Penzance line.

Polperro

Prettier than Looe, Polperro is another ancient fishing village, a picturesque jumble of narrow lanes and fishing cottages around

DEVON & CORNWALL

a tiny harbour, best approached along the coastal path from Looe or Talland. It's very popular with day-trippers so visit in the evening or during the low season.

Polperro was once heavily involved in pilchard fishing by day and smuggling by night; the small **Heritage Museum** *(☎ 01503-272423; The Warren; adult/child £1/50p; open 10am-6pm daily Easter-Oct)* features 17th-century smuggling memorabilia.

Fowey
☎ 01726 • pop 1900

With its graceful terraces and tiny alleys overlooking the estuary of the same name, Fowey (pronounced foy) is almost like a mini St Ives. It has a long maritime history, and in the 14th century conducted raids on French and Spanish coastal towns. This led to a Spanish attack on Fowey in 1380; for defence, Henry VIII later built **St Catherine's Castle** *(EH; admission free; open daily)*, the remains of which overlook Readymoney Beach south of the centre. The town later prospered by shipping Cornish china clay, although yachts mainly fill its harbour today. Stop to check out the fine Norman front of **St Fimbarrus Church**, founded in the 6th century but upgraded in 1336 and 1460.

The **TIC** *(☎ 833616, fax 834939; e info@fowey.co.uk; 4 Custom House Hill; open 9am-5.30pm Mon-Fri, 9am-5pm Sat, 10am-5pm Sun Easter-Sept, closes Sun & 12.30pm Sat Oct-Easter)* is in the post office.

Fowey is at the southern end of the Saints' Way, a 26-mile (42km) waymarked trail running to Padstow on the northern coast. It's also a pleasant base for short walks south around the estuary. Ferries cross the river to Bodinnick (50p) every few minutes to access the 4-mile (6km) Hall Walk to Polruan, from where ferries sail back to Fowey (70p).

Golant YHA Hostel *(☎ 0870 770 5832, fax 832947; e golant@yha.org.uk; Penquite House; adult/child £11.25/8; open Feb-Oct)* is a substantial Georgian house overlooking the estuary 4 miles (6km) north of Fowey. Bus No 24 from St Austell (40 minutes, every 30 minutes) stops in Castle Dore, 1½ miles (2.5km) from the hostel.

The Globe Posting House Hotel *(☎ 833322; e theglobefowey@yahoo.com; 19 Fore St; B&B per person from £15)* is a good deal, as it's a small, friendly place

right in the centre of town with an excellent seafood bistro.

The Ship Inn *(☎ 839431, fax 834935; Trafalgar Square; B&B doubles with/without en suite £55/40)* was built in 1570 by local legend John Rashleigh; it's got bar snacks, good St Austell beer and charm in buckets.

Boutique **Marina Hotel** *(☎ 833315, fax 832779; e themarinahotel@dial.pipex.com; The Esplanade; B&B per person from £58; mains £16-26)* has style, fantastic views, and a seriously talented chef cooking fish and seafood.

Bus No 24 from St Austell (45 minutes, every 30 minutes) runs to Fowey and also passes Par, the closest train station.

Lanhydrock House
Amid parkland above the River Fowey, Lanhydrock *(NT; ☎ 01208-73320; house admission £7, garden & grounds only £3.80; house open 11am-5.30pm Tues-Sun Apr-Sept, 11am-5pm Tues-Sun Oct, garden open 10am-6pm daily year round)* was a substantial 16th-century manor devastated by a fire in 1881 but rebuilt in sympathetic style. A magnificent plaster ceiling depicts Old Testament scenes in the 17th-century Long Gallery, which survived the fire, but the house is mainly of interest for its portrayal of *Upstairs Downstairs* life in Victorian England. The kitchens are particularly fascinating, complete with gadgets that were mod cons 100 years ago.

Lanhydrock is 2½ miles (4km) southeast of Bodmin. Bus No 55 runs from Bodmin Parkway train station, 1¾ miles (3km) from Lanhydrock.

Restormel Castle
Perched on a high mound overlooking the River Fowey, 1½ miles north of Lostwithiel, the Norman keep of this ruined 13th-century castle *(☎ 01208-872687; adult/child £1.90/1; open 10am-6pm daily Apr-Sept, 10am-5pm daily Oct)* gives spectacular views over the countryside; you can see why Edward, the Black Prince, chose it as his home.

Charlestown
☎ 01726

Despite its size, St Austell isn't particularly exciting. However, it's worth making a detour to the little port of Charlestown, a marvellously picturesque village and harbour built by Charles Rashleigh between 1790 and 1815. On occasion the harbour is filled with magnificent square-rigged ships.

The **Shipwreck & Heritage Centre** (☎ 69897; w www.shipwreckcharlestown.com; adult/child £4.95/free; open 10am-5pm daily Mar-Oct) exhibits artefacts from over 150 shipwrecks and has fascinating displays of diving equipment dating back to 1740, as well as illustrating aspects of 19th-century Cornish village life with animated models.

T'Gallants (☎ 70203; 6 Charlestown Rd; en-suite singles/doubles £30/45) is an elegant Georgian B&B with a pleasant tea garden.

Pier House Hotel (☎ 67955, fax 69246; e pierhouse@cornwall-county.com; en-suite B&B singles/doubles from £45/70), right on the quayside, was originally two farm cottages; now it's a comfortable hotel with a good restaurant.

Bus No 31 makes the short hop from St Austell hourly.

TRURO
☎ 01872 • pop 19,000
Made wealthy by the distribution of Cornish tin, Truro is the county's administrative centre and a surprisingly lively place to visit, despite the paucity of attractions. Lemon St has some fine Georgian architecture, and the relatively recent (late-19th-century) **cathedral** is worth a look; built in neogothic style, it was the first new cathedral to be built in England since St Paul's in London.

The **TIC** (☎ 274555, fax 263031; w www .truro.gov.uk/pages/welcome.html; Municipal Buildings, Boscawen St; open 9am-5.30pm Mon-Fri, 9am-5pm Sat) is near the covered market. **Guided tours** (☎ 271257), costing £3/1.50 per adult/child, depart from the TIC at 11am every Wednesday.

The **Royal Cornwall Museum** (☎ 272205; w www.royalcornwallmuseum.org.uk; River St; adult/child £3/2; open 10am-5pm Mon-Sat), the county's largest, has exhibits on Cornish history and archaeology, as well as excellent displays of ceramics and minerals. Its extensive fine-art collection includes pieces by Constable, Caravaggio and Blake.

Places to Stay & Eat
The Fieldings (☎ 262783; e averil@fieldings intruro.com; 35 Treyew Rd; B&B singles/ doubles from £18/32) is a pleasant Edwardian house with good views of the town.

Inside its imposing Georgian exterior, the **Royal Hotel** (☎ 270345, fax 242453; e re ception@royalhotelcornwall.co.uk; Lemon St; singles/doubles from £59/80) is chic and modern; its excellent **Mannings Restaurant** (mains £7-17) cooks up good seafood and steak.

Saffron (☎ 263771; Quay St; mains £7-10.50; closed Sun & Mon evening) serves interesting seafood specials such as roast Porbeagle shark and spider crab chowder.

MI Bar (☎ 277214; Lemon Quay; mains £5-8) is a zippy café-bar with decent tapas and terrace seating.

Old Ale House (☎ 271122; Quay St; bar meals £4.50-6.50) is a low-ceilinged pub with generously sized snacks and fine ales.

Getting There & Away
Truro is 246 miles (394km) from London, 26 miles (42km) from St Ives and 18 miles (29km) from Newquay.

Many National Express services require a change at Plymouth. There are direct coaches to London (£41 economy return, seven hours, four daily), Penzance (£4.75, 1½ hours, five daily) and St Ives (£4, one hour, two daily).

Truro is on the main rail line between London Paddington (£63 saver return, 4¾ hours, every two hours) and Penzance (£11.80, 45 minutes, every two hours). There's a branch line to Falmouth (£2.30 single, 20 minutes, every two hours Monday to Saturday).

ROSELAND PENINSULA
South of Truro, the lovely Roseland Peninsula gets its intriguing name not from flowers (although there are plenty) but from the Cornish word ros, meaning promontory. Head for coastal villages such as **Portloe**, a wreckers' hang-out on the South West Coast Path, or **Veryan**, awash with daffodils in spring and entered between two thatched roundhouses.

St Mawes has an unusual clover-leaf-plan **castle** (EH; ☎ 01326-270526; adult/child £2.90/1.50; open 10am-6pm daily Apr-Sept, 10am-5pm daily Oct, 10am-1pm & 2pm-4pm Wed-Sun Nov-Mar), the best preserved of Henry VIII's coastal fortresses.

St Just-in-Roseland boasts what must be one of the most beautiful churchyards in the country, full of flowers and tumbling down to a creek with boats and wading birds.

SOUTHWEST CORNWALL
Falmouth
☎ 01326 • pop 20,300

Falmouth is a seaside resort, a working dock and a student town, and these three elements combine well: there's plenty to see and do but it's not merely a tourist ghetto and it has a lively vibe. The port came to prominence in the 17th century as the terminal for the Post Office Packet boats taking mail to America. The dockyard is still important for repairs and shipbuilding.

The **TIC** (☎ 312300, fax 313457; **w** www .falmouth-cornwall.org; 28 Killigrew St; open 9.30am-5.30pm Mon-Sat Apr-Sept, Mon-Fri Oct-Mar, plus 10am-2pm Sun Jul & Aug) is opposite the bus terminal.

Things to See & Do On the end of the promontory is **Pendennis Castle** (EH; ☎ 316594; admission £4; open 10am-6pm daily Apr-Sept, 10am-5pm daily Oct, 10am-4pm daily Nov-Mar), Cornwall's largest, with superb views from the ramparts. The hands-on Discovery Centre explores the castle's 450-year history, while the sights, sounds and smells of battle are recreated in the gun tower, with cannons firing and gunsmoke billowing.

The impressive **National Maritime Museum** (☎ 313388, fax 317878; **w** nmmc.co.uk; Discovery Quay; adult/child £5.90/3.90; open 10am-5pm daily Feb-Dec) opened by the docks in late 2002. The Flotilla Gallery houses up to 40 boats from the large national collection, while the Cornwall Galleries cover the county's shipbuilding, fishing and seafaring history.

From the Prince of Wales pier, **King Harry Ferries** (☎ 862312; car/person £3.50/20p) cross to St Mawes every 20 minutes. In summer, boat trips run to a 500-year-old smuggler's cottage upriver (around £3) and on to Truro (around £6/3 adult/child return, one hour). The pier is lined with boat companies' booths; try **Enterprise Boats** (☎ 374 241) or **Cornish Belle** (☎ 01872-850309).

Places to Stay & Eat B&Bs and small hotels line Melvill Rd and Avenue Rd near the train station.

Trevoil Guest House (☎ 314145; 25 Avenue Rd; singles/en-suite doubles £17/38) is a friendly, simple B&B just back from the harbour.

Chellowdene (☎ 314950; Gyllingvase Hill; en-suite B&B per person from £20) is an unusual character house overlooking Falmouth Bay and Gyllingvase Beach.

Entering 19th-century **De Wynn's** (☎ 219259; Church St; open 10am-5pm Mon-Sat, 11am-4pm Sun) feels as though nothing's changed since sea captains converged here 200 years ago for cakes and seafood pie (£6.50).

Pipeline (☎ 312774; 21 Church St; mains £4-8; closed Sun) dishes up Mexican, Caribbean and Italian morsels in a colourful, surfy space.

No 33 (☎ 211914; 33 High St; mains £11-15; dinner only Mon-Sat) is relaxed and rustic, but cooks up a storm with fish and seafood.

Good pubs include cosy, local **Mason Arms** (☎ 311061; 31 Killigrew St) and the nautical-themed **Chain Locker** (☎ 311685, Quay St) on the waterfront, for that genuine fishing-town feel.

Getting There & Away National Express coaches run to London (£41 economy return, eight hours, daily) and Penzance (£4.75, one hour, daily). Strangely, Cornish destinations such as St Ives and Newquay are poorly served. Bus No 2 runs to Penzance (every 30 minutes). Bus No T8 runs to Truro (£3.60 return, 1¼ hours, five daily Monday to Saturday).

Falmouth is at the end of the branch railway line from Truro (£2.30 single, 20 minutes, every two hours Monday to Saturday).

The Lizard
☎ 01326

Mainland England's most southerly point, the Lizard peninsula feels like a pleasantly remote backwater, a counterpoint to the commercial excesses of Land's End. A wonderful section of the South West Coast Path winds its way around the coastline, much of it owned by the NT. Rare plant species flourish and there are stretches of unusual red-green serpentine rock; keep an eye out for seals, sharks and dolphins. For more information on this unique area, visit **w** www.lizard-peninsula.co.uk.

In 1901 Marconi transmitted the first transatlantic radio signals from Poldhu. The Lizard is still associated with telecommunications and is dominated by the white satellite dishes of the **Goonhilly Earth Station**

(☎ 0800 679593; W www.goonhilly.bt.com; adult/child £5/3.50; open 10am-5pm daily Oct-June, 10am-6pm daily July-Sept), the largest satellite station on earth. The multimedia visitor centre explores the history of international communications.

Across the north of the Lizard flows the beautiful **River Helford**, lined with ancient oak trees and hidden inlets: the perfect smugglers' hideaway. Secluded **Frenchman's Creek**, the inspiration for Daphne Du Maurier's novel of the same name, can be reached on foot from the car park in **Helford** village.

On the northern bank of the river is **Trebah** (☎ 250448; W www.trebah-garden.co.uk; adult/child £4.50/2.50; open 10.30am-5pm daily), touted as Cornwall's 'Garden of Dreams'. First planted in 1840, it's dramatically situated in a steep ravine filled with giant rhododendrons, huge Brazilian rhubarb plants and Monterey pines.

Near Gweek, at the western end of the river 6 miles (10km) east of Helston, is the **National Seal Sanctuary** (☎ 221361; W www.sealsanctuary.co.uk/corn1.html; adult/child £7.50/4.50; open 9am-5pm daily May-Sept, 9am-4pm Oct-Apr), which cares for sick, injured and orphaned seals before returning them to the wild. There are also otters and sea lions to up the 'aww' factor.

Coverack YHA Hostel (☎ 0870 770 5780, fax 280119; Parc Behan, School Hill, Coverack; adult/child £10.25/7; open Apr-Oct) is a lonesome country house out on a limb 12 miles (19km) southeast of Helston.

Three miles (5km) west of Helston is **Porthleven**, another quaint fishing port with excellent beaches nearby.

Cadgwith is the quintessential Cornish fishing village, with thatched, whitewashed cottages and a small harbour. **Lizard Point** is a 3½-mile (6km) walk along the South West Coast Path from here.

At the peninsula's very tip are the twin towers of the **Lizard Lighthouse** (☎ 290065; adult/child £2.50/1.50; open 11am-5pm daily July & Aug, Sun-Fri June & Sept, Sun-Thur Apr, May & Oct), built in 1751 to replace an earlier erection from 1619. Guided tours take you round the engine room and to the top of the tower, offering spectacular views.

Helston The gateway to the Lizard, on 8 May Helston stages the **Furry Dance**, when the town takes to the streets in a remnant celebration of a pagan festival commemorating the coming of spring and the passing of winter. Housed in the old butter market, **Helston Folk Museum** (☎ 564027; Church St; adult/child £2/50p; open 10am-5pm Mon-Sat) tells of these strange happenings, displaying a hearty mishmash of heritage artefacts, including a 5½-ton cider press from 1750.

The **TIC** (☎ 565431, fax 572803; e info@helstontic.demon.co.uk; 79 Meneage St; open 10am-1pm & 2pm-4.30pm Mon-Fri, 10am-1pm Sat, until 4pm Sat Aug) has visitor information.

Getting There & Away The Lizard's transportation hub is Helston, served by **Truronian buses** (☎ 01872-273453; W www.truronian.co.uk). Bus No T1 runs from Truro via Helston (45 minutes) to the village of Lizard (1½ hours, roughly hourly, four Sunday). It's just under a mile from the village to Lizard Point. Bus No T2 runs from Helston to Goonhilly (20 minutes), Coverack (25 minutes) and St Keverne (40 minutes, 10 daily Monday to Saturday). Bus No T4 runs from Helston to Falmouth (70 minutes) via Gweek (25 minutes) and Trebah (45 minutes, every two hours Monday to Saturday, four Sunday). A Day Rover ticket valid on all Truronian buses costs £4.50/2.50 per adult/child.

St Michael's Mount

Perched on a rocky island and cut off from the mainland at high tide, St Michael's Mount (NT; ☎ 01736-710507; admission £4.60; open 10.30am-5.30pm Mon-Fri Apr-Oct) is impressive, its priory buildings rising loftily above the crags. Named after a fisherman's vision of the archangel Michael, in 1070 the mount was granted to the monks who built Mont St Michel off the Normandy coast and this became an important place of medieval pilgrimage. Since 1659 the St Aubyn family has lived in the ex-priory buildings. The dramatic 12th-century castle features a rococo Gothic drawing room, an armoury and the fascinating 14th-century priory church. There are also subtropical hanging gardens (admission £2.50). Last admission is at 4.45pm.

At low tide, you can walk across from Marazion but at high tide in summer there's a **ferry** (☎ 01736-710265; adult/child £1/50p).

Bus No 2 passes Marazion as it travels from Penzance to Falmouth.

DEVON & CORNWALL

PENZANCE
☎ 01736 • pop 19,700

Penzance is many things to many people: the end of the line from London, a seaside resort, a stopover for ferry passengers and a hippy chill-out zone. Objectively, it's a pleasant enough town, with pockets of interest between the shops and opportunities for diving and windsurfing.

Orientation & Information

The harbour spreads along Mount's Bay, with the ferry terminal to the east, the train and bus stations just to the north and the main beach to the south. **Newlyn**, out on the western edge of Penzance, was the centre of a community of artists in the late 19th century; these days it's one of the country's busiest fishing ports (not saying much!) and has some good restaurants and B&Bs.

The **TIC** (☎ 362207, fax 363600; e pztic@ penwith.gov.uk; Station Approach; open 9am-6pm Mon-Sat, 10am-1pm Sun May-Sept, 9am-6pm Mon-Fri, 10am-1pm Sat Oct-Apr) is in the car park by the train and bus stations. **Ghost Tours** (☎ 331206; adult/child £3/2) depart from the TIC at 8.30pm on Thursdays and Sundays, April to September (plus 10.15pm July and August).

Polyclean Laundrette (☎ 364815; 4 East Terrace; open 7.30am-7.30pm daily) doubles as an Internet café; access costs 5p/minute.

Things to See & Do

Penzance has some attractive Georgian and Regency houses in the older part of town around Chapel St, where you'll also find the exuberant early-19th-century **Egyptian House** with its bizarre, florid front.

The **Trinity House National Lighthouse Centre** (☎ 360077; Wharf Rd; adult/child £3/1; open 10.30am-4.30pm daily Apr-Oct) relates the history of lighthouses that have helped keep ships off this dangerous coast.

Fine examples of the Newlyn school of painting are exhibited in the **Penlee House Gallery & Museum** (☎ 363625; Morrab Rd; adult/child £2/free, all free Sat; open 10am-5pm Mon-Sat May-Sept, 10.30am-4.30pm Mon-Sat Oct-Apr), while the museum displays western-Cornish artefacts from the Stone Age to today.

The collection of automata at **Round the Bend** (☎ 332211; The Barbican, Battery Rd;

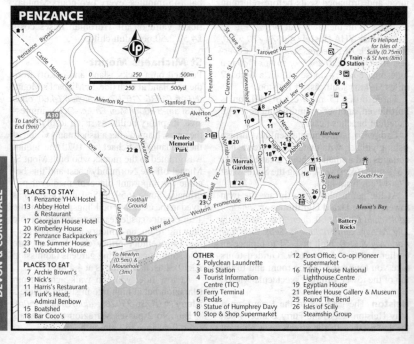

PENZANCE

PLACES TO STAY
1 Penzance YHA Hostel
13 Abbey Hotel & Restaurant
17 Georgian House Hotel
20 Kimberley House
22 Penzance Backpackers
23 The Summer House
24 Woodstock House

PLACES TO EAT
7 Archie Brown's
9 Nick's
11 Harris's Restaurant
14 Turk's Head; Admiral Benbow
15 Boatshed
18 Bar Coco's

OTHER
2 Polyclean Laundrette
3 Bus Station
4 Tourist Information Centre (TIC)
5 Ferry Terminal
6 Pedals
8 Statue of Humphrey Davy
10 Stop & Shop Supermarket
12 Post Office; Co-op Pioneer Supermarket
16 Trinity House National Lighthouse Centre
19 Egyptian House
21 Penlee House Gallery & Museum
25 Round The Bend
26 Isles of Scilly Steamship Group

DEVON & CORNWALL

adult/child £2.50/1.50; open 11am-5pm daily) is unique: an array of modern mechanical toys, sculptures and cartoons, it's bound to entertain and amaze kids (and parents).

The 25-mile (40km) section of the South West Coast Path around Land's End between Penzance and St Ives is one of the most scenic parts of the whole route. The walk can be broken at the Land's End YHA hostel at St Just-in-Penwith, and there are plenty of cheap farm B&Bs along the way.

Places to Stay

Penzance YHA Hostel *(☎ 0870 770 5992, fax 362663;* e *penzance@yha.org.uk; Castle Horneck, Alverton; adult/child £11.25/8)* is an 18th-century mansion on the outskirts of town, with great views. Bus Nos 5B, 6B and 10B run from the train station to the hostel; it's a 500m walk from the bus stop.

Penzance Backpackers *(☎ 363836;* e *pz backpack@ndirect.co.uk; The Blue Dolphin, Alexandra Rd; bunk beds £10, doubles £24)* is a friendly place and one of the cleanest hostels you'll see. Bus Nos 1, 1A, 5A and 6A go there from the TIC or train station.

Penzance's accommodation is concentrated along the Western Promenade, Alexandra Rd and Morrab Rd.

Kimberley House *(☎ 362727; 10 Morrab Rd; singles/doubles from £20/40)* is a modern, friendly B&B with a commendable absence of chintz. Most rooms have an en suite.

Woodstock House *(☎/fax 369049;* e *wood stocp@aol.com; 29 Morrab Rd; B&B per person £18-25)* is more traditional but eminently comfortable.

Close to good restaurants and pubs, **Georgian House Hotel** *(☎/fax 365664; 20 Chapel St; en-suite doubles £46)* is an elegant B&B with spacious rooms.

The Summer House *(☎ 363744, fax 360959;* e *summerhouse@dial.pipex.com; Cornwall Terrace; en-suite doubles from £65; 3-course dinner £22.50)* is a beautiful Grade-II-listed house, with superb Mediterranean-influenced cuisine.

The elegant 17th-century **Abbey Hotel** *(☎ 366906, fax 351163;* e *glyn@abbeyhotel .fsnet.co.uk; Abbey St; B&B singles/doubles from £75/100)* has sumptuous bedrooms and huge bathrooms, and there's a charming walled garden, views of St Michael's Mount and a restaurant for fine dining.

You can rent a floor of the **Egyptian House** (see Things to See & Do previously) from the **Landmark Trust** *(☎ 01628-825925);* in a three-person apartment, four-night winter breaks start at £126, while a week in summer costs from £473.

Places to Eat

The Summer House and **Abbey Hotel** *(☎ 330680)* both have excellent restaurants (see Places to Stay).

Nick's *(☎ 363814; 5 Alverton St; pizza £5-10, specials £12-15)* is a relaxed Italian restaurant with lunch-time snacks and more satisfying seafood dinners.

Archie Brown's *(☎ 362828; Bread St; mains £3-6; open 9.30am-5pm Mon-Sat)* is a popular vegetarian café just behind Market Jew St.

Chapel St hosts two well-known pubs. The cavernous, kitsch **Admiral Benbow** *(☎ 363448; 46 Chapel St; mains £7.50-16)* and the snug **Turk's Head** *(☎ 363093; 49 Chapel St; mains £7.25-13)*, both serving excellent seafood; the Admiral also has an extensive vegetarian selection.

Harris's Restaurant *(☎ 364408; 46 New St; mains £15-26; closed Sun)* is the place for seriously classy seafood. Smoked salmon cornets with fresh crab will sate the appetite.

Bar Coco's *(☎ 350222; 13 Chapel St; tapas £2-5; closed Sun)* is a flamboyant café-bar with decent tapas and Mediterranean dishes, although most come for the *cerveza* (beer).

Boatshed *(☎ 368845; Wharf Rd; mains £5-12.50)*, a modern waterside café-bar, has pizzas, seafood and an upstairs club where hip-hop and jazzy sounds rule till 2am at weekends.

Getting There & Around

Penzance is 281 miles (450km) from London, 9 miles (14km) from Land's End and 8 miles (13km) from St Ives.

National Express coaches run to London (£41 economy return, nine hours, six daily) and Heathrow airport, Bristol (£36, 6½ hours, two daily), Exeter (£22, five hours, two daily), Plymouth (£7.25, 3½ hours, seven daily), Truro (£4.75, 1½ hours, five daily), Newquay (£5.50, 1¾ hours, three daily) and St Ives (£3.25, 25 minutes, five daily). There are daily First Western National services to Land's End (one hour) on bus No 1, hourly during the week, less frequently at the weekend.

The train offers an enjoyable if pricey way to get to Penzance from London Paddington (£63 saver return, five hours, eight daily). There are a few direct trains from Penzance to St Ives (£2.80 single, 20 minutes, hourly), with connections at St Erth.

Pedals (☎ 360600; e pedalsbikes@hotmail .com; Wharf Rd; open 9am-5pm daily) rents mountain bikes (£11 for 24 hours).

WEST CORNWALL

Tourism in this area is coordinated by Penwith District Council; its website (w www .go-cornwall.com) is a useful resource.

Mousehole
☎ 01736

Once a pilchard-fishing port, cottages cluster round the edge of the harbour at Mousehole (pronounced mowsel). Described by Dylan Thomas as 'the loveliest village in England', it's certainly delightful but it's popularity is boosted by its proximity to Penzance so it's very busy in summer. Like St Ives, the village attracts artists and there are interesting craft shops.

The Old Coastguard (☎ 731222, fax 731720; e bookings@oldcoastguardhotel.co.uk; en-suite B&B singles/doubles from £35/70) is a beautifully modernised hotel, with a pleasant bar-diner overlooking the sea.

The cosy **Ship Inn** (☎ 731234; South Cliff, Mousehole; en-suite B&B singles/doubles £32.50/55; mains £7-12.50), nestled down by the harbour, does good seafood and fresh fish.

Bus Nos 5A/5B and 6A/6B run the 20-minute journey to Penzance every half-hour.

Minack Open-Air Theatre

Surely the world's most spectacularly located open-air theatre, Minack (☎ 01736-810181; performances adult £5.50-7, child £2.75-3.50) perches on the edge of the cliffs overlooking Porthcurno Bay. The **visitor centre** (adult/child £2.50/1; open 9.30am-5.30pm daily Apr-Sept, 10am-4pm Oct-Mar) recounts the story of Rowena Cade, the indomitable local woman who did much of the construction herself until her death in 1983, and the growth from a local open-air production in 1929 to the current 17-week annual season (mid-May to mid-September). The centre is closed when there's a matinee performance.

Minack is south of Porthcurno, 3 miles (5km) from Land's End and 9 miles (14km)

from Penzance. Bus No 1 from Penzance to Land's End stops at Porthcurno, Monday to Saturday.

Land's End

The coast on either side of Land's End is some of the most spectacular in England. Standing at the very tip of this island, gazing out over the vast expanse of the Atlantic Ocean, is quite a magical experience.

At least, we assume it was before the **Legendary Land's End** (☎ 0870 458 0099; w www.landsend-landmark.co.uk; open 10am-5pm daily summer, 10am-3pm winter) theme-park development began drawing in the hordes. Bring a full wallet: here, you can have your photo taken by the signboard listing your home town and its distance from this famous spot for £5, or visit 'attractions' such as the multimedia Return to the Last Labyrinth (adult/child £4/2.50) or the Air Sea Rescue experience in a moving cinema (adult/child £2.50/1.50). Tickets covering every attraction cost £10/6 per adult/child, and it costs £3 to park. On the plus-side, the complex does provide 250 jobs in an unemployment black spot.

Land's End Hotel (☎ 01736-871844, fax 871599; B&B per person from £48) is a decent enough place, and allows you to stroll around the headland once the donut sellers and munchers have departed in the evening.

Land's End is 9 miles (14km) from Penzance, 886 miles (1418km) from John o'Groats and 3147 miles (5035km) from New York. Bus No 15, usually open-top in summer, runs along the coast to St Ives (1½ hours, four daily), and bus Nos 1, 1A and 1C (one hour) run hourly from Penzance.

Westward Airways (☎ 788771) offers sightseeing flights over Land's End from the airfield at St Just; a seven-minute hop costs from £17.

Sennen
☎ 01736

Just 1½ miles northeast of Land's End are the twin settlements of Sennen and, on the coast, Sennen Cove. Sennen village has a backpackers, several B&Bs and 'England's Last Pub', while Sennen Cove boasts a sandy beach, excellent surf and fantastic ice-cream shops.

Whitesands Lodge (☎ 871776; e info@ whitesandslodge.co.uk; Sennen Village; dorm

WEST CORNWALL

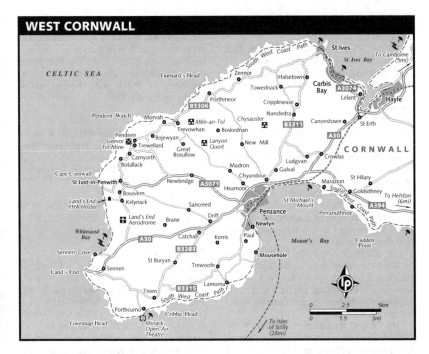

beds £10, singles/doubles from £18/36) is an excellent backpackers. There's a funky café, yoga sessions, and surfing and climbing lessons arranged by the owners.

Old Success Inn (☎ 871232, fax 871457; e oldsuccess@sennencove-fsbusiness.co.uk; Sennen Cove; en-suite B&B doubles £80), a characterful 17th-century fishermen's hostelry, serves good bar food.

At friendly **Myrtle Cottage** (☎ 871698; Old Coastguard Row, Sennen Cove; B&B per person with/without en suite from £22.50/16) all rooms have sea views and there are delicious cream teas (£2.95) and snacks.

St Just-in-Penwith
☎ 01736

The nondescript appearance of remote St Just, six miles (9km) north of Land's End, belies its past as a centre for tin and copper mining in Victorian days. **Geevor Tin Mine** (☎ 788662; w www.geevor.com; adult/child £6/3.50; open 10am-5pm Sun-Fri Easter-Oct, 10am-4pm Mon-Fri Nov-Mar) at Pendeen, north of St Just, finally closed in 1990 and is now open to visitors; claustrophobes beware the tours of tiny 18th-century mine-

shafts. St Just is also a base for walks west to Cape Cornwall or south along the South West Coast Path to Land's End.

The area between St Just and St Ives is littered with standing stones and other mysterious ancient remains alongside abandoned engine-houses. If prehistory is your thing, track down **Lanyon Quoit**, the **Mên-an-Tol** and **Chysauster Iron Age Village**.

Land's End YHA Hostel (☎ 0870 770 5906, fax 787337; Letcha Vean; adult/child £10.25/7; open daily July & Aug, Mon-Sat Apr-June, Tues-Sat Sept & Oct) is about half a mile south of the village; it's tricky to find (call for directions) but wonderfully isolated, near the coast path.

Kelynack Caravan & Camping Park (☎/fax 787633; e steve@kelynackholidays.co.uk; tent sites per person £3.50, barn bunk bed £7) is an exceptionally friendly place a mile (1.6km) south of St Just; call for a pick-up. The small bunk barn (eight beds) is clean and comfortable, with its own kitchen.

Bosavern House (☎/fax 788301; e marcol@ bosavern.u-net.com; per person with en suite from £23, tent site & 2 people £8.50; campsite open Mar-Oct; B&B year round) is a pleasant B&B with a camping area (and sinful cream teas).

Bus No 15 runs regularly from St Ives (one hour, four daily), while bus Nos 10, 10A, 10B and 11A go from Penzance (30 minutes, every 30 minutes).

Zennor
☎ 01736

A stunning 6-mile (10km) stretch of the South West Coast Path runs from St Ives to the little village of Zennor, where DH Lawrence wrote part of *Women in Love*. **St Senara's Church** dates from at least 1150. Look for the medieval carved Mermaid Chair; legend tells of a beautiful, mysterious woman who lured a chorister into the sea at Mermaid's Cove, where you can still hear them singing.

The excellent **Wayside Folk Museum** (*☎ 796945; adult/child £2.50/1.50; open 10.30am-5.30pm Sun-Fri May-Sept, 11am-5pm Sun-Fri Apr & Oct*) crams a surprising number of local-heritage artefacts into various period rooms.

Old Chapel Backpackers Hostel (*☎/fax 798307; dorm beds £10, tent sites per person £3.50; baguettes £3-4, pizza £4*) is a tidy little hostel with a fine café and a camping field.

Snug **Tinners Arms** (*☎ 792697; ploughman's lunch £5.50*) pleases with ploughman's lunches and excellent Cornish beer.

Bus Nos 8A, 8B and 15 run from St Ives (20 minutes, four daily Monday to Saturday).

ST IVES
☎ 01736 • pop 10,100

Captivating St Ives has a photogenic harbour which must have been important once but now seems almost forgotten, eclipsed by other attractions. The iridescent sea, fine beaches and steep alleyways don't just draw tourists, either. These attributes are magnetic to artists, who've been painting and sculpting here since Turner visited in 1811. In 1993 Tate St Ives, a branch of the famous art gallery, opened and countless galleries and craft shops line the streets. There are also plenty of great restaurants and guesthouses.

In summer St Ives gets unbelievably crowded: avoid July and August weekends.

Orientation
The built-up area above St Ives' harbour merges into Carbis Bay to the south. Fore

St, the main shopping strip, is set back from the wharf and crammed with eateries. The north-facing section of the town, overlooking Porthmeor Beach, hosts Tate St Ives and many guesthouses. The train station is by Porthminster Beach, with the bus station nearby up Station Hill.

Information
The **TIC** (*☎ 796297, fax 798309;* **e** *ivtic@ penwith.gov.uk; Street-an-Pol; open 9am-6pm Mon-Sat Easter-Sept, 10am-1pm Sun Easter-June & Sept, 10am-4pm Sun July & Aug, 9am-5pm Mon-Fri, 10am-1pm Sat Oct-Easter*) is in the Guildhall.

Computers Plus (*☎ 798166; 1 Chapel St; open 9am-5pm Mon-Fri, 9am-1pm Sat*) has Internet access for £2 per hour.

Tate St Ives
Opened in 1993 in a remarkable £3-million building, Tate St Ives (*☎ 796226;* **w** *www .tate.org.uk; Porthmeor Beach; adult/child £4.25/free; open 10am-5.30pm daily Mar-Oct, 10.30am-4.30pm Tues-Sun Nov-Feb*) is a showcase for the St Ives school of art; wide central windows frame the surfing scene on Porthmeor Beach below. The collection is small and exclusive, with works by Ben Nicholson, Barbara Hepworth, Naum Gabo, Terry Frost and other local artists. Changing exhibitions featuring major contemporary artists complete the picture.

The café on the roof is almost as popular as the gallery itself.

A joint ticket with the Barbara Hepworth Museum costs £6.95/3.50 per adult/child.

Barbara Hepworth Museum & Sculpture Garden
One of the 20th century's greatest sculptors, in the 1930s Barbara Hepworth, with friend Henry Moore and Ben Nicholson (her then-husband), was part of a leading group of artists with an interest in abstraction, influenced by the likes of Piet Mondrian. While Moore's sculpture tended to the human, Hepworth avoided representational styles and aimed for abstract beauty. She moved to Cornwall in 1939 and lived in St Ives from 1949 until her death in a fire in 1975.

The studio (*☎ 796226; Barnoon Hill; adult/child £3.95/free*) is maintained much as it was in the 1950s. It's managed by Tate St Ives, and has the same opening times.

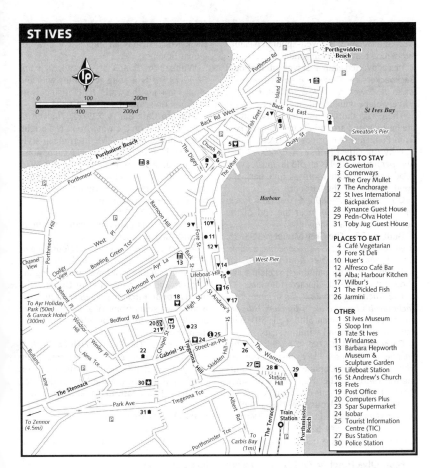

ST IVES

PLACES TO STAY
2 Gowerton
3 Cornerways
6 The Grey Mullet
7 The Anchorage
22 St Ives International
   Backpackers
28 Kynance Guest House
29 Pedn-Olva Hotel
31 Toby Jug Guest House

PLACES TO EAT
4 Café Vegetarian
9 Fore St Deli
10 Huer's
12 Alfresco Café Bar
14 Alba; Harbour Kitchen
17 Wilbur's
21 The Pickled Fish
26 Jarmini

OTHER
1 St Ives Museum
5 Sloop Inn
8 Tate St Ives
11 Windansea
13 Barbara Hepworth
   Museum &
   Sculpture Garden
15 Lifeboat Station
16 St Andrew's Church
18 Frets
19 Post Office
20 Computers Plus
23 Spar Supermarket
24 Isobar
25 Tourist Information
   Centre (TIC)
27 Bus Station
30 Police Station

The beautiful garden forms a perfect backdrop for some of Hepworth's larger works.

St Ives Museum

The local heritage museum (☎ 796005; Wheal Dream; adult/child £1.50/50p; open 10am-5pm Mon-Fri, 10am-4pm Sat Easter-Oct) has an interesting collection of bits relating to blacksmithery, fishing and shipwrecks.

Beaches

There are several excellent beaches in the area. **Porthmeor** is the surfing beach to the north of the town. Just to the east is tiny, sandy **Porthgwidden**.

There are sandy areas in the sheltered harbour but most families head south to **Porthminster**, which has half a mile of sand and a convenient car park. **Carbis Bay**, to the south-east, is also good for children. **Porth Kidney Sands**, the next beach along, is only safe for swimming if you stay between the flags. It's dangerous to swim in the Hayle estuary.

Windansea (☎ 794830; 25 Fore St) rents wetsuits and surfboards (£5 each per day).

Organised Tours

A variety of walking tours lasting 1½ to two hours run during summer, most costing £3/2 per adult/child. **Walkabout** (☎ 810287) tells historical tales of the town, while **Ghost Walks** (☎ 331206) unearths the spooky side.

Places to Stay

Ayr Holiday Park (☎ 795855, fax 798797; w www.ayrholidaypark.co.uk; Higher Ayr; tent

DEVON & CORNWALL

sites & 2 people £7.10-11.40), half a mile west of the centre, is a well-appointed campsite which rents caravans and cabins.

In a converted chapel, **St Ives International Backpackers** (☎ 799444; e stives@backpack ers.co.uk; Lower Stennack; dorm beds £8-12) is a lively place with excellent facilities.

There's no shortage of guesthouses above the harbour and around the road into St Ives from Penzance. All prices are B&B.

Toby Jug Guest House (☎ 794250; 1 Park Ave; per person £20) is an old favourite, with good-value en-suite rooms, a bike park and good views over the harbour.

Gowerton (☎ 796805; 6 Sea View Place; en-suite doubles £45), near the end of the headland, also has fine views.

Built in 1776, **The Grey Mullet** (☎ 796635; e greymulletguesthouse@lineone.net; 2 Bunkers Hill; singles/doubles from £22/48) has walls covered with paintings, sketches and photos; it's a central, characterful place.

The Anchorage (☎ 797135; e james@the anchoragebb.fsnet.co.uk; 5 Bunkers Hill; per person £20-25) is even older (c.1730), with snug little rooms and window seats.

Cornerways (☎ 796706; e bryan.pyecroft@ lineone.net; Bethesda Place; en-suite doubles from £38) hosted Daphne du Maurier during the 1940s; it's been updated a bit since then but still has an air of elegance.

Kynance Guest House (☎ 796636; e en quiries@kynance24.co.uk; 24 The Warren; en-suite doubles £44-52), an attractive old tin-miners' cottage, is handy for restaurants and the bus station.

Pedn-Olva Hotel (☎ 796222, fax 797710; e pednolva@westcountryhotelrooms.co.uk; Porthminster Beach; per person £40-58), a not-quite-boutique beachside hotel, has a small swimming pool and an excellent seafood restaurant.

Ivy-clad **Garrack Hotel** (☎ 796199, fax 798955; e garrack@accuk.co.uk; Burthallen Lane; singles/doubles from £63.50/106; 4-course dinner £24.50) feels like an exclusive country club, with charming grounds, an indoor pool and an acclaimed restaurant.

Places to Eat

Fore St Deli (30 Fore St) is a great place to stock up on home-made pies, bread, cheeses (and booze) for picnics.

Café Vegetarian (☎ 793621; Island Square; lunch £3-5, dinner mains £8.50-9.50), up-

stairs in a cosy whitewashed cottage off Back Rd East, has an impressive array of global flavours.

Wilbur's (☎ 796663; St Andrew's St; mains £7.50-13.50) is a snug restaurant with old photos gracing the walls. Its British cuisine is strong on seafood and fresh fish.

Alfresco Café Bar (☎ 793737; The Wharf; mains £10-14), on the waterfront, is a bright, lively place with a Mediterranean-style menu and lots of fish and vegetarian options.

The name **Jarmini** (☎ 797975; The Warren; mains £10.95) is Punjabi for purple, and this vibrant, friendly restaurant is *very* purple. Cuisine is adventurous fusion.

Huer's (☎ 797999; The Wharf; mains £9-13) does the contemporary seafood thing in an understated space.

Alba (☎ 797222; Old Lifeboat House; mains £12-17), on the wharf, is sleek and sharp, with huge picture windows overlooking the harbour, and tempting modern British cuisine. **Harbour Kitchen** (☎ 798937), the barbistro downstairs from Alba, shares the chef and love of seafood but offers fusion and more-modest snacks.

The chef at **The Pickled Fish** (☎ 795100; 3 Chapel St; mains £11-15; open 7pm-10pm Mon-Sat) has done time at the finest London hotels and it shows in the Euro-influenced cuisine at this smart, informal restaurant.

Entertainment

Isobar (☎ 796042; Tregenna Hill; open to 2am) is St Ives' hippest spot, a lively bar with a nightclub playing garage, uplifting house and dance.

The walls of 14th-century **Sloop Inn** (☎ 796584; The Wharf) are hung with paintings by local artists, but on summer evenings most people ignore them and drink out by the harbour.

Chilled café-bar **Frets** (☎ 799652; 7 High St; open 10am-midnight) serves pasta and paella during the day, cocktails and live jazz by night.

Getting There & Away

St Ives is 8 miles (13km) from Penzance and 277 miles (443km) from London. National Express operates coaches to London (£41 economy return, 8¼ hours, three daily), and to Newquay (£5.50, 1¼ hours, three daily), Penzance (£3.25, 25 minutes, five daily), Plymouth (£7.25, three hours, four daily) and Truro (£4, one hour, two daily). There's one service daily direct to Exeter (£22, 4¼ hours) but surprisingly it's sometimes quicker to change at Plymouth.

There's a three-times-daily bus service (No 15) from St Ives to Land's End via Zennor, St Just-in-Penwith and Sennen Cove in summer, open-top if weather permits. In winter, you must go via Penzance.

St Ives is on a scenic branch railway line from St Erth (£1.60 single, 13 minutes, hourly), on the main London–Penzance line.

A Park & Ride train service operates from the Lelant Saltings Rail Halt 2 miles (3km) south of town.

AROUND ST IVES
Industrial Discovery Centre

The tin mines and engines dotted around are a reminder of Cornwall's past importance (and, poignantly, of the role the industry's decline played in its current economic problems). At the Industrial Discovery Centre (☎ 01209-315027; W www.trevithicktrust .com/cornmnen.htm; Pool, Camborne; adult/ child £5/3; open 11am-5pm Sun-Fri Apr-Oct, 11am-5pm daily Aug) you'll see two working mine engines (albeit now electrically powered) and an excellent interpretative gallery, a film covering the history of mining, and exhibits exploring the social implications of the industry here and abroad. Staff are enthusiastic and knowledgeable.

Pool is off the A30 12 miles (19km) east of St Ives.

NEWQUAY
☎ 01637 • pop 17,400

Newquay is the kind of place you either love or loathe. It's a confused, if enjoyable, blend of surf gossip, family holidays and testosterone-driven lad hell; there are great beaches and full-on nightlife, as well as 'family' (read: slightly tacky) attractions. Whatever your opinion, it's indisputably the foremost surfing spot in England and a good place to learn. There's talk of building an artificial reef at the main beach to ensure more consistent surf.

Much of Newquay is modern but on the cliff north of Towan Beach stands the whitewashed 14th-century **Huer's House**, a lookout for approaching pilchard shoals; every Cornish fishing village had such a watchtower and a huer directing netting op-

erations. Until they were fished out early in the 20th century, these shoals were enormous: one St Ives catch of 1868 netted a record 16.5 million fish.

Information

The **TIC** (☎ 854020, fax 854030; e info@ newquay.co.uk; Marcus Hill; open 9.30am-5.30pm Mon-Sat, 10am-2.30pm Sun late May–mid-Sept, 9.30am-4.30pm Mon-Fri, 9.30am-12.30pm Sat mid-Sept–late May) is near the bus station in the centre.

Tad & Nick's Talk'n'Surf (☎ 874868; 72 Fore St; open 10am-6pm daily) is a bright-and-breezy cybercafé (access costs £4 per hour) with good stuffed pittas (£2.95). **Cyber Surf** (☎ 875497; 2 Broad St; open 10am-late daily) is another option (access is 7p per minute).

There's a **laundrette** (☎ 875901; 1 Beach Parade, Beach Rd) nearby.

Things to See & Do

If the weather's bad (occasionally!) or you don't fancy sunbathing, there are countless theme parks, pools and other 'attractions'.

Blue Reef Aquarium (☎ 878134; W www .bluereefaquarium.co.uk; Towan Promenade; adult/child £4.95/3.25; open 10am-5pm daily), right on the main beach, is a modern, well-presented collection of Cornish and tropical sea-life.

Newquay Waterworld (☎ 853828; W www .newquaywaterworld.co.uk; Trenance Park; adult/child £4/3.10) has a tropical fun pool (with obligatory slides) and a 25m swimming pool. Hours vary but the fun pool is open at least 10am to 5pm Saturday and Sunday, and 11am to 8pm Monday to Friday, mid-February to August.

Also in Trenance Park, **Newquay Zoo** (☎ 873342; W www.newquayzoo.co.uk; adult/ child £6.25/3.95; open 9.30am-6pm Apr-Oct) is hot on 'cute' beasties (meerkats, penguins, tamarins) and has some big cats and macaques, too.

Trenance Park is approximately 500m southeast of the centre.

Beaches

Fistral Beach, to the west of the town round Towan Head, is England's most famous surfing beach. There are fast hollow waves, particularly at low tide, and good tubing sections when there's a southeasterly wind.

Watergate Bay is a 2-mile-long sandy beach on the eastern side of Newquay Bay. At low tide it's a good place to learn to surf. A mile (or 3 miles by car) southwest of Newquay, **Crantock** is a small northwest-facing sheltered beach, where the waves are best at mid- to high tide.

Surfing

Surf shops hire boards and wetsuits for around £5 each per day. Try **Fistral Surf Co** (☎ 850520; 8 Beacon Rd • ☎ 850808; 19 Cliff Rd; open 9am-6pm daily) or **Tunnel Vision Surf Shop** (☎ 879033; 6 Alma Place; open 9am-7pm daily).

Surf schools abound; all-inclusive, half-day beginner's lessons cost £20 to £25. Try **British Surfing Association** (☎ 850737; w www.nationalsurfingcentre.com; Fistral Beach • ☎ 851487; Tolcarne Beach) or **Offshore Extreme** (☎/fax 877083; w www.offshore-extreme.co.uk).

Places to Stay

There are several campsites in the area. **Porth Beach Tourist Park** (☎ 876531, fax 871227; e info@porthbeach.co.uk; Porth; tent sites & 2 people £6-12), a mile (1.5km) north-east of the centre, has excellent facilities.

There are more hostels than you can shake a stick at. Most cater for surfers and stag parties; some are mere flophouses, while others have better standards, secure board storage and links with surf schools.

Newquay Surf Lodge (☎ 851143; w www.newquaysurflodge.co.uk; 8 Springfield Rd; dorm beds per week Aug £99, outside peak season per night/week £6/35) is a well-kept, friendly spot that doesn't seem to attract the riotous crowds. **Newquay Reef Surf Lodge** (☎ 878088; 5/7 Springfield Rd), owned by the same people, has en-suite dorms and twins.

Home Surf Lodge (☎ 873387; e home.surflodge@btinternet.com; 18 Tower Rd; B&B dorm beds £17.50) is a big, clean place with slightly cramped dorms but good facilities, including free Internet access.

Base Surf Lodge (☎ 874852; w www.basesurflodge.com; 20 Tower Rd; dorm beds £10-20) is a new, spotless option with a licensed bar (but no kitchen; breakfast is included) and reasonably spacious dorms.

Busy **Newquay International Backpackers** (☎ 879366; e newquay@backpackersco.uk;

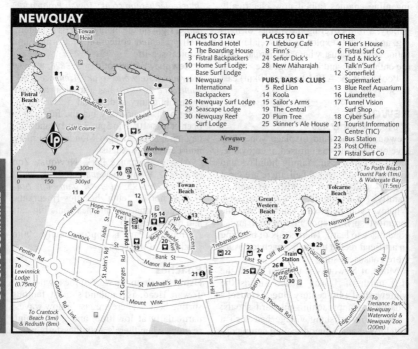

NEWQUAY

PLACES TO STAY
1 Headland Hotel
2 The Boarding House
3 Fistral Backpackers
10 Home Surf Lodge;
    Base Surf Lodge
11 Newquay
    International
    Backpackers
26 Newquay Surf Lodge
29 Seascape Lodge
30 Newquay Reef
    Surf Lodge

PLACES TO EAT
7 Lifebuoy Café
8 Finn's
24 Señor Dick's
28 New Maharajah

PUBS, BARS & CLUBS
5 Red Lion
14 Koola
15 Sailor's Arms
19 The Central
20 Plum Tree
25 Skinner's Ale House

OTHER
4 Huer's House
6 Fistral Surf Co
9 Tad & Nick's
    Talk'n'Surf
12 Somerfield
    Supermarket
13 Blue Reef Aquarium
16 Laundrette
17 Tunnel Vision
    Surf Shop
18 Cyber Surf
21 Tourist Information
    Centre (TIC)
22 Bus Station
23 Post Office
27 Fistral Surf Co

DEVON & CORNWALL

69-73 Tower Rd; dorm beds off season £8, en-suite twins peak season £32) has good facilities, and arranges discounts on board hire, food and club entry.

Over at Fistral, excellent **The Boarding House** *(☎ 873258; w www.theboarding house.co.uk; 32 Headland Rd; dorm beds £13-17.50)* has en-suite rooms with TVs and board lockers, and a large café-bar area with a pool table and terrace.

Fistral Backpackers *(☎ 873146; 18 Headland Rd; dorm beds £6.50-12, doubles £27)*, with a home cinema for film buffs, is large and a bit chaotic, but well positioned.

Streets running back from the main beach are full of guesthouses, but book ahead if you're planning to stay in July and August.

Seascape Lodge *(☎ 874215; e info@sea scapelodge.co.uk; 1 Tolcarne Rd; en-suite rooms per person £25)* is a lively place close to the action. Rates don't include breakfast.

Headland Hotel *(☎ 872211; fax 872212; e office@headlandhotel.co.uk; Fistral Beach; B&B singles £70-99, doubles £100-158)* is an imposing edifice perched on the headland above Fistral Beach. Rooms are tastefully furnished, and there are two pools, tennis courts and a nine-hole golf course.

Places to Eat

Lifebuoy Café *(☎ 878076; Lower Tower Rd; mains £4.50-12)* is a colourful spot, with fine breakfasts and a host of global dishes.

Señor Dick's *(☎ 851601; East St; mains £7-12)* is a popular Mexican joint in the thick of the bar scene.

New Maharajah *(☎ 877377; 39 Cliff Rd; mains £5-9; open 5.30pm-late daily)* is the top Indian place, with fine views and a good vegetarian selection.

Finn's *(☎ 874062; The Old Boat House, South Quay Hill; mains £10-16)*, in a fabulous position on Towan Beach, picks the freshest fish straight off the boats for its modish cuisine.

Lewinnick Lodge *(☎ 878117; Pentire Headland; mains £6.50-12.50)* is the kind of cool bar-diner you just wouldn't expect here; European-influenced seafood dishes complement amazing views over Fistral.

Entertainment

Newquay is crammed with pubs, bars and (often dodgy) clubs, making it a great place for a night out.

The Central *(☎ 878310; 11 Central Square)* is a spacious, noisy bar with an outdoor terrace that is nevertheless usually heaving.

Cavernous **Red Lion** *(☎ 872195; North Quay Hill)* is *the* surfers' hangout. Check which clubs are hip or stick around for live bands Friday and Saturday.

Skinner's Ale House *(☎ 876391; 58 East St)* is a spit-and-sawdust (literally!) pub for people who like real Cornish beers; there's live music Thursday to Sunday.

Plum Tree *(☎ 872814; 19 Bank St)*, the latest pre-club option, offers DJs and lethal cocktails.

Sailor's Arms *(☎ 872838; Fore St)* is a bar and club playing cheesy house.

Koola *(☎ 873415; w www.thekoola.com; Beach Rd)* plays underground tunes and is currently the hippest venue.

Getting There & Away

Newquay is 32 miles (51km) from St Ives and 252 miles (403km) from London. National Express has direct buses to London (£41 economy return, seven hours, three daily), Exeter (£16.50, 3½ hours, two daily), Plymouth (£6, 1½ hours, four daily), Penzance (£5.50, 1¾ hours, three daily) and St Ives (£5.50, 1¼ hours, three daily).

There are four trains daily between Newquay and Par (£4.30 single, 45 minutes), on the main London–Penzance line.

AROUND NEWQUAY
Trerice

Escape the cultural void of Newquay at Trerice *(NT; ☎ 01637-875404; admission £4.40; open 11am-5.30pm Wed-Fri, Sun & Mon Apr-Sept, Sun-Fri late July-early Sept)*, a charming Elizabethan manor. Built in 1571, much of the structure and elaborate plasterwork is original, and there is some fine oak and walnut furniture from the 17th and 18th centuries. An oddity is the lawn-mower museum in the barn, with more than 100 grass-cutters going back over a century.

Trerice is 3 miles (5km) southeast of Newquay. During summer, bus No 50 runs directly here several times a day.

NORTHERN CORNWALL

Some of England's best beaches and most endearing fishing villages face the Atlantic along the north coast, but getting around this area without wheels requires patience. From

Newquay, the coastal road passes **Bedruthan Steps**, a series of rock stacks along a sandy beach, faintly reminiscent of the 12 Apostles in Victoria, Australia. At **Constantine Bay** there's a wide, sandy beach, good for surfing.

Padstow
☎ 01841 • pop 2500

Gourmet capital of Cornwall, Padstow is a popular fishing village on the Camel estuary, famous for its **May Day Festival** (see the boxed text 'My Kingdom for an Oss' in this section). There are some wonderful stone cottages and excellent accommodation, although these days, TV chef Rick Stein has the place pretty much sewn up.

The **TIC** (☎ 533449, fax 532356; **e** pad stowtic@visit.org.uk; Red Brick Building, North Quay; open 9.30am-5pm Mon-Sat, 10am-3.30pm Sun, closed winter) charges £3 to book accommodation.

Above the village is **Prideaux Place** (☎ 532411; adult/child £6/2; open 1.30pm-4pm Sun-Thur mid-May–Sept), a lavish manor house built in 1592 by the Prideaux-Brune family, purportedly descendants of William the Conqueror, who still reside here. Its grand plasterwork ceilings and stately grandeur have been acknowledged by countless film directors who've used it as a location for numerous period dramas.

The Camel Trail is a disused railway line, good for walking or cycling, starting at the south end of Padstow and running east through Wadebridge (5¾ miles, 9km) and Bodmin (11 miles, 17km); it's possible to continue north to Poley's Bridge (16¾ miles, 26km). Bicycles can be hired from **Padstow Cycle Hire** (☎ 533533; South Quay; open 9am-5pm daily) costing from £8 per day and **Brinhams** (☎ 532594; South Quay; open 9am-5pm daily) for £6 per day.

Places to Stay & Eat South of town, **Dennis Cove Camping** (☎ 532349; car, tent sites & 2 people £9.70-13.50; open May-Sept) is a small, well-appointed site overlooking the estuary.

Treyarnon Bay YHA Hostel (☎ 0870 770 6076; Tregonnan; adult/child £10.25/7) is located above a popular surfer's beach about 4½ miles (7km) west of Padstow. Bus No 55 from Padstow occasionally stops at nearby Constantine.

There are umpteen B&Bs in Padstow.

Snug little **Althea Library** (☎/fax 532717; **e** enquiries@althealibrary.co.uk; 27 High St; en-suite B&B doubles £54-60) is a delightful, Grade II–listed cottage offering vegan and vegetarian breakfasts.

Tregea Hotel (☎ 532455, fax 533542; **e** tim@tregea.co.uk; 16-18 High St; en-suite B&B doubles £72-92) is another excellent place – friendly, stylish and immensely comfortable.

The Seafood Restaurant (☎ 532485; **w** www.rickstein.com; Riverside; mains £16.50-28) is Rick Stein's sleek flagship establishment. There's no denying the calibre of the cuisine, but his fame ensures you'll need to book months in advance.

Don't have the booking (or the brass)? Get Steined at **St Petroc's Hotel & Bistro** (☎ 532700; 4 New St; mains £13.50-14.50) or **Rick Stein's Café** (☎ 532700; Middle St; mains £10.50; closed Sun). If all else fails, at **Stein's Seafood Deli** (South Quay; open 9.30am-5pm Tues-Sat) a delectable crab pasty will set you back £2.95. There's classy accommodation and cooking courses too – check the website.

Escaping the Stein gravity, **London Inn** (☎ 532554; 6/8 Lanadwell St; mains £7-13) is a cosy local with good Cornish beers and daily fish specials.

Bus No 55 runs to Bodmin Parkway (50 minutes) and the Eden Project (£5.20 return, 1½ hours) hourly till 6pm. Bus No 555 goes

---

My Kingdom for an Oss

May Day festivities take place in many parts of Britain but Padstow's raucous fertility rite, featuring the fabled Obby Oss (hobby horse), is believed to be the oldest such event in the country. The ritual begins just before midnight on 30 April, as villagers sing to the innkeeper at the Golden Lion with the news that summer is 'a-come'. Then, at 10am the next morning the Blue Ribbon Oss – a man garbed in a huge hooped sailcloth dress and wild-looking horse headdress – erupts to dance around the town, grabbing any woman close enough and daubing her with coal (or, often, pinching her – it's believed to aid childbearing!). He's followed at 11am by the Old Original (or Red) Oss and the madness continues until late.

to Truro (£4 return, 1¾ hours, four daily Monday to Saturday), while bus No 556 serves Newquay (£4 return, 1¼ hours, five daily Monday to Saturday, four Sunday).

Port Isaac

A steep-sided cove and natural harbour gives Port Isaac picture-postcard looks. The old village has several welcoming pubs and galleries, but it's far from overrun by tourists so well worth a visit.

The Old School Hotel & Restaurant (☎ 01208-880721; e oldsch.hotel@eclipse .co.uk; Fore St; B&B en-suite singles/doubles from £30/60; mains £13-20) is a beautifully converted schoolhouse overlooking the harbour; the restaurant serves excellent seafood.

Tintagel

☎ 01840

Tintagel village today is a morass of tearooms, souvenir shops and day-trippers but even mass tourism can't detract from the surf-battered grandeur of Tintagel Head. Crossing the bridge to the island and its 13th-century **castle ruins** (EH; ☎ 770328; admission £3; open 10am-6pm daily Apr-Sept, 10am-5pm daily Oct, 10am-4pm daily Nov-Mar), you enter the world of knightly lore. Storytellers will occasionally spin yarns about the Knights of the Round Table and King Arthur who, legend has it, was born here in the late 5th century to beautiful Queen Igraine.

Back in the village, **The Old Post Office** (NT; ☎ 770024; Fore St; admission £2.30; open 11am-5.30pm daily Apr-Sept, 11am-4pm daily Oct) is a fascinating, higgledy-piggledy 14th-century house that served as a post office in the 19th century.

The **TIC** (☎ 779084; e tintagelvc@ukonlin .co.uk; Bossiney Rd; open 10am-5pm daily Mar-Oct, 10.30am-4pm daily Nov-Feb) has a small exhibit about Arthur and local history.

Places to Stay & Eat Headland Caravan Park (☎ 770239, fax 770925; e headland .cp@virgin.net; Atlantic Rd; tent sites & 2 people £8.50; open Easter-Oct) is at the village's northern edge.

Tintagel YHA Hostel (☎ 0870 770 6068, fax 770733; Dunderhole Point; adult/child £10.25/7; open mid-Mar–mid-Oct) is a tiny whitewashed cottage in a spectacular cliff-top setting on the South West Coast Path, three-quarters of a mile south of the village.

Ye Olde Malthouse Inn (☎ 770461; B&B per person £23-25) is a 14th-century pub with good Cornish beer and bar food.

The Old Millfloor (☎ 770234; B&B from £22), in a delightful brookside dell, is idyllic beyond words, with simple, comfortable rooms in a 17th-century mill cottage. It's about 3 miles (5km) west of Tintagel; follow the signs to Trebarwith Strand.

Getting There & Away Bus No 122/124 runs from Wadebridge (1¼ hours, eight daily Monday to Friday) and the No X10 comes from Exeter (2¼ hours, four daily Monday to Saturday); both go on to Boscastle (10 minutes).

Boscastle

☎ 01840

The gorgeous natural harbour that made Boscastle a suitable fishing port attracts visitors in droves. It's also worth hunting out **Minster Church** in a wonderful wooded valley about a mile southeast of the visitor centre. The **harbour wall** dates from 1584 and was built on the orders of Sir Richard Grenville, captain of Elizabeth I's ship *The Revenge*.

The **visitor centre** (☎/fax 250010; e visi torcentre@boscastlevc.fsnet.co.uk; Cobweb Inn Car Park; open 10am-5pm daily Easter-Oct, 10.30am-4pm daily Nov-Easter) houses a small local history exhibition.

The **Museum of Witchcraft** (☎ 250111; The Harbour; adult/child £2/1; open 10.30am-5.30pm Mon-Sat, noon-5.30pm Sun) is a fascinating glimpse into the world of Wicca and associated beliefs. It aims to educate rather than convert or titillate, and is well presented and thought-provoking.

Boscastle Harbour YHA Hostel (☎ 0870 770 5710, fax 250615; adult/child £10.25/7; open Apr-Sept) is perfectly positioned right by the harbour.

Sunnyside (☎ 250453; e mail@siford34 .freeserve.co.uk; B&B per person with/without en suite £25/19) is a homely, attractive harbourside cottage.

For bus information, see the previous Tintagel section.

Bodmin Moor

Cornwall's 'roof' is a high heath pock-marked with bogs and with giant tors like those on Dartmoor rising above the wild landscape – Brown Willy (419m) and Rough Tor (400m) are the highest. It's a desolate place that works on the imagination; the Beast of Bodmin, a large black catlike creature, has been seen regularly for many years. The murder of Charlotte Dymond in 1844 is another story that's still discussed; you can participate in a recreation of the trial of her alleged killer, Matthew Weeks, at **Bodmin Shire Hall** (*☎ 01208-76616; Mount Folly; adult/child £3/2; open 11am-3pm Mon-Sat*).

Bodmin lies in the southwest of the moor. The **TIC** (*☎/fax 01208-76616; e bodmintic@ visit.org.uk; Shire House, Mount Folly; open 10am-5pm Mon-Sat*) has leaflets on exploring the moor; the small **Town Museum** (*☎ 01208-77067; Mount Folly; admission free; open 10.30am-4.30pm Mon-Sat Apr-Sept*) is opposite. The bizarre **Bodmin Jail** (*☎ 01208-76292; Berrycombe Rd; adult/child £3.90/2; open 10am-6pm Mon-Sun, 11am-6pm Sat*) exhibition, in the old county prison dating from 1776, is very amateurish but the accounts of true crimes of old are strangely enthralling. Look out for William Hocking, hanged for bestiality: the angst-ridden face of the 'sheep' is worth the admission price!

The A30 cuts across the centre of the moor from **Launceston**, which has a ruined 11th-century **castle** (*EH; ☎ 01566-772365; admission £2; open 10am-6pm daily Apr-Sept, 10am-5pm daily Oct, 10am-1pm & 2pm-4pm Fri-Sun Nov-Mar*) perched above it, and a granite **church** with extensive carvings.

At **Bolventor** is **Jamaica Inn** (*☎ 01566-86250, fax 86177; B&B singles/doubles with en suite from £37/55*), made famous by Daphne Du Maurier's novel of the same name. On a misty winter's night the place still feels atmospheric, and the accommodation's comfortable. The inn also manages **Daphne du Maurier's Smugglers** (*adult/child £2.50/2; open 10am-5pm daily Easter-Oct, 11am-4pm Nov–mid-Jan & mid-Feb–Easter*), an animated series of scenes from the book with some nautical and smuggling relics for show. Bolventor is a good base for walks on the moor. About a mile to the south is **Dozmary Pool**, said to have been where Arthur's sword, Excalibur, was thrown after his death. It's a 4-mile (6km) walk northwest of Jamaica Inn to Brown Willy.

Bodmin has bus connections with St Austell (No 29, one hour, hourly Monday to Saturday), as well as Bodmin Parkway (No 56, 15 minutes, hourly Monday to Saturday), a station on the London to Penzance line farther south. Bus No 76/X76 runs from Launceston to Plymouth (1½ hours, hourly Monday to Saturday).

Bude
☎ 01288 • pop 3700

Just this side of the Cornwall-Devon border, Bude is a popular bucket-and-spade resort with great surf. Crooklets Beach is the main surfing area, just north of town. Nearby Sandymouth is good for beginners, and Duckpool is also popular. Summerleaze, in the centre of Bude, is a family beach.

Bude Visitor Centre (*☎ 354240, fax 355769; e budetic@visit.org.uk; The Crescent; open 10am-5pm Mon-Sat, plus 10am-4pm Sun June–mid-Sept*) has accommodation information.

There are plenty of surf schools; try **Outdoor Adventure** (*☎ 361312; w www.outdoor adventure.co.uk; Atlantic Court*), charging £16/30 for half/full-day lessons.

Upper Lynstone Camping Park (*☎ 352017, fax 359034; e reception@upperlynstone.co.uk; tent sites & 2 people £7-11*) is a peaceful spot three-quarters of a mile west of town.

Downs View, back from Crooklets Beach, is wall-to-wall B&Bs. Despite the name, **Surf Haven** (*☎ 353923; e info@surfhaven.info; 31 Downs View; per person with en suite £17-26*) isn't run by blonde Australians in wetsuits, but is comfortable and friendly.

Life's a Beach (*☎ 355222; Summerleaze Beach; lunch £2.75-4.50, 2/3-course dinner £16.50/18.50*) transforms from snack stop to contemporary bistro at night, with mouth-watering global seafood dishes. You can also hire surfboards (£12 per day) and wetsuits (£6 per day).

As you'd expect, surfers here get thirsty. **JJ's Bar** (*☎ 352555; The Headland*), just back from Summerleaze Beach, is currently the wildest watering hole.

National Express coaches run from Exeter (£7.80 economy return, 1¾ hours, five daily), as does local bus No X9 (two hours, six daily).

ISLES OF SCILLY
☎ 01720 • pop 2000

It's no exaggeration to say that the Isles of Scilly, 140 rocky islands dangling 28 miles (45km) southwest of mainland Cornwall,

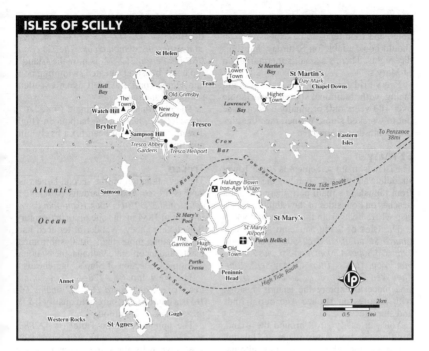

seem stuck in a time warp. It's 4000 years since the first settlers arrived; Bronze Age relics can still be seen scattered around the islands and, though the tools have changed, traditional industries (fishing and low-level agriculture) continue much the same. The pace of life is slow and everyone knows everyone else; many share surnames and are related in one way or another.

The mild climate that enables the islanders to cultivate bulbs and subtropical plants for export also draws holiday-makers who develop a lasting attachment to the wide, white beaches; most come back year after year, which adds to the community feel. Clear, cool water attracts divers keen to explore the many wrecks, while sailors and windsurfers take to the waves and anglers fish for cod, megrim and porbeagle shark. Walkers enjoy the rugged coastal scenery, twitchers search for puffins and shearwaters, and others trip to the off-islands to visit seal colonies.

Of the islands, St Mary's, Tresco, St Martin's, St Agnes and Bryher are inhabited. St Mary's is the largest (2½ miles by 1¾ miles; 4km by 3km) and most populous.

Information

The **Isles of Scilly Tourist Board** (☎ 422536, fax 422049; e tic@scilly.gov.uk; Wesleyan Chapel, Porthcressa Bank, Hugh Town; open 8.30am-5.30pm Mon-Thur, 8.30am-5pm Fri & Sat Easter-Oct, plus 10am-noon Sun June-Sept, closes noon Sat Nov-Dec, closed all day Sat & Sun Jan-Easter) is on St Mary's. The Standard Guidebook, Isles of Scilly (£3) is a detailed fold-out map with text; a simple double-sided map (30p) is adequate for most needs.

A commercial website (w www.scilly online.co.uk) provides a lot of useful background information, while the TIC website (w www.simplyscilly.co.uk) helps with accommodation listings.

Accommodation should be booked well in advance. Many places close between November and May. All prices provided are en suite, per person, per night. Each island, except Tresco, has a simple, reasonable campsite. There are plenty of self-catering options; the TIC has listings. The biggest operator is **Island Properties** (☎ 422211; w www.isles-of -scilly.co.uk/island-properties.html); flats start at £200 per week.

Many visitors eat dinner at their B&B or hotel, and food tends to be expensive. You should book a table on Saturday and Sunday nights. There's a small **supermarket** on St Mary's.

Every Friday evening you can watch **gig racing**, with traditional six-oar boats (some over 100 years old) originally used to race out to wrecked ships. Women race the gigs on Wednesday in summer.

St Mary's

The islands' main settlement is Hugh Town, straddling an isthmus separating the Garrison from the island's main part; there are good beaches on both sides of the isthmus. This is also where boats from the mainland dock.

The **Isles of Scilly Museum** (☎ 422337; Church St; adult/child £2/50p; open 10am-12pm & 1.30pm-4.30pm Mon-Sat, plus 7.30pm-9pm Mon, Tues & Thur-Sat May-Sept, 2pm-4pm Wed Oct-Apr, or by arrangement) is a fine place to explore the islands' history, with features on Bronze Age burial finds and shipwrecks.

You can easily stroll around the island, spotting the Iron Age village at Halangy Down and the other ancient sites; alternatively, **Scilly Walks** (☎ 423326; w www.scillywalks.co.uk) leads three-hour archaeological tours, costing £3.50/2 per adult/child. **Island Wildlife Tours** (☎ 422212; e william.wagstaff@virgin.net; 42 Sally Port) concentrates on the islands' ornithological wealth; full-day tours cost £7.

Underwater Island Safaris (☎ 422732; Nowhere, Old Town) will guide divers to wrecks and reefs for £30/40 with/without your own equipment.

Above-water-sports enthusiasts head for **Rat Island Sailboat Company** (☎ 422060; Porthmellon), where windsurf hire starts at £10 per hour, sailing lessons £27.

The **campsite** (☎ 422670; e tedmoulson@cs.com; Tower Cottage, Garrison Farm; tent sites per person per night £4.50-6.55) is west of Hugh Town.

Evergreen Cottage (☎ 422711; The Parade; B&B per person £24.50-29.50) is a charming 300-year-old captain's cottage, cosy but not twee.

The Wheelhouse (☎/fax 422719; Porthcressa; B&B per person £32-38, half-board £42-48) is immensely popular, a spacious guesthouse next to a fine beach.

Built as part of a fort in 1593, **Star Castle Hotel** (☎ 422317, fax 422343; w www.starcastlescilly.demon.co.uk; The Garrison; B&B per person £52-97) is now the island's top hotel, boasting a heated swimming pool and tennis courts, as well as an excellent seafood restaurant.

The oh-so-nautical **Mermaid** (☎ 422701; mains £6-10), next to the harbour in Hugh Town, is the place to head for a lively pint and fine pub grub.

Tresco

The key attraction on the second-largest island is **Tresco Abbey Gardens** (☎ 424105; adult/child £7.50/free; open 10am-4pm daily), laid out in 1834 on the site of a 10th-century Benedictine abbey. Wonderful terraced gardens feature more than 5000 subtropical plants, and incorporate **Valhalla**, the National Maritime Collection of Ship's Figureheads.

The **New Inn** (☎ 422844; e newinn@tresco.co.uk; half-board £64-107; mains £6-16) is a comfortable pub, with quality B&B, pizza, steak and seafood.

The upmarket **Island Hotel** (☎ 422883; e islandhotel@tresco.co.uk; half-board £99-236), owned by the same company, has a heated swimming pool and attractive beachside gardens.

Bryher

Much of the landscape on the smallest inhabited island is rugged coastal heath; Hell Bay in an Atlantic gale is a powerful sight. There are good views over the islands from the top of Watch Hill, and Rushy Bay is one of the finest Scilly beaches. From the quay, occasional boats cross to deserted Samson Island, where abandoned settlers' cottages tell a story of hard subsistence living.

The **campsite** (☎ 422886; tent sites £4.50-6) is near the quay. **Hell Bay Hotel** (☎ 422947, fax 423004; e hellbay@aol.com; half-board £79-132), with spacious, tasteful rooms, is mere steps from a fine beach.

St Martin's

Known for its beautiful beaches, St Martin's is the most northerly of the main islands. A walk east along the windswept northern cliffs leads to the **Day Mark**, a red-and-white candy-striped landmark built in 1687.

There's excellent diving among seals and wrecks. **Isles of Scilly Dive School** (☎ 422848;

e *jo.allsop@ukgateway.net; Higher Town)* charges from £25 per dive.

The **campsite** *(☎ 422888;* **e** *chris@stmartinscampsite.freeserve.co.uk; Middle Town; tent sites £4-6)* is near Lawrence's Bay at the west of the island.

Polreath *(☎ 422046; Higher Town; B&B per person £35-45),* a cosy, well-appointed cottage, is one of the few B&Bs.

St Martin's on the Isle *(☎ 422090, fax 422298;* **e** *stay@stmartinshotel.co.uk; B&B per person £85-120),* the only hotel, is arguably the best on the islands, with a renowned seafood restaurant.

St Agnes
England's most southerly community somehow transcends even the tranquillity of the other islands; it's an ideal spot to stroll, unwind and reflect. The islanders call themselves Turks.

The **campsite** *(☎ 422360; Troy Town Farm; tent sites £4-6)* is at the southwest of the island. **Covean Cottage** *(☎ 422620; B&B per person £23.50-30.50)* is a little stone cottage offering excellent cream teas.

The Turk's Head *(☎ 422434; mains £6-10)* is everyone's dream pub, with lovely views, fine beers and good seafood.

Getting There & Away
There's no transport to or from the islands on a Sunday.

Air The **Isles of Scilly Skybus** *(☎ 0845 710 5555;* **w** *www.ios-travel.co.uk)* flies between St Mary's and Land's End (£85/95 return October to March/April to September, 15 minutes) and Newquay (£102/114, 30 minutes) up to five times daily, Monday to Saturday year round, and to Exeter (£170/190, 50 minutes) and Bristol (£220/240, 70 minutes) daily between March and October. Children under 12 pay half-price, and short breaks of up to three nights cost around 20% less.

British International *(☎ 01736-363871, fax 332253;* **w** *www.scillyhelicopter.co.uk)* helicopters fly to St Mary's (20 minutes, at least six daily Monday to Saturday April to October, three daily Monday to Saturday November to March) and Tresco (20 minutes, at least three daily Monday to Saturday April to October, one or two daily November to March) from Penzance heliport. Adult/child return fares are £100/50; short breaks of up to four nights cost £72/36 per adult/child, and other deals are sometimes available. It costs £2 per day to leave your car at the heliport, and a minibus from Penzance train station connects with flights (£1.25 one way, 10 minutes).

Boat The **Isles of Scilly Steamship Group's** *(☎ 0845 710 5555;* **w** *www.ios-travel.co.uk) Scillonian* sails between Penzance and St Mary's (£65/72 return October to March /April to September, two hours 40 minutes, daily Monday to Saturday). Children under 12 pay half-price, and short breaks of up to three nights cost £55/50 adult/child return.

Getting Around
Boats sail to the four off-islands from St Mary's harbour at least daily in summer, several times daily to Tresco. A return trip to any island costs £5.80, while a triangular return (eg, St Mary's–Tresco–Bryher–St Mary's) costs £7.50. Fares for boat trips to the uninhabited islands to see the seals and sea birds vary but are usually around £6.

The airport bus service (£2.50) departs from The Strand in Hugh Town 40 minutes before each flight. A circular bus service runs around St Mary's several times daily in summer (£1 to all destinations). There are tours of St Mary's by **vintage 1948 bus** *(☎ 422 387)* for £5, or **1929 Riley open-top car** *(☎ 422479)* for £15/20/22 per 2/3/4 people.

Bikes are available at **Buccabu Hire** *(☎ 422289; Porthcressa, Hugh Town)* for £6 per day and **Tresco Bicycle Hire** *(☎ 422807)* for £8 per day.

The Marches

The Marches – where little England merges with wild and woolly Wales – is a beautiful strip of the country, blessed with a wealth of rustic charms, and hardly touched by time or tainted by mass tourism. There are some outstanding urban attractions here, although it's the Marches rural personality, a charming blend of English and Welsh, that makes it such a rewarding alternative to the beaten track. This is ideal touring country whether you're driving, cycling, walking or even canoeing, and provides the perfect opportunity to absorb the simple pleasures of English country life.

The sweeping landscapes are studded with castles and ruins, laying testament to the many ferocious battles and struggles that were played out across this stage over time. In the 8th century the Anglo-Saxon King Offa of Mercia built an earthwork barricade along the border with Wales to try and quell the tensions. It was known as Offa's Dyke, and much of it is still traceable as a popular walking route today.

It was under the Normans in the 11th century that these bordering counties first emerged as a separate entity. In an effort to subdue the fiercely independent Welsh, William the Conqueror established small independent kingdoms here under the rule of his most loyal supporters. These rulers were called Marcher Lords after the Anglo-Saxon word *mearc*, meaning boundary. Ten centuries later, the areas – principally the counties of Shropshire and Herefordshire, with Worcestershire thrown in for geographical good measure – are still known collectively as the Marches.

Shropshire is the jewel in the Marches' crown, with the handsome Tudor town of Shrewsbury as its capital, the fascinating industrial-heritage site of Ironbridge Gorge its star attraction and the south Shropshire Hills the back garden that all its neighbours covet. Herefordshire contains the picturesque River Wye, with its wealth of water-based activities, a glorious sweep of black-and-white villages and the marvellous medieval Mappa Mundi. Meanwhile, muddying your hiking boots on the illustrious hills of Malvern is a highlight of any visit to Worcestershire.

Highlights

- Strolling around the atmospheric streetscapes of Shrewsbury, England's most picturesque Tudor town

- Stepping back through time at Ironbridge Gorge, the cradle of the Industrial Revolution

- Rambling through the gentle hills and tranquil valleys of Shropshire's Long Mynd

- Navigating the extraordinary 13th-century Mappa Mundi

- Taking a summer tour through the bewitching historical house of Hellens

- Taking in the stunning views and water adventures on the River Wye at Symonds Yat

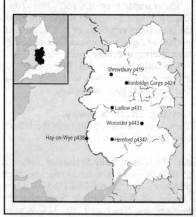

ACTIVITIES

The Marches is a region perfect for gentle walking, cycling and other outdoor activities, with hundreds of miles of paths and tracks snaking through pastoral idylls, wooded valleys and gentle hills. This section provides a few ideas to get you started, with more information given in the Activities chapter near the start of this book. Regional tourism websites contain walking and cycling information, and all Tourist Information Centres (TICs) stock free leaflets plus maps and guides (usually £1 to £5) covering walking, cycling and other activities.

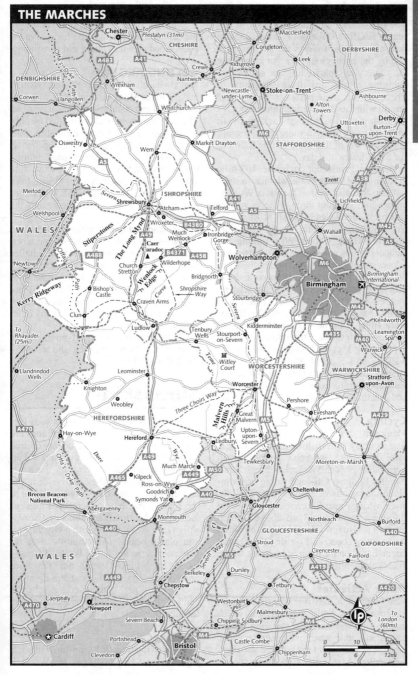

THE MARCHES

Chester
To Prestatyn (31mi)
Macclesfield
CHESHIRE
Congleton
Leek
DERBYSHIRE
A6
A483
A41
Crewe
Kidsgrove
Corwen
Nantwich
Newcastle-
under-Lyme
Stoke-on-Trent
Ashbourne
DENBIGHSHIRE
Llangollen
Wrexham
Alton
Towers
Derby
Whitchurch
Uttoxeter
Burton-
upon-Trent
Oswestry
Wem
Market Drayton
STAFFORDSHIRE
A50
A5
Trent
A38
Meifod
SHROPSHIRE
M6
Lichfield
Severn
Shrewsbury
Atcham
Telford
A41
A5
Welshpool
Wroxeter
B4380
M54
Walsall
M42
WALES
Stiperstones
The Long Mynd
A49
Much
Wenlock
Ironbridge
Gorge
A5
Newtown
A488
Caer
Caradoc
B4371
A458
Wolverhampton
M6
Birmingham
International
Church
Stretton
Wilderhope
M42
Bishop's
Castle
Wenlock Edge
Corve
Bridgnorth
Birmingham
Kerry Ridgeway
Shropshire
Way
Stourbridge
Severn
To
Rhayader
(25mi)
Clun
Craven Arms
Kenilworth
Llandrindod
Wells
Ludlow
Tenbury
Wells
Stourport-
on-Severn
Kidderminster
Leamington
Spa
A435
A40
Knighton
Leominster
Teme
Witley
Court
WORCESTERSHIRE
M40
Warwick
A425
WARWICKSHIRE
Stratford-
upon-Avon
Weobley
HEREFORDSHIRE
Three Choirs Way
Worcester
Pershore
Evesham
A470
Hay-on-Wye
Malvern Hills
Great
Malvern
M5
Hereford
Wye
Ledbury
Upton-
upon-
Severn
Moreton-in-Marsh
A49
Much Marcle
M50
Tewkesbury
Kilpeck
A449
A465
Ross-on-Wye
Goodrich
Cheltenham
Brecon Beacons
National Park
Dove
Symonds Yat
A40
Northleach
Burford
Abergavenny
Monmouth
Gloucester
A40
OXFORDSHIRE
GLOUCESTERSHIRE
Stroud
Cirencester
Fairford
WALES
Severn Way
M5
A419
A420
Berkeley
Dursley
Tetbury
A449
Chepstow
Westonbirt
Malmesbury
M4
Caerphilly
A470
Newport
Severn Beach
Chipping Sodbury
To
London
(60mi)
Cardiff
Portishead
Clevedon
M4
Castle Combe
Chippenham
Bristol
Avon
0   10   20km
0   6   12mi

Walking

The best-known long-distance walk in this region is **Offa's Dyke**, a 177-mile (285km) national trail that follows the ancient ditch dug by the eponymous Mercian king in the 9th century to separate England and Wales. Running south–north from Chepstow to Prestatyn, this route passes through varied terrain with lots of historical interest but it's surprisingly hilly, so best tackled by fit hikers. If you want a more gentle stroll, short sections of this route can be followed for a few hours or a day.

Another gentle option is the 107-mile (172km) **Wye Valley Walk**, which also starts in Chepstow and follows the River Wye upstream into England through Herefordshire and back into Wales to finish at Rhayader. Yet another favourite is the 106-mile (170km) **Three Choirs Way** linking the cathedral cities of Hereford, Worcester and Gloucester. As with all long routes, these can be followed for just a short section and still provide a great snapshot of Marches scenery.

Areas ideal for shorter walks include the idyllic English countryside of the **Shropshire Hills**, with the well-known ridges of Wenlock Edge, the Stiperstones and the lovely Long Mynd. The region's other main walking area is the **Malvern Hills**, which straddle the boundary between Worcestershire and Herefordshire, offering easy paths and breathtaking views.

Cycling

Many parts of the Marches make good cycling country. Shropshire in particular is ideal for touring, and you can rent bikes in Shrewsbury, Much Wenlock, Church Stretton and Ludlow. Off-road riding areas include the woods of Hopton near Ludlow, and Eastridge near Shrewsbury. High-level riding on the Long Mynd above Church Stretton is also rewarding. In Herefordshire, the **Ledbury Loop** is a 17-mile (27km) rural circuit based on the town of Ledbury, where bikes can be hired.

Other Activities

Near Monmouth, the River Wye runs through a narrow valley called Symonds Yat, which makes a perfect base for canoeing (either easy-grade white water, or longer river trips), while other sections of the Wye are also regular paddlers' haunts. Rocky buttresses above the river mean rock climbing is also popular at Symonds Yat. Farther north, if you've got the cash and the courage, the Long Mynd is a renowned area for gliding and paragliding.

GETTING AROUND

For all its charms relatively few visitors make it to the Marches, as without your own transport it can be infuriatingly inaccessible. The main towns are well connected by public transport, but exploring rural attractions this way needs time, planning and patience.

The A49 is the main road running north–south and you never have to venture very far from it. Railway lines radiate from the county capitals of Shrewsbury, Hereford and Worcester, although they serve only the largest towns.

First Midland Red (☎ 01905-763888) and **Arriva** are the region's main bus operators, although a bewildering array of smaller local companies connect rural centres. TICs stock timetables. A Day Rover pass with First Midland Red costs £4.60/3.60 per adult/child and allows travel anywhere on its system and on routes run by many other smaller companies.

Useful national transport numbers are ☎ 0870 608 2608 for coach and ☎ 08457 484950 for rail inquiries.

Shropshire

Spread across the rolling hills between Birmingham and the Welsh border, Shropshire is a large, sparsely populated county centred on the attractive town of Shrewsbury and bisected, roughly east to west, by the River Severn. To the north the countryside is flat and uninspiring but the Shropshire Hills to the south – the 'blue remembered hills' of local scribe AE Housman, author of *A Shropshire Lad* – are peppered with pretty villages and placid peaks. The county's most remarkable attraction is the World Heritage–listed Ironbridge Gorge, not far from Shrewsbury. Towards the southern tip of the county you'll find Ludlow, cute as a button and teeming with historical architecture and terrific restaurants.

Walking

Walking in the bucolic Shropshire Hills is a joy. The best-known ridges are Wenlock

Edge, the Long Mynd and the Stiperstones, all around 500m high and taken in by the 136-mile (218km) **Shropshire Way**, which loops from Shrewsbury south to Ludlow.

Cycling

Shropshire is a picture from the saddle, and a good 100-mile (161km) five- or six-day cycle route takes in its most appealing features. The route goes from Shrewsbury to Ironbridge (14 miles, 23km), Much Wenlock (5 miles, 8km), Ludlow (20 miles, 32km), Clun (17 miles, 27km), Church Stretton and the Long Mynd (15 miles, 24km), and back to Shrewsbury (16 miles, 26km) alongside roads parallel to the busy A49. You can rent bikes in most towns and some villages, and TICs stock lists of cycle

hire firms. The larger ones will also stock *Cycling for Pleasure in the Marches*, which has comprehensive route maps and notes.

Getting Around

There are useful rail services from Shrewsbury to Church Stretton, Craven Arms and Ludlow. The invaluable *Shropshire Bus & Train Map*, available free from TICs, shows all bus routes.

SHREWSBURY

☎ 01743 • pop 60,000

When Charles Dickens lodged in Shrewsbury in the 19th century, he looked from his hotel window 'all downhill and slantwise at the crookedest black and white houses, all of many shapes except straight shapes'. The

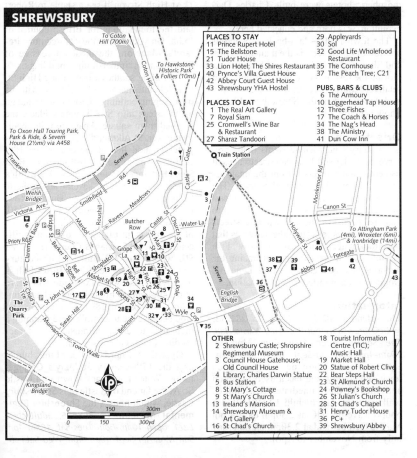

SHREWSBURY

PLACES TO STAY
11 Prince Rupert Hotel
15 The Bellstone
21 Tudor House
33 Lion Hotel; The Shires Restaurant
40 Prynce's Villa Guest House
42 Abbey Court Guest House
43 Shrewsbury YHA Hostel

PLACES TO EAT
1 The Real Art Gallery
7 Royal Siam
25 Cromwell's Wine Bar & Restaurant
27 Sharaz Tandoori
29 Appleyards
30 Sol
32 Good Life Wholefood Restaurant
35 The Cornhouse
37 The Peach Tree; C21

PUBS, BARS & CLUBS
6 The Armoury
10 Loggerhead Tap House
12 Three Fishes
17 The Coach & Horses
34 The Nag's Head
38 The Ministry
41 Dun Cow Inn

OTHER
2 Shrewsbury Castle; Shropshire Regimental Museum
3 Council House Gatehouse; Old Council House
4 Library; Charles Darwin Statue
5 Bus Station
8 St Mary's Cottage
9 St Mary's Church
13 Ireland's Mansion
14 Shrewsbury Museum & Art Gallery
16 St Chad's Church
18 Tourist Information Centre (TIC); Music Hall
19 Market Hall
20 Statue of Robert Clive
22 Bear Steps Hall
23 St Alkmund's Church
24 Powney's Bookshop
26 St Julian's Church
28 St Chad's Chapel
31 Henry Tudor House
36 PC+
39 Shrewsbury Abbey

streetscapes have changed little over the centuries and visitors today are still enamoured by the higgledy-piggledy charms of England's finest Tudor town.

Set within a horseshoe loop of the River Severn, the town's defensive potential first appealed to the Saxons in the 5th century. After the Norman Conquest, the settlement came under the control of Roger de Montgomery, who built the castle perched above the train station. For many years Shrewsbury was pivotal in keeping the Welsh in tow while it prospered from the region's wool trade and successful merchants built many of the black-and-white buildings that crown the town today. It became an important staging post on the London to Holyhead route in the 18th century, when many of the town's atmospheric hotels were built. Charles Darwin, who rocked the world with his theory of evolution, was born and educated here.

The town itself – laid-back, prosperous and full of character – is the main attraction and Shrewsbury makes a good base for exploring the rest of the county. It is quiet and relatively tourist-free, apart from a week in mid-August when the Shrewsbury Flower Show is held.

Orientation

Shrewsbury's near-island status helps preserve the Tudor and Jacobean streetscapes of its centre and protects it from the unattractive urban sprawl of surrounding areas. The train station is a five-minute walk northeast of the centre and is as far as you'll need to venture. Many of the old winding streets still bear names reflecting the activities that once took place there – Butcher Row, Fish St and Milk St are obvious but tracing the histories of Gay Meadow, Grope Lane and Dogpole takes a little more imagination.

Information

The splendid **TIC** (☎ 281200, fax 281213; e tic@shrewsburytourism.co.uk; Music Hall, The Square; open 10am-6pm Mon-Sat, 10am-4pm Sun Jun-Sept, 10am-5pm Mon-Sat Oct-late May) provides information on town and county, and has a useful map on activities in the immediate area. Guided walking tours (adult/child £2.50/1.50, 1½ hours) leave the TIC at 2.30pm daily from May to October and at 2.30pm on Saturday only from November to April.

Powney's Bookshop (☎ 369165; w www.powneysbookshop.demon.co.uk; 4-5 Alkmund's Place) is a good source for walking maps.

You can check your emails – but that's about it – at **PC+** (☎ 242135; 11 Abbey Foregate) for £4 per hour.

Walking Tour

Start from the TIC, in the old **Music Hall** built in 1839. Opposite, in the square, is the **Market Hall** (☎ 351067), an open-sided building erected in 1596 and where Shrewsbury's wool merchants, or 'drapers', traded until the mid-19th century. On the insides of the pillars at the northern end you can still see the holes the markers used to record the number of fleeces sold.

At High St you'll see a statue to Robert Clive, former mayor of Shrewsbury, who laid the foundations for British control of India. On your left is the 16th-century **Ireland's Mansion**, the most impressive of Shrewsbury's timber-framed buildings.

Travelling southeast back along High St, turn left into narrow Grope Lane with its overhanging buildings. Cross Fish St and go up the steps into St Alkmund's Place, the original town square. Apart from its medieval tower, **St Alkmund's Church** was completely remodelled at the end of the 18th century. The restored 14th-century **Bear Steps Hall** (open 10am-4pm daily) is worth a gander, and there are several atmospheric black-and-white houses along Butcher Row, including the **Abbot's House**, built in 1450.

You should be able to see the spire – one of the highest in England – of the magnificent, medieval **St Mary's Church** (St Mary's St), which has a beautiful 15th-century angel roof and stained glass. Best of all is the great Jesse window, made from rare mid-14th-century English glass. The original spire collapsed in 1894 – thrown down by God because the townsfolk were planning a memorial to anticreationist Darwin (according to the vicar's sermon).

Opposite the northern side of the church, past the 17th-century **St Mary's Cottage**, follow Water Lane back down into Castle St. At the far end of Castle St is **Shrewsbury Castle**, which houses the **Shropshire Regimental Museum** (☎ 358516; adult/child £2/1; open 10am-5pm Tues-Sat, 10am-4pm Sun-Mon Apr-Sept, 10am-4pm Wed-Sat Feb-

Mar), although the view is more worthwhile than the collection. There's no charge to walk around the grounds. The entrance gate of the castle is Norman but much of the castle was remodelled by Edward I, and restored by the Scottish engineer Thomas Telford in the late 18th century.

Down the alley near the entrance to the castle is the Jacobean-style **Council House Gatehouse**, dating from 1620. Beyond it is the **Old Council House**, where the Council of the Welsh Marches used to meet to administer the area.

Across the road from the castle is the **library**, surely one of the grandest in the land, with a **statue of Charles Darwin** outside. Returning to St Mary's St, follow it into Dogpole. At the end of Dogpole, turn right onto Wyle Cop, which is Welsh for 'hill top'. The **Lion Hotel** was where Dickens stayed on his visit to the town; a 200-year-old gilded lion marks its entrance. Henry VII is said to have stayed in the **Henry Tudor House**, on the other side of Barracks Passage, before the Battle of Bosworth.

If you turn around and walk back down Wyle Cop then bear left, you'll reach the graceful 18th-century **English Bridge**, widened and reconstructed in 1927 and offering magnificent views of the town's skyline. **Shrewsbury Abbey** is ahead of you.

Double back over the bridge, down the steps and stroll left along the river to **The Quarry Park** and its undulating and fragrant manicured gardens, which host the annual **Flower Show**. Wander up to the impressive **St Chad's Church**, built in 1792, and into the tranquil church grounds and you will see – the first flat stone on your left – the cracked and spookily authentic **gravestone of Ebenezer Scrooge**. When a version of Dickens' *A Christmas Carol*, starring George C Scott, was made here in 1984, one of the old headstones was adapted for the film's final scene when the Ghost of Christmas Future shows the miserly bean-counter his grave.

Shrewsbury Abbey

The large red-sandstone Shrewsbury Abbey *(w www.shrewsburyabbey.com; Abbey Foregate; admission £2 donation; open 9.30am-5.30pm daily Apr-Oct, 10.30am-3pm daily Nov-Mar)* is what's left of the Benedictine monastery founded by Roger de Montgomery in 1083. The architecture is in three different styles – Norman, Early English and Victorian – and you can measure and compare the prowess of the early British builders, as well as admire the 14th-century west window of heraldic glass, among other historical features.

A controversial and compelling sculpture, *The Naked Christ* by local artist Michelle Coxon, caused a national stir when it was unveiled in 2001. It portrays a crucified and decomposing Christ – the decay said to symbolise the Saviour's suffering – with what's left of his genitals exposed.

The abbey is renowned for its acoustics and a notice board inside provides information on choral society and Hill Organ recitals (1pm on Wednesday is a reliable slot).

Shrewsbury Museum & Art Gallery

Shrewsbury's main museum *(☎ 361196; Barker St; admission free; open 10am-5pm Tues-Sat year round, 10am-4pm Sun & Mon June-Sept)* is housed in restored 16th- and 17th-century buildings and exhibits a mixed bag of contemporary art and two levels packed with costumes and antiquities from as far back as the Middle Ages.

Places to Stay

Whatever your means, Shrewsbury has a good range of accommodation. Hotels abound in the centre, while you'll find several B&Bs around Abbey Foregate.

Oxon Hall Touring Park *(☎ 340868, fax 340869; w www.morris-leisure.co.uk/oxon hall.html; Welshpool Rd; tent sites per person from £7.25)* is a five-star facility catering for caravanners and campers who like nature and comfort in equal doses. It's next to Shrewsbury's Park and Ride, 2½ miles (4km) from the town centre, and has a kiddies-free section.

Shrewsbury YHA Hostel *(☎ 0870 770 6030, fax 0870 770 6031; e shrewsbury@ yha.org.uk; The Woodlands, Abbey Foregate; open Mon-Sat Apr-Aug, Tues-Sat Sept-Oct; dorm beds £9.50)* is a pleasant spot in a Victorian ironmaster's house, about a mile from the train and bus stations.

Abbey Court Guest House *(☎ 364416, fax 358359; 134 Abbey Foregate; B&B per person with/without en suite £25/20)* has bright and cheerful rooms and is the pick of the town's B&Bs.

Prynce's Villa Guest House (☎ 356217; 15 Monkmoor Rd; singles/doubles from £20/35), off Abbey Foregate, has spacious quarters with old-fashioned decor.

Tudor House (☎ 351735; 2 Fish St; singles/doubles from £30/60), dating from 1460, is centrally located on a quiet medieval street and has pretty beamed rooms.

The Bellstone (☎ 242100, fax 242103; w www.bellstone-hotel.co.uk; Bell Stone; rooms £37.50), with slick and well-priced accommodation, offers some character despite being modern.

Lion Hotel (☎ 353107, fax 352744; w www.regalhotels.co.uk/thelion; Wyle Cop; singles/doubles from £79/99), the most atmospheric accommodation in town, is a classic 17th-century coaching inn where many a passing luminary wined, dined and reclined. You can take the Dickens Suite, where the author stayed while on a reading tour for A Christmas Carol in the 1880s. The room is furnished with antique bits and bobs and a Victorian bed (with mattress c. 2002). Ask to see the magnificent ballroom, where Thomas de Quincy is said to have kipped when the guest rooms were full.

Prince Rupert Hotel (☎ 499955, fax 357306; w www.prince-rupert-hotel.co.uk; Butcher Row; singles/doubles £75/95, often cheaper at the weekends), Shrewsbury's smartest address, provides luxurious lodgings in a tastefully converted 12th-century building. 'Shearing' specials in summer mean it's often full of old age pensioners.

Places to Eat

Good Life Wholefood Restaurant (☎ 350455; Barracks Passage; meals £3-6), in a cosy little nook off Wyle Cop, is fantastic for healthy, hearty and delicious fare, including a choice of nine salads that will help put the romp back in your stomp.

The Cornhouse (☎ 231991; 59a Wyle Cop; meals £8-13) has innovative, seasonal British cuisine. The weekend brunch menu accommodates late risers, and Sunday blues top off the weekend nicely.

The Peach Tree (☎ 355055; 21 Abbey Foregate; bar snacks £4-6, meals £9-12) is by far the most cosmopolitan joint in Shrewsbury and provides consistently good food.

The Bellstone (☎ 242100; mains £8-12) is smart casual and has a tasty menu ranging from tapas to steaks.

Cromwell's Wine Bar & Restaurant (☎ 361440; 11 Dogpole; mains £7-11) is Tudor chic with an ever-changing cavalcade of international flavours served in a tastefully restored 15th-century building. There's a lovely, if rather reserved, rear patio.

The Shires Restaurant (☎ 353107, fax 352744; Wyle Cop; meals £8-12), in the Lion Hotel, has crisp white linen, impeccable service and terrific traditional British food.

Sharaz Tandoori (☎ 351744; 79 Wyle Cop; meals £5-8) is our pick of the Indian restaurants and serves rustic fare accompanied by Bollywood anthems until midnight weekdays and 1am at the weekend.

Royal Siam (☎ 353117; Butcher Row; meals £7-11) dishes up passable versions of Thai classics in an atmospheric 14th-century timber-framed building.

Sol (☎ 340560; w www.solrestaurant.co.uk; 82 Wyle Cop; 3-course meals £30), with a Michelin star, is the gastronomic pride of the town, renowned for its sumptuous food but not for its decor and ambience, which don't match the lofty standards of the kitchen.

The Real Art Gallery (☎ 270123; 24 Meadow Place; open 10am-5.30pm Tues-Sat, 11am-5pm Sun), not far from the castle, has the best coffee, while **Appleyards** (☎ 240180; 85 Wyle Cop) is an outstanding deli.

Entertainment

Locals lament a time when there was a different pub for every day of the year, although there are still several good drinking dens. On weekend nights, it pays to choose your venue warily because the centre of town can get very rowdy.

Loggerhead Tap House (Church St) is the traditional pub with the most character, and has a splendid selection of ales and not a hint of affectation.

The Coach & Horses (Swan Hill) is a rival for best pub: it's a wonderful inn with bonhomie by the barrel. There's a handy poster of the Shropshire Hills and their altitudes, along with good game roasts.

The Nag's Head (Wyle Cop) is livelier, smokier and louder than most. It boasts a big beer garden that actually has a patch of lawn and a jukebox last updated when David Essex was a bright prospect.

Three Fishes (4 Fish St) is a more refined, smoke-free hostelry that serves wholesome ales at scrawny prices.

Dun Cow Inn (171 Abbey Foregate), just past the Abbey, is full of clutter but manages to be extremely cosy and is a local institution.

The Armoury (Welsh Bridge) is a huge open shell of a pub that features considerate lighting, and assorted pics and antiquities on the walls. It is flanked by two dodgy clubs where bouncers compete with young drinkers for predominance.

C21 (☎ 355055; 21 Abbey Foregate), attached to The Peach Tree, is the place for a bit of city glamour and a welcoming flirty smile whatever your orientation. Sunday and Monday are gay and lesbian nights.

The Ministry (Abbey Foregate; cover charge £4) has theme nights – everything from disco to garage – and free lollipops from behind the bar.

Getting There & Away

Shrewsbury is 150 miles (241km) from London, 68 miles (109km) from Manchester, 43 miles (69km) from Chester and 27 miles (43km) from Ludlow.

Bus National Express has two connections daily with London (£18.50, 4½ hours) via Telford and Birmingham (1½ hours). Bus No 96 serves Ironbridge on its way from Shrewsbury to Telford, approximately every second hour Monday to Saturday. Bus No 420 goes to Birmingham twice daily, bus No 435 travels to Ludlow via Church Stretton and bus No 553 heads to Bishop's Castle on Friday and Saturday evenings only.

Train There are no direct trains connecting Shrewsbury and London – you must change at Wolverhampton for the most direct route, and journey times vary from three to 6½ hours. There are regular trains from Cardiff to Manchester via Ludlow.

Shrewsbury is a popular starting point for two scenic routes into Wales: one loop taking in Shrewsbury, northern Wales and Chester; the other, **Heart of Wales Line** (☎ 01597-822053), runs southwest to Swansea (£15.80, four hours) and connects with the Cardiff to Fishguard main line.

AROUND SHREWSBURY
Attingham Park

The grandest of Shropshire's stately homes, this late-18th-century mansion (☎ 01743-708162; admission to house & grounds £4.60;

open 1pm-4.30pm Fri-Tues late Mar-Oct, grounds open daily until dusk year round), owned by the National Trust (NT), combines elegance and ostentation in equal measures. Behind its imposing neoclassical facade, you'll find a picture gallery by John Nash and magnificent Regency interiors containing Grand Tour paintings and impressive collections of Regency silver and lavish Italian furniture. It is set in 92 hectares of landscaped grounds that shelter a herd of deer and provide pleasant walks along the River Tern.

Attingham Park is 4 miles (6km) southeast of Shrewsbury at Atcham on the B4380. Bus No 81 (Shrewsbury–Edgmond) runs five times daily Monday to Friday, less on weekends, and stops near the end of the Attingham Park driveway. A taxi from Shrewsbury will cost about £7.

Wroxeter Roman City

Wroxeter (☎ 01743-761330; admission £3.60; open 10pm-6pm daily Mar-Sept, 10pm-5pm Oct, 10am-1pm & 2pm-4pm Nov-Mar), run by English Heritage (EH), has the ancient name Viroconium and was the fourth-largest city in Roman Britain. It survived modern development because its successor, Shrewsbury, was built on a separate site. Unfortunately, most of the city lies under farmland and all you can see are the extensive remains of the public baths and a few archaeological finds in the small museum.

Remote-sensing techniques have made it possible – without turning a sod of earth – to map the city remains, which are believed to be as big as Pompeii. The costs of excavation are prohibitive so, for the time being at least, you'll need to use a lot of imagination to picture the site's former greatness.

Wroxeter is 6 miles (10km) southeast of Shrewsbury, just off the B4380 on the way to Ironbridge. Bus No 81 stops nearby (see Attingham Park for details).

IRONBRIDGE GORGE
☎ 01952

The World Heritage Site of Ironbridge Gorge was the Silicon Valley of the 18th century, and the birthplace of the Industrial Revolution. It was here, in 1709, that Abraham Darby pioneered the technique of smelting iron ore with coke, a process that transformed the town into the dynamo that

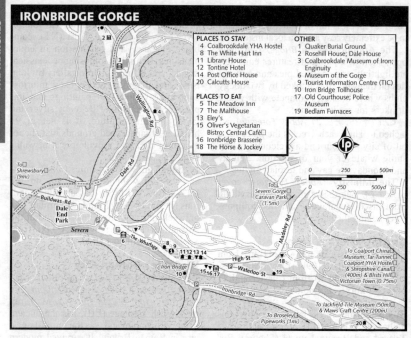

IRONBRIDGE GORGE

PLACES TO STAY
4   Coalbrookdale YHA Hostel
8   The White Hart Inn
11 Library House
12 Tontine Hotel
14 Post Office House
20 Calcutts House

PLACES TO EAT
5   The Meadow Inn
7   The Malthouse
13 Eley's
15 Oliver's Vegetarian
    Bistro; Central Café
16 Ironbridge Brasserie
18 The Horse & Jockey

OTHER
1   Quaker Burial Ground
2   Rosehill House; Dale House
3   Coalbrookdale Museum of Iron;
    Enginuity
6   Museum of the Gorge
9   Tourist Information Centre (TIC)
10 Iron Bridge Tollhouse
17 Old Courthouse; Police
    Museum
19 Bedlam Furnaces

drove industrial progress for the rest of the century. His innovation led to the production of the first iron wheels, iron rails, the steam locomotive and the first iron bridge, which was constructed here by Abraham Darby III in 1779 and remains the centrepiece of this most prestigious of industrial sites today. Abraham Darby II, no slouch himself, invented the forging process, which enabled single beams of iron to be produced.

There is a wealth of prestigious industrial relics housed in 10 engaging museums scattered around the picturesque setting of the gorge. Even if industrial archaeology doesn't ring your bell, Ironbridge is an absorbing detour (although it sometimes appears so quaint, the locals could be actors on the TIC's payroll).

Orientation

It would be ideal if you had your own transport here because the sights are far-flung, hills are steep, there is no bike hire and buses are scarce. It's 3 miles (5km) from Blists Hill Victorian Town to the Coalbrookdale Museum of Iron. Parking can be a bother around the bridge, although there are a few pay-and-display spots nearby and most of the museums have their own spaces.

Information

If you're relying on public transport, get help from the enthusiastic **TIC** (☎/fax 432166; ⓦ www.ironbridge.org.uk; The Wharfage; open 9am-5pm Mon-Fri, 10am-5pm Sat & Sun), located near the bridge. You can exchange money here and in the post office, while the old police station houses the only ATM.

Things to See & Do

If you intend visiting all or most of Ironbridge's museums, purchase a passport ticket from the TIC, which will admit you to all of the sites and is valid indefinitely until you've done the lot. The combined ticket costs £12.95/8.25 per adult/child, a saving of more than £20 on what it would cost otherwise. Bear in mind that many sites have reduced opening hours in winter and some close from November to March.

Museum of the Gorge This former warehouse (☎ 432166; The Wharfage; adult/child £2/1) houses a small exhibition covering the history of the gorge and includes a 12m model of the river valley as it would have looked during its heyday in 1796. A good way to begin your visit is with the absorbing video, which sets the museum in its historical context and provides an overview of the Industrial Revolution. The rest of the centre focuses on the environmental consequences of industrialisation.

Coalbrookdale Museum of Iron It was here that Abraham Darby first succeeded in smelting iron ore with coke, and you can see his furnace, now lovingly restored. The converted foundry *(adult/child £4.20/2.40)* today houses some of the extraordinary products of iron-making and a history of the Coalbrookdale company.

The Darby Houses About 90m up the hill from the Coalbrookdale Museum of Iron, 18th-century **Rosehill House** *(☎ 433521; adult/child £2.90/1.60)* was built by the Darbys but is maintained as it was when it was home to an early-19th-century ironmaster. Next door in the partly restored **Dale House** is the office where Darby would have pored over his designs for the bridge. Combined admission to the Coalbrookdale Museum of Iron and the Darby Houses costs £5/3.15.

Iron Bridge & Tollhouse As well as providing a crossing over the river, Abraham Darby III's world-first iron bridge promoted the area and his technological prowess. It was closed to vehicles in 1934, and the tollhouse *(admission free)* now houses an exhibition about the bridge's history.

Blists Hill Victorian Town This 20-hectare open-air museum *(☎ 433521; Legges Way, Madeley, Telford; adult/child £8/5)* is set up like a Victorian theme park, with reconstructed buildings and craftspeople demonstrating skills of the era. If you have any pounds left after paying the hefty admission, you can exchange them for shillings to spend in the shops, restaurant, pub and gift shop (you get the idea). It's jam-packed in summer and you should allow at least half a day if this sounds like your cup of afternoon tea.

Coalport China Museum When iron-making moved elsewhere, Coalport china

slowed the region's decline until it, too, moved in 1926. This museum *(adult/child £4.20/2.40)* exhibits all sorts of elaborate pottery and depicts the hardships of factory life at the time; there is a children's gallery and demonstration workshops.

Tar Tunnel A short stroll alongside the Shropshire Canal brings you to this remarkable phenomenon *(adult/child £1.10/55p)* where natural bitumen oozes from the walls.

Jackfield Tile Museum Across the river from Coalport, this old factory *(adult/child £4.20/2.40)* has a wonderful display of thousands of decorative tiles, mainly from Victorian times, as well as a drop-in workshop.

Broseley Pipeworks Two miles from the iron bridge – and worth the detour if you've got your own transport – this was the home of one of Britain's most prolific pipe makers. Production stopped in 1957, when cigarettes had all but replaced pipes, and the factory's doors were closed, sealing 350 years of tradition. The building *(adult/child £2.90/1.60; open 1pm-5pm June-Sept)* is largely as it was when the last worker turned out the lights. There's a lively exhibition exploring a potted history of smoking.

Enginuity Ironbridge's most recent attraction *(adult/child £4.95/3.50)*, which opened in July 2002 and cost £7 million to build, is a hands-on, feet-on, full-on exploration of design and engineering in modern life. It allows visitors – the young and the young at heart – to become apprentice engineers and discover many of the hows, whys and what fors of technology.

Places to Stay
Severn Gorge Caravan Park *(☎/fax 684789; Bridgnorth Rd, Tweedale; tent sites per person from £3.60)*, just less than a mile north of Blists Hill, is the best place to pitch your tent.

YHA has two hostels at either end of Ironbridge Gorge. **Coalport YHA Hostel** *(☎ 0870 770 5882, fax 0870 770 5883; e ironbridge@yha.org.uk; John Rose Building, High St, Coalport; dorm beds £11.25)*, near the China Museum, is the place to make bookings for both. **Coalbrookdale YHA Hostel** *(Paradise Rd, Coalbrookdale)* is near the Museum of Iron.

The White Hart Inn (☎ 432481; The Wharfage; beds per person £23) isn't touting for tourists – normally contractors – but if you're after something cheap and central then you might consider this basic place.

Post Office House (☎ 433201; 6 The Square; singles/doubles from £34/44) has three pleasantly furnished rooms (one with en suite) above the village post office.

Calcutts House (☎ 882631, fax 882951; ⓦ www.calcuttshouse.co.uk; Calcutts Rd, Jackfield; singles/doubles with en suite £49/59), away from the relative hubbub, is an 18th-century pad with opulent rooms named after the celebrated ironmasters who lived here over the years.

Library House (☎ 432299, fax 433967; ⓦ www.libraryhouse.com; 11 Severn Bank; singles/doubles £50/60) has luxurious lodgings in a distinguished Georgian mansion set back off the road.

Places to Eat
There are **cafés** at the Museum of Iron and Blists Hill (and a pub too), as well as in the Maws Craft Centre in summer.

The White Hart Inn (☎ 432481; The Wharfage; meals £4-6) is the place for central, inexpensive and mediocre pub grub served in big portions.

Eley's (☎ 432030), on the square, does an excellent, really porky pork pie for committed carnivores, a mean pastie for vegetarians and lots of savouries for everyone in between.

Old Courthouse (☎ 433838; Waterloo St), above the Police Museum, is the most interesting of the teashops, where you sip with the ghosts of Victorian judge and jury.

Oliver's Vegetarian Bistro (☎ 433086; 33 High St; mains around £6; open 7pm-11pm Tues-Fri, noon-3pm Sat, noon-5pm Sun) is an excellent spot with creative, moderately priced vegetarian fare.

Ironbridge Brasserie (☎ 432716; 29 High St; meals from £15; open Tues-Sun) serves robust British cuisine at elevated prices, and is the choice for summer alfresco.

The Malthouse (☎ 433712; The Wharfage; 3-course meals around £20) is a wonderful spot, with quick and tasty snacks in the bar and slow and scrumptious contemporary creations in the restaurant. There's regular live jazz in the bar.

The Meadow Inn (☎ 433193; Buildwas Rd) is one of the best pubs in Shropshire, with terrific, award-winning home-made pub grub, a splendid garden and unique views of the colossal cooling towers.

The Horse & Jockey (☎ 433798; 15 Jockey Bank) is a lovely, relaxed traditional pub and a firm favourite with the locals. It has the best steak pie in the land – according to the body established to promote British meat – which more than makes up for the steep 10-minute walk to get here.

Getting There & Away
Ironbridge is 14 miles (23km) from Shrewsbury. Coming from the other direction, it's well signposted from junction 4 on the M54. The nearest train station is 5 miles (8km) away at Telford. Bus No 96 runs hourly between Shrewsbury and Telford, via Ironbridge, Monday to Saturday.

BRIDGNORTH
☎ 01746
Tumbling down a sandstone bluff, Bridgnorth has a dramatic location above the River Severn and is most interesting for its railways. It's the northern terminus of the **Severn Valley Railway** (☎ 01299-403816), whose trains chug down the picturesque valley to Kidderminster. A unique funicular, the **Bridgnorth Cliff Railway** (☎ 762052; ⓦ www.bridg northcliffrailway.co.uk; ticket 70p; open 8am-8pm Mon-Sat, noon-8pm Sun May-Sept, 8am-6.30pm Mon-Sat, noon-6.30pm Sun Oct-Apr), scales the cliff separating High Town, at the top of the bluff, and Low Town below.

Lovers should check out the pleasingly potty **The Hundred House Hotel** (☎ 730353, fax 730355; ⓦ www.hundredhouse.co.uk; singles/doubles £75/99, meals £9-15), 6 miles (10km) north of Bridgnorth, which has antique beds, lavender-scented sheets and swings in the rooms. The food, enriched with fresh garden herbs, is fabulous.

Getting There & Away
Bus No 436 runs from Shrewsbury to Bridgnorth eight times a day Monday to Saturday (five times on Sunday), and you can catch the steam train from any of the stations in the Severn Valley.

MUCH WENLOCK
☎ 01952
Much Wenlock is an attractive town, with a patchwork of historical buildings and, we

kid you not, strong claims to being the birthplace of the modern Olympics (see the boxed text below).

The **TIC** (☎ 727679; High St; open 10.30am-1pm & 2pm-5pm Mon-Sat year round, plus Sun July-Aug) shares a 19th-century building with a museum filled with historical bits and bobs.

Things to See & Do

The TIC provides a free map to the town's sights of historical interest, starting with the enchanting ruins of the 13th-century **Much Wenlock Priory** (☎ 727466; adult/child £3/1.50; open 10am-6pm daily Apr-Sept, 10am-5pm daily Oct, 10am-4pm Wed-Sun Nov-Mar), set in beautiful grounds that are studded with pine and cherry trees and adorned with wildflowers sprouting out from crumbling foundation stones. There's also a display of kooky Victorian topiary: squirrels and teddy bears the last time we looked. Productions of Shakespeare's plays are staged here on July and August evenings.

You can also get a pamphlet, *The Olympian Trail*, which takes you on a pleasant 1½ mile (2km) walking tour of the town, and explores the link between the village and the modern Olympics.

Places to Stay & Eat

Stokes Bunkhouse Barn (☎ 727293, fax 728130; e c.h.hill.and.son@farmline.com; Newton House Farm; dorm beds £7), signposted from the A458, is a converted 19th-century threshing barn comprising a kitchen,

one cottage and two bedrooms catering for up to six.

The Raven Hotel (☎ 727251, fax 728416; w www.ravenhotel.com; singles/doubles £65/85, 3-course meals £20) is country chic, with bright and spacious rooms in converted stables set around a courtyard brimming with pansies; it's also worth booking in for dinner.

The Talbot Inn (☎ 727077; w www.the-talbot-inn.com; 13 High St; singles/doubles £45/70; meals £5-14) is wonderfully atmospheric, with colossal beams and cavernous fireplaces – great on a cold or wet day. Rooms above the pub are pleasant, if a tad overpriced, and the grub is reliable.

The Gaskell Arms (☎ 727212; w www.thegaskellarmshotel.activehotels.com; singles/doubles £48/70, meals £8-14), at the top of High St away from the TIC, is a charming 17th-century coaching inn with splendidly old-fashioned rooms and an atmospheric oak-beamed restaurant.

The George & Dragon Inn (☎ 727312; 2 High St) is the place where you'll find the most local character.

You may be surprised to see weekend queues streaming down the High St of this quiet little place. The reason is **A Ryan & Son** traditional butchers, and if you're a British tourist you won't want to leave town without a few of Paddy's pies under your arm.

Getting There & Away

Much Wenlock is about 7 miles (11km) northwest of Bridgnorth. Bus Nos 435 and

---

Granddaddy of the Modern Olympics

Local doctor and sports enthusiast William Penny Brookes fused his knowledge of the ancient Olympics and rural British pastimes to launch the Much Wenlock Olympic Games in 1850. They were largely intended as a distraction for the town's young population, who, at the time, were spending most of their energies drinking and fighting.

The games became an annual event and pricked the interest of the like-minded Baron Pierre Coubertin, who came to Much Wenlock in 1890 to see them for himself. He and Brookes became firm friends with the shared dream of reviving the ancient Olympics. Coubertin, of course, went on to launch the modern Olympics in Athens in 1896, which featured many of the events he had seen in Much Wenlock (although chasing a greased pig around town never really caught on). Brookes was invited to the event but, alas, he died before the games opened, aged 86.

The good doctor never really got his share of the Olympic limelight until almost a century later when International Olympic Committee President JA Samaranch visited his grave in Much Wenlock to 'pay tribute and homage to Dr Brookes, who really was the founder of the Modern Olympic Games'. The Much Wenlock Olympics are still held every July.

436 run from Shrewsbury to Ludlow via Much Wenlock approximately every two hours from Monday to Saturday, with a reduced service on Sunday.

AROUND MUCH WENLOCK
Wenlock Edge

This steep limestone escarpment stretches 15 miles (24km) from Much Wenlock to Craven Arms and provides terrific walking country with superb views across rolling farmland to the Long Mynd and Shropshire plains. The National Trust owns much of the ridge, and there are many waymarked trails starting from car parks dotted along the B4371. You need your own transport or time to walk.

The Wenlock Edge Inn (☎ 01746-785678; W www.wenlockedgeinn.co.uk; Hilltop; singles/doubles £45/70), about 4½ miles southwest of Much Wenlock on the B4371, was named 'best pub in Britain 2002'. It's a very ordinary pub – part of its charm – with a relaxed atmosphere and hearty home-made fare. Jack, the friendly ghost, adds a little edge to the storytelling (biggest liar) night on the second Monday of the month. Accommodation is modest but cosy.

Wilderhope Manor YHA Hostel (☎ 0870 770 6090, fax 0870 770 6091; e wilderhope@ yha.org.uk; Longville-in-the-Dale; open Feb-Oct; dorm beds £11.25), a grand, gabled Elizabethan manor house 7 miles (11km) southwest of Much Wenlock, is a wonderful spot set deep in lush countryside. The 16th-century building was saved and restored thanks to the kindness of local walker WA Cadbury – yes, he of the fruit and nut chocolate – who purchased the run-down dwelling and donated it to the NT in 1935. You can catch buses from Ludlow and Bridgnorth to Shipton, a half-mile walk from Wilderhope, or catch the weekend Wenlock Wanderer shuttle bus from Church Stretton (£2 return; contact TICs for more details).

CHURCH STRETTON
☎ 01694

Church Stretton – recently awarded town status, to the delight of those in the TIC – is a picturesque settlement in a deep valley formed by the Long Mynd and the Caradoc Hills. Apart from the lack of a decent boozer, it makes a terrific base for exploring the surrounding hills and has quite a few interesting old buildings, including an early-12th-century Norman church.

The TIC (☎ 723133; Church St; open 10am-1pm & 2pm-5pm Mon-Sat Apr-Sept) has stacks of useful walking information.

You can hire mountain bikes and tandems from Terry's Cycles (☎ 723302; 6 Castle Hill, All Stretton) for £10 and £20 per day respectively, and bikes can be delivered and collected for an extra charge.

Places to Stay

Brookfields Guest House (☎ 722314; Watling St North; singles/doubles with en suite £30/50) is a good choice if you want to stay in the town. It's close to the train station and has very comfortable and spacious rooms.

Staying on or near the hills is a better option if you're here to ramble (see also Around Church Stretton following). Cwmdale Farm (☎ 722362; Cwmdale Valley; accommodation per person £20), nestled in an idyllic valley, feels like the rainbow's end. It's a 10-minute walk from town and one step from the Long Mynd, and has picture-postcard views, cosy rooms and just the right amount of farm atmosphere. The friendly owners will collect you from the train station.

Longmynd Hotel (☎ 722244, fax 722718; W www.longmynd.co.uk; Cunnery Rd; singles/doubles from £60/110), perched above Church Stretton, has granny decor, spa facilities and a breakfast room with breathtaking views of the Stratton Hills.

Places to Eat

There are several excellent eateries open by day but it's more difficult to eat well and inexpensively at night.

Berry's Coffee House (☎ 724452; 17 High St; meals £4-7) doesn't seem so flash at first but linger a while and you'll see why it was recently named best teahouse in Shropshire. The home-made desserts will make your knees wobble, and there's also an Internet terminal to check up on your email.

The Acorn (☎ 722495; 26 Sandford Ave; meals £4-7; open Thur-Mon) is a wonderful wholefoods café and does a mouthwateringly good line in mainly vegetarian fare.

Jaipur (☎ 724667; 6 Sandford Ave; meals £8-11) does exquisitely rustic Indian cuisine.

The Studio (☎ 722672; 59 High St; meals £9-15) is to fine dining what the Long Mynd is to serenity.

Getting There & Away

Church Stretton is on the A49, the main road running through the region. There are about a dozen trains to Shrewsbury daily (£3.40, 20 minutes) and bus No 435, which runs between Shrewsbury and Ludlow several times daily, stops here.

AROUND CHURCH STRETTON
The Long Mynd

The Long Mynd is the most famous of Shropshire's hills and one of the best walking areas in the Marches. The Victorians called the area Little Switzerland, promoting it as a health resort and bottling the local spring water.

Walking

The entire heathlands are webbed with walking trails, and you can ramble wherever you like and enjoy memorable views. Just a 10-minute walk from Church Stretton, the **Carding Mill Valley** trail leads up to the 517m (1695ft) summit of the Long Mynd, with views of the Stiperstones to the east. There's an information centre and tearoom in the summer, and an information kiosk year round that provides details on what flora and fauna to expect. This trail can get very busy at weekends and in summer, so you might prefer to pick your own peak or cross the A49 and climb towards the 459m (1506ft) summit of Caer Caradoc.

You can drive part of the way up the Carding Mill Valley, although the NT would rather you took the **Long Mynd Shuttle bus** *(return trip £2; 5 times daily Nov-Mar, weekends only Apr-Oct)* from Beaumont Rd or the station. However, you don't have far to walk until you're in among it, so to speak.

Places to Stay & Eat

For daytime eats, head to Church Stretton.

Bridges Long Mynd YHA Hostel *(☎ 01588-650656, fax 650531; Ratlinghope; dorm beds £8.75; open Apr-Oct)* is basic and beautiful, with mainly big dorms. It's 5 miles (8km) from Church Stretton in an old village school at Ratlinghope. Boulton's bus No 551 comes here from Shrewsbury on Tuesday only.

Stretton Hall Hotel *(☎ 723224, fax 724365; w www.strettonhall.co.uk; All Stretton; singles/doubles from £50/80, meals £8-15)*, in the tiny village of All Stretton 1 mile (1.5km) north of Church Stretton, is a friendly, peaceful and dignified establish-

ment, offering elegant rooms, top-notch traditional British grub and relaxing pints in an elegant Georgian house. The **Yew Tree** pub is opposite...in every respect.

The Station Inn *(☎ 781208; Marshbrook; meals £5-10)* is the best place for pub grub in the vicinity. If you have the means to make the 3km trip from Church Stretton along the road to Craven Arms, you should dash down for sublime steak-and-mushroom pie, and other hearty home-made treats.

Jinlye Guest House *(☎/fax 723243; w www.jinlye.co.uk; Castle Hill, All Stretton; rooms per person £27)* is an excellent, award-winning 16th-century property atop the Long Mynd, 2 miles (3km) north of Church Stretton. Most of the eight bright, cosy and feminine rooms have baths and views.

CRAVEN ARMS

The only reason to venture here – apart from the fact that it has a train station – is the new **Shropshire Hills Discovery Centre** *(☎ 01588-676030; w www.shropshire-cc.gov.uk/discover .nsf; open 10am-5.30pm daily Apr-Sept, 10am-4.30pm Tues-Sun Nov-Mar)*, and then only on a wet day. The exhibits, including a simulated balloon flight, are intended to give an insight into the history and geology of the region but they seem to be pitched at the very young and the very old. The centre's grass roof is its most interesting feature and you can get a look at that from the pub next door. The Discovery Centre is located at the southern end of town.

For transport details see the Church Stretton Getting There & Away section earlier.

BISHOP'S CASTLE
☎ 01588

This invigorating little town, in frontier country near the Welsh border, is famed not for its castle – which no longer exists – but for a couple of pub breweries that usually manage to keep visitors for longer than they'd intended (see Breweries later in this section).

Tourist information and accommodation options are available from the beguilingly batty **Old Time** *(☎ 638467; e jane@tan-house .demon.co.uk; 29 High St; open 10am-10pm Mon-Sat, 10am-2pm Sun)*.

The picturesque 16th-century **House on Crutches** *(☎ 630007; admission 50p; open noon-4pm Sat & Sun, 11am-3pm bank holidays*

THE MARCHES

Apr-Sept) houses the town's museum, which depicts local history.

Walking

After becoming acquainted with the breweries, you can walk off your indulgences along the **Shropshire Way**, which runs through the town and joins up with the **Offa's Dyke Path** to the south; the **Kerry Ridgeway** to the south; or head north and risk the forbidding ridges of the **Stiperstones**, where Satan is said to hold court.

Breweries

The Three Tuns (☎ 638797; Salop St; singles/doubles £45/75) is legendary and offers a 20-minute tour of an old Victorian brewery (which costs £1 although they usually forget to collect the cash). Each stage of the brewing process descends from floor to floor, which is probably what you'll do if you develop a taste for either of the regular potent bitters. There is also good pub grub and comfy split-level accommodation.

Six Bells Inn (☎ 638930; Church St; meals £5-10), the village's *other* brewery and the locals' choice, is a modern, recycled affair attached to an inn that's had a licence since 1720. There's excellent and well-proportioned pub grub, and tours of the brewery if you call in advance.

Places to Stay & Eat

Green Caravan Park (☎ 650605; Wentnor; open mid-Mar–Oct; tent sites £7) is not far beyond Bishop's Castle along the B4385 in the Onny Valley, another good spot for walking.

Old Time (☎ 638467; e jane@tan-house .demon.co.uk; 29 High St; B&B per person £20) offers B&B and the owner is full of beans and local information.

The Poppy House (☎ 638181; 20 Market Square; singles/doubles £22/44; snacks £3-7) is a nonsmoking café, gallery and guesthouse abounding in china, cards and cuddly toys. Cute accommodation is provided in the large, rambling house, which comes with the requisite low beams.

The Castle Hotel (☎ 638403; The Square; singles/doubles £37.50/65; meals £3-8) is a lovely, relaxed early-18th-century tavern that's not nearly as 'hotelish' as it looks from the outside. The six comfortable rooms – soon to be eight – are situated around an attractive Georgian staircase (room No 8 is the

most atmospheric). There are three bars to choose from; the one with leather chairs and a grandfather clock is a memorable spot to savour the polished pub cuisine.

Getting There & Away

Bishop's Castle is just off the A488 main road 26 miles (42km) south of Shrewsbury. Craven Arms, 12 miles (19km) away, is the nearest train station. Bus No 553 runs to and from Shrewsbury (one hour) approximately every two hours daily.

CLUN
☎ 01588

It's always Sunday afternoon in Clun, described by the poet AE Housman as one of the quietest places under the sun. It's 6 miles south of Bishop's Castle and has the pummelled ruins of a Norman castle as its focal point. The **Museum of Clun** (open 11am-1pm & 2pm-5pm Sat & Tues Easter-Oct) has an interesting collection of bric-a-brac from Roman times to the present, and is a reminder of the extraordinary history even a place this small can conceal from the casual tourist.

Clun is in the heart of more good walking territory, and it's as good a place as any to join **Offa's Dyke**, just a few miles west of the village.

You can get tourist info from the **Clun Garage**, a petrol station on the way into the village from Craven Arms.

Clun Mill Youth Hostel (☎ 0870 770 5916, fax 0870 770 5766; dorm beds £9.50; open late March-Aug), a restored water mill on the northern outskirts of the village, has en-suite dorms. Phone to check other opening times.

The Sun Inn (☎ 640277; High St; singles/doubles £25/50, meals £4-8) is a jovial tavern with adequate rooms and hearty pub fare. Check out the size of the farmers in the bar to get an idea how big meal portions will be.

Getting There & Away

Bus No 745 runs this way from Ludlow, while a more limited service connects to Bishop's Castle. Services to Ludlow leave roughly every two hours, but there are just two on Saturday and none on Sunday.

LUDLOW
☎ 01584 • pop 7500

Ludlow, set around the rambling ruins of a Norman castle and chock-a-block with historical architecture, is the most handsome Marches town. It is also the culinary capital of the west, with three Michelin-starred restaurants, although you don't have to dig particularly deep to eat well here. Geography helps Ludlow coyly guard its charms from flocks of suitors and it remains a lot less crowded than similar towns in the Cotswolds (outside of festival times, see later in this section).

Ludlow prospered from the sale of fleeces and the manufacture of woollen cloth since the times of the medieval wool trade, and it was the administrative centre of the Council of the Welsh Marches until 1689.

Ludlow's **TIC** (☎ 875053; e ludlow.tour ism@shropshire-cc.gov.uk; Castle St; open 10am-1pm & 2pm-5pm Mon-Sat Easter-Oct, 10.30am-1pm & 2pm-5pm Sun June-Aug) is in the 19th-century **assembly rooms**, which also house a small museum with some diverting exhibits, such as a model of the world's oldest spider – a trigonotarbid arachnid – which would be 415 million years old if it was still climbing bathroom walls today.

There is a busy calendar of festivals throughout the year, the biggest being the **Ludlow Festival** (☎ 872150; w www.ludlow festival.co.uk), a fortnight of theatre and music that takes place in June and July. The **Ludlow Marches Food & Drink Festival** (w www.foodfestival.co.uk) is promoted as Britain's foremost, and takes place over a long weekend in September. Accommodation can be nigh impossible to find during these festivals, especially during the former.

Things to See & Do

The impressive **Ludlow Castle** (☎ 873355; w www.ludlowcastle.com; Castle Square; adult/child £3.50/1.50; open 10am-5pm daily May-Sept, 10am-4pm daily Oct-Dec & Feb-Apr, 10am-5pm Sat & Sun Jan), perched above the Rivers Teme and Corve, was built by Roger de Lacy around 1090, one of a line of fortifications built along the Marches to ward off the marauding Welsh. It was transformed into a palace by Roger Mortimer in the 14th century; its chequered history is reflected in the different architectural styles, including Norman, medieval and Tudor. Although the Mortimers remained firmly royalist during the Civil War, the castle was surrendered to the Parliamentarians

and thus saved from demolition. The round chapel in the inner bailey was built in 1120 and is one of few surviving. There is a wonderfully evocative **audio tour** (50p) and the castle grounds provide an attractive setting for productions during the Ludlow Festival.

The **Church of St Laurence** (King St), one of the largest parish churches in Britain, was extensively rebuilt in the 15th century but has some original Early English features, along with a lofty tower, fine stained glass and some extraordinary, ornate medieval misericords, ranging from the pious to the seemingly profane.

The TIC can provide information on the waymarked 30-mile (48km) **Mortimer's Trail** to Kington, which starts just outside the castle entrance.

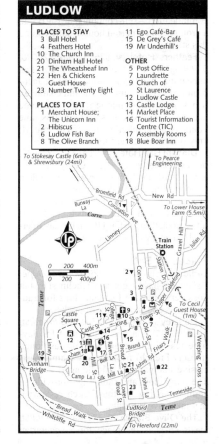

LUDLOW

PLACES TO STAY
3 Bull Hotel
4 Feathers Hotel
10 The Church Inn
20 Dinham Hall Hotel
21 The Wheatsheaf Inn
22 Hen & Chickens Guest House
23 Number Twenty Eight

PLACES TO EAT
1 Merchant House; The Unicorn Inn
2 Hibiscus
6 Ludlow Fish Bar
8 The Olive Branch

11 Ego Café-Bar
15 De Grey's Café
19 Mr Underhill's

OTHER
5 Post Office
7 Laundrette
9 Church of St Laurence
12 Ludlow Castle
13 Castle Lodge
14 Market Place
16 Tourist Information Centre (TIC)
17 Assembly Rooms
18 Blue Boar Inn

Places to Stay

Accommodation in Ludlow tends to be expensive, especially if you try winging it on arrival.

Hen and Chickens Guest House (☎ 874 318; W www.hen-and-chickens.co.uk; 103 Old St; rooms per person from £25), housed in a former pub, has a good location, ample parking, a homely atmosphere and comfortable rooms – it's about the best of the cheaper B&Bs.

The Wheatsheaf Inn (☎ 872980, fax 877990; Lower Broad St; singles/doubles from £30/45), practically built into the old town walls, is a gorgeous 17th-century inn with smallish but bright, tastefully furnished rooms and sumptuously soft linen.

Number Twenty Eight (☎ 876996, fax 876860; W www.no28.co.uk; 28 Lower Broad St; rooms from £75) provides refined accommodation – self-contained or B&B – in a group of small period houses dotted along this street.

Feathers Hotel (☎ 875261, fax 876030; Bull Ring; singles/doubles from £70/90) is an unbearably handsome timber-framed Jacobean property, oozing charm and character. It has magnificent public rooms and some luxurious guest quarters, but don't assume yours is a chamber of historical import; only one-third of the rooms are original.

Dinham Hall Hotel (☎ 876464, fax 876019; singles/doubles £75/130), a Georgian property right beside the castle, combines modern comfort with period design and traditional manners. On Monday to Friday from October to April, you can get the rooms for half-price if you book through the TIC on the day of arrival – a deal well worth checking out.

Places to Eat

Ludlow Fish Bar (☎ 879300; 14 Upper Galdeford) hasn't got a Michelin star, but does very passable fish and chips for traditionalists and those light of pocket.

De Grey's Café (☎ 872764; 5-6 Broad St; meals £7-10) is a reasonable spot for daytime teas, light meals and old-fashioned (loosely French) frippery in the almost exclusive company of middle-aged women. The ivory cloth and candlelight provide an ambient setting for the French restaurant that takes over at night.

The Olive Branch (☎ 874314; 2-4 Old St; meals £5-8) is the place for a vegetarian lunch, with a variety of hot meals, brisk salads and delectable desserts sure to launch you on a calorie-crunching walk of the town.

The Unicorn Inn (☎ 873555; Lower Corve St; meals £6-9) has oak panelling, red velvet and beams galore, as well as the best pub grub for miles.

The Church Inn (☎ 872174, fax 877146; The Buttercross, Church St; rooms from £60; meals £6-8) is the oldest tavern in town and is full of original beams and wonky floors – the food is reasonable.

Ego Café-Bar (☎ 878000; Quality Square; 3-course meals £18), off Castle Square, does top-notch Continental cuisine and coffee.

Hibiscus (☎ 872325; 17 Corve St; set menus £32.50) serves up contemporary cuisine with a strong French accent, and is the pick of the Michelin mob. The other two high-achievers are **Merchant House** (☎ 875438; W www.merchanthouse.org; Lower Corve St; set menus £32.50) and **Mr Underhill's** (☎ 874431; W www.mr-underhills .co.uk; Dinham Weir; singles/doubles £70/75, 3-course meals £30).

Getting There & Away

Ludlow is on the A49, 29 miles (47km) south of Shrewsbury and 24 miles (39km) north of Hereford. Trains go regularly direct to Shrewsbury (£7.80, 30 minutes), Church Stretton (£4.90, 15 minutes) and Hereford (£6.20, 25 minutes). Bus routes radiate from Ludlow to Hereford and Birmingham (bus Nos 192 and 292) and Shrewsbury (bus No 435).

AROUND LUDLOW
Stokesay Castle

Lawrence of Ludlow, England's most successful wool merchant, built Stokesay Castle (EH; ☎ 01588-672544; admission including audio tour £4.40; open 10am-6pm daily Apr-Sept, 10am-5pm daily Oct, 10am-1pm & 2pm-4pm Wed-Sun Nov-Mar) in the 13th century. It is actually a fortified manor house – designed more for domestic comforts than military defence – and features a stunning timber-framed Jacobean gatehouse sure to send you reaching for your camera. There's also an enchanting garden that's hardly been touched since the original owners first pitched their medieval forks.

Inside the impressive Great Hall, with its original timber staircase, admire the gabled windows and consider that glass was so expensive around the 17th century that the family would carry the panes with them whenever they moved between manors.

Stokesay Castle is 7 miles (11km) northwest of Ludlow, just off the A49. Bus No 435 runs infrequently to Stokesay from Shrewsbury and Ludlow; drivers will drop you at the bottom of the lane leading to the castle. Alternatively, you catch the train to Craven Arms just over a mile away.

Croft Castle

The sturdy exterior of the Croft family residence (NT; ☎ 01568-780246; admission £3.80; open 1.30pm-5.30pm Wed-Sun May-Sept, 1.30pm-5.30pm Sat & Sun Apr, 1.30pm-4.30pm Sat & Sun Oct, also open bank holidays) dates from the 14th century, although most of its flamboyant and decorative interior is 18th and 19th century and includes fine plasterwork ceilings, a splendid Georgian staircase and rare furniture. The castle has a lovely avenue of 350-year-old Spanish chestnuts, a pleasant walled garden, an interpretive centre and tearooms.

The castle is 9 miles (14km) south of Ludlow – actually in Herefordshire – off the B4362. Bus No 492 from Hereford or Ludlow runs eight times a day (including Sunday) and stops at Gorbett Bank, 2 miles away.

Herefordshire

Bounded by the Malverns to the east and Wales to the west, Herefordshire (w www .herefordshiretourism.co.uk) is a sleepy county of fields and hedgerows, virtually untainted by tourism. Hereford is the regional capital, home to the remarkable Mappa Mundi, one of the highlights of the Marches. The River Wye meanders its way through the county, providing unforgettable scenery and opportunities for water adventures galore. Herefordshire can also claim at least a slither of the remarkable town of Hay-on-Wye (straddling the Welsh border), offering the world's largest second-hand book browse.

Activities

Several long-distance walking paths pass through this area (see the Activities section at the beginning of this chapter). The **Offa's Dyke Path** runs along the western border with Wales, while the 107-mile (172km) **Wye Valley Walk** begins in Chepstow (Wales) and follows the river's course upstream into England through Herefordshire and back into Wales to Rhayader. The **Three Choirs Way** is a 100-mile (160km) route connecting the cathedrals of Hereford, Worcester and Gloucester, where the music festival of the same name has been celebrated for more than three centuries.

Getting Around

There are railway stations at Hereford, Leominster and Ledbury with good links to the major English cities.

Numerous local and national bus companies provide services in Herefordshire but, fortunately, **Herefordshire Council** (☎ 01432-260211; e public.transport@herefordshire .gov.uk; Public Transport Information, Herefordshire Council, PO Box 236 Hereford HR4 9ZH) publishes comprehensive timetable booklets, available from TICs and bus stations. Alternatively, there's always the **National Traveline** (☎ 0870 608 2608).

If you are heading to south Wales consider a Network Rider (£4.50) for a day's unlimited travel on Stagecoach and most other bus services in the area.

HEREFORD

☎ 01432 • pop 48,400

Hereford is a humdrum regional capital on the banks of the River Wye and is most interesting for the Mappa Mundi, a magnificent medieval map kept in the town's patched-together cathedral. The town – also famous for producing cider and a famous breed of cattle – has a smattering of historic buildings and secondary sights, and makes for a pleasant day trip or a forgettable overnighter.

The Saxons built Hereford (literally, Army Ford) as a defence against the Welsh. It became a religious centre after the Saxon king Ethelbert was murdered nearby. Legend has it that the ghost of Ethelbert wasn't happy about being *buried* 'nearby' so he spooked the authorities into reinterring him in Hereford. His posthumous valour endeared him to Hereford's military-minded, who built the cathedral in his honour. The Welsh burned it down a few hundred years later and it's the second cathedral – built on the same site in the 11th century – that towers over the town today.

THE MARCHES

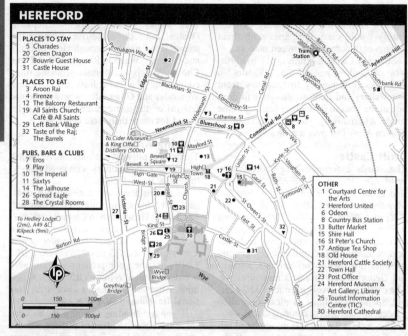

HEREFORD

PLACES TO STAY
5 Charades
20 Green Dragon
27 Bouvrie Guest House
31 Castle House

PLACES TO EAT
3 Aroon Rai
4 Firenze
12 The Balcony Restaurant
19 All Saints Church;
   Café @ All Saints
29 Left Bank Village
32 Taste of the Raj;
   The Barrels

PUBS, BARS & CLUBS
7 Eros
9 Play
10 The Imperial
11 Saxtys
14 The Jailhouse
26 Spread Eagle
28 The Crystal Rooms

OTHER
1 Courtyard Centre for
   the Arts
2 Hereford United
6 Odeon
8 Country Bus Station
13 Butter Market
15 Shire Hall
16 St Peter's Church
17 Antique Tea Shop
18 Old House
21 Hereford Cattle Society
22 Town Hall
23 Post Office
24 Hereford Museum &
   Art Gallery; Library
25 Tourist Information
   Centre (TIC)
30 Hereford Cathedral

Orientation

The triangular, pedestrianised High Town is the heart of the city. The cathedral is a few blocks south towards the river, while the bus and train stations lie to the northeast, off Commercial Rd.

Information

The hugely helpful **TIC** (☎ 268430; 1 King St; open 9am-5pm Mon-Sat year round, 10am-4pm Sun June-Sept) is opposite the cathedral. There are guided **walking tours** (☎ 266867) at 10.30am Monday to Saturday and at 2.30pm on Sunday, from June to September (£2/1 per adult/child).

You can access the Internet for free at the **library**, which has two computers reserved for visitors. You can use them in half-hour blocks, although you can normally charm your way to a longer slot.

Hereford Cathedral

The purple-red cathedral (☎ 374200; **w** www.herefordcathedral.co.uk; 5 College Cloisters, Cathedral Close) – although first built around the end of the 11th century and therefore one of England's oldest – looks nothing like the

original and is a fusion of different architectural styles that pleases some as much as it disappoints others. The biggest changes came after the west tower collapsed into the nave on Easter Monday 1786. In the choir is the 14th-century bishop's throne and King Stephen's chair, which was warmed by the regal buns of the king himself. In the northern transept, a classic example of Early English architecture, is the shrine of St Thomas Cantilupe, a 13th-century Hereford bishop. The Victorians – as was their want – gave the cathedral a thorough going over and most of the decoration you see today is theirs.

The cathedral is best known for two ancient treasures, the most famous being the **Mappa Mundi** (☎ 374209; adult/child £4/3.50; open 10am-4.15pm Mon-Sat, 11am-3.15pm Sun May-Sept, 11am-3.15pm Mon-Sat Oct-Apr), a map that was drawn on a piece of vellum (treated animal hide) in the late 13th century and records how scholars of the time saw the world in spiritual as well as geographical terms. It is the largest and best-preserved example of this type of cartography and a fascinating pictorial encyclopedia of the times.

On the same ticket you can visit another ancient treasure, the largest surviving **chained library** in the world, containing a unique collection of some 1800 rare books and 227 manuscripts dating from the 8th to the 19th century, some of which are always on display. From the Middle Ages up to the 18th century, books were often chained in such a way that they could be taken from the shelves and read but not removed from the library. The oldest book in the collection – and the oldest artefact in the cathedral – is the *Hereford Gospels*, created around here in the 8th century.

At the time of publication the cathedral was scheduled to host the **Three Choirs Festival** (*w www.3choirs.org*), an event it shares with Gloucester and Worcester Cathedrals, in the summer of 2003. You can catch evensong at 5.30pm Monday to Saturday and 2.30pm on Sunday. There's a café in the cloister, with standard salads and stuff.

Old House

Marooned in the middle of High Town, the Old House (*☎ 260694; admission free; open 10am-5pm Tues-Sat year round, 10am-4pm Sun Apr-Sept*) is a marvellous black-and-white, three-storey wooden house, built in 1621 and fitted with 17th-century wooden furnishings showing the typical domestic arrangements of the time. Note the murals of the Muses on the 1st floor.

Cider Museum & King Offa Distillery

Herefordshire is the home of British cider and produces more than half of the country's total output. Just off the A438 to Brecon, or a dreary 10-minute walk from the centre, you can visit the Cider Museum & King Offa Distillery (*☎ 354207; Pomona Place; adult/child £2.60/2.10; open 10am-5.30pm daily Apr-Oct, 11am-3pm Tues-Sun Nov-Mar*), based in a former cider works. It explores the history of the drink and exhibits an assortment of machinery and paraphernalia. A **tour** that costs £10 per guide, regardless of how many people are in the group, can help bring the otherwise rather dry exhibits alive; book in advance. They recommended making cider brandy here in 1984 after a 250-year gap – sample a sip and appreciate that there really was no hurry.

Hereford Museum & Art Gallery

This museum and art gallery (*☎ 260692; open 10am-5pm Tues-Sat, 10am-4pm Sun*) is located above the library on Broad St and displays a diverse range of exhibits; you should expect anything from Roman antiquities and English watercolours to Saxon combs and a hive of bees.

Hereford Cattle Society

If you want to learn more about Herefords, the incredibly resilient breed of cattle this town has exported worldwide, pop into the friendly Hereford Cattle Society (*☎ 272057; 3 Offa St*), which has oodles of information and a rather fetching line in bovine paraphernalia. Not one herd of Herefords – noted for their survival instincts – was infected in the foot-and-mouth epidemic that devastated the English countryside in 2001.

Places to Stay

Accommodation can often be scarce during the week, so book in advance.

Charades (*☎ 269444; 34 Southbank Rd; en-suite rooms per person £30*) is an outstanding B&B in a lovely Georgian house offering comforts that really ought to cost more. The rooms are bright and elegant but, despite what anyone tells you, it's at least a 10-minute walk from the city.

Bouvrie Guest House (*☎ 266265; 26 Victoria St; singles/doubles £20/40*) isn't much to look at but, despite being on a very busy main road, has the best location of any of the cheaper places in town, just a short walk from the cathedral. Contractors are the staple but the rooms are reasonable and the welcome is warm whatever your circumstances.

Hedley Lodge (*☎ 277475; Belmont Abbey; singles/doubles £33.50/56*), not far out of town on the A465, is the celestial choice, with pleasant and peaceful lodgings in an old abbey tended entirely by monks.

The **Green Dragon** (*☎ 272506, fax 352139; w www.heritage-hotels.com; Broad St; singles/doubles from £65/80*) is a handsome and very central Georgian hotel, although the rooms – due for renovation – are slightly gloomy and overpriced.

Castle House (*☎ 356321, fax 266460; w www.castlehse.co.uk; Castle St; singles/doubles £90/165*), once the bishop's residence, combines style and matter-of-fact sophistication, and is a wonderful place to stay.

Places to Eat

Café @ All Saints (☎ 370415; High St; meals £5-8), set inside a working church, is *the* most atmospheric place to eat and the church's novel way of reviving flagging attendances. You can enjoy wholesome and mostly vegetarian fare – from toasties to creative casseroles – beneath England's largest weathercock and a medieval carving of a gentleman mooning.

Firenze (☎ 270183; 21 Commercial Rd; meals £7-11) is a pretty good Italian joint with an overly expensive restaurant but more reasonable pizzeria. There is a string of **fish and chip shops** along this street.

Aroon Rai (☎ 279971; 60 Widemarsh St; meals £6-8; open Mon-Sat), which means sunrise, has a wide range of authentic Thai dishes and some ridiculously large banquets.

Taste of the Raj (☎ 351076; St Owen's St; meals £7-10) is rustic *and* refined, and provides the best Indian food on the Wye.

Left Bank Village (☎ 340200; W www.left bank.co.uk; Bridge St) is a slick development incorporating a bakery, café, ice-cream parlour, delicatessen and two restaurants. The problem is it's overpriced, devoid of personality and feels like an arcade, although **Floodgates Brasserie** (dinners £30), **La Rive Restaurant** and **Charles Cocktail Bar** (small/large tapas £3/6) have lovely balconies overlooking Wye Bridge, the river and the cathedral; the food is generally first-rate.

Castle House (Castle St; mains £13-20) is one of the best fine-dining experiences in the Marches. The elegant dining room is worthy of chef Stuart McLeod's sophisticated brand of modern British cuisine. Set lunch is a very reasonable £19.

Entertainment

The Barrels (St Owen's St) is an ever-lively pub with stained glass on the windows depicting scenes of Wye Valley life, and much table football, pool and merriment within. It is home to the Wye Valley Brewery, in converted stables out back, and some welcoming locals as permanent (and often as plastered) as the walls.

Saxtys (Widemarsh St) is a laid-back, 30-something wine bar.

The Crystal Rooms (☎ 267378; W www.naughtybutnice.org; 13 Bridge St; cover charge £6) is Hereford's most renowned club and the place for a big night on the tiles. There are good local DJs and national names visit occasionally.

Eros (☎ 353868; 100 Commercial Rd), not quite as dodgy as it sounds, gets a lively crowd of 18- to 30-year-olds.

Play (☎ 270009; 51-55 Blue School St; open 9pm-1.30am Fri-Sat) is even less sophisticated, but fun if you're in the mood. Food, drinks and cover charge come to £8 – yes, it's that kind of place.

The Jailhouse (☎ 344354; 1 Gaol St) features live music from local bands.

Courtyard Centre for the Arts (☎ 359252; W www.courtyard.org.uk; Edgar St) has two venues staging a busy and varied schedule of events, from comedy to theatre and film to poetry. Alternatively, there's one screen at the **Odeon** cinema next door to Eros.

Getting There & Away

Hereford is 25 miles (40km) from Worcester and 140 miles (225km) from London.

There are four through trains daily (fewer on Saturday and Sunday) from Hereford to London Paddington (£33, approximately three hours), also serving Worcester (£5.20, 50 minutes). There are also hourly trains to Birmingham (95 minutes) via Worcester.

National Express (☎ 08705 808080) operates three services daily from London (£14.50, four hours) via Heathrow, Gloucester and Ross-on-Wye or Ledbury.

Bus services run from St Peter's Square to Leominster (bus No 492 every hour Monday to Saturday and every two hours on Sunday) and Worcester (bus Nos 419/420 every hour Monday to Saturday, three journeys on Sunday). From the Country bus station in Commercial Rd, bus No 38 runs to Gloucester via Ross-on-Wye (hourly Monday to Saturday, every two hours on Sunday) and bus No 476 connects to Ledbury (twelve daily Monday to Saturday, fewer on Sunday).

AROUND HEREFORD
Leominster

Leominster (lem-ster), 14 miles north of Hereford on the A49, is a quiet market town renowned for its antiques; dealers and browsers will find everything from high-quality period pieces to charming curios at the numerous shops lining the town's attractive, half-timbered centre. If antiques aren't your style, you can explore the Norman **Priory Church**, made enormously wide by three naves (well, two naves and an aisle) built in successive centuries.

The **TIC** (☎ 01568-616460; 1 Corn Square), in the centre of town, can provide the lowdown on where to shop, stay and eat.

Leominster is on the Cardiff–Manchester rail line. There are 16 trains a day (seven on Sunday) to Shrewsbury, Ludlow and Hereford. Bus No 492 runs to Hereford hourly; bus No 495/496 connects to the black-and-white villages (see boxed text) every two hours Monday to Friday, less on weekends.

The Golden Valley

The Golden Valley, at the foot of the Black Mountains, was made famous by the author CS Lewis and the film *Shadowlands*. It follows the course of the meandering River Dore and boasts beautiful unspoilt rural vistas, studded by historical ruins evoking the border valley's tumultuous past. *This* is why you brought the car.

Kilpeck Church

Deep within lush Herefordshire countryside is the tiny hamlet of Kilpeck, where you'll find an astonishing church that remains practically unchanged since the Normans built it in the 12th century. Inside there is a pamphlet guide to the remarkable corbels, or original carvings, ringing the building. They range from the profound to the comical and include a famous Sheela Na Gig (a Celtic figure representing the sexual and procreative power of women) on the south side.

Just 9 miles (14km) from Hereford, Kilpeck is less than 2 miles (3km) off the A465 and well worth a detour.

HAY-ON-WYE
☎ 01497 • pop 1400 • elevation 203m

The tiny town of Hay is the used-book capital of the world, a bonanza for browsers and only a quill's length over the border in Wales.

Some 40 shops stock hundreds of thousands of volumes covering every subject ever committed to paper.

On 1 April 1977 the town famously declared itself independent from Britain, earning a furious rebuff from the local council and marking itself indelibly on the map. Orchestrating the insurrection was the self-styled King of Hay, bookseller Richard Booth, the man responsible for Hay's metamorphosis and owner of the 900-year-old

---

Black-&-White Villages

Northwest Herefordshire's black-and-white villages make for a wonderful tour of historical England and its country life. The tourism authority promotes a 40-mile (64km) circular circuit through the most popular spots, taking in handsome timber-framed buildings, old churches, convivial pubs and idyllic villages. The **Black-and-white Village Trail** starts at Leominster and climaxes at Eardisland, the most picturesque village of all, and you can pick up a guide from any Tourist Information Centre (TIC) for 50p. **Pembridge** is another gem with a huddle of classic houses, and its useful **Black & White Villages Centre** (☎ 01544-388761; open 9am-6pm daily) has a TIC, tearooms, a gift shop and cycle hire.

---

part-ruined Hay Castle, as well as the largest bookshop in town.

Hay becomes the epicentre of the literary universe for a week in May/June when it hosts the **Hay Festival of Literature**. National and international scribes gather to scratch their chins and occasionally kick up their heels. The population of the town swells 50-fold, and bed space is as unlikely as Salman Rushdie becoming mayor of Tehran.

Even if you're not into bookish pursuits, Hay is a pretty place where you can soak up the village atmosphere, explore the surrounding countryside and clear the holiday cobwebs with canoeing and walking.

Orientation & Information

The English-Welsh border runs roughly 300m from Hay's compact centre, where you'll find most points of interest.

The **TIC** (☎ 820144; Oxford Rd; open 10am-1pm & 2pm-5pm daily Easter-Oct, 11am-1pm & 2pm-4pm daily Nov-Easter) is up a hill on the edge of town by the main car park. When we visited it was run by a couple of silver-haired ladies who would clearly prefer to be playing bridge and baking than dispensing information to bothersome tourists.

Activities

On the northeastern corner of **Brecon Beacons National Park**, Hay is an excellent base for exploring western Herefordshire and the Black Mountains of Wales. The **Offa's Dyke**

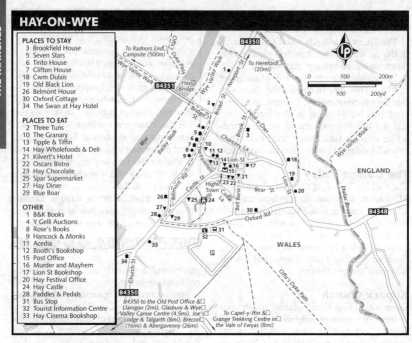

HAY-ON-WYE

PLACES TO STAY
3 Brookfield House
5 Seven Stars
6 Tinto House
7 Clifton House
18 Cwm Dulais
19 Old Black Lion
26 Belmont House
30 Oxford Cottage
34 The Swan at Hay Hotel

PLACES TO EAT
2 Three Tuns
10 The Granary
13 Tipple & Tiffin
14 Hay Wholefoods & Deli
21 Kilvert's Hotel
22 Oscars Bistro
23 Hay Chocolate
25 Spar Supermarket
27 Hay Diner
29 Blue Boar

OTHER
1 B&K Books
4 Y Gelli Auctions
8 Rose's Books
9 Hancock & Monks
11 Acedia
12 Booth's Bookshop
15 Post Office
16 Murder and Mayhem
17 Lion St Bookshop
20 Hay Festival Office
24 Hay Castle
28 Paddles & Pedals
31 Bus Stop
32 Tourist Information Centre
33 Hay Cinema Bookshop

walking route passes nearby. For fun on the River Wye, you can hire kayaks and Canadian canoes (the Volvos of the river) from **Paddles & Pedals** (☎ 820604; *Castle St*), which, despite the name, doesn't do bikes. Canoe hire is £18/28 for a half/full day and kayak hire £12/18.

Bookshops

The TIC and most shops stock the indispensable pamphlet guide to the town's 40 general and specialist bookshops, where (even buffs generally concede) quantity rules over quality. The most famous depository is **Booth's Bookshop** (☎ 820322; *44 Lion St*), followed by the excellent **Hay Cinema Bookshop** (☎ 820071; *Castle St*) in the old picture house.

Places to Stay

Outside of the festival, accommodation options are generally plentiful and good value.

Radnors End Campsite (☎ 820780; *per person £3.50*) is 500m from the bridge over the River Wye on the road to Clyro.

Clifton House (☎ 821618; **w** *www.clifton househay.co.uk*; *Belmont Rd; per person £20*) has pleasant doubles and a really cosy

lounge. The owners can provide local maps and arrange walks.

Seven Stars (☎ 820886; **w** *www.hay-on -wye.co.uk/sevenstars; 11 Broad St; singles/ doubles £48/55*) has comfortable rooms – all with new beds – and a sauna and 14m heated swimming pool; nonguests can book the sauna for £3.50 per person, per hour.

Old Black Lion (☎ 820841; **w** *www .oldblacklion.co.uk; Lion St; singles/doubles £35/80*) has pleasant and spacious rooms, each of which comes with its own teddy bear, propped up to greet you on arrival.

The **Old Post Office** (☎ 820008; *singles/ doubles from £18/56*), less than 2 miles from Hay on the B4350 to Brecon, is the best place to stay if you've got your own wheels. It's a gorgeous pad, with a polished oak floor, sumptuous king-size beds and a terrific vegetarian breakfast. The same people recently opened the more basic Oxford Cottage (same telephone number) in Hay itself.

Places to Eat

During the festival – and at the height of summer – **Hay Wholefoods & Deli** (☎ 820708; *1 Lion St*) supplies terrific picnic hampers (there's a veggie option), which include baskets and crockery. Give staff a day's notice and tell them how much you want to spend.

Hay Chocolate *(☎ 821880; 19 High Town)* is the place to indulge in sweet treats shaped as all things literary. For a laugh, tell them their bookworms look like caterpillars.

Tipple & Tiffin *(☎ 821932; The Pavement; cheeseboard £6; open Tues-Sun)* feels like a village wine bar and is a good spot for a postbrowse sip or (tiny) snack.

The Granary *(☎ 820790; Broad St; dinners around £8; open 12pm-10pm May-Sept, 12pm-5.30pm Nov-Apr)* is delightfully dithery and has delicious wholesome fare of the sort your nana used to make.

Kilvert's Hotel *(☎ 821042; Bull Ring; singles/doubles from £50/70; bar/restaurant meals £4/9)* has consistently good tucker in the oak-beamed bar and à la carte restaurant. The accommodation is also good.

Blue Boar *(☎ 820884; Castle St; mains around £12)* has reasonable food, although it's still only pub grub and the atmosphere needn't be so stuffy, sir.

Old Black Lion *(☎ 820841; Lion St; bar snacks/mains £7/13)* is another tavern providing upmarket pub grub, although, in this case, the mutton isn't being dressed up as lamb. The dining room is charming, the atmosphere convivial, and the Black Lion Ale memorable (the first few at least).

Three Tuns *(Broad St; open 1pm-3pm & 7.15pm-11pm Mon-Sat)*, a wonderful, tiny old pub and cider house, is much loved by locals. It's run by an adorable landlady, Lucy, who's been here for more than 40 years, serving customers with a radiant smile, and regaling them with stories. Descending the steps of her tavern is like stepping back in time.

Getting There & Away
Hay is 20 miles (32km) west of Hereford, where you'll find the nearest train station. If you're driving, allow time to cruise because the countryside is spellbinding.

Bus No 39 from Hereford (£6.60, 55 minutes) and from Brecon (£6.60, 45 minutes) runs five times daily, and bus No 40 has four services on Sunday.

ROSS-ON-WYE
☎ 01989 • pop 8300
Ross-on-Wye – although seeming a little forlorn these days – provides a reasonable

base for exploring this picturesque stretch of the River Wye, which wriggles its way through woods and meadows down through Symonds Yat to Monmouth.

Accommodation is plentiful, there are several excellent eateries and a couple of atmospheric pubs.

The **TIC** *(☎ 562768, fax 565057; Swan House, Edde Cross St; open 9am-5.30pm Mon-Sat, 10am-4pm Sun)* can help with information on activities and walks in and around the area. You can hire bikes from **Revolutions** *(☎ 562639; 48 Broad St)* from £10 per day.

Places to Stay & Eat
The nearest hostel is 6 miles (10km) south of Ross at Welsh Bicknor (see Goodrich in Around Ross-on-Wye later in this section).

Brookfield House *(☎ 562188;* W *www .brookfieldhouse.co.uk; Overross St; accommodation per person £22)* has shared bathrooms and basic comforts.

The Rosswyn *(☎ 562733; High St; singles/ doubles £40/70)* is a lovely, gregarious pub with attractive wood panelling and an original Jacobean staircase leading up to the homely, en-suite rooms.

King's Head Hotel *(☎ 763174, fax 769578;* W *www.kingshead.co.uk; 8 High St; singles/doubles from £45/75; 3-course dinners £17.50)* is a comfortable place with a congenial bar and luxurious leather armchairs, the perfect tonic after a day on your feet. The restaurant and bar meals are standard, but the Roy Orbison soundtrack is unpalatable.

Oat Cuisine *(☎ 566271; 47 Broad St; lunches £5-7)* is a reliable and inexpensive wholefood café and shop.

Meaders *(☎ 562803; 1 Copse Cross St; meals £7-10)* is vaguely Hungarian – the menu has a Magyar dash here and there – but clearly one of the best eateries in Ross, with massive tasty portions and a relaxed atmosphere.

Yaks 'n Yetis *(☎ 564963; Broad St; meals £6-10)* is an ambitious, and bizarre, mix of Tibetan, Nepalese, Thai and Mexican cuisine that occasionally hits the mark.

The Pheasant at Ross *(☎ 565751; 52 Edde Cross St; 3-course dinners £25; open Tues-Sun)* does fine English cuisine for dedicated carnivores.

Cloisters *(☎ 567717; 24 High St; meals £8-12)* has candles, red tablecloths, exposed walls and excellent fish dishes, and is the best bet for an intimate evening.

Getting There & Away

Ross is 14 miles (23km) from Hereford and 16 miles (26km) from Gloucester, with bus links to Lodon via Cheltenham and Cirencester. From the Cantilupe Rd terminus, bus Nos 38 and 33 run hourly Monday to Saturday to and from Hereford and Gloucester respectively.

AROUND ROSS-ON-WYE
Goodrich

From the roof of the keep at **Goodrich Castle** *(EH; ☎ 01600-890538; admission £3.60; open 10am-6pm daily Apr-Sept, 10am-5pm Oct, 10am-1pm & 2pm-4pm Wed-Sun Nov-Mar)* you get spectacular views of the Wye Valley and can appreciate how important – and impenetrable – this sandstone fortress would have been when it was built as a border stronghold in the 12th century. Cromwell's troops laid siege to the castle for over four months during the Civil War and eventually defeated it, although there's still plenty left to see. It's often a muddy walk from the car park: don't wear white shoes here after rain. There's a rather dry 45-minute audio tour.

From the village, it's a steep 1½-mile hill-hugging climb up to **Welsh Bicknor YHA Hostel** *(☎ 0870 770 6086, fax 0870 770 6087; e welshbicknor@yha.org.uk; dorm beds £11.25; open Apr-Oct)*, a Victorian rectory standing in 10 hectares of gorgeous riverside grounds.

Goodrich is 5 miles (8km) south of Ross off the A40. Bus No 34 stops here every couple of hours on its way between Ross and Monmouth.

Symonds Yat
☎ 01600

Symonds Yat, 2½ miles (4km) south of Goodrich, is an awesome little spot on the River Wye and a perfect base for river activities. It is crammed in summer and totally off-limits on sunny Sundays and bank holidays, but well worth a visit at quieter times. 'Yat' means gap or gate, and Symonds was the name of the high sheriff of Herefordshire, who would have controlled the gate and therefore all the river trade.

Symonds Yat East, a pretty little hamlet hugging the east bank of the river, is simply gorgeous. Symonds Yat West, at least the bit immediately opposite, is equally pretty but the upper part has a big and tacky fairground with kiss-me-quick hats and an entirely different vibe, although you might be interested in the Jubilee Puzzle Hedge Maze or the tropical world of butterflies.

An ancient hand ferry connects the two sides of the village. It costs 60p, singing included. At one time there were said to be more than a hundred of these ferries along the Wye; now there are only two.

Activities This area is exceptionally well endowed with activities to stimulate mind, body and soul, and is especially renowned for canoeing and rock climbing. The **Wyedean Canoe Centre** *(☎ 01594-833238; w www .wyedean.co.uk)* has a solid reputation for organising kayaking and white-water trips, and can also arrange caving and climbing. As flat as it may look, the river has a strong current and is not suitable for swimming.

From Symonds Yat East, it's a steep but easy walk – at least on a dry day – up 504m to the crown of the region, **Symonds Yat Rock**, which provides tremendous views of the river and valley as it twists around on itself. You can see two pairs of rare peregrine falcons that nest in the cliffs opposite, under the telescopic glare of friendly RSPB volunteers and visitors. Keep your dogs and kiddies on a short lead up here; there's a 90m drop over a harmlessly low-looking wall. The Forestry Commission maintains a little gift, refreshment and light meals shack in the clearing, which opens from 10am until everybody nicks off.

Places to Stay & Eat There is a string of accommodation and feeding options on the east side, starting with the atmospheric **Saracen's Head** *(☎ 890435; w www.saracenshead inn.co.uk; singles/doubles £40/60; meals £8-13)* in the heart of the bustle, where rooms and food are fine (if nothing special).

Rose Cottage *(☎ 890514; singles/doubles £24.50/43; light meals £5-8)* has three small rooms overlooking the river and a busy café on the front terrace. **Garth Cottage** *(☎ 890 364; rooms per person £25)*, next door, is small, quiet and friendly.

The Royal Hotel *(☎ 890238, fax 890777; w www.royalhotel-symondsyat.com; singles/ doubles from £35/80; meals £11-16, BBQ* *from £6)* is an old hunting lodge at the end of the strip and one of the best places to stay in all of the Marches. Run by a friendly and spirited Australian family, it has a welcoming atmosphere, superb food – including a gourmet Aussie barbecue on Sunday afternoon – lovely gardens, and a range of comfortable rooms.

Getting There & Away Symonds Yat is about 3 miles (5km) south of Goodrich, signposted from the A40, and beyond the reach of public transport.

LEDBURY
☎ 01531 • pop 7000 • elevation 147m
This handsome market town has antique shops, a wealth of historical architecture and perversely uncomfortable street benches.

The helpful **TIC** *(☎ 636147, fax 634313; e tourism@herefordshire.gov.uk; 3 The Homend; open 10am-5pm Mon-Sat)* can provide details on the **Ledbury Poetry Festival**, which takes place for 10 days in July and attracts bards from near and far.

You can hire bikes from the friendly **Saddle Bound Cycles** *(☎ 633433; 3 The Southend)* for £5 per day, and also get your map of the Ledbury Loop, a lovely 17-mile (27km) circular ride along secondary roads through rural Herefordshire.

Things to See
Ledbury's centrepiece is the delightfully dainty **Market House** *(open 11am-1pm & 2pm-4pm Mon-Fri, 2pm-5pm Sun)*, a 17th-century, black-and-white timber-framed structure in Market Place. From here, you can wander up the creaky and cobbled **Church Lane**, chock-a-block with notable architecture, including the **Painted Room** *(open 11am-1pm & 2pm-4pm Mon-Fri, 2pm-5pm Sun)*, with 16th-century floral frescoes.

Still in Church Lane, the **Butcher's Row Houses** *(☎ 632040; admission free; open 11am-5pm daily Easter-Sept)* is an engaging folk museum with displays ranging from 19th-century school clothing to a remarkable 18th-century communal 'Boot' bath that used to be carted from door to door for the poor to scrub in.

At the far end of the lane is the 12th-century parish church of **St Michael and All Angels**, with its splendid 60m spire and tower, which are separate from the church,

something you don't see everyday. The spire was a 1733 addition to the Norman nucleus. A free pamphlet inside points out the interesting features.

Places to Stay & Eat
Unlike some other large towns in this region, weekends are the busiest time for mid-range accommodation in Ledbury.

The **Feathers Hotel** *(☎ 635266; w www.feathers-ledbury.co.uk; High St; singles/doubles from £71.50/95)* is a fetching and homely establishment with a convivial bar, a comfortable tea lounge, charming rooms and the absurdly named **Fuggles** restaurant (named after a locally grown hop that hangs from virtually every pub ceiling in town).

The **Talbot Hotel** *(☎ 632963; New St; singles/doubles £27.50/49.50; meals £7-13)* has a wonderful dining room containing one of the finest examples of oak panelling in England. The only blemishes are the bullet holes left by inconsiderate Cavaliers and Roundheads who had a fight here during the Civil War and accidentally killed a barmaid. The rooms are small, adequate and inexpensive; the food is a little rich.

Mrs Muffin's *(☎ 633579; 1 Church Lane)* is a fabulous place for afternoon tea in a warm, cosy atmosphere, although the exceedingly good cakes will do your waistline no good at all.

The **Prince of Wales** *(☎ 632250; Church Lane; meals £4-7)* offers the best value on a plate. The landlord is friendly, the locals raucous, the atmosphere smoky and the shepherd's pie ridiculously good for £4.45.

Ceci Paolo *(☎ 632976; w www.cecipaolo.com; 21 High St)* is a food emporium comprising a superb deli, wine and kitchen shops and an excellent café that combines city chic with country portions.

Getting There & Away
Ledbury is 16 miles (26km) from Hereford, 10 miles (16km) from Great Malvern and not far from the M50 at the junction of the A417, A449 and A438 roads. The train station, to the north of the town, is on the Hereford to Birmingham railway line and has hourly trains to Hereford, Great Malvern, Worcester and Birmingham.

Bus No 476 runs from Hereford hourly (every two hours on Sunday) and bus Nos 678, 417 and 675 have regular services

THE MARCHES

from Market House to Gloucester, Worcester and Great Malvern respectively.

AROUND LEDBURY
Eastnor Castle
Eastnor Castle (☎ 01531-633160; adult/child £5.50/3, grounds only £3.50/2; open 11am-5pm Sun-Fri July & Aug, plus Sun & bank holidays Apr-early Oct) looks like it leapt from the pages of a fairy tale and is very popular for weddings and corporate events. Even when the castle is closed the extensive grounds, which include a deer park and arboretum of rare trees, are worth a look. The castle itself was built in the early 19th century, using Norman and Gothic styles, and has undergone much renovation work over recent years. Its rooms are rich in Italianate and Gothic furnishings.

The castle is a short distance from junction 2 of the M50 and just over 2 miles (3km) east of Ledbury on the A438.

Much Marcle
The village of Much Marcle is a tiny and remarkable place, home to two of the most impressive tourist attractions in the Marches.

First up is the enthralling historical house of **Hellens** (☎ 01531-660504; adult/child £4/2), one of the oldest houses in Britain and still occasionally inhabited by descendants of the family who built it in the 13th century. The largely 17th-century interior has been almost perfectly preserved through benign neglect; fortunately for us, down the ages the family were too busy squabbling over ownership to think about renovating. A wonderful tour (2pm, 3pm and 4pm Wednesday, Saturday and Sunday from April to September) takes you on a mesmerising journey through the house and its history. You can gather your thoughts with tea and cakes afterwards, or take a walk through the garden, which includes a lovely brick dovecote.

You're deep in cider country here and can celebrate the fact with a visit to **Westons Cider Mills** (☎ 01531-660233; **w** www.westons-cider.co.uk; The Bounds). Henry Weston started making cider for friends and family on this site in the 1870s. The local MP soon persuaded him to go commercial and got Westons cider put on tap in the parliament bar (where it still bears influence on the affairs of the state today).

You don't have to be a cider drinker to enjoy a visit, and tours of the mill (£3, 1½ hours, 2.30pm on Monday, Wednesday and Friday) are as relaxing as they are informative. Admission to the Edwardian-style garden and museum is free.

Much Marcle is 5 miles (8km) southwest of Ledbury, just off the A449, but you need your own wheels to get there.

Worcestershire

Worcestershire is a county of contrasts, where the rural idyll of little England clashes with the urban sprawl of big Britain. The north and east of the county consist of flat plains that blend into the industrial Midlands and offer little in the way of attractions, while the largely rural west and south are fringed by the Malvern Hills and the Cotswolds respectively. The Rivers Wye, Severn and Avon flow through the county and there are several attractive riverside market towns, particularly Upton-upon-Severn. Binding the county together is the regional capital of Worcester, a worthwhile base only if you're relying on public transport.

Activities
The **Severn Way** walking route winds its way through Worcestershire, passing through Worcester and Upton-upon-Severn. The **Three Choirs Way** links Worcester to Hereford and Gloucester.

Cyclists should pick up *Elgar Ride Variations* from TICs, which has a choice of routes around the Malverns.

Getting Around
Regular rail links are thin on the ground, while Kidderminster is the southern railhead of the popular Severn Valley Railway.

The **Wye Valley Wanderer** (☎ 01432-260948) is a popular bus linking Pershore and Worcester with Ledbury, Ross-on-Wye and Hereford on summer Sundays and bank holiday Mondays. Also see the Getting Around section at the start of this chapter.

WORCESTER
☎ 01905 • pop 75,500
Worcester (**woos**-ter) is known the world over for china and cricket. It is also home to the impressive cathedral where King John of

Magna Carta fame is buried, and is closely associated with Edward Elgar, Britain's greatest music composer, who was born nearby and popped his proverbial clogs here. Given the familiarity, it's all the more disappointing then to discover Worcester a disjointed and uninviting town, the charms of which are suppressed like so much of its Tudor and Georgian architecture. Good-value accommodation is scarce, and you'll be hard pushed to eat well on a budget.

Orientation

The main part of the city lies on the east bank of the River Severn, the cathedral rising above it. Friar and New Sts run into one another to create the city's prettiest thoroughfare; it's along here you'll find most of the pubs, eateries and other signs of life.

Information

The reliable **TIC** (☎ 726311, fax 722481; **w** www.cityofworcester.gov.uk; Guildhall, High St; open 9.30am-5pm Mon-Sat) provides information for the whole county. Walking tours (adult/child £3/1.50, 1½ hours) leave from the TIC at 11am Monday to Friday and 2.30pm on Wednesday, May to August. Bikes can be hired from **Peddlers** (☎ 24238; 46 Barbourne Rd) for £8 per day or £30 per week.

Worcester Cathedral

The first cathedral to grace this site, on the banks of the River Severn, was built in the 10th century. The current cathedral (☎ 28854; **e** info@worcestercathedral.org.uk; requested donation £3; open 7.30am-6pm daily) was begun in 1084 by Bishop – later Saint – Wulfstan but now encapsulates a medley of different styles displaying renovators' skills down through the ages. The atmospheric crypt, the largest Norman crypt in the country, dates from the time of Wulfstan, while the choir and Lady Chapel were built in 13th-century Early English style. Highlights include an impressive 12th-century circular chapterhouse, one of the first of its kind, and some splendid Victorian stained glass.

Wicked King John, whose treachery towards his brother Richard left the country in turmoil at his death, is buried in the choir (apart from his thumb which was nicked as a souvenir). Knowing he stood only the

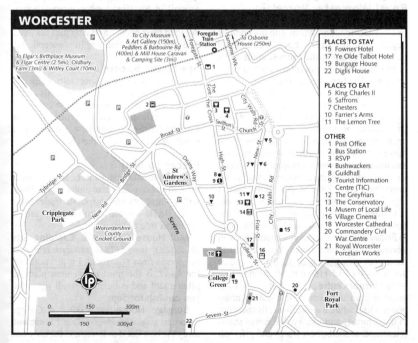

WORCESTER

To City Museum & Art Gallery (150m), Peddlers & Barbourne Rd (400m) & Mill House Caravan & Camping Site (3mi)

To Elgar's Birthplace Museum & Elgar Centre (2.5mi), Oldbury Farm (3mi) & Witley Court (10mi)

Foregate Train Station

To Osborne House (250m)

The Cross

Broad St

Swithun's St

Church

The Foregate

City Walls Rd

New St

St Andrew's Gardens

Deans Way

High St

Friar St

City Walls

Tybridge St

Bridge St

New Rd

Severn

Cripplegate Park

Worcestershire County Cricket Ground

College St

College Green

Fort Royal Park

Severn St

PLACES TO STAY
15 Fownes Hotel
17 Ye Olde Talbot Hotel
19 Burgage House
22 Diglis House

PLACES TO EAT
5 King Charles II
6 Saffrons
7 Chesters
10 Farrier's Arms
11 The Lemon Tree

OTHER
1 Post Office
2 Bus Station
3 RSVP
4 Bushwackers
8 Guildhall
9 Tourist Information Centre (TIC)
12 The Greyfriars
13 The Conservatory
14 Musem of Local Life
16 Village Cinema
18 Worcester Cathedral
20 Commandery Civil War Centre
21 Royal Worcester Porcelain Works

0   150   300m
0   150   300yd

flimsiest chance of making it through the Pearly Gates, the dying king asked to be buried disguised as a monk.

If you're fit and fond of a view, there are tours up the 249 steps (60m) of the tower for £1.50. The best views of the cathedral are from either bank of the river, particularly from the County Cricket Ground opposite. The cathedral choir sings evensong at 5.30pm Monday to Wednesday, Friday and Saturday, and at 4pm Sunday.

Commandery Civil War Centre

Not far from the cathedral, the Commandery *(☎ 361821; W www.worcestercitymuseums.org.uk; adult/child £4/2.85; open 10am-5pm Mon-Sat, 1.30pm-5pm Sun)* is a splendid Tudor building used by Charles II as his headquarters during the momentous Battle of Worcester (1651), the final major conflict of England's traumatic Civil War. The centre details the ins and outs of this and many other battles that raged in 17th-century England and gives a wonderful overview of the Civil War in general by way of computer, audio and visual exhibits.

Royal Worcester Porcelain Works

In 1751 Doctor John Warne and his buddies began making ornate bone china as a hobby; the result is the longest continuous production of any porcelain company in England. The firm was granted a royal warrant in 1789 and still supplies HRH with some of her preferred crockery.

The Royal Worcester Porcelain Works *(☎ 746000; W www.royal-worcester.co.uk; open 9am-5.30pm Mon-Sat, 11am-5pm Sun)* moved to its current 4-hectare site in 1840 and has an entire visitor complex, with tours, shops, a restaurant and a museum. A ticket for everything costs £8/6.75 per adult/child, a significant saving if you're this way inclined.

Guided one-hour factory tours – of the bone china only – are available from Monday to Friday and cost £5, but you should book in advance during busy times. You also get to paint your own plate with the help of one of the artists for £3.50 (no cost for children).

The **Visitor Centre** *(adult/child £2.25/1.75)* gives you an impression of a 19th-century potter's life, while a short film tells the story of the company and factory. A series of shops (clearance, seconds, best wares and gift) sell everything from a 23-piece 'best' dinner service for nearly £1000 to seconds for just a few quid.

The **Museum of Worcester Porcelain** *(adult/child £3/2.25; open 9.30am-5pm Mon-Fri, 10am-5pm Sat)* tells the factory's story through an intricate and extravagant collection of works from the company's very first pieces to its most recent creations. When groups of old ladies are visiting, if you listen very carefully you can sometimes hear their knees knock together in excitement.

Historical Properties

For an impression of what Worcester looked like before modern planners got their filthy paws on it, stroll down New St and Friar St, both flanked by fine Tudor and Elizabethan buildings.

Built in 1480, **The Greyfriars** *(NT; ☎ 23571; Friar St; admission £3; open 2pm-5pm Wed, Thur & Mon bank holidays Easter-Oct)* is an attractively restored, timber-framed Tudor house, full of textiles and furnishings, with a pretty walled garden.

The splendid **Guildhall** *(High St)* is a Queen Anne building of 1722, designed by a pupil of Sir Christopher Wren, Thomas White, who died in poverty after the city dragged their heels on paying him his dues. The period decoration within is exceptional.

Spectator Sports

If sport is more your spectacle, there are spring and summer racing carnivals at the nearby **Worcester racecourse** *(☎ 0870 220 2772)*, while the central **Worcestershire County Cricket Ground** *(☎ 748474)* is a lovely spot to cheer on the chaps.

Places to Stay

Lodgings in Worcester can be hard to come by midweek, when many places are filled with contractors and corporate trade. Most of the B&Bs – a fairly grim bunch – are on the north side of town.

Mill House Caravan & Camping Site *(☎ 451283, fax 754143; Hawford; tent sites per person from £6)*, about 3 miles north on the A449, is the most convenient place to pitch a tent and is beside a small river that you can fish for 50p.

Burgage House *(☎ 25396; 4 College Precincts; singles/doubles £30/55)* is far and away the best B&B in town, and the only one that makes you feel like you're on holiday. It has huge and comfortable rooms with bath or shower – the front ones with views of the cathedral – and is on a quiet cobbled street.

Osborne House *(☎/fax 22296;* e *enquiries@ osbornehouse.freeserve.co.uk; 17 Chestnut Walk; B&B rooms with en suite from £36)* is another popular B&B, as good as any in this area, although not particularly cheerful. Barbourne Rd, farther north of the centre, has a glut of drab B&Bs along the same block.

Ye Olde Talbot Hotel *(☎ 612760; Friar St; singles/doubles £60/70)* is part of a reasonable chain and, pound for pound, one of the best places in town to rest your head.

Fownes Hotel *(☎ 613151, fax 23742; City Walls Rd; singles/doubles Mon-Fri from £90/95, Sat & Sun £55/70)*, in a converted glove factory, is a huge and dishevelled old place popular with blue-collar business folk.

Diglis House *(☎ 353518, fax 767772;* w *www.diglishousehotel.co.uk; Severn St; singles/doubles from £80/90)*, located on the banks of the River Severn, offers comfortable rooms, many with river views.

Oldbury Farm *(☎ 421357; Lower Broadheath; rooms per person £25)*, about 3 miles (5km) out of town, is a lovely Georgian farmhouse with fishing rights and stables, next to Elgar's birthplace.

Places to Eat

It's much of a muchness with Worcester's eateries and you may as well go for a wander down Friar and Mew Sts and see what tickles your fancy.

King Charles II *(☎ 22449; 29 New St; 3-course lunches £9.95, evening meals £9-17)* is atmospheric and historical, and offers good Continental cuisine. It was through the back door of this 16th-century house that King Charles II is said to have fled to exile in France during the Battle of Worcester in 1651. Low lights, lace tablecloths and crystal glasses provide the ambience.

Chesters *(☎ 611638; 51 New St; meals £6-10)*, nearby, is vaguely Mexican with a little bit of everything else thrown in. The food is only OK; the chirpy surroundings are popular with groups.

Saffrons *(☎ 610505; 15 New St; meals £10-15)* offers a global tour from Thai to modern British.

The Lemon Tree *(☎ 27770; 12 Friar St; lunches around £10, dinners around £20)* offers modern British cooking with a distinctly international flavour in intimate surroundings.

Farrier's Arms *(Fish St)* is an old and popular local near the cathedral that does a satisfying line in home-cooked grub, and has a huge and free-ranging German shepherd that looks like Tina Turner.

Entertainment

RSVP *(☎ 723035; The Cross; food served from 8am-9.30pm)* is an old church where the original pulpit is incorporated into the staircase. It's always lively but the food is ordinary.

Ye Olde Talbot Hotel *(☎ 612760; Friar St)* is the best pub in the centre of town but it gets totally swamped before and after the flicks (directly opposite).

The Conservatory *(Friar St)* is nice and relaxed, with a varied crowd and a warmer atmosphere than most.

Bushwackers *(Trinity St)* is a napkin-for-beermat Aussie theme bar that draws huge numbers of all shapes and sizes. There's a huge beer terrace, should the sun come out, and ladies drink free on Monday night.

Getting There & Away

Worcester is 25 miles (40km) from Hereford, 57 miles (92km) from Oxford and 113 miles (182km) from London.

Worcester Foregate station, approximately 500m north of the cathedral, is the most central station in the city and has about a dozen trains daily to and from London Paddington (£22.80, 2¼ hours) and Hereford (£5.60, 40 minutes). The odd train goes only as far as the city's other station, Shrub Hill, about the same distance again from the cathedral.

National Express has two coaches daily between Crowngate bus station and Victoria bus station, London (£23, 4½ hours). Bus No 44 has hourly services daily to Great Malvern, bus No 372 goes to Gloucester via Upton every two hours and bus No 417 has four journeys to Ledbury Monday to Saturday.

AROUND WORCESTER
Elgar's Birthplace Museum

About 3 miles (5km) west of Worcester is Lower Broadheath, the birthplace of Sir Edward Elgar (1857–1934), England's greatest composer. You can visit the cottage (☎ 01905-333224; adult/child £3.50/1.75, open 11am-4.15pm daily) where he was born and see his gramophone, writing desk, musical manuscripts and various personal mementos. The **Elgar Centre**, next door, is a museum of Elgar memorabilia and, more importantly, the place to listen to his music and appreciate what all the fuss is about.

Bus Nos 311 and 317 go from Worcester to Broadheath Common, a short walk away from the museum, three times daily Monday to Saturday.

Witley Court

Arguably the most venerable and romantic ruin in England, Witley Court (EH; ☎ 01299-896636; admission £4; open 10am-6pm daily Apr-Oct, 10am-4pm Wed-Sun Nov-Mar) was one of Britain's most extravagant private homes when it was built in the mid-19th century. It was sadly neglected over the years but saved from total demolition by EH. Even derelict, the house is stunning and the gardens are well on their way back to their former Victorian glory. The spectacular fountains – including one depicting Perseus and Andromeda, which used to spout water 30m into the air – are due to be finished by spring 2003.

The adjacent **Great Witley Church** is widely considered to be one of the finest baroque churches in England, its rather simple exterior belying a sumptuous interior featuring exquisite paintings by the likes of Antonio Bellucci and some exceptionally ornate carving and glasswork. The church doubles as a wonderful music hall and houses regular classical concerts throughout the summer (call ☎ 01299-896437 for details).

Witley Court is 10 miles (16km) northwest of Worcester on the A443 and the nearest train station is at Droitwich Spa, about 8 miles (13km) away. Bus No 758 from Worcester or Kidderminster to Tenbury Wells pass this way infrequently.

GREAT MALVERN
☎ 01684 • pop 30,000

Great Malvern is the biggest and best known of a cluster of settlements along the slopes of the Malvern Hills, which rise from the flat plains of Worcestershire. It became popular as a Victorian resort and today is well-heeled and a tad snooty; it has lots of

cedars, pines and monkey-puzzle trees, Victorian fittings and incredibly steep streets.

The tidy **TIC** (☎ 892289, fax 892872; e malvern.tic@malvernhills.gov.uk; 21 Church St; open 10am-5pm daily) has all you need to know about the town and the hills. At 10.30am on Saturday, there's a TIC **guided tour** of Victorian Great Malvern, which costs £2 and lasts for 1½ hours.

Malvern Priory

The priory church, founded in 1085 and with original Norman pillars still lining the nave, is packed with remarkable features. Here you'll find the greatest collection of stained glass from the 15th century, the zenith of English glass. The choir features 1200 medieval tiles, the oldest and finest collection in England, while you can also see many fine misericords under the tip-up seats of the monks' stalls. They depict mythology and various domestic scenes from the 14th century and feature an almost complete set of the labours of the months from the 15th century.

A shop inside the priory has a handy pamphlet pointing out the features of interest.

Malvern Museum of Local History

For the story of the town, venture into the Malvern Museum of Local History (☎ 567 811; open 10am-5.30pm daily Easter-Oct, except Wed during school term), housed in the impressive Priory Gatehouse (1470) of the town's former Benedictine abbey. By way of introduction, as you enter there are two large embroidered murals depicting all of the things for which Great Malvern is renowned, from spring water to radar.

Malvern Theatres (☎ 892277; Grange Rd) is one of Britain's leading provincial theatres and hosts many outstanding shows. It is based in the Winter Gardens Complex and, despite the not-so-recent name change, is still known locally as the Winter Gardens.

The **Theatre of Small Convenience** (☎ 568 933; Edith Walk) is in a converted Victorian men's lavatory, and is recognised by the Guinness statisticians as the world's smallest theatre. It seats 12 and hosts varied (mainly amateur) arts from puppetry to poetry.

Walking

The Malvern Hills – about 9 miles (14km) long and never more than 5 miles (8km) wide – straddle the boundary between Worcestershire and Herefordshire. There are 18 named hills, each affording spectacular views. The highest points are Worcestershire Beacon (419m), North Hill (397m) and the Herefordshire Beacon or British Camp (334m). The entire length of the hills is open to ramblers and they are crisscrossed by more than 100 miles of paths. The TIC stocks the *Malvern Map Set* (£1.50), with five maps covering the chain of hills. You can fill up your water bottle at any of around 70 springs dotted around the hills.

Places to Stay
There's lots of excellent accommodation in Great Malvern, although, in keeping with the neighbourhood, it tends to be pricey. Head to the smaller villages for cheaper options.

Malvern Hills YHA Hostel *(☎ 0870 770 5948, fax 0870 770 5949; e malvern@yha .org.uk; 18 Peachfield Rd; dorm beds £10.25; open mid-Feb–Oct)* is in Malvern Wells, 1½ miles (2.5km) south of Great Malvern on the A449 (take bus No 675 from Great Malvern to British Camp).

The Foleys Arms *(☎ 573397, fax 569665; 14 Worcester Rd; singles/doubles from £74/98)* is a large and graceful Georgian hotel that aims to please, with little comforts like fluffy towels and soothing sofas. There are good ales and bonhomie in the handsome **Bolly and Bass** bar.

The Abbey Hotel *(☎ 892332, fax 578006; w www.sarova.com; Abbey Rd; singles/doubles from £100/110)* is a jolly good place with elegant rooms and a striking ivy-covered facade.

The Cottage in the Wood Hotel *(☎ 575859, fax 560662; w www.cottageinthe wood.co.uk; Holywell Rd; singles/doubles from £78/144)*, 3 miles (5km) from Great Malvern, is on a secluded ledge above Malvern Wells and has spectacular views. There is a range of lodgings in three separate buildings and dinner in the outstanding restaurant is a bargain at £30.

Malvern Link, a tiny village on the other side of the hills to Great Malvern, is a good base for walkers. **The Firs** *(☎ 564016; 243 West Malvern Rd; singles/doubles £25/50)* combines cockney hospitality with comfy rooms and wonderful views, while **Harcourt Cottage** *(☎ 574561; 252 West Malvern Rd;*

singles/doubles £30/40) is a French version where the owner cooks evening meals.

Places to Eat
Blue Bird Tea Rooms *(☎ 561166; 9 Church St; meals £4-6)*, almost next door to the TIC, feels like being at your nana's place. Quiche and salads are staples but there's cream tea if you fancy a little après-hike treat.

The White Seasons *(☎ 575954; 27 Church St; meals £10-17)* specialises in fish and seafood, and is the place for a special evening meal. Don't expect much change out of £30 for three courses; vegetarians shouldn't expect much at all.

Lady Foley's Tearoom *(☎ 893033; Imperial Rd; lunches £4-7)* serves simple and inexpensive vegetarian lunches and teas on the quaintly atmospheric platform of the Victorian train station. There doesn't seem to be much coming and going but it's very atmospheric nonetheless.

Anupam *(☎ 573814; 85 Church St; meals £7-12)* is an innovative Indian restaurant just off the main drag.

Getting There & Away
Great Malvern is 8 miles (13km) from Worcester (£3.50, 15 minutes) and 15 miles (24km) from Hereford (£4.70, 30 minutes), and regular trains come from both.

National Express runs one bus daily between Great Malvern and London (£23, 4½ hours) via Worcester – there's an information and ticket window at the Post Office. Bus No 44 connects Worcester with Great Malvern every half-hour daily, while bus No 675 has regular services to Ledbury from Monday to Saturday.

UPTON-UPON-SEVERN
☎ 01684
Upton is a bonny little town with an eye-catching jumble of Tudor and Georgian architecture, lively pubs and a penchant for festivals (including the popular Oliver Cromwell jazz festival that takes place at the end of June).

For information, contact the **TIC** *(☎ 594200, fax 594185; e upton.tic@malvernhills.gov.uk; 4 High St; open 10am-5pm Mon-Sat, 10am-4pm Sun)*. Map enthusiasts should beat a path to **The Map Shop** *(☎ 593146; 15 High St)*, which has one of the best selections outside London.

Places to Stay & Eat

Old Street B&B (☎ 594242; 35 Old St; singles/doubles £22.50/45) is an exceedingly cute cottage and a jolly good place to repose, half way along the main street.

The White Lion (☎ 592551, fax 593 333; w www.whitelionhotel.biz; 21 High St; singles/doubles £53/77) is a lovely, la-de-da pub offering old-fashioned hospitality and comforts. The older rooms have oodles more character than the recently renovated ones.

The Pepperpot Brasserie (High St; meals £12-14) is a lovely, oak-beamed restaurant serving little portions at big prices.

The Upton thing is to pub-crawl; a grand idea in a pedestrian-friendly place stacked with atmospheric bars dating back to when the town was an important river crossing:

Swan Hotel (☎ 592299; Waterside; singles/ doubles £40/65; meals £6-10) is the pick of the riverside taverns and has expansive views, as well as a gregarious bar with low beams, exposed walls and a sassy welcome. The food is a cut above your normal pub fare.

The Little Upton Muggery (Old St) is a quaint tavern with more than 500 beer mugs hanging from the ceiling and good pub grub coming from the kitchen. A Desperate Dan Pie will cost you £6.50, a Diddy Dan Pie – if you can stand the ignominy – costs £4.50.

Fans of the TV series *The League of Gentlemen* should head to the nearby village of Hanley Castle for the **Three Kings Inn** (☎ 592686), an ancient and well-loved 'local' that gets its real ales from small independent breweries. It pongs a little and you'd need to be very hungry to partake in the toasted sandwiches, but it's undeniably atmospheric and has dangerously comfy 1920s brown leather chairs. It's about 2 miles (3km) north of Upton, just off the B4211, in a tiny hamlet beside a school.

Getting There & Away

Upton is 11 miles (18km) south of Worcester, just over 1 mile (2km) from the A38 and 5 miles (8km) from the M5. Bus No 372 runs between Upton and Worcester seven times daily from Monday to Saturday; there's a reduced Sunday service on bus No 372.

Oxfordshire, Gloucestershire & the Cotswolds

Welcome to Middle England. This isn't quite a geographic term, because the area covered by this chapter lies a bit to the south and slightly to the west of the country, but a social, political and cultural one, for it is in the counties of Oxfordshire and Gloucestershire (that are straddled by the beautiful Cotswolds) that you will find the hearth and heart of a quasi-mythical England. This is an idyll made up of rolling fields and charming towns topped by church spires, where butter is churned and farm labourers drink home-made cider.

Inevitably, this idyll has proved popular with growing numbers of London-weary professionals who are looking for a bigger slice of the good life, and these days you're most likely to encounter an ex-banker running an antique shop than a field hand straight out of *Jude the Obscure*.

ACTIVITIES

The picture-postcard villages and gentle rolling farmlands of the Cotswold counties are ideal for walking and cycling, and this section provides a few ideas to point you in the right direction. Information is also provided in the main Activities chapter near the start of this book, with suggestions for specific walks and rides given throughout this chapter. Regional tourism websites all contain walking and cycling information, and Tourist Information Centres (TICs) stock leaflets (free) plus maps and guides (usually £1 to £5) covering walking, cycling and other activities.

Walking

Of the long-distance routes in this region, the **Cotswold Way** is an absolute classic and justifiably popular. It runs south to north from Bath to Chipping Campden, with most people covering the 108 miles in about a week. You can also do the route north to south or just cherry-pick a section for a few days. Most people prefer the northern half as it has more typical Cotswold scenery, while the southern half is quieter and has a slightly (but only slightly) harder edge.

Highlights

- Admiring the overwhelming beauty of Oxford University
- Visiting Blenheim Palace and its superb gardens
- Appreciating the muted elegance of Regency Cheltenham
- Exploring Gloucester Cathedral and its magnificent cloisters
- Seeing the honey-hued stone villages of the Cotswolds, particularly Stow-on-the-Wold
- Checking out the Cheltenham Festival in March, a highlight of the social and racing calendar

Another very popular long-distance route that starts in this region is the **Thames Path** national trail, which follows Britain's best-known river downstream from the source near Cirencester all the way to London. The whole 173-mile route usually takes walkers about two weeks, but a very enjoyable five-day section runs from the start near Cirencester across to Oxford (you can trim this to four days by going from Cricklade to Oxford), giving a perfect taste of the eastern part of this region.

For shorter walks, the **Cotswold Hills** offer endless opportunities, with gentle paths

449

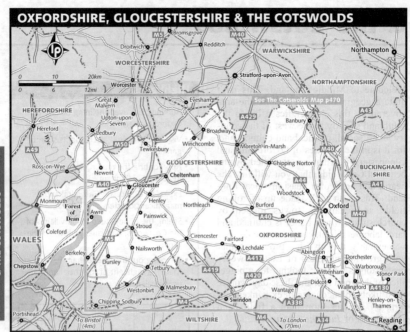

OXFORDSHIRE, GLOUCESTERSHIRE & THE COTSWOLDS

leading through woods and fields, alongside clear-flowing rivers or up to viewpoints on the western escarpment overlooking the Severn Valley. Towns that make good bases for walking include the marvellously named trio of Moreton-in-Marsh, Stow-on-the-Wold and Bourton-on-the-Water.

Cycling

The Cotswold counties are good for cycling, with plenty of quiet country lanes and generally mild but rewarding gradients. The Cotswold Hills themselves are especially scenic, although the steep western escarpment can be a bit of a shock for the unwary.

In the eastern part of the region, Oxford is a famously bike-friendly city, with several bike-rental outfits. Waymarked long distance routes in the region include the **Thames Valley Cycle Way**, which starts in Oxford and leads eventually to London. This is part of the National Cycle Network (see the main Activities chapter for more details).

The **Cotswolds** and **Chilterns** both have many bridleways open to mountain bikers, and the local people here are (quite rightly) very keen on keeping off-roaders off the footpaths too. In the west of the region, the **Forest of Dean** has many dirt-track options, and some dedicated mountain bike trails.

Oxfordshire

To many visitors, Oxfordshire *is* Oxford, the world-famous university town that millions of tourists flock to so they can wander around its beautiful colleges and photograph each other in the elegant quads or ornate doorways. Oxford can be a pretty hard act to follow.

Luckily, the rest of the county doesn't have to. Beyond Oxford's city limits lies the gentle charm of pastoral England – unruffled yet intensely conscious of its own appearance, an increasingly urbane but stubbornly rural county that prides itself on its history, culture and social gatherings. This is particularly true of the towns- and villages-on-Thames, that famous river that meanders elegantly through the centre and south of the county.

As well as the colleges, museums and gardens of Britain's oldest university, no-one should miss Blenheim Palace, the spectacular birthplace of Sir Winston Churchill.

ACTIVITIES

As well as the national trails mentioned in the main chapter introduction, other long walking routes in this county include the **Oxfordshire Way** – a 65-mile waymarked trail connecting the Cotswolds with the Chilterns, running from Bourton-on-the-Water to Henley-on-Thames. As with all long routes, though, you can easily do just a short section for a couple of hours or a full day, and leaflets available from local TICs divide the route into 16 walks of between 2 and 8 miles in length.

Oxfordshire is also good cycling country, with many quiet roads and few extreme gradients; Oxford is a centre for bike rental if you don't have your own wheels. Cycling routes through the county include the **Oxfordshire Cycleway**, taking in Woodstock, Burford and Henley.

GETTING AROUND

For all public transport information, call **Traveline** (☎ 0870 608 2608). Oxford is the hub of a fairly comprehensive bus service. TICs stock a useful free *Bus & Rail Map* showing routes and giving contact numbers for each operator. The main companies are **Stagecoach** (☎ 01865-772250) and the **Oxford Bus Company** (☎ 01865-785400).

Both these companies offer good day- and week-long bus passes that can save you plenty, especially if you plan on doing a lot of bus travelling. See Getting Around in the following Oxford section for more details.

From Oxford, **Cotswold Roaming** (☎ 018 65-250640) runs guided bus tours to several places around Oxford between April and October, including Blenheim Palace (half-day tour, adult/child £16/10), which includes admission to the palace; Bath & Castle Combe (full-day tour, adult/child £30/18); and the Cotswolds (full-day tour, adult/child £32.50/20).

Oxfordshire has a reasonable rail network, with Oxford and Banbury the main stations. There are services on the Cotswolds and Malvern line between London Paddington and Hereford, and between London Euston and Birmingham. Call **National Rail Enquiries** (☎ 08457 484950) for details.

OXFORD

☎ 01865 • pop 115,000

Tweed-jacketed 20-somethings discussing the meaning of 'pathos' on a perfectly manicured lawn...wide-eyed tourists poring over maps oblivious to the bus bearing down on them...locals pretending not to hear when asked where Mag-daleen is...it must be Oxford, a city that is virtually synonymous with academic excellence and – these days – large-scale tourism.

Oxford should be high on your list of must-dos in Britain, but remember that it's up there on everyone else's too. They come to see the university, spread across the town centre among 39 separate colleges that range in age from 50 to over 600 years old. The most beautiful of these are sumptuous and elegant examples of the best of British architecture: handsome, honey-coloured buildings jealously guarding gorgeous quadrangles, courtyards and gardens.

Oxford thrives on tourism, and the university has gone to great lengths to ensure that it remains one of the world's foremost centres of third-level education, rather than a giant academic theme park, by consistently restricting access to its colleges.

Still, there's enough here to keep you occupied for a week, and if you can ignore the infernal tour buses and the unsightly reminders of Oxford's industrial past (these days it is heavily reliant on the services industry), it is pure pleasure to let yourself get lost in the small lanes and alleys that crisscross the university.

History

Oxford was a fairly key Saxon town thanks to its strategic location at the point where the River Cherwell meets the Thames (called the Isis round these parts, from the Latin name *Tamesis*), and was heavily fortified by Alfred the Great in the war against the Danes.

Oxford's importance, however, grew dramatically after 1167, when all Anglo-Norman students were expelled from the then centre of European scholastic life, the Sorbonne in Paris. They cast off the sophistication and revelry of the Parisian high life in favour of an Augustinian abbey in not-so-trendy Oxford.

Undaunted by the lack of distractions, students came in droves but managed to create a lasting enmity between themselves and the local townspeople, culminating in

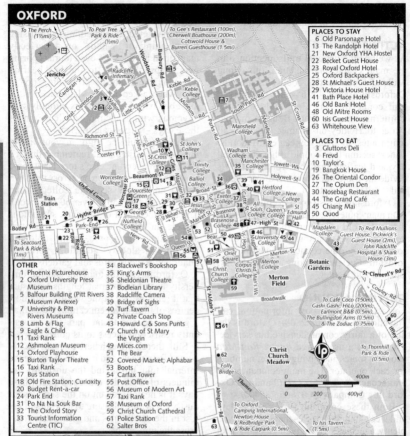

OXFORD

To The Perch (1½mi)
To Pear Tree Park & Ride (½mi)
To Gee's Restaurant (100m), Cherwell Boathouse (200m), Cotswold House & Burren Guesthouse (1.5mi)

Jericho
Radcliffe Infirmary

Train Station

Botley Rd

To Seacourt Park & Ride (1mi)

To Red Mullions Guest House, Pickwick's Guest House (2mi), John Radcliffe Hospital & Shark House (3mi)

To Café Coco (150m), Gashi Gashi, HiLo (200m), Earlmont B&B (0.5mi), The Bullingdon Arms (0.5mi) & The Zodiac (0.75mi)

To Thornhill Park & Ride (0.5mi)

To Isis Tavern (1.5mi)

To Oxford Camping International, Newton House & Redbridge Park & Ride Carpark (0.5mi)

Christ Church Meadow

PLACES TO STAY
6 Old Parsonage Hotel
13 The Randolph Hotel
21 New Oxford YHA Hostel
22 Becket Guest House
23 Royal Oxford Hotel
25 Oxford Backpackers
28 St Michael's Guest House
29 Victoria House Hotel
41 Bath Place Hotel
46 Old Bank Hotel
48 Old Mitre Rooms
60 Isis Guest House
63 Whitehouse View

PLACES TO EAT
3 Gluttons Deli
4 Frevd
10 Taylor's
19 Bangkok House
26 The Oriental Condor
27 The Opium Den
30 Nosebag Restaurant
44 The Grand Café
45 Chiang Mai
50 Quod

OTHER
1 Phoenix Picturehouse
2 Oxford University Press Museum
5 Balfour Building (Pitt Rivers Museum Annexe)
7 University & Pitt Rivers Museums
8 Lamb & Flag
9 Eagle & Child
11 Taxi Rank
12 Ashmolean Museum
14 Oxford Playhouse
15 Burton Taylor Theatre
16 Taxi Rank
17 Bus Station
18 Old Fire Station; Curioxity
20 Budget Rent-a-car
24 Park End
31 Po Na Na Souk Bar
32 The Oxford Story
33 Tourist Information Centre (TIC)
34 Blackwell's Bookshop
35 King's Arms
36 Sheldonian Theatre
37 Bodleian Library
38 Radcliffe Camera
39 Bridge of Sighs
40 Turf Tavern
42 Private Coach Stop
43 Howard C & Sons Punts
47 Church of St Mary the Virgin
49 Mices.com
51 The Bear
52 Covered Market; Alphabar
53 Boots
54 Carfax Tower
55 Post Office
56 Museum of Modern Art
57 Taxi Rank
58 Museum of Oxford
59 Christ Church Cathedral
61 Police Station
62 Salter Bros

the St Scholastica's Day Massacre in 1355 (see boxed text later in this chapter). Thereafter, the king, eager to keep an eye on student activity, ordered that the university be broken up into colleges, each of which then developed its own traditions.

The first colleges, built in the 13th century, were Balliol, Merton and the imaginatively named University. At least three colleges were built in each of the following three centuries, and more followed, though at a slower rate. The newer colleges, such as Keble, were added in the 19th and 20th centuries to cater for an ever-expanding student population. Today there are about 15,000 undergraduates spread among 39 colleges. So many brains in the one place didn't necessarily bring enlightenment though, and it

wasn't until the opening of Lady Margaret's Hall in 1878 that women were admitted to the university. However, until 1920 they had to content themselves with the seemingly pointless exercise of swotting hard for four years without being awarded a degree. Today the colleges are open to everyone and almost half the students are female.

First-time visitors to Oxford will be surprised at just how industrialised the city is. In 1790 Oxford was linked by canal to the Midlands' industrial centres, but the city's real industrial boom came when William Morris began producing cars here in 1912. The Bullnose Morris and the Morris Minor were both produced in the Cowley factories and Oxford's academic reputation was overshadowed by its manufacturing importance.

St Scholastica's Day Massacre

Ever since the arrival of the first fresh-faced students to Oxford after 1167, there has been friction with the local townspeople. Most of the time it involved a bit of name-calling and the odd slight but occasionally it erupted into full-scale violence, most notably in 1209 and 1330, when a bunch of battered scholars, tired of being whipping boys for the local bullies, abandoned Oxford for Cambridge and Stamford in Lincolnshire respectively, founding universities on their arrival. What happened on February 10–11 1355, however, was to make the two previous riots seem like an innocent pillow fight.

Two drunken students, Walter Sprynghouse and Roger de Chesterfield, were celebrating St Scholastica's Day and stumbled into the Swyndlestock Tavern on Carfax. One of them began complaining about the quality of the wine, whereupon he threw his glass into the landlord's face. A fist-fight ensued, which quickly developed into a full-scale street brawl between students and townspeople. When he got wind of what was going on, the chancellor ordered the pealing of the bells of St Mary the Virgin and every student who heard it rushed to arm himself and join the fight. By the end of the day the fight had somewhat petered out and an uneasy truce was established; the students returned to the university to celebrate a victory.

The next morning, however, it all went horribly wrong. The townspeople were still furious and they enlisted the help of villagers from the surrounding countryside, who arrived armed with pickaxes, shovels and pikes. Baying for student blood, they went on a rampage and at the end of the second day of fighting 63 students lay dead alongside 30 or so townspeople. By this stage, King Edward III had ordered troops to quell the riot and after reviewing the situation decided in the students' favour.

The king drew up a charter that essentially brought the town under the control of the university, but if that wasn't humiliating enough, he also ordered that the mayor and burgesses (citizens) attend a service on the anniversary of the riot and pay the vice chancellor a yearly recompense of a penny for every student killed.

Incredibly, this practice continued until 1825 when the mayor, Alderman Grubb, flatly refused to pay the fine. To the locals' intense chagrin, the university would not agree to the elimination of the practice and every year thereafter the mayor had to pointedly refuse to pay what was blatantly a ridiculous and humiliating affair finally came to an end in 1955, when Mayor William Richard Gowers, MA, Oriel, was awarded an honorary Doctorate of Civil Law, the first mayor in Oxford's history to receive such a distinction. The olive branch was finally extended...600 years after the event.

Orientation

The city centre is surrounded by rivers and streams to the south, east and west, and can easily be covered on foot. Carfax Tower, at the junction of Queen and Cornmarket Sts and St Aldate's, makes a good central landmark, but watch out for tour buses: they seem intent on scaring the pants off every wide-eyed pedestrian visitor who isn't careful.

There are frequent buses to Carfax Tower from the train station to the west. Alternatively, turn left into Park End St and it's a 15-minute walk. The bus station is nearer the city centre, off Gloucester Green.

University buildings are scattered throughout the city, with the most important and architecturally interesting in the centre. It will take more than a day to do justice to

them all but, if pushed for time, try to visit Christ Church, New and Magdalen colleges.

The big student areas in town are Jericho, in the northwest city centre, and Cowley Rd, about a mile southeast of Carfax.

Information

Tourist Offices The TIC (☎ 726871; 15-16 Broad St; open 9.30am-5pm Mon-Sat year round plus 10am-3.30pm Sun Easter-Sept) recently moved to new, larger premises on account of the sheer volume of daily traffic, particularly in summer. We hope the move improves the mood of the staff, who were fairly curt when we visited.

The TIC stocks a Welcome to Oxford brochure, which has a walking tour with college opening times. For further information, check out the official website at **w** www.vis itoxford.org.

Money Every major bank & ATM is represented on or near Cornmarket.

Post & Communications The main **post office** (☎ 223344; St Aldate's) is open 9am to 6pm Monday to Saturday.

You can check email at **Mices.com** (☎ 726364; 118 High St); access is £2.50 for 30 minutes.

Bookshops Our favourite of Oxford's many bookshops is **Blackwell's** (☎ 333606; 48-51 Broad St), which looks pretty compact from the front, but wait until you hit the basement. If there's an English book or manual in print, chances are it will be there.

Medical Services The **John Radcliffe Hospital** (☎ 741166; Headley Way, Headington) is 3 miles (5km) east of the city centre.

Boots (☎ 247461; 6 Cornmarket) is one pharmacy in the city centre.

Emergency The **police station** (☎ 266000) is on St Aldate's.

Carfax Tower

At the top of St Aldate's in the city centre, Carfax Tower (adult/child £1.20/60p; open 10am-5.30pm Mon-Sat, 11am-5pm Sun May-Oct, 10am-3.30pm daily Nov-Apr), with its quarterjacks (figures who hammer out the quarter hours on bells), is the sole reminder of medieval St Martin's Church. The name comes from the Latin quadri furcus, meaning 'four forks', and indeed it stands at the junction of four streets. There's a fine view from the top of the tower that is good for orientating yourself. The telescope at the top has been broken for years, so you don't need to stick the required 20p in to get a good view.

Museum of Oxford

This museum (☎ 815559; St Aldate's; admission £2.50; open 10am-4pm Tues-Fri, 10am-5pm Sat, noon-4pm Sun) introduces the city's history. There's everything you need to know about Oxford here and exhibits range from a mammoth's tooth (which had nothing to do with the foundation of Oxford) to a Morris Minor (which played a huge part in the city's manufacturing boom).

Museum of Modern Art

This marvellous gallery space, commonly referred to as MOMA (☎ 722733; Pembroke St; adult/child £2.50/free; open 11am-5.30pm Tues-Wed & Fri-Sun, until 8pm Thur), is one of the best contemporary art museums outside of London. The focus is on 20th-century painting, sculpture and photography, with a healthy emphasis on other cultures. If you're into abstract installations and six-figure doodles, you'll definitely enjoy this.

Ashmolean Museum

Established in 1683, the Ashmolean (☎ 278 000; admission £3 donation; open 10am-5pm Tues-Sat, 2pm-5pm Sun & bank holiday Mon) is the country's oldest museum, based on the collections of the gardening Tradescant family (John Tradescant was Charles I's gardener) and Dr Elias Ashmole who presented their possessions to the university. It's a little musty these days, but it's got plenty of character and the curators are veritable founts of information.

The Beaumont St building is one of Britain's best examples of neo-Grecian architecture and dates from 1845. It houses extensive displays of European art (including works by Raphael and Michelangelo) and Middle Eastern antiquities. The music room has a Stradivarius violin that is reputed to be the best exemplar of its kind in the world. It's hard to tell, though, as it's encased in glass.

Curioxity

If you're dragging kids around and somehow they can't appreciate the subtle beauty of Oxford's architecture and history, a visit to this hands-on science centre (☎ 247004; 40 George St; adult/child £2.50/2; open 10am-4pm daily June-Sept & Easter, by organised tour at other times) should sort them out. Two-way mirrors, optical illusions and other fun stuff are intended to be educational, but we suspect it's just a smoke screen for what is essentially a hi-tech kids' playground.

Oxford University Press Museum

Located in the main building of the world-famous Oxford University Press in Jericho, this museum (☎ 556767; admission free; open 9.30am-5pm Mon-Fri) is one of Oxford's less-visited attractions. Half-hour tours of the museum reveal the history of printing from the beginning right up to the modern day. The most interesting story, however, tells of the creation of the Oxford English Dictionary (see 'The Brains Behind the OED' boxed text).

University & Pitt Rivers Museums

Housed in a superb Victorian Gothic building, the University Museum *(☎ 272950; Parks Rd; admission free; open noon-5pm daily)* is devoted to natural science. The dodo relics, along the wall to the left as you enter the museum, are particularly popular.

It was in the museum's library, in 1860, that the great Darwinist debate reached its climax when the Bishop of Oxford William Wilberforce asked biologist and philosopher TH Huxley (who coined the term 'agnostic') whether it was from his grandfather's or grandmother's side that he was descended from monkeys. Amid laughter Huxley answered that he would rather be descended from monkeys than a Wilberforce. Needless to say, history has sided with Huxley.

You can reach the Pitt Rivers Museum *(☎ 270927; admission free; open 12pm-4.30pm Mon-Sat, 2pm-4.30pm Sun)* through the University Museum. It's the kind of place Indiana Jones would be perfectly at home in: the glass cases at the Pitt Rivers are crammed with everything from a sailing boat to a gory collection of shrunken South American heads. There are said to be over one million items, and some (mainly weird and wonderful musical instruments) have been moved to an annexe, the **Balfour Building** *(Banbury Rd)*. Every Wednesday at 6pm the Oxford Gamelan Society puts on a recital using the instruments. Call ☎ 723645 for details.

The Oxford Story

Across from Balliol College is The Oxford Story *(☎ 790055; Broad St; adult/child £5.70/ 4.70; open 9.30am-5pm Apr-Oct, 10am-4.30pm Nov-Mar)*, which is incredibly popular with tourists but derided by locals and students as cheesy rubbish. Basically, it's a 40-minute ride through the university's history in carriages designed to look like college desks, with an audio commentary by ex-Mastermind presenter Magnus Magnusson.

The Brains Behind the OED

In 1878 the Oxford University Press agreed to fund the century's biggest literary project, the compilation of what was then called *The New English Dictionary of Historical Principles*. In order to create a comprehensive dictionary, editor James Murray issued a circular asking for a corps of volunteers, who between them would read every book ever published and make precise notes on the words used therein.

Of the thousands of volunteers who signed up to the mammoth project, the most enthusiastic of all was Dr WC Minor, a US Civil War surgeon whose address was Broadmoor, Crowthorne in Berkshire. Over the next 20 years, he contributed more than any other volunteer to the point that Murray considered him his most valued contributor and in 1891 made a point of travelling to meet him.

Broadmoor is a hospital for the criminally insane, and Murray had long assumed that his venerable Dr Minor was employed there. He couldn't have been more wrong. Minor was actually the asylum's longest-serving inmate, a schizophrenic committed in 1872 for the motiveless murder of a man in London. While he was providing invaluable knowledge on word origins and usages, he was also consistently demonstrating the destructive nature of his illness. At one point he was convinced that women were visiting him at night and having sex with him; he was so repulsed by his own lasciviousness that he severed his own penis.

Yet Murray was deeply taken by Minor's complete devotion to his dictionary project and continued to work with Minor until the latter was transferred to a hospital in the USA in 1910.

The Oxford English Dictionary – a 12-volumed masterpiece – was finally completed in 1928. With 414,825 words defined and 1,823,406 illustrative quotations used, it was the most comprehensive lexicographical project ever undertaken. Sadly, Murray never saw its completion, having died in 1915; nor did Minor, who expired five years later. Although numerous supplements were published thereafter, a full second edition did not appear until 1989, but Minor's and Murray's fingerprints are still the most obvious of all.

OXFORDSHIRE, GLOUCESTERSHIRE & THE COTSWOLDS

The Shark House

The owner of 1 New High St, Headington, just three miles east of Oxford city centre off the main London road, must have felt that his plain, terraced house was just too similar to the ones around it. The option of painting it a funky colour was just too mundane, and there wasn't enough room to add Doric columns or a veranda. The answer, of course, is to jam a life-size model of a great white shark through the roof, so it looks like it just crashed into the house from above. This is probably Oxford's most bizarre attraction, and one that should definitely make the photo album.

To get there, take Stagecoach bus No 5 to Headington.

University Buildings & Colleges

Pembroke College Often described as the coal scuttle of Christ Church (because it's directly across from it), Pembroke (☎ 276444; St Aldate's) was founded in 1624. Traditionally, students were either poor scholars known as 'servitors' or wealthy ones called gentlemen commoners. Dr Samuel Johnson was a servitor in the 18th century, and he remarked that the difference between them was that 'servitors are men of wit and no fortune while gentlemen commoners were men of fortune and no wit'. Johnson was notoriously lazy while studying here, preferring to sit in his rooms drinking copious amounts of tea rather than attend a lecture. His massive teapot (which apparently holds 20 cups) is on display in the small museum. Admission to this college is by appointment only in groups accompanied by an official guide.

Christ Church College The grandest and most popular of all of Oxford's colleges, Christ Church (☎ 276150; St Aldate's; adult/child £4/3; open 9am-5.30pm Mon-Sat, noon-5pm Sun) is also known as The House. It was founded in 1525 by Cardinal Thomas Wolsey – who suppressed 22 monasteries to acquire the funds – and called Cardinal's College. In 1546 Henry VIII decided to take it over himself and rechristened it Christ Church. Ever since then, it has maintained close ties with suc-

cessive English monarchs, who usually stay here when visiting.

Christ Church has educated some pretty big names. Philosopher John Locke and William Penn, the founder of Pennsylvania, were students at the same time but were both expelled. Poet WH Auden and mathematician Charles Dodgson (the sometime-storyteller better known as Lewis Carroll) fared a little better and managed to last the four years of their studies.

The main entrance is below **Tom Tower**, so called because it is dedicated to St Thomas of Canterbury. The upper part of the tower, designed by Sir Christopher Wren in 1682, rests on a Tudor base. Great Tom, the seven-ton tower bell, chimes 101 times each evening at 9.05pm, the time when the original 101 students were called in. Since Oxford is five minutes west of Greenwich, this is actually 9pm Oxford time.

Visitors, however, must enter through the smaller gate further down St Aldate's. Immediately to the left is the cloisters, which gives way to **Christ Church Cathedral**, the smallest cathedral in the country. Christ Church has been Oxford's Anglican cathedral since the reign of Henry VIII and was founded on the site of the nunnery of St Frideswide, whose shrine was a focus of pilgrimage until it was partly destroyed at Henry VIII's orders. The shrine was reconstructed in the 19th century. Beside it is a **Watching Loft** for the guard, who made sure no-one walked off with the saint's relics. The Lady and Latin chapels boast some particularly fine windows.

From the cathedral, you enter the wonderful **Tom Quad**, the largest quadrangle in Oxford. During the Civil War, royalist forces turned it into a cattle pen. To the south side is the **Great Hall**, the college's dining room. If you look at the door under the staircase, you'll notice the words 'No Peel' burnt into it. This graffiti dates from the mid-17th century, when the college doctor prescribed raw potato peels to counteract the effects of an outbreak of plague. The cure didn't work and the students, sick of their enforced diet, took hot knife to wood.

You can also explore another two quads and the **Picture Gallery**, with its modest collection of Renaissance art. One particularly appealing painting features the biblical Judith holding the severed head of Holofernes.

Corpus Christi College This small and beautiful college (☎ 276600; Merton St; admission free; open 1.30pm-4.30pm daily) is sandwiched between Christ Church and Merton colleges. It was founded in 1517 by Bishop Richard Fox, but he never saw its completion on account of blindness. It is said that students walked him around the small front quad 23 times to make it seem bigger than it actually was.

In the middle of the front quad is a **pelican sundial**, which can calculate the time by the sun *and* the moon, although it's always five minutes fast. From the garden at the back of the college there are terrific views of Fellows' garden, Christ Church gardens and the meadows. Corpus Christi has a reputation for being the friendliest and most liberal of all of Oxford's colleges.

Merton College Small, smart and rich, Merton College (☎ 276310; Merton St; admission free; open 2pm-4pm Mon-Fri, 10am-4pm Sat & Sun) was one of the original three colleges founded in 1264 and represents the earliest form of collegiate planning.

The 14th-century **Mob Quad** was the first of the college quads. The **Old Library** leading off it is the oldest medieval library in use, with some books still chained up, an ancient antitheft device. The library owns several 15th-century astrological instruments, and an astrolabe that may have been used by Chaucer. JRR Tolkien (who taught here) undoubtedly spent many a day leafing through the dusty tomes in search of arcane runes and old Saxon words that helped shape *The Lord of the Rings*.

Tolkien's fame may have been cemented recently by the successful movie version of his classic, but he is not the only literary giant associated with Merton. TS Eliot was a student here, only we don't think that a film version of *The Wasteland* would do as well at the box office.

A really delightful way of visiting the college is by attending the candlelit concerts put on in the chapel on summer evenings.

Magdalen College Whatever you do, don't pronounce it phonetically. Magdalen (pronounced mawd-len; ☎ 276000; High St; adult/child £2/1 Apr-Sept only, free rest of year; open noon-6pm daily July-Sept, 2pm-dusk Oct-June), near the handsome Magdalen Bridge, is Oxford's wealthiest and probably most beautiful college. It has its own deer park (behind St Swithun's Quad) and a stunning cloisters, whose strange gargoyles and other carved figures inspired CS Lewis' stone statues in *The Chronicles of Narnia*.

The college was founded in 1458 by William of Waynflete, the bishop of Winchester. The chapel, with its 43m-high bell tower, dates from the late 15th century.

Oscar Wilde was a student here and legend has it that he found out about his first-class honours degree while reading the *Times* in an Oxford tavern. Sir John Betjeman, the poet laureate, and actor Dudley Moore were also students.

Opposite Magdalen are the **Botanic Gardens** (☎ 276920; open 9am-4.30pm daily), founded in 1621 by Henry Danvers for the study of medicinal plants.

St Edmund Hall This small college (☎ 279000; Queen's Lane; open daylight hours), also known as Teddy College, was officially declared one in 1957 but has been in existence since 1269; it is the sole survivor of the original medieval halls – the teaching institutions that preceded colleges in Oxford. The Mohawk chief Oronhyatekha studied here in 1862 (and eloped with the principal's daughter), but the best-remembered student is Paul Methuen, who in 1703 signed a treaty with Portugal that introduced port wine to the English market and dramatically increased the popularity of after-dinner conversations in the library.

May Day Morning

Sometime in the late 15th century, a bunch of choristers decided to practise their hymns from the top of Magdalen Tower...at 4am. The local townspeople, bemused as much as interested, gathered to listen, and a tradition was launched. Every May Day, the singing begins at 6am, but more importantly the bars open at 4am. The whole town discovers a need to drink in the middle of the night and then proceeds down to the tower, where they listen, cheer and chat before chucking themselves into the Cherwell. It's the best way to ensure that you get soaked both inside and out.

Its small chapel was decorated by William Morris and Edward Burne-Jones.

Queen's College Named after the wife of Edward III, Queen Philippa, Queen's (☎ 279121; High St) was founded in 1341 but the current buildings are all in classical style. Like most colleges, it preserves some idiosyncratic traditions: students are summoned to meals with a trumpet call and at Christmas a boar's head is served to commemorate a time when a scholar fought off an attacking boar by thrusting a volume of Aristotle down its throat, shouting *Graecum Est* as he killed the animal (the last words of the book). To visit the college, you must join an official tour (see Organised Tours later in this section).

University College Now famous as the college where Bill Clinton *didn't* inhale when smoking a joint, University (☎ 276602; High St; closed to the public) was founded in 1249, although documents 'proving' that the college had actually been founded by King Alfred in the 10th century were held as gospel truth until the 19th century.

Its most famous monument is a memorial to Percy Bysshe Shelley (1792–1822), who was expelled for publishing a pamphlet entitled *The Necessity of Atheism* in 1811. Over the years this pretty gaudy statue (a nude, dead Shelley with the muse of poetry looking up at him longingly) has been messed with for the sake of a few laughs: his penis has been painted in different colours and, on one occasion, the wardens walked in to find the *Times* crossword on his lap. To prevent more student japes, the statue was cordoned off, but it's still worth seeing.

Shelley's little misdemeanour, however, pales in comparison to the practices of physician Thomas Southwell, who founded the College of Physicians in 1441. While renting rooms here in 1420, he was caught in an act of necrophilia with the late Duchess of Gloucester. He was arrested and sent to the Tower of London, where he died the night before his execution.

Besides the US ex-president, another luminary to have studied here is Stephen J Hawking, the astrophysicist who managed the incredible feat of making black holes a popular topic of conversation at dinner parties.

All Souls College This quiet college (☎ 279379; High St; admission free; open 2pm-4pm Mon-Fri) is easily the oddest college of all. It was founded in 1438 as a centre of prayer and learning, and the souls in question were those of the dearly departed (English) soldiers of the Hundred Years' War – making this the most elaborate war memorial in England.

All Souls has only four undergraduates, who have been accepted to the college following an examination of such weirdness and rigour – a 'question' to one candidate involved eating a cherry tart and then disposing of the stones in an 'appropriate' manner of his own choosing – that most fail. The rest are fellows, or graduates, who were elected to the college. Basically, to get in you have to be a genius with perfect table manners.

The college's reputation for oddity is further demonstrated in the tradition of 'All Souls Mallard', which takes place on 14 January. The warden leads a procession to look for a mythical duck that appeared when the college foundations were being dug, all the while singing the 'mallard song'.

The college **chapel** is worth seeing. The poet WB Yeats, though not a fellow, loved the chapel and composed the poem *All Souls Night* in tribute to it.

Church of St Mary the Virgin This beautiful church (cnr High & Catte Sts; adult/child £1.60/80p; open 9am-7pm daily July-Aug, 9am-5pm daily Sept-June) has a 14th-century tower offering splendid views.

Radcliffe Camera One of Oxford's best-known and most photographed buildings, the Radcliffe Camera (Radcliffe Square) is a spectacular circular library ('camera' means room in Italian) built in 1748 in the Palladian style. It's not open to the public.

Brasenose College Dating from the 16th century, Brasenose College (☎ 277830; admission £1; open 10am-11.30am & 2pm-4.30pm daily) is entered from Radcliffe Square. It takes its name from an 11th-century snout-like door knocker that was stolen in 1334 by students from Stamford College, Lincolnshire, and only returned to Brasenose in 1890 when the college bought the whole of Stamford College so as to reacquire the door knocker. It now hangs above the high table in the dining hall. Next to it is a portrait of Alexander Nowell, a college principal, whose claim to fame is the 'invention' of bottled beer. A keen angler, he used to bottle his ales for fishing trips, and once buried a bottle to keep it cool. When he dug it up, it was fizzy.

Former students include William Golding, author of *Lord of the Flies*, John Buchan, who wrote *The Thirty-Nine Steps*, and Michael Palin, of Monty Python fame.

New College To reach this college *(☎ 279555; cnr Holywell St & New College Lane; admission £2 Apr-Sept, free Oct-Mar; open 11am-5pm Easter-Oct, 2pm-4pm daily Nov-Easter)*, turn down New College Lane under the **Bridge of Sighs**, a 1914 copy of the famous bridge in Venice. New College was founded in 1379 by William of Wykeham, bishop of Winchester, and its buildings are fine examples of the perpendicular style. Don't miss the chapel, which has superb stained glass, much of it from the 14th century. The west window is a design by Sir Joshua Reynolds, and Sir Jacob Epstein's disturbing statue of Lazarus is also here. The gardens contain a section of Oxford's medieval wall.

A former college warden was William Spooner, whose habit of transposing the first consonants of words made his name part of the English language: a spoonerism. It's claimed that he once reprimanded a student with the words, 'You have deliberately tasted two worms and can leave Oxford by the town drain.'

Sheldonian Theatre The university's main public building *(☎ 277299; Broad St; adult/child £1.50/1; open 10am-12.30pm & 2pm-4.30pm Mon-Sat)* was commissioned by Gilbert Sheldon, Archbishop of Canterbury, and entrusted in 1667 to Christopher Wren, at that time Professor of Astronomy. It was his first major work.

Bodleian Library One of England's three copyright libraries, the Bodleian Library *(cnr Broad St & Parks Rd)* is off the Jacobean-period **Old Schools Quadrangle**. **Library tours** *(☎ 277000)* take place at 10.30am, 11.30am, 2pm and 3pm daily, and show off Duke Humfrey's library (1488). They book

up fast and cost £3.50 (no children under 14). Also not to be missed is the **Divinity School** *(open 9am-5pm Mon-Fri, 9am-12.30pm Sat)*, which is attached to the library and has a superb vaulted ceiling. It is renowned as a masterpiece of 15th-century English Gothic architecture.

Trinity College This college *(☎ 279900; Broad St; admission £1; open 10.30am-noon & 2pm-4pm daily)* was founded in 1555, but the existing buildings mostly date from the 17th century. Trinity has traditionally maintained a heated rivalry with Balliol, which usually takes the form of absurd practical jokes.

Balliol College One of the oldest of all the colleges, Balliol *(☎ 277777; Broad St; admission £1; open 2pm-5pm daily)* was founded in 1263, but most of the buildings date from the 19th century. The wooden doors between the inner and outer quads still bear scorch marks from when Protestant martyrs were burned at the stake in the mid-16th century.

Lincoln College Lincoln *(☎ 279800; Turl St; admission free; open 2pm-5pm Mon-Sat, 11am-5pm Sun)* was founded by bishop Richard Fleming in 1427 to defend the 'mysteries of the sacred page against those ignorant laics who profane with swinish snouts its most Holy pearls', but its most famous student and Fellow was John Wesley, the founder of Methodism, who came here at the turn of the 18th century. Bishop Fleming would surely have objected, but his ghost will have to settle for the enmity with which Wesley was held by his fellow students, who despised him for his phenomenal devotion to his studies and the fact that he is said to have delivered over 40,000 sermons.

Wesley's former rooms are open for visitors.

Exeter College This college *(☎ 279600; admission 50p; open 2pm-5pm daily)* is known for its elaborate 17th-century dining hall. The chapel includes a William Morris tapestry *(The Adoration of the Magi)*; Morris was also an undergraduate, along with his Arts & Crafts friend Edward Burne-Jones, in 1853. Other notables to have passed through here include the actor Richard Burton.

Jesus College This college (☎ 279700; Turl St; admission free; open 2pm-4.30pm daily) was originally established in 1571 to train Welsh scholars in 'good letters'. Many of today's students are still drawn from Wales, but despite what students of other colleges say, they don't grow leeks on one side of the front lawn and breed goats on the other. Famous folk from here include TE Lawrence (that man of Arabia) and former Labour prime minister Harold Wilson. A less well-known student was Sir Lewis Morris, whose mediocre poetry sold poorly, leading him to complain to Oscar Wilde that he thought there was a 'conspiracy of silence' against him. Wilde is thought to have advised him to 'join in this conspiracy'.

Punting

You may have to contend with four score other tourists flapping about on the Cherwell, but one of the best ways of soaking up the local atmosphere is by taking to the river in a punt. It's easier said than done, but the secret to controlling these flat-bottomed boats is to push *gently* on the pole to get the punt moving and then use it as a rudder to keep on course.

Punts are available from Easter to September and hold five people, including the punter. Both the Thames and the Cherwell are shallow enough for punts, but the best advice is to bring a picnic and head upstream along the Cherwell. You can rent a punt from **Howard C & Sons** (☎ 202643; High St), by Magdalen Bridge, for £10 per hour (£25 deposit), or from the **Cherwell Boat House** (☎ 515978), farther upstream at the end of Bardwell Rd, for £8 per hour (£50 deposit) on weekdays and £10 per hour (£60 deposit) at weekends.

Alternatively, follow the Cherwell downstream from Magdalen Bridge for views of the colleges across the Botanic Gardens and Christ Church Meadow.

Organised Tours

Oxford City Council and the **TIC** (☎ 726871) run two-hour, guided walking tours of the colleges from the TIC at 10.30am, 11am, 1pm and 2pm daily, Easter to September; they cost £6/3 per adult/child. Tours (£6.50/3.50 per adult/child) based on the incredibly popular detective Inspector Morse (based on books written by Colin Dexter

and played on TV by actor John Thaw), who solved crimes all around town, are also very popular, leaving the TIC every Saturday at 1.30pm. If you fancy a ghost tour, they depart from the TIC at 8pm Friday and Saturday, July to September (and Halloween night). They cost £8/4 per adult/child.

Guide Friday (☎ 790522) runs a hop-on, hop-off city bus tour every 15 minutes from 9.30am to 7pm between April and October, less often in winter. It leaves from the train station and costs £9/2.50 per adult/child.

Blackwell's (☎ 333606) runs literary tours (2pm Tuesday and Saturday, 11am Thursday), civil war tours (2pm Sunday) and a Tolkien tour (11.45am Wednesday). All tours depart from the Broad St branch of the bookshop, and all cost £6/5 per adult/child.

Places to Stay

Accommodations in Oxford are relatively expensive, and unless you plan on bunking down in the youth hostel, expect to pay at least £30 for even the most basic single with a shared bathroom. Between May and September beds fill up very quickly, so book in advance or join the queue at the TIC and pay £3 for help.

The main areas are on Abingdon Rd to the south, Cowley and Iffley Rds to the east, and Banbury Rd to the north. All are on bus routes, but Cowley Rd has the best selection of places to eat.

Camping Conveniently located by the Park & Ride car park, **Oxford Camping International** (☎ 244088; 426 Abingdon Rd; camping per person £7, per tent site £5) is 1½ miles (2.5km) south of the city centre.

Hostels The most convenient hostel, **Oxford Backpackers** (☎ 721761; 9A Hythe Bridge St; dorm beds £12) is a short walk from the train station. There are 80 beds, mostly in dorms, and good cooking facilities. From April to September you need to book a week in advance and leave a deposit.

New Oxford YHA Hostel (☎ 0870 770 5970, fax 251182; 2a Botley Rd; dorm beds £18.75) has better facilities and also includes breakfast.

University Accommodation Over the holidays it is possible to find a room in empty student accommodation.

Isis Guest House *(☎ 248894; 45-53 Iffley Rd; rooms per person with/without en suite £28/26; open July-Sept)* is what St Edmund Hall turns into from July to September, offering student digs as superior B&B accommodation.

Old Mitre Rooms *(☎ 279821; Brasenose Lane; singles/doubles £26/48; open July-Aug)* does pretty much the same as the Isis Guest House, with rooms that are similar in size and quality.

B&Bs & Hotels – Central Refurbished in 2002, **Becket Guest House** *(☎ 724675; 5 Becket St; standard singles/doubles from £35/48, en-suite singles/doubles £40/58)* is now a pleasant – if basic – guesthouse a stone's throw from the train station.

St Michael's Guest House *(☎ 242101; 26 St Michael's St; singles/doubles without en suite £40/55)*, just off Cornmarket St, is extremely central and therefore very popular. Rooms are comfortable and clean, and usually booked out weeks in advance.

Victoria House Hotel *(☎ 727400, fax 727402;* e *info@victoriahousehotel.co.uk; 29 George St; singles/doubles £75/85)* is a brand new hotel that will undoubtedly prove popular with business travellers. Rooms are thoroughly modern and very comfortable. The business tariff is £5 cheaper.

Royal Oxford Hotel *(☎ 248432, fax 250049; Park End St; singles/doubles £99/119)* is probably the best of Oxford's mid-level quality hotels, with beautifully appointed rooms that also cater to the business traveller.

Oxford's choicest accommodation is also centrally located.

The Randolph Hotel *(☎ 0870 400 8200; Beaumont St; singles/doubles £140/170)*, Forte's hotel opposite the Ashmolean Museum, was built in 1864 in neogothic style. It is Oxford's most famous and – we think anyway – most overrated hotel.

Old Parsonage Hotel *(☎ 310210; 1 Banbury Rd; singles/doubles £130/165)* is a delightful, wisteria-clad place with elegantly furnished rooms. If you're looking for luxury, this is the place to go.

Bath Place Hotel *(☎ 791812; 4-5 Bath Place; singles/doubles from £90/140)* is a luxurious, 10-room retreat in which all rooms have different styles, and some have four-poster beds.

Old Bank Hotel *(☎ 799599; 92 High St; singles/doubles from £135/155)* brings the designer hotel to Oxford at designer prices. Rooms are plush and lush, and some have great views over All Souls College.

B&Bs & Hotels – East East of the city centre there are B&Bs in the student area around Cowley and Iffley Rds, but your best bet is to head for Headington Rd – which is only a short walk from Headington's New High St and the Shark House.

Earlmont *(☎ 240236; 233 Cowley Rd; singles/doubles from £35/50)* is the only B&B left on Cowley Rd, and it's pretty basic at that. Rooms are small and a little dirty, but it's the cheapest place you'll find in town.

Red Mullions Guest House *(☎ 742741, fax 769944;* e *redmullion@aol.com; 23 London Rd; rooms from £60)* is a large guesthouse on London Rd (the continuation of Headington Rd), about 2 miles (3km) northeast of town. The rooms are a little frayed around the edges but they're comfortable nonetheless.

Pickwick's Guest House *(☎ 750487; 15-17 London Rd; rooms from £60)* is another good choice in the area, with large, comfortable rooms.

B&Bs & Hotels – North There are several B&Bs along Banbury Rd, north of the city centre.

Cotswold House *(☎ 310558; 363 Banbury Rd; singles/doubles with en suite from £45/66)* is an excellent B&B about 2 miles (3km) north of the city centre. It's worth the effort.

Burren Guest House *(☎ 513513; 374 Banbury Rd; singles/doubles from £33/48)* is fairly basic, but it's perfect if all you're looking for is a place to bunk down for the night.

B&Bs & Hotels – South A good-value place, **Whitehouse View** *(☎ 721626; 9 Whitehouse Rd; singles/doubles from £20/35)* is closest to the city centre, on a side road off Abingdon Rd.

Newton House *(☎ 240561; 82 Abingdon Rd; singles/doubles from £50/60)* is a large and comfortable house with clean rooms.

Places to Eat

Not surprisingly, Oxford abounds with cafés, restaurants and other eateries, where you can get everything from snacks to full-blown gourmet meals. The trick here, however, is finding somewhere that isn't bent on ripping off its customers by assuming that they're either the wealthy parents of students or gormless tourists.

Restaurants Typically appealing to the more studious of Oxford's inhabitants, patrons of **Nosebag Restaurant** (☎ 721033; 6-8 St Michael's St; cakes £1.60-1.80) come here for the good soups, fine selection of cakes and suitably grumpy mood of the staff.

HiLo (☎ 725984; 68-70 Cowley Rd; mains around £6) is a ramshackle Jamaican restaurant with no fixed menu and a penchant for charging whatever it can get away with. Nevertheless, it is incredibly popular with students, who may love it for its late-night drinking. It's a far cry from Oxford sophistication, and all the better for it.

The Oriental Condor (☎ 250988; 20 Park End St; mains around £6) is a typically sparse Chinese restaurant (good food, crap decor) that is very popular with Oxford's Chinese community.

Bangkok House (☎ 200705; 42A Hythe Bridge St; set meals for 2 people £15.50), out towards the station, is one of our favourite restaurants in town; try the mushroom and galangal soup, which is sublime.

Gashi Gashi (☎ 200789; 96 Cowley Rd; mains around £8) is an excellent Japanese restaurant that specialises in fresh sushi.

The Opium Den (☎ 248680; 79 George St; mains from £7.95) is considered one of the best Chinese restaurants in town, and offers a series of set menus for those who like to pick and mix.

Quod (☎ 202505; 92 High St; mains from £8) is incredibly popular with the local set for stylish Italian cuisine in comfortable surroundings.

Chiang Mai (☎ 202233; 130a High St; mains around £10) is an excellent Thai restaurant inside a beautiful Tudor building.

Gee's Restaurant (☎ 553540; 61 Banbury Rd; mains from £10) is a fabulous Mediterranean restaurant housed inside an old conservatory, complete with hanging plants and – in the evening – fairy lights that make for a brilliant atmosphere.

The Cherwell Boathouse (☎ 552746; Bardwell Rd; mains from £10) is simply the best place to eat in summer. With a perfect location on the river and a mouthwatering

selection of dishes (including great veggie selections), it's the perfect spot for a postpunt meal.

Cafés Oxford's most elegant coffee house, **The Grand Café** (☎ 204463; 84 High St) is a definite must for visitors, if only to sit over a latte in the opulent surroundings.

Frevd (☎ 311171; 119 Walton St) is, simply, one of the most beautiful places in town. This converted church is now a café-bar that thankfully has retained its stained-glass windows and artwork. The cocktails are pricey.

Café Coco (☎ 200232; 23 Cowley Rd; mains around £6) is a popular student hangout at the town end of Cowley Rd. The menu offers mostly pizza, fish and salad.

There are dozens of places to get a takeaway sandwich, and we recommend these two: **Taylor's** (☎ 558853; 31 St Giles St), which has delicious sandwiches as well as really good cakes, and **Gluttons Deli** (110 Walton St), which does the best meat sandwiches.

Market The **Covered Market** (Market St) is the perfect spot for the self-caterer. It's more like a French market than your average English one: full of wonderful foods and produce, from sausage and beans to imported patés.

Entertainment

Pubs It's a student town, so there's no lack of good bars and pubs.

Turf Tavern (☎ 243235; 4 Bath Place), a perennial student favourite, is hidden down a city centre alley and has been featured in the Inspector Morse TV series based on Colin Dexter's books.

Eagle & Child (☎ 310154; 49 St Giles') is where JRR Tolkien and CS Lewis used to meet for readings from The Hobbit and The Chronicles of Narnia. It's a 17th-century place where academics loosen up.

The Bear (☎ 721783; Alfred St), just off High St, is thought to be the oldest pub in the city. It has incredibly low ceilings, an outrageously sloping floor and a traditional wooden interior, and is one of our favourite pubs in town. On Tuesday nights it runs a really difficult pub quiz.

King's Arms (☎ 242369; 40 Hollywell St) is a crowded student pub in the heart of the city, opposite the Sheldonian Theatre.

Lamb & Flag (☎ 515787; 12 St Giles'), once the haunt of Graham Greene and Thomas Hardy, is now a popular student bar with the atmosphere of an old Victorian drawing room.

Isis Tavern (Iffley Lock, Iffley Village), a 1½-mile (2.5km) walk along the towpath from Folly Bridge, is the perfect place to go on a sunny day provided you don't mind the crowds.

The Perch (☎ 240386; Bisney Rd), by the river in Bisney, is a beautiful thatched-roof pub that is a 25-minute walk from the city centre; from Walton St, take Walton Well Rd and cross Port Meadow.

Also worth a look, on weekdays at least, are a couple of the university bars, particularly those in **New College** and **Magdalen**. Weekends can be tough, as bouncers usually check student IDs to keep numbers down.

Clubs Good clubs are surprisingly thin on the ground, especially considering that the city was the birthplace of Radiohead, Ride and Supergrass.

The Bullingdon Arms (☎ 244516; Cowley Rd), better known as the Bully, features a mix of 70s disco and happy House on Friday, while Saturday gets a little harder with trance and the occasional techno beat.

Park End (☎ 250181; 37 Park End St) is Oxford's largest – and most frequented – nightclub, complete with three floors of shirt-drenching dance music that rarely moves out of the safe, commercial genre. In summer, it gets some top-name DJs.

Po Na Na Souk Bar (☎ 249171; 13-15 Magdalen St) is part of a Moroccan-style chain club that features jazzy beats and other kinds of interesting down-tempo, alternative flavours. It's the best club in town.

The Zodiac (☎ 420042; 190 Cowley Rd) is a pretty groovy club that appeals to a wide range of musical tastes, from heavy metal to hardcore dance. It also hosts live gigs, usually guitar-thrashing indie bands kicking off their England tours.

Theatre & Cinema The **Oxford Playhouse** (☎ 798600; Beaumont St) puts on a mixed bag of theatre, music and dance. The **Old Fire Station** (☎ 794490; George St) stages mainly classical plays, while the **Burton Taylor Theatre** (☎ 798600; Gloucester St) goes for more offbeat student productions.

The most interesting films tend to get a screening at the **Phoenix Picturehouse** (☎ 554909; Walton St).

Getting There & Away

Oxford is 57 miles from London, 74 miles from Bristol and 33 miles from Cheltenham.

Bus Several bus lines compete for business on the route to London. Oxford Tube goes to London's Victoria coach station every 12 minutes but also stops at Marble Arch, Notting Hill Gate and Shepherd's Bush. An overnight return to Victoria costs £9; the journey takes around 1½ hours and the service operates 24 hours a day. It also stops on St Clements St, near Cowley Rd.

National Express has numerous buses to central London, Heathrow and Gatwick airports.

There are also five buses daily to Birmingham (£10.20, 1½ hours), three buses to Cambridge (£16, 2¾ hours), one service to Bath (£10.25, two hours) and Bristol (£13.50, 2¼ hours), and two to Gloucester (£8.25, 1½ hours) and Cheltenham (£7.75, one hour).

The Oxford Bus Company's London Express bus No X80 runs every 20 minutes (£9); Gatwick Express bus No X80 runs hourly (£19); and the Heathrow Express bus No X70 runs every half-hour (£12).

Stagecoach serves most of the small towns in Oxfordshire. If you're planning a lot of bus journeys we recommend you purchase a saver pass: the Megarider Plus pass gives you unlimited bus travel in Oxford and the rest of the county for seven days for £9, while the Countryrider pass gives you unlimited seven-day travel in Oxfordshire alone (excluding Oxford) for £7.

If you're visiting Oxford by private coach tour, all buses stop just outside St Edmund's Hall on High St.

Train There are half-hourly services to London Paddington (£16.70, one hour); and hourly trains to Coventry (£18.80, one hour), Birmingham (£19, 1½ hours), Worcester (£14.60, 80 minutes) and Hereford (£17.50, two hours) via Moreton-in-Marsh (£7.70, 35 minutes).

To connect with trains to the southwest you have to change at Didcot Parkway (£3.50 single, 15 minutes). There are plenty of connections to Bath (£13.20, 1½ hours). Change at Swindon for another line running into the Cotswolds (Kemble, Stroud and Gloucester).

Car & Motorcycle The M40 provides fast access from London but Oxford has a serious traffic problem and parking is a nightmare. We highly recommend that you use the Park & Ride system: as you approach the city follow the signs for the four car parks – Redbridge to the south, Thornhill to the southeast, Pear Tree to the northwest and Seacourt to the west – which are all situated off the ring road. Parking is free, but the buses to the city centre cost £1 return. They leave every 10 minutes throughout the day, Monday to Saturday. The Oxford Bus Company bus No 300 serves Redbridge and Pear Tree every six minutes Monday to Saturday (every 15 minutes Sunday), while bus No 400 serves the other two just as frequently. You can buy a 12-ride pass for £7. If you want to know more about parking in Oxford, call ☎ 785400.

Getting Around

Bus Oxford was one of the world's first cities to introduce battery-operated electric buses. They run every 12 minutes from the train station into the city centre from 8am to 6pm Monday to Saturday for a flat fare of 30p.

The city has fallen victim to the worst excesses of bus deregulation, with so many competing buses plying Cornmarket St that it can be difficult to cross the road. Citylink bus No 4 serves Iffley Rd and bus No 5 serves Cowley Rd. The information office in the bus station has full details. Stagecoach's Dayrider Plus pass (£3.80) gives you unlimited bus travel in Oxford for 24 hours.

Taxi There are taxis outside the train station and near the bus station, as well as on St Giles', George St and St Aldate's. A taxi to Blenheim Palace costs around £15.

Bicycle Students have always espoused pedal power and there are cycle lanes along several streets. The *Cycle into Oxford* map, available from the TIC, shows all the local cycle routes.

Beeline Bikes (☎ 246615) rents bikes for £10/£65 per day/week (£50 deposit).

Boat For boat trips, **Salter Bros** (☎ 243421) offers several interesting jaunts from Folly

Bridge from May to September, including a two-hour trip to Abingdon (one way/return £6.80/10.40).

WOODSTOCK
☎ 01993 • pop 1200

The village of Woodstock owes its fame and prosperity to glove-making and the Churchill family. Although people usually come here en route to Blenheim Palace, there's also a fine collection of 17th- and 18th-century buildings, particularly the Bear Hotel and the town hall, built at the duke of Marlborough's expense in 1766. The church has an 18th-century tower tacked onto a medieval interior.

Opposite the church, Fletcher's House accommodates the **Oxfordshire County Museum** *(☎ 811456; Park St; adult/child £2.50/ 50p; open 10am-5pm Tues-Sat, 2pm-5pm Sun)*, which has displays and dioramas on the environment and history of Oxfordshire.

The **TIC** *(☎ 813276; Park St; open 9.30am-5.30pm Mon-Sat, 1pm-5pm Sun)* is attached to the museum.

Blenheim Palace

This extraordinary palace *(☎ 811325; adult/child £10/5; open 10.30am-5pm mid-Mar–Oct, park open 9am daily year-round)* – one of Europe's largest – was designed by Sir John Vanbrugh and Nicholas Hawksmoor between 1705 and 1722. The palace – and a cash award of £240,000 – was given as a 'well done and thanks' gift by Queen Anne to John Churchill, Duke of Marlborough, for his role in defeating the French at the Battle of Blenheim in 1704. Blenheim (pronounced blennum) is still the Churchill family pile, home of the 11th duke and duchess.

Living in a Unesco World Heritage Site is a pretty costly business and involves footing the considerable bill required to open the house up to visitors for part of the year. You can even visit the private apartments used by the duke and duchess – so long as they're not in town – as part of a 30-minute guided tour (extra charge per adult/child £4/2). There are free guided tours of the rest of the house every few minutes, but you can wander around on your own if you like.

You enter this remarkable baroque fantasy through the **Great Hall**, which has 20m-high ceilings embossed with a painting (1716) by Sir James Thornhill of the first duke of Marlborough at the battle that earned him the house. The elaborate lock on the main door, a complicated brass affair, was copied from a lock on the gates of Warsaw.

You proceed to the **Churchill Exhibition**, four rooms devoted to the life, work and writings of Sir Winston, who was born at Blenheim in 1874. According to a notice on the wall he was born prematurely, but historians have long since discounted this as a necessary lie in the face of Victorian opprobrium – it seems Winnie's folks got a little ahead of themselves and couldn't wait until the wedding day. Amid photos of the world's most famous cigar-chomper at rest and letters written to friends and family, you can see a pair of the great man's slippers and even locks cut from his five-year-old head. Churchill and his wife, Lady Clementine Spencer-Churchill, are buried in nearby Bladon Church, whose spire is visible from the Great Hall.

On your way to the drawing rooms you'll pass the **China Cabinet**, which has entire collections of Meissen (Dresden) and Sèvres porcelain; the former collection was a present from the king of Poland in exchange for a pack of staghounds.

Although the other rooms in the house are all magnificent, the most impressive of all is the 55m **Long Library**, with books collected by the 9th duke – and where the 10th and 11th dukes probably did their homework.

The palace is surrounded by over 800 hectares of grounds, some of which is parkland landscaped by Lancelot 'Capability' Brown. JMW Turner painted here, and George III thought the grounds the most beautiful he had ever seen. Blenheim Park railway leads to the herb garden, the butterfly house and a large maze.

Places to Stay & Eat

Plane Tree House (☎ 813075; 48 Oxford St; singles/doubles £45/60) is an upmarket B&B in a renovated Cotswolds stone house. The comfortable rooms are decorated in a rustic style.

Feathers Hotel (☎ 812291, fax 813158; e enquiries@feathers.co.uk; Market St; singles/doubles £99/135) has luxuriously appointed rooms in a 17th-century building.

Bear Hotel (☎ 0870 400 8202, fax 813 380; e bear@heritage-hotels.co.uk; singles/doubles from £98/158) is a 13th-century

coaching inn that is top of the heap in terms of luxury and ambience.

Harriet's Tearooms (20 High St; pastries from £1.30) is a nice little teashop with some of the best French pastries this side of Calais.

Brotherton's Brasserie (☎ 811114; 1 High St; mains around £9) has a fair range of Mediterranean favourites, plus a healthy wine list.

Getting There & Away

From Oxford, catch Stagecoach bus No 20/A from Oxford bus station Monday to Saturday. They don't run a Sunday service any more, leaving the four buses in the hands of **Pete's Travel** (☎ 0121-505 3245). **Cotswold Roaming** (☎ 308300) offers organised excursions to Blenheim from Oxford, departing at 10am and returning at 1.50pm daily. The cost is £16/10 per adult/child, and includes admission to Blenheim and a guided tour.

AROUND WOODSTOCK
Oxford Bus Museum

You'd want to be pretty keen, but this museum (☎ 883617; Old Station Yard, Long Hanborough; adult/child £2/1; open 10.30am-4.30pm Sun year-round, plus 1.30pm-4.30pm Sat Easter-Oct) has the largest collection of public buses in England. There are over 40 of them dating back more than 100 years, all fully restored with more on the way. At 3.30pm every Sunday there are free bus rides on one of these classics.

Long Hanborough is about 2 miles (3km) southwest of Woodstock on the A4095. The museum is next door to the train station, about a 10-minute ride from Oxford.

ABINGDON
☎ 01235 • pop 30,000

The elegant market town of Abingdon straddles the Thames about 6 miles (10km) south of Oxford. Until 1536 the town was dominated by a powerful abbey (founded in the 7th century) that was larger than the one at Westminster. It was destroyed following the dissolution of the monasteries and nothing now remains except a few buildings that were constructed around it.

The helpful **TIC** (☎ 522711; 25 Bridge St; open 9.30am-5pm Mon-Sat) has plenty of information.

The impressive **County Hall** building was built between 1678 and 1682 by Christopher Kempster, who was one of Wren's masons for St Paul's Cathedral in London. It now houses a local museum. Wider than it is long, **St Helen's Church** is a fine example of perpendicular architecture.

Places to Stay & Eat

Barrow's End (☎/fax 523541; 3 The Copse; singles/doubles from £25/44) is a modern architect's version of a traditional bungalow. Rooms are extremely comfortable and beautifully appointed.

The Upper Reaches (☎ 0870 400 8101, fax 555182; Thames St; singles/doubles £140/160) is a splendidly restored mill house with rooms straight out of a fantasy book. It sits on the river and has its own mooring dock. It also has a very good **restaurant** (mains around £13).

Fallowfields Country House Hotel (☎ 820416, fax 821275; Faringdon Rd, Kingston Bagpuize with Southmoor; singles/doubles from £120/140) is the former home of the Begum Aga Khan. Today it's a splendid guesthouse where luxury is a given. It's about 3 miles (5km) west of Abingdon on the A4115.

If you just fancy a drink, the **Nag's Head** (☎ 536645; Thames St) straddles the bridge and has a lovely outdoor area overlooking the river.

Getting There & Away

The nicest way to reach Abingdon from Oxford is by boat (see the Boat section in Oxford earlier in this chapter). Alternatively, the **Oxford Bus Company** (☎ 01865-785400) runs bus No X3 between Abingdon and Oxford (30 minutes, £1.80 single) every 15 minutes (30 minutes on Sunday). The slower bus Nos 4 and 35 stop in various towns along the way. Stagecoach bus Nos 31 and 31X link Abingdon, Oxford and Wantage, while bus Nos 32, 32A and 32B link Abingdon, Wantage, Didcot, Harwell, Oxford and the A34 turnoff.

AROUND ABINGDON
Didcot

Little is left of the old town of Didcot, the skyline is dominated by the giant cooling towers of a power station. However, the town's saving grace – and not just for trainspotters – is the **Didcot Railway Centre** (☎ 01235-817200; Train Station; adult/child £7.50/5; open 10am-5pm daily), a marvellous shrine to the Great Western Railway (GWR), the line that ran from Bristol to London through Didcot. It was designed by Isambard Kingdom Brunel and completed in 1841; until 1892 its train ran on a unique, broad-gauge track and retained its independence until the nationalisation of the railways in 1948.

The museum, housed in and around the old engine shed, features a collection of original steam engines and a beautiful re-creation of an old country station, complete with a level crossing. So-called 'steam days' are held throughout the year, when visitors can ride the old engines and learn a thing or two about the old Victorian signalling system. Call for details.

Didcot is 10 miles south of Abingdon. Bus Nos 32, 32A and 32B link the town with Abingdon, Oxford and Wantage. You can also get here by frequent trains from Oxford (£2.30, 15 minutes).

Dorchester-on-Thames

A street of old coaching inns and a magnificent medieval church are more or less all there is of Dorchester-on-Thames, although in Saxon times there was a cathedral here. In the 12th century an abbey was founded on the site. Following the Reformation it became the parish church of Sts Peter and Paul, and it's worth stepping inside to see the rare Norman lead font with figures of the apostles; a wonderful Jesse window with carved figures and stained glass tracing Christ's ancestry; and a 13th-century monument of a knight. There's a small museum and café in the **Abbey Guest House**, which also dates back to the Middle Ages.

Bus No X39 connects Dorchester with Oxford and Abingdon.

Warborough

If you're looking for the kind of rural village that Thomas Hardy might have set one of his novels in, Warborough is as close as you'll get. At the centre of everything is the village green, which doubles up as the cricket pitch. Around it are a number of attractive buildings, including a beautiful thatched cottage.

There are no museums to visit or churches of note to admire, just a gorgeous village that seems oblivious to the passing of time.

The Cricketer's Arms (☎ 01865-858192; 145 Thame Rd; singles/doubles £28/40) is a marvellous old inn with three rooms that are comfortable and well appointed. It also does a fair selection of pub grub for around £5 to £6, but it's best for a good pint and a chat.

Warborough is 6 miles (10km) southeast of Abingdon on the A329. Perhaps a reason for its timelessness is that there are virtually no public transportation services to/from the village; a shopper's bus runs to Wallingford (9 minutes, £2.80 adult return), 4½ miles (7km) away, every Friday but that's it. From Oxford, the hourly bus No 105 runs to Wallingford (1 hour, £2.25), stopping in all the villages (but not Warborough), while the faster bus No X39 takes only 25 minutes, also departing hourly.

Little Wittenham

This secluded village is well known in the area for its beautiful cottages and **St Peter's Church**, a gorgeous stone building where inside are buried Sir William Dunch, the much-despised medieval MP for Wallingford, and his wife, the aunt of Oliver Cromwell.

The village lies at the bottom of the Sinodun Hills, basically two hills topped by trees and known as Wittenham Clumps (and irreverantly as the Berkshire Bumps or Mother Dunch's buttocks, after Sir William's wife), which for centuries was an important defensive position overlooking the Thames. It is believed that a Saxon tribe called the Atrebati fought off Julius Caesar's armies here in the 1st century BC.

The hills in this area are now part of the **Little Wittenham Nature Reserve** (☎ 01865-407792; admission free), which is spread over 100 hectares of woodland and grassland.

WANTAGE

☎ 01235 • pop 9700

Wantage lies at the foot of the Downs, 15 miles (24km) southwest of Oxford. Alfred the Great was born here in 849, and his statue dominates the main square (for more on King Alfred see the Winchester section in the Southeast England chapter). The Ridgeway is less than 3 miles (5km) to the south.

The **TIC** (☎ 760176; open 10am-4.30pm Mon-Sat, 2.30pm-5pm Sun) is located in the museum. The **Vale & Downland Museum Centre** (☎ 771447; Church St; adult/child £2/1.50; open 10am-4.30pm Mon-Sat, 2.30pm-5pm Sun), in a converted 16th-century cloth merchant's house, has information about King Alfred and life around the Ridgeway.

Places to Stay & Eat

Ridgeway Youth Hostel (☎ 760253; Court Hill; beds per adult/child £10/7.50; open daily May–early Sept), about 2 miles (3km) south of Wantage, was created out of several old barns set round a courtyard.

Alfred's Lodge (☎ 762409; 23 Ormond Rd; singles/doubles from £18/36) is an elegant Victorian house with comfortable (if a little small) rooms that are clean and tidy.

The Bell Inn (☎ 763718, fax 224391; 38 Market Place; singles/doubles £35/50) is a beautiful 16th-century inn with comfortable rooms and a **restaurant** (mains around £7) that serves good, home-cooked food.

Ridgeway House B&B (☎ 751538; e rob ertsfamily@compuserve.com; West St; singles/doubles £30/50) is an excellent option, with very modern rooms that are stocked with fresh flowers and fruit.

You can get bar meals in **The Shears** (Mill St; mains £5-8). The **Flying Teapot**, beside the church, does good snacks.

Getting There & Away

Stagecoach (☎ 01865-772250) bus Nos 31 and 32 serve Wantage about five times an hour from Didcot and Abingdon.

AROUND WANTAGE
Uffington White Horse

The stylised image of a white horse cut into the side of what is now called White Horse Hill is, along with Stonehenge, one of the most remarkable and mysterious of England's ancient sites, but incredibly gets nowhere near the same amount of visitors.

This extraordinary chalk figure, which measures 114m long and 49m wide, was carved into the turf about 2000 years ago, but what exactly it is supposed to represent remains anyone's guess. The most accepted legend was propagated by GK Chesterton, who claimed that King Alfred cut the figure to celebrate his victory over the Danes at the nearby Battle of Ashdown in 871. More recently, scholars have uncovered a number of burial sites in the area leading them to assume that it had some kind of religious function, but they've little evidence to back up the theory.

Whoever did carve it, though, did a pretty good job. The figure was cut into the turf to the depth of 1m and then filled with white chalk, but what is really amazing is that the lines of perspective are such that the horse is best viewed from a distance (see the boxed text 'White Lines' in the Wessex chapter for more details).

Just below it is **Dragon Hill**, so-called because it is believed that St George slew the dragon here, leading to another legend that the horse was George's own mount, a fanciful notion that sounds terrific in theory but doesn't really stand up to scrutiny.

Above the chalk figure are the grass-covered earthworks of Uffington Castle. From the Ridgeway Youth Hostel, near Wantage, a wonderful 5-mile walk leads along the Ridgeway to the White Horse.

Thomas Hughes, author of *Tom Brown's Schooldays*, was born in Uffington village. His house is now a museum. **The Craven** (☎ 01367-820449; singles/doubles from £25/ 48) is a thatched farmhouse offering B&B.

HENLEY-ON-THAMES
☎ 01491 • pop 11,000

If it wasn't for the world-famous regatta, Henley would be just another of those pleasant towns along the Thames dotted with pretty stone houses and a few elegant Tudor offerings. And it is, except for the first week in July, when the gathering of boaters and blazers draws the cream of English society to its river bank for what is in essence a week-long posh picnic hosted by the high ranks of the corporate entertainers. If boys and their boats are not your thing, the Henley Festival, which usually takes place in the week following the regatta, may appeal: it's a four-day pageant of drama and music.

The **TIC** (☎ 578034; The Barn, King's Rd; open 9.30am-5pm Mon-Sat, 11am-4pm Sun) is next to the Town Hall. Between May and September there's also an information booth in Mill Meadows.

Stately High St is dominated by **St Mary's Church**, which dates back to the 13th century. Above the arches of Henley Bridge, built in 1786, are sculptures of Isis and Father Thames. Two fine coaching inns, the Red Lion and the Angel, stand sentinel at the High St end of the bridge. Both predate their 18th-century heyday and have played

host to many eminent people, from the duke of Wellington to James Boswell.

Henley Royal Regatta
In 1829 the first Oxford and Cambridge boat race took place between Hambledon Lock and Henley Bridge. Ten years later the regatta was developed to enhance Henley's growing reputation.

Each year, in the first week of July, the regatta still plays host to the beau monde. Despite its peculiar mix of pomposity and eccentricity, it's a serious event that attracts rowers of the highest calibre.

There are two main areas for spectators – the stewards' enclosure and the public enclosure – although most people appear to take little interest in what's happening on the water. Epicurean picnics are consumed, large quantities of Pimm's (an alcoholic fruit drink) and champagne are drunk, and it's still an important fixture in the social calendar. Those with contacts in the rowing or corporate worlds can get tickets to the stewards' enclosure; others pay £8 for a day ticket to the public enclosure on Wednesday and Thursday, or £12 on Friday and Saturday. Tickets for the Sunday final are £10.

River & Rowing Museum
Henley has a purpose-built museum, designed by minimalist architect David Chipperfield, displaying paintings and artefacts associated with the history of Henley and rowing on the River Thames. Like all modern museums, the River & Rowing Museum (☎ 415600; Mill Meadows; adult/child £4.95/ 3.75; open 10am-6pm Mon-Sat, 10.30am-6pm Sun) harnesses modern technology to liven up its story.

Henley Festival
Surprisingly for such a conservative town, the Henley Festival features a vibrant and diverse programme, ranging from opera to avant-garde French percussionists, including jazz, rock, poetry and theatre. It's held at closed and open-air venues all over town. The main events take place on a floating stage on the Thames, and a grandstand is erected at the riverside. Tickets range from £7 for the car park to £68 for front row of the grandstand – although the latter tend to be block-booked by the corporate sharks long before the event. Call ☎ 843404 for details.

Places to Stay

During regatta and festival weeks, rooms here are impossible to find, so book well in advance.

Camping A quarter of a mile out of Henley, **Swiss Farm International Camping** (☎ 573419; Marlow Rd; per adult/tent £5/2) is a family-owned farm.

B&Bs & Hotels Conveniently located, **No 4 Riverside** (☎ 571133; 4 River Terrace; singles/doubles from £40/50) has comfortable, well-appointed rooms facing the river.

Old School House (☎ 573929, fax 680501; e adrian.lake@btinternet.com; 42 Hart St; singles/doubles from £35/50) is a stunning brick and flint building with really cosy, comfortable rooms.

The Rise (☎ 579360; Rotherfield Rd; singles/doubles £45/60) is a large Georgian house with elegant bedrooms and a bit of luxury.

Apple Ash (☎ 574198; e aidan@mills-thomas.freeserve.co.uk; Woodlands Rd, Harpsden Woods; singles/doubles from £40/55) is a gorgeous Edwardian house about 3 miles (5km) out of town (and only accessible by car) but worth the effort: the rooms are huge, beautifully appointed, and the service is top-notch and friendly.

Thamesmeade Hotel (☎ 574745, fax 579944; e thamesmead@supanet.com; Remenham Lane; singles/doubles £105/125) is a splendidly posh hotel overlooking the town's cricket green.

Red Lion Hotel (☎ 572161, fax 410039; e reservations@redlionhenley.co.uk; Hart St; singles/doubles £99/145) is the town's best hotel, a 17th-century, wisteria-clad former coaching inn where breakfast costs £12.95 extra (£8.50 if you want the continental).

Places to Eat

Good food is surprisingly hard to come by in Henley. There are a few good pubs, but most eateries are boring chain restaurants.

Near the TIC, the **Three Tuns** (5 Market Place; lunch around £7) does good bar meals, including Sunday lunch.

Thai Orchid (☎ 412227; 6 Hart St; mains around £9) is a fancy Thai restaurant that also does set three-course meals for £19.95.

The Old Rope Walk (22 Hart St; mains around £6) is a nice coffee shop and restaurant that does a good Yorkshire pudding for £6.15. It also does a fabulous high tea.

Getting There & Away

Henley is 21 miles (34km) southeast of Oxford on the A423 and 40 miles (64km) west of London. **Thames Travel** (☎ 874216) bus No X39 links Henley with Oxford and Abingdon hourly.

To get from Henley to Oxford by train you must change at Twyford or Reading. Henley to London Paddington takes about one hour and costs £8.20 per adult.

Getting Around

Henley is the perfect place to indulge in a bit of messing about on the river, and plenty of boat companies near the bridge are ready to help you enjoy yourself. On summer Sundays, **Hobbs & Son** (☎ 572035) organises cruises from £25 a head. Shorter trips to Hambledon Lock and back cost about £5/4 per adult/child. To hire a five-seater rowing boat costs £12 an hour, or for a four-seater motorboat it's £22.

AROUND HENLEY-ON-THAMES
Stonor Park

Stonor Park (☎ 01491-638587; admission house & gardens £5.50, gardens only £3.50; open 2pm-5.30pm Sun Apr, 2pm-5.30pm Wed & Sun July-Aug) is the Camoy family pile, descendants of the Stonor family who first acquired the estate in the 13th century. The Stonors remained staunchly Catholic after the Reformation, refusing to acknowledge the sovereign as the head of the new Church of England. Although the estate became a temporary haven for the anti-Reformation movement, the family were soon arrested and their lands confiscated. They were later reinstated, and continued pretty much as before.

The house has a fine collection of paintings, including works by Tintoretto and Lodovico Carracci. The chapel frieze – carved out of wooden boxes by a Polish artist during WWII – was a present from Graham Greene, a friend who stayed here to write *Our Man in Havana* (1958; made into a film by Karol Reed in 1959 starring Alec Guinness).

The extensive hillside gardens are covered in daffodils, narcissi, irises and roses.

Stonor Park is 5 miles (8km) north of Henley. You need your own transport to get here.

The Cotswolds

Straddling the western edge of Oxfordshire and the eastern side of Gloucestershire are the Cotswolds, a low-rise ridge of limestone hills that rise steeply from the Severn Valley in the west and slope gently eastward toward the Oxford vale.

During the Middle Ages most of the Cotswolds were open sheep runs, providing an important source of wealth for the towns and villages that grew prosperous on the backs – literally – of their woolly friends. The wealth accrued from wool, and later the sale of manufactured cloth, is still in evidence in the wonderful churches and manor houses to be found in the elegant market towns.

For additional information on most Cotswold towns and villages, check out the website at **w** www.completely-cotswold.com.

ACTIVITIES

The 105-mile (170 km) Cotswold Way meanders gently from Chipping Campden to Bath, with no major climbs or difficult stretches. Ordnance Survey (OS) Outdoor Leisure Map 45 (£5.95) covers the walk between Chipping Camden and Winchcombe, while OS Explorer Map 79 (£3.95) covers it between Woodmancote to Stroud.

Cycling is equally popular in the Cotswolds. Bartholomew's *Cycling in the Cotswolds* (£8.99) provides the full details. **Cotswold Country Cycles** (☎ 01386-438706) rents bikes for £12 a day from

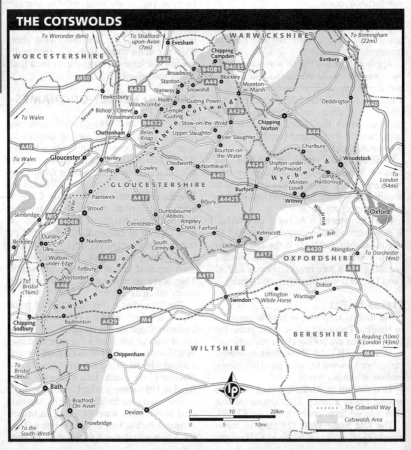

THE COTSWOLDS

Chipping Campden. Several companies offer guided or unguided walking tours; try **Cotswold Walking Holidays** (☎ *01242-254353;* e| *walking@star.co.uk; 10 Royal Parade, Bayshill Rd, Cheltenham*).

GETTING AROUND
Limited as it is, the Cotswolds bus service is still more comprehensive than the rail network, which only skims the northern and southern borders. The Gloucestershire public transport inquiry line (☎ 01452-425543) or the national Traveline (☎ 0870 608 2608) has details of all public transport in the Cotswolds.

CIRENCESTER
☎ 01285 • pop 13,500 • elevation 134m
The quiet and refreshingly unpretentious town of Cirencester, clustered around an impressive parish church, offers little as a reminder of its bygone importance when, as Corinium, it was England's second-largest Roman town after London and had one of the largest amphitheatres in the country. For this we have the Saxons to thank, who destroyed the town in the 6th century – you can see the grassed over remains of the amphitheatre on Cotswold Ave – and rebuilt it as a series of smaller settlements renamed Cirencester. It regained a measure of importance in the Middle Ages, when it became the most important wool town in the area.

Today it's a fairly affluent place that likes to call itself the capital of the Cotswolds. It's a lovely place to while away a day.

The town's centre is Market Square, where you'll find the church and **TIC** (☎ *654 180; Corn Hall; open 9.30am-5.30pm Apr-Dec, 9.30am-5pm Jan-Mar*). Weekly markets still take place every Monday and Friday.

Church of St John the Baptist
One of England's largest churches, St John's seems more like a cathedral. It has a magnificent perpendicular-style tower, built with the reward given by Henry IV to a group of earls who foiled a rebellion. The highlight of the exterior, however, is the three-storey south porch, which faces the square. Built as an office by late-15th-century abbots, it subsequently became the medieval town hall.

Inside the church several memorial brasses record the matrimonial histories of import-ant wool merchants. A 15th-century painted stone pulpit comes complete with hourglass and the east window contains fine medieval stained glass. A wall safe displays the **Boleyn Cup**, made for Anne Boleyn, second wife of Henry VIII, in 1535. The church is also notable for the oldest 12-bell peal in the country, and continues to observe the ringing of the 'pancake bell' on Shrove Tuesday and the celebration of the Restoration on 29 May.

Corinium Museum
This museum (☎ *655611; Park St; adult/child £2.50/1; open 10am-5pm Tues-Sat, 2pm-5pm Sun*) has a reconstructed Roman kitchen, and an impressive collection of Roman artefacts and other bits and bobs. The museum was scheduled to close in September 2002 for a major refurbishment, so check with the TIC or call before visiting.

Cirencester Park & Swimming Pool
On the western edge of town, this park features magnificent geometrical landscaping, designed with the help of the poet Alexander Pope. The Broad Ride makes an excellent short walk.

The **house** was built by the first earl of Bathurst between 1714 and 1718, and hides behind one of the world's highest yew hedges. It's not open to the public.

Adjacent to the park is the **open-air swimming pool** (☎ *653947; Thomas St; adult/child £2.20/1; open 9.30am-6.30pm daily mid-May–Aug*), one of the oldest swimming pools in England (1869). The water in the pool is from a local well (you swim in the treated version).

The Brewery Arts Centre
Just off Cricklade St, this is a thriving arts centre (☎ *657181; admission free; open 9.30am-5pm daily*) occupied by 12 artists whose studios are open to the public. There's a small crafts shop where you can buy their work. The centre also hosts a series of excellent concerts throughout the year, featuring anything from jazz to classical. Check with the TIC for details of upcoming events.

Places to Stay
Camping If you're prepared to tolerate the lack of facilities for a cheap stay, you'll

enjoy **Abbey Home Farm** (☎ 652808, 656969; per person with bicycle/car £1.50/ 2.50), an organic farm a mile north of Cirencester on the Northleach road.

Hostels Five miles (8km) northwest of Cirencester, **Duntisbourne Abbots Youth Hostel** (☎ 821682; beds £9; open Mon-Sat Apr-Oct) is in a Victorian vicarage. The hostel is renowned for its good food.

B&Bs & Hotels Victoria Rd has several B&Bs and guesthouses.

The Corner House (☎ 641958; 101a Victoria Rd; singles/doubles £30/40) has large, clean and comfortable rooms that are well worth the price.

Wimborne House (☎ 653890; 91 Victoria Rd; singles/doubles £30/40) is a large Victorian house with elegant rooms and a friendly atmosphere – one of the bedrooms has a beautiful four-poster bed.

White Lion Inn (☎ 654053; 8 Gloucester St; en-suite singles/doubles from £39.50/47) is a 17th-century coaching inn five minutes' walk from the town centre.

The Fleece Hotel (☎ 658507, fax 651017; Market Place; singles/doubles £82/97) is the top place in town. Breakfast is an extra £10.

Places to Eat

Black Jack Coffee House (Black Jack St) is a good place to pause for refreshment, while the **Swan Yard Café** (6 Swan Yard) does mouthwatering cakes. For putting together a picnic you can't do better than **Jeroboams**, beside the church, where it claims to 'build' sandwiches rather than make them.

Getting There & Away

National Express buses run hourly from Cirencester to London (£13, 2¼ hours), Cheltenham Spa (£2.70, 25 minutes) and Gloucester (£5, 50 minutes).

Stagecoach bus No 51 runs to Cheltenham, 12 miles to the north, hourly at 20 minutes past the hour between 9.20am and 6.20pm (single/return £2.10/3.15, 40 minutes). Swanbrook Coaches runs five buses daily (two on Sunday) to Gloucester (single/return £1.55/2.30, 40 minutes).

NORTHERN COTSWOLDS

The northern Cotswolds are characterised by charming villages of soft, mellow stone, built in folds between the rolling wolds. Although they owe their existence to the medieval wool industry, most now rely on tourism for a living. A handful have been overwhelmed, but even these are worth a look. Unfortunately, public transportation between many of the towns is limited at best.

Burford
☎ 01993 • pop 800

One of the loveliest of Cotswold villages, Burford has a long street of handsome stone houses and attracts crowds of tourists in summer. It boasts fine 14th- to 16th-century houses and a medieval bridge over the River Windrush. The **TIC** (☎ 823558; Sheep St; open 9.30am-5.30pm Mon-Sat, 10.30am-3pm Sun) is by the Lamb Inn.

The 16th-century **Tolsey Museum** (Toll House; High St; admission 75p) houses a small museum on Burford's history; there's also an 18th-century dollhouse.

Places to Stay & Eat The cheapest option in town, **Chevrons** (☎ 823416; High St; en-suite singles/doubles from £30/40) has clean and basic rooms that are fairly well appointed.

Lamb Inn (☎ 823155; Sheep St; en-suite rooms per person Mon-Fri from £55.50, Sat & Sun from £60.50), dating from the 15th-century and Burford's oldest pub, is now a very comfy place to stay, with beamed ceilings and creaking stairs. Short breaks are better value.

Bay Tree Hotel (☎ 822791, fax 823008; Sheep St; doubles from £145) is the best place in town, and a fabulous hotel it is too: exposed beams, overhanging wisteria and flagstone floors give it plenty of 16th-century character, although the services are thoroughly modern.

Bould Farm (☎/fax 01608-658850; B4450 near Idbury; singles/doubles £30/50) is one of the best places you'll find anywhere in the Cotswolds for the price. It's a working farm about 5 miles (8km) northeast of Burford (and only reachable by private transport), and has four superb rooms with beautiful furnishings and plenty of space. To get there, travel north on the A424 toward Stow-on-the-Wold, take a right onto the B4450 and go through the hamlet of Idbury. The farm is on your right. We highly recommend it.

Burford has several good pubs. The characterful **Mermaid** *(High St)* and the **Golden Pheasant** *(High St)* do bar snacks and full meals.

High St has several tearooms: **Huffkins** has the most incredible selection of cakes and is always busy, while **Priory Tea Rooms** has tables outside during summer.

Getting There & Away From Oxford, Swanbrook runs four buses a day (two on Sunday) to Burford (single/return £2.20/3.30, 45 minutes) via Witney. Stagecoach bus No X3 runs to Burford, also via Witney, nine times a day, Monday to Saturday only (£2.70, 55 minutes)

Witney
☎ 01993 • pop 22,000
Witney is the eastern gateway to the Cotswolds. Since 1669, the town has specialised in the production of blankets. Sheep on the Cotswolds and the local downs provided the wool, while the River Windrush provided the water. High-quality blankets continue to be made here; the Queen still orders hers from Early's of Witney.

The **TIC** *(☎ 775802)* is in the 18th-century town hall in Market Square.

Although the town's grown to absorb the demands of Oxford commuters and light industry, the centre retains character despite its proximity to Oxford. On High St, blankets were formerly weighed and measured in the 18th-century baroque Blanket Hall. In Market Place stands the 17th-century Buttercross, originally a covered market.

Clearly signposted in the suburbs of Witney is the **Cogges Manor Farm Museum** *(☎ 772602; adult/child £4.20/2.10; open 10.30am-5.30pm Tues-Fri, noon-5.30pm Sat & Sun late Mar–Nov)*, where domestic farm animals roam the grounds of a 13th-century manor house, which was drastically altered in the 17th and 18th centuries. Here you can sample cakes and scones freshly baked on the old range. Jump off the Oxford to Witney bus (£1.70, 30 minutes; see the previous Burford section) at the Griffin Pub and walk down Church Lane.

Places to Stay & Eat A salmon-coloured, 17th-century coaching inn, **The Court Inn** *(☎ 703338, fax 700980; 43 Bridge St; singles/doubles £26/42)* has good quality rooms.

The Witney Hotel *(☎ 702137, fax 705337; 7 Church Green; singles/doubles £30/52)* is a beautiful, family-run B&B in a listed building. The rooms are exceptionally well appointed.

The Marlborough Hotel *(☎ 776353, fax 702152; 28 Market Square; singles/doubles from £56/80)* is the top spot in Witney, a Georgian coaching inn that has been converted into a charming hotel with modern luxuries.

Bistro 35 *(☎ 703540; 35 High St; mains from £7)* is about as interesting as food gets here; the menu has an assortment of continental dishes that are all pretty good.

Getting There & Away Swanbrook runs four buses Monday to Saturday (two on Sunday) between Cheltenham and Oxford via Witney (from Oxford: £2.10, 30 minutes; from Cheltenham: £4.90, one hour). This service also goes to Gloucester (£5.50, 1½ hours) and serves a number of Cotswold towns along the way, including Northleach, Minster Lovell and Burford.

Minster Lovell
This gorgeous little village in the valley of the River Windrush was one of William Morris' favourite spots in the Cotswolds, and it's not hard to see why. The walks along the river are particularly beautiful.

On the village outskirts are the ruins of **Minster Lovell Hall**, the family home of Viscount Francis Lovell (1454–c.1487), who fought with King Richard III against the Earl of Richmond (later Henry VII) at the Battle of Bosworth in 1485. After Richard's defeat and death, Lovell organised a rebellion against the new king but was soundly beaten in 1487 at the Battle of Stoke. He disappeared from the battlefield and was never seen again. In 1708 a skeleton seated at a table was discovered inside a secret vault in the house; it is thought that Lovell died here while in hiding.

Hill Grove *(☎ 703120, fax 700528; Crawley Dry Lane; singles/doubles £28/48)* is a pleasant working farm with large, well-appointed rooms above the River Windrush, about 1½ miles (2.5km) east of town off the B4047.

In the heart of the village, **The Swan** is a beautiful old pub that does pretty decent food for about £6.

Minster Lovell is 3 miles (5km) west of Witney, off the A40, and 5 miles (8km) southeast of Burford. Swanbrook coaches stop here on the Oxford to Cheltenham run (see the previous Witney section).

Chipping Norton
☎ 01608 • pop 5400 • elevation 165m

Chipping Norton is an attractive market town that grew rich on wool and, later, tweed. The **Church of St Mary** is a classic example of the wool churches seen throughout the Cotswolds, while the old glove factory off the road to Moreton-in-Marsh is a striking monument to the industrial architecture of the 19th century.

The small local history **museum** (☎ 658 518; 4 High St; adult/child £1.25/75p; open 2pm-4pm Tues-Sun Easter-Oct) is in the old hall opposite Town Hall. It has displays on the town's wool manufacturing traditions.

The Old Vicarage (☎ 641567; 5 Church St; singles/doubles £30/50) is just that: a 16th-century vicarage that has been converted into a beautiful B&B with large, homey rooms.

About 3 miles (5km) southwest of town in the hamlet of Churchill is **The Forge** (☎ 658173, fax 659262; B4450, Churchill; singles/doubles £45/55), a superb, 200-year-old country house that does top-notch B&B. One of the rooms has a Jacuzzi and four have four-poster beds.

Northleach
☎ 01451 • pop 1000 • elevation 154m

Clustered around a gorgeous market square, Northleach is a wonderful mixture of architectural styles and evocative names, and is home to perhaps the finest of the wool churches, a masterpiece of the Cotswold perpendicular style, with an unrivalled collection of medieval memorial brasses.

The **TIC** (☎ 860715; Fosse Way), on the A249, is in the old Northleach House of Correction, once a model 19th-century prison. Also here is the **Cotswold Heritage Centre** (adult/child £2.50/1; open 10.30am-5pm Mon-Sat, noon-5pm Sun Apr-Oct only), fronted by a superb collection of old carts and shepherds' vans. Inside, you can watch some truly interesting colour films from the 1930s that offer a great vision of what Northleach was once like. Cars and colours may be different today, but the town hasn't changed all that much.

Near the square is Oak House, a 17th-century wool house that contains **Keith Harding's World of Mechanical Music** (☎ 860181; adult/child £5/2), a collection of clocks and musical boxes. The one-hour tour (included in the admission price) is a lot of fun, and you can get to hear Rachmaninoff played on a piano roll.

About 4 miles (6.5km) southwest of Northleach, run by the National Trust (NT), is **Chedworth Roman Villa** (☎ 01242-890256; adult £3.80; open 10am-5pm daily Apr-Oct, 11am-4pm Tues-Sun Feb-Mar & Nov, closed rest of year), one of the best exposed Roman villas in England. Built around 120 for a wealthy landowner, it contains some wonderful mosaics illustrating the seasons.

Places to Stay & Eat A 400-year-old former wool merchant's cottage, **Cotteswold House** (☎ 860493; Market Square; rooms with en suite from £50) has exposed beams and original panelling. The three rooms have all been refurbished to a pretty high standard.

The **Sherborne Arms**, the charming **Red Lion** and the **Wheatsheaf**, all around Market Square, are the readiest sources of sustenance, solid or liquid.

Getting There & Away Northleach is 9 miles from Burford and 13 miles from Cheltenham off the A40. Swanbrook runs four buses Monday to Saturday (two on Sunday) between Cheltenham and Oxford via Northleach (from Oxford: single/return £3.50/5.25, one hour; from Cheltenham: £2/3.25, 30 minutes).

Bibury
☎ 01285 • pop 500

Described by William Morris as 'the most beautiful village in England', Bibury is a delightful place that prospered during the 17th and 18th centuries thanks to the wool trade. Its steady demise throughout the 19th century led to hard times and plenty of rioting, with the result that a substantial number of its inhabitants were shipped off to the penal colonies in Australia.

There are some lovely houses, most notably on **Arlington Row**, which is perhaps the most photographed street in all of Britain with it's line of NT-owned weavers' cottages, spawning countless calendars and postcards.

Opposite is Rack Isle, where cloth was once dried after weaving and fulling (compressing) in the 17th-century **Arlington Mill** (☎ 740368; adult/child £2/1.20; open 10am-5.30pm), which was converted in 1913 to aid the wartime effort. Today it houses a folk museum, and you'll also find a small tearoom and gift shop.

Places to Stay & Eat A supremely elegant house, **Cotteswold House** (☎/fax 740609; e cotteswold.house@btclick.com; Arlington; singles/doubles £35/48) has three large and beautifully appointed rooms, all en suite.

Bibury Court Hotel (☎ 740337, fax 740660; e info@biburycourt.co.uk; singles/doubles £100/125) is the top spot in town, a simply enormous Tudor home set in 2½ gorgeous hectares of parkland. Luxury abounds.

Jenny Wren's Tearoom (High St; afternoon tea £5.95) offers an afternoon tea so filling you won't need dinner.

Getting There & Away Swanbrook runs two buses daily (except Sunday) between Lechlade-upon-Thames and Cirencester (£3.40, 45 minutes), passing through Bibury.

Bourton-on-the-Water
☎ 01451 • pop 2600 • elevation 148m
Bourton is certainly attractive, with the River Windrush passing beneath a series of low bridges in the village centre and an array of handsome houses in Cotswold stone, but a word of warning: the town seems to be entirely given over to the tourist industry – particularly of the octogenarian coach tour kind. The best time to enjoy this village is in the evening, when the coach tours have gone, or in winter, when there are fewer of them.

To justify the large area set aside for coaches and cars, a number of specific attractions (the model railway and village, perfume exhibition and maze) have opened in the village. There's also a serious bird conservation project, **Birdland** (☎ 820480; adult/child £4.25/2.50; open 10am-5pm daily May-Sept, 10am-3pm daily Oct-Apr), which started after the owner purchased two islands in the Falklands to save the local penguin colonies.

Places to Stay & Eat There's no shortage of places to stay, and considering that most coach tours leave town before dark, you

should have few problems finding somewhere to bunk down.

Fairlie (☎ 821842; Riverside; doubles £38) is a gorgeous house built in Cotswold stone with large, attractive rooms.

Kingsbridge Inn (☎ 820371, fax 810179; Riverside; singles/doubles £49/64) is a truly elegant affair, with three beautifully appointed rooms. The breakfast is sensational.

Tearooms and restaurants, all serving similar fare, line the main street.

The Slaughters
Upper and Lower Slaughters have pretty off-putting names, but along with Bourton-on-the-Water they are the most famously picturesque villages in the Cotswolds. Which also means that you'll have trouble taking a decent picture for the numbers of visitors that descend on them once the weather gets warm. Incidentally, their name derives from an old Saxon word meaning 'place of sloe trees' (and not some gruesome murder!).

The Slaughters are best reached on foot from Bourton, an hour away. Following part of the Warden's Way from Bourton will take you across the Fosse Way, over a meadow and along a path into Lower Slaughter. Continuing past the **Victorian flour mill** (adult/child £1.50/75p; open 10am-6pm daily Mar-Oct), the route crosses meadows and goes behind the Manor House into Upper Slaughter.

Alternatively, you can opt to do one of the **Guide Friday** (☎ 01789-294466) 45-minute round-trip tours, which run between April and September. Tours are held every hour or so daily, departing from the war memorial in Bourton. They cost £4.50/1 per adult/child.

Stow-on-the-Wold
☎ 01451 • pop 2000 • elevation 240m
The highest town in the Cotswolds, Stow-on-the-Wold is also our favourite in the area, a genuinely elegant town at the heart of which is a large square that resembles an Italian piazza. There are no museums worth visiting, no major (or minor) attractions: it is just a place to walk around, and wander in and out of its 32 antique shops. Although it gets its fair share of visitors, you'll only notice their numbers if you don't book accommodation in advance.

The **TIC** (☎ 831082; Hollis House) is on Market Square.

Places to Stay & Eat On the eastern side of Market Square, **Stow-on-the-Wold Youth Hostel** (✆ 0870 770 6050, fax 870017; The Square; beds per adult £12.75; open daily Apr-Sept, Fri-Sat only Nov-Dec, closed Jan, closed Sun mid-Feb–Mar & Oct) is a top-class hostel, with clean six-bed dorms, all en suite.

Number Nine (✆ 870333; 9 Park St; singles/doubles £40/55) is a wonderful guesthouse with beautifully furnished rooms, all done in minimalist style.

Stow Lodge Hotel (✆ 830485, fax 831671; e enquiries@stowlodge.com; The Square; doubles from £95) is the pick of the bunch, a converted rectory and coach house set back from the main square on its own grounds. The rooms are excellent.

The Royalist Hotel (✆ 830670, fax 870048; e info@theroyalisthotel.co.uk; Digbeth St; singles/doubles from £50/90) is another contender for top spot. It was founded in 947, therefore claiming to be England's oldest inn – and has carbon dated some timbers to prove it. The real attraction, however, is the food served in the **947 Restaurant**, which is simply divine. The fish cake with caviar (£8.95) is delicious. If this wasn't praise enough, the adjoining Eagle & Child bar was voted the eighth-best pub in England by the *Independent*.

Fox Inn (✆ 870555, fax 870669; Lower Oddington; rooms £58-85), about 3 miles (5km) east of Stow on the A436 to Chipping Norton, is a creeper-clad inn with simply stunning rooms. Each is carefully decorated in period furniture and features antique wooden beds. It is a pub, but the food (mains around £10) is divine.

Peggums (✆ 830102; Church St) is a gorgeous little tearoom that serves good sandwiches for around £2.50.

Getting There & Away Pulhams Coaches operates daily services linking Stow with Moreton-in-Marsh (80p, 15 minutes), and a Monday to Saturday service to Cheltenham (£1.70, 45 minutes).

The nearest train stations are 4 miles away at Kingham and Moreton-in-Marsh.

Moreton-in-Marsh
✆ 01608 • pop 2600 • elevation 144m
Straddling the Fosse Way, the old Roman road between Cirencester and Leicester, Moreton may not be the most attractive Cotswold town but it does have some of the best transport connections. Its name is a corruption of the Saxon word 'march', which means boundary. If you're here during the week, you should check out the large **Tuesday market**, which takes place in the middle of town and has over 200 stalls selling all kinds of excellent junk and good produce.

About 1½ miles (2.5km) west of Moreton is the spectacular, Mogul-style **Sezincote House** (admission house adult £5.50, garden adult/child £3.75/1; garden open 2pm-6pm Thur-Fri Jan-Sept), built in 1810 by Charles Cockerell of the East India Company and thought to have inspired Brighton Pavilion. There are tours of the house on Thursday and Friday afternoons in May, June, July and September. Children are not admitted to the house.

Places to Stay & Eat An utterly charming Cotswold stone house, **Acacia** (✆ 650130; 2 New Rd; rooms with/without en suite £40/36) has small, comfortable rooms (only one en suite).

The Bell Inn (✆ 651688, fax 652195; High St; singles/doubles £39.50/75) has five large, luxurious rooms in a converted stable block.

Manor House Hotel (✆ 650501, fax 651481; e bookings@cotswolds-inns-hotels -co.uk; High St; singles/doubles from £90/115) is top-notch, with superbly appointed rooms that have all the frills.

Pubs include the atmospheric **White Hart Royal** (✆ 650731; High St) and the **Black Bear** (✆ 652992; High St), known for its excellent hot beef sandwiches.

Getting There & Away Pulhams Coaches operates a daily service (limited on Sunday) between Moreton and Cheltenham (12 Monday to Saturday, two on Sunday, £1.90, one hour) via Stow-on-the-Wold (15 minutes) and Bourton-on-the-Water (20 minutes). Many surrounding villages put on market-day buses. Bus Nos M21 and M22 run hourly to Stratford (11 Monday to Saturday only, £2.60, 1¼ hours) via Broadway (£1.60, 20 minutes) or Chipping Campden alternately (£1.60, 40 minutes).

There are trains roughly every hour to Moreton from London Paddington (£23.90, 1¾ hours) via Oxford (£12.80, 30 minutes) and on to Worcester (£13.50, 40 minutes) and Hereford (£17.40, 1¾ hours).

Chipping Campden
☎ 01386 • pop 2000 • elevation 145m

In an area filled with exquisite villages, Chipping Campden, with its thatched roofs, neatly clipped hedges and gorgeous gardens, seems straight out of *The Wind in the Willows*. The unspoiled main street is flanked by a succession of golden-hued terraced cottages, each subtly different from the next.

The **TIC** *(☎ 841206; Noel Arms Courtyard)* is off High St. Across the road, the gabled Market Hall dates from 1627. At the western end is **St James**, a very fine Cotswold wool church with some splendid 17th-century monuments. Nearby are the Jacobean lodges and gateways of the vanished manor house, and opposite is a remarkable row of **almshouses**.

About 4 miles (6.5km) northeast of Chipping Campden, in secluded Hidcote Bartrim, are **Hidcote Manor Gardens** *(NT; ☎ 438333; adult £5.80; open 10.30am-6.30pm Sat-Wed Mar-May & Aug-Sept, 10.30am-6.30pm Sat-Thur June-July, 10.30am-5.30pm daily Oct-Nov, closed Dec-Feb)*, a series of six gardens designed by Major Lawrence Johnston in the 1920s. They rank as one of the finest examples of Arts & Crafts landscaping in Britain (for more details on the Arts & Crafts movement see The Midlands chapter).

Places to Stay & Eat A timber-framed 15th-century house, **Badgers Hall** *(☎ 840839;* e *badgershall@talk21.com; High St; doubles £60)* has comfortable rooms.

Marnic House *(☎ 840014, fax 840441;* e *marnic@zoom.co.uk; Broad Campden; singles/doubles from £36/44)*, 1 mile outside town, is an award-winning, fairly modern house with really comfortable rooms and a friendly atmosphere.

Eight Bells *(Church St; mains around £8)* is an excellent restaurant with a British and continental menu.

Badger Bistro *(☎ 840520; The Square)* does Sunday lunch for under £6, while **Joel's Restaurant** *(☎ 840598; High St)* has a selection of pastas and a modern British menu. For a cream tea try **Badgers Hall** *(High St)* or **Bantam Tearooms** *(High St)*.

Getting There & Away Bus No 569 runs hourly to Stratford or Moreton. On Tuesday the market bus runs from Moreton, otherwise a taxi will cost about £8.

Getting Around You can hire a bike from **Cotswold Country Cycles** *(☎ 438706; Longlands Farm Cottage)* for £12/60 per day/week.

Broadway
☎ 01386 • pop 2000 • elevation 140m

Just over the border in Worcestershire, this well-known and much-visited village is strung out along a broad street, beneath the crest of an escarpment. Undeniably handsome, and largely unspoiled despite its fame, it has inspired writers, artists and composers, from JM Barrie to Edward Elgar. A new bypass has brought some relief from through traffic, but coaches still manage to cause maximum chaos in high summer.

The **TIC** *(☎ 852937; 1 Cotswold Court; open 11am-1pm & 2pm-5pm Mon-Sat)* is in a shopping arcade off the northern end of High St.

The lovely medieval **Church of St Eadburgha** is signposted from the town, a 30-minute walk away. For a longer walk, take the footpath opposite the church that leads up to **Broadway Tower** *(☎ 852390; adult/child £3/2.20; open 10am-5.30pm daily)*, a crenellated, 18th-century folly that stands above the town with a small William Morris exhibition on one floor. On a clear day you can see 12 counties from the top.

Olive Branch Guest House *(☎ 853440, fax 859070; 78 High St; singles/doubles from £36/55)* is a listed 16th-century guesthouse with comfortable, elegant rooms.

The Cotswolds Olimpicks

Founded by one Robert Dover in 1612, the Cotswolds Olimpicks is one of the most entertaining and bizarre sporting competitions in England. Events originally included welly wanging (throwing boots), shin-kicking, the sack race and climbing a slippery pole.

The competition was reinstated in 1951 and – incredibly – has earned the official sanction and support of the British Olympic Association. Most of the old disciplines are included, except for shin-kicking, which somehow isn't deemed a worthwhile event. Held at the beginning of June and running over the Spring Bank Holiday, they take place on Dover's Hill, on the edge of town, and the whole affair ends in a big dancing festival.

The Lygon Arms (☎ 852255, fax 858611; e info@the-lygon-arms.co.uk; High St; singles/ doubles from £149/190), now owned by the ultraswish Savoy Group, is not just the best place in town, but probably the top hotel in all of the Cotswolds.

Try **Garford's** (☎ 858522; High St; mains £6.50) for a mean steak-and-kidney pie.

Getting There & Away Broadway is 9 miles (14km) from Moreton-in-Marsh. Take bus No 559 to Evesham (eight Monday to Saturday) and bus No 606 to Cheltenham (six Monday to Saturday, 1½ hours).

Snowshill

Furnished with an extraordinarily eclectic collection of items, **Snowshill Manor** (NT; ☎ 01386-852410; adult £6; open noon-5pm Wed-Sun Apr-Oct, also Mon July-Aug) is worth visiting if only to get a glimpse inside the mind of the marvellously eccentric Charles Paget Wade, who stocked his house with everything from Japanese armour to Victorian perambulators. The walled gardens are particularly delightful and the restaurant has wonderful views. Timed tickets are issued for the cramped house. It's an uphill walk to get here from Broadway, about 3 miles (5km) south.

Stanton

☎ 01386 • pop 340 • elevation 183m
This tiny village doesn't really figure on many itineraries, as it's out of the way and doesn't have any attractions worth making the effort for.

However, if you're looking for somewhere to enjoy a good pint of local ale on a summer's day, you won't find a more pleasant pub than the **Mount Inn** (☎ 584316; mains around £6), which has marvellous views of the surrounding countryside from its perch on the edge of the village. It also has a modest menu: nothing fancy, just good old pub grub.

Stanton is 3 miles (5km) south of Broadway on the B4632.

Stanway

There isn't much in this blink-and-you'll-miss-it hamlet except for the elegant **Stanway House** (☎ 01386-584469; adult/child £3.50/1.50; open 2pm-5pm Tues & Thur), a handsome Jacobean property with an elaborate gatehouse and a beautiful, baroque water garden that is one of the finest in the country. There is a pyramid cascade and a 25m fountain.

Stanway is 2 miles (3km) south of Stanton along the B4632.

Hailes

Once one of England's most important Cistercian monasteries, there's little else left of **Hailes Abbey** (NT; ☎ 01242-602398; adult £2.80; open 10am-6pm daily Easter-Oct, 10am-6pm Sat & Sun rest of year) save its foundations, but the ruins are quite evocative. Before it was dissolved by Henry VIII, pilgrims would come from all over the country to worship the phials of Christ's blood that were kept here, but these were exposed to a mixture of honey and saffron at the time of the dissolution. The site is now run by the NT in conjunction with English Heritage (EH).

The small neighbouring **church**, with medieval stained glass, murals and heraldic tiles, is delightful. A short walk away are the organic **Hailes Fruit Farm** (good cider) and **Orchard Tea Room**.

Hailes is about 3 miles (5km) northeast of Winchcombe along the Cotswold Way.

Winchcombe

☎ 01242 • pop 5000 • elevation 137m
Saxon Winchcombe was the capital of its own county and the seat of Mercian royalty. Its Benedictine abbey was one of the country's main pilgrimage centres.

These days its main attraction is **Sudeley Castle** (☎ 604357; adult/child £6.50/3.50; open 10.30am-5.30pm daily Easter-Oct), once a favoured retreat of Tudor and Stuart monarchs. Henry VIII's last wife, Catherine Parr, came to live here after she married Thomas Seymour, Lord of Sudeley (and ancestor of actress Jane Seymour), following the king's death. Her tomb is in the chapel and one of her teeth is displayed inside the house, along with paintings by Constable and Turner.

The house was badly damaged by parliamentarians during the Civil War because Charles I used to seek refuge here, but it was rebuilt in the 19th century by the Dent family in a more contemporary style. The real treat is the truly beautiful **Queen's Garden**.

In the village proper, splendid **St Peter's Church** is noted for its fine gargoyles. The **TIC** (☎ 602925; High St) has information about other local walks.

Gloucestershire Warwickshire Railway

This cunningly named steam railway has appropriated the initials of the most famous railway line in Britain, the Great Western Railway (GWR). Unfortunately this GWR (☎ 621405; return adult/child £7/4) doesn't travel such a useful route as Bristol to London; instead it goes from Toddington to Gotherington via Winchcombe. The railway is operated completely by volunteers. Ring ahead to find out what days it is running, or visit its website at **w** www.gwsr.plc.uk.

Places to Stay & Eat A beautiful half-timbered Tudor building, **Wesley House** (☎ 602366, fax 609046; High St; singles/doubles £55/80) does an excellent two-course dinner in the restaurant for £19.50.

Blair House (☎ 603626, fax 604214; 41 Gretton Rd; singles/doubles from £25/42) is a friendly place farther out of town, but within walking distance.

Wincelcumbe Tearooms (☎ 603578; 7 Hailes St) does soup with tasty rosemary and raisin bread, and classic cream teas for about £3.50.

Old White Lion (North St) is a lovely 15th-century pub.

Getting There & Away Castleways Coaches runs 10 buses daily, Monday to Saturday (two on Sunday), from Winchcombe to Cheltenham (£1.30, 25 minutes) or Broadway (£1.50, 40 minutes).

SOUTHERN COTSWOLDS

Just as beautiful as their northern neighbours, the southern Cotswolds are nevertheless quite different: the stone is more soberly coloured, the valleys are steeper and the whole area is generally less reliant on tourism. Which means that if you want to get away from the camera-clicking and the coach tours, the southern villages are the place to be.

Painswick

☎ 01452 • pop 2800 • elevation 153m
Incredibly, the picture-perfect village of Painswick, often called the 'Queen of the Cotswolds', is not overrun by tourists, at least not usually. Instead, you'll have to settle for an overabundance of yew trees, especially in the graveyard of **St Mary's Church**, where they share space with the

table-top (raised) tombs of rich wool merchants who made the town prosperous from the 17th century.

Curiously, for many centuries there were only 99 yew trees in the grounds, as legend had it that should the hundredth be allowed to grow, the devil would appear and shrivel it. To celebrate the millennium, however, they went ahead and planted it anyway – so far, no sign of the Wicked One.

The streets behind the church are lined with handsome merchants' houses. Bisley St, with several 14th-century houses, was the original thoroughfare, while New St is a medieval addition. Rare iron spectacle stocks stand in the street just south of the church.

The **TIC** (☎ 813552; The Library, Stroud St; open 10am-4.30pm Tues-Fri, 10am-1pm Sat & Sun Easter-Oct) is staffed by enthusiastic volunteers who'll tell you everything you want to know about this lovely town.

Painswick Rococo Garden The gardens of Painswick House (☎ 813204; adult/child £3.75/2; open 11am-5pm daily Jan-Oct), half a mile north of the town, are a restored version of original gardens designed in the 1740s by Benjamin Hyett. They're best visited in February or March for the spectacular snowdrop displays.

Places to Stay & Eat A converted early 18th-century corn mill, **Hambutts Mynd** (☎ 812352; Edge Rd; singles/doubles from £27/48) has retained most of its original characteristics. It caters especially for Cotswold Way walkers.

Cardynham House (☎ 814006; The Cross; singles/doubles from £36/46) is right in the middle of town and has nine rooms, all with four-poster beds; the building dates back to the 15th century.

Thorne (*☎ 812476; Friday St; doubles £60*) is a 16th-century place that also incorporates a 15th-century market building. It has only two doubles.

The Falcon Inn (*☎ 814222, fax 813377; New St; singles/doubles from £42.50/65*) is another excellent choice, with fully refurbished rooms. It also has a pretty good **restaurant** (*mains around £8*).

Painswick Hotel (*☎ 812160; Kemps Lane; singles/doubles from £80/115*), a former Georgian rectory, is now the best hotel in town, with luxurious rooms decorated with beautiful antiques.

The March Hare (*☎ 813452; Tibbiwell St; set dinner £21.50*) is a terrific Thai restaurant that does a really tasty six-course dinner.

The Royal Oak (*☎ 813129; St Mary's St*) is a beautiful old bar that is popular with locals, as is the bar in the **Falcon Inn**.

Getting There & Around Bus No 46 connects Cheltenham and Stroud with Painswick hourly. Swanbrook has a better service for Gloucester. Those with their own vehicles watch out – the streets are extremely narrow.

Stroud
☎ 01453 • pop 37,800 • elevation 158m

The narrow, steep-sided Stroud Valley stands out from the rest of the southern Cotswolds and was the last area in the Cotswolds to hold onto its wool industry. Stroudwater scarlet, once famous throughout the world, is produced in very small quantities these days, and many of the old mills have been reconverted to other uses.

Stroud is built around a spur above the River Frome; it's a pleasant town to spend an afternoon. Walk around Stroud's hilly streets to take in the old **Shambles market** (Wednesday, Friday and Saturday), **Tudor town hall** and **Stroud Museum**. The Stroud Subscription Rooms on George St houses the **TIC** (*☎ 760960; open 10am-5pm Mon-Sat*).

London Hotel (*☎ 759992; standard singles/doubles from £32/45, with en suite £45/57*), opposite the town centre car park, offers B&B.

Fern Rock House (*☎ 757307; 72 Middle St; singles/doubles £22/40*) is a tidy, comfortable B&B.

Pelican (*Union St*) serves pub lunches and there are several cafés in the pedestrianised High St, behind the TIC. Our favourite is **The Old Lady Teashop** (*Threadneedle St*), above a bakery. It has a pretty good selection of cakes and sandwiches.

Bus No 46 runs hourly to Painswick and Cheltenham. Bus No 93 operates half-hourly to Gloucester.

Uley
☎ 01453

This tiny, picturesque village 6 miles (10km) southwest of Stroud was once a prosperous weaving centre that was renowned for its blue dye, but today is little more than a dormitory for nearby Dursley.

Extending the length of ridge above the village are the overgrown remains of the largest Iron Age hill fort in England, **Uley Bury**. To get there on foot, follow the steep path that runs from the village church; if you have your own wheels, you can drive right up to the car park by the fort entrance. The site is closed off so you can't clamber over the ruins, but the 2-mile (3km) perimeter walk affords some stunning views of the surrounding countryside.

One mile (1.5km) east of the village is **Owlpen Manor** (*☎ 860261; adult/child £4.50/2; open 2pm-5pm Tues-Sun Apr-Sept*), one of the most enticing Tudor mansions in southern England. It was built in stages between 1450 and 1616, but lay derelict for nearly 100 years until 1926, when it was partially refurbished by Norman Jewson, a Cotswolds Arts & Crafts architect and follower of William Morris. Today the house is the property of the Mander family and features some interesting painted textiles, family portraits, and a good collection of Cotswold Arts & Crafts furniture and fittings. The magnificent Tudor **Grand Hall** has been fully restored to its original best.

Surrounding the house are the formal seven-terraced **gardens**, first developed in 1723. The fabulous yew trees, old roses and box parterres were much admired for their 'old English' style by the top gardeners of the 20th century, including Gertrude Jekyll, Geoffrey Jellicoe and Vita Sackville-West.

You should consider spending a night in one of the estate's nine **holiday cottages** (*☎ 860261; rooms per person from £26*) that carry inviting names such as Summerfield,

Peter's Nest and Marlings End. Inside, they do not disappoint: they are all exquisitely decorated in largely Victorian style, and all have a kitchen, bathroom and sitting room.

The **Cyder House Restaurant** (☎ 860816; mains around £9; open lunch & dinner daily Easter-Sept, Sat evening only rest of year), also on the estate, has earned kudos for its elegant cuisine, a mix of classic English with some interesting continental touches.

There are hourly buses to Uley from Stroud (£2.30, 20 minutes) daily, except Sunday.

Slimbridge

Eleven miles southwest of Gloucester, the village of Slimbridge sits between the busy M5 motorway and the River Severn. Just outside the village is the **Slimbridge Wildfowl & Wetlands Trust** (☎ 01453-891900; adult/child £6/3.50; open 9.30am-4.30pm daily Oct-Mar, 9.30am-5.30pm daily rest of year), established in 1946 by the late Sir Peter Scott. It's now Britain's largest wildfowl sanctuary, and serves as an important breeding ground for geese, swans, ducks and flamingos. Many of these birds are migratory and it is just as interesting in winter, when flocks of swans arrive here from the frozen Russian steppes, as it is in summer.

Admission is discounted if you stay the night before at **Slimbridge Youth Hostel** (☎ 0870 770 6036, fax 890625; beds £12; open Mar-Aug), half a mile south across the Sharpness Canal.

Bus No 308 links Bristol with Gloucester and passes by the Slimbridge crossroads, 2 miles (3km) from the town centre.

Berkeley

☎ 01453 • pop 1550

This quiet Georgian town is best known for **Berkeley Castle** (☎ 810332; adult/child £5.70/3.10, grounds only £2/1; open 11am-5pm Mon-Sat, 2pm-5pm Sun June-Sept, 2pm-5pm Tues-Sun Apr-May, 2pm-4.30pm Sun only Oct), a beautiful medieval fortress set in terraced Elizabethan gardens surrounded by lawns. It was here, in 1327, that Edward II was imprisoned and then murdered by order of his wife Queen Isabella and her lover. The last days of his life have become the stuff of gruesome legend: he was thrown into a dank, dirty dungeon whose only ventilation came from a shaft

An Unfinished Masterpiece

In 1852 work began on a mansion at Woodchester, 1 mile (1.5km) north of Uley. But instead of completing yet *another* stately home, the workers downed tools in 1868, walked out and never came back. What they left behind was 16 years of labour and a massive Victorian house with 27 unfinished rooms. Doors lead nowhere, fireplaces are stuck halfway up a wall and corridors end at ledges with views of the ground below. The mansion is undergoing some pretty serious maintenance, but the end result is to leave it exactly as it is: not one extra brick is going to be added.

The **house** (☎ 750455; adult/child £4/2; open 11am-4pm Sun Easter-Oct, also 11am-4pm Sat July-Aug) also features an impressive set of gruesome gargoyles and is home to one of England's largest colonies of greater horseshoe bats, as well as around 200 lesser horseshoes. It is said that the house is home to a headless horse and a floating coffin, but they *would* say that about a mysterious Victorian mansion...

that led directly to a pit where the rotting carcasses of dead animals were kept. He was then impaled on a red-hot poker.

The **Butterfly Farm** (adult/child £2/1) across the car park opens one hour after the castle.

A path winds through **St Mary's** churchyard, with its unusual detached bell tower, to the **Jenner Museum** (☎ 810631; adult/child £2.50/1; open Tues-Sun), in the house where Edward Jenner performed the first smallpox vaccination in 1796. Opening hours are similar to the castle's.

Berkeley is 6 miles (10km) southwest of Slimbridge. Badgerline's bus No 308 from Bristol to Gloucester passes this way.

Tetbury

☎ 01666 • pop 4500 • elevation 114m

On the A433, Tetbury has an interesting 18th-century Gothic church with a graceful spire and wonderful interior. The 17th-century Market House was used for wool trading. The **TIC** (☎ 503552; Long St; open 9.30am-4.30pm Mon-Sat) is at Old Court House.

The village of Westonbirt is 2½ miles (4km) southwest of Tetbury, and the nearby

Westonbirt Arboretum (☎ 880220; adult/child £4.50/1.50; open 10am-dusk daily) boasts a magnificent selection of temperate trees. Walks through the vast grounds are particularly stunning in spring and autumn.

Bus No 29 serves Tetbury every two hours from Stroud (£2.10, 30 minutes) before transforming itself into No 620 and proceeding toward Bath (£4, 1¼ hours), making a stop at the Westonbirt Arboretum en route.

Lechlade-on-Thames
☎ 01367 • pop 350

At the highest navigable point of the River Thames, Lechlade is graced by the spire of **St Lawrence's Church**, described as an 'aerial pile' by Shelley in his 1815 poem *A Summer Evening Churchyard, Lechlade, Gloucestershire*. A wool church, it was rededicated to the Spanish saint by Catherine of Aragon, who held the manor in the 16th century.

About 3 miles (5km) east of Lechlade off the Faringdon road, **Kelmscot Manor** (☎ 252486; adult/child £6/3; open 11am-1pm & 2pm-5pm Wed Apr-Sept) was home to William Morris, the poet, artist and founder of the Arts & Crafts movement. It opens on the occasional summer Saturday. The **Memorial Cottages** nearby feature a beautiful carving of Morris seated under a tree.

Another worthwhile side-trip from Lechalde is **Buscot Park** (NT; ☎ 240786; admission £5, grounds only £4; open 2pm-6pm daily), a Palladian mansion that is home to the Faringdon art collection, which includes paintings by Rembrandt, Reynolds, Rubens, Van Dyck and Murillo, as well as a comprehensive series of pre-Raphaelite British works. The house is 2½ miles (4km) southeast of Lechlade on the Faringdon road.

Close to Buscot Park, the **Apple Tree Guest House** (☎ 252592; Buscot Village; singles/doubles £26/42) is a comfortable B&B in a listed property. The rooms are very tastefully decorated.

Cambrai Lodge (☎ 253173; Oak St; singles/doubles £29/47) is a modern, comfortable guesthouse in the heart of Lechlade.

There are three buses daily from Lechlade to Cirencester (£2.70, 20 minutes).

Fairford
The only reason to stop in Fairford (and you can do so on your way from Lechlade to Cirencester) is to visit **St Mary's Church**, home of England's only complete set of medieval stained-glass windows. They're the work of Barnard Flower, master glass-painter to Henry VII, who created them around 1480.

The Lechlade to Cirencester bus stops along the High St.

Gloucestershire

Bisected by the River Severn, Gloucestershire is a county of stunningly pretty stone villages, remarkable views and the source of the traditional picture of rustic, rosy-cheeked England. Some of the villages are extremely popular; the best way to escape the commercialism is to explore on foot or by bike.

Nestled in the Severn Vale are the county capital, Gloucester, with its magnificent cathedral; elegant Cheltenham, one of England's best preserved Regency towns; and Tudor Tewkesbury, with a once-powerful but still beautiful abbey. To the west, and geographically part of Wales, are the Forest of Dean and the beautiful Wye Valley bordering Wales (see The Marches chapter for more information).

ACTIVITIES
Gloucestershire is perfect for walking and cycling, with plenty of footpaths and quiet roads, mild yet rewarding gradients and fine pubs for refreshment. TICs stock a stack of walking guides and a useful pack called *Cycle Touring Routes in Gloucestershire*.

Campus Holidays (☎ 01242-250642) organises mountain-bike tours of the region, starting from Cheltenham.

GETTING AROUND
Most TICs stock local bus timetables, or you can phone the Gloucestershire public transport inquiry line for details (☎ 01452-425543).

GLOUCESTER
☎ 01452 • pop 106,600

The county capital Gloucester (pronounced glo-ster) was originally founded as Glevum by the Romans as a retirement home for Cirencester's centurions. Despite beginning life in service of those at the end of theirs, the town became an important Saxon garrison and then a key Norman town; so import-

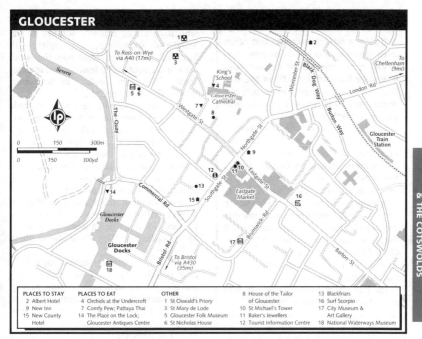

GLOUCESTER

PLACES TO STAY	PLACES TO EAT	OTHER	8 House of the Tailor	13 Blackfriars
2 Albert Hotel	4 Orchids at the Undercroft	1 St Oswald's Priory	of Gloucester	16 Surf Scorpio
9 New Inn	7 Comfy Pew; Pattaya Thai	3 St Mary de Lode	10 St Michael's Tower	17 City Museum &
15 New County	14 The Place on the Lock;	5 Gloucester Folk Museum	11 Baker's Jewellers	Art Gallery
Hotel	Gloucester Antiques Centre	6 St Nicholas House	12 Tourist Information Centre	18 National Waterways Museum

ant that Henry III was crowned in St Peter's Abbey in 1216 and Edward II was buried here after his murder in 1327. His tomb proved so popular with medieval royal watchers that Gloucester became a centre of pilgrimage. During the Civil War, the strongly Puritan town attracted a more hostile kind of royal attention, doggedly withstanding a 26-day siege by the king's forces.

In modern times, Gloucester prospered firstly on the back of the Forest of Dean's iron, coal and timber industries, and in the 20th century as manufacturer of heavy industry, including railway rolling stock, aircraft and motorcycles. Although it retains some of its medieval character, particularly in its cruciform-shaped historic centre and magnificent Norman cathedral, Gloucester today bears too many scars of its industrial past and for many years has lived in the shadow of its more glamorous neighbour, Cheltenham. The much touted dockland development scheme, which promises restaurants, cafés and boutiques centred on the Severn, is, at the time of writing, some way off completion. Still, the town is definitely worth a visit – even as a day trip from Chel-

tenham – if only to wander about the cathedral and exquisite cloister, which is one of the most stunningly beautiful you'll see anywhere in England.

Orientation & Information

The city centre is based around Northgate, Southgate, Eastgate and Westgate Sts, which all converge on The Cross. The **TIC** (☎ 396572; 28 Southgate St; open 10am-5pm Mon-Sat year-round, also 11am-3pm Sun July-Aug) sells the *Via Sacra* town trail (the route of the original pilgrimage) and a leaflet outlining the route of the 26-mile (42km) Glevum Way around the city outskirts. It also runs a 1½-hour guided walk of the historic centre, departing from the TIC at 2.30pm daily, mid-June to mid-September, which costs £2.50.

Surf Scorpio (☎ 528030; 135 Eastgate St; open 9.30am-6pm Mon-Sat) should take care of all your email needs. It charges £1 for 30 minutes of Internet time.

Gloucester Cathedral

The city's most extraordinary building is the magnificent Gothic cathedral (☎ 528095;

Surfing the Severn Bore

A 'bore' is a tidal phenomenon that occurs when flood-tides pour into the wide mouth of an estuary in greater volume than can easily flow along the normal channel of the river. The incoming tide then sweeps over the slower river flow and pushes upstream, flooding the riverbanks as it goes.

In Britain the most striking bore occurs on the River Severn, the country's longest river. At its deepest point the Severn Bore can be 2.75m deep, although in October 1966 a bore measuring 2.82m and travelling at 13 miles an hour was recorded.

In recent years a new sport of bore-surfing has developed, with surfers, body-boarders and canoeists lining up to catch the wave. If they time it right they can ride for 1½ miles (2.5km) upriver, much to the irritation of traditionalists who think they're spoiling a great natural phenomenon.

The best places to see the Severn Bore are between Awre, where the estuary narrows, and Gloucester. The Gloucester TIC will be able to tell you the dates to go borewatching. Wear wellies, as the water floods the surrounding roads.

College Green; admission £2.50 donation; open 7am-6pm daily), the first outstanding example of the English perpendicular style. Although the Saxons founded St Peter's Abbey here in 681, in 1069 a group of Benedictine monks began the construction of their own church, albeit attached to the original abbey.

The first church, finished in 1100, was large but hardly splendid. Its conversion to the magnificent building visible today began after the murder of Edward II in 1327, when income generated as a result of the church's new role as a centre of pilgrimage was set aside to do the job. Henry VIII was said to be so impressed by the new Gothic church that he conferred the status of cathedral on it no sooner than he'd ordered that St Peter's Abbey be dissolved in 1541, and the new cathedral became the centre of the Gloucester diocese.

Inside, the cathedral skilfully combines the best of Norman and Gothic design. The nave has retained much of its original character, from the thick, sturdy columns that lend it an air of gracious solidity, to the wonderful Norman arcading, replete with beautiful mouldings. Note how the south wall of the south aisle leans out of true because of the defensive ditch of the Roman town (Glenvum) beneath.

The newly restored eastern window, made in 1349 to commemorate local participation in the Battle of Crecy, is the largest in England, while the wooden choir stalls date from 1350. Above them soars wonderfully elaborate lierne vaulting. The late-15th-century Lady Chapel represents the final flowering of the perpendicular style.

In the southern ambulatory is an effigy of Robert, William the Conqueror's eldest son. Edward II's magnificent tomb, surmounted by an alabaster effigy, is in the northern ambulatory.

The northern transept, containing a 13th-century reliquary, leads into the treasury and also gives access to the tribune gallery, where there is an **exhibition** *(admission £2; open 10.30am-4pm Mon-Fri, 10.30am-3.30pm Sat Apr-Oct)* on the cathedral's history. The whispering gallery is particularly effective here, and you can pick up even the quietest of murmurs across the vaulting. In the northern aisle is a memorial to John Stafford Smith, a Gloucester composer who wrote the tune for the US national anthem.

At the western end stands a statue of Edward Jenner (1749–1823), who discovered how to vaccinate people against smallpox at nearby Berkeley.

The magnificent 69m-high tower was constructed from 1450 to replace the 13th-century spire.

The **Great Cloister**, complete in 1367, is the first example of fan vaulting in England and is only matched in beauty by Henry VIII's Chapel at Westminster Abbey. On one side is the monks' *lavorium* (wash basin); check out the niches for their towels across the way. You (or your kids) might recognise the cloister from the *Harry Potter* films: it was used in the corridor scenes at Hogwart's School, while the students of the attached King's School were used as extras.

Guided tours of the cathedral are available by arrangement.

Every third year Gloucester Cathedral hosts the Three Choirs Festival. It will be Gloucester's turn in 2004.

Other Things to See & Do

In recent years the historic **Gloucester Docks** have undergone a massive restoration that has brought a semblance of activity back to a moribund area that in the 19th century was Britain's largest inland port, servicing up to 600 ships a year. Fifteen Victorian warehouses have been restored and refurbished, and now house museums, restaurants and offices.

The most interesting of these is Llanthony, the largest warehouse, which houses the excellent **National Waterways Museum** (☎ 318054; adult/child £5/4; open 10am-5pm daily), which has a varied collection of historic vessels and imaginative displays.

Antiquarians and fans of wonderful old junk should definitely visit the **Gloucester Antiques Centre** (☎ 422900; 1 Severn Rd; open 10am-5pm Mon-Sat, 1pm-5pm Sun), a huge, four-storey warehouse literally packed with antiques, collectables and other knick-knacks. For some, it's literally a day out.

The **Gloucester Folk Museum** (☎ 526467; 99 Westgate St; adult/child £2/free; open 10am-5pm Mon-Sat, 10am-4pm Sun) is in a 16th-century former clothier's house. Displays include a dairy, an ironmonger's shop and a Victorian schoolroom. A new interactive gallery called The Portal helps brings the city's rich history to life.

St Nicholas House, next door, was the family home of the Whittingtons of pantomime fame. Nearby are the remains of **St Oswald's Priory** and **St Mary de Lode**, Gloucester's oldest church.

At 5 Southgate St, **Baker's Jewellers** is an Edwardian shop that boasts a curious mechanical clock, with figures to represent the four countries making up the United Kingdom. **Blackfriars** (Ladybellgate St; admission free; open daily) is Britain's finest surviving example of a Dominican priory. There are free guided tours of the priory at 3pm on Sunday during July and August.

Along Eastgate St are the 15th-century **St Michael's Tower** (currently under repair), **Eastgate Market** (pop inside to inspect the Beatrix Potter clock) and the remains of the East Gate itself. The **City Museum & Art Gallery** (☎ 524131; Brunswick Rd; adult/child £2/free; open 10am-5pm Mon-Sat, 10am-4pm Sun) is worth dropping by to see the beautiful Birdlip Mirror dating back to the 1st century AD.

Fans of Beatrix Potter will love the **House of the Tailor of Gloucester** (☎ 422856; adult/child £1.50/free; open 10am-5pm Mon-Sat), off Westgate St, established in the shop that inspired the story of the same name. The exhibition includes a very popular gift shop.

Places to Stay

The Albert Hotel (☎ 502081; 56 Worcester St; singles/doubles from £27/42) is near the town centre in a charming listed property.

New Inn (☎ 522177; 16 Northgate St; singles/doubles £35/50) is our favourite hotel in town. It's a historic place reckoned to have been in the hospitality business since 1455. The rooms are very comfortable.

New County Hotel (☎ 307000; 44 Southgate St; doubles with en suite from £65) is a clean, comfortable and characterful three-star hotel only five-minutes' walk from the town centre.

The Tailor of Gloucester

Beatrix Potter's own favourite story was apparently *The Tailor of Gloucester*, the famous children's story she wrote and illustrated in 1901 as a Christmas present for a friend.

While visiting some cousins at Harescombe Grange, near Stroud, she heard a story about a real-life tailor, John Prichard of Gloucester. As in her tale, he'd been asked to make a waistcoat for the city's mayor. So busy was he that the Saturday before the Monday when the garment was due, he had only reached the cutting stage. But when he returned to the shop on Monday, he found it complete, bar a single buttonhole. A note pinned to it read, 'No more twist'.

Mystified (but commercially minded), he placed an advert in his window imploring people to come to Prichard's where the 'waistcoats are made at night by the fairies'. Later it transpired that the tailor's assistants had finished the waistcoat after sleeping in the shop because they'd stayed out too late to get home.

John Prichard died in 1934 and his tombstone at Haresfield records that he was the Tailor of Gloucester. In Potter's version, the young tailor became an old one, and the fairies became mice.

Places to Eat

Orchids at the Undercroft *(Gloucester Cathedral; lunch £6.99)*, part of the former monastery hall, is a great place for lunch or afternoon tea.

Also near the cathedral are **Comfy Pew** *(☎ 415648; College St; mains £5)*, which does teas and cakes, light lunches and à la carte dinners, and **Pattaya Thai** *(☎ 520739; College St; set lunches around £4.95)* – both restaurants are housed in beautiful old timbered buildings.

The Place on the Lock *(☎ 330253)*, on the 1st floor of the Gloucester Antiques Centre, is a cafeteria-style place.

Getting There & Away

Gloucester is 105 miles (170km) from London, 49 miles (80km) from Oxford, 45 miles (70km) from Bath and 16 miles (25km) from Cirencester. National Express has all the usual connections, and buses every two hours to London (£14, 3½ hours). An Explorer ticket to use the Gloucestershire bus network for a day costs £5/3.50 per adult/child. There are buses every 15 minutes to Cheltenham, but the quickest way to get there is by train (£2.30, 10 minutes).

AROUND GLOUCESTER
The Forest of Dean

Formerly a royal hunting ground, the Forest of Dean occupies a triangular plateau between Gloucester, Ross-on-Wye and Chepstow. This 42-sq-mile forest (including 28 sq miles of woodland) is subject to ancient forest law. Writer Dennis Potter was born here (describing it as 'a heart-shaped land') and JRR Tolkien visited often; the forest land is said to have inspired the setting for *The Lord of the Rings*. In 1978 it was designated a National Forest Park, the first in England.

Few tourists make it to the forest, even though it's an excellent area for walking or cycling. The main **TIC** *(☎ 01594-836307, for accommodation bookings ☎ 832889; High St, Coleford)* stocks walking and cycling guides and also books accommodations (free).

St Briavels Castle Youth Hostel *(☎ 0870 770 6040, fax 01594-530849; Lydney; beds £12)*, an imposing, moated place, was once a hunting lodge used by King John. It's west of the forest above the Wye Valley.

Clearwell Caves *(☎ 01594-832535; adult/child £3.50/2.50; open 10am-5pm daily Mar-*

Oct), near Coleford, have been mined for iron since the Iron Age, and you can wander through nine dank, spooky caves and inspect the paraphernalia of the mine workings alongside pools and rock formations. Every Halloween something akin to an underground rave takes place in Barbecue Churn, the largest cave; book ahead to get in.

Scatterford Cottage *(☎ 01594-835527;* e *simbar@supranet.com; The Butts, Clearwell; rooms per person from £17.50)* is a small cottage with just two rooms and a shared bathroom. They're comfortable and cosy.

Less than 3 miles (5km) away is the pretty village of **Newland**, dominated by All Saints, the so-called 'Cathedral of the Forest'. In the Greyndour Chantry look for the brass depicting a miner with a *nelly* (tallow candle) in his mouth, a pick in his hand and a *billy* (backpack) on his back.

Cherry Orchard Farm *(☎ 01594-832212; B&B per person without en suite from £20)* is a large Victorian farmhouse on a working dairy farm. The rooms are big and the atmosphere is very friendly.

At the Beechenhurst Enclosure near Cinderford you can follow the easy Forest of Dean **sculpture trail**.

The **Dean Heritage Museum** *(☎ 822170; adult/child £3.50/2; open 10am-6pm daily Apr-Sept, 10am-5pm Feb, Mar & Oct)*, in an old mill at Soudley near Cinderford, tells the history of the forest and free miners. The **Dean Heritage Kitchen** has lunches and teas.

Buses run from Gloucester and Monmouth to Coleford and the smaller villages. Trains also run to Lydney Junction. On Wednesday, Thursday, Saturday and Sunday from April to September steam trains run five times daily on the Dean Forest Railway from Lydney to Norchard. Tickets cost £2.70/5 single/return. For details phone ☎ 01594-843423.

Newent
☎ 01531 • pop 5160

The unspoilt small town of Newent has some attractive architecture and the **Shambles Museum of Victorian Life** *(☎ 822144; adult/child £4/2; open 10am-6pm Tues-Sun Easter-Dec)*, with assorted Victorian-style shopfronts around a tearoom.

At the **National Birds of Prey Centre** *(☎ 820286; adult/child £6/3.50; open 10.30am-5.30pm daily Feb-Nov)*, on the outskirts of Newent, you can watch hawks and owls in free flight during daily displays.

The **TIC** *(☎ 822468; 7 Church St; open 9am-5pm Mon-Sat)* is almost opposite the museum. Good food with English wine can be sampled in the restaurant at the **Three Choirs Vineyard** *(☎ 890223)*, where self-guided tours are available for £2.50/1.50 per adult/child.

Stagecoach bus No 32 runs here from Gloucester.

CHELTENHAM
☎ 01242 • pop 88,000

This elegant example of Regency town planning was just another Cotswolds town until 1716, when pecking pigeons were discovered to be eating salt crystals from a spring and Cheltenham quickly developed into the definitive spa, a rival to its more illustrious sibling Bath. These days, however, less people come for the waters than for the National Hunt Festival in March, when 40,000 punters a day come to bet their bankrolls on England's premier steeplechase event.

Equine attractions aside, Cheltenham has retained much of the gentility that came with being a spa town. Its handsome squares, colourful public gardens and elegant early-19th-century architecture exude a certain class and culture.

Cheltenham also plays host to the Music and Cricket festivals in July and the Literature Festival in October. With plenty of accommodations and some of the best dining to be found in the Cotswolds, the town is an excellent base for exploring the area.

History
When the famous pigeons appeared to develop extra vigour after a little foraging in the field where the Cheltenham Ladies' College now stands, a pump room was built and the town began attracting the sick and hypochondriac in ever-increasing numbers (including George III in 1788, who was both sick and a hypochondriac). The king's visit sealed the spa's future and new wells were built, as well as houses to accommodate the hordes of visitors, among them Handel and Jane Austen.

These days, most people just go to their local GPs, but Cheltenham's architecture has ensured that the town still gets its fair share of visitors. It's hard to resist the beautifully proportioned terraces, mostly creamy white and decorated with wrought-iron balconies

and railings. Believe it or not, many of these attractive, imposing terraces were the prefabs of the early 19th century, built by property speculators with an eye for a quick buck. By the 1960s, many were sinking under their own weight and millions of pounds have been spent just to keep them standing.

Orientation
Cheltenham train station is out on a limb to the west; bus F or G will run you to the town centre for 70p. The bus station is behind The Promenade in the town centre.

Central Cheltenham is eminently walkable. The not-too-attractive High St runs roughly east–west; south from it is The Promenade, the most elegant shopping area ('the Bond St of the West'). The Promenade extends into Montpellier, a 19th-century shopping precinct where you'll now find most of the good B&Bs and restaurants, beyond which lie Suffolk Square and Lansdowne Crescent. Pittville Park and the old Pump Room are a mile north of High St.

Information
The **TIC** *(☎ 522878; 77 The Promenade; open 9.30am-5.15pm Mon-Sat)* sells all sorts of Cotswold walking and cycling guides, as well as *The Romantic Road*, a guide to a 30-mile circular driving tour of the southern Cotswolds. It also runs a free accommodations service. After hours, a box just outside the main door has lists of B&Bs with available rooms and their prices.

There are good, informative **walking tours** of Regency Cheltenham lasting 1¼ hours from the TIC at 11am daily. Tickets cost £2.50.

You can check email at **Equals** *(☎ 237292; 287 High St)*, which charges £2 for half-an-hour's access.

The Promenade
The Promenade is the heart of Cheltenham and is at its best in summer, when its hanging baskets are full of flowers.

The **Municipal Offices**, built as private residences in 1825, are among the best features of one of Britain's most beautiful thoroughfares. In front of the offices stands a **statue of Edward Wilson** (1872–1912), a Cheltenham man who went on Captain Scott's ill-fated second expedition (1910–12) to the South Pole and died in Antarctica.

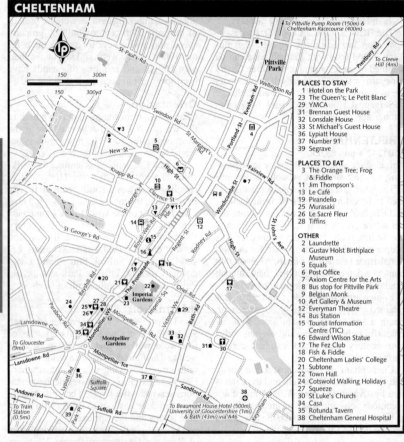

CHELTENHAM

To Pittville Pump Room (150m) &
Cheltenham Racecourse (400m)

To Cleeve
Hill (4mi)

St Paul's Rd

Pittville
Park

Prestbury Rd

St Margaret's Rd

0   150   300m
0   150   300yd

Swindon Rd

Wellington Rd

Evesham Rd

New St

High St

Knapp Rd

Clarence St

St George's Pl

St George's Rd

Royal Well Rd

Crescent Pde

Regent St

The Promenade

Baghill Rd

Parabola Rd

Lansdowne Cres

To Gloucester
(9mi)

Lansdowne Rd

Montpellier Wk

Montpellier St

Montpellier Spa Rd

Imperial
Gardens

Montpellier
Gardens

Montpellier Tce

Lypiatt Rd

Suffolk
Square

Andover Rd

To Train
Station
(0.5mi)

Park Pl

Suffolk Rd

Sandford Rd

Imperial Sq

Oriel Rd

Victoria Wk

Bath Rd

To Beaumont House Hotel (500m),
University of Gloucestershire (1mi)
& Bath (43mi) via A46

Portland St

Fairview Rd

Winchcombe St

St John's Ave

High St

Rodney Rd

Keynsham Rd

PLACES TO STAY
1 Hotel on the Park
23 The Queen's; Le Petit Blanc
29 YMCA
31 Brennan Guest House
32 Lonsdale House
33 St Michael's Guest House
36 Lypiatt House
37 Number 91
39 Segrave

PLACES TO EAT
3 The Orange Tree; Frog
   & Fiddle
11 Jim Thompson's
13 Le Café
19 Pirandello
25 Murasaki
26 Le Sacré Fleur
28 Tiffins

OTHER
2 Laundrette
4 Gustav Holst Birthplace
   Museum
5 Equals
6 Post Office
7 Axiom Centre for the Arts
8 Bus stop for Pittville Park
9 Belgian Monk
10 Art Gallery & Museum
12 Everyman Theatre
14 Bus Station
15 Tourist Information
   Centre (TIC)
16 Edward Wilson Statue
17 The Fez Club
18 Fish & Fiddle
20 Cheltenham Ladies' College
21 Subtone
22 Town Hall
24 Cotswold Walking Holidays
27 Squeeze
30 St Luke's Church
34 Casa
35 Rotunda Tavern
38 Cheltenham General Hospital

Following The Promenade towards Montpellier, you come to the **Imperial Gardens**, built to service the Imperial Spa.

Pittville Pump Room

Set in a delightful area of villas and parkland a mile from the town centre, the Pump Room (*Pittville Park; admission free; open 10am-5pm Wed-Mon*) is the town's finest Regency-style building. Built between 1825 and 1830, it was constructed as a spa and social centre for Joseph Pitt's new estate. Upstairs, there are occasional art exhibitions in the former library and billiard rooms. Downstairs (where you can still taste the spa water if you so desire), the former ballroom is now used for concerts. The park itself is also used for Sunday concerts ('Pittville on Sunday') throughout the summer.

Art Gallery & Museum

Cheltenham's history is imaginatively displayed at the Art Gallery & Museum (*☎ 237431; Clarence St; admission free; open 10am-5.30pm Mon-Sat*), which has excellent sections covering Edward Wilson, William Morris and the Arts & Crafts movement, and Dutch and British art. There's a temporary exhibition gallery on the ground floor.

Gustav Holst Birthplace Museum

The Victorian house (*☎ 524846; 4 Clarence Rd; adult/child £2.50/2; open 10am-4pm Tues-Sat*), where composer Gustav Holst (1874–1934) was born, displays Holst memorabilia alongside descriptions of life 'below stairs' (ie, in the servants' quarters) at the turn of the century. You get to listen to music as you go round too (usually *The Planets*).

Cleeve Hill
About 4 miles (6km) north of Cheltenham, Cleeve Hill, at 325m, is the highest point of the Cotswolds and lowland England, and offers fine views over Cheltenham. Buses run up the hill roughly once an hour on weekdays from the town centre.

Cheltenham Racecourse
On Cheltenham's northern outskirts, Prestbury is reputedly Britain's most haunted village and home to the Cheltenham racecourse, one of the country's top courses. The **Hall of Fame museum** *(☎ 513014; admission free; open 8.30am-5.30pm Mon-Fri)* is dedicated to its history.

Tickets for the National Hunt Festival, which takes place over four days in March, can be booked by calling ☎ 226226. Each day costs about £20.

Places to Stay
Although accommodations are plentiful, at festival time the chance of getting a room are about as good as picking seven winners in a row. If you're here for any of the festivals (particularly the racing), you'd better have booked long in advance.

Hostels The **YMCA** *(☎ 524024; e housing@cheltenhamymca.claranet.co.uk; 6 Victoria Walk; beds £16)* is in an elegant but run-down building close to the town centre. The beds are clean and tidy, and the rate includes breakfast.

University of Gloucestershire *(☎ 532774; e cgconferenceservices@chelt.ac.uk; beds £20)* also lets rooms at its three sites over the Easter and summer holidays.

B&Bs & Hotels The Montpellier area, just southwest of the town centre, is the best spot for good B&Bs.

Segrave *(☎ 523606; 7 Park Place; singles/doubles £18/35)* is a small B&B, set in a sturdy Regency property with secure parking.

Lonsdale House *(☎ 232379; Montpellier Dr; singles/doubles from £23/46)* is a pristine B&B set in a charming town house and has well-appointed rooms.

St Michael's Guest House *(☎ 513587; 4 Montpellier Dr; singles/doubles £28/45)* is smaller but equally popular, and has really comfortable rooms.

Number 91 *(☎ 579441; 91 Montpellier Terrace; singles/doubles from £28/50)*, where Wilson of the doomed 1912 Antarctic expedition was born (see The Promenade section earlier), has beautifully furnished rooms.

Brennan Guest House *(☎ 525904; 21 St Luke's Rd; singles/doubles from £22/40)*, a friendly, centrally located place, has six rooms with shared bathroom.

Lypiatt House *(☎ 224994, fax 224996; Lypiatt Rd; singles/doubles from £58/68)* is a pretty extravagant Victorian villa with luxurious rooms.

Beaumont House Hotel *(☎ 245986, fax 520044; 56 Shurdington Rd; en-suite singles/doubles from £46/66)* has a couple of rooms with opulent four-poster beds for £87. The other rooms are fairly well-appointed too.

Hotel on the Park *(☎ 518898, fax 511526; e stay@hotelonthepark.co.uk; 38 Evesham Rd; singles/doubles from £88.50/126.50)* is a luxurious Regency hotel, between the town centre and Pittville Park, with a good restaurant and 12 well-appointed rooms.

The Queen's *(☎ 0870 400 8107, fax 224145; e queens@heritage-hotels.co.uk; The Promenade; singles/doubles from £110/130)* is a gracious Victorian place where some rooms have fine views across the Imperial Gardens. Edward VII, Elgar and Arthur Conan Doyle all stayed here. The restaurant (see Places to Eat, following) is excellent.

Places to Eat
There's some fine dining to be had in Cheltenham.

Le Sacré Fleur *(☎ 525230; The Promenade; mains around £12)* is a small, slick French restaurant with a carefully prepared menu of classic French dishes.

Le Petit Blanc *(☎ 266800; The Queen's; 3-course meals £17)*, a not-so-poor-man's introduction to the sort of food the other half eat at Raymond Blanc's famed Manoir de Quatre Saisons in London, has fantastic entry level three-course meals but hearty eaters will not find the portions up to the presentation.

Murasaki *(☎ 227757; 8 The Courtyard; 2-course lunch £9.95, dinner mains around £13)* is a tastefully decorated Japanese restaurant with excellent sushi.

Pirandello (☎ 234599; 103 The Promenade; mains around £13) is a popular Italian restaurant with good, solid cooking.

Jim Thompson's (☎ 246060; 40 Clarence St; sandwiches £5, mains £8), a theme bar and restaurant, has Arabic lattice-work and flaming torches outside. The menu is mostly Asian fusion, even though it advertises itself as (and looks like) a bazaar. Bizarre, more like it, but interesting nonetheless.

Le Café (1 Royal Well Rd; breakfast £2.50) is a cheap 'caff' behind the bus station.

Tiffins (☎ 222492; 4 The Promenade) is a popular place with moving and shaking locals, and offers a dazzling array of sandwiches to eat in or take away.

The Orange Tree (☎ 234232; 317 High St) is an inviting vegetarian restaurant. Axiom Centre for the Arts' (see Theatre & Music under Entertainment following) vegetarian café (☎ 253183) serves veggie shepherd's pie.

Entertainment

Pubs, Bars & Clubs A sophisticated café-bar, **Casa** (Montpellier Walk) is where some of Cheltenham's bright, young things like to gather. **Squeeze Bar** (☎ 573666; 21 The Courtyard) is another trendy bar with a pumping, commercial soundtrack.

The Fish & Fiddle is a funky little place just off The Promenade; on Friday nights there's drum 'n' bass and hip-hop; Saturday night it's funk, soul and jazz.

Belgian Monk (Clarence St) has an excellent array of strong stuff for those more worried about beer than atmosphere.

Rotunda Tavern (Montpellier Walk) is more like the pub visitors expect from England. One last place worth a stop is the **Frog & Fiddle** (High St) down at the architecturally challenged end of High St, an up-and-coming part of town.

Dedicated clubbers might find Cheltenham lacking, but **The Fez Club** (☎ 262925; 12-14 Bath Rd) was, at the time of writing, the most popular club in town, with queues down the block to get in.

Subtone (☎ 575925; 117 The Promenade) gets a steady crowd and draws occasional big-name DJs from London.

Theatre & Music The **Everyman Theatre** (☎ 572573; Regent St) stages anything from comedy and panto to Shakespeare. **Pittville Pump Room** often hosts classical music con-

certs, while the **Town Hall** (☎ 227979; Imperial Square) offers the more popular stuff. The **Axiom Centre for the Arts** (☎ 690243; 57 Winchcombe St) has a regular programme of less mainstream theatrical events and music.

Getting There & Away

Cheltenham is 100 miles (160km) from London, 43 miles (70km) from Oxford, 40 miles (65km) from Bristol and 9 miles (15km) from Gloucester.

Bus National Express runs buses between Cheltenham and London (£11, 2¾ hours), Oxford (£7.75, 1¼ hours) and all other places on the National Express network. Swanbrook Coaches also has buses to Oxford (£5, 1½ hours).

Buses to Gloucester run every 10 minutes (£1.10, 30 minutes), Monday to Saturday. There are buses every two hours to Cirencester (30 minutes).

Pulhams Coaches operates daily buses to Moreton (one hour) via Bourton and Stow. Castleways Coaches runs regularly between Cheltenham and Broadway (45 minutes) via Winchcombe, Monday to Saturday.

Train Cheltenham is on the Bristol to Birmingham line, with hourly trains to London (£37.50, 2½ hours), Bristol (£9.70, 45 minutes), Bath (£14.70, one hour), and regular departures for Gloucester (£2.50, 10 minutes).

Getting Around

Compass Holidays (☎ 250642) has bicycles for hire for £12 per day at Cheltenham train station.

TEWKESBURY

☎ 01684 • pop 9500

Tudor-heavy Tewkesbury is living proof that 16th-century architects didn't know how to draw a straight line, so the town is endowed with buckled timber-framed buildings that look like they can barely sustain their own weight. But they have done – for 500 years – and the town is made all the more attractive by the wonderful alleys and courts that separate the wonky buildings. Church St, Mill St and Mill Bank are particularly worth exploring.

The town's biggest draw, however, is the magnificent, medieval abbey church, which dominates the town just off Church St.

The **TIC** (☎ 295027; Barton St) is in the **museum** (Barton St; admission 75p). The **John Moore Countryside Museum** (☎ 297174; 41 Church St; adult/child £1/50p; open 10am-1pm & 2pm-5pm Tues-Sat Apr-Oct) features a natural history collection, basically a bunch of stuffed predators and rodents. It's named after local conservationist and writer John Moore, who in the 1930s wrote prophetically on the need for conservation before there was any sense of urgency about the matter. There's a small farmer's market from 7am to 4pm every second Saturday in a car park next to the abbey entrance.

Tewkesbury Abbey

The town's focal point is the church of the former Benedictine abbey (☎ 850959; admission £2 donation; open 9.30am-6pm daily), the last of the monasteries to be dissolved by Henry VIII. Stone to build it was brought by sea and river from Normandy in the 12th century. Tewkesbury's fortunes depended on the wool industry because the abbey owned land and sheep all over the Cotswolds. When the abbey was dissolved, the church survived because the townspeople bought it.

One of Britain's largest churches, with a 40m-high tower, it has some spectacular Norman pillars lining the nave, 14th-century stained glass above the choir and an organ dating from 1631. Don't miss the tombs of Edward, Baron Le Despenser, who fought at Poitiers in 1356, and John Wakeman, the last abbot, who is shown as a vermin-ridden skeleton.

On Saturday between June and September, the abbey hosts classical recitals. They begin at 7.30pm and cost £6.

A **visitors centre** (open 10am-4pm Mon-Sat) by the gate houses an exhibition on the abbey's history, and the Abbey Refectory, which does tea, coffee and lunches.

Places to Stay

The nicest places to stay are all near the abbey on Church St.

Crescent Guest House (☎ 293395; 30 Church St; beds per person £20) is pretty basic, with three small, clean rooms that all share a bathroom.

Two Back of Avon (☎ 298935; Riverside Walk; rooms per person from £22) is a tiny, family-run B&B with three beautifully appointed rooms. It is so small, however, that it feels more like a homestay.

Abbey Hotel (☎ 294247; 67 Church St; singles/doubles from £40/52) is a comfortable and spacious Tudor hotel that is slightly frayed around the edges.

Bell Hotel (☎ 293293, fax 295938; ensuite singles/doubles from £60/80) is a splendid Tudor hotel, with comfortable, elegant rooms.

Jessop House Hotel (☎ 292017; 65 Church St; singles/doubles £55/75) is in a Grade II listed building. The rooms are well appointed and there's a nice courtyard out the back.

Tudor House (☎ 297755, fax 290306; 51 High St; singles/doubles/suite £55/75/110) has a giveaway name, and indeed it is true to type: a wonderful hotel with a slightly dilapidated look but some fine rooms. The four-poster suite is particularly luxurious.

Places to Eat

My Great Grandfather's (☎ 292687; 85 Church St; mains around £8) is a homey restaurant and tearoom that is one of the most popular spots in town.

Abbey Tea Rooms (☎ 292215; 59 Church St; mains £5) is a charming Tudor tearoom that serves roasts.

Aubergine (☎ 292703; 73 Church St; starters £5, mains £7.50) is an elegant café with a world fusion menu – you'll find everything from salmon and dill fish cakes to Moroccan lamb tagine.

New World (☎ 292225; 61 High St; mains £6) is a superb Vietnamese restaurant run by a former resident of Hanoi – the food is very authentic and reasonably priced.

Royal Hop Pole (☎ 294517; 95 Church St; starters £4.95, mains £10.95-14.95), mentioned in Dickens' Pickwick Papers, is a popular pub, restaurant and **hotel** (singles/doubles £75/84). The food is none too imaginative, but very well prepared.

If you fancy a postprandial pint, try the incredibly old **Berkeley Arms** (Church St).

Getting There & Away

The easiest way to get to Tewkesbury is by bus No 41 from Clarence St in Cheltenham, which runs hourly.

You can also get from Cheltenham to Tewkesbury by train, but Ashchurch train station is about 3 miles (5km) out of town.

The Midlands

Fact: the Midlands is not top of the hit list of most visitors to Britain.

And that's what is so great about it. Stratford-upon-Avon and Warwick aside, the region boasts few big-name sights so, in general, doesn't suffer from the crowds that afflict the tourist magnets. It also has a reputation for consisting of dreary industrial settlements – one not entirely unfounded, as a trip up the M1 on a wet and windy day will confirm. The region has traditionally been England's manufacturing powerhouse, resulting in the development of some deeply unattractive towns. The end of the Industrial Revolution didn't mean a reversion to quaint cottages and rural idylls and, frequently, what the growth of industry didn't destroy, WWII bombing polished off.

Of course, each industrial centre has a hinterland, and the hinterlands of most Midlands towns are delightful. Ten miles outside Nottingham you can be winding through charming villages as pheasants flap off the road, while in Birmingham you can hop on a canal narrowboat and wend your way west along the peaceful arteries that once fed the industrial heart. The vibrant centres of population – Birmingham, Nottingham and Leicester – also offer some of the best restaurants and nightlife in the country, making them ideal bases for exploring the region.

The southern Midlands boasts two of England's most popular tourist sites: Warwick Castle, one of the finest medieval buildings in England, and Stratford-upon-Avon, a place of pilgrimage for Shakespeare lovers from around the world.

In contrast, the northern Midlands is often dismissed as England's industrial backyard. This is where the working-class did their working before industrial decline; there's a wide gap in living standards between northern cities such as Stoke and those south of Birmingham. However, tucked away amid the urban sprawl of the northern reaches are rambling Cannock Chase and part of the Peak District National Park, with endless opportunities for walking, cycling and other outdoor activities in some of the wildest countryside around.

So there's a mini north-south divide here, and east-west, too: talk football and you'll

Highlights

- Visiting the Bard's den in Stratford-upon-Avon
- Mixing it up in the bars and clubs of Nottingham
- Reliving medieval days at Warwick Castle
- Going underground among stalactites and gemstones in the 'showcaves' of Buxton and Castleton
- Feeling stately in the grand houses of Chatsworth and Keddleston
- Walking, cycling or climbing in the great outdoor playground of the Peak District

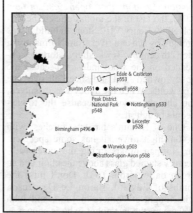

Edale & Castleton p553
Buxton p551 ● ● Bakewell p558
Peak District National Park p548
● Nottingham p533
Birmingham p496 ●
● Leicester p528
● Warwick p503
●Stratford-upon-Avon p508

hear forlorn tales of the former dominance of Leicester City and Nottingham Forest (east Midlands), while Birmingham and West Bromwich Albion (west) are joyfully back in the top flight. This is important stuff in these parts.

A trip to the Midlands isn't really about a castle or a museum or a mountain. It's a window onto the unique, proud and enduring character of each town or region you visit.

ORIENTATION & INFORMATION

It's perhaps appropriate that it's easiest to orientate yourself here by motorways. The M1 winds north from London, demarking the eastern third of the region (which is bounded to the east by the A1) and running parallel with a line of the east Midlands'

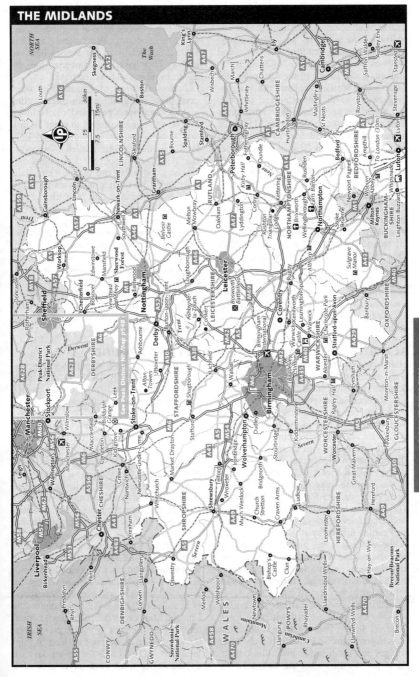

THE MIDLANDS

major towns: Bedford, Northampton, Leicester, Derby and Nottingham, in that order. The M40 does the same for the south and west Midlands, passing Stratford-upon-Avon and Warwick on its way to the M42 and Birmingham, in the middle of the region. Routes spider out from Birmingham, the M6 running east towards Coventry and the M1, and northwest up towards Wolverhampton, Stafford and Stoke-on-Trent; the M54 splits off at Wolves to head over to Telford and Shrewsbury. The Peak District is midway between M1 and M6.

Centralised tourist information for the region (plus southwest to Gloucestershire, Herefordshire and Worcestershire, and up to Lincolnshire) is provided by the **Heart of England Tourist Board** (☎ *01905-761100;* **w** *www.visitheartofengland.com*); it offers information on places that we just couldn't squeeze in, and is a good place to start your planning.

Note that, unless otherwise stated, admission prices given are per adult/child. Other concessionary rates (seniors, students, group discounts) often apply – it's always worth asking.

ACTIVITIES

Many parts of the Midlands are predominantly urban, and the opportunities for outdoor activities are limited among the factories and streets. But elsewhere in the region, conditions are good, and the **Peak District National Park** is one of the finest areas in Britain for walking and cycling – more details are given in the introduction to the Peak District section later in this chapter.

The Peak District is also home to the start of the **Pennine Way** national trail, which leads keen walkers for 260 miles through Yorkshire and Northumberland into Scotland. Under development, but open in places, the **Pennine Bridleway**, runs roughly parallel to the walking route, and is designed for horse riding and off-road cycling. But these long-distance epics are the tip of the iceberg; the Peak District is criss-crossed with a vast network of paths for walkers, country lanes for touring cyclists, and tracks and bridleways for mountain bikers – with something for every level of ability, from mile-eating rides to gentle strolls. Ideal bases include the villages and small towns of Matlock Bath, Edale and Castleton, or the national park

centre at Fairholmes on the Derwent Reservoirs. Bikes can be hired at Fairholmes, and at various other points around the Peak District, especially in the areas where old railway lines have been converted into delightful walking and cycling tracks.

In the south of the Midlands region, other good places for gentle walking and cycling include **Cannock Chase** and the **National Forest**, an ongoing project to plant 30 million trees across this part of central England. The main centre (called Conkers) is near Ashby-de-la-Zouch in Leicestershire.

Also good is **Rutland Water**, a large lake surrounded by cycling and walking trails, with an information and bike hire centre. This is also a great place for water sports such as sailing and windsurfing.

More information is given in the Activities chapter and some suggestions for shorter walks or cycle rides are given throughout this chapter. Regional tourism websites all contain walking and cycling information, and Tourist Information Centres (TICs) stock leaflets (free) plus maps and guides (usually £1 to £5) covering walking, cycling and other activities.

GETTING AROUND

For information on transport, see the individual county entries. The SCB travel guide (**w** *www.scbeastmidstravel.co.uk*), which displays many bus timetables, is useful.

National Express (☎ *08705 808080;* **w** *www.gobycoach.com*) has extensive coach services in the Midlands; Birmingham is a major hub.

Stagecoach (☎ *01788-535555*) sells Explorer tickets (£5.99) allowing a day's bus travel around the south Midlands area (including Birmingham, Coventry, Kenilworth, Leamington, Northampton, Stratford-upon-Avon and Warwick) and to places further afield.

Day Ranger tickets cover train travel after 9am weekdays, all day Saturday and Sunday: in the west Midlands (adult/child £12.50/6.25) in a triangle formed by Northampton, Stoke and Hereford, and over to Shrewsbury; or in the east Midlands (£20/10) bounded by Lincoln, Matlock, Crewe, Nuneaton, Leicester and Peterborough. If you're going to be travelling a lot, check out the Heart of England Rover (£64/42.25 for seven days, or £49/32.35 for three days travel in seven), with the same validity. See w www.national rail.co.uk for details. There's a 34% discount for railcard holders.

For the more remote, rural areas where buses are few and far between, having your own wheels can save you hours or days. There are plenty of car hire companies in the area, most charging from around £30 per day for a small vehicle. At **EasyCar** (☎ 0906 333 3333; w www.easycar.co.uk; Horse Fair Car Park, Bristol St, Birmingham) you can book cars online costing from as little as £7 per day – obviously you have to book well in advance to get this price.

Birmingham

☎ 0121 • pop 966,000 • elevation 134m

Ah, radiant Birmingham! England's second-largest city has been slighted so often and so widely that a visit should be mandatory just to dispel any residual prejudice. Its reputation for being aesthetically challenged, once largely justified, is being reversed by some cutting-edge developments, and there are still some older cultural and architectural joys to be unearthed in and around the place. Retaining much manufacturing industry, it never lost its fierce pride and, once again, the bounce is back in the city, with stylish shops, excellent restaurants and some of the country's best bars and clubs to delight residents and visitors alike. It's as if the city has wearied of trying to prove its detractors wrong and is simply out to enjoy itself.

One of the great centres of the Industrial Revolution, Birmingham was home to inventors such as steam pioneers James Watt (1736–1819) and Matthew Boulton (1728–1809), and chemist Joseph Priestley (1733–1804). By the mid-19th century, though, the 'workshop of the world' exemplified everything that was bad about industrial development. Under enlightened mayors such as Joseph Chamberlain (1836–1914) the city became a trendsetter in civic regeneration, but WWII air raids undid their good work and post-war town planners completed the vandalism by designing the ring roads and motorways that virtually obliterated the old city centre, bar a few gems. Fortunately, the likes of the award-winning Brindleyplace, the Mailbox and Millennium Point are revitalising hitherto disastrously unwelcoming areas.

The Birmingham accent is consistently rated England's most unattractive. Colloquially, the city is known as Brum, the inhabitants as Brummies and the dialect as Brummie.

Orientation

The endless ring roads, roundabouts and underpasses make Birmingham a confusing city to navigate, particularly for motorists.

The city centre is the pedestrian precinct in front of the huge Council House. Head west from here to Centenary Square, the International Convention Centre and Symphony Hall, and the development at Gas St Basin and Brindleyplace.

Southeast of the Council House, most of Birmingham's shops can be found along pedestrianised New St and in the modern City Plaza, Pallasades and Pavilions shopping centres; the latter is overlooked by the landmark Rotunda office block.

After dark the underpasses linking New St station with Digbeth coach station can seem alarming, especially for lone women.

The good news is that work is currently under way to redevelop the ghastly Bull Ring into a new shopping and leisure area, due for completion in late 2003 (for details, see w www.bullring.co.uk). In the meantime, the locale around what was St Martin's Circus remains a colossal building site with tricky road diversions: motorists beware.

Information

The central **TIC** (☎ 643 2514, fax 616 1038; w www.birmingham.org.uk; 2 City Arcade; open 9.30am-5.30pm Mon-Sat) is the most useful, although there's a second **TIC** (☎ 780 4321, fax 780 4260; e piazza@marketing birmingham.com; open 9am-5.15pm Mon-Fri) in the National Exhibition Centre, midway between Birmingham and Coventry and near Birmingham airport.

Museum enthusiasts should check w www .bmag.org.uk, providing information on most of the city's museums and galleries, including opening hours, admission costs and forthcoming exhibitions.

Various free magazines litter hotel lobbies, bars and restaurants, providing handy updates on current exhibitions, the best eateries and the hippest bars and clubs. Pick of the bunch is probably the fortnightly What's On (free at the TIC, elsewhere 80p).

THE MIDLANDS

BIRMINGHAM

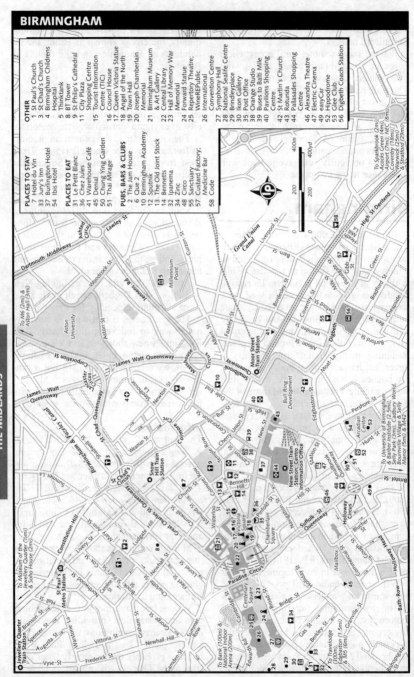

PLACES TO STAY
7   Hotel du Vin
33 Jury's Inn
37 Burlington Hotel
54 Ibis Hotel

PLACES TO EAT
31 Le Petit Blanc
36 Chez Jules
41 Warehouse Café
45 Denial
50 Chung Ying Garden
51 Thai Mirage

PUBS, BARS & CLUBS
2   The Jam House
6   Que 2
10 Birmingham Academy
12 Sputnik
13 The Old Joint Stock
14 Bennetts
32 Ipanema
34 Zinc
48 Circo
55 Sanctuary
57 Custard Factory;
    Medicine Bar
58 Code

OTHER
1   St Paul's Church
3   St Chad's Church
4   Jury's Church
5   Birmingham Childrens
    Hospital
5   Thinktank
8   BT Tower
9   St Philip's Cathedral
11 City Plaza
    Shopping Centre
15 Tourist Information
    Centre (TIC)
16 Council House
17 Queen Victoria Statue
18 Angel of the North
19 Town Hall
20 Joseph Chamberlain
    Memorial
21 Birmingham Museum
    & Art Gallery
22 Central Library
23 Hall of Memory War
    Memorial
24 Forward Statue
25 Repertory Theatre;
    WineREPublic
26 International
    Convention Centre
27 Symphony Hall
28 National Sealife Centre
29 Brindleyplace
30 Ikon Gallery
35 Post Office
38 Orange Studio
39 Buses to Balti Mile
40 Pavilions Shopping
    Centre
42 St Martin's Church
43 Rotunda
44 Pallasades Shopping
    Centre
46 Alexandra Theatre
47 Electric Cinema
49 easyCar
52 Hippodrome
53 Glee Club
56 Digbeth Coach Station

Orange Studio (☎ *0800 790 0909;* w *www .orangestudio.co.uk; 7 Cannon St; open 8.30am-6.30pm Mon-Fri, 10am-6.30pm Sat)* is a hip Internet café off New St charging £3 per hour, and it has DJs upstairs.

Town Centre
The central pedestrian precinct of Victoria and Chamberlain Squares features a statue of Queen Victoria, a fountain, a memorial to Joseph Chamberlain and some of Birmingham's most eye-catching architecture. The imposing **Council House** forms the north-eastern face of the precinct. The precinct's northwestern corner is formed by the modernist Central Library, reminiscent of an inverted ziggurat, with the Paradise Forum shop and café complex next to it.

To the south stands the **Town Hall**, designed by Joseph Hansom (creator of the hansom cab, forerunner to London's black taxis) in 1834 to look like the Temple of Castor and Pollux in Rome. For those who won't make it to Gateshead to see Antony Gormley's *Angel of the North* statue (see Newcastle-upon-Tyne in the Northeast England chapter), his wingless *Iron Man* (1993), on Victoria Square, is a step in the same direction.

West of the precinct, Centenary Square is another pedestrian square closed off at the western end by the International Convention Centre and the Symphony Hall, and overlooked by the Repertory Theatre. In the centre is the **Hall of Memory War Memorial** and a monolithic, Soviet-style statue titled *Forward*, depicting Brummie workers.

Birmingham Museum & Art Gallery
This impressive building (☎ *303 2834; Chamberlain Square; admission free; open 10am-5pm Mon-Thur & Sat, 10.30am-5pm Fri, 12.30pm-5pm Sun)* houses displays of local and natural history, fine archaeology and ethnography exhibits, and a renowned collection of Pre-Raphaelite paintings (see the boxed text 'The Pre-Raphaelites & the Arts and Crafts Movement' following). Other highlights include works by Degas, Braque, Renoir and Canaletto. The charming Edwardian tearoom is worth a stop for cake and coffee, too.

St Philip's Cathedral
England's smallest cathedral, St Philip's (☎ *236 4333; Colmore Row; donations requested; open 7am-7pm Mon-Fri, 9am-5pm Sat & Sun)* was built in neoclassical style between 1709 and 1715. The Pre-Raphaelite artist Edward Burne-Jones was responsible for the magnificent stained-glass windows: the *Last Judgement* at the western end, the *Nativity, Crucifixion* and *Ascension* at the eastern end.

Brindleyplace & The Mailbox
Birmingham sits on the hub of England's canal network (the city has more canals than

---

The Pre-Raphaelites & the Arts and Crafts Movement

The Pre-Raphaelite Brotherhood was formed in 1848 by three young British artists: Dante Gabriel Rossetti, William Holman Hunt and John Everett Millais. Four other artists soon joined them in their rejection of contemporary English art in favour of the directness of art prior to the High Renaissance, especially the work preceding that of Raphael.

Often unashamedly romantic in its view of the past, their work was characterised by almost photographic attention to detail, a combination of hyper-realism and brilliant colours; the themes and methods attracted criticism at the time, but ensured the movement's popularity to this day.

Birmingham Museum & Art Gallery has one of the best collections of works by the Pre-Raphaelites. If you get the bug, there are more fine paintings in the Lady Lever Art Gallery at Port Sunlight near Liverpool.

The Arts and Crafts movement followed Pre-Raphaelitism in yearning for a pure, idealised mode. The socialist William Morris, the movement's leading light, was a close friend of Pre-Raphaelite Edward Burne-Jones and projected the same ideals into tapestries, jewellery, stained glass and textile prints, following the principles of medieval guilds, in which the same artists designed and produced the work. Cheltenham Art Gallery & Museum has a fine display of Arts and Crafts furniture, as does Arlington Mill in Bibury, Gloucestershire. Those passing through Birmingham must call on Wightwick Manor, an Arts and Crafts masterpiece complete with original William Morris wallpaper and fabrics.

Venice) and visiting narrow boats can moor in the Gas St Basin right in the heart of the city.

During the 1990s the creation of Brindleyplace, a waterfront development of trendy shops, restaurants and bars, transformed the area west of Centenary Square. A similar development to the southeast, the Mailbox, is rather more style-conscious, bristling with designer boutiques and sleek eateries.

The **National Sealife Centre** (☎ 633 4700; W www.sealife.co.uk; 3a Brindleyplace; adult/child £8.50/6; open 10am-5pm daily), a state-of-the-art facility designed by Sir Norman Foster, is the largest inland aquarium in England, with more marine creatures than you could imagine. The otter sanctuary is a particular favourite with kids.

The **Ikon Gallery** (☎ 248 0708; W www .ikon-gallery.co.uk; 1 Oozells Square, Brindleyplace; admission free; open 11am-6pm Tues-Sun) features changing exhibitions of modern art, sometimes impressive, often utter nonsense, depending on one's taste. There is also a lively little tapas-centric café.

Jewellery Quarter

Birmingham is a major jewellery manufacturing centre and the Jewellery Quarter is packed with manufacturers and showrooms. The TIC provides a free guide to the area, which includes plenty of information about the industry and details of two walking trails around the district.

In the **Museum of the Jewellery Quarter** (☎ 554 3598; 75-79 Vyse St; adult/child £2.50/2; open 10am-4pm Mon-Fri, 11am-5pm Sat), the Smith & Pepper jewellery factory is preserved as it was on the day it closed in 1981 after 80 years of operation. You can explore the history of jewellery-making in Birmingham since the Middle Ages and watch demonstrations of the art.

The Jewellery Quarter is about three quarters of a mile (1km) northwest of the centre; catch one of a host of buses (No 101 is the easiest), or take the metro from Snow Hill or the train from Moor St to Jewellery Quarter station.

Millennium Point & Thinktank

East of the centre, the Millennium Point development is promoted as a purveyor of technology for the people. The focal point is Thinktank (☎ 202 2222; W www.thinktank.ac; Curzon St; adult/child £6.50/4.50; open 10am-

5pm Sat-Thur), a substantial and ambitious attempt to make science accessible (primarily to kids), with varying degrees of success. Interactive displays cover topics such as the body and medicine, wildlife, future technology and industrial history. There's also Birmingham's first **Imax cinema** (☎ 202 2222; W www.imax.ac; adult/child £6/4) with a five storey–high screen.

Soho House

The industrialist Matthew Boulton lived in Soho House (☎ 554 9122; Soho Ave, Handsworth; adult/child £2.50/2; open 10am-5pm Tues-Sat, noon-5pm Sun) from 1766 to 1809. It has been painstakingly restored to reflect the styles of Boulton's era, and features displays on the life and associates of the great man, including James Watt. Soho House is walking distance from the Jewellery Quarter; bus Nos 74, 78 and 79 pass near by, or take the metro to Benson Rd station from Snow Hill.

Barber Institute of Fine Arts

A visit to the Barber Institute (☎ 414 7333; admission free; open 10am-5pm Mon-Sat, 2pm-5pm Sun) is, for art lovers, the highlight of a visit to Birmingham. The collection takes in Renaissance masterpieces, paintings by old masters such as Rubens and Van Dyck, British greats including Gainsborough, Reynolds and Turner, an array of impressionist pieces and modern classics by the likes of Picasso and Schiele.

The Barber Institute is at the University of Birmingham, 2½ miles (4km) south of the city centre. Take bus No 61, 62 or 63, or the train from New St to University station.

Aston Hall

Built between 1618 and 1635, this Jacobean mansion (☎ 327 0062; Trinity Rd, Aston; admission free; open 2pm-5pm daily Easter-Oct) boasts some impressive friezes and ceilings, and houses fine vintage furniture, paintings and textiles from the Birmingham Museum's collections. It's about 3 miles (5km) north of the city centre. Get there on bus No 65 or 104, or take a train to Aston station from New St.

Organised Tours

Canal boat trips are operated by **Second City Canal Cruises** (☎ 236 9811) costing adult/

child £3/2 and **Sherborne Wharf** (☎ 455 6163; **w** www.sherbornewharf.co.uk) who charge £4.25/3.25. The TIC provides two helpful leaflets on the city's canals for those wishing to explore in a bit more depth.

Places to Stay

Birmingham has no hostels. Central hotels court business visitors and usually reduce prices at the weekend: ask at the TIC, which also makes accommodation bookings.

Few B&Bs are central, but many are within a 3-mile radius of the centre. Acocks Green (to the southeast) and the area stretching from Edgbaston to Selly Oak are popular areas.

Ashdale House Hotel (☎ 706 3598, fax 707 2324; **w** www.ashdalehouse.co.uk; 39 Broad Rd, Acocks Green; B&B en-suite/shared singles £28/20, doubles £48/40) is a friendly place in a Victorian house overlooking a park.

Awentsbury Hotel (☎/fax 472 1258; **e** ian@awentsbury.com; 21 Serpentine Rd, Selly Park; singles/doubles from £36/50) is a peaceful B&B in a detached Victorian house close to the university.

Ibis Hotel (☎ 622 6010, fax 622 6020; Arcadian Centre, Ladywell Walk; doubles Mon-Thur/Fri-Sun £45/35), a bland but good-value chain hotel, is next to Chinatown and eateries aplenty.

There's more of the same at **Travelodge** (☎ 191 4564; 230 Broad St; doubles Mon-Thur/Fri-Sun £52.95/49.95), ideally placed for exploring Brindleyplace's nightlife.

Jurys Inn (☎ 606 9000, fax 606 9001; **e** jurysinn_birmingham@jurysdoyle.com; 245 Broad St; doubles £99), also near Brindleyplace, has plush rooms; weekend discounts are sometimes available.

Burlington Hotel (☎ 643 9191, fax 628 5005; **e** mail@burlingtonhotel.com; Burlington Arcade, 126 New St; singles/doubles Sun-Thur £145/155, Fri & Sat £77/97) is grand and classy, one of the best of the central options.

Hotel du Vin (☎ 236 0559, fax 236 0889; **e** info@birmingham.hotelduvin.com; Church St; doubles/suites from £110/175) is the sleekest boutique hotel in town, with a fine bistro, a health spa, a humidor and an amazing cave du vin (wine cellar).

Places to Eat

Birmingham's contribution to cuisine is the balti, a Pakistani dish that has been adopted by curry houses across the country. The heartland is the Birmingham Balti Triangle in Sparkbrook, 2 miles (3km) south of the centre. Pick up a complete listings leaflet in the TIC (or see **w** www.thebaltiguide.com) and head out on bus No 4, 5 or 6 from Corporation St. One of the best is **Al Frash** (☎ 753 3120; 186 Ladypool Rd; mains £3-8; open 5pm-midnight Sun-Thur, 5pm-1am Fri & Sat), winning awards for its baltis and with more tasteful decor than the average.

Back in the centre, **Warehouse Café** (☎ 633 0261; 54-57 Allison St, Digbeth; mains £3-6; open noon-2.30pm Mon-Fri, noon-3pm Sat), a great choice for a vegan or vegetarian lunch, has speciality Irish and jazz nights.

Chez Jules (☎ 633 4664, fax 633 4669; 5a Ethel St; mains £8.50-13, 2-course lunch £5.90) is a refreshingly unpretentious faux-rustic French place with decent regional standards.

The area around the Arcadian Centre (a kind of mini-Brindleyplace with trendy bars and restaurants) just south of New St is Birmingham's Chinatown.

Chung Ying Garden (☎ 666 6622; 17 Thorpe St; mains £7.50-13) cooks up excellent Cantonese cuisine, wheeling out 70 varieties of dim sum.

Thai Mirage (☎ 622 2287; 41-43 Hurst St; mains £5-20) has an extensive menu of Thai classics and a refined interior.

Brindleyplace offers wall-to-wall eateries, with many of the big chains represented and a couple of special places.

Bank (☎ 633 4466; 4 Brindleyplace; 3-course pre-concert meal £12.50, mains £9.50-20) has a sophisticated atmosphere and draws the punters with mod-Brit dishes.

Le Petit Blanc (☎ 633 7333; 9 Brindleyplace; 2-course/3-course set menu £12.50/15.50, mains £8.50-15.75) offers a taste of Raymond Blanc's cuisine, with traditional Francophile favourites such as foie gras, and a substantial wine list.

Nearby **wineREPublic** (☎ 644 6464; **e** wine-republic@necgroup.co.uk; Centenary Square; bar menu £4-7, mains £8-14; closed Sun), the Rep theatre's restaurant, is bright, sharp and airy, and the food comes in for plenty of praise.

The Mailbox also offers a range of up-market options.

Denial (☎ 643 3080; 120-122 Wharfside St; mains lunch/dinner £8.50/14.95; lunch only Sun) is a sleek, highly rated canalside

THE MIDLANDS

eatery serving up modern British cuisine with a Mediterranean slant.

Entertainment

As with the eating scene, the world of drinking, dancing, and culture-dunking is massive and constantly changing. Keep an eye on the magazines and flyers in bars for the latest news.

Pubs, Bars & Clubs Chain bars are the norm here; finding an honest-to-god 'pub' in the centre is tricky, but there are many bars worth checking out, including two impressive banks-turned-boozers.

Bennetts (☎ 643 9293; 8 Bennetts Hill) is a massive space, like the interior of a regency hall; there's a mellow 'library' area if the grand surroundings get too much.

The Old Joint Stock (☎ 200 1892; 4 Temple Row West) serves up fine Fuller's ales in an awesome venue with gilt mouldings and a glass-domed ceiling.

Sputnik (☎ 643 7510; Upper Temple St) has that grungy feel licked: a basement bar displaying B-movie posters and surprisingly varied tunes (reggae, drum'n'bass, funk and house), plus good beers and a friendly vibe.

The dividing line between restaurant, bar and club is blurred. Many eateries become popular watering-holes at night, while bars welcome DJs and get the punters pogoing.

Circo (☎ 643 1400; 6 Holloway Circus) is a cool café-bar with DJs and stomach-lining tapas if required.

Zinc (☎ 200 0620; Regency Wharf, Gas St Basin; open 10am-midnight Mon-Thur, to 2am Fri & Sat, to 10.30pm Sun) is a Conran bar-diner; there's an enticing menu, and the cool, relaxed space lends itself to chilling to the jazz and funk soundtrack.

The **Custard Factory** on Gibb St in Digbeth is a remarkable and expanding arts and media centre that is taking the city by storm; it houses a gallery, recording studios, and dance and theatre spaces. (The name? The building was constructed a century ago by custard magnate Sir Alfred Bird).

Medicine Bar (☎ 693 6001) is the night hotspot of the Custard Factory, where the hip and the curious drink till late to the sounds of the region's upcoming DJs.

Ipanema (☎ 643 5577; 9 Brindleyplace) doles out tapas, a mellow vibe, guest DJs and the chance to brush up on your salsa skills.

Code (☎ 665 6333; W www.code-europe .co.uk; Heath Mill Lane, Digbeth) is currently the club most likely. The Godskitchen night features biggies such as Fatboy Slim, Paul Oakenfold and Carl Cox.

Sanctuary (☎ 246 1010; 78 Digbeth High St) is a sizable club proper with drum'n'bass a speciality.

Que 2 (☎ 212 0550; 212 Corporation St) is an incredible venue housed in a former Methodist church. Club nights such as Prosession and Sundissential inspire a religious following.

Glee Club (☎ 0870 241 5093; Hurst St) hosts stand-up comedians several nights a week.

Music Ultramodern **Symphony Hall** (☎ 780 3333; Broad St) hosts performances by the City of Birmingham Symphony Orchestra and other classical and pop shows.

National Exhibition Centre Arena (☎ 909 4133), out by Birmingham international airport, hosts major rock and pop acts, as does its sister venue, the **National Indoor Arena** (☎ 909 4144; King Edwards Rd) behind Brindleyplace.

The Jam House (☎ 200 3030; W www.the jamhouse.com; 1 St Paul's Square) is a classy music bar featuring live swing, jazz, r'n'b and rock and roll; admission charges apply some nights.

Birmingham Academy (☎ 262 3000; W www.birmingham-academy.co.uk; 52-54 Dale End) is the best rock-and-pop venue. Acts that don't gig in Birmingham usually play **Civic Hall & Wulfrun** in Wolverhampton (see the following Around Birmingham section).

Theatre & Cinema Theatres include the **Hippodrome** (☎ 0870 730 1234; W www .birmingham-hippodrome.co.uk; Hurst St), hosting the Birmingham Royal Ballet as well as musicals; the **Alexandra Theatre** (☎ 0870 607 7533; Station St), offering everything from Puccini to panto; and the **Birmingham Repertory Theatre** (The Rep; ☎ 236 4455; W www.birmingham-rep.co.uk; Centenary Square, Broad St), with serious drama and new plays straight from London's best theatres.

Electric Cinema (☎ 643 7277; W www .electricbirmingham.co.uk; Station St; members/nonmembers £3.50/4.50) is the city's art-house cinema, often showing cult movies.

Getting There & Away

Air Birmingham has an increasingly busy international airport (☎ 767 5511; W www .bhx.co.uk) with flights to numerous European destinations and New York. It's on the outskirts of Birmingham, about 7 miles (11km) east of the centre.

Bus National Express runs coaches between dreary Digbeth coach station and destinations around Britain including London (£17 economy return, 2¾ hours, hourly), Oxford (£11.75, 1½ hours, five daily) and Manchester (£13, 2½ hours, 11 daily). Bus X20 runs to Stratford-upon-Avon (£3.40/4.05 single/return, 1¼ hours, hourly Monday to Saturday, eight on Sunday).

Train New St station is beneath the Pallasades shopping centre. Trains to Birmingham international station serve both the National Exhibition Centre and Birmingham airport.

Most national trains run from New St, including those to/from London (£22 three-day advance return, 1¾ hours, every 30 minutes), Oxford (£22.10 saver return, 1½ hours, hourly), Bristol (£32.30 saver return, 1½ hours, hourly), Manchester (£24.70 saver return, 1¾ hours, every 30 minutes) and Edinburgh (£78.50 saver return, 4¾ hours, roughly hourly). Some services, such as those to Stratford-upon-Avon (£4.80 single, 50 minutes, hourly), run from Snow Hill and Moor St stations.

In July and August, the **Shakespeare Express** steam train (☎ 707 4696; W www. vintagetrains.co.uk; adult/child single £10/3, return £15/5) operates between Birmingham Snow Hill and Stratford-upon-Avon twice each Sunday. Journeys take one hour.

Metro Birmingham's tram system (the Metro; W www.travelmetro.co.uk) runs from Snow Hill to Wolverhampton via the Jewellery Quarter, West Bromwich and Dudley. Fares start at 60p and rise to £1.80 for the full length. A day pass costs £3.50.

Getting Around

Bus No 900 runs to the airport (£1.35, 45 minutes, every 20 minutes). Trains for the airport run between New St and Birmingham international station (£2.45, 45 minutes, every 10 minutes). A taxi (☎ 782 3744) from the airport to the centre costs about £16.

Centro (☎ 200 2700; W www.centro.org.uk), the transport authority for the Birmingham and Coventry area, provides general travel advice and a comprehensive guide to getting around the west Midlands for those with mobility difficulties. The Daytripper ticket (£4/2.45) gives all-day travel on buses and trains after 9.30am; if you need to start earlier, buy a Centrocard (£5).

Local trains operate from Moor St station, which is only a few minutes' walk from New St: follow the red line on the pavement.

AROUND BIRMINGHAM
Cadbury World & Bournville Village

Chocoholics head for **Cadbury World** (☎ 0121 451 4159; W www.cadburyworld .co.uk; adult/child £8.50/6.40), off Linden Rd, a lip-smacking exploration into the production, marketing and (naturally) consumption of chocolate, with interactive gizmos and plenty to keep kids entertained. Not surprisingly, you must book ahead by phone. Opening hours are complicated; it's closed for much of December and January and open from 10am to 3pm or 10am to 4pm for most of the rest of the year (phone or check the website for details).

Cadbury World is part of pretty Bournville village, designed for early 20th-century factory workers by the Cadbury family; large houses, each unique, are set around a green. **Selly Manor** (☎ 0121 472 0199; Maple Rd; adult/child £2/50p; open 10am-5pm Tues-Fri year round, 2pm-5pm Sat & Sun Apr-Sept only), dating from at least 1327, was carefully taken apart and reconstructed by George Cadbury when threatened with destruction; it now houses 18th-century furnishings and has a Tudor garden.

To get to Bournville take a train from Birmingham New St, or catch bus No 83, 84 or 85.

The Black Country

The industrial region west of Birmingham is known as the Black Country, a 19th-century epithet bestowed because of the smoke from its foundries and factories. Though it's been cleaned up, it's still not a tourist hotspot. **Walsall** has a worthy attraction in the **New Art Gallery** (☎ 01922-654400; Gallery Square; admission free; open 10am-5pm Tues-Sat, noon-5pm Sun), home

Running from the Republicans

Charles II (1630–85), England's merry monarch who 'never said a foolish thing, nor ever did a wise one', was almost captured by parliamentarians following his defeat at the Battle of Worcester in 1651. His father, Charles I, had already lost his head to the House of Commons, and Charles II, had he been captured, would likely have lost his too. However, he escaped to the Continent with help from supporters along the way and two of the houses that harboured him, Boscobel House, run by English Heritage (EH), and Moseley Old Hall, run by the National Trust (NT), are open to visitors.

Boscobel House (☎ 01902-850244; Brewood; admission £4.40; open 10am-6pm daily Mar-Sept, 10am-5pm daily Oct, 10am-4pm Wed-Sun Nov), a modest 17th-century timber-framed house, is home to the so-called Royal Oak, the tree up which Charles hid when parliamentarians searched the house. It is 8 miles (13km) northwest of Wolverhampton, over the border in Shropshire.

Moseley Old Hall (☎ 01902-782808; Fordhouses; admission £4.20; open 1pm-5pm Sat, Sun & Wed Apr-Oct) was a second house that saved the king and has a small priest-hole where Charles was able to hide. It is 4 miles (6km) north of Wolverhampton; take bus No 613 or 870–2.

After his escape, Charles II wandered Europe in exile for many years, scheming and plotting his return with help from Catholic monarchs. A settlement was eventually negotiated returning him as king in 1660. He ruled until 1685, a volatile monarch with a combative attitude towards parliament, unsurprising given the treatment of his father. During the last four years of his rule, parliament was dissolved.

to the eclectic Garman Ryan collection including works by Picasso, Rembrandt, Modigliani and Van Gogh.

Wolverhampton West of Birmingham, Wolverhampton's population of 258,000 has an accent unique even in the west Midlands: if you were having trouble understanding Brummies, you'll find things get harder here.

The **TIC** (☎ 01902-556110, fax 556111; w www.wolverhampton.gov.uk/tic; 18 Queen Square; open 9.30am-5.30pm Mon-Fri, 9.30am-1pm & 1.30pm-5pm Sat Apr-Sept, 10am-4pm Mon-Fri, 10am-1pm & 1.30pm-4pm Sat Oct-Mar) provides information on the area.

As well as **Wolverhampton Art Gallery** (☎ 01902-552055; Lichfield St; admission free; open 10am-5pm Mon-Sat), boasting fine collections of pop art and 18th- and 19th-century landscape paintings, Wolverhampton is home to **Wightwick Manor** (☎ 01902-761400; admission £5.60; open 1.30pm-5pm Thur & Sat Mar-Dec). Run by the National Trust (NT), it is an Arts-and-Crafts masterpiece, complete with original William Morris wallpaper and fabrics, Kempe glass and de Morgan tiling.

The **Civic Centre & Wulfrun** (☎ 01902-552121; w www.wolvescivic.co.uk; North St) are arguably the west Midlands' top venues for rock, pop and alternative bands. Check the website for upcoming gigs.

Black Country Living Museum This extensive, lively museum (☎ 0121 557 9643; w www.bclm.co.uk; Tipton Rd, Dudley; adult/child £8.25/4.75; open 10am-5pm daily Mar-Oct, 10am-4pm Wed-Sun Nov-Feb) features a coal mine, village and fairground, re-created as they would have been in the industrial heyday of the 19th century. It's a great place for a day out, with a full programme of mine trips, Charlie Chaplin films and opportunities to watch glass-cutters and sweet-makers in action.

To get there from Birmingham city centre, take the No 126 bus from Corporation St and ask to be let off at Tipton Rd. It's a 10-minute walk along Tipton Rd to the museum, or you can catch bus No 311 or 313. Alternatively, take the train from Birmingham New St to Tipton, 1 mile (1.5km) from the museum. A Daytripper ticket will cover the entire bus or train journey.

Warwickshire

History books, play-acting and castle-builders have made otherwise unremarkable Warwickshire home to two of England's biggest tourist attractions: Shakespeare's home at Stratford-upon-Avon and Warwick's superb castle. If you prefer your castles in pieces, head to Kenilworth; if more recent history's your bag, Coventry's modern cathedral and motor heritage will please. Elsewhere the county has plenty of museums, historic houses and gently pleasant countryside.

Orientation & Information

Warwickshire is roughly kidney shaped, with Coventry sitting between the lobes. Kenilworth, Leamington Spa and Warwick lie in the line running south from Coventry; Stratford-upon-Avon sits on the other side of the M40 motorway bisecting the southern lobe.

Much of the county lays claim to the title 'Shakespeare Country', and tourism is coordinated accordingly. Contact individual TICs, or check the website (**w** www.shakespeare-country.co.uk) for details. Stratford and Warwick are good bases for exploring.

Getting Around

The Warwickshire transport site (**w** www.warwickshire.gov.uk/transport) has details of local bus and train services, as well as news on roads. Coventry is a major transport hub with rail connections to London Euston, Birmingham New St and Leicester.

A good ticket option is the Shakespeare Country Explorer (one day £25/12.50, three days £30/15), which allows return train travel from London Marylebone or Paddington to Stratford, Warwick or Leamington Spa, plus unlimited travel between these towns for the duration of the ticket and discounted admission to attractions.

WARWICK

☎ 01926 • pop 22,500

Even without the massive inducement of its fine castle, the sedate county town has other historic buildings and a general air of gentility to make it an attractive destination.

Orientation & Information

Warwick is simple to navigate; the A429 runs right through the centre with Westgate at one end and Eastgate at the other. The old town centre lies just north of this axis, the castle just south.

The **TIC** (☎ 492212, fax 494837; **w** www.warwick-uk.co.uk; Court House, Jury St;

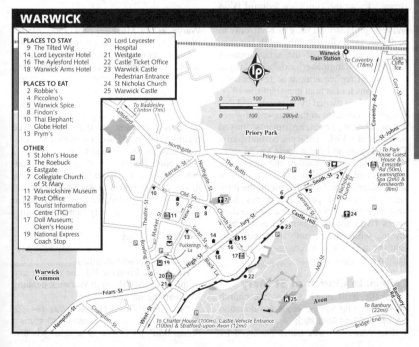

WARWICK

PLACES TO STAY
9 The Tilted Wig
14 Lord Leycester Hotel
16 The Aylesford Hotel
18 Warwick Arms Hotel

PLACES TO EAT
2 Robbie's
4 Piccolino's
5 Warwick Spice
8 Findon's
10 Thai Elephant;
   Globe Hotel
13 Prym's

OTHER
1 St John's House
3 The Roebuck
6 Eastgate
7 Collegiate Church
   of St Mary
11 Warwickshire Museum
12 Post Office
15 Tourist Information
   Centre (TIC)
17 Doll Museum;
   Oken's House
19 National Express
   Coach Stop
20 Lord Leycester
   Hospital
21 Westgate
22 Castle Ticket Office
23 Warwick Castle
   Pedestrian Entrance
24 St Nicholas Church
25 Warwick Castle

THE MIDLANDS

open 9.30am-4.30pm daily), near the junction with Castle St, sells the informative *Warwick Town Trail* leaflet (50p).

Warwick Castle

With its strategic position, Warwick has been the site of fortifications since the 10th century. Later, William the Conqueror ordered the construction of a wooden motte-and-bailey fort here in 1068, but the magnificent medieval castle (☎ 0870 442 2000; w www .warwick-castle.co.uk; adult/child £10.75/ 6.55 mid-Sept–Apr, £12.50/7.40 May–mid-Sept; open 10am-6pm daily Apr-Sept, 10am-5pm Oct-Mar) is largely the 14th-century work of Thomas de Beauchamp, with 17th- to 19th-century interior embellishments. Lancelot Capability Brown landscaped the splendid grounds in 1753. The result is one of the most substantial and impressive castles in England: be prepared to spend hours wandering and wondering (and, in summer, queuing; it's very popular).

One of the key characters in the castle's fluctuating fortunes was Warwick the King-maker, Richard Neville, the 16th earl (1428–71). Having replaced the ineffectual Henry VI with the king's son Edward IV in 1461, Neville then fell out with Edward IV and brought Henry VI back in 1470, only to be defeated and killed by Edward IV less than a year later. Much of the action centres around the 'Kingmaker' exhibition, using models and replica armour to re-create his preparations for his final great battle in 1471.

The castle is owned by Tussauds, and that influence is evident in the waxwork figures that populate the private apartments, arrayed as for a late 19th-century weekend party. The packaging and sheen doesn't in any way mask the highlights, though: the superb furnishings and sheer splendour of the interior are fascinating, and a walk around the ramparts rewards with panoramic views. Kids love the arrays of weighty armour, the dungeons (with torture chamber) and 'ghost tower', while the recently restored 19th-century mill house offers an insight into early power generation.

Collegiate Church of St Mary

Originally built in 1123, this fine church (☎ 403940; Old Square; requested donation £1; open 10am-6pm daily Apr-Oct, 10am-4.30pm Nov-Mar) was badly damaged by the so-called Great Fire of Warwick in 1694, and rebuilt in a mishmash of styles. The remarkable perpendicular Beauchamp Chapel (built 1442–60 at a cost of £2400, a huge sum for the time) survived the fire, and the magnificent bronze effigy of Richard Beauchamp, 13th earl of Warwick, graces the centre of the chapel. Richard 'Kingmaker' Neville is the sinister-looking figure on the corner of the tomb.

Don't miss the 12th-century crypt with remnants of a medieval dunking stool, used to drench scolding wives.

Lord Leycester Hospital

At the Westgate end of the town, the road cuts through a sandstone cliff above which perches the impressive Lord Leycester Hospital (☎ 491422; High St; adult/child £3.20/ 2.20, garden only £1.50; hospital open 10am-5pm Tues-Sun Apr-Sept, 10am-4pm Tues-Sun Oct-Mar), made an almshouse in 1571 by Robert Dudley, earl of Leicester and favourite of Queen Elizabeth I. Housed in a group of 14th-century timber-framed buildings, it has a beautiful courtyard, a fine chapel and a guildhall built by 'Kingmaker' Neville.

Museums

Warwickshire Museum (☎ 412500; Market Place; admission free; open 10am-5pm Tues-Sat year round, 11.30am-5pm Sun Apr-Sept), in the 17th-century market building, has displays on natural history and archaeology.

The **Doll Museum** (☎ 495546; Castle St; adult/child £1/75p; open 10am-5pm Tues-Sat, 11.30am-5pm Sun Apr-Sept, 10am-4pm Sat only Oct-Mar), in the half-timbered medieval Oken's House, contains a fine collection of early dolls and toys.

St John's House (☎ 412132; St John's; admission free; open 10am-5pm Tues-Sat year round, 2.30pm-5pm Sun Apr-Sept), a charming Jacobean mansion, features reconstructed Victorian rooms and a regimental museum.

Places to Stay

The nearest hostel is in Stratford-upon-Avon (see that section later).

B&Bs line Emscote Rd, the eastern end of the main road through Warwick heading for Leamington Spa.

Park House Guest House (☎/fax 494359; 17 Emscote Rd; en-suite doubles £40-45) is a decent B&B in a Gothic-looking town house.

The Tilted Wig (☎ 410466, fax 495740; e tiltedwig@tiscali.co.uk; 11 Market Place; en suite doubles £58) is a pleasant pub in the centre, with B&B, decent food and an outdoor area for summer dining.

Warwick Arms Hotel (☎ 492759, fax 410587; 17 High St; B&B en-suite singles/ doubles £55/65), an early 18th-century coaching inn, has the history and the comfort.

Lord Leycester Hotel (☎ 491481, fax 491561; e reception@lord-leycester.co.uk; 17 Jury St; en-suite singles/doubles from £55/70) has modern, comfortable rooms (some with four-poster beds). Downstairs is **Knights** restaurant, offering standard British fare, and a bar.

Charter House (☎ 496965, fax 411910; e penon@charterhouse8.freeserve.co.uk; 87-91 West St; en-suite singles/doubles from £56/ 80) is a small, outstanding B&B, with period rooms and four-poster beds.

The Aylesford Hotel (☎ 492799, fax 492817; e aylesford@freeuk.com; 1 High St; en-suite singles/doubles/four-posters £55/ 75/95), opposite the TIC, has great rooms, a bistro and a good medieval-styled cellar restaurant.

Places to Eat

Piccolino's (☎ 491020; 31 Smith St; pizza & pasta £5-7.50) is deservedly popular, with a real trattoria atmosphere and delicious seafood pasta.

Warwick Spice (☎ 491736; 24 Smith St; mains £4.50-10; evenings only) is a relaxed place serving up Indian and Bangladeshi dishes.

Thai Elephant (☎ 410688, fax 407170; 8 Theatre St; mains £7-10), in the Globe Hotel, has exuberant decor and northeastern Thai specialities.

Robbie's (☎ 400470; 74 Smith St; mains £13-15.50; open 7pm-late Tues-Sat) is a mellow, intimate spot, with Med-influenced flavours and jazz tunes.

Prym's (☎ 439504; 48 Brook St; mains £10-16; closed Sun dinner) looks like a café but serves up fine, game-heavy specialities such as guinea fowl and venison.

Smart and sophisticated **Findon's** (☎ 411755; 7 Old Square; lunch dishes £4.95, 2-course dinner £15.95) is arguably Warwick's top fine-dining option.

The Roebuck (☎ 494900; Smith St) plugs itself as an 'ale shrine'; it's a friendly, snug pub with a selection of good cask beers and photos of old Warwick.

Getting There & Away

National Express coaches operate from Puckerings Lane on Old Square; there are three coaches daily from London (£16.50 economy return, 2¾ hours). Local bus Nos X16 and X18 run to Coventry (£2.75/4.50 single/return, 55 minutes), Stratford-upon-Avon (£2.55/3.30, 20 minutes) and Leamington Spa (£1.45/2.45, 15 minutes) from Market Square (hourly Monday to Saturday, every two hours on Sunday).

Trains operate to Birmingham (£3.90 single, 30 minutes, every half-hour), Stratford-upon-Avon (£3.30 single, 20 minutes, hourly) and London (£23.20 saver return, 1½ hours, hourly).

AROUND WARWICK
Baddesley Clinton

Baddesley Clinton (NT; ☎ 01564-783294; admission £5.80, grounds only £2.90; house open 1.30pm-5pm Wed-Sun Mar, Apr Oct & Nov, 1.30pm-5.30pm Wed-Sun May-Sept), an enchanting 13th-century moated house, has hardly altered since the death of Squire Henry Ferrers in 1633 and boasts fine Elizabethan interiors. Three priest-holes demonstrate its role as a refuge for persecuted Catholics in the 16th century. Baddesley Clinton is 7½ miles northwest of Warwick, just off the A4141. Bus No 60 passes nearby travelling between Warwick and Solihull.

LEAMINGTON SPA
☎ 01926 • pop 57,000

Although not awash with attractions, central Leamington is attractive enough, with broad shopping streets and fine Regency architecture. It's a less-busy alternative to staying in Stratford or Warwick when exploring the area.

The **TIC** (☎ 742762, fax 742766; e leamington@shakespeare-country.co.uk; The Parade; open 9.30am-5pm Mon-Sat year round, 11am-4pm Sun Apr-Oct, 11am-3pm Oct-Mar) is in the Royal Pump Rooms and sells a handy Walk Around Leamington Spa guide (50p).

The Pump Rooms also house a **Museum & Art Gallery** (☎ 742700; w www.royal-pump-rooms.co.uk; admission free; open 10.30am-5pm Tues, Wed, Fri & Sat, 1.30pm-8pm Thur, 11am-4pm Sun) featuring a varied programme of exhibitions and a restored Victorian Turkish baths room.

Jephson Gardens, opposite the Pump Rooms, are being upgraded; historic buildings are being restored and there will be a new public greenhouse.

Places to Stay & Eat

There are several B&Bs on Avenue Rd near the station.

Charnwood Guest House (☎ 831074; 47 Avenue Rd; £20-25 per person) is a friendly B&B in a handy spot.

Dell Guest House (☎ 422784; e dell .house@virgin.net; 8 Warwick Place; shared/en suite per person £22/28) is a comfortable B&B near the munching and shopping district; vegetarian breakfasts are available.

Adams Hotel (☎ 450742, fax 313110; e enquiries@adams-hotel.co.uk; 22 Avenue Rd; en-suite singles/doubles from £56/68) offers quality B&B in one of Leamington's large Regency villas.

Casa Valle (☎ 741128; e info@casavalle .co.uk; mains £8-16; closed Sun) has a simple menu steering clear of formulaic pasta and pizza; there's also a mouthwatering deli counter.

Broadsheet food critics love **Solo** (☎ 422422; 23 Dormer Place; 2/3-course lunch £15/18, 3-course dinner £25-28), Leamington's best restaurant: expect truffle oil and pan-European cuisine.

Moo (☎ 337763; Russell St) is a retro-chic bar with a mellow vibe and tasty snacks.

Getting There & Away

National Express coaches run three times daily to London (£16.50 economy return, 2¾ hours). Bus No X12 runs to Coventry every 20 minutes, while X14, X16 and X18 go there hourly (Nos X16 and X18 also serve Stratford-upon-Avon and Warwick). Trains run to Birmingham New St (£4.20 single, 40 minutes, every 20 minutes), London Marylebone or Paddington (£23.20 saver return, 1¾ hours, every 30 minutes) and Stratford-upon-Avon (£3.70 single, 30 minutes, roughly hourly).

KENILWORTH

☎ 01926 • pop 22,000

Famed for its ruined medieval castle, villagey old Kenilworth is away from (but walking distance to) the new town, which

has accommodation and eateries but not much else; that said, it's not unpleasant despite effectively existing as a dormitory town for nearby Coventry.

The **TIC** (☎ 852595, fax 864503; The Library, 11 Smalley Place; open 9am-7pm Mon, Tues, Thur & Fri, 9.30am-4pm Sat) handles visitor inquiries.

Kenilworth Castle

Dramatic, red-sandstone Kenilworth Castle (☎ 852078; adult/child £4.40/2.20; open 10am-6pm daily Apr-Sept, 10am-5pm Oct, 10am-4pm Nov-Mar), managed by English Heritage (EH), was founded around 1120 and enlarged in the 14th and 16th centuries; it's been owned and inhabited by an array of powerful men, including John of Gaunt, Simon de Montfort and Robert Dudley, and attracted several visits from Elizabeth I. The castle was deliberately ruined in 1644 after the Civil War, but the huge 12th-century keep and extensive Norman walls remain; history is brought to life as you take an audioguided tour around the atmospheric ruins. Various events and performances take place here throughout the year; call for details.

Stoneleigh Abbey

This impressive Georgian abbey-mansion (☎ 858535; w www.stoneleighabbey.org; admission £5, one child free with each adult, extra child £2.50; guided tours 11am, 2pm & 3pm Tues-Thur & Sun Easter-Oct), founded in 1154, is undergoing restoration, but a large chunk is open to the public. The splendid Palladian West Wing, completed in 1726, contains richly detailed plasterwork ceilings and panelled rooms; the medieval gatehouse, dating from 1346, is also worth a look, as are the grounds, landscaped by Repton and Nessfield. Stoneleigh is about 2 miles (3km) east of Kenilworth town centre off the B4115.

Places to Stay & Eat

There are several B&Bs on Priory Rd.

Ferndale Guest House (☎ 853214, fax 858336; 45 Priory Rd; singles/doubles £26/40) has very comfortable en-suite rooms.

Castle Laurels Hotel (☎ 856179, fax 854954; w www.castlelaurelshotel.co.uk; Castle Rd; singles/doubles £38/59) is a superior B&B, more like a small, exclusive hotel, by the castle.

Raffles (☎ 864300; 57 Warwick Rd; 2/3-course lunch £12.50/15, 2/3/4-course dinner £18.50/21.50/23.50) is a classy place serving Malaysian cuisine and authentic Singapore Slings (£4.25).

The Clarendon Arms (☎ 852017; 44 Castle Hill) is opposite the castle; it's renowned for its pub food and has a garden and courtyard for summer supping.

The Virgins & Castle (☎ 853737; 7 High St) is a cosy pub with plenty of nooks and crannies and a menu of Filipino specialities.

Getting There & Away

National Express coaches run daily from London (£16.50 economy return, 2¾ hours). To get to Stratford-upon-Avon (£2.95/4.50 single/return, 50 minutes), Warwick (£2.10/3.55, 20 minutes), Coventry (£1.55/2.55, 25 minutes) or Leamington Spa (£1.55/2.55, 15 minutes) take bus No X16 or X18 (bus Nos X12 and X14 also run to Leamington Spa and Coventry), which each run hourly.

STRATFORD-UPON-AVON
☎ 01789 • pop 22,000

Would this small market town have preserved its many historic buildings, timber-framed houses and tourist appeal if fate hadn't cast the die and selected Stratford as the birthplace of world-famous Elizabethan playwright William Shakespeare? Well, possibly: it's in a convenient spot near Coventry, and Warwick and Kenilworth Castles, the Cotswolds are within striking distance, and its good accommodation and eating options make it a handy base. Some feel that the incessant bard-linked marketing and coach-loads of tourists detract from its appeal, but there's plenty to see; visit and make up your own mind.

Orientation & Information

Arriving by coach or train, you'll find yourself within walking distance of the town centre, which is easy to explore on foot. Transport is only really essential for visiting Mary Arden's House.

Close to the river on Bridgefoot, the **TIC** (☎ 293127, fax 295262; e stratfordtic@shakespeare-country.co.uk; open 9am-6pm Mon-Sat, 10.30am-4.30pm Sun Apr-Oct, 9am-5pm Mon-Sat, 10am-3pm Sun Nov-Mar) has plenty of information but gets frantically busy in summer. Every Saturday (plus Sun-

day during July, August and September) free two-hour **guided walks** (☎ 412602) depart from outside the TIC at 10.30am.

Cyber Junction (☎ 263400; 28 Greenhill St; open 10am-5.30pm Mon-Thur & Sat, 10am-6pm Fri, 10am-5pm Sun) offers Internet access at £5/3 per one/half-hour and game play as well as snacks.

Sparklean (☎ 269075; 74 Bull St) is a handy laundrette.

The Shakespeare Houses

The **Shakespeare Birthplace Trust** (☎ 204016; w www.shakespeare.org.uk) manages five buildings associated with Shakespeare. In summer crowds are enormous and the small Tudor houses are packed; visit out of season if possible. Note that wheelchair access to the properties is very restricted.

Three of the houses are central, one is a short bus ride away, and the fifth a drive or bike ride out. A £12/6 ticket offers access to all five properties, or £8.50/4.20 for the three town houses. To pay for each place individually would cost nearly twice as much. Opening times are complex, but generally the properties open 9am or 9.30am to 5pm Monday to Saturday and 9.30am or 10am to 5pm Sunday, June to August; times are more variable during the rest of the year. Phone or visit the website for more information.

Shakespeare's Birthplace The number-one Shakespeare attraction (Henley St; adult/child £6.50/2.50) has a modern exterior (so changed, in fact, it's doubtful the Bard would recognise it, if indeed he was born here – there's no concrete evidence) but inside it's very much 'olde'. It's been a tourist hotspot for three centuries; you'll see the evidence of famous 19th-century visitor-vandals who scratched their names on one of the windows. Family rooms have been re-created in the style of Shakespeare's time, and there's a 'virtual reality' display downstairs for visitors unable to gain access to the upper areas. A ticket includes admission to the adjacent **Shakespeare Exhibition** where well-devised interpretative displays give the lowdown on Stratford's famous son.

New Place & Nash's House The wealthy retired Shakespeare bought a fine home at New Place on the corner of Chapel St and Chapel Lane; the house was demolished in

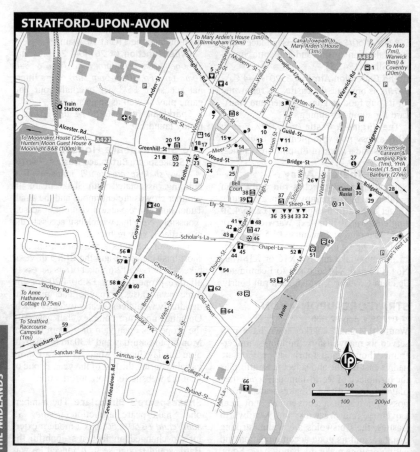

STRATFORD-UPON-AVON

1759, and an attractive Elizabethan knot garden occupies part of the grounds. Displays in the adjacent Nash's House (adult/child £3.50/1.70), where his granddaughter Elizabeth lived, tells the town's history and contains a collection of 17th-century oak furniture and tapestries.

Hall's Croft Shakespeare's daughter Susanna married the eminent doctor John Hall, and their fine Elizabethan town house (Old Town; adult/child £3.50/1.70) stands near Holy Trinity Church. The main exhibition is a fascinating insight into medical practice in Shakespeare's time.

Anne Hathaway's Cottage Before their marriage, Shakespeare's wife lived in Shot-

tery, a mile (1.5km) west of the centre, in a pretty thatched farmhouse (adult/child £5/2). As well as contemporary furniture there's an orchard and **Shakespeare Tree Garden**, with examples of all the trees mentioned in Shakespeare's plays. A footpath (no bikes allowed) leads to Shottery from Evesham Place, or catch a bus (☎ 404984) from outside the NatWest Bank on Wood St to the end of Cottage Lane.

Mary Arden's House The home of William's mother now houses the **Shakespeare Countryside Museum** (adult/child £5/2.50) with exhibits tracing local country life over the past four centuries. Since there's also a collection of rare farm animals and a turn-of-the-20th-century farm-

STRATFORD-UPON-AVON

house, you'll probably spend more time here than at the other properties.

Mary Arden's House is at Wilmcote, 3 miles (5km) west of Stratford. If you cycle there via Anne Hathaway's Cottage, follow the Stratford-upon-Avon Canal towpath to Wilmcote rather than retracing your route or riding back along the busy A3400. The easiest way to get there otherwise is on a bus tour (see Getting Around later in this section).

Holy Trinity Church

Holy Trinity Church (☎ 266316; Old Town; suggested donation for chancel £1/50p; church open 8.30am-6pm Mon-Sat, 12.30pm-5pm Sun Apr-Oct; 9am-4pm Mon-Sat, 12.30pm-5pm Sun Nov-Mar) has transepts from the mid-13th century and many later additions (the spire dates from 1763), but it's the Bard connections that draw crowds. In the chancel are photocopies of Shakespeare's baptism and burial records, the graves of Will and his wife, and a bust created seven years after Shakespeare's death but before his wife's and thus assumed to be a good likeness.

Harvard House

The exuberantly carved Harvard House (☎ 204016, fax 296083; High St; adult/child £1.50/50p, free to holders of Shakespeare Houses multiple tickets; open 11.30am-4.30pm Thur-Mon July-Sept, Fri-Sun May, June & Sept-Nov) was home to the mother of John Harvard, after whom Harvard University in the USA was named in the 17th century. It now houses a **Museum of British Pewter**.

Other Things to See & Do

The **Royal Shakespeare Company Gallery** (☎ 412617; adult/child £1.50/1; open noon-6.30pm Mon-Fri, 9.30am-6.30pm Sat, noon-4pm Sun), inside the Swan Theatre, features changing displays of the RSC's collection of props, costumes and theatrical paraphernalia. **Theatre tours** (☎ 403405; adult/child £4/3 including admission to RSC Gallery) operate at 1.30pm and 5.30pm Monday to Saturday (11am and 5.30pm matinee days) and noon, 1pm, 2pm and 5.30pm Sunday.

Falstaffs Experience (☎ 298070; W www.falstaffsexperience.co.uk; 40 Sheep St; adult/child £3.50/1.50; open 10am-5.30pm Mon-Sat, 11am-5pm Sun), an old timbered building housing recreations of a witches' glade and a plague cottage, is like an extended stationary ghost train, with some history thrown in; mordant kids (and grown-ups) will love it.

THE MIDLANDS

Stratford Tales (☎ 404600; Cox's Yard, Bridgefoot; adult/child £3.95/2.50; open 10am-5pm daily) features dioramas of scenes from the town's past with recorded commentaries. The over-marketed Cox's Yard development also includes a pub with its own microbrewery.

The **Teddy Bear Museum** (☎ 293160; 19 Greenhill St; adult/child £2.50/1.50; open 9.30am-5.30pm daily), founded, bizarrely, by former politician and broadcaster Gyles Brandreth, is popular with youngsters and those who would never have kicked teddy out of the bed.

The **Guild Chapel** (cnr Chapel Lane & Church St) dates from 1269, though it was rebuilt in the 15th century; it's not open to the public except for services (10am Wednesday and noon Saturday April to September). Next door is **King Edward VI School**, which Shakespeare probably attended; it was originally the Guildhall.

Places to Stay

Camping There are a few campsites near town. **Stratford Racecourse** (☎ 267949, fax 415850; Luddington Rd; 2-person pitches £10; open Easter-Sept) is just off the Evesham Rd a mile to the west, while **Riverside Caravan & Camping Park** (☎ 292312, fax 415330; Tiddington Rd; e info@stratfordcaravans.co .uk; pitches £5-9) is a similar distance east.

Hostels Central **Stratford Backpackers Hotel** (☎ 263838; e stratford@hostels.co.uk; 33-34 Greenhill St; beds in dorms/twin rooms £12/15) has a good reputation among travellers. Book well ahead in summer.

Stratford-upon-Avon YHA Hostel (☎ 0870 770 6052, fax 205513; e stratford@yha.org.uk; Hemmingford House, Alveston; B&B singles/ doubles £24/36) is a large old house 1½ miles (2.5km) east of the town centre along Tiddington Rd. Bus Nos X18 and 77 run to Alveston from Bridge St.

About a Bard

Possibly the greatest dramatist of all time, William Shakespeare was born in Stratford-upon-Avon in 1564, the son of a local glovemaker. At the age of 18 he married Anne Hathaway, eight years his senior, and their first daughter, Susanna, was born about six months later. Boy and girl twins, Hamnet and Judith, followed two years later.

Did the sheen of domestic bliss wear thin then? Around this time Shakespeare moved to London and began to write for the Lord Chamberlain's Company. This successful ensemble boasted the finest theatre (the Globe) and the best actors. It wasn't until the 1590s that Shakespeare's name appeared on his plays; before that, the company's name was regarded as more important than the dramatist's.

Shakespeare's 37 plays made novel and inventive use of the English language, often to ribald comic effect (although generations of schoolchildren would doubtless disagree), and boasted superb plot structures and deep insights into human nature – characteristics that have ensured not only their survival over the centuries but also their popularity in other languages. Early writings included comedies such as The Comedy of Errors, historical accounts such as Henry VI and Richard III, and tragedies including Romeo & Juliet. The new century saw his great tragedies: Hamlet, Othello, King Lear and Macbeth.

Around 1610 Shakespeare retired, moved back to Stratford, and lived in comfortable circumstances until his death in 1616, whereupon his body (and a legacy of mass tourism) was conferred on the parish church. His wife outlived him by seven years.

Despite Shakespeare's prodigious output of plays, no letters or other personal writing have survived and the little that is known about him and his family has been pieced together from birth, death and marriage files and other official records (including the will in which he left his wife his 'second-best bed'!). This paucity of information has bred wild theories that Shakespeare didn't actually write the plays. Since none have survived in manuscript form, there's no handwriting evidence to prove they're his. Nonbelievers speculate that Shakespeare's origins and education were too humble to have provided the background, experience and knowledge to write the plays. Their favourites for the 'real' Shakespeare are the earl of Derby or the earl of Oxford who, they claim, may have had reasons for wanting to remain anonymous.

B&Bs Stratford's B&Bs generally offer a good standard, and most are in attractive Victorian houses. Prime hunting grounds are Evesham Place, Grove Rd, Broad Walk and Alcester Rd. Accommodation can be hard to find during summer; if you're stuck, the TIC charges £3 plus 10% deposit to find something.

Arrandale (*☎ 267112; 208 Evesham Rd; per person £16-18)* is one of the cheapest options; it's a 10-minute walk from the centre.

Grosvenor Villa (*☎ 266192;* e *marion@ grosvenorvilla.com; 9 Evesham Place; per person £20-25, doubles with bath £50)* is a fine choice: spotless, very friendly and less flowery than some.

Dylan Guest House (*☎ 204819;* e *thedy lan@lineone.net; 10 Evesham Place; per person £22-28)* is another friendly, clean and comfortable (but slightly more chintzy) place.

Virginia Lodge (*☎/fax 292157; 12 Evesham Place; per person £18-24)* is similar; all rooms have an en suite and one has a four-poster bed.

Carlton Guest House (*☎ 293548; 22 Evesham Place; singles with shared facilities £18-22, doubles with shower/bath £40/48)* has light, airy rooms; even the singles are big and pleasant.

The owners of **Quilts & Croissants** (*☎ 267629, fax 551651;* e *rooms@quilt-crois sants.demon.co.uk; 33 Evesham Place; rooms £18-25)* have travelled widely themselves; they're extremely amiable and go far to make you comfortable.

Stay at **Twelfth Night** (*☎ 414595; 13 Evesham Place; en suite per person £26-32)* for an extra touch of class: breakfast is served on bone china.

Woodstock Guest House (*☎/fax 299881;* e *woodstockhouse@compuserve.com; 30 Grove Rd; en suite per person £28)* is a highly rated, award-winning B&B.

There are several places on Alcester Rd, near the train station.

Moonlight (*☎ 298213; 144 Alcester Rd; per person £16-19)* is one of the cheapest B&Bs.

Hunters Moon Guest House (*☎ 292888, fax 204101;* e *thehuntersmoon@ntlworld .com; 150 Alcester Rd; per person £20-26)* is a nonsmoking place with good vegetarian breakfasts.

Moonraker House (*☎ 267115, fax 295504;* e *moonrakerleonard@aol.com; 40 Alcester Rd; singles £40-55, doubles £55-70, 4-poster*

bed suites £80) is, as you'd expect for the price, something special; B&Bs don't come much classier.

Hotels The top-end hotels cater to international package tours (or businesspeople during the week) and tend to be booked out. All rooms have an en suite.

Stratheden Hotel (*☎/fax 297119;* e *rich ard@stratheden.fsnet.co.uk; 5 Chapel St; B&B doubles/twins £32-35)*, an old building (parts c.1673) in the thick of the Shakespeare action, is tastefully furnished, very friendly and good value for the location.

Payton Hotel (*☎ 266442, fax 294410;* e *info@payton.co.uk; 6 John St; B&B per person from £28)* is another small, genteel place, again good value for the standard.

At **The White Swan** (*☎ 297022, fax 268773;* e *whiteswan@work.gb.com; Rother St; singles/doubles £70/85)* beams, oak panelling and four-posters abound, although most rooms are modern. It's just a few steps from the Birthplace.

The Shakespeare (*☎ 0870 400 8182, fax 415411;* e *shakespeare@macdonald-hotels .co.uk; Chapel St; singles/doubles from £57.50/ 115)*, with its beautiful historic buildings, is a four-star establishment; true to form, some rooms have four-poster beds.

Falcon Hotel (*☎ 279953, fax 414260; Chapel St; singles/doubles £110/130)* is a charming place with rooms in an old timber-framed building; there's also a more modern wing. Special deals are sometimes available.

Thistle Stratford-upon-Avon (*☎ 294949, fax 415874;* e *stratford.uponavon@thistle .co.uk; Waterside; singles/doubles from £126/ 146)*, one of Stratford's finest, is immediately across the road from the Swan Theatre. Discounts of 50% or more are sometimes available in the low season.

Places to Eat

Shakespeare clearly makes you hungry: there's no shortage of eateries in town.

Havilands (*☎ 415477; 5 Meer St; cream tea £3.95; open 9am-5pm Mon-Sat)* is a small, cosy spot for lunch or just to indulge in coffee and home-made cake.

Lemon Tree (*☎ 292997; 2 Union St; panini & baguettes £3.50; closed Sunday)* is a happy, breezy kind of lunch spot.

Sheep St is wall-to-wall eateries, generally with a refined but relaxed ambience and a range of cuisines. Mains in all of Stratford's non-chain dinner restaurants tend to cost between £8 (for vegetarian options) to £16 (for steak or seafood).

Opposition (☎ 269980; 13 Sheep St) is a popular Italian place; it's trendy but not snobby.

Lambs (☎ 292554; 12 Sheep St) is highly regarded, with an extensive wine list; the menu is influenced by various world cuisines. This is where you'd take the parents-in-law to impress.

Vintner Wine Bar (☎ 297259; 5 Sheep St; open 10am-late daily) is the best bet for lively vegetarian options.

Stylish **Edward Moon's** (☎ 267069; 9 Chapel St) has a tasty menu from around the globe, and sinful desserts including a tempting sticky-toffee pudding.

Coconut Lagoon (☎ 293546; 21 Sheep St) serves up delicious South Indian regional specialities in a bright, modern space.

Georgetown (☎ 204445; 23 Sheep St), next door, is very upmarket, very sleek and very Malaysian; it has a good selection of vegetarian options.

Other Asian restaurants include award-winning **Usha** (☎ 297348; 28 Meer St; mains £5.50-11), blending Bangladeshi and Indian cuisine; **Relax** (☎ 293522; 29 Meer St; mains £5-7; open to midnight Mon-Sat), with various regional Chinese dishes; and **Thai Kingdom** (☎ 261103; 11 Warwick Rd; mains £6-11; closed Sunday), which has been pleasing punters with quality Thai classics for 10 years.

De:alto (☎ 298326; 13 Waterside) announces itself with a neon sign. That's neon as in art, not tack: this Italian restaurant near the river is one of *the* places to be seen.

Restaurant Margaux (☎/fax 269106; 6 Union St; mains £8-18; closed Sunday) prepares a variety of fine French-influenced food in equally fine surroundings.

Russons (☎ 268822; 8 Church St; closed Sun & Mon) is the place to come for seafood and fresh fish. It's classy but not stiff, with pleasantly rustic decor.

Named one of the best restaurants outside London, **Desport's** (☎/fax 269304; e booking@desports.co.uk; 13-14 Meer St; closed Sun & Mon) creates international cuisine with the finest ingredients, and there's a well-thought-out wine list to boot. The deli downstairs is a good option for lunch or picnic treats.

On that note, there are a couple of shops worth checking out if you fancy making your own meal.

Wholefood (☎ 292353; Greenhill St) sells delicious vegetarian pastries, sandwiches and the like.

Paxton & Whitfield (☎ 415544; 13 Wood St) has been selling cheeses to the discerning (including the royals) since 1797; entering the shop is like reaching a very strong-smelling nirvana.

Entertainment

Pubs & Bars A pint at the riverside **Dirty Duck** (☎ 297312; Waterside), aka the Black Swan, is an essential Stratford experience for thespians and theatre-goers alike.

Windmill Inn (☎ 297687; Church St) is reputedly the oldest pub in town; despite the 'historic' tag it's lively and serves fine ales.

Garrick Inn (☎ 292186; 25 High St), steeped in history, is worth visiting just to marvel at the low ceilings, dark wood beams and, well, age.

Bar Humbug (☎ 292109; 1 Guild St) has school desks and a beer garden, and avoids both the 'olde' and 'too-hip' cliches. It also cooks up great pies (£5.95).

Tonic (☎ 262233; 1 Shakespeare St), a relaxed, retro-styled bar-diner, has mellow tunes and of-the-minute food; it's the best spot in town to wind down with a cocktail.

Theatre & Cinema Seeing a **Royal Shakespeare Company** production is a must. Performances take place in the main **Royal Shakespeare Theatre**, the adjacent **Swan Theatre** or, nearby, **The Other Place**.

The **box office** (☎ 0870 609 1110, fax 403413; w www.rsc.org.uk; open 9.30am-8pm Mon-Sat) is in the Royal Shakespeare Theatre. Tickets normally cost from £6 to £42 depending on the performance and venue, but there's a bewildering array of offers for under-25s, students, seniors and other selected groups, plus discounts for previews; it's best to call or check the website for details. There are always a few tickets sold on the day of performance, and available only to personal callers, so it's worth checking if you haven't booked.

Stratford Picture House (☎ 415500; w www.picturehouse-cinemas.co.uk; Windsor St; adult/child £5/3.50) shows mainstream, international and art-house films.

Getting There & Away

Stratford-upon-Avon is 93 miles (150km) from London, 40 miles (64km) from Oxford and 8 miles (13km) from Warwick. Bus services are a lot better than train connections to most parts of the country.

Bus National Express destinations from Stratford's Riverside Bus Station include Birmingham (£7.25 economy return, one hour, daily), Oxford (£9.25, one hour, daily) and London Victoria (£16.50, 3½ hours, three daily).

Buses run to Warwick (X16 and X18, £2.55/3.30 single/return, 20 minutes, hourly), Coventry (X16 and X18, £3.20/ 4.50, 1¼ hours), Leamington Spa (X16 and X18, £2.95/4.50, 40 minutes) and Birmingham (X20, £3.40/4.05 single/return, 1¼ hours, hourly Monday to Saturday, eight on Sunday).

Train Stratford-upon-Avon station is on Station Rd, a few minutes' walk west of the centre. There are only a few direct services from London Paddington (£23.20 saver return, two hours), but some services from Marylebone that require a change at Banbury or Leamington Spa are almost as quick.

From the north, transfer at Leamington Spa or Birmingham Moor St station (£4.80 single, 50 minutes, hourly).

In July and August, the **Shakespeare Express** steam train (☎ 0121-707 4696; w www .vintagetrains.co.uk; single adult/child £10/3, return £15/5, 1 hr, twice each Sunday) operates between Birmingham Snow Hill and Stratford.

Getting Around

Bus Open-top buses of **City Sightseeing** (☎ 299123; w www.city-sightseeing.com) circuit past the TIC and the five Shakespeare properties every 15 minutes during peak summer months (usually April to September), less frequently over winter; fares are £8.50/2.50 per adult/child. They operate on a jump-on-jump-off basis, so you can spend as long as you like at each attraction, and are a convenient way of getting to the out-of-town houses.

Bicycle Stratford is small enough to explore on foot, but a bicycle is good for getting out to the surrounding countryside or the rural Shakespeare properties. The canal towpath

offers a fine route to Wilmcote. **Warwickshire County Council** (☎ 01827-872660) produces leaflets detailing cycling routes.

Pashley Cycles (☎ 205057; Guild St) hires bikes from £10/5 per day/half-day.

Boat Punts, canoes and rowing boats are available from **Rose's Boathouse** (☎ 267073) by Clopton Bridge. Hire row boats and punts for £2.50/1.50 per hour. **Bancroft Cruises** runs half-hour trips (☎ 269669; e captain@ bancroftcruises.co.uk) for adults/children £3/2, daily, from April to October, leaving from the Moat House Hotel pier.

AROUND STRATFORD-UPON-AVON

Stratford is ringed by pretty villages, atmospheric pubs and stately homes. It's a pleasant walk or cycle to Birmingham along the Stratford-upon-Avon Canal towpath.

Charlecote Park

Sir Thomas Lucy is said to have caught the young Shakespeare poaching deer in the grounds of Charlecote Park (NT; ☎ 01789-470277; e charlecote@smtp.ntrust.co.uk; admission £5.80; open noon-5pm Fri-Tues Apr-Oct); deer still roam the park, landscaped by Capability Brown. Built around 1551, the interior was redesigned in Elizabethan style in the early 19th century; the Victorian kitchen and the Tudor gatehouse are particularly interesting. Charlecote is in Wellesbourne, around 5 miles (8km) east of Stratford-upon-Avon. Bus X18 runs from Stratford, Warwick and Coventry hourly.

Ragley Hall

The family home of the Marquess and Marchioness of Hertford (☎ 01789-762090; w www.ragleyhall.com; adult/child £6/4.50; open noon-5pm Thur-Sun Apr-Sept) is a grand Palladian mansion built between 1679 and 1683, with a later baroque plasterwork ceiling and some good modern paintings. The intriguing South Staircase Hall with its murals and ceiling painting was restored between 1968 and 1982. Ragley is 2 miles (3km) southwest of Alcester off the A435/A46.

Heart of England Balloons

If you're tired of looking at historic landmarks and greenery from the ground, Heart of England Balloons (☎ *01789-488219;* w *www.ukballoons.com; Cross Lanes Farm, Walcote),* based near Alcester, offers the chance to soar above it all in a hot-air balloon. One-hour flights cost £139 per person.

COVENTRY
☎ 024 • pop 299,300

Nobody would claim that Coventry is an attractive town. There are a few Georgian town houses and medieval cottages, and the modern cathedral is a masterpiece, but WWII bombing raids and subsequent thoughtless redevelopment have left a city centre that is essentially a ghastly shopping precinct within a ring road. That said, there's enough here to justify a day trip from Stratford, Warwick (which both have better accommodation options) or Birmingham.

During the 14th century, the wool trade made Coventry one of the largest towns in England. Decline set in and Coventry was still essentially a medieval town when the Industrial Revolution hit. It was one of the most inventive of the Victorian industrial centres, claiming to be the birthplace of the modern bicycle and going on to become the heart of Britain's car- and aircraft-manufacturing industries until they disintegrated in the 1970s.

Coventry is probably best known for Lady Godiva, a medieval member of the elite who, legend has it, rode through the city naked to force her husband Leofric to help the poor: a kind of 'Stripping Hood'. You'll see monuments to her and Leofric around town.

Orientation & Information
Central Coventry is encircled by a ring road with most points of interest tucked inside. Medieval Spon St, west of the centre, has several half-timbered buildings relocated from elsewhere in the city.

The TIC (☎ *0800 777220, fax 7622 7255;* w *www.coventry.org; Bayley Lane; open 9.30am-5pm Mon-Fri, 10am-4.30pm Sat & Sun),* facing the cathedrals, provides self-guided tours of the historic centre (audio handset or brochure; both £1.75) and books accommodation.

Cathedrals
Founded in the 12th century and rebuilt from 1373, St Michael's was one of England's largest parish churches when it became a cathedral in 1918, its spire topped only by those of Salisbury and Norwich cathedrals. Then, in 1940, a Luftwaffe raid gutted the cathedral, leaving only the outer walls and the spire standing amid the ruins.

After the war, the ruins were left as a reminder. Designed by Sir Basil Spence, the adjacent St Michael's Cathedral (☎ *7622 7597;* e *information@coventrycathedral.org; requested donation £3)* was built between 1955 and 1962, one of the few examples of post-war British architecture to inspire popular affection. It's noted for the soaring etched glass screen wall at the western end, for the Graham Sutherland tapestry above the altar, for Piper's lovely stained glass and for Epstein's sculpture of St Michael subduing the devil beside the entrance steps.

The old cathedral spire (☎ *7626 7070; adult/child £1.50/75p)* still looks down on the ruins and its 180 steps lead up to magnificent views; opening hours are irregular, so call to check.

Other Things to See & Do
St Mary's Guildhall (*Bayley Lane; admission free; usually open 10am-4pm Sun-Thur)* is a

---

Stripping Away the Myth

Lady Godiva is to Coventry what Robin Hood is to Nottingham, a real historical character whose story has been embellished through the ages. Godiva, wife of Leofric, mean-minded earl of Mercia and lord of Coventry in the 11th century, was a compassionate woman who begged her husband to relieve the tax burden on the region's poor. Leofric jested that he would do so only if she rode naked on a horse from one end of town to the other. Surprisingly she did just that, although only on agreement from the townsfolk that they remain indoors. One young voyeur called (Peeping) Tom couldn't resist the temptation for an eyeful, and was struck blind.

Myths aside, Lady Godiva certainly played an important role in the history of Coventry. Unfortunately for romantics, it is unlikely that Leofric would have allowed his wife to demean herself in such a way. However, for Coventry it is an excuse for a celebration and every year a parade is held in early June to commemorate the original stripper.

marvellous, rambling building dating from 1342. The various rooms, with sloping floors, carved dark wood walls, stained-glass windows and 14th-century heraldic bosses, house treasures such as the Tournai tapestry, commissioned in 1500 and depicting kings, queens, lords, ladies and saints. Phone the Herbert Art Gallery (☎ 7683 2381) to check opening times.

Holy Trinity Church (☎ 7622 0418; *Trinity St; open 10am-4pm daily*) dates from the 12th century and its 67m spire has long been a landmark of the city. Above the chancel arch is a unique fresco from c.1420, now restored to its former glory. Smaller **St John's Church** at the end of Spon St is famous for giving the world the expression 'sent to Coventry'. Royalist prisoners of war were interned here during the Civil War, out of touch with their friends and family.

The **Priory Visitor Centre** (☎ 7655 2242; *Priory Row; admission free; open 10am-5.30pm Mon-Sat, noon-4pm Sun*) highlights the history of the original cathedral and priory, founded by the omnipresent Leofric 1000 years ago, with artefacts and computer-generated reconstructions.

Coventry's chequered history is explored at **Herbert Art Gallery & Museum** (☎ 7683 2381; *Jordan Well; admission free; open 10am-5.30pm Mon-Sat, noon-5pm Sun*) with some excellent interactive displays, a range of medieval artefacts and changing contemporary exhibitions, as well as a gallery devoted to paintings of Lady Godiva.

The **Museum of British Road Transport** (☎ 7683 2425; **w** www.mbrt.org.uk; *Hales St; admission free; open 10am-5pm daily*) has a huge collection of bicycles, motorcycles, racing cars and rally cars and even Thrust 2 (once the world's fastest car) alongside traditional family cars, and charts the evolution of some of Britain's finest makes and models.

Crammed in the **Coventry Toy Museum** (☎ 7622 7560; *36-37 Much Park St; adult/child £1.50/1; open 1pm-5pm daily*), housed in the 1352 Whitefriars Gate, is an incredible mass of toys, games, bikes and assorted juvenilia: fascinating and faintly creepy.

Places to Stay
Hollyfast Caravan Park (☎ 7633 6411; *Wall Hill Rd, Allesley; per tent £8*) is the handiest campsite, about 3 miles (5km) northwest of

the centre. Bus Nos 7 and 75 run to the end of Browns Lane, from where it's another 500m walk.

There's no hostel. **Priory Halls of Residence** (☎ 7623 6015; *Priory St; per person £17; open July & Aug*) provides accommodation during university holidays.

Coventry has many B&Bs, most clustered around St Patrick's Rd and Park Rd, both close to the noisy ring road; nearby Stratford offers better value. It's often hard to find a room here. The **TIC** offers a free accommodation booking service (☎ 0800 243748).

Crest Guest House (☎ 7622 7822; **e** *alan harve@aol.com; 39 Friars Rd; B&B per person from £26.50*) offers a good standard of comfort.

Chez Hugh (☎/fax 7622 3210; *9 Park Rd; per person from £20*) is a modern, family-run B&B with a bar and restaurant.

Ibis Coventry South (☎ 7625 0500; *Mile Lane; doubles Mon-Thur/Fri-Sun £42/35*) is a central option offering modern, standard rooms.

Menzies Leofric Hotel (☎ 7622 1371, fax 7655 1352; **e** *leofric@menzies-hotels.co.uk; Broadgate; singles/doubles £79/99*) is a four-star option in the centre. Don't be put off by the ugly exterior: it's much nicer inside.

Coombe Abbey (☎ 7645 0450, fax 7663 5101; *Brinklow Rd, Binley; singles/doubles from £125/140*), in the suburbs, is the city's finest hotel, once an 11th-century abbey.

Places to Eat
Browns (☎ 7622 1100; *Earl St; all meals £5*) is a big, airy space with a gallery area and an extensive menu, including plenty of vegetarian options. A popular bar by night, DJs ply their trade at the weekend, when it's open till 1am.

Etna Restaurant (☎ 7622 3183; *57 Hertford St; mains £7-14; closed Sun*) is favoured by locals for its Italian cuisine and fine fresh fish.

Medieval Spon St (and yes, that adjective is always used!) has several eateries.

Despite the distressed wooden beams and medieval venue, **1450 Café Bar** (☎ 7622 9274; *21 Spon St; mains £7-15*) is a bright, lively place serving up steak, fish and a range of terrifyingly strong Belgian beers.

Kakooti (☎ 7622 1392; *16 Spon St; mains £8-13; open noon-2pm Tues, Thur & Sat, 6pm-10.30pm Tues-Sat*) is an excellent place serving imaginative international seafood and vegetarian dishes.

There are some good balti restaurants in Coventry, and the Foleshill Rd remains one of the most popular hunting grounds.

Moonlight Balti (☎ 7663 3414; 196-198 Foleshill Rd; mains £3-7; open 5pm-1am daily) has a regular following, perhaps because of the late opening hours.

Entertainment

Pubs & Bars With two universities, Coventry has a thriving nightlife, although the centre is plagued with uninteresting chain bars.

Relaxed **Golden Cross** (☎ 7622 2311; 8 Hay Lane), nestled beneath the cathedrals in Hay Lane, is one of Coventry's oldest pubs, dating from the 16th century. DJs play indie and funk Wednesday to Saturday.

Old Windmill (☎ 7652 5183; 22-23 Spon St), aka Ma Browns, is a good spot for ale enthusiasts, hosting two beer festivals a year.

Whitefriars Olde Ale House (☎ 7625 1655; 114-115 Gosford St), a refreshing change from the noisy student bars nearby, is a medieval building with stained glass, cosy snugs and an amazing range of draught beers.

Inspire Café Bar (☎ 7655 3355; New Union St) is a fantastic venue in the base of the old Christchurch spire, retaining the old pews and Gothic ambience but adding outdoor tables, a range of world beers and nibbles.

Theatre & Cinema The **Arts Centre** (☎ 7652 4524; w www.warwickartscentre .co.uk; Gibbett Hill Rd) at the University of Warwick, 4 miles (6km) south of the city, is the largest outside London, with an extensive array of dance, theatre and comedy, and a popular cinema showing left-field foreign films and cult classics. Bus Nos 12, X12 and X14 run here from the centre.

Belgrade Theatre (☎ 7655 3055; w www .belgrade.co.uk; Belgrade Square) stages musicals, concerts and drama.

Getting There & Away

Air Birmingham international airport (☎ 0121-767 5511; w www.bhx.co.uk) is close to Coventry.

Bus National Express coaches run to London (£15.50 economy return, 2½ hours, nine daily) and Oxford (£10.75, 1¾ hours, two daily).

West Midlands bus services are coordinated by **Centro** (☎ 7655 9559). Pool Meadow bus station has closed, and regional services run from various stops around town. Bus Nos 157 (£3.50, every 30 minutes) and X67 (hourly) run to Leicester (one hour) from The Burges, while bus Nos X16 and X18 run to Kenilworth (£1.55/2.55 single/return, 25 minutes), Leamington (£2.20/2.75, 40 minutes), Warwick (£2.85/4.50, 55 minutes) and Stratford (£3.20/4.50, 1¼ hours) from Trinity St hourly.

There are plenty of buses to Birmingham, but the train is much quicker.

Train The train station is just across the ring road, south of the centre. Coventry is on the main rail route to London Euston (£22 three-day advance return, 1½ hours; every 30 minutes); the standard single fare is £42, but big savings can be made by booking just a few days ahead. Birmingham (£2.95 single, every 10 minutes) is less than 30 minutes away.

Getting Around

Bus No 900 runs to Birmingham international airport (£1.60, 40 minutes, every 20 minutes).

Phone Centro (☎ 7655 9559) for local bus service information. A Coventry Daysaver ticket (£2/1.40) is valid for bus travel for one day, while a Daytripper ticket (£4/2.45) gives you a day's use of local bus and train services in the Centro area at weekends and after 9.30am Monday to Friday.

Staffordshire

If you heard that this semi-forgotten county fits between Birmingham and the southern fringes of Manchester, it might not seem too appealing, but Staffordshire features rolling Cannock Chase and parts of the Peak District (covered later in this chapter) such as the rocky outcrops of The Roaches, as well as Lichfield's wonderful cathedral and stately Shugborough. In between are rolling hills criss-crossed with narrow winding lanes linking charming villages and market towns.

Orientation & Information

Staffordshire's attractions are spread fairly evenly around the county: Stoke to the northwest; the Peak District and Leek northeast, with Alton Towers just south; Lichfield to the southeast, and Stafford just southwest of the centre.

For general tourist information, contact **Staffordshire Tourism** (☎ 0870 500 4444; w www.staffordshire.gov.uk/tourism). Particularly useful is the *Canal County* leaflet, giving ideas for boating, cycling or walking along the county's delightful waterways.

Getting Around

For information on Staffordshire buses, call the **Busline** (☎ 01782-206608). The **Moorlands Traveller 21** (☎ 01538-386888) is a flexible bus service linking the northeastern moorlands villages with Leek. **Virgin trains** (☎ 0845 722 2333; w www.virgin.com/trains) serve the county. Stoke-on-Trent, Stafford and Lichfield are the best transport hubs.

LICHFIELD
☎ 01543 • pop 28,700

The kind of small, handsome market town where tearooms outnumber bus stops, Lichfield's cobbled streets, attractive gardens and towering red-brick cathedral lure snappers as well as shoppers.

The **TIC** (☎ 308209, fax 308211; w www .lichfield-tourist.co.uk; Donegal House, Bore St; open 9am-5pm Mon-Fri, 9am-4.30pm Sat Apr-Sept; 9am-4.45pm Mon-Fri, 9am-2pm Sat Oct-Mar) handles visitor inquiries.

The **Lichfield Festival** (☎ 306543; w www .lichfieldfestival.org), held in the first half of July, features mostly classical and world music, cinema and theatre.

Lichfield Cathedral

The fine cathedral (☎ 306100; requested donation £3; open 7.30am-6.15pm daily) is instantly recognisable by its three spires, and boasts a fine Gothic west front adorned with exquisitely carved statues of the kings of England from Edgar through to Henry I, plus the major saints. Most of what you see dates from the various rebuildings of the Norman cathedral between 1200 and 1350. The gold-leafed skull of St Chad, the first bishop of Lichfield, was once kept in St Chad's Head Chapel, just to the west of the south transept.

A superb illuminated manuscript from AD 730, the *Lichfield Gospels*, is displayed in the beautifully vaulted mid-13th-century chapterhouse. Don't miss the effigy of George Augustus Selwyn, first Bishop of New Zealand in 1841, in the Lady Chapel (which boasts 16th-century Flemish stained glass), or Sir Francis Chantrey's *Sleeping Children* at the eastern end of the south aisle, a poignant memorial to two young girls who died in tragic circumstances.

A stroll round **Cathedral Close**, which is ringed with imposing 17th- and 18th-century houses, is also rewarding.

Other Things to See & Do

The **Samuel Johnson Birthplace Museum** (☎ 264972; Breadmarket St; adult/child £2.20/1.30; open 10.30am-4.30pm daily Apr-Sept, noon-4.30pm daily Oct-Mar) is in the house where the pioneering lexicographer was born in 1709. His dictionary, together with the biography written by his close friend James Boswell *(The Life of Samuel Johnson)*, established him as one of the great scholars, critics and wits of the English language. You can inspect the famous dictionary using the computer in the bookshop in the lobby, and learn about his life and work through the museum's exhibits.

Grandfather of the more famous Charles, Erasmus Darwin was himself a remarkable autodidact, doctor, inventor, philosopher and poet, influencing the Romantics. The **Erasmus Darwin Centre** (☎ 306260; Beacon St; adult/child £2.50/2; open 10am-4.30pm Thur-Sat, noon-4.30pm Sun) commemorates his life with a video, pictures and personal items; it's in the house where he lived from 1756 to 1781. Exhibits and displays illustrate his varied work and association with luminaries such as Wedgwood, Boulton and Watt.

The **Heritage Centre & Treasury** (☎ 256 611; St Mary's Centre; adult/child £3/2.50; open 10am-5pm daily), on the Market Square, houses an audiovisual presentation covering 1300 years of Lichfield history; the treasury exhibits a small but attractive display of civic, ecclesiastical and regimental silverware. Climb the tower (£1/80p) for fine views of the city.

Places to Stay

The TIC makes bookings free of charge.

There are several B&Bs on Beacon St, round the corner from Cathedral Close. **32 Beacon St** (☎ 262378; singles/doubles from £22/38) is a cosy town house with two en-suite rooms.

For a little more, you can stay on The Close itself: **No 8** (☎ 418483; **e** gilljones@talk21.com; B&B shared/en-suite singles £26/32, doubles £46/52) is an excellent place with three rooms, some with a great view of the cathedral.

Angel Croft Hotel (☎ 258737, fax 415605; Beacon St; singles/doubles Mon-Thur £65/80, Fri-Sun £52.50/63.50) is an imposing Georgian house opposite Cathedral Close.

The George Hotel (☎ 414822, fax 415817; **e** mail@thegeorgelichfield.co.uk; B&B singles /doubles Mon-Thur £95/106, Fri-Sun £55/80) is the top option, an 18th-century coaching inn right in the heart of the city.

Places to Eat

Cathedral Coffee Shop (☎ 306125; 19 The Close; sandwiches £1.70-3; open 9.30am-4.45pm Mon-Sat, noon-4.45pm Sun), set in a charming 18th-century house, is a good place for a snack or a full Sunday lunch (£5.99).

The Eastern Eye (☎ 415047; 19 Bird St; mains £5.50-11, vegetarian thali £9.50; open 5pm-midnight daily) is a popular Indian restaurant with an award-winning chef.

Thai Rainbow (☎ 264209; 15 Bird St; mains £5.50-8.50) is a peaceful place serving up tasty Thai favourites.

Don Paco (☎ 300789; 28 Bird St; mains £7-13; open 6.30pm-11pm Mon-Sat) is a pleasantly rustic Spanish restaurant with plenty of steak, fish and (naturally) paella.

Chandlers Grande Brasserie (☎ 416688; 2/3-course dinner £11.75/15), in the old Corn Exchange, is locally renowned for continental cuisine and a fine ambience.

Entertainment

Samuel Johnson described Lichfield folk as 'the most sober, decent people in England'; that was 250 years ago and there are pubs-a-plenty these days.

The King's Head (☎ 256822; 21 Bird St) is a traditional pub with a conservatory area and a courtyard for sunbathing while supping.

Joott (☎ 410022; 13 Bird St; open noon-2am Mon-Sat, noon-12.30am Sun) is the place to head for late-night frolics, a comfortable café-bar with leather sofas and a balcony terrace.

Getting There & Away

National Express coaches run daily to/from London (£16.50 economy return, 3½ hours).

Bus No 112 runs to Birmingham (£2.05/3.50 single/return, 1¼ hours, hourly), while No 825 serves Stafford (£2.25/3.50 single/return, 1¼ hours, hourly).

There are two train stations: central Lichfield City and Lichfield Trent Valley. Trains run to both from Birmingham New St station (£3 single, 30 minutes, every 15 minutes). Journeys to London Euston involve changing at either Birmingham or Nuneaton.

STOKE-ON-TRENT

☎ 01782 • pop 266,500 • elevation 132m

If you're in Stoke, chances are you're into porcelain: Staffordshire's industrial heart, historically important in the production of pottery of all kinds, is none too appealing itself (though no worse than other manufacturing towns). You could visit on a day trip from any of six or seven nearby centres, though you'd want a whole day to really explore the potteries. Arnold Bennett left memorable descriptions of the area in its industrial heyday in his novels *Clayhangar* and *Anna of the Five Towns* – something of a misnomer since Stoke actually consists of six towns.

Orientation & Information

Stoke-on-Trent is made up of Tunstall, Burslem, Hanley, Stoke, Fenton and Longton, together often called the Potteries. Hanley is the official 'city centre'. Stoke-on-Trent train station is south of Hanley, but buses from outside the main entrance run there in minutes. The bus station is in the centre of Hanley.

The **TIC** (☎ 236000, fax 236005; **e** stoke.tic@virgin.net; Quadrant Rd, Hanley; open 9.15am-5.15pm Mon-Sat), in the Potteries shopping centre, stocks an informative map with the locations of the various showrooms, factory shops and visitor centres, of which Wedgwood, Spode and Royal Doulton are the pick.

Things to See & Do

Even if you're bored by bone china, the **Wedgwood Story Visitor Centre** (☎ 204218; **w** www.thewedgwoodstory.com; Barlaston; adult/child £6.95/4.95; open 9am-5pm Mon-Fri, 10am-5pm Sat & Sun), set in wonderful parklands, offers a fascinating insight into the production process, with an extensive collection of historic pieces to gawp at. Almost more interesting are the film and dis-

THE MIDLANDS

plays on the life of founder Josiah Wedgwood (1730–95). An innovative potter, he was also a driving force behind the construction of Britain's canals and the abolition of slavery; altogether a remarkable man. Bus Nos 62 and 63 run to Wedgwood, and trains between Stafford and Stoke stop at Wedgwood station.

The **Potteries Museum & Art Gallery** (*☎ 232323; Bethesda St, Hanley; admission free; open 10am-5pm Mon-Sat, 2pm-5pm Sun Mar-Oct; 10am-4pm Mon-Sat, 1pm-4pm Sun Nov-Feb)* covers the history of the Potteries and houses an extensive collection of ceramics as well as some fine art (Picasso, Degas) and high-profile touring exhibitions.

Constructed round Stoke's last remaining bottle kiln and its yard, the wonderful **Gladstone Pottery Museum** (*☎ 319232; Uttoxeter Rd, Longton; adult/child £4.95/3.50; open 10am-5pm daily)* is an evocative reconstruction of a typical small pottery in the early 20th century. A highlight for those of scatological bent is the Flushed With Pride exhibition, charting the story of the toilet from chamber pots and shared privy holes (with smell effects!) to modern high-tech conveniences. Bus Nos 6, 7 and 8 serve Longton from Hanley.

Places to Stay & Eat

Leek Rd, just off Station Rd, is convenient for the train station and has a few B&Bs.

L Beez Guest House (*☎ 846727; 46 Leek Rd; per person from £17.50)* is a clean, reasonably priced B&B.

In Burslem the family-run **George Hotel** (*☎ 577544, fax 837496; e georgestoke@btinternet.com; Swan Square, Burslem; singles/doubles from £65/85)* is handy for the Doulton factory shop.

North Stafford Hotel (*☎ 744477, fax 744580; Winton Square; singles/doubles Mon-Thur £97/115, B&B per person Fri-Sun £39)*, opposite the station, offers more comfort. It has all the trimmings expected of a three-star place.

The museums and visitor centres all have eateries; they all feel more like tearooms than restaurants, but the **Sir Henry Doulton Gallery Restaurant** (*☎ 292451; Nile St, Burslem)*, **Ivy House** and **Josiah's Bistro** (both at the Wedgwood Story) are pretty good.

Shaffers (*☎ 206030; 63 Piccadilly, Hanley; mains £5.50-8.50; open 6pm-1am daily)*,

'curry house of the stars', serves award-winning Kashmiri cuisine and baltis.

Portofino (*☎ 209444; 38 Marsh St, Hanley; mains £6-18)*, the leading Italian restaurant, backs up the regulation pizza and pasta with good regional specialities.

Churrasco (*☎ 206201; 39 Albion St, Hanley; baguettes £2-3.50, mains £5-10.50)* is a bar with good lunchtime snacks, varied dinners with fresh ingredients and plenty of fish, and a relaxed atmosphere for a drink later.

Entertainment

La Bodega (*☎ 273322; 66 Piccadilly, Hanley)* and **Bar la de Dah** (*☎ 272775; 62-64 Piccadilly, Hanley)* are adjacent and similar: bright, lively places for a drink and a nibble, the former concentrating on tapas.

The Sugarmill (*☎ 214991; Brunswick St, Hanley)* is the area's top venue for up-and-coming bands and indie dance nights.

Regent Theatre (*☎ 213800; Piccadilly, Hanley)* is an Art Deco surprise in central Hanley, staging plays and musicals.

Getting There & Around

Stoke is 162 miles (259km) from London. National Express coaches run to/from London (£19.50 economy return, 4 hours, five daily) and Manchester (£5.50, 1½ hours, eight daily). Local bus No 101 runs to Stafford (£2.30 single, 1¼ hours) every 30 minutes. The TIC has city bus timetables, also online (**w** www.ukbus.co.uk).

Trains run hourly to London (£41.60 saver return, 1¾ hours).

AROUND STOKE-ON-TRENT
Biddulph Grange Gardens

These gorgeous Victorian gardens *(NT; ☎ 01782-517999; adult/child £4.50/2.40; open noon-5.30pm Wed-Fri, 11am-5.30pm Sat & Sun Apr-Oct)* boast Chinese, Egyptian and Italian corners: it's a botanical world tour. A highpoint is the Rainbow, a huge bank of rhododendrons that flower simultaneously. The gardens are 7 miles (11km) north of Stoke; take bus No 66 from Stoke train station (40 minutes, every 20 minutes).

Little Moreton Hall

England's most spectacular black-and-white timber-framed house *(☎ 01260-272018; adult/child £4.50/2.25; open 11.30am-5pm Wed-Sun late Mar-Oct, 11.30am-4pm Sat &*

Sun Nov-late Dec) dates back to the 16th century; it contains important wall paintings and an indefinable sense of romance. Little Moreton is off the A34 south of Congleton.

Alton Towers
It's big, it's brash, but if you can look past the incredible commercialism, Alton Towers (☎ 0870 500 1100; w www.altontowers.com; adult/under-12 £18.50-25/15.50-20, open 9.30am-5pm daily Oct–mid-Mar, longer hrs mid-Mar–Sept) is a bundle of fun; England's most popular theme park is a must for white-knuckle fiends. There are over 100 rides, including vertical drops, flying roller coasters, log flumes and more; it's pointless naming the biggest buzz, because new thrills are introduced frequently. Prices vary depending on arcane 'seasons', being most expensive during school holidays.

The nearest campsite is **Star Caravan & Camping Site** (☎ 01538-702219; Star Rd, Cotton; w www.starcaravanpark.co.uk; per tent/person £4/2), 2 miles (3km) north of Alton off the B5417.

Dimmingsdale YHA Hostel (☎ 01538-702304; Oakamoor; adult £9.50) is 2 miles (3km) northwest of the park.

There's an expensive hotel within the park, but most visitors opt to stay in nearby villages; helpfully, the park's website features a list of accommodation options. Alton itself is an attractive village with several B&Bs.

Old School House (☎ 01538-702151; e old_school_house@talk21.com; Castle Hill Rd, Alton; en suite per person from £28) is an exceptional B&B in a Grade II–listed house dating from 1845.

Alton Towers is east of Cheadle off the B5032. Public transport is sketchy, but various train companies periodically offer all-in-one packages from London and other cities; check the website for current details.

Drayton Manor Park
Southern Staffordshire's answer to Alton Towers, Drayton Manor (☎ 01827-287979; w www.draytonmanor.co.uk; adult/child £15-17.50/11-13.50; open 10.30am-5pm Easter-Oct, longer hrs May-Sept) is another massive theme park with huge rides. Rides include **Apocalypse**, a 54m 'stand up' drop from a tower and **Stormforce 10**, a 'wet-knuckle ride'. Again, prices are highest at weekends

and during school holidays. The park is near Junctions 9 and 10 of the M42 on the A4091. Bus No X76 runs daily from Birmingham.

LEEK
☎ 01538 • pop 20,000 • elevation 215m
Leek is an appealing market town that makes a good base for visiting the Potteries and the Peak District. It's also a gateway to the Staffordshire moorlands (in particular the Roaches, popular with climbers) and has a few worthy attractions, and some interesting markets and antique shops to explore.

The **TIC** (☎ 483741, fax 483743; e tourism .smdc@staffordshire.gov.uk; 1 Market Place; open 9.30am-5pm Mon-Fri, 10am-4pm Sat) provides information on attractions and accommodation.

St Edward's Church (Church St; open 10am-4pm Wed, 10am-noon Fri & Sat), completed in 1306, has a beautiful rose window by William Morris.

All Saint's Church (☎ 370786; Compton; open 1am-4pm Wed & Sat) was described by John Betjeman as 'one of the finest churches in Britain'; the Morris & Co stained glass windows at the eastern end are from designs by Edward Burne-Jones, and the Arts and Crafts wallpainting is rich and ornate.

Brindley Mill (☎ 483741; Mill St; adult/child £1.50/1; open 2pm-5pm Mon-Wed mid-July–Aug, 2pm-5pm Sat & Sun Easter-Sept) was built in 1752 by canal pioneer James Brindley. It's been beautifully restored and once again mills corn; inside is a small museum to Brindley and the art of millwrighting.

The Green Man (☎ 388084; 38 Compton; singles/doubles £28/45) offers comfortable, en-suite rooms in a cosy annexe.

Den Engel (☎ 373751; St Edward St) is a Flemish bar serving mussels, *genevers* (Dutch gins) and those dangerous Belgian beers.

The Roebuck (☎ 372179; 18 Derby St) dates back to 1626, although some say it was originally built in Shrewsbury and moved to Leek later. It's a smoky, traditional pub with a friendly atmosphere.

Bus Nos 16 and 18 run to Leek from Hanley (Stoke-on-Trent).

STAFFORD
☎ 01785 • pop 60,000
The county town of Staffordshire, once a crossroads for travellers, is a pleasant though

fairly anonymous place, with a couple of attractions worth a look on your way through. The **TIC** (☎ 619619; Market St; open 9.30am-5pm Mon-Fri, 10am-5pm Sat) is behind the town hall.

The **Ancient High House** (☎ 619619; Greengate St; admission free; open 10am-5pm Mon-Sat) is the largest timber-framed town house in the country and has period rooms containing displays on the history of the house since its construction in 1595.

Stafford Castle (☎ 257698; Newport Rd; admission free; visitor centre open 10am-5pm Tues-Sun Apr-Oct, 10am-4pm Nov-Mar), built by William the Conqueror, is no more than a ruin but hosts various special events and affords sweeping views. There's a small visitor centre.

AROUND STAFFORD
Shugborough

This regal, neoclassical mansion (☎ 01889-881388; admission to whole site £8/5, house & museum £6/4; open 11am-5pm Tues-Sun Apr-Sept, 11am-5pm Sun Oct) is the ancestral home of Lord Lichfield, renowned photographer (there's an exhibition of his work here). Started in 1693 and considerably extended during the 18th and 19th centuries, Shugborough has marvellous state rooms and a fine collection of Louis XV and XVI furniture. The estate is famous for the monuments within its grounds, including a Chinese House, Doric temple and the Triumphal Arch. There is also the Staffordshire County Museum, exploring life 'below stairs' for servants, and a farm.

Shugborough is 6 miles (8km) east of Stafford on the A513; bus No 825 runs nearby.

Bedfordshire

Bedfordshire is compact, peaceful and largely agricultural; as a tourist destination it's low key, with one major town and the fine stately home at Woburn. The River Great Ouse winds across the fields of the north and through Bedford; the M1 motorway runs across the semi-industrial south. For information on buses around the county, phone the **Traveline** (☎ 0870 608 2608) or check the website of **Stagecoach** (w www.stagecoachbus.com), the main regional bus company.

BEDFORD
☎ 01234 • pop 73,900

The county town is best known as the home of John Bunyan (1628–88), the 17th-century Nonconformist preacher and author of *The Pilgrim's Progress*. Places with links to John Bunyan are in and around the town, which boasts an attractive riverside setting and an impressive art gallery but is otherwise bland. It's an easy day trip from London.

The **TIC** (☎ 215226, fax 217932; e tic@bedford.gov.uk; 10 St Paul's Square; open 9.30am-5pm Mon-Sat, also 11am-3pm Sun May-Sept) stocks a free guide to places with a Bunyan connection. Guided walks depart the TIC at 2.15pm on summer Sundays.

Things to See & Do

The **Bunyan Meeting Free Church** (☎ 213722; Mill St; open 10am-4pm Tues-Sat Mar-Oct) was built in 1849 on the site of the barn where Bunyan preached from 1671 to 1678. The church's bronze doors, inspired by Ghiberti's doors for the Baptistry in Florence, show scenes from *The Pilgrim's Progress*. One famous stained-glass window shows Bunyan in jail (he spent 12 years in prison for preaching).

THE MIDLANDS

The purpose-built **John Bunyan Museum** (☎ 213722; admission free; open 11am-4pm Tues-Sat Mar-Oct) next door offers an insight into the author's life, and visitors can admire some 169 editions of *The Pilgrim's Progress* from around the world.

Cecil Higgins Art Gallery (☎ 211222; Castle Close) houses a splendid collection of glass, porcelain and colourful Victorian furniture, and an enviable collection of watercolours by Blake, Turner, Rosetti and Millais. **Bedford Museum** (☎ 353323), with archaeological and historical exhibits, is next door. It opens 11am to 5pm Tuesday to Saturday, 2pm to 5pm Sunday, and admission to both is £2.10/free.

Places to Eat

Vol-au-Vent (☎ 360320; 27 St Peters St; mains £6.95-13.50) is a well-regarded French restaurant.

Bar Citrus (☎ 409294; 29 Harpur St; mains £4.95-6.95; food served to 6pm) is a light, airy place with a relaxed atmosphere and daily specials.

The central area offers a range of chain bars, and a few more-interesting options.

The Flower Pot (☎ 302500; 25 Tavistock St; mains £4-8) is a snug little pub serving good ales and food, just back from the main shopping area.

Getting There & Away

Bedford is 50 miles (80km) north of London and 30 miles (48km) west of Cambridge.

National Express runs direct coaches to Cambridge (£8.50 economy return, one hour, three daily). The hourly X5 runs to Oxford (£5.99 day return) and Cambridge (£5 day return) daily. The X2 runs to Northampton (one hour) hourly Monday to Saturday, irregularly on Sunday. The bus station is half a mile (1km) west of High St.

There are frequent trains from King's Cross Thameslink (£17.20 Cheap Day return, one hour, every 15 minutes) to Bedford's Midland station, a well-signposted 500m walk west of High St.

WOBURN ABBEY & SAFARI PARK

A grand stately home built on the site of a Cistercian abbey, **Woburn Abbey** (☎ 01525-290666, fax 290271; w www.woburnabbey .co.uk; adult/child £8/3.50; open 11am-4pm daily late Mar-Sept, Sat & Sun Jan-late Mar &

Oct) has been the seat of the dukes of Bedford for almost 400 years. The present house dates mainly from the 18th century and is stuffed with 18th-century furniture, porcelain, silver and paintings by luminaries such as Rembrandt, Gainsborough and Reynolds.

The 12-sq-km park, landscaped by Humphrey Repton, is home to the largest breeding herd of Père David's deer, extinct in their native China for a century (although a small herd was returned to Beijing in 1985).

Although it's easily accessible by car off the M1 motorway, trains from King's Cross Thameslink only run to Flitwick, leaving you to take a taxi for the last 5 miles (8km) to the abbey.

A mile from the house is **Woburn Safari Park** (☎ 01525-290407; w www.woburnsafari .co.uk; adult/child £12.50/9, £1 more during school holidays; open 10am-5pm daily Mar-Oct, 11am-3pm Sat & Sun only Nov-Feb), the country's largest drive-through animal reserve, boasting lions, tigers, rhino and a host of other creatures. If you visit the abbey first you qualify for a 50% discount.

WHIPSNADE

Whipsnade Wild Animal Park (☎ 01582-872171; w www.whipsnade.co.uk; adult/child £9.90/7.50; open 10am-6pm Mon-Sat, 10am-7pm Sun), the free-range branch of London Zoo, was originally established to breed endangered species in captivity and aims to release 50 animals into the wild for every one captured. The 2500 animals (including tigers, giraffes and wallabies) on the 2.4-sq-km site in pleasingly large enclosures can be viewed by car, on the park's railway or on foot.

It costs an additional £8.50 for a car if you want to drive around the park.

Whipsnade is about 5 miles (8km) southwest of Luton. **Green Line** (☎ 0870 608 7261) bus No 758 departs Bulleid Way, London Victoria, at 9am, to Hemel Hempstead, from where bus No 43 serves Whipsnade (£8.60/4.30 return), returning at 3.30pm.

Northamptonshire

Some pious Saxons, a homicidal humpbacked king and Doc Marten: what do these people have in common? Answer: Northamptonshire, one of those Midlands counties with many delightful spots to visit but no single major drawcard pulling in the hordes. In many ways this makes it an ideal touring region: the history and culture are here, but you get to see them without having to peer over anyone's shoulder. The countryside is dotted with stately homes, ancient churches and Tudor mansions as well as a few more offbeat attractions.

Orientation & Information
Northamptonshire is roughly 50 miles long and 20 wide, running southwest to northeast. The M1 motorway cuts diagonally across the county just below Northampton, which lies in the middle; attractions are scattered widely. For general information about the county, check the website **w** www.visitnorthamptonshire.info. Northampton's TIC stocks plenty of information about the whole county.

Getting Around
Buses run to most places of interest from Northampton and other nearby towns; some services run only a few times daily, so it's best to check times with the operator. **Stagecoach** (**w** www.stagecoachbus.com) has timetables on the Internet, or call the **Traveline** (☎ 0870 608 2608). Driving is the way to see the most of the county; turning a corner on a winding country lane and coming across a sleepy village is one of the joys of the region. All the major car rental companies have branches in Northampton.

NORTHAMPTON
☎ 01604 • pop 179,600
A modern town with pockets of history, Northampton doesn't see a whole lot of tourists but why complain? There's enough here to keep you occupied for a day, and it's a good base for trips around the county.

Although nothing significant remains of it, Thomas à Becket was tried for fraud in Northampton Castle in 1164. The Industrial Revolution made the town a shoe-manufacturing centre and around town are numerous factory shops knocking out cheap Doc Martens and, for serious gentlemen, Churches also has some bespoke outlets.

The town is centred on the Market Square, with the main pedestrianised shopping route Abington St running east from it, which becomes the Kettering Rd, with its hotels and bars. To the south of Market Square is the Guildhall and TIC, and the bus station is north.

The helpful **TIC** (☎ 622677, fax 604180; **w** www.northampton.gov.uk/tourism; Guildhall Rd; open 10am-5pm Mon-Sat, 2pm-5pm Sun, 10am-2pm bank holidays) is in the Central Museum and has a huge amount of information about surrounding attractions. The free *Historic Town Trail* leaflet describes a walking tour of the town's hidden treasures.

The town is at its busiest during the annual festival in August, featuring concerts, displays and hot-air balloons.

Things to See & Do
Central Museum & Art Gallery (☎ 639415; Guildhall Rd; admission free; open 10am-5pm Mon-Sat, 2pm-5pm Sun) has a huge, well-presented collection of shoes from the 14th century to the present to make foot fetishists drool, as well as some fine paintings and special exhibitions.

The **Church of the Holy Sepulchre** (☎ 754782) has curiosity value as one of only four round churches in the country; founded after the first earl of Northampton returned from the Crusades in 1100, it's a close facsimile of its namesake in Jerusalem. Opening hours are irregular; call for details.

St Peter's Church (Mayfair) is a marvellous Norman edifice built in 1150 and restored in the 19th century by Gilbert Scott. The detail on the original capitals is outstanding. For rock-nuts: William Smith, known as the father of modern geology, is buried here. Get the key from the Black Lion pub next door.

Places to Stay & Eat
Aarandale Regent Hotel (☎ 631096; **e** info@aarandale.co.uk; 6-8 Royal Terrace, Barrack Rd; singles/doubles from £32/46) is a friendly, family-run B&B close to the centre.

Coach House Hotel (☎ 250981, fax 234248; 10 East Park Parade; **e** info@coach-house-hotel.com; en-suite singles/doubles from £55/65), a row of converted Victorian houses on the Kettering Rd, has modern, comfortable rooms.

Lime Trees Hotel (☎ 632188, fax 233012; **e** info@limetreeshotel.co.uk; 8 Langham Place; singles/doubles Mon-Thur £69/82, Fri-Sun £49/72) is a fine option, an attractive Georgian house about half a mile (1km) north of the centre.

Miraj (☎ 637659; e) the_miraj@amserve
.net; 28-34 Wellington St; mains £4.95-
11.95) is an upmarket Indian place, a cut
above the norm.

Joe's Diner (☎ 620022; 104a Abington St;
mains £6.75-16.95; closed Sun) breaks the
mould of the American theme eatery with a
huge range of quality burgers, friendly staff
and a healthy dearth of tacky 'memorabilia'.

The Vineyard (☎ 633978; 7 Derngate;
mains £12.95-16.95; closed Sun & lunch Fri)
is a smart place popular with businesspeople
and the pre-theatre crowd, offering French-
influenced options and fresh fish dishes.

Entertainment
The city centre is awash with the usual Rats,
Slugs, Moons and Hogs.

The Malt Shovel (☎ 234212; 121 Bridge
St), a Campaign for Real Ale (Camra)
favourite, offers a taste of local spirit. There
are always guest beers as well as a huge
international selection of bottled beers.

Picturedrome (☎ 230777; w www.thepic
turedrome.com; 222 Kettering Rd) is a vibey
bar hosting fortnightly comedy nights, live
music and other events.

Roadmender (☎ 604222; w www.road
mender.org; 1 Ladys Lane) is a local landmark,
a unique venue featuring up-and-coming
bands, theatre, comedy and club nights.

Derngate and **Royal Theatre** (☎ 624811;
w www.northamptontheatres.com; Guildhall
Rd) are managed together. The former is
Northampton's arts centre and hosts anything
from Tom Jones to Tom Thumb; the latter is
an impressive Victorian structure staging
local and quality West End productions.

Getting There & Away
Northampton is 68 miles (109km) from London. National Express coaches run to London
(£11.75 economy return, two hours, five
daily), Nottingham (£11.75, 2½ hours, daily)
and Birmingham (£6, 1½ hours, two daily).
Bus X38 serves Oxford (£5.99 day return, 1½
hours, four daily Monday to Saturday, two on
Sunday), while bus X7 heads to Leicester
(£5.99 day return, 80 minutes, hourly, five on
Sunday). Plenty of buses run to Kettering.
Greyfriars bus station is on Lady's Lane, just
north of the Grosvenor shopping centre.

Northampton has excellent rail links with
Birmingham (£11.50 saver return, one hour,
hourly) and London Euston (£21.60, one

hour, at least every 30 minutes). The train
station is about half a mile (1km) west of
town along Gold St.

AROUND NORTHAMPTON
Althorp
The late Diana, Princess of Wales, is commemorated in a memorial and museum in
the grounds of her ancestral home, Althorp
Park (bookings ☎ 0870 167 9000; w www
.althorp.com; adult/child £10.50/5.50, plus
£2.50 access to house; open 10am-5pm daily
July-Sept). The 16th-century mansion itself
houses works by Rubens, Gainsborough
and Van Dyck. Profits from ticket sales go
to her Memorial Fund. The limited number
of tickets must be booked by phone or on
the website. Incidentally, Althorp should be
pronounced altrup.

Althorp is off the A428 northwest of
Northampton. There are four buses daily linking Althorp with Northampton train station.

Stoke Bruerne
The Canal Museum (☎ 01604-862229;
w www.thewaterwaystrust.co.uk; adult/child
£3/2; open 10am-5pm daily Apr-Oct, 10am-
4pm Tues-Sun Nov-Mar), on a pretty stretch
of the Grand Union Canal at Stoke Bruerne,
8 miles (13km) south of Northampton, is an
excellent centre exploring the development
of English canals from the 17th century with
the aid of models, photos, costumes, panor-
amas and pieces of vintage equipment.

If the displays catch your eye, take a
cruise on the **Indian Chief** (☎ 01604-
862428), run by the Boat Inn; trips range
from 25 minutes (adult/child £2/1.50) to six
hours (£12/8).

Waterways Cottage (☎ 01604-863
865; e) wendycox@waterways.junglelink.com;
Bridge Rd; en-suite double £45) is a comfortable B&B behind The Boat Inn.

The Boat Inn (☎ 01604-862428; e) en
quiries@boatinn.co.uk, w www.boatinn.co.uk;
mains £2.95-10.95) is a charming thatched
canalside pub, one of several in the village.

Bus No 37 from Northampton to Milton
Keynes calls at Stoke Bruerne (£1.90/3.30
single/return, 30 minutes, four daily Monday to Saturday).

Sulgrave Manor
Built by Lawrence Washington after he was
sold the property by Henry VIII in 1539,

Sulgrave Manor (☎ 01295-760205; w www .stratford.co.uk/sulgrave; adult/child £5/2.50; open 2pm-5.30pm Tues-Thur, Sat & Sun Apr-Oct) is a well-preserved Tudor mansion; unsurprisingly, the fact that 250 years later a certain family descendant named George Washington became the first president of the USA bolsters the interest of overseas visitors. The family lived here for 120 years before Colonel John Washington moved to Virginia in 1656. Admission includes a guided tour.

Sulgrave Manor is just off the B4525, 7 miles (11km) northeast of Banbury.

All Saints, Brixworth

All Saints (☎ 01604-880286; usually open 10am-6pm Apr-Sept, 10am-4pm Oct-Mar) is England's largest relatively intact Saxon church (which doesn't mean it's huge!). Although the church itself is fascinating, it's almost more evocative viewed from the sheep-inhabited churchyard. Built on a basilica plan around AD 680, it incorporates Roman tiles from an earlier building. The tower and stair turret were added after 9th-century Viking raids, and the spire was built around 1350.

Brixworth is 6 miles (10km) north of Northampton off the A508. Bus X7 runs from Northampton (10 minutes, hourly Monday to Saturday, five on Sunday).

All Saints, Earls Barton

This wonderful (and still very active) worship-place (☎ 01604-810045; open 10.30am-12.30pm & 2pm-4pm Mon-Sat Apr-Sept, by appt Oct-Mar) is notable for its solid Saxon tower with patterns seemingly imitating earlier wooden models. Probably built during the reign of Edgar the Peaceful (r. 959–75), the 1st-floor door may have offered access to the tower during Viking raids. Around 1100 the Norman nave was added to the original tower; other features were added in subsequent centuries.

Earls Barton is 8 miles (13km) east of Northampton. Bus Nos 45 to 47 run from Northampton (10 minutes, every 20 minutes, seven on Sunday).

Rushton Triangular Lodge

To call the lodge (EH; ☎ 01536-710761; adult/child £1.95/1; open 10am-6pm daily Apr-Sept, 10am-5pm daily Oct) a folly is to underestimate the power of faith on the mind of Sir Thomas Tresham. He designed a number of buildings in the area (and was imprisoned more than once for expressing his Catholic beliefs). With three of everything, from sides to floors to gables, the lodge is Tresham's enduring symbol of the trinity, built at the end of the 16th century. Mysterious, esoteric inscriptions and a magical setting among rapeseed fields gives a visit a surprising impact.

The lodge is 4 miles (7km) northwest of Kettering. Bus No 19 from Kettering stops in Desborough, 2 miles away (20 minutes, every 30 minutes Monday to Saturday, every two hours on Sunday).

Kirby Hall

Once one of the finest Elizabethan mansions, known as the 'Jewel of the English Renaissance', the construction of Kirby Hall (EH; ☎ 01604-735400; adult/child £3.30/1.70; open 10am-6pm daily Apr-Sept, 10am-5pm daily Oct, 10am-4pm Sat & Sun Nov-Mar) was begun in 1570, with additions being made up to the 19th century. Abandoned and fallen into disrepair, it's still a remarkable, atmospheric site, with fine filigree stonework, ravens cawing in the empty halls and peacocks roaming its restored formal parterre gardens.

Kirby Hall is 4 miles (7km) northeast of Corby.

Oundle

Its streets and squares graced with the honey-coloured Jurassic limestone and Colleyweston slate roofs of 16th- and 17th-century buildings, Oundle is the photogenic face of Northamptonshire. It's also a good base for visiting nearby **Fotheringhay**, birthplace of Richard III (demonised by the Tudors and Shakespeare) and execution place of Mary, Queen of Scots, in 1587. The castle in which these events took place is now merely a small hillock, but Fotheringhay is a charming village with thatched cottages and a pub with much-lauded food, the **Falcon** (☎ 01832-226254).

Oundle's **TIC** (☎ 01832-274333, fax 273326; e oundletic@east-northamptonshire .gov.uk; 14 West St; open 9am-5pm Mon-Sat, also 1pm-4pm Sun Easter-Aug) sells a Walking Trail leaflet (£1) for exploring the quaint streets.

Haunted **Talbot Inn** (☎ 01832-273621, fax 274545; New St; B&B en-suite singles/doubles £70/95; bar food £3.85-6.35; served 11am-6pm), built in 1626, allegedly incorporates the staircase from nearby Fotheringhay Castle which Mary descended on the way to her execution; her executioner is reputed to have stayed here before he gave her the chop. Its pleasantly refurbished rooms retain the atmosphere of the old inn, and there's an upmarket restaurant.

Bus X4 runs hourly from Northampton (£3 single, 1½ hours, four on Sunday) and Peterborough (£2.50 single, 30 minutes).

Leicestershire & Rutland

Despite the recent marketing push, Leicestershire doesn't yet have the strongest tourism gravity; in some ways it's not surprising – locals themselves tend to play down the attractions of the county. However, in typical Midlands' fashion, it boasts some interesting small towns, a rich industrial heritage and a few key historic sites, plus magnificent Belvoir Castle. The county town has danceterias and drinking-holes worth a look, too.

Tiny Rutland was merged with Leicestershire in 1974, but in April 1997 regained its 'independence' as a county. With magnificent Rutland Water and charming settlements, it appeals to lovers of water sports and quaint villages.

Orientation & Information

Leicestershire and Rutland together look like an upside-down map of Australia. Leicester is virtually bang in the centre of its county, with the M1 motorway running north–south just to the west, dividing the largely industrial towns and National Forest of the west from the more rural east, including Belvoir Castle. Rutland's little solar system, east of Leicester and tucked away between four counties, revolves around central Rutland Water.

For general county-wide information, contact **Leicestershire Tourism** (☎ 0116-265 7302; e tourism@leics.gov.uk).

Getting Around

Bus services in Leicestershire are operated by **Arriva Fox County** (☎ 0116-264 400); it's

best to get timetable information from the **Traveline** (☎ 0870 608 2608). A steam train runs between Leicester and Loughborough; see the Leicester Getting There & Away section for details.

LEICESTER
☎ 0116 • pop 318,500

Like many a Midlands' town, Leicester (**lester**) suffered reversals of fortune at the hands of the Luftwaffe, thoughtless urban planners and industrial decline. Although nobody would call Leicester beautiful, it's taken the best of post-war changes and made good, reinventing itself as an environmentally progressive, ethnic melting pot that could teach other, bigger centres a thing or two about multiculturalism. The modern town has a large and vibrant Asian community and there are Hindu, Muslim, Jain and Sikh temples as well as some excellent Asian restaurants. Many of the city's most interesting events are staged around festivals such as Holi, Diwali and Eid-ul-Fitr. Nightlife, though not as diverse or noted as in neighbouring Nottingham, is definitely on the up.

The city's history dates back to Roman times. Later, it was one of the five Danelaw towns and was the traditional home of Shakespeare's tragic King Lear and his daughters. In 1239 Simon de Montfort, earl of Leicester, captured the castle. Medieval Leicester became a centre for manufacturing stockings but remained a small town until the rapid industrial growth of the 19th century.

Orientation & Information

Leicester is initially difficult to navigate as there are few landmarks, but the pedestrianised central area around the market and clock tower makes things a little simpler. For drivers, it's plagued by the usual maze of one-way streets and forbidden turns. Although there isn't a ring road as such, the A594 does almost a whole circuit and most attractions flank or are contained within it.

The centre of the Asian community, Belgrave Rd (the 'Golden Mile') is about a mile northeast of the centre. Castle Park, with many of the historic attractions, lies immediately west of the centre, beside De Montfort University.

The **TIC** (☎ 299 8888, fax 225 4050; w www.discoverleicester.com; 7-9 Every St; open 9am-5.30pm Mon-Wed & Fri, 10am-

5.30pm Thur, 10am-5pm Sat) is on Town Hall Square. Walking tours run from the TIC a couple of times a week, costing adult/child £2.50/2. Call the TIC for details.

There are three reasonably priced Internet cafés. **Ice Mango** (☎ 262 6255; 4 Market Place; open 9am-7pm Mon-Sat, 11am-5.30pm Sun) is the most central charging £1/1.80 per half-/one hour, while **J:Café** (☎ 254 9927; 49 Braunstone Gate; open 11am-7.30pm Mon-Sat, noon-6pm Sun) is in the hip bar district and costs £2 per hour. **CyberCuts** (☎ 285 6661; 122 Granby St; open 7am-9pm Mon-Sat, 10am-9pm Sun) is an interesting option: a barber's shop where you surf for £1/1.50 per half-/one hour while you await your trim.

Jewry Wall & Museums
Leicester's museums (**w** www.leicestermuseums.ac.uk) are free and open 10am to 5pm Monday to Saturday and 1pm to 5pm Sunday April to September (10am to 4pm daily October to March).

Despite its name, **Jewry Wall** is one of England's largest Roman civil structures and has nothing to do with Judaism. You can walk among excavated remains of the Roman public baths (around AD 150), of which the wall was part. Notwithstanding its grim external appearance, the **Jewry Wall Museum** (☎ 247 3021; St Nicholas Circle) contains wonderful Roman mosaics and frescoes, as well as an interactive exhibition, The Making of Leicester, with lots of artefacts and models.

New Walk Museum & Art Gallery (☎ 255 4100; New Walk) houses a collection of fine Victorian, German and decorative art as well as Egyptian mummies, natural history displays and changing exhibitions.

Newarke Houses Museum (☎ 247 3222; The Newarke) contains a surprisingly varied collection in two 16th-century buildings. There are some reconstructed period shops, displays of various oddities (an extensive selection of truncheons covers 1796–1886!) and exhibitions on two of Leicester's best-known citizens: Daniel Lambert (see the boxed text 'Leicester's Weightiest Citizen' following) and Thomas Cook, the package-holiday pioneer.

In the late 14th-century **Guildhall** (☎ 253 2569; Guildhall Lane), reputedly the most haunted building in Leicester, you can peer

Leicester's Weightiest Citizen
Born in 1770, Daniel Lambert, the one-time keeper of Leicester Gaol, started life as a normal baby but soon began to tip the scales at ever more alarming totals. Despite eating only one meal a day, by age 23 he weighed 32 stone (202kg) and by 39 an astounding 52 stone 11lb (333kg), making him, as the Dictionary of National Biography puts it, 'the most corpulent man of whom authentic record exists'.

When he died in Stamford in 1809 one wall of the house had to be dismantled to remove the coffin, and 20 pallbearers were needed to carry it to the graveyard. A whole room in Leicester's Newarke Houses Museum is devoted to Lambert's memory.

into old police cells and inspect a copy of the last gibbet used to expose the body of an executed murderer. There are also small temporary exhibitions.

National Space Centre
This centre (☎ 0870 607 7223; **w** www.spacecentre.co.uk; Exploration Dr; adult/child £7.95/5.95; open 9.30am-6pm Tues-Sun, plus Mon during Leicester school holidays, last entry 4.30pm) is a spectacular and successful attempt to bring space science to us ordinary mortals. Interactive displays cover cosmic myths, the history of astronomy and of course the development of space travel; in the Space Now! area you can check on the status of all current space missions. Films in the domed Space Theatre (included in admission price) launch you to the far reaches of the galaxy, and you can come back to earth with a coffee in **Boosters** café, sitting beneath huge booster rockets. The centre is off the A6 about 1½ miles (2.5km) north of the city centre. Take bus No 54 from Charles St or 61 from Haymarket bus station.

Temples
Materials were shipped in from India to convert a disused church into a **Jain Centre** (☎ 254 3091; **w** www.jaincentre.com; 32 Oxford St; open 8.30am-8.30pm Mon-Sat, 8.30am-6.30pm Sun). The building is faced with marble, and the temple (the first outside the subcontinent and the only one in

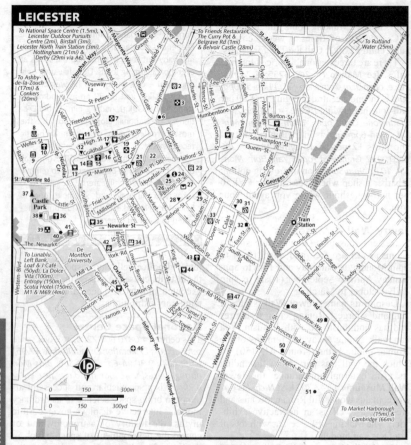

LEICESTER

Europe) boasts a forest of beautifully carved pillars inside. Jainism evolved in India at around the same time as Buddhism.

Close to the Jewry Wall is the Sikh **Guru Nanak Gurdwara** (☎ 262 8606; 9 Holy Bones; open 1pm-4pm Thur or by arrangement). There is a small museum, which contains an impressive model of the Golden Temple in Amritsar.

Activities

The **Leicester Outdoor Pursuits Centre** (☎ 268 1426; W www.lopc.homestead.com; Loughborough Rd) is the place to head for canoeing, abseiling, archery and all manner of pastimes for the over-energetic. All activities cost £55 for two hours, except quad-biking (£90 for two hours).

Special Events

Leicester hosts numerous cultural and religious festivals throughout the year; contact the TIC for details. The Asian community celebrates **Diwali** during autumn and the celebration, the largest of its kind outside India, draws visitors from all around the world.

During August the city hosts the biggest **Caribbean Carnival** (☎ 225 7770; W www.lccarnival.org.uk) outside London's Notting Hill Carnival. The **Comedy Festival** (☎ 291 5511; W www.comedy-festival.co.uk) in February is now the largest in the country, drawing big names and new talent.

Places to Stay

The TIC makes bookings for £2.

LEICESTER

PLACES TO STAY		18	The Globe	24	Tourist Information Centre
29	Ramada Jarvis Hotel	35	The Charlotte		(TIC)
32	YMCA; The Y	44	Weavers	25	The Bike Park
48	Belmont House Hotel	45	Swan & Rushes	26	Town Hall
49	Park Hotel			27	Post Office
50	Spindle Lodge	**OTHER**		31	Cyber Cuts
		1	St Margaret's Bus Station	33	Little Theatre
PLACES TO EAT		2	Haymarket Theatre; Dino's	34	Phoenix Arts Centre
12	Noodle Bar	3	Haymarket Shopping Centre	36	St Mary de Castro Church
16	Opera House	6	Clock Tower	37	Richard III Statue
17	Liquid	7	Shires Shopping Centre	38	Courthouse
20	The Case	8	Guru Nanak Gurdwara	39	Castle Motte
28	Whole Truth Café	9	Jewry Wall Museum	40	Turret Gate
30	Bossa	10	St Nicholas Church	41	Newarke Houses Museum
		14	Guildhall	42	Jain Centre
PUBS, BARS & CLUBS		15	St Martin's Cathedral	43	Holy Cross Church
4	J21	19	St Martin's Shopping Centre	46	Royal Infirmary
5	Attic	21	Ice Mango	47	New Walk Museum & Art
11	Orange Tree	22	Market		Gallery
13	Po Na Na	23	Jongleurs Comedy Club	51	De Montfort Hall

The **YMCA** (☎ 255 6507; 7 East St; singles £12) is just across from the train station; long-stay rates are lower.

Leicestershire Backpackers Hostel (☎ 267 3107; 157 Wanlip Lane, Birstall; tents £5, beds per night/week £10/48) is an odd little place 3 miles north of the centre; it takes under-26 travellers only, cooking is communal and rates include a basic breakfast. Bus services are variable; phone the hostel for details.

There are some cheap B&Bs on and near London Rd and Saxby St, south of the train station, although this is not the most salubrious area.

Park Hotel (☎ 255 4329; 125 London Rd; singles/doubles with shared facilities £25/35, with bath £35/45) is a reasonable, if rather unexciting, place.

Westcotes Dr, off Narborough Rd, is a better hunting ground.

Scotia Hotel (☎/fax 254 9200; e scotiahotel@amserve.com; 10 Westcotes Dr; en-suite singles/doubles £27/42) is a friendly, old-school B&B; it's much nicer inside than out.

Moving up a notch, **Spindle Lodge** (☎ 233 8801, fax 233 8804; e spindlelodgeleicester@orange.net; 2 West Walk; en-suite singles/doubles from £40/65) is a charming Victorian town house with a restaurant and bar. Rooms with shared bathroom are cheaper.

Belmont House Hotel (☎ 254 4773, fax 247 0804; e info@belmonthotel.co.uk; De Montfort St; singles/doubles Sun-Thur £95/105, Sat & Sun £55/80) is a Georgian-style building but with modern, comfortable rooms.

Ramada Jarvis Hotel (☎ 255 5599, fax 254 4736; e sales.leicester@ramadajarvis.com; Granby St; singles/doubles Sun-Thur from £110/124, B&B Fri-Sun £49/78), a central, Grade II–listed establishment, is the city's top option.

Places to Eat

The 'Golden Mile' on Belgrave Rd, a mile (1.5km) to the north of the centre (take bus No 22 or 37 from Haymarket bus station), is noted for its fine Indian and vegetarian restaurants.

Friends (☎ 266 8809; 41-43 Belgrave Rd; mains £5-12; closed Sun lunchtime), an award-winning tandoori eatery, serves excellent northern-Indian food, with a range of fish and vegetarian dishes.

The Curry Pot (☎ 253 8256; e mail@the currypot.co.uk; 78-80 Belgrave Rd; mains £5-13; closed Sun) has an unusual angle: both Indian and Portuguese cuisines are on the menu in a funky, bright space.

Back in town, **Noodle Bar** (☎ 262 9029; 1 St Nicholas Place; noodles £4; closed Sun lunchtime) draws students and time-pressed suits with tasty, filling, good-value Chinese food.

Whole Truth Café (☎ 254 2722; 19 Belvoir St; lunch £3-6; open 9am-4pm Mon-Sat) is a lively vegetarian place with a creative menu. Works by local artists grace the walls.

Liquid (☎ 261 9086; 5 Guildhall Lane; toasted baguettes £2; open 8.30am-6pm Mon-Sat, plus Sun Dec) is a cool juice bar for

THE MIDLANDS

mid-shop munching. Wash down your sun-dried tomato and mozzarella baguette with a banana lassi (£1.60 to £2).

Bossa (☎ 233 4544; 110 Granby St; toasties £1) has cheap toasted sarnies in a cheerful, almost European atmosphere, and pavement tables for hot days. At night it draws a gay crowd.

La Dolce Vita (☎ 254 0006; 36 Narborough Rd; pasta £6-8; open 7pm-11pm Tues-Sat) is a small, local Italian joint with decent pastas and specialities such as *Trota* (oven-baked trout with garlic and lemon sauce £10.95).

Opera House (☎ 223 6666; 10 Guildhall Lane; 2/3-course lunch £11.75/13.50, dinner mains £15-19) wins awards for its modern British cuisine (with a hint of French influence); it's one of the swankier places in town.

Dino's (☎ 262 8308; 13 Garrick Walk; 3-course lunch £9, mains £8.50-15; closed Sun), next to the Haymarket Theatre, offers Mediterranean and Pacific Rim cuisine in a modern, sleek environment.

The Case (☎/fax 251 7675; 4-6 Hotel St; mains £7-16; closed Sun) epitomises stylish contemporary dining, in a bright, airy first-floor space. Food is fashionable (pan-fried calf liver, wild boar sausages, scallops) and competent; the basement Champagne Bar serves cheaper snacks.

Most bars offer good food.

Entertainment

Pubs & Bars Leicester has a thriving nightlife, due partly to the huge student population at Leicester and De Montfort Universities. Places come and go by the month; check the website **w** www.leicesterguide.co.uk/bars for up-to-the-minute tips. The centre has some good boozers and a few hip bars, as well as the inevitable rash of chain pubs.

The Globe (☎ 262 9819; 43 Silver St) is that rare beast, a traditional old pub (built 1720) in the centre with fine draught ales, a warm atmosphere and decent bar snacks.

You like beers? How many beers? **Swan & Rushes** (☎ 233 9167; 19 Infirmary Square) has five ales on tap and over 100 bottled options, plus unusual European snacks (continental meats and cheeses).

The Orange Tree (☎ 223 5256; 99 High St) is a chilled, cool little café-bar; the skylights and comfy sofas lend a relaxed air.

The left bank of the canal is an up-and-coming area; Braunstone Gate, Narborough Rd and Hinckley Rd are wall-to-wall bars and eateries.

Left Bank (☎ 255 2422; 26 Braunstone Gate) set the pace in this district, and offers good Euro-centric food.

Loaf (☎ 299 9424; 58-64 Braunstone Gate) has newspapers, bottled beers and the immortal motto 'it is better to have loafed and lost, than never to have loafed at all'.

Entropy (☎ 225 9650; 42 Hinckley Rd) has cool, minimal decor, subtle lighting and smooth tunes; it also does good bar food and an all-day breakfast (from £6). Look for the H North sign.

Lunablu (☎ 255 1911; 54 Braunstone Gate) is the pre-club bar of choice, with DJs and a late licence at the weekend.

Clubs & Gigs At **J21** (☎ 251 9333; 13 Midland St), one of Leicester's biggest clubs, big-name DJs play loud house.

Po Na Na (☎ 253 8190; 24 Careys Close), along with sister lounge bar Bam Bu Da, is currently red hot, pleasing those in the know with funk, house and sleazy vibes.

Attic (☎ 222 3800; Free Lane), a smallish venue off Halford Lane, drops hip-hop, breakbeat, latin electronica and indie.

Weavers (☎ 254 0004; 54 King St) is undergoing a bit of a renaissance with discerning clubbers, especially the gay scene.

The Charlotte (☎ 255 3956; **w** www.thecharlotte.co.uk; 8 Oxford St) is Leicester's legendary venue that has played host to the biggies, including Oasis and Blur, before they became megastars. It's a small place with a late licence and regular club nights.

Bands that are just too big to squeeze in these days usually play at **De Montfort Hall** (☎ 233 3111; **w** www.demontforthall.co.uk; Granville Rd), southeast of the centre, which also stages classical concerts.

Theatre & Comedy The **Phoenix Arts Centre** (☎ 255 4854; **w** www.phoenix.org.uk; Newarke St) hosts art-house films, fringe plays, comedy and dance events.

Venues for plays also include **Little Theatre** (☎ 255 1302; **w** www.thelittletheatre.net; Dover St). **Haymarket Theatre** (☎ 253 9797; **w** leicesterhaymarkettheatre.org; 1 Belgrave Gate) has more mainstream fare. **The Y** (☎ 255 6507; 7 East St) is a multipurpose theatre/bar venue attached to the YMCA, hosting concerts, poetry, plays and other 'events'.

Jongleurs Comedy Club (☎ 0870 787 0707; w www.jongleurs.com; 30-32 Granby St) often hosts big-name acts.

Getting There & Away

Bus National Express operates from St Margaret's bus station on Gravel St, north of the centre, to London (£19 economy return, three hours, nine daily) and Birmingham (£6.50, one hour, six daily). Express bus No 777 runs to Nottingham (£3.50 day return, one hour, eight daily Monday to Saturday), while Nos X67 (£3.50, one hour, hourly) and 157 (every 30 minutes) run to Coventry.

Train There are trains running to London St Pancras (£35.70 saver return, 1½ hours, every 30 minutes), Birmingham (£11, one hour, every 30 minutes) and Cambridge (£32.30, two hours, hourly).

More tourist jaunt than serious transport option, **The Great Central Railway** (☎ 01509-230726; w www.gcrailway.co.uk) operates steam locomotives between Leicester North station on Redhill Circle and Loughborough Central, the route along which Thomas Cook ran his original package tour in 1841. The 8-mile (13km) trip runs every weekend and daily, May to August. The return trip costs adult/child £9.50/6.50. Take bus No 37, 61 or 61A from Haymarket bus station.

Getting Around

Central Leicester is fairly flat and easy to get around on foot. As an alternative to local buses, **Discover Leicester** (☎ 299 8888; adult/under-15 £3.50/2.50) runs a jump-on-jump-off bus around the city and up to Belgrave Rd, the Great Central Railway and the National Space Centre every 30 minutes from 10am to 5pm on Saturday, Sunday and school holidays from May to October.

The Bike Park (☎ 299 1234; Town Hall Square; open 8am-6.30pm Mon-Fri, 8.30am-6pm Sat) offers a great service, including bike hire (£7.50/4 per day/half-day), bike parking (30p/£1 per hour/day), showers (65p), information and cycle maps.

AROUND LEICESTER
Bosworth Battlefield

The **Battlefield Visitor Centre** (☎ 01455-290429; adult/child £3/2; open 11am-5pm daily Apr-Oct, Sun only Nov & Dec, Sat & Sun March) features an exhibition about the Battle of Bosworth Field, where Richard III was defeated by the future Henry VII in 1485, ending the Wars of the Roses; 'a horse, a horse, my kingdom for a horse', was his famous death cry (at least, according to the Bard). Richard III may be known as a villain for his supposed role in the murder of the 'princes in the tower', but Leicester has adopted him as something of a folk hero, not the hunchback of Shakespearean spin. The battle is re-enacted annually.

The battlefield is 16 miles (24km) southwest of Leicester at Sutton Cheny. Bus No 153 runs hourly from Leicester to Market Bosworth, 2 miles (3km) to the north.

Ashby-de-la-Zouch

☎ 01530 • pop 10,600 • elevation 146m

Itself a mildly appealing market town, Ashby's draw is the **castle** (EH; ☎ 413343; admission £3; open 10am-6pm daily Apr-Sept, 10am-5pm daily Oct, 10am-4pm Wed-Sun Nov-Mar). Built in Norman times and owned by the Zouch family until 1399, it was extended in the 14th and 15th centuries and then reduced to its present picturesque ruined state in 1648 after the Civil War; a lively audioguide introduces the characters and details the history. Bring a torch (flashlight) to explore the underground passageway connecting the tower with the kitchen.

For town information contact Ashby-de-la-Zouch **TIC** (☎ 411767, fax 560660; North St; open 10am-5pm Mon-Fri, 10am-3pm Sat). Ashby is on the A511 about 15 miles (24km) northwest of Leicester. Bus No 118 (No 218 Sun) runs hourly from St Margaret's bus station in Leicester.

Conkers & The National Forest

The National Forest is an ongoing project to plant 30 million trees in a swathe from Leicester through Derbyshire and into Staffordshire. Central to the scheme is Conkers (☎ 01283-216633; w www.visit conkers.com; Rawdon Rd, Moira; adult/child £5.25/3.25; open 10am-5pm daily), a purpose-built visitor centre with a range of interactive displays on woodland life, biology and environmental issues. There's lots of touching, smelling and hearing: it's a multisensory experience designed to captivate children but fascinating for all. Conkers is northwest of Leicester off the A444; it's tricky to get to by public transport.

Belvoir Castle

In the wilds of the county is Belvoir (**bee-ver**) Castle (☎ 01476-870262; W *www.belvoir castle.com; adult/child £7/4.50; open 11am-5pm daily May-Sept, selected days in Apr, Sun only Oct*), a magnificent baroque and Gothic fantasy rebuilt in the 19th century after suffering serious damage during the Civil War, and home to the duke of Rutland. A hefty portion of the sumptuous interior is open to the public, and collections of weaponry, medals and art (including masterpieces by Reynolds, Gainsborough, Holbein and Rubens) are highlights. There are marvellous views across the countryside, and peacocks roam the delightful gardens. Belvoir is 6 miles (10km) west of Grantham, off the A1.

RUTLAND

Rutland's motto is 'Multum in Parvo' ('so much in so little') and it is England's smallest county, much of it formed by **Rutland Water**, a vast and attractive reservoir offering ample opportunity for water sports and activities of all kinds, including climbing, bird-watching and sailing. The **Rutland Belle** (☎ 01572-787630; W *www.rutlandwater cruises.com; The Harbour, Whitwell Park*) offers pleasure cruises every afternoon, May to September, costing adult/child £4.50/3.50. The **Watersports Centre** (☎ 01780-460154; *Whitwell*) organises windsurfing, canoeing and sailing. **Rutland Sailing School** (☎ 01780-721999; W *www.rutlandsailingschool.co.uk; Edith Weston*) offers tuition to sailors of all abilities. For bike hire contact **Rutland Water Cycling** (☎ 01780-460705; W *www.rutland cycling .co.uk; Whitwell Car Park*).

The sleepy county town of **Oakham** has a famous school and **Oakham Castle** (*admission free; open 10am-1pm & 1.30pm-5pm Mon-Sat, 1pm-5pm Sunday, shorter hours Nov-Feb*), really the Great Hall, sole standing remnant of a Norman structure. Oakham's **TIC** (☎/fax 01572-724329; *34 High St; open 10am-4pm Tues-Sat*) handles visitor inquiries; there is another branch (☎ 01572-653026; *Sykes Lane, Empingham*) by Rutland Water. Bus No 2 runs from Nottingham (£2.60, 1¼ hours, hourly); trains run roughly hourly from Leicester (day return £5.90) and Peterborough (£5.90).

South of Oakham is the village of Lyddington, 6 miles (10km) north of Corby, home to the **Bede House** (EH; ☎ 01572-822438; *adult/child £3/1.50; open 10am-6pm daily Apr-Sept, 10am-5pm daily Oct*). Originally a wing of the medieval rural palace of the Bishops of Lincoln, in 1600 it was converted into almshouses. Although the interior is sparsely furnished now, fine interpretative displays and an excellent free audioguide fill in the gaps.

Nottinghamshire

Most famous for a man in tights (Robin Hood, his merry men and the Sheriff of Nottingham are still totems of business and tourism alike), Nottinghamshire is a lot more than Lincoln green and fat friars. Nottingham itself draws the movers and shakers, in business as in clubbing, and there are several other places with historical or literary connections that beg a visit.

Listen out for the peculiar Brum-cum-Yorkshire accent, and don't be alarmed if you're greeted with a hearty 'eyupmeduck'.

Orientation & Information

Nottinghamshire is tall and thin, spreading a surprising distance north of Nottingham to finish level with Sheffield, though most of the county's attractions are in the southern half, with Newstead and Eastwood just north of Nottingham, Sherwood Forest in the county's centre and Newark and Southwell to the east.

Tourism is organised by district and town, although there's a website providing county-wide information at W www.notting hamshiretourism.co.uk.

Getting Around

Useful journey planners with details of bus transport around the county can be found on W www.ukbus.co.uk and W www.utc .nottscc .gov.uk. **Sherwood Forester buses** (☎ 0115-977 4268) operate to tourist attractions all over Nottinghamshire on Sundays and bank holidays in summer. An unlimited-travel Ranger Ticket for £5/2.50 gives discounted admission to some attractions.

NOTTINGHAM
☎ 0115 • pop 270,200

Nottingham is the surprise package of the east Midlands, home to a vibrant fashion, music and sporting scene that competes with

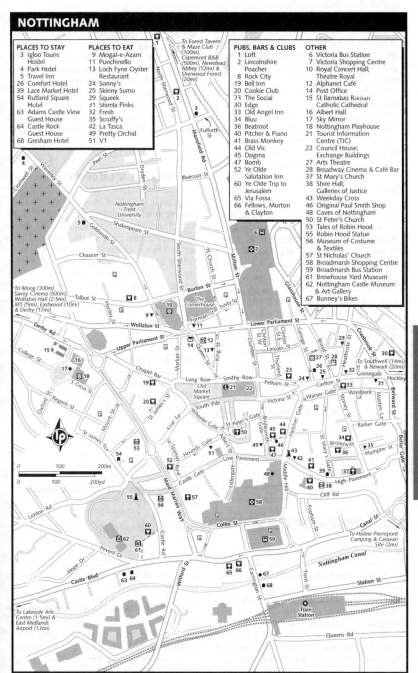

NOTTINGHAM

PLACES TO STAY
3 Igloo Touris Hostel
4 Park Hotel
5 Travel Inn
26 Comfort Hotel
39 Lace Market Hotel
54 Rutland Square Hotel
63 Adams Castle View Guest House
64 Castle Rock Guest House
68 Gresham Hotel

PLACES TO EAT
9 Mogal-e-Azam
11 Punchinello
13 Loch Fyne Oyster Restaurant
24 Sonny's
25 Skinny Sumo
29 Squeek
31 Shimla Pinks
32 Fresh
35 Scruffy's
42 La Tasca
49 Pretty Orchid
51 V1

PUBS, BARS & CLUBS
1 Loft
2 Lincolnshire Poacher
8 Rock City
19 Bell Inn
20 Cookie Club
23 The Social
30 Edge
33 Old Angel Inn
34 Bluu
36 Beatroot
40 Pitcher & Piano
41 Brass Monkey
44 Old Vic
45 Dogma
47 Bomb
52 Ye Olde Salutation Inn
60 Ye Olde Trip to Jerusalem
65 Via Fossa
66 Fellows, Morton & Clayton

OTHER
6 Victoria Bus Station
7 Victoria Shopping Centre
10 Royal Concert Hall; Theatre Royal
12 Alphanet Café
14 Post Office
15 St Barnabas Roman Catholic Cathedral
16 Albert Hall
17 Sky Mirror
18 Nottingham Playhouse
21 Tourist Information Centre (TIC)
22 Council House; Exchange Buildings
27 Arts Theatre
28 Broadway Cinema & Café Bar
37 St Mary's Church
38 Shire Hall; Galleries of Justice
43 Weekday Cross
46 Original Paul Smith Shop
48 Caves of Nottingham
50 St Peter's Church
53 Tales of Robin Hood
55 Robin Hood Statue
56 Museum of Costume & Textiles
57 St Nicholas' Church
58 Broadmarsh Shopping Centre
59 Broadmarsh Bus Station
61 Brewhouse Yard Museum
62 Nottingham Castle Museum & Art Gallery
67 Bunney's Bikes

THE MIDLANDS

The Legend of Robin Hood

In the Middle Ages most of Nottinghamshire was covered in forest, stomping ground (legend has it) of Robin Hood and his merry men, trying to stymie the wicked Sheriff of Nottingham in the name of absentee 'good' King Richard I.

Sites associated with Robin abound. Nottingham Castle obviously played a key role, as did St Mary's Church in the Lace Market. Robin is said to have married Maid Marian in Edwinstowe church, while Fountaindale, near Blidworth, is the supposed site of his battle with Friar Tuck.

But did Robin ever really exist? As long ago as 1377 William Langland made fleeting reference to him in his poem *Piers Plowman*, but it was only in the early 16th century that the story began to be fleshed out, most notably in the ballad *A Geste of Robyn Hoode*. In 1795 Joseph Ritson collected all the known accounts of Robin into one volume, since then innumerable authors (including Scott and Tennyson) have produced torrid novels and poems, while heart-throbs such as Errol Flynn, Kevin Costner and, um, Jason Connery have portrayed the robber-of-the-rich on silver and square screens.

Disappointingly, researchers have failed to turn up any hard evidence that the outlaw actually existed. He is, for example, said to have been born in Lockesley in Yorkshire or Nottinghamshire, but no such place appears on any map. Optimists point to a Loxley in Staffordshire where Hood's father supposedly owned land. But it may be that 'Robin' is no more than a jumbled memory of ancient ideas about forest fairies, or a character made up to give voice to medieval resentments.

the best in England. Long a centre of industry known for Raleigh bikes, the Boots pharmacy empire and (ahem) cigarette production, the old manufacturing base is diminished; however, fashion designer Paul Smith is a leading light, the clubs and bars are some of the liveliest in the country, and Trent Bridge remains a major draw for cricket fans. It's also a mecca for shopaholics drawn from miles around, a remarkably appealing town, as shopping centres go.

The Saxon city bore the less than charming name of Snotingham, but modern Nottingham had its moment of glory in the 19th century when the lace industry transformed the city centre. Lace-making declined during the 1890s and was virtually killed off by WWI, although the tourist industry supports some small-scale lace production.

Nottingham's famed Goose Fair dates back to the Middle Ages; these days it's an outsized funfair, which takes place in the Forest Recreation Ground.

Orientation & Information

Like other Midlands' cities, Nottingham is chopped in pieces by an inner ring road enclosing most of the attractions, eateries and bars. The train station is south of the canal on the southern edge of the centre. There are two bus stations: Victoria bus station is hidden away behind the Victoria shopping centre, just north of the city centre, while Broadmarsh bus station is behind Broadmarsh shopping centre to the south.

The **TIC** (☎ 915 5330, fax 915 5323; w www.visitnottingham.com; 1-4 Smithy Row; open 9am-5.30pm Mon-Fri, 9am-5pm Sat year round, 11am-3pm Sun May-Sept) is in the Council House on Old Market Square.

Discount tandem tickets are available for some attractions: for example, admission to both the caves and Tales of Robin Hood costs adult/child £8.50/6.

Alphanet Café (☎ 956 6988; 4 Queen St; open 9.30am-8.30pm Mon-Thur, 9.30am-7pm Fri & Sat) is the central option for coffee and cyberculture charging £2 for 30 minutes.

Nottingham Castle Museum & Art Gallery

Nottingham Castle was demolished after the Civil War and replaced with a mansion in 1674. The 'castle' itself is nothing to get excited about, but is worth visiting for the museum (☎ 915 3700; adult/child £2/1 Sat & Sun, free Mon-Fri; open 10am-5pm daily Mar-Oct, 10am-5pm Sat-Thur Nov-Feb) opened inside the castle shell in 1875. Nottingham's history is vividly described, and some of the medieval alabaster carvings for which Nottingham was noted are displayed. Upstairs there's an art gallery with changing exhibitions and some fine permanent pieces (Lowry, Delacroix and Rosetti).

There's a stylish café and an excellent shop. Events including a Shakespeare Festival and Robin Hood Pageant are held here; call for details.

An underground passageway, known as Mortimer's Hole, leads from the castle to Brewhouse Yard. Roger Mortimer, who arranged Edward II's murder, is said to have been captured by supporters of Edward III who entered via this passage. Tours of Mortimer's Hole take place at 2pm and 3pm Monday to Friday (adult/child £2/1).

Caves of Nottingham
Nottingham stands on a plug of Sherwood sandstone that is riddled with constructed caves dating back to medieval times. Rather surprisingly, the entrance to the most fascinating, readily accessible caves (☎ 924 1424; adult/child £3.75/2.75; open 10am-5pm Mon-Sat, 11am-5pm Sun) is inside Broadmarsh shopping centre. These contain an air-raid shelter, a medieval underground tannery, several pub cellars and a mock-up of a Victorian slum dwelling.

The Tales of Robin Hood
The Tales (☎ 948 3284; w www.robinhood .uk.com; 30-38 Maid Marian Way; adult/child £6.50/4.50; open 10am-6pm daily May-Sept, 10am-5.30pm daily Oct-Apr) is a sub-Tussauds-style attraction (almost a fairground ride in places) that takes you through models of Nottingham Castle and Sherwood Forest in the days when Robin was battling it out with the sheriff. Afterwards you can find out more about the reality behind the legend. It's quite commercialised, but fun.

Wollaton Hall
Built in 1588 by Sir Francis Willoughby, land and coal mine owner, Wollaton Hall (☎ 915 3900; Wollaton Park, Derby Rd; open 11am-5pm daily Apr-Oct, 11am-4pm daily Nov-Mar) is a fine example of Tudor architecture at its most extravagant. Architect Robert Smythson was also responsible for the equally avant-garde Longleat (see the Wessex chapter). The hall now houses a decent natural history museum.

The Industrial Museum (open 10am-5pm daily Apr-Oct), in the 18th-century stable block, displays lace-making equipment, Raleigh bicycles, a gigantic 1858 beam engine and oddities such as a locally invented,

1963 video recorder that never got off the ground.

Wollaton Park, surrounding the hall, is a popular picnic spot.

Admission to either museum is free Monday to Friday, £1.50/80p on Saturday and Sunday, adult/child £2/1 for a combined ticket to both museums. Wollaton Hall is on the western edge of the city, 2½ miles (4km) from the centre; get there on bus No 35, 36 or 37.

Brewhouse Yard Museum
Housed in five 17th-century cottages virtually below the castle, this museum (☎ 915 3600; Castle Boulevard; adult/child £1.50/80p Sat & Sun, free Mon-Fri; open 10am-4.30pm daily) re-creates everyday life in Nottingham over the past 300 years with particularly fine reconstructions of traditional shops, and hosts good temporary exhibitions.

Museum of Costume & Textiles
Arranged in period rooms, this intriguing museum (☎ 915 3500; Castle Gate; admission free; open 10am-4pm Wed-Sun & bank holidays) displays costumes from 1790 to the mid-20th century, as well as tapestries and lace. Again, it's housed in a row of 17th- and 18th-century houses and is worth a look even if needlework isn't your bag.

Galleries of Justice
In the impressive Shire Hall building on High Pavement, the Galleries of Justice (☎ 952 0555; w www.galleriesofjustice.org.uk; High Pavement; adult/child £6.95/5.25, £1 discount if booked at TIC; open 10am-5pm Tues-Sun Apr-Oct, 10am-4pm Tues-Sun Nov-Mar) takes you through the history of the judicial system from medieval ordeals by water or hot iron to modern crime detection. You're guided through much of the action by 'jailers' and 'prisoners', and it's highly interactive: you may find yourself sentenced to death in a Victorian courtroom!

Organised Tours
The knowledgeable guides of The Nottingham Experience (☎ 911 5005; e nottingham .exp@orangenet.co.uk) whisk visitors from the castle gatehouse on a 30-minute tour of the city (adult/child £4/3.50), recounting the stories behind the sights. Longer themed group tours are also available.

THE MIDLANDS

The **Original Nottingham Ghost Walk** (☎ 01773-769300; **w** www.ghost-walks.co.uk; adult/under-12 £4/2; 7pm Sat Jan-Nov) departs from Ye Olde Salutation Inn (see Pubs & Bars) to explore the spooky underbelly of the city's past.

Places to Stay

The nearest campsite is **Holme Pierrepont Camping & Caravan Site** (☎ 982 4721; Adbolton Lane; tents £5.75-7.50; open Mar-Oct), at the National Watersports Centre 2 miles (3km) southeast of the centre off the A52. Bus No 11 runs from the city to within a quarter mile of the site every 15 minutes (No 11C runs past the site on Sunday).

Igloo Tourist Hostel (☎ 947 5250; **e** reception@igloohostel.co.uk; 110 Mansfield Rd; dorm beds £12), a short walk north of Victoria bus station, is a decent backpackers. The entrance is on Fulforth St.

There are a host of B&Bs on or near Mansfield Rd as it enters Sherwood, north of the centre.

Claremont (☎ 960 8587; 2 Hamilton Rd; en-suite singles £32-38, doubles £45-55) is a large, comfortable B&B on a quiet side road.

Adams Castle View Guest House (☎ 950 0022; 85 Castle Boulevard; singles/doubles £22.50/45) and **Castle Rock Guest House** (☎ 948 2116; 79 Castle Boulevard; doubles from £39) are just below the castle; both are smallish, basic places.

There are some cheap B&Bs near the train station; some are OK, but don't expect too much in this part of town.

Gresham Hotel (☎ 950 1234; 109 Carrington St; singles/doubles from £20/38) is large and handy; it's reasonable for the price.

Park Hotel (☎ 978 6299, fax 942 4358; **e** enquiries@parkhotelcitycentre.co.uk; 5-7 Waverley St; singles/doubles from £48/68), often hosts sports teams. It tends to be lively.

Travel Inn (☎ 0870 238 3314, fax 908 1388; **w** www.travelinn.co.uk; Goldsmith St; en-suite doubles £52.95) is another clean, faceless chain hotel that's worth considering, for location and value.

Comfort Hotel (☎ 947 5641, fax 948 3292; **e** admin@gb620.u-net.com; George St; en-suite doubles £67) is not a bad deal, considering its location in the thick of the action in Hockley.

Rutland Square Hotel (☎ 941 1114, fax 955 9494; **e** rutlandsquare@zoffanyhotels.co.uk; St James St; singles/doubles £93/110) is a central business-class hotel with style and serious discounts at the weekend (from £35 per person).

Lace Market Hotel (☎ 852 3232, fax 852 3223; **e** reservations@lacemarkethotel.co.uk; 29-31 High Pavement; singles/doubles £89/99) is an exclusive boutique hotel that sometimes offers reduced weekend rates.

Places to Eat

Good news for vegetarians: choices now range from burgers to haute cuisine.

V1 (☎ 941 5121; **w** www.v-1.co.uk; Hounds Gate; meals £3.90-4.90; open 8am-6pm Mon-Sat, noon-4pm Sun) does true fast food, but without the meat.

The area around Carlton St to the east of the centre is currently the epicentre of eating (and drinking). Most of the café-bars here and in the Lace Market do chic chow (see Entertainment later).

Cool-but-friendly **Squeek** (☎ 955 5560; 23-25 Heathcoat St; mains £8.95; open 5.30pm-midnight Mon-Sat) dishes up fabulous vegetarian and vegan cuisine.

Fresh (☎ 924 3336; 15 Goose Gate; dinner mains £9-12; open 8am-5.30pm Mon & Tues, 8am-9pm Wed-Fri, 9am-9pm Sat) is bright and confident, serving world cuisine all day and good snacks at lunch. There are tasty vegetarian and fish selections.

Skinny Sumo (☎ 952 0188; 11-13 Carlton St; mains £7, sushi £1.50-3.50) has a sushi bar conveyor-belt and a variety of authentic Japanese dishes; look out for speciality nights (curry, noodles) during the week.

Broadway Cinema Cafebar (☎ 952 1551; 14-18 Broad St; specials £5.25) is ideal for soup or baguettes at lunchtime, more substantial fare in the evening and drinks with hip sounds and visuals later.

Shimla Pinks (☎ 958 9899; 38 Goose Gate; mains £6-12; open evening only Sat & Sun) is part of an expanding chain offering fine contemporary Indian cuisine in a lush, sleek interior.

Mogal-e-Azam (☎ 947 3820; 7-9 Goldsmith St; mains £6-15), located beside the Theatre Royal, is another acclaimed Indian restaurant.

Scruffy's (☎ 911 6333; 47 Stoney St; mains £7-14; open evenings only except Sun), in a dungeon-like cellar, is more diner than bar, serving up steaks, pasta, pies and attitude.

La Tasca (☎ 959 9456; 9 Weekday Cross; tapas £2-4, paella £7.50-9.50) is large, lively, bright and a lot of fun; grab your sangria and head to the upstairs cushions overlooking the Weekday Cross.

Loch Fyne Fish Restaurant (☎ 988 6840; 17 King St; fish mains £7-15) is a branch of the excellent Scottish oyster-and-seafood company. Half a dozen oysters cost £5.95.

Pretty Orchid (☎ 958 8344; 12 Pepper St; lunch £5.90, dinner mains £6-13; closed Sun) is a top-notch Thai place just off Bridlesmith Gate.

Punchinello (☎ 941 1965; 35 Forman St; mains £7.50-13) claims to be Nottingham's oldest restaurant. A charming place, it's been pleasing diners with Med-influenced fare for as long as we can remember.

Sonny's (☎ 947 3041; 3 Carlton St; mains £10-15.50) is a classy place with a bright and imaginative menu of modern British dishes (and large windows so you can see and be seen).

Entertainment

The **Cornerhouse** (Forman St), opposite Theatre Royal, is a spanking modern development that has everything you might or might not want: glitzy clubs, chain restaurants (including Wagamama, TGI Fridays and a host of themed eateries), bars and a 15-screen **Warner Village cinema** (☎ 0870 240 6020; w www.warnervillage.co.uk).

Pubs & Bars Tucked into the cliff below the castle, **Ye Olde Trip to Jerusalem** (☎ 947 3171; Brewhouse Yard, Castle Rd) is one of England's best (and oldest) pubs, supposedly host to thirsty crusaders pre-departure; today's drinkers sup in the same nooks and crannies in the upstairs bar, cut into the rock.

Ye Olde Salutation Inn (☎ 988 1948; Maid Marian Way), just over the ring road, is another oldie (c.1240) with decent beers and no pretensions.

Lincolnshire Poacher (☎ 941 1584; 161-163 Mansfield Rd) will appeal to real-ale fiends. It's a brilliant pub with well-kept beer.

Forest Tavern (☎ 947 5650; 257 Mansfield Rd), just up the hill, has a selection of Belgian beers; the happening little **Maze Club** (270 North Sherwood St), part of the same venue, is behind.

Bell Inn (☎ 947 5241; 18 Angel Row) is one of the few places right in the centre where you can get a decent beer and relax on a weekend night. Not trendy, not quaint, just fine.

Old Angel Inn (☎ 950 2303; Woolpack Lane) is a popular student pub with funky tunes and great beer.

Fellows, Morton & Clayton (☎ 950 6795; 54 Canal St) is an excellent brewpub overlooking the redeveloped and re-emergent canalside area of town.

Via Fossa (☎ 947 3904; Castle Wharf, 44 Canal St), nearby, is one of the places to go in town and heaves during summer. Luckily it has a huge interior with off-the-wall furnishings, as well as plenty of space outside.

Pitcher & Piano (☎ 958 6081; The Unitarian Church, High Pavement), surely one of the boldest church conversions in the country, draws the faithful daily (and nightly: it opens till midnight Friday and Saturday).

Sometimes it seems as if the whole of the Lace Market area is one huge, hyper-hip café-bar. They come and go, some are cooler than others, but they tend to follow the same pattern: brown leather sofas for lounging, subdued lighting for smooching and smooth-talking, sleek food for feeding, an unspoken dress code and DJs for added cred. Picking the best is risky, but the current cream are probably **Brass Monkey** (☎ 840 4101; 11 High Pavement) for cocktails till 1am, **Dogma** (☎ 988 6830; 9 Byard Lane) for its big basement space, and **Bluu** (☎ 950 5359; 5 Broadway; open to midnight Sun-Tues, 1am Wed-Sat) for live bands, great food and a friendly vibe.

Other pre-club bars worth checking out further from the scene are **Loft** (☎ 924 0213; 217 Mansfield Rd) and **Moog** (☎ 841 3830; Newdigate St), off Alfreton Rd, both with retro-chic styling and cutting-edge DJs.

Clubs Again, the number and variety of clubs means that trying to pick the best is like trying to catch rhinos with a popgun.

The Social (☎ 950 5078; 23 Pelham St), sibling of the equally cool London joint, has DJs and live guests, and is one of the places to be seen.

Cookie Club (☎ 950 5892; 22 St James St), just west of Market Square, is a friendly little club with alternative nights and fair prices.

Bomb (☎ 950 6667; 45 Bridlesmith Gate) is small on the outside (blink and you'll miss it), a funky club with few rules and wide-ranging tunes.

Beatroot (☎ 924 0852; 6-8 Broadway), an old-timer, still packs 'em in with a mellow feel, happy house and a chill-out room.

Edge (☎ 910 6880; 1265 Lower Parliament St) gets the gay crowd going with dirty house.

Rock City (☎ 941 2544; w www.rock -city.co.uk; 8 Talbot St) is the major live venue for bands, and has popular indie, rock and student club nights.

The Old Vic (☎ 910 0009; w www.just thetonic.com; Fletcher Gate) hosts arguably the best comedy nights in the Midlands on Saturdays and Sundays.

Theatre, Cinema & Classical Music

The city's art-house film centre is **Broadway Cinema** (☎ 952 6611; w www.broad way.org.uk; 14-18 Broad St).

The **Savoy** (☎ 947 5812; 233 Derby Rd; adult/child £4.25/3.25) is a vintage cinema with double seats and an interval for ice-cream consumption.

Lakeside Arts Centre (☎ 846 7777; w www.lakesidearts.org.uk; DH Lawrence Pavilion, University Park) is a multi-purpose venue hosting films, classical music, comedy and dance.

Theatres include the **Arts Theatre** (☎ 947 6096; w www.artstheatre.org.uk; George St) and the **Nottingham Playhouse** (☎ 941 9419; w www.nottinghamplayhouse.co.uk; Wellington Circus), a respected venue outside which sits *Sky Mirror*, a superb Anish Kapoor sculpture.

Royal Concert Hall and **Theatre Royal**, staging musicals and big acts, share a booking office (☎ 989 5555; w www.royalcentre -nottingham.co.uk; Theatre Square) and an imposing building close to the centre.

Getting There & Away

Nottingham is 131 miles (210km) from London.

Air East Midlands Airport (☎ 01332-852852; w www.eastmidlandsairport.com) is off the A453 near Kegworth, about 13 miles (22km) southwest of Nottingham, and handles flights to domestic and European destinations.

Bus National Express buses operate from the Broadmarsh bus station to London

(£20.50 economy return, three hours, eight daily), Leeds (£13.50, 2¼ hours, seven daily) via Sheffield, and Manchester (£15.50, 3¼ hours, two daily). Dunn Line (☎ 08700 121212) Express bus No 777 runs to Leicester (£3.50 day return, one hour, eight daily Monday to Saturday).

Trent Buses (☎ 01773-712265; w www .trentbuses.co.uk) operate a TransPeak service from Broadmarsh bus station to Derby (£3, 30 minutes) and through the Peak District to Manchester (£7.10, 3¼ hours), every two hours daily.

Train Nottingham isn't on the main line through the Midlands, but trains run frequently from London St Pancras (£42.80 saver return, 1¾ hours, every 30 minutes), Birmingham (£15, 1¼ hours, every 30 minutes) and Sheffield (£13.30, one hour, hourly).

Getting Around

For information on buses within Nottingham, call ☎ 950 3665 or check the website (w www.nctx.co.uk). A Day Rider ticket gives you unlimited travel for £2.20.

The most convenient bus for the airport is No 5 (£1.20, one hour), which runs from Victoria bus station hourly (every two hours on Sunday).

A tram system is being built to run from Bulwell through the centre and Hockley to the train station; it's due for completion by 2004.

Bunney's Bikes (☎ 947 2713; 97 Carrington St), near the train station, hires bikes from £8 per day (plus deposit); bike parking is 60p.

AROUND NOTTINGHAM
Newstead Abbey

With its attractive gardens, romantic lakeside ruins and notable connections with scoundrel-poet Lord Byron (1788–1824), whose country pile it was, Newstead Abbey (☎ 01623-455900; w www.newsteadabbey .org.uk; adult/child £4/1.50, gardens only £2/1.50; house open noon-5pm daily Apr-Sept, garden open 9am-dusk daily year round) is a popular weekend destination for tourists and local families alike.

Founded as an Augustinian priory around 1170, it was converted into a home after the dissolution of the monasteries in 1539.

Beside the still-imposing facade of the priory church are the remains of the manor. It now houses some interesting Byron memorabilia plus Victorian paintings and furnishings in the extant chambers.

The house is 12 miles (19km) north of Nottingham, off the A60. The Sherwood Forester bus runs right there on summer Sundays. Bus Nos 737, 747 and 757 run from Nottingham (25 minutes, every 20 minutes, hourly on Sunday) to the abbey gates.

DH Lawrence Heritage

The **DH Lawrence Birthplace Museum** *(☎ 01773-717353; 8a Victoria St, Eastwood; open 10am-5pm daily Apr-Oct, 10am-4pm Nov-Mar)*, home of Nottingham's controversial author (1885–1930), has been reconstructed as it would have been in Lawrence's childhood, with period furnishings. Down the road, the **Durban House Heritage Centre** *(Mansfield Rd)*, with the same telephone number and opening hours, sheds light on the background to Lawrence's books by re-creating the life of the mining community at the turn of the 20th century. Admission to each museum costs adult/child £2/1.20, or £3.50/1.80 for both. Eastwood is about 10 miles (16km) northwest of the city; take Trent Buses service No 1.

Sherwood Forest

Don't expect to lose yourselves like outlaws; the skimpy fragments remaining in Sherwood Forest Country Park are thronged with tourists most of the time, although there are still a few peaceful spots. The **Sherwood Forest Visitor Centre** *(☎ 01623-823202; w www .sherwood-forest.org.uk; admission free; open 10.30am-5pm daily Apr-Oct, 10am-4.30pm daily Nov-Mar)* houses Robyn Hode's Sherwode (sic), a slightly cheesy exhibition describing the lifestyles of bandits, kings, peasants and friars in radical Rob's day. A major attraction is the Major Oak, where Robin is supposed to have hidden. If ever there was a case for plant euthanasia, this is it: the tree has almost more supports than branches these days. The Robin Hood Festival is a massive medieval re-enactment that takes place every August.

Sherwood Forest YHA Hostel *(☎ 0870 770 6026, fax 01623-825796; e sherwood@ yha.org.uk; Forest Corner, Edwinstowe; adult £12.75)* is a modern hostel with comfortable dorms just a short distance from the visitor centre.

Sherwood Forester buses run the 20 miles (32km) to the park from Nottingham on Sunday; catch bus No 33 from Nottingham Monday to Saturday.

Southwell

☎ 01636 • pop 6400

One of those archetypal sleepy market towns bursting with tearooms and antique shops, Southwell is a key stop for another reason: **Southwell Minster** *(☎ 812649; suggested donation £2/1; open 8am-7pm daily May-Sept, 8am-dusk Oct-Apr)* is a Gothic cathedral unlike any other in England, its two heavy, square front towers belying the treats within. The nave dates from the 12th century, although there is evidence of an earlier Saxon church floor, itself made with mosaics from a Roman villa. A highlight of the building is the chapterhouse, filled with incredible naturalistic 13th-century carvings of leaves, pigs, dogs and rabbits. The library is also a fascinating place, housing manuscripts and heavy tomes from the 16th century and earlier.

A visit to **Southwell Workhouse** *(NT; ☎ 817250; Upton Rd; admission £4; open noon-5pm Wed-Sun mid-Mar–Oct, 11am-5pm Aug)* is a sobering but fascinating experience. An audioguide, narrated by 'inmates' and 'officials', describes the life of paupers in the mid-19th century to good effect, despite the fact that most of the rooms are empty.

Bus Nos 101 and 201 run from Nottingham (£2, 40 minutes, every 20 minutes, hourly on Sunday) and on to Newark (£1.50, 25 minutes, hourly, every two hours on Sunday).

Newark-upon-Trent

☎ 01636 • pop 35,000

Another market town with a historical pedigree, key evidence of its past importance is ruined **Newark Castle** *(admission to grounds free; open to dusk year round)*, one of the few to hold out against Cromwell's men during the Civil War – only for Charles I to order surrender, condemning the building to rapid destruction. An impressive Norman gate remains, part of the structure in which King John died in 1216. Entry to the gate itself is by guided tour (adult/child £2/1) only; contact the TIC for details.

The TIC (☎ 655765, fax 655767; e gilstrap@ newark-sherwooddc.gov.uk; The Gilstrap Centre, Castlegate; open 9am-6pm daily Apr-Sept, 9am-5pm Oct-Mar) houses a small display on the town's history. Pick up the *Walkabout Tour* leaflet and explore.

The town has a large, cobbled square overlooked by the fine, timber-framed 14th-century Olde White Hart Inn (now a building society) and the Clinton Arms Hotel (now a shopping mall), from where former prime minister Gladstone made his first political speech and where Lord Byron stayed while his first book of poems was published.

Near the TIC, **Gannets Daycafe** (☎ 702066; 35 Castlegate; snacks £2-5) scoops the lunchtime trade with good coffee and cream teas. The modern cuisine at smart **Café Bleu** (☎ 610141; 14 Castlegate; mains £9.50-14; closed Sun dinner) is not noticeably French, but accomplished, with good seafood and fish options.

Bus Nos 91, 101 and 201 run to Nottingham (£2.60, 1¼ hours, hourly, every two hours Sunday); No 91 runs via Southwell (£1.50, 25 minutes).

Derbyshire

Much of Derbyshire is within the Peak District National Park, and for many visitors the two areas are synonymous – although the park overlaps several other counties, and the parts of Derbyshire beyond the national park boundary contain many more attractions.

Inside and outside the park, the Derbyshire countryside is a delightful mix of beautiful wild moors, cosy green valleys, lonely farms and ancient villages. Within this rural setting stand the industrial city of Derby, the spa resort of Buxton, sturdy market towns and some wonderful stately homes – including unforgettable Chatsworth. Together, all this justifiably makes Derbyshire one of the most visited counties in England.

Activities

Outdoor activities available in Derbyshire include walking, cycling, rock climbing, caving and paragliding, to name but a few. Many take place inside the Peak District National Park, and are covered under the Activities heading in that section, following.

Getting There & Around

Derbyshire takes public transport seriously, and of the buses, the TransPeak service is very handy, running two-hourly between Nottingham and Manchester, right across Derbyshire, via Derby, Matlock, Bakewell and Buxton. The operator, **Trent Buses** (☎ 01773-712265; w www.trentbuses.co.uk), knows about service and has won several awards. 'Zig-zag' tickets (£3.50) allow a day's unlimited rides in Derbyshire (although it's not valid north of Bakewell).

By train, it's easy to reach Derby, Matlock and Buxton – and these all make good gateways. Another excellent launch pad is the Hope Valley railway between Sheffield and Manchester, which runs through the Peak District via many small villages where you can hike to the hills straight from the station platform.

The Derbyshire Wayfarer day-pass covers buses and trains throughout the county and beyond (eg, to Manchester and Sheffield). It costs £7.50 per adult (and one child free) or £12 for a family, and you also get discounts at local attractions. For details contact **Traveline** (☎ 0870 608 2608) or check w www.derbybus.net.

DERBY
☎ 01332 • pop 224,000

Once a sleepy market town, Derby was transformed by the Industrial Revolution into a major manufacturing centre – first silk, then china, then railways, and finally world-famous Rolls-Royce aircraft engines. Anyone keen on ornaments and tableware, or the historical side of English engineering, should definitely consider a visit.

Orientation & Information

Central Derby has some dull pedestrianised shopping streets, although the old part of town is quite attractive: a partly-cobbled thoroughfare called Irongate has a few good pubs and cafés, and leads to the cathedral.

Off Irongate branch a couple of narrow old streets with several good options for eating and drinking (caffeine or something stronger), and some of Derby's more interesting shops selling books, CDs, surf gear, jewellery and designer clothes.

For more information on Derby, or ideas on accommodation if you decide to stay, contact the TIC (☎ 255802; Market Place).

Things to See

Derby's 18th-century **cathedral** *(Queen St; open daily)* boasts a 64m-high tower and magnificent wrought-iron screens. Recently built (for an English cathedral) its unusual interior of creamy white plasterwork and large windows make it very light and airy. Among the many memorials, you can't miss the huge tomb of Bess of Hardwick – one of Derbyshire's most formidable residents in days gone by; for details see Hardwick Hall in the Around Chesterfield section.

From the cathedral, stroll down the wonderfully named Amen Alley, and cross the road to see the statue of **Bonnie Prince Charlie**; he got this far from Scotland in the Jacobite Rebellion of 1745. A cannon left by his troops can still be seen at Kedleston Hall – see the Around Derby section following.

Next to the River Derwent, in a former Silk Mill, **Derby Industrial Museum** *(☎ 255 308; Silk Mill Lane; admission free; open 11am-5pm Mon, 10am-5pm Tue-Sat, 2pm-5pm Sun & Bank Holidays)* tells the city's manufacturing history; if you're into trains and – especially – aero-engines, this is heaven.

The factory of **Royal Crown Derby** *(☎ 712841; Osmaston Rd; open 9am-5pm Mon-Sat, 10am-4pm Sun)* turns out some of the finest bone china in England. There's no charge to visit the demonstration area to see workers skilfully make delicate china flowers, using little more than a hat-pin, spoon handle and head-lice comb! There's also a shop, piled high with teapots, collectable paperweights and various bargains, and a café. For the full inside view, the factory **tour** *(four daily, Mon-Fri; phone for times and reservations; adult £5)* is fascinating, even if china isn't your cup of tea; you'll see the entire process, from vats of raw powder and bone-mix through to the final touches of liquid gold decoration.

Places to Eat & Drink

For a cheap bite in central Derby, **Acropolis** *(Market Place)* is a no-frills place, with a menu so large it fills a whole window. Nearby, Sadlers Gate and Old Blacksmith's Yard (off Sadlers Gate) between them boast half-a-dozen modern café-bars, with tables on the pavement ideally arranged for people-watching, and a couple of decent restaurants.

Around the cathedral are some more choices, including **Ye Olde Dolphin Inne** *(Queen St; snacks and meals £2-5)*, traditional and intimate (OK, cramped), with four little bars and good pub grub. Nearby, the **Silk Mill** *(Full St)* is a roomier pub, also doing food (including breakfast), while **Vida** *(Queen St; mains £4)* is a small café-bar with a good view of the cathedral.

For a traditional town atmosphere, Derby's best pubs are near the train station. The justifiably award-winning **Brunswick Inn** *(Railway Terrace)* is worth a journey, with first-class beer (some brewed on-site), and good, no-nonsense food. Nearby, the **Alexandria Hotel** *(Siddals Rd)* is similarly excellent, and continues the railway theme, with numerous loco-photos and a tongue-in-cheek 'no train spotters' sign at the door.

Getting There & Away

Derby's dismal bus station is close to the centre. The TransPeak bus (No TP) runs every two hours between Nottingham and Manchester, via Derby, Matlock, Bakewell and Buxton. Between Derby and Nottingham takes 30 minutes; between Derby and Bakewell takes an hour (£4.95).

The train station is southwest of the centre. From London, there are trains to Derby (£40, two hours, about hourly), continuing to Chesterfield, Sheffield and Leeds.

AROUND DERBY
Kedleston Hall

Sitting proudly in vast landscaped parkland, the superb neoclassical mansion of **Kedleston Hall** *(NT; ☎ 01332-842191; admission £5.30; open noon-4pm Sat-Wed Easter-Oct)* is a must for all stately-home aficionados. The Curzon family has lived here since the 12th century and Sir Nathaniel Curzon tore down an earlier house in 1758 so this stunning masterpiece could be built. Meanwhile, the poor old peasants in Kedleston village had their humble dwellings moved a mile down the road as they interfered with the view!

You enter the house through a grand portico to reach the breathtaking Marble Hall, with its massive alabaster columns and statues of Greek deities. Curved corridors on either side offer splendid views of the park – don't miss the arc of floorboards, specially cut from bending oak boughs. Other highlights include richly decorated bedrooms, and a circular saloon with a domed roof, modelled on the Pantheon in Rome.

Things turned full circle when another great building, Government House in Calcutta (now Raj Bhavan), was modelled on Kedleston Hall, as a later Lord Curzon was viceroy of India around 1900. His collection of oriental artefacts is on show, as is his wife's 'peacock' dress – made of gold and silver thread and weighing 5kg. They were tough in the days of the Empire!

Kedleston Hall is 5 miles (8km) northwest of Derby. By bus, service No 109 between Derby and Ashbourne goes within about 1½ miles of Kedleston Hall (20 minutes, seven daily Monday to Saturday, five on Sunday), and on sunny days walking the rest is no hardship. On Sunday and Bank Holidays the bus loops right up to the house.

Calke Abbey

Ten miles south of Derby sits the house and grounds of **Calke Abbey** (NT; ☎ 01332-863822; adult/child £5.40/2.70; open 1pm-5.30pm Sat-Wed Apr-Oct). This is no normal stately home. Built around 1703, a dynasty of eccentric and reclusive baronets meant very little has changed – especially since about 1880. The result is a ramshackle maze of rooms crammed with ancient furniture, mounted animal heads, shelves of books, thousands of stuffed birds, and endless piles of bric-a-brac from the last three centuries. Some rooms are in fabulous condition, others are deliberately untouched, complete with crumbling plaster and mouldy wallpaper. A stroll round the gardens is a similar time-warp experience – in the potting sheds, nothing has changed since about 1930, but it looks like the gardener left only yesterday.

Admission to Calke Abbey house is by timed ticket. On summer weekends it's wise to phone ahead and check there'll be space. You can enter the gardens and grounds at any time. Visitors coming by car must enter via the village of Ticknall. Bus Nos 68 and 69 from Derby to Swadlincote stop at Ticknall (40 minutes, hourly) and from there it's a 2-mile walk through the park.

Ashbourne

The thriving little market town of Ashbourne is about 15 miles (24km) northwest of Derby, on the road towards Buxton, at the very southern tip of the Peak District National Park. Fine old buildings from ages past line the market place and the main street, a great many now turned into antique and art shops drawing crowds of eager browsers at weekends. (Things get even busier once a year when the game of Shrovetide Football is rigorously pursued – see the boxed text 'Ancient Customs' later.)

The **TIC** (☎ 01335-343666; Market Place; open 9.30am-5pm Mon-Sat, 10am-4pm Sun) can provide leaflets or advice on B&Bs in the area. Ashbourne also has many teashops and pubs. Our favourites include: **One for the Pot** (Market Place), a colourful little café; the **Gingerbread Shop** (St John's St), a bakery and tearoom in a half-timbered building (Ashbourne is famous for its gingerbread); **Smith's Tavern** (St John's St), a popular pub with traditional ambience plus good food and beer; and **The Horns** (Victoria Sq), another fine old pub, with outdoor seating on the square for when the sun shines.

For outdoor activity fans, Ashbourne is the southern terminus of the Tissington Trail, a former railway-line and now a wonderful easy-gradient path for walkers and cyclists cutting through fine west Derbyshire countryside. The Tissington Trail takes you north towards Buxton, and connects with the High Peak Trail running south towards Matlock Bath – for more details on circular route possibilities see Activities in the Peak District National Park section, following. About a mile outside town along Mapleton Lane **Ashbourne Cycle Hire** (☎ 01335-343156) is on the Tissington Trail, with a huge stock of bikes and trailers for all ages, plus free leaflets showing the route with pubs and teashops along the way.

To get to Ashbourne by bus, there are numerous services from Derby; the trip takes about 30 to 45 minutes. Direct buses include No 107 (hourly Monday to Saturday), No 111 (three per day on Sunday and Bank Holidays), and No X1 (five daily Monday to Friday, four daily Saturday and Sunday), which continues to Manchester.

Dovedale

About 3 miles (5km) northwest of Ashbourne, the River Dove winds through the steep-sided valley of Dovedale. It's one of the most beautiful parts of Derbyshire, so can get crowded on summer weekends – especially near the famous stepping stones – but midweek it's a lovely place for a walk. The quaint Dovedale Guide (£1.25), avail-

Ancient Customs

Shrove Tuesday comes before Ash Wednesday, the first day of Lent – the Christian time of fasting. So Shrove Tuesday is the day to use up all your rich and fattening food, which led to the quaint tradition of Pancake Day in England, and the rather less staid Mardi Gras festival elsewhere in the world.

On Shrove Tuesday, various English towns celebrate with pancake races, but in Ashbourne they go for something much more energetic. Here they play Shrovetide Football – but it's nothing like the football most people are used to. For a start, the goals are 3 miles apart, the 'pitch' is a huge patch of countryside, and the game lasts all afternoon and evening (then starts again the day after). There are two teams, but hundreds of participants, and very few rules indeed. A large leather ball is fought over voraciously as players maul their way through fields and gardens, along the river, and up the main street – where shop windows are specially boarded over for the occasion. Visitors come from far and wide to watch, but only the brave should take part!

About 8 miles up the road from Ashbourne, in the Staffordshire village of Wetton, another 'traditional' event takes place on an early weekend each June – the World Toe Wrestling Championship. It all started in 1976, when talk at Ye Olde Royal Oak Inn turned to sport. Depressed at England's inability to dominate in any global event, regulars decided to invent a sport that the home country would always win (because nobody else knew about it). The plan was sundered in 1977 by a random Canadian strolling in and beating the local champion. Game over. Resurrected in 1990, the annual event now pulls in hefty crowds (and serious money for charity), with men and women sitting on a 'toedium' attempting to force their opponent's toe onto the side of the 'toesrack'.

able from Ashbourne TIC, has more background, and a map showing footpaths.

Romantic travellers 'ventured' to Dovedale in the Victorian era, bestowing fanciful names on the natural features, so today we can admire hills and rocky buttresses called Thorpe Cloud, Dovedale Castle, Lovers' Leap, the Twelve Apostles, Tissington Spires, Reynard's Kitchen and Lion Head Rock. Another early visitor was Izaak Walton, the 17th-century fisherman and author of *The Compleat Angler*. The **Izaak Walton Hotel** at the southern end of Dovedale is named in his honour, and the public bar or pretty garden here make it well worth a stop for after-walk refreshment.

MATLOCK BATH
☎ 01629 ● pop 1800
Roughly in the centre of Derbyshire, on the southeastern edge of the Peak District National Park, are the twin towns of Matlock and Matlock Bath. Matlock is pleasant, but has little in the way of sights, although it's a very handy gateway to the scenic dales on this side of the park. The reason to come is for Matlock Bath, an unashamedly brash and delightfully tacky little place, like a lost seaside resort, complete with a promenade of amusement arcades, an aquarium, cafés,

pubs and souvenir shops – some with stock apparently unchanged since Victorian times.

Every weekend – and all through the summer – groups of local lads and lasses, couples, families, kids and grannies come here from miles around, and there's a totally no-frills buzz about the place. At weekends, Matlock Bath is also especially popular with motorcyclists, so the buzz is sometimes a roar, but the throb of engines and parading leather-clad enthusiasts all add to the general good-time atmosphere.

Orientation & Information
Matlock Bath is 2 miles (3km) south of Matlock. Everything revolves around North Parade and South Parade, a line of seaside-style shops, attractions and eateries along one side of the main road through town, with the River Derwent on the other side, standing in for the sea. Matlock Bath's **TIC** (☎ 55082; **w** www.derbyshire.gov.uk; *The Pavilion; open 9.30am-5pm daily Mar-Oct, weekends only Nov-Feb*) has friendly staff, and plenty of leaflets and local guidebooks.

Things to See & Do
Item one on the agenda: buy some chips or candyfloss and just stroll around. Then cross the river to stroll some more in the

park on the other side, where some steep paths lead to great cliff-top viewpoints.

At the **Mining Museum** (☎ 583834; The Pavilion; adult/child £2.50/1.50; open 10am-5pm daily) you can clamber through shafts and tunnels, and for £1.50 extra go down **Temple Mine** and try panning for 'gold'.

For a different view, go to the **Heights of Abraham** (☎ 582365; adult/child £7.30/5; open 10am-5pm daily Mar-Oct, Sat & Sun Feb-Mar), a wholesome family attraction, with underground caverns, adventure playground, woodland nature trails and an audiovisual show. The price includes a spectacular cable-car ride up from the valley floor.

Near the cable-car base, the **Whistlestop Centre** (admission free; open 10am-5pm daily Apr-Oct, weekends only Nov-Mar), at the old train station, has wildlife and natural garden exhibits, and children's activities in the summer.

For the finest views, from the cable-car base, walking trails lead up to airy viewpoints on top of **High Tor**; you can see down to Matlock Bath and over to **Riber Castle**, a Victorian folly.

Gulliver's Kingdom (☎ 01925-444888; admission £6.80; open 10am-5pm daily late May-early Sept, weekends and holidays Oct-Apr) is a junior theme park. Kids aged four to 10 will like it, while mum and dad can grimace at the junk food they consume, and the detritus others leave behind.

A mile south of Matlock Bath is **Masson Mill** (☎ 581001; adult/child £2.50/1.50; open 10am-4pm Mon-Sat, 11am-4pm Sun), built in 1783 for pioneering industrialist Richard Arkwright, and acknowledged as a masterpiece of the era. Today it's an intriguing working museum, with renovated looms and weaving machines, and the world's largest collection of bobbins. If that's not draw enough, the attached 'shopping village' (three floors of High Street textile and clothing names) might pull you in.

From late August to October, don't miss the **Matlock Illuminations** (Pavilion Gardens; evenings from dusk Fri-Sun), with endless streams of pretty lights and outrageously decorated boats on the river, plus occasional firework displays.

Places to Stay

Matlock YHA Hostel (☎ 0870 770 5960; e matlock@yha.org.uk; 40 Bank Rd; beds £11, rooms from £39) is 2 miles from Matlock Bath.

Matlock Bath has several B&Bs in the heart of things on North Parade and South Parade, and a few places just out of the centre. There are also more choices in nearby Matlock.

Ashdale (☎ 57826; 92 North Parade; doubles £45) is a neat and tidy place in a large old house.

Fountain Villa (☎ 56195; 86 North Parade; doubles £45) has comfortable rooms, very nicely decorated with antiques and period furniture.

Sunnybank Guesthouse (☎ 584621; Clifton Rd; per person from £23) is a friendly little B&B on a quiet road just outside Matlock Bath.

Temple Hotel (☎ 01629 583911; Temple Rd; singles/doubles £47/78) has a slightly dated seaside guesthouse feel – perfect for Matlock Bath – and the downstairs bar does good beer and pub food.

Hodgkinson's Hotel & Restaurant (☎ 582 170; w www.hodgkinsons-hotel.co.uk; 150 South Parade; singles £38, doubles £68-88) is a wonderfully quirky place, oozing history, packed with Victorian furniture and with a very relaxed and welcoming atmosphere.

Places to Eat & Drink

North Parade and South Parade are lined end-to-end with cafés, teashops and takeaways, all serving up standards like chocolate cake, fish and chips, fried chicken, pies and burgers – hear those arteries scream! For something more elaborate, **The Balti** (☎ 55069; 265 Dale Rd; mains £6-10) offers fair curries and other eastern specialities; it's busy, verging on rushed, at summer weekends. (Dale Rd is the northern extension of North Parade.)

Of the pubs, the **Princess Victoria** (South Parade) is lively, the **County & Station** (Dale Rd) is relatively quiet, and **The Fishpond** (South Parade) has great live music. Up on the hillside, the bar at the **Temple Hotel** (listed in Places to Stay) does good pub food, and the terrace outside is a great place to watch the firework displays that tie in with the Matlock Illuminations (late August to October).

Getting There & Away

Matlock and Matlock Bath are both on the route of the TransPeak bus service (No TP) between Nottingham and Manchester, with buses two-hourly, via Derby, Bakewell and Buxton. Matlock to Bakewell takes about 30 minutes. You can also reach Matlock Bath by train from Derby (25 minutes, at least eight daily).

AROUND MATLOCK BATH

From just outside Matlock town centre, about 2½ miles from Matlock Bath, steam trains and scenic railcars trundle along **Peak Rail** (☎ 01629-580381; ⓦ www.peakrail.co.uk; *nine services daily weekends, Sun only Nov-Mar, extra weekday services Jun-Sept; return fares adult/child £6/4)* via stops at Darley Dale to the northern terminus near the village of Rowsley. For train buffs and families it's a great ride. There are long-term plans to ex-

tend the line to Bakewell and Buxton, reinstating the 'missing link' through the heart of Derbyshire that was cut in the 1960s. The line of the railway currently forms the basis of the Monsal Trail – a path for walkers – described in the Bakewell section following.

From Rowsley train station a riverside path leads to **Caudwell's Mill** *(adult/child £3/1; open 10am-6pm daily Mar-Oct, weekends Nov-Feb)*, a huge and fascinating flour mill, full of working belts, shafts and other machinery – some almost a century old. There's a tearoom here, several craft-workers, and a shop selling gifts and…flour. You can also reach Rowsley direct from Matlock by bus, as it's on the road to Bakewell (see Getting There & Away in that section for details).

The Derwent National Heritage Corridor

Flowing through the heart of Derbyshire, the River Derwent is not the best known of England's rivers, but it has a vitally important place in English history. Textile mills established here to exploit water-power in the 18th century were a pivotal kick-start for the Industrial Revolution, which eventually made Britain a world power in Victorian times. Do you remember learning about Hargreave's 'spinning jenny' and Arkwright's 'water frame' in school history lessons? These machines transformed manufacturing processes across the world, but the humble Derwent Valley is where they came from.

Today, many mills are preserved as fascinating museums and visitor centres, while the Derwent Valley is also home to numerous historical villages, wildlife sites and various tourist attractions – from the high hills of the Pennines to the industrial city of Derby. The whole lot has been rolled into a bundle called the National Heritage Corridor, and in 2001 the section from Matlock Bath to Derby was declared a World Heritage Site by Unesco. Whatever your interest, a day or two here is bound to be rewarding.

A small selection of things to see is given in the following text. Most are covered in more detail in the Derbyshire and Peak District sections of this chapter. For more information, you can get leaflets from local TICs.

Derwent Reservoirs – tiny streams flow off the moors to form the fledgling River Derwent; three large dams hold back the water, making a perfect centre for outdoor activities.

Chatworth House – grand stately home, with the Derwent flowing through the landscaped grounds.

Matlock – Derbyshire market town, and southern terminus for cheery Peak Rail steam trains.

Matlock Bath – weekender favourite, with many family attractions, including Masson Mill, a major landmark in Derwent's industrial development. Nearby Cromford Mill was the world's first water-powered cotton spinning mill.

Belper – bustling little town, and the site of North Mill, built in 1805 as the most technologically advanced of its time – a gem of the industrial era. Today the visitor centre is the focus of the World Heritage Site.

Derby – capital of Derbyshire; the Derwent-side Silk Mill is one of England's oldest sites and now an industrial museum showcasing early textile manufacture and the city's later products – trains and aero-engines.

Shardlow Marina – where the Derwent meets the River Trent; colourful jetties, narrowboats and river-port heritage centre.

CHESTERFIELD
☎ 01246 • pop 72,000

The 'capital' of northeast Derbyshire, Chesterfield is best known for the remarkable **Crooked Spire** of St Mary and All Saints Church that overlooks the town. Dating from 1360, the spire twists and leans – a giant corkscrew 68m high and 3m out of true – and no-one is really sure why (see the boxed text 'Chesterfield's Crooked Spire' following for some theories).

The church can be visited at any time, but if you want to go inside the spire, and get great views over the town, **tours** *(adult/child £2.50/1)* are arranged most days. There's no fixed timetable, you simply ask the verger if he's got time to show you around. On summer weekends there are at least two or three tours a day.

Next to the church, is Chesterfield's **Museum & Art Gallery** *(St Mary's Gate; open 10am-4pm Mon-Tues & Thur-Sat)*. Pride of place goes to a huge medieval winding wheel used to build the famous spire long before the days of tower-cranes, while a builder's mug that sat forgotten on a beam for 250 years is a reminder of the human touch.

If Chesterfield features on your itinerary, it's worth linking a visit to the large and lively **market** *(High St)*, held every Monday, Friday and Saturday (as it has since the 12th century). Thursdays see a huge 'flea market' of antiques and oddities. The helpful **TIC** *(☎ 345777; Low Pavement)* is nearby.

The easiest way to get here is by train; Chesterfield is between Nottingham–Derby (20 minutes) and Sheffield (10 minutes), with services about hourly.

AROUND CHESTERFIELD
Hardwick

If you're weighing up which stately homes to see, **Hardwick Hall** *(NT; ☎ 01246-850430; admission £6.40, open 12.30pm-5pm Wed-Thur & Sat-Sun Apr-Oct)* should be high on your list. This was home to the 16th century's second-most famous woman, Elizabeth countess of Shrewsbury – known to all as Bess of Hardwick. Unashamedly modelling herself on the era's *most* famous woman – Queen Elizabeth I – Bess gained power and wealth by marrying four times, upwards each time.

When her fourth husband died in 1590, Bess had a huge fortune to play with, and built Hardwick Hall with the very best designs of the time. Glass was a status symbol, so she went all-out on the windows, and a contemporary ditty quipped 'Hardwick Hall – more glass than wall'. Also astounding are the magnificent High Great Chamber and Long Gallery; these and many other rooms and broad stairways are decorated with fabulous large and detailed tapestries.

This place is special because after Bess died her descendants rarely used Hardwick Hall, and over the centuries it escaped the modernisation that befell many other grand houses. What you see is truly Elizabethan.

Next door is **Hardwick Old Hall** *(EH; admission £3; open 11am-6pm Mon, Wed, Thur, Sat & Sun Apr-Sept; 11am-5pm Mon, Wed, Thur, Sat & Sun, Oct)*, Bess's first house, now a romantic ruin. A combined ticket for both halls is available.

Also fascinating are the formal gardens, again virtually unchanged for centuries, and around the hall spreads the great expanse of **Hardwick Park** with short and long walking trails leading across fields and through woods. Pick up a map (free) at the ticket office. A point to aim for is the **Hardwick Inn**, which does food. You can also bring a picnic. All in all it's a great day out.

Hardwick Hall is 10 miles (16km) southeast of Chesterfield, just off the M1. By public transport, a special historic coach runs from Chesterfield (Sunday only June to August, £5, with half-price entry at Hardwick), out in the morning, back in the afternoon, giving about three hours at Hardwick. The bus also passes **Stainsby Mill** – a quaint

Chesterfield's Crooked Spire

Why is the church spire at Chesterfield twisted and bent? Reasons given for this ecclesiastical anomaly include the following: it's because the devil once flew by and got his tail caught; it's because a virgin once got married here and the spire was so surprised it bent down to have a look; it's because many craftsmen were killed off by the Black Death and cowboy builders did the job; it's because heavy lead tiles were fixed over a poorly seasoned timber frame. Whatever the real reason, the people of Chesterfield prefer version two, and say that when another virgin gets married here, the spire will straighten up again.

working flour-mill dating from 1245 – and ends at **Bolsover Castle**, yet another stately home. For details, contact the TIC in Chesterfield, or see **w** www.cosycoach.co.uk.

Peak District

The Peak District National Park is a remarkable region, with pretty villages, historic sites, grand houses, fascinating limestone caves, the southernmost hills of the Pennines, and some of England's most wild and beautiful scenery. On the map you'll see it smack bang in the middle of one of the most densely populated parts of England, but when you're out in the moors and valleys, the cities seem very far away.

The Peak (as it's called – not from the hills, which are quite rounded, but from the name of an early British tribe that once lived here) is one of the country's best-loved national parks. So loved, that it's the busiest in Europe, and the second busiest in the world after Mount Fuji. Now there's a claim to fame. To escape the crowds, you should avoid summer weekends, but even then, with a bit of imagination, it's still easy enough to enjoy this wonderful area in relative peace and solitude.

Orientation & Information

The Peak District is principally in Derbyshire but spills into five adjoining counties (including Yorkshire, Staffordshire and Cheshire) and is one of the largest national parks in England. This 555-sq-mile protected area is divided into two distinct zones: the harsher, higher, wilder Dark Peak to the north, characterised by peaty moors and dramatic gritstone cliffs called 'edges'; and the lower, prettier, more pastoral White Peak to the south, with green fields marked by drystone walls, and divided by deep-cut dales.

There are TICs (those run by the national park are called visitor centres) in Buxton, Bakewell, Castleton, Edale and other locations, all overflowing with maps, guidebooks and leaflets detailing walks, cycle rides and other ideas to keep you occupied. For general information, the *Peak District* newspaper (free from TICs) and the official park website at **w** www.peakdistrict.org cover transport, activities, local events, guided walks and so on.

Well-Dressed Derbyshire

The tradition of 'dressing' (decorating) wells or springs in thanksgiving for a good supply of water is unique to the county of Derbyshire, and probably dates from Celtic times. Each year between May and September about 60 village wells are dressed with large and intricate mosaics of flower petals and leaves depicting scenes from the Bible, local history or events, or more modern issues such as rainforest protection. The event often includes a church service, or a village carnival, with displays such as country dancing. Over the centuries many Derbyshire villages have become mining towns or even city suburbs – but the festival still takes place. June and July are the main months, and each village's well (or wells) are dressed for a week only. Pick up a *Well Dressing* leaflet in any Tourist Information Centre in Derbyshire for dates and locations.

Activities

Walking The Peak District is one of the most popular walking areas in England, crossed by a vast network of footpaths and tracks – especially in the White Peak – and you can easily find a walk of a few miles or longer, depending on your energy and interests. If you want to explore the higher realms of the Dark Peak, which often involves the local art of 'bog trotting', make sure your boots are waterproof and be prepared for wind and rain – even if the sun is shining when you set off.

The Peak's most famous walking trail is the **Pennine Way**, with its southern end at Edale and its northern end over 250 miles away in Scotland. If you don't have a spare three weeks to cover this route, from Edale you can follow the trail north across wild hills and moors for just a day or two. An excellent three-day option is to Hebden Bridge – a delightful little town described in the Yorkshire chapter of this book.

The 46-mile **Limestone Way** winds through the Derbyshire countryside from Castleton to Rocester in Staffordshire on a mix of footpaths, tracks and quiet lanes. The northern section of this route, through the White Peak between Castleton and Matlock, is 26 miles, and hardy folk can do it over a long summer day, but two days is better. The

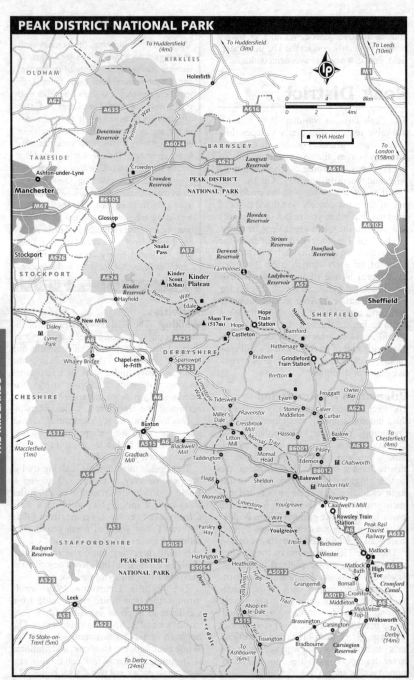

PEAK DISTRICT NATIONAL PARK

route goes via Miller's Dale, Monyash, Youlgreave and Bonsall, with YHA hostels and B&Bs along the way, plus ample pubs and cafés. TICs have a detailed leaflet.

The YHA in Derbyshire produces a handy set of *Youth Hostel Walking Routes* (20p each) describing walks around and between Peak District and Derbyshire hostels.

Various shorter walks are described throughout this section. All the villages make good bases for exploring the surrounding area, and Fairholmes at the Derwent Reservoirs is great for getting deep into the hills. The High Peak and Tissington Trails described in the Cycling section following are equally popular with walkers.

Cycling The Peak District is a very popular cycling area, especially the White Peak and the parts of Derbyshire south of here around Matlock and Ashbourne, which has a network of quiet lanes, plus many tracks for mountain-bikers. In the Dark Peak there are fewer roads, and they are quite busy with traffic, although there are some good off-road routes. A good place to start any ride is a TIC – all stock maps, books and leaflets for cyclists and mountain-bikers.

In the Dark Peak, Edale is a popular start-point for mountain-bikers, and around the Derwent Reservoirs is also good. In the White Peak, all the villages mentioned in this section make good bases for cycle tours.

For easy traffic-free riding, head for the 17½-mile **High Peak Trail**, a route for cyclists and walkers on the mostly flat track of an old railway. You can join the trail at Cromford, near Matlock Bath, but it starts with a very steep incline, so if you seek easy gradients a better start is Middleton Top, a mile or so north. The trail winds beautifully through hills and farmland to a village called Parsley Hay, and continues on for a few more miles towards Buxton. At Parsley Hay another former-railway-turned-walking-and-cycling-route, called the **Tissington Trail** heads south for 13 miles to Ashbourne. You can go out and back as far as you like, or make it a triangular circuit, following the busy B5053 or (preferably) the quiet lanes through Bradbourne and Brassington.

There are several **Cycle Hire Centres** in the Peak District, including: **Fairholmes** (☎ 01433-651261), for the Derwent area; **Parsley Hay** (☎ 01298-84493) and **Middleton**

Top (☎ 01629-823204) for the Tissington and High Peak Trails. TICs have a leaflet detailing all other hire centres, opening times etc. Charges are around £10 to £15 per day for adult bikes (deposit and ID required), and kids' bikes and trailers are also available.

Caving & Climbing The Peak District limestone is riddled with caves and caverns – including 'showcaves' open to the public in Castleton, Buxton and Matlock Bath (described in the sections on those places elsewhere in this chapter). For serious caving (or pot-holing) trips, TICs can provide a list of accredited outdoor centres, and if you know what you're doing, Castleton makes a great base. For guidebooks, gear (to buy or hire) and a mine of local information, contact **Hitch n Hike** (☎ 01433 651013; **w** www .hitchnhike.com; *Mytham Bridge, North Bamford, Hope Valley, Derbyshire*) a specialist caving and outdoor activity shop in Bamford, near Castleton. The website also has more info about caving in the area.

If you'd rather be on top of the rock, the Peak is a popular climbing area, and has long been a training ground for England's top mountaineers. There are multipitch routes on limestone faces such as High Tor, overlooking Matlock Bath, and a great range of short climbing routes on the famous gritstone edges of Froggatt, Curbar and Stanage.

Places to Stay
TICs have lists of hotels, B&Bs or campsites – whatever suits your budget. Walkers may appreciate the 13 **camping barns** (*per person from £3.50*) dotted around the Peak. Usually owned by farmers, booking is organised centrally through the **YHA** (☎ 0870 870 8808). Or pick up a *Camping Barns in England* leaflet at TICs.

Getting There & Around
The Peak District authorities are trying hard to wean visitors off their cars, and TICs stock the excellent *Peak District Timetable* (60p) covering local buses and trains. For more details, see Getting There & Around in the Derbyshire section.

BUXTON
☎ 01298 • pop 20,000 • elevation 270m
Buxton is just outside the border of the Peak District National Park, and makes a handy

gateway for the northern and western areas. With its grand Georgian architecture, leafy parks and busy tourist ambience the town is frequently compared to Bath, and just like Bath, Buxton also has a natural warm-water spring discovered by the Romans. The town's heyday was in the 18th century when 'taking the waters' was highly fashionable.

Today, Buxton still attracts many visitors, and is almost – but not quite – genteel. Away from the historical sights, it's just like many other north-country market towns, although none the worse for that. Every Tuesday and Saturday, the Market Place is full of colourful stalls and has a great atmosphere. Around town, there's also a vast selection of shops selling crafts, books and antiques, perfect for a day of idle browsing.

Orientation & Information

Buxton has two centres: the historical area, with The Crescent, Opera House and Pavilion; and the Market Place, surrounded by pubs and restaurants. The TIC (☎ 25106; e tourism@highpeak.gov.uk; w www.peak district-tourism.gov.uk; The Crescent) can help you find a place to stay, and has useful leaflets (50p) on walks in the town and surrounding countryside.

The Post Office (Spring Gardens; open 9am-6pm Mon-Fri, 9am-3pm Sat) is in the co-op, and Internet access at Northwest Computers (11 Bridge St; 9am-5pm Mon-Sat) costs £4 per hour. There are several banks with ATMs on The Quadrant.

Things to See & Do

It has to be said, Buxton was not at its best when we visited in 2002; some wonderful old buildings were slightly tacky and in dire need of TLC. Several major renovation projects are planned however, and hopefully by the time you read this, things will look a lot better.

Buxton's flagship Opera House (☎ 0845 1272190; w www.buxton-opera.co.uk) is a century old and was recently restored to full glory. Naturally, it's the centre for Buxton's famous Opera Festival (held every July, and the largest of its kind in England), but for rest of the year enjoys a full programme of drama, dance, concerts and comedy. Tours of the auditorium and backstage areas are available at 11am most Saturday mornings.

Next to the Opera House is The Pavilion, a giant palace of glass built in 1871, which overlooks Pavilion Gardens – a pleasant park with lawns, ponds and a miniature train. Broad Walk is a traffic-free road alongside the edge of the gardens, ideal for an evening perambulation.

Perhaps Buxton's grandest building is The Crescent, a graceful curve of houses modelled on the Royal Crescent in Bath. Just east of here is Cavendish Arcade, formerly a thermal bathhouse (you can still see the chair used for lowering the infirm into the restorative waters) with several craft and book shops and a striking coloured glass ceiling.

On the other side of The Crescent, the TIC is in the old Natural Mineral Baths where you can still see the source of the mineral water – now Buxton's most famous export. A small display tells the full story.

Across from the TIC, the Pump Room, which dispensed Buxton's spring water for nearly a century, now hosts temporary art exhibitions. Just outside is St Ann's Well, a fountain where you can fill up on free mineral water.

Opposite The Crescent, a small park called The Slopes rises steeply in a series of grassy terraces. From the top there are views over the centre and across to the grand old Palace Hotel and the Devonshire Hospital, Buxton's most eye-catching edifice, complete with towers and a massive dome that Jerusalem might envy.

Poole's Cavern (☎ 26978; adult/child £5.20/2.75; open 10am-5pm daily Mar-Oct) is a splendid showcave about a mile from the centre. Amiable and enthusiastic guides will take you deep underground to see an impressive selection of stalactites (including the longest in England) and stalagmites (including unique 'poached egg' formations). In spring and autumn, running water makes the cave even more dramatic.

From near the cave entrance, a 20-minute walk leads up through Grin Low Wood to Solomon's Temple, a small tower with fine views over the town and surrounding Peak District.

A longer walk is the Monsal Trail, which leads all the way to Bakewell – see that section for details.

Places to Stay

Most B&Bs are in the suburbs, just a short walk from the centre.

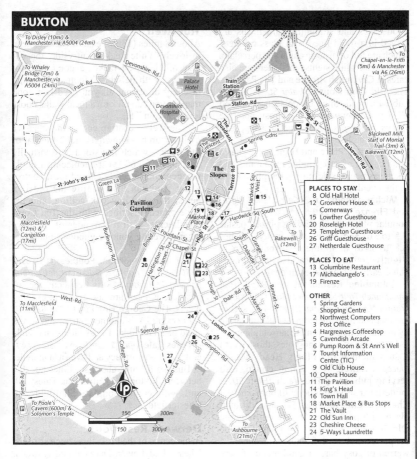

BUXTON

To Disley (10mi) & Manchester via A5004 (24mi)

To Whaley Bridge (7mi) & Manchester via A5004 (24mi)

Devonshire Rd

Park Rd

Palace Hotel

Train Station

Station Rd

To Chapel-en-le-Frith (5mi) & Manchester via A6 (26mi)

Devonshire Hospital

The Quadrant

Bridge St

Bakewell Rd

To Blackwell Mill, start of Monsal Trail (3mi) & Bakewell (12mi)

Park Rd

Spring Gdns

St John's Rd

Green La

The Crescent

The Slopes

Terrace Rd

Hardwick Sq West

Pavilion Gardens

To Macclesfield (12mi) & Congelton (17mi)

Burlington Rd

Broad Wk

Fountain St

St James' Tce

Hatrington St

Chapel St

Market Place

High St

Hardwick Sq South

South Ave

Dale Rd

Grange Rd

Hardwick Sq

To Bakewell (12mi)

Bennet St

New Market St

Dateside

Clough St

To Macclesfield (11mi)

West Rd

Spencer Rd

London Rd

College Rd

Temple Rd

Compton Rd

Green La

To Poole's Cavern (600m) & Solomon's Temple

To Ashbourne (21mi)

0   150   300m
0   150   300yd

PLACES TO STAY
8 Old Hall Hotel
12 Grosvenor House & Cornerways
15 Lowther Guesthouse
20 Roseleigh Hotel
25 Templeton Guesthouse
26 Griff Guesthouse
27 Netherdale Guesthouse

PLACES TO EAT
13 Columbine Restaurant
17 Michaelangelo's
19 Firenze

OTHER
1 Spring Gardens Shopping Centre
2 Northwest Computers
3 Post Office
4 Hargreaves Coffeeshop
5 Cavendish Arcade
6 Pump Room & St Ann's Well
7 Tourist Information Centre (TIC)
9 Old Club House
10 Opera House
11 The Pavilion
14 King's Head
16 Town Hall
18 Market Place & Bus Stops
21 The Vault
22 Old Sun Inn
23 Cheshire Cheese
24 5-Ways Laundrette

Templeton Guesthouse (☎ 25275; 13 Compton Rd; per person £18.50) has a choice of standard and en-suite rooms.

Griff Guesthouse (☎ 23628; 2 Compton Rd; per person £20) is no-frills and noted for its food.

Lowther Guesthouse (☎ 71479; 7 Hardwick Sq West; per person £21) is a quiet, friendly place, and a good choice in this range.

Netherdale Guesthouse (☎ 23896; 16 Green Lane; doubles £60) is a smart and comfortable place on a leafy street.

There are hundreds of hotels in Buxton, many dating from the Georgian and Victorian heydays. Around Pavilion Gardens and along Broad Walk are several particularly fine atmospheric places.

Grosvenor House (☎ 72439; **e** grosvenor .buxton@btopenworld.com; 1 Broad Walk; doubles £50-75) is a friendly family-run hotel.

Roseleigh Hotel (☎ 24904; **e** enquiries@ roseleighhotel.co.uk; 19 Broad Walk; singles/ doubles from £25/52) has charming rooms, and a comfortable lounge full of travel books and deep leather armchairs.

Old Hall Hotel (☎ 22841; The Square, singles/doubles £65/96) is a grand establishment and claims to be the oldest hotel in England. Former guests include Mary Queen of Scots and Daniel Defoe.

Places to Eat & Drink

Spring Gardens, an otherwise uninspiring pedestrianised shopping street, has several cheap cafés. At **Hargreaves Coffeeshop** good cakes and straightforward meals are served in a room lined with glass cabinets, which are full of historic china and porcelain. For a break while sightseeing, there are also cafés at **Cavendish Arcade** and **The Pavilion**. The **Old Club House** *(Water St)*, is a large pub with inside and outside seats, and food all day. **Cornerways** at the Grosvenor (see Places to Stay) is a nice quiet teashop, with pavement tables.

The Market Place and High St area has a good choice of cafés, pubs, restaurants and takeaways, and is definitely the place to be in the evening.

Michaelangelo's *(☎ 26640; Market Place)* and **Firenze** *(☎ 72203; Market Place)* are popular places, both serving pizzas, pastas (£5 to £6) and Mediterranean-style dishes (£8 to £10) in intimate surrounds (read slightly cramped); both also offer good-value early-evening special deals.

Columbine Restaurant *(☎ 78752; Hall Bank; lunch Thur-Sat, dinner Mon-Sat; lunches around £5, dinner mains £10-12)* serves highly rated food, including a full vegetarian menu, in calm and intimate surroundings.

Of the many watering-holes, those worth a stop include the **King's Head** *(Market Place)* favoured by a young crowd, also serving pub grub; the **Vault** *(High St)*, a modern bar serving food until 6pm; and the **Cheshire Cheese** *(High St)*, a traditional place with pool table. Our favourite is the **Old Sun Inn** *(High St)*, which could just be the perfect pub, with friendly atmosphere, a warren of cosy bars, a good menu of very fine food, and a range of well-kept beer to go with it.

Getting There & Away

All buses leave from/arrive at the Market Place. From Manchester or the Peak District, the handiest bus is the two-hourly TransPeak service (No TP) between Nottingham and Manchester, via Derby, Bakewell and Buxton. Between Bakewell and Buxton takes 30 minutes. Other services include Chesterfield to Buxton (£4.70, one hour, seven daily).

Trains run from Manchester to Buxton (£5.70, 50 minutes, hourly) via New Mills. (Buxton is the end of the line.) Change at New Mills to get to Sheffield via Edale and the Hope Valley line.

AROUND BUXTON
Tideswell

About 8 miles (13km) east of Buxton, deep in lovely White Peak countryside, the village of Tideswell makes a good base for walking, with delightful footpaths leading in every direction; all you need is a good map, or you can pick up a local walks booklet at Buxton TIC.

Tideswell's centrepiece is the massive parish church – known as the **Cathedral of the Peak** – which has stood here virtually unchanged for 600 years; replacing a single wooden door recently caused local controversy. You can also admire the old box pews, the ship-like oak ceiling, and the huge panels inscribed with the Ten Commandments, a firm reminder of the days when coveting your neighbour's maid just wasn't on.

For accommodation, **Poppies** *(☎ 01298-871083;* **e** *poptidza@dialstart.net; Bank Square; B&B from £18)* is frequently recommended, and can provide excellent evening meals. The **George Hotel** *(☎ 01298 871382; per person £25)* is another option, and serves good beer and food. Tideswell also has **Hills & Dales Cafe** *(open 10am-5pm Fri-Sun)*, several shops, a pharmacy and even a laundrette.

Bus No 65 runs about six times per day between Buxton and Calver, via Tideswell, and with connections to Sheffield and Chesterfield.

Derwent Reservoirs

In the centre of the Peak, three huge artificial lakes – Ladybower, Derwent and Howden, together known as the Derwent Reservoirs – collect water for the cities of Derbyshire and the Midlands. They are also focal points for walking and mountain-biking.

The place to aim for is Fairholmes, a national park centre which has a **TIC** *(☎ 01433-650953)*, car park, snack-bar and cycle hire. From here, numerous walks are possible, from gentle strolls along the lakeside to more serious outings on the moors above the valley. For cycling, a lane leads up the west side of Derwent and Howden reservoirs (it's closed to car traffic at weekends) and a dirt track comes down the east side making a good 12-mile circuit, while challenging off-road routes lead deeper into the hills. The TIC stocks a very good range of route-leaflets, maps and guidebooks.

Getting There & Away

Fairholmes is 2 miles (3km) north of the A57, the main road between Sheffield and Manchester. By car, access is easy. By bus, No 273 goes once daily (four on Sunday) between Sheffield (30 minutes) and Castleton (15 minutes), via Fairholmes. Bus No 257 runs from Sheffield to Fairholmes (eight times daily weekends April to October) and continues up to the end of the road on the west side of Howden Reservoir – an excellent way to reach the high hills and one of the wildest parts of the Peak District.

EDALE

☎ 01433 • pop 350 • elevation 230m

The Edale Valley marks the border of the White and Dark Peak areas, and contains the tiny rustic village of Edale – one of the most popular bases for walking in the park. The **TIC** (☎ 670207; open daily) has a small exhibition about the park, and can supply all the leaflets, maps and guides you'll need. The local tourism association's website at w www.edale-valley.co.uk is also very useful.

Walking

Edale is most famous for being the southern terminus of the Pennine Way, but endless walks of varying length are possible in the surrounding area. Heading south, a great walk from Edale takes you up to Hollins Cross, a point on the ridge that runs south of the valley. From here, you can aim west to the top of Mam Tor and watch the hang-gliders

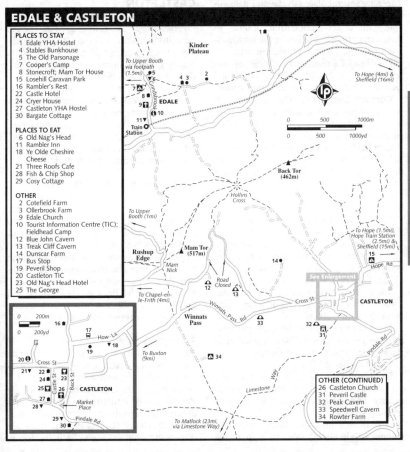

EDALE & CASTLETON

PLACES TO STAY
1 Edale YHA Hostel
4 Stables Bunkhouse
5 The Old Parsonage
7 Cooper's Camp
8 Stonecroft; Mam Tor House
15 Losehill Caravan Park
16 Rambler's Rest
22 Castle Hotel
24 Cryer House
27 Castleton YHA Hostel
30 Bargate Cottage

PLACES TO EAT
6 Old Nag's Head
11 Rambler Inn
18 Ye Olde Cheshire Cheese
21 Three Roofs Cafe
28 Fish & Chip Shop
29 Cosy Cottage

OTHER
2 Cotefield Farm
3 Ollerbrook Farm
9 Edale Church
10 Tourist Information Centre (TIC); Fieldhead Camp
12 Blue John Cavern
13 Treak Cliff Cavern
14 Dunscar Farm
17 Bus Stop
19 Peveril Shop
20 Castleton TIC
23 Old Nag's Head Hotel
25 The George

OTHER (CONTINUED)
26 Castleton Church
31 Peveril Castle
32 Peak Cavern
33 Speedwell Cavern
34 Rowter Farm

THE MIDLANDS

swoop around above. Or go east along the ridge, with great views on both sides, past the cliffs of Back Tor to reach Lose Hill (which, naturally, faces Win Hill). Or you can continue south, down to the village of Castleton (described in the next section).

From Edale you can also walk north onto the Kinder Plateau – dark and brooding in the mist, gloriously high and open when the sun's out. Weather permitting, a fine circular walk starts by following the Pennine Way through fields to Upper Booth, then up a path called Jacobs Ladder, and along the southern edge of Kinder, before dropping down to Edale via the steep rocky valley of Grindsbrook Clough, or the ridge of Ringing Roger.

Places to Stay & Eat
There are several places to stay in Edale village, and we list a selection here. There are many more accommodation options in farms and remote cottages in the surrounding area – the TIC can provide details.

Fieldhead Campsite (☎ 670386; per person £3.50) is neat and compact, with good facilities, and near the TIC and train station.

Cooper's Camp (☎ 670372; per person £3) is a larger place at the upper end of the village larger; facilities are good and there's a shop and café attached.

Cotefield Farm Camping Barn (☎ 0870 870 8808; per person £4) is bookable through the YHA, while **Stables Bunkhouse** (☎ 670235; Ollerbrook Farm; per person £8) is another good cheap option. Both places are less than a mile east of the village centre.

Edale YHA Hostel (☎ 0870 770 5808; e edale@yha.org.uk; dorm beds £11) is a large old country house 1½ miles east of the village centre. It's also an activity centre and very popular with youth groups.

The Old Parsonage (☎ 670232; Grindsbrook; B&B per person from £16) is straightforward but clean and tidy, and a long-time favourite with walkers.

Mam Tor House (☎ 670253; Grindsbrook; B&B per person around £18) is a good mid-range place. If it's full, the owners can direct you to other B&Bs.

Stonecroft (☎ 670262; Grindsbrook; B&B per person from £26-30) offers excellent quality food and accommodation, and very friendly service.

For filling no-frills food, head for **Cooper's Café** near Cooper's Camp, or the

café at the train station; both are open from breakfast-time to 5pm.

Edale has two pubs, the **Old Nag's Head** and the **Rambler Inn**; both serve passable pub grub, but neither place is at all inspiring. Still, that's your only choice, and they know it. If you've got wheels, the **Cheshire Cheese**, about 2½ miles east of Edale towards the neighbouring village of Hope, is a much better option.

Getting There & Away
By far the easiest way to reach Edale is by train on the line between Sheffield and Manchester (about eight per day Monday to Friday, about five per day at weekends). Trains also stop at several other Peak villages.

CASTLETON
☎ 01433 • pop 900 • elevation 180m
Overshadowed by 517m-high Mam Tor, the neat little settlement of Castleton has a central square, a couple of narrow lanes with sturdy gritstone houses and colourful gardens, and a good collection of cosy country pubs. Oh yes – and about a million tourists on summer weekends. But don't let that put you off. Come here at a quieter time to enjoy good walks in the surrounding area, and marvel at the famous 'showcaves', where a semi-precious stone called Blue John has been mined for centuries.

Orientation & Information
Castleton stands at the western end of the Hope Valley. The main route through the village (Cross St, the A6187) used to switchback up the side of notoriously unstable Mam Tor, but frequent landslips destroyed the road, and traffic now goes up the narrow, spectacular (and much older) Winnats Pass. On or just off Cross St are pubs, shops, cafés, B&Bs, the YHA hostel, and the **TIC** (☎ 620679; open 10am-5.30pm daily Easter-Oct, weekends only Oct-Apr).

Things to See
On the hillside above Castleton stands ruined **Peveril Castle** (EH; ☎ 620613; adult/child £2.40/1.20), well worth the steep walk up from the village. It was built by William Peveril, son of William the Conqueror, and the central keep (about all that remains) was added by Henry II in 1176. The ruins are interesting, but the view from the top is

stunning: straight down to Castleton's medieval street grid, and north to Mam Tor with the Dark Peak beyond.

The area around Castleton is riddled with caves, and four are open to the public. Although mostly natural, they have been extensively mined for Blue John, as well as lead and silver, and so have been enlarged over the centuries. All charge £5 to £6 for adults, and half price for children.

Peak Cavern *(☎ 620285; open 10am-4pm daily April-Oct, weekends only Nov-Mar)*, is easily reached by a pretty stream-side walk from the village centre. The cave entrance is the largest in England, known (not so prettily) as the Devil's Arse.

Speedwell Cavern *(☎ 620512; open 10am-4.30pm daily, 10am-3pm Oct-Apr)* is a former mine near Winnats Pass and contains a unique flooded tunnel which you travel along by boat to reach an underground lake called the 'bottomless pit'.

Treak Cliff Cavern *(☎ 620571; open 10am-5.30pm daily Mar-Oct, 10am-3pm daily Nov-Feb)* is a short walk from Castleton, with exposed veins of Blue John and great stalactites, including the much-photographed 'stork' (which actually looks more like a dinosaur with a stomach complaint).

Blue John Cavern *(☎ 620638; open 9.30am-5pm daily)* is an impressive set of multi-coloured chambers and passageways – a main source of Blue John. You can get here on foot up the closed section of the Mam Tor road.

Walking
Castleton is the northern terminus of the Limestone Way, which includes narrow, rocky Cave Dale, far below the east wall of the castle. Information on the whole 26-mile northern section of this route between Castleton and Matlock is given under Activities at the start of this section.

If you feel like a shorter walk, you can follow the Limestone Way up Cave Dale for a few miles, then loop round on paths and tracks to the west of Rowter Farm to meet the Buxton Rd. Go straight (north) on a path crossing fields and another road to eventually reach Mam Nick, where the road to Edale passes through a gap in the ridge. Go up steps here to reach the summit of Mam Tor, for fine views along the Hope Valley. (You can also see the fractured remains of

the old main road.) The path then aims northwest along the ridge to another gap called Hollins Cross, from where paths and tracks lead back down to Castleton. This 6-mile circuit takes three to four hours.

A shorter option from Castleton is to take the path direct to Hollins Cross, then go to Mam Tor, and return by the same route. (About 4 miles, two to three hours.) From Hollins Cross, you can extend any walk by dropping down to Edale, or you can walk direct from Castleton to Edale via Hollins Cross. (For details on Edale, see that section earlier.)

Places to Stay
For campers, the nearest place is well-organised **Losehill Caravan Park** *(☎ 620636; Hope Rd; per site £5-6, plus per adult £4-5)*.

Rowter Farm *(☎ 620271; per person £3)* is a simple campsite up on the hills about 1 mile west of Castleton. Drivers should approach via Winnats Pass; if you're on foot you can follow paths from Castleton village centre, as described in the Walking section earlier.

Castleton YHA Hostel *(☎ 0870 770 5758; e castleton@yha.org.uk; Castle St; dorm beds £11, rooms from £40)* is large and often busy, with knowledgeable management, and a good choice of dorms and smaller rooms.

Cryer House *(☎ 620244; Castle St; B&B per person £24)* is a long-standing favourite with affable hosts, and a popular garden tearoom out front.

Bargate Cottage *(☎ 620201; Market Place; B&B per double room £43)* is bright and full of character, and often recommended.

Rambler's Rest *(☎ 620125; Mill Bridge; doubles per person £17.50, en suite £22)*, as the name implies, offers a special welcome to walkers. This friendly place also has a large en-suite room with three or four beds (£22 per person), ideal for small groups or people with kids.

Castle Hotel *(☎ 620578; Castle St; rooms Mon-Thur £50, weekends £60)* offers comfortable pub accommodation, as well as tasty good-value meals and very efficient service.

Places to Eat & Drink
For hot drinks, snacks and lunches, teashops abound in Castleton. Those worth a visit include **Cosy Cottage** *(Market Place)* for scones piled with cream, **Cryer House**

(Castle St), favoured for its pretty garden and conservatory and **Three Roofs** (Cross St) which is especially good for breakfast.

For a hot takeaway, there's a **fish and chip shop** round the corner from the YHA hostel – usually open lunchtime and evening at weekends. Near the bus stop, **Peveril Shop** (How Lane) sells food and groceries, and also does sandwiches to take away – ideal for a day on the hills or a long bus ride.

Castleton is also very well supplied with pubs. Our favourites include **The George** (Castle St; mains around £7) which serves up good filling food and is especially popular with walkers, and the **Cheshire Cheese** (Hope Rd), an excellent traditional pub of character. Also good for food is the **Olde Nag's Head Hotel** (☎ 620451; bar meals £7-9) a friendly place which also offers romantic candlelit suppers for £17.95 and Sunday lunches for £12.95, plus B&B for £30 per person if you eat so much you can't leave.

Getting There & Away
You can get to Castleton from Bakewell on Bus No 173 (45 minutes, five per day Monday to Friday, three per day at weekends), via Hope and Tideswell.

The nearest train station is Hope, about 1 mile east of Hope village (a total of 3 miles east of Castleton) on the line between Sheffield and Manchester. At summer weekends a bus runs between Hope station and Castleton tying in with the trains.

EYAM
☎ 01433 • pop 900 • elevation 200m
The village of Eyam (pronounced ee-em, or eem) is a quaint little spot, and most famous for a fatal incident in 1665 when a consignment of cloth from London delivered to a local tailor brought with it the dreaded disease known simply as the plague. As it spread through Eyam, the rector convinced the inhabitants to quarantine themselves rather than transmit it further. This they did, and by the time the plague ended in late 1666, around 250 of the village's 800 inhabitants had died, while people in surrounding villages remained relatively unscathed. But even without this poignant story, Eyam is well worth a visit, with its streets of old cottages backed by rolling green hills forming a classic Peak District view.

Walking
Apart from the historical attractions described in Things to See following, Eyam makes a great base for walking and cycling in the surrounding White Peak area. A short walk for starters leads up Water Lane from the village square, then up through fields and a patch of woodland to meet another lane running between Eyam and Grindleford; turn right here and keep going uphill, past another junction to **Mompesson's Well** where food and other supplies were left during the plague time for Eyam folk by friends from other villages. The Eyam people paid for the goods using coins sterilised in vinegar. You can retrace your steps back down the lane, then take a path which leads directly to the church. This 2-mile circuit takes about 1½ hours.

Things to See
The **church** dates from Saxon times and has many reminders of the plague, including a cupboard said to be made from the box that carried the infected cloth to Eyam. More sobering is the plague register, recording those who died, name by name, day by day. Many plague victims were buried in the churchyard, but only two headstones from the time exist – one for Catherine Mompesson, the rector's wife.

Also in the churchyard, but from a much earlier era, the 8th-century **Celtic cross** is one of the finest in England. Before leaving, check your watch against the **sundial** on the church wall.

In the church you can buy the *Eyam Map* (£2.50), and smaller leaflets (20p) which describe the village's history and all the sites associated with the plague. You can also find a leaflet describing some of the monuments and headstones in the churchyard.

Around the village, many buildings have information plaques attached; these include the **plague cottages**, where the tailor lived, next to the church.

Eyam Hall (☎ 631976; adult/child £4.25/3; open 11am-4pm Wed, Thur & Sun Jun-Aug) is a fine old 17th century manor house, and the courtyard contains a tearoom and numerous craft workshops.

Eyam Museum (W www.eyammuseum.demon.co.uk; adult/child £1.50/1; open 10am-4.30pm Tues-Sun Easter-Oct) is well worth a stop. Of course, the plague is the main story, but there are neat little exhibits on geology,

Saxon history, and the village's time as a lead mining and silk weaving centre.

Look out too for the **stocks** on the village green – somewhere handy to leave the kids perhaps, while you look at the church.

Places to Stay & Eat
Eyam YHA Hostel (☎ 0870 770 5830; e eyam@yha.org.uk; Hawkhill Rd; dorm beds £11, twin rooms from £43) is in a fine old Victorian house on the village edge. If it's full **Bretton YHA Hostel** is only 1½ miles away.

Crown Cottage (☎ 630858; Church St; B&B per double room £50) is also known as the Old Rose & Crown. The very friendly people here welcome walkers and cyclists and can advise on routes in the area.

Miner's Arms (☎ 630853; Water Lane; B&B per person £30-40) is a fine old pub, with amiable management, good beer, decent food and very comfortable rooms.

Eyam has two cafés: **Peak Pantry**, on the village square, has good cakes and coffee; **Eyam Tearooms**, just up the road, is slightly more twee, but the cakes are just as good (and B&B is also available).

Getting There & Away
Eyam is 7 miles (11km) north of Bakewell, 12 miles (19km) east of Buxton. Regular buses from Bakewell towards Sheffield or Chesterfield go to Calver, from where you can walk along the main road to Stoney Middleton, then take a path up the steep valley side to Eyam (2 miles). From Buxton, bus No 65 runs about six times per day to/from Calver, via Eyam.

BAKEWELL
☎ 01629 • pop 3800 • elevation 120m
After Buxton, this is the largest town in the Peak District (though it's hardly a metropolis) and a good base for walking, cycling or touring. It's also a notorious traffic bottleneck on summer weekends, but at quieter times it's worth a stop to see some interesting sights and the various shops which claim to be the birthplace of the world-famous Bakewell pudding. Two of the Peak District's most famous stately homes are nearby, and the town is surrounded by some fine countryside.

Orientation & Information
The centre of town is Rutland Square, from where roads radiate to Matlock, Buxton and

Plague Survivor Mystery

A mysterious aspect of the plague (and similar epidemics) that has long interested scientists is – to put it bluntly – why it didn't kill everyone, given its notoriously contagious nature. A possible answer came to light in 2001 when a fascinating study conducted by American scientists discovered that many local Eyam people descended from plague survivors carry a distinctive rare gene.

The same research then located a gay man in California who expected to contract AIDS, yet remained immune, also carrying this same rare gene (possibly inherited from a Derbyshire forebear). The next challenge for the scientists is to isolate the 'Eyam gene' and use it in the ongoing quest for a cure for AIDS.

Sheffield. The **TIC** (☎ 813227; Bridge St; open daily), in the old Market Hall, has racks of leaflets and books about Bakewell and the national park.

Things to See & Do
Bakewell's weekly **market** is on Monday, when the square behind the TIC is very lively. Up on the hill above Rutland Square, **All Saints Church** has some ancient Norman features, and even older Saxon stonework remains, including a tall cross in the churchyard, which sadly has suffered at the hands of time.

Near the church, **Old House Museum** (Cunningham Place; adult/child £2.50/1; open 1.30pm-4pm daily Easter-June & Oct; 11am-4pm daily Jul-Sept) displays local miscellany, including a Tudor loo.

A stroll from Rutland Square down Bridge St brings you – not surprisingly – to the pretty **medieval bridge** over the River Wye, from where riverside walks lead in both directions. Go upstream through the water meadows, and then along Holme Lane to reach **Holme Bridge**, an ancient stone structure used by Peak District packhorses for centuries.

Walking & Cycling
On the northern edge of Bakewell, a former railway line has been converted to a walking and cycling track called the **Monsal Trail**. From Bakewell you can cycle about

3 miles north and 1 mile south on the old railway itself – and there are numerous other tracks and country lanes nearby. **Bakewell Cycle Hire** (☎ 814004) at the old station has mountain bikes for £11 per day; opening times depend on the weather, so phone ahead if possible.

Walkers on the Monsal Trail follow alternate sections of the old railway and pretty footpaths through fields and beside rivers (to avoid tunnels, now closed). From Bakewell, an excellent out-and-back walk (3 miles each way) goes to the dramatic viewpoint at Monsal Head – where there's a good pub and a friendly café. Allow three hours for the round trip. (Longer if you have a good lunch.)

If you're out for the day, from Monsal Head you can keep following the Monsal Trail northwest towards Buxton. A good point to aim for is Miller's Dale where impressive viaducts cross the steep-sided valley (and there's another good café), or you can go all the way to Blackwell Mill (3 miles east of Buxton) – a total distance of about 9 miles – and get a bus back. Alternatively, get a bus to Buxton, and walk back to Bakewell. The TICs at Bakewell and Buxton have a *Monsal Trail* leaflet (free) with all the details.

Other walking routes go to the stately homes of Haddon Hall and Chatsworth House (see Around Bakewell, following). You could take a bus or taxi there and walk back, so you don't put mud on the duke's carpet.

Places to Stay

Bakewell YHA Hostel (☎ 0870 770 5682; Fly Hill; dorm beds £10) is a modern building just out of the centre at the top of a very steep hill.

Easthorpe and **Melbourne** (☎ 815357; Buxton Rd; B&B per person from £23) are run as one unit on either side of a busy road, with plenty of rooms and friendly service.

Croft Cottage (☎ 814101; e croftco@bt internet.com; Coombs Rd; B&B per person around £25) is a quaint old building near the bridge.

Long Meadow (☎ 812500; Coombs Rd; B&B per single or double £50) offers very comfortable accommodation in a separate wing of a renovated old house.

Castle Inn (☎ 812103; Bridge St; rooms £45) is one of the better pubs in Bakewell, with good rooms (single, double or family of four) all the same rate, plus £4 to £6 for breakfast.

Rutland Arms Hotel (☎ 812812; e rut land@bakewell.demon.co.uk; Rutland Sq; rooms per person £40-55) is a venerable establishment, cashing in fully on its history (see the boxed text 'Which Bakewell

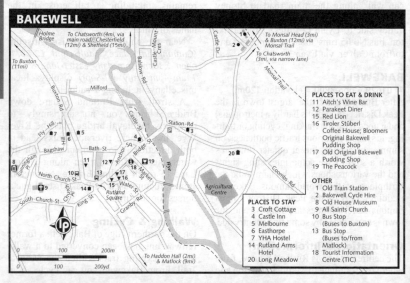

BAKEWELL

Holme Bridge
To Chatsworth (4mi, via main road); Chesterfield (12mi) & Sheffield (15mi)
Castle Mount Cres
Castle Dr
To Buxton (11mi)
To Monsal Head (3mi) & Buxton (12mi) via Monsal Trail
To Chatsworth (3mi, via narrow lane)
Monsal Trail
Milford
Balslow Rd
Buxton Rd
Castle St
Station Rd
Fly Hill
Bath St
Anchor Sq
Bagshaw
Cunningham Pl
Bridge St
Market St
North Church St
Church St
Wye
South Church St
Water St
Rutland Square
King St
Cranby Rd
Coombs Rd
Agricultural Centre
To Haddon Hall (2mi) & Matlock (9mi)

0 100 200m
0 100 200yd

PLACES TO EAT & DRINK
11 Aitch's Wine Bar
12 Parakeet Diner
15 Red Lion
16 Tiroler Stüberl Coffee House; Bloomers Original Bakewell Pudding Shop
17 Old Original Bakewell Pudding Shop
19 The Peacock

OTHER
1 Old Train Station
2 Bakewell Cycle Hire
8 Old House Museum
9 All Saints Church
10 Bus Stop (Buses to Buxton)
13 Bus Stop (Buses to/from Matlock)
18 Tourist Information Centre (TIC)

PLACES TO STAY
3 Croft Cottage
4 Castle Inn
5 Melbourne
6 Easthorpe
7 YHA Hostel
14 Rutland Arms Hotel
20 Long Meadow

THE MIDLANDS

Pudding?'), and especially popular with coach tour groups. Front rooms overlook the square but can be noisy.

Places to Eat & Drink

Bakewell's streets are lined with cutesy teashops and bakeries, most with 'pudding' in the name, and all selling the town's eponymous cake. There are several fish-and-chip shops too.

Parakeet Diner *(Anchor Sq; open daily)* is a straightforward café, popular with walkers and cyclists, offering snacks, meals and fry-up breakfasts.

Tiroler Stüberl Coffee House *(Water St; open daily)* dares to be different, offering Austrian sausage and apple strudel alongside coffee, scones and snacks.

Aitch's Wine Bar *(☎ 813895; Buxton Rd; lunches £5-7, evening mains £11-15)* is a long-standing place with a highly rated and imaginative menu: 'around the world in eighty plates'.

Of the pubs, the **Red Lion** *(Bridge St)* is cheap and cheerful; the **Castle Inn** (see Places to Stay) does decent pub-grub, and **The Peacock** has a good atmosphere, with beer and food to match.

Getting There & Away

Bakewell is easily reached on the TransPeak bus (No TP), which runs two-hourly between Nottingham and Manchester, via Derby, Buxton, Bakewell and Matlock.

AROUND BAKEWELL
Haddon Hall

Described as a medieval masterpiece, Haddon Hall *(☎ 01629-812855; adult/child £6.75/3.50; open 10.30am-5pm daily Apr-Sept, Thur-Sun Oct)* was originally owned by William Peveril, son of William the Conqueror (see Castleton earlier in this chapter), and what you see today dates mainly from the 14th to 16th centuries. Haddon Hall is special because it was abandoned right through the 18th and 19th centuries, and escaped the 'modernisation' enjoyed by so many other country houses. Highlights include the Chapel, steeped in history, the Long Gallery, truly stunning and skilfully bathed by natural light, and the vast Banqueting Hall, virtually unchanged since the days of Henry VIII. The popular film about Henry's daughter *Elizabeth* was shot here,

Which Bakewell Pudding?

Bakewell blundered into the recipe books around 1860 when a cook at the Rutland Arms Hotel made strawberry tart, but mistakenly (some stories say drunkenly) spread the egg mixture on top of the jam instead of stirring it into the pastry, thus creating the Bakewell pudding (pudding, mark you, not tart). It now features regularly on local dessert menus and is certainly worth sampling.

Two of Bakewell's many pudding-selling establishments are locked in battle over whose is the original recipe, and both have records dating back to 1889. **Bloomers Original Bakewell Pudding Shop** *(Water St)* insists it's 'the first and only', while the **Old Original Bakewell Pudding Shop** *(Bridge St)* is adamant that its recipe is older. The latter certainly pulls in more trade thanks to its position on the main thoroughfare.

History dictates that you should visit them both and do a comparison. It's good for fair play, if not for your waistline.

and, not surprisingly, Haddon Hall made a perfect backdrop. Outside are beautiful gardens and courtyards.

The house is 2 miles south of Bakewell on the A6. You can get there on any bus heading for Matlock (about hourly) or walk – the footpath through the fields mostly on the east side of the river is much more pleasant than following the busy main road. The TIC in Bakewell can help with more details.

Chatsworth

The great stately home, manicured gardens and perfectly landscaped park of Chatsworth together form a major highlight for many visitors to England – as the great line of tour buses parked here in summer will testify. But it's no accident – this is truly one of the finest stately homes in England. To get full value, plan on spending a whole day here.

The main draw is sumptuous **Chatsworth House** *(☎ 01246-582204; adult/child £8/3; open 11am-4.30pm daily Easter-Oct, shorter hrs/days Nov & Dec)*. Known as the 'Palace of the Peak', this vast edifice has been occupied by the dukes of Devonshire for centuries. The original house was started in

1551 by the inimitable Bess of Hardwick (see Around Chesterfield earlier in the chapter) and a little later, Chatsworth's most famous guest was Mary Queen of Scots. She was imprisoned here between 1570 and 1581 at the behest of Elizabeth I, and under the guard of Bess's fourth husband, the earl of Shrewsbury.

The house was extensively altered between 1686 and 1707, and again enlarged and improved in the 1820s, and much of what you see dates from these periods. Among the prime attractions, crane your neck to admire the amazing painted and decorated ceilings, although the 30 or so rooms are all treasure-troves of splendid furniture and magnificent artworks.

The house is surrounded by 40 sq km of **gardens** (entry is adult/child £4.50/2 if you don't go in the house), complete with a fountain so high it can be seen when you're miles away in the hills of the Dark Peak, and a great stairway cascade down which water tumbles and flows.

For the kids an **adventure playground** (admission £3.50) and other attractions provide hours of fun. Beyond that is another 400 hectares of parkland, originally landscaped by Capability Brown, and now open to the public all year for walking and picnicking.

Chatsworth is 3 miles (5km) northeast of Bakewell. If you're driving, it's £1 to park. Bus No 179 runs twice daily (Monday to Saturday) and No 211 four times daily (Sunday). Virgin Trains runs a bus between Macclesfield, Buxton and Bakewell (two per day) which extends to Chatsworth June through September.

Your other options are to walk or cycle from Bakewell. Start out on the quiet lane that leads uphill from the old train station; then walkers can take footpaths through Chatsworth park via the remarkable mock-Venetian village of Edensor (pronounced Ensor), and cyclists can pedal via Pilsley. The TIC in Bakewell has maps and local walks leaflets, and will help with more advice on routes or transport to and from Chatsworth.

Eastern England

Eastern England, that not-quite-remote but oh-so-distinct area of the country covered by the counties of Suffolk, Norfolk, Cambridgeshire and Lincolnshire, doesn't really have a flair for the dramatic. Once upon a time (and a very long time ago it was), the part of this region known as East Anglia (Norfolk, Suffolk and east Cambridgeshire) was the economic epicentre of England, where huge wealth was generated on the back of the wool-and-cloth trade, but in recent centuries the region seems to have settled almost comfortably into semi-retirement. Which is precisely the reason that – with the exception of one world-famous university town – mass tourism has given this part of the country a wide berth, preferring York over Lincoln, Bath over Bury St Edmunds and Canterbury over Ely.

In so doing they are missing out on a fascinating region that can be extraordinarily beautiful. Traditionally separate from the rest of England by the Fens (reclaimed marshlands) and the Essex forests (virtually nonexistent these days), here you'll find picturesque market towns straddling a gently undulating landscape, crisscrossed by waterways and marshland and bordered by some stunning coastlines. But history is not quite dead and gone, and in the midst of this pastoral idyll you will find plenty of evidence of eastern England's busy medieval past.

Highlights

- Reliving the past in medieval Lavenham
- Boating on the beautiful Norfolk Broads
- Dreaming of being a Nobel laureate while strolling around the University of Cambridge
- Enjoying Choral Evensong at King's College Chapel, Cambridge; a truly uplifting experience
- Trying to punt on the River Cam
- Hiking up Steep Hill to Lincoln's superb cathedral

- Lincoln p605
- King's Lynn p585
- Norwich p577
- Ely p602
- Bury St Edmunds p570
- Cambridge p588

HISTORY

East Anglia was a major Saxon kingdom, consisting of the northern people (Norfolk) and the southern ones (Suffolk). Raedwald, who died sometime between AD 616 and 628, was the first East Anglian king of whom anything is known, but the discovery of the Sutton Hoo ship and all its treasures in 1939 suggest that he and his ilk knew something of the good life.

From the early Middle Ages, East Anglia became a major centre for wool and the manufacture of woollen products. Then, in the 14th century, Edward III invited Flemish weavers to settle in the area, and for the next four centuries Norwich was England's most important weaving town. Evidence of the region's links with the Low Countries is visible throughout eastern England; long

drainage canals, windmills and the architecture (particularly in King's Lynn) have more than a hint of Dutch influence about them. The wealth this connection brought built scores of churches and helped subsidise the development of Cambridge.

By the 17th century the emergence of a work-happy urban bourgeoisie growing ever-richer on successful trade with continental Europe, coupled with a fairly strong sense of religious duty, resulted in the twin principles of parliamentarianism and Puritanism that would climax in the Civil War. Oliver Cromwell, the uncrowned king of the parliamentarians, was a small-time merchant residing in Ely when he answered God's call to become his very own Englishman and take up arms against the fattened and corrupt monarchy of Charles I.

EASTERN ENGLAND

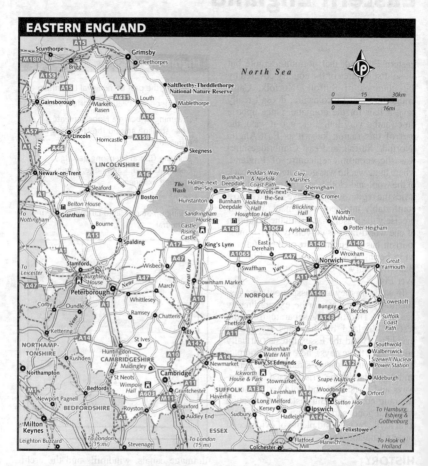

EASTERN ENGLAND

By the middle of the 18th century, however, eastern England's fortunes were on the wane. The Industrial Revolution had begun in earnest, but it was all happening to the northwest.

While Manchester was building enormous mills to process Indian calico for sale in Europe and the American colonies, the cottage industries of East Anglia slowly began to go out of business. By the end of the 19th century, the only weaving done in the region was on a tiny, specialist scale.

Today the region's economy is predominantly rural, though crops – especially barley – have replaced sheep as the mainstay. Market gardening is also a major earner, while most of the towns have developed some form of light industry.

ORIENTATION & INFORMATION

Norwich, King's Lynn, Cambridge and Lincoln are all easily accessible from London by train and bus. Ely, Peterborough and King's Lynn are on a direct train line from Cambridge. The **East of England Tourist Board** (☎ *01473-822922*; **w** *www.eastofenglandtouristboard.com*) can provide further information.

ACTIVITIES

It has to be said, eastern England is not renowned as an outdoor activities destination, but dig beneath the surface and there are some good options here, and this section provides a few ideas. More information is given in the Activities chapter, and suggestions for shorter walks and rides are given throughout this chapter. Regional tourism websites all contain walking, cycling and sailing information, and TICs all stock leaflets (free) plus maps and guides (usually £1 to £5) covering walking, cycling and other activities.

Walking

Eastern England is not classic walking country. To put it bluntly, there aren't enough hills. But if that's not a worry, then the area is perfect for easy rambles through gentle farmland, or alongside rivers and small lakes in the Norfolk Broads. For more salt-watery flavours, the coasts of Norfolk and Suffolk are both followed by footpaths.

The region's best-known long-distance walk is the **Peddars Way and Norfolk Coast Path** a six-day, 88-mile (142km) national trail. It follows an ancient Roman road for its first half, then meanders along the beaches, sea walls, salt marshes and fishing villages of the coast for the second half. Any part of the route can be done just as a day or weekend option; this is much easier on the coast section, and especially rewarding if you're into bird-watching as there are some top-quality nature reserves along this stretch.

Farther south, the 50-mile **Suffolk Coast and Heaths Path** runs between Felixstowe and Lowestoft, via Snape Maltings, Aldeburgh, Dunwich and Southwold. As with all long routes, even if you don't want to go the whole way, it makes the perfect focus for shorter walks and rambles.

Cycling

With a long history of human settlement, but little in the way of urbanisation, Norfolk, Suffolk, Lincolnshire and Cambridgeshire all have networks of quiet country lanes. Eastern England is also famous for being flat, and thus makes perfect country for gentle cycle-touring – as long as the wind is minimal or behind you. If you're heading east into cold winds you'll realise there are no hills to deflect it between here and the Urals. But with an eye on the weather, and judicious use of the cycle-friendly local train service, you can have a great time on two wheels.

There's gorgeous riding along the Suffolk and Norfolk coastlines, and in the Fens. In the northern part of the region, King's Lynn and Hunstanton make good bases, and bike hire is available. In the south of the region,

Cambridge is an excellent base for cycle tours, and bikes can be hired here too.

For mountain bikers, Thetford Forest, near Thetford, is an ideal place to start, and much of the **Peddars Way** mentioned in the Walking section consists of lanes and bridleways, which are also open to cyclists, and makes a mixed on- and off-road route. (The contiguous Norfolk Coast Path is strictly for walkers only.)

Other Activities

On the coast and Norfolk Broads **sailing** is popular; there are several sailing centres where you can hire boats or arrange lessons. Alternatively, many people tour the Broads in **motorboats** these days. At towns like Wroxham you can hire boats – anything from large cabin cruisers for a week, to little craft with phut-phut outboards for a couple of hours gentle messing about on the river. More watery fun is available in Cambridge, where a visit is incomplete without a spot of **punting**. If you want to keep your feet dry, **land-yachting** takes place on some of the long, wide, and frequently empty, beaches of the Norfolk Coast.

GETTING AROUND
Bus

Bus transport around the region is slow and disorganised but there are many local companies linking all but the smallest hamlets.

For national and local timetable information, phone ☎ 0870 608 2608. Specify which county you want transport information for and you'll be transferred to the appropriate operator. There are also direct regional transport information lines in operation for Norfolk and Suffolk (see the following section).

Train

From Norwich you can catch trains to the Norfolk coast and Sheringham but there's an unfortunate gap between Sheringham and King's Lynn (you could take the bus) that prevents a rail loop back to Cambridge. The Anglia Plus pass offers travel for three days out of seven for £20, one day for £9. These are valid from 8.45am Monday to Friday and all day on weekends. For all train information phone ☎ 08457 484950 or check the website at **w** www.angliarail ways.co.uk.

Suffolk

Like so much of East Anglia, the great trading boom that made Suffolk an economic powerhouse during the Middle Ages has been confined to history, leaving the county bereft of industry and big cities. Today Suffolk is something of a rural backwater, and is all the better for it as far as visitors are concerned. The county is a good example of that kind of England described by George Orwell as a place where you'd find 'cycling spinsters, cricket and warm beer'. In keeping with the general topography of East Anglia, the county is pretty flat but the landscape has a serene beauty in parts.

The painter Constable enthused about the county's 'gentle declivities, its woods and rivers, its luxuriant meadow flats sprinkled with flocks and herds, and its well-cultivated uplands, with numerous scattered villages and churches, farms and picturesque cottages'. The description still holds true for much of the county today.

The region's economic boom as a wool trading centre lasted until the 16th century and has left the county with its magnificently endowed 'wool' churches, many built to support much larger populations than live here now. Some of the villages have changed little since then and Suffolk buildings are famous for their *pargeting* – decorative stucco plasterwork.

Getting Around

Suffolk has a great network of local bus companies, which should allow you to travel between towns without too many hassles. There's a regular train service linking Ipswich, Sudbury and Bury St Edmunds. For travel information within the county, call Suffolk County Tourism on ☎ 0845 958 3358.

IPSWICH

☎ 01473 • pop 129,600

Once a principal player in the Saxon world and a major trading centre during the Middle Ages, modern Ipswich barely registers on the list of England's most important towns. Yet the county capital is still an important commercial and shopping centre, as well as the county's transport hub. The town centre is a compact and relatively pleasant warren of small streets where you'll find a couple of beautiful examples of the Tudor style (Ancient House and Christchurch Mansion). Also worth checking out is the Wet Dock quayside, which is a thoughtful modern development.

The **TIC** (☎ 258070, fax 432017; e tourist@ipswich.gov.uk; open 9am-5pm Mon-Sat) is in St Stephen's Church, off St Stephen's Lane, near the bus station and Ancient House. The TIC organises 90-minute guided tours (adult/child £2/1.50) of the town at 2.15pm every Tuesday and Thursday. There are also guided ghost tours at 8pm on the first Thursday of every month, leaving from the TIC; call ☎ 462721 for prices and availability.

The train station is a 15-minute walk southwest of the TIC along Princes St and across the roundabout.

Things to See & Do

The 17th-century **Ancient House** (☎ 214144; 40 Buttermarket; shop open 9am-5.30pm Mon-Sat) is now a branch of Lakelands kitchen outfitters, and you can wander in to take a look at the exquisite hammer-beam roof on the first floor. The external decor, completed around 1670, is an extravagant example of the Restoration style, with plenty of stucco and some of the finest examples of pargeting in the country. The house is about 50m north of the TIC, just off St Stephen's Lane.

The **Unitarian Meeting House** (☎ 218217; Friars St; admission free; open noon-4pm Tues-Thurs, 10am-4pm Sat, May-Sept) is a Grade I listed building built in 1699. It is one of the finest Dissenting Meeting Houses in the country.

The **Ipswich Museum** (☎ 433550; High St; admission free; open 10am-5pm Tues-Sat) has exhibits on natural history, geology and archaeology. There's a good collection of British birds.

Set in a 26-hectare park about 300m north of town, **Christchurch Mansion** (☎ 433554; Soane St; admission free; mansion & gallery open 10am-5pm Tues-Sat, 2.30pm-4.30pm Sun Mar-Sept; 10am-4pm Tues-Sat, 2.30pm-4.30pm Sun Oct-Feb) is a fine Tudor mansion built between 1548 and 1550. The exterior is awash with Dutch-style gables, while the enormous interior is decorated with period furniture and the walls are adorned with an extensive collection of works by Constable and Gainsborough. The Wolsey Art Gallery hosts contemporary art exhibitions at the mansion. To get there, walk north from the TIC along St Stephen's Lane, which becomes Tower St. Turn right onto St Margaret's St and then take a left at the fork onto Soane St.

Places to Stay & Eat

Cliffden Hotel (☎ 252689, fax 461077; e cliffden.hotel@virgin.net; 21 London Rd; singles/doubles from £21/36) is a comfortable, family-run hotel about a 10-minute walk west of the TIC along Tavern St.

Redholme Guest House (☎ 250018, fax 233174; 52 Ivry St; singles/doubles from £29/46) is an elegant Victorian house near Christchurch Mansion. The four en-suite rooms are huge and well appointed.

Pipps Ford (☎ 01449-760208, fax 01449-760561; e b&b@pippsford.co.uk; Needham Market; singles/doubles from £35/65) is an exquisite Tudor farmhouse beside the River Gipping. Patchwork quilts, antiques, inglenook fireplaces…it's just perfect for that cottagey stay. You'll need your own transport; it's 10 miles (16km) from Ipswich, just off the A14 to Bury St Edmunds.

Great White Horse Hotel (☎ 256558, fax 253396; e gwh@keme.co.uk; Tavern St; singles/doubles from £50/60) was used by Dickens in *Pickwick Papers*. The 'mouldy, ill-lighted rooms' have been replaced by comfortable, well-appointed ones that cater to the modern business traveller.

There are some good places to eat by the Wet Dock.

Il Punto (☎ 289748), aboard a pleasure boat docked along the quayside, is one of several good places to eat by the Wet Dock. The food is French and you can eat well for around £17.

Getting There & Away

National Express runs daily coaches to Ipswich from a number of destinations, including London (£8.90, 2¾ hours) and Cambridge (£7.25, 1½ hours). **Beestons** (☎ 823243) runs buses every half-hour to Sudbury (£2, one hour), Monday to Saturday. On Sunday **Chambers** (☎ 01787-227233) runs two services between the towns. First Eastern Counties runs buses every 30 minutes to Bury St Edmunds (£5.60, 1¼ hours).

There are half-hourly trains to London's Liverpool St station (£24.20, 1¼ hours) and Norwich (£14.90, 50 minutes); and 12 trains daily to Bury St Edmunds (£5, 30 minutes).

AROUND IPSWICH
Sutton Hoo

In 1939 archaeologists digging in and around a group of burial mounds close to the River Deben, 2 miles (3km) east of Woodbridge and 6 miles (9.5km) northeast of Ipswich, uncovered the hull of an Anglo-Saxon ship and a haul of other Saxon artefacts that rank as one of the most important discoveries in British history. In March 2002 a new **exhibition hall** (☎ 01394-389700; Woodbridge; adult/child £3.50/2; open 10am-5pm daily June-Sept, 10am-5pm Wed-Sun Easter-May & Oct, Sat only rest of year), administered by the National Trust (NT), opened to display these extraordinary finds, which include a full-scale reconstruction of King Raedwald's burial chamber and the Sutton Hoo ship. Other treasures recovered at the site, including a warrior's helmet and shield, gold ornaments and Byzantine silver, are on display in London's British Museum.

There's a video introduction and a guided tour of the burial site. First Eastern Counties runs 12 buses to Woodbridge, Monday to Saturday (10 minutes, 50p); ask the driver to stop at Sutton Hoo.

Located in Woodbridge itself is **Seckford Hall** (☎ 01394-385678, fax 01394-380610; e reception@seckford.co.uk; singles/doubles from £79/120), a lavish Tudor country house set in 14 hectares of woodland. The rooms are luxurious, there's an indoor pool and an adjacent 18-hole golf course.

STOUR VALLEY

Running along the border between Suffolk and Essex, the River Stour flows through a soft, pastoral landscape that has inspired numerous painters, the most famous being Constable and Gainsborough. The beautiful houses and elegant churches of some of the sedate villages along the Stour are a lasting legacy of a time when these were major operators in the medieval weaving trade. By the end of the 15th century the Stour Valley was producing more cloth than anywhere else in England. Within 100 years, production had shifted to the bigger towns like Colchester, Ipswich and Norwich and the villages receded into industrial obscurity. By the end of the 19th century the Stour Valley was a rural backwater, ignored by the Industrial Revolution and virtually everyone else – a curse for the locals but a godsend for visitors looking for a genuine experience of the gentle English countryside. While some of the more picturesque towns, such as Lavenham and Sudbury, are attracting visitors in greater numbers, the area is still quiet enough to ensure that you'll be able to explore it.

For Dedham Vale, the area known as Constable country, see the Essex section in the Southeast England chapter.

Long Melford
☎ 01787 • pop 2800
Known for its 2-mile (3km) long High St (the longest in England, the locals like to claim) and the lovely timber-framed buildings that line it, Long Melford has a magnificent church with some fine stained-glass windows, two stately homes and the obligatory antique shops.

Built in 1578, **Melford Hall** (NT; ☎ 880 286; adult £4.40; open 2pm-5.30pm Wed-Sun May-Sept, 2pm-5.30pm Sat & Sun Apr & Oct, phone for other times) is a turreted Tudor mansion in the centre of the village. There's an 18th-century drawing room, a Regency library, a Victorian bedroom and a display of paintings by Beatrix Potter, who was a relative of the Parker family, owners of the house from 1786 to 1960, when it passed into the hands of the Treasury.

On the edge of the village, at the end of a tree-lined avenue, lies **Kentwell Hall** (☎ 310207; w www.kentwell.co.uk; adult/child £6.50/3.50; open noon-5pm daily Apr-Oct), another redbrick Tudor mansion but one that's privately owned and makes much more of its origins. Once described in Country Life magazine as 'the epitome of many people's image of an Elizabethan house', this is not a museum but a house where the furnishings and decor have been meticulously restored over the past 30 years. In 2001 it won the Heritage Building of the Year award, given by the Good Britain Guide. The house is surrounded by a moat, and there's a brick-paved Tudor rose maze and a rare-breeds farm.

Although the house is a delight to visit at any time of year, the real treat occurs between mid-June and mid-July, when over 200 Tudor enthusiasts abandon their contemporary cynicism and don their traditional hose and velvet jackets to recreate and live out a certain year in the Tudor calendar. Admission is more expensive during the historical re-enactment period.

The **Great Church of the Holy Trinity** has lunch-time recitals at 1.10pm every Wednesday from mid-May to mid-September. For details of what's on, contact **Mrs Jilly Cooper** (☎ 281836).

Places to Stay & Eat Large and salmon-coloured, **High Street Farm House** (☎/fax 375765; e anroy@lineone.net; singles/doubles £36/56) is a 16th-century building at the northern end of town. The rooms are large and comfortable, and an excellent breakfast is served in the oak-beamed dining room.

The Crown Hotel (☎ 377666, fax 379005; Hall St; singles/doubles from £35/60) is a good choice; the rooms are all well appointed and the atmospheric bar serves excellent ales.

The Black Lion Hotel & Restaurant (☎ 312356, fax 374557; The Green; singles/doubles £71/93) has simply gorgeous rooms and an excellent restaurant (mains around £8). It's right on the village green.

Melford Valley Indian Cuisine (☎ 310079; Hall St; mains around £8) is a great choice for quality sub-continental food.

The Bull (☎ 378494; Hall St; mains around £8) is a half-timbered Elizabethan joint that specialises in traditional roasts and grills.

Scutcher's Bistro (☎ 310200; Westgate St; mains £12.90-15) is not just the top spot in town, but one of the most renowned restaurants in the Stour Valley. The exquisite menu features classic British cuisine with continental touches. It's just west of the Green, near the Black Lion.

Shopping Long Melford is littered with antique shops.

Country Antiques (☎ 310617; Westgate St) has plenty of 18th- and 19th-century bric-a-brac.

Patrick Marney (☎ 880533; Gate House, Melford Hall) is an exclusive shop that specialises in barometers. Viewing appointments are required.

Getting There & Away Chambers Buses runs 12 buses from Monday to Saturday between Long Melford and Bury St Edmunds (£2.20, one hour) calling at Sudbury (£1, five minutes). It also runs a circular bus route between Long Melford and Sudbury (£1.10, 10 minutes) at 10 and 40 minutes past the hour from Monday to Saturday.

Sudbury
☎ 01787 • pop 17,800

Recreated by Charles Dickens as Eatanswill in *The Pickwick Papers* (1836–7), Sudbury is the largest town in the western half of the Stour Valley. The groundwork for its success was laid back in the Middle Ages, when the town grew from strength to strength on the back of a roaring trade in wool.

Like the rest of East Anglia, sheep have given way to crops, but Sudbury continues to maintain a key link with the manufacture of cloth, especially silk weaving.

It isn't a bad place to while away an afternoon, but most visitors drop in to visit the birthplace of the town's most famous son, portrait and landscape painter Thomas Gainsborough (1727–88).

The **TIC** (☎ 881320, fax 374314; **e** sud burytic@babergh.gov.uk; open 9am-5pm Mon-Fri year round, 10am-4.45pm Sat Apr-Sept, to 2.45pm Oct-Mar) is in the town hall.

Gainsborough's House The birthplace of one of England's most celebrated artists has been preserved as a shrine and is now a museum (☎ 372958; 46 Gainsborough St; **w** www.gainsborough.org; adult/child £3/ 1.50, admission free in Dec; open 10am-5pm Tues-Sat, 2pm-5pm Sun) with the largest collection of his work in the country. The house features a Georgian facade built by Gainsborough's father, while the mulberry tree in the garden features in some of the son's paintings. Inside, the extensive collection features his earliest known work, *A Boy and a Girl in a Landscape*, now in two separate parts (the author of the separation is unknown), a portrait of *Reverend Tobias Rustat* and the exquisite *Lady Tracy*. This last work is particularly beautiful for its delicate portrayal of drapery and its folds. Gainsborough's studio features original furniture as well as his walking stick and pocket watch. In the parlour is a statue of a horse, the only known sculpture the artist ever produced.

Celebrity Duel: Thomas Gainsborough vs Sir Joshua Reynolds

Although Thomas Gainsborough (1727–88) was undoubtedly one of the major English painters, his professional life was marked by a fairly intense but mutually respectful rivalry with the pre-eminent portrait artist of the 18th century, Sir Joshua Reynolds (1723–92).

For starters, while they may have both been accomplished painters, Gainsborough was in most ways the antithesis of Reynolds. Whereas Reynolds was sober-minded and the complete professional, Gainsborough (even though his output was prodigious) was much more easy-going and often overdue with his commissions, writing that 'painting and punctuality mix like oil and vinegar'. Although eager to advance his career, Gainsborough was lazier than Reynolds, who was an expert at currying favour with the rich and powerful. He always ensured that the dignity (and looks) of his sitters were enhanced by basing their poses along classical lines, whereas Gainsborough preferred looser poses, often setting his subjects against a rich landscape, which sometimes took the focus away from the subject. Furthermore, Gainsborough was never exclusively a portraitist (the best path towards advancement in the vainglorious 18th century), stating that while he painted portraits by profession he painted landscapes by choice.

Ever mindful of the successes of the other, the two painters' careers took similar strides. In 1768 both were founding members of the Royal Academy, and while Reynolds went on to be its president and George III's Principal Painter, Gainsborough's skill with the brush ensured that he soon became a favourite at the Royal Court. One story has it that at a Royal Academy dinner, Reynolds proposed a toast to 'Gainsborough, the best landscape painter in Britain' to which a fellow academician replied, 'and the best portrait artist too!'. Reynolds, whose speciality was portraiture, was suitably incensed.

The two rivals were united, however, at Gainsborough's deathbed. The dying man asked specifically for Reynolds to come and see him, and after his death Reynolds paid tribute to his rival in his 14th *Discourse*. Recognising the fluid brilliance of his brushwork, Reynolds praised 'his manner of forming all the parts of a picture together' and wrote of 'all those odd scratches and marks' that 'by a kind of magic, at a certain distance…seem to drop into their proper places'. Gainsborough, who disdained literature and preferred music, would have been grudgingly impressed.

The Gallery and Weaving Room are home to constantly changing exhibits of modern art, while in summer the garden hosts sculpture exhibitions. See the boxed text 'Celebrity Duel: Thomas Gainsborough vs Sir Joshua Reynolds'.

Places to Stay The **Old Bull Hotel** (☎ 374120, fax 379044; Church St; singles/doubles from £42/52) is a family-run hotel in a 16th-century building with nine rooms, all decorated differently.

Boathouse Hotel (☎/fax 379090; Ballingdon Bridge; singles/doubles from £36/50) is on the water and the hotel rents out rowing boats. Rooms are clean and well appointed.

Getting There & Away Bus travel in and out of Sudbury is quite tricky. See Getting There & Away in the Long Melford section for details of Chambers Bus services. Beestons runs eight buses daily, Monday to Friday (seven on Saturday), to Ipswich (£2.90, one hour). To get most anywhere else involves a few changes. For Cambridge, you first have to get to Haverhill; Beestons has nine buses per day Monday to Friday (£1.80, 45 minutes), seven on Saturday and five on Sunday. From Haverhill, **Stagecoach Cambus** (☎ 01233-423554) runs buses roughly every 30 minutes to Cambridge (£2.50, one hour) from Monday to Saturday and every two hours on Sunday.

Sudbury also has a train station with an hourly service to London (£24.80, 1¼ hours).

LAVENHAM
☎ 01787 • pop 1700

Best – and rarely – enjoyed without the caravans of tour buses obscuring the view, Lavenham is the prettiest village in Suffolk, hence the buses. It's a beautifully preserved example of a medieval wool town, with over 300 listed buildings. Some are timber-framed, others decorated with pargeting. There are cosy, pink, thatched cottages, crooked houses, antique shops and art galleries, quaint tearooms and ancient inns. When the wool industry moved to the west and north of England in the late 17th century, none of Lavenham's inhabitants could afford to build anything more modern.

The **TIC** (☎ 248207; e lavenham@ babergh .gov.uk; Lady St; open 10am-4.45pm daily Apr-Oct, 11am-3pm Sat-Sun Mar & Nov) has re-cently introduced guided walks (adult/child £3/free) around the village departing from the TIC at 2.30pm on Saturday and 11am and 2.30pm on Sunday. It also has a list of places to stay.

Market Place, off High St, is dominated by the handsome **guildhall** (NT; ☎ 247646; admission £3; open 11am-5pm daily Apr-Oct, 11am-4pm Sat & Sun Mar & Nov), a superb example of a close-studded, timber-framed building, dating back to the early 16th century. It's now a local history museum with displays on the wool trade.

Little Hall (High St; adult/child £1.50/free; open 2pm-5.30pm Wed, Thur, Sat & Sun Apr-Oct), which has soft ochre plastering and grey timber, is a private house that is open to the public.

At the southern end of the village, opposite the car park, is the **Church of St Peter and St Paul**. Its soaring steeple is visible for miles around. The church bears witness to Lavenham's past prosperity as a centre of the local wool trade.

Places to Stay & Eat With all the earmarks of an architect's own design, **The Island House** (☎ 248181; e islandhouse@dial.pipex. com; Lower Rd; room £55) is simply gorgeous. The one guest room has its own private sitting room and a terrace with great views of the surrounding countryside. It's near the Market Place.

Lavenham Priory (☎ 247404, fax 248472; w www.lavenhampriory.co.uk; Water St; singles/doubles from £59/79) is easily the most attractive option in town. Once the home of Benedictine monks, then medieval cloth merchants, it's now an upmarket B&B.

Swan Hotel (☎ 247477, fax 248286; High St; singles/doubles from £79/158) is one of the county's best-known hotels, a late medieval building that has been exquisitely restored and updated with modern amenities.

There are numerous **teashops** offering light lunches.

The Angel (☎ 247388, Market Place; mains around £14) serves excellent modern British cuisine, with smoked fish the speciality of the house.

Getting There & Away Chambers Buses connect Lavenham with Bury St Edmunds (£1.70, 30 minutes) and Sudbury (£1.50, 20 minutes) with an hourly bus (until 6pm Monday to Saturday, no service on Sunday) from Bury St Edmunds to Colchester via Sudbury and Lavenham. There are no direct buses from Cambridge; you must go via Sudbury, also the location of the nearest train station (see that section earlier in the chapter).

KERSEY
☎ 01473 • pop 240

If Lavenham has a rival for the title of most photogenic village in Suffolk, then Kersey is it, although 'village' is a slight exaggeration; it's little more than a one-street hamlet. Many of the handsome Tudor-style, timber-framed houses have been bought up by city folk looking for a weekend getaway in Merry Olde Englande, who have paid handsomely for the privilege. Kersey is genuinely charming, but there is little to do here save admire the architecture and marvel at the fact that the village's only street (appositely named 'The Street') dips and disappears into a shallow ford (known as the Water Splash) before reappearing on the other side!

Kersey Pottery (☎ 822092; The Street; open 10am-5.30pm Tues-Sat & 11am-5pm Sun year round) is a well-respected potter's studio and shop where you can browse and buy handmade stoneware.

The 14th-century, oak-timbered **Bell Inn** (☎ 823229) and the **White Horse** (☎ 824418) are good spots for a pint or a bit of pub grub.

Kersey is 8 miles (13km) southeast of Lavenham off the A1141. There are three buses daily between Kersey and Ipswich (£2.10, one hour) from Monday to Saturday. The twice daily Sunday service also serves Sudbury (£1.50, 20 minutes). From Lavenham, the only way to get here is by taxi; **Granger's Cars** (☎ 01787-247456, 0589-409 237) charges between £7 and £8. The trip takes about 20 minutes.

HADLEIGH
☎ 01473 • pop 6595

During the Middle Ages, Hadleigh was one of the largest wool and market towns in eastern England, outranked only by Ipswich and Bury St Edmunds. Today, the town remains relatively prosperous, but its heyday is long gone and it has to content itself with being an attractive, largish town with a rich architectural heritage.

At the centre of it all is the wonderful, 15th-century **guildhall** (☎ 827752; adult/child

£1.50/1; open 2pm-5pm Thur & Sun June-Sept), topped by a splendid crown post roof. The building has been managed by the Hadleigh Market Feoffment (elected management committee) continuously since 1432. Admission includes a guided tour. In good weather, tea and scones (£2) are served in the guildhall garden.

Next door, the soaring **St Mary's Church** (Church St) is one of the largest parish churches in East Anglia, and its features date from the late 12th-century tower to the nave altar, which was completed in 1971.

To the west of the church is the **Deanery Tower** (not open to public), built in 1495 by Archdeacon William Pykenham as a gatehouse for a projected mansion nearer the river (he died before it could be built). The battlements and machicolation over the oriel window are purely ornamental, but they appear a little odd considering this was basically a clergyman's house. The building is also where the Oxford Movement was launched in 1833, which sought to reassert Catholic teaching within the Church of England.

Hadleigh is also the headquarters of the **East of England Tourist Board** (☎ 822922, fax 823063; e eastofenglandtouristboard@ compuserve.com; Toppesfield Hall), just off the High St. It is not a walk-in office, so all inquiries should be by telephone. It can, however, provide comprehensive lists of what to see and do in the region, as well as where to stay and eat.

There are a couple of decent pubs in town. The **Cock Inn** (☎ 822879; 89 George St; mains around £5) is a typical country pub that serves a limited menu of bar food.

Hadleigh is 2 miles (3km) southeast of Kersey. There are hourly buses from Ipswich (£1.80, 30 minutes) and Sudbury (£1.50, 35 minutes).

BURY ST EDMUNDS
☎ 01284 • pop 30,500

Suffolk's most attractive large town straddles the Lark and Linnet Rivers amid gently rolling farmland. It has a distinct Georgian flavour, with street upon street of handsome, 18th-century facades that hark back to a period of great prosperity. It's now a busy agricultural centre and cattle, vegetable and fruit markets are held at Angel Hill every Wednesday and Saturday. Greene King, the famous Suffolk brewer, is based here.

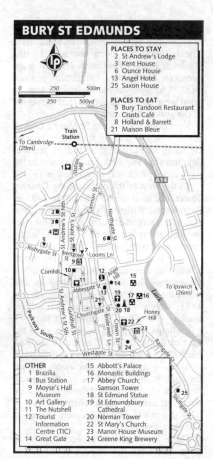

BURY ST EDMUNDS

PLACES TO STAY
2 St Andrew's Lodge
3 Kent House
6 Ounce House
13 Angel Hotel
25 Saxon House

PLACES TO EAT
5 Bury Tandoori Restaurant
7 Crusts Café
8 Holland & Barrett
21 Maison Bleue

OTHER
1 Brazilia
4 Bus Station
9 Moyse's Hall Museum
10 Art Gallery
11 The Nutshell
12 Tourist Information Centre (TIC)
14 Great Gate
15 Abbott's Palace
16 Monastic Buildings
17 Abbey Church; Samson Tower
18 St Edmund Statue
19 St Edmundsbury Cathedral
20 Norman Tower
22 St Mary's Church
23 Manor House Museum
24 Greene King Brewery

Centrally placed, Bury is a convenient point from which to explore western Suffolk. Worth seeing is the ruined abbey, set in a beautiful garden. There's also a fascinating clock museum, and recommended guided tours of the brewery.

History

Bury's motto 'Shrine of a King, Cradle of the Law' recalls the two most memorable events in its history. The Danes decapitated Edmund, a Christian prince from Saxony who was destined to be the last king of East Anglia, in 855 and his body was brought here for reburial in 903. The shrine to this king (who later became a saint) was to be the focal point of a new Benedictine monastery called St Edmundsbury, around which the town grew.

The abbey, now ruined, became one of the most famous pilgrimage centres in the country and, until the dissolution of the monasteries in 1536, was the wealthiest in the country.

The second memorable episode in Bury's early history took place at the abbey. In 1214 at St Edmund's Altar, the English barons drew up the petition that formed the basis of the Magna Carta.

Orientation & Information

Bury is an easy place to find your way around because it has preserved Abbot Baldwin's 11th-century grid layout.

The train station is a quarter of a mile north of the town centre; there are regular bus connections to the centre (50p). The bus station is in the heart of town in St Andrew's St North. The TIC (☎ 764667, fax 757084; e tic@stedsbc.gov.uk; 6 Angel Hill; open 9am-5.30pm daily Easter-Oct, 9am-5.30pm Mon-Sat Nov-Easter) has plenty of information on the town and is also the starting point for guided walking tours (adult/child £3/free) that depart at 2.30pm daily except Sunday, Easter to September.

There are tours of the **Greene King Brewery** (☎ 763222; Crown St) at 2.30pm Monday to Thursday. Tickets cost £7; tours are popular, so you'll need to book ahead.

The Abbey & Park

Although the abbey (admission free; open daily to sunset) is very much a ruin, it's a spectacular one set in a beautiful garden. After the dissolution of the monasteries, the townspeople made off with much of the stone – even St Edmund's grave and bones have disappeared.

You can enter the abbey grounds through the main **Great Gate**, built sometime between 1327 and 1346, or farther up along Angel Hill via the older **Norman Tower**, built between 1120 and 1148 and designed to serve as the belfry for the adjacent church of St James (now St Edmundsbury Cathedral). These are the best-preserved buildings of the whole complex and give an impression of how imposing the whole pile must have been.

Just inside the Great Gate is the **Great Court**, which was once completely surrounded by buildings where the practical affairs of the abbey were conducted. Today it is an elegant formal garden. Just beyond the court is a dovecote that marks the only remains of the **Abbot's Palace**; his gardens have been transformed into a bowling green.

The most solid remains of the once powerful and mighty abbey church are part of the western front and **Samson Tower**, which since the dissolution have had houses built into them. In the small garden in front of Samson Tower is a beautiful statue of St Edmund by Elizabeth Frink (1976). The rest of the abbey church spreads eastward like a fallen skeleton, with bits of stonework and the odd pillar giving a clue of its immense size. You can guide yourself around the ruins using the information boards, which help to show what a large community this must have been; just north of the church lie the ruined remains of a cluster of monastic buildings that at one time served as a dormitory, a monastic lavatory, the prior's house and an infirmary.

St Edmundsbury Cathedral

Also known as St James', the cathedral *(open 8.30am-8pm daily Apr-Oct, 8.30am-7pm Nov-Mar)* dates from the 16th century but the eastern end was added between 1945 and 1960 and the northern side was not completed until 1990. It was made a cathedral in 1914.

The architecture of the entrance porch has a strong Spanish influence, a latter-day tribute to the devotion of Abbot Anselm (1121–48), who instead of making a pilgrimage to Santiago de Compostela in Galicia chose to stay and build a church dedicated to St James (Santiago in Spanish) on the abbey grounds.

The interior is light and lofty with a gorgeous painted hammer-beam roof. The Spanish theme continues in the Lady Chapel in the south transept, while the north transept houses a particularly beautiful sculpture of *Christ Crucified* by Elizabeth Frink. The cathedral is currently undergoing a massive restoration thanks to an award of £8 million from the Millennium Commission; the work should be finished by 2004.

St Mary's Church

Built around 1430 St Mary's contains the tomb of Mary Tudor (Henry VIII's sister and one-time queen of France). A curfew bell is still rung, as it was in the Middle Ages.

Manor House Museum

Near St Mary's is Manor House *(☎ 757072; 5 Honey Hill; adult/child £3/2; open 10am-5pm*

Tues-Sun), a magnificent museum of horology, art and costume housed in a Georgian building. It is worth being here around noon, when all the clocks strike.

Art Gallery & Moyse's Hall Museum

Bury's only **art gallery** *(☎ 762081; Cornhill; adult/child £1/free; open 10.30am-5pm Tues-Sat)* is in a Grade I listed building designed in 1774 by Robert Adam, originally as a theatre. Inside there are eight annual exhibitions of contemporary art.

Nearby is the newly refurbished **Moyse's Hall Museum** *(☎ 706183; Cornhill; admission free; open 9am-5.30pm Mon-Sat)* with a new wing housing an exhibit dedicated to the Suffolk Regiment – its history, feats of bravery and uniforms.

The rest of the museum is devoted to local archaeology, complete with interactive displays. Frankly, the building itself, which dates from the 12th century and is probably East Anglia's oldest domestic building, is more interesting.

Places to Stay

Kent House *(☎ 769661; e lizkent@supanet .com; 20 St Andrew's St North; singles/doubles from £25/42)* is a small town house with even smaller rooms. Nevertheless, they are clean and relatively comfortable.

St Andrew's Lodge *(☎ 756733; 30 St Andrew's St North; singles/doubles £35/50)* is a larger place than Kent House, with motel-style rooms that are comfortable but characterless. There is, however, in-house parking.

Saxon House *(☎ 755547; 37 Southgate St; singles/doubles £55/60)* opened in 2002 with two gorgeously appointed rooms in a fully restored, 15th-century timber-frame building that was once an almshouse.

Ounce House *(☎ 761779, fax 768315; e pott@globalnet.co.uk; Northgate St; singles/ doubles with bath from £60/85)* is an elegant guesthouse with large, tastefully appointed rooms. Ask for a room with a garden view.

Angel Hotel *(☎ 753926, fax 750092; e sales@theangel.co.uk; 3 Angel Hill; singles/ doubles from £69/89, weekends per person from £53, with dinner £60)*, in the centre of Bury, once lodged Charles Dickens and is where Mr Pickwick enjoyed an 'excellent roast dinner'. It's the best hotel in town.

EASTERN ENGLAND

Places to Eat

Maison Bleue *(☎ 760623; 31 Churchgate St; mains £9-17.50, set menu £19.95; open Mon-Sat)* is a highly recommended seafood restaurant. Mains include such dishes as brill, sea bass, monkfish and so on.

Holland & Barrett *(☎ 706677; 6 Brentgovel St; most dishes around £3; open to 5.30pm Mon-Sat)* is a vegetarian restaurant and café.

Crusts Café *(☎ 763293; 13 Brentgovel St; mains around £4)* is a lovely café serving a wide range of dishes, from lasagne to steak and kidney pie.

Bury Tandoori Restaurant *(☎ 724222; 108 Risbygate St; mains around £8.50)* is the best Indian in town, with the usual menu of sub-continental dishes.

Entertainment

In a word, there isn't much of it. The pubs are pretty bland, and the only one we can recommend is the **Nutshell** *(The Traverse)*, the best-known pub in Bury – because it claims to be Britain's smallest. It is tiny.

At weekends the kids flock to **Brazilia** *(☎ 769655; Station Hill)*, which is open Thursday to Saturday only, and features a popular mix of '70s disco (Thursday) and commercial house and trance (the other two nights). Dress up as jeans and trainers (sneakers) will leave you in the cold. Admission costs between £4 and £7, depending on the night.

Getting There & Away

Bury is 75 miles (120km) from London, 35 miles (56km) from Norwich and 29 miles (46km) from Cambridge.

There's a daily National Express bus to London (£11.25 day return, two hours and 20 minutes). From Cambridge, Stagecoach Cambus runs buses to Bury (£4.50, 35 minutes) hourly from Monday to Saturday; the last bus back to Cambridge leaves at 5.05pm. First Eastern Counties runs buses every 30 minutes to Ipswich (£5.60, 1¼ hours).

Bury is on the Ipswich (£7.10, 20 minutes) to Ely (£9.90, 30 minutes) railway line so trains to London (£27.10, 1¾ hours) go via these towns virtually every hour. From Cambridge, there are trains every two hours to Bury (£9.90, 45 minutes).

AROUND BURY ST EDMUNDS
Ickworth House & Park

Three miles (5km) southwest of Bury on the A143, Ickworth House *(NT; ☎ 01284-735270; house & park adult/child £5.95/2.60, park only £2.70/80p; house open 1pm-5pm daily mid-Mar–Oct, park open 7am-7pm daily year round)* is the eccentric creation of the 4th Earl of Bristol and Bishop of Derry Frederick Hervey (1730–1803; see the boxed text 'The Eccentric Earl'). It's an amazing structure, with an immense oval rotunda dating back to 1795. It contains a fine collection of furniture, silver and paintings (by Titian, Gainsborough

---

The Eccentric Earl

The Hervey family had such a reputation for eccentricity that it was said of them that when 'God created the human race he made men, women and Herveys'. Perhaps the biggest weirdo of them all was the creator of Ickworth House, Frederick, the third son of the 3rd earl. As Bishop of Derry, he was renowned not for his piety but for his agnosticism, vanity and oddity: he would force his clergymen to race each other through peat bogs in the middle of the night, sprinkle flour on the floor of his house to catch night-time adulterers, champion the cause of Catholic emancipation (he was, after all, a Protestant bishop) and earn himself the sobriquet of 'wicked prelate' from George III.

Not content with his life in Ireland, in later years Frederick took to travelling around Europe, where he indulged each and every one of his passions: women, wine, art and intrigue. He tried to pass himself off as a spy in France, and for his trouble he was rewarded with a nine-month prison sentence in a Napoleonic jail. While in Italy, he horrified visiting English aristocrats with his dress sense and manners; he often dressed in military garb and once chucked a bowl of pasta onto a religious procession because he hated the sound of tinkling bells.

For many years, it was believed that the highly prestigious Bristol hotels, present in virtually every major European city, were named after him. Unfortunately, it is not the case, but it would have been a most satisfactory (though ill-fitting) tribute to one of the oddest aristocrats in English history.

and Velasquez). Outside, there's an unusual Italian garden and a park designed by Lancelot 'Capability' Brown, with way-marked trails, a deer enclosure and a hide.

First Eastern Counties runs a bus service (£1.35) at 12.35pm and 4.10pm daily bound for Garboldisham (No 304), leaving from outside Bury train station.

Pakenham Water Mill

England's only remaining parish water mill and windmill (☎ 01359-230275; adult/child £2/1.75; open 2pm to 5.30pm Wed, Sat & Sun Good Friday-Sept) still in operation is in the small village of Pakenham, 6 miles (9.5km) northeast of Bury St Edmunds along the A143. Corn has been ground here for over 900 years, and the mill makes an appearance in the Domesday Book survey of 1086. The mill ceased production in 1974, but it was taken over four years later by the Suffolk Preservation Society, who sponsored a painstaking restoration. During the restoration a Tudor mill was uncovered on the site of the present building, which dates from the late 18th century. Visitors get a guided tour of the building and can observe the grinding process from start to finish; you can also buy ground corn produced on the premises.

There are four buses daily from 1.05pm (No 337 to Thetford), Monday to Friday and three on Saturday (£1.50, 20 minutes). The bus stops in front of the Fox pub; the mill is just up the street.

ALDEBURGH

☎ 01728 • pop 2800

The sea is closing in on Aldeburgh, where the beach is now only yards from the village. The place is best known for the Aldeburgh Festival which takes place in June (see 'The Aldeburgh Festival' boxed text).

The TIC (☎/fax 453637; e atic@suffolk coastal.gov.uk; High St; open 9am-5.15pm daily Easter-Oct, 10am-4pm Mon-Sat Nov-Easter) can help with information.

Walking

The Suffolk Coast and Heaths Path passes through Aldeburgh, and you can follow it northwards beside the sea for a few miles, and enjoy the salt air. Alternatively, from Aldeburgh follow the path inland for a lovely walk towards the village of Snape Street, 3 miles (5km) up the Alde River, past some

pleasant wooded areas and fields. Just south of Snape Street, where a road crosses the river, are the large buildings of the Maltings (see 'The Aldeburgh Festival' boxed text).

Places to Stay & Eat Blaxhall Youth Hostel (☎ 688206; beds per adult/under-18 £12/8.75) is 4½ miles (7km) from Aldeburgh, near Snape Maltings.

Ocean House (☎ 452094, fax 453909; 25 Crag Path; singles/doubles from £40/65, sea-facing room extra £5) is a delightful guest-house overlooking the sea in the middle of town. The rooms are all in period style.

White Lion Hotel (☎ 452720, fax 452986; Market Cross Place; singles/doubles from £73.50/114), overlooking the shingle beach, is Aldeburgh's oldest, but has recently received a 21st-century facelift. We recommend a sea-facing room; they cost £10 extra.

The Captain's Cabin (☎ 452520; 170-172 High St; mains around £7) is a cosy, waterfront restaurant that serves a mix of dishes from breaded plaice fillet to sausages and mash.

The Lighthouse (☎ 453377; 77 High St; mains around £9) is one of Aldeburgh's most celebrated eateries and a big favourite with visiting Londoners. The imaginative menu features a range of eclectic dishes, with a particular emphasis on fish.

Café 152 (☎ 454152; 152 High St; mains around £11; closed Mon-Tues Nov-Mar) is the best restaurant in town. Seafood is the order of the day, be it char-grilled squid on a bed of salad leaves or a less exotic (but equally delicious) grilled sole.

Getting There & Away First Eastern Counties runs hourly buses between Ipswich and Aldeburgh (£3.20/5.60 single/return, 80 minutes).

AROUND ALDEBURGH

The coast on either side of Aldeburgh is one of great contrasts with traditional seaside resorts such as Lowestoft in the north, the busy port of Felixstowe (now freight only – passenger ferries all go from Harwich) in the south, and some of the least-visited sections of coastline in England in-between, but it is certainly worth taking the time to explore. It's a heritage coastline that's being gradually whittled away by the sea – the old section of the village of Dunwich – including its 12 churches – now lies completely underwater.

The Aldeburgh Festival

The world-famous Aldeburgh Festival is a most serious affair. For three weeks in June, a variety of venues in Aldeburgh and nearby Snape Maltings, 3 miles (5km) upriver host a series of concerts, recitals, films and plays drawn from the uppermost end of the creative canon. The brainchild of Benjamin Britten, singer Peter Pears and writer/producer Eric Crozier, the first festival took place in 1948, and in 2002 it celebrated its 55th year with a truly outstanding programme of events, including the premiere of Gerard Barry's opera *The Triumph of Beauty and Deceit* and the screening of three of Samuel Beckett's plays on film: *Play, Catastrophe* and *Film*, all set to the author's favourite piece of music, Schubert's *Death and the Maiden*. All very highbrow indeed.

Tickets for the three-week festival range in price from £8 to £17, though several of the events are free. For information and bookings, phone the **box office** (☎ 453543) or check out the website at **W** www.aldeburgh.co.uk.

About 4 miles (6.5km) north of Aldeburgh is Sizewell, a nuclear power plant topped by what is most kindly described as a giant golf ball. Its anomalous presence along this stretch of coast has been a major cause of concern for environmentalists and a host of other nuclear nay-sayers, but the plant's two reactors won't be ceasing their atom-bashing activities any time soon.

With public transport virtually nonexistent in places it can be tough to get around if you don't have your own wheels, but an excellent country walk and the quiet serenity of some of the seaside villages make this a good spot to idle away a few lazy days.

Orford

Few visitors get to this little village, 6 miles (9.5km) south of Snape Maltings, but there are several worthwhile attractions. The ruins of **Orford Castle** (☎ 01394-450472; adult/child £2.70/1.50; open 10am-5pm daily Apr-Oct, shorter hrs Nov-Mar), run by English Heritage (EH), date from the 12th century; only the keep has survived.

The spit of land outside the village (and only accessible by ferry from Orford Quay) is **Orford Ness** (NT; ☎ 01394-450900; adult

£5.60 including ferry crossing; open 10am-5pm Tues-Sat July-Sept, Sat only Mar-June & Oct), a national nature reserve that, between 1913 and the mid-1980s, was a secret military testing ground.

It is the largest vegetated shingle spit in Europe, home to a variety of rare birds, animals and plants, including avocets, oyster-catchers and migratory waders. There's a 3-mile (5km) path lined with information boards, as well as abandoned military installations. The last ferry departs from Orford Quay at 2pm and from the reserve at 5pm.

Also from Orford Quay, **MV Lady Florence** (☎ 0831 698298) takes diners on all-inclusive, 2½-hour brunch cruises (9am to 11.30am) or four-hour lunch or dinner cruises, year round. The brunch cruise costs £19 all-inclusive (the menu is fixed), while the lunch and dinner cruises cost £11 per person for the boat plus whatever you choose from the menu: mains cost from £7.50 to £9.50.

SOUTHWOLD
☎ 01502 • pop 4070

As Dunwich began disappearing into the sea in the middle of the 16th century, so Southwold, perched safely atop a cliff about 4 miles (6.5km) to the north, began to prosper as a fishing town. Although it too has seen better days, at least as a trading centre, it remains one of the prettiest resort towns on this stretch of coastline, with a gorgeous, sandy beach that is a perennial Blue Flag (ie, clean beach) award winner.

The **TIC** (☎ 724729; 69 High St; open 10am-5.30pm Mon-Sat, 11am-4pm Sun Apr-Sept; 10.30am-5pm Mon-Fri, to 5.30pm Sat Oct-Mar) is in the heart of town.

The town's most interesting architectural landmark is the **Church of St Edmund** (Church St; admission free; open 9am-6pm daily June-Aug, to 4pm rest of year), a 15th-century building with a superbly proportioned nave.

The **Southwold Museum** (☎ 726817; Victoria St; admission free; open 10.30am-noon daily Aug & 2pm-4pm daily year round) has a good display on the town's history, with a particular emphasis on the Battle of Solebay (1672), fought between the English, French and Dutch fleets just off the coast. There were 132 ships and 50,000 troops involved, so it was one hell of a fight.

And of course there is the **pier**, originally built in 1899. It hasn't had the luckiest of histories: it was badly damaged by storms in 1934, 1955 and 1979 before eventually closing in 1998 for safety reasons. It recently reopened after a complete renovation and has the usual selection of bars, fast-food outlets and amusement arcades.

Places to Stay & Eat
Amber House (☎ 723303; North Parade; singles/doubles from £26/40) is a spacious, Victorian terraced house with cosy, comfortable rooms.

Victoria House (☎ 722317; 9 Dunwich Rd; singles/doubles £25/50) is equally good, and the rooms are just that little bit bigger.

Saxon House (☎ 723651; 86 Pier Ave; singles/doubles £45/60) is a mock-Tudor house with bright, airy rooms that are clean and comfortable. It is about 100m from the pier.

The Dutch House (☎ 723172; Ferry Rd; mains around £7; closed Mon) is a good spot for a bite of lunch or dinner.

Southwold is also home to the Adnams Brewery, and you should try some of its creamy ales in one of town's pubs. We recommend the **Red Lion** (South Green).

Getting There & Away
First Eastern Counties buses stop here on the Ipswich to Great Yarmouth run.

AROUND SOUTHWOLD
Walberswick
☎ 01502 • pop 1800
Hard to believe, but the pretty village of Walberswick was a busy port from the 13th century right up to WWI where cheese, bacon, corn, timber and fish were traded in abundance. You can still buy fresh fish, but that's about it: today the village is a sleepy little getaway where well-to-do holiday-makers come to chill out. The English Impressionist Philip Wilson Steer (1860–1942) set the trend in the late 19th century, moving here to paint some of the finest landscapes of the day.

The only excitement occurs in July, when the village hosts the **British Open Crabbing Championships**, where contestants have 90 minutes to land the heaviest crab with only a single line and bait. Anyone can enter, but the competition is pretty fierce, with baits being a closely guarded secret. For more information, call ☎ 722359.

The 600-year-old **Bell Inn** (☎ 723109, fax 722728; singles/doubles £50/80) is the best option if you're looking to stay over; rooms are large and comfortable. The inn also houses a pretty good seafood restaurant (mains around £8 to £9) with flagged floors, low beams and open fires.

Walberswick is less than a mile south of Southwold. From Southwold, there are two ways to get here. Pick up the path at the southern end of High St to eventually reach a bailey bridge (for pedestrians and cyclists only), which spans the Blythe River. Alternatively, a summer **ferry** (50p; 10am-12.30pm & 2pm-4.30pm daily, June-Aug, weekends only Easter-May) crosses the Blythe at half-hourly intervals.

Norfolk

Noel Coward once remarked that 'Norfolk is very flat'. It is, but Mr Coward was not referring to its geography, and the county has long endured a reputation for dullness, with no sign of abating: it is no accident that comedian Steve Coogan's chillingly boring creation, Alan Partridge, lives in the county. However, it is the lack of frenetic activity that makes Norfolk so worthwhile, a tranquil haven for those looking for a bit of relaxation. Bird-watchers and their binoculars are attracted by its several nature reserves, while its superb, unspoilt coastlines draw a limited number of tourists eager to escape the cheesy, 'holiday-by-the-sea' feel that has afflicted so many of England's beaches.

Norfolk's inhabitants have also got a reputation for bloody-mindedness; there's a story that tells of the appointment of a new bishop to the diocese, who was told by his predecessor that if he wanted to lead someone in this part of the world, he should first find out where they were going and then walk in front of them. It is this doggedness that undoubtedly helped make the region such a commercial success in the Middle Ages.

Today however, Norfolk is much quieter and less populated than it was 500 years ago. Norwich, the county town, is a very pleasant place with an interesting castle and cathedral, as well as the best nightlife in the whole region (bar Cambridge) – due for the most part to the presence of the university, which means that the town is overrun by students.

EASTERN ENGLAND

The Norfolk Broads is a network of inland waterways that have long been popular for boating holidays, and King's Lynn is a historic port on the River Ouse. The whole area is easily accessible from Cambridge.

For a truly comprehensive guide to what's on in Norfolk, check out w www.visitnorfolk.co.uk and w www.norfolkcoast.co.uk. A particularly useful leaflet called *Independent Traveller's Norfolk* and an associated website w www.itnorfolk.co.uk cover various activities in this county, as well as information on hostels, campsites and local transport.

Activities

Several waymarked walking trails cross the county, the best known being the Peddars Way and Norfolk Coast Path national trail, mentioned in the Activities section at the start of this chapter. Other long routes include the Weavers Way, a 57-mile (92km) walk from Cromer to Great Yarmouth via Blickling and Stalham, and the Angles Way, which follows the valleys of the Rivers Waveney and Little Ouse for 70 miles (113km).

The Around Norfolk Walk is a 220-mile (354km) circuit which combines the Peddars Way and Norfolk Coast Path, the Weavers Way and the Angles Way. Any of these routes can be followed for just an hour or two or a day or two, and TICs have leaflets, route maps and other inspirational literature for walkers – and even more material for cyclists.

Getting Around

The county public transport phone line (☎ 08453 006116) has information on bus routes and fares. In Norwich, the **Norfolk Bus Information Centre** (*NORBIC;* ☎ 01603-285007) has information and tickets for bus travel throughout the county.

Norwich, King's Lynn, Cromer and Great Yarmouth are easily accessible by rail.

NORWICH

☎ 0121 • pop 966,000

Norfolk's county town (pronounced nor-ritch) was a major player in the medieval world, when it was even larger than London. Historians and economists may ruefully study the town's golden epoch, when its prosperity was based on trade with the Low Countries, and wonder what exactly went wrong, but to our minds the town seems to have got much of it just right. Norwich's his-torical importance is evident throughout the town, while the in the last few years a major programme of urban rejuvenation – culminating in the opening of the impressive Forum in November 2001 – has made it one of the most attractive in eastern England.

History

The East Angles built the village of Northwic on a gravel terrace above the River Wensum, and by the time a bunch of marauding Danes sacked the new-and-improved town of Norwich in 1004, it was already an important market centre. Shortly after their invasion in 1066 the Normans built the splendid castle keep, now the best-preserved example in the country. In 1336 Edward III encouraged Flemish weavers to settle here; their arrival helped establish the wool industry that would ensure Norwich's provincial importance until the end of the 18th century, when it was overtaken by the growth of the industrial cities of the north.

Norwich's links with the Low Countries were further tightened in the 16th century, when a mass immigration flooded the town with more weavers and textile workers: in 1579 more than a third of the town's 16,000 citizens were foreigners. Of a staunch Protestant stock, which proved beneficial during the Civil War, as the town's close ties with the parliamentary cause ensured that Norwich saw virtually no strife.

Modern Norwich remains one of England's most important centres of footwear manufacturing, as well as one of the country's largest agricultural and livestock markets.

Orientation

The castle is in the centre of Norwich and the TIC is two blocks west. Below the castle lies what has been described as the most complete medieval English city. Clustered round the castle and Anglican cathedral, within the circle of river and city walls, are more than 30 parish churches. The other, Roman Catholic, cathedral lies to the west of the centre.

At the heart of the city is the **market** *(open roughly 8am-4.30pm daily)*, a patchwork of stall awnings known as tilts. This is one of the biggest and longest-running markets in the country. It was moved here 900 years ago from its original site in Tombland by the now Anglican cathedral.

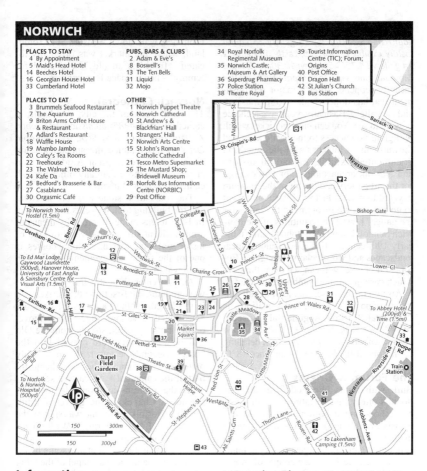

NORWICH

PLACES TO STAY
4 By Appointment
5 Maid's Head Hotel
14 Beeches Hotel
16 Georgian House Hotel
33 Cumberland Hotel

PLACES TO EAT
3 Brummels Seafood Restaurant
7 The Aquarium
9 Briton Arms Coffee House
   & Restaurant
17 Adlard's Restaurant
18 Waffle House
19 Mambo Jambo
20 Caley's Tea Rooms
22 Treehouse
23 The Walnut Tree Shades
24 Kafe Da
25 Bedford's Brasserie & Bar
27 Casablanca
30 Orgasmic Café

PUBS, BARS & CLUBS
2 Adam & Eve's
8 Boswell's
13 The Ten Bells
31 Liquid
32 Mojo

OTHER
1 Norwich Puppet Theatre
6 Norwich Cathedral
10 St Andrew's &
   Blackfriars' Hall
11 Strangers' Hall
12 Norwich Arts Centre
15 St John's Roman
   Catholic Cathedral
21 Tesco Metro Supermarket
26 The Mustard Shop;
   Bridewell Museum
28 Norfolk Bus Information
   Centre (NORBIC)
29 Post Office

34 Royal Norfolk
   Regimental Museum
35 Norwich Castle;
   Museum & Art Gallery
36 Superdrug Pharmacy
37 Police Station
38 Theatre Royal

39 Tourist Information
   Centre (TIC); Forum;
   Origins
40 Post Office
41 Dragon Hall
42 St Julian's Church
43 Bus Station

Information

The **TIC** (☎ 727927, fax 765389; ⓦ www.nor wich.gov.uk; open 10am-6pm Mon-Sat & 10.30am-4pm Sun Apr-Oct, 10am-5.30pm Mon-Sat Nov-Mar) is just inside the new Forum on Millennium Plain. A number of guided walking tours (adult/child £2.50/1, 1½ hours) take place at various times, including the evening – check with the TIC for details.

There are a couple of **post offices** (☎ 220228; 13-17 Bank Plain • ☎ 761635; 84-85 Castle Mall) in the city centre. If you need to check email, there is an **Internet point** (☎ 760808) in Row B of the market that charges £1 for 15 minutes.

Gaywood Launderette (☎ 624891, 24 Earlham Rd; open 7.30am-11pm daily) is just opposite EdMar Lodge.

Superdrug Pharmacy (☎ 619179; 25 Gentleman's Walk; open 8.30am-6pm Mon-Sat) should take care of all your needs. The **Norfolk & Norwich Hospital** (☎ 286286; Wessex St) is about 500m south of Unthank Rd.

The **police station** (☎ 768769; Bethel St) is southwest of the market.

Norwich Castle Museum & Art Gallery

The massive Norman castle keep was built in about 1160 and measures 28m square by 21m high – a solid sentinel on the hill overlooking the medieval and modern cities. It's the best surviving example of Norman military architecture after the Tower of London and has worn pretty well, although it was refaced in 1834.

The castle (☎ 493636; castle & museum adult/child £2.90/2.25, art gallery & natural history exhibit £2.90/2.25, art gallery & museum & art gallery £4.70/3.50; open 10.30am-6.30pm Mon-Sat June-Sept, to 4.30pm Oct-May) has recently reopened after a major refurbishment that has done wonders to its museum and art gallery. Basically, you have a choice of what to see. You can buy one ticket which will grant you access to the castle keep and the museum – which has well-presented and documented exhibits of natural history and Norfolk archaeology – or you can opt for the art gallery and the bit of the museum devoted to natural history. If you only want to go for one, we recommend the latter, for the gallery houses the paintings of the Norwich School. Founded by John Crome in the early 19th century, this group painted local landscapes and won acclaim throughout Europe. Of course, you can see everything, in which case go for the combination ticket.

Also on the premises, in the Shirehall (entrance opposite the Anglia TV station), is the **Royal Norfolk Regimental Museum** (☎ 493649; adult/child £1.80/90p; open 10am-5pm Mon-Sat, 2pm-5pm Sun), detailing the history of the local regiment since 1830.

The Forum & Origins
Built with funds obtained from the National Lottery, the extraordinary all-glass, horseshoe-shaped **Forum** is the most impressive building to hit Norwich's skyline in many decades. It is three storeys high and is home to Norfolk's largest library, a number of cafés, the TIC and a couple of shops.

It's also where you'll find **Origins** (☎ 727 920; adult/child £4.95/3.50; open 10am-6pm Mon-Sat, 10.30am-4.30pm Sun) an interactive museum devoted to 2000 years of Norfolk and Norwich history. A 40m-long, two-storey-high screen shows 180-degree images of the area's past, a particularly enthralling experience for kids. Other highlights include trying to speak the original Norfolk dialect and flooding the Norfolk Fens. It's not an in-depth look at the area's history, but it's a lot of fun and sure to impress.

Elm Hill
Thanks to imaginative restoration, this street has retained its medieval charm and atmosphere and is, appropriately enough, the centre of the local antique business. It's

one of the most attractive parts of the city. From here walk down Wensum St to Tombland, where the market was originally located. 'Tomb' is an old Norse word for 'empty' – hence space for a market.

Norwich Cathedral
The focal point of the city, the Anglican cathedral (☎ 764385; admission free; open 7.30am-7pm daily May-Sept, 7.30am-6pm Oct-Apr) has retained the appearance and characteristics of a great Anglo-Norman abbey church more than any other English cathedral except Durham.

The foundation stone was laid in 1096, and the building took 40 years to complete. In 1463 it was made fireproof by means of a magnificent stone lierne vault (a kind of inside roof) that, with its sculpted bosses, is one of the finest achievements of English medieval masonry.

As you enter the cathedral through the western door, the first thing that strikes you is the length of the nave. Its 14 bays are constructed in yellow-beige stone. Above, on the amazing vault, stories from the Old and New Testament are carved into the bosses. Beyond the tower, which is richly patterned, is probably the most beautiful part of the cathedral – the eastern section.

At the eastern end, outside the War Memorial Chapel, is the grave of Edith Cavell, a Norfolk nurse who was shot by the Germans in Belgium during WWI for helping POWs to escape.

The cathedral close contains some handsome houses and the old chapel of the King Edward VI School (where Nelson was educated). Its current students make up the choir, which usually performs in at least one of the three services held daily here.

St Julian's Church
Tucked away in a tiny alley is St Julian's Church (☎ 624738; St Julian's Alley; admission free; open 7.30am-5.30pm daily Apr-Sept, to 4pm Oct-Mar), where a shrine to Julian of Norwich is a centre for pilgrimage. Julian (also known as Juliana, 1342–c.1416) wrote down her religious visions in a collection called *The Revelations of Divine Love*, which is unparalleled in English literature for the clarity and depth of perception. Although she was never beatified, she is still considered a saint, due to an occasion when, questioning

her place in the world, God was reputed to appear to her and speak the words 'All shall be well'. Inspired by these words, pilgrims have been visiting her shrine for centuries, though the cell where she wrote the book was torn down during the Reformation, and they have had to content themselves with a small chapel that was built after WWII.

Other Museums
About 200m north of the castle are three museums in the same area. The Mustard Shop has a small **museum** (☎ 627889; 15 Royal Arcade; admission free; open 9.30am-5pm Mon-Sat, 11am-4pm bank holidays, closed Sun) that tells the story of Colman's Mustard, a famous local product. Nearby is **Bridewell Museum** (☎ 667227; Bridewell Alley; adult/ child £2/1; open 10am-5pm Mon-Sat), which has surprisingly interesting displays of local industries throughout the past 200 years. Formerly a merchant's house, in the 14th century it served as an open prison for vagrants (a bridewell).

Strangers' Hall (☎ 629127; £2.50/1.50; open 9am-5pm Mon-Sat) is 250m west of here, along St Andrew's St and Charing Cross. It's a medieval town house with rooms furnished in period styles from Tudor to Victorian. Highlights include the stone vaulted undercroft, dating from 1320, the fine Georgian Dining Room and the Tudor Great Hall with its stone-mullioned window and screen.

There are tours (£2.50 per person, maximum 15 people) of the museum at 11am, 1pm and 3pm on Wednesday and Saturday. Call for bookings.

Dragon Hall (☎ 663922; 115-123 King St; adult/child £2.50/1; open 10am-4pm Mon-Sat Apr-Oct, 10am-4pm Mon-Fri Nov-Mar) is another medieval town house with a superb crown post roof and impressive, timber-framed great hall.

Sainsbury Centre for Visual Arts
To the west of the city, on the university campus (a 20-minute bus trip from Castle Meadow), this gallery (adult/child £2/1; open 11am-5pm Tues-Sun) is remarkable both for the building itself and the art it contains. It was designed by Norman Foster and is filled with an eclectic collection of works by Picasso, Moore, Bacon and Giacometti, displayed beside art from Africa, the Pacific and the Americas.

Places to Stay
Camping & Hostels A mile south of the centre, **Lakenham Camping** (☎ 620060; Martineau Lane; pitches per person £5; open Easter-Oct) is beside the A146.

Norwich YHA Hostel (☎ 0870 770 5976, fax 629075; e norwich@yha.org.uk; 112 Turner Rd; beds per adult/under-18 £10/6.90; open daily Apr-Oct) is 2 miles (3km) from the train station on the western edge of the city. From November to March, it runs the Rent-a-hostel scheme, which caters to large groups only; phone for information. In addition to dorm beds, there are family rooms with two to six beds.

B&Bs & Hotels Most of the B&Bs and cheaper hotels are outside the ring road, along Earlham and Unthank Rds to the west, and around the train station.

The closer the B&Bs along Earlham Rd are to the centre the more expensive they are.

Hanover House (☎ 667402; e aylmus@ clara.co.uk; 60 Earlham Rd; doubles £40) has just two doubles, but they're comfortable and well appointed.

EdMar Lodge (☎ 615599, fax 495599; e edmar@cwcom.net; 64 Earlham Rd; en-suite singles/doubles from £35/40) is an excellent place.

Georgian House Hotel (☎ 615655, fax 765 689; e reception@georgian-hotel.co.uk; 32-34 Unthank Rd; singles/doubles from £52.50/76) is a really elegant Victorian house directly opposite St John's Roman Catholic Cathedral. The rooms are beautiful.

Beeches Hotel (☎ 621167, fax 620151; e reception@beeches.co.uk; 2-6 Earlham Rd; singles £64-69, doubles £82-94) has luxury accommodations in three separate Grade II–listed Victorian houses, collectively known as the Beeches. They're all terrific, but try to get a room in The Plantation, if only because of its wonderful garden.

On the far side of town, close to the train station, are plenty of budget B&Bs.

Abbey Hotel (☎/fax 612915; 16 Stracey Rd; singles/doubles £20/40) is our favourite in a row of B&Bs behind the station. The rooms are not particularly big, but the place has a nice, friendly atmosphere.

Cumberland Hotel (☎ 434550, fax 433 3355; e Cumberland@paston.co.uk; 212-216 Thorpe Rd; singles/doubles £49.50/69.50) is a pleasant, family-run hotel near the train station. It's not particularly beautiful, but the careful touches, such as hanging baskets and big, wooden beds, give it a comfortable, homely feel.

By Appointment (☎ 630730; 25-29 St George's St; singles/doubles £70/95) is one of our favourite hotels in all of eastern England. It may have an odd name but this 15th-century listed building has some of the most beautifully appointed rooms you'll find anywhere in the region.

Maid's Head Hotel (☎ 209955, fax 613688; Tombland; singles/doubles weeknights £100/120, weekends per person £47) is a comfortable 700-year-old former coaching inn in the centre. There is a minimum two-night stay at weekends.

Places to Eat

Norwich has a wide selection of excellent restaurants and nice cafés.

Adlard's Restaurant (☎ 633522; 79 Upper St Giles St; 4-course dinner £35; open dinner Mon, lunch & dinner Tues-Sat), offering classic French cuisine, is good for a splurge.

Brummels Seafood Restaurant (☎ 625 555; 7 Magdalen St; 2-course menu £22) operates on the 'eat fish, live longer' premise – the catch is always fresh and the prices discreet.

The Walnut Tree Shades (☎ 620166; Old Post Office Court), in the city centre, is a fabulous little restaurant specialising in all things beefy; the steak Diane (£12.50) will have carnivores drooling.

The Aquarium (☎ 630090; 22 Tombland; mains around £9) specialises mostly in English cuisine, but there are the inevitable French and continental influences.

Treehouse (☎ 763258; 14 Dove St; mains around £5 & £6.50; open Mon-Sat), above a health food shop, is an excellent vegetarian restaurant serving such delicacies as nut and moonbeam pate. Main courses come in two sizes at two prices.

Briton Arms Coffee House & Restaurant (☎ 623367; 9 Elm Hill; mains £5-9) is in a lovely thatched cottage with its own little garden. The food is traditional English with some clever modern touches.

Casablanca (☎ 624620; 66 London St; mains around £8) is a good Moroccan restaurant where everything is cooked to order – and diners are occasionally entertained by belly dancers.

Mambo Jambo (☎ 666802; 14-16 Lwr Goat Lane; mains around £7) explores the hot and spicy taste of Creole, Cajun and Mexican cuisine.

Waffle House (☎ 612790; 39 St Giles St; waffles £2.95-7) specialises in savoury and sweet Belgian waffles. There's a wide selection of fillings.

Kafe Da (☎ 622836; 18 Bedford St; dishes £4.50-7) is a trendy café themed around international espionage: the subs are named after Bond movies, the sandwiches after Russian leaders.

Bedford's Brasserie & Bar (☎ 666869; 1 Old Post Office Yard; mains £6-7) is almost opposite Kafe Da. On the menu are sauteed king prawns with chilli jam in a light puff pastry (£6.50) – not run-of-the-mill pub grub!

Orgasmic Café (☎ 676650; 6 Queen St; mains around £6) is a new spot that serves really good gourmet food and has a superb selection of wine by the glass.

Caley's Tea Rooms (☎ 629364; Guildhall, Market Square) is where you'll find some of the nicest chocolate in all of England. Chocoholics, prepare yourselves!

There's a convenient **Tesco Metro** supermarket on Market Square for self-catering.

Entertainment

ArtEast is a useful, free Norfolk listings magazine published bimonthly. You can pick it up in the TIC and most cafés.

Pubs There's live jazz or blues most nights at **Boswells** (☎ 629099; 20 Tombland) wine bar.

Adam & Eve's (Bishopgate) is for serious beer drinkers.

The Ten Bells (76 St Benedict's St) is popular with students.

Nightclubs Norwich's club scene is the only one in East Anglia to rival Cambridge. All nightclubs run from 9pm or 10pm to 2am.

Mojo (☎ 622533; 62 Prince of Wales Rd; admission £4) features soul, breaks, hip-hop and r'n'b.

Time (☎ 767649; Riverside; admission £2-5), about a mile west of town on the Yare, is the biggest club in town, with a capacity of 1700. The music is hard house and other dance anthems. Admission varies depending on the night. Trainers (sneakers) and jeans are no-nos.

Liquid (☎ 611113; Prince of Wales Rd; admission £5) is a high-tech dance club with a suitable soundtrack of techno and hard house.

Theatre & Concerts Theatre Royal (☎ 630 000; Theatre St) features programmes by touring drama and ballet companies.

Norwich Arts Centre (☎ 660352; Reeves Yard, St Benedict's St) has a wide-ranging programme of drama, concerts, dance, cabaret and jazz.

St Andrew's and Blackfriars' Halls (☎ 628477; St Andrew's Plain), once home to Dominican Blackfriars, now serve as an impressive civic centre where concerts, antique and craft markets, the Music and Arts Festival, and even the annual beer festival are held; there's also a café in the crypt.

Norwich Puppet Theatre (☎ 629921; St James, Whitefriars; adult/child tickets around £6/4) is popular, particularly with children.

Getting There & Away

National Express has a daily bus to London (£13, three hours). First Eastern Counties runs hourly buses to King's Lynn (£3.70, 1½ hours) and Peterborough (£3.70, 2 hours 40 minutes); and half-hourly buses to Cromer (£1.90, 1 hour). There are five buses daily to Bury St Edmunds (£3.90, 1½ hours) and an hourly service to Great Yarmouth (£2.20, 45 minutes).

There are no bus services to Cambridge, on account of a new direct rail link that was to be operational by autumn 2002.

There are hourly rail services to King's Lynn (£9, 40 minutes) and Ely (£12.60, 1¼ hours). There is a half-hourly service to London Liverpool St (£31.20, two hours); hourly trains to Great Yarmouth (£4.40, ½ hour) and Cromer (£3.80, 50 minutes). To get to Cambridge you'll need to go to Ely.

AROUND NORWICH
Blickling Hall

There has been a manor house here since 1057 when Harald, earl of the East Saxons (later King Harald) built the first Blickling. In 1437 the house was bought by Geoffrey Boleyn and later inherited by his grandson Thomas, whose daughter Anne was born and raised here – at least according to tradition. Historians aren't so sure. Anne, of course, made the fatal mistake of marrying Henry VIII, which led to her execution in 1533, and

it is said that on the anniversary of her execution a coach drives up to the house – drawn by headless horses, driven by headless coachmen and containing the queen with her head on her lap.

The current house (NT; ☎ 01263-733084; admission £6.50; hall open 1pm-4.30pm Wed-Sun Apr-July, Sept & Oct, & Tues Aug, gardens open 10.30am-5.30pm Wed-Sun Easter-Oct, 11am-4pm end of year) was almost entirely rebuilt by Robert Lyminge at the behest of Sir Henry Hobart, James I's chief justice. It is filled with Georgian furniture, pictures and tapestries. There's an impressive Jacobean plaster ceiling in the long gallery. The house is surrounded by parkland offering good walks.

Blickling Hall is 15 miles (24km) north of Norwich. **Saunder's Coaches** (☎ 01692-406020) runs hourly buses here from Norwich from June to August (£1.30, 20 minutes). Aylsham is the nearest train station, 1¾ miles away.

NORFOLK BROADS

The Norfolk Broads is an area of navigable rivers, lakes, marshland, nature reserves and bird sanctuaries – 125 miles (200km) of lock-free waterways – in eastern Norfolk. The area, measuring some 117 sq miles (303 sq km), has 'national protected status', which is equivalent to being a national park. It is also an official Area of Outstanding Natural Beauty (AONB).

There's little variety of scenery but the ecology of the area means that it's a wonderful place for nature lovers and for people who like being on or near the water. The habitat includes freshwater lakes, slow-moving rivers, water meadows, fens, bogs and saltwater marshes, and the many kinds of birds, butterflies and water-loving plants that inhabit them.

How Hill, a mere 12m above sea level, is the highest place in the Broads. Since there's nothing to impede the path of sea breezes, this is a good area for wind power. Many wind pumps (which look like windmills) were built to drain the marshland and to return the water to the rivers.

Orientation

The Broads form a triangle with Norwich–Cromer road, the Norwich–Lowestoft road and the coastline as the three sides.

The Origin of the Broads

For many years the origin of the Norfolk Broads was unclear. The rivers were undoubtedly natural and many thought the lakes were too – it's hard to believe they're not when you see them – but no-one could explain how they were formed.

The mystery was solved when records were discovered in the remains of St Benet's Abbey (on the River Bure). They showed that from the 12th century certain parts of land in Hoveton Parish were used for peat digging. The area had little woodland and the only source of fuel was peat. Since East Anglia was well populated and prosperous, peat digging became a major industry.

Over a period of about 200 years, approximately 1040 hectares were dug up. However, water gradually seeped through causing marshes, and later lakes, to develop. The first broad to be mentioned in records is Ranworth Broad in 1275. Eventually, the amount of water made it extremely difficult for the diggers and the peat-cutting industry died out. In no other area of England has human effort changed the natural landscape so dramatically.

Wroxham, on the A1151 from Norwich, and Potter Heigham, on the A1062 from Wroxham, are the main centres. Along the way there are plenty of waterside pubs, villages and market towns where you can stock up on provisions, and stretches of river where you can feel you are the only person around.

Information

The **Broads Authority** (☎ 01603-610734; **w** www.broads-authority.gov.uk/broads/indexie.html; Thomas Harvey House, 18 Colegate, Norwich NR3 1BQ) can give details on conservation centres and Royal Society for the Protection of Birds bird-watching hides at Berney Marshes, Bure Marshes, Cockshoot Broad, Hickling Broad, Horsey Mere, How Hill, Ranworth, Strumpshaw Fen and Surlingham Church Marsh.

You can also obtain information about the Broads from the Norwich TIC. *The Broadcaster* is a visitors' magazine, published annually.

Getting Around

Two companies that operate boating holidays are **Blakes** (☎ 01603-782911) and **Hoseasons** (☎ 01502-501010). Costs depend on the boat size, the facilities on the boat, the time of year and the length of the holiday. A boat for two to four people costs £525 to £850 for a week including fuel and insurance. Short breaks (three to four days) during the off-season are much cheaper.

Many boat yards (particularly in the Wroxham and Potter Heigham areas) have a variety of boats for hire by the hour, half-day or full day. These include the traditional flat-bottom boats known as wherries. Charges still vary according to the season and the size of the boat but they start from £12 for one hour, £32 for four hours and £50 for one day.

No previous experience is necessary but remember to stay on the right side of the river, that the rivers are tidal, and to stick to the speed limit – you can be prosecuted for speeding. If you don't feel like piloting your own boat, Broads Tours runs 1½-hour pleasure trips from April to September, with a commentary, for £5.80/4.20 per adult/child. There are two bases for **Broads Tours** (☎ 01603-782207; The Bridge, Wroxham • ☎ 01692-670711; Herbert Woods, Potter Heigham).

GREAT YARMOUTH
☎ 01493 • pop 54,800

Norfolk's most popular seaside resort has gone the way of so many others and is overrun by tacky amusement arcades, greasy spoon cafés and cheap B&Bs. It's also an important port for the North Sea oil and gas industries. Hardly an inviting feature. Yet Great Yarmouth does have a couple of genuine lures: a wide, sandy beach and a number of interesting buildings in the old town.

The **TIC** (☎ 846345, fax 846221; open 9am-5pm Mon-Fri year round) is in the town hall in the centre of town. There's also another **office** (☎ 842195; Marine Parade; open 9.30am-5.30pm daily Easter-end Sept).

The **Elizabethan House Museum** (☎ 745 526; South Quay; adult/child £2/1; open 10am-5pm Sun-Fri) was a merchant's house and now contains a display of 19th-century domestic life. The **Tollhouse Museum** (☎ 858900; Tolhouse St; adult/child £1.30/1; open 10am-5pm Mon-Fri, 1.15pm-5pm Sat & Sun) was once the town's courthouse and jail; prison cells can be seen and there's a display covering the town's history. There's also a small **maritime museum** *(Marine Parade)* near the TIC. It has the same opening hours and admission prices as the Tollhouse.

The **Norfolk Nelson Museum** *(☎ 850698; 26 South Quay; adult/child £2/1; open 10am-5pm Mon-Fri)* opened in 2002 to celebrate the life and times of the one-eyed hero of Trafalgar, who was a regular visitor to Great Yarmouth (Great Yarmouth seems proud of the fact that they beat London by 24 years in their tribute to him, erecting their statue on the South Denes in 1819).

Also worth checking out is the **Maritime Festival**, which takes place on the newly refurbished South Quay in September. Celebrating the town's rich seafaring heritage, it is a weekend-long shindig of music, crafts and visiting vessels. Check with the TIC for details.

There are numerous B&Bs, and **Great Yarmouth Youth Hostel** *(☎ 0870 770 5840, fax 856600; 2 Sandown Rd; beds per adult £10.25)* is three-quarters of a mile from the train station, near the beach. **Tunstall Camping Barn** *(☎ 700279; Manor Farm, Tunstall, Halvergate; beds £6)* is an independent hostel with 20 sleeping platforms in a barn. It's about 6 miles (9.5km) from Great Yarmouth, on the Norwich road.

Great Yarmouth has bus and rail connections to Norwich: First Eastern Counties runs an hourly bus service (£2.85, 40 minutes); Wherry Lines runs trains roughly every half-hour (£4.30, 25 minutes) daily except Sunday, when there are hourly departures between 8.20am and 5.20pm only.

CROMER
☎ 01263 • pop 4500

In the late Victorian and Edwardian eras, Cromer was transformed into the most fashionable resort on the coast. It's now somewhat run down, but with its elevated seafront, long sandy beach and scenic coastal walks, it's still worth visiting. Cromer has long been famous for its crabs, and they're still caught and sold here. The **TIC** *(☎ 512497, fax 513613; open 9.30am-6pm Mon-Sat, 9.30am-5pm Sun mid-July–Aug, 10am-5pm Mon-Sat Sept–mid-July)* is by the bus station.

Two miles (3km) southwest of Cromer, **Felbrigg Hall** *(NT; ☎ 837444; adult/child £5.90/2.90; open 1pm-5pm Sat-Wed Mar-*

Oct) is one of the finest 17th-century houses in Norfolk. It contains a collection of 18th-century furniture; outside is a walled garden, orangery and landscaped park.

Cromer is one of the few coastal resorts with a train station linked to Norwich. There are 13 trains daily Monday to Saturday and six on Sunday (£3.40, 45 minutes).

CLEY MARSHES

Between Cromer and Wells, Cley Marshes is one of the top bird-watching places in Britain, with over 300 species recorded. There's a **visitor centre** *(☎ 740008)* built on high ground to give good views over the area. But probably the best spot for birdwatching is among the reeds, where there are some excellent hides.

WELLS-NEXT-THE-SEA
☎ 01328 • pop 2400

Set back from the sea, Wells is both a holiday town and a fishing port. It's a pleasant place, with streets of attractive Georgian houses, flint cottages and interesting shops. The **TIC** *(☎ 710885, fax 711405; Staithe St; open 10am-5pm Mon-Sat, 10am-4pm Sun Easter–mid-July, Sept & Oct; 9.30am-6pm Mon-Sat, 9.30am-5pm Sun mid-July–Aug)* can help with visitor inquiries.

A narrow-gauge steam railway runs 5 miles (8km) to **Little Walsingham**, where there are Catholic shrines and the ruins of an Augustinian abbey that have been an object of pilgrimage for almost 1000 years.

Wells YHA Hostel *(☎ 0870 770 6084, fax 711748; Church Plains; beds £11.25)* is a new hostel in a beautiful Victorian building.

AROUND WELLS-NEXT-THE-SEA

Situated in a 1200-hectare deer park 2 miles (3km) from Wells, **Holkham Hall** *(☎ 710227; adult/child £5/2.50; open 1pm-5pm Sun-Thur late May-Sept)* is an extraordinarily grand Palladian mansion. The grounds were designed by Capability Brown. Admission includes the Bygones Museum (a small museum of local folklore and artefacts) and the park, which is open throughout the year.

Burnham Deepdale
☎ 01485 • pop 1100

This gorgeous place is actually two villages in one and includes the hamlet of Brancaster Staithe. There's nothing particularly to visit, but there's plenty to do, including all kinds of water sports, and it makes a good base for walking or cycling. **Northshore Sports & Leisure** (☎ 210236; The Boatyard, Brancaster Staithe), can fulfil all your equipment needs, from kayaking to windsurfing.

The **TIC** (☎ 210256; open 10am-4pm Thur-Mon) has plenty of information on activities and places to visit in the surrounding area, and also runs a free accommodation booking service.

Marsh Barn (☎ 210036) is half a mile east of town, just off the A149 coast road. The four barns are used for a variety of local events, including art exhibitions, lectures and a jazz festival featuring local players that runs in late August.

Deepdale Granary (☎ 210256; e deep daleinformation@deepdalefarm.co.uk; beds £9.50) is a marvellous hostel spread across a 17th-century converted stables and barn, and the management is a good source of local information.

The nearest train station is King's Lynn. Bus No 411 runs here (£1.40, 15 minutes) from Cromer.

KING'S LYNN
☎ 01553 • pop 37,500

One of England's most important medieval ports, King's Lynn (or Lynn, as the locals call it) is perfectly situated about 3 miles (5km) from the sea on the Great River Ouse, which was wide and deep enough to serve as a natural base for fishing fleets. Their crews, meanwhile, descended on the town where their tendencies to wreak havoc were kept in check by the staunchly pious citizens, who shared their town with a number of religious foundations. The old town is still a fascinating mixture of these elements and Lynn is still a port today, though much less busy than it once was. Away from the port, the modern town is sadly sterile, with the main streets clogged with chain stores and bland architecture.

There are three market days a week: Tuesday (the major market, with everything from clothing to bric-a-brac and fish), Friday (with a limited selection of flowers and vegetables) and Saturday (a food market selling fish, fruit, flowers and vegetables). The Tuesday market takes place in the suitably named Tuesday Market Place, while the Friday and Saturday markets are held in Saturday Mar-

ket Place, in front of St Margaret's Church. The markets open by 8am and usually run until 4pm, depending on the weather. In July there's the popular King's Lynn Festival of Music and the Arts (see that section later).

Orientation
The old town lies along the eastern bank of the river. The train station is on the eastern side of the town. Modern Lynn and the bus station are between them.

Information
The **TIC** (☎ 819440, fax 819441; e kings -lynn.tic@west-norfolk.gov.uk; open 9.15am-5pm Mon-Sat, 10am-5pm Sun Apr-Oct, 10.30am-4pm daily Nov-Mar) is in the **Custom House** (Purfleet Quay).

The **post office** (☎ 692185; Baxter's Plain; open 9am-5.30pm Mon-Fri, 9am-12.30pm Sat) is in the centre of town.

Gaywood Launderette (☎ 770078; 21 St Faith's Drive; open 6.30am-9pm daily) is east of the town centre, just off Gaywood Rd. Service washes, available daily except Sunday, cost a minimum of £6.

Jai Chemists (☎ 772828; 68 High St; open 9am-5.30pm Mon-Sat) is a central pharmacy. All chemists in town operate on a rota system, whereby once every two weeks or so they are open until 6.30pm. Check with the TIC for details of whose turn it is. The **Queen Elizabeth Hospital** (☎ 613613; Gayton Rd) is at the Hunstanton bypass, about 2½ miles (4km) east of the town centre.

The **police station** (☎ 691211) is on St James Rd.

Walking Tour
This walk takes around 2½ hours. Start in the Saturday Market Place at **St Margaret's** parish church, founded in 1100 with a Benedictine priory. Little remains of the original buildings but the church is impressive for its size (72m long) and contains two Flemish brasses that are among the best examples in the country. By the west door there are flood-level marks – 1976 was the highest but the 1953 flood claimed more lives.

Walk south down Nelson St to see a fine collection of domestic and industrial buildings. Their frontages are 17th and 18th century but their interiors are much older. On the corner of St Margaret's Lane, and dating back to the 15th century, is a restored build-

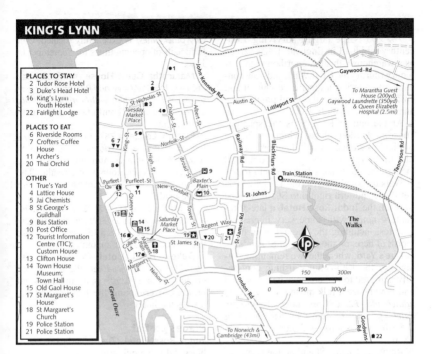

KING'S LYNN

PLACES TO STAY
2 Tudor Rose Hotel
3 Duke's Head Hotel
16 King's Lynn
   Youth Hostel
22 Fairlight Lodge

PLACES TO EAT
6 Riverside Rooms
7 Crofters Coffee
   House
11 Archer's
20 Thai Orchid

OTHER
1 True's Yard
4 Lattice House
5 Jai Chemists
8 St George's
   Guildhall
9 Bus Station
10 Post Office
12 Tourist Information
   Centre (TIC);
   Custom House
13 Clifton House
14 Town House
   Museum;
   Town Hall
15 Old Gaol House
17 St Margaret's
   House
18 St Margaret's
   Church
19 Police Station
21 Police Station

ing that was once the warehouse or 'steel-yard' of the Hanseatic League (the Northern European merchants' group). Now known as **St Margaret's House**, it is home to a number of civic offices, including the Education League, the Weights & Measures department and the town registrar. In theory, access is restricted to those offices alone, but you can wander in and have a look at the interior. If there's a group of you, you're better off seeking permission by calling the **Education League** (☎ 669200).

Continue northwest on Margaret Plain to College Lane and the former Thoresby College, which was founded in 1508 to house priests and is now the youth hostel (see Places to Stay later). Across Queen St is the **town hall**, dating back to 1421. Next to it is the **Town House Museum** (☎ 773450; 46 Queen St; adult/child £1.90/1.50; open 10am-5pm Mon-Sat, 2pm-5pm Sun May-Sept, 10am-4pm Mon-Sat Oct-Apr). Inside you will find exhibits charting life in the town from the Middle ages up to the 1950s.

Next door the **Old Gaol House** (☎ 774297; adult/child £2.40/1.75; open 10am-5pm daily Easter-Oct, 10am-5pm Fri-Tues Nov-Easter)

has been converted into a tourist attraction with self-guided audio tours. The town's priceless civic treasures, including the 650-year-old King John Cup, can be seen in the basement. Last entry is at 4.15pm.

Continuing down Queen St you pass **Clifton House**, with its quirky barley-sugar columns and waterfront tower, which was used by merchants scanning the river for returning ships. Its interior is in dire need of restoration so access is restricted to groups organised by the TIC.

Walk down the lane to the river past the sturdy, red floodgates. The stately Bank House is on your right. Opposite the square is **Purfleet Quay**, in its heyday the principal harbour. The quaint building with the lantern tower is the **Custom House** (housing the TIC), which dates back to 1683.

Turn into King St, where the second medieval town begins. It was planned in the latter half of the 12th century and had its own church, guildhall, market and friary. There are many interesting buildings in King St, especially on the left-hand (western) side, where the wealthier merchants built their homes and warehouses on reclaimed land. **St George's Guildhall** *(NT; ☎ 767557)* is the largest surviving 15th-century guildhall in England. It has served as a warehouse, theatre, courthouse and armoury (during the Civil War), and now contains art galleries, a theatre, restaurant and coffee house. This is the focal point of the annual King's Lynn festival.

At the end of King St is the spacious **Tuesday Market Place**, which fulfils its original role once a week. It's bordered by old buildings, including the Corn Hall (1854) and the Duke's Head Hotel (1689).

Walk diagonally across the Tuesday Market Place and turn right into St Nicholas St to reach the **Tudor Rose Hotel**, a late-15th-century house with some very interesting features, including the original main door. North of here, on the corner of St Ann's St, is **True's Yard**, where the two remaining cottages of the 19th-century fishing community that used to be here have been restored and now house a **folk museum** *(☎ 770479; adult/child £2.50/1.50; open 10am-5pm daily Apr-Sept, to 4pm Oct-Mar)* detailing the life of a shellfish fisherman around 1850.

Return to Chapel St and on the corner of Market Lane is an attractive building known as **Lattice House** dating from the 15th century that now houses a restaurant.

King's Lynn Festival of Music & the Arts

The King's Lynn Festival – East Anglia's most important cultural gathering – was the brainchild of Lady Ruth Fermoy and offers a diverse programme of concerts and recitals of all kinds of 'serious' music, from medieval ballads to Jamaican jazz.

It usually takes place in the last week of July. There are also lectures and plays (Molière featured in the 2002 festival). Since 2001 the main festival has been preceded by the **Festival Too**, which usually takes place in and around Tuesday Market Place and puts the onus firmly on rock and pop music.

For details of programmed events, contact the **administrative office** *(☎ 767557, fax 767688; e enquiries@klfestival.freeserve.co .uk)* or the **box office** *(☎ 764864)*.

Places to Stay

King's Lynn Youth Hostel *(☎ 0870 770 5902, fax 764312; Thoresby College, College Lane;* *beds £9.25; always open 1 July-31 Aug, hours vary other times)* is excellently located. Call for details of opening times for September to June.

Maranatha Guest House *(☎ 774596, fax 763747; 115-117 Gaywood Rd; rooms per person from £18, doubles with/without en suite £44/40)* is a large, comfortable house with clean rooms.

Fairlight Lodge *(☎ 762234, fax 770280; 79 Goodwins Rd; singles/doubles £20/35, with bath £25/44)* is a comfortable guesthouse with seven rooms, four with en suite. The complimentary biscuits in each room are home-made.

Tudor Rose Hotel *(☎ 762824, fax 764894; e kltudorrose@aol.com; St Nicholas St; singles/doubles from £30/60)* is a 15th-century house that has modern, well-appointed rooms.

Duke's Head Hotel *(☎ 774996, fax 763556; Tuesday Market Place; singles/doubles from £50/90)* is a fine classical building overlooking the market, and the town's top hotel.

Places to Eat

Tudor Rose Hotel *(Tuesday Market Place)* has good value pub grub.

Riverside Rooms *(☎ 773134; mains £14.95-18)* is right by the river, near the undercroft.

Thai Orchid *(☎ 767013; 33-39 St James St; lunch £6.95, evening mains from £6)* is a good restaurant. The lunch menu features a rotating selection of 15 classic Thai dishes.

Archer's *(☎ 769177; Purfleet St; many dishes £4-5.95; open Mon-Sat)* is a pleasant, friendly place with a good range of coffees.

There are several places for teas or light meals.

Crofters Coffee House *(King St; open 9.30am-5pm Mon-Sat)*, in the guildhall undercroft at the Arts Centre, is recommended.

Getting There & Away

King's Lynn is 43 miles (69km) north of Cambridge on the A10.

First Eastern Counties runs an hourly bus service to Norwich (£4.85, 1½ hours) Monday to Saturday; on Sunday the service runs every two hours from 8.25am with the last bus at 6.55pm.

There are hourly trains from Cambridge (£13.80, 50 minutes) and Norwich (£14.50, 45 minutes).

AROUND KING'S LYNN
Castle Rising Castle
The amazingly well-preserved keep of this castle *(EH; ☎ 01553-631330; adult £3.25; open 10am-6pm daily Apr-Oct, 10am-4pm daily Nov-Mar)*, built between 1138 and 1140, is set in the middle of a massive earthwork. It was once the home of Queen Isabella, who arranged the gruesome murder of her husband Edward II at Berkeley Castle in Gloucestershire.

Bus No 411 runs here (£1.50, 19 minutes) every hour from King's Lynn bus station, 6 miles (9.5km) to the south.

Sandringham House
The Queen's country pile *(☎ 01553-772675; adult/child £6/3.50, grounds & museum only £5/3; open 11am-4.45pm daily Apr-Sept unless royal family is present)* is set in 25 hectares of landscaped gardens and lakes, and it's open to the hoi polloi when the court is not in residence.

Queen Victoria bought the house and an 8000-hectare estate in 1862 so as to give her son, the Prince of Wales (later Edward VII), somewhere to call his official residence, but he wasn't altogether happy with the Georgian building Mummy had bought for him. Over the next eight years, the house was redesigned in a style that would eventually bear his name.

The current crop of royals spend about three weeks a year here from mid-July to the first week in August, but they don't have the run of the whole estate. About half of the remaining 7975 hectares is leased out to farm tenants (a royal living doesn't pay for itself, you know), while the remaining hectares are managed by the Crown Estate as forestry.

The house itself is home to a museum that contains a collection of vintage cars and other royal trinkets. There are guided tours (£3.50) of the formal gardens on Friday and Saturday at 2pm.

There is also a yearly programme of special events, including a craft fair in September. Check with the office for details of upcoming events or write to Sandringham House, The Estate Office, Sandringham, Norfolk PE35 6EN.

First Eastern Counties bus No 411 (which also goes to Castle Rising Castle) runs here from King's Lynn bus station (£1.80, 25 minutes), 10 miles (16km) southwest.

Houghton Hall
Built for Sir Robert Walpole in 1730, Houghton Hall *(☎ 01485-528569; adult/child £6.25/3.25; open 1pm-5.30pm Thur-Sun Easter-Sept)* in the Palladian style is worth seeing for the ornate state rooms alone. It's 14 miles (22.5km) northeast of King's Lynn. Last admission is at 5pm.

Unfortunately, the house is not served by public transport; if you don't have your own wheels you'll have to get here from King's Lynn by taxi, which should cost between £11 and £12.50. A reputable service in King's Lynn is **Ken's Taxis** *(☎ 01553-766166)*.

Cambridgeshire

If you're in Cambridgeshire, chances are you're here for one reason: to walk and poke around the hallowed cobbled streets of one of the world's most famous university towns. Indeed, Cambridge has few rivals in a number of categories besides prestige, not least in sheer beauty.

Yet the rest of the county should not go unexplored. Basically a flat, fertile and once-submerged plain known as the Fens, Cambridgeshire is wonderful cycling country that you can explore with great ease. From Cambridge, a towpath winds 15 miles (24km) to Ely where the superb cathedral, on ground slightly higher than the surrounding plain, is known as the 'ship of the fens'.

In the north of the county there's another fine cathedral at Peterborough, which carries the questionable title of England's shopping capital.

Activities
Short strolls and city ambles are suggested throughout this section. For longer walks, the TIC in Cambridge stocks a number of guides, including *Walks in South Cambridgeshire*.

Getting Around
Public transport centres on Cambridge, which is only 55 minutes by rail from London. This line continues north through Ely to terminate at King's Lynn in Norfolk.

From Ely, branch lines run east through Norwich, southeast into Suffolk and northwest to Peterborough and into Lincolnshire.

The main buses operating in the area are **Stagecoach Cambus** *(☎ 01223-423554)* between Cambridge, Bury St Edmunds and Ely; **Cambridge Coach Services** (☎ *01223-423900*), Cambridge to Norwich; and **Stagecoach United Counties** (☎ *01604-620077*), Cambridge to Huntingdon and Peterborough.

The useful *Cambridgeshire and Peterborough Passenger Transport Map* is available at all TICs.

CAMBRIDGE
☎ 01223 • pop 88,000

Often described as the only true university town in England, Cambridge is an extraordinary place, a city unlike no other in the country in that it is almost completely dominated by that venerable institute of higher learning. It received its royal charter only a couple of years before the arrival of the first

students in 1209, and ever since the town and university have grown together, with the latter always retaining the upper hand.

Although Cambridge is smaller than 'the other place' (as Oxford is referred to here), the university's pervasive influence has ensured that it is more architecturally unified and – to most observers – more aesthetically pleasing. The city's trump card is the choir and chapel of King's College, which is one of the highlights of any trip to England. The rest of the city isn't half-bad either, a stunning mix of medieval buildings, elegant courtyards and expansive parkland, particularly the 'Backs', through which meanders the gentle River Cam.

Cambridge's position and lack of heavy industry gives it a rustic flavour, but Cambridge

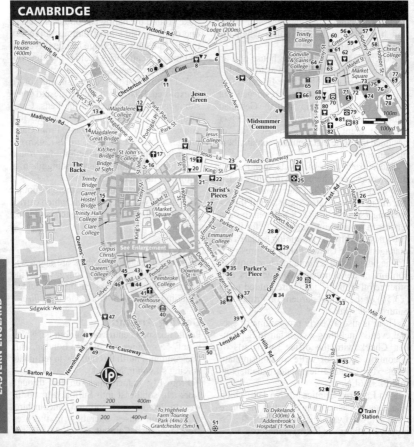

CAMBRIDGE

is hardly rural. A busy market town brimming with history and antiquity, Cambridge is confidently striding into the new millennium. Its streets are lined with elegant designer shops and fancy boutiques and there is no shortage of overpriced continental-style cafés and trendy restaurants, all clamouring for a share of tourists' and students' bulging wallets. Yet it is Cambridge's tranquil, ageless appearance which is hardest to match, and which the visitor will remember best.

History

At first a Roman fort and later a small Saxon settlement, Cambridge was just a tiny rural backwater until 1209, when the university town of Oxford exploded in a riot between scholars and townspeople, forcing a group of students to quit while their heads were still intact and move up to Cambridge to found a new university. The facts surrounding the foundation are a little hazy, undoubtedly due to another riot in 1261 between 'town and gown', when the university records were burnt. At the rioters' trial, the judges ruled in favour of the students,

setting a precedent that would last for centuries. The new university had found favour with the law and began to establish a firm footing within the town.

The collegiate system, unique to Oxford and Cambridge, came into being gradually with the first college, Peterhouse, founded in 1284 by Hugo de Balsham (later Bishop of Ely). The plan was for tutors and students to live together in a community, much as they would in a monastery.

From the 14th century on, a number of colleges were founded by royalty, nobility, leading church figures, statesmen, academics and trade guilds – all for men only. In 1869 and 1871, however, women were finally accorded the right to study here with the founding of women-only Girton and Newnham colleges – although they had to wait until 1948 before they were allowed to graduate.

The honour roll of famous graduates reads like an international who's who of high achievers and a list of their accomplishments in a wide variety of fields could fill a couple of thick volumes. So far, the university has produced 78 Nobel Prize

CAMBRIDGE

PLACES TO STAY
1 Antony's
2 Acorn Guest House
3 Hamilton Hotel
9 Aaron House
10 Arundel Guest House
26 The Ark
28 Warkworth House
34 YMCA
36 De Vere University Arms Hotel
44 Garden House (Moat House)
50 Lensfield Hotel
52 Tenison Towers Guest House
53 Cambridge Youth Hostel
55 Sleeperz

PLACES TO EAT
4 Midsummer House
7 Twenty-Two
14 Michel's Brasserie
20 Yippee
21 Clowns
32 Al Casbah
33 Trattoria Pasta Fresca
35 Hobb's Pavilion
39 The Gulshan
42 Fitzbillies
45 Nadia's (Silver St)
48 Choice's Café
58 Tatties

68 Nadia's (King's Parade)
69 Rainbow

PUBS, BARS & CLUBS
5 Fort St George
8 Boathouse
12 Henry's
18 Po Na Na
22 Champion of the Thames
23 St Radegund
24 Sophbeck Sessions
38 Venue
47 Granta (and Punt Hire)
62 Fez
63 Bar Ha! Ha!
73 Fifth Avenue
80 The Eagle

OTHER
6 Cleanomat Dry Cleaners
11 Riverboat Georgina
13 Kettle's Yard
15 Trinity Punt Hire
16 Vantage Pharmacy
17 Round Church
19 All Saints Church
25 Grafton Centre
27 Drummer St Bus Station
29 Police Station
30 Mike's Bikes

31 CB1
37 HSBC (Bank)
40 Fitzwilliam Museum
41 Little St Mary's Church
43 Ben Hayward Cycles
46 Scudamore's Punt Hire
49 Cambridge Recycles
51 University Botanical Gardens
54 Geoff's Bike Hire
56 Galloway & Porter
57 American Express
59 Dillions
60 Heffer's Bookshop
61 Heffer's Music
64 Heffer's Children's Bookshop
65 Senate House
66 King's College Chapel
67 Great St Mary's Church
70 Arts Theatre
71 Tourist Information Centre (TIC)
72 Boots
74 WH Smith
75 Heffer's Plus
76 Thomas Cook
77 Abbey National (Bank)
78 Post Office
79 International Telecom Centre
81 Saxon Tower
82 Church of St Bene't
83 Corn Exchange

EASTERN ENGLAND

Cambridge, aka...

It seems quite ironic that in a city renowned for its academic excellence and the superior quality of its scholarly research, there is still doubt over how exactly Cambridge got its name. One thing, however, is certain: at the heart of the matter are two rivers, the Cam and its tributary the Granta, although until at least AD 1000 it was the latter that was deemed more important. Britain's first historian, the venerable Bede, made reference to the settlement of *Grantacaestir* in around AD 730, while 15 years later Felix of Crowland wrote of *Grontricc*. In 875 the Anglo-Saxon Chronicle mentioned *Grantebrycge*, but from 1107 the town was known variously as *Caumbrigge*, *Caumbregge*, *Caumberage* and *Cantabrigia*. The first line of Chaucer's *Reeve's Tale*, written at the end of the 14th century, reads: 'At Trumpington, not fer fro Cantebrigge'. But still the town's name continued to change. In 1478 it was Camebrygge, finally becoming Cambridge during Elizabethan times.

winners (29 from Trinity College alone), 13 British prime ministers, nine archbishops of Canterbury, an immense number of scientists, a healthy host of poets and other scribblers... And this is but a limited selection. Today the university remains at the top of the research league in British universities. It owns a prestigious publishing firm and a world-renowned examination syndicate; it is the leading centre for astronomy in Britain; its Fitzwilliam Museum contains an outstanding art collection; and its library is used by scholars from around the world.

Orientation

The colleges and university buildings comprise the centre of the city. The central area, lying in a wide bend of the River Cam, is easy to get around on foot or by bike. The best-known section of the Cam is the Backs, which combines lush river scenery with superb views of six colleges, including King's College Chapel. The other 25 colleges are scattered throughout the city.

The bus station is central on Drummer St, but the train station is a 20-minute walk to the south. Sidney St becomes St Andrew's St to the south and Bridge and Magdalene Sts to the north, and is the main shopping street.

Information

Tourist Offices The TIC (☎ 322640, fax 457588; ⓦ www.cambridge.gov.uk; Wheeler St; open 10am-6pm Mon-Fri, 10am-5pm Sat, 11am-4pm Sun Apr-Oct; 10am-5.30pm Mon-Sat Nov-Mar) organises walking tours at 1.30pm every day, year round, with extra tours at 10.30am, 11.30am and 2.30pm from May to September. Group sizes are limited so buy your ticket in advance.

Tours costs £7.25 and include King's College; £6.25 if King's College is closed, in which case the tour includes St John's College. In summer 2002 the TIC began running 1½-hour drama tours of historic Cambridge, complete with actors in Tudor costumes.

Adult/child tickets cost £4.50/2.25 and tours depart from the TIC at 6.30pm on Tuesday, July to August only.

Post & Communications Send mail at the **main post office** (☎ 323325; 9-11 St Andrew's St; open 9am-5.30pm Mon-Sat). To check email or make cheap international phone calls go to the **International Telecom Centre** (☎ 357358; open 9am-10pm daily) directly opposite the TIC; Internet charges are 99p per hour (but the computers are slow). **CB1** (☎ 576306; 32 Mill Rd; open 10am-8pm daily) is an Internet café with walls stacked with second-hand books. Access costs £3.25 per hour.

Money There are plenty of banks with ATMs around the city centre. Try **Abbey National** (☎ 350495; 60 St Andrew's St) or **HSBC** (☎ 314822; 75 Regent St). There's also a branch of **American Express** (☎ 345203; 25 Sidney St) and **Thomas Cook** (☎ 543100; 8 St Andrew's St).

Bookshops Booksellers do a roaring trade in Cambridge. The largest chain of all is Heffers, which has branches throughout the city. For academic books, the **main branch** (☎ 568582; 20 Trinity St) is directly across from Trinity College. **Heffers Plus** (☎ 568596; 31 St Andrew's St) sells general paperbacks and guidebooks. **Heffers Children's Bookshop** (☎ 568551; 29-30 Trinity St) does what it says on the tin, while **Heffers Music** (☎ 568562; 19 Trinity St) is renowned throughout England for its excellent selection of classical CDs, particularly of the choral kind.

There are also branches of **Dillons** *(☎ 351 688; 22 Sidney St)* and **WH Smith** *(☎ 311313; 26 Lion Yard)*. An excellent second-hand bookshop is **Galloway & Porter** *(☎ 367876; 30 Sidney St)*, which does mostly remaindered and damaged stock.

Laundry The **Cleanomat Dry Cleaners** *(☎ 464719; 10 Victoria Ave)* is just north of the bridge and near Chesterton Rd. You can drop off your laundry or do it yourself.

Medical Services The **Addenbrooke's Hospital** *(☎ 245151)* is about half a mile south of the train station, just off Hills Rd. There are plenty of pharmacies dotted around the city centre, including two outlets of **Boots** *(☎ 350213; 28 Petty Cury • ☎ 350213; Grafton Centre)*. **Vantage Pharmacy** *(☎ 353002; 66 Bridge St)* is another.

Emergency The **police station** *(☎ 358966; Parkside)* is just across Parker's Piece from the city centre.

The University of Cambridge

The university has three eight-week terms: Michaelmas (October to December), Lent (mid-January to mid-March) and Easter (mid-April to mid-June). Exams are held from mid-May to mid-June. There's general mayhem for the 168 hours following exams – the so-called May Week. Most colleges are closed to visitors for the Easter term and all are closed for exams. Precise details of opening hours vary from college to college and year to year, so contact the TIC for up-to-date information. Five colleges (King's, Queen's, Clare, Trinity and St John's) charge admission to tourists (£1.50 to £3.80). You may, however, find that tourists are now denied admission at some of the colleges described in this section. Each year more colleges decide that the tourist bandwagon is just too disruptive. For all university-related inquiries, call the university's **central office** *(☎ 337733)*.

Walking Tour One

This 3-hour walk visits King's College Chapel and the most central colleges, and includes a stretch along the river.

From the TIC, walk west to King's Parade, turn right and continue north to **Great St**

Mary's Church *(☎ 741716; Senate House Hill)*. This university church, built between 1478 and 1519 in the late-Gothic perpendicular style, has a feeling of space and light inside thanks to its clerestory, wide arch and woodcarving. The traditional termly university sermons are preached here. To get your bearings, climb the 123 steps of the **tower** *(admission £2)* for a good view of the city. The building across King's Parade, on the right-hand side of the square, is the **Senate House**, designed in 1730 by James Gibbs. It's the most beautiful example of pure classical architecture in the city; graduations are held here.

Gonville & Caius Now walk onto Trinity St, head north, and turn left into the first gateway to reach this fascinating old college *(☎ 332400)*. It was founded twice, first by a priest called Gonville, in 1348, and then again by Dr Caius (pronounced keys), a brilliant physician and scholar, in 1557. Of special interest here are the three gates: Virtue, Humility and Honour. They symbolise the progress of the good student, since the third gate (the *Porta Honoris*, a fascinating confection with a quirky dome and sundials) leads to the Senate House and thus graduation. Walk through the gate, turn right, then left, to reach King's College Chapel.

King's College Chapel All the college chapels are individually remarkable but King's College Chapel *(☎ 331100)* is supreme in its grandeur. It's one of the finest examples of Gothic architecture in England and is comparable with Chartres cathedral in France.

The chapel was conceived as an act of piety by Henry VI and dedicated to the Virgin Mary. The king laid its foundation stone in 1446 and building was completed around 1516. Henry VI's successors, notably Henry VIII, glorified the interior (and themselves in doing so). Services are led by its choir, originally choristers from Eton College, another of Henry VI's foundations. The choir's Festival of the Nine Lessons and Carols on Christmas Eve are heard all over the world.

Enter by the southern porch. Despite the original stained-glass windows, the atmosphere inside is light. Cromwell's soldiers destroyed many church windows in East Anglia but it is believed that, having been a Cambridge student, their leader spared King's.

The stunning interior of 12 bays is about 11m wide, 22m high and 80m long. This vast expanse is the largest in the world canopied by fan vaulting. It's the work of John Wastell, and is a miracle of beauty and skill. Upon seeing it, Christopher Wren reputedly stated that he could have built it, but only if someone had shown him where to set the first stone.

The elaborate carvings, both in wood and stone, include royal coats of arms, intertwined initials, the royal beasts of heraldry, and flowers that were the emblems of Tudor monarchs and related families. Among the Yorkist roses on the western wall is one containing the figure of a woman. Some claim she is Elizabeth of York but it's more likely that she's the Virgin Mary.

The antechapel and the choir are divided by the superbly carved **wooden screen**, another gift from Henry VIII. Designed and executed by the king's master carver Peter Stockton, the screen bears Henry's initials entwined with those of Anne Boleyn, who supposedly inspired Henry's act of generosity. Almost concealed by the mythical beasts and symbolic flowers is one angry human face: perhaps it is Stockton's jest for posterity?

Originally constructed between 1686 and 1688, the magnificent organ has been rebuilt and developed over the years, and its pipes now top the screen on which they rest.

The **choir stalls** were made by the same craftsman who worked on the screen but the canopies are Carolingian. Despite the dark wood, the impression is still of lightness as one approaches the **high altar**, which is framed by Rubens' *Adoration of the Magi* and the magnificent east window.

The excellent **Chapel Exhibition** *(adult/child £3.50/2.25)* is in the northern side chapels, to the left of the altar. Here, you can see the stages and methods of building chapel set against the historical panorama from inception to completion. On display are costumes, paintings, illuminated manuscripts and books, plans, tools and scale models, including a full-size model showing how the fan vaulting was constructed.

The vergers are helpful with information and there are occasional guided tours on the weekend. Weekday tours can be arranged at the TIC. The chapel comes alive when the choir sings; even the most pagan heavy-metal fan will find **Choral Evensong** an extraordin-ary experience. Evensong is at 5.30pm, Tuesday to Saturday (men's voices only on Wednesday, a cappella on Friday) and there are two services on Sunday, at 10.30am and 3.30pm. There are services from mid-January to mid-March, mid-April to mid-June, mid-July to late July, early October to early December and on 24 and 25 December.

Trinity College From King's College Chapel, return to King's Parade and follow it north into Trinity St; the entrance to Trinity College *(☎ 338400; admission £1.75)* is on the left opposite Heffers bookshop. Henry VIII founded Trinity in 1546 but it was left to Dr Nevile, Master of Trinity (1593–1615) in Elizabeth's reign, to fulfil his wishes, as Henry died six weeks after founding the college.

As you walk through the impressive brick gateway (1535), have a look at the statue of Henry that adorns it. His left hand holds a golden orb, while his right grips a table leg, put there by students who removed the golden sceptre years ago. As you enter the **Great Court**, scholastic humour gives way to a gaping sense of awe, for it is the largest of its kind in the world. The place is literally dripping with history: to the right of the entrance is a small tree, planted in the 1950s and reputed to be a descendant of the apple tree made famous by Trinity alumnus Sir Isaac Newton.

The square is also the scene of the run made famous by the film *Chariots of Fire* – 350m in 43 seconds (the time it takes the clock to strike 12). Although plenty of students have a go, Harold Abrahams (the hero of the film) never actually attempted it and his fictional run wasn't even filmed here. If you fancy your chances remember that you'll need Olympian speed to even come close to making it in time (we tried and failed miserably!).

The Gothic antechapel to the right of the gate is full of huge statues of famous Trinity men, such as Tennyson and Newton. The vast hall has a hammer-beam roof and lantern. Beyond the hall are the cloisters of Nevile's Court and the dignified **Wren Library** *(open to visitors noon-2pm Mon-Fri year round, 10am-6pm Mon-Fri & 10.30pm-12.30pm Sat during term)*. It contains 55,000 books printed before 1820 and over 2500 manuscripts, including AA Milne's original *Winnie the Pooh*. Both he and his son Christopher Robin were graduates. The library is certainly worth visiting, though you may have to queue.

Along the Backs Walk out of the cloisters and turn right to look at St John's New Court on the western bank. It's a 19th-century residence block connected with the rest of **St John's College** by two bridges: Kitchen Bridge and the **Bridge of Sighs** (built in 1831, a replica of the original in Venice). Cross Trinity Bridge and turn left, following the footpath until you come to Garret Hostel Bridge. Pause on top to watch the punts below and look upstream to the bridge at **Clare College**. It's ornamented with decorative balls and is the oldest (1639), most interesting bridge on the Backs. Its architect was paid the grand total of 15p for his design so, feeling aggrieved at such a measly fee, he cut a slice out of one of the balls adorning the balustrade (the next to last one on the left) thus ensuring that the bridge would never be 'complete'. Or so the story goes. Walk on, then turn right into Trinity Hall.

Trinity Hall College This is a delightfully small college *(☎ 332500)*, wedged among the great and the famous. Despite the name, it has nothing to do with Trinity College. It was founded in 1350 as a refuge for lawyers and clerics escaping the ravages of the Black Death, thus earning it the nickname of the 'Lawyers' College'. You enter through the newest court, which overlooks the river on one side and has a lovely Fellows' garden on another. Walking into the next court, you pass the 16th-century library, which has original Jacobean reading desks and books chained to the shelves to prevent their permanent removal – the 16th century's equivalent of electronic bar codes.

Old Schools As you walk out of the first court, you'll see a tall, historic gate, which gets little attention. It's the entry to Old Schools, the administrative centre of the university. The lower part dates back to 1441 and the upper part was added in the 1860s. You are now back in the heart of the university.

Walking Tour Two

This walk visits Christ's College, Jesus College, the Round Church and Magdalene College. The walk should take about two

hours and you could continue afterwards to see the Kettle's Yard art gallery. Start outside Christ's, on the corner of St Andrew's and Hobson Sts. Christ's only opens to visitors from 10.30am to 12.30pm and 2pm to 4pm, so plan your walk accordingly.

Christ's College Christ's *(☎ 334900)* was founded in 1505 by that pious and generous benefactress, Lady Margaret Beaufort, who also founded St John's. It has an impressive entrance gate emblazoned with heraldic carving. The figure of the founder stands in a niche, hovering over all like a guiding spirit. Note the stout oak door leading into First Court, which has an unusual circular lawn, magnolias and wisteria creepers. The court is a mixture of original buildings and 18th-century facings and windows. The hall was rebuilt in neogothic style in the 19th century and the chapel's early sections include an oriel window that enabled the founder to join in services from her 1st-floor room.

The Second Court has an interesting Fellows' building, dating back to 1643. Its gate leads into a Fellows' garden, which contains a mulberry tree under which Milton (who came up to the college in 1628) reputedly wrote *Lycidas*. Continuing through Iris Court you're confronted by the stark, grey, modern students' block, which seems totally out of place. Look at the little theatre tucked into the right-hand corner, then walk out past New Christ's into Hobson St; turn right, then left and right into Jesus Lane. You'll pass Westcott, another theological college (not part of the university), then All Saints Church – dubbed St Op's (St Opposite) by Jesus students. Charles Darwin studied here.

Jesus College The approach to Jesus *(☎ 339339)*, founded 1496, via the long 'chimney' is impressive, as is the main gate, which is under a rebus of the founder, Bishop Alcock. A rebus is a heraldic device suggesting the name of its owner: the bishop's consists of several cockerels. The spacious First Court, with its redbrick ranges, is open on the western side – an unusual feature.

The best parts of Jesus are the tiny, intimate cloister court to your right and the chapel, which dates back to the St Radegund nunnery. The bishop closed the nunnery, expelled the nuns for misbehaving and founded the new college in its place.

The chapel is inspiring and reflects Jesus' development over the centuries. It has a Norman arched gallery from the nunnery building, a 13th-century chancel and beautiful restoration work and Art Nouveau features by Pugin, Morris (ceilings), Burne-Jones (stained glass) and Madox Brown.

The other buildings in Jesus are rather an anticlimax but the extensive grounds, which include a cricket pitch, are pleasant to walk through.

Round Church Turn right out of Jesus College, go up Jesus Lane, turn right into Park St and left into Round Church St. At the top of this street is the amazing Round Church, or Church of the Holy Sepulchre (☎ 518219). It was built in 1130 to commemorate its namesake in Jerusalem and is one of only four in England. It's strikingly unusual, with chunky, round Norman pillars that encircle the small nave. The rest of the church was added later in a different style; the conical roof dates from just the 19th century. No longer a parish church, it's now a **brass-rubbing centre** (☎ 871621; open 10am-6pm daily in summer, 1pm-4pm daily in winter). Depending on the size of the brasses, this costs from £5 to £24.

Magdalene College Turn right down Bridge St. It was around Magdalene Bridge that the Romans built the bridge that marked the origins of Cambridge. Boats laden with cargo tied up and unloaded where the block of flats now stands on the riverbank. Facing you across the river is Magdalene (pronounced mawd-lin), which you enter from Magdalene St.

Originally a Benedictine hostel, the college (☎ 332100) was re-founded in 1542 by Lord Audley. It has the dubious honour of being the last college to allow women students; when they were finally admitted in 1988, male students wore black armbands and flew the college flag at half-mast.

Its river setting gives it a certain appeal but its greatest asset is the Pepys Library, housing the magnificent collection of books the famous diarist bequeathed to his old college – he was a student here between 1650 and 1653.

Walking Tour Three

Taking in the colleges just to the south of the centre, including Corpus Christi, Queen's and Emmanuel, this walk takes about 2½ hours.

Corpus Christi From King's Parade, turn into Bene't (short for Benedict) St to see the oldest structure in Cambridgeshire – the Saxon tower of the Franciscan **Church of St Bene't** (☎ 353903), built in 1025. The rest of the church is newer but full of interesting features. The round holes above the belfry windows were designed to offer owls nesting privileges; their services were valued as mice-killers. It was here in 1670 that parish clerk Fabian Stedman invented change-ringing (the ringing of bells with different peals in a sequential order). The church also has a bible that belonged to Thomas Hobson, owner of a nearby livery stable who insisted that customers renting a horse take the one nearest the door because that had rested longest – hence the term 'Hobson's choice', meaning no choice at all.

The church served as chapel to Corpus Christi (☎ 338000), next door, until the 16th century when the college built its own. There's an entrance to the college leading into Old Court, which has been retained in its medieval form and still exudes a monastic atmosphere. The door to the chapel is flanked by two statues; on the right is Matthew Parker, who was college master in 1544 and archbishop of Canterbury for much of the reign of Elizabeth I. A pretty bright lad, Mr Parker was known for his curiosity, and his endless questioning gave us the term 'nosey parker'. Playwright Christopher Marlowe (1564–93), author of *Dr Faustus* and *Tamburlaine*, was a Corpus man, as a plaque, next to a fascinating sundial, bears out. New Court, beyond, is a 19th-century creation.

The college library has the finest collection of Anglo-Saxon manuscripts in the world that, with other valuable books, were preserved from destruction at the time of Henry VIII's dissolution of the monasteries.

Queens' College Queens' (☎ 335511; admission £1.20), one of the Backs' colleges, was the first Cambridge college to charge admission. This was initiated to pay for soundproofing its vulnerable site on this busy street. It takes its name from the two queens who founded it – Margaret of Anjou (wife of Henry VI) and Elizabeth of Woodville (wife of Edward IV), in 1448 and 1465 respectively – yet it was a conscientious rector of St Botolph's Church who was its real creator.

The college's main entrance is off Queens' Lane. The redbrick gate tower and Old Court, which immediately capture your attention, are part of the medieval college. So is Cloister Court, the next court, with its impressive cloister and picturesque, half-timbered President's Lodge (president is the name for the master). The famous Dutch scholar and reformer Erasmus lodged in the tower from 1510 to 1514. He wasn't particularly enamoured of Cambridge: he thought the wine tasted like vinegar, the beer was slop and the place too expensive, but he did write that the local women were good kissers. The Cam is outside Cloister Court, and is crossed by the wooden Mathematical Bridge which brings you into the 20th-century Cripps Court.

Peterhouse College Founded in 1284 by Hugo de Balsham, later Bishop of Ely, Peterhouse (☎ 338200) is the oldest and smallest of the colleges. It stands to the west of Trumpington St, just south of the Church of St Mary the Less (better known as **Little St Mary's**). St Peter's-without-Trumpington-Gate was the church's original odd-sounding name (because it stood outside, or 'without', the old gate) and it gave the college its name. Inside is a memorial to Godfrey Washington, an alumnus of the college and a great-uncle of George Washington. His family coat of arms was the stars and stripes, the inspiration for the US flag. A walk through Peterhouse gives you a clear picture of the 'community' structure of a Cambridge college though, unusually, the master's house is opposite the college, not within it. The college's list of notable alumni includes the poet Thomas Grey, who came up in 1742, and Henry Cavendish, the first person to measure the density of water. He also calculated the weight of the planet: if you must know, Earth weighs six thousand million million tonnes.

First Court, the oldest, is small, neat and bright, with hanging baskets and window boxes. The 17th-century chapel is on the right, built in a mixture of styles that blend well. Inside the luminous 19th-century stained-glass windows contrast with the older eastern window.

The Burrough range, on the right, is 18th century and the hall, on the left, a restored, late 13th-century gem. Beyond the hall are sweeping grounds extending to the Fitz-william Museum. Bearing right, you enter a court with an octagonal lawn, beyond which are the library, theatre and First Court.

Pembroke College Pembroke (☎ 338100) has several courts linked by lovely gardens and lawns. It was founded in 1347 by Marie de St Pol de Valence, the widowed countess of Pembroke. At 17 she'd married the 50-year-old earl, but he was killed in a joust on their wedding day, making her 'maid, wife and widow all in one day'. As usual, the oldest court is at the entrance. It still retains some medieval corner sections. The chapel, on the extreme right, is an early Wren creation (1665): his uncle Mathew Wren, bishop of Ely, had spent 18 years imprisoned in the Tower of London courtesy of Oliver Cromwell, and had promised that if released he would build a chapel in his old college.

Crossing Old Court diagonally, walk past the handsome Victorian dining hall and into charming Ivy Court. Walk through and round the corner to see a sweeping lawn with an impressive statue of Pitt the Younger (prime minister in the 18th century) outside the ornate library clock tower.

Continue through the garden past the green where students play croquet after exams in summer, and out, right, into Pembroke St.

Emmanuel College Founded in 1584, this is a medium-sized college (☎ 334200; St Andrew's St), comprising a community of some 600 people.

If you stand in Front Court, one of the architectural gems of Cambridge faces you – the Wren chapel, cloister and gallery, completed in 1677. To the left is the hall; inside, the refectory-type tables are set at right angles to the high table.

The next court, New Court, is round the corner. It has a quaint herb garden reminiscent of the old Dominican priory that preceded the college.

There are a few remnants of the priory in the *clunch* (chalk) core of the walls of the Old Library. Turn right to re-enter Front Court and go into the chapel. It has interesting windows, a high ceiling and a painting by Jacopo Amigoni. Near the side door is a plaque to a famous scholar, John Harvard (BA 1632), who was among 30 Emmanuel men who settled in New England. He left money to found the university that bears his name in the Massachusetts town of Cambridge. His portrait also features in one of the stained-glass windows but, as the artist had no likeness of Harvard from which to work, he used the face of John Milton, a contemporary of Harvard's at the college.

Fitzwilliam Museum

This massive neoclassical edifice (☎ 332900; Trumpington St; admission free; open 10am-5pm Tues-Sat, 2.15pm-5pm Sun) with its vast portico takes its name from the seventh Viscount Fitzwilliam, who bequeathed his fabulous art treasures to his old university in 1816. The building in which they are stored was begun by George Basevi in 1837, but he did not live to see its completion in 1848: while working on Ely Cathedral he stepped back to admire his handiwork, slipped and fell to his death. It was one of the first public art museums in Britain.

In the lower galleries are ancient Egyptian sarcophagi and Greek and Roman art, as well as Chinese ceramics, English glass and illuminated manuscripts.

The upper galleries contain a wide range of paintings, including works by Titian, Rubens, the French Impressionists, Gainsborough, Stubbs and Constable, right up to Cézanne and Picasso. It also has fine antique furniture. There are guided tours at 2.30pm on Sunday.

How to Punt

Punting looks pretty straightforward but, believe us, it's not. No sooner had we dried off and hung our clothes on the line, we thought it was a good idea to offer a couple of tips on how to move the boat and stay dry.

1. Standing at the end of the punt, lift the pole out of the water at the side of the punt.
2. Let the pole slide through your hands to touch the bottom of the river.
3. Tilt the pole forward (that is, in the direction of travel of the punt) and push down to propel the punt forward.
4. Twist the pole to free the end from the mud at the bottom of the river, and let it float up and trail behind the punt. You can then use it as a rudder to steer with.
5. If you've not yet fallen in, raise the pole out of the water and into the vertical position to begin the cycle again.

Kettle's Yard

This house (cnr Northampton & Castle Sts; admission free; open 11.30pm-5pm Tues-Sun) was the home of HS 'Jim' Ede, a former assistant keeper at the Tate Gallery in London, and his wife Helen. In 1957 they opened their home to young artists with a view toward creating 'a home and a welcome, a refuge of peace and order, of the visual arts and of music'. Their efforts resulted in a beautiful collection of 20th-century art, furniture, ceramics and glass by such artists as Henry Moore, Henri Gaudier-Brzeska and a host of other Britons. In 1966 they donated their home and collection to the university, which opened it as a museum (☎ 352124; admission free; open 2pm-4pm Tues-Sun) but didn't touch the arrangement of the pieces. In the adjoining exhibition gallery (opened 1970) there are temporary exhibits of contemporary art.

Punting

Taking a punt along the Backs is sublime, but it can also be a wet and hectic experience, especially on a busy weekend. Look before you leap.

If you do wimp out, you can opt for a chauffeured punt, and if the water doesn't attract you at all, the Backs are also perfect for a walk or a picnic.

There's a host of places where you can rent punts. Trinity Punts (☎ 338483), behind Trinity College, charges £8 per hour (plus £30 deposit). The Granta pub (see Entertainment) also charges £8 per hour with a £40 deposit. Down by Silver St, Scudamore's (☎ 359750) charges £12 per hour plus £60 deposit or a credit card imprint. Chauffeured punts here cost £40 per punt and the trip lasts 45 minutes. Due to the traffic on the Cam, between 1 and 6pm the punts carry a maximum of 12 people; at other times they can carry up to 18.

Punting the 3 miles (5km) up the river to the idyllic village of Grantchester makes a great day out.

Walking & Cycling Routes

One of the prettiest walks in the whole region is the 3-mile (5km) walk to Grantchester from Cambridge along the River Cam. More of a gentle stroll than a walk, all you have to do is follow the meander of the river as it winds its way southwest – in fine weather the river is full of punts.

For tootling around town by bike, the flat topography makes things easy, although beyond the city the scenery can get a bit monotonous. The TIC stocks the useful guide *Cycle Routes and the Cambridge Green Belt Area*, and the *Cambridge Cycle Route Map*.

Organised Tours
Guide Friday/City Sightseeing (☎ 362444) runs five hop-on hop-off tour buses around the city, calling at the train station. Tours are daily, year round. Tickets cost £7.50/3.

Riverboat Georgina (☎ 500111) runs two-hour cruises from the river at Jesus Lock for £7/8.50 day/evening. From April to September there are departures at 1pm and 6pm, with more frequent departures in mid-season.

Places to Stay
Camping & Hostels Highfield Farm Touring Park (☎/fax 262308; Long Rd, Comberton; 2-person tents Apr-June, Sept & Oct £7.75, July & Aug £9.25; open Apr-Oct) is 4½ miles (7km) southwest of Cambridge.

Cambridge YHA Hostel (☎ 0870 770 5742, fax 312780; 97 Tenison Rd; dorm beds adult members £12.75, nonmembers £14.75) has small dormitories and a restaurant near the train station.

B&Bs There are numerous B&Bs to choose from at any time of the year, even more during university holidays from late June to late September.

YMCA (☎ 356998, fax 312749; Gonville Place; singles/doubles £23/37, per week £130/224) has bargain weekly rates; the rooms are clean and very tidy.

Tenison Towers Guest House (☎ 363924; 148 Tenison Rd; rooms per person £22-30) is an excellent B&B with clean, comfortable rooms and attentive service.

The Ark (☎ 311130; 30 St Matthew's St; singles/doubles from £27/38) has prettily appointed rooms painted in bright, airy colours. The service is friendly and very courteous.

Warkworth House (☎ 363682, fax 369655; Warkworth Terrace; singles/doubles from £39/56) is a lovely Victorian terraced house just off Parkside, with comfortable rooms. The breakfast is delicious and the owner is extremely friendly. It is popular with students from overseas.

There are plenty of B&Bs north of the city around Chesterton Rd.

Antony's (☎ 357444; 4 Huntingdon Rd; singles/doubles/triples from £20/30/44) is spacious and comfortable, with four singles, four doubles and three triples.

Benson House (☎/fax 311594; 24 Huntingdon Rd; singles/doubles from £30/45) is elegant, with well-equipped doubles with en-suite showers.

Dykelands (☎ 244300, fax 566746; e dyke lands@fsbdial.co.uk; 157 Mowbray Rd; singles/doubles from £30/38) is an excellent choice, albeit a little far from the action, just south of the train station. The rooms, all furnished in pine, are extremely comfortable. Its location will be no problem to cyclists.

Aaron House (☎ 314723; 71 Chesterton Rd; singles £30-34, doubles £48-64) is a Victorian home that was the birthplace of a former Archbishop of Canterbury, Arthur Ramsey. All rooms have an en suite.

Acorn Guest House (☎ 353888, fax 350527; 154 Chesterton Rd; singles £35-50, doubles £50-70), farther east along Chesterton Rd, has spotless rooms, all with en-suite bathroom.

Carlton Lodge (☎ 367792, fax 566877; e info@carltonlodge.co.uk; 245 Chesterton Rd; singles/doubles from £19/38) is run by widely travelled, friendly people. The rooms are comparatively large and well appointed.

Hotels Sleeperz (☎ 304050, fax 357286; e info@sleeperz.com; Station Rd; singles/doubles from £30/45), right outside the train station, is an attractively converted railway warehouse. Rates include breakfast. Rooms with a double bed are larger; all others have cabin-style bunk beds.

Hamilton Hotel (☎ 365664, fax 314866; e enquiries@hamiltoncambridge.co.uk; 156 Chesterton Rd; singles £25-48, doubles £45-68) is a little shabby and the singles are tiny, but it's a clean, budget hotel that offers value for money.

Arundel House Hotel (☎ 367701, fax 367 721; e info@arundelhousehotels.co.uk; 53 Chesterton Rd; singles £67.50-89.50, doubles £85-115) is in a large Victorian terrace overlooking the Cam. It's an elegant place, with beautiful rooms, all have an en suite.

Lensfield Hotel (☎ 355017, fax 312022; e enquiries@lensfieldhotel.co.uk; 53 Lensfield Rd; singles/doubles from £55/89), in the south near the Fitzwilliam Museum, has 32 well-appointed rooms. The service is terrific.

Garden House (*Moat House;* ☎ *259988, fax 316605; Granta Place, Mill Lane; singles/ doubles £169/200*) is a posh place in the centre right on the Cam with its own private garden. There are 117 luxurious bedrooms that have all been recently refurbished. Rates exclude breakfast. There are serious discounts on weekend rates.

De Vere University Arms Hotel (☎ *351241, fax 461319;* e *devere.uniarms@airtime.co.uk; Regent St; singles/doubles from £130/190*) is a huge Victorian mansion overlooking Parker's Piece. The elegant rooms were given a make-over in 2001, confirming the hotel's status as the best in town.

Places to Eat

There are literally hundreds of eateries in Cambridge, from gourmet restaurants to cheap 'n' cheerful cafés. Following is a list of our favourites.

Restaurants Overlooking the river on Midsummer Common, **Midsummer House** (☎ *369299; set lunch around £30.50, set dinner £46; open lunch Tues-Fri & Sun, dinner Tues-Sat*) is a smart, sophisticated place with a superb menu, and said to have one of the most comprehensive wine lists outside Paris. You may need to book several weeks in advance.

Twenty-two (☎ *351880; 22 Chesterton Rd; set dinner £29.95*), cleverly disguised in amongst the row of B&Bs, is probably the best restaurant in town. The gourmet menu is outstanding (mostly French) and the service is top notch.

Michel's Brasserie (☎ *353110; 21 North-ampton St; set lunches £8.95*) has set lunches and more expensive à la carte dinners. The French menu is excellent.

Mill Rd has many good restaurants, mostly of the North African and Indian variety.

Trattoria Pasta Fresca (☎ *352836; 66 Mill Rd; mains around £7*) is our favourite Italian restaurant in Cambridge: unpretentious, award-winning, very popular with every-one…need we say more? Yes, the food is simply delicious.

Al Casbah (☎ *579500; 62 Mill Rd; mains £6-9*) is a tasty Algerian restaurant with a really good couscous for £8.95. The food is cooked on an indoor barbecue.

The Gulshan (☎ *302330; 106 Regent St; mains from £5.95*) is our choice for Indian food in Cambridge, especially curry.

Rainbow (☎ *321551; 9a King's Parade; mains around £7*) is a good vegetarian restaurant with a wide range of options. It's across the road from King's College.

Yippee (☎ *518111; 7-9 King St; mains around £8*) is a newish Asian fusion place that has quickly become one of the best restaurants in town. Book at weekends.

Hobb's Pavilion (☎ *367480; Park Terrace; mains around £8; open Tues-Sat*) occupies the old cricket pavilion and specialises in filled pancakes. In summer, it's the best place in town.

Cafés **Clowns** (☎ *355711; 54 King St; sand-wiches around £2.50*) is a long-time student favourite and serves good-value light meals and sandwiches. It's a great spot for reading the newspaper.

Fitzbillies (☎ *352500; 52 Trumpington St*) is a brilliant bakery-café. The Chelsea buns (85p) are an outrageous experience and so is the chocolate cake beloved by generations of students, but there are many other tempta-tions in addition to the usual sandwiches and pies – stock up before you go punting. Cakes and buns are also available by mail order.

Tatties (☎ *323399; 11 Sussex St; everything £1-2.95*) has long been a budget favourite. It specialises not only in baked potatoes stuffed with a variety of tempting fillings but also in breakfasts, filled baguettes, salads and cakes.

Nadia's (*King's Parade • Silver St*) is a small chain of bakeries that are excellent value (for example, bacon sandwich and coffee for 95p before 10.30am). A smoked ham and Em-mental cheese baguette is £1.05.

Choices Café (☎ *360211; Newnham Rd*) will make up picnic hampers for punters for about £5 per person.

Entertainment

Pubs & Bars Punting is a big deal in Cam-bridge, at least with a certain section of the university population, and despite the fact that they have earned themselves somewhat of a reputation for being rowdy in the pub after a day's rowing, the punting pubs – where rowers hang out and tourists can rent punts – are definitely worth checking out.

Fort St George (*Midsummer Common*) is said to be the oldest pub on the Cam, dating from the 16th century. The location is perfect: on the river at the north end of Midsummer

Common, it's a popular spot, particularly in summer. You can rent punts from here.

Granta *(Newnham Rd)* is another pub with punt hire beside it. Inside, it's a popular rower's pub.

Boathouse *(14 Chesterton Rd)* can be visited by punt and even has its own mooring place.

Away from the Cam, Cambridge has plenty of atmospheric pubs and trendy bars.

The Eagle *(Bene't St)* appealed to Nobelprize-winning scientists Crick and Watson, who spent equal time in the laboratory and here, so perhaps Greene King, the Suffolk brewers, played a part in the discovery of the structure of DNA. This 16th-century pub was also popular with American airmen in WWII; they left their signatures on the ceiling.

Champion of the Thames *(68 King St)* is not remotely connected with punting, despite the name. This is just an old-style traditional pub, with live music on Tuesday. It's a wonderful spot for a pint of ale.

St Radegund *(127 King St)* is a tiny, gorgeous pub that's popular with locals.

If you're looking for bars with a more contemporary feel, there's plenty of choice.

Henry's *(Quayside)*, in the warm weather, overflows with students enjoying a full on party by the Cam.

Bar Ha! Ha! *(17 Trinity St)* is popular with the trendy young things.

Venue *(66 Regent St)* is a bar above a restaurant of the same name, and where you'll find the best cocktails in town.

Sophbeck Sessions *(14 Tredgold La)* is an oddly named Cajun-style bar in the northeast of town that's popular among students and visitors alike as a good place to have a drink and enjoy some jazz and soul.

Clubs The place to go if clubbing is your thing, **Fez** *(☎ 519224; 15 Market Passage; admission £2-7, free before 9pm Mon & Wed; open 8pm-2pm Mon-Sat)* has queues most nights and the music is loud and thumping. Admission varies depending on the night.

Po Na Na Souk Bar *(☎ 323880; 7b Jesus Lane; admission £1.50; open to 2am)* is a terrific bar and club in the basement of a neoclassical building. The style is Moroccan kasbah, and the DJs spin a mix of Latin, house and other funky rhythms.

Fifth Avenue *(☎ 364222; Heidelburg Gardens, Lion Yard; admission around £7)* is also

popular; it's a bit of a meat market, but shopping can be good fun. It's a slice of Ibiza in Cambridge.

Theatre Corn Exchange *(☎ 357851)*, near the TIC, is the city's main centre for arts and entertainment, attracting the top names in pop and rock as well as more classical artists, such as the English National Ballet.

Arts Theatre *(☎ 503333; 6 St Edward's Passage)* is Cambridge's only real theatre, putting on everything from pantomime to serious dramatic works.

The King's College Choir is unique to Cambridge – don't miss it. See the King's College Chapel entry in the earlier Walking Tour One section.

Getting There & Away

Cambridge can easily be visited as a day trip from London (although it's worth staying at least a night) or en route north. It's well served by trains, though not so well by bus.

Bus National Express has hourly buses to London (£8, 2½ hours), and four buses per day to/from Bristol (£21, six hours). Unfortunately, connections to the north aren't straightforward. To get to Lincoln or York you'll have to change at Peterborough or Nottingham, respectively. King's Lynn is also only accessible via Peterborough – it's easier to take a train.

Airlink/Jetlink *(☎ 0870 5757747)* runs the Inter-Varsity Link via Stansted airport (£6) to Oxford (£16, three hours, six per day). It also runs buses to Heathrow (£22) and Gatwick (£26) airports.

Train There are trains every 30 minutes from London's King's Cross and Liverpool St stations (£24.60, 55 minutes). There are also hourly connections to Bury St Edmunds (£9.90, 45 minutes), Ely (£3.60, 15 minutes) and King's Lynn (£13.80, 50 minutes). You can connect at Peterborough with the main northbound trains to Lincoln, York and Edinburgh. If you want to head west to Oxford or Bath you'll have to return to London first.

Getting Around

Most vehicles are now banned from the centre of Cambridge. It's best to use the five, well-signposted Park & Ride car parks (£1.25) located on the outskirts of town.

EASTERN ENGLAND

Shuttle buses run between the centre and the car parks between 7am and 7pm daily.

Bus A free, gas-powered shuttle stops at Emmanuel St in the centre. Four bus lines (85p to £1.25) run around town from Drummer St, including bus No 3 from the train station to the town centre. Dayrider passes (£2.50) offer unlimited travel on all buses within Cambridge for one day; megarider passes (£7) are valid for one week.

Taxi For a taxi, phone **Cabco** (☎ 312444). Unless you have a lot of luggage, it's not really worth taking one from the train station to the centre. It costs between £3.50 and £3.80 and takes about 10 minutes; you can walk it in about 25 minutes.

Bicycle It's easy enough to get around Cambridge on foot but, if you're staying out of the centre, or plan to explore the Fens, a bicycle can be useful. You don't need a flash mountain bike because there are few hills; most places rent three-speeds. **Ben Hayward Cycles** (☎ 355229; w www.benhaywardcycles .com; 69 Trumpington St) rents bikes for £12 per day from mid-May to mid-October. You can book online. **Geoff's Bike Hire** (☎ 365629; 65 Devonshire Rd), near the youth hostel, charges £8 per day and £16 per week but gives a 10% discount to YHA members. **Cambridge Recycles** (☎ 506035; 61 Newnham Rd) charges £8 to £10 per day. **Mike's Bikes** (☎ 312591; 28 Mill Rd) also charges £8 per day or £10 per week (plus £50 deposit) for a bike with no gears.

AROUND CAMBRIDGE
Grantchester
Three miles (5km) southeast from Cambridge, Grantchester is a delightful village of thatched cottages and flower-filled meadows beside the Granta River.

Its quintessential Englishness was recognised by the poet Rupert Brooke, who was a student at King's before WWI, in the immortal lines: 'Stands the church clock still at 10 to three, And is there honey still for tea?' Grantchester's most famous resident is the novelist Jeffrey Archer, who nominally lives at the Old Vicarage but is currently residing At Her Majesty's Pleasure for perjury (although he will probably have been released by the time you read this).

The Fens

The Fens were strange marshlands that stretched from Cambridge north to The Wash and beyond into Lincolnshire. They were home to people who led an isolated existence fishing, hunting and farming scraps of arable land among a maze of waterways. In the 17th century, however, the duke of Bedford and a group of speculators brought in Dutch engineer Sir Cornelius Vermuyden to drain the Fens and the flat, open plains with their rich, black soil were created. The region is the setting for Graham Swift's excellent novel *Waterland*.

As the world's weather pattern changes and the sea level rises, the Fens are beginning to disappear underwater again. It's estimated that by the year 2030 up to 400,000 hectares could be lost.

There are teashops, some attractive pubs and the **Orchard Tea-garden**, where cream teas are served under apple trees. The best of the pubs is the **Red Lion**, near the river, which has a very pleasant garden.

Walk here via the towpath or hire a punt.

American War Cemetery
Four miles (6.5km) west of Cambridge, at Madingley, is a very moving cemetery (☎ 01954-210350; open 8am-5.30pm daily 16 Apr-30 Sept, 8am-5pm Oct-15 Apr) with neat rows of white-marble crosses stretching down the sloping site to commemorate 3811 Americans killed in battle while based in Britain. The latest soldier to be buried here died during the Gulf War in 1991.

You can visit the cemetery as part of a City Sightseeing tour (see Organised Tours under Cambridge earlier).

Imperial War Museum
Military hardware enthusiasts should head for this war museum (☎ 01223-835000; adult/child £8/4; open 10am-6pm daily mid-Mar–Sept, 10am-4pm Oct–mid-Mar) in Duxford, 9 miles (14.5km) south of Cambridge right by the motorway. The museum is housed in an airfield that played a significant role in WWII, especially during the Battle of Britain. It was the home of the famous Dambuster squadron of Lancasters, and today is home to the Royal Airforce's

Red Arrows squadron, which performs all kinds of celestial trickery at air shows throughout the world.

Here you'll find Europe's biggest collection of historic aircraft, ranging from WWI biplanes to jets, including Concorde. The American Air Museum, designed by Norman Foster, is also on the site. It has the largest collection of American civil and military aircraft outside of the United States. Air shows are frequently held here and battlefield scenes are displayed in the land warfare hall, where you can check out WWII tanks and artillery. Kids will enjoy the adventure playground and the flight simulator.

The museum runs courtesy buses – the price of the journey is included in the admission – from Cambridge train station every 40 to 50 minutes between 9.40am and 3.40pm (until 2.20pm October to mid-March); they also stop outside the Crowne Plaza Hotel by the Lionyard.

Wimpole Hall

A large, gracious, 18th-century mansion set in 140 hectares of beautiful parkland, Wimpole Hall (NT; ☎ 01223-207257; adult/child £6.20/2.80, including Home Farm £9/4.50; farm open 10.30am-4pm Tues-Thur, Sat & Sun Mar-Nov; 10.30am-5pm July & Aug; hall open 1pm-5pm Tues-Thur, Sat & Sun) was the home of Rudyard Kipling's daughter until her death in 1976. Wimpole Home Farm, next to it, was established in 1794 as a model farm; today, it preserves and shows rare breeds.

Wimpole Hall is 8 miles (13km) south of Cambridge on the A603. There's no charge to just walk in the park, which is open dawn til dusk year round.

Whippet service No 175 passes this way from Cambridge. Alternatively, you could try walking the Wimpole Way, a 13-mile (21km) waymarked trail from Cambridge. A leaflet is available from the TIC in Cambridge.

ELY

☎ 01353 • pop 9000

Ely (pronounced ee-lee) is an unspoilt, gracious market town with neat Georgian houses, a river port and one of the country's great cathedrals. Today it stands in the centre of the Fens, but at one time it was an island, and derived its name from the eels that swam in the surrounding waters.

Orientation & Information

Ely is tiny, so you'll have no problems getting around.

The **TIC** (☎ 662062, fax 668518; 29 St Mary's St; open 10am-5.30pm daily Apr-Sept, 10am-5pm Mon-Sat, 11.15am-4pm Sun Oct-Mar) is in Oliver Cromwell's House.

A combined ticket, the 'passport to Ely', is available for £9 (£7 for students) for the main sights – Ely Cathedral, the stained glass museum, Ely Museum and Oliver Cromwell's House. There's a farmer's market held in Market Place from 8.30am to 3.30pm on Saturday twice a month; check with the TIC for details.

The **police station** is at the corner of Egremont St and Lynn Rd, and there's a branch of **Lloyd's TSB** bank, with ATM, on High St.

Ely Cathedral

The origins of the cathedral (☎ 667735; admission £4; open 7am-7pm daily Easter-Aug, 7.30am-6pm Mon-Sat, 7.30am-5pm Sun Sept-Easter) stem from a remarkable queen of Northumbria, Etheldreda. She had married twice but was determined to pursue her vocation to become a nun. She founded an abbey in 673 and, for her good works, was canonised after her death. The abbey soon became a pilgrimage centre.

It was a Norman bishop, Simeon, who began the task of building the cathedral. It was completed in 1189 and remains a splendid example of the Norman Romanesque style. In 1322 – after the collapse of the central tower – the octagon and lantern, for which the cathedral is famous, were built. They have fan vaulting and intricate detail.

Other features of special interest include the Lady Chapel, the largest of its kind in England, which was added in the 14th century. The niches were rifled by iconoclasts but the delicate tracery and carving remain intact. There's an amazing view from just inside the western door – right down the nave, through the choir stalls and on to the glorious eastern window – no clutter, just a sublime sense of space, light and spirituality.

Ely was the first cathedral in the country to charge admission and, with funds gathered since 1986, it has managed to restore the octagon and lantern tower. There are free guided tours of the cathedral and also an octagon and roof tour (£4 extra). There's a **stained glass museum** (adult/child £3.50/2.50) in the south

EASTERN ENGLAND

602 Cambridgeshire – Ely

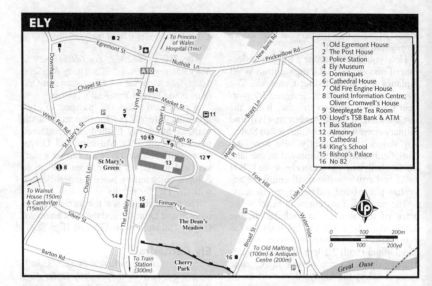

triforium. Choral Sunday service is at 10.30am and evensong is at 5.30pm Monday to Saturday, 3.45pm on Sunday.

Other Things to See & Do

The area around the cathedral is historically and architecturally interesting. There's the Bishop's Palace, now a nursing home, and King's School, which supplies the cathedral with choristers.

Oliver Cromwell's House (☎ 662062; *adult/child £3.50/2.75*) stands to the west, across St Mary's Green. Cromwell lived with his family in this attractive, half-timbered, 14th-century house from 1636 to 1646, when he was the tithe collector of Ely. The TIC, occupying the front room in the house, offers an audiovisual presentation and an interesting tour of the rooms.

The history of the town is told in **Ely Museum** (☎ 666655; *adult/child £2/ free; open 10.30am-5.30pm daily May-Oct, 10.30am-4.30pm daily Nov-Apr*), in the Old Gaol House.

It's worth walking down to the river by following the signs. There is an interesting **antiques centre** near the river. The **Old Maltings** (☎ 662633; *Ship Lane*), which stages exhibitions and has a café (the Waterfront Brasserie) is nearby.

River Great Ouse is a busy thoroughfare – swans and ducks compete with boats

for river space. The towpath winds up and downstream: for a quiet walk, turn left; turn right for the pub and tea garden. If you continue along this path you'll see the Fens stretching to the horizon.

Places to Stay

There are few budget options in Ely. There are several B&Bs on Egremont St.

Old Egremont House (☎ 663118, fax 666 968; *31 Egremont St; singles/doubles £45/54*) is an attractive house with a large garden.

The Post House (☎ 667184; *12a Egremont St; singles/doubles £20/40*) is unmissable with the Union flag raised outside; the rooms are plain but comfortable.

No 82 (☎ 667609, fax 667005; *82 Broad St; singles/doubles £20/40*) is a pleasant Georgian house with four neat rooms.

Walnut House (☎ 661793, fax 663519; e walnuthouse1@aol.com; *1 Houghton Gardens; singles/doubles £25/50*) is large and gorgeous, with beautifully appointed rooms.

Cathedral House (☎/fax 662124; e farm dale@cathedralhouse.co.uk; *17 St Mary's St; singles/doubles £35/50*) offers very comfortable B&B accommodation.

Places to Eat

Eels are a local delicacy served in several of the restaurants.

Old Fire Engine House (☎ 662582; St Mary's St; mains about £12; open Mon-Sat), Ely's best restaurant, is a good place to try eels. It's more like the comfortable house of a friend than a restaurant, with excellent food.

Dominiques (☎ 665011; St Mary's St; mains around £5) serves cream teas, as well as lunches and set dinners. Totally non-smoking, it has good vegetarian choices.

Steeplegate Tea Room (☎ 664731; 16 High St) is right beside the cathedral, upstairs from a craft shop. Light lunches and baked potatoes from £2.50 are available.

Almonry (☎ 666360), to the left of the Lady Chapel, close to Steeplegate Tea Room, is virtually in the grounds of the cathedral. This attractive garden restaurant has a wide range of teas and coffees.

Getting There & Away

Ely is on the A10, 15 miles (24km) northeast of Cambridge and an easy day trip. Following the Fen Rivers Way (map available from TICs); it's a 17-mile (27km) walk.

Bus Nos X11 and X12 run every half-hour from Cambridge's Drummer St bus station (£3.30, one hour). The X8, which runs hourly to King's Lynn from Cambridge, is quicker, taking only 45 minutes to reach Ely.

By train, there are hourly departures from Cambridge (£3.60, 15 minutes). From Ely, there are hourly trains to Peterborough (£7.20, 35 minutes) and half-hourly trains to King's Lynn (£9, 1½ hours) and Norwich (12.10, 55 minutes).

PETERBOROUGH

☎ 01733 • pop 156,600

Peterborough likes to advertise itself as the capital city of shopping and, while this may do wonders for the retail trade, it does precious little for tourism, especially the kind familiar with British shopping centres and high-street chain stores. Yet Peterborough is home to a wonderful cathedral that is worth visiting, but only just. Luckily, it's an easy day trip from Cambridge.

The cathedral precinct is an extension of the busy Cowgate, Bridge St and Queensgate. The TIC (☎ 452336, fax 452353; e tic@peterborough.gov.uk; 45 Bridge St; open 8.45am-5pm Mon-Wed & Fri, 10am-5pm Thur, 10am-4pm Sat), is nearby. The bus and train stations are within walking distance of the TIC, just west of the city centre.

Peterborough Cathedral

In Anglo-Saxon times, when the region was part of the kingdom of Mercia, King Peada, a recent convert to Christianity, founded a monastic church here in 655. This was sacked and gutted by the Danes in 870. In 1118 the Benedictine abbot John de Sais founded the present cathedral (☎ 343342; requested donation £3; open 9am-6.15pm daily) as the monastic church of the Benedictine abbey. It was finally consecrated in 1237.

As you enter the precinct from Cathedral Square you get a breathtaking view of the early 13th-century western front, one of the most impressive of any cathedral in Britain.

On entering you're struck by the height of the nave and the lightness, which derives not only from the mellow Barnack stone (quarried close by and transported via the River Nene) but also from the clerestory windows. The nave, with its three storeys, is an impressive example of Norman architecture. Its unique timber ceiling is one of the earliest of its kind in England (possibly in Europe) and its original painted decoration has been preserved.

The Gothic tower replaced the original Norman one, but had to be taken down and carefully reconstructed after it began to crack in the late 19th century.

In the northern choir aisle is the tombstone of Henry VIII's first wife, the tragic Catherine of Aragon, buried here in 1536. Her divorce, engineered by the king because she could not produce a male heir, led to the Reformation in England. Her only child (a daughter) was not even allowed to attend her funeral. Every 29 January there is a procession in the cathedral to mark the death of Catherine.

Directly opposite, in the southern aisle, two standards mark what was the grave of Mary Queen of Scots. On the accession of her son, James, to the throne, her body was moved to Westminster Abbey.

The eastern end of the cathedral, known as the New Building, was added in the 15th century. It has superb fan vaulting, probably the work of master mason John Wastell, who worked on King's College Chapel in Cambridge.

Places to Stay & Eat

Anchor Lodge (☎ 312724; 28 Percival St; singles/doubles £44/54) is a gorgeous B&B

with large, well-appointed rooms close to the city centre.

Bull Hotel (☎ 561364, fax 557304; Westgate; singles/doubles £99/110), about 200m from the train station, is a good spot for business travellers, with very comfortable, functional rooms. Breakfast is extra.

Central Peterborough is full of eateries. The **Nip In Café** (☎ 603835; Hereward Cross; mains around £4.50) is a pretty nice place for a bite.

Getting There & Away

Peterborough is 37 miles (60km) north of Cambridge. **Stagecoach United Counties** (☎ 01604-620077) and National Express run buses from Cambridge (£7.25, one hour); some services require a change in Huntingdon. There are hourly trains from Cambridge (£9.60, 55 minutes).

Lincolnshire

Sneering southerners tend to dismiss Lincolnshire as dull and dour, but chances are they've never actually set foot in the county. What they would discover, however, is just the contrary, as Lincolnshire is not just pretty, but pretty friendly too.

This is particularly true of Lincoln, the county capital. At the heart of the gorgeous old town is the cathedral, one of the finest Gothic buildings in Europe, built on the proceeds of a flourishing wool trade. Lincolnshire's commercial acumen is also evident in the lovely, unspoilt towns spread throughout the rest of the county. Beautiful parish churches – for which the county is famous – stand cheek-to-jowl with solid stone-built houses with red-tiled roofs to create an 'olde Englande' look that has attracted a number of film companies looking for an appropriate period setting in which to shoot.

Lincolnshire is also thought of as pretty flat, but the landscape is actually quite diverse. The county is made up of several distinct landscapes, from the hilly countryside of the western county to the flat marshlands of the east. The Lincolnshire Wolds, to the north and east of Lincoln, are comprised of low rolling hills and small market towns. To the southeast, the flat Lincolnshire Fens is fertile agricultural land reclaimed from the sea. The whole area is crisscrossed by a network of rivers and dykes, while the coastline to the east is marked by wide sandy beaches as well as salt marshes, dunes and pools.

It's easy cycling and walking country, and the weather is a great plus: Lincolnshire receives only half the national average of rainfall, hence the county's slogan, 'the drier side of Britain'.

Activities

Lincolnshire is not renowned as a walking area, but if you want a long route, from the sea to the Midlands in the footsteps of history, try the Viking Way; a 140-mile (225km), waymarked trail that runs from the Humber Bridge, through the Lincolnshire Wolds, to Oakham in Leicestershire. For a short taster, you can focus on the section in Lincolnshire Wolds and use the route as a base for a day-walk.

Renting a bike in Lincoln, or bringing one with you, is an excellent idea. TICs stock sets of *Lincolnshire Cycle Trails*.

Getting There & Away

Stamford and Lincoln are easily reached by bus from London, as are Glasgow and Birmingham. However, Lincolnshire is not quite on the well-trodden transport trail, and your best bet for getting here from the south is probably by train, although if you're planning to visit the county from Cambridge you'll most likely have to change in Peterborough.

Getting Around

Regional transport is poor but the main routes are well enough served by train or bus. The national **Travel Line** (☎ 0870 608 2608) has details of bus and rail times for the county; once you've dialled, press option 4.

LINCOLN

☎ 01522 • pop 81,987

Lincoln is tougher to get to than York, so many visitors give Lincoln a miss and rush to marvel at its great rival's wonderful cathedral instead. Unfortunately, they are losing out on Lincoln's own 900-year-old mother church, the third largest in England and one of the finest examples of Early English architecture in the country. Lincoln's unattractive and depressing suburbs don't do the city's tourist authorities any favours, but hidden inside the bland outskirts is a compact medieval centre with some won-

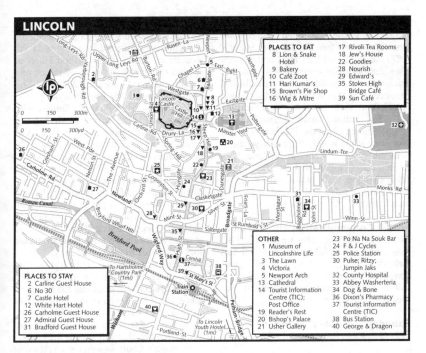

LINCOLN

PLACES TO EAT
8 Lion & Snake Hotel
9 Bakery
10 Café Zoot
11 Hari Kumar's
15 Brown's Pie Shop
16 Wig & Mitre
17 Rivoli Tea Rooms
18 Jew's House
22 Goodies
28 Nourish
29 Edward's
35 Stokes High Bridge Café
39 Sun Café

PLACES TO STAY
2 Carline Guest House
6 No 30
7 Castle Hotel
12 White Hart Hotel
26 Carholme Guest House
27 Admiral Guest House
31 Bradford Guest House

OTHER
1 Museum of Lincolnshire Life
3 The Lawn
4 Victoria
5 Newport Arch
13 Cathedral
14 Tourist Information Centre (TIC); Post Office
19 Reader's Rest
20 Bishop's Palace
21 Usher Gallery
23 Po Na Na Souk Bar
24 F & J Cycles
25 Police Station
30 Pulse; Ritzy; Jumpin Jaks
32 County Hospital
33 Abbey Washerteria
34 Dog & Bone
36 Dixon's Pharmacy
37 Tourist Information Centre (TIC)
38 Bus Station
40 George & Dragon

derful Tudor architecture and one of the steepest urban climbs this side of San Francisco. The people, largely spared the tourist hordes, are particularly friendly, while the presence of a university means that there are plenty of young people around.

History

For the last 2000 years, most of Britain's invaders have recognised the potential of this site and made their mark. Lincoln's hill is of immense strategic importance, giving views for miles across the surrounding plain. Communications were found to be excellent – below it is the River Witham, navigable to the sea.

The Romans established a garrison and a town they called Lindum. In AD 71 it was given the status of a colonia, or chartered town (Lindum Colonia); hence Lincoln. Gracious public buildings were constructed and it became a popular place for old soldiers past their prime to spend their twilight years.

The Normans began work on the castle in 1068 and the cathedral in 1072. In the 12th century the wool trade developed and wealthy merchants established themselves.

The city was famous for the cloth known as Lincoln green, said to have been worn by Robin Hood. Many of the wealthiest merchants were Jews but, following the murder of a nine-year-old boy in 1255 for which one of their number was accused, they were mercilessly persecuted, many being driven out.

During the Civil War the city passed from Royalist to Parliamentarian and back again, but it began to prosper as an agricultural centre in the 18th century. In the following century, after the arrival of the railway, Lincoln's engineering industry was established. Heavy machinery produced here included the world's first tank, which saw action in WWI.

Orientation & Information

The cathedral stands imperiously on top of the hill in the centre of the old part of the city, with the castle and most of the other attractions located conveniently nearby. Three-quarters of a mile down from the cathedral (a 15-minute walk) lies the new town, and the bus and train stations. Joining the two is the appositely named Steep Hill, and believe us, they're not kidding. Even locals stop to catch their breath.

EASTERN ENGLAND

Tourist Offices The TIC (☎ 873213, fax 873214; 9 Castle Hill; open 9am-5.30pm Mon-Fri & 10am-5pm Sat-Sun year round • ☎ 873256, fax 873257; 21 The Cornhill; open 10am-5pm Mon-Sat year round) is in the old black-and-white building near the cathedral entrance. It has recently opened a second branch down in the new town, near the river.

Guided walking tours (adult/child £3/ 1.50, 1½ hours) from the TIC in Castle Hill take place at 11am and 2.15pm daily June to September, and at weekends in June, September and October. New in 2002 was a 1¼-hour ghost walk (adult/child £3/2) on Wednesday, Friday and Saturday at 7pm, also from the TIC in Castle Hill.

Post & Communication The post office (☎ 526031; 90 Bailgate) is next to the TIC. You can check email at the excellent **Sun Café** (☎ 579067; 7 St Mary's St; open 8am-8pm daily), directly across from the train station. Internet access costs £2 for 30 minutes (see also Places to Eat).

Laundry The **Abbey Washeteria** (☎ 530 272; 197 Monks Rd) charges £5.50 per load.

Medical Services There are plenty of pharmacies in town, including a branch of **Dixon's** (☎ 524821; 194 High St). The **County Hospital** (☎ 573103) is half a mile east of the TIC, just off Greetwell Rd.

Emergency The **police station** (☎ 882222) is on West Parade.

Cathedral

This superb cathedral (☎ 544544; adult/child £3.50/3; open 7.15am-8pm Mon-Sat, 7.15am-6pm Sun June-Aug; 7.15am-6pm Mon-Sat, 7.15am-5pm Sun Sept-May) is the county's greatest attraction. Its three great towers dominate the city and can be seen from miles around. The central tower stands 81m high, which makes it the third-highest in the country after Salisbury Cathedral (123m) and Liverpool's Anglican Cathedral (101m). While this is impressive enough, imagine it twice as high, which it was until toppled by a storm in 1547.

Lincoln Cathedral was built on the orders of William the Conqueror and construction began in 1072. It took only 20 years to complete the original building, which was 99m

long with two western towers, but in 1185 an earthquake caused severe damage. Only the western front of the old cathedral survived. Rebuilding began under Bishop Hugh of Avalon (St Hugh) and most of the current building dates from the late 12th to late 13th centuries, in the Early English style.

The entrance is below the famous mid-12th-century frieze on the **western front**. Emerging into the **nave**, most people are surprised to find a substantial part of the cathedral empty, but this is actually how it would have looked back in 1250 when it was completed. Medieval cathedrals and churches, like mosques and Hindu temples today, did not have pews. This open area is now used for concerts and plays; services take place in St Hugh's choir. The stained glass in the nave is mostly Victorian, but the **Belgian marble font** dates back to the 11th century.

There are interesting stained-glass windows at each end of the transepts. The **Dean's Eye** contains glass that has been here since the 13th century; the glass in the **Bishop's Eye** dates from the 14th century. High above in the central tower, Great Tom is a 270kg bell that still sounds the hours.

St Hugh's Choir was the first section of the church to be rebuilt. The vaulting above is arranged at odd angles, but the canopied stalls of the choir are beautifully carved and over 600 years old.

The **Angel Choir**, named after the 28 angels carved high up the walls under the highest windows, was built as a shrine to St Hugh. Modern pilgrims search for the famous **Lincoln Imp**, a stonemason's joke that has become the city's emblem. The legend goes that this malevolent being was caught trying to chat up one of the 28 angels and was turned to stone.

There are free, one-hour tours of the cathedral at 11am, 1pm and 3pm daily; there's also a tour of the roof (one hour, maximum 14 people) beginning at 2pm.

There's evensong daily except Wednesday at 5.15pm (3.45pm on Sunday), and sung Eucharist at 9.30am on Sunday.

Bishops' Palace

Just south of the cathedral are the impressive ruins of the medieval Bishops' Palace (EH; ☎ 527468; admission £3; open 10am-6pm daily Apr-Sept, to 5pm Oct-Mar), which, had it not been gutted by parliamentary forces during the Civil War, would still be one of Lincoln's most imposing structures. It was begun in 1150 and in its day was the administrative centre of the largest diocese in England. The East Hall range, with its superb vaulted undercroft, was built by Bishop St Hugh around 1200 as his private residence.

The walled **terrace garden** is part of English Heritage's Contemporary Heritage Gardens scheme, and affords lovely views of the town below.

Lincoln Castle

Begun in 1068, just four years before the cathedral, the castle (*☎ 511068; adult/child £2.50/1; open 9.30am-5.30pm Mon-Sat, 11am--5.30pm Sun Apr-Sept, to 4pm daily Oct-Mar*) was built over the original Roman town and incorporates some of the old Roman walls. As well as the usual views from the battlements one expects from a castle, the old prison is particularly interesting. Public executions used to draw crowds of up to 20,000 people, and took place in front of Cobb Hall, a horseshoe-shaped tower in the northeastern corner that served as the city's prison for centuries. The redbrick building on the eastern side replaced it and was used until 1878.

In the same building as the chapel, Lincoln's copy of the Magna Carta is on display. There are free tours of the castle at 11am and 2pm daily, from April to September.

Walking Tour

After looking around the cathedral and the castle, leave by the castle's western exit. Across the road is **The Lawn** (*☎ 873622; Union Rd; open 9am-5pm Mon-Fri, 10am-5.30pm Sat & Sun; shorter hrs Nov-Feb*), a former lunatic asylum that now houses a concert hall and several exhibition areas. The **Sir Joseph Banks Conservatory**, in this complex, is a tropical glasshouse containing descendants of some of the plants brought back by this Lincoln explorer who accompanied Captain Cook to Australia.

A short walk up Burton Rd is the **Museum of Lincolnshire Life** (*☎ 528448; adult/child £2/60p; open 10am-5.30pm daily May-Sept, & 2pm-5.30pm Sun Oct-Apr*). It's a fairly interesting museum of local social history – displays include everything from an Edwardian nursery to a WWI tank built here.

Return to Westgate and continue east to Bailgate. Turn left to see the **Newport Arch**.

Built by the Romans, this is the oldest arch in Britain that still has traffic passing through it. Walk back along Bailgate and continue past the TIC down **Steep Hill**. There are several shops to tempt the tourist, including second-hand bookshops (the **Reader's Rest** is good) and teashops.

As well as the black-and-white Tudor buildings on Steep Hill, **Jew's House** is of particular interest, being one of the best examples of 12th-century domestic architecture in Britain. It's now an upmarket restaurant (see Places to Eat later). A few doors down is **Goodies** (*☎ 525307; 4 Steep Hill*), a traditional sweet shop that has 300 varieties in stock – bull's eyes, pear drops, sherbet lemons and humbugs. (Goodies is Lincs dialect for sweets/chocolate.)

Located one block east of Jew's House is the **Usher Gallery** (*☎ 527980; Lindum Rd; adult/child £2/50p, admission free on Fri; open 10am-5.30pm Mon-Sat, 2.30pm-5pm Sun*), the city's art gallery. Inside, the main focus is on the paintings and drawings of Peter de Wint (1784–1849) and on memorabilia associated with Lincolnshire-born Alfred Lord Tennyson (1809–92), the poet laureate.

Organised Tours

Besides the excellent tours laid on by the tourist office (see Information), there are also **Guide Friday bus tours** (*☎ 01789-294466*) of the town daily from April to September (£6/2.50).

Places to Stay

Camping & Hostels About 3 miles (5km) southwest of the train station you'll find **Hartsholme Country Park** (*☎ 873577; Skellingthorpe Rd; site & 2 people £4-8; open 31 Mar-31 Oct*). To get here, take the R66 bus from the main bus station in the direction of Birchwood Estate; ask the driver to drop you off (it's about a 20-minute ride).

Lincoln Youth Hostel (*☎ 0870 770 5918, fax 567424; 77 South Park Ave; beds per adult £11, doubles £19, 5-bed dorms £46.50; open daily Feb-Oct, Fri & Sat Nov & Dec*) provides good budget accommodation in various sized rooms.

B&Bs & Hotels Carholme Rd, just west of the town centre, has some excellent B&Bs.

Carholme Guest House (*☎ 531059, fax 511590; 175 Carholme Rd; singles/doubles*

£25/40) has five well-appointed rooms – all with en suite.

Admiral Guest House *(☎/fax 544467; 16-18 Nelson St; singles/doubles £25/38)* is a lovely 100-year-old house just off Carholme Rd with really comfortable rooms. Unusually, smokers can puff away in their rooms.

No 30 *(☎ 521417; 30 Bailgate; singles/ doubles £25/45)* has just two rooms in a beautiful Georgian town house about 250m from the cathedral. This is an excellent choice, but be sure to book as early as possible as it's always full.

Bradford Guest House *(☎ 523947; 67 Monks Rd; singles/doubles £25/40)* is another good choice. The neat and tidy rooms all have en-suite showers.

Carline Guest House *(☎/fax 530422; 1-3 Carline Rd; singles/doubles £30/44)* is more upmarket. The 12 rooms have been individually appointed and all have a private bathroom.

Castle Hotel *(☎ 538801, fax 575457; Westgate; singles/doubles from £62/84)*, directly across from the TIC, is in a restored 19th-century building. It's fancy and comfortable.

White Hart Hotel *(☎ 526222, fax 531 798; e heritagehotels-lincoln.white-hart@ forte-hotels.com; Bailgate; doubles £115)*, by the cathedral, is Lincoln's top hotel. It's a luxurious place with 48 beautifully appointed rooms.

Places to Eat

Lincoln has a number of excellent restaurants with fine gourmet menus, but cheaper cafés are also in plentiful supply.

Jew's House *(☎ 524851; Steep Hill; mains around £9)*, occupying a 12th-century building that's an attraction in its own right, is Lincoln's top restaurant.

Hari Kumar's *(☎ 537000; 80 Bailgate; mains £7-12)* is a stylish restaurant serving mostly Thai food, but with a couple of English dishes on the menu.

Brown's Pie Shop *(☎ 527330; 33 Steep Hill)* is close to the cathedral and popular with tourists. It's still worth eating here since pies are a Lincolnshire speciality. Rabbit pie with Dorset scrumpy costs £9, but there are cheaper options.

Café Zoot *(☎ 536663; 5 Bailgate; mains £4.95, specials £8)* is a pleasant café-style eatery near the TIC. The continental cuisine is excellent.

Lion & Snake Hotel *(☎ 523770)* was founded in 1640, which makes it Lincoln's oldest pub. Situated on the Bailgate, it's probably better known for its real ale and good-value, home-made bar food.

Wig & Mitre *(☎ 535190; 29 Steep Hill; mains around £8)* is near Brown's Pie Shop. It's a pub with a restaurant.

Edward's *(☎ 519144; 238 High St; mains £7-9)* is a large bar-brasserie where you can get everything from a coffee or a beer to a full meal.

Nourish *(☎ 576277; 1 Newland; all mains around £2.50; open 8am-3pm Mon-Fri, to 2pm Sat)* is a wonderful little café that uses only organic ingredients. The quiche (£1.99) is particularly good.

Sun Café *(☎ 579067; 7 St Mary's St)* serves up backpacker favourites like scrambled eggs on toast (£1.25) and pancakes (£1.50), but it's more of a gathering place where you can just hang out. There are monthly readings, African drum lessons, and art talks. If ever there was a Southeast Asian–style backpacker café in England, then this is it.

Rivoli Tea Rooms *(☎ 537909; 18 Steep Hill)* is the place for cream teas.

Stokes High Bridge Cafe *(☎ 513825; 207 High St; open 9am-5pm Mon-Sat)* is popular with tourists since it's in a 16th-century timbered building right on the bridge over the River Witham. You can get lunches and teas.

There's also a good **bakery** *(cnr Westgate & Bailgate)*.

Entertainment

Pubs Every guided tour makes a stop at (or at least acknowledges) the **Victoria** *(6 Union Rd)*. Lincoln's most famous public house doesn't disappoint: it's a terrific bar with a huge selection of beers.

Dog & Bone *(10 John St)* is a distinctive bar with a fine selection of ales east of High St, just off Monks Rd.

George & Dragon *(100 High St)* is one of the more popular pubs in town, and what it lacks in original character it more than makes up for in friendly ambience – though it can get very crowded at weekends.

Clubs Jumpin Jaks/Pulse/Ritzy *(☎ 522314; Silver St; open Wed-Sun only)* is three clubs in one. The music is charty, loud and attracts Lincoln's younger crowd. Admission to all three varies from £3 to £8, depending on the night, but there are discount fliers handed out throughout many of the city's bars.

Po Na Na Souk Bar (☎ 525828; 280-1 High St) is a much more serious club, though just as fun. The tunes are deeper, with a good mix of soulful house, eclectic funk and other esoteric sounds.

Getting There & Away
Lincoln is 142 miles (229km) from London, 94 miles (151km) from Cambridge and 81 miles (130km) from York.

Bus National Express operates a daily direct service (at 7.35am) between Lincoln and London (£17.50, 4½ hours), via Stamford (£8.25, 1½ hours). There are also direct services to Birmingham (£10.75, 2¾ hours) and Glasgow (£38.50, nine hours). For Cambridge (£16.25, three hours) you must change at Peterborough, which usually involves a lengthy wait.

The main local bus company is Lincolnshire Roadcar. It runs hourly buses between Lincoln and Grantham (£2.70, 1¼ hours), Monday to Saturday, and between Lincoln and Skegness (£3.60; 1¾ hours). Stamford is also served by **Kimes Coaches** (☎ 01529-497251), albeit on Saturday only with a departure at 4pm (£3.50 return, one hour, 40 minutes). From Lincoln to Boston (£3.70, 1¾ hours) there are nine buses, Monday to Saturday only.

Train To get to and from Lincoln usually involves a change. Hourly trains to Boston (£13.30, 1¼ hours) and Skegness (£15.60, two hours) include a change at Sleaford. For Cambridge (£30.10, 2½ hours), you must change at Peterborough (£17.40, 1½ hours) and Ely (£26.50, two hours 20 minutes). There are hourly departures throughout the day. Grantham (£8.70, 40 minutes) is on the main London to Glasgow line; there are about 20 trains per day.

Getting Around
Bus The city bus service is efficient. From the bus and train stations, bus No 51 runs past the youth hostel and Nos 7 and 8 link the cathedral area with the lower town (60p).

Bicycle You can rent everything from a three-speed to a mountain bike from **F&J**

Cycles (☎ 545311; 41 Huntgate), but 21 speeds are hardly an essential requirement for cycling in this flat county. Rent an 18-speed from £8 to £10 per day, and up to £30 per week.

GRANTHAM
☎ 01476 • pop 31,000
Anyone old enough to remember the eventful reign of Lady Margaret Thatcher, who served as British prime minister from 1979 to 1990, will find a good example of her vision for Britain in the pleasant redbrick town where she was born. Baroness Thatcher lived at 2 North Parade, above her father's grocery shop; today it's a chiropractor's clinic. The only other noteworthy inhabitant was Sir Isaac Newton, who received his early education here. There's a statue of him in front of the guildhall – a statue of the former Conservative prime minister might eventually grace the town but this book will have gone through several more editions before it does.

For the time being, the Iron Lady will have to content herself with a section devoted to her in the town's **museum** (St Peter's Hill; admission free; open 10am-5pm Mon-Sat). Another section is devoted to Newton and frankly, unless you really want to see the famous handbag with which the Iron Lady saluted the press after her 1979 electoral victory, it is by far the more interesting.

The **TIC** (☎/fax 406166; Avenue Rd; open 9.30am-5pm Mon-Sat) is by the guildhall.

The town has an interesting parish church, **St Wulfram's**, with a 85m-high spire, the sixth-highest in England. It dates from the late 13th century. Inside there's a chained library (with the books attached to the shelves by chains) which Isaac Newton used while studying there.

Three miles (5km) northeast of Grantham on the A607 is **Belton House** (NT; ☎ 566116; bus Nos 601 & 609; admission £5.50; open 1pm-5pm Wed-Sun Apr-Oct), one of the finest examples of Restoration countryhouse architecture. Built in 1688 for Sir John Brownlow, and set in a 400-hectare park, the house is known for its ornate plasterwork ceilings and wood carvings attributed to the Dutch carver Grinling Gibbons.

Places to Stay & Eat
Red House (☎ 579869, fax 401597; 74 North Parade; singles/doubles £25/48), in a listed

Georgian building in the town centre, has three en-suite rooms.

The Coach House (☎/fax 573636; e coach housenn@cwcom.net; rooms per person £25), just outside Belton House, is a listed building; rates include breakfast. Smokers will have to exercise their lungs in the large garden – it's a smoke-free joint.

Beehive (☎ 404554; Castlegate) is best known for its pub sign – a real beehive full of live South African bees! The bees have been here since 1830, which makes them one of the oldest populations of bees in the world. Good, cheap lunches are available, and the bees stay away from the customers.

Getting There & Away

Grantham is 25 miles (40km) south of Lincoln. Lincolnshire Roadcar runs buses every hour between the two, Monday to Saturday, and four times on Sunday (£2.80, one hour 10 minutes). It also runs a service (four daily, Monday to Saturday) to Stamford (£2.40, 1½ hours); National Express runs one bus daily, Monday to Saturday.

By train (£8.70, 40 minutes), you'll need to change at Newark to get to Lincoln. There is at least one train per hour throughout the day. Direct trains run from London King's Cross to Grantham (£30, 1¼ hours) hourly throughout the day.

STAMFORD

☎ 01780 • pop 16,000

This beautiful town of stone buildings and cobbled streets was made a conservation area in 1967 and is one of the finest stone towns in the country. The **TIC** (☎/fax 755611; open 9.30am-5pm Mon-Sat year round, & 10am-3pm Sun Apr-Oct) is in the **Stamford Arts Centre** (27 St Mary's St).

It's best to simply wander round the town's winding streets of medieval and Georgian houses, but the **Stamford Museum** (☎ 766 317; Broad St; admission free; open 10am-5pm Mon-Sat year round, plus 2pm-5pm Sun Apr-Sept) is certainly worth visiting. As well as displays charting the history of the town, there's a clothed model of local heavyweight Daniel Lambert, who tipped the scales at 336kg before his death in 1809. After his death his suits were displayed in a local pub where Charles Stratton, better known as Tom Thumb, would put on a show by fitting into the suit's armholes. Hilarious, apparently.

Places to Stay & Eat

St George's B&B (☎ 482099; 16 St George's Sq; singles/doubles £25/40), not to be confused with the George hotel, is a gorgeous 19th-century house with Victorian fireplaces and antiques. It also has a private garden.

Martin's (☎ 752106, fax 482691; 20 St Martin's Rd; singles/doubles £32/54.50) is another great B&B, just beyond the bridge over the Welland River, only a couple of minutes' walk from the centre of town.

There are a number of historic pubs that also offer accommodation.

Bull & Swann Inn (☎ 763558; High St; singles/doubles with bath £35/45) does good meals.

George (☎ 750750, fax 750701; e george hotelofstamford@btinternet.com; 71 St Martin's St; singles/doubles from £85/120), across the street from the Bull & Swann, is the top place to stay. It's a wonderful old coaching inn, parts of the building date back a thousand years. There's a cobbled courtyard and luxurious rooms. There's also an excellent restaurant that also serves upmarket pub grub: if you want anything fancier expect to fork out at least £20.

Getting There & Away

Stamford is 46 miles (74km) from Lincoln and 21 miles (34km) south of Grantham.

National Express serves Stamford from London (£9.75, 2¾ hours) via Lincoln (£7.75, 1½ hours). Lincolnshire Roadcar operates four buses daily, Monday to Saturday only, between Stamford and Grantham (£2.60, 1½ hours). National Express also runs one bus daily.

There are 15 trains daily to Cambridge (£13.90, 1¼ hours) and Ely (£8.70, 55 minutes). Norwich (£15.20, one hour 50 minutes) is on the same line, but there are fewer direct trains; you will most likely have to change at Ely.

AROUND STAMFORD
Burghley House

Just a mile (1.6km) south of Stamford, this immensely grand Tudor mansion (☎ 01780-752451; w www.burghley.co.uk; adult/child £6.75/3.50, 1 child free per paying adult; open 11am-5pm daily Apr-early Oct), pronounced Bur-lee, is the home of the Cecil family. It was built between 1565 and 1587 by William Cecil, Queen Elizabeth's adviser.

It's an impressive place with 18 magnificent state rooms. The Heaven Room was painted by Antonio Verrio in the 17th century and features floor-to-ceiling gods and goddesses disporting among the columns. There are over 300 paintings, including works by Gainsborough and Brueghel; state bedchambers, including the four-poster Queen Victoria slept in; and cavernous Tudor kitchens.

It's a pleasant 15-minute walk through the park from Stamford train station. The Burghley Horse Trials take place here over three days in early September and are of international significance.

BOSTON
☎ 01205 • pop 34,000

A major port in the Middle Ages, Boston lies near the mouth of the River Witham, in the bay known as The Wash. By the end of the 13th century the town was one of the most important wool trading centres in the country, exporting the fleeces of three million sheep annually. Boston's other claim to fame came in the 17th century, when it temporarily imprisoned a group of religious separatists looking to settle in the virtually unknown territories of the New World. These later became known as the Pilgrim Fathers, the first white settlers of the US. Word of their success made it back to the English Boston, whereupon a crowd of locals decided to sail across the Atlantic, where they founded a namesake town in the new colony of Massachusetts.

Today the town is but a shadow of its former self, but it has retained much of its medieval appearance, down to the street grid, whereby the two main streets flank both sides of the river and are linked by small foot bridges. It's an easy place to wander about in, and has a number of interesting sites.

The TIC (☎/fax 356656; Market Place; open 9am-5pm Mon-Sat year round) is under the Assembly Rooms on Market Place. Market days are Wednesday and Saturday; you can buy pretty much everything from a fish to a bicycle.

As you walk around the town, be sure to check out Shodfriars Hall (South St; not open to the public), a marvellous Tudor building that has been faithfully restored.

St Botolph's Church

In keeping with its high-flying status, the town ordered the construction of an impressive church in 1309: the result was St Botolph's (☎ 362864; church admission free, tower adult/child £2/1; open 9am-4.30pm Mon-Sat, Sun between services) and its 88m-high tower – known as the Boston Stump – the tallest in the country. The fenland on which it's built was not firm enough to support a thin spire, hence the sturdy tower. Climb the 365 steps to the top to see (on a clear day) Lincoln, 30 miles away.

Inside there is a splendid 17th-century pulpit from which John Cotton, the fiery vicar of St Botolph's, delivered five-hour catechisms and two-hour sermons during the 1630s. By all accounts, it was he who convinced his parishioners to follow in the footsteps of the Pilgrim Fathers and emigrate.

The Guildhall

It was from Boston that the Pilgrim Fathers made their first break for the freedom of the New World in 1607. They were imprisoned in the guildhall (☎ 365954; admission £1.50; open 10am-5pm Mon-Sat, & 1.30pm-5pm Sunday May-Sept), where the cells that held them are now a fairly extensive visitor centre with multimedia exhibits on the town's history and a eulogising display on the struggles of the Pilgrim Fathers.

Places to Stay & Eat

Park Lea (☎/fax 356309; 85 Norfolk St; singles £22-24, doubles £32-36) is a five-minute walk from the marketplace. There is only one double without bathroom.

Bramley House (☎/fax 354538; e bramley house@ic24.net; 267 Sleaford Rd; singles/ doubles from £20/38.50), an old 18th-century farmhouse, is about half a mile west of town along the Sleaford road. It has nine comfortable rooms and also does pub grub.

There are many other eateries dotted about town, but we recommend you check out Maud's Tea Rooms (☎ 352188; Maud Foster Windmill, Willoughby Rd; mains £5-6), about half-a-mile northeast of Market Place. This is a fully functional mill, and the tearooms serve good vegetarian dishes. You can also buy the local produce: organic flour.

Getting There & Away

From Lincoln it's easier to get to Boston by train than by bus, but even that involves a change at Sleaford. Trains run from Lincoln hourly (£13.30, 1¼ hours).

EASTERN ENGLAND

SKEGNESS

☎ 01754 • pop 18,000

If you like amusement arcades and cheap fun fair rides, then 'Skeggy' – the east coast's classic seaside resort – is the place for you. Tens of thousands of Britons holiday here every year, mostly because it's cheaper than going to Spain, it's by the sea and every night offers up some kind of hands-in-the-air entertainment – from bingo to bad cabaret. Virtually every inch of the Grand Parade, which skirts the six-mile-long (9.5km) beach, is covered in amusement arcades, fish and chip shops, pubs and B&Bs. It's loud, phenomenally tacky and frankly a bit of a dump.

The **TIC** (☎ 764821; Grand Parade; open 9.30am-5pm daily, Apr-Sept, 10m-4pm Mon-Fri, Oct-Mar) is directly opposite the **Embassy Centre** (☎ 768333), home of Skeggy's cabaret scene and where you can watch your favourite Abba tribute band in all its glory; shows usually kick off at around 7.30pm. From July to September, this stretch of beach is anointed with 25,000 light bulbs, which come on in the evening to celebrate the Skegness Illuminations.

B&Bs are not hard to find, and are generally quite cheap, starting from around £18 per person. The TIC will help you find a room if you need one.

Skegness is pretty easy to get to by either bus or train. From Boston, Lincolnshire Roadcar runs five buses daily, Monday to Saturday (£2.60, 1¼ hours). **Brylaine Travel** (☎ 01205-364087) runs three daily along the same route. Tickets, however, are only valid on the service provided by the issuing company. From Lincoln, Lincolnshire Roadcar buses run hourly, Monday to Saturday, and five on Sunday (£3.60, 1¾ hours).

There are 15 trains daily, Monday to Saturday, and eight on Sunday, between Skegness and Boston (£4.20, 35 minutes). Although there is an hourly train link between Skegness and Lincoln (£15.60, two hours) it involves a change at Sleaford; you're better off getting the bus.

LOUTH

☎ 01507 • pop 14,500

East Lincolnshire's largest market town, the largely Georgian Louth sits on the banks of the River Lud between the Wolds to the west and the marshes of the Lincolnshire coast. A curious fact about Louth is that it has two

---

The Pilgrimage of Grace

The revolt against Henry VIII's reformation of the church began in Louth in 1536. Deeply annoyed by Henry's plans to dissolve all of the monasteries and appoint new bishops to every diocese, northerners were pushed over the edge by Henry's minister Thomas Cromwell, who at the same time decided to pursue some fairly radical land reform programmes in the northern counties. On 1 October, the crown commissioners arrived in Louth to fulfil Henry and Cromwell's orders, but they were attacked by an angry mob. What was a protest was now a full rebellion, later called the Pilgrimage of Grace. Lincoln was occupied and the rebels demanded an end to dissolution, Cromwell's resignation and the dismissal of the newly appointed heretical bishops. Henry, however, was unmoved and the rebellion petered out on 19 October.

Although the Louth rebellion was a bit of a damp squib, it inspired a more serious rebellion in Yorkshire by Robert Aske, a gentleman farmer who gathered 30,000 men and engaged the crown forces and forced Henry to consider the rebels' demands. He did, or pretended to, and Aske eventually disbanded his forces. The government reacted swiftly by arresting and executing the ringleaders in early 1537, and the rebellion was finally at an end.

♔♔♔♔♔♔♔♔♔♔♔♔♔♔

---

hemispheres – east and west – as the zero longitude line cuts right through the town.

Dominating the town is the soaring spire of **St James' Church** (open 10am-4.30pm Easter-Christmas), added to the medieval church between 1500 and 1515. The dramatic buttresses and battlements of the church exterior – described by Sir John Betjemen as 'one of the last great medieval Gothic masterpieces', belie a fairly inconsequential interior, however, although the lovely wooden roof, built in the early 19th century, is undoubtedly a feature. You can climb the tower (£1.50) for marvellous views of the town and surrounding countryside.

The **TIC** (☎/fax 609289; New Market Hall, off Cornmarket; open 9am-5pm Mon-Sat) has all the information you'll need.

The most elegant street in town is Westgate, which is lined with Georgian houses. The mid-17th-century **Church Precincts** at

No 47 and the grander No 45 are particularly handsome. Just opposite is Westgate Place, and through the archway you will find a row of terraced houses, one of which bears a plaque commemorating Tennyson's residence here between 1816 and 1820.

Places to Stay & Eat

The Ramsgate Hotel (☎ 602179; 15 Ramsgate; singles/doubles £20/30) has pretty comfortable rooms, and it's very central.

The Priory (☎ 602930, fax 609767; Eastgate; singles/doubles £45/69) is a magnificent building from 1818 that has been converted into a simply gorgeous hotel. This all-white, half-castle, half-residence is easily the top spot in town. For an extra £15, you can get dinner at the excellent restaurant.

Besides the Priory, Louth has a surprisingly good selection of restaurants.

Taipan Tai (☎ 602332; 138 Eastgate; mains around £8) has a wonderful menu of Thai specialities.

Ferns (☎ 603209; 40 Northgate; mains around £9) is a good choice is you're after solid English cuisine.

Getting There & Away

Louth is 23 miles (37km) northeast of Lincoln, from where there are buses every couple of hours (£3.50, 45 minutes).

AROUND LOUTH
Saltfleetby-Theddlethorpe National Nature Reserve

Ten miles (16km) east of Louth along the B1200, which meanders its way through the Fens, is one of the most attractive nature reserves (☎ 01507-338611) in this part of the country. Spread over 5 miles (8km) of sand dune, fresh- and saltwater marsh, it is best appreciated in early summer, when the stunning marsh orchids are in full bloom. In spring and autumn, migratory wildfowl flock to the reserve. There are dozens of trails crisscrossing the whole area, which helps to keep your feet dry as you negotiate the myriad lagoons.

You'll need your own transport to get here. At the end of the B1200, take a right on to the A1031 and, about three quarters of a mile farther on, follow the signs for the nature reserve.

Yorkshire

The first thing you notice about Yorkshire is that it's *big*. So big, that it's split into four separate counties – South Yorkshire, West Yorkshire, North Yorkshire and the East Riding of Yorkshire – but there's still a definite homogeneity and a confident 'national' pride, which is lacking in many other parts of England. This surely comes from the feelings of space and freedom that go hand-in-hand with sheer size. Yorkshire folk call it 'God's own country' and can get away with such claims when people in areas such as Kent, Essex or Lincolnshire simply can't.

Maybe it's this sense of statehood (quips about the People's Republic of South Yorkshire during the militant 1980s were only half a joke) that gives Yorkshire people a reputation for a straight-talking, no-nonsense attitude. Or maybe it's the landscape of dark moors and rocky outcrops, or the background of generations struggling to earn a living from the land or the factories, but whatever, Yorkshire people just don't sit on the fence. Whether it's football, clubs, books or theatre, or just life generally – things are either great or terrible. There's no in-between.

Historically, Yorkshire really was a separate country once. In the 9th century the Danish Vikings made York their capital and ruled the Danelaw – pretty much all of northern and eastern England. (See the History section in Facts about England for more details of this turbulent time.) After the Norman Conquest of 1066, William the Conqueror found the north rebellious and difficult, and responded with brutal thoroughness; his army destroyed towns and villages, murdered thousands and devastated the countryside. Twenty years later, royal commissioners collecting data for the Domesday Book recorded the simple, but frighteningly eloquent, 'waste' beside many parish names. It took the region generations to recover, and fanciful historians might even trace the roots of England's north–south divide to this period.

The Danish heritage survives today, especially in the language (words such as fell (hillside) and dale (valley) have Nordic origins, as do place-names including *kirk* or *by*), and DNA samples taken in some Yorkshire villages show 'the blood of the Vikings' still flows here.

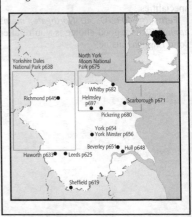

Highlights

- Exploring York's winding medieval streets, awe-inspiring minster and delightful museums

- Strolling down green valleys or hiking over high moors in the Yorkshire Dales

- Shopping, eating, drinking and dancing, then shopping some more in Leeds – the Knightsbridge of the north

- Walking in the footsteps of Captain Cook and Count Dracula in the narrow streets of Whitby

- Riding steam trains at Haworth and Pickering, or admiring the scenic Esk Valley and Settle–Carlisle railway lines

- Staring out to sea from the dramatic high cliffs of the North York Moors

In later centuries Yorkshire prospered on the medieval wool trade, which sponsored the great cathedral at York and the enormous monasteries, such as Rievaulx and Fountains, which can still be seen today. A few more centuries passed, and the cities of Leeds, Bradford and Sheffield became powerhouses of the Industrial Revolution.

Against this human story, the Yorkshire countryside is a grand backdrop, containing two of England's best national parks, the Yorkshire Dales and the North York Moors; some beautiful countryside; and a spectacular coastline. The cities, too, attract their share of visitors, with museums, galleries, pubs and bars – not to mention top-class football teams – while Sheffield and Leeds boast some of the best nightclubs in the country. All in all, there's something for everyone, and if your tour of England takes you beyond London and the southeast, then Yorkshire should definitely be on the schedule.

ORIENTATION & INFORMATION

Yorkshire covers a large part of northern England, and a vast range of landscapes. From the Pennine Hills on the western side of the region (separating Yorkshire from age-old rival Lancashire), you can travel through the green valleys of the Yorkshire Dales, across the plains of the Vale of York and the rolling hills of the North York Moors and Yorkshire Wolds, to finally end at the dramatic east coast.

The major north–south transport routes – the M1 and A1 motorways and the main London to Edinburgh railway line – run through the middle of Yorkshire following the flat lands between the Pennines and the Moors, and serving the key cities of Sheffield, Leeds and York.

For regional information, the **Yorkshire Tourist Board** (☎ 01904-707070, fax 701414; ⓦ www.yorkshirevisitor.com; 312 Tadcaster Rd, York YO24 1GS) has plenty of general leaflets and brochures. For more detailed information, contact the local Tourist Information Centres (TICs) listed throughout this chapter. As well as the main website, which helps locate accommodation (among other things), you might also want to look at ⓦ www.yorkshirefarmbreaks.com (which covers rural accommodation) and ⓦ www .yorkshireonscreen.com (which covers – you've guessed it – the Yorkshire locations of a surprisingly large number of movies and TV soaps).

ACTIVITIES

Within Yorkshire are high peaks, wild hills, tranquil valleys, farmland, moorland and a stupendous coastline. With this fantastic selection, not surprisingly, it's a great place for outdoor activities.

Walking

The most famous walk that passes through Yorkshire is the **Pennine Way**, stretching over 250 miles (400km) from Edale in the Peak District to Kirk Yetholm near Kelso in Scotland. The Yorkshire section starts on day two, and runs for over 100 miles (160km), via Hebden Bridge, Malham, Horton-in-Ribblesdale and Hawes, passing near Haworth and Skipton too – all places covered in this book. An even more popular long-distance route is the 190-mile (306km) **Coast to Coast Walk**, which crosses northern England eastward from the Lake District, through the Yorkshire Dales and North York Moors. Doing just the Yorkshire sections would take a week to 10 days and offers some of the finest walking of its kind in England.

Other long-distance walks in Yorkshire include: the venerable **Cleveland Way**, a moor-and-coast classic (details in the North York Moors section); the charming and not-too-strenuous **Dales Way**, which leads from the Yorkshire Dales to the Lake District (details in the Yorkshire Dales section); and the beautiful but oft-overlooked **Wolds Way,** which winds through the most scenic part of eastern Yorkshire (see the East Riding section).

For shorter walks and rambles, the best area is the **Yorkshire Dales**, with a great selection of hard and easy walks through scenic valleys or over wild hilltops, with even a few peaks thrown in for good measure. The **Yorkshire Wolds** hold hidden delights, while the quiet valleys and dramatic coasts of the **North York Moors** also have many good opportunities, although the broad ridges of the high moors can be a bit featureless and less attractive for keen walkers.

For general information get the *Walk Yorkshire* brochure from TICs or see ⓦ www.walkyorkshire.com. All TICs stock a mountain of leaflets (free or up to £1) on local walks, and sell more detailed guidebooks and maps. At train stations and TICs, it's worth looking out for leaflets produced by companies such as Northern Spirit, detailing walks from train stations. Some tie in with train times, so you can walk one way and ride back.

Cycling

Cycling is a great way to see Yorkshire; there's a vast network of country lanes, although the most scenic areas are also attractive to car drivers, so even some minor roads can be busy at weekends. The **Yorkshire Dales** is a good place to start, especially the quieter areas in the north around

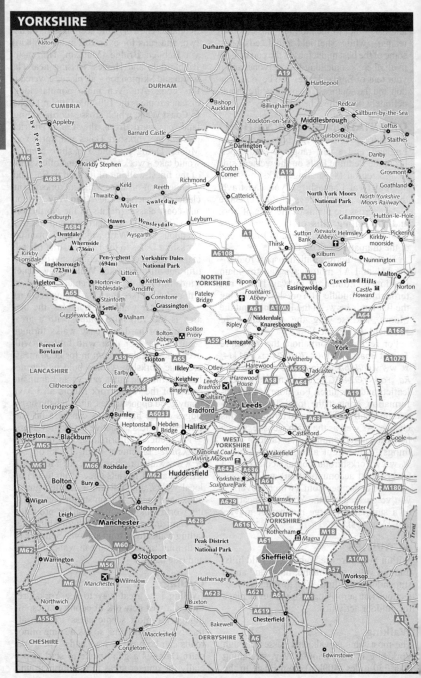

YORKSHIRE

Swaledale and Wensleydale, and the west around Dentdale. The areas just outside the park are great too – Nidderdale for example.

The **National Cycle Network** (see the Activities chapter) in Yorkshire includes the **White Rose Cycle Route**, a 120-mile (193km) cruise from Hull to York to Middlesbrough, via the rolling Yorkshire Wolds and the dramatic edge of the North York Moors, and a traffic-free section on the old railway between Selby and York.

Other traffic-free routes include **Whitby to Scarborough** – another disused railway line, and an effortless way to tour this rugged coastline.

For off-road riding, Yorkshire has several options. A good place to start is the **North York Moors**, where networks of bridlepaths, former railways and disused mining tracks are now turned over to two-wheel use. For mixed on and off road, the **Yorkshire Dales** has an excellent network of old 'drove roads' (formerly used for driving cattle to market) which wind across lonely hillsides, and tie in neatly with the narrow country lanes in the valley bottoms.

GETTING THERE & AROUND

Yorkshire's main gateway cities by road and rail are Sheffield in the far south, Leeds for the west and York for the centre and north. If you're coming by sea from northern Europe, Hull (in the East Riding) is the region's main port. More specific details for each area are given under Getting There & Away in the separate sections throughout this chapter. For inquiries, the national **Traveline** (☎ *0870 608 2608*) covers buses and trains all over Yorkshire.

Bus

Long-distances buses and coaches run by **National Express** (☎ *08705 808080*) regularly service most cities and large towns in Yorkshire from London, the south of England, the Midlands and Scotland. For example, to York there are services from London (£27, five hours, three daily), Birmingham (£27, three hours, one daily) and Edinburgh (£34.50, six hours, one daily). More details are given under Getting There & Away in the individual town and city sections.

Bus transport around Yorkshire is frequent and efficient, especially between major towns. Services are more sporadic in the national parks but still perfectly adequate for reaching most places – particularly in the summer months (June to September).

Train

The main line between London (£63.20, two hours 10 minutes) and Edinburgh (£56, 2½ hours) runs through Yorkshire with at least 10 services per day, via York and Doncaster – where you might change to reach other places in Yorkshire. There are also direct services; eg, London to Sheffield (£48, around 10 daily, 2½ hours), London to Leeds (£62, hourly, two hours), and Manchester to Leeds (£13.90, one hour). One of England's most famous and scenic railways is the Settle–Carlisle Line (SCL), which crosses the Yorkshire Dales via a spectacular series of tunnels and viaducts. Trains start/end in Leeds, and Carlisle is a good stop on the way to Scotland (for details see the Yorkshire Dales section). Call **National Rail Enquiries** (☎ 08457 484950) forl timetable details.

Boat

Details on passenger ferries to Hull from northern Europe are given in the main Getting There & Away chapter.

Sheffield

☎ 0114 • pop 431,000 • elevation 100m
To most people, the word 'Sheffield' means two things: steel and *The Full Monty*. For hundreds of years, England's fourth-largest city has been a major steel producer, rolling out everything from bomb-proof plate for battleships to delicate medical instruments, and was especially renowned for its cutlery. 'Sheffield steel' embossed on your knife and fork stood for quality around the world. Then came the 1980s and '90s and many steel mills closed, forcing thousands of workers onto the dole. That's where the surprise smash-hit film *The Full Monty* came in – a tale of unemployed Sheffield steelworkers who turned to stripping to raise some cash. It was a feel-good film, and it suddenly put Sheffield on the map, even though the hard truth (six blokes getting their kit off can't solve a city's economic slump) was skimmed over.

But the late 1990s saw an upturn in Sheffield's fortunes – maybe helped by the movie – and today's visitors find a city work-

ing hard to reinvent itself. Smart hotels and galleries are springing up, the whole centre is revelling in a major facelift, and several new attractions based on the industrial past are well worth a visit. On the entertainment side, there's a buzz that hasn't been seen for a long while, powered in no small way by an exuberant and ever-growing student population. A few years ago, a much-trumpeted survey of English student cities showed that Sheffield ranked first in terms of 'good times'. Since then, it's got better, although the effect of this lively selection of pubs and clubs on academic achievement has yet to be researched.

Sheffield makes a good stopover if you need a burst of city life while travelling between south and north England, and is a very handy gateway for the Peak District National Park, which brushes up against the western outskirts. Chesterfield, with its famous twisted spire, and several top-class stately homes (all with Sheffield connections), are also just a train or bus hop away.

Orientation & Information

Sheffield's bus and train stations are ringed by busy roads and grotty high-rise buildings, so neither gives a good first impression. Major renovations are planned though – so the place could look swish by the time you arrive, or be a massive construction site.

The most interesting central area is around Church St, Tudor Square, Fargate and a square called Barker's Pool. Just west of here Division St and Devonshire St have hip clothes and record shops, popular restaurants and trendy bars. A block north is West St, also with restaurants and bars, especially popular with students, and lively rather than trendy here. West St becomes Glossop Rd and leads westwards to the University of Sheffield main campus.

Tourist Offices The friendly **TIC** (☎ 221 1900; **w** www.sheffieldcity.co.uk; Tudor Sq; open 9.30am-5.15pm Mon-Fri, 9.30am-4.15pm Sat) has a good stock of leaflets and local guidebooks. Staff can help with accommodation bookings, and don't mind being asked if the *Full Monty* bus tour is still available. (It isn't.)

Post & Communications The handiest **post office** (Norfolk Row; open 8.30am-5.30pm Mon-Fri, 8.30am-3pm Sat) is be-

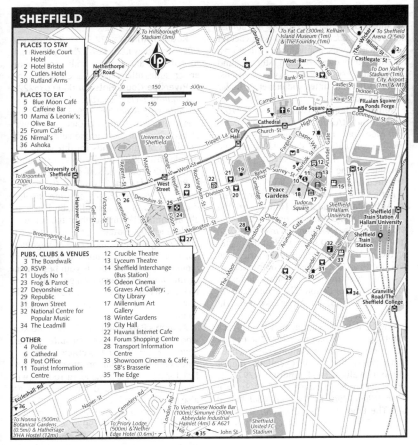

SHEFFIELD

PLACES TO STAY
1 Riverside Court Hotel
2 Hotel Bristol
7 Cutlers Hotel
30 Rutland Arms

PLACES TO EAT
5 Blue Moon Café
9 Caffeine Bar
10 Mama & Leonie's; Olive Bar
25 Forum Café
26 Nirmal's
36 Ashoka

PUBS, CLUBS & VENUES
3 The Boardwalk
20 RSVP
21 Lloyds No 1
23 Frog & Parrot
27 Devonshire Cat
29 Republic
31 Brown Street
32 National Centre for Popular Music
34 The Leadmill

12 Crucible Theatre
13 Lyceum Theatre
14 Sheffield Interchange (Bus Station)
15 Odeon Cinema
16 Graves Art Gallery; City Library
17 Millennium Art Gallery
18 Winter Gardens
19 City Hall
22 Havana Internet Cafe
24 Forum Shopping Centre
28 Transport Information Centre
33 Showroom Cinema & Café; SB's Brasserie
35 The Edge

OTHER
4 Police
6 Cathedral
8 Post Office
11 Tourist Information Centre

tween the TIC and Fargate. **Havana Internet Cafe** (☎ 249 5453; 32 Division St; open 10am-6pm daily) charges £1.25 for 15 minutes.

Things to See & Do
Pride of place goes to the **Winter Gardens**, a wonderfully ambitious public space with glass roof, exotic plants and soaring wood-clad arches. The 21st-century architecture contrasts sharply with the Victorian **town hall** next door, and is further enhanced by the nearby **Peace Gardens** – complete with fountains, sculptures and lawns of lunching office workers whenever there's a bit of sun.

Sheffield's cultural revival is spear-headed by the **Millennium Galleries** (☎ 278 2600; Arundle Gate; admission free; open 10am-5pm Mon-Sat, 11am-5pm Sun). Dis-

plays cover Sheffield steel and metalworking, contemporary art, craft and design, and an eclectic collection established and inspired by Victorian artist, writer, critic and philosopher John Ruskin.

Nearby, **Graves Art Gallery** (☎ 278 2600; Surrey St; admission free; open 10am-5pm Mon-Sat) has a neat and accessible display of British and European art, plus works from the temporarily closed Mappin Gallery.

The **cathedral** on Church St has wonderful stained glass (ancient and modern), a memorial to the crew of the HMS *Sheffield* lost during the Falklands conflict and the grave of the earl of Shrewbury, famous for being the jailer of Mary Queen of Scots and husband to Bess of Harwick (see the Derbyshire section of The Midlands chapter).

A mile (1.6km) from the centre, the **Botanical Gardens** (*Clarkehouse Rd; admission free; open daily 8am-dusk*) is a peaceful haven, with lawns, ponds, plant collections, families, sunbathers, revising students and three grand crystal-palace-style pavilions, built in Victorian times and currently under loving restoration.

Kelham Island Museum (☎ 272 2106; *Alma St; adult/child £3.50/2; open 10am-4pm Mon-Thur, 11am-4.45pm Sun*) is a fascinating celebration of Sheffield's industrial heritage, complete with steam-powered machines – one the size of a house that's still fired up a few times a day.

For a view of steel from an earlier era, go to **Abbeydale Industrial Hamlet** (☎ 236 7731; *adult/child £3/free; open 10am-4pm Mon-Thur, 11am-4.45pm Sun mid-Apr–Oct*). It's 4 miles (6.5km) southwest of the centre on the A621 (towards the Peak District) and well worth a stop. In the days before factories, metalworking was a cottage industry, just like wool or cotton. These rare (and restored) houses and machines take you right back to that era.

Sheffield is the capital of English **rock climbing**. All the real rock is in the nearby Peak District, but if it's raining (or you need instruction) there are excellent indoor climbing walls at **The Foundry** (☎ 279 6331; *45 Mowbray St; adult/child £5.30/3; open 10am-10pm Mon-Fri, 10am-6pm Sat & Sun*) and **The Edge** (☎ 275 8899; *John St; adult/child £5/4; open 10am-10pm Mon-Fri, 10am-8pm Sat & Sun*).

Places to Stay

Hostels Within easy reach of Sheffield by train, **Hathersage YHA Hostel** (☎ 0870 770 5852; *Castleton Rd; dorm beds £10*) is 12 miles (19.5km) away in the Peak District village of Hathersage.

University of Sheffield (☎ 222 0260; *rooms per person £12*) offers functional comfortable rooms in self-catering flats during July and August, when students clear out for the summer holidays. Most flats are in the suburb of Broomhill, about a mile (1.6km) west of the centre, and the minimum stay is two nights.

B&Bs & Hotels Sheffield has some central accommodation options, and a large cluster of B&Bs southwest of the centre along Wostenholm Rd and Montgomery Rd in the suburb of Nether Edge.

Rutland Arms (☎ 272 9003; *86 Brown St; singles/doubles from £24/37*) is a fine traditional pub, and very central; some rooms are en suite, others have shared bathrooms.

Riverside Court Hotel (☎ 0800 0352228; e *enquire@riversidecourt.co.uk; 4 Nursery St; en-suite singles/doubles £29/39*) is a good, clean, efficient, budget choice, in a down-at-heel area, but close to the centre. Breakfast is £3.50, and rooms for three/four/five people cost £49/59/69. There's a restaurant-bar, laundry room and self-service kitchens.

Priory Lodge (☎ 258 4670; *40 Wostenholm Rd, Nether Edge; en-suite singles/doubles £26/38*), is a small suburban hotel about a mile (1.6km) south of the centre.

Nether Edge Hotel (☎ 255 4363; w *www.nether-edge-hotel.co.uk; 21-23 Montgomery Rd; en-suite singles/doubles £35/45, family rooms per person £22.50*) is your best choice in this area and budget range, with clean airy rooms and friendly management. The downstairs bar serves snacks and evening meals.

Andrews Park Hotel (☎ 250 0111; *48 Kenwood Rd, Nether edge; en-suite singles/doubles £40/50*), a neat, efficient, friendly place on a quiet suburban street, has breakfast for an extra £4. Standard rooms (with shared bathrooms) and family rooms are also available, and special discounted room-and-breakfast deals are sometimes offered.

Cutlers Hotel (☎ 273 9939; e *enquiries@cutlershotel.co.uk; George St; singles £45-59, doubles £60-69*) is very central, catering for business travellers and thespians from the nearby Lycium. It's a touch old-fashioned, but offers good service and cheaper rates at weekends.

Hotel Bristol (☎ 200 4000; e *sheffield@bhg.co.uk; Blonk St; doubles Fri-Sun £52, Mon-Thur £69*) is a former office block, now providing modern minimalist style and efficient service. It's good value in this range, although they should've gone easy on the dark paint.

Places to Eat

For a wide range of city centre options, you can't go wrong on Division St, Devonshire St, West St and Glossop Rd. There are cafés, takeaways, pubs and bars doing food, and a wide range of restaurants.

Forum Café *(127 Division St; lunch about £5; open 10am to 1am daily)* is open and airy, with coffees, snacks, newspapers, art on the wall and customers who wander in from the vaguely alternative Forum Shopping Centre next door. In the evening, it's more bar-like, with lower lights and louder music.

Blue Moon Café *(off Church St; snacks £1-3, lunches £3-5)* moved to this new location because space was short at the old place and the number of customers kept growing. A good sign indeed. Come here for tasty cakes, soups, salads and some lovely veggie lunch creations, served in a friendly atmosphere.

Caffeine Bar *(Norfolk Row; sandwiches £2-4, mains around £5; open 8.30am-6pm Mon-Sat)* serves fine coffee, and good fresh snacks and meals, with not a microwave in sight.

Olive Garden *(above Wicker Herbal Stores, Surry St; open 9am-4.30pm Mon-Sat)* serves all your favourite healthy bakes and flans.

Mama & Leonie's *(☎ 272 0490; Norfolk St; mains £5-7)* is a long-standing pizza and pasta favourite, popular with pre- and post-theatre-goers.

Nirmal's *(☎ 2724054; 189 Glossop Rd; starters £2-4, mains £5-7)* proudly serves 'food from Delhi', earning many accolades from local curry fans.

The Showroom *(Paternoster Row; bar – snacks £3-4, mains around £6; café-bar – mains £8.50)* has a lively bar (see Entertainment), while the café-bar does good food, but the soulless setting does it no justice.

SB's Brasserie *(☎ 275 1966; 4 Leadmill Rd; open noon-2.30am Mon-Fri, evening only Sat & Sun)*, under the Showroom, is a deservedly popular Indian restaurant, also serving steak-and-chips type meals.

Southwest of the centre, London Rd and Eccleshall Rd are lined with shops, pubs, bars and eateries. London Rd is no-frills but up-and-coming, Eccleshall Rd is smarter and has a studenty feel. Take a stroll and take your pick. Our favourites include the following.

Simunye *(229 London Rd; open 11am-6pm Mon-Sat)* is a friendly little multicultural café, with good coffees, ciabattas (£1.50), magazines to read and world music CDs for sale.

Vietnamese Noodle Bar *(☎ 258 3608; 200 London Rd; open noon-midnight daily; mains £5-7)* serves up a range of steaming bowls and sizzling plates; it's particularly busy at weekends, when service may slip a little.

Ashoka *(☎ 268 3029; 307 Eccleshall Rd; starters £3, mains £4-8, sides £2)* is a long-standing and award-winning favourite, producing tasty curries and other treats from India, Pakistan and Bangladesh.

Nonna's *(☎ 268 6166; 539-541 Ecclesall Rd; lunches around £5, evening pastas around £8, other mains £10-15)* is buzzy and stylish, producing food highly-rated by locals, in a European café-bar-restaurant atmosphere. Come for coffee and the papers, or a full Italian job.

Entertainment

To keep up with Sheffield's vibrant club and live music scene, and everything else that's happening, the listings section in the weekly *Sheffield Telegraph* (50p, every Friday) is invaluable.

Pubs & Bars The city centre has many options, especially concentrated around Division St and West St. A tiny selection is listed here to start you off.

Frog & Parrot *(Division St)* a no-frills but very popular pub, serving up pub grub and a range of beers, including infamous 'Roger & Out' – the strongest beer in the world, brewed on-site, and served in small glasses for health and safety reasons.

Lloyds No 1 *(Division St)* is a large bar, with good service, cheap drinks and decent food, bulging at the seams each evening.

RSPV *(Division St)* is a spacious bar, good for a quiet drink during the day, or a loud and lively pre-club warm-up in the evening.

Devonshire Cat *(Wellington St)* neatly combines a modern bar atmosphere with a wonderful selection of top-notch beer from around England and the world; and jolly decent home-cooked food too.

Rutland Arms *(86 Brown St)* is a traditional pub, with good cheap beer, no-nonsense bar-food at lunchtime and in the early evening, and a popular Sunday lunch.

Showroom Bar *(Paternoster Row)*, originally aimed at film fans, now has a life of its own, with a slightly arty, slightly hip clientele. The ambience is good, and so is the food, but the service is horribly slow. Out of term-time the slothful moonlighting students go home and real bar-staff pour the drinks.

Fat Cat *(☎ 249 4801; 23 Alma St)* is outside the centre, but easily one of Sheffield's finest pubs, and well worth the walk or taxi ride. Or pull in here for refreshment after admiring

Kelham Island Museum next door. There's a wide range of real ales (some brewed on the premises), three bars (one nonsmoking), good pub grub, a roaring fire in winter and a delightfully unreconstructed interior. Don't miss the fascinating exhibit on local sanitation in the men's toilets.

Clubs & Venues It's official – Sheffield has some of the best clubs in England. Just ask the bus-loads of punters who come from miles around every weekend, or those bleary-eyed students recovering in pubs Sunday lunchtimes. Even the queues are legendary. Club nights change from month to month, so check the listings to locate hip-hop, funky house, indie or whatever else floats your boat.

For live music, the smaller venues are listed here. Big names play at **Sheffield Arena** or **Don Valley Stadium** – also a major sporting venue.

Republic (☎ 276 6777; 112 Arundel St) is a major crowd-puller, rated as one of the best clubs in the north, with deep cred and Gatecrasher links.

Brown St (☎ 279 6959; Paternoster Row) is a café-bar during the day, and a club after dark, placed among the world's top five by *The Face*.

The Leadmill (☎ 275 4500; Leadmill Rd) offers a mix of club nights and live bands; it's seen the fashions come and go for 20 years, and still jumps with the best of them.

The Boardwalk (☎ 279 9090; Snig Hill) is an institution, and excellent for live music; local bands, old rockers, up-and-coming stars, world music, the obscure, the novel and the downright weird – they all play here. No real music fan should miss checking what's on.

Sheffield City Hall (☎ 278 9789; Barker's Pool) is a grand old performance venue, attracting middle-sized names of all sorts – comedy, rock, operatic recitals – and appreciative audiences. Downstairs, a livelier bunch makes use of the sprung dance floor on weekend club nights.

National Centre for Popular Music (Paternoster Row) is a striking building and unintentional monument to Millennium excess, which disappointed crowds in 2000, as it had little connection with pop. So the exhibits were mothballed, and the space used for live performances and club nights. In 2002 these were mothballed too, so look out for posters locally to see what takes their place.

Theatre & Cinema The **Crucible** and **Lyceum** theatres on Tudor Square share the same **box office** (☎ 276 9922). Both are home to excellent regional drama, and the Crucible's respected resident director draws in the big names; a highlight of 2002 was Kenneth Brannagh's breathtaking *Richard III*.

Showroom Cinema (☎ 275 7727; Paternoster Row) is the largest independent cinema in England, with a great mix of art-house, offbeat and not-quite-mainstream films on four screens. For everything else, there's the **Odeon** (☎ 272 3981; Arundle Gate).

Spectator Sports

Sheffield has two main football teams – Sheffield United and Sheffield Wednesday. Both currently play in Division 1, and while interfan rivalry is razor sharp, it's generally good-natured. United plays at the Bramall Lane stadium, just south of the city centre, while Wednesday's home is Hillsborough (one of the largest stadiums in the country), about 3 miles (5km) north of the centre. Fans of football history will love to know that Sheffield is also home to the two oldest teams in the world – Sheffield FC and Hallam FC, although both are now in minor leagues. They played each other in the first ever club football match, way back in 1860.

Getting There & Away

Sheffield is 160 miles (260km) from London, 40 miles (65km) from Manchester, and 36 miles (60km) from Leeds. If you can't bring yourself to stay the night, there are lockers at the bus station. Call ☎ 01709-515151 for information on all public transport in Sheffield and South Yorkshire.

Air Signs proudly show Sheffield City Airport (☎ 201 1998), but services are limited mainly to private business charter planes and helicopters, plus Channel Island holiday flights in the summer.

Bus Sheffield's bus station (called the Interchange) is on the eastern edge of the city centre, just 100m north of the train station. National Express services link Sheffield with London (£18.50, eight per day, 4 hours) and other major centres in the north. There are frequent buses to/from Leeds (£7, 1½ hours), and various rural services linking Sheffield and the Peak District.

Train Services from London St Pancras to Sheffield (£48, around 10 daily, 2½ hours), go via Derby or Nottingham. The trains run at least hourly to/from: Leeds (£8, 30 minutes), Manchester Piccadilly (£14, one hour), York (£14, 80 minutes) and Manchester airport (£18.50, 70 minutes).

If you're heading for the Peak District (and you should be), local services on the Hope Valley line between Sheffield and Manchester take you deep into the hills. The scenery is gorgeous, even if you don't get off the train. (For more details see the Peak District section in The Midlands chapter.)

Getting Around
The main hubs for local bus services to the western and southern suburbs are dreary High St and pleasant Pinstone St. 'Overground' buses run every ten minutes during the day (Monday to Saturday). Sheffield also boasts a modern Supertram which trundles through the city centre.

For a day of sightseeing (see Around Sheffield), a South Yorkshire Peak Explorer pass (£5.25) is valid for one day on all of the buses, trams and trains of South Yorkshire and north Derbyshire. Buy passes on your first bus, or at the helpful **transport information centre** (open 9am-5pm Mon-Sat) just off Pinstone St.

AROUND SHEFFIELD
About 10 miles (16km) south of Sheffield is **Chesterfield**, famous for its church with a twisted spire, and **Hardwick Hall**, an impressive stately home. For details see the Derbyshire section of the Midlands chapter.

Northeast of Sheffield, just off the M1 motorway near Rotherham, it's well worth aiming for **Magna** (☎ 01709-720002; w www .magnatrust.org.uk; Sheffield Rd, Rotherham; adult/child £8/6; open 10am-5pm daily). An unashamed celebration of heavy industry and high technology, this place is billed as a 'science adventure centre' – and that's just what it is. Split into four main themes – earth, air, fire and water – you can stand in a tornado (or try to), mess around with real JCB mechanical diggers, see steel being forged, blast away with water canons or simply fly through the air (well, nearly). Did the earth move for you? It will here, in the virtual earthquake. One of our research assistants, Matthew (aged 10), said it was 'ace' and 'wicked'. Sure, it's hid-

den learning, but it's all jolly good fun for kids – and grown-ups too.

To reach Magna from Sheffield, take bus No 69 (four per hour Monday to Saturday, hourly on Sunday, 20 minutes) towards Rotherham. It'll drop you at the dor.

Farther north, and also easily reached from Sheffield, is another industrial heritage site, the **National Coal Mining Museum**, and for a different perspective there's the **Yorkshire Sculpture Park**. Both sites are just over the border in West Yorkshire, and covered in the Around Leeds section, later in this chapter.

West Yorkshire

For centuries West Yorkshire's prosperity depended on textiles. Wool and cloth manufacturing flourished from the Middle Ages, but exploded in the Industrial Revolution, when a cottage industry – traditionally employing women spinning downstairs while their men wove away upstairs – quickly gave way to large factories.

By the early 20th century West Yorkshire, particularly Leeds and Bradford, dominated the wool industry, and the landscape is still characterised by its relics. Long rows of weavers' cottages and workers' houses built along ridges overlook the towering chimneys of the mills in the valleys, all separated by the wild, bleak stretches of moorland so vividly described by the Brontë sisters – West Yorkshire's most renowned literary export.

Since the end of WWII the vast textile industries have almost completely disappeared, leaving architectural landmarks and a culturally diverse legacy – thanks to the labourers who came to the mills from all over the world, particularly the Indian subcontinent – that still dominate the region today.

Activities
Walking The Pennine chain strides through West Yorkshire as a series of wild hilly moors, cut by steep-sided valleys where streams and rivers rush eastwards towards the great cities, where they once provided power to the mills that characterise the area. Today, the valleys and moors make good walking country, although the South Pennines (as this area's called) is wedged between the Peak District and the Yorkshire Dales, and has to defer to these areas in terms of sheer quality.

The **Pennine Way**, one of England's longest trails, follows the watershed through the area, and some good walks are possible following it for just a day or two. Between the towns of Hebden Bridge and Haworth is a popular option, and to get back you can follow another route called, not surprisingly, the **Haworth to Hebden Bridge Path**, which passes through quiet farmland and scenic wooded valleys. Hebden Bridge and especially Haworth make ideal bases for circular walks too, with several long and short options. The TICs all have leaflets and guidebooks on local walks, or see the sections on those towns, following, for more ideas.

Cycling To be blunt, West Yorkshire isn't great country for cycle touring; many roads are too urban in flavour, and the hills are darned steep too. The **National Cycle Network** (see the main Activities chapter) in West Yorkshire includes the short but traffic-free Leeds to Shipley route, which mostly follows a canal-side path (passing Saltaire, covered in this section), with plans to extend to Bradford by 2005.

Getting There & Around

The Metro is West Yorkshire's highly efficient train and bus network, centred on Leeds and Bradford – which are also the main gateways to the county. For transport details call **Metroline** (☎ 0113-245 7676; **W** www.wymetro.com) or the national **Traveline** (☎ 0870 608 2608). Metro DayRover passes (£4.50) are good for travel on buses and trains after 9.30am on weekdays and all day at weekends. There's a thicket of additional DayRovers covering buses and/or trains, plus heaps of useful Metro maps and timetables, all available at TICs.

LEEDS

☎ 0113 • pop 726,100

Leeds buzzes and bursts with services. Its heart is lined with busy pedestrianised streets, packed with shops and restaurants, upstanding Victorian edifices and arcades, and decadent clubs and bars. It's a see-and-be-seen place: shopping, eating, drinking and dancing are the main attractions, although it also boasts the impressive hardware of the Royal Armouries on its spruced-up canal bank.

Once pulsing with textile manufacturing and trade, this one-time driving industrial force is now pretty much dead, with memorials scattered over the city. Contemporary Leeds is the biggest financial centre in the country outside London, and, on a converse tip, has one of the biggest nightlife scenes. Many bars have late licences, lending the whole proceedings a relaxed flavour. Some legendary club nights have been honing their brand of hedonism for more than a decade, while new venues and versions pop up every time you blink.

The city is also a good base for excursions to Haworth, Hebden Bridge and Bradford.

Orientation

The city is strung out along the north bank of the River Aire and the Leeds–Liverpool Canal. The train and bus stations are central but the cheaper hotels are a bus ride away. It's best to explore the city centre on foot.

The **University of Leeds** (☎ 243 1751) and **Leeds Metropolitan University** (☎ 283 2600) are both just northwest of the centre.

Information

The large **Gateway to Yorkshire TIC** (☎ 242 5242, fax 246 8246; **W** www.leeds.gov.uk; PO Box 244, LS1 1PL, The Arcade; open 9am-5.30pm Mon-Sat, 10am-4pm Sun) is in the train station.

Leeds' **main post office** (open 9am-5.30pm Mon-Sat) is on City Square and **Internet Exchange** (☎ 242 1093; 29 Boar Lane; open 9.30am-8pm Mon-Fri, 10am-7pm Sat, 11am-6pm Sun), where Internet access costs £1 for 30 minutes, is near the train station.

Waterstone's (☎ 244 4588; 97 Albion St) is a large shop with a good selection of maps.

Leeds General Infirmary (☎ 243 2799) is the huge local hospital. It is west of Calverley St in the city centre.

Things to See & Do

A purpose-built, castle-like building houses the impressive **Royal Armouries** (☎ 220 1916, recorded information ☎ 220 1999; **W** www.armouries.org.uk; Armouries Drive; bus No 95; admission free; open 10.30am-5pm daily), on the banks of the Leeds–Liverpool Canal. The interior, painted a curiously unwarlike peach colour, includes four floors of exhibits centred on the themes of war, tournaments, self-defence, hunting and the Orient. Interpreters and interactive exhibits fill in the historical background and help put life

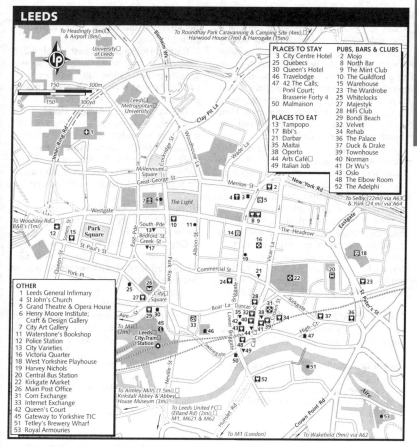

LEEDS

To Headingly (3mi),
& Airport (8mi)

To Roundhay Park Caravanning & Camping Site (4mi),
Harwood House (7mi) & Harrogate (15mi)

University
of Leeds

Blenheim Wk.

Leeds
Metropolitan
University

Clay Pit La

Woodhouse La

Wade La

Cockridge St.

Inner Ring Rd.

Millennium
Square
Great George St.

Merrion St.

New York Rd

Westgate

The Light

To Woodsley Rd,
B&B's (1mi)

Somers St.

St Paul's St.

Park
Square

South Pde

Bedford St.

Greek St.

Eastgate

Queen St.

York Pl.

Albion St.

Park Row

Commercial St.

Vicar La

The Headrow

St Peter's La

To Selby (22mi) via A63
& York (24 mi) via A64

City
Square

Aire St.

To M1
(2mi)

Leeds
City Train
Station

Boar La

Duncan St

Briggate

Kirkgate

High Ct.

Call La

Lower Briggate

Crown St

Swinegate

Neville St.

To Armley Mills (1.5mi),
Kirkstall Abbey & Abbey
House Museum (3mi)

To Leeds United FC
(Elland Rd) (2mi),
M1, M621 & M62

Hunslet Rd

Aire

Crown Point Rd

To M1 (London)

To Wakefield (9mi) via A62

PLACES TO STAY	PUBS, BARS & CLUBS
3 City Centre Hotel	2 Mojo
25 Quebecs	8 North Bar
30 Queen's Hotel	9 The Mint Club
46 Travelodge	10 The Guildford
47 42 The Calls;	15 Warehouse
Pool Court;	23 The Wardrobe
Brasserie Forty 4	25 Whitelocks
50 Malmaison	27 Majestyk
	28 HiFi Club
PLACES TO EAT	29 Bondi Beach
13 Tampopo	32 Velvet
17 Bibi's	34 Rehab
21 Darbar	36 The Palace
35 Maitai	37 Duck & Drake
38 Oporto	39 Townhouse
44 Arts Café	40 Norman
49 Italian Job	41 Dr Wu's
	43 Oslo
	48 The Elbow Room
	52 The Adelphi

OTHER	
1 Leeds General Infirmary
4 St John's Church
5 Grand Theatre & Opera House
6 Henry Moore Institute;
Craft & Design Gallery
7 City Art Gallery
11 Waterstone's Bookshop
12 Police Station
13 City Varieties
14 Victoria Quarter
18 West Yorkshire Playhouse
19 Harvey Nichols
20 Central Bus Station
22 Kirkgate Market
26 Main Post Office
31 Corn Exchange
33 Internet Exchange
42 Queen's Court
45 Gateway to Yorkshire TIC
51 Tetley's Brewery Wharf
53 Royal Armouries

into the instruments of death. There are numerous demonstrations throughout the day (pick up a schedule when you arrive) and outside from Easter to October you can see displays of jousting and falconry in the Tiltyard. The Royal Armouries is about half a mile from the TIC.

City Art Gallery (☎ 247 8248; w www.leeds .gov.uk/artgallery; The Headrow; admission free; open 10am-5pm Mon, Tues, Thur-Sat, 10am-8pm Wed, 1pm-5pm Sun) has a good collection of 20th-century art, including works by Stanley Spencer and Anthony Gormley. One of the last century's greatest sculptors, Henry Moore (1898–1986) was a Leeds School of Art graduate and the adjoining **Henry Moore Institute** (☎ 246 7467) stages exhibitions of 20th-century sculpture.

Tucked away off northern Briggate is the redundant but lovingly nurtured **St John's Church** (☎ 244 1689; open 9.30am-5.30pm Tues-Sat), a one-off masterpiece of 17th-century design, full of elaborate oak box-pews. A wonderful screen presents huge carvings of the coat of arms of James I and of Charles I as Prince of Wales.

Leeds' industrial past is displayed at **Armley Mills** (☎ 263 7861; adult/child £2/ 50p; open 10am-5pm Tues-Sat, noon-5pm Sun), a huge old textile mill built in 1805. The exhibits are a good overview of the Industrial Revolution, and the huge, mostly silent machines are resonant reminders of a lost industry. Bus Nos 14, 66 and 67 stop close by, or it's a peaceful stroll along the canal path.

In 1152 Cistercian monks from Fountains Abbey in North Yorkshire began work on a new abbey, later called **Kirkstall Abbey** (☎ 263 7861; Abbey Rd; admission free; open dawn to dusk daily). The dark, severe Norman ruins are striking and romantic, and make for an evocative wander. The complex reached its peak in the early 16th century when work on the **crossing tower** was completed. Then Henry VIII made his moves against the church and the roof literally fell in.

Across the road, the **Abbey House Museum** (☎ 230 5492; adult/child £3/1; open 10am-5pm Tues-Fri & Sun, noon-5pm Sat), once the Great Gate House to the abbey, contains meticulously reconstructed shops and houses to evoke Victorian Leeds. The impressive attention to detail is lit by flickering candlelike-light. Children will enjoy it, and there are displays giving an interesting insight into monastic life as well.

It's a turning off the A65, 3 miles (5km) southwest of Leeds. Various buses pass nearby, including Nos 733, 737 and 50.

Places to Stay
The TIC makes bookings for accommodation and has numerous special offers.

Camping Roundhay Park Caravanning & Camping Site (Elmet Lane, Roundhay; ☎ 266 1850; camping per person £4.40; bus Nos 98 & 99; open May-Sept), 4 miles (6.5km) to the northwest, is the most convenient site.

B&Bs Leeds B&Bs tend to be basic, and good taste nipped off for a long weekend a few decades ago and hasn't been seen since. The handiest B&Bs for the centre are behind the University of Leeds. To get here, take bus No 56, 58 or 60 from the city centre.

Manxdene Hotel (☎ 243 2586; 154 Woodsley Rd; singles/doubles from £27/40) is amenable, with plain rooms.

Moorlea Hotel (☎ 246 5393; 146 Woodsley Rd; singles/doubles from £27/40, with en suite £35/48) is basic and friendly; the pint-sized bar could have escaped from a low-budget sitcom.

There's another batch of B&Bs on Cardigan Rd, Headingley, backing onto the cricket ground; take bus No 74 or 75 from Infirmary St.

Boundary Express (☎/fax 275 7700; 42 Cardigan Rd; doubles from £39.95, with en suite £49.95) has halls decked with cricket memorabilia; the rooms are cheaply furnished but fine.

Trafford House & Budapest Hotel (☎ 275 2034, fax 274 2422; 16-18 Cardigan Rd; singles/doubles/triples £30/46/69, with en suite £44/60/87) has rooms with good cricket-ground views; three have balconies.

The very friendly **Butlers Hotel** (☎/fax 274 4755; w www.butlershotel.co.uk; en-suite singles/doubles from £64.95/69.95), adjoining the Boundary Express, has cluttered rooms with fittings such as old-fashioned telephones. Former guests include Catherine Zeta-Jones in her D-list days.

Hotels As Leeds is a business destination; standard prices are quoted here – but most hotels are cheaper at weekends.

City Centre Hotel (☎ 242 9019; 51 New Briggate; en-suite singles/doubles from £27/50) is well located with simple rooms and pea-sized bathrooms.

Travelodge (☎ 244 5793, fax 246 0076; Blayds Court, Swinegate; rooms with en suite £52.95) offers basic rooms and is nicer than it appears from the outside. Breakfast is extra.

Malmaison (☎ 398 1000, fax 398 1002; e leeds@malmaison.com; Sovereign St; singles/doubles from £75/105) is self-consciously stylish. Rooms have lovely canal views and electric curtains so you don't have to strain yourself to see them.

Quebecs (☎ 244 8989, fax 244 9090; w www.etontownhouse.com; 9 Quebecs St; rooms £80-250) is the former Victorian Leeds and County Liberal Club and has elaborate wood panelling and brilliant heraldic stained-glass windows. Rooms are decorated in neutral colours with varying degrees of success; one of the deluxe rooms has a dramatic spiral staircase.

Queen's Hotel (☎ 243 1323, fax 242 5154; City Square; singles/doubles from £80/105) is a huge old railway hotel that has been spruced up to cater to a business crowd.

42 The Calls (☎ 244 0099, fax 234 4100; 42 The Calls; rooms from £99) is in a converted Victorian grain mill overlooking the river. Its over-designed rooms are endearingly proportioned.

Places to Eat
Oporto (☎ 243 4008; 31-33 Call Lane; mains £7.50-15) is informal and popular, with

poppy-red sofas, exposed brickwork and tasty food.

Arts Café *(☎ 243 8243; 42 Call Lane; mains around £10)*, with a bohemian vibe, offers unpretentious modern British cooking amid warm yellow walls.

Pool Court, attached to 42 The Calls (see Hotels earlier), is Michelin-starred, with starched white tablecloths and outside seating overlooking the canal.

Brasserie Forty 4 *(☎ 234 3232; 42 The Calls; 3-course meal around £22)* is less formal with excellent food, but curiously decorated with a mismarriage of leaf and leopard skin.

Tampopo *(☎ 245 1816; 15 South Parade; rice & noodle dishes around £5.95-7.95)* offers tantalising Southeast-Asian cuisine. It's spacious, buzzing and minimalist with communal tables.

Maitai *(☎ 243 1989; 159 Briggate; dishes around £7-9)* serves reasonable and tasty Thai dishes in unflashy surroundings.

Darbar *(☎ 246 0381; 16 Kirkgate; mains from £8.75)* is a large, opulent restaurant serving delicious Indian specialities.

Italian Job *(☎ 242 0185; 9 Bridge End; dishes around £6)* has a traditional, unfussy interior and offers a good range of Italian standards.

Bibi's *(☎ 243 0905; 16 Greek St; mains around £7-18)*, at the higher end of the price range, is a neoclassical local favourite serving Italian classics and modern renditions.

Harvey Nichols *(☎ 204 8000; 107-11 Briggate)* has a ground-floor **espresso bar** with tables out under the cover of the Victoria Quarter arcade, ideal for all-weather posing. Upstairs, the light, bright **Fourth Floor Café** *(bar snacks £6; mains from £11; cocktails £7)* is a serene place to muse how to break the news of your purchase to your bank, and has innovative casual lunches and formal dinners.

In Headingly – student central – the **Ferret Hall Bistro** *(☎ 275 8613; w www.ferrethall bistro.co.uk; starters around £5, mains from around £11)* is a homely, intimate choice, with mismatched wooden tables and a Creole-influenced menu. Or try the perennially packed, glass-fronted **Citrus Café** *(☎ 274 9002; North Lane; mains £6-9; BYO)*.

Entertainment

Leeds takes its nights on the town seriously – get the monthly *Leeds Guide* (£1.70) or *Absolute Leeds* (£1.50) for current listings. Glammed-up hoards crawl the clusters of venues around Boar Lane and Call Lane. There's even an entertainment complex – **The Light** *(The Headrow)*, which contains various bland, carefully pitched venues, such as **Tiger Tiger**, aimed at the over-25s.

Pubs It may be a 21st-century city, but Leeds has some great traditional pubs. **Whitelocks** *(☎ 245 3950; Turk's Head Yard)*, dating from 1715, has courtyard tables and pub grub such as giant Yorkshire pudding (£1.95).

The Adelphi *(☎ 245 6377; 3-5 Hunslet Rd)* was built around 1898 and has changed little since, with fine wood panelling, tiles and engraved glass.

Duck & Drake *(☎ 246 5806; 43 Kirkgate)* has high ceilings, obligatory pub characters, real ales and regular live music – mainly jazz.

The Guildford *(☎ 244 9204; The Headrow)* is an attractive Art Deco classic featuring tall, stained-glass windows and solitary men pondering their pints.

The Palace *(☎ 244 5882; Kirkgate)* has one large room dating from the 1930s, possibly the widest choice of ales and a good beer garden.

Bars Most bars open till at least 2am, with an admission charge of £2 to £4, up to £6 at weekends.

Dr Wu's *(☎ 242 7629; 35 Call Lane)*, black-leather panelled and small, has an intriguing pebbledash corner; different DJs nightly vary the vibe, but it's bound to be studiously cool whatever.

The Elbow Room *(☎ 245 7011; w www .elbow-room.co.uk; 64 Call Lane; bar snacks £8-10)* is effortlessly appealing, with pop art and purple pool tables and laid-back music.

Mojo *(☎ 244 6387; 18 Merrion St)* is easygoing, trendy but not try-hard and has walls plastered with groovy maestros from Frank Zappa to the Dalai Lama.

Norman *(☎ 234 3988; 36 Call Lane)* is ferociously stylish, with lipstick-red seating and crazy-paving mirrors.

North Bar *(☎ 2424540; 24 New Briggate)* is a busy, refreshingly unglitzy bar with a background of rare groove, soul and jazz. It offers a formidable Belgian beer selection to an artsy crowd.

Oslo *(☎ 245 7768; Lower Briggate)* has curvaceous terracotta nooks and crannies lit

YORKSHIRE

by deep blue lights, perhaps so-named due to its oh-so-cool reputation for laid-back house nights.

QC (☎ 245 9449; Lower Briggate; open till 4am Mon-Sat) and **Bar Fibre** (☎ 200888; w www.barfibre.com; 168 Lower Briggate) are almost interchangeable chrome-and-glass gay bars, next door to each other, both spilling out into the cannily named Queen's Court.

Townhouse (☎ 219004; Assembly St) is a three-level venue decorated with ashen wood, burly bouncers and dapper characters eyeing up each other's understated labels.

Velvet (☎ 242 5079; 11-13 Hirst's Yard), nearby, is a classy, light and airy gay bar-restaurant upstairs (mains £6 to £15; open Tuesday to Saturday and Sunday lunch).

The Wardrobe (☎ 383 8800; w www.the -wardrobe.co.uk; St Peter's Square) has a long bar, high ceilings, frequent live music and a buzzing, eclectic crowd. A basement with a cochineal-red interior and sunken dance floor is a great environment for live jazz (tickets £8 to £12).

Clubs The tremendous Leeds club scene attracts people from miles around. In true northern tradition, people brave the cold wearing next to nothing, even in winter, which is a spectacle in itself.

HiFi Club (☎ 242 7353; w www.thehifi club.co.uk; 2 Central Rd) is intimate, with a fun, heaving, student-heavy atmosphere and specialises in funk, hip-hop and soul.

Mint Club (☎ 244 3168; w www.themint clubleeds.co.uk; 8 Harrison St) is small, with a big reputation, and hosts house nights with a cosy feel.

Rehab (2 Waterloo House, Assembly St), in a 17th-century building with a clinical theme, hosts Basics once a week, a hard-house institution that's been responsible for many a Monday-morning 1000m-stare.

Space (☎ 246 1030; Hirsts Yard; admission £10), a white-walled, packed-out, starkly modern venue, is where house music's big guns frequently play.

Warehouse (☎ 246 8287; 19-21 Somers St) hosts the mixed bootie-shaker **Speed Queen** event (w www.speedqueen.co.uk), featuring an outrageous crowd against a hi-energy soundtrack.

For mainstream pop from the cheese counter and alcohol-fuelled mating rituals try **Majestyk** (☎ 242 4333) or **Bondi Beach** (☎ 243 4733), both on City Square.

Theatre & Cinema One of England's last old-fashioned music halls dating from 1865, Leeds' **City Varieties** (☎ 243 0808; w www.cityvarieties.co.uk; Swan St) has hosted Chaplin and Houdini. Today it offers anything from clairvoyants to art-house neo-country musicians.

West Yorkshire Playhouse (☎ 213 7700; Quarry Hill Mount; under-26 tickets £3 Mon-Wed) has a sturdy reputation for excellent live drama.

The **Grand Theatre & Opera House** (☎ 222 6222; w www.leeds.gov.uk/grandtheatre; 46 New Briggate; tickets from £8) presents opera, musicals and plays, including performances by acclaimed **Opera North** (☎ 244 5326; w www.operanorth.co.uk).

Hyde Park Picture House (☎ 275 2045; w www.leeds.gov.uk/hydepark; Brudenell Rd; adult/child £3.50/2) is an Edwardian cinema in student central showing a meaty range of art-house and mainstream choices. Take bus No 56 or 63 from the city centre.

Spectator Sports Elland Road is the home of Premier Division **Leeds United Football Club** (tickets ☎ 226 1000; e tickets@ lufc.co.uk). You could tout your soul to see a top-flight game, but it's unlikely to help. Tickets for less-popular matches go on sale to the public about a month in advance. You can also tour the ground; call ☎ 367 6223 for details. To get there, take bus No 51, 52 or 54 from Kirkgate Market.

The first cricket match played at Headingly was in 1890, and it's still a venue for test matches and home ground of the **Yorkshire County Cricket Club** (tickets ☎ 278 7394; w www.yorkshireccc.org.uk; test match from £20). To get here, take bus No 74 or 75 from Infirmary Street or catch a train to Burley Park station.

Shopping

The designer-ridden **Victoria Quarter** (☎ 245 5333) arcades on Briggate are mosaic paved and stained-glass roofed. **Harvey Nichols** (☎ 204 8000; 107-11 Briggate) stocks an upmarket range of clothes for those with equivalent wallets, and has a couple of cafés.

Closer to earth, **Kirkgate Market** (☎ 214 5162; open 9am-5pm Mon-Sat, to 1pm Wed;

open-air market Thur-Tues), once home of Marks, who later joined Spencer, sells fresh produce and cheap goods.

The circular **Corn Exchange** (☎ 234 0363; open daily), built in 1865 to house the grain trade, has a wonderful, wrought, armadillo-like lid, and is the place to come for one-off clothes, eclectic jewellery or records.

Getting There & Away

Air Eight miles (13km) north of the city via the A65, **Leeds-Bradford airport** (☎ 250 9696) offers domestic and charter flights, plus international flights to a few major European cities. The Airlink 757 bus operates at least hourly between the airport and the bus and train station (£1.60, 40 minutes). A taxi costs around £15.

Bus National Express has services between Leeds and most British cities including London (£21.50, 4½ hours, nine daily) and Manchester (£9.25, one hour, nine daily).

Yorkshire Coastliner has useful services linking Leeds, York, Castle Howard, Goathland and Whitby (Nos 840, 842 and X40). It also links Leeds, York and Scarborough (Nos 843, 845 and X45). A Coastliner Freedom Ticket allows unlimited travel on any of these services (adult/child £10/5 per day).

Train Leeds City station has hourly services from London King's Cross (£62, two hours). There are also services to Sheffield (£8.90, 45 minutes), Manchester (£13.90, one hour) and York (£6.80 single, 30 to 40 minutes).

Leeds is also the start-point for services on the famous Settle–Carlisle line. For more details see the Yorkshire Dales section.

Getting Around To get around Leeds, Metro buses go from the Central Bus Station to most parts of the city and to the suburbs. Many also stop on or near City Square. Ask the TIC staff or bus drivers about the various DayRover tickets that cover trains and/or buses around the city, and for reaching Bradford, Haworth and Hebden Bridge as well. For more details see the West York-shire Getting Around section earlier.

AROUND LEEDS

A day out from Leeds opens up a fascinating range of options: stately splendour at Harewood, dust and darkness at the Na-tional Coal Mining Museum, or technology and poppadoms at Bradford, to name but a few. Places are listed roughly in order of distance from Leeds, first to the west and north, then to the south.

Bradford

☎ 01274 • pop 290,000 • elevation 150m

The centre of Bradford is just 9 miles west of the centre of Leeds, and the outer edges merge so the two cities are effectively united on the ground – although not when it comes to football, or much else, come to that. Leeds sees Bradford as the poor relative, while Bradford thinks Leeds has pretensions above its station. They both could be right.

For centuries Bradford was world capital of the wool trade, but the industry collapsed in the 1950s, and the city still struggles to find a new role. A large population of Pakistanis and Bangladeshis settled here throughout the 20th century and – despite occasional racial tensions – have helped reinvigorate the city and give it new energy. A high point of the year is a colourful celebration of Asian music and dance called the *Mela*, part of the annual Bradford festival which is held every June.

Things to See The top sight for any visit to Bradford is the **National Museum of Photography, Film & Television** (NMPFT; ☎ 202030; admission free; special events & cinemas about £3; open 10am-6pm Tues-Sun & bank holidays). Five floors are packed with exhibits – from 19th-century cameras and early animation to digital technology and the psychology of advertising. There's lots of hands-on stuff too; you can film yourself in a bedroom scene or play at being a TV newsreader. The museum also houses a massive IMAX screen and two other cinemas with a mix of offbeat and mainstream films.

The oft-overlooked **Colour Museum** (☎ 390955; Providence St; adult/child £1.50/1; open 10am-4pm Tues-Sat) is a little gem, just a 10-minute walk from the centre. Aimed mainly at school groups, it tells the story of Bradford's wool-dying trade, and has a fascinating section on how our eyes perceive colour, including a display contrasting the visual sense of different species (what's blue to you isn't blue to Fido).

Bradford Industrial Museum (☎ 435900; Moorside Rd, Eccleshill; admission free; open 10am-5pm Tues-Sat, noon-5pm Sun), 3 miles out of the centre, gives a hint of what a Yorkshire textile spinning mill was like at the peak of the Industrial Revolution. Other exhibits include various steam engines (sometimes working), transport from the last 100 years, and a horse-drawn tram to give a quick 'step back in history' round the car park.

About a mile (1.6km) from the industrial museum is **Undercliffe Cemetery** *(Undercliffe Lane; admission free; open daylight hrs daily)*, one of England's best collections of tombs for the 19th-century rich and famous. If you're into Victorian funerary art, it's wonderful, or (as they say locally) dead good.

Places to Eat Bradford is famous for its curries, so if you're still here in the evening, don't miss trying one of the city's hundred or so restaurants.

Kashmir *(☎ 726513; 27 Morley St; open evenings to 2am; mains around £4)*, just round the corner from the NMPFT, claims to be the oldest in town. It's no-frills and authentic with bare tables, no cutlery, no beer – just good filling food. To wash it down (or work up a hunger) there are several pubs nearby; those around the Alhambra theatre are a good start.

Koh-I-Noor *(☎ 737564; Simes St, Westgate; mains £5-8)* is a smarter place, northwest of the centre, with outrageous decor, slick staff and excellent food. A good place for a fun night out.

Getting There & Away Reaching Bradford from Leeds by Metro train is easy; there are very frequent services every day.

Saltaire

A landmark from the Victorian era, Saltaire was built in 1851 by philanthropic woolbaron Titus Salt as a 'village' for his factory workers. Overlooking the rows of neat honey-coloured cottages, the factory (the largest in the world at the time) had heating, ventilation and good light, and today has been nominated for Unesco World Heritage status.

Saltaire's **TIC** *(☎ 01274-774993; 2 Victoria Rd; open 10am-5pm daily)* has maps of the village and runs free guided walks.

The factory is now **Salt's Mill** *(☎ 01274-531163; w www.saltsmill.org.uk; admission free; open 10am-6pm daily)* a splendidly bright and airy cathedral-like building where the main draw is an exhibition of

work by Bradford-born artist David Hockney (1937–). There are also shops of books and crafts, and a café-diner.

Saltaire is 9 miles west of Leeds centre, and 3 miles north of Bradford centre (effectively an outer suburb of Bradford). Getting here is easy: Saltaire has its own train station on the Metro rail network, with regular services from Bradford and Leeds.

Harewood

On the map, Harewood appears as a cluster of houses about 7 miles (11.5km) north of Leeds, but the reason people come is to visit the great park, sumptuous gardens and mighty edifice of **Harewood House** *(☎ 0113-218 1010; w www.harewood.org; adult/child £9/5, Sun & Bank Hols £10/5.50; grounds open 10am-6pm, house 11am-4.30pm daily Mar-Oct)*. As an outing from Leeds you can easily fill a day here, and if you're heading for Harrogate, stopping off is highly recommended.

Harewood House was built between 1759 and 1772 and absolutely no expense was spared when it came to hiring the big names of the time. Lancelot 'Capability' Brown laid out the grounds, Thomas Chippendale supplied the furniture (the largest commission he ever received, costing £10,000 two centuries ago), John Carr designed the exterior, Robert Adams designed the interior, and Italy was raided to create an appropriate art collection. The end result is 100% classic stately home.

As well as the grand paintings inside the house, the separate **Terrace Gallery** displays touring exhibitions of contemporary work. Nearby are the formal **gardens**, with statues and geometric flowerbeds laid out on a broad terrace overlooked by the windows, steps and pillars of the house.

Many locals come to Harewood just to relax or saunter through the grounds, without even thinking of going inside the house. It's especially popular with families, and on summer weekends there's almost a beach atmosphere. Hours of entertainment can be had in the **Bird Garden**, with many colourful species including penguins (feeding time at 2pm is a highlight), and there's also a boating lake, café and adventure playground. For more activity, there's a network of walking trails around the lake or through the parkland.

From Leeds, use bus No 36 (at least half-hourly Monday to Saturday, hourly on Sunday) which continues to Harrogate. Visitors coming by bus get half-price admission too (so hang on to your ticket). From the main gate, it's a 2-mile (3km) walk through the grounds to the house and gardens. At busy times there's a free shuttle service.

National Coal Mining Museum

For centuries the driving force of industrial West and South Yorkshire was coal, and until the closures of the 1980s there were many mines in this area. Now there's less than a handful. To remember that era, Claphouse Colliery is now the **National Coal Mining Museum for England** (☎ *01924-848806;* **w** *www.ncm.org.uk; Overton, near Wakefield; open 10am-5pm daily; admission free).*

Highlight of a visit is the tour underground; complete with helmet and head-torch you ride in a 'cage' almost 150m down, then follow passages all the way to the coal seam where massive drilling machines now stand idle. Former-miners now work as guides, and explain the details – sometimes with a suitably authentic and almost impenetrable mix of local dialect and technical terminology.

Up on top, there are modern audiovisual displays, some fascinating memorabilia (including sketches by Henry Moore – see the Yorkshire Sculpture Park section, following), plus exhibits about trades unions, strikes and the wider mining communities – only slightly over-romantic in parts. You can also stroll round the pit-pony stables (with their equine inhabitants also now retired) or the slightly eerie bath-house, totally unchanged since the miners scrubbed off the coal dust and emptied their lockers for the last time. There are also longer nature trails in the surrounding fields and woods.

The museum is about 10 miles (16km) south of Leeds, on the A642, which drivers can reach from the M1. By public transport, take a train from Leeds to Wakefield (at least hourly, 15 minutes), and then bus No 232 towards Huddersfield can drop you outside the museum (hourly, 25 minutes). Bus No 231 (hourly on Sunday) from Wakefield goes to Bretton Park (see the Yorkshire Sculpture Park section following) then continues to the National Coal Mining Museum.

Yorkshire Sculpture Park

The vast grounds of Bretton Park have been turned into a wonderful outdoor gallery, where representational statues and intriguing abstract works sit among lawns, trees and fields. This is the **Yorkshire Sculpture Park** (☎ *01924-830302;* **w** *www.ysp.co.uk; Bretton, near Wakefield; open 10am-5pm daily, 11am-4pm Nov-Mar; admission free).* There's also an indoor gallery, café and gift shop, and you can easily spend a few hours here. If the weather is good, this a great place for a day out – take a stroll, take a picnic, take in the art...

Artists represented include: Ronald Rae, who carves wonderful animals *in* (not out of) huge blocks of granite (there's 100 tons-worth of his work here); Anthony Caro, whose massive steel *Promenade* sculpture invites exploration inside and out; plus Barbara Hepworth and Antony Gormley. Numerous works are by Yorkshire's own Henry Moore, perhaps the best-known English sculptor, who was largely influenced by the outdoors, and preferred his art to be sited in the landscape, rather than indoors. He certainly got his wish here.

The Yorkshire Sculpture Park is about 12 miles (19.5km) south of Leeds, and about 18 miles (29km) north of Sheffield, just west of the M1 motorway, so access is easy for drivers. By public transport, take a train from Leeds to Wakefield (at least hourly, 15 minutes), or from Sheffield to Barnsley (at least hourly, 20 minutes); then bus No X41 runs between Barnsley and Wakefield via Bretton Park (hourly Monday to Saturday, 25 minutes). Bus No 231 (hourly on Sunday) from Wakefield goes to Bretton Park then continues to the National Coal Mining Museum (see the section earlier).

HEBDEN BRIDGE

☎ 01422 • pop 3700 • elevation 100m

Deep in the valley of Calderdale, surrounded by high South Pennine hills, Hebden Bridge was once a textile mill-town like many others in this part of Yorkshire. But where others have slumped, Hebden Bridge has turned into an attractive and slightly alternative, slightly trendified little tourist centre, spoilt only by busy traffic on the main through route. There's a surprising number of craft shops, organic cafés, second-hand book and record shops, some good traditional pubs and friendly modern cafés, and it's home to a two-week Arts Festival in July.

As well as the honest-to-God Yorkshire folk who have lived here for years, the

YORKSHIRE

population today includes university academics, Manchester commuters and hardcore hippies, and there's also a large gay community. In recent years Hebden Bridge has become such a desirable place to live that house prices have rocketed, and many new-comers now head for nearby Todmorden instead.

Up on the hillside above Hebden Bridge is the much older village of **Heptonstall**, its narrow cobbled street lined with 500-year-old cottages, and a beautiful churchyard that has even older origins. It's like Haworth without the crowds, and if you like a literary link you'll be pleased to know that the renowned poet Ted Hughes grew up near Hebden Bridge and wrote many poems about the area. His wife and fellow-poet Sylvia Plath is buried in Heptonstall's Methodist church.

Information
The TIC (☎ 843831; e hebdenbridge@ytbtic .co.uk; 1 Bridge Gate; open around 10am-5pm daily, shorter hrs mid-Oct–mid-Mar) has a good stock of maps and leaflets on local walks and history.

Things to See & Do
On the canal-side, just out of the centre, the **Alternative Technology Centre** (☎ 842121; open 10am-5pm Mon-Fri, shorter hrs Sat & Sun) has a few solar and wind-powered displays and a shop full of green gear.

From the centre of Hebden Bridge, near the old **packhorse bridge** (built 1510), a steep path leads up to Heptonstall giving excellent views of the valley. If the spirit is weak, local bus No H2 takes the road way round, hourly. In Heptonstall, you can visit the ruined **Old Church** (dating from the 13th century), the **New Church** (1854), the small **museum** (open 1pm-5pm weekends Easter-Oct) of local history, the **Methodist church**, the oldest in England, and the ancient **Cloth Hall** – once a centre for Yorkshire's famous weaving cottage industries.

For a flat walk from the centre of Hebden Bridge, you can follow the **Rochdale Canal**, which runs through the town, complete with locks and brightly painted narrowboats: go east for a taste of countryside; or go west for a more urban feel, and heave-to at the excellent **Stubbing Wharf** pub.

Hardcastle Crags is the name of two unspoilt wooded valleys run by the National Trust (NT), 1½ miles northwest of town off the A6033. There are streams and waterfalls, and numerous walking trails, some of which link to the Pennine Way, and another which takes you all the way to Haworth.

Places to Stay
High Greenwood Campsite (☎ 842287; around £3 per person) is about 3 miles (5km) northwest of town, reached on the lane that runs through Heptonstall. It's just off the footpath between Hebden Bridge and Haworth, near Hardcastle Crags, and the Pennine Way runs nearby too, so it's very popular with walkers.

Mankinholes YHA Hostel (☎ 0870 770 5952; e mankinholes@yha.org.uk; beds £10) is in a grand old manor house, 4 miles (6.5km) southwest of Hebden Bridge, and half a mile from the Pennine Way – so it's also a walkers' favourite.

There are many B&Bs and small hotels in Hebden Bridge and more in the surrounding countryside.

Myrtle Grove (☎ 846078; Old Lees Rd; rooms per person £20-25) is small and neat, and the friendly owner is a mine of information on local places to walk, eat or drink – and can also direct you to other B&Bs if this one is full.

Angeldale Guesthouse (☎ 847321; e enq@ angeldale.co.uk; Hangingroyd Lane; rooms per person £22-27) is a spacious place with helpful and welcoming hosts, just outside the centre.

White Lion Hotel (☎ 842197; Bridge Gate; rooms per person £25-30) is a large 400-year-old coaching inn, very central, with neat rooms, busy bars and a restaurant downstairs.

Places to Eat & Drink
Crown Fisheries (Crown St; open daily to 6.30pm; mains around £4) serves up a great fish supper (fish, chips, bread and butter and tea), and also does takeaways.

Gustibus (☎ 846913; St George's Sq; snacks & light meals £3, mains around £5; open for lunch & dinner) is an excellent deli-café-restaurant with a Mediterranean flavour.

Hebdens (☎ 843745; Hangingroyd Lane; pizzas £7, mains around £10; open evenings Wed-Sun) is a modern and well-regarded Italian-leaning restaurant. Come early midweek for discounts on pizzas and pastas.

In the heart of town, the **White Swan** (bar food around £4) is a good straightforward pub, often busy. Just up the road, the **White Lion** (☎ 842197; Bridge Gate) is a smarter, pricier option with recommended food.

Getting There & Away
Getting here by train is easy: Hebden Bridge is on the line between Leeds and Manchester Victoria (services about every 30 minutes Monday to Saturday, hourly on Sunday, about 45 minutes), part of the Metro train network based on Leeds. (Get off at Todmorden for Mankinholes YHA Hostel.)

HAWORTH
☎ 01535 • pop 5000 • elevation 175m
Former home to the 19th century's novel-writing Brontë sisters, Haworth rivals Stratford-upon-Avon as England's most important literary shrine. Here is the parsonage where the literary classics *Jane Eyre* and *Wuthering Heights* were penned, and there are numerous other Brontë memorials around the small town. Even without this bookish link, Haworth would still draw visitors: the dark-stone houses of cobbled Main St, running steeply down from the parish church, provides a quintessential West Yorkshire view.

On top of the Brontës, Haworth's festival calendar has a bygone feel. Events include the 1940s weekend each May (with everyone dressed in WWII uniforms, Vera Lynn on the wireless etc) and a Victorian-style Christmas torchlight procession.

Information
The **TIC** (☎ 642329; e haworth@ytbtic.co.uk; 2-4 West Lane; open 9am-5.30pm Apr-Sept, 9am-5pm daily Oct-Mar) has an excellent supply of information on the village, the surrounding area and, of course, the Brontës. Another good source of information is w www.brontecountry.co.uk.

Main St is lined with cafés, tearooms, pubs and shops selling everything imaginable (and more) bearing the Brontë name. Handy stops might include: the **post office** (open 9am-5.30pm Mon-Fri, 9am-12.30pm Sat), which also changes money; **Venables & Bainbridge**, selling used books, including many vintage Brontë volumes; and **Spooks**, selling tarot cards, aromatherapy oils, and books on serious magic and local folklore.

Things to See
Your first stop should be **Haworth Parish Church** (open daily; admission free), a lovely old place of worship, built in the late 19th century, on the site of the 'old' church that the Brontë sisters knew, which was demolished in 1879. In the surrounding churchyard, gravestones are covered in moss, or thrust to one side by growing trees, which gives the whole place a tremendous feeling of age.

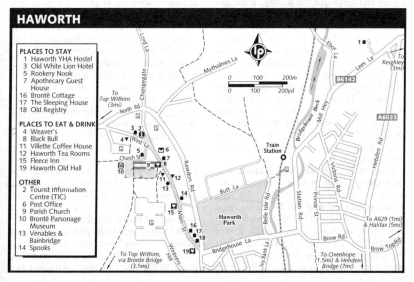

HAWORTH

PLACES TO STAY
1 Haworth YHA Hostel
3 Old White Lion Hotel
5 Rookery Nook
7 Apothecary Guest House
16 Brontë Cottage
17 The Sleeping House
18 Old Registry

PLACES TO EAT & DRINK
4 Weaver's
8 Black Bull
11 Villette Coffee House
12 Haworth Tea Rooms
15 Fleece Inn
19 Haworth Old Hall

OTHER
2 Tourist Information Centre (TIC)
6 Post Office
9 Parish Church
10 Brontë Parsonage Museum
13 Venables & Bainbridge
14 Spooks

The Brontës of Haworth

The Rev Patrick Brontë and his family moved to Haworth Parsonage in 1820, but his wife died soon after, and the children – Emily, Charlotte and Anne, and the lone boy Branwell – were brought up by their aunt. As soon as they could draw and write, the children conjured up mythical heroes and countries, and produced miniature home-made books. It was an auspicious start for the three famous Brontë sisters who stand out today as major figures in the pantheon of English literature.

Emily Brontë's best-known novel is *Wuthering Heights*, an epic tale of obsession and revenge, while Charlotte Brontë's most famous book, *Jane Eyre*, revolves around the central character's dilemma over a choice of husband, and is a wonderful celebration of the independent female spirit. Anne Brontë wrote *The Tenant of Wildfell Hall*, yet another classic of melodrama, mystery and love.

In all the Brontë sisters' works, the landscape surrounding Haworth was a great influence, and the austere Yorkshire moors always have a presence as strong as any of the leading characters.

Set in a pretty garden overlooking the church and graveyard, the **Brontë Parsonage Museum** (☎ 642323; w www.bronte.org.uk; adult/child £4.80/1.50; open 10am-5.00pm daily Apr-Sept, 11am-4.30pm Oct-Mar, closed Jan) is where the Brontë family lived from 1820. Rooms are meticulously furnished and decorated, exactly as they were in the Brontë era, with many personal possessions on display. There's also a neat and informative exhibition, which includes the fascinating miniature books the Brontës wrote as children. If you're with kids, the *Scribblemania* leaflet lets your offspring emulate these protegés.

Haworth is on the **Keighley & Worth Valley Railway** (KWVR; ☎ 645214; w www.kwvr .co.uk) – home to several steam and classic diesel engines and very popular with holiday crowds. It's also loved by film crews seeking old-world locations; even though it was decades ago, *The Railway Children* is still the most famous movie shot here. Trains operate around hourly at weekends all year; in holiday periods they're daily. Adult rover tickets (which let you stop at other stations – such as Oakworth, home of Mr Perks) cost £9. Standard one-way or return tickets are also available, and children travel half-price.

Walking

Haworth is surrounded by the moors of the South Pennines – immediately familiar to Brontë fans – and the TIC has leaflets on local walks to endless Brontë features. A 6½-mile (10.5km) favourite leads to Top Withins, a ruined farm thought to have inspired *Wuthering Heights*. Other walks can be worked around the Brontë Way, a longer route linking Bradford and Colne via Haworth. Alternatively, the Pennine Way runs west of Haworth and can be followed south to Hebden Bridge (see earlier). There's also a direct walking route between Haworth and Hebden Bridge, via the scenic valleys of Hardcastle Crags.

Places to Stay

Haworth YHA Hostel (☎ 0870 770 5858; e haworth@yha.org.uk; Longlands Drive, off Lees Lane; dorm beds £10, rooms from £39; open daily Feb-Nov, Fri-Sat only Nov-Jan) is in a big old house on the northeastern edge of town.

Rookery Nook (☎ 643374; 6 Church St; room per person from £15-22), rubbing shoulders with the church, is a good first choice; the best rooms are spacious with New Age decor, and the budget rooms are cramped but good value. Breakfast (£2.50 to £3.50) is served in the room.

Apothecary Guest House (☎ 643642; e apot@sisley.freeserve.co.uk; 86 Main St; en-suite singles/doubles from £20/40) is friendly and popular, with well-equipped rooms, a bit heavy on the chintz, but right in the centre of things.

Old Registry (☎ 646503; w www.oldreg istry.com; 2-4 Main St; en-suite singles/doubles £25/42) is very comfortable and stylishly rustic (or rustically stylish), complete with four-poster beds. In the same row of houses you'll find four more B&Bs, all with en suites or standard rooms from £18 to £25, including the **Sleeping House** and **Brontë Cottage**.

Old White Lion Hotel (☎ 642313; w www .oldwhitelionhotel.com; West Lane; singles/ doubles around £50/70) is a large rambling place in the heart of town. Attached is a highly rated restaurant (mains £10 to £12), and a bar that's old-fashioned and quiet (like most of the clientele), which also serves up good pub food (around £7).

Several pubs and tearooms also offer accommodation; some are listed under Places to Eat & Drink.

Places to Eat & Drink

Among the many cafés on Main St, **Villette Coffee House** *(115 Main St; snacks £1-3, mains £4)* is always popular, with a fine range of cakes and meals of the scampi-and-chips variety, plus high-calorie all-day breakfasts at £3.

Haworth Tea Rooms *(68 Main St; snacks £1-3, mains £4)* has friendly management and many good healthy options including baked spuds and veggie nachos. Upstairs is a small guesthouse with singles/doubles from £30/50.

Black Bull *(119 Main St; snacks around £3, mains £6.50)* is a large pub most famous for being Branwell Brontë's local. Today, it caters more for the tourist trade, serving up adequate bar food, and also offering accommodation. The nearby **Kings Arms** is livelier, does food at similar rates, and also has an interesting history; as well as a pub it's been a courthouse and a mortuary, and by sheer chance it now tends to be the locals' choice – but beware of karaoke night.

Fleece Inn *(51 Main St; meals around £8)* is an old favourite, although a recent revamp means the traditional ambience has gone, but it's still worth a stop for good beer and fine pub food.

Haworth Old Hall *(☎ 642709; Sun St; snacks £3, salads £6, mains £6-10)* is a highly-rated inn, with decent food, wine and beer, all served in convivial surroundings. The steak and ale pie is a classic. If you want to linger longer, comfortable doubles cost £50.

Weaver's *(☎ 643822; 15 West Lane; open Tues-Sat; bar suppers £4-10, 3-course restaurant-meal £20-25)* is smart, stylish and comfortable, with simply the best food in town and a menu featuring local specialities. Get there early to try the tasty two-course bar 'sampler' menu (£10.50). Rooms are also available (singles/doubles £50/75).

Getting There & Away

From Leeds, the easiest approach to Haworth is via Keighley, which is on the Metro train network (see the Leeds section). Bus No 500 runs between Keighley and Haworth (six daily, 15 minutes), and also serves Todmorden and Hebden Bridge. From Keighley you can also reach Haworth on the K&WV Railway, especially handy at summer weekends when roads are jam-packed.

ILKLEY

☎ 01943 • pop 20,000 • elevation 220m

Originally established as a village on a packhorse route across the Yorkshire Dales, Ilkley grew into a wealthy market centre in the Middle Ages, with much of the trade based on wool. Today, this town still exudes an air of 'old money' and quiet comfort, with plenty of hanging baskets and antique shops, those reliable indicators of well-to-do neighbourhoods, always much in evidence. There

---

Ilkley Moor Baht'at, Wi't Boots

In times gone by, to go walking in the damp misty hills of Ilkley Moor without a hat (*baht'at* in local dialect) was a recipe for bad health, and the warnings are forever remembered in *Ilkley Moor Baht'at* – a traditional English folk song and Yorkshire's national anthem. These days, Ilkley Moor can often be damp and misty, but if the sun is shining it's a lovely place for a walk. So get your boots on, get the *Walks from Ilkley* leaflet (30p) from the TIC and head for the hills.

From town it's a short walk to White Wells, a former spring and Victorian bathing place (there's now a teashop to revive flagging spirits), and then up past Cow and Calf Rock for great views over the town (the nearby Cow and Calf pub might further revive spirits, but can be very crowded at weekends). For something longer, from White Wells you can go right over the top of Ilkley Moor – especially fine in August when the heather is turning purple – to another popular pub called Dick Hudson's. To return you can retrace your steps, or come back part way, then zigzag around on paths which eventually take you east, past ancient Horncliff's Well, to finally come out by the Cow and Calf, and then it's all downhill to Ilkley. A great day out – but don't forget your hat!

are plenty of exclusive shops and boutiques, and the roads are lined with fancy cars. For visitors, the plus side is some decent pubs and restaurants.

Ilkley is a pleasant place to stop over for a night, and a handy gateway to the Yorkshire Dales National Park, especially if you're on the way from Leeds or Harrogate. The packhorse days are gone, but there are footpaths along the lovely River Wharf, ideal for a short stroll or a longer walk as far as Bolton Priory or Grassington (see the Walking section).

Information

Ilkley's **TIC** (☎ 602319; open 9.30am-5pm Mon-Sat) is in the town hall opposite the bus and train stations. There's a good stock of leaflets and books covering walks and things to see in the local area.

Things to See

Ilkley's understated **Manor House Museum** (☎ 600066; Church St; open 11am-5pm Wed-Sat, 1pm-4pm Sun; admission free) is a beautiful old Elizabethan building behind the church, dating from the 15th and 16th centuries. Inside, displays include two Roman gravestones, and photos of more recent bygone days.

Just outside the museum is the even more understated ruin of a **Roman Fort**. As part of Empire's attempt to quell unruly northerners, it once covered much of the churchyard and nearby Riverside Gardens, although today it's reduced to some grass-covered former walls and sections of rampart.

Walking

For a short stroll, from the centre of Ilkley, go down to the 'new' bridge (built 1904) over the River Wharfe. Don't cross this bridge but go left down some steps and through a park called Riverside Gardens to reach the attractive Old Bridge. Cross this then follow a path back along the north bank to the New Bridge.

For something longer, from the Old Bridge you can take the Dales Way (look for the signpost that says, misleadingly, 'Bowness 73 miles') through fields and woods 3 miles (5km) to the village of Addingham. Keeping on the Dales Way, you can follow footpaths (and a nasty few hundred metres of busy main road) to bypass the village of Bolton Abbey, and reach the ruins of Bolton Priory – see the next section for more details. From Ilkley to Bolton Abbey is about 7 miles (11.5km) on the paths, and takes two to three hours. An even longer option is to continue along the Dales Way from Bolton Abbey to Grassington (see the Yorkshire Dales section).

If you want to get out of the valley, and onto the hills, one of the most popular destinations is Ilkley Moor – see the boxed text 'Ilkley Moor Baht'at, Wi't Boots'.

Places to Stay

There are many places to stay in town, and more in the surrounding countryside.

Roberts Family B&B (☎ 817542; e petraroberts1@activemail.com; 63 Skipton Rd; singles £25-30, doubles £36-40) offers a very friendly and typically Yorkshire straight-talking welcome; the more expensive rooms have en suites.

One Tivoli Place (☎ 600328; e tivolipl@aol.com; 1 Tivoli Pl; singles/doubles £25/50) is a smart, calm and friendly B&B, just half a mile out of the centre, handily placed for walks on Ilkley Moor.

The Riverside Hotel (☎ 607338; Bridge Lane; singles/doubles from £40/57) is a slightly old-fashioned place in a quiet position, off the main road, next to (not surprisingly) the River Wharf and the Old Bridge (see the Walking section). Rooms are airy, comfortable, and very pink.

Grove Hotel (☎ 600298; e res@grovehotel.org; The Grove; en-suite singles/doubles from £47/64) has just six rooms, and combines professional service with a modern homely feel.

The Crescent Hotel (☎ 600012; w www.crescenthotelilkley.co.uk; Brook St; singles/doubles £62/82) built, naturally, in a grand curve at the heart of Ilkley, has 20 rooms and a bar and restaurant downstairs, which gives things a bustling atmosphere. Front rooms overlook a busy junction, and can be noisy, but the view's better.

Places to Eat & Drink

Ilkley's most famous café is **Betty's** (The Grove) – linked to the eponymous upmarket honeypots in Harrogate and York. They take their tea and coffee seriously here; it's over £5 a pot with a scone and cream. Nearby, **Sweet Indulgence** is a more down-to-earth bakery and café, with a traditional sweet shop downstairs, still selling goodies by weight from big glass jars.

The Riverside Hotel (Bridge Lane; snacks £2-3, mains £4-6) is a large friendly pub, very popular at weekends, as clients stroll in from the nearby park. The grub is fine, though the sandwiches are unappealing, but with good beer and happy hour from 4pm to 8pm, maybe drinking is a priority here.

Negreski's (☎ 605900; 1 New Brook St; lunch £6, dinner £10-12) serves up good modern French and fusion; come early for two-course specials at £8.

Bar Tat (7 Cunliffe Rd; snacks £4, mains £6-8) is a smart and slightly trendy 'ale and wine bar', with fine beer, lunches and evening meals. In contrast, **The Midland** (Station Rd) is a good traditional no-frills town pub, while **Johnstones** (Brook St) is a modern bar, also serving food, which becomes more of a club in the evening. For something more serene, the bar at the **Crescent Hotel** (Brook St) is good; it has a small courtyard patio, and a decent attached restaurant.

Getting There & Away
Bus No X84 runs between Leeds and Skipton (three per hour) via Ilkley. (To/from Skipton takes 30 minutes.) From Leeds, it's even easier to reach Ilkley by train – there are services at least hourly every day (30 minutes).

BOLTON ABBEY
The tiny village and country estate of Bolton Abbey is about 5 miles (8km) northwest of Ilkley, and the big draw here is the ruined church of **Bolton Priory** (admission free; open 9am-6pm/dusk daily) a beautiful old place built in the 12th century. With soaring arches and huge windows looking frail against the sky, these grand remains have inspired artists such as Wordsworth and Turner, and part of the building is still used as a church today.

As well as the priory ruins, the main attraction here is the scenic River Wharfe, which flows through the grounds, and there's a network of footpaths and walking trails beside the river and through the surrounding area. It's very popular with families (part of the riverbank looks like a beach at weekends), and you can buy teas and ice creams in the Cavendish Pavilion, a short walk from the priory. Other highlights include the stepping-stones (with a large gap between two stones in the middle of the

river, frequently forcing faint-hearted walkers to turn around and use the bridge) and The Strid, a narrow, wooded, picturesque gorge just upstream from the pavilion.

The shop and information centre in the village has leaflets (free) with walking maps and more details or you can check **w** www.boltonabbey.com.

Yorkshire Dales National Park

The Yorkshire Dales is a wonderful area of high hills and moors, cut by broad valleys where rivers of clear water flow over creamy limestone beds. Some hills have steep sides, exposed cliffs and even occasional pointy summits, but much of the landscape is smooth and less foreboding.

On the grassy moors the overwhelming impression is of space and openness, while the valleys contain remains of ancient settlements, simple stone villages and lonely farmsteads, with endless pale grey drystone walls dividing patchwork fields or snaking wildly over the slopes. This is the region made famous by James Herriot and *All Creatures Great and Small* (he lived in Thirsk, east of the park) and the landscapes he described, which later featured in films and TV series, remain pretty much unchanged today.

So the number-one reason to come to the Dales is for the scenery, and it's understandably one of the most popular areas in England for walking and cycling. Car drivers love it too, and as a result the roads can get extremely crowded. If you can't avoid busy summer weekends, try to come by bus or train, and even then it's well worth getting off the beaten track.

Orientation & Information
The 683-sq-mile (1770 sq km) Yorkshire Dales National Park divides into two parts: In the north, two main valleys run west to east – broad expansive Wensleydale (home of the famous cheese) and narrow secretive Swaledale. In the south, the main valleys – Ribblesdale, Malhamdale, Littondale and Wharfedale – all run north–south and are the most popular areas for tourists.

The main Dales gateways are Skipton in the south, and Richmond in the northeast.

YORKSHIRE

Good bases in the park itself include Settle, Grassington and Hawes. All have excellent TICs (some are called park visitor centres), stocking a mountain of local guidebooks and maps, and providing accommodation details.

To the northwest and west, the towns of Kirkby Stephen and Kirkby Lonsdale can also make handy jumping-off points, although both these spots are outside the national park boundary, and actually in the county of Cumbria (despite definite Dales affiliations) – so they're covered in that chapter in this book.

The *Visitor* newspaper, available from TICs, lists local events and walks guided by park rangers, as well as many places to stay and eat. The official park website at **w** www .yorkshiredales.org.uk is similarly useful.

Activities

Walking The Yorkshire Dales has a vast footpath network, with options for everything from easy strolls to challenging hikes; we suggest a few options throughout this section. Look out at TICs for leaflets on organised walks from train stations, notably on the Settle–Carlisle Line.

Two of England's most famous long distance routes cross the Dales. The Pennine Way goes through the rugged western half of the park. If you haven't got the three weeks required to cover all 259 miles (417km), a few days in the Dales, between Malham and Hawes for example, will repay the effort. The Coast to Coast Walk (a 190-mile/306km classic) goes through lovely Swaledale in the northern Dales. Following

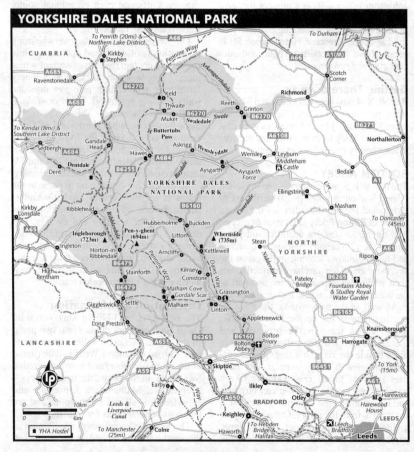

the route for a few days is highly recommended – see the Richmond section for more details.

Another long-distance possibility is the Dales Way, which begins in Ilkley, follows the River Wharfe through the heart of the Dales, and finishes at Bowness-on-Windermere in the Lake District. If you start at Grassington, it's an easy five-day 60-mile (97km) journey.

Cycling Outside busy summer weekends, this is excellent cycling country. Most roads follow the rivers along the bottom of the Dales so, although there are still some steep climbs, there's also plenty on the flat. TICs stock maps and leaflets with suggested routes (on-road and off-road) for a day or longer.

Just one example is the Yorkshire Dales Cycle Way, an energetic and exhilarating 130-mile (210km) loop, taking in the best of the park. Skipton is a convenient start, from where you ride up Wharfedale, then steeply over Fleatmoss to Hawes. From here turn east along Wensleydale to Aysgarth, then north over the wild hills to Reeth. The roads are steep but the scenery is breathtaking. Follow Swaledale westwards, through remote Keld and down to the market town of Kirkby Stephen. Then it's south to Sedbergh, and up beautiful Dentdale to pop out at Ribblehead. It's plain sailing now, through Horton-in-Ribblesdale to Stainforth, one more climb over to Malham, and finally back to Skipton for tea and medals.

Places to Stay

There are many villages in and around the park with a good range of hotels, B&Bs, hostels and campsites. Most rural pubs also do B&B. Walkers and hardy outdoor types can take advantage of **camping barns**. Usually owned by farmers, booking is organised centrally through the **YHA** (☎ 0870 870 8808). For details, TICs have a *Camping Barns in England* leaflet.

Getting There & Around

The main gateway towns of Skipton and Richmond are well served by public transport, and local bus services radiate out from there. Get hold of the very useful *Dales Explorer* timetable from TICs – as well as covering every bus in the region it contains maps, B&B listings, local information and

an excellent selection of walks that tie in with bus services.

Going by train, the best and most interesting access to the Dales is via the famous Settle–Carlisle Line (see the boxed text). From the south, trains start in Leeds and pass through Skipton, Settle, and numerous small villages, offering unrivalled access to the hills straight from the station platform. Of course, if you're coming from the north, Carlisle is the place to get on board.

SKIPTON
☎ 01756 • pop 13,500 • elevation 130m
Just outside the national park, Skipton is a large and busy market town. The **TIC** (☎ 792809; e skipton@ytbtic.org.uk; 35 Coach St; open 10am-5pm Mon-Fri, 9am-5pm Sat) is central and well stocked.

Skipton Castle (☎ 792442; adult/child £4.60/2.30; open 10am-6pm Mon-Sat, noon-6pm Sun), at the top of main street, is one of the best-preserved medieval castles in England – a fascinating contrast to the ruins you'll see elsewhere – and well worth a visit.

Places to Stay & Eat
There's a strip of B&Bs just outside the centre on Keighley Rd. All those between Nos 46 and 57 are worth trying.

Westfield House (☎ 790849; 50 Keighley Rd; singles from £23, doubles from £42) has very friendly management and good facilities.

Bizzie Lizzies (☎ 793189; 36 Swadford St; mains £5-6) is a large modern restaurant overlooking the canal, locally celebrated for the quality of its fish and chips. There's also an attached takeaway.

Of the pubs, **The Black Horse** (Coach St), is a large place with an outside terrace and meals daily, but our favourite is the **Narrow Boat** (Victoria St), a traditionally-styled place with good beer, friendly service and bar food (not on weekends).

Getting There & Away
Reaching Skipton is effortless by train from Leeds; it's the last stop on the Metro network (at least hourly, 40 minutes). For heading into the Dales, see the boxed text 'The Settle–Carlisle Line'. For Grassington, take bus No 72 (£4, six per day Monday to Saturday, 30 mins) or No 67 (hourly, Sunday); most go via the train station.

GRASSINGTON

☎ 01756 • pop 1200 • elevation 180m

The attractive little town of Grassington is 6 miles (9.5km) north of Skipton. It's thronging in summer but the local people never seem too busy to give a friendly welcome to tourists. The cobbled square is surrounded by cafés and shops, and the town is surrounded by idyllic countryside, so Grassington makes a great base for south Dales jaunts.

Your first stop should be (and if you come on the bus it will be) the TIC (☎ 752774; open 9.30am-5pm daily Apr-Oct, shorter hrs Nov-Mar) at the big car park on the edge of town. There's a good stock of maps and guides, and a nice little display that puts the surrounding scenery in context.

Places to Stay & Eat

The nearest YHA Hostel (☎ 0870 770 5920; beds £10) is a mile south of Grassington, in the picturesque hamlet of Linton.

There are several B&Bs along and just off Main St.

Town Head Guesthouse (☎ 752811; Low Lane; rooms per person from £26) is a quiet, neat and tidy place in a good position.

Foresters Arms (☎ 752349; Main St; singles/doubles £30/60) offers exceedingly friendly service, good pub grub and a range of rooms.

Black Horse Hotel (☎ 752770; fax 753452; Garrs Lane; B&B per person from £30) has a traditional no-frills bar, smarter restaurant and comfortable rooms.

Getting There & Away

To reach Grassington, details are given in the Skipton section earlier. For onward travels the No 72 continues up the valley to the nearby villages of Kettlewell and Buckden.

AROUND GRASSINGTON

North of Grassington, narrow roads lead up the beautiful valley of Wharfedale. Drivers take the road on the west side of the river; if you're cycling, take the quieter east-side option. If you're walking, follow the charming stretch of the Dales Way long-distance footpath (see the Activities section) through a classic Yorkshire Dales landscape of lush meadows surrounded by drystone walls, with traditional field-barns dotting the hillsides.

About 7 and 11 miles respectively from Grassington, the villages of Kettlewell and Buckden make good places to aim for, between them offering a good choice of campsites, B&Bs, teashops and pubs (all doing food and accommodation). Our favourite hostelries include the Blue Bell Inn and The Racehorses (which has a nice riverside garden) in Kettlewell, and the Buck Inn in Buckden. A few miles beyond Buckden, in the tiny settlement of Hubberholme, the friendly George Inn is also worth a stop. Another option is a triangular route taking in Kettlewell, Buckden and the village of Litton in the little valley of Littondale, to the west of Wharfedale, where the Queens Arms is another fine historical inn.

Check at Grassington TIC about the local buses that trundle up and down Wharfedale daily in the summer months (weekends in winter) – ideal for bringing home weary walkers.

MALHAM

☎ 01729 • pop 350 • elevation 200m

At the northern end of the quiet and beautiful valley of Malhamdale, this traditional village is well worth a stop, not only for its charm but also for the natural wonders nearby – all easily reached by foot (and covered in the Walking section following).

The excellent TIC (☎ 830363; e mal ham@ytbtic.co.uk; open 10am-4pm daily Apr-Oct, Fri-Sun Nov-Mar) has the usual wealth of information, local walks leaflets, maps and guidebooks.

Walking

The 5-mile (8km) Malham Landscape Trail (the TIC has details) takes in Malham Cove, a huge rock amphitheatre that was once a waterfall to rival Niagara, and Gordale Scar, a deep limestone canyon with scenic cascades and the remains of an Iron Age settlement.

For something longer, you can follow various paths eastwards through remote farmland for anything between 6 miles (9.5km) and 11 miles (17.5km) to reach Grassington, or head west on a great 6-mile (9.5km) hike over the hills to Settle. An even better option is a two day-hike between Grassington and Settle via Malham.

The long-distance Pennine Way passes right through Malham, and you can go north or south for as many days as you like. A day's walk away is Horton-in-Ribblesdale, described later in this section.

Places to Stay & Eat

Malham YHA Hostel (☎ *0870 770 5946;* **e** *malham@yha.org.uk; dorm beds £11.25, rooms from £39*) is right in the village centre.

Beck Hall (☎ *830332; rooms per person £21-28*) is a charming old house on the edge of the village, with a stream flowing through the garden.

Lister Arms (☎ *830330; listers@globalnet .co.uk; rooms per person from £28*) is a 17th-century coaching inn with excellent beer, fine pub food and comfortable rooms.

SETTLE

☎ 01729 • pop 3000 • elevation 140m

The little town of Settle sits east of the main A65, and retains much of its traditional character, with narrow cobbled streets leading out from the central market square (which still sees stalls and traders every Tuesday), surrounded by shops and some good pubs. Access is easy, and there are plenty of accommodation options. The **TIC** (☎ *825192;* **e** *settle@ytbtic.co.uk; Town Hall; open 9.30am-4.30pm daily*) has maps and guidebooks, and an excellent range of local walks leaflets (free).

Places to Stay & Eat

Stainforth YHA Hostel (☎ *0870 770 5946;* **e** *stainforth@yha.org.uk; dorm beds £11.25, rooms from £39*) is 2 miles (3km) north of Settle on the B6479 to Horton-in-Ribblesdale.

Liverpool House (☎ *822247; Chapel Sq; rooms per person £20-24*) offers a charming welcome and a range of rooms in a quiet street just off the centre.

Station House (☎ *822533;* **e** *station house@byinternet.com; double room £45*) is a friendly place and, as the name suggests, right by the famous railway line – a must for train spotters.

Golden Lion Hotel (☎ *822203; Duke St; rooms per person from £25; lunches £3-5, evening mains £7-9*) is central with a nice ambience, old-style bar and good interesting menus.

Royal Oak Hotel (☎ *822561; Market Place; rooms per person £28.50; bar meals from around £5*) is a good pub with an oak-panelled bar, a popular restaurant and comfortable rooms.

Around the square are several cafés, including **The Shambles**, noted for filling fish-and-chip suppers (£5.30) and the **Old Naked Man** with a bakery, cakes, snacks, ice cream, and not a French loaf joke in sight.

Getting There & Away

The easiest way to get here is by train. From the south, trains from Leeds or Skipton heading for Carlisle (see the 'Settle–Carlisle Line' boxed text) stop at the station near the town centre; those heading for Morecambe (on the west coast) stop at Giggleswick, about 1½ miles (2.5km) outside town.

AROUND SETTLE
Horton-In-Ribblesdale

☎ 01729

Five miles (8km) north of Settle, the little village of Horton is a favourite spot for walkers, cyclists and cavers. Everything centres round the **Pen-y-ghent Cafe** (☎ *860333; open Wed-Mon*), which serves up filling meals , home-made cakes, and pint mugs of tea. The friendly owners sell maps, guidebooks and walking gear, and the café acts as the village **TIC** (**e** *horton@ytbtic .co.uk*). There's also a **post office shop** for groceries and takeaways.

Holme Farm Campsite (☎ *860281; per tent £1, per person £2*) is a good simple place near the main road.

Dub-Cote Farm Camping Barn (☎ *860 238;* **w** *www.threepeaksbarn.co.uk; bunk beds £7.75*) is half a mile southeast of the village, well equipped with self-catering facilities.

There are several B&Bs in and around Horton.

The Knoll (☎ *860283; rooms per person £20*) is neat and efficient, and near the village centre.

Rowe House (☎ *860212; doubles per person £19-23, singles from £24*), on the north side of the village, offers excellent service.

Crown Hotel (☎ *860209;* **e** *minehost@ crown-hotel.co.uk; rooms per person £22-27*) is a homely place with a bar and a range of meals.

Golden Lion (☎ *860206; bunkroom per bed £7, B&B per person £18-21*), unmissable in lurid green, is a livelier pub offering breakfast, packed lunches, bar-food and evening dinners.

The Three Peaks

The countryside north of Settle is dominated by the Three Peaks – Whernside (735m),

Ingleborough (723m) and Pen-y-ghent (694m) – and the summits are linked by a long circular route that has been a classic walk for many years. The traditional start is the Pen-y-ghent Café in Horton-in-Ribblesdale and walkers try to complete the whole 25-mile (40km) route in under 12 hours. Others knock it off in six hours or less. Even faster are the fell-runners in the annual Three Peaks Race, who do it in about 2½ hours. If you're looking for a challenge, this might be one for you. If you like to actually enjoy your walking, doing a section of this route is perfectly feasible (for example

The Settle–Carlisle Line

The Settle–Carlisle Line (SCL), is one of the greatest rail engineering achievements of the Victorian era, and takes passengers across some of the best countryside in northern England. It's a working part of the national rail network (not a touristy set-up, although steam train specials do occasionally run), but the views from the windows are amazing and it's one of the best ways get to the heart of the Dales.

History

The SCL was the last major railway to be built by gangs of navvies using picks and shovels and involved some amazing work. The Ribblehead Viaduct has 24 arches, the tallest about 50m high, and the viaducts at Dent Head and Arten Gill are almost as impressive. The longest tunnel is under Blea Moor and over a mile (1.6km) long. Altogether there are 325 bridges, 21 viaducts and 14 tunnels.

The line was created by the Midland Railway Company. Legend has it that the company chairman looked at a map of Yorkshire, saw the big gap that was the Dales and drew a line across it, saying 'That's where I'll have my railway'. Reality was harsher: the line took 5000 men more than seven years to build, and cost over £3.5 million (a vast sum) and 100 lives (an even greater cost), thanks to accidents and appalling conditions in the workers' camps.

In the 1970s British Rail decided the expense of repairing the line was unjustifiable and the line was threatened with closure, but the ensuing public outcry has ensured its survival, at least for the time being. Today, it's a major tourist attraction, as well as a working railway. Even if you don't go on the train it's well worth visiting the lovingly maintained stations at places like Settle and Ribblehead.

Schedules and Fares

There are trains between Leeds and Carlisle via Settle, running along the SCL, about eight times per day. The entire journey takes two hours 40 minutes and some sample return fares in the Dales area are: Leeds–Skipton £5; Leeds–Settle £8; Settle–Carlisle £16.40. Various hop-on hop-off passes for one or three days are also available.

From most stations in Yorkshire, you can pick up the SCL timetable (free), which also includes a colour map of the line and brief details of places of interest. You can get more information from National Rail Enquiries (☎ 08457 484950) or for some background have a look at [W] www.settle-carlisle-railway.org.uk and [W] www.settle-carlisle.co.uk.

The Journey

The first section of the journey from Leeds is along the Aire Valley, with a stop at **Keighley**, where the Keighley & Worth Valley Railway branches off to Haworth (of Brontë fame, and covered in the West Yorkshire section). Next is **Skipton** – gateway to the southern Dales – and then your first sight of proper moors as the train arrives in the attractive market town of **Settle**. The train chugs up the valley beside the River Ribble, through **Horton-in-Ribblesdale**, across the spectacular Ribblehead Viaduct and then plunges through Blea Moor Tunnel, to pop out above Dentdale, where **Dent** station is one of the highest in the country. (Dent village is a couple of miles away down in the valley.) Next stop **Garsdale** (just a few miles west of Hawes), then the train reaches its highest point (356m) at Ais Gill, before leaving the Dales behind and trundling down to **Kirkby Stephen**. The last halts are **Appleby** then **Langwathby,** just northwest of Penrith (a jumping-off point for the Lake District), then the train finally pulls into **Carlisle**. What a ride!

walking from Horton as far as Ribblehead, and returning by train) and still highly recommended.

HAWES

☎ 01969 • pop 1300 • elevation 220m

The bustling little town of Hawes sits at the heart of Wensleydale – the home of the world-famous cheese – and makes a good base for exploring the northern Yorkshire Dales. Two stone bridges cross a rushing stream that flows through the town centre, and the wide main street and narrow lanes are lined with old-style shops, some small supermarkets, banks with ATMs, outdoor shops, half a dozen pubs, even more cafés, a couple of smart restaurants, some basic fish and chip takeaways, endless craft and pottery studios, a laundrette and a post office. What more could you want?

The **TIC** (☎ 667450; **e** hawes@ytbtic.co.uk; open 10am-5pm daily Easter-Oct, shorter hrs Nov-Apr) shares the Old Station building with the **Dales Countryside Museum** (same phone & hrs as TIC; adult/child £3/free) – a beautifully presented social history of the area. There's still an old train in the yard too.

The **Wensleydale Creamery Visitor Centre** (☎ 667664; open 10am-4pm daily; adult/ child £2/1.50) is billed as a major tourist attraction. It's briefly interesting, but watching guys shovel tons of cheese around quickly palls. Come before 3pm, as after that they're cleaning up. It's free to enter the shop, which sells – guess what – cheese and other produce, plus souvenirs of Wallace and Grommet, the cartoon characters who went to the moon for something to put on their crackers.

Places to Stay & Eat

Campers can aim for the well-organised, friendly **Bainbridge Ings Caravan & Camp Site** (☎ 667354; **w** www.bainbridge-ings.co .uk; per car, tent & 2 adults £7.50, hikers & cyclists per person £3), in spacious farmhouse fields about half-a-mile east of town.

Hawes YHA Hostel (☎ 0870 770 5854; **e** hawes@yha.org.uk; Town Head; dorm beds £10) is a modern place, just west of the centre.

There are many B&Bs in town; the following is a small selection.

Laburnum House (☎ 667717; The Holme; rooms per person from £21) is a quaint cottage in the centre, with a busy tearoom and terrace downstairs serving tea and scones (£2), hearty sandwiches (£3) and meals (£5).

Brandymires (☎ 667482; Muker Rd; doubles per person £20, singles £28) is a fine old tall-windowed house on the north side of town, with a no-nonsense atmosphere but good service and comfortable rooms.

Old Station House (☎ 667785; Hawdraw Rd; en-suite doubles £45) is a neat and tidy place next to – you guessed it – the old station (now the TIC).

Steppe Haugh (☎ 667645; Town Head; rooms per person £27) is a smart and comfortable place on the main road, near the YHA hostel.

There are plenty of pubs, including **The Fountain** (☎ 667206; Market Place; B&B per person £30; bar food around £5) with a lively bar and good en-suite rooms. The traditional **White Hart** (Market Place) is also good for a pint or a bar-meal (around £6)

Bulls Head Hotel (☎ 667437; **w** www .bullsheadhotel.com; Market Place; rooms per person £25-30) is a real surprise; it's a pub no more, but a stylish little hotel with a range of en-suite and standard rooms.

Getting There & Away

Hawes is not especially well served by public transport. From Northallerton, bus Nos 156 and 157 run to Hawes (about hourly Monday to Friday, two hours) via Leyburn, where you can connect with transport to/from Richmond. On Sunday (March to October) there are buses to Hawes from Manchester (No X43) via Skipton and Grassington, and from Leeds (No 806). Between Hawes and the Lake District, bus No 112 runs to/from

---

Yorkshire Pride

A local poem reads:
'Whernside, Ingleborough and Pen-y-ghent,
The highest hills twixt Tweed and Trent.'
But hold on there. The River Trent is in Nottinghamshire and the Tweed on the Scottish border, while Scafell – England's highest mountain – is only about 40 miles (64.5km) west of the Dales in the Lake District. Although Yorkshire people are known to be proud of their county, this might be just a tad too much hype!

YORKSHIRE

Kendal (once daily, 90 minutes), very early in the morning, with a few extra services on some other weekdays. The TIC can advise on other bus services aimed at visitors.

RICHMOND
☎ 01748 • pop 7900 • elevation 110m

Richmond is one of the most charming towns in England, and surprisingly few people know it. Cobbled streets and alleyways, lined with Georgian buildings or old stone cottages, radiate from the large market square, and give exhilarating glimpses of the surrounding hills and dales. To complete the scene, a massive ruined castle perches high on a rocky outcrop overlooking the town on one side and the rushing River Swale on the other.

Orientation & Information

Richmond is east of the Yorkshire Dales National Park but makes a good gateway for the northern area. Centre of everything is Trinity Church Square (with market day on Saturday). Just north of here, the **TIC** *(☎ 850 252;* **e** *richmond@ytbtic.co.uk; Victoria Rd; open 9.30am-5.30pm daily)* has friendly staff and the usual maps and guides, plus several leaflets (around 50p) showing walks in town and the surrounding countryside. Helpful **Castle Hill Books** *(Castle Hill)* is another place for guides and reading material.

Things to See

Top of your list must be **Richmond Castle** *(EH; ☎ 822493; admission £2.90; open 10am-6pm daily Apr-Sept, 10am-4pm Oct-Mar).* It was founded in 1070 by an aide of William the Conqueror to help subdue the north – one of the first in England since Roman times to be built of stone. It's had many uses through the years, including a stint as a prison for conscientious objectors during WWI (there's a small and sobering exhibition about their part in the castle's history). The best part of a visit is the view from the top of the remarkably well-preserved 30m-high tower; you can look down on the market place or over the surrounding hills, and truly imagine yourself king of the castle.

For a more recent look at military might, **Green Howards Museum** *(☎ 822133; Trinity Church Sq; adult/child £3/2; open 10am-4pm Mon-Sat Feb-Nov, Sun also Apr-Oct)* has three floors of exhibits telling the story of this famous Yorkshire regiment, from the Crimea to Kosovo.

In a totally different vein, **Richmondshire Museum** *(☎ 825611; Ryder's Wynd; adult/ child £1.50/1; open 11am-5pm daily Easter-Oct)* is a delightful little gem, with very informative staff and local history exhibits including an early Yorkshire cave-dweller, James Herriot's surgery, and informative displays on lead mining, which forever altered the Swaledale landscape a century ago.

Walking & Cycling

West from Richmond you can follow paths along the River Swale, upstream and downstream from the town. A longer option is along the north side of Swaledale, following the famous long-distance Coast to Coast route, all the way to Reeth. For a grand day out, take the first bus (£2) from Richmond to Reeth then walk back; the TIC has route and bus time details.

Cyclists can also follow Swaledale: as far as Reeth may be enough, while a trip to Keld, then over the high wild moors to Kirkby Stephen is a more serious but very rewarding 33-mile (53km) undertaking.

For more details, see Around Richmond, following.

Places to Stay

Windsor House *(☎ 823285; 9 Castle Hill; rooms per person £18)* is a rambling old place and an excellent no-frills choice.

There's a batch of pleasant places along a street called Frenchgate, and several more on Maison Dieu and Pottergate (the road into town from the east).

Pottergate Guesthouse *(☎ 823826; 4 Pottergate; rooms per person £19)* is very friendly and good value.

Emmanuel House *(☎ 823584; 41 Maison Dieu; rooms per person £20)* is a modern house with quiet, efficient service.

66 Frenchgate *(☎ 823421;* **e** *paul@ 66french.freeserve.co.uk; 66 Frenchgate; ensuite rooms per person from £22)* is an old house, modern in style, with great views from the back rooms.

Willance House *(☎ 824467; 24 Frenchgate; rooms per person from £25)* is a good traditional place.

Frenchgate Hotel *(☎ 822087, fax 823596; 59-61 Frenchgate; singles/doubles around £39/70)* is a small, smart, comfortable hotel.

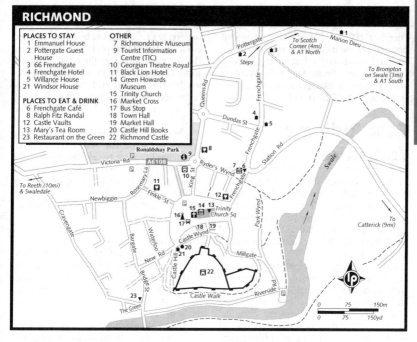

RICHMOND

PLACES TO STAY
1 Emmanuel House
2 Pottergate Guest House
3 66 Frenchgate
4 Frenchgate Hotel
5 Willance House
21 Windsor House

PLACES TO EAT & DRINK
6 Frenchgate Café
8 Ralph Fitz Randal
12 Castle Vaults
13 Mary's Tea Room
23 Restaurant on the Green

OTHER
7 Richmondshire Museum
9 Tourist Information Centre (TIC)
10 Georgian Theatre Royal
11 Black Lion Hotel
14 Green Howards Museum
15 Trinity Church
16 Market Cross
17 Bus Stop
18 Town Hall
19 Market Hall
20 Castle Hill Books
22 Richmond Castle

Places to Eat & Drink

Trinity Church Square and the surrounding streets have a huge choice of pubs, teashops, cafés and takeaways.

Mary's Tea Room (5 Trinity Church Sq; lunches under £4) offers delicious baked snacks and cakes.

Frenchgate Café (☎ 824949; 29 Frenchgate; lunches around £3, evening mains £7-10) offers sandwiches and coffees through the day, then becomes a bistro in the evening, serving imaginative European-style food.

Restaurant on the Green (☎ 826229; The Green; open Fri & Sat dinner only; mains around £10) has a good interesting menu, and also offers B&B, with just two rooms at £25/40 for a single/double.

Surprisingly, despite a vast choice, few of the pubs in Richmond are up to much. After extensive research, the best we found was the **Black Lion Hotel** (☎ 823121; Finkle St; bar food £5, mains in restaurant around £7), with cosy bars, low beams, good beer and food, plus B&B. Other options include the low-key **Castle Vaults** (Trinity Church Sq) and the large **Ralph Fitz Randal** (Queens Rd) where cheap food and drinks attract a boisterous crowd.

Getting There & Away

From Darlington (on the railway between London and Edinburgh) it's easy to reach Richmond on bus No 34 (£4, hourly, 30 minutes; four on Sunday). All buses stop in Trinity Church Square.

AROUND RICHMOND
Swaledale

West of Richmond, the River Swale flows through Swaledale – the quietest and least-visited of the Dales – with a wild and rugged beauty to contrast sharply with the softer, greener places farther south. It's hard to imagine, but only a century ago this was a major lead mining area. When the price of ore fell in the 19th century many people left Swaledale for good. Some went to England's burgeoning industrial cities, and others emigrated – especially to Wisconsin in the USA – leaving Swaledale almost empty, a legacy that remains today, with just a few small lonely villages scattered along its length.

Reeth

In the heart of Swaledale is the pretty village of Reeth – a great base for exploring

Swaledale, with shops, cafés and some good pubs dotted around a large sloping green. There's a **TIC** (☎ 01748-884059; e reeth@ytbtic.co.uk) and many B&B options. To understand Swaledale's fascinating history, the dusty little **Swaledale Folk Museum** (☎ 01748-884373; admission £1; open 10.30am-5pm daily Easter-Oct) is well worth a look.

East Riding of Yorkshire

In the 9th century the conquering Danes divided Yorkshire into three administrative regions, or ridings – from the Danish *thridings*, meaning third. The west and north ridings have become West Yorkshire and North Yorkshire, but the East Riding has retained its Viking title.

Hull is the region's biggest city, stolidly seated between the broad horizons of the Humber and Hull Rivers. Long a busy port and commercial centre, it has a gruff, plain appearance to match, but some excellent sights. North of the city is Beverley, a small market town, with lots of 18th-century character, and an enormous medieval religious and cultural legacy.

The expanse of the River Humber, with its soaring, delicate, powerful bridge, flows massively to meet the sea by a flat, deserted coast and the strange protuberance of Spurn Head. Farther north up the coast, there are some classic, small, brash seaside settlements: Bridlington and the rather-more-restrained Filey, and beyond that the drama of the Flamborough cliffs and Bempton Cliffs Nature Reserve.

The countryside inland is largely flat and nondescript – much of it drained marshland, which has been intensively farmed. Respite from the prairies comes in the form of the Yorkshire Wolds, an area of gently rolling chalky hills between Hull, York and the coast; it's an attractive area, in a low-key kind of way.

Activities

The low, chalky, rolling hills of the Yorkshire Wolds are ideal for gentle walks and cycle tours. Whether you're on two feet or two wheels, the town of Beverley makes a good base, and the northern Wolds can also be easily reached from York.

The area's main long-distance walk is the 80-mile (130km) **Wolds Way**. This national trail starts at **Hessle**, a riverside town 4 miles (6.5km) west of Hull, close to the

---

An Appalling Calling – Drystone Walling

The endless lines of pale grey limestone dry-stone walls that snake across the hills are a major part of the Yorkshire Dales landscape, and make good use of one of the area's most ubiquitous features – stones. Their construction may seem rudimentary – no mortar is used, and the stones are fitted together like a complex 3D jigsaw – but as with so many classic designs, the walls are the result of elegant engineering that has proved remarkably resilient to the tough Yorkshire weather, and the oldest date from the 16th century.

The busiest era for wall-building was the 18th and 19th centuries, when an experienced builder – or waller – could complete about six to seven metres of wall a day. Given the absence of any mechanical aid, this meant lifting about 12 tonnes of stone. Heavy work indeed.

To conserve energy, wallers realised that trying to change the shape of stones was pointless. Instead, every type of stone had a specific role. The largest stones formed the foundation along the ground. Above this two parallel walls were built with medium-sized stones both tilting slightly inwards. To prevent a total collapse, small stones were used as filler. Large flat stones were used every few layers as throughstones to link the two sides, and large rounded coping stones cap off the top. Experienced wallers could size up a stone by eye and feel and usually put it straight into place. True experts could boast that they never had to handle a stone twice.

In the 20th century traditional drystone walls fell out of favour, as cheap wire fencing could be erected with minimal cost and effort. But in recent times, the aesthetic and cultural importance of drystone walls has been recognised, and national park grants encourage landowners to once again build and restore of these vital elements of the classic Dales landscape.

Humber Bridge, and leads northwards through farmland, hills and quiet villages, to end at the tip of Filey Brigg, a peninsula on the east coast just north of the town of Filey. Billed as 'Yorkshire's best-kept secret', it takes five days, and is an excellent beginners' walk, as the landscape is not high and conditions not too strenuous.

The **Cleveland Way** (see the North York Moors section) also ends at Filey, and for a shorter walk in bracing sea-air you can follow the Cleveland Way along a scenic stretch of coast northwards from Filey to Scarborough.

Getting There & Around

Hull is easily reached by rail from Leeds, York, Beverley, Filey and Scarborough, and is also the hub for regional bus services. There's a useful website at w www.getting around.eastriding.gov.uk.

HULL

☎ 01482 • pop 333,000

Determinedly unaffected by the exotic trade that has passed through its docks, Hull (its full official name, Kingston-upon-Hull, is rarely used) feels like it will suffer no nonsense. It seems apt that jaundiced, rueful poet Philip Larkin (1922–85) presided over its university library for many years. Hemmed in by the blue mass of the river Humber, the city of Hull has been a major port for centuries, and so it remains in today's diminished terms.

It was badly bombed during World War II, and has its share of grimy post-war developments, but the Old Town retains a sense of the prosperous Victorian era. Perched on the waterfront, overlooking the endless Humber, is The Deep – a huge aquarium resembling a glinting mothership, and there are lots of other attractions around town if you look hard enough.

Orientation & Information

The Old Town of Hull is bounded by Fensway and Freetown Way and the Rivers Humber and Hull, with the marina and The Deep just to the south. It's all walkable.

Hull's **TIC** (☎ 223559, fax 613959; e hull paragon@ytbtic.co.uk; Carr Lane; open 10am-5pm Mon-Sat, 11am-3pm Sun) is surrounded by the imposing buildings of Queen Victoria Square. The **Central Library** (☎ 223 344; Albion St) has free Internet access.

Lunn Poly (☎ 227456; 17 King Edward St; open 9am-5.30pm Mon-Sat) will exchange money and has a travel agency. You can send mail at the **post office** (57 Jameson St; open 9am-5.30pm Mon-Sat).

Waterstones (☎ 580234; 19-21 Jameson St) is probably the best local option for books.

The Deep

Thousands of visitors have taken a state-of-the-art dip in **The Deep** (☎ 381000; w www .thedeep.co.uk; adult/child £6/4; open 10am-6pm daily) since it opened in 2002. This colossal, angled monolith stands at the edge of the port, with great views across the Humber. Inside it's just as dramatic, as echoing commentaries and computer-generated interactives run you through the formation of seas, and onwards. The largest aquarium contains 2.5 million litres of water and even has a glass lift. To get a good view of the tank's 19 different types of sharks and such, it's best (if more pedestrian) to take the stairs, as the lift ride is complete almost as you register that it's started. And it's rare you see a pod full of people zoom through a tank.

Other Things to See

Hull has a remarkable collection of city-run **museums** (☎ 613902; w www.hullcc.gov .uk/museums; open 10am-5pm Mon-Sat, 1.30pm-4.30pm Sun). All share the same phone number and opening hours and are free unless otherwise stated.

The serene **Ferens Art Gallery** (Queen Victoria Sq), built in 1927, has a decent collection that includes works by Stanley Spencer and Peter Blake.

The dusty-feeling but interesting **Maritime Museum**, in the former dock offices (1871), celebrates Hull's long maritime traditions, and includes some daunting whale skeletons.

The well-preserved High St has three eclectic museums. Attractive, Georgian **Wilberforce House** (1639) was the birthplace in 1759 of the antislavery crusader William Wilberforce. It covers the history of slavery and the campaign against it. Behind it is the **Artic Corsair** (☎ 613902; w www.artic-cor sair.co.uk; open 10.30am-3pm Wed & Sat, 1.30pm-3pm Sun); tours demonstrate the hardships of trawling in the Arctic Circle.

Streetlife Transport Museum has recreated 1930s streets, all sorts of historic vehicles to get on and off, and a pleasant

YORKSHIRE

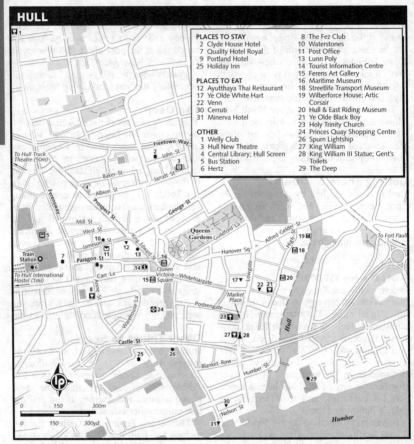

HULL

PLACES TO STAY
2 Clyde House Hotel
7 Quality Hotel Royal
9 Portland Hotel
25 Holiday Inn

PLACES TO EAT
12 Ayutthaya Thai Restaurant
17 Ye Olde White Hart
22 Venn
30 Cerruti
31 Minerva Hotel

OTHER
1 Welly Club
3 Hull New Theatre
4 Central Library; Hull Screen
5 Bus Station
6 Hertz

8 The Fez Club
10 Waterstones
11 Post Office
13 Lunn Poly
14 Tourist Information Centre
15 Ferens Art Gallery
16 Maritime Museum
18 Streetlife Transport Museum
19 Wilberforce House; Artic Corsair
20 Hull & East Riding Museum
21 Ye Olde Black Boy
23 Holy Trinity Church
24 Princes Quay Shopping Centre
26 Spurn Lightship
27 King William
28 King William III Statue; Gent's Toilets
29 The Deep

garden. The **Hull & East Riding Museum** traces local history from Roman times to the present, with new Anglo-Saxon, medieval and geology galleries.

At the heart of the Old Town, **Holy Trinity Church** (☎ 324835; open 11am-2pm Tues-Fri Oct-Mar, 11am-3pm Mon-Fri, 9.30am-noon Sat Apr-Sept, services Sun year round) is a magnificent 15th-century building with a striking central tower, and a long, tall, unified interior worthy of a cathedral. It features huge areas of windows, built to keep the weight of the walls down as the soil here is unstable.

Moving to some more prosaic architectural treasures, southeast of the church are some famous rare Art Nouveau **gents toilets** (Market Place) that have been relieving the

pressure since 1902. The nearby **King William III Statue** (Market Place) was erected in 1734 in honour of William of Orange, who besides being king also has the distinction of introducing England to gin, which he brought from his native Holland. The statue's proximity to the toilet is pure coincidence.

Built in 1927, the **Spurn Lightship** is now anchored in the marina. It once provided guidance for ships navigating the notorious Humber estuary.

Around 6 miles (9.5km) east of the centre, along the A1033, **Fort Paull** (☎ 893 339; ⓦ www.fortpaull.co.uk; adult/child £4.50/3; open 10am-6pm Apr-Oct, 11am-4pm Nov-Mar) is a grand, lavishly restored fort. The 1860s structure, with its underground labyrinths, is interesting, while stilted waxworks and warlike stuff document the fort's history from the AD 910 Viking landing onwards.

Walking

The TIC sells a brochure called *The Seven Seas Fish Pavement Trail* (40p), a delightful, historic self-guided tour of the Old Town, following fish shapes embedded in the pavement. Kids love it.

Guided walks *(adult/child £2.50/1; 2pm Mon-Sat, 11am Sun Apr-Oct)* leave from outside the TIC.

Places to Stay

Hull International Hostel *(☎ 216409; 4 Malm St; bus No 9 or 68; dorm bed £10, single £12)* has one single and one four-bedded room in a small house a mile west of the centre.

Clyde House Hotel *(☎ 214981; 13 John St; singles/doubles from £24/40)* is the best budget choice near the Old Town. It is next to leafy Kingston Square and has simple rooms.

Holiday Inn *(☎ 0870 400 9043, fax 386302; Castle St; rooms £120-145, Fri & Sat £60-80)* is the nicest place to stay. It overlooks the marina, and has well-equipped rooms, many with balconies.

Portland Hotel *(☎ 326462, fax 213460; Paragon St; singles/doubles £110/125, Fri & Sat £58/68)* is a modern place with smart rooms.

The **Quality Hotel Royal** *(☎ 325087, fax 323172; 170 Ferensway; singles/doubles £90/100, Fri & Sat rooms from £50)* is part of the train station complex. Fortunately it's less bleak, with reasonable, run-of-the-mill rooms.

Places to Eat

Ye Olde White Hart *(☎ 326363; 25 Silver St; mains around £4)* dates from the 1700s and has a good range of beer and food. Upstairs is the Plotting Parlour, where reputedly the decision was taken to deny King Charles I the city in 1642. Ask about the skull residing above one of the bars.

Ayutthaya Thai Restaurant *(☎ 219544; 47 Jameson St; open Mon-Sat; dishes £4.50-18.50)* is well thought of and has all the usual Thai-restaurant regalia.

Cerruti *(☎ 328501; 10 Nelson St; mains £9.95-26.50; open Mon-Fri lunch, Mon-Sat dinner)* is an attractive and respected Italian place, specialising appropriately in seafood.

Minerva Hotel *(☎ 326909; Nelson St; lunch daily, dinner Mon-Thur)* has a lot of charm, a fine pier-side location and possibly the smallest pub room in the country.

Venn *(☎ 224004; W www.venn.biz; 21 Scale Lane; open Tues-Sat; starters £5-9, mains £9-20)*, with a brasserie and small restaurant, has muted, cool decoration. Food is complex modern British, but, this being Hull, it's refreshingly pose free.

Entertainment

At weekends, locals party in intimidating, rowdy – mainly single-sex – groups, all dressed to kill. There's a corresponding number of intimidating, rowdy bars and clubs, with a few notable exceptions.

King William *(☎ 227013; 41 Market Place)*, with live music three nights a week and a beer garden out the back, is a decent pub that's busy day and night.

The Fez Club *(☎ 212507; Anne St; admission £2-7; open till 3am Mon-Sat)* has diverse nights including student-pleasing indie and hands-in-the-air house.

Welly Club *(☎ 326131, 221676; 105-7 Beverley Rd; admission free-£5; open till 2am, closed Wed & Sun)* shakes a leg to everything from ska to soul, and there's a Saturday residency by home-grown Steve Cobby of local heroes Fila Brazillia.

Ye Olde Black Boy *(☎ 326516; 150 High St)* has a site dating from 1337, and is smoke-stained and plush-seated in the great English pub tradition.

Hull Truck Theatre *(☎ 323638; W www.hulltruck.co.uk; Spring St)* is home to acclaimed down-to-earth playwright John Godber and presents vibrant drama, comedy and Sunday jazz.

Hull New Theatre *(☎ 226655; W www.hullnewtheatre.co.uk; Kingston Square)* is a traditional regional theatre hosting popular drama, concerts and musicals.

Shopping

Princes Quay Shopping Centre *(☎ 586622; W www.princes-quay.co.uk)*, an imposing glass building set in a moat facing the modern marina, is filled with chain stores of every kind.

Getting There & Away

The bus station is on Ferensway, just north of the train station. National Express has buses to/from London (£30, five hours 50 minutes, four daily) and Manchester (£18.50, four hours 20 minutes, one daily). Both National Express and Bus No X46 run frequently to/from York (£3.80 single, one hour 50 minutes). Local services also leave from here.

The train station is west of Queen Victoria Square, in the town centre. Hull has good rail links north and south, and west to York (£15.50, one hour, hourly) and Leeds (£14.90, one hour, hourly).

The ferry port is 3 miles (5km) east of the centre at King George Dock. A bus to/from the train station connects with the ferries. **P&O North Sea Ferries** (☎ *0870 129 6002, fax 706438;* **w** *www.mycruiseferries.co.uk*) has daily ferries to/from Rotterdam and Zeebrugge (both £48 to £67, 14 hours).

Getting Around
Hull's city centre is walkable, but if you need a motor there's a **Hertz** (☎ *323906*) office at the train station.

AROUND HULL
Humber Bridge
The graceful, concrete and metal Humber Bridge swoops 1410m across the broad river – the world's third-longest single-suspension bridge – seemingly hung by fine threads. It has linked Yorkshire and Lincolnshire since 1981, opening up what was an often-overlooked corner of the country.

Near the base of the bridge on the north side is a small park with nature trails that run from the parking area all the way down to the riverbank. The park can be reached from the bridge access roads. The park is also home to the **Humber Bridge TIC** (☎*/fax 01482-640852; open 9am-5pm Mon-Fri, 9am-6pm Sat & Sun May-Sept, 10am-3pm Nov-Feb, 9am-4pm Mar, Apr & Oct*). It handles information requests for all of East Riding of Yorkshire and the Wolds Way and has a display documenting the construction of the bridge.

The bridge is 1 mile (1.6km) west of the small riverside town of **Hessle**, about 4 miles (6.5km) west of Hull and effectively an outer suburb. Bus Nos 66, 67 and 68 run regularly from Hull's centre (£1.90, 30 minutes) to Hessle, and this is also a stop for local trains on the line from Hull to Leeds, Doncaster and Sheffield.

BEVERLEY
☎ 01482 • pop 19,500
Beverley feels undiscovered. It's an unspoilt market town, filled with a harmonious collection of 18th-century buildings. Approaching Beverley, its magnificent medieval minster rises from the small tangle of town, providing a sense of timeless pilgrimage. And Beverley not only boasts this, but another rich medieval church as well as a charming rambling pub – Nellie's.

Orientation & Information
Beverley is small and easily walked to from either the train or bus stations.

Helpful Beverley **TIC** (☎ *391672;* **e** *beverley@ytbtic.co.uk; 34 Butcher Row; open 9.30am-5.15pm Mon-Fri, 9.30am-4.45pm Sat, 10am-2pm Sun June-Aug*) handles visitor inquiries.

Send mail at the **post office** (*Register Square; open 9am-5.30pm Mon-Fri, 9am-12.30pm Sat*).

The **library** (☎ *885355; Champney Rd; open 9.30am-5pm Mon & Wed, 9.30am-7pm Tues, Thur & Fri, 9am-1pm Sat*) also has a small art gallery with changing exhibitions. The **Beverley Bookshop** (☎ *0800 616 394; 16 Butcher Row*) is a good locally owned bookshop.

There's a large market in the main square on Saturday.

Beverley Minster
The first church on this site was built in the 7th century when a monastery was established. The present building (☎ *868540;* **w** *www.beverleyminster.co.uk; requested donation £2; open 9am-7pm daily May-Sept, 9am-5pm daily Mar-Apr & Oct-Nov, 9am-4pm Dec-Feb*) dates from 1220 but construction continued for two centuries, spanning the Early English, Decorated and Perpendicular periods. Hailed for its unity of forms, the church has a magnificent Gothic perpendicular west front (1390–1420).

Inside, the nave is strikingly high. Extraordinary medieval faces and demons peer down from every possible vantage point, while expressive stone musicians play silent instruments. Note particularly a 10th-century frith stool (Old English for 'peace chair') relating to the minster's sanctuary arrangements; the fruit- and angel-laden Gothic canopy of the Percy Tomb; the 68 medieval

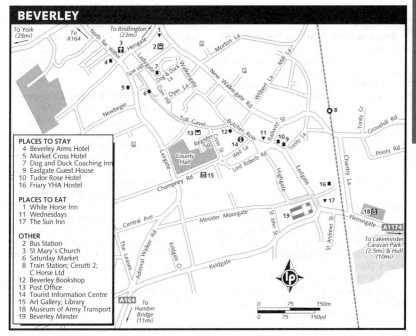

BEVERLEY

To York (28mi)
To A164
To Bridlington (23mi)
North Bar Within
Hengate
Ladygate
Sow Hill Rd
Dog & Duck La
Corn Hill
Dyer La
Walkergate
New Walkergate Rd
Wilbert La
Morton La
Mill La
Newbegin
Toll Gavel
Butcher Row
Railway St
Trinity La
Grovehill Rd
Priory Rd
Register Sq
Cross St
Well La
Lord Roberts Rd
Highgate
Eastgate
Chantry La
Champney Rd
County Hall
Flemingate
A1174
St John St
Minister Moorgate
St Andrews St
Central Ave
The Leases
Admiral Walker Rd
Keldgate Cl
Keldgate
A164
To Humber Bridge (11mi)
To Lakeminster Caravan Park (2.5mi) & Hull (10mi)

PLACES TO STAY
4 Beverley Arms Hotel
5 Market Cross Hotel
7 Dog and Duck Coaching Inn
9 Eastgate Guest House
10 Tudor Rose Hotel
16 Friary YHA Hostel

PLACES TO EAT
1 White Horse Inn
11 Wednesdays
17 The Sun Inn

OTHER
2 Bus Station
3 St Mary's Church
6 Saturday Market
8 Train Station; Cerutti 2; C Horse Ltd
12 Beverley Bookshop
13 Post Office
14 Tourist Information Centre
15 Art Gallery; Library
18 Museum of Army Transport
19 Beverley Minster

0   75   150m
0   75   150yd

misericords (the largest collection in the country) and the late Norman font (c.1170).

There's an interesting display showing the history of the minster and town. Check out the rebuilt treadwheel crane, where workers ground around like hapless hamsters to lift the huge loads necessary to build such medieval structures.

St Mary's Church

St Mary's (☎ 865709; ⓦ www.stmarysbever ley.org.uk; admission free; open 9am-5pm Mon-Sat Mar-Apr, 9am-6pm Mon-Sat May-Sept, 9am-4pm Mon-Sat Dec-Feb, noon-4pm Sun, sometimes open later June-Aug) inevitably plays second fiddle to the minster, but is a glorious church, built in stages between 1120 and 1530. In the North Choir Aisle look out for a carving (c.1330) thought to have inspired Lewis Carroll's White Rabbit. The Chancel dates from 1280, with a rare painted ceiling depicting English kings (1445). The church was built by the Beverley minstrel guilds and this patronage is honoured in the lavish carvings of musicians and instruments. The West Front is considered one of England's finest (early 15th century).

Museum of Army Transport

All manner of military transport is on display at the Museum of Army Transport (☎ 860445; adult/child £4.50/3; open 10am-5pm daily). The exhibits are indoors, cover almost a hectare and include trains, planes and trucks – lots and lots of trucks. You can board various army vehicles, and there are displays to put them into context.

The museum is just east of the minster at Flemingate.

Places to Stay

Lakeminster Caravan Park (☎ 882655; Hull Rd; tent pitches £10) has camping facilities. It is 2½ miles (4km) east of town. Bus Nos 121 and 122 (hourly) will drop you by the park.

Friary YHA Hostel (☎ 0870 770 5696; Friar's Lane; admission £8.75; open Mon-Sat Easter-end Oct) is in a beautiful 14th-century Dominican friary.

Eastgate Guest House (☎ 868464; 7 Eastgate; singles/doubles from £26/39, with en suite £39/47) is a friendly B&B with floral, simple rooms.

Market Cross Hotel (☎ 679029; 12-14 Lairgate; singles/doubles £25/45) has blowsy rooms in a Georgian building close to the main square.

Dog and Duck Coaching Inn *(☎ 886079; 33 Ladygate; en-suite singles/doubles £25/38)* is a pleasant pub with a wing of modern rooms for rent that open onto a garden.

Tudor Rose Hotel *(☎ 882028; Wednesday Market; singles/doubles £39/49)* has comfortable rooms above a good pub and restaurant.

Beverley Arms Hotel *(☎ 869241, fax 870907; North Bar Within; singles/doubles from £85/100)* is a dignified Georgian inn; ask for a room in the old building.

Places to Eat
Tudor Rose Hotel *(Wednesday Market; mains around £6-9)* – see Places to Stay – serves appetising and intriguing Polish specialities.

Cerutti 2 *(☎ 866700; Station Square; mains £9-17; open Mon-Sat)* does excellent Italian and is a remarkable place to find in a train station. **C Horse Ltd**, at the other side of the station, is a fine-food deli run by the same folk.

Wednesdays *(☎ 869727; 8 Wednesday Market; starters £3.50, mains £7.50-15; open lunch & dinner Mon-Sat)* has a good reputation and an adventurous Euro menu cooked with interesting ingredients and spices.

The Sun Inn *(☎ 881547; 1 Flemingate)* claims to be Beverley's oldest pub (was formerly the Tap and Spile). It's well located across from the minster and has good real ale.

White Horse Inn *(☎ 861973; 22 Hengate)*, or Nellie's, is a lovely, dimly lit place, with rambling rooms, open fires and tables outside. There's regular live music and poetry.

Getting There & Away
The train station lies east of the town centre. The bus station is north on Sow Hill.

Bus No X46/X47 links Beverley with York (£3.35 single, one hour 10 minutes, hourly). There are frequent buses to Hull (Nos 121, 122, 246 and X46/X47, £1.90, 30 minutes).

There are regular trains to/from Scarborough via Filey (£10.20, one hour 30 minutes). Trains to/from Hull (£4.60, 20 minutes) run at least hourly.

Details on boats to Hull from northern Europe are given in the main Getting There & Away chapter.

EAST YORKSHIRE COAST
The coast of the East Riding of Yorkshire has long unpeopled stretches, and ranges from the fine blustery cliff tops at Flamborough and Bempton to the strange long sandy outpost of Spurn Head, via Bridlington, a small, brash and entertaining seaside resort.

The places in this section are described north to south.

Bempton Cliffs Nature Reserve
Run by the Royal Society for the Protection of Birds, Bempton Cliffs Nature Reserve *(☎ 01262-851179; pedestrian/car free/£3; visitor centre open 10am-5pm daily Mar-Nov, 10am-5pm Sat & Sun Dec & Feb)* is a delightful place for non-twitchers too. Around 3 miles (5km) of paths (open at all times) skirt the top of the imposing chalk cliffs, which are home to over 200,000 nesting sea birds – the largest colony in England – every spring and summer. There are many other feathered residents in place the rest of the year as well. The species flapping about include gannets, auks, guillemots, razorbills, kittinakes and ever-popular puffins.

There is a good visitor centre with a small snack bar set back from the cliffs. Binoculars can be rented for £2.50 and there are usually volunteers on hand to provide guidance.

The reserve is a well-marked 1¼ miles (2km) from the village of Bempton and the B1229. By public transport, take one of the frequent trains on the Hull–Scarborough line and then walk.

Flamborough
The small village of Flamborough is 3 miles (5km) east of Bridlington. Fine views soar out from the milk-coloured cliffs at Flamborough Head, 2 miles (3km) east of the village.

Seabirds *(☎ 01262-850242; meals £5-12)* is at the junction of the B1255 and the B1229. It is a classic country pub with several rooms, open fires and a beer garden. The real ale selection is good and the seafood lunches and dinners excellent.

Bridlington
☎ 01262 • pop 31,138

The little town of Bridlington presents a roll call of the English seaside's usual suspects, with all the tawdry charm that such diversions involve. The promenade has a small funfair, candyfloss, arcades, all-day-breakfasts, palmists, lager specials and often windswept people. There's a long, sandy attractive beach.

The **TIC** (*☎ 01262-673474; 25 Prince St; open 9.30am-5.30pm Mon-Sat, 11am-3pm Sun*) is near the north beach and has short-term parking at the front. It can book a vast array of rooms.

Bridlington is on the line from Hull to Scarborough with frequent trains to the former (£8, 45 minutes) and the latter (£5.20, 45 minutes).

Spurn Head

Spurn Head (*admission per car £2.50*) is a narrow sandbank that dangles off the coast on the north side of the Humber estuary. It has a long military history and is an important nature reserve.

In 1804 gun batteries were built on Spurn Head in case the French came calling. In following decades the fortifications were greatly expanded to meet various threats. By WWII there were guns of all sizes mounted in heavy concrete emplacements. After the war, the odds of some enemy force arriving in assault boats faded and the guns were removed, although remnants of the many concrete emplacements and roadways survive.

A benefit of the years of military use is that Spurn Head was spared commercial development. Today it is made up of large rolling sand dunes covered with various sea grasses. Most of the land is now part of the **Spurn National Nature Reserve**.

There are two TICs. One has a café and is at the end of the B1445 in Kilnsea, the last village on the mainland. Called the **Blue Bell Tea Room** (*☎ 01964-650139; open 11am-4.30pm daily July-Sept, 11am-5pm Sat & Sun Sept-June*), it is close to the beach, and allows free camping on its grassy land. It has a collection of materials outlining the unusual nature of the sandbank. *Spurn's Moving Story* details the shifting nature of the sands and shows how one good storm could wash the entire head away. The other is run by the **Yorkshire Wildlife Trust** (*open 10am-5pm Sat & Sun*) and is a mile farther south along the Spurn Head access road.

The single-track road to the point is 2½ miles (4km) long. There are many good walks, and at the tip of the head, you can see the spurting tides of the Humber as well as the busy shuttle boats used by the pilots of the many passing freighters.

Back in Kilnsea, along the B1445, the **Crown and Anchor** (*☎ 01964-650276; en*-suite singles/doubles £30/39; mains £5-8.50) is a fine pub with good food, and a dramatic, isolated, waterside location.

Public transport to Kilnsea and Spurn Head is nonexistent. It's about 28 miles (45km) east of Hull. The flat roads are good for bikes.

York

☎ 01904 • pop 123,000

York is a fascinating city of extraordinary cultural and historical wealth. Its medieval spider's web of narrow streets is enclosed by a magnificent circuit of 13th-century walls. At its heart lies the immense, awe-inspiring minster, with an exterior like craggy lace. The city is thick with museums tracing its long history – from ancient times, to the Viking era, to the heyday of the railway. The streets themselves present a cornucopia of heritage as well as every kind of restaurant and myriad traditional pubs with centuries of pint pouring experience.

Unsurprisingly, the city's a tourist honey pot, and July and August can be crowded.

History

It's thought that the Brigantes tribe had a settlement at the confluence of the Rivers Foss and Ouse before the Romans arrived to set up a walled garrison, Eboracum, in AD 71.

Eboracum was strategically important, and a civilian settlement prospered around the large fort. But by AD 400, the Roman Empire was disintegrating, and the legions were withdrawn. In the 5th century the Anglo-Saxons founded Eoforwic on the Roman ruins, the capital of the independent kingdom of Northumbria.

In 625 Christianity was brought here by Paulinus, a Roman priest, who succeeded in converting the Saxon king of Northumbria, King Edwin, and his nobles. The first wooden church was built in 627 and in the 7th and 8th centuries the city became a centre of learning that attracted students from around Europe.

The Danish Vikings captured the city in 866, making it their capital, Jorvik, for nearly 100 years and sharing out the Northumbrian lands between themselves. Despite their marauding reputation, the period was relatively peaceful and the city became an important trading port. In 954 King Eadred of Wessex

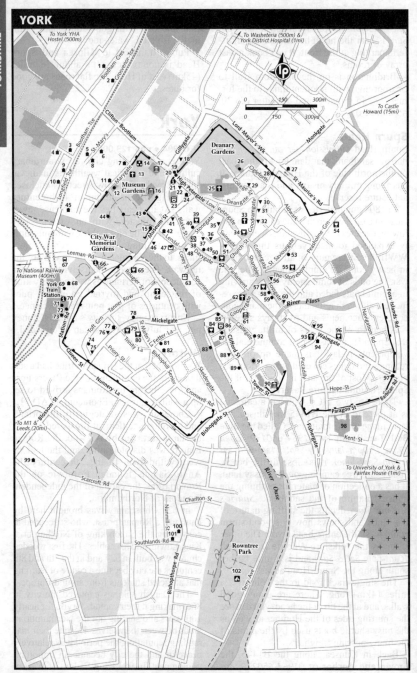

YORK

To York YHA
Hostel (500m)

To Washeteria (500m) &
York District Hospital (1mi)

To Castle
Howard (15mi)

Deanary
Gardens

Museum
Gardens

City War
Memorial
Gardens

To National Railway
Museum (400m)

York
Train Station

To M1 &
Leeds (20mi)

Mickelgate

River Foss

To University of York &
Fairfax House (1mi)

River Ouse

Rowntree
Park

YORK

PLACES TO STAY
1 Gables Guest House
2 Brontë House
3 Elliotts Hotel
4 Alcuin Lodge
5 Crook Lodge
6 Treetops Guest House
7 Coach House Hotel
8 23 St Mary's
9 Martins Guest House
10 Briar Lea Guest House
11 Jorvik Hotel
24 Dean Court Hotel
27 Monkbar Hotel
42 Judges Lodging Hotel
45 Abbey Guest House;
   Riverside Walk
68 Royal York Hotel
77 York Backpackers
82 York Youth Hotel
94 St Denys Hotel
99 Wheatlands Lodge
100 Nunmill House
101 Acorn Guest House
102 Rowntree Park Camping

PLACES TO EAT
18 Café No 8
22 Plunkets; Café Concerto
29 St William's College/
   Restaurant
30 La Piazza
31 Lime House
32 Siam House
35 El Piano; Priestleys Vintage
   Clothing
36 Oscar's Wine Bar & Bistro
37 Rubicon
41 Ask; Grand Assembly Rooms
46 Pizza Express

48 Betty's
51 VJ's Artbar
56 Rish
60 Blue Bicycle
75 Jinnah
76 Blake Head Bookshop &
   Vegetarian Café
88 Fiesta Mexicana
95 The Tapas Tree

PUBS & CLUBS
34 Old White Swan
39 Ye Olde Starre
52 The Roman Bath
54 Black Swan
55 Fibbers
57 Blue Bell
65 The Maltings
79 Ziggy's
80 The Ackhorne
84 King's Arms
96 Spread Eagle

OTHER
12 St Mary's Lodge
13 St Olave's Church
14 St Mary's Abbey
15 Museum Gardens Lodge
16 Yorkshire Museum
17 York City Art Gallery
19 Bootham Bar; Steps to
   City Walls
20 Bootham Tower
21 Tourist Information Centre
23 York Theatre Royal
25 York Minster
26 Treasurer's House
28 Monk Bar; Richard III
   Museum; Steps to City Walls;
   Bob Trotter Bicycle Hire

33 Holy Trinity, Goodramgate
38 Internet Exchange
40 AmEx
43 Multangular Tower
44 Gatehall; Hospitium
47 Post Office
49 Borders
50 Nevisport
53 Archaelogical Resource
   Centre
58 Merchant Adventurer's
   Hall
59 Jack Duncan Books
61 Jorvik Viking Centre
62 All Saints Pavement
63 City Screen; City Screen
   Café-Bar
64 All Saints, North St
66 York Travel Bus Info Centre
67 Local Bus Stops
69 York Model Railway
70 Tourist Information Office
71 Station Taxis
72 Hertz
73 Europcar
74 York Brewery
78 Wildcat Records; Ken
   Spellman Booksellers
81 Practical Car & Van Rental
83 Yorkboat River Trips
85 Thomas Cook
86 Grand Opera House
87 York Dungeon
89 Eddie Brown Tours
90 York Castle Museum
91 Clifford's Tower
92 Fairfax House
93 St Denys Church
97 Walmgate Bar
98 York Barbican Centre

managed to drive out the last Viking ruler, reuniting Danelaw with the south, but a turbulent period followed. In 1066 King Harold II was forced to quell a Norwegian invasion-rebellion at Stamford Bridge, east of York, just before he got trounced by William the Conqueror at the Battle of Hastings.

William built two wooden castles in York. After they were briefly captured by an Anglo-Scandinavian army, he burnt York and Durham and laid waste to the countryside in retribution. In the 11th century the Normans started to rebuild the city, beginning the construction of the minster. Despite being decimated by fire in 1137, York thrived over the next three centuries, prospering through royal patronage, textiles, trade and the church to become England's second city.

But by the time the minster was complete in the 15th century, the city was in recession. The textile industry moved elsewhere, and Hull took over as the region's main port. The Reformation, and associated decline of the church's power and wealth, hit York hard. However, Henry VIII established a branch of the King's Council here to help govern the north, and this was to contribute to the city's recovery under Elizabeth I and James I.

The council was abolished during Charles I's reign, but York's garrison meant it was an important Royalist stronghold during the Civil War. In April 1644 York was besieged, finally falling in June 1644. Fortunately, the commander of the Parliamentarian forces, Sir Thomas Fairfax, a local man, prevented the troops pillaging the minster.

York recovered its former prominence in the 18th century, as it became a fashionable social centre, dominated by the aristocracy, drawn by its culture and new racecourse, and many fine Georgian buildings were added to its architectural wealth. The coming of the railway in 1839 transformed the city again, employing thousands of people, alongside other developing industries such as confectionery manufacture. Since the decline of these in the latter half of the 20th century, the main trade has been tourism.

Orientation

Remember that, in York, *gate* means street and *bar* means gate. The city is circled by a ring road. There are five major landmarks: the wall enclosing the small city centre; the minster at the northern corner; Clifford's Tower at the southern end; the River Ouse that cuts the centre in two; and the train station to the west.

Information

The main **TIC** (☎ 621756, fax 551888; De Grey Rooms, Exhibition Square; open 9am-6pm Mon-Sat, 10am-5pm Sun Apr-Sept; 9am-5pm Mon-Sat, 10am-4pm Sun Oct-Mar) is north of the river near Bootham Bar. There's also a small **TIC** (open 9am-6pm Mon-Sat, 10am-5pm Sun Apr-Sept; 9.30am-5pm Mon-Sat, 10am-4pm Sun Oct-Mar) at the train station.

American Express (☎ 676501; 6 Stonegate; open 9am-5.30pm Mon-Fri, 9am-5pm Sat) has an exchange service.

Send mail at the **post office** (22 Lendal; open 8.30am-5.30pm Mon & Tues, 9am-5.30pm Wed-Sat). **Internet Exchange** (☎ 638 808; 13 Stonegate; open 9am-7pm Mon-Sat, 11am-6pm Sun) charges £1.50 for 15 minutes online.

Thomas Cook (☎ 653626; 4 Nessgate) is a travel agent offering a full service.

Well-stocked **Borders** (☎ 653300; 1-5 Davygate; open 9am-9pm Mon-Sat, 11am-5pm Sun) occupies part of a 19th-century chapel. There's a wealth of second-hand and antiquarian bookshops (see Shopping).

You can do a load at the **Washeteria** (☎ 623379; 124 Haxby Rd).

York District Hospital (☎ 631313; Wiggington Rd) is a mile north of the centre.

York Minster

York Minster (☎ 624426; **w** www.yorkminster.org; suggested donation adult/child £3.50/1, undercroft £3.80/1, tower adult/child £3/1; open 7am-6pm Mon-Sat, from 1pm Sun Jan-Mar, Nov & Dec, to 6.30pm Apr, to 7.30pm May, to 8.30pm June-Aug, to 8pm Sept & to 7pm Oct, undercroft & tower open 10am-4.30pm Mon-Sat Jan, Feb, Nov & Dec, noon-6pm Mar, 10am-5.30pm Apr, Oct, 10am-6pm May & Sept, 9.30am-6.30pm

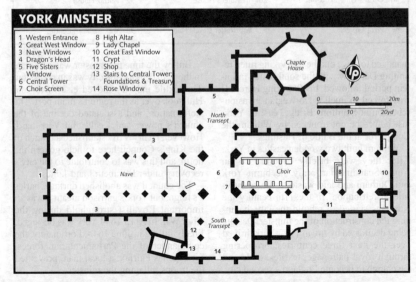

YORK MINSTER

1 Western Entrance
2 Great West Window
3 Nave Windows
4 Dragon's Head
5 Five Sisters Window
6 Central Tower
7 Choir Screen
8 High Altar
9 Lady Chapel
10 Great East Window
11 Crypt
12 Shop
13 Stairs to Central Tower; Foundations & Treasury
14 Rose Window

Chapter House

North Transept

Nave

Choir

South Transept

June-Aug, from 12.30pm Sun), or the Cathedral & Metropolitan Church of St Peter, is one of Europe's largest medieval cathedrals. It's the seat of the archbishop of York, the Primate of England, second only in importance to the archbishop of Canterbury, the Primate of *All* England.

The minster incorporates the remains of seven buildings. It is most famous for its extensive medieval stained-glass, particularly the work in the enormous Great East Window (1405–8).

The first church on the site was a wooden chapel built for Paulinus' baptism of King Edwin on Easter Day 627; its site is marked in the crypt. With deliberate symbolism, the church was built on the site of a Roman basilica, a vast central assembly hall; parts can be seen in the foundations. A stone church was started but fell into disrepair after Edwin's death. St Wilfred built the next church but this was destroyed during William the Conqueror's brutal suppression of the north. The first Norman church was built in stages to 1080; you can see surviving fragments in the foundations and crypt.

The present building, built mainly from 1220 to 1480, manages to represent all the major stages of Gothic architectural development. The transepts were built in Early English style between 1220 and 1255; the octagonal chapter house was built between 1275 and 1290 in the Decorated style; the nave from 1291 to 1340, and the west towers, west front and central, or lantern, tower were built in Perpendicular style from 1470 to 1472.

You enter from the western end. The nave is unusually tall and wide. Although the aisles (to the side) are roofed in stone, note that the central roof is wood painted to look like stone. On both sides of the nave are shields of the nobles who met Edward II at a parliament in York. Also note the **dragon's head** projecting from the gallery – it's a crane believed to have been used to lift a font cover. There are several fine **windows** dating from the early 14th century, but the most dominating is the **Great West Window**, from 1338, with beautiful stone tracery.

The transepts are the oldest part of the building above ground and the **Five Sisters Window**, with five lancets over 15m high, is the minster's oldest complete window; most of its tangle of glass dates from around

1250. In 1984 the south transept was damaged by a fire and is now fully restored.

The 13th-century **chapter house** is a magnificent example of the Decorated style. Sinuous stonework surrounds a wonderful uninterrupted space. There are more than 200 expressive carved heads and figures.

The minster's heart is dominated by the awesome **central tower**. The 15th-century **choir screen** depicts the 15 kings from William I to Henry VI.

The **lady chapel** behind the **high altar** is dominated by the huge **Great East Window**. It illustrates the beginning and end of the world as described in Genesis and the Book of Revelations.

Entered from the southern choir aisle, the **crypt** contains fragments from the Norman cathedral. The font shows King Edwin's baptism and marks the site of Paulinus' original wooden chapel.

In the south transept, the **Rose Window** commemorates the union of the royal houses of Lancaster and York, through the marriage of Henry VII and Elizabeth of York, which ended the Wars of the Roses and began the Tudor dynasty.

The entry to the stairs up to the tower and down to the foundations and treasury is also in the south transept. Despite sometimes long queues for the tower, the view over York and the surrounding countryside is worth both the wait and the steep, claustrophobic climb (275 steps) to the top.

The **foundations** and **treasury** shouldn't be missed. In 1967 the foundations were excavated when the central tower threatened to collapse; while engineers worked frantically to save the building, archaeologists uncovered Roman and Norman ruins that attest to the site's ancient history – one of the most extraordinary finds is a Roman culvert, still carrying water to the Ouse. The treasury houses 11th-century artefacts, including relics from the graves of medieval archbishops.

To see everything could easily absorb the best part of a day. The worthwhile guided tours are free.

Around the Minster

Owned by the minster since the 15th century, **St William's College** (☎ 637134; *College St)* is an attractive half-timbered Tudor building housing an excellent restaurant (see Places to Eat).

The **Treasurer's House** (NT; ☎ 624247; Minster Yard; admission £3.80; open 11am-4.30pm Sat-Thur Apr-Oct) was home to the minster's medieval treasurers. Substantially rebuilt in the 17th and 18th centuries, the 13 rooms house a fine collection of furniture and supply a good insight into 18th-century life.

City Walls

You can get onto the walls, built in the 13th century, via steps by **Bootham Bar** (on the site of a Roman gate) and follow them clockwise to Monk Bar, a walk offering particularly beautiful views of the minster. There are oodles more access points including off Station Rd and Monkgate.

Monk Bar is the best preserved medieval gate, with a small **Richard III Museum** (☎ 634191; adult/child £2/1; open 9am-5pm daily Mar-Oct, 9.30am-4pm daily Nov-Feb) upstairs. The museum sets out the case of the murdered 'Princes in the Tower' and invites visitors to judge whether their uncle, Richard III, killed them.

Walmgate Bar is England's only city gate with an intact barbican (an extended gateway to ward off uninvited guests), and was built during the reign of Edward III.

Museum Gardens

The Museum Gardens (open dawn-dusk daily) make a peaceful 4-hectare city-centre oasis. Assorted picturesque ruins and buildings include **Museum Gardens Lodge** (Victorian Gothic Revival) dating from 1874 and a 19th-century working **observatory**. The **Multangular Tower** was the western tower of the Roman garrison's defensive wall. The small Roman stones at the bottom have been built up with 13th-century additions.

The classical **Yorkshire Museum** (☎ 629 745; adult/child £3.95/2.95; open 10am-5pm daily) has some interesting Roman, Anglo-Saxon, Viking and medieval exhibits and good temporary exhibitions.

The ruins of **St Mary's Abbey** (founded 1089) date from 1270 to 1294. The ruined **Gatehall** was its main entrance, providing access from the abbey to the river. The adjacent **Hospitium** dates from the 14th century, although the timber-framed upper storey is a much-restored survivor from the 15th century; it was used as the abbey guesthouse. **St Mary's Lodge** was built around 1470 to provide VIP accommodation.

St Olave's Church (open 9am-5.15pm Mon-Fri) dates from the 15th century, but there has been a church dedicated to Norway's patron saint here since at least 1050.

Merchant Adventurers' Hall

Built between 1357 and 1361, the outstanding Merchant Adventurers' Hall (☎ 654818; Fossgate; adult/child £2/70p; open 9am-5pm Mon-Sat, noon-4pm Sun Easter-Sept, 9.30am-3.30pm Mon-Sat Oct-Easter), with its massive oak timbers, testifies to the power of the medieval guilds. They controlled all foreign trade into and out of York – a handy little monopoly.

Jorvik Viking Centre

From 1976 to 1981 excavations in Coppergate uncovered Jorvik, the 9th-century Viking settlement that preceded modern York. Jorvik Viking Centre (☎ 543403; w www.vikingjorvik.com; Coppergate; adult/child £6.95/5.10; open 9am-5.30pm daily Apr-Oct, 10am-4.30pm Nov-Mar) is one of York's most popular attractions and you may have to queue. You are transported back to the past in a 'time car', and a commentary guides you through a smells-and-all re-creation of what the Viking town probably looked like, with bad-hair-day fibreglass figures speaking a language derived from modern Icelandic. At the end of the ride there's a chance to inspect finds from the site. It's less corny than it sounds and well worth a visit.

The Jorvik people also run the **Archaeological Resource Centre** (ARC; ☎ 654324; St Saviourgate) in an old church. It has various programmes that allow for hands-on exploration of archaeology. Call for details.

Clifford's Tower

Around 1068 William the Conqueror built two mottes (mounds) crowned with wooden towers. The original one on this site was destroyed by fire during anti-Jewish riots in 1190 when 150 Jews sheltering in the castle took their own lives. It was then rebuilt into the keep for York Castle using a highly unusual figure-eight design. There's not much to see inside (EH; ☎ 646940; admission £2.10; open 10am-6pm daily Apr-June & Sept, 9.30am-7pm July & Aug, 10am-5pm Oct, 10am-4pm Nov-Mar) but the views over the city are excellent.

York Castle Museum

Located in the centre of York near Clifford's Tower, the popular York Castle Museum (☎ 653611; adult/child £5.95/3.50; open 9.30am-5pm daily Apr-Oct, 9.30am-4pm Nov-Mar) contains displays of everyday life, with reconstructed domestic interiors, and a less homely prison cell where you can try out the condemned man's bed. There's a bewildering array of evocative everyday objects from the past 400 years and worthwhile changing exhibitions and special events.

National Railway Museum

This museum (☎ 621261; W www.nrm.org.uk; Leeman Rd; admission free; open 10am-6pm daily), east of the train station, is one of the world's biggest railway museums and winner of the Egg award in 2001 (best museum in Europe). Remarkably popular with lone men, it focuses on the all-too-distant past when England was a leader in railway technology. You can peer inside many gleaming carriages (including Queen Victoria's saloon) and locomotives (including the speed-record-breaking *Mallard*), and wander around a vast annexe including the restoration workshops. Allow two hours to do the museum justice.

Medieval Churches

Of York's 41 pre-16th-century churches, 20 still survive, many with their stained glass intact. The finest is **All Saints, North St** (☎ 728122; call for opening hrs), easily spotted by the octagon rising above its tower. It has wonderful 14th-century glass – one bit depicts a man wearing glasses.

The wonky lines inside **Holy Trinity, Goodramgate** (☎ 613451; open 10am-5pm Tues-Sat, May-Sept, to 4pm Oct-Apr) almost induce seasickness. The church was started in the 13th century and added to over the next 200 years. Rare 17th- to 18th-century box pews surround a two-tier pulpit.

Perpendicular **All Saints Pavement** (☎ 631116; open 9am-4.30pm Mon-Sat), between High Ousegate and Coppergate, has a graceful octagonal lantern tower (its lamp acted as a beacon to medieval travellers) and 14th-century stained glass.

St Denys Church (☎ 633261; Walmgate; open 10am-4.30pm Apr-Oct) was a fishmongers' church. It dates from the 12th century, but has been much adapted. There's a fine 14th-century window.

Other Things to See & Do

Fairfax House (☎ 655543; W www.fairfax house.co.uk; Castlegate; adult/child £4.50/ 1.50; open 11am-5pm Mon-Thur & Sat, 1.30pm-5pm Sun, guided tours 11am & 2pm Fri late Feb–early Jan) is a beautiful restored Georgian house with elaborate stucco work. It's survived incarnations as a gentleman's club, dancehall, cinema and army billet.

The 19th-century **York City Art Gallery** (☎ 551861; W www.yorkbrew.demon.co.uk; Exhibition Square; adult/child £2/1.50; open 10am-5pm daily) includes works by Reynolds, Nash, Boudin and Lowry.

York Brewery (☎ 621162; 12 Toft Green; adult/14-17 yrs £4.25/3) has tours of its small plant and all-important tastings throughout the day.

York Dungeon (☎ 632599; W www.the dungeons.com; 12 Clifford St; adult/child £6.50/4.95; open 10am-6pm daily Apr-Sept, 10.30am-5.30pm Oct-Mar) is a series of exultantly gruesome historical reconstructions. For the especially hardened there's a lovely bit on the plague.

In the heart of York, the quaintly cobbled **Shambles** hints at what a medieval street might have looked like if it was overrun with people told they have to buy something silly and be back on the tour bus in 15 minutes. It takes its name from the Saxon word *shamel*, meaning slaughterhouse.

If modern British train technology has failed you and you have time to kill at the station, you might find the **York Model Railway** (☎ 630169; adult/child £3.20/2; open 9.30am-6pm daily Mar-Oct, 10.30am-5pm Nov-Feb) diverting. It's right next to the station entrance and comprises a huge set-up where, at least in this miniature world, the trains always run on time.

Organised Tours

Bus For a good overall introduction to the city you might consider one of the open-top buses that trundle about town. Tours leave from Exhibition Square outside the main TIC.

York Citysightseeing (☎ 692505; W www .city-sightseeing.com; day tickets adult/child £6/free) does a hop-on hop-off service calling at all the main sights; buses leave every 15 minutes.

Guide Friday (☎ 640896; W www.guide friday.com; tours mid-Feb–Nov; day tickets *adult/child £7.50/2.50)* operates essentially the same service. Competition between the two is fierce – the usual fare is often heavily discounted.

Eddie Brown *(☎ 640760; 8 Tower St)* runs a range of good-value day bus tours into the surrounding countryside and farther afield, including Ilkley and Haworth for £7.50.

Boat YorkBoat River Trips *(☎ 628324; W www.yorkboat.co.uk; Lendal Bridge)* runs Ouse cruises. One-hour return trips *(adult/senior/child £6/5.50/3)* depart from King's Staith (behind the fire station) and Lendal Bridge (next to the Guildhall, under the bridge) from 10.30am daily from February to the end of November. From April to October, there's the obligatory ghost cruise at 6.30pm daily (and 8pm in July and August) from King's Staith (adult/child £6.50/3.50).

Walking Yorkwalk *(☎ 622303; W yorkwalk .netfirms.com; adult/child £5/1)* offers a series of two-hour themed walks on Roman York, the snickelways (alleys) and many more. Walkers get a £1 discount for Guide Friday tours and Guide Friday ticket holders get a 50p discount for walks. Walks depart from Museum Gardens Gate on Museum St.

The **Association of Voluntary Guides** *(☎ 640780)* has free two-hour walking tours of the city from Exhibition Square in front of York City Art Gallery at 10.15am daily, year round. There is also a 2.15pm tour from April to October and a 6.45pm tour from June to August.

The **Complete York Tour** *(☎ 706643)* is a walk around the city and the minster that can be adapted to your preferences. Call for details.

Roam'in Tours of York *(☎ 07931 668935; W www.roamintours.co.uk)* offers history and specialist tours (adult/child £2/50p) or you can take its DIY audio tour (£3).

York has many companies offering ghost walks. The following are the rattling bare bones: the **Original Ghost Walk of York** *(☎ 01759-373090; 8pm daily)* leaves from the King's Arms; the **Ghost Hunt of York** *(☎ 608700; W www.ghosthunt.co.uk; 7.30pm daily)* starts at the Shambles; and **Mad Alice Ghost Tours** *(☎ 425071; 7.30pm Tues-Sat)* leaves from Clifford's Tower. All cost adult/child £3/2 and last about 1½ hours; you should phone first.

Places to Stay

Despite the prevalence of hotels and B&Bs, it can be difficult to find a bed in midsummer. Prices also jump significantly in the high season. The TIC's efficient accommodation booking service charges a hefty £4.

Camping & Hostels The closest site, **Rowntree Park Camping** *(☎ 658997; Terry Ave; adult/tent/car £4.75/2/1.50)*, is a 20-minute walk southeast of the station in a park by the river. There are a few pitches for backpackers. There's little grass on the sites so you'll need something soft to sleep on.

York YHA Hostel *(☎ 0870 770 6102/3, fax 651230; W www.york-yha.org.uk; Water End, Clifton; B&B adult £16; open year round)* is large but busy, so book ahead. Once the Rowntree (Quaker confectioners) mansion, it has mainly four-bed dorms. It's about a mile northwest of the TIC; turn left into Bootham, which becomes Clifton (the A19), then left into Water End. There's a riverside footpath from Lendal Bridge, but it's ill lit so avoid it after dark.

York Youth Hotel *(☎ 625904; W www .yorkyouthhotel.demon.co.uk; 11 Bishophill Senior; dorm beds £9-15, singles £20-25)*, within the city walls, has a good range of rooms, including singles.

York Backpackers *(☎/fax 627720; W www .yorkbackpackers.mcmail.com; 88-90 Micklegate; dorm beds/doubles from £11/30)*, in a stately Georgian building, gives a friendly welcome. Internet access costs £1 for 15 minutes and it has a bar open till 1am.

Fairfax House *(☎ 434784; e central-reser vations@york.ac.uk; 99 Heslington Rd; bus No 4; singles per person £20)* is an ivy-covered building, part of the University of York (accommodation only available during holidays), 2 miles (3km) southeast of the city.

B&Bs – Northwest There are lots of B&Bs and hotels in the streets north and south of Bootham (the A19 to Thirsk), to the northwest of the city.

Martins Guest House *(☎ 634551; e mar tinsbandb@talk21.com; 5 Longfield Terrace; singles/doubles £22/25, with en suite per person £23/25)* is friendly, with average rooms, one of several B&Bs in a long Victorian row.

Briar Lea Guest House *(☎ 635061; W www.briarlea.co.uk; 8 Longfield Terrace;*

en-suite singles/doubles per person from £24/35) offers refreshingly simple rooms.

Alcuin Lodge *(☎ 632222; e alcuinlodge@ aol.com; 15 Sycamore Place; en-suite doubles per person from £25)* has decent doubles in a cluttered Victorian house.

Abbey Guest House *(☎ 627782; 14 Earlsborough Terrace; singles £35, doubles £55-58.50)* is attractive, with river views.

Riverside Walk *(☎ 620769; 9 Earlsborough Terrace; singles £35, doubles £55-58.50)*, also overlooking the river, is bright and likeable, with a fair amount of flounce.

The Gables Guest House *(☎ 624381; 50 Bootham Crescent; en-suite rooms per person from £28)* has basic rooms with pine furniture.

Treetops Guest House *(☎ 658053; 21 St Mary's; en-suite singles £29, doubles from £54)* is a tall Victorian house; some rooms have views across rooftops to the minster.

Brontë House *(☎ 621066; w www.bronte -guesthouse.com; 22 Grosvenor Terrace; en-suite singles/doubles from £32/56)* has charming rooms with lovely leafy outlooks.

Crook Lodge *(☎ 655614; w www.crook lodge.co.uk; 26 St Mary's; en-suite rooms per person from £30)* is creeper-shrouded, with comfortable rooms.

23 St Mary's *(☎ 622738; 23 St Mary's; singles/doubles from £36/65)*, opposite, is a smart and stately townhouse, with a prevalence of lace and chintz.

B&Bs – Southwest There are B&Bs clustered around Scarcroft Rd, Southlands Rd and Bishopthorpe Rd.

Acorn Guest House *(☎ 620081; 1 Southlands Rd; en-suite rooms per person from £23)* is decent, with a stripe-meets-floral decor.

Nunmill House *(☎ 634047; e info@nun mill.co.uk; 85 Bishopthorpe Rd; doubles with en suite per person from £25)* has fine, well-kept rooms and stencilling throughout.

Wheatlands Lodge *(☎ 654318; e wheat lodge@aol.com; 75 Scarcroft Rd; en-suite singles/doubles from £28/40)* comprises a row of attractive, listed Victorian villas, with 60 bright rooms.

Hotels – Northwest Large, high-ceilinged rooms are available at friendly **Elliotts Hotel** *(☎ 623333; w www.elliottshotel.co.uk; 2-4 Sycamore Place; en-suite singles/doubles per person £35/30)*.

The Coach House Hotel *(☎ 652780; 20/22 Marygate; rooms per person from £29.50, with en suite from £32; meals around £10)* offers 12 pleasant rooms in a quiet spot across from the city walls.

Jorvik Hotel *(☎ 653511; w www.jorvik hotel.co.uk; 50-52 Marygate; en-suite singles £35-40, doubles per person £29-32)* has a walled garden, and 23 comfortable rooms.

Minster Hotel *(☎ 621267, fax 654719; w www.minsterhotel.co.uk; 60 Bootham; singles £70, doubles £60-100)* has 30 well-equipped but bland rooms in a modern annexe, and a restaurant and bar in a Georgian townhouse.

Hotels – Centre Smart, cosy rooms can be found at **St Denys Hotel** *(☎ 622207, fax 624800; w www.stdenyshotel.co.uk; St Denys Rd; en-suite singles/doubles from £45/55)*.

Judges Lodging Hotel *(☎ 638733, fax 679947; 9 Lendal; singles/doubles £75/100)* has tasteful rooms – despite one having a Queen Mother theme – in a Georgian mansion, some with spa bath.

Dean Court Hotel *(☎ 625082, fax 620305; e deancourt@btconnect.com; Duncombe Place; low season singles/doubles from £95/ 128, high season £105/145)* has a commanding position across from the minster – rooms with views are best but they're all very comfortable.

Monkbar Hotel *(☎ 638086, fax 629195; w www.monkbar-hotel.co.uk; St Maurice's Rd; singles/doubles from £90/130)* is a smart, bland hotel just outside the gate, with a courtyard garden.

Royal York Hotel *(☎ 653681, fax 623503; w www.lemeridien.com; Station Rd; rooms per person from £69)* is a huge, grand, Victorian railway hotel. Some rooms have minster views.

Places to Eat

Many York pubs serve food; they're listed in the Entertainment section.

Restaurants There's live music on Wednesday at **VJ's Artbar** *(☎ 673788; w www .v-js.co.uk; 1 Finkle St; open 10am-11pm Mon-Sat, 11am-6pm Sun; burgers about £5)*, a funky burger joint with a bar and a mural-decked covered courtyard.

Pizza Express *(☎ 672904; 17 Museum St; pizzas £5-7.75)* serves the usual presentable pizzas in an elegant former gentlemen's club, with tall windows overlooking the Ouse.

Fiesta Mehicana (☎ 610243; **w** www.fiesta mehicana.co.uk; 14 Clifford St; burritos £8.45), popular with students, is a Tex-Mex, with all the subtlety and sour cream that entails.

La Piazza (☎ 642641; 45 Goodramgate) has excellent Italian food, including pizzas from £5.50.

Oscar's Wine Bar & Bistro (☎ 652002; 8 Little Stonegate; sandwiches £4, mains £6-10) has a heated courtyard and Spanish-leaning dishes.

The Rubicon (☎ 676076; **w** www.rubicon restaurant.co.uk; 5 Little Stonegate; tapas £2.50, mains around £5) is an airy vegetarian restaurant with an array of healthy options.

Siam House (☎ 624677; 63a Goodramgate; most dishes £7-9; open Tues-Sat lunch, Mon-Sat dinner) has fresh, fragrant Thai food in a lovely upstairs room.

Jinnah (☎ 659999; 105-7 Micklegate; dishes around £7; open to midnight) is a fine Indian restaurant. The dishes are carefully prepared and creatively served.

The Tapas Tree (☎ 674848; 48 Walmgate; tapas around £3; open Tues-Sat dinner) is a lively, intimate place, with a good array of Spanish morsels.

Ask (☎ 637254; Blake St; pasta & pizza £6-7), a reliable chain, resides in the glorious Grand Assembly Rooms, with lofty ceilings, columns and potted palms.

Lime House (☎ 632734; 55 Goodramgate; mains £8.95-13.25; open Wed-Sun), pocket-sized and candle-lit, serves up aromatic modern British stuff.

St William's College/Restaurant (☎ 634 830; starters £2.95, mains £9.50-14; open 10am-10pm), in a building dating from 1461, does fine food. There's a beautiful, cobbled courtyard.

Blue Bicycle (☎ 673990; 34 Fossgate; mains around £12), in a former brothel, is one of York's finest restaurants, romantic and candle-lit and serving tasty French seafood dishes.

Plunkets (☎ 637722; 9 High Petergate; mains £9-13.50) offers cuisine influenced by the American southwest in a dimly lit 1640 timber-framed building, and has the Rolling Stones' signatures in lipstick in the upstairs bar.

Rish (☎ 622688; 7 Fossgate; mains around £10-18) serves delicious, original modern

British cooking in a serene, small, stylish restaurant.

Cafés A calm, neutrally coloured space dotted with sofas, **Café No 8** (☎ 653074; 8 Gillygate; sandwiches & salads about £3; open Mon-Sat) serves lunch, coffee and snacks.

Betty's (☎ 659142; St Helen's Square; sandwiches around £4, cream tea £5.45; open 9am-9pm) is a very popular shrine to tea. A pianist plays from 6pm. Or you can try **Little Betty's** (☎ 622865; 46 Stonegate; 9am-5.30pm), where an afternoon high tea costs £9.65 and would feed a village.

Café Concerto (☎ 610478; 21 High Petergate; cakes £2-3, starters £4-6, mains £9.80-12.50), with walls papered by sheet music, and a plant-filled front facing the minster, is a café by day and bistro by night, with divine food.

El Piano (☎ 610676; **w** www.elpiano.co.uk; 15 Grape Lane; open 10am-12.30am Mon-Sat; dishes around £5, BYO) has interesting chat to overhear, and regular live music, in an original, colourful, vegetarian Hispanic café.

Blake Head Bookshop & Café (☎ 623767; 104 Micklegate; mains around £5.50; 9.30am-5pm Mon-Sat, 10am-5pm Sun) is a soothing vegetarian eatery with an imaginative, child-friendly menu.

City Screen Café-Bar (☎ 541144; 13-17 Coney St; snacks 80p-£5.75, mains £4.90-7.20) is a laid-back, artsy place offering great river views, outside seating and tempting bites; there's another bar downstairs that hosts original live music and DJs in the evening.

Entertainment

The Ackhorne (☎ 671421; 9 St Martin's Lane) is tucked away from beery Micklegate and is as comfortable as old slippers. A few locals have taken root.

Black Swan (☎ 686911; Peasholme Green) was once the mayor's house and is a welcoming, dark-beamed place with rambling rooms and live folk music on Thursday.

Blue Bell (☎ 654904; 53 Fossgate) is a tiny pub; first opened in 1798, it has not changed much since.

King's Arms (☎ 659435; King's Staith; lunch about £5) is a creaky place with a central, scenic location and riverside tables.

The Maltings (☎ 655387; **w** www.maltings .co.uk; Tanners Moat), below Lendal Bridge, has a great beer selection, a fine atmosphere and live music on Monday and Tuesday evenings.

Ye Olde Starre (*☎ 623063; 40 Stonegate*), although in tourist central, is popular with locals – it was used as a morgue by the Roundheads, but the atmosphere's improved since then. It has decent ales and outside tables overlooked by the minster.

Old White Swan (*☎ 540911; 80 Goodramgate*), centred around a courtyard, has a range of live music, from jazz to polka to rock.

The Roman Bath (*☎ 620455; St Sampson's Square*) has a…Roman bath in the basement, discovered when building a new cellar in 1928–30. You can visit it for adult/child £1/50p; ask at the bar.

Fibbers (*☎ 651250; 8-12 The Stonebow*), in a hideous building, has lively gigs every night, including local bands, tenuous tribute options, and some vaguely familiar names.

Spread Eagle (*☎ 635868; 98 Walmgate; meals around £6*) is wall-to-wall with locals who enjoy the good beer selection and decent menu of typical bar chow. There's a garden at the back.

York Theatre Royal (*☎ 623568; St Leonard's Place*) stages well regarded productions of theatre, opera and dance.

York Barbican Centre (*☎ 656688; Barbican Rd*) stages big-name concerts in a partly pyramidal, modern building.

City Screen (*☎ 541144; w www.picture house-cinemas.co.uk; 13-17 Coney St*) shows mainstream and art-house films; there are a couple of bars too (see Places to Eat).

Ziggy's (*☎ 620602; 53-55 Micklegate; 10pm-2am Tues-Sat*) is a relaxed club with theme nights ranging from Goth to disco.

Grand Opera House (*☎ 671818; Clifford St*), despite its name, puts on a wide range of productions.

Shopping

Coney St and its adjoining streets are the hub of York shopping.

Nevisport (*☎ 639567; 8 St Sampson Square*) sells walking and camping gear as well as maps and guides.

Wildcat Records (*☎ 625156; 76 Micklegate*) has an offbeat selection of used and new CDs and vinyl.

Priestleys Vintage Clothing (*☎ 631565; 11 Grape Lane*) is tucked away and has some lovely, if pricey, old clobber, beautifully presented.

York has many second-hand and antiquarian bookshops. They are clustered in two main areas, Micklegate and Fossgate. **Ken Spellman Booksellers** (*☎ 624414; 70 Micklegate*) has been selling rare, antiquarian and second-hand books since 1910. **Jack Duncan Books** (*☎ 641389; 36 Fossgate*) sells cheap paperbacks and unusual books.

Getting There & Away

Bus There are bus stops along Rougier St (off Station Rd, inside the city walls on the western side of Lendal Bridge) but National Express, and some local and regional buses leave from outside the train station.

The very useful **York Travel Bus Info Centre** (*☎ 551400; 20 George Hudson St; open 8.30am-5pm Mon-Fri*) has complete schedule information and sells local and regional tickets.

The TICs sell National Express tickets. There are services to London (£27, five hours, three daily), Birmingham (£27, three hours, one daily) and Edinburgh (£34.50, six hours, one daily).

Train York train station is a spectacular masterpiece of Victorian engineering, a great curving structure of brick, glass and iron, over a quarter of a mile long. It's also well served by trains. There are numerous services from London's King's Cross (£63.20, two hours 10 minutes) and Edinburgh (£56, 2½ hours). Trains also connect with Peterborough (£39, one hour 50 minutes) for Cambridge and East Anglia. There are good connections with southern England including Oxford (£59.50, 4¾ hours), via Birmingham (£38, 2½ hours).

Local trains from Scarborough take 45 minutes (£13.20).

Car & Motorcycle By road York is about 200 miles (322km) from London and Edinburgh and 25 miles (40km) from Leeds and Helmsley. For getting away from York to tour the surroundings there are several options.

Europcar (*☎ 656161*) is right by platform 1 in the station. Besides a full range of cars, it rents bicycles and stores luggage (£3 per 24 hours).

Hertz (*☎ 612586*) is near platform 3 in the station.

Practical Car & Van Rental (*☎ 624848; Tanners Moat*) often has good deals.

Getting Around

York is easily walked on foot. You're never really more than 20 minutes from any of the major sights or areas.

Bus The local bus service is provided by First York, which sells a day pass valid on all of its local buses, for £2.10. The Bus Info Centre has service details (see Bus in the Getting There & Away section).

Car & Motorcycle York gets as congested as most English cities in summer and parking in the centre can be expensive (up to £8 for a day); but most guesthouses and hotels have access to parking.

Taxi Try **Station Taxis** (☎ 623332), which has a kiosk outside the train station.

Bicycle You can hire bicycles for £7.50 per day from **Bob Trotter** (☎ 622868; 13 Lord Mayor's Walk) outside Monk Bar. Europcar in the train station rents bikes from £10 per day. The Bus Info Centre has a useful free map showing York's bike routes.

If you're energetic you could pedal out to Castle Howard (15 miles/24km), Helmsley and Rievaulx Abbey (12 miles/19.5km) and

Medieval Guilds

A feature of York in medieval times was the rise of the guilds established by groups of craftsmen and tradesmen (and they were all men) – the forerunner of today's trade unions or professional associations.

Crafts and trades were restricted to the members of an appropriate guild – except at markets (which were usually weekly) or fairs (usually annual) – and guilds checked the quality of the work, investigated complaints and regulated prices. While those first two activities may have actually served their customers, the regulation of prices was at the heart of the guilds' existence. Prices were fixed at levels that allowed for comfortable margins and a fat and happy existence. If there's any doubt about the profits these monopolistic practices allowed, just look at some surviving guild buildings, such as York's Merchant Adventurers' Hall or St Mary's Church in Beverley.

Thirsk (another 12 miles/19.5km), and then catch a train back to York. There's also a section of the Trans-Pennine-Trail cycle path from Bishopthorpe in York to Selby (15 miles/24km) along the old railway line. The TICs have maps.

AROUND YORK
Castle Howard

There are few buildings in the world that are so perfect that their visual impact is almost a physical blow – Castle Howard (☎ 01653-648333; w www.castlehoward.co.uk; adult/child house & grounds £8/5, grounds £5/3; house open 11am-4.30pm daily, grounds 10am-6.30pm daily mid-Mar–Oct) is one. Made famous by its staring role in *Brideshead Revisited*, this stately home is a work of supreme theatrical grandeur and audacity, set in the rolling Howardian Hills, with wandering peacocks on its terraces. In the 1750s, a team of 30 gardeners was employed to take care of its folly-dotted landscaped grounds.

The earl of Carlisle made a brave choice in 1699 when he picked a successful playwright and army captain, Sir John Vanbrugh, as architect. It's hard to conceive that this was Vanbrugh's very first work. Vanbrugh in turn chose Nicholas Hawksmoor, who had worked for Christopher Wren, as his clerk of works. This successful collaboration was repeated at Blenheim Palace.

Unsurprisingly, Castle Howard draws crowds of visitors. Outside weekends, however, it's surprisingly easy to find the space to appreciate this hedonistic marriage of art, architecture, landscaping and natural beauty. Wandering about the grounds, views open up over the hills, Vanbrugh's playful Temple of the Four Winds and Hawksmoor's stately Mausoleum, but the great Baroque house with its magnificent central cupola is an irresistible visual magnet. Inside, it is full of treasures, such as the chapel's Pre-Raphaelite stained glass.

Castle Howard is 15 miles (24km) northeast of York, 4 miles (6.5km) off the A64. You could spend the whole day here. There are a couple of twee cafés, but it's best to take a picnic.

Castle Howard can be reached by several tours from York. Check with the TIC for up-to-date schedules. Yorkshire Coastliner has a useful bus service that links Leeds, York,

Castle Howard, Pickering and Whitby (No 840). A day return from York costs £4.40, while a Coastliner Freedom ticket (adult/senior/family £10/7/26) is good for unlimited rides all day; buy tickets on the bus.

Nunnington Hall

This 17th-century manor house *(NT; ☎ 01439-748283; admission £4.50; open 1.30pm-4.30pm Wed-Sun Apr-Oct, also Tues June-Aug)* is a good example of how one could live when one had plenty of serfs to do the heavy lifting out on the estate. A forest of hardwoods went into the rich panelling of the public spaces. Outside, the walled garden is a perfect refuge from the demands of running the house. The combination of the River Wye, the orchards and the various water fowl is magical.

Nunnington Hall is in the tiny village of Nunnington, which is just off the B1257, 4½ miles (7km) southeast of Helmsley. It's easily combined with a visit to Castle Howard, which is 7 miles (11.5km) south via Slingsby.

North Yorkshire

North Yorkshire contains some of England's most magnificent monuments, two beautiful national parks (see the Yorkshire Dales and North York Moors sections) and the glorious city of York (see earlier). To the west of the county stretch out beautiful dales, cut through by rugged stone walls and spotted with extravagant houses and the faded, spectral grandeur of monastic ruins. The Dales run into the moors, that roll on gently to the steep drop of cliffs edging the east coast.

Unlike much of northern England, the landscape is unmarked by the looming mills and mines that remain elsewhere – hallmarks of the Industrial Revolution. The county's industries, such as lead mining, did not warrant huge increases in production, so the countryside remained largely untouched. Since the Middle Ages it's been mainly dominated by sheep, and the great houses, prosperous towns and rich abbeys were often built with the fortunes made from wool. The landscape and climate do not encourage crop cultivation, another reason for the untamed quality of the land.

The towns and cities of North Yorkshire share a particularly powerful sense of the past, with well-preserved buildings that reflect their respective glory days, from the genteel spa of Harrogate, to the blowsy, dramatically situated resorts of Scarborough and Whitby, to the splendour of York, resonant with centuries of its significance.

Activities

The best walking and cycling is in the Yorkshire Dales and the North York Moors. See the separate sections on these national parks for more details.

Getting There & Around

The main gateway town is York and a web of buses and trains connect places in North Yorkshire. More specific details on the Yorkshire Dales and the North York Moors are given in those sections following. For county-wide information, call **Traveline** *(☎ 0870 608 2608)* for information. There are various Explorer passes, and individual bus and train companies also offer their own saver schemes, so it's always worth asking for advice on the best deal when you buy your ticket.

THIRSK

☎ 01845 • pop 4162

Thirsk is a market town with tidy, attractive streets and a large central square, where large markets are held on Monday and Saturday. It has a prime location between the Yorkshire Dales and North York Moors national parks. What it's really famous for, though, is as the fictional 'Darrowby' of James Herriot's stories of life as a Yorkshire vet.

Thirsk's **TIC** *(☎ 522755; e thirsk@ytbtic .co.uk; 49 Market Place; open 11am-4pm Mon-Sat, noon-4pm Sun)* is on the main square.

World of James Herriot

His real name was Alfred Wight but to millions of fans he's James Herriot, the wry Yorkshire veterinarian whose adventures were recorded in *All Creatures Great and Small*, several other books, and a much-loved 1970s TV show. The building at 23 Kirkgate where the real Dr Wight lived, worked and wrote his books has been turned into the World of James Herriot *(☎ 524234; adult/child £4.50/3.50; open 10am-6pm daily Apr-Sept, 11am-4pm Nov-Mar)*. It has been restored to its 1940s appearance, complete with vintage copies of trade journals such as *Tail-Wagger* lying about.

But there's more here than just Wight artefacts (he used a pen-name because his professional organisation said that writing of his practice under his real name would be 'marketing'). There's a video documentary on his life and a re-creation of the TV show sets. It's all quite well done and you'll be in the company of true fans, many of whom have that look of pilgrimage on their faces. Note that although animals are celebrated inside, they're required to stay outside.

Thirsk Museum

Housed in the home where Thomas Lord (of Lord's Cricket Ground fame) was born in 1755, the tiny museum (☎ 527707; w www .thirkmuseum.org; 14-16 Kirkgate; adult/child £1.50/75p; open 10am-4pm Mon-Wed, Fri & Sat) has a small collection of items from Neolithic times to the Herriot era.

Places to Stay & Eat

The TIC books B&Bs and has a handy accommodation list.

The Three Tuns Hotel (☎ 523124, fax 526 126; Market Place; en-suite singles/doubles from £45/65; mains from £6) hosted the Wordsworths on their honeymoon and has decent rooms.

Golden Fleece (☎ 523108, fax 523996; Market Place; en-suite singles/doubles from £65/85; mains from £8) has spacious rooms and creative food.

Getting There & Away

There are frequent daily buses from York (45 minutes).

Thirsk is well served by trains on the line between York and Middlesbrough. However, the train station is a mile (1.6km) west of town and the only way to cover that distance is on foot or by cab (☎ 522473).

AROUND THIRSK
Ripon
☎ 01765 • pop 13,000

A small city with a big cathedral, Ripon has winding streets and a broad, symmetrical market place lined by Georgian houses. Every evening at 9pm the Ripon Hornblower 'sets the watch' with a bit of trumpeting by the central obelisk. This used to signal when the night watchmen took over

security, and reputedly has been taking place for over 1000 years. There's a busy market on Thursday. The **TIC** (☎ 604625; Minster Rd; open 10am-1pm & 1.30pm-5.30pm Mon-Sat, 1pm-4pm Sun) is near the cathedral and has information on local walks, and will book accommodation.

Ripon Cathedral (☎ 602072; w www.ripon cathedral.org.uk; suggested donation £3, treasury 50p; open 8am-5.30pm, evensong 5.30pm) is well worth exploring. The first church on this site was built in 660 by St Wilfred, and its rough, humble crypt lies intact beneath today's soaring edifice. Above ground, the building dates from the 11th century, with its noble and harmonious Early English west front clocking in at 1220. Medieval additions have resulted in the medley of Gothic styles throughout, culminating in the rebuilding of the central tower – work that was never completed. It was not until 1836 that this impressive parish church got cathedral status. Look out for the fantastical creatures decorating the animated medieval misericords, believed to have inspired Lewis Carroll – his father was Canon here (1852–68).

Until 1888 Ripon was responsible for its own peacekeeping, and this has resulted in a grand array of punishing attractions. **Law & Order Museums** (☎ 690799; 7-day combined ticket adult/child £3.50/free; open 11am-4pm daily Apr-June, 11am-4.30pm July & Aug, 1pm-4pm Sept, noon-3pm Oct) combine the **Courthouse Museum**, a 19th-century courthouse (recognisable from sappy TV series *Heartbeat*), the **Prison & Police Museum**, which includes the medieval punishment yard and the clammy cells where no-good Victorians ended up, and the **Workhouse Museum**, which shows the grim treatment of poor vagrants from the 19th century to WWII.

Bus No 36 comes from Leeds via Harrogate every 20 minutes.

Fountains Abbey & Studley Royal Water Garden

Sheltered in the secluded valley of the River Skell is Yorkshire's only World Heritage Site. Memorable and timeless, it should not be missed. The strangely obsessive and beautiful formal water gardens, with their wild natural backdrop, are punctuated by many eclectic buildings. All this is set around the huge, stately abbey ruins and the whole site has an extraordinary sense of vast green space. A very tranquil day could easily slip by here.

The site includes the sublime wreck of Fountains Abbey, Jacobean Fountains Hall, the exuberantly Victorian St Mary's Church and a number of follies.

Fountains Abbey began as a small breakaway group of 13 monks from a Benedictine abbey in York. In 1132 the Archbishop of York granted them land in what was virtual wilderness. Lacking assistance from any established abbey or order, they turned to the Cistercian order for help. In 1147 the monastery was devastated by fire – only the church was spared. It was rebuilt immediately, then expanded in the early 13th century to accommodate its population. Later changes date from the late 15th century.

The Cistercians were often called the White Monks because they wore a habit of undyed wool, reflecting the austerity and simplicity of their order. They were committed to long periods of silence and eight daily services. This didn't leave much time for practical matters, so the Cistercians ordained lay brothers who lived within the monastery but pursued the abbey's ever-growing business interests – wool, lead mining, quarrying, animal breeding and so on.

After economic collapse in the 14th century following the Black Death, the monks rented their lands to tenant farmers and replaced lay brothers with servants. By the early 16th century a desultory 30 monks rattled around the abbey.

After the dissolution the estate was sold into private hands and between 1598 and 1611 Fountains Hall was built with stone from the abbey ruins. The hall and ruins were united with the Studley Royal Estate in 1768.

The main house of Studley Royal burnt down in 1946 but the superb landscaping, with its serene artificial lakes, survives hardly changed from the 18th century. Studley Royal was owned by John Aislabie (once Chancellor of the Exchequer), who dedicated his life to creating the park after a financial scandal saw him expelled from parliament.

Orientation & Information Fountains Abbey (NT; ☎ 01765-608888; w www.foun tainsabbey.org.uk; admission to abbey, hall &

garden per adult £4.80; open 10am-4pm daily Jan-Mar & Oct-Dec, 10am-5pm Apr-Sept) lies 4 miles (6.5km) west of Ripon off the B6265. The deer park (admission free) opens during daylight hours. St Mary's Church (open 1pm-5pm Apr-Sept) features occasional concerts. There are free one-hour **guided tours** (11am & 2.30pm, Apr-Oct & 3.30pm Apr-Sept, garden 2pm Apr-Oct).

Public transport is limited to summer Sunday services; call for details of any buses that might be running.

HARROGATE
☎ 01423 • pop 64,000

A Victorian spa town, Harrogate feels prim, pretty and immaculate, pervaded by an old-fashioned Englishness, with its ornate architecture and flowerbeds. Once people flocked here for health cures, when sulphur water was all the rage, but now they head for its sweeter-smelling massive flower shows, which alongside frequent conventions have helped the town maintain its prosperity. Floral displays are at their height in spring and autumn, but there are extensive gardens all around town that make for a beautiful stroll at any time of year, and one that takes you back to another era. Agatha Christie ended up in hiding here after her marriage broke down, and Harrogate's lace-curtained facade feels an appropriate setting for the queen of quintessentially English crime. The episode is immortalised in the film Agatha starring Vanessa Redgrave and Dustin Hoffman (1977).

The town is also close to the eastern edge of Yorkshire Dales National Park, and has many good hotels, B&Bs and restaurants. The glorious Turkish baths are not to be missed.

Orientation & Information
Harrogate is almost surrounded by gardens including the 80-hectare Stray in the south. The main shopping streets – Oxford St and Cambridge St – are lined with smart shops and are mostly pedestrianised. There's a **Conference Centre** (☎ 500500) on Kings Rd.

Harrogate's **TIC** (☎ 537300; w www.har rogate.gov.uk/tourism; open 9am-6pm Mon-Sat, 10am-1pm Sun Apr-Sept, 9am-5pm Mon-Fri, 9am-4pm Sat Oct-Mar) is in the **Royal Baths Assembly Rooms** (Crescent Rd).

Send mail at the **post office** (11 Cambridge Rd; open 9am-5.30pm Mon-Sat).

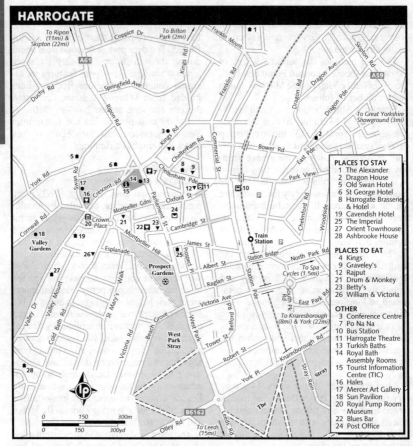

HARROGATE

To Ripon (11mi) & Skipton (22mi)

To Bilton Park (2mi)

Coppice Dr

Franklin Mount

■ 1

Skipton Rd

A61

Kings Rd

Franklin Rd

Dragon Rd

Dragon Ave

A59

Springfield Ave

Ripon Rd

Duchy Rd

Kings Rd

3 ●

Cheltenham Rd

Commercial St

Bower Rd

East Pde

Dragon Pde

To Great Yorkshire Showground (3mi)

● 2

5 ■

6 ■

4 ▼

Park View

Swan Rd

Crescent Rd

Cheltenham Pde

7 ▼

8 ●

9 ●

24 ▼

12 ▼ □ 11

□ 10

Park View

Chelmsford Rd

Woodside

York Rd

17 ●

16 ●

14 ●

13 ●

Oxford St

Montpellier Gdns

Parliament St

23 ▼

Cambridge St

Cornwall Rd

□ 20 Crown Place

21 ●

22 □ ▼

Montpellier Hill

James St

Train Station

Station Bridge

North Park Rd

18 ●

Valley Gardens

■ 19

Esplanade

26 ▼

● 25

Albert St

Prospect Pl

Station Pde

To Spa Cycles (1.5mi)

East Park Rd

27 ●

Prospect Gardens

Raglan St

Valley Dr

Valley Mount

Cold Bath Rd

St Mary's Walk

Victoria Ave

Belford Rd

To Knaresborough (8mi) & York (22mi)

Knaresborough Rd

Stray Rein

The Stray

28 ●

West Park Stray

Victoria Rd

Beach Grove

West Park

Tower St

Robert St

York Pl

B6162

Otley Rd

To Leeds (15mi)

Leeds Rd

LP

0   150   300m
0   150   300yd

The Waters

A visit should start at the ornate **Royal Pump Room Museum** (☎ 556188; Crown Place; adult/child £2/1.25; open 10am-5pm Mon-Sat, 2pm-5pm Sun Apr-Oct, to 4pm daily Nov-Mar), built in 1842 over the most famous of the sulphur springs. It gives an insight into how the phenomenon created the town and the illustrious visitors that it attracted, and there's a chance to tuck into some stinky spa water.

You can experience the waters first-hand while stepping back in time at the restored **Turkish Baths** (☎ 556746; �}w www.harrogate .co.uk/turkishbaths; admission £10; open 9am-9pm daily) in the Royal Baths Assembly Rooms. The mock Moorish facility is gloriously Victorian and offers a range of

watery delights – steam rooms, saunas, and so on. A visit should last at least two hours.

There's a complicated schedule of opening hours that are at turns single sex and mixed pairs – call for more details. You can pre-book a range of reasonably priced massages and other therapies.

Mercer Art Gallery

The Mercer Art Gallery (☎ 556188; Swan Rd; admission free; open 10am-5pm Tues-Sat, 2pm-5pm Sun) is a serene, stately space, home to locally produced works of art and visiting shows.

Gardens

The **Valley Gardens** are beautiful, with quintessentially English lawns and flowerbeds, overlooked by the vast, ornate, glass-domed **Sun Pavilion** (☎ 522588; w www.harrogate .co.uk/sunpavilion; Cornwall Rd), built in 1933. The nearby bandstand houses concerts on Sunday afternoons from June to August.

The **West Park Stray** is another fine garden and park, south of the centre.

Walking
There are free historical walking tours offered daily from Easter to October; check with the TIC for details.

Special Events
The immense **Harrogate Flower Show** (☎ 0870 758 3333; w www.flowershow.org .uk) is held in April at the Great Yorkshire Showground.

The **Great Yorkshire Show** (☎ 541000; w www.greatyorkshireshow.org) is the major annual exhibition staged in July by the Yorkshire Agricultural Society (also held at the showground). It's a real treat, with all manner of farm critters competing for prizes and last year's losers served up in a variety of ways.

Places to Stay
Bilton Park (☎ 863121; e tony@bilton -park.swinternet.co.uk; Village Farm, Bilton; adult/car £8/4; open Apr-Oct), 2 miles (3km) north of town, has pitches for tents. Take bus No 201, 203 or 204 from the bus station.

Dragon House (☎ 569888; 6 Dragon Parade; singles/doubles £20/40, en-suite doubles £45), in a quiet, leafy street, is welcoming and has basic rooms.

The Alexander (☎ 503348; 88 Franklin Rd; rooms per person £25) is a fully restored Victorian mansion with immaculate, unstintingly floral rooms.

Cavendish Hotel (☎ 509637; 3 Valley Dr; singles/doubles from £35/55, four-poster £70) has comfortable rooms with a touch of flounce, some overlooking the Valley Gardens.

Ashbrooke House (☎/fax 564478; 140 Valley Dr; singles/doubles £27/50), close to Valley Gardens, has attractive rooms with some original Victorian features.

Old Swan Hotel (☎ 500055, fax 501154; Swan Rd; rooms per person from £48) is an ivy-coated 18th-century coaching house set in 2 hectares of gardens. The interior has an innately English, 1920s feel. This is where Agatha Christie chose to bolt to in 1926.

Harrogate Brasserie & Hotel (☎ 505041, fax 722300; w www.brasserie.co.uk/brasserie; 28-30 Cheltenham Parade; singles/doubles from £48.50/75) has 14 stylish rooms, an excellent restaurant and frequent live jazz.

Orient Townhouse (☎ 565818; w www .orienttownhouse.com; 51 Valley Drive; singles/ doubles £65/80) has bright, harmonious rooms favouring Eastern-influenced design. No chintz in sight.

The Imperial (☎ 565071, fax 500082; Prospect Place; singles/doubles from £85/100) is a grand hotel with good Stray views. Cheap weekend deals are available.

St George Hotel (☎ 561431, fax 530037; 1 Ripon Rd; singles/doubles from £95/120), an Edwardian place, has a commanding position across from the TIC. The rooms are warmly decorated and there's an indoor pool.

Places to Eat
Harrogate Brasserie & Hotel (☎ 505041; 30 Cheltenham Parade; 2-course meal £12.50) has a French dinner menu in a deep red setting with chequered flooring. There's a good wine list and regular live jazz.

Drum & Monkey (☎ 502650; 5 Montpellier Gardens; mains around £6; open Mon-Sat), with its curvaceous windows, offers hugely popular, traditional seafood.

Rajput (☎ 562113; 9-11 Cheltenham Parade; dishes £5.50-7.50; open to 11pm) has tiptop Indian food.

Kings (☎ 568600; 24 Kings Rd; starters £5.50, mains around £13) is a light and airy restaurant set in an old Victorian house offering inventive fish dishes and some succulent meat options.

Betty's (☎ 502746; w www.bettysandtay lors.co.uk; 1 Parliament St; mains under £7; open 9am-9pm) is a classic tearoom dating from 1919, founded by a Swiss immigrant confectioner who got on a wrong train, ended up in Yorkshire and decided to stay. It heaves with scone groupies (tea and scones around £5). A pianist tinkles among the teacups from 6pm.

Graveley's (☎ 507093; 8-10 Cheltenham Parade) serves tasty takeaway fish and chips (£3.50), and there are outside tables. The main restaurant has a long and varied menu with many fish dishes (£6 to £9).

Harrogate Theatre (Oxford St; open 10am-6pm Mon-Sat) has a grand old café that's popular at lunchtime.

William & Victoria (☎ 506883; Downstairs, 6 Cold Bath Rd; starters £3-7, mains £7-14; open Mon-Fri lunch, Mon-Sat dinner) is a dark and cosy, wood-lined wine bar that serves traditional British food.

Entertainment

Blues Bar (☎ 566881; 2 Montpellier Parade) has a good, lively atmosphere, popular with laid-back locals primed with regular live jazz and blues sessions.

Hales (☎ 725571; 1-3 Crescent Rd) is a traditional pub serving meals. The wooden interior is lit by flickering vintage gas lighting.

Po Na Na (☎ 509758; 2 Kings Rd; free before 11pm; open 10pm-2am Wed-Sat) is the most refined club on offer, proffering some funky stuff, from 70s disco to house.

Harrogate Theatre (☎ 502116; w www.har rogatetheatre.com; Oxford St) stages drama, comedy and music in Art Deco surroundings.

Getting There & Away

Harrogate is between Leeds (15 miles/24km) and York (22 miles/35.5km) and on the rail line that runs between Leeds (£4.30, 50 minutes, about half-hourly) and York (£4.10, 45 minutes, 10 to 12 daily).

National Express bus No 561 runs from Leeds (£4.25, 50 minutes, four daily). Bus No 383 comes from Ripon (£4.25, 25 minutes, three daily). Bus Nos 36 and 36A also run regularly between Ripon, Harrogate and Leeds.

Getting Around

Harrogate is walkable (a healthy stroll is in keeping with local traditions).

Spa Cycles (☎ 887003; 1 Wedderburn Rd), about 1½ miles (2.5km) east of Harrogate station, rents bicycles from £10 to £15 per day.

SCARBOROUGH

☎ 01723 • pop 37,000

Scarborough is spectacularly set above two beautiful white-sand bays. Topped by a hulk of a castle, elaborate Georgian, Victorian and Edwardian buildings line its streets. However, there's a disconsolate sense of former, unobtainable splendours and the town feels at times deflated, for all its tawdry attempts to beguile punters with seaside kitsch: fish and chips! Arcades! Donkeys on the beach! But the combination of its setting, some fine sights and the quintessential English seaside experience make it a good place to spend a few days, and its renowned theatre is the base of England's popular playwright, Alan Ayckbourn, whose plays always premier here.

History

The headland separating the bays has an impressive defensive position and has been occupied since Celtic times. The Vikings established a fishing village in the 9th century by what is now known as the Old Harbour. The Normans built their castle around 1130 and it survived until 1648 when it was badly damaged by the Parliamentarians. It was also bombarded by a German battleship in 1914.

The medieval fishing and market town grew up around the Old Harbour. It was transformed into a fashionable spa town following the discovery of mineral springs in 1620. It became one of the first places in England where sea bathing was popular and from the mid-18th century was a successful seaside resort, hence all the fine buildings. It has just about survived the impact of cheap package holidays to the Mediterranean.

Orientation

Modern suburbs sprawl west of the town centre, which is above the old town and the South Bay. The town is on a plateau above the beaches; cliff lifts, steep streets and footpaths provide the links. The Victorian development to the south is separated from the town centre by a steep valley, which has been landscaped and is crossed by high bridges.

The main shopping street, Westborough, has a dramatic view of the castle rising in the distance. The North Bay is home to all the tawdry seashore amusements; the South Bay is more genteel. The old town lies between St Mary's Church, the castle and the Old Harbour.

Information

The **TIC** (☎ 373333, fax 363785; e scarbor oughtic@scarborough.gov.uk; Unit 3, Pavilion House, Valley Bridge Rd; open 9.30am-6pm daily May-Sept, 10am-4.30pm Mon-Sat Oct-Apr) is busy; there is a Harbourside Information Centre as well. There's a Yorkshire Coast and Country website at w www.ycc.org.uk covering this and the surrounding area.

Send mail at the **post office** (11-15 Aberdeen Walk; open 9am-5.30pm Mon-Fri,

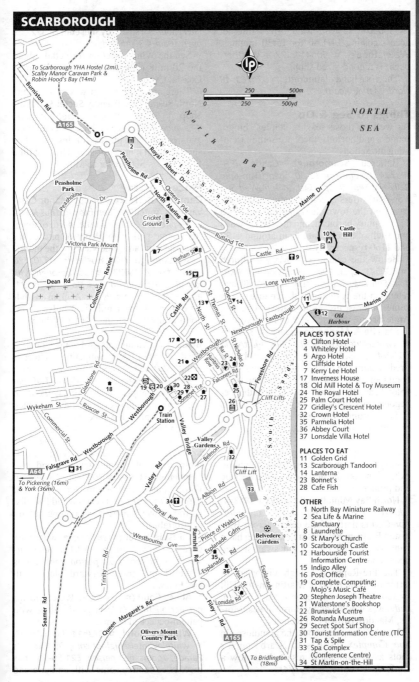

SCARBOROUGH

To Scarborough YHA Hostel (2mi),
Scalby Manor Caravan Park &
Robin Hood's Bay (14mi)

NORTH
SEA

North Bay

Castle
Hill

Peasholme
Park

Cricket
Ground

Victoria Park Mount

Dean Rd

Long Westgate

Old
Harbour

Cliff Lifts

Train
Station

Valley
Gardens

To Pickering (16mi)
& York (36mi)

Cliff Lift

Belvedere
Gardens

Olivers Mount
Country Park

To Bridlington
(18mi)

PLACES TO STAY
3 Clifton Hotel
4 Whiteley Hotel
5 Argo Hotel
6 Cliffside Hotel
7 Kerry Lee Hotel
17 Inverness House
18 Old Mill Hotel & Toy Museum
24 The Royal Hotel
25 Palm Court Hotel
27 Gridley's Crescent Hotel
32 Crown Hotel
35 Parmelia Hotel
36 Abbey Court
37 Lonsdale Villa Hotel

PLACES TO EAT
11 Golden Grid
13 Scarborough Tandoori
14 Lanterna
23 Bonnet's
28 Cafe Fish

OTHER
1 North Bay Miniature Railway
2 Sea Life & Marine
   Sanctuary
8 Laundrette
9 St Mary's Church
10 Scarborough Castle
12 Harbourside Tourist
   Information Centre
15 Indigo Alley
16 Post Office
19 Complete Computing;
   Mojo's Music Café
20 Stephen Joseph Theatre
21 Waterstone's Bookshop
22 Brunswick Centre
26 Rotunda Museum
29 Secret Spot Surf Shop
30 Tourist Information Centre (TIC
31 Tap & Spile
33 Spa Complex
   (Conference Centre)
34 St Martin-on-the-Hill

YORKSHIRE

9am-12.30pm Sat). **Complete Computing**
(☎ 500501; 14 Northway) offers Internet
access costing £1/1.50 for 15/30 minutes.
Waterstone's (☎ 500414; 97-8 Westborough) is a good-sized shop.

There's a handy **laundrette** (☎ 375763; 48
North Marine Road).

Things to See & Do
As well as those seaside staples: bingo,
burgers and buckets, there are some fascinating attractions.

Battered **Scarborough Castle** (EH;
☎ 372451; admission £2.80; open 10am-6pm
daily Apr-Sept, to 5pm Oct, to 4pm Wed-Sun
Nov-Mar) offers excellent views across the
bays and the town. It is approached via a
13th-century barbican, and the curtain walls
and shell of a keep date from around 1130
and 1160 respectively.

Below the castle is **St Mary's Church**
(☎ 500541; open 10am-4pm Mon-Fri, 1pm-
4pm Sun May-Sept) dating from 1180 and
rebuilt in the 15th and 17th centuries, with
some interesting 14th-century chapels.
Anne Brontë is buried in the churchyard.

Sea Life & Marine Sanctuary (☎ 376125;
w www.sealife.co.uk; Scalby Mills; adult/child
£6.50/4.75; open 10am-6pm daily), although
tired-seeming, explores the Jurassic seas,
coral reefs and the world of the octopus with
aplomb, and the rescue work done with woe-
begone seals and sea turtles is lovely to see.

The **Rotunda Museum** (☎ 374839; Vernon Rd; adult/child £2/1.50; open 10am-5pm
Tues-Sun June-Sept, 11am-4pm Tues, Sat &
Sun Oct-May) traces local matters from prehistory to the present, and has changing
exhibitions on themes such as the seaside
and pirates.

North Bay Miniature Railway (☎ 381344;
adult/child £2.50/1.60; open daily mid-
Apr–Oct) is north of the centre across Burniston Rd from **Peasholm Park**, which has a
vaguely oriental theme and swan-shaped
pedal-boats.

The Pre-Raphaelite, high Victorian interior of **Church of St Martin-on-the-Hill**
(☎ 360437; Albion Rd; open 7.30am-5.30pm
daily) was worked on by Burne-Jones, Morris, Maddox Brown and Rossetti.

Nearby along the shore, the grandiose old
Spa Complex testifies to Scarborough's
roots as a fashionable resort. It is now a
conference centre (☎ 376774).

The Old Mill Hotel (see Places to Stay
later) houses a small **toy museum** (☎ 372735;
open 10am-4.30pm daily).

See the Whitby section for details about
the 20-mile (32km) Whitby–Scarborough
Coastal Cycle Trail.

There are some decent waves out in the
North Sea and the friendly **Secret Spot Surf
Shop** (☎ 500467; w www.secretspot.co.uk;
4 Pavilion Terrace) can advise on conditions
and recommend places for lessons. The
shop rents all manner of gear. The best time
for waves is September to May.

Places to Stay
Camping & Hostels Scalby Manor Caravan Park (☎ 366212; Burniston Rd; bus No 12
or 21; pitches £6-11) is 3 miles north of town.
It's a large park with plenty of pitches for
vans and tents and good views of the moors.

Scarborough YHA Hostel (☎ 0870 770
6022, fax 7706023; e scarborough@yha
.org.uk; Burniston Rd; bus No 3, 12 or 21;
adult £10.25; open daily Apr-Aug), in an idyllic converted water mill, is 2 miles (3km)
north of town along the A166 to Whitby.

B&Bs If something stays still long enough in
town, it'll offer B&B; competition is intense
and it's difficult to choose between places.

Kerry Lee Hotel (☎ 363845; 60 Trafalgar
Square; rooms per person with/without en
suite from £15/13) is one of the best-value
places with plain but cheery rooms.

Argo Hotel (☎ 375745; 134 North Marine
Rd; rooms per person with/without en suite
from £20/17) has pleasant, small, floral
rooms overlooking the cricket ground.

Inverness House (☎ 369770; 22 Aberdeen
Walk; rooms per person Apr-Sept from
£16.50, Oct-Mar £10) is central and friendly,
its rooms won't merit a card home but are
comfortable.

Cliffside Hotel (☎ 361087; w www.york
shirecoast.co.uk/cliffside; 79-81 Queen's Parade; en-suite rooms per person from £20) is
a well-kept, straightforward place with
good views.

Abbey Court (☎ 360659; 19 West St; rooms
per person from £21) is good value, with
pattern-bedecked rooms.

Whiteley Hotel (☎ 373514, fax 373007;
e whiteleyhotel@bigfoot.com; 99 Queen's
Parade; rooms per person £21.50-25) has
nice, twee rooms, some with en suite and

Swan Theatre, Stratford-upon-Avon

Punting on the River Cam, Cambridge

Pub, Lavenham, Suffolk

Chatsworth House, Derbyshire

York Minster, York

North York Moors National Park, Yorkshire

Drystone walls and fields, Yorkshire

good sea views, if you can stomach the charmless welcome.

Hotels A friendly, stately place, **Lonsdale Villa Hotel** (☎ 363383; e lonsdale@scarborough.co.uk; Lonsdale Rd; en suite singles/doubles from £25/24 per person) has comfortable rooms.

Parmelia Hotel (☎ 361914; w www.parmeliahotel.co.uk; 17 West St; rooms per person with/without en suite £21/19.5), in a darkly formal Victorian building, has a cheery host.

Old Mill Hotel (☎ 372735, fax 377190; w www.windmill-hotel.co.uk; Mill St; rooms per person Nov-Mar/Apr-Oct from £23/26) is set around a converted 18th-century windmill. There's a small toy museum (see Things to See & Do earlier).

Clifton Hotel (☎ 375691, fax 364203; Queen's Parade; singles/doubles per person from £55/45, with view £65/55) is substantial and Victorian, with great views over North Bay; Wilfred Owen wrote several war poems while staying here – but this isn't a reflection of the conditions.

Palm Court Hotel (☎ 368161, fax 371547; St Nicholas Cliff; singles/doubles per person from £42/39) is old-fashioned with well-equipped rooms.

Gridley's Crescent Hotel (☎ 360929, fax 354126; w www.crescent-hotel.co.uk; The Crescent; singles/doubles from £46.50/85) is in a fine building with views over Crescent Gardens.

Crown Hotel (☎ 373491, fax 362271; Esplanade; singles/doubles per person from £60/55, with sea view £70/65) has views of the castle and South Bay.

The Royal Hotel (☎ 364333, fax 500618; St Nicholas St; singles/doubles from £57.50/105) has a lavish Regency interior, grand staircase for Shirley Bassey–style entrances, and smart rooms, some with views.

Places to Eat

Lanterna (☎ 363616; 33 Queen St; mains £12-28; open Mon-Sat), a snug Italian, specialises in fresh local seafood.

Cafe Fish (☎ 500301; 19 York Place; mains around £13) is informal and serves fresh local fish in a variety of ways, but usually with a rich sauce.

Stephen Joseph Theatre restaurant (Westborough; ☎ 368463; mains £9; open Mon-Sat)

has interesting modern British fare. Lunch is a bargain, with sandwiches under £2.

Golden Grid (☎ 360922; 4 Sandside; cod from £5), on the foreshore, has been doling out fish and chips since 1883. It's bright and traditional, with starched white tablecloths.

Bonnet's (☎ 361033; 38-40 Huntriss Row; soup £2, mains from £5; café open 9am-5.30pm, restaurant open Fri & Sat dinner) is an excellent tearoom, open since 1880, with delicious cakes, a serene courtyard, and adjoining shop selling hand-made chocolates.

Mojo's Music Café (☎ 351983; 18-20 Northway; bagels & soups around £4; open 10am-5.30pm Tues-Sat) combines a CD shop with a retro diner, complete with leather booths and chequered floor.

Scarborough Tandoori (☎ 352393; 50-52 St Thomas St; dishes around £4), dark and cosy, serves up laudable Indian dishes, making a refreshing change from all that golden batter.

Entertainment

Indigo Alley (☎ 375823; North Marine Rd) is an excellent, small and welcoming pub, with a good range of beers. There's regular live jazz and blues and Monday theatre in a limpet-sized curtained-off space.

Tap & Spile (☎ 363837; 94 Falsgrave Rd) is a relaxed pub with a few rooms and a good selection of Yorkshire ales. It has folk music on many nights.

Stephen Joseph Theatre (☎ 370541; w www.sjt.com; Westborough; tickets around £9) stages a good range of drama. Much-renowned chronicler of middle-class mores, Alan Ayckbourn, premiers his plays here. It also has a fine restaurant (see Places to Eat).

Getting There & Away

Scarborough is a good transport hub. It's 230 miles (370km) from London, 70 miles (113km) from Leeds, 16 miles (26km) from Pickering and 20 miles (32km) from Whitby.

There are reasonably frequent Scarborough & District buses (No 128) along the A170 from Pickering (£4.60, one hour) and Helmsley (£5.25, 1½ hours). They leave from Westborough.

There are regular buses, Nos 93 and 93A (via Robin Hood's Bay), from Whitby (£4.50, one hour). No 843 comes from Leeds (£13, eight to 12 daily) via York (£9.50).

There are regular trains from Leeds (£16.50, one hour 20 minutes) via York and

Harrogate; the journey traverses a good cross section of Yorkshire. There's a service from York (£9.80, 45 minutes, hourly). Frequent trains serve Hull (£9.50, one hour 20 minutes) via Beverley.

Getting Around

Victorian funicular lifts slope up and down Scarborough's steep cliffs to the beach daily from February till the end of October.

Local buses leave from the western end of Westborough and outside the train station.

For a cab, call ☎ 361009; £3.50 should get you to most places in town.

FILEY

☎ 01723 • pop 6619

Filey is a quiet beach town with a respectable, vaguely refined air. Formerly a fishing village, since the 18th and 19th centuries it's been providing a more sedate and genteel alternative to its brasher neighbours, Bridlington and Scarborough. An important walking centre, it's the hub for the Cleveland Way, and the Wolds Way finishes here, at the dramatic coastal outcrop of Filey Brigg (for more details, see the East Riding of Yorkshire section earlier). Five miles of sandy beach offer ample scope for paddling weary feet. Murray St is lined with shops and links the train and bus stations to the beach.

Filey's TIC (☎ 518000; e fileytic@scarboroughbc.gov.uk; John St; open 10am-5.30pm daily May-Sept, 10am-12.30pm & 1pm-4.30pm Oct-Apr) is well appointed and helpful, booking local accommodation.

Filey is served by trains on the line between Hull and Bridlington to the south and Scarborough to the north (every two hours). The bare-bones station is about a mile (1.6km) west of the beach. The town is 7 miles (11km) south of Scarborough on the A165. Bus Nos 120 and 121 come from Scarborough (30 minutes, hourly).

North York Moors National Park

The North York Moors is a wild and frequently windswept area of rolling whaleback hills, cut by deep green valleys sheltering farms, villages, castles and the occasional ruined abbey. From the ridge-top roads and high open moors there are great views, while in the east the countryside gives way abruptly to a dramatic coastline of sheer cliffs, sheltered bays and long sandy beaches.

One of the principal glories of the moors is the vast expanse of heather, which flowers in an explosion of pink and mauve from July to early September. Outside the flowering season, the browns-tending-to-purple on the hills – in vivid contrast to the deep greens of the Dales – give the park its characteristic moody appearance.

Orientation & Information

The park covers 553 sq miles (1432 sq km), with hills and steep escarpments forming the northern and western boundaries, and the eastern limit marked by the North Sea coast. The southern border runs roughly parallel to the A170 Thirsk–Scarborough road, and the main gateway towns are Helmsley and Pickering in the south, and Whitby in the northeast – all with good TICs. The national park also runs TICs (called visitor centres) at Sutton Bank, Danby and Robin Hood's Bay. Although outside the park, Scarborough is another good gateway (see the North Yorkshire section for details.)

The national park produces the very useful *Moors & Coast* visitor guide (50p), available at TICs, hotels etc, with information on things to see and do and an accommodation listing. The park website at w www.northyorkmoors-npa.gov.uk is even more comprehensive.

Activities

Several ideas for short walks and rides (from a few hours to all day) are suggested in this section, and TICs stock an excellent range of walking leaflets (around 50p), as well as more comprehensive walking and cycling guidebooks.

Walking A network of footpaths spreads across the moors, and there are many excellent walking opportunities – especially along the western escarpment and the cliff-tops on the coast. The green and tranquil valleys are also ideal for a spot of relaxed rambling, although for avid walkers, the broad ridges and rolling high ground of the moors can be a bit featureless after a few hours and for that reason this area is not as popular as the Yorkshire Dales or the Lake District – a plus if you're looking for peace and quiet.

For long-distance walks, the famous Coast to Coast route strides across the park and the Cleveland Way covers three sides of the moors' outer rim on its 109-mile (175km), nine-day route from Helmsley to Filey, through a wonderful landscape of escarpments and coastline.

The Cook Country Walk, named for explorer Captain Cook, who was born and raised in this area, links several monuments commemorating his life. This 40-mile (64km) three-day route follows the flanks of the Cleveland Hills from Marton (near Middlesbrough), then the superb coast from Staithes south to Whitby.

Cycling Once you've puffed up the escarpment, the North York Moors make fine cycling country, with ideal quiet lanes through the valleys and scenic roads over the hills. There's also a great selection of tracks and former railways for mountain bikes.

Places to Stay
The national park is ringed with towns and villages, all with a good range of accommodation – although options thin out in the central area. Walkers and outdoor fans can take advantage of the network of **camping barns**. Most are on farms, with bookings administered by the **YHA** (☎ 0870 870 8808). For more details TICs have a *Camping Barns in England* leaflet.

Getting There & Around
If you're coming from the south, from York (15 miles/24km outside the park) there are regular buses to Helmsley, Pickering, Scarborough and Whitby.

From the north, head for Middlesbrough, then take the Esk Valley railway line through the northern moors to Whitby, via Grosmont and several other villages which make useful bases. A second line, the North Yorkshire Moors Railway (NYMR), runs through the park from Pickering to Grosmont. Using these two railway lines, much of the moors area is easily accessible for those without wheels.

The highly useful Moorsbus network (**w** www.moorbus.net) operates on Sunday from May to October, daily mid-July to late August or early September, and is ideal for reaching out-of-the-way spots. Pick up a

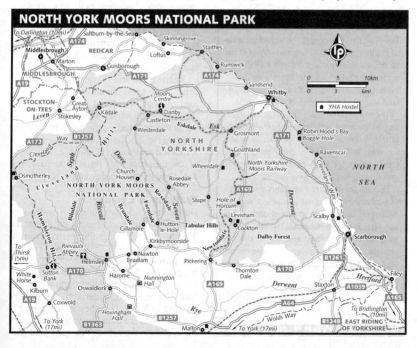

NORTH YORK MOORS NATIONAL PARK

YORKSHIRE

timetable and route-map from TICs. A standard Moorsbus day-pass costs £2.50, and for £12.50 the pass covers you on the Esk Valley and NYMR trains too – a good deal if you plan to really make a day of it. Family tickets and one-off fares for short journeys are also available.

Call the national **Traveline** (☎ *0870 608 2608*) for all public bus and train information.

HELMSLEY
☎ 01439 • pop 1500

Helmsley is a classic North Yorkshire market town, with a central square of proud old houses and historic coaching inns. There's a busy market here every Friday. Overlooking the town is a fine Norman castle, and nearby are the superb ruins of Rievaulx Abbey, overlooked by the grassy expanse of Rievaulx Terrace. With several good walks in the area (many taking in historical sights), Helmsley makes a good base for exploring this beautiful southwest corner of the Moors.

Orientation & Information
The centre of everything is the Market Place; all four sides are lined with twee shops, cosy

pubs and several cafés. The helpful **TIC** (☎ *770173*; e *helmsley@ytbtic.co.uk; open 9.30am-5.30pm daily Mar-Oct, 10am-4pm Fri-Sun Nov-Feb*) is also here selling maps and books, and can help with accommodation.

Things to See
Just southwest of the Market Place stands the impressive ruin of **Helmsley Castle** (*EH; ☎ 770442; admission £2.50; open 10am-6pm daily Apr-Oct, 10am-4pm Wed-Sun Nov-Mar*). Most striking are the massive 'earthworks' (deep ditches and banks) dating from the 12th century, to which later rulers added thick stone walls and defensive towers – one still stands like a giant tooth against the sky. There are great views from the battlements over nearby Dumcombe Park, and kids love the 'dungeons', although they're actually just boring old cellars.

Just outside the castle, **Helmsley Walled Garden** would be just another plant and produce centre, were it not for its dramatic position and its fabulous selection of flowers, fruits and vegetables – some of which are quite rare – not to mention the herbs, including 40 varieties of mint. If you're into horticulture with a historical twist, this is Eden.

South of the castle stretches the vast landscape of **Duncombe Park** with the grand stately home of **Duncombe Park House** (☎ *770213; house & grounds £6, park only £2; open 11am-5.30pm Thur-Sun late Apr-Oct*) at its heart. From the house and formal gardens, wide grassy walkways and terraces lead through woodland to mock-classical temples, while longer walking trails are set out in the parkland – now protected as a nature reserve. The house, ticket office and information centre are 1½ miles (2.5km) south of town, an easy walk through the park. You could easily spend a day here.

Walking & Cycling
Duncombe Park has numerous walks (see earlier), and for something a bit longer the 3½-mile route along the pretty river to Rievaulx Abbey is an absolute must. The TIC can provide route leaflets, and advise on buses if you don't want to walk both ways. This route is also the overture to the Cleveland Way (described under Activities earlier). Cycling to Rievaulx Abbey is also possible, but the roads are quite busy; a better option for cyclists is the network of quiet (and rela-

---

Heather & Grouse

The North York Moors is the largest expanse of heather moorland in England. When in full bloom it's stunning and it's also a vitally important habitat for wildlife. Worldwide there's more tropical rainforest than heather moorland – so treat this rare stuff with respect!

There are three main species of heather: ling is the most widespread, has a pinkish-purple flower and is most spectacular in late summer; bell heather is deep purple; and cross-leaved (or bog) heather prefers wet ground and tends to flower earlier.

Perhaps the heather moorlands' most famous inhabitant is the red grouse – a popular field-sport target. The grouse-shooting season lasts from the 'Glorious Twelfth' of August to 10 December, and the heather is periodically burned (giving managed moorland a patchwork effect) to encourage new growth, as the grouse nests among mature plants but feeds on new shoots. That is, of course, until someone comes along and blasts it out of existence.

YORKSHIRE

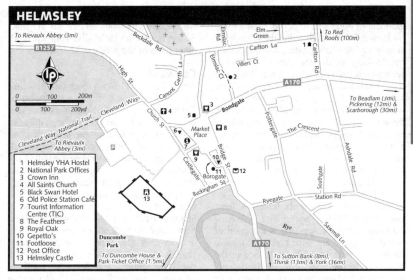

HELMSLEY

To Rievaulx Abbey (3mi)

B1257

Beckdale Rd

Elmslac Rd

Elm Green

Carlton La

To Red Roofs (100m)

Villiers Ct

High St

Canons Garth La

Elmslac Ct

Carlton Rd

A170

To Beadlam (3mi), Pickering (12mi) & Scarborough (30mi)

Cleveland Way

Church St

Bondgate

Pottergate

The Crescent

Ashdale Rd

Cleveland Way National Trail

To Rievaulx Abbey (3mi)

Market Place

Castlegate

Bridge St

Borogate

Buckingham Sq

Southgate

Station Rd

Duncombe Park

Ryegate

Rye

Sawmill Ln

To Duncombe House & Park Ticket Office (1.5mi)

A170

To Sutton Bank (8mi), Thirsk (13mi) & York (36mi)

0   100   200m
0   100   200yd

1 Helmsley YHA Hostel
2 National Park Offices
3 Crown Inn
4 All Saints Church
5 Black Swan Hotel
6 Old Police Station Café
7 Tourist Information Centre (TIC)
8 The Feathers
9 Royal Oak
10 Gepetto's
11 Footloose
12 Post Office
13 Helmsley Castle

---

tively flat) country lanes east of Helmsley. **Footloose** (☎ 770886; Borogate) is a friendly outdoor shop, with maps for sale and bikes for rent (£7.50 per day, booking preferred).

Places to Stay & Eat
For camping **Wrens of Rydale** (☎ 771260; Gale Lane, Nawton; per car, tent & 2 adults £8, cheaper rates for hikers) is a small, quiet, neat site about 3 miles (5km) east of Helmsley, south of Beadlam.

Helmsley YHA Hostel (☎ 0870 7705860; [e] helmsley@yha.org.uk; Carlton Lane; beds £9.50) is a modern place with a suburban feel just outside the centre.

Red Roofs (☎ 770175; 3 Carlton Lane; rooms per person £20) offers straightforward B&B in single and double rooms.

Crown Inn (☎ 770297; Market Place; rooms per person £36; mains £8) is old-fashioned, with a homely atmosphere, an older, quieter clientele, three bars and good food.

The Feathers (☎ 770275; [e] feathershotel@aol.com; Market Place; singles/doubles from £40/60; mains around £7) is a traditional inn with four-poster beds and other historical trimmings, and a large, busy bar downstairs, serving a range of bar meals.

Black Swan Hotel (☎ 0870 4008112; Market Place; doubles around £80) has upscale rooms and lovely back gardens, plus a bar and smart restaurant.

Royal Oak (Market Place) is the liveliest of the town's pubs, with good beer and bar-meals.

As well as the pubs, the Market Place has several cafés, including the quaint **Old Police Station** (Market Place).

Gepetto's (☎ 770479; 8 Bridge St), just south of Market Place, is a great Italian restaurant with an open kitchen, and pizzas for £6 to £7.

Getting There & Away
All buses stop in the Market Place. From York to Helmsley, take bus Nos 31, 31A and 31X (£4.20, three per day Monday to Saturday, 1½ hours). Between Helmsley and Scarborough, bus No 128 (£6, hourly, 1½ hours; four on Sunday) goes via Pickering.

AROUND HELMSLEY
Rievaulx
About 3 miles (5km) west of Helmsley is the little village of Rievaulx (pronounced ree-voh) and the famous remains of **Rievaulx Abbey** (EH; ☎ 798228; admission £3.60; open 10am-6pm daily Apr-Sept, 10am-4pm Oct-Mar). This is everything a ruin should be: battered enough by the passage of time to give a venerable air, but with enough beautiful stonework, soaring pillars and graceful arches remaining so you can imagine how it looked in its 13th century heyday.

Rievaulx may not have the overwhelming grandeur of Fountains Abbey, or the stunning position of Whitby Abbey, but the site is quite simply idyllic – a secluded, wooded valley overlooking fields and the River Rye – with a view pretty much as it was 900 years ago, when Cistercian monks first arrived. And it seems they enjoyed the scenery just as much as we do today: one abbot, St Aelred, famously described the abbey's surroundings as 'everywhere peace, everywhere serenity'. For your own spiritual refreshment, the ruins surrounded by neat lawns and shady trees. For nourishment of another sort, it's also a great place for a picnic, especially if you've walked over from Helmsley.

Near the abbey, **Rievaulx Terrace & Temples** (NT; ☎ 798340; admission £3.30; open 10.30am-5pm daily Apr-Oct) is a section of wooded escarpment once part of extensive Duncombe Park (see Things to See in the Helmsley section). In the 1750s landscape-gardening fashion favoured a natural or gothic look, and many aristocrats had mock ruins built in their parks. The Duncombe family went one better, as their lands contained a genuine medieval ruin – Rievaulx Abbey – and the half-mile-long grassy terrace was built, with classical-style temples at each end, so lords and ladies could stroll effortlessly in the 'wilderness' and admire the ruins in the valley below. Today, we can do the same, with views over Ryedale and the Hambleton Hills forming a perfect backdrop.

A visit to these two historic sites makes a great day out from Helmsley, but note that there's no direct access between the abbey and the terrace. Their entrance gates are about a mile apart and easily reached along a lane – steeply uphill if you're going from the abbey to the terrace.

Sutton Bank

Sutton Bank is a dramatically steep escarpment 8 miles (13km) west of Helmsley. If you're driving, this may be your entry to the North York Moors. And what an entry. The road climbs steeply up, with magnificent views westwards across the Pennines and Yorkshire Dales. At the top, there's a **TIC** (☎ 01845-597426; open 10am-5pm daily Apr-Oct, 11am-4pm daily Nov, Dec & Mar, 11am-4pm Sat & Sun Jan & Feb) with exhibitions about the moors, books and maps for sale, and handy leaflets on short walks to nearby

view-points. If you don't have your own wheels, the Moorsbus service No M3 links Sutton Bank with Helmsley, from where all other parts of the park can be reached.

Coxwald

About 7 miles (11.5km) southwest of Helmsley, and the same distance southeast of Thirsk (covered in the North Yorkshire section), Coxwald is an immaculate village of golden stone with a serene sense of symmetry, nestling in beautiful countryside. It may be in the north but it shouts middle England (it even *sounds* like Cotswold), and Yorkshire accents are pretty scarce hereabouts.

Apart from the quiet picture-postcard beauty of the place, the main attraction is **Shandy Hall** (☎ 01347-868465; gardens/house adult £4.50/2.50; gardens open 11am-4.30pm daily May-Sept, house 2pm-4.30pm Wed, 2.30pm-4.30pm Sun May-Sept), built in the 15th century, and home to ebullient eccentric Laurence Sterne (1713–68), author of *Tristram Shandy*, when he was parson here. The house is full of 'Sterneana', with lots of information on this entertaining character, so outrageous that he who would sometimes write wearing 'a purple jerkin and yellow slippers, without either wig or cap'.

Nearby is **Byland Abbey** (EH; ☎ 01347-868614; admission £1.70; open 10am-1pm & 2pm-6pm daily Apr-Sept, to 5pm Oct), the elegant remains of a fine Cistercian creation, now a series of lofty arches surrounded by open green slopes.

For a place to stay or eat, the **Fauconberg Arms** (☎ 01347-868214; Main St; en-suite singles/doubles £35/60; mains £7-15) is a cosy local in the heart of the village, with good food and simply-furnished but comfortable rooms.

Newburgh House (☎ 01347-868177; singles/doubles £40/60) is a smart, tranquil place close to a small lake, and serving excellent breakfasts.

Wombwell Arms (☎ 01347-868280; Wass; mains £8-11), is a refined little pub in the village of Wass, about a mile from Coxwald on the Byland Abbey road, which offers excellent and substantial meals.

HUTTON-LE-HOLE

☎ 01751

The little village of Hutton-le-Hole is a delightful collection of quaint old stone cottages, seemingly deep in the heart of the North York Moors, but in reality just 2½ miles (4km) north of the main A170 road, about equidistant from the market towns of Helmsley and Pickering.

The main feature here is the village green, an undulating grassy expanse kept trim by nibbling sheep, with a stream creating a small valley that divides the village in two, although it's easily crossed by a neat white footbridge. The dips and hollows on the green might give the village its name – it was once called simply Hutton Hole, but prim Victorians added the Frenchified 'le', which the locals defiantly pronounce 'lee'.

Linguistics notwithstanding, this is a fine place for a stroll, or a spot of light rustic souvenir shopping followed by tea and scones. The TIC (☎ 417367; open 10am-5.30pm daily mid-Mar–early Nov) has leaflets on walks in the area, including a 5-mile (8km) circuit to the nearby village of Lastingham.

Things to See

Attached to the TIC is the **Ryedale Folk Museum** (☎ 417367; adult/child £3.25/1.75; open 10am-5.30pm daily mid-Mar–early Nov), a fascinating collection of traditional North York Moors buildings from different eras, including a medieval manor house, simple farmers' houses, a blacksmith's forge and a row of 1930s village shops – complete with enamel signs for Brasso and Kiwi boot polish. Inside some of the buildings are demonstrations of traditional crafts such as chair-weaving, lace-making and glass-blowing. It's easy to spend a few hours here marvelling at the skills of Moors residents past and present. There are also sheds of old farming equipment, some fascinating exhibits and old photos from the days when ironstone mines and railways crossed the landscape (many now turned to trails for walkers and cyclists), an archaeology section, and a revealing display of underwear through the ages.

Places to Stay & Eat

Hutton-le-Hole has a small choice of places to stay in the village itself, and the TIC can help with more suggestions if you want B&B on a farm in the surrounding countryside.

Moorlands House (☎ 417548; e welcome@moorlandshouse.com; double rooms £65) is an excellent choice for stylish

B&B and convivial atmosphere. The well-travelled hosts delight in meeting guests from around the world or just up the road, and can advise on walks or places to eat in the surrounding area.

The Barn Hotel (☎ 417311; rooms per person £30) was indeed once a farm-building, then a humble row of cottages, now with comfortable rooms and a suitably old-fashioned feel.

The Crown (bar meals £6-7) is the village pub, a straightforward spot that's popular with locals and visitors. The main street also boasts at least three **teashops**, all offering drinks, snacks and lunches.

Getting There & Away

Moorsbus services (see the North York Moors Getting There & Away section) through Hutton-le-Hole include No M3 between Helmsley and Danby (seven per day) and Nos M1 and M2 between Pickering and Danby (eight per day). Outside times when the Moorsbus runs, you'll need your own transport to get here. Alternatively catch bus No 128 along the A170 (see the Helmsley section for details), drop off at the junction east of Kirkbymoorside and walk the 2½ miles (4km) up the lane to Hutton-le-Hole.

PICKERING
☎ 01751 • pop 6000

The attractive market town of Pickering has been a busy trading centre for centuries. It's particularly lively these days as it stands on the crossroads between York, Thirsk, Whitby and Scarborough, and it's also the southern terminus of the North Yorkshire Moors Railway (NYMR), where puffing steam trains attract great crowds.

Orientation & Information

The main drag is the Market Place, lined with a quaint and quirky collection of shops, pubs and cafés, and most of the town is within a five-minute walk from here. The main A170 passes just south of the centre.

The **TIC** (☎ 473791; e pickering@ytbtic.co.uk; open 9.30am-5.30pm Mon-Sat, 9.30am-4pm Sun Mar-Oct, 10am-4pm Mon-Sat Nov-Feb), on a street called The Ropery, can provide details on accommodation in Pickering and at villages along the NYMR. Next door, the library offers a free Internet service.

YORKSHIRE

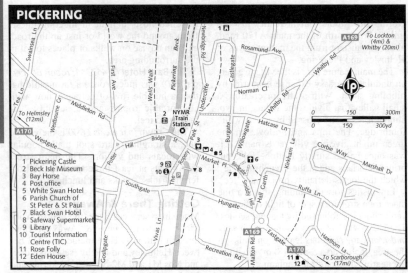

PICKERING

1 Pickering Castle
2 Beck Isle Museum
3 Bay Horse
4 Post office
5 White Swan Hotel
6 Parish Church of
   St Peter & St Paul
7 Black Swan Hotel
8 Safeway Supermarket
9 Library
10 Tourist Information
    Centre (TIC)
11 Rose Folly
12 Eden House

Things to See

Well worth a look is **Pickering Castle** *(EH; ☎ 474989; admission £2.50; open 10am-6pm daily Apr-Sept, 10am-4pm daily Oct-Mar)*, founded by William the Conqueror and much improved by later kings. It looks just like the diagrams you drew in school history lessons – thick stone outer walls circling the keep, perched atop a 12m-high motte (mound) with great views of the surrounding country.

As well as the fine castle, if history is your thing, don't miss the **Parish Church of St Peter & St Paul**, where the inside walls are covered with medieval murals. Once common, but destroyed elsewhere during the Reformation, these Biblical stories-in-pictures are very rare.

For history of a secular sort, **Beck Isle Museum** *(☎ 473653; Bridge St; adult/child £3/1.50; open 10am-5pm daily Apr-Oct)* has re-created old shops (including printing and cobbling emporia) and boasts a surprisingly large collection of miscellany from bygone Pickering.

Places to Stay & Eat

About 4 miles (6.5km) north of Pickering, straightforward **Lockton YHA Hostel** *(☎ 0870 7705938; beds £7.75)* is accessible by bus (towards Whitby) or NYMR train (via Levisham, then a 2-mile/3km walk).

There are a few choices in the centre and a strip of B&Bs on Eastgate (the A170 to/from Scarborough).

Eden House *(☎ 472289; e edenhouse@ breathemail.net; 120 Eastgate; rooms per person £22-24)* is a neat, traditional place.

Rose Folly *(☎ 475067; e gail@rosefolly .freeserve.co.uk; 112 Eastgate; rooms per person £23-25)* offers a friendly welcome and pretty garden.

The Black Swan Hotel *(☎ 472286; Birdgate; singles/doubles £32/54; snacks £3-5, meals £6-7)* is a popular traditional pub with fine beer, good food and cosy accommodation.

The White Swan Hotel *(☎ 472288; e welcome@white-swan.co.uk; Market Place; singles/doubles £70/100, Fri & Sat £80/110; mains £9-15)* skilfully combines a smart-but-not-swanky pub, a highly rated restaurant and a luxurious small inn, all with professional friendly service.

There are several cafés and teashops on Market Place, and for drinks of another sort the **Bay Horse** *(Market Place)* is a good no-nonsense pub.

Getting There & Away

Bus No 128 between Helmsley (40 minutes) and Scarborough (50 minutes) runs hourly via Pickering. Yorkshire Coastliner (Nos 840, 842 and X40) services run to/from York (£8.50, hourly, 70 minutes).

For train details, see the North Yorkshire Moors Railway, following.

AROUND PICKERING
North Yorkshire Moors Railway

Pickering is the southern terminus of the privately owned North Yorkshire Moors Railway (NYMR), which runs for 18 miles (29km) through beautiful countryside to the village of Grosmont. Lovingly restored steam locos pull period carriages, resplendent in polished brass and bright paintwork, and the railway appeals to train buffs and day-trippers alike. For visitors without wheels, it's excellent for reaching out-of-the-way spots. Even more useful, Grosmont is also on the main railway line between Middlesbrough and Whitby, which opens up yet more possibilities for walking or sightseeing.

Pickering, the railway, and the surrounding countryside can easily absorb a day. At all stations there's information about waymarked walks, lasting between one and four hours. For more information, call **Pickering Station** (☎ 01751-472508), or see the **recorded timetable** (☎ 01751-473535), or see w www .northyorkshiremoorsrailway.com. Generally, there are four to eight trains daily between April and October. The full journey takes an hour, and tickets allowing you to get on and get off as much as you like cost £10. (It's £5 for children and a range of family deals are also available.)

From Pickering the line heads northeast through a river valley, and the first stop is **Levisham station**, 1½ miles (2.5km) west of beautiful Levisham village, which faces Lockton across another steep valley.

Next along is **Newton Dale**, ideal for walkers heading for the impressive crater-like bowl in the hills called the Hole of Horcum; it's a request stop only, so let the guard know if you want to get off here.

A few miles farther is **Goathland**, a picturesque village surrounded by heather-clad moors. It attracts many visitors because it's 'Aidensfield' in the British TV series *Heartbeat*, and more recently was a set for a *Harry Potter* film. There are several good walks from the station, including along a pretty trail to Grosmont. If you want to halt for a while, there are several hotel and B&B options plus a campsite.

At the northern end of the line is the sleepy little village of **Grosmont** (pronounced gro-

mont), although it comes alive when the steam trains pull across the level crossing on the main street. There are some B&B options here, plus a nice café and a pub doing food, and that's about it. All change please.

Getting There & Away You can start your train ride in Pickering, or in Grosmont, which is easily reached from Whitby by 'normal' train along the Esk Valley line (see the Whitby section for details). A grand day out from Pickering combines the NYMR, the Esk Valley Line between Grosmont and Whitby and the bus over the moors between Whitby and Pickering.

DANBY
☎ 01287 • pop 400 • elevation 140m

Danby is a tiny village deep in the moors at the head of Eskdale, where the surrounding countryside is particularly beautiful. It makes a good base, as the **Moors Centre** (☎ 660654; open 10am-5pm daily Apr-Oct, 11am-4pm Sat & Sun Nov-Mar), the park headquarters, is just half a mile from the village, and has displays, information, a café, an accommodation-booking service and a huge range of local guidebooks, maps and leaflets.

There are several short circular walks from the centre, but first on your list should

---

Horsepower & History

The railway from Pickering to Whitby was built in the 1830s, coming only 10 years after the pioneering Stockton–Darlington line. Steam power was still in its infancy, and initially carriages were pulled by horses, except where one steep incline was conquered by a balancing system of water-filled tanks. On downhill stretches the train freewheeled, and the horses got to ride in their own carriage!

The first steam locomotive was introduced in 1847, and trains continued to run up and down for more than a century, until the line was closed in the infamous 'rationalisation' of the 1960s.

But the railway didn't remain idle for long. In 1967 a volunteer preservation society was formed to restore and operate the Grosmont–Pickering line. Their efforts were successful and today the NYMR carries over 300,000 passengers a year.

YORKSHIRE

be Danby Beacon; it's a stiff 2 miles up-hill to the northeast, but the stunning 360° views across the moors make the sweat sweet.

Places to Stay & Eat

Danby Mill Farm (☎ 660330; rooms per person £16), by the train station, offers a friendly welcome and straightforward camping for £3 per person and equally no-frills B&B. Some other farms in the area also do accommodation – the Moors Centre staff can advise.

The Duke of Wellington (☎ 660351; e landlord@dukeofwellington.freeserve.co.uk; rooms per person from £28) in the village centre is a fine traditional pub, serving good beer and meals.

Getting There & Away

Using the delightful Esk Valley railway, access is easy. There are five trains daily: Whitby is 20 minutes east; Middlesbrough one hour west (£4).

WHITBY

☎ 01947 • pop 14,000

The coastal town of Whitby could be just another tacky beach resort, but it magnificently transcends the crowds, and remains a most interesting and attractive town, easily ranking among the highlights of any trip to the north. It's a wonderful, lively combination of a working harbour complete with colourful fishing boats, a maze of narrow medieval streets lined with restaurants and pubs, a vista of redbrick houses spilling down a headland, and a cacophony of coaches, amusement arcades, fish-and-chip shops and other seaside paraphernalia, all topped by the imposing silhouette of an ancient ruined abbey. And there's an equally colourful mix of people – good-time girls and boys, retirees, young families, hikers, bikers and the occasional goth – with everyone just having a great time.

As well as the delights of the town itself, Whitby is the perfect base for exploring nearby cliffs, coves and fishing villages, or as a gateway to the North York Moors that surround the town on three sides. On the fourth side, of course, is the sea. And you'll never have any doubt that you're close to the water, thanks to boat-horns, occasional mists, and the constant shrieks of seagulls.

Whitby is also a major draw for fans of history and literature: the abbey enjoys one

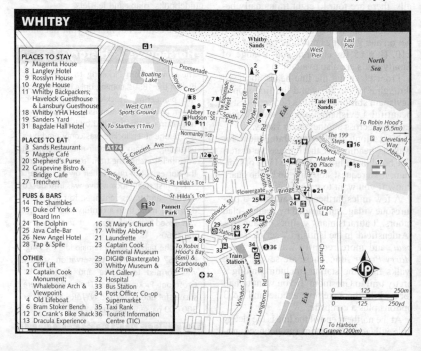

WHITBY

PLACES TO STAY
7   Magenta House
8   Langley Hotel
9   Rosslyn House
10 Argyle House
11 Whitby Backpackers;
    Havelock Guesthouse
    & Lansbury Guesthouse
18 Whitby YHA Hostel
19 Sanders Yard
31 Bagdale Hall Hotel

PLACES TO EAT
3   Sands Restaurant
5   Magpie Café
20 Shepherd's Purse
22 Grapevine Bistro &
    Bridge Cafe
27 Trenchers

PUBS & BARS
14 The Shambles
15 Duke of York &
    Board Inn
24 The Dolphin
25 Java Cafe-Bar
26 New Angel Hotel
28 Tap & Spile

OTHER
1   Cliff Lift
2   Captain Cook
    Monument;
    Whalebone Arch &
    Viewpoint
4   Old Lifeboat
6   Bram Stoker Bench
12 Dr Crank's Bike Shack
13 Dracula Experience
16 St Mary's Church
17 Whitby Abbey
21 Laundrette
23 Captain Cook
    Memorial Museum
29 DIGI@ (Baxtergate)
30 Whitby Museum &
    Art Gallery
32 Hospital
33 Bus Station
34 Post Office; Co-op
    Supermarket
35 Taxi Rank
36 Tourist Information
    Centre (TIC)

Captain Cook – Whitby's Famous Son

Although he wasn't actually born in Whitby, the town has adopted the famous explorer Captain James Cook, and since the first tourists got off the train in Victorian times, local entrepreneurs have mercilessly cashed in on his memory, as endless 'Endeavour Cafés' and 'Captain Cook Chip Shops' testify.

Whitby's own link with the sea is much older. The Romans built a lighthouse here and from the Middle Ages the town became a major maritime centre, with Whitby-built and Whitby-crewed ships serving generations of traders, whalers and fisherfolk.

The young James Cook started his apprenticeship in 1746, working on Whitby 'cats' – unique, flat-bottomed ships carrying coal from Newcastle to London. Nine years later he joined the navy, and in 1768 began the first of three great voyages of discovery, during which he reached Australia. Cook returned to Europe with detailed charts, vast notebooks full of etchings and observations, numerous plant and animal samples, and a vast wealth of knowledge garnered from these long journeys. His ships on all three voyages, including the *Endeavour*, were based on the design of 'cats', and in this small but vital way Whitby played a part in world exploration and 18th-century scientific understanding.

---

of the most stunning locations in England, and the town was the launch-pad for the maritime career of Captain James Cook, one of the world's greatest explorers, while Bram Stoker based some of his gothic fantasy novel *Dracula* here. (See the boxed text 'Whitby's Gothic Heritage'.)

And Whitby's final claim to fame – the best fish and chips in the country.

Orientation & Information

Whitby is divided in two by the harbour and River Esk estuary. On the east bank is the older part of town; the newer (19th-century) town grew up on the western side.

The **TIC** (☎ 602674; Langborne Rd; open 9.30am-6pm daily May-Sept, 10am-4.30pm daily Oct-Apr) has a wealth of information on the town and the surrounding moors and coast.

The **post office** (open 8.30am-5.30pm Mon-Sat) is across from the TIC inside the Co-op Supermarket. Other services include Internet access at **Java Cafe-Bar** (Flowergate) for £6 per hour or **Digi** (Baxtergate) at £3 per hour, and a **laundrette** (72 Church St).

An intriguing feature of Whitby is that many streets have two names. For example, Abbey Terrace and Hudson St are opposite sides of the same street, as are West St and The Esplanade.

Festivals

The good citizens of Whitby put on a full programme of festivals throughout the year, when the town is particularly lively (although accommodation can be hard to find so it's always wise to book ahead). These include the folk music festival, the world music festival, and the famous Gothic festival – when anyone in town not wearing black or false fangs is definitely a weirdo.

Whitby Abbey & St Mary's Church

There are ruins, and then there's **Whitby Abbey** (EH; ☎ 603568; admission £3.60; open 10am-6pm daily Apr-Sept, to 4pm Oct-Mar). Dominating the town, in a simply stunning location, this ancient holy place dates from the 11th to 14th centuries, with huge solid pillars, soaring arches and gaping windows made all the more dramatic with the North Sea sky behind. Nearby, **St Mary's Church** (open 10am-5pm daily Apr-Oct, to 4pm Nov-Mar) has an atmospheric interior full of skewed and tilting galleries and box pews.

You reach the abbey and the church via the famous 199 steps up the cliff side. Take time out to catch your breath and admire the fantastic view.

Captain Cook Memorial Museum

Dedicated to the memory of Whitby's famous son, the Captain Cook Memorial Museum (☎ 601900; Grape Lane; adult/child £2.50/1.80; open 9.45am-5pm daily Apr-Oct, 11am-3pm Sat & Sun Mar) is in a house once occupied by the ship-owner to whom Cook was apprenticed. Highlights include Cook's own maps and writings, etchings from the

South Seas and a wonderful model of the *Endeavour*, with all the crew and stores laid out for inspection.

Whitby Museum & Art Gallery

In a quiet park overlooking the town, Whitby Museum (☎ 602908; *Pannett Park; adult/child £2.50/1, art gallery admission free; open 9.30am-5.30pm Mon-Sat, 2pm-5pm Sun May-Sept, shorter hrs Oct-Apr)* is a quaint traditional place with glass cabinets of fossils (including a dinosaur), Cook memorabilia, ships in bottles, plus weird stuff like a suitably gothic amputated hand and an invention for weather forecasting using live leeches. The gallery contains work by the Staithes group of artists.

Dracula Experience

Always looking for a way to sink their teeth into tourists, local entrepreneurs have set up the Dracula Experience (☎ 601923; *9 Marine Parade; adult/child £1.95/1.50; open 10am-10pm daily May-Sept, noon-5pm Sat & Sun Oct-Apr)*. With lots of lights and mirrors, some electrical trickery and a small cast of real live actors, it puts on a show loosely inspired by the Bram Stoker novel (see the boxed text 'Whitby's Gothic Heritage'). It's corny, but what the hell. It's fun too.

Captain Cook Monument

At the top of the cliff near East Terrace, the Captain Cook Monument shows the great man looking out to sea, usually with a seagull perched on his head. Nearby is the Whalebone Arch (it's just that), remembering Whitby's days as a whaling port, and a scruffy viewpoint with telescopes.

Tours

Several companies along the harbourside offer **boat-rides** and **fishing trips**, out to sea or up the estuary. The cost is about £2.50 for three hours.

Two **open-top buses** cruise the streets daily via all the major sights with commentary and hop-on hop-off service. The fare is £4, valid all day.

Walking & Cycling

Although it's hardly tranquil, a walk up the main road to the new bridge high above the Esk is worth it for great views. For something a bit longer, the 5½-mile (9km) cliff-top walk south to Robin Hood's Bay is a real treat (allow three hours). Or head north for 10 miles (16km) to reach Staithes (five hours). A local bus will get you home again; see Around Whitby for more details.

First choice for a bike ride is the excellent 20-mile (32km) Whitby to Scarborough Coastal Cycle Trail, which starts a few miles outside town, following the route of an old railway line. It's particularly good for reaching Robin Hood's Bay. Bikes can be hired from **Dr Crank's Bike Shack** (☎ 606661; *20 Skinner St)*.

Places to Stay

Whitby YHA Hostel (☎ 0870 7706089; e *whitby@yha.org.uk; Church Lane; beds £10.25)* is in an old house overlooking the town, next to the abbey – a position hip hotels would die for.

Harbour Grange (☎ 600817; e *back packers@harbourgrange.onyxnet.co.uk; Spital Bridge; dorm beds £9)* is a very neat and tidy place on the waterfront, also with family rooms and an 11.30pm curfew.

Whitby Backpackers (☎ 601794; e *mar tin@warrener65.freeserve.co.uk; 28 Hudson St; beds £10, rooms per person from £26)* has good facilities and a friendly relaxed ambience. The helpful owner is a wealth of information on local walks and evening entertainment, and gives discounts for longer stays.

Hudson St is the centre of B&B-land, and on the surrounding streets if a place isn't offering accommodation it's probably been abandoned. Most offer a range of rooms and rates; en-suite facilities usually cost a few pounds more than a 'standard' room.

Magenta House (☎ 820915; *7 The Esplanade; B&B per person £20, room only £15)* is a good budget choice.

Havelock Guesthouse (☎ 602295; *30 Hudson St; rooms per person £17.50-20)* is a large place with good rooms.

Lansbury Guesthouse (☎ 604821; *29 Hudson St; rooms per person £20-24)* has neat, comfortable rooms and friendly service.

Others to try include **Argyle House** (☎ 602733; *18 Hudson St; rooms per person £20-22)* and **Rosslyn House** (☎ 604086; *11 Abbey Terrace; rooms per person £20-25)*.

The Langley Hotel (☎ 604250; *16 Royal Crescent; en-suite singles/doubles £32/58)* offers friendly service, a faint whiff of Victorian splendour and excellent sea-views.

Sanders Yard (☎ 825010; 95 Church St; rooms per person £30-35) offers a change from the usual – imaginative and comfortable decor in rooms overlooking a flower-filled courtyard (which is a vegetarian café during the day).

Bagdale Hall Hotel (☎ 602958, fax 820714; 1 Bagdale; rooms per person £49-59, lodge rooms £45) is a lovely old-world place, with comfortable rooms and good service. Just up the road, doubles and family rooms at the more straightforward lodge are a bargain in this range.

Places to Eat & Drink

Magpie Café (☎ 602058; 14 Pier Rd; open lunch & dinner; mains £7-9) has a reputation for the best fish and chips in the world but unfortunately most of the world knows, so there are often long queues.

Trenchers (☎ 603212; New Quay Rd; open lunch & dinner; mains £7-9) is less traditional than the Magpie but with very slick service and usually shorter queues.

There are numerous other places in town where a fish and chip supper (ie, served with peas, bread and tea) will cost about £5 to £6. Of these, **Bridge Cafe** (Bridge St) is recommended, while **Sands Restaurant** (☎ 603500; Khyber Pass) is noted for its sea views.

Many pubs also serve food, including, of course, fish and chips or crab sandwiches. A good first choice is the popular **Duke of York** (Church St), with plentiful food and quick service, while next door the smaller **Board Inn** is another place with views, good beer and seafood. **The Dolphin** (Bridge St) has tables inside or out on the pavement, while **The Shambles** (Market Pl) is modern and spacious with huge picture windows overlooking the harbour.

Shepherd's Purse (☎ 820228; 95 Church St, mains around £5) is a veggie place behind a wholefood shop with the same name, with a great range of healthy, interesting snacks and meals, and a very nice courtyard.

Grapevine Bistro (☎ 820275; 2 Grape Lane) is a Mediterranean-style place, highly rated by locals, offering snacks and baguettes at lunchtime, and in the evening tapas dishes for around £5, plus excellent evening meals.

Java Cafe-Bar (Flowergate; open 7.30am-11pm) is modern, small and stylish with excellent coffee, good breakfasts, snacks and newspapers.

Entertainment

As befitting a holiday town, there are several lively pubs. The **New Angel Hotel** (☎ 602943; New Quay Rd) has a young and boisterous crowd, and music or live bands at weekends. The **Tap & Spile** (☎ 603937; New Quay Rd), is a straightforward place with good local rock and folk bands.

Getting There & Away

Whitby is 230 miles (370km) from London and 45 miles (72km) from York.

Bus Nos 93 and 93A run to/from Scarborough (£3, one hour, about hourly), and to Middlesbrough (about hourly), with fewer services on Sunday. Yorkshire Coastliner (Nos 840 and X40) runs between Whitby and Leeds (£9, seven per day, three hours) via Pickering and York.

Whitby's Gothic Heritage

The famous story of Dracula, inspiration for a thousand lurid movies, was written by Bram Stoker while staying at a B&B in Whitby in 1897. Although most Hollywood versions of the tale concentrate on deepest, darkest Transylvania, much of the original book was set in Whitby, and many sites can still be seen today.

The events are remembered at Whitby's annual Gothic Festival (every October/November, with a smaller event in April). It's Rocky Horror at the seaside – the town is full of people in black, and the atmosphere is fun and relaxed, but quite bizarre.

The TIC sells an excellent Dracula Trail leaflet (50p) but a few sites you shouldn't miss include the stone jetty in the harbour, where the Russian boat chartered by Dracula was wrecked as it flew in ahead of the huge storm. You'll need more imagination in the car park in front of the train station; this was once sidings for freight cars, and it's from here that Dracula left Whitby for London in one of his boxes of dirt.

After the town sites, you can climb the same 199 stone steps that the heroine Mina ran up when trying to save her friend Lucy. At the top of the steps is moody St Mary's Church, where Mina first saw Lucy sitting next to a suspicious black being. By that time, of course, it was too late. Cue music. The End.

If you're coming from the north, you can get to Whitby by train along the Esk Valley line from Middlesbrough (£9.50, four per day, 1½ hours), one of the most attractive lines in the country – even more scenic than the North Yorkshire Moors Railway (see the section earlier). From the south, it's easier to get a train from York to Scarborough, then a bus from Scarborough to Whitby.

Getting Around

Whitby is a compact place and those 199 steps help burn off the fish and chips. But if you need one, there's a taxi rank near the TIC.

AROUND WHITBY
Robin Hood's Bay

Just 5 miles (8km) south of Whitby, Robin Hood's Bay has a lot more to do with smugglers than the Sherwood Forest hero, but this picturesque haven is well worth a visit, although like so many places it's very busy on summer weekends.

A single main street called New Rd winds through the old part of town, dropping steeply down from the cliff-top to the sea. (There's compulsory parking at the top – don't even think about driving down as there's hardly room to turn at the bottom.) Off New Rd there's a honeycomb of cobbled alleys, secret passages and impossibly small houses. There are giftshops, teashops and a trail of pubs (it might be safer to start from the bottom and work your way up) many with seats outside, so this is an excellent place to just sit and watch the world go by.

The **visitors centre** (☎ 01947-885900), in the restored 19th-century Old Coastguard Station right at the foot of the main street, provides local information and has good exhibits on the ecology of the moors and coast. Also worth searching out is the tiny volunteer-run **museum** (off New Rd; admission 50p; usually open daily in summer), packed with miscellany from the sea and

the town, and the **Old Chapel** that now houses an excellent second-hand bookshop and a delightful vegetarian café with a terrace overlooking the sea.

Among the pubs, our favourite for ambience is the old **Dolphin**, the **Victoria Hotel** has the best beer and good food, and the **Bay Hotel** is notable for being the end of the famous Coast-to-Coast long-distance walk. Some pubs do B&B and there are several other accommodation options – the TIC in Whitby can advise.

It's eminently possible to walk or cycle here from Whitby. Also, bus Nos 93 and 93A run hourly between Whitby and Scarborough via Robin Hood's Bay – the bus stop is at the top of the hill, in the new part of town.

Staithes

About 11 miles (18km) by road from Whitby, tucked beneath high cliffs and running back along the steep banks of a river, the small fishing town of Staithes seems to hide from the modern world, focusing still on its centuries-old battle with the sea. It's like Robin Hood's Bay, but with a more authentic feel: the houses are less prettified, you can see fishermen's jackets drying on lines, and seagulls the size of vultures swoop down the narrow alleys that lead off the main street.

The town's claim to fame is that explorer James Cook worked as a grocer here when a boy. Legend says that fishermen's tales of the high seas, and bad treatment by his master, led him to steal a shilling and run away to Whitby. The rest of the tale is told in great detail in the fascinating and lovingly maintained **Captain Cook & Staithes Heritage Centre** (admission £2.50; open 10am-5.30pm daily), packed to the gunwales with nautical relics.

To get here from Whitby, buses to Middlesbrough can drop you in Staithes at the top of the hill. If you're feeling fit, walking one way and bussing the other makes for a great day out.

Northwest England

The northwest is not just a part of England's once-mighty industrial heartland; it was its very engine room. It was here that the Industrial Revolution was born and raised into the overwhelming force of capitalism; it was here that the world's first modern city was designed; and it was here that the endless possibilities of the Age of Reason were put through their original paces.

If the thought of jam-packed urban conurbations sounds less than appealing, we urge you to think again, for in Manchester you will find one of England's most interesting and vibrant cities, living testimony to the genius of contemporary urban planning and the indomitable desire of people to live well. Close by and not far behind, Liverpool is not just the birthplace of The Beatles but a city that is well on the way towards revitalising itself after decades of adversity.

South of both, Chester is a Tudor treasure with a 2-mile (3km) ring of Roman walls, while to the north, Blackpool is England's most famous seaside resort and a compelling example of the tacky brashness that defines the traditional holiday by the sea. If you're looking for some quiet time away from the traffic and the nightlife, the wonderful scenery of the Ribble Valley and the Isle of Man can be explored with ease.

ORIENTATION & INFORMATION

The towns and cities covered in this chapter are all within easy reach of each other, and are well linked by public transport. The two main cities, Manchester and Liverpool, are only 34 miles (55km) apart and are linked by hourly bus and train services. Chester is only 18 miles (29km) south of Liverpool, but is also easily accessible from Manchester by train or via the M56 motorway. Blackpool is 50 miles (80km) to the north of both cities, and is also well connected.

England's Northwest Tourist Office (☎ 0870 609 2002; Portland St, Manchester; open 10am-5.30pm Mon-Sat) recently opened in conjunction with the city's hosting of the 2002 Commonwealth Games, but at the time of research was planning to continue to provide information on the region for the foreseeable future.

Highlights

- Visiting the top-class museums and getting a taste for Manchester's extraordinary nightlife
- Walking Chester's City Walls and the wonderful Rows
- Riding stomach-churning roller coasters at Blackpool's Pleasure Beach, fun for both young and old
- Discovering the quirky and beautiful Isle of Man: it's not just for tax-dodgers and petrol-heads
- Taking the ferry across the Mersey: you should at least hum the song while enjoying the best views of Liverpool
- Browsing through the Lady Lever Art Gallery in Port Sunlight

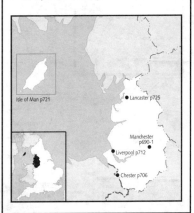

ACTIVITIES

The northwest of England is a predominantly urban area, and good places for activities like walking or cycling are thin on the ground. Well worth a look though is the Ribble Valley, which includes the frequently overlooked Forest of Bowland. Also covered in this chapter is the Isle of Man, a world apart, with top-notch walking and cycling opportunities. Regional tourism websites all contain walking and information, and TICs all stock leaflets (free) plus maps and guides (usually £1 to £5) covering walking, cycling and other activities.

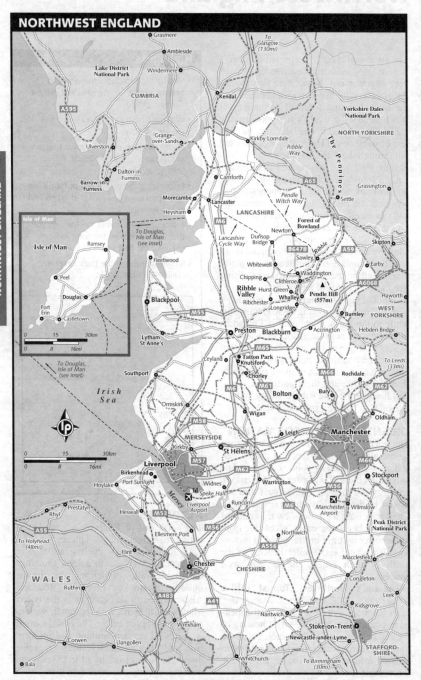

NORTHWEST ENGLAND

Manchester

☎ 0161 • pop 74,000

If London has a regional rival, then Manchester is it. The uncrowned capital of the north, the world's first industrial city has thoroughly reinvented itself in the last decade and is now one of the most exciting and interesting cities in England. To many, the city is best known for its enormously successful football team and the extraordinary nightlife that earned it the moniker 'Madchester', but Manchester is also where you'll find a wealth of fascinating museums, rich and varied dining and some of the best shopping anywhere outside of London.

Yet perhaps the most admirable element to this transformation is the firm belief among urban planners that form must follow function, and that cities are first and foremost human dwellings. The historian AJP Taylor wrote that Manchester was 'the only place in England which escapes our characteristic vice of snobbery', and that it is the only city 'which can look London in the face…as a rival version of how people should live in a community'. We couldn't agree more. Testament to this belief is the remarkable life on show at street level: from the trendy bars and boutiques of the bohemian Northern Quarter to the loud-and-proud attitude of the Gay Village and the chic, self-possessed stylings of the Castlefield area. Spend enough time here and you too will be infected with the palpable confidence of a city that knows it's onto a good thing.

History

Manchester first saw light as a Roman colony, but it was the arrival of Flemish weavers in the 14th century that was the nucleus of its later expansion. In 1762 the Manchester–Worsley canal was built, allowing for the easy transport of cheap coal, and in 1769 Richard Arkwright (1732–92) patented a steam-powered cotton mill that allowed for the mass production of cotton yarn. The Industrial Revolution was now in full flow, and Manchester was at its heart. The extension of the canal to the Mersey and Liverpool in 1776 ensured that Manchester now had direct access to a sea port, and as the cotton flowed out, the money really began to flow in. By 1800 Manchester was known as 'Cottonopolis'. It was, in George Orwell's phrase, the 'belly and guts of the nation'.

So much expansion, however, brought enormous social problems. Conditions in the mushrooming cotton mills were abominable. In 1819 agitation in favour of parliamentary reform and the abolition of the hated Corn Law (that kept corn prices artificially high) led to a mass gathering of 60,000 workers in St Peter's Fields, a site now occupied by the Free Trade Hall. Although the crowd was entirely well behaved, the authorities panicked and soldiers charged the crowd, killing 11 and injuring 500.

The massacre came to be known as Peterloo – after Waterloo only four years earlier – and it provided a rallying point in the battle for reform. In 1821 the weekly *Manchester Guardian* was founded to foster parliamentary reform and free trade; in 1955 it dropped 'Manchester' from its title and became simply *The Guardian*.

Manchester's precocious growth, however, was untenable. Textile efforts suffered due to the growing competition from the USA and continental Europe, and though Manchester was still the financial and commercial nucleus of the industry, trading cotton on the floor of the Royal Exchange, the city's manufacturing base was in decline. Not even the opening of the Ship Canal in 1894 between Liverpool and Manchester, which for a time made the city Britain's fourth-largest port, was enough to staunch the bleeding, and by the end of WWII Manchester was in deep industrial trouble.

Despite the decline of the manufacturing industries and the rise in unemployment, Manchester remained an important financial centre with a thriving cultural life, though this was hardly reflected in the city's appearance. Then, in 1996, the IRA blew up most of the commercial centre around the Royal Exchange and the Arndale Centre in the worst explosion ever on the British mainland, though miraculously no-one was killed. Rather than patch up the damage, however, the city embarked on an ambitious programme of urban rejuvenation that has once again restored the city to a position of primacy.

In 2002 Manchester hosted the Commonwealth Games, which were a resounding success and a fitting tribute to a city in rebirth.

MANCHESTER

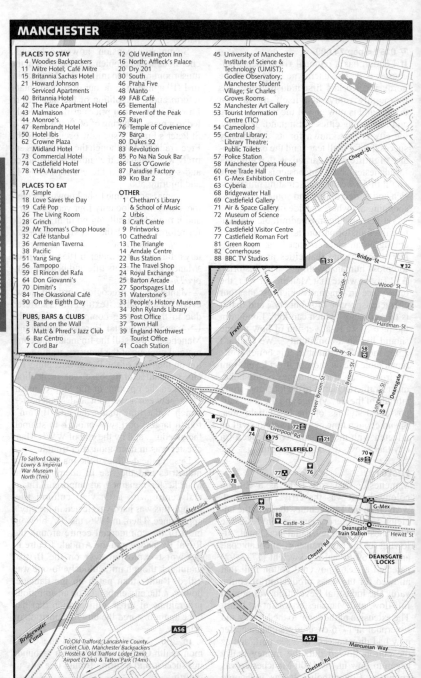

PLACES TO STAY
4 Woodies Backpackers
11 Mitre Hotel; Café Mitre
15 Britannia Sachas Hotel
21 Howard Johnson Serviced Apartments
40 Britannia Hotel
42 The Place Apartment Hotel
43 Malmaison
44 Monroe's
47 Rembrandt Hotel
50 Hotel Ibis
62 Crowne Plaza Midland Hotel
73 Commercial Hotel
74 Castlefield Hotel
78 YHA Manchester

PLACES TO EAT
17 Simple
18 Love Saves the Day
19 Café Pop
26 The Living Room
28 Grinch
29 Mr Thomas's Chop House
32 Café Istanbul
36 Armenian Taverna
38 Pacific
51 Yang Sing
56 Tampopo
59 El Rincon del Rafa
64 Don Giovanni's
70 Dimitri's
84 The Okassional Café
90 On the Eighth Day

PUBS, BARS & CLUBS
3 Band on the Wall
5 Matt & Phred's Jazz Club
6 Bar Centro
7 Cord Bar

12 Old Wellington Inn
16 North; Affleck's Palace
20 Dry 201
30 South
46 Praha Five
48 Manto
49 FAB Café
65 Elemental
66 Peveril of the Peak
67 Rain
76 Temple of Convenience
79 Barça
80 Dukes 92
83 Revolution
85 Po Na Na Souk Bar
86 Lass O'Gowrie
87 Paradise Factory
89 Kro Bar 2

OTHER
1 Chetham's Library & School of Music
2 Urbis
8 Craft Centre
9 Printworks
10 Cathedral
13 The Triangle
14 Arndale Centre
22 Bus Station
23 The Travel Shop
24 Royal Exchange
25 Barton Arcade
27 Sportspages Ltd
31 Waterstone's
33 People's History Museum
34 John Rylands Library
35 Post Office
37 Town Hall
39 England Northwest Tourist Office
41 Coach Station

45 University of Manchester Institute of Science & Technology (UMIST); Godlee Observatory; Manchester Student Village; Sir Charles Groves Rooms
52 Manchester Art Gallery
53 Tourist Information Centre (TIC)
54 Cameolord
55 Central Library; Library Theatre; Public Toilets
57 Police Station
58 Manchester Opera House
60 Free Trade Hall
61 G-Mex Exhibition Centre
63 Cyberia
68 Bridgewater Hall
69 Castlefield Gallery
71 Air & Space Gallery
72 Museum of Science & Industry
75 Castlefield Visitor Centre
77 Castlefield Roman Fort
81 Green Room
82 Cornerhouse
88 BBC TV Studios

NORTHWEST ENGLAND

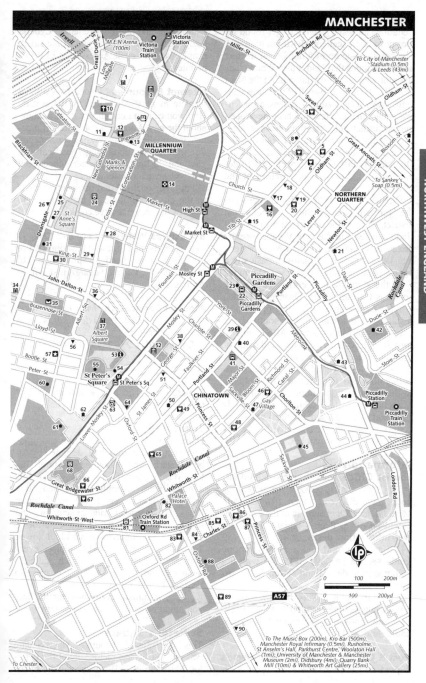

MANCHESTER

Orientation

Central Manchester is easy to get round on foot or by the excellent Metrolink tramway. The city is made up of a number of distinct neighbourhoods that lend it the vibrant character for which it is now famous. At the heart of it all – if only because all of the buses converge on it – is Piccadilly Gardens, a gardenless square that has recently been developed into an aesthetically charming urban space.

Immediately west and just south of the cathedral is the newly named Millennium Quarter, which has been spectacularly developed following the destruction of the 1996 bomb.

Directly north of Piccadilly Gardens lies the Northern Quarter, the city's bohemian district, while a few blocks southeast you'll find Canal St and the Gay Village (see the boxed text 'Gay & Lesbian Manchester', later). Next to it is Chinatown, basically a couple of streets full of Chinese restaurants.

In the southwestern corner of the city centre is Castlefield and Deansgate Locks, a hyper-trendy area with some of the best restaurants in town. Farther south is the University of Manchester (UMIST; on Oxford St/Rd), where you'll also find some of the best clubs and bars. Farther west, near the Bridgewater Canal, are two stadiums, both called Old Trafford; the first is home to the world's most famous football team, Manchester United, while the second is a cricket ground used by the Lancashire county team and, occasionally, by the national team for test matches.

Information

Tourist Office The extremely helpful TIC (☎ 234 3157, fax 236 9900; e visitor_centre@ notes.manchester.com; open 10am-5.30pm Mon-Sat, to 4.30pm Sun), is in the town hall extension off St Peter's Square. There are two **information desks** (☎ 489 6412, 489 6412) at the airport and a 24-hour **phone guide service** (☎ 0891 8715533) with accommodation details and so on. Calls cost 60p a minute.

The TIC sells tickets for all sorts of guided walks. These operate most weekends and almost daily year round. They cost adult/child £5/4.

Post & Communication Of course there's a **post office** (Brazennose St; open 9am-

5.30pm Mon-Fri) or you can keep in touch with friends and family via email at **Cyberia** (Oxford St) at the northern end of the street, near Lower Mosley St. Access costs £1 for 15 minutes.

Internet Resources Manchester's official website at is w www.manchester.gov.uk. Here you can find out all you need to know about the city. Another good source of practical information is w www.manchester.com. For information pertaining specifically to gay and lesbian Manchester, check out w www.gaymanchester.co.uk.

For a personalised and often funny guide to the city's multitude of bars, log on to w www.tmossey.freeserve.co.uk.

Bookshops Waterstone's (☎ 832 1992; 91 Deansgate) is the biggest in the country. For all things sport, head to **Sportpages Ltd** (☎ 832 8530; Barton Square) just off St Anne's Square.

Medical Services The **Manchester Royal Infirmary** (☎ 276 1234; Oxford Rd) is south of the city centre.

Cameolord (☎ 236 1445; St Peter's Square; open 10am-10pm daily) is a late-night chemist.

Emergency The **police station** (☎ 872 5050; Bootle St) is near the town hall.

Town Hall

Dominating Albert Square is the enormous Victorian Gothic **town hall**, designed by Albert Waterhouse (of London's Natural History Museum fame) between 1868–77. It is a magnificent example of the neogothic style, which was very trendy in Victorian times. The interior is rich in sculpture and ornate decoration, while the exterior is crowned by an impressive 85m-high tower. Tours of the building (£4) take place every Saturday at 2pm between March and September, departing from the TIC. You can also visit the building on your own, but as it's a working administrative centre for the city you might be denied access to certain areas.

St Peter's Square

This busy square just south of Albert Square was once St Peter's Fields, site of the Peterloo Massacre in 1819. In the middle of the square is the elegant **Central Library** (☎ 234 1900; admission free; open 10am-8pm Mon-Thur, 10am-5pm Fri-Sat), built in 1934 by Vincent Harris, who used the Pantheon in Rome as his influence. With over 20 miles (32km) of shelves, it is the largest municipal library in Britain. The building is also home to the **Library Theatre** (see Entertainment later).

Just off the square is the **Free Trade Hall**, completed in 1856 and the only public building in Britain to be named after a principle. It's built on the precise spot where the massacre took place. It is currently closed as it is being turned into a fancy hotel.

Manchester Art Gallery

The city's foremost gallery (☎ 235 8888; Mosley St; admission free; open 10am-5pm Tues-Sun) reopened in May 2002 after a £35 million make-over; if its forebear was impressive, this one is spectacular.

The gallery is divided into three distinct sections, which are all joined by a stunning new atrium. The first is the original gallery, designed by Charles Barry (the architect of the Houses of Parliament) in 1834. The impressive permanent collection on the first floor covers post 18th-century art, with artists represented including Gainsborough, Canaletto, Constable, Turner, Pisarro, Gaugin and Rodin. In another set of rooms is one of the country's finest collections of Pre-Raphaelite art, including Holman Hunt's *Hireling Shepherd*, Ford Madox Ford's *Work* and John Everett Millais' *Autumn Leaves*. The ground floor also contains a café, restaurant and the ubiquitous gift shops.

The new gallery, a wonderfully bright, airy space created by Michael Hopkins & Associates, has a permanent collection devoted to British art of the 20th century, with paintings by Lucien Freud, Francis Bacon, David Hockney and Stanley Spencer among others. There is also a separate room for visiting exhibitions, which will mainly show international, contemporary art.

The third section is housed within the Athenaeum, joined to the rest of the gallery via an atrium. Also designed by Charles Barry, it opened in 1837 as a 'gentleman's' club, and its main feature is the impressive former lecture hall, designed by architects Clegg & Knowles in 1873. It is now home to the new Gallery of Craft & Design, which features an international collection of varied items including textiles, toys and dolls' houses dating from 1000 BC to the modern day. Also in the Athenaeum is the permanent collection of pre-17th-century art, with works predominantly from the Dutch and early Renaissance masters.

Urbis

It is fitting that the world's first industrial city, today consumed with redefining itself as a city of the future, should be the site of this stunning new museum (☎ 907 9099; City Park, Corporation St; adult/child £5/3.50; open 10am-6pm daily, to 8pm Sat) devoted to cities and the way humans react to them.

The building, designed by Ian Simpson Architects, is easily one of the city's most distinctive: a huge, frosted-glass triangle that boldly paves the way for future architectural development. Ironically, it is built on the site of a 19th-century urban slum called Little Gibraltar, whose appalling living conditions were described in all their shocking colour by Engels in *The Condition of the Working Classes in England*.

You begin your interactive tour at the top floor, in the appositely named Arrive, which recreates the shock of landing in a city for the first time. You move downwards through Change, which features a 200-year timeline of Manchester's immigration, and then on to Order, which is perhaps the most interesting section of all. Here, in sometimes unnerving detail, you discover how cities work – and sometimes don't work. The final section is called Explore, where urban life is examined in detail. The exhibits are all very eye-catching and interesting, while the pedantic self-importance of so many modern museums is thankfully avoided through humour and a clever dose of wit.

John Rylands Library

Probably Manchester's most beautiful building, this stunning library (☎ 834 5343; 35 Deansgate; admission free; open 10am-5pm Mon-Fri, 10am-1pm Sat) was built in memory of the wealthy cotton manufacturer. It is an excellent example of Victorian Gothic, and its breathtaking **reading room**, designed by architect Basil Champneys to appear like a monastic library, should on no account be missed. The library has a fine collection of early printed books (including a Gutenberg Bible, several Caxtons and manuscripts dating back to 2000 BC). Tours every Wednesday at noon cost £1.

Chetham's Library & School of Music

The city's oldest complete structure, the library (☎ 834 7861; Long Millgate; admission free; open 9am-12.30pm & 1.30pm-4pm Mon-Fri) was built in 1421 to house the clergy from the nearby collegiate church (now the cathedral). After the dissolution of the monasteries it fell into disrepair, but it was purchased in 1653 by a wealthy merchant called Humphrey Chetham, who converted it into a charity school for orphaned boys and a free library for scholars. In the mid-19th century these scholars included Engels and Marx, whose favourite seats were by the large bay window in the main reading room; it is likely that the revolutionary *Communist Manifesto* was formulated here. The library is the only part of the building that is open to visitors, as the rest of it is a national school for young musicians.

Castlefield Urban Heritage Park

Castlefield, in the southwestern corner of the city centre, was the site of the first Roman fort built in AD 79. Its real importance however, dates to the 18th and 19th centuries, when it was the site for a number of industrial firsts, including the opening of the Bridgewater Canal in 1761 and the construction of the first passenger train station on Liverpool Rd in 1834. This was the heart of industrial Manchester, and its legacy is an industrial landscape of enormous weather-stained brick and rusting cast-iron relics of canals, viaducts, bridges, warehouses and market buildings.

Sensing an opportunity, the city has skilfully redeveloped all of this into an interesting heritage park (visitor centre: ☎ 834 4026, fax 839 8747; e enquiries@castlefield.org.uk; 101 Liverpool Rd; open 10am-4pm Mon-Fri, noon-4pm weekends). You'll find a number of museums and galleries here as well as trendy pubs and restaurants (see Places to Eat and Entertainment).

Museum of Science & Industry At the heart of the heritage park is the city's largest museum (☎ 832 1830; Liverpool Rd; admission free; open 10am-5pm daily), spread across 2.8 hectares that include the former Liverpool Rd

train station – part of which has been preserved for posterity. If there's anything you want to know about the industrial (and post-industrial) revolution and Manchester's key role in it, you'll find it among the collection of steam engines and locomotives, factory machinery from the mills, and the excellent exhibition telling the story of Manchester from the sewers up. There's also an **Air & Space Gallery** featuring historic aircraft and a planetarium.

A recent refurbishment has seen the addition of **Xperiment!**, a hands-on, interactive science centre aimed primarily at kids, while 2003 will see the opening of a **Science Gallery** dedicated to Manchester's trailblazing role in industrial development. Allow at least three hours.

Castlefield Gallery This excellent gallery (☎ 832 8034; 2 Hewitt St, Knott Hill; admission free; open 1pm-6pm Wed-Sun, to 8pm Thur) has been fully refurbished and is the place to see the best of the northwest's offerings in contemporary art.

Imperial War Museum North

Although it had not opened at the time of research, we managed a sneak preview of Manchester's newest museum (☎ 877 9240; Trafford Wharf Rd; admission free; open 10am-6pm daily). It is truly impressive, beginning with the aluminium-clad showpiece designed by acclaimed architect Daniel Libeskind. It is divided into three shards, the tallest of which is 55m-high, that are intended to symbolise the three theatres of war since 1900: air, sea and land. Whereas so many war museums focus on the generally sterile military hardware used in past conflicts, this one adopts a more humane stance, examining people's experience of a world destroyed by war (although there is also some military hardware on show).

To get there, take the Metrolink (£1.90) to Broadway or Harbour City.

The Lowry

One of the most dramatic buildings of Manchester's cityscape, the Lowry (☎ 876 2020; w www.thelowry.com; Pier 8, Salford Quays; Lowry Day Pass adult/child £6/5.50; open 9.30am-midnight daily), is a sight to behold. Designed by Michael Wilford, it caused quite a stir when it opened in 2000, but has proved an unqualified success, attracting over a million visitors a year. It is an enormous glass-and-steel construction that looks like a giant, futuristic ship in permanent dock; indeed, the only comparison is with Bilbao's Frank E Gehry–designed Guggenheim Museum.

The complex is named after one of England's favourite artists, LS Lowry, who is mostly noted for his industrial landscapes and impressions of northern towns, and contains over 300 of his paintings and drawings. It also encapsulates two theatres, the 1750-capacity Lyric and 460-capacity Quays (which resembles Shakespeare's Globe in London); a number of galleries, including the mildly interesting **Artworks** *(adult/child £3.75/free; open 11am-5pm Sun-Wed, 11am-7.30pm Thur-Fri, 10am-7.30pm Sat)*, which attempts to examine art through technology; shops, restaurants and bars. The theatres host a diverse range of performances, from dance to comedy. To find out more call the **box office** *(☎ 876 2000)*.

The Lowry Day Pass is a good deal as it offers free admission into all of the galleries, knocks £2 off theatre ticket prices and includes a free **guided tour**, which usually costs £2.50. To get here, take the Metrolink from the centre to either Broadway or Harbour City. A return ticket costs £1.90.

University of Manchester

About a mile (1.6km) south of the city, the University of Manchester is one of England's most extraordinary institutions, and not just because it is a top-class university with a remarkable academic pedigree and a great place to party. It is also home to two marvellous museums that are well worth seeing.

Regular buses run from the centre down Oxford St to the university.

Manchester Museum A city institution for over 100 years, the Manchester Museum *(☎ 275 2634; University of Manchester, Oxford Rd; admission free; open 10am-5pm Mon-Sat, 11am-4pm Sun year round)* is an extensive and fascinating mix of natural history and social sciences. It has galleries devoted to Archaeology, Archery, Botany, Ethnology, Geology, Numismatics, Oriental Studies and Zoology, but the real treat here is the Egyptology section. The museum has been one of the forerunners in the study of Egyptology since a number of objects from the town sites of Kahun and Gurob were donated in 1890, including plenty of mummies and everyday artefacts. One particularly interesting section is devoted to the work of Dr Richard Neave, who has rebuilt faces of people who have been dead for over 3000 years, pioneering

NORTHWEST ENGLAND

A Mancunian Heroine

One of the city's most cherished daughters was Emmeline Pankhurst (1858–1928), the militant champion of women's rights and the leader of the Women's Social and Political Union (WSPU), which she founded here in 1903 and was popularly known as the Suffragettes.

Their basic aim was to achieve voting equality for women, and to that end Pankhurst was not averse to using some fairly radical tactics, particularly against the Liberal Party, which she identified as the main obstacle to suffrage reform. She campaigned ceaselessly against Liberal candidates, and on numerous occasions issued pamphlets calling for an assault on the House of Commons, which landed her and her fellow activists in prison. In 1910 the Liberals promised to introduce a 'conciliation' bill into the Commons but then reneged, and thereafter the WPSU turned to extreme militancy. Pankhurst's daughter Christabel directed a series of arson attacks (from a safe haven in Paris) on public buildings throughout much of 1912–13. Emmeline was arrested 12 times during that time, but refused to back down until the outbreak of WWI in 1914, when she suspended operations for the duration of the war.

She emigrated to North America at the end of the war, where she lectured continuously on women's suffrage. In 1926 she returned to England where she campaigned as a Conservative candidate, but her health failed before she could be elected. A few weeks after her death the Representation of the People Act (1928), establishing voting equality for men and women, was passed.

You can visit Pankhurst's childhood home, now the **Pankhurst Centre** *(☎ 273 5673; 60-62 Nelson St; admission free; open 10am-5pm Mon-Fri year round)*, which has excellent displays and photographs on her remarkable life and political struggles.

techniques that are now used in criminal forensics.

Whitworth Art Gallery Manchester's second-most important art gallery (☎ 275 7450; University of Manchester; Oxford Rd; admission free; open 10am-5pm Mon-Sat & 2pm-5pm Sun year round) has a wonderful collection of British watercolours. It also houses the best selection of historic textiles outside London's Victoria & Albert Museum and a number of galleries devoted to the work of artists from Dürer and Rembrandt to Lucien Freud and David Hockney.

Well worth investigating are the surprisingly interesting rooms dedicated to wallpaper, proof that bland pastels and horrible flowery patterns are not the final word in wall decoration.

Godlee Observatory

This little-visited observatory (☎ 200 4977; Floor G, Main Building, UMIST, Sackville St; admission free; open 7pm-10pm Thur, guided tours by arrangement) is one of the most interesting places in all of Manchester. Built in 1902, it is a fully functioning observatory with its original Grubb telescope in place; even the rope and wheels that move the telescope are original. Not only can you glimpse at the heavens (if the weather allows), but the views of the city from the balcony are exceptional.

People's History Museum

This excellent museum (☎ 839 6061; Bridge St; adult/child £1/free, free to all Fri; open 11am-4.30pm Tues-Sun), in an Edwardian pumping station that provided hydraulic power to the city from 1909 to 1972, has well-laid-out exhibits devoted to social history and the labour movement. There are plenty of exhibits touching on such diverse themes as the Peterloo Massacre, the suffragette movement, the rise of trade unions and a particularly good exhibit on working class pastimes, with special emphasis on football. Also in the museum is the desk at which Thomas Paine (1737–1809) wrote *Rights of Man* (1791).

Places to Stay

It's hardly surprising, but the closer you get to the centre, the more you'll pay for a room. That said, Manchester's hotels – which cater mostly to the business traveller – offer a dizzying range of deals, mostly at weekends, so prices can fluctuate wildly. We recommend that you use the TIC's accommodation service (£3) in order to find the kind of place you want for the best price. Remember that during the football season (August to May), rooms can be almost impossible to find if Manchester United are playing at home.

Hostels The **YHA Manchester** (☎ 839 9960, fax 835 2054; e manchester@yha.org.uk; Potato Wharf; beds £19), a stunning place near the Museum of Science & Industry in the Castlefield area, has comfortable four-bed dorms.

Manchester Student Village & Sir Charles Groves Rooms (☎ 236 1776; Lower Chatham St; doubles £40) are part of UMIST, with excellent accommodation available between mid-June and mid-September. The university also has budget accommodation from £13.50 per person, £9 if you're a student, in **St Anselm's Hall** (☎ 224 7327; 14 Kent Rd East, Victoria Park) and **Woolaton Hall** (☎ 224 7244; Whitworth Lane, Fallowfield). Visitors will only be accommodated if they make their booking before 5pm, either by phone or in person.

Manchester Backpackers' Hostel (☎ 865 9296; 64 Cromwell Rd; beds from £12, doubles £34), 2 miles (3km) south of the centre, is a good private hostel in Stretford with cooking facilities, a TV lounge and some doubles. The closest Metrolink stop is Stretford.

Woodies Backpackers (☎ 228 3456; e backpackers@woodiesuk.freeserve.co.uk; 19 Blossom St; dorm beds £12) is a 10-minute walk northeast of Piccadilly Gardens. It's pretty comfortable and offers Internet access.

B&Bs & Hotels – Central Liverpool Rd in Castlefield offers two good accommodation options. **Commercial Hotel** (☎ 834 3504; 125 Liverpool Rd; singles/doubles £27/45) is a traditional pub close to the museum and **Castlefield Hotel** (☎ 832 7073, fax 837 3534; 3 Liverpool Rd; singles/doubles weekends £36/49) is a modern hotel with excellent amenities, including a fitness centre that guests can use at no extra cost.

Mitre Hotel (☎ 834 4128, fax 839 1646; Cathedral Gates; rooms without bathroom per person from £30) is an excellent city-centre option, just next to the cathedral. The rooms are large if a little spartan, but comfortable nonetheless.

Monroe's (☎ 236 0564; 38 London Rd; singles/doubles £25/36), opposite Manchester Piccadilly train station, is popular with a gay clientele.

Rembrandt Hotel (☎ 236 1311, fax 236 4257; e therembrandthotel@aol.com; 1 Sackville St; singles/doubles with bathroom £40/57) is in the heart of the gay village and is the favoured spot for the older, more distinguished crowd.

Hotel Ibis (☎ 234 0600, fax 234 0610; 96 Portland St • ☎ 272 50 00, fax 272 5010; Charles St; rooms weekday/weekend £42/45), the popular French chain-hotel group, has two hotels in the city centre.

Britannia Sachas Hotel (☎ 228 1234, fax 236 9202; e brit-sachas@connectfree.co.uk; Tib St; singles/doubles weekends from £50/80) looks run down, but once inside you'll find that it is a thoroughly modern, luxurious hotel.

Britannia Hotel (☎ 228 2288; e sales@britannia-man.itsnet.co.uk; Portland St; singles/doubles from £40/75), once a cotton warehouse, has been converted into a luxury four-star hotel.

Crowne Plaza Midland Hotel (☎ 236 3333, fax 932 4100; e sales@basshotels-uknorth.co.uk; Peter St; doubles weekdays from £85, weekends £125), a sumptuous Edwardian place opposite the G-Mex Exhibition Centre, is where Mr Rolls and Mr Royce supposedly met.

Malmaison (☎ 278 1000, fax 278 1002; e manchester@malmaison.com; Joshua Hoyle Building, Auburn St; rooms £120), across the road from Piccadilly station, is an award-winning hotel with stylish, spacious rooms that have all been individually appointed.

B&Bs & Hotels – Suburbs Didsbury, 4 miles (6.5km) from central Manchester, is an attractive southern suburb, with good local pubs and frequent buses into the city. Wilmslow and Palatine Rds have many hotels in converted Victorian houses.

Elm Grange Hotel (☎/fax 445 3336; e elmgrange.hotel@virgin.net; 561 Wilmslow Rd, Didsbury; singles/doubles from £26/40) is a pleasant spot with well-furnished rooms.

Old Trafford Lodge (☎ 874 3333, fax 874 3399; e sales.lancs@ecb.co.uk; Talbot Rd;

rooms weekends £49) has modern, functional rooms that fill up when a cricket match is on.

Self-Catering Apartments Better value (and more beautiful) than a top-end hotel are Manchester's self-catering apartments.

Howard Johnson Serviced Apartments (☎ 236 8963; fax 238 8767; e sales@manchester.premgroup.com; 3 Dale St; 1/2-bed apartments per night from £55/75) has comfortable, well-appointed apartments with a full range of services, including maid service and food delivery. It's in the trendy Northern Quarter.

The Place Apartment Hotel (☎ 778 7500, fax 778 7507; e info@theplaceforliving.com; Ducie St; 2-bed apartments from £80) has the kind of stunning loft-style apartments you'd hire an interior designer to decorate.

Places to Eat
Restaurants The most distinctive restaurant zones are Chinatown in the city centre and Rusholme in the south. The restaurants listed here are just the orange sauce on the duck.

Yang Sing (☎ 236 2200; Princess St), specialising in Cantonese cuisine, is highly acclaimed. During the day there is a set menu for £9.50 but expect to pay twice that in the evening.

Pacific (☎ 228 6668; 58 George St; mains around £9) is a highly rated Thai/Chinese restaurant serving up fantastic food.

El Rincón del Rafa (☎ 839 8819; Longworth St; mains from £8.75) is a superb Spanish restaurant with a mouth-watering selection of tapas and a marvellous tortilla Espanola.

Simple (☎ 835 2526; Tib St; mains around £8) is just as the name says, a thoroughly minimalist restaurant that serves up solid English cuisine. Try the bangers and mash.

Rusholme, on Wilmslow Rd, the extension of Oxford St/Rd, is more commonly known as Curry Mile and has a concentration of Indian/Pakistani restaurants unsurpassed in Europe.

Sanam Sweet House & Restaurant (☎ 224 3852; 145 Wilmslow Rd) is worth trying for its excellent Karachi chicken (£5.75) and its array of mouth-watering sweets.

Darbar (☎ 224 4394; 65-67 Wilmslow Rd; most mains £6.50-8) is not only cheap (student discounts are available) but exceptionally good. Bring your own booze.

Grinch (☎ 907 3210; 5-7 Chapel Walks; mains around £8) is a refreshingly good chain restaurant that is popular with business folk and gourmets alike, who come for the excellent English cuisine.

Don Giovanni's (☎ 228 2482; 11 Oxford St; mains around £8.50) is our choice for good Italian cuisine. The portions are massive.

Mr Thomas's Chop House (☎ 832 2245; 52 Cross St; dishes from £6.50) has probably the best pub food in town and they pour great real ale.

Tampopo (☎ 819 1966; 16 Albert Square; mains from £7) is wonderful. It is a minimalist noodle bar that has become a Manchester institution.

Armenian Taverna (☎ 934 9025; 3-5 Princess St; open Tues-Sun), in the basement, has really tasty near-Eastern cuisine. It will

do you a *couscous bidaoui* for £7.90 or a Tbilisi kebab for £8.75.

Café Istanbul (☎ 833 9942; Bridge St; mains around £8.50), farther west of the Armenian Taverna, may have gaudy blue decor, but the kitchen serves up the best Turkish cuisine in town. For local wine, try the invitingly named Buzbag.

The Living Room (☎ 832 0083; Deansgate; mains £9-13) is a bar-restaurant dressed up to look vaguely North African (think Humphrey Bogart and Ingrid Bergman), even if the food is strictly continental.

At the time of writing it was one of the favourite eateries of a number of Manchester United players.

Vegetarians could try next to the Metropolitan University or the pleasant **Dimitri's** (☎ 839 3319; Campfield Arcade) which serves

The Madchester Sound

It is often claimed that Manchester is the engine room of British pop. In 1976 the legendary Sex Pistols played two gigs in the Free Trade Hall. Moshing with the rest of the crowd were a bunch of names that would literally grab English music by the scruff of the neck and imprint the words 'Made in Manchester' on the best of what was to come. First there was Howard Devoto, lead singer with local band The Buzzcocks, who would later quit and form the band Magazine. Then there was Mark E Smith, a sneering, cynical teenager whose band, The Fall, first offered up the distinctive guitar and vocal sound for which Manchester would become famous.

Also there were Bernard Sumner and Peter Hook, who joined up with a shy young singer called Ian Curtis to form Joy Division in 1978. They were signed to Tony Wilson's fledgling label, Factory Records, and provided two songs for the label's first release, *A Factory Sampler*. Their music was dark and threatening, chronicling the hopelessness and despair that was afflicting so much of Britain's youth at the time. In 1980, after just one album release *(Unknown Pleasures)*, Curtis took his own lyrics a little too seriously and committed suicide, apparently hanging himself with a piano wire. Distressed but undaunted, Hook and Sumner changed the band's name to New Order and in 1983 released the anthemic *Blue Monday*, which successfully fused the guitar-driven sound of punk with a pulsating dance beat. This ground-breaking single is still the biggest-selling 12" in British history.

Another fan who watched the Sex Pistols in 1976 was Morrissey, who in 1982 teamed up with guitarist Johnny Marr to form The Smiths. Morrissey's brilliant lyrics and laconic delivery, coupled with Marr's driving guitar and catchy riffs, earned them a cult following that would eventually make them the best-loved of all of Manchester's bands.

By 1989 Manchester was in the throes of a musical revolution. New Order's commercial success had allowed Tony Wilson to open his own club in 1982, called the Haçienda, a platform not just for local bands but for a brand new sound coming out of Chicago and Detroit: House. DJs Mike Pickering, Graeme Park and Jon Da Silva were the music's most important apostles, and when Ecstasy hit the scene toward the end of the decade, it seemed that every kid in town was 'mad for it'.

Heavily influenced by these new arrivals, the city's guitar bands took notice and began shaping their sounds to suit the clubbers' needs. The most successful were The Stone Roses, who in 1989 released *Fools' Gold*, a pulsating hit with the rapid shuffle of James Brown's *Funky Drummer* and a druggie guitar sound that drove dancers wild. Around the same time the Happy Mondays, fronted by the laddish Shaun Ryder and the wacked-out Bez (whose only job was to lead the dancing from up a mixture of Greek, Italian and Spanish food. A quick lunch will cost £3.

Cafés Attached to the hotel of the same name (see Places to Stay), **Café Mitre** (☎ 834 4128; Cathedral Gates; sandwiches £2.50) is a wonderful place to have a sandwich, delivered with great friendliness and courtesy.

On the Eighth Day (☎ 273 4878; 107-111 Oxford Rd; mains £2.50-4), next to the Metropolitan University, is a vegetarian stalwart that is favoured by UMIST students.

Café Pop (☎ 237 9688; Oldham St; salads £3) is typical of the Northern Quarter: bohemian, colourful and slightly kitsch. It serves excellent fruit milkshakes (£2.50) and does a wonderful range of salads.

Love Saves the Day (☎ 832 0777; Tib St; house salad £4.90) is the most popular of the Northern Quarter's cafés and it also includes a deli and a small supermarket. They even make their own coffee.

The Okassional Café (62 Charles St; mains £3-5) is a run-down spot that prides itself on only serving fair trade dishes. From the outside it looks like an abandoned shack, but it's very popular with Manchester's more intellectual crowd, who come here to discuss matters of the utmost gravity.

Entertainment

Manchester's nightlife is simply legendary. No matter what your taste, the city can satisfy it somehow. In order to make sense of Manchester's bewildering choice of entertainment, we strongly suggest you buy a copy of the fortnightly *City Life* (£1.60), available most anywhere.

NORTHWEST ENGLAND

The Madchester Sound

the stage), hit the scene with the infectious *Hallelujah*. The other big anthems of the day were *The One I Love* by The Charlatans, A Guy Called Gerald's *Voodoo Ray* and *Pacific* by 808 State, all local bands and producers. The party known as Madchester was officially declared.

By 1992 however, it was all but over. Over-danced and over-drugged, the city woke up with a terrible hangover. The Haçienda went bust, Shaun Ryder's legendary drug intake stymied his musical creativity and the Stone Roses withdrew in a haze of post-party depression, not to be heard of again until 1994, when they released *Second Coming*, but it just couldn't match their eponymous debut album. They lasted another two years before breaking up. The fertile crossover scene, which had seen clubbers go mad at rock gigs and rock bands play the kind of dance sounds that kept the floor thumping until the early hours, virtually disappeared and the two genres withdrew into a more familiar isolation.

Manchester's creative buzz, however, couldn't be quashed so easily. The city's musical pioneers struck gold again in 1994 when local band Oasis released their debut album *Definitely Maybe*. Their follow-up album, *(What's the Story) Morning Glory* hit the shelves in 1995, selling more copies than all of the Manchester bands that preceded them. Yet despite songwriter Noel Gallagher's great ear for a catchy tune and his brother Liam's in-your-face posturings and delivery, Oasis were doomed to a limited run because they relied far too much on the chord structures and infectious melodic lines created by The Beatles 25 years earlier. They're still going, but their one-time claims of being the most famous band in the world seem sadly out of date today.

A number of bands have replaced them in the critics' canon. The Verve (from nearby Wigan) released *Urban Hymns* in 1997, with the chart-topping *Bitter Sweet Symphony* leading the charge, but singer Richard Ashcroft broke the band up in 2000 to go solo. In 2001 Badly Drawn Boy's debut album, *The Hour of the Bewilderbeast*, picked up the top prize at that year's Mercury Music Awards and he went on to write the soundtrack for *About a Boy*, the 2002 film based on Nick Hornby's book. On the dance scene, local producer Mr Scruff has earned kudos for his excellent jazzy house beats, while the presence of over 20 different record labels in Manchester is proof that there's still plenty going on. The last big thing may have faded, but the next one may be just around the corner.

If you missed the party, you can get a terrific sense of what it was like by watching Michael Winterbottom's *24-Hour Party People*, released in 2002, which perfectly captures the hedonism, extravagance and genius of Madchester's cast of characters, particularly Tony Wilson, played with uncanny accuracy by English comedian Steve Coogan.

Pubs & Bars Manchester has shown itself more than capable of cashing in on a trend. At the moment, that trend is super-trendy café-bars, and here you'll find more than you'll ever need. Still, there are plenty of great, more traditional pubs in which to enjoy a pint of ale – in Manchester's case, usually Boddington's.

Lass O'Gowrie (☎ 273 6932; 36 Charles St), off Oxford St, is a popular student and BBC hang-out – it's across the street from the Beeb's Manchester HQ – with an excellent small brewery on the premises and good-value bar meals.

The Old Wellington Inn (☎ 830 1440; 4 Cathedral Gates), one of the oldest buildings in the city, was severely damaged twice by bombing in 1940 and then in 1996, but still manages to stay on its feet. It's a Manchester institution and a lovely spot for a pint of genuine ale.

Peveril of the Peak (☎ 236 6364; 127 Great Bridgewater St) is another unpretentious pub with wonderful Victorian glazed tilework outside.

Rain (☎ 235 6500; 80 Great Bridgewater St), opposite Peveril of the Peak, is a relaxed drinkers joint with a huge balcony out back. It was an umbrella factory (hence the name).

Dry 201 (☎ 236 5920; 28 Oldham St), or rather its predecessor Fac 201, was the first and best of Manchester's pre-club bars (it was owned by the same crowd that owned the Haçienda), and while these days it has many rivals, it won't give up its top spot that easily.

Barça (☎ 839 7099; Catalan Square) is a terribly trendy café-bar frequented by the beautiful people; it still manages to be unpretentious.

Cord Bar (☎ 832 9494; Dorsey St), in a tiny street off Tib St, is a friendly and trendy bar decorated with fittings filched from the Haçienda when it closed.

Bar Centro (☎ 835 2863; 72-74 Tib St) is another popular bar in the Northern Quarter, particularly with trendies and the cool, bohemian set.

Dukes 92 (☎ 839 8646; 2 Castle St) is one of the best spots in town on account of its unpretentious atmosphere, even if the service is painfully slow.

Temple of Convenience (☎ 288 9834; Great Bridgewater St) is a tiny basement pub with a terrific atmosphere located in…a former public toilet.

Kro Bar (☎ 274 3100; 325 Oxford Rd), the favoured watering hole of UMIST students, has minimalist decor and an ultra-cool atmosphere. A second bar – Kro Bar 2 – was scheduled to open farther on down the road closer to the city centre.

Clubs Manchester may have moved on from the legendary, drug-fuelled halcyon

Gay & Lesbian Manchester

The city's gay scene is unsurpassed outside London, and caters to every taste. The useful *Gay & Lesbian Village Guide*, available from the TIC, lists numerous gay bars, clubs, galleries and groups. For other information, check with the **Manchester Gay Centre** (☎ 274 3814; Sydney St) and the **Lesbian & Gay Switchboard** (☎ 274 3999; 4pm-10pm daily). *All Points North* is a good free monthly paper covering the north of England and Scotland.

At the heart of it all is the Gay Village, centred on gorgeous Canal St. Here you will find bars, clubs, restaurants and hotels that cater almost exclusively to the pink pound.

Manto (46 Canal St) was the first openly gay bar in the area, and is still popular, if a little drunk on its own success. Directly across the canal is **Metz**, a lovely café-bar that has become more fashionable than Manto. **Praha Five** (Canal St) is a large café-bar that becomes a nightclub after 11pm. On Friday there's a women-only night at the upstairs bar at the **Rembrandt Hotel** (see Places to Stay).

The club scene is very fickle and changes all the time, but the granddaddy of them all is the fabulous **Paradise Factory** (☎ 273 5422; 112-116 Princess St), an institution with the gay community. It throws up a good mix of happy house, disco and other party tunes.

Britain's biggest gay and lesbian arts festival, It's Queer Up North (IQUP), takes place every two years – the next in spring 2004. The Manchester Mardi Gras (**W** www.mardigras.co.uk) kicks off around the end of August each year and attracts over 500,000 people.

days of the late 1980s and early 1990s, but the party goes on, albeit in more muted fashion.

Clubs host a forever-changing mixture of dance nights, so check *City Life* for what's on when you're in town. What follows is but a toe-poke in the vast ocean of clubs spread about the city.

South (☎ 831 7756; 4A South King St) really kicks off the weekend: on Friday night you can hear everything from northern soul to Britpop, while Saturdays feature a more soulful selection of funk and disco.

Sankey's Soap (☎ 661 9085; Jersey St, Ancotes) stands in the middle of the industrial wasteland that is Ancotes, but that doesn't deter the hard-nose clubbers who come for the superb selection of techno (Laurent Garnier is a regular) and uplifting house.

North (☎ 839 1989; Tib St) is an excellent nightclub, so long as you have your dancing shoes on and glow-sticks at hand. The music is hard, fast and generally of a very high calibre.

The Music Box (☎ 236 9971; 65 Oxford St) is a basement club (beneath Jilly's Rockworld) that has hosted some of the best Madchester nights. The place gets really full, and very sweaty.

Elemental (☎ 236 7227; 69 Oxford St) offers commercial music during the week, but weekends feature garage and house. It's a lot of fun.

FAB Cafe (☎ 236 2019; 111 Portland St) is a place to check out if you're a big fan of *Thunderbirds*.

The music is loud but best of all are the Thunderbirds models and puppets decorating the club. FAB Virgil!

Live Music The 'Manchester Sound' may have become somewhat subdued in recent years, but there are plenty of bands willing to crank it up again.

Band on the Wall (☎ 834 1786; 25 Swan St), one of the best live music venues, hosts everything from jazz to blues, folk and pop.

Matt & Phred's Jazz Club (☎ 661 7494; Oldham St) is an absolute must on a night out. There's live jazz every night, and the atmosphere is simply terrific.

M.E.N. Arena (☎ 950 5000; Great Ducie St) is a giant arena that hosts large-scale rock concerts (as well as being the home of the city's ice hockey and basketball teams).

Classical Music Manchester is home to two world-famous symphony orchestras, the cash-strapped Halle and the BBC Philharmonic.

Bridgewater Hall (☎ 907 9000; Lower Mosley St), enormous and impressive, is home to the Halle (Britain's longest established professional symphony orchestra), but also hosts more contemporary offerings.

Manchester Opera House (☎ 242 2509; Quay St) has lately turned its attentions to staging lavish musicals like *The King And I* and *Singing in the Rain*.

Theatre, Cinema & Exhibitions Green Room (☎ 236 1677; 54 Whitworth St West) is the premiere fringe venue and also has a good café-bar.

There's nearly always something interesting on at the **Royal Exchange** (☎ 833 9833; St Anne's Square) or the **Library Theatre** (☎ 236 7110; St Peter's Square).

Cornerhouse (☎ 228 2463; 70 Oxford St) has a decent cinema, gallery and café.

The **G-Mex Exhibition Centre** (☎ 834 2700), cleverly converted from the derelict Central train station, is opposite the Bridgewater Hall and hosts exhibitions, concerts and indoor sporting events.

Printworks (☎ 0870 010 2030; Printworks, Exchange Square) is where you'll find **Filmworks**, an ultra-modern, 12-screen cinema complex that also includes an IMAX theatre. Tickets cost £4.50.

Spectator Sports

To all but the most avid sports fan, spectator sports in Manchester begin and end with football. How could it not, as the city is home to the world's wealthiest and most famous football team?

Manchester United Their stars are treated like gods (and paid like them too), their stadium is worshipped as holy ground and their successes are considered the just rewards that only the best deserve. It's all enough to make opposition fans turn into 'ABUs' (Anyone But United) and Manchester United into the most hated club in England. English loathing notwithstanding, they remain the most famous club in the world, followed as passionately in Asia and South America as they are in Old Trafford's Stretford End.

NORTHWEST ENGLAND

A comprehensive history of the club can be explored in the **Old Trafford museum** (*adult/child £5.50/3.75, including tour £8.50/ 5.75; open 9.30am–5pm daily*), which also features a state-of-the-art call-up system so that you can view your favourite goals.

The best part of a visit, however, is the **tour** (☎ *868 8631; every 10 minutes, 9.30am–4.30pm daily except match days*). This includes a stop in the changing rooms, a peak at the players' lounge (from which the manager is banned unless invited in by the players) and a walk down the tunnel to the pitchside, which is as close to ecstasy as many of the club's diehard fans will ever get. Truly avid fans can even get married here.

As far as match tickets are concerned – good luck getting one at retail prices for even a meaningless pre-season friendly.

Manchester City The city's best-supported club locally (see the boxed text below) has been yo-yoing through the divisions for more time than any fan cares to remember. In 2002–3 they will play their last season at their Maine Road stadium before moving to the City of Manchester Stadium, built for the Commonwealth Games in 2002.

Due to their impending move, it is unclear what facilities the new stadium will offer in terms of tours or museums, but you can call ☎ 828 1201 to find out.

Lancashire County Cricket Club Cricket is a big deal here, and the Lancashire club (☎ *282 4000; Warwick Rd*), founded in 1816 as 'The Aurora' before changing its name in 1864, is one of the most beloved of all England's county teams, despite not having won the county championship since 1930. The really big match in Lancashire's calendar is the Roses match against Yorkshire, but if you're not around for that one, the other games in the **county season** (*ad-*

Opposites *Don't* Attract

A favourite Mancunian joke tells of a man standing on the roof of Old Trafford, preparing to jump to the pitch below. The police are called, and one shouts up:

'What are you doing up there?'

'I'm going to kill myself!' comes the desperate reply.

'Why?'

'Because Manchester City are going to be relegated.'

'But,' says the cop, 'you're standing on the roof of Man United's ground. Why don't you go to Maine Road? For one, it's higher...'

'You must be joking,' says the jumper. 'Have you seen the size of the queue over there?'

In 1937 Manchester City won their first English League title. That same year, their great cross-city rivals Manchester United were relegated to the second division. *Sic transit gloria mundi:* for City fans it's been downhill ever since.

United's home ground is Old Trafford, re-christened the 'Theatre of Dreams' by the PR men; a hi-tech, modern temple to the game on the outskirts of the city. City's Maine Road is a dated stadium bang in the middle of the redbrick, terraced housing and high-rise flats of Moss Side (although they are moving into a luxurious, modern stadium of their own at the end of the 2002–03 season). Only 3 miles (5km) separate the stadia, but the city's two clubs now occupy different worlds. Today, United are the world's wealthiest and most famous club and the Champagne just keeps flowing, thanks to 14 league titles (seven in the last decade alone), 10 FA Cups and two European Cups. Meanwhile, City's name has become a byword for spectacular failure in English football. Ex-United manager Tommy Docherty was asked after he was fired what he would do on Saturday afternoons. He told reporters that he wanted to take a break from football, so he would probably just go to Maine Road.

Yet, somehow, the City fans who pack the Kippax Stand every week even during the worst of times (1999: United win the treble, City are relegated for the second successive year) have managed to turn losing into an art. Bump into a young fan wearing the sacred blue and white and observe the pride in his face. United might be the most supported team in the universe, but any City fan will tell you that if you throw a stick down Deansgate on a Saturday night, the last thing you'll hit is a United fan.

mission £10-12), which runs throughout the whole summer, are a great day out.

International test matches are also played here occasionally.

Shopping

Manchester is second only to London as a shopper's paradise. Most designer shops can be found in the **West End**, made up of Deansgate, King and Bridge Sts. At the top of Deansgate are the **Royal Exchange Shopping Centre** and St Anne's Square, home of the **Barton Arcade**, two luxurious shopping arcades. In the Millennium Quarter is the mightily impressive **Triangle**, while across the street, just off Exchange Square, the eagerly anticipated opening of **Harvey Nichols** is due to take place in 2003.

Affleck's Palace *(Oldham St)* is a restored warehouse full of stalls, shops and cafés selling clubbing gear from young designers, second-hand clothes, crystals, leather gear, records – you name it. This is a thriving, buzzy place with a great atmosphere.

One hundred metres north of Affleck's Palace is Manchester's impressive **Craft Centre** *(☎ 832 4274; Oak St; open 10am-5.30pm Mon-Sat)*, housed in the old fish and poultry market building. Be sure to wander around the rest of the neighbourhood, which has some terrific, quirky shops.

Getting There & Away

Manchester is about 200 miles (320km) from London, 250 miles (400km) from Glasgow, 60 miles (100km) from York and 34 miles (55km) from Liverpool.

Air Twelve miles (19.5km) south of the city, **Manchester airport** *(☎ 489 3000)* is the largest outside London, serving 35 countries. A train to the airport costs £2.80, a coach £2.50.

Bus National Express serves most major cities from Chorlton St coach station in the city centre. Buses leave almost hourly for Liverpool (£5, one hour) and Leeds (£6, 1¼ hours). A coach to London costs £17 (4¾ hours).

Train Manchester Piccadilly is the main station for trains to and from the rest of the country, although Victoria station serves Halifax and Bradford. The two stations are linked by Metrolink. Trains run every half-hour to Liverpool Lime St (£9.50, 45 minutes) and Blackpool (£11.50, 1¼ hours); there is also an hourly service to Chester (£10.20, one hour). There are at least six trains daily to London (£49.50, three hours), Glasgow (£48.40, three hours) and Newcastle (£47.40, three hours).

Getting Around

Day Saver tickets allow one day's travel throughout the Greater Manchester area and cover a range of transport combinations: bus only (£3.30), bus and train (£3.80), bus and Metrolink (£4.50), train and Metrolink (£5) and all three (£6.50). For inquiries about local transport, including night buses, phone ☎ 228 7811 (8am to 8pm daily).

Bus Centreline bus No 4 provides a free service around the heart of Manchester every 10 minutes. Pick up a route map from the TIC. Most local buses start from Piccadilly Gardens, where you'll also find the Travelshop, which has timetables but no fares, forcing you to consult each bus driver individually.

Metrolink The Metrolink trams operate on a mixture of disused rail tracks and tracks laid along the city-centre streets. There are frequent links between Victoria and Piccadilly train stations and G-Mex (for Castlefield). Buy tickets at the machines on the platforms. For information phone ☎ 205 2000. A return to the Lowry Centre or Old Trafford is £1.90.

Train Castlefield is served by Deansgate station with rail links to Piccadilly, Oxford Rd and Salford Crescent stations.

AROUND MANCHESTER
Quarry Bank Mill

In Wilmslow, 10 miles (16km) south of Manchester, you can visit an 18th-century cotton mill *(☎ 01625-527468; adult/child £5/3.40, including Apprentice House £6.50/3.70; mill open 10.30am-5.30pm daily, Apr-Sept, 10.30am-5pm Tues-Sun Oct-Mar; Apprentice House open 2pm-4.30pm Tues-Fri, from 11am weekends year round)* in beautiful Styal Country Park.

Now administered by the National Trust (NT), you can see the old waterwheel that powered the mill and some of the old machinery. Costumed guides in the Apprentice

The War of the Roses

The War of the Roses was nothing more than a protracted quarrel between two factions, the House of Lancaster (whose symbol was a red rose) and the House of York (represented by a white one), over who would rule England.

It began with the Lancastrian Henry VI (1422–61 and 1470–71), who was terrific as a patron of culture and learning, but totally inept as a ruler, and prone to bouts of insanity. During the worst of these he had to hand power over to Richard, Duke of York, who served as protector but acted as king. Henry may have been nutty, but his wife Margaret of Anjou was anything but, and in 1460 she put an end to Richard's political ambitions by raising an army to defeat and kill him at the Battle of Wakefield. Round one to Lancaster.

Next it was the turn of Richard's son Edward. In 1461 he avenged his father's defeat by inflicting one of his own on Henry and Margaret, declaring himself Edward IV (1461–70 and 1471–83) as a result. One all.

But Edward's victory owed much to the political machinations of Richard Neville, Earl of Warwick – appropriately nicknamed 'the kingmaker' – but the throne proved an amnesiac and in time Eddie forgot his friends. In 1470 Warwick jumped ship and sided with the Lancastrians. Edward was exiled and Henry, Margaret and Warwick were all smiles. Half-time and the score was two-one to Lancaster.

Edward came back strongly a year later. He first defeated and killed Warwick at the Battle of Barnet before crushing Henry and Margaret at Tewkesbury. Henry was executed in the Tower of London and Margaret ransomed back to France, where she died in poverty. Just to make sure, Edward also killed their son.

The Yorkists were back in the game, and Edward proved to be a good and popular king. When he died (apparently worn out by his sexual excesses), power passed to his brother Richard, who was to rule as regent until Edward's 12-year-old son came of age. Two months after the king's death, Richard arranged for the 'disappearance' of his nephew and he was crowned Richard III. The Yorkists, however, had scored an own goal, as when rumours of Dickie's dastardly deed became known, he was as popular as a bad smell. In 1485, the Lancastrians, led by the young Henry Tudor, defeated Richard at the Battle of Bosworth, leaving the fallen king to offer his kingdom in exchange for a horse. Final result: victory to Lancaster.

The coronation of Henry VII, and his subsequent marriage to Edward IV's daughter Elizabeth, put an end to the fighting and ushered in the Tudor dynasty, but it didn't end the rivalry.

They may not be fighting with swords and lances, but one of the great enmities in English football today is that between Lancashire's Manchester United – who wear red – and Yorkshire's Leeds United, who wear all-white.

House will give you a depressing insight into the life of some of the mill's younger workers – a life of shared beds, and brimstone and treacle cures. To get there take a train (except Sunday) to Styal station and walk for half a mile, or catch the free No 200 bus from Manchester airport. The car park costs £2.50.

Wigan

Home to one of Britain's top rugby league teams and an excellent yearly jazz festival, Wigan is otherwise a fairly quiet and unexciting town, famous mainly because George Orwell used it as the basis for his book, *The Road to Wigan Pier*.

But forget any thought of fortune-telling booths and kiss-me-quick hats – this pier was never more exciting than a contraption used for tipping coal into barges on the Leeds and Liverpool Canal.

Nevertheless, the site has been used to create a fine **heritage centre** (☎ 01942-323666; adult/child £7.50/5.95; open 10am-5pm Mon-Thur, 11am-5pm Sat & Sun) that attempts to recreate the lives of workers in a mine in the late 1800s – the conditions were appalling. You can also see inside an old textile mill, whose machinery can still be set working for visitors.

For 10 days in July, Wigan hosts a top-notch international **jazz festival** (☎ 01942-

Castlerigg Stone Circle, Lake District National Park, Cumbria

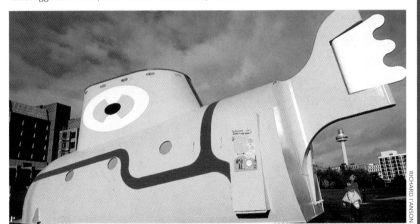
Yellow Submarine, Liverpool

Manchester United's stadium, Old Trafford, Manchester

Puffins, Farne Islands

Hadrian's Wall, Northumberland

Angel of the North, Gateshead

Tyne and Swing Bridges, Newcastle-upon-Tyne

825677; W www.wiganjazz.net) which attracts the best of contemporary jazz as well as a few classic players; in 2002 Woody Herman was one of the featured acts. Also on the bill are a number of workshops and seminars.

There's also a **TIC** (☎ 01942-825677) in the mill building that provides an accommodation service. To get there, take bus No 32 from Cannon St in Manchester city centre (1¼ hours), or take a train to Wigan station from Victoria station (Manchester) or Liverpool.

Cheshire

There's plenty to see in Cheshire; a largely agricultural county where black-and-white Friesian cows graze in close proximity to the black-and-white half-timbered farmhouses that give an indication of Cheshire's rich Tudor heritage. You can scan the stars with the gigantic radio telescope at Jodrell Bank, investigate the canals at the wonderful waterways museum at Ellesmere Port, or try to track down the mock-Tudor homes of Manchester United's and Liverpool's biggest stars, but when it comes down to it, Cheshire is all about Chester.

CHESTER
☎ 01244 • pop 82,000
Chester is one of England's most beautiful cities, an elegant collection of Tudor and Victorian buildings ringed by an almost continuous, 2-mile-long (3km) red sandstone wall originally built by the Romans. Once a thriving commercial centre, the city has long been overtaken by its larger neighbours in economic importance, but for sheer aesthetic kudos it has no local rivals.

History
Chester was originally founded in AD 79 as Castra Devana, the largest Roman fortress in Britain. The Romans abandoned it in the 5th century, after which it became a prosperous Mercian settlement, but it really prospered under the Normans, who took control of the town in 1071. By the 14th century it was the northwest's busiest port. It suffered extensive destruction during the Civil War, when Cromwell's forces kept it under siege for 18 months (1644–46), but the real damage was

natural: the gradual silting of the River Dee eventually diminished its importance and by the 18th century it had been overtaken by Liverpool as the region's primary port.

The construction of the railway in the 19th century once again made Chester an important commercial centre, but today Chester is primarily a tourist attraction, as well as the administrative centre for the county.

Orientation
Most places of interest are inside the walls where the Roman street pattern is relatively intact. From the High Cross (the stone pillar which marks the town centre), four roads fan out to the four principal gates.

Information
Tourist Offices You'll find the **TIC** (☎ 402 111; e tis@chestercc.gov.uk; Northgate St; open 9am-5.30pm Mon-Sat, 10am-4pm Sun May-Oct, 10am-5pm Mon-Sat Nov-Apr) in the town hall opposite the cathedral.

Chester Visitors' Centre (☎ 351609; Vicar's Lane; open 10am-5.30pm Mon-Sat, 10am-4pm Sun May-Oct, 10am-5pm Mon-Sat Nov-Apr), just east of the city walls, has exhibits on the town's history plus the usual tourist information and brochures.

The TIC runs a number of excellent walking tours. The Pastfinder Tour, which takes you around all of the attractions in the medieval city, departs at 10.30am and 2.15pm from the visitor centre and 10.45am and 2.30pm from the town hall, June to September (morning tours only the rest of year); they cost adult/child £3/2.50.

Between June and October, there are the increasingly ubiquitous ghost tours departing at 7.30pm from the town hall Thursday to Saturday only, costing adult/child £3.50/3.

Our favourite tour, however, is the Roman Soldier Patrol, where a centurion in full battle gear takes you on a patrol of the city walls. These run at 1.45pm from the visitor centre (2pm from the town hall), Thursday to Saturday only, from June to August and cost adult/child £3/2.50.

Post & Communications There's a **post office** (2 St John St; open 9am-5.30pm Mon-Sat) just outside the city walls. Internet access at a cost of £2 per half-hour is available at **i-station** (☎ 401680; Rufus Court),

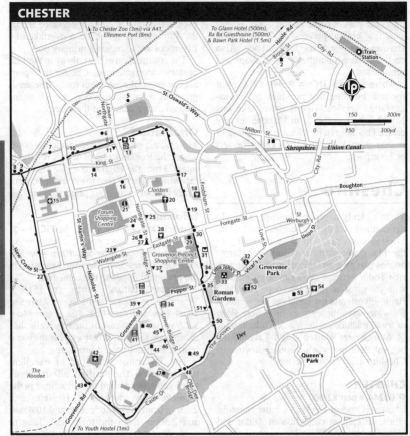

CHESTER

entered off Abbey Gardens, or in the **public library** next to the TIC.

Medical Services & Emergency The **Chester Royal Infirmary** (☎ 365000) is on St Martin's Way.

The **Cheshire Constabulary** (☎ 350000; Castle Esplanade) is close to the castle.

Disabled visitors should head for the very helpful **Dial House** (☎ 345655; Hamilton Place; open 10am-4pm Mon-Fri, closed Wed afternoon), which gives advice and has a café.

A Tour of the City Walls

Chester's walls were originally built around AD 70 to protect the Roman fort of Deva. Over the following centuries they were

often altered but their present position was established around 1200. After the Civil War the walls were rebuilt as a fashionable promenade.

Nowadays the 2-mile (3km) circuit of the walls is a great introduction to Chester and should take 1½ to two hours. This suggested circuit proceeds clockwise from **Eastgate** at the prominent **Eastgate Clock**, built for Queen Victoria's Diamond Jubilee in 1897.

The **Thimbleby Tower**, also known as the Wolf Tower, was destroyed during the Civil War and never rebuilt. From here you can look down on the foundations of the southeastern angle tower of the old Roman fort. Just beyond is the **Newgate**, added in 1938 but in medieval style. From here the origin-

CHESTER

PLACES TO STAY		PUBS, BARS & CLUBS		21	Tourist Information Centre
1	Ormonde Guest House	12	Alexander's Jazz Theatre		(TIC); Town Hall
2	Aplas Guest House	18	Yates's Wine Lodge	22	Watergate
3	Mill Hotel	28	Boot Inn	24	Dial House
14	Chester Town House	54	Boat House	27	High Cross
26	Commercial Hotel			30	Eastgate Clock
29	Chester Grosvenor Hotel		**OTHER**	31	Post Office
40	Grosvenor Place	4	King Charles' Tower	32	Chester Visitors' Centre
	Guest House	5	Davies Bros. Cycles	33	Roman Amphitheatre
44	Castle House	6	Blue Coat Hospital	34	Thimbleby Tower
49	Recorder Hotel		(School)	35	Newgate
53	Grove Villa	7	Northgate Locks	36	Toy & Doll Museum
		8	Water Tower	38	Dewa Roman
	PLACES TO EAT	9	Bonewaldesthorne's		Experience
11	Cathedral Refectory		Tower	41	Grosvenor Museum
23	Katie's Tea Rooms	10	Morgan's Mount	42	Police Station
25	The Blue Bell	13	i-station	43	Roman Harbour Wall
37	Boulevard de la Bastille	15	Chester Royal Infirmary	47	Agricola's Tower
39	Francs	16	Public Library	48	Bridgegate
45	Ruffino's Deli	17	Kaleyards Gate	50	Wishing Steps
46	Vincent's	19	Bell Tower	52	St John the Baptist
51	The Albion	20	Cathedral		Church

al Roman fortress walls ran westwards, a course roughly followed by the modern ring road. From Newgate the remains of part of the **Roman Amphitheatre** can be seen.

Outside the walls, the **Roman Gardens** contain a collection of Roman stonework brought here from excavations around Chester. Descend the **wishing steps** at the corner of the wall.

They were added in 1785 and local legend claims that your wish will come true if you can run up and down the steps while holding your breath.

Continue past the Recorder Hotel to the **Bridgegate** beside the **Old Dee Bridge**. This oft-rebuilt bridge dates from 1387, although parts of it are centuries newer. Just inside the gate is the 1664 **Bear & Billet** pub, once a tollgate into the city.

Beyond Bridgegate, the walls disappear for a short stretch. Inside the walls, **Agricola's Tower** is virtually all that remains of the medieval castle. Turn the corner beside the castle ruins.

Cross Grosvenor Rd to where the wall runs alongside the **Roodee**, Chester's ancient horse racing track built on grassland left when the river changed course. The Roodee hosts Britain's oldest horse race which, uniquely, is run anticlockwise. The city wall stands a-top a stretch of **Roman Harbour Wall**. Cross **Watergate** and look

left to the **Watergate Inn**, where the river once passed.

Continue to the northwestern corner, where a short peninsula of wall leads out to the **Water Tower**. Actually on the corner, **Bonewaldesthorne's Tower** once guarded the river at this point but when it shifted course in the 14th century the extension to Water Tower had to be built. In subsequent centuries the river has moved even farther west leaving both towers high and dry.

A little farther on, below the walls, you can see the **Northgate Locks**, a short but steep series of locks built in 1779 by Thomas Telford, the pioneering canal engineer. Continue past **Morgan's Mount** where a Captain Morgan defended the city during the Civil War. Across the canal is the **Blue Coat Hospital (School)**, now closed.

From **Northgate** the walls tower above the **Shropshire Union Canal** which runs in what was once a moat-like ditch constructed by the Romans outside the walls. From **King Charles' Tower** at the corner, Charles I looked out to see his defeated army straggling back from battle in 1645.

Cross the 1275 **Kaleyards Gate** through which monks would go to work in their vegetable gardens outside the walls; it's still ceremonially locked every night at 9pm. Traces of the original Roman wall are visible from outside the walls just south of

Kaleyards Gate. Continue past **Chester Cathedral** and the **Bell Tower** and you'll be back at the Eastgate Clock.

Chester Cathedral

A Saxon church dedicated to St Werburgh was built here in the 10th century but in 1092 it became a Benedictine abbey and a Norman church replaced the earlier construction. The abbey was closed in 1540 with Henry VIII's dissolution of the monasteries and a year later the building became a cathedral (☎ 324756; admission by £2 donation; open 7.30am-6.30pm daily). The 12th-century cloister and its surrounding buildings are essentially unaltered and retain much of the structure from the early monastic years.

The present cathedral was built between 1250 and 1540 but there were later alterations and a lot of Victorian reconstruction. There are 1¼-hour guided tours (adult/child £2.50/1.50) between 9.30am and 4pm Monday to Saturday, but they must be booked in advance.

The Rows

The four streets stretching out from the Cross feature Chester's most eye-catching architecture, the two-level galleried arcades known as the Rows. As the Roman walls slowly crumbled, medieval traders built their shops against the resulting rubble banks, while later arrivals built theirs on top.

Between Easter and September, at noon on Tuesday to Saturday, you can watch the town crier (in medieval dress of course) flamboyantly welcome visitors in a 15-minute spiel from the middle of the Cross.

Dewa Roman Experience

Off Bridge St, this museum (☎ 343407; Pierpoint Lane; adult/child £4.20/2.50; open 9am-5pm daily) aims to show what life was like in Roman times.

Your tour begins in a reconstructed galley after which you move into a Roman street and watch an entertaining audiovisual presentation.

Museums

The **Grosvenor Museum** (☎ 402008; Grosvenor St; admission free; open 10.30am-5pm Mon-Sat, 2pm-5pm Sun), has excellent

displays on Roman Chester. The Stuart, mid-Georgian and Victorian period rooms are also worth seeing.

'All things toys' is the idea behind the **Toy & Doll Museum** (☎ 346297; Lower Bridge St; adult/child £2/1; open 10am-5.30pm Mon-Sat, 11am-5pm Sun), which displays an eclectic array of antique toys and dolls.

St John the Baptist Church

Directly opposite the visitors centre stands St John the Baptist Church (Vicars Lane; open 9.15am-6pm daily), built on the site of an older Saxon church in 1075. It started out as a cathedral of Mercia before being rebuilt by the Normans. The foundations could not have been too sound as the northwestern tower has collapsed twice in its history, in 1573 and 1881. The eastern end of the church, abandoned in 1581 when St John's became a parish, now lies in peaceful ruin and includes the remains of a Norman choir and medieval chapels.

Along the River

Beyond the city walls, The Groves is a popular riverside promenade leading to Grosvenor Park. You can hire rowing boats (£4.50 per hour), pedal boats (£4 per half-hour) or motor boats (£5 per half-hour), or take a short cruise (adult/child £3/2 per half-hour). Boats are available from 9am to 6pm daily, April to September.

Chester Zoo

Chester is home to England's largest zoo (☎ 380280; adult/child £10.50/8.50; open from 10am daily), noted for its pleasant garden setting.

The zoo is on the A41, 3 miles (5km) north of the city centre. Bus Nos 11C and 12C run between the town hall and zoo (£1.85 return, every 15 minutes Monday to Saturday, twice-hourly on Sunday).

Places to Stay

Most of Chester's numerous places to stay are outside the city walls but within easy walking distance of the centre.

Outside the Walls A mile from the city centre, the **Chester YHA Hostel** (☎ 0870 770 5762, fax 681204; 40 Hough Green; beds £11.50) is across Grosvenor Park Bridge in a pleasant Victorian house.

Brook St near the train station has a couple of good-value B&Bs from around £19 per person.

The friendly and accommodating **Ormonde** (☎ 328816; 126 Brook St) and the comfortable **Aplas Guest House** (☎ 312401; 106 Brook St) are both less than five minutes' walk from the train station.

Hoole Rd, a 10- to 15-minute walk from the centre and leading beyond the railway tracks to the M53/M56, is lined with low- to mid-price B&Bs.

Bawn Park Hotel (☎ 324971, fax 310951; 10 Hoole Rd; B&B per person from £20) is cosy.

Ba Ba Guest House (☎ 315047; e reservations@babaguesthouse.freeserve.co; 65 Hoole Rd; rooms per person from £22) is worth the extra few pounds as it's comfortable and very friendly.

Glann Hotel (☎ 344800; 2 Stone Place; rooms per person from £26), off the Hoole Rd, is an attractive Victorian house.

Grove Villa (☎ 349713; e grove.villa@tesco.net; 18 The Groves; en-suite rooms per person £20), a Victorian place with views of the River Dee, is one of the better B&Bs in town and has beautiful rooms.

Mill Hotel (☎ 350035, fax 345635; e reservations@millhotel.com; Milton St; singles/doubles from £49/65), larger than Grove Villa on the other side of the canal, boasts a health club, swimming pool and canal cruises.

Inside the Walls Centrally situated, **Grosvenor Place Guest House** (☎ 324455, fax 400225; 2-4 Grosvenor Place; singles/doubles with bathroom £40/50) has fairly large, comfortable rooms.

Castle House (☎ 350354; 23 Castle St; rooms per person from £26), dating from the 16th century, is near Grosvenor Place Guest House and has comfortable rooms (some with bathroom).

Commercial Hotel (☎ 320749, fax 348318; St Peter's Churchyard; rooms per person from £40) is a popular choice as it has spotless, modern rooms in a very central location.

Recorder Hotel (☎ 326580; e ebbs@compuserve.com; 19 City Walls; rooms per person from £42), eager-to-please, is just off Lower Bridge St, right on the walls and near the river. The comfortable rooms are lovely.

Chester Town House (☎ 350021; e davidbellis@chestertownhouse.co.uk; 23 King St; en-suite singles/doubles £40/55) in its quiet, pleasantly old-world surroundings, dates from 1680.

Chester Grosvenor Hotel (☎ 324024; e chesgrove@chestergrosvenor.co.uk; 58 Eastgate St; singles/doubles low season £125/160) has an incredible location right on Eastgate. It's a classy, old-style hotel with modern conveniences.

Places to Eat

Chester is packed with all kinds of restaurants and cafés.

Francs (☎ 317952; 14 Cuppin St; mains around £7), deservedly popular, serves traditional French food every day.

Boulevard de la Bastille (Bridge St Row; sandwiches around £2.50) is one of the best cafés in town, as well as one of the nicest.

Ruffino's Deli (46 Lower Bridge St) does excellent sandwiches for around £4.

Vincent's (☎ 310854; 58-60 Lower Bridge St; mains £8-14) is a colourful place with Caribbean cuisine.

The Blue Bell (☎ 317758; Northgate St) serves up better quality food than The Pied Bull or Ye Olde Custom Inn; escalope of calves livers costs £13.25.

The Albion (☎ 340345; 4 Albion St; mains around £8), a fine Edwardian pub, serves reliable English food, without chips or fry-ups, and the best real ale in town.

The **cathedral refectory** (☎ 313156; Abbey Square) serves soup of the day for £2 but the stone-walled **Katie's Tea Rooms** (☎ 400322; Watergate St), spread over three floors of an historic building, gives it a run for its money as the best place for a light lunch.

Entertainment

The pubs mentioned under Places to Eat are all equally good for a pint or two.

With great views overlooking the river, the **Boat House** (The Groves) is a good spot, as is the **Boot Inn** (Eastgate Row), where 14 Roundheads were killed. If you're looking for live music try **Yates's Wine Lodge** (☎ 344813; Frodsham St) which attracts a noisy, young crowd at night.

Alexander's Jazz Theatre (☎ 340005; Rufus Court) is a combination of wine bar, coffee bar and tapas bar. Admission is sometimes free before 10pm otherwise it costs £3 to £8, depending on who's performing.

NORTHWEST ENGLAND

Getting There & Away

Chester is 188 miles (303km) from London, 85 miles (137km) from Birmingham, 40 miles (64km) from Manchester and 18 miles (29km) from Liverpool. It has excellent transport connections, especially with North Wales.

Bus Just north of the city inside the ring road is the National Express bus station. It has services to Manchester (£4.75, 1¼ hours, six daily), Bristol (£18, four hours, six daily), Llandudno (£5.75, 1¾ hours, three daily), Liverpool (£5, one hour, four daily), Birmingham (£8.25, 2½ hours, five daily) and London (£17, 5½ hours, nine daily).

For information on local bus services, ring the **Cheshire Bus Line** (☎ 602666). Local buses leave from the Town Hall Bus Exchange. On Sunday and bank holidays a Sunday Adventurer ticket gives you unlimited travel in Cheshire for adult/child £3.50/2.50.

Train The train station is a 15-minute walk from the city centre via Foregate St and City Rd, or Brook St. City-Rail Link buses are free for people with rail tickets, and stop outside the station and on Frodsham St.

There are hourly trains to Manchester (£10.20, 1 hour), Liverpool (£3.30, 40 minutes), London Euston (£46.50, three hours) and Holyhead (£19.40, two hours), via the North Wales coast, for Ireland.

Getting Around

Much of the city centre is closed to traffic from 10.30am to 4.30pm so a car is likely to be a hindrance. Anyway, the walled city is easy to walk around and most places of interest are close to the wall.

City buses depart from the Town Hall Bus Exchange. Call ☎ 602666 for details. **Guide Friday** (☎ 347457) offers open-top bus tours of the city; an all-day ticket costs adult/child £6.75/2.50 (£8.75/3 if you want a half-hour river cruise included).

Davies Bros Cycles (☎ 371341; 5 Delamere St), has mountain bikes for hire at £11 per day.

AROUND CHESTER
Ellesmere Port

The superb **Boat Museum** (☎ 0151-355 5017; adult/child £5.50/3.70; open 10am-5pm daily Apr-Oct, 11am-4pm Sat-Wed Nov-

Mar), 8 miles (13km) north of Chester on the Shropshire Union Canal, has a large collection of canal boats as well as indoor exhibits.

Take Bus No 4 from the Town Hall Bus Exchange in Chester (45 minutes) or it's a 10-minute walk from Ellesmere Port train station.

KNUTSFORD
☎ 01565 • pop 13,700

Fascinating Knutsford would be a typical lowland English market town if it wasn't for the eccentric philanthropy of Richard Watt (1842–1913), a millionaire glove manufacturer with his own personal vision of Mediterranean architecture. The weird and wonderful buildings that he commissioned for the town make it one of the most interesting places in Cheshire.

Although Watt's influence was certainly greater, Knutsford makes the biggest deal of its links with Elizabeth Cleghorn Gaskell (1810–65), who spent her childhood here and used the town as the model for *Cranford* (1853), her most noteworthy novel.

The **Knutsford Heritage Centre** (☎ 650506; 90a King St; admission free; open 1.30pm-4pm Mon-Fri, noon-4pm Sat & 2pm-4.30pm Sun) is a reconstructed former smithy that has plenty of information on Gaskell, including the *Cranford Walk Around Knutsford* (80p), a leaflet about her local haunts. Our favourite displays, though, are on Watt and his quirky contributions to English architecture.

You can see the best example of these along King St, which is a fine example of the splendidly haphazard harmony of English urban architecture.

The eye-catching **Gaskell Memorial Tower**, which incorporates the swanky Belle Epoque restaurant (see Places to Stay & Eat) and the **King's Coffee House** (meant to lure the men from the pubs) is the best example of Watt's peculiar genius. The **Ruskin Reading Room** (Drury Lane) is also worth a look.

The **TIC** (☎ 632611; Toft Rd; open 9am-5pm Mon-Fri & 9am-1pm Sat) is in the council offices opposite the train station. It has a comprehensive accommodation list.

Special Events

The biggest event in Knutsford's calendar is **Royal May Day**, inaugurated in 1864. The main festivities take place on the Heath, a large area of common land, and include morris dancing, brass bands and a pageant of historical characters from fiction and fact. Perhaps the most interesting tradition, though, is that of 'sanding', when the streets are covered in colourful messages written in sand. Legend has it that the Danish King Canute, while crossing the marsh between Over and Nether Knutsford, scrawled a message in the sand wishing happiness to a young couple on the way to their wedding. The custom is also practised on weddings and feast days.

Places to Stay & Eat

Cross Keys Inn (☎ 750404; King St; singles/doubles £69/85), rebuilt by Watt in 1909, is a lovely pub with large, comfortable rooms and excellent service. The ale served in the bar is the best in town.

The Belle Epoque (☎ 633060; fax 634150; 60 King St; rooms from £60), part of Richard Watt's Gaskell Memorial Tower, has seven gracious rooms that are all beautifully appointed, but it's best known for its excellent brasserie (mains around £10), which offers top French nosh in luxurious surroundings.

Treasure Village (☎ 651537; 84 King St; mains around £8) is an outstanding restaurant specialising in Peking and Cantonese cuisine.

Getting There & Away

Knutsford is 15 miles (24km) northwest of Manchester and is on the Manchester (£6.10, 30 minutes) to Chester (£9.70, 40 minutes) train line so there are frequent connections to both.

The train station is on Adams Hill, at the southern end of King St.

AROUND KNUTSFORD
Tatton Park

King St in Knutsford ends at the southern entrance to the 400-hectare Tatton Park estate (NT; ☎ 01625-534400; open 10am-7pm daily). One mile (1.6km) into the estate is the 19th-century **Wyatt House** (adult £3; open 1pm-5pm Tues-Sun Apr-Oct), a fine Regency house with a wonderful medieval great hall, a 1930s-style working farm (adult £2.80) and a series of gardens. Car admission to the park costs £3.80.

On Sunday bus No X2 links Tatton Park with Chester (one hour).

NANTWICH
☎ 01270 • pop 12,000

Cheshire's second-best example of black-and-white Tudor architecture after Chester is the elegant town of Nantwich. The town was rebuilt from scratch after a devastating fire in 1583, thanks to a nationwide appeal by Elizabeth I (as well as a personal donation of £1000) who deemed the town's salt production so important that she had to intercede to help.

Her generosity is proudly commemorated with a plaque on the appositely named **Queen's Aid House** (High St), itself a striking Tudor building.

The rest of the largely pedestrianised centre has plenty of fine examples of the black-and-white style, although it's a wonder how so many of them stay standing, such is their off-kilter shape and design.

Only a handful of buildings survived the fire, the most important of which is 14th-century **Church of St Mary** (☎ 625268; open 9am-5pm daily), a fine example of medieval architecture.

Apart from salt, the town grew up around cheese and leather production, and all three are depicted in the **Nantwich Museum** (☎ 627104; Pillory St; admission free; open 10am-4.30pm Mon-Sat Apr-Sept, Tues-Sat only Oct-Mar).

The helpful **TIC** (☎ 610983, fax 610880; Church Walk; open 9.30am-5pm Mon-Sat, 10am-4pm Sat & 11am-3pm Sun) is near the main square.

Places to Stay & Eat

The Limes (☎/fax 624081; 5 Park Rd; rooms per person from £24) is a good, comfy B&B with spacious rooms.

Crown Hotel (☎ 625283, fax 628047; High St; singles/doubles from £59/72) is easily the best place to stay in town, a gorgeous half-timbered hotel built soon after the fire. It also has an excellent Italian restaurant (mains around £10).

Pillory House & Coffee Shop (☎ 623524; Pillory St; sandwiches £2.50) is an old-style tearoom that serves sandwiches and inexpensive hot dishes and perfect for that quick lunchtime filler.

Getting There & Away

Arriva Midlands operates an hourly bus service from Nantwich to Chester (£4.70,

1 hour) from the bus station on Beam St, two minutes' walk north of the TIC.

Nantwich is on the Manchester to Cardiff line so there are regular trains to Manchester (£10.20, 1¼ hours). The train station is about a five-minute walk south of the centre.

Liverpool

☎ 0151 • pop 510,000

Of all the northwestern cities, Liverpool has perhaps the strongest sense of its own identity, a hard-bitten industrial port that has long been known for its radical politics and struggle to stave off the worst effects of the economic decline that has afflicted it for the last 50 years.

The last 20 years have been particularly tough, as spiralling unemployment, the partial demise of the once all-powerful labour movement and the disenfranchisement of the radical left that for so long flavoured local politics have cast long shadows on a city that was once a major force in the Empire.

Yet Liverpool cannot be dismissed so easily, and in recent years the proliferation of EU funds and local investment has seen the beginnings of a dramatic turnaround in its economic fortunes.

The city is in the midst of a major programme of urban redevelopment, which has already begun to reanimate the decrepit streets and convert the once boarded-up city centre buildings into shops, restaurants, cafés and fancy apartments.

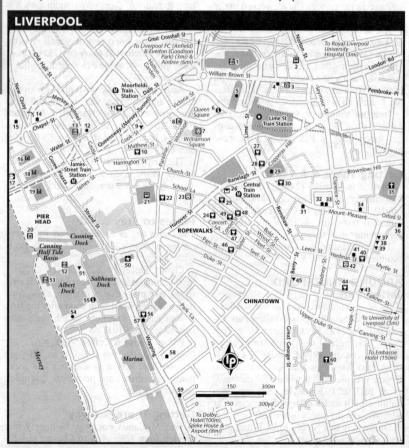

It's well worth setting aside time to explore Liverpool properly. The Albert Dock, the Western Approaches Museum, the twin cathedrals and the city streets themselves offer vivid testimony to the city's rugged history, while its nightlife is rich and varied enough to guarantee a good time.

History

Like Bristol, 18th-century Liverpool prospered on the back of the triangular trading of slaves for raw materials. From 1700 ships carried cotton goods and hardware from Liverpool to West Africa, where they were exchanged for slaves.

The slaves were, in turn, carried to the West Indies and Virginia, where they were exchanged for sugar, rum, tobacco and raw cotton.

As a great port, the city attracted thousands of immigrants from Ireland and Scotland and its Celtic influences are still apparent. However, between 1830 and 1930 nine million emigrants – mainly English, Scots and Irish, but also Swedes, Norwegians and Russian Jews – sailed from Liverpool for the New World.

The start of WWII led to a resurgence of Liverpool's importance. Over one million American GIs disembarked here before D-Day and the port was, once again, hugely important as the western gateway for transatlantic supplies. The arriving GIs brought with them the latest American records, which made Liverpool the first European port of call for the new rhythm and blues that would eventually become rock and roll. Within 20 years, the Mersey Beat was *the* sound of British pop and four mop-topped Scousers had formed a skiffle band that would become mildly successful.

Orientation

Liverpool stretches north–south along the River Mersey estuary for more than 13 miles (21m). The main visitor attraction is the Albert Dock on the waterfront west of the city centre. The centre, including the two cathedrals to the east, is quite compact and easy to explore on foot.

Lime St, the main train station, is just to the east of the city centre. It is also one of the four city centre stops for the Merseyrail system, which also goes to Central Station, just to the south (see Getting Around). The National Express **coach station** *(cnr Norton & Islington Sts)* is 300m north. The **bus station** *(Paradise St)* is in the centre.

NORTHWEST ENGLAND

LIVERPOOL

PLACES TO STAY		
14	Thistle	
15	Crowne Plaza Liverpool	
29	Britannia Adelphi Hotel	
31	YMCA	
32	Belvedere	
33	Aachen Hotel	
34	Feathers Hotel	
36	University of Liverpool	
41	nternational Inn	
57	YHA Liverpool International	
58	Hotel Ibis	
59	Campanile Hotel	

PLACES TO EAT	
9	Casa Bella
37	Everyman Bistro & Theatre
38	I Macho
39	Becher's Brook
43	Number Seven Café
45	Far East
51	Blue

PUBS, BARS & CLUBS	
10	Cavern Club
11	G-Bar
22	Escape-E2
24	Bar Ça Va
25	Revolution
27	American Bar
28	Vines
30	Sunrise@Sound Factory
40	Philharmonic
44	Ye Cracke
46	Cream; Mello Mello
47	Society
48	Modo
49	Baa Bar
56	The Baltic Fleet

OTHER	
1	Liverpool Museum; Walker Art Gallery
2	National Express Coach Station
3	Planet Electra
4	Mars
5	St George's Hall
6	Tourist Information Centre (TIC)
7	Liverpool Playhouse
8	Conservation Centre
12	Town Hall
13	Western Approaches Museum
16	Royal Liver Building
17	Pier Head Ferry Terminal
18	Cunard Building
19	Port of Liverpool Building
20	Museum of Liverpool Life
21	us Station & Parking
23	Bluecoat Arts Centre
26	Post Office
35	Metropolitan Cathedral
42	Unity Theatre
50	Merseyside Police Headquarters
52	Merseyside Maritime Museum
53	Tate Gallery Liverpool
54	The Beatles Story
55	Tourist Information Centre (Albert Dock)
60	Anglican Cathedral

Information

Tourist Offices The helpful TIC (☎ 709 5111; e askme@visitliverpool.com; open 9am-5.30pm Mon-Sat, 10.30am-4.30pm Sun), is in the Queen Square Centre, and there's a **branch** in the Albert Dock (☎ 708 8574; open 10am-5.30pm daily). Both have a free accommodation booking service. Alternatively, try their **accommodation hotline** (☎ 0845 601 1125).

Look for the excellent **Liverpool Heritage Walk**, an illustrated guide to the city's landmarks, identified by numbered metal markers set in the footpath.

Both TICs sell tickets for city bus tours. The hop-on hop-off bus tour has 11 stops (adult/child £6/4.50). The new duck tour, in rebuilt and updated WWII amphibious vehicles, takes to the water at Albert Dock as well as showing the main sights on the waterfront.

It costs adult/child £9/6 and lasts one hour. There's also the highly recommended 2¼-hour Beatles tour (see the boxed text 'Doing The Beatles to Death').

Check out w www.visitliverpool.com for online information.

Post & Communications There's a **post office** (Ranelagh St; open 9am-5.30pm Mon-Sat) in the city centre. **Planet Electra** (☎ 708 0303; 36 London Rd) doubles as a regular and Internet café; access is £1.25 per half-hour.

Medical Services & Emergencies The closest hospital to Liverpool centre is the **Royal Liverpool University Hospital** (☎ 706 2000; Prescot St), about 3 miles (5km) east. If you require a late-night pharmacy, **Mars** (☎ 709 5271; 68 London Rd) is open until 10pm nightly.

Merseyside Police Headquarters (☎ 709 6010) is opposite Albert Dock on Canning Place.

Dangers & Annoyances The city centre can get quite dodgy after dark, so be sure to exercise care if walking alone. Under no circumstances should you leave anything of value in your car; local thieves are like magpies and will swoop in and clean you out before you can turn around.

City Centre

The **town hall**, at the end of Castle St, was designed by John Wood the Elder of Bath and completed in 1754. Both the dome and the impressive portico and balcony, where The Beatles were received by the Lord Mayor in 1964, were added later.

The confusing **Clayton Square** is a modern shopping centre opposite the Central station. **Bold St**, south of Central station, marks the northern boundary of the area known as **Ropewalks**, where rope was manufactured for visiting ships during the 18th and 19th centuries.

Once considered one of the world's most luxurious hotels, the **Britannia Adelphi Hotel** (Lime St) was completed in 1912 to serve wealthy passengers staying overnight before or after the Atlantic crossing. Situated farther north along the road is the superb Edwardian pub **Vines**, with its luxurious interior (built in 1907), and the welcoming **American Bar**, favoured by the US forces during WWII. In the 19th century, Lime St was famous for prostitution and was immortalised in the John Lennon song 'Maggie Mae'.

A group of Liverpool's most impressive buildings are clustered together opposite Lime St station, although traffic funnelling into the city and the entrance of the Queensway Mersey Tunnel makes it difficult to appreciate them. Built as a concert hall in 1854 **St George's Hall** (admission £2.50; open 10.30am-4.30pm Mon-Sat) is considered one of the world's greatest neoclassical buildings; its exterior is Grecian, its interior Roman. Tours take place daily, except Sunday, from mid-July to August for £2.

Liverpool Museum & Walker Art Gallery

Liverpool Museum (☎ 478 4399; William Brown St; admission free; open 10am-5pm Mon-Sat, noon-5pm Sun) is a traditional museum covering everything from archaeology to natural history. It also has a planetarium and hosts interesting temporary exhibitions. As well as its renowned collection of Pre-Raphaelite art, the Walker Art Gallery (☎ 478 4199; admission free; open 10am-5pm Mon-Sat, noon-5pm Sun) has an important collection of Italian and Flemish paintings and some interesting impressionists and post-impressionists, including a Degas, Cézanne and Matisse. It's recently undergone a partial refurbishment that's resulted in new exhibition spaces for contemporary art; in 2002 the big show was 'The Art of Paul McCartney'. There's a pleasant café on the ground floor.

The museum and gallery are side by side.

Western Approaches Museum

The Combined Headquarters of the Western Approaches (☎ 227 2008; 1 Rumford St; adult/child £4.75/3.45; open 10.30am-4.30pm Mon-Thur & Sat Mar-Oct), the secret command centre for the Battle of the Atlantic, was buried under yards of concrete beneath an undistinguished building behind the town hall in Rumford Square. At the end of the war the bunker was abandoned with virtually everything left intact.

Conservation Centre

The Conservation Centre (☎ 478 4999; admission free; open 10am-5pm Mon-Sat, noon-5pm Sun), in the disused Midland Railway Goods Depot in Old Haymarket, is a state-of-the-art exhibition telling the story behind the conservation of the items on display in local museums and art galleries. Hand-held wands allow you to tune into different stories as you walk around – you'll probably be surprised to discover how much fun it all is.

Metropolitan Cathedral

According to Sir Edwin Lutyens' original plans, Liverpool's Roman Catholic cathedral (☎ 709 9222; off Mount Pleasant; open 8am-6pm daily, to 5pm Sun Oct-Mar) would have been larger than St Peter's in Rome. Unfortunately, WWII and Liverpool's decline forced the priests to lower their sights. The present church-in-the-round (locally referred to as 'Paddy's Wigwam') was completed in 1967 according to the design of architect Sir Frederick Gibberd, and incorporates Lutyens' crypt. The soaring exterior is strikingly successful and the interior space is mightily impressive.

Anglican Cathedral

Work on the red sandstone, neogothic Anglican cathedral (☎ 709 6271; Hope St; voluntary donation £2; open 8am-6pm daily) started in 1902 and was finally completed in 1978, by which time it was only exceeded in size by St Peter's and the cathedrals of Milan and Seville. Almost everything about the place is larger than life, including the central bell,

which is the world's third largest. The cathedral was the life work of Sir Giles Gilbert Scott (1880–1960). Scott was also responsible for the design of the old red telephone booth, which explains why one of these is tucked away upstairs.

Even those who don't usually care for neogothic are likely to be awed by this great, austere sea of space. There are terrific views of Liverpool from the top of the 101m tower (adult/child £2/1; open 11am-3pm Mon-Sat).

Beside the porch steps, there's a **memorial** to the 96 Liverpool football fans who died in the crush at Hillsborough Stadium in 1989.

Albert Dock

Built between 1841 and 1848 the Albert Dock was one of the earliest enclosed docks in the world. Now 2¾ hectares of water are ringed by a colonnade of enormous cast-iron columns and impressive five-storey warehouses. The whole complex is the city's biggest tourist attraction, with 4.5 million visitors annually.

In the 1980s the warehouses were restored and now house several outstanding museums, numerous shops and restaurants, offices, studios for Granada TV, a branch of the TIC and several tacky tourist attractions.

Merseyside Maritime Museum This museum (☎ 478 4499; admission free; open 10am-5pm daily) has a large range of imaginatively developed exhibits. Major displays are Emigrants to a New World, the WWII Battle of the Atlantic, and Builders of Great Ships.

There is also an absorbing Transatlantic Slave Gallery that describes the shameful trade and its repercussions in the form of modern racism.

Museum of Liverpool Life This museum (☎ 478 4080; admission free; open 10am-5pm daily) celebrates the city in all its guises; from its multiculturalism and advocacy of trade unionism to its role in the British Army.

The Mersey Culture exhibit looks at Liverpool's contribution to sport and music, including the Grand National, its football teams and the explosion of the Mersey beat in the 1960s.

Tate Gallery Liverpool It's particularly appropriate that Liverpool should have been chosen as home to this extension (*admission free*) of the London Tate Gallery – Henry Tate (benefactor of the original gallery) co-founded the famous Tate & Lyle sugar business here. The newly refurbished **Albert Dock Gallery** (☎ *702 7400; open 10am-5.50pm Tues-Sun*) hosts high-quality changing exhibitions. The **Tate and the Albert Dock Gallery** (*open 10am-5.50pm Tues-Sun*) is the special exhibition part of the Tate.

The Beatles Story Despite its promising name this attraction (☎ *709 1963; adult/child £7.95/5.45; open 10am-6pm daily Mar-Oct, 10am-5pm daily Nov-Feb*) fails to capitalise on its subject's potential. Fanatics won't discover anything they don't already know and, aside from some old TV clips and John Lennon's famous white grand piano, there's little to kindle excitement for later generations. A Beatles Combo ticket costing £15.50 gets you into the exhibition and a seat on the Magical Mystery Tour (see the boxed text 'Doing The Beatles to Death').

North of Albert Dock The area to the north of Albert Dock is known as **Pier Head**, after a stone pier built in the 1760s. This is still the departure point for ferries across the River Mersey (see Getting Around later), and was, for millions of migrants, their final contact with European soil.

Today this area is dominated by a trio of self-important buildings dating from the days when Liverpool's star was still ascending. The southernmost, with the dome mimicking St Paul's Cathedral, is the **Port of Liverpool Building**, completed in 1907. Next to it is the **Cunard Building**, in the style of an Italian palazzo, once HQ to the Cunard Steamship Line. Finally, the **Royal Liver Building** (pronounced lie-ver) was opened in 1911 as the head office of the Royal Liver Friendly Society. It's crowned by Liverpool's symbol, the famous 5.5m copper Liver Bird. It was originally an eagle but over time artists' representations came to look more like a seagull or cormorant. **Tours** (☎ *236 2748*) of the building are free but must be pre-booked.

Places to Stay

Note that beds can be hard to find when Liverpool or Everton football clubs are playing at home. You'll also be lucky to find anything if you haven't booked ahead for the third week of August when The Beatles annual convention comes to town.

Camping & Hostels **Wirral Country Park** (☎ *648 4371; Station Rd, Thurataston; per person including tent £4.50*) is 9 miles (14.5km) southwest of the city on the Wirral Peninsula. It has all the facilities, including a barbecue stand and picnic facilities.

Doing The Beatles to Death

Between March 1961 and August 1963, The Beatles played a staggering 275 gigs in a club on Mathew St called the Cavern, which was essentially a basement with a stage and a sound system. They shared the stage with other local bands who helped define the 'Mersey Beat', but it was John, Paul, George and Ringo who emerged into the sunlight of superstardom, unparalleled success and crass marketing.

Forty years later, the club is gone, the band has long broken up and two of its members are dead, but the phenomenon lives on. Walk down Mathew St today and you will be overwhelmed by the businesses cashing in on their name and success. There's an Abbey Rd Oyster Bar, an Abbey Rd Shop, a Lucy in the Sky With Diamonds café and a Lennon Bar…and that's before you stumble on Cavern Court and the Cavern Walks shopping mall. Even the Cavern was brought back to life, with the same name but a different location (see Entertainment).

If you want to join an official tour of all Beatles-related sites, both TICs sell tickets for the **Magical Mystery Tour** (☎ *709 3285*), a 2¼-hour bus trip taking in Penny Lane, Strawberry Fields and many other landmarks. It departs from opposite the Pumphouse pub in Albert Dock at 2.20pm and from the main TIC at 2.30pm daily. In July and August, there are also Saturday tours at 11.50am. Tickets cost £10.95. Better value is The Beatles Combo ticket at £15.50, which covers admission to **The Beatles Story** (☎ *709 1963*) and a seat on the Magical Mystery Tour.

If you'd rather do it yourself, the TICs also stock the *Discover Lennon's Liverpool* guide and map, and *Robin Jones' Beatles Liverpool*.

Embassie Hostel (☎ 707 1089, fax 707 8289; 1 Falkner Square; dorm beds £13.50), an excellent and welcoming place, is to the east of the Anglican cathedral but still within walking distance of the centre. Facilities include a laundry and TV lounge.

The International Inn (☎ 709 8135; South Hunter St; dorm beds £15), a new hostel just off Hardman St, is in the city centre. All rooms are clean, tidy and have en suites.

YHA Liverpool International (☎ 0870 770 5924, fax 709 0417; 25 Tabley St; beds £18.50) is a purpose-built facility across the road from Albert Dock, 600m south of James Street station. The four- and six-bed dorms are all in pristine condition. Rates include breakfast.

YMCA (☎ 709 9516; 56 Mount Pleasant; B&B per person £15.50) offers plain but comfortable B&B.

University of Liverpool (☎ 794 3298, fax 794 3816; rooms per person £16) has self-catering rooms at **Mulberry Court** (Oxford St), near the Metropolitan Cathedral. It also has a **B&B** (☎ 794 6440; Greenbank Lane; B&B from £17) over Easter and from mid-April to mid-May and mid-June to mid-September.

B&Bs & Hotels There's a handy group of hotels on Mount Pleasant, between the city centre and the Metropolitan Cathedral.

Belvedere (☎ 709 2356; 83 Mount Pleasant; singles/doubles £20/40) is a small, B&B-style hotel (like staying in a family home) with cosy rooms. This is the cheapest option you'll find so close to the city centre.

Dolby Hotel (☎ 708 7272, fax 708 7266; 36-42 Chaloner St; rooms £36) is the kind of place you might find along a European motorway – all convenience but little character. Still, the rooms are pretty good for the price, and the hotel is well situated close to Albert Dock.

Aachen Hotel (☎ 709 3477, fax 709 1126; 89-91 Mount Pleasant; singles/doubles £30/40), an award-winning place, has well-equipped rooms, most with showers.

Feathers Hotel (☎ 709 9655, fax 709 3838; e feathershotel@feathers.uk.com; 119-125 Mount Pleasant; singles/doubles from £34/44) is a good mid-range hotel. Try to avoid the really small singles, but make the most of the all-you-can-eat buffet breakfast.

Campanile Hotel (☎ 709 8104, fax 709 8725; cnr Wapping & Chaloner Sts; rooms £42) is a purpose-built hotel with modern, comfy rooms just opposite the Albert Dock. Breakfast is not included.

Hotel Ibis (☎ 706 9800, fax 706 9810; 27 Wapping; rooms £42) is an excellent choice as far as mid-price chain hotels go. All rooms are modern, comfortable and very clean. It is right on the waterfront, a short walk from Albert Dock.

Britannia Adelphi Hotel (☎ 709 7200, fax 708 0743; Ranelagh Place; singles/doubles £45/60), Liverpool's largest hotel, was considered one of the world's most luxurious hotels when it opened in 1912, complete with marble floors and crystal chandeliers. Its opulence has definitely faded and the rooms are not quite as grand as they were, but it remains one of the city's most distinctive landmarks.

Thistle (☎ 227 4444, fax 236 3973; Chapel St; singles/doubles from £80/90), is virtually beside the Royal Liver Building and is a modern, five-star, multistorey hotel with good views over the River Mersey. Good-value weekend breaks are available.

Crowne Plaza Liverpool (☎ 243 8000, fax 243 8111; St Nicholas Place, Princes Dock, Pier Head; rooms from £125), a modern and luxurious spot right on the waterfront, is the top hotel in town these days.

Places to Eat

It's taken a while, but dining options in the city have finally started to get interesting. The area around Slater, Hardman and Bold Sts is worth trying for a reasonable choice of places to eat.

Number Seven Café (☎ 709 9633; 7 Falkner St; mains around £6) is a very popular restaurant with a mixed menu of fish, meat, salads and various vegetarian options.

Everyman Bistro (☎ 708 9545; 5 Hope St; closed Sun), underneath the Everyman Theatre, is highly recommended as a place to tuck into cheap, good food (pizza slices for £2 and delicious desserts).

El Macho (☎ 708 6644; 23 Hope St; most mains around £9.50) has a cheerful atmosphere and enormous servings of spicy Mexican food. The lunch menu is cheaper, including nachos for £3.50.

Becher's Brook (☎ 707 0005; 29A Hope St; mains around £10), a few doors south of El Macho, does classy modern British cookery and is one of the better restaurants in town.

NORTHWEST ENGLAND

Casa Bella (☎ 258 1800; 25 Victoria St) is a good, cheap Italian serving pizza and pasta from £6.30.

Liverpool's Chinatown has declined since its glory days, but there are still several Chinese restaurants around Berry St and it does have the largest Chinese gate in Europe.

Far East (☎ 709 3141; 27-35 Berry St; mains around £8), is your best bet in town for good Cantonese food. There are set menus from £15.95, and delicious *dim sum* from noon to 6pm.

The Albert Dock is also a good place to look for something to eat.

Blue (☎ 709 7097; 17 Edward Pavilion; mains around £8) is where you can enjoy comfortable couches, a view of the dock, and choose from a selection of good continental dishes.

The **refectory** (☎ 707 1722; St James Mount) in the Anglican cathedral serves great-value hot lunches for around £4. There are also excellent **cafés** in the Walker Art Gallery and the Conservation Centre.

Entertainment

Liverpool has a thriving, and changeable, nightlife. Wander around Mathew St and southeast to Bold, Seel and Slater Sts and you'll stumble upon an amazing array of pubs and clubs catering to every imaginable taste. To find out what's on where, look out for the free monthly entertainment guide *In Touch*.

Pubs & Bars Philharmonic (☎ 707 2837; 36 Hope St), on the corner of Hardman St, was built in 1897 by the same shipwrights who designed the *Lusitania* and the original *Queen Elizabeth* and is one of Britain's most extraordinary pubs.

The interior is resplendent with etched and stained glass, wrought iron, mosaics and ceramic tiling – and if you think that's good, just wait until you see inside the marble toilets.

The Baltic Fleet (☎ 709 3116; 33 Wapping) is a little more ordinary than the Philharmonic but still wonderful. It's next to the youth hostel (see Places to Stay), and pours a superb traditional ale.

Ye Cracke (☎ 709 4171; 13 Rice St) has long been favoured by students from the nearby College of Art, including one John

Lennon The atmosphere is terrific, as is the little circular snug in the middle of the bar.

The last decade has seen a flourishing of the late-night bar, where the emphasis is on cool surroundings and DJs who really know how to crank up the music. The following all stay open until 2am.

Modo (☎ 709 8832; Concert Square) is one of the coolest bars in town, with a great mix of people and a terrific atmosphere.

Revolution (☎ 707 2727; 18-22 Wood St) is a popular Russian theme bar that specialises in vodka.

Mello Mello (☎ 707 0898; 40-42 Slater St), the city's hippest bar in the early 1990s, may have lost some of its shine but still has some of the best DJs you'll hear in town.

Baa Bar (☎ 707 0610; 43-45 Fleet St) was the first – and best – of Liverpool's new-style bars. It too is a little faded, but it's a great spot nonetheless. It's mainly popular with students.

Bar Ça Va (☎ 709 9300; 4a Wood St) is an unpretentious watering hole covered in posters that pulls in a mixed crowd of students, office types and others in search of a good night out.

G-Bar (☎ 255 1148; 1-7 Eberle St; closed Mon-Tues), in a small lane off Dale St behind Moorfields train station, is the city's premier gay bar and club, even though it attracts a mixed crowd. Wednesday nights are mostly gay, while weekends are for uplifting house and trance. No matter what night, the music is top notch.

Clubs No English city worth its salt can do without a good selection of clubs, and in Liverpool you'll find one of the best in the country, as well as others to satisfy virtually every taste, mostly in the area between Hanover and Slater Streets. Most clubs open until 4am and charge between £4 and £10.

Nation (☎ 709 1693; 40 Slater St/Wolstenholme Square), once the weekly home of Cream, England's most famous club night, still draws them in – 3000 a night – from all over. These days it is home to a number of excellent nights, including Bugged Out! and Medication, which fill the floor to the sounds of progressive house, trance and UK Garage. For once, the hype is spot on: it's a fantastic night out.

The bouncers enforce a strict dress code: absolutely no sportswear.

Society (☎ 258 1230; 47 Fleet St) is the students' favourite danceteria. The sounds are commercial and camp, the lighting is terrific and the smoke machine works overtime to create the atmosphere. For a change, the comfortable upstairs balcony is open to everyone and not just questionable VIPs.

Sunrise@Sound Factory (☎ 709 9586; 1 Mount Pleasant) is an after-hours dance club for serious dancers. There's no alcohol served (most are fuelled by other substances), just hardcore trance music, and it runs from 2am until 6am every Sunday morning.

Cavern Club (☎ 236 1964; 8-10 Mathew St) is not where the original was, but it is a pretty faithful reconstruction of the legendary original – basically a brick cellar. It hosts a surprisingly good disco on Friday night and many of the bands that perform here on other nights are top quality, although you're wasting your time if you're looking for the next fab four.

Escape – E2 (☎ 708 8809; 41-45 Paradise St) is Liverpool's only real gay club. Happy house, disco and other party tunes are the order of the night. The best night is Thursday.

Theatre & Classical Music One of Britain's most famous repertory theatres, **Everyman Theatre** (☎ 709 4776; Hope St) has featured the works of local playwright Alan Bleasdale, among others.

Liverpool Playhouse (☎ 709 8363; Williamson Square) or **The Empire** (☎ 709 1555; Lime St) could be staging anything from straight plays to musicals.

Bluecoat Arts Centre (☎ 709 5279; School Lane) and the **Unity Theatre** (☎ 709 4988; Hope Place) host innovative, small-scale companies.

Philharmonic Hall (☎ 709 3789; Hope St) is where the Royal Liverpool Philharmonic Orchestra plays.

Creamfields Festival The August Bank Holiday (the second week in August) belongs to Cream and its world-famous festival of music. The best acts in dance music, as well as some of the world's top DJs, put on an unforgettable show. For information and schedule information, call ☎ 709 1693.

Spectator Sports

Football to some may be as crucial as life and death, but in Liverpool it's a little bit more than that. There is no other city in England where the fortunes of its football clubs are so inextricably linked with those of its inhabitants. The city has two clubs, Liverpool and Everton, whose Anfield and Goodison Park grounds are separated by the stretch of Stanley Park in the not quite salubrious northeast of the city. Plans, however, are afoot for both clubs to move to new stadiums; Liverpool to a larger stadium about 400m from the current ground sometime between 2003 and 2004, and Everton to a purpose-built stadium in King's Dock, although the plan is only in development.

Liverpool is also home to the world's most famous steeplechase event, the Grand National, run in the first weekend in April at the Aintree course in the north of the city.

Liverpool FC Liverpool FC (☎ 263 9199, ticket office ☎ 220 2345; Anfield Rd) is the most successful club in British history and for most of the 1970s and 1980s was virtually unbeatable. The 1990s proved to be a nightmare, as they failed to win much of anything while their hated rivals Manchester United couldn't put a foot wrong. The new millennium has seen the club back on the winning trail and they're challenging for the championship once again, last won in 1990.

Tickets for home games are notoriously difficult to obtain, so you might have to settle for a **tour** (☎ 260 6677; with museum adult/child £8.50/5.50; every couple of hours except match days) of the Anfield stadium and/or a visit to the small **museum** (adult/child £5/3), which features memorabilia from Liverpool's glory years.

Everton FC The city's 'other' team, the blues of Everton (☎ 330 2400, ticket office ☎ 330 2300; Goodison Park), haven't had much to sing about since 1987 when they won the championship, but they have spent more years in the top flight than any other club (100 in 2002–3).

Tours (☎ 330 2277; adult/child £5.50/3.50; 11am & 2pm, Sun-Wed & Fri) of Goodison Park run throughout the year except on the Friday before home matches.

The Grand National England's most beloved race is a permanent and important fixture on the country's social calendar. It is an incredible spectacle, too, as 40-odd horses clamber over the most difficult jumps in world racing, including the Chair, Becher's Brook and the Canal Turn.

You can book **tickets** (☎ 523 2600) for the actual event, or visit the **Grand National Experience** (☎ 522 2921; admission £7), a visitor centre that includes a race simulator – those jumps are very steep indeed.

To get here, take the Merseyrail to Aintree.

Getting There & Away
Liverpool is 210 miles (338km) from London, 100 miles (160km) from Birmingham, 75 miles (121km) from Leeds and 34 miles (55km) from Manchester.

Air Liverpool John Lennon Airport (☎ 288 4000), 8 miles (13km) south of the city centre, has services to a variety of European destinations. Bus No 80A or 180 departs from Paradise St Station every 20 minutes, while

Airportxpress 500 runs between the airport and the city centre (outside Lime St station) every 30 minutes (£2) from 7am to 10pm daily.

Bus National Express services link Liverpool to most major towns. There are seven buses daily from London (£17, five hours) and two daily from Manchester (£4.50, 1¼ hours).

To get to the town centre from the coach station, turn right up Seymour St and then right again along London Rd. To get to Chester catch bus No X8 from Queen Square in the city centre.

Train Numerous services run to Lime St station, including trains from Wigan (£5.80, 50 minutes), Chester (£3.30, 40 minutes), Manchester (£9.50, 45 minutes) and London (£49.80, three hours).

Boat The Isle of Man Steam Packet Company (☎ 0870 552 3523; w www.steam -packet.com) operates a service between Douglas and Liverpool (Pier Head) every weekend throughout the year and daily between March and mid-November.

The journey time is 4¼ hours by ferry or 2½ hours by catamaran. Foot passenger fares start at £28 single but are cheaper at off-peak times. Bicycles are transported free but a car will cost from £85 each way.

Getting Around
Local public transport is coordinated by **Merseytravel** (☎ 236 7676). Zonal tickets are also sold at post offices. An all-zone all-day ticket for bus, train and ferry (except cruises) costs £4.50. Most local buses leave from Queen Square to the east of St George's Hall. Smart Bus Nos 1 and 5 link Albert Dock with the city centre and the university every 20 minutes. If you don't fancy the ferry across the Mersey (see later), the suburban Merseyrail network will take you under the river. As well as Lime St, trains call at Central Station – as the name suggests, it's a useful stop for the central shops and bars. The other stops in the city are Lime St, James St (handy for Albert Dock) and Moorfields Station (near the Western Approaches Museum).

Mersey Cabs (☎ 298 2222) operates tourist taxi services and has some cabs adapted for disabled visitors. The famous ferry across the River Mersey (adult/child £1.10/90p), started 800 years ago by Benedictine monks but immortalised by Gerry & the Pacemakers, still offers one of the best views of Liverpool. Boats for Woodside and Seacombe depart from Pier Head Ferry Terminal, next to the Liver Building to the north of Albert Dock. Special 50-minute commentary cruises depart hourly, 10am to 3pm on weekdays and until 6pm at weekends year round and cost adult/child £3.75/1.90. Phone ☎ 630 1030 for more information.

AROUND LIVERPOOL
Port Sunlight
Southwest of Liverpool across the River Mersey on the Wirral Peninsula, Port Sunlight is a picturesque 19th-century village created by the philanthropic Lever family to house workers in its soap factory. The main reason to come here is the wonderful **Lady Lever Art Gallery** (☎ 478 4136; off Greendale Rd; adult/child £3/1.50; open 10am-5pm Mon-Sat, noon-5pm Sun) where you can see some of the greatest works of the Pre-Raphaelite Brotherhood, as well as some fine Wedgwood pottery.

Also in the village is the **Heritage Centre** (☎ 644 6466; 95 Greendale Rd; adult/child 80/50p; open 10am-4.30pm daily, 11am-4.30pm Sat & Sun Oct-Mar), which tells the story of the creation of Port Sunlight.

Trains run from Lime St station to Port Sunlight.

Speke

Six miles (9.5km) south of Liverpool is the plain suburb of Speke, but what draws the visitors is **Speke Hall** *(NT; ☎ 427 7231; adult/ child £5/3; open 1pm-5pm Wed-Sun)*, a marvellous black and white half-timbered hall. It contains several priest's holes where 16th century Roman Catholic priests could hide when they were forbidden to hold Masses.

Bus No 80 or 82 from Lime St station will drop you within a mile of Speke Hall. Visitors to Speke Hall can also go by minibus to another NT-owned property at **20 Forthlin Rd**, Liverpool, once home to Sir Paul McCartney. It's been restored to its 1950s' look although there's little linked to the great Macca. Tours leave Speke Hall at 3.10pm and 4pm Wednesday to Saturday, from Easter to October. A combined ticket with Speke Hall costs adult/child £5.50/2.80. Pre-book by phoning ☎ 0151-486 4006. Tours also run from The Beatles Story at Albert Dock.

Isle of Man

☎ 01624 • pop 78,000

The Isle of Man is a quirky world of its own. Thought of as a weird place by many mainlanders, most of them have never actually seen the lush valleys, barren hills and rugged coastlines of the island, which make for great walking, cycling and driving. And anyone familiar with motor sports will know that the island is famous for its Tourist Trophy (TT) motorcycle races, which every May and June add 45,000 to the island's small population. The island's other great industry is tax avoidance – wealthy Brits can shelter their loot here without having to move to Monte Carlo or the Cayman Islands.

Home to the world's oldest continuous parliament, the Isle of Man enjoys special status in Britain, and its annual parliamentary ceremony honours the 1000-year history of the Tynwald (a Scandinavian word meaning meeting field). Unfortunately, Douglas, the capital, is a run-down relic of Victorian tourism with fading B&Bs. The tailless Manx cat and the four-horned loghtan sheep are unique to the Isles.

Orientation & Information

Situated in the Irish Sea, equidistant from Liverpool, Dublin and Belfast, the Isle of

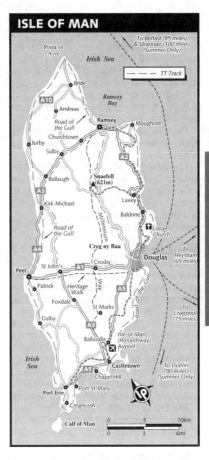

NORTHWEST ENGLAND

Man is about 33 miles (53km) long by 13 miles (21km) wide. Ferries arrive at Douglas, the port and main town on the southeast coast. Flights come in to Ronaldsway airport, 10 miles (16km) south of Douglas. Most of the island's historic sites are operated by Manx National Heritage, which offers free admission to NT or English Heritage (EH) members. Unless otherwise indicated, Manx Heritage (MH) sites open 10am to 5pm daily, Easter to October. The phone number for all inquiries is ☎ 648000.

Walking & Cycling

There are plenty of walking trails. Ordnance Survey (OS) Landranger Map 95 (£3.95) covers the whole island, while the free *Walks on the Isle of Man* is available from the TIC in Douglas. The Millennium Way is a walking path that runs the length of the island amid some spectacular scenery. The most demanding of all walks is the 90-mile (145km) Raad ny Foillan, or Road of the Gull, a well-marked path that makes a complete circuit of the island and normally takes about five days to complete. Other routes are detailed under the relevant sections following.

There are six designated off-road cycling tracks on the island, each of varying range of difficulty.

The island is also home to the International Cycling Week Festival, which takes place in mid-July. It's a pretty serious affair, attracting top cyclists from around the world as well as enthusiastic Sunday racers. Check with the TIC in Douglas for details.

DOUGLAS
☎ 01624 • pop 22,200

Looking across the Irish Sea towards Blackpool, Douglas is not particularly endearing. Half the Victorian seafront terraces look ready for demolition, renovation or a good coat of paint. More modern buildings look to have been designed by some of Britain's least inspired architects on their off days.

The **Manx Museum** *(MH; admission free; open 10am-5pm Mon-Sat year round)* gives an introduction to everything from the island's prehistoric past to the latest TT race winners.

The **TIC** *(☎ 686766; open 9am-7pm May-Sept, to 5pm rest of year)*, in the Sea Terminal Building, makes free accommodation bookings.

Feegan's Internet Lounge *(☎ 679280; 22 Duke St)*, can handle all your emailing needs for £1 per 15 minutes.

Places to Stay

The TIC's camping information sheet lists sites all around the island. Everything is booked out for TT week and the weeks each side of it, often for years ahead.

The seafront promenade is shoulder-to-shoulder with B&Bs where you should find a half-decent room for about £25 per head (but count on paying up to £50 for a room with a sea view).

Two reasonable places are the **Curnard Hotel** *(☎/fax 676728; 28-29 Loch Promenade; rooms from £28)* and, more expensive, the **Modwena Hotel** *(☎ 675728; 39-40 Loch Promenade; rooms per person from £32)*.

Sefton Hotel *(☎ 645500; Harris Promenade; rooms per person £40)* is more upmarket, with comfortable rooms.

Places to Eat

Even the big fast-food outlets skip round Douglas, leaving a choice of fish and chip shops, Chinese takeaways and a handful of restaurants.

Blazer's *(☎ 673222; cnr North Quay & Bridge St)*, set in a stone building overlooking the quay, is a wine bar with pub-style food.

L'Expérience *(☎ 623103; Summerhill)*, at the bottom of Summerhill, is a smart French restaurant serving *queenies* (local scallops).

There are a few good pubs around, including the popular local hang-out **Tramshunter** on the promenade and the originally named **Rovers Return** *(☎ 676459; 11 Church St)* specialising in the local brew Bushy Ales.

AROUND DOUGLAS

You can follow the TT course up and over the mountain or wind around the coast. The mountain route takes you close to the summit of **Snaefell** (621m), the island's highest point. It's an easy walk up to the summit or you can take the electric tram from Laxey on the coast. The tram stops by the road where **Murray's Motorcycle Museum** displays motorcycles and TT memorabilia.

On the edge of Ramsey is the **Grove Rural Life Museum** *(MH; adult/child £3/2)*. The church in the small village of **Maughold** is on the site of an ancient monastery; a small shelter houses quite a good selection of stone crosses and ancient inscriptions.

Describing the **Laxey Wheel** *(MH; adult/child £3/2)*, built in 1854 to pump water from a mine, as a 'great' wheel is no exaggeration; it measures 22m across and can draw 250 gallons (1140L) of water per minute from a depth of 550m. The wheel-headed cross at **Lonan Old Church** is the island's most impressive early Christian cross.

CASTLETOWN

At the southern end of the island is Castletown, a quiet harbour town which was originally the capital of the Isle of Man. The town is dominated by the impressive 13th-century **Castle Rushen** *(MH; adult/child £4.50/2.50)*. The flagtower affords fine views of the town and coast. There's also a small **Nautical Museum** *(MH; adult/child £3/2)* displaying, among other things, its pride and joy *Peggy*, a boat built in 1791 and still housed in its original boathouse. A school dating back to 1570 in **St Mary's church** *(MH; admission free)* is behind the castle.

AROUND CASTLETOWN
Between Castletown and Cregneash, the Iron-Age hillfort at **Chapel Hill** encloses a Viking ship burial site.

On the southern tip of the island, the **Cregneash Village Folk Museum** *(MH; adult/child £3/2)* recalls traditional Manx rural life. The **Calf of Man**, the small island just off Cregneash, is a bird sanctuary. **Calf Island Cruises** *(☎ 832339)* run between the islands regularly during the summer. Visits cost adult/child £10/5 from Port Erin.

Port Erin, another Victorian seaside resort, plays host to the small **Railway Museum** *(adult/child £1/50p; open 9.30am-5.30pm daily Apr-Oct)* depicting the history of steam railway on the island.

Places to Stay & Eat
Port Erin has a good range of accommodation, as does Port St Mary.

Aaron House *(☎ 835702;* e *aaron_house _iom@yahoo.com; the Promenade; rooms per person £28)*, in Port St Mary, is a splendid Victorian-style B&B with sea views.

Whistle Stop Coffee Shop *(☎ 833802)* in the Port Erin train station makes filling sandwiches for around £3 and lovely home-made cakes.

PEEL
The west coast's most appealing town, Peel has a fine sandy beach but its real attraction is the 11th-century **Peel Castle** *(MH; adult/ child £3.50/2)*, stunningly positioned atop St Patrick's Island and joined to Peel by a causeway.

The excellent **House of Manannan** *(MH; adult/child £5/2.50; open year round)* museum uses interactive displays to explain Manx history and its seafaring traditions.

A combined ticket for both costs adult/child £8/4.

Places to Stay & Eat
Peel has several B&Bs including the **Fernleigh Hotel** *(☎ 842435; Marine Parade; rooms per person from £22)*, which has twelve bedrooms and prices include breakfast.

Creek Inn *(☎ 842216 fax 843359; East Quay; rooms from £34)*, opposite the House of Manannan, offers self-catering rooms. It's also popular for food, serving Manx queenies (scallops) for £7.

AROUND PEEL
Three miles (5km) east of Peel is **Tynwald Hill** at St John's, where the annual parliamentary ceremony takes place on 5 July.

Getting There & Away
Air Manx Airlines *(☎ 0845 725 6256)* has frequent connections with much of Britain and Ireland, as does **Jersey European** *(☎ 0870 567 6676)* but there are also other smaller operators. Weekend return flights from London generally cost £130 but fares can be as low as £70 from Liverpool.

Boat The **Isle of Man Steam Packet** *(☎ 0870 552 3523;* w *www.steam-packet .com)* operates regular car ferries and high-speed SeaCat catamarans to Douglas from Dublin, Belfast, Heysham, Fleetwood, Liverpool and Ardrossan. Foot passenger fares start at £28 single but you'll have to pay from £85 to take a car across. At times it can be cheaper to fly and hire a car on arrival. The crossing from Liverpool takes 2½ hours by SeaCat or four hours by ferry. From time to time you can get special fares so it's worth calling ahead or checking out the website.

Getting Around
A taxi from the airport into Douglas will cost about £16.50 compared with £1.90 by bus. There are several car rental operators at the airport and in Douglas, charging from £29 upwards for a day's rental. The Isle also has a comprehensive bus service; the TIC in Douglas has timetables and fares. In Douglas bicycles can be hired at **Eurocycles** *(☎ 624 909; 8A Victoria Rd)*. The charge is £11 for the first day, £10 per day for three-day hire and £8.50 per day for five-day hire. The whole of the island is suitable for cycling.

There are several interesting **rail services** *(☎ 663366)* that operate from Easter to September. These include the Douglas–Laxey–Ramsey electric tramway (£6 return); a steam train operating from Douglas via Castletown to Port Erin (£3.10 return); the Snaefell Mountain Railway running between Laxey and Summit (£6 return); and the narrow-gauge Groudle Glen Railway (£4 return). A ticket covering rides on all these trains for three days in seven costs adult/child £18/9.

Inevitably, the Isle of Man is petrol-head heaven, with plenty of scenic, sweeping bends that make for some exciting driving, either by motorbike or in a car. Outside of the towns, there is no speed limit on the island, so you can speed away to your heart's content. Naturally, the most popular drive is along the TT route.

Lancashire

Lancashire is bordered by the River Mersey in the south, the sea in the west, the Pennines in the east and the Lake District in the north. Manchester and Liverpool, the region's great ports, are administered separately. Of the traditional seaside resorts serving Manchester and Liverpool, Blackpool lives splendidly, if tackily, on, while the once-popular Morecambe is worth visiting for the lovely bay and its magnificent sunsets.

The county town, Lancaster, has notable Georgian architecture.

LANCASTER
☎ 01524 • pop 46,300
Although it dates back as far as Roman times, Lancaster's heyday was the 18th century, when it was an important port in the slave trade. The port is much quieter now, but the town's rows of handsome Georgian buildings make this a pleasant stopover on the way to the Ribble Valley.

Information
The TIC (☎ 841656, fax 847615; 29 Castle Hill; open 9am-5pm Mon-Sat) stocks a comprehensive free guide to Lancaster and Morecambe. The staff will help with accommodation bookings. The main post office (85 Market St; open 9am-5.30pm Mon-Fri, 9am-12.30pm Sat) is in the centre of town. Internet access is available in the City Library (Market Square; free).

Lancaster Castle & Priory
Lancaster's imposing castle (☎ 64998; admission free; open 10am-5pm daily) was originally built in 1150. Later additions include the Well Tower, more commonly

known as the Witches' Tower as it was used to incarcerate the accused of the famous Pendle Witches Trial of 1612, and the impressive, twin-towered gatehouse, both of which were added in the 14th century. Most of what you see today, however, dates from the 18th and 19th centuries, when the castle was substantially altered to suit its new role as a prison, which it remains today.

Regular 45-minute tours take in the elegant, neogothic Shire Hall courtroom. It was here in 1975 that the Birmingham Six (Irish men accused of planting a devastating bomb in a Birmingham pub) were tried and wrongfully convicted to life imprisonment (they were eventually released in 1991). Also on the tour is Hadrian's Tower, which has a display of instruments of torture and a dungeon. A full tour costs adult/child £4/2.50, less at times when court sittings curtail the tours. Immediately next to the castle is the equally fine priory church (☎ 65338; admission free; open 9.30am-5pm daily), founded in 1094 but extensively remodelled in the Middle Ages.

Other Things to See
The Maritime Museum (☎ 64637; St George's Quay; adult/child £2/1; open 11am-5pm daily, Easter-Oct, 12.30pm-4pm Nov-Easter), in the 18th-century Custom House, recalls the days when Lancaster was a flourishing port at the centre of the slave trade.

The City Museum (☎ 64637; Market Square; admission free; open 10am-5pm Mon-Sat), has a mixed bag of local historical and archaeological exhibits.

The Judges' Lodgings (☎ 32808; adult/child £2/1; open 10.30am-1pm & 2pm-5pm Mon-Fri, 2pm-5pm Sat July-Sept, 2pm-5pm Mon-Sat Oct-June), off China St, is a 17th-century townhouse containing a Museum of Childhood and some fine furnishings. The Cottage Museum (☎ 64637; 15 Castle Hill; adult/child £1/50p; open 2pm-5pm daily Apr-Sept) has been furnished to show life in an artisan's house in the early 19th century.

Places to Stay & Eat
Lancaster lacks a youth hostel but over Easter and in summer 400 beds are available for B&B at £18.80 per head in the accommodation block at the University College of St Martin's (☎ 384460; Bowerham Rd). St Mary's Parade on Castle Hill has two good B&Bs.

Castle Hill House (☎ 849137; 27 St Mary's Parade; singles/doubles £27/42) is a lovely refurbished Victorian town house.

The Priory (☎ 845711; 15 St Mary's Parade; singles/doubles £30/50) is equally as beautiful as Castle Hill and charges slightly more.

Wagon & Horses (☎ 846094; 27 St Georges Quay; singles/doubles £30/45), next to the Maritime Museum, is a relaxed pub offering rooms with river views.

Pizza Margherita (☎ 36333; 2 Moor Lane) is a relaxed place with great pizzas at a reasonable price, including Calzone Mexicana for £5.95.

Simply French (☎ 843199; 27A St George's Quay) next to the Maritime Museum, serves a filling two-course lunch for £6 and jugs of sangria for £5.95 to liven up the place.

Folly Cafe (☎ 388540; 27 Castle Park) serves dishes such as Morecambe Bay potted shrimps (£4.95) in a building that doubles as a small art gallery.

From Easter to October, teas and lunches are available in the **Priory Refectory** (☎ 65338; Priory Church).

A reasonable student population makes Lancaster a lively place during term.

Water Witch Pub (Aldcliffe Rd) has a good spot on the canal.

Friary & Firkin (St Leonardgate), originally a church, has enough room to accommodate the regular mobs and live music.

Getting There & Away

Lancaster is on the main west-coast railway line and on the Cumbrian Coast Line. Trains

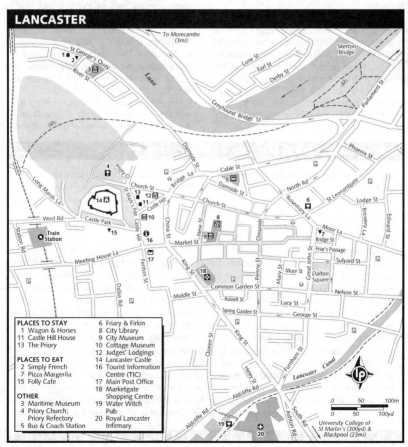

LANCASTER

PLACES TO STAY
1 Wagon & Horses
11 Castle Hill House
13 The Priory

PLACES TO EAT
2 Simply French
7 Pizza Margherita
15 Folly Cafe

OTHER
3 Maritime Museum
4 Priory Church;
  Priory Refectory
5 Bus & Coach Station

6 Friary & Firkin
8 City Library
9 City Museum
10 Cottage Museum
12 Judges' Lodgings
14 Lancaster Castle
16 Tourist Information
  Centre (TIC)
17 Main Post Office
18 Marketgate
  Shopping Centre
19 Water Witch
  Pub
20 Royal Lancaster
  Infirmary

NORTHWEST ENGLAND

serve Kendal (£7.40, 30 minutes), Windermere (£9.20, one hour) and Carlisle (£19.40, 3½ hours). There are also National Express links with most local towns.

MORECAMBE
☎ 01524 • pop 44,500

Only 5 miles (8km) west of Lancaster, Morecambe was a quiet little fishing village until the mid-19th century when it developed into a full-blown seaside resort, thanks to the construction of the railway, which brought holidaying mill workers from the surrounding towns in their droves.

Its popularity has irrevocably waned, however, since WWII, when bolder and brasher Blackpool to the south became *the* west coast resort for the bucket-and-spade brigade.

The **TIC** *(☎ 582808; Old Station Buildings; open 9.30am-5pm Mon-Sat, year round, & 10am-4pm Sun June-Sept)* is on Central Promenade and runs a free accommodation service. Also in the same building is the **Platform Arts Centre** *(☎ 582803; admission free; open 10am-5pm Mon-Sat)*, a pleasant gallery exhibiting local artists' work.

The old harbour has been refurbished and all that remains is the **stone jetty**, which is adorned with bird sculptures, a tribute to the glorious bay, which is considered Britain's most important wintering site for wildfowl (mainly terns) and wading birds such as ducks and geese. Sunsets here can be quite spectacular. Farther down the promenade is the town's most famous statue (by Graham Ibbeson), that of Ernie Bartholomew, better known as Ernie Morecambe, one half of comic duo Morecambe and Wise (see boxed text).

Trains run hourly from Lancaster (£1.90, 10 minutes).

THE RIBBLE VALLEY

Lancashire's most attractive landscapes lies trapped between the brash tackiness of Blackpool to the west and the sprawling urban conurbations of Preston and Blackburn to the south.

The northern half of the valley is dominated by the sparsely populated moorland of the Forest of Bowland, which is great for walks, while the southern half features the rolling hills, attractive market towns and ruins through which flows the River Ribble.

The Ribble Way, a 70-mile (113km) footpath that follows the River Ribble from its source to the estuary, is one of the more popu-

---

Lancashire's Laurel & Hardy

Britain has never been short of comic talent, but perhaps the greatest comic duo of them all were John Eric Bartholomew (1926–84) and Ernest Wiseman (1925–99), better known as Morecambe and Wise.

As a child, Lancaster-born Bartholomew used to spend his summers in Morecambe. When he decided as a teenager to pursue a career as an entertainer, he took the name of his favourite seaside town and, with his partner Ernie Wise (who merely abbreviated his), made them two of the most famous names in Britain.

Modelled on Laurel and Hardy's brand of clever slapstick comedy punctuated by brilliant one-liners, Morecambe and Wise became a stage sensation in 1941 before transferring their talents to television in the early 1950s. Their humour was clean, innocent and very clever, and much of their success was predicated on their adoption of two distinct characters: Wise as the naive, gullible dreamer and Morecambe as the quick-witted schemer who always seemed to come out on top.

Throughout the 1960s they were the unquestioned kings of British comedy, and audiences tuned into their shows in ever-increasing numbers. Even in the 1970s, when comedy took a quirkier, more cerebral turn with the arrival of the likes of Monty Python's Flying Circus, Morecambe and Wise remained sentimental favourites, a comic duo that had become a veritable institution.

In 1977 they performed many of their old sketches in a once-off Christmas special on BBC that was watched by 28 million people – a record audience and a testament to their popularity. In one particularly memorable scene, Morecambe is standing by a window, staring out on to the street. We hear the sound of an ambulance screeching by at full blast and Morecambe turns to Wise and deadpans, 'He'll never sell ice creams going at that speed'. They just don't write 'em like they used to.

lar walks in the area and passes through Clitheroe.

For online information check out **w** www .lancashirehillcountry.co.uk.

Getting There & Around

Buses regularly run from Preston and Blackburn to Clitheroe and there are hourly trains from Manchester (£7.70, 70 minutes) and Preston (£5.30, 50 minutes).

Your own wheels are the best way to get around. The Bowland Pathfinder Bus only operates on Sunday and bank holidays but connects Clitheroe and Longridge via Chipping, Dunsop Bridge, Newton, Slaidburn and Waddington. A day ticket for adult/child £3.50/2 gives unlimited travel on the service. Contact the TIC in Clitheroe for details.

Pedal Power (☎ 422066; Waddington Rd, Clitheroe) has bicycles for hire, as does **Bowland Cycle Hire** (☎ 446670; Slaidburn) for around £12 per day, £60 per week.

Clitheroe

☎ 01200 • population 13,200

The Ribble Valley's largest market town is best known for its impressive **Norman keep** (admission free; open dawn-dusk daily), built in the 12th century and now standing sadly empty (although there are great views of the river valley below). The extensive grounds are home to the **castle museum** (☎ 424635; adult/child £2/50p; open 11am-5pm daily May-Sept, Sat-Wed only Oct-Dec & Feb-Apr, closed Jan), which has a mildly interesting display on the castle's history.

The rest of the town has a number of pleasant **shops** and **pubs** that can keep you occupied for a few hours.

For information on the town and surrounding area, including a pretty informative leaflet on Pendle Hill (see later), the **TIC** (☎ 425566; fax 426339; 14 Market Place; open 9am-5pm Mon-Sat) is the place to go.

The 17th-century **White Lion Hotel** (☎ 426955; 11 Market Place; rooms from £21), right opposite the TIC, has fairly comfortable rooms.

Brooklyn Guest House (☎ 428268; 32 Pimlico Rd; singles/doubles from £27/42) is a traditional B&B with cosy rooms.

Halpenny's of Clitheroe (☎ 424478; Old Toll House, 1-5 Parson Lane; mains around £5) is a traditional teashop that serves sandwiches and dishes like Lancashire Hot Pot.

Cycling the Ribble Valley

The Ribble Valley is perfect cycling country. It is well covered by sections of the North Lancashire Cycle Way, created in 1982. For more information, contact the **Blazing Saddles Mountain Club** (☎ 01442-844435).

The TIC in Clitheroe (see later) has three useful publications: Bowlands by Bike (free), Mountain Bike Ribble Valley Circular Routes (£2) and Mountain Bike Rides in Gisburn Forest (£1.50).

Pendle Hill

A couple of miles east of Clitheroe is the hill (558m) made famous by the so-called Pendle Witches, 10 women who allegedly practised all kinds of malevolent witchcraft until they were convicted on the sole testimony of one child and hanged in 1612. Local tourist authorities make a big deal of the mythology surrounding the unfortunate women, and every Halloween a pseudomystical ceremony is performed here to commemorate their 'activities'.

If that wasn't enough, the hill is also renowned as the spot where George Fox had a vision in 1652 that led him to found the Quakers. Whatever your thoughts on witchcraft and religious visions, the hill is a great spot to walk to.

Ribchester

West along the river from Clitheroe is the small town of Ribchester, which has an interesting **Roman Museum** (☎ 01254-878261; adult/child £2/1; open 9am-5pm Mon-Fri, noon-5pm weekends) on the site of a fort established in AD 78.

The White Bull (☎ 01254-878303; Church St; singles/doubles £30/45), near the museum, has comfortable rooms.

Forest of Bowland

☎ 01200

This vast, grouse-ridden moorland is somewhat of a misnomer. The use of 'forest' is a throwback to an earlier definition, when it served as a royal hunting ground. Today it is an Area of Outstanding Natural Beauty (AONB), which makes for good walking and cycling, including the Pendle Witch Way, a 45-mile (72km) walk from Pendle Hill to northeast of Lancaster that cuts right through the area, and the North Lancashire Cycle Way that runs along the eastern border. The forest's main town is Slaidburn, about 9 miles (14.5km) north of Clitheroe on the B6478.

Other villages worth exploring are Newton, Whitewell and Dunsop Bridge.

Places to Stay YHA Youth Hostel (☎ 0870 770 6034, fax 446656; King's House; beds £9.50) is in the middle of Slaidburn, in a converted 17th-century village inn.

More luxurious accommodation is limited. **Hark to Bounty Inn** (☎ 446246, fax 446361; Townend; singles/doubles £29.50/59.50), in Slaidburn, is a 13th-century place with wonderfully atmospheric rooms and a pretty good restaurant (mains around £5.75 to £13). It specialises in homemade herb breads.

Elsewhere, we can recommend the **Inn at Whitewell** (☎ 448222, fax 448298; Whitewell Village; singles/doubles from £60/80), once the home of the Forest Keeper, a remarkable place set amid 1.2 hectares of grounds. The rooms are wonderful. The restaurant (mains around £11) specialises in traditional English game dishes.

Camping Barns

For basic, cheap accommodation, camping barns are a good option. Facilities vary between barns, but generally you'd expect to find a shared sleeping area, flush toilet, shower, some type of cooking facility and a place for preparing food.

To check the availability or to make a reservation for any of the barns contact the **Camping Barns Reservation Office** (☎ 420102, fax 420103, e campingbarnsyha@enterprise.net; 6 King St, Clitheroe). The following barns all charge £4.50 per night per person.

Chipping Barn (☎ 01995-61209) is half a mile west of the village of Chipping and handy for the moors. Breakfast can be booked if required.

Hurst Green Barn (☎ 01254-826304), 1½ miles (2.5km) west of Hurst Green village, has metered electricity supply and is well placed for walks in the Forest of Bowland.

Downham Barn (☎ 441242) is at the foot of Pendle Hill and is strategically placed near the Pendle, Ribble and Lancashire Ways.

BLACKPOOL
☎ 01253 • pop 150,600

The unchallenged doyen of the tacky British seaside resort, Blackpool has stubbornly refused to fade in spite of the challenge of budget holidays to southern Spain and other destinations where the sun is guaranteed to shine.

Basically, Blackpool offers little else but unadulterated fun. Its famous 'golden mile' is packed with amusement arcades, fairground rides, fish-and-chip shops, pubs and bingo halls that are aimed to distract and divert with almost complete abandon. It's not sophisticated, but the aggressive marketing strategy that backs it all up certainly is: it cleverly combines the time-tested 'tradition' of a British holiday by a British sea with the high-tech, 21st-century amusements that are bound to thrill even the most unresponsive kid.

Blackpool is famous for its tower, its three piers, its Pleasure Beach and its **Illuminations**, a successful ploy to extend the brief summer holiday season. From early September to early November, 5 miles (8km) of the Promenade are illuminated with thousands of electric and neon lights.

Orientation & Information

Blackpool is surprisingly spread out but can still be managed easily without a car – trams run the entire 7-mile (11.5km) length of the seafront Promenade.

The helpful **TIC** (☎ 478222, fax 478210; e tourism@blackpool.gov.uk; 1 Clifton St; open 8.30am-5pm Mon-Sat, 9am-4pm Sun May-Oct, 8.45am-4pm Mon-Sat Nov-Apr) books local accommodation for free. There's a **branch** (☎ 403223) in Pleasure Beach and by the North Pier (open in summer only).

For online information check out the website w www.blackpooltourism.com.

Blackpool Tower

Built in 1894 this metal tower (☎ 622242; adult/child £11/7; open 10am-11pm daily Easter-Sept, 10am-6pm Sun-Fri & 10am-11pm Sat Oct-Easter) was the second of its kind in Europe and is now Blackpool's best-known symbol. It's over 150m high and houses a vast entertainment complex that should keep the kids happy, including a Dinosaur Ride, jungle gym and an indoor circus that is one of the best in Britain.

The highlight is the magnificent, rococo **ballroom**, with extraordinary sculptured and gilded plasterwork, murals and chandeliers. Couples still glide across the floor to the melodramatic tones of a huge Wurlitzer organ from 2pm to 11pm every day. *Saturday Night Fever* might never have happened.

Blackpool Pleasure Beach & The Sandcastle

The UK's most visited outdoor attraction, drawing over seven million visitors a year, the Pleasure Beach (☎ *0870 444 5566; admission free; open from 10am daily Apr-early Nov, Sat & Sun only early Nov-Mar*) is a 16-hectare collection of over 70 stomach-churning roller coasters, funfair rides and other entertainments.

They include the Big One, the tallest and fastest roller coaster in Europe, reaching a top speed of 85mph (137km/h) before hitting a near-vertical descent of 75m, and the Ice Blast, which delivers you up a 65m steel tower before returning to earth at 80mph (130km/h).

While the hi-tech modern rides will draw the biggest queues, spare a moment to check out the marvellous collection of older 'woodies', as the old-style wooden roller coasters are called. Here you can see the world's first Big Dipper (1923), but be sure to have a go on the Grand National (1935), whose carriages trundle along a 1½-mile (2.5km) long track in an experience that is typically Blackpool – complete with riders waving their hands.

Rides are divided into categories and you can buy tickets for individual categories or for a mixture of them all. An unlimited ticket to all rides costs £25 for one day, £40 for two.

There are no set times for closing, it depends on how busy they are.

Across the road is The Sandcastle (☎ *343 602; admission before/after 2pm £5.20/ 2.50; open from 10am daily May-Oct, Sat & Sun only Nov-Feb*), an indoor water complex complete with its own rides.

Sea Life Centre

Near the Central Pier is this state-of-the-art aquarium (☎ *622445; New Bonny St; adult/child £7/5; open 10am-8pm daily*), which features eight-foot sharks and a giant octopus.

Places to Stay

Blackpool has over 2500 hotels, B&Bs and self-catering units, showing just how popular a holiday destination it is. Even with so many places to stay, it is worth booking ahead during the Illuminations. Competition is fierce so you should have no trouble finding somewhere to stay for around £18 a head, except at the height of summer, when the cheapest rooms go for about £25. The TIC also produces an accommodation guide specifically for gay and lesbian holidaymakers. Good places to start looking are Albert and Hornby Rds, 300m back from the sea but close to the tower, pubs and discos. B&Bs, in Albert Rd, charging around £20 a head include the comfortable **Boltonia Hotel** (☎ *620248, fax 299064; 124-126 Albert Rd*). Nearby, is the pleasant **Hotel Bambi** (☎ *343 756; Bright St; rooms per person £18.50*).

Quiet Gynn Ave, about half a mile north of North Pier is lined with B&Bs charging around £19 per person. Possibilities include the **Bramleigh Hotel** (☎ *351568; 15 Gynn Ave*), the **Haldene Private Hotel** (☎ *353763; 4 Gynn Ave*) or **The Austen** (☎ *351784; 6 Gynn Ave*).

Clifton Hotel (☎ *621481; rooms per person weekdays/weekends £32/40*) at the base of the North Pier with superb sea views, is more upmarket.

Places to Eat

Forget gourmet meals – the Blackpool experience is all about stuffing your face with burgers, hot dogs, doughnuts and fish and chips. Most people eat at their hotels where roast and three vegetables often costs just £4 a head.

There are a few restaurants around Talbot Square (near the TIC) on Queen St, Talbot Rd and Clifton St. The most interesting possibility is the Afro-Caribbean **Lagoonda** (☎ *293837; 37 Queen St; starters around £4, mains £9*), a friendly, no-nonsense eatery that serves up colourful (and often spicy) dishes with a tropical flavour.

Getting There & Away

Blackpool is approximately 50 miles (80km) from both Liverpool and Manchester and 250 miles (400km) from London.

Bus National Express has services to most major towns in Britain. The central coach station is on Talbot Rd, near the town centre. There are five buses daily from London to Blackpool (6 hours, £21), three buses daily from Manchester to Blackpool (1½ hours, £5.25) and Liverpool to Blackpool (1½ hours, £5.25).

Train The main train station is Blackpool North, about five blocks east of the North Pier on Talbot Rd. Trains arrive here from

Preston, Manchester and Liverpool. To get to Blackpool you often have to change in Preston (£5.10, 30 minutes). Trains also run from London (£52.20, four hours).

Getting Around

A one day travel card covering trams and buses costs adult/child £4.75/4.25. With more than 14,000 car parking spaces in Blackpool you'll have no problems parking.

Cumbria

Cumbria is England's most intensely eclectic and beautiful county. At its centre, the Lake District National Park gets most of the attention, with its hulking mountains merging into mirror-topped lakes and its rose-decked towns and villages. But the Eden Valley, to the east, is rolling, verdant and less explored, and the Cumbrian coastline offers unexpected broad strands of open white sand and interesting small towns.

The jam-packed scenic diversity was caused by glacial movements carving the volcanic landscape after the Ice Age. The county's geology is reflected in its kaleidoscope of building materials – from the red sandstone of Carlisle, Penrith and St Bees, to the green slate of Borrowdale, and the light-grey limestone of Kendal.

Cumbria had for a long time an agricultural economy, and its ancient and continuing farming heritage has moulded its landscape. Ever since the championing of the 18th-century Romantic poets – who initiated walking for pleasure rather than practical reasons – and the Victorian arrival of the railway, the Lake District has been a major tourist centre.

In 2001 the foot-and-mouth epidemic closed the countryside, and the entire region took a severe battering, but the following year visitors flooded back.

The M6 and the west-coast railway divide the county into the less-visited eastern third, which runs into the Yorkshire Dales, and Pennines, and the western two-thirds, which includes the Lake District National Park and England's highest mountains. For regional information contact the **Cumbria Tourist Board** (☎ *015394-44444;* ⓦ *www.cumbria-the-lake -district.co.uk; Ashlea, Holly Rd, Windermere*).

ACTIVITIES

Cumbria is dominated by the Lake District National Park, renowned as one of the finest walking areas in Britain – and also great for cycling (off and on road), rock climbing, sailing and much more. This section provides a few tempting ideas; more information is given in the main Activities chapter near the start of this book, with suggestions for shorter walks and rides given throughout this chapter. Regional tourism websites all contain walking and cycling in-

Highlights

- Advancing tentatively over the silver thread of the Hardknott Pass

- Exploring the countryside through the eyes of Wordsworth, Ruskin, Ransome or Potter

- Messing about on Windermere, Coniston Water, Grasmere or Derwent Water

- Surveying the scene while rising to the challenge of Helvellyn, Scafell Pike or the Old Man, to name a few

- Making it out to the vacant wilds of Wasdale

- Discovering the redbrick towns and quiet, verdant pastures of the Eden Valley

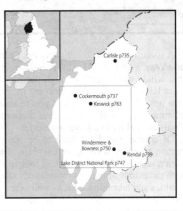

formation, and Travel Information Centres (TICs) all stock leaflets (free) plus maps and guides (usually £1 to £5) covering walking, cycling and other activities.

Walking

There's no official national trail through Cumbria, but one of Britain's most famous long-distance walks, the **Coast to Coast**, strides west to east through the region, and then goes on to conquer the Yorkshire Dales and the North York Moors as well. The route's total length is 191 miles (307km). To do just the Cumbria section, the 82 miles (132km) from St Bees to Shap, takes five days and is an excellent introduction to the region for fit walkers.

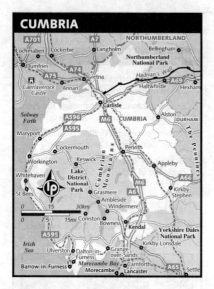

CUMBRIA

A more manageable option is the **Cumbria Way**, a 68-mile (115km) five-day route that winds south–north through the region from Ulverston to Carlisle, keeping mainly (but not wholly) to valleys. If you're short of time, the middle three days between Coniston and Keswick are wonderful.

Of course you don't have to be super-human to enjoy walking in Cumbria. The region is crossed by a network of footpaths, with thousands of options for relaxed valley rambles and lakeside walks, as well as more challenging one-day routes to mountain summits such as Scafell Pike (the highest peak in England), Fairfield, Skiddaw, Helvellyn or the Old Man of Coniston. And don't forget the area outside the National Park – there are many more walks along the often-overlooked Cumbria coast.

Cycling

Cumbria is a good area for cycling, but the steep hills and narrow lanes that sometimes get clogged with traffic can be off-putting. Nevertheless, keen cyclists could consider the waymarked 259-mile (432km) circular **Cumbria Cycle Way**; it can be done in five days, but a full week is better.

Another possibility is the 140-mile (225km) **Sea To Sea Cycle Route** (known as the C2C). This popular route is fast becoming a classic, going west–east across northern

England from Whitehaven or Workington, on the Cumbria coast, through the northern part of the Lake District, and then over the wild North Pennines to finish at Newcastle-upon-Tyne or Sunderland.

Most people will need five days to complete the whole route, and doing just the Cumbria section – as far as Penrith – would be a great weekend outing.

There's also a branch of the route up to Carlisle so you could finish there instead. Established as part of the National Cycle Network (see the main Activities chapter for more detail), the C2C is aimed at road bikes, but there are several optional off-road sections along the way.

For serious mountain biking, or a mix of on and off road, Cumbria has some excellent routes, but (unlike the Yorkshire Dales, for example) the area has few ridable high-level bridleways. Many are former miners' tracks; they lead into the hills and then stop, so you have to come back the same way. The best destination is **Grizedale Forest**, which has a good network of tracks, and you can admire some weird and wonderful open-air sculptures as you ride along.

Other Activities

The mountains of the Lake District offer top-quality **rock climbing**, from steep single-pitch routes to longer and less-demanding classics that experienced climbers can tackle solo.

As befitting a region of lakes, **sailing** is also popular here – notably on Windermere, Derwent Water and Coniston (where canoes and kayaks can also be hired).

GETTING AROUND

Traveline (☎ 0870 608 2608; **w** www.traveline-cumbria.co.uk; open 7am-8pm daily) provides travel information. TICs give away the invaluable Getting Around Cumbria booklet, with timetables for buses, trains and ferries.

Bus

The main operator is **Stagecoach**. Its Explorer tickets (adult/child £7/5 one day, £16/12 four days, £23/16.50 seven days; available on the bus) give unlimited travel on its services in both Cumbria and Lancashire.

Tours

Mountain Goat (☎ 015394-45161; **w** www.mountain-goat.com; Victoria St, Windermere)

offers half-day (£14) and full-day escorted tours (£26) of Cumbria and the Lake District in minivans. If you don't have your own transport this is a good way of getting to some of the more remote areas, especially out of season. There are lots of pick-up points.

CARLISLE
☎ 01228 • pop 72,500

Carlisle is a handsome, sedate town with lots of rosy red sandstone buildings. It has a rich and rollicking history and a small but lively student population.

Its stormy location near the Scottish border has left it with a wealth of historical sights, and you can use it as a springboard for Northumberland, Hadrian's Wall and the beautiful Scottish Borders, as well as for the Lake District.

Five beautiful train journeys start from here (see Getting There & Away later in this section).

History
A Celtic camp or *caer* (preserved in the modern name of Carlisle) possibly provided a site for the Romans, who built a military station here.

Hadrian's Wall was later built a little to the north, and Carlisle became the Roman northwest administrative centre. But even the mighty Roman Empire was hard-pressed to maintain control and the Picts sacked the town in AD 181 and 367.

Carlisle survived into Saxon times under constant pressure from the Scots and was ravaged by Danish Vikings in 875. In 1092 the Normans seized it from the Scots, and William Rufus began construction of the castle and town walls.

The Scots fought back, and took charge of the city from 1136. In 1157 the English were once again ascendant, and Henry II grasped back power. From 1173 to 1461 the Scots attacked nine times, only prevailing once, in 1216 (they were later paid to leave).

From the Middle Ages to the mid-16th century, the Scottish Borders, or the Debateable Lands as they were known, were dominated by great families with complex blood feuds who mercilessly fought and robbed the English, the Scots and each other.

The English developed Carlisle as a military stronghold from where they launched their attacks on the Scots. The city walls,

A Cottage of Your Own

If you're after some Cumbrian self-catering serenity, a good place to start your search is on the Net.

W www.cumbrian-cottages.co.uk
W www.lake-district-cottages.com
W www.cottages4you.co.uk
W www.holidays-in-lakeland.co.uk
W www.heartofthelakes.co.uk
W www.lakelandcottages.co.uk

citadels (two rotund structures to the south of the centre) and the great gates that slammed shut every night got an awful lot of use.

During the Civil War, Carlisle was Royalist and was eventually taken, battered and starving, by the Roundhead Scottish army after a nine-month siege (1644–45). In 1745 Bonnie Prince Charlie swept into town, and proclaimed his father king at the market cross, but it only took a few weeks for the city to be restored to the English.

After the Restoration, a strange thing happened. Peace came at last to Carlisle. So, eventually, did industry, cotton mills and railways.

Orientation & Information
The train station is south of the city centre, a 10-minute walk from Town Hall Square (also known as Greenmarket) and the TIC. The bus station is on Lonsdale St, about 250m east of the square.

The **TIC** (☎ 625600; W *www.historic -carlisle.org.uk; Town Hall Square; open 9.30am-5pm Mon-Sat, 10.30am-4pm Sun May, June & Sept; 9.30am-6pm Mon-Sat, 10.30am-4pm Sun July & Aug; 10am-4pm Mon-Sat Oct-Apr)* is well appointed and has Net access (£1/1.50 for 15/30 minutes).

Open Book Visitor Guiding (☎ 670578; W *www.greatguidedtours.co.uk)* offers various tours of Carlisle and the surrounding area from April to September. Prices range from £1.80/90p to £3/2. It also provides free on-board guides four times daily on the weekend from June to September on the AD122 bus (see Getting There & Around under Hadrian's Wall in the Northeast England chapter for details).

There's a **post office** (*20-34 Warwick Rd)* close to the train station. **Ottakar's Bookstore**

CUMBRIA

(☎ 542300; 66 Scotch St) covers a good selection of topics.

In an emergency, the **Cumberland Infirmary** *(☎ 523444; Newtown Rd)* is half a mile west of the city centre. The **police headquarters** are north of Town Hall Square off Scotch St.

The website **w** www.historic-carlisle.org .uk is a good source of online information.

Carlisle Castle

English Heritage's (EH) dark and brooding Carlisle Castle *(☎ 591922; adult £3.20; open 9.30am-6pm daily Apr-Sept, 10am-4pm Oct-Mar)* was probably built on the site of British and Roman fortresses. The fine Norman keep was built in 1092 by William Rufus, and Mary Queen of Scots was briefly imprisoned here in 1568 after losing the Scottish throne. There's a maze of passages and chambers – it's possible to see stones in the dungeon that prisoners licked to keep themselves hydrated – and great views from the ramparts. It also houses the **Kings Own Royal Border Regiment Museum**, which tells you all you'd ever want to know about Cumbria's Infantry Regiment. There are castle tours daily (£1.50/50p; April to October).

Carlisle Cathedral

The high-vaulted, red sandstone cathedral *(☎ 548151; requested donation £2; open 7.30am-6.15pm Mon-Sat, 7.30am-5pm Sun)* was originally constructed as a priory church in 1122, becoming a cathedral in 1133. During the 1644–45 siege, two-thirds of the nave was torn down to help repair the city wall and castle.

Serious restoration didn't begin until 1853, but a surprising amount survives, including the east window and part of the original Norman nave.

Features to look out for are 15th-century misericords, the fine 14th-century east window, some medieval graffiti, the lovely Brougham Triptych in the north transept, choir carvings and the impressive treasury.

Surrounding the cathedral are other priory relics, including the 16th-century **Fratry** (see Places to Eat) and the **Prior's Tower**.

Tullie House Museum

This excellent museum *(☎ 534781; Castle St; adult/child £5/2.50; open 10am-5pm Mon-Sat, noon-5pm Sun year round)* describes the city's development with flair. Particularly strong on Roman Carlisle, it has lots of information on Hadrian's Wall. The pesky Border Reivers (bandits; see the boxed text later) who used to terrorise the area are given a lively audio-visual treatment.

The Millennium Gallery covers architecture and archaeology, and includes a luminescent glass wall that plays local stories through miniature speakers. Outside, the separate Georgian house has a **gallery of childhood** *(admission free; same hours as museum)*. It's worth dropping into the small art gallery afterwards.

Guildhall Museum

The Guildhall Museum *(☎ 532781; Town Hall Square; admission free; open noon-4.30pm Tues-Sun Apr-Oct)* covers local history. The bulging building itself rewards a look. It was built as a town house in about 1405 but was left to the city and occupied by Carlisle's trade guilds.

Places to Stay

Dalston Hall Caravan Park *(☎ 710165; bus No 91; 2 people, tent & car £6.50-8; open Mar-Nov)* is a grassy 60-pitch site, just off the B5299 to the south of the city. Dalston train station is half a mile away.

Carlisle YHA Hostel *(☎ 0870 770 5752; e dee.carruthers@unn.ac.uk; Bridge Lane; adult £13.50; open mid-July–mid-Sept)* is housed in the Old Brewery Residences (university halls), next to the castle.

Chatsworth Guest House *(☎ 524023; Chatsworth Square; rooms per person £25)* is a charming place and elaborately Victorian, with lovely rooms.

Cornerways Guest House *(☎ 521733; 107 Warwick Rd; rooms with/without en suite per person from £18/16)* is welcoming, with a large tiled hallway, tall ceilings and big windows.

East View Guest House *(☎/fax 522112; w www.eastviewguesthouse.com; 110 Warwick Rd; en-suite rooms per person from £20)* has spacious, straightforward rooms.

Howard Lodge *(☎ 529842; 90 Warwick Rd; en-suite singles/doubles £25/40)* proffers airy, plain rooms.

Langleigh Guest House *(☎ 530440; Howard Place; en-suite singles/doubles from £20/44)* has pretty rooms, with lots of dark wooden furniture.

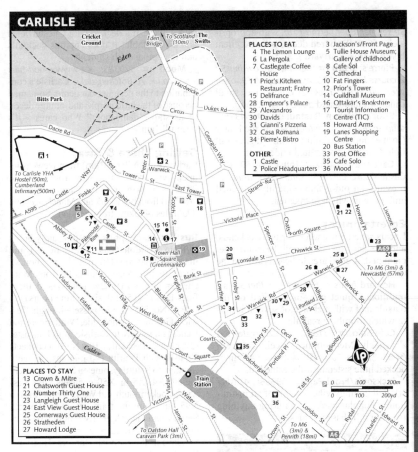

CARLISLE

PLACES TO EAT
4 The Lemon Lounge
6 La Pergola
7 Castlegate Coffee House
11 Prior's Kitchen Restaurant; Fratry
15 Delifrance
28 Emperor's Palace
29 Alexandros
30 Davids
31 Gianni's Pizzeria
32 Casa Romana
34 Pierre's Bistro

OTHER
1 Castle
2 Police Headquarters

3 Jackson's/Front Page
5 Tullie House Museum; Gallery of childhood
8 Cafe Sol
9 Cathedral
10 Fat Fingers
12 Prior's Tower
14 Guildhall Museum
16 Ottakar's Bookstore
17 Tourist Information Centre (TIC)
18 Howard Arms
19 Lanes Shopping Centre
20 Bus Station
33 Post Office
35 Cafe Solo
36 Mood

PLACES TO STAY
13 Crown & Mitre
21 Chatsworth Guest House
22 Number Thirty One
23 Langleigh Guest House
24 East View Guest House
25 Cornerways Guest House
26 Stratheden
27 Howard Lodge

Stratheden (☎ 520192; 93 Warwick Rd; *en-suite singles/doubles £17/38*) is a friendly place, in a small, heritage-listed town house.

Number Thirty One (☎/fax 597080; e bestpep@aol.com; 31 Howard Place; *en-suite singles/doubles from £55/90; open Mar-Oct*), much-lauded, on a leafy, quiet street, has immaculate and spacious rooms.

Crown & Mitre (☎ 525491, fax 514553; w www.crownandmitre-hotel-carlisle.com; *English St; singles/doubles from £95/119*) is Edwardian and overlooks Town Hall Square. The highlight is its hall, backed by stained-glass windows; rooms are plush and plain.

Places to Eat

Alexandros (☎ 592227; 68 Warwick Rd; *mezze around £3, mains £9-11; open Mon-*

Sat) is a cheery, small, delicious Greek restaurant, with yellow-orange walls and maverick, occasionally dancing, staff.

Emperor's Palace (☎ 402976; Warwick Rd; *mains around £8*) is a redbrick, upmarket and tasty Chinese restaurant.

Italian restaurants offer some bargains.

Casa Romana (☎ 591969; 44 Warwick Rd; *mains around £5*) provides food among heavy garlands.

Gianni's Pizzeria (☎ 521093; 3 Cecil St; *mains around £5*) is lantern lit and popular.

La Pergola (☎ 531081; 28 Castle St; *pizza & pasta £4-6*) is a popular place in the basement of an attractive old town house.

Davids (☎ 523578; 62 Warwick Rd; *mains around £10*) offers more refined Italian food.

CUMBRIA

The Lemon Lounge (☎ 546363; 18 Fisher St; set menu per person £18), with appropriately citrus-flavoured decor, is an excellent bistro with a courtyard.

Pierre's Bistro (☎ 515111; 6a Lowther St; 2-course lunch £4.90, mains around £9; open Wed-Sat lunch, Tues-Sat dinner) has small candle-lit tables and good French food.

Prior's Kitchen Restaurant (☎ 543251; soup around £3; open Mon-Sat), in the Fratry (former monks' dining room), dishes out light lunches in a vaulted undercroft.

Castlegate Coffee House (☎ 592353; Castle Court, Castle St; sandwiches from £2) provides an old-fashioned, frilly-curtained ambience in which to take tea.

Entertainment

Locals save their energy for the weekends, and the bars just south of the centre get crammed. A good area to head is around the cathedral.

Howard Arms (☎ 598941; Lowther St) is a traditional, quiet pub, nicely tiled on the outside and with a choice of several rooms in which to imbibe real ale.

Cafe Solo (☎ 631600; 1 Botchergate) has a vaguely Mediterranean feel. **Cafe Sol** (☎ 522211; 31 Castle St) is its nice painting-decked little sister, near the cathedral.

Jackson's/Front Page (☎ 596868; 4 Fisher St), with a dingy vibe, is a bit of an institution; a popular bar/club featuring anything from drum'n'bass to blues.

The Border Reivers

The Reivers were brigands whose backgrounds differed but who had in common a complete disregard for the governments of England and Scotland. For the Reivers, sheep rustling and burning the homes of their enemies were a way of life. As a result, northern Cumbria and Northumberland, the southern Scottish Borders, and Dumfires and Galloway are littered with minor castles and towerhouses, as people struggled to protect themselves.

It wasn't until James VI of Scotland succeeded Elizabeth I of England and united the two countries that order was finally re-asserted. The Reivers are credited with giving the words 'blackmail' and 'bereaved' to the English language.

Fat Fingers (☎ 511774; 48 Abbey St) is a funky place. It's decked with Chesterfields and a pool table; it does copious cocktails and is popular with students.

Mood (☎ 520383; W www.mood-bars-food.co.uk; 70 Botchergate) is Carlisle's contribution to the designer-bar genre. So-named because of the lurid purple-and-orange decor, or its staff's demeanour? Who cares – it's open till 1am.

Getting There & Away

Carlisle is 58 miles (93km) from Newcastle-upon-Tyne, 95 miles (153km) from Glasgow, 98 miles (158km) from Edinburgh, 115 miles (185km) from both York and Manchester and 295 miles (475km) from London.

Bus National Express runs four daily buses to/from London (£34, seven hours) and many to Glasgow (from £17, two hours). Three to five buses run daily from Manchester (from £19, 2¾ hours) and three from Bristol (£50.50, six to nine hours).

Bus No 555 or 556 passes through Keswick, Grasmere, Ambleside, Windermere and Kendal on its way to Carlisle from Lancaster (3¾ hours, three daily). Bus No 104 connects Carlisle with Penrith (40 minutes, 13 daily Monday to Saturday, nine on Sunday), where the No X4, X5 or X50 connects with Keswick, Cockermouth and Workington. Bus No X95 runs from the train station to Hawick, Selkirk and Galashiels (two hours 10 minutes, 11 daily Monday to Saturday, four on Sunday) in the Scottish Borders. Hadrian's Wall bus AD122 (four daily June to September and Saturday and Sunday in May and October) connects Hexham and Carlisle. The No 685 (11 daily Monday to Saturday, eight on Sunday from June to early September) connects Carlisle with Haltwhistle, Hexham, Corbridge and Newcastle.

Train Regular trains come from London Euston (from £70, four hours, nine to 11 daily).

Carlisle is the terminus for five famous picturesque railways; phone ☎ 08457 484950 for timetable details and information on Day Ranger passes.

Cumbrian Coast Line Follows the coast in an arc around to Lancaster (£18.80 single, 3½ hours; see under Cumbrian Coast later in the chapter), with views over the Irish Sea

Glasgow–Carlisle Line The main route north to Glasgow and gives you a taste of the spectacular Scottish landscape – the service run by ScotRail follows the most scenic route (from £20.50, 1½ hours)

Lakes Line Branches off the main north–south Preston and Carlisle line at Oxenholme (£19.10, 45 minutes), outside Kendal, for Windermere

Settle–Carlisle Line Cuts southeast across the Yorkshire Dales through unspoilt countryside (£18.30 single; see the Yorkshire chapter for more details)

Tyne Valley Line Follows Hadrian's Wall to/from Newcastle-upon-Tyne (£9.30 single, 1½ hours; see Hadrian's Wall in the Northeast England chapter)

Getting Around

Carlisle's centre is eminently walkable, but if you need a cab call **Shankland Taxis** (☎ 526253).

COCKERMOUTH

☎ 01900 • pop 7702 • elevation 101m

grew up around the confluence of the Cocker and Derwent rivers. Small cobbled alleys lead off its quiet, leafy streets. Despite its bunch of museums (including Wordsworth's boyhood home) and proximity to the National Park, it hasn't taken off as a tourist centre in the way of the Lake District towns, and has a pleasantly uneventful feel. If you are thinking of heading

off to Buttermere and Borrowdale, it's a good starting point.

Information

The **TIC** (☎ 822634; **e** *email@cockermouth -tic.fsnet.co.uk*; open 9.30am-4.30pm Mon-Sat Apr-June & Oct; 9.30am-4pm Jan-Mar, Nov & Dec; 9.30am-5pm & 10am-2pm Sun July-Sept) is in the town hall. There's Net access at the **library** (☎ 325990; Main St), £1 for 30 minutes, but you'll need to book.

The **main post office** (open 8am-6pm Mon-Sat) is in Lowther Went shopping centre.

Wordsworth House

This Georgian country house (☎ 824805; Main St; admission £3.50; open 10.30am-4.30pm Mon-Fri Apr-Oct, Sat June-Aug), built in 1745, was the early home of William Wordsworth and his sister Dorothy; it's now operated by the National Trust (NT). The walled garden has a terrace where it meets the riverbank, immortalised in *The Prelude*.

The house is furnished as it would have been in the 18th century, and holds some Wordsworth memorabilia. The flagstoned kitchen contains a snug café (scone £1.80).

Other Things to See

Beerphiles will enjoy Mr Jenning's products, brewed here for over 170 years. **Jenning's Brewery** (☎ 821011; adult/child £4.50/1.50),

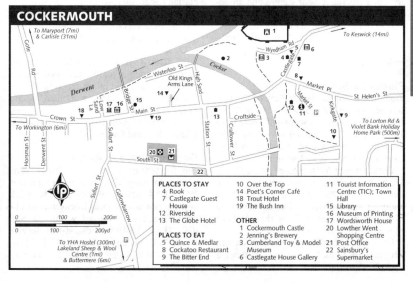

COCKERMOUTH

To Maryport (7mi) & Carlisle (31mi)

To Keswick (14mi)

To Workington (6mi)

To Lorton Rd & Violet Bank Holiday Home Park (500m)

To YHA Hostel (300m) Lakeland Sheep & Wool Centre (1mi) & Buttermere (6mi)

0   100   200m
0   100   200yd

PLACES TO STAY	10 Over the Top	11 Tourist Information
4 Rook	14 Poet's Corner Café	Centre (TIC); Town
7 Castlegate Guest	18 Trout Hotel	Hall
House	19 The Bush Inn	15 Library
12 Riverside		16 Museum of Printing
13 The Globe Hotel	OTHER	17 Wordsworth House
	1 Cockermouth Castle	20 Lowther Went
PLACES TO EAT	2 Jenning's Brewery	Shopping Centre
5 Quince & Medlar	3 Cumberland Toy & Model	21 Post Office
8 Cockatoo Restaurant	Museum	22 Sainsbury's
9 The Bitter End	6 Castlegate House Gallery	Supermarket

CUMBRIA

alongside the River Cocker, offers 1½-hour tours that finish up in the bar. Tours take place at 11am and 2pm Monday to Saturday between March and October; 11am, 12.30pm, 2pm and 3.30pm daily July and August; 2pm January, February, November and December. Children aged under 12 are not admitted.

The **Museum of Printing** (☎ 824984; w www.printinghouse.co.uk; Main St; admission £2.50; open 10am-4pm Mon-Sat) crams in a range of exotic presses and equipment. It's certainly a lesson in how easy computers have made things.

Cumberland Toy & Model Museum (☎ 827606; w www.toymuseum.co.uk; Banks Court; adult/child £3/1.50; open 10am-5pm daily Feb-Nov) is a labour of love. Its small display cases burst with dusty dollhouses, meccano, and much more.

Castlegate House Gallery (☎ 822149; w www.castlegatehouse.co.uk; admission free; open 10.30am-5pm Mon, Tues, Fri & Sat, 10.30am-7pm Wed, 2pm-5pm Sun), opposite Cockermouth Castle, has changing exhibitions of local artists' work in stately Georgian surroundings, and sculpture in its pretty, walled garden.

Lakeland Sheep & Wool Centre (☎ 822673; Egremont Rd; sheep shows adult/child $4/3; open 9.30am-5.30pm, 4 shows daily Sun-Thur Mar-Nov) comprises the Western Lake District Visitor Centre and an eccentric series of sheep shows – a kind of *One Man and his Dog* without the action.

The mainly ruined **Cockermouth Castle** dates from the 12th century, but is a private residence.

Places to Stay

Violet Bank Holiday Home Park (☎ 822169; Simonscales Lane; 2 people, tent & car £7.20-8.20), off Lorton Rd, is about half a mile from the centre and surrounded by rolling hills. Take the local bus from Main St to Rose Lane, from where it's a five-minute walk.

Cockermouth YHA Hostel (☎ 0870 770 5768; e reservations@yha.org.uk; Double Mills; adult £8.75; open daily Apr-Oct) is secluded and pretty, and has 26 beds in a 17th-century water mill on the southern edge of town.

From Main St follow Station St, then turn left into Fern Bank Rd; the hostel is down a track off Fern Bank Rd.

Castlegate Guest House (☎ 826749; 6 Castlegate; rooms per person with/without en suite £20/17.50) is a beautiful Georgian town house.

Riverside (☎ 827504; 12 Market St; rooms per person with/without en suite £20/18.50), well placed on the river, is friendly.

Rook (☎ 828496; 9 Castlegate; en-suite singles £20-22, doubles £34-38) has copious paintings and uneven angles, and is recommended. Rates include breakfast.

The Globe Hotel (☎ 822126; Main St; singles/doubles £28.50/52.50) is mustily traditional. It accommodated Robert Louis Stephenson when he visited Cockermouth in 1871.

Places to Eat

The Bitter End (☎ 828993; Kirkgate) is Cumbria's smallest brewery and a great tucked-away pub with decent food.

Bush Inn (☎ 822064; Main St; lunch £3.95-5.75) is a popular place to mull over a pint, and offers straightforward pub grub.

Cockatoo Restaurant (☎ 826205; 16 Market Place; starters £4-5.50, mains £11-15; open Wed-Mon lunch, Wed-Sat & Mon dinner) does excellent, elaborately, rich dishes.

Quince & Medlar (☎ 823579; 13 Castlegate; starters around £5.50, mains £11.50; open dinner Tues-Sat) is wood-panelled, candlelit, and one of the country's best vegetarian restaurants.

Trout Hotel (☎ 823591; Crown St; mains £5-10) offers good-value traditional bar meals in an upmarket hotel.

Over the Top (☎ 827016; 36 Kirkgate; open 10am-4pm & 7.30pm-9pm Wed-Sat) is a tiny, popular café, furnished with a wooden dresser and mismatched tables.

Poet's Corner Café (☎ 828676; 1 Old Kings Arms Lane; sandwiches £2-3; open 9am-4.30pm Mon-Sat), off Main St, is down a little alley and has outside seating.

Getting There & Away

Bus No 600 travels to/from Carlisle (one hour, eight daily Monday to Saturday). Nos X5 and X4 between Workington, Keswick and Penrith also stop at Cockermouth (14 daily Monday to Saturday, six on Sunday). Bus No 949 is a **dial-a-ride service** (☎ 822795) between Cockermouth and Buttermere (20 minutes, Monday to Thursday and Saturday).

KENDAL

☎ 01539 • pop 24,785

Synonymous with a certain minty, calorific snack, Kendal is a lively town that has had a market since 1189. Its grey-stone streets have a plain charm, and it is home to an exceptional art gallery and collection of museums. The busy, prosperous town was a wool and weaving centre from the Middle Ages to around the 18th century. Pre-mint cake, Kendal was best known for a type of cloth – 'misbegotten knaves in Kendal-green' appear in Shakespeare's *Henry IV Part I*.

The **TIC** *(☎ 725758, fax 734457; *w* www .kendaltown.org; Highgate; open 9am-5pm Mon-Sat Sept-June, 9am-6pm Mon-Sat July-Aug, plus 10am-4pm Sun Apr-Oct)* is in the town hall. There's a **post office** *(open 9am-5.30pm Mon-Sat)* on the main street, Stricklandgate.

Access the Net across the road at the **library** *(☎ 773522)*, at £1 for 30 minutes, or at the YHA Hostel (see Places to Stay).

Things to See & Do

Kendal has three noteworthy **museums** *(adult/child £3.50/1.75; open 10.30am-5pm daily Apr-Oct; 10.30am-4pm Feb, Mar, Nov & Dec)*. Once you've visited one you can see the others for £1 each.

The **Museum of Lakeland Life** *(☎ 722464; *w* www.lakelandmuseum.org.uk)* is a delight, with reconstructed period shops and rooms from different eras, a model of a local mine and lots of information on lost local industries such as bobbin-making. One room recreates the study of Arthur Ransome, author of *Swallows & Amazons*.

Across the courtyard, in the illustrious surroundings of a Palladian mansion, the fine **Abbot Hall Art Gallery** *(☎ 722464; *w* www.abbothall.org.uk)* has a surprisingly rich collection, displaying watercolours, portraits by local man George Romney, and a good small 20th-century collection. The gallery has links with the Tate, so has some superb temporary exhibitions. The nice café serves wholesome grub.

The **Kendal Museum** *(☎ 721374; *w* www .kendalmuseum.org.uk; Station Rd)* houses local archaeological finds, tells the story of Kendal Castle and has a natural history section where stuffed animals glare accusingly from the walls. Alfred Wainwright, of *Pictorial Guide* fame, was honorary curator from

KENDAL

To Staveley (4.5mi) & Windermere (9mi) via A591
Windermere Rd
To Kendal Climbing Wall (1mi) & M6 North
Train Station
Queens' Road
Strickland
Sandes Ave
Fellside
Blackhall
Kent
Stramongate
Finkle St
New Road
Allhallows La
Lowther St
Aynam Road
Beast Banks
Highgate
Captain French La
Gillingate
Kirkland Rd
Parr St
Sunnyside
To Oxenholme (2mi)
To Sizergh Castle (3mi); Levens Hall (5mi) & M6 South (7mi)
Park Side Rd

PLACES TO STAY	20 The Lobster Pot
1 Lakeland Natural Vegetarian Guest House	21 The Moon
2 Martindales	**OTHER**
5 Bridge House	3 Kendal Museum
16 YHA Youth Hostel	6 Post Office
19 Highgate Hotel	7 Library
	8 Bus Station
PLACES TO EAT	13 Tourist Information Centre (TIC)
4 Castle Dairy	14 Burgundy's Wine Bar
9 Chang Thai Restaurant	17 Castle Howe
10 1657 Chocolate House	22 Kendal Castle
11 Olde Fleece	23 Museum of Lakeland Life
12 Paulo Gianni's	24 Abbot Hall Art Gallery; Café
15 Waterside Wholefoods	
18 Brewery; Green Room & Vats Bar	

1945 to 1974. Shrinelike, his office and some possessions are preserved.

Kendal Climbing Wall *(☎ 721766; *w* www.kendalwall.co.uk; Lake District Business Park, Mint Bridge Rd; adult/child £6/5)* has a huge indoor wall and offers courses for all levels. It's worth also clambering up to the 13th-century ruins of **Kendal Castle**, to the east of the river, owned for a long time by the family of Katherine Parr (Henry VIII's last wife), or to the site of **Castle Howe**, a grassy mound – the remains of a Norman motte and bailey – to the west.

Places to Stay

Kendal YHA Hostel *(☎ 0870 7705893; *e* kendal@yha.org.uk; 118 Highgate; adult £13.50, 2-bed rooms £33; open Tues-Sun*

CUMBRIA

The Climbers' Friend

Kendal town will be best known to many as home of Kendal Mint Cake – the high-energy snack that sustained Sir Edmund Hillary and Tensing Norgay on their successful attempt on the summit of Everest in 1953.

These days Kendal seems legally bound to disseminate mint cake, whether brown, white or even chocolate-coated.

---

mid-Feb–Oct, Fri & Sat Nov–mid-Feb) is in part of the 19th-century brewery building. It's pleasant, with pool tables and Net access (five minutes for 50p).

Bridge House *(☎ 722041; w www.bridge house-kendal.co.uk; shared singles/doubles per person £16/18, en-suite doubles per person £25)* is a Georgian place with homely rooms and leafy outlooks.

Lakeland Natural Vegetarian Guest House *(☎ 733011; Low Stack, Queen's Rd; w www .lakelandnatural.co.uk; singles/doubles/triples £37/63/85; 3-course dinner £15.95)* is a high-up, bacon-free Victorian homestead with sweeping views.

Martindales *(☎ 724028; 9/11 Sandes Ave; en-suite singles/doubles with bath £30/47)*, is friendly, with floridly floral rooms, some with river outlooks.

Highgate Hotel *(☎/fax 724229; w www .highgatehotel.co.uk; 128 Highgate; singles/ doubles £30/48)*, welcoming and heritage listed, with a monochrome front, has comfortable rooms.

Places to Eat & Drink

Brewery *(☎ 725133; Highgate; w www.brew eryarts.co.uk)* is a wonderful arts complex in a rambling building that once kept Westmorland in beer. Its **Green Room & Vats Bar** *(mains from £5)* has outside seating, a laid-back atmosphere and good food.

Castle Dairy *(☎ 730334; 26 Wildman St; open Tues-Sat, Sun lunch only)*, in a lovely 14th-century house, specialises in evening roasts but does lighter daytime meals.

Chang Thai Restaurant *(Stramongate; dishes £7-8)* has dark red walls and a warmly lit, romantic atmosphere.

The Lobster Pot *(☎ 729696; 167-169 Highgate; fish & chips £4)*, opposite Highgate Hotel, has fine takeaway fish and chips.

The Moon *(☎ 729254; 129 Highgate; mains £8.75-13.75; open Wed-Sun)*, small and in cheerful hues of blue, does good modern British.

Paulo Gianni's *(☎ 736581; 21a Stramongate; mains around £5-8)* is a lively, cosy restaurant, popular with local office workers, serving admirable pizza and pasta.

Kendal groans with good cafés. Try **1657 Chocolate House** *(☎ 740702; w www.the chocolatehouse.co.uk; 54 Branthwaite Brow)*, with its low beams and faded chintz.

Waterside Wholefoods *(☎ 729743; Kent View, Waterside; open 8.30am-4.30pm Mon-Sat)* serves up tasty, imaginative veggie food by the river.

Burgundy's Wine Bar is a popular, rambling bar with table football – it's the place to go for local ale. **Olde Fleece** *(Highgate)* is a refurbished, comfortable pub.

Getting There & Around

Kendal station is on the branch train line from Windermere (15 minutes) to Oxenholme. But Oxenholme is only 2 miles (3km) to the south of town, with trains from Carlisle (£16, one hour) and London Euston (£60, 3¾ hours).

Bus No X35 runs from Barrow, via Ulverston (1¼ hours, 12 daily Monday to Saturday, three on Sunday). Bus No 555 or 556 (five to 10 daily) stops at Kendal, Windermere, Ambleside, Grasmere and Keswick.

Bike hire is available at **Askew Cycles** *(☎ 728057; Old Brewery, Wildman St)* for £12 per day.

AROUND KENDAL
Sizergh Castle

Signposted 3½ miles (5.5km) south of Kendal off the A590 is Sizergh Castle *(NT; ☎ 560070; bus No 555/556 from Kendal; admission £5, garden only £2.50; castle open 1.30pm-5.30pm Sun-Thur Easter-Oct, garden open from 12.30pm)*, home of the Strickland family for over 700 years. Central to its construction is a 14th-century *pele* tower (fortified dwelling).

Much of the interior is Elizabethan, with some stunning carved wooden chimney pieces.

The pride and joy is the inlaid chamber panelling, which was sold to London's Victoria & Albert Museum during hard times, and returned after 100 years.

Levens Hall

Another 2 miles (3km) south is Levens Hall (☎ 60321; w www.levenshall.co.uk; bus No 555/556; house & garden adult/child £6.50/ 3.20, gardens only £5/2.50; house open noon-5pm, gardens 10am-5pm Sun-Thur Apr– mid-Oct), an Elizabethan mansion built around a c. 1350 *pele* tower. The beautifully kept house contains some wonderful paintings and Jacobean furniture. The shapely topiary garden, unchanged in design since 1694, resembles a backdrop for *Alice in Wonderland* and is alone worth the stop.

Cumbrian Coast

The sweep of Morecambe Bay has an unnerving sense of space, with some interesting towns in the hills above: genteel Grange, medieval Cartmel and lively Ulverston. Northwards along the coast there's some striking scenery tempered by declining industrial towns. Calm Ravenglass is the starting point for *La al Ratty*, a small train that will shift you into wild and lovely Eskdale – the gateway to remote Wast Water. Less-charming Sellafield, a nuclear power station, dominates the next part of the coast, and beyond it is the straggling town of St Bees, and Whitehaven – a sleepy, historic port.

Most of the places covered in this section can be found on the Lake District National Park map.

Getting Around

The Cumbrian Coast railway line loops 120 miles from Carlisle to Lancaster (both cities are on the main line between London and Glasgow). Trains run about hourly, and a single costs £18.80. Phone ☎ 08457 484950 for full details. Although most of it lies outside the park boundary, the line provides useful access points for the western lakes.

The railway line's famous Carnforth station was immortalised in David Lean's 1945 film, a classic of English restraint, *Brief Encounter* – the original clock still hangs near where Trevor Howard bumped into Celia Johnson.

GRANGE-OVER-SANDS
☎ 015395 • pop 4041

Sedate Edwardian Grange sits surrounded by hilly greenery, above the broad expanse of beautiful Morecambe Bay. It's possible to walk across the endless flats at low tide but only with the official Queen's guide (a role established in 1536), as the crossing is otherwise dangerous, fraught with tides and quicksand. Once this was a popular shortcut to the Lake District. Cartmel monks moonlighted as guides for travellers, and horse-drawn coaches plied the route till 1857. The attractive resort town grew up around the flow of travellers. Today there's not much to keep you here unless you're after a peaceful haven for your twilight years. The crossing (8 miles, 13km; w www.morecambebay.org.uk) takes around 3½ hours.

The TIC (☎ 34026; Victoria Hall, Main St; open 10am-5pm daily Easter-Oct) grudgingly supplies all sorts of local information.

Places to Stay & Eat

Arnside YHA Hostel (☎ 01524-761781; e arnside@yha.org.uk; Redhills Rd, Arnside; adult £10.25; open Feb-Nov) is a tree-shaded stone house. It's a mile from Arnside station, which is a 10-minute train ride from Grange, or you can take bus No 552 (£5.80, 30 minutes, seven daily Monday to Friday, five daily on Saturday).

Kents Bank Rd, running south of Grange's centre, is full of places to stay.

Thornfield House (☎ 32512; w www.thorn fieldhouse.co.uk; rooms per person £22.50-25) is welcoming, with mighty fine bay views.

Grange Hotel (☎ 33666; w www.grange -hotel.co.uk; Station Square; rooms per person from £59, bay view extra £7.50-15), on the hill across from the train station, is grand and upmarket.

Grange has numerous teashops, but is lacking in restaurants.

Higginsons (☎ 34367; Keswick House; Main St), one of England's best butchers, serves up the finest pies and pasties for miles around.

The Coffee Pot (☎ 33269; Main St; sandwiches around £3), across from the TIC, has views of Morecambe Bay.

Getting There & Away

Both the train station and bus stop are a short walk north of the TIC. Bus No X35 from Kendal costs £3 (25 minutes, 12 daily), but it's more fun and scenic to take the train to Grange, which is on the Cumbrian Coast Line, with frequent connections to Lancaster

CUMBRIA

(£4.75, 25 minutes, hourly) and Carlisle (£49, three hours, hourly). Bus No 532 runs from Cartmel (£2.40, 25 minutes, six daily) from Monday to Saturday, and No X35 from Barrow (£3, 50 minutes, 12 daily Monday to Saturday) via Ulverston.

AROUND GRANGE
Cartmel
☎ 015395 • pop 1938

A mile west of Grange-over-Sands, captivating Cartmel is a village with medieval buildings, a small market square and a n enormous and magnificent 12th-century church.

Fortunately the church, **Cartmel Priory** *(☎ 36261; open 9am-5.30pm May-Oct, 9am-3.30pm Nov-Apr)*, wasn't demolished during the dissolution of the monasteries in the 16th century, due to intervention by parishioners – parish churches frequently escaped destruction. It survives as one of the finest in the northwest. The 45-foot-high 15th-century east window is luminous, although much of the original glass was destroyed. The intricately carved choir stalls date from 1440, and the surviving half of the finely worked Harrington tomb from the 13th century. Skulls and hourglasses, *momento mori*, are carved in the floor – 17th- and 18th-century reminders of mortality. It has guided tours (adult/child £2/1) at 11am and 2pm Wednesday from May to October. The concerts on summer Saturdays are recommended.

Cartmel Heritage Centre *(☎ 36874; Market Square; adult/child £2/50p; open 10am-4pm Wed-Sun Apr-Oct, 10am-4pm Sat & Sun Nov-Mar)*, in the 14th-century priory gatehouse, has quirkily put-together displays offering a brief glimpse into local history, as well as a medieval privy.

Apart from the priory, Cartmel is famous for its racecourse – the smallest in the country – and sticky-toffee pudding. Set by the River Eea, the course comes alive on race days (last weekend in May and in August) and the town is packed to the gunnels (accommodation must be booked well ahead).

Places to Stay & Eat Just south of the village, **Cartmel Caravan & Camping Park** *(☎ 36270; Wells House Farm; 2-person tent sites & car £8-10)* occupies a tranquil site.

Bank Court Cottage *(☎ 36593; rooms per person £18.50)* is quiet, tucked away down an alleyway off Market Square.

Bluebell House *(☎ 36658; Devonshire Square; en-suite rooms per person from £25)* is a former coaching inn built around 1660, with views of the priory and comfortable rooms.

The pubs are the best place for a bite to eat. **Kings Arms** *(☎ 36220; lunch £4-7, dinner £7-12)* is multiroomed with tables spilling out onto the pretty square.

Cavendish Arms *(☎ 36240; B&B per person £30-40, mains £8-12)* is the oldest village pub, an ivy-covered 16th-century inn with great food and its own excellent beer. It's also possible to stay the night in cosy, old-fashioned rooms.

You can stock up on mouth-watering sticky-toffee pudding at the **Cartmel Village Shop** *(☎ 36201)* on the square.

Getting There & Away On a regular basis, Monday to Saturday, bus No 532 runs from Grange to Cartmel (25 minutes, 10 daily) via Cark, 2 miles (3km) to the southwest, which is the nearest train link.

Holker Hall & Lakeland Motor Museum

Set in undulating, formal gardens, Holker Hall *(☎ 58328; adult/child £8.75/4.65, house & grounds only £6.90/4.20, grounds only £3.95/2.25; house open 10.30am-4.30pm Sun-Fri, grounds 10am-6pm, last admission 4.30pm)* dates from the 16th century but is mainly a confident Gothic Victorian creation. The interior offers more high Victoriana, with lots of dignified drapery and grand woodcarving. There's a stately deer park, and the stables house the Lakeland Motor Museum *(adult/child £6.90/4.20; open 10.30am-4.45pm)*, with truckloads of classic cars, including a replica of Donald Campbell's Bluebird.

ULVERSTON
☎ 01229 • pop 11,866

Ulverston's sloping, charismatic, cobbled streets radiate out from a small, lively marketplace. There's a cheery, friendly air about the town, with a palpable sense of community. This is enhanced by the numerous annual festivals, which feature lots of visitor-pleasing English traditions, such as morris dancing – that most sexless of fertility rites. Ulverston is also the starting point for the Cumbria Way.

The helpful **TIC** (☎ *587120, fax 582626;* **W** *www.ulverston.net; Coronation Hall, County Square; open 9am-5pm Mon-Sat)* can help with booking accommodation along the Cumbria Way. Access the Internet at the **library** (☎ *894151; Kings Rd)*; 30 minutes for £1.minutes for £1.

Things to See
Comedian Stan Laurel was born at 3 Argyle St in 1890. Fans will want to make the pilgrimage to the **Laurel & Hardy Museum** (☎ *582 292; 4c Upper Brook St; adult/child £2/1; open 10am-4.30pm daily Feb-Dec)*, which has floor-to-ceiling memorabilia and shows some of their movies too.

A tower on top of Hoad Hill is visible from all around town, and provides good views. It commemorates local hero Sir John Barrow (1764–1848), explorer and author of *Mutiny of the Bounty* (1831). Part of the town's **Heritage Centre** (☎ *583811; John Barrow's Cottage; admission free; open 11am-4pm Sat, noon-4pm Sun)* is housed in the tiny yeoman's cottage, dating from 1549, where he was born, with some 16th-century-style furnishings. By the time you read this, the rest of the heritage centre may've found a home; contact the TIC for details.

Conishead Priory (☎ *584029;* **W** *www .manjushri.org.uk; temple open to public 2pm-4pm Sat & Sun)* is a dramatic 19th-century Gothic mansion 2 miles (3km) south of Ulverston on the A5087 coast road. The site dates back to 1160, when there was a leper hospital here. The priory has been home to a Manjushri Buddhist Centre since 1977, with a permanent community of around 100. It has been beautifully restored and a 24-square-metre Buddhist temple, housing some of the largest Buddhist statues in Europe, has been added to the grounds.

Tours (adult/child £2/1) leave at 2.30pm and 3.45pm, and weekend meditation retreats are available throughout the year. Bus No 11 makes regular trips from Ulverston to Barrow-in-Furness via the priory (12 daily Monday to Saturday).

Places to Stay
Walkers Hostel (☎/fax *585588;* **W** *www .walkershostel.freeserve.co.uk; Oubas Hill; B&B dorm rooms £12, B&B plus dinner £18)* is cheery and a mine of information on local and Lake District walks. It's a 10-minute walk from the centre on the A590 to Kendal.

Cheap B&B is also available in private rooms.

Church Walk House (☎ *582211; Church Walk; en-suite singles/doubles from £25/45)* has big, bright rooms, right in the centre of town.

Rock House (☎ *586879; 1 Alexander Rd; rooms per person £20)* is a large, well-kept Victorian place.

Trinity House Hotel (☎ *587639;* **W** *www .training hotel.co.uk; Princes St; B&B singles Mon-Fri £52-58, doubles £64-76, rooms only Sat & Sun £44)* has high-ceilinged, comfortable rooms.

The Whitehouse (☎ *583340; Market St; en-suite singles/doubles £25/44)*, a wonderful maze of a house, is a superbly renovated 300-year-old cottage.

Places to Eat
Farmers Arms (☎ *584469; Lowick Garden; mains from £6)* spills out into the marketplace and serves elaborate pub food.

Rose & Crown (☎ *583094; King St; mains around £5)* is a convivial, cosy pub with several rooms, excellent food and enormous servings.

Ugly Duckling Restaurant (☎ *581573; 1 Buxton Place; mains around £12.95; open evenings only Tues-Sat)* serves upmarket cuisine in a lace-curtained setting.

Hot Mango Cafe (☎ *584866; 27 King St; sandwiches from £4.95; open Tues-Sat)*, filled with wooden tables, is a buzzing place for a snack.

Moonshadow Gallery Café (☎ *588828; 46 Market St; sandwiches £3.55; open Tues-Sat)* is a calm space above a gallery, serving vegetarian wholefood.

Getting There & Away
Regular trains from Carlisle (£29.80, 2½ hours) and Lancaster (£8.60, 40 minutes) stop at Ulverston station, five-minutes' walk south of the centre. To reach Cartmel by bus, you have to change at Grange (eight daily Monday to Saturday).

BARROW-IN-FURNESS
☎ 01229 • pop 70,100
Stolid-looking even on the sunniest day, homely Barrow has wide streets and lots of 1960s blocks, interspersed with redbrick Victorian dock buildings. Developed in 1849 to supply the railway with iron and

CUMBRIA

steel, it later became a busy port. Ships are still fitted down at the docks. Despite its unpromising appearance, it's a friendly place, and there are some interesting sights.

The slightly bewildered TIC (☎ 894784; Forum 28, Duke St; open 9.30am-5pm Mon-Wed & Fri, 10.30am-5pm Thur year round, & 10am-4pm Sat Apr-Oct, 10am-2pm Sat Nov-Mar) is opposite the town hall and books accommodation.

Barrow's **Dock Museum** (☎ 89444; w www.dockmuseum.org.uk; admission free; open 10am-5pm Tues-Fri, 11am-5pm Sat & Sun Apr-Oct; 10.30am-4pm Wed-Fri, 11am-4pm Sat & Sun Nov–mid-Apr) is housed in a modern building built over a heritage-listed dry dock. It has a thought-provoking history of the town, and shows its fast development from a village to a huge shipbuilding port and industrial centre, with lots of anecdotal colour.

Getting There & Away
There are frequent connections from Carlisle (£30, 2½ hours, hourly) and Lancaster (£9.30, one hour, hourly) as Barrow is on the Cumbrian Coast Line. There is also a direct rail link from Manchester airport to Barrow (two hours). Bus No 618 runs to Barrow from Ambleside via Ulverston and Windermere (70 minutes, five daily Monday to Saturday, three on Sunday). Bus No X35 runs from Kendal (1¼ hours, 12 daily Monday to Saturday) via Grange and Ulverston.

AROUND BARROW-IN-FURNESS
Furness Abbey
The romantic rose-coloured ruins of Furness Abbey (EH; ☎ 823420; admission £2.80; open 10am-6pm daily Apr-Sept, 10am-5pm Oct, 10am-4pm Wed-Sun Nov-Mar) are hidden away in the green and shady 'Vale of Deadly Nightshade', 1½ miles (2.5km) north of Barrow-in-Furness. Beautifully carved arches and elegant vaulting run throughout the dramatic remnants, and the infirmary chapel is particularly well preserved. A small museum on site relates the story of the abbey and contains a superb collection of stone carvings, including two rare 13th-century effigies of knights in armour.

The abbey was founded by Savignac monks after a donation of land by Stephen (later king), Earl of Mortain in 1127. Following a merge with the Cistercian order,

the abbey became among the most powerful in the north and its wealth attracted many visitors, some unwelcome, such as the Scots who raided it twice. It survived until 1537 at which time Henry VIII dissolved the monasteries for his own benefit.

The redbrick **Abbey Inn** (☎ 825359; Abbey Approach; mains around £5.50), just outside the abbey entrance, will feed you up.

You can pick up bus No 6 or 6A from Barrow, which passes by the abbey on a regular basis.

Piel Castle
Small and mysterious, Piel Island is visible from the shore of so-called Roa Island (attached to the mainland). It's home to some dark castle ruins, a lifeboat station, a lone pub and a couple of houses.

Piel Castle was built by the monks of Furness Abbey as a defensive outpost against raids. It served as a fortified warehouse for trading and smuggling goods to Ireland – the abbey was a large player in such manoeuvres. The landlord of the Ship Inn is traditionally called the 'King of Piel', which dates from when Lambert Simnel declared himself king on landing here in 1487.

The windswept island and overgrown castle (which dates from the 14th century) are normally accessible by ferry from Roa Island, 5 miles (8km) southeast of Barrow. The **ferry** (☎ 835809) runs 11am to 5pm Monday to Saturday and 11am to 6pm Sunday, Easter to September (adult/child single £1.50/75p) – but telephone in advance.

You can grab a bite to eat at **Bosun's Locker Cafe** (sandwiches £1.60; open Tues-Sun) next to the ferry landing on the mainland.

Bus No 11 runs to Ulverston from Barrow-in-Furness via Roa Island regularly.

South Lakes Wild Animal Park
This park (☎ 466086; w www.wildanimalpark.co.uk; adult/child £7/5; open 10am-5pm daily), 5 miles (8km) north of Barrow near Dalton-in-Furness, is no caged-up zoo. It's designed with animals, rather than visitors, in mind. Trenches and ditches are used rather than cages and it's possible to get up close to a number of animals. Monkeys and lemurs jump from tree to tree with few restrictions.

The park showpiece has to be tiger feeding at 2.30pm daily. Unique to Europe, enrichment feeding (making the tigers climb and 'hunt' for their food) is quite a sight and shows just how agile and strong these big cats are. You can also check out spectacled bears and the world's largest collection of kangaroos.

From June to September a bus links the zoo to both the Dalton and Askam rail stations; call the zoo for details.

RAVENGLASS & AROUND
Ravenglass
It's difficult to envisage the little coastal village of Ravenglass, a remote and quiet seaside cluster of houses, 27 miles (44km) north of Barrow, as an important Roman naval port. The Romans were drawn to its sheltered harbour, but all that remains of their substantial fort are the unusually intact walls of a 4th-century **Bath House** that stand 3.75m high, about half a mile from the train station down a signposted track. Ravenglass itself is on the Cumbrian Coast Line so there are frequent links north and south along the coast.

At Ravenglass you can swap from the normal train line to the private narrow-gauge **Ravenglass & Eskdale Railway** (☎ 01229-717171; W www.ravenglass-railway.co.uk; adult/child £7.40/3.70), affectionately known as La al Ratty, originally built in 1875 to carry iron ore. There's an interesting little museum at the station, and a Wainwright booklet called Walks from Ratty (£1.50) available from the railway.

Ratty beautiful 7-mile (11km) journey runs up into Eskdale and the foothills of the Lake District mountains. From Eskdale by car you can drive over the thrilling and beautiful Hardknott Pass and Wrynose Pass down into Little Langdale (see later in the chapter). But, be warned: the road takes sharp bends without warning. The grade is 1 in 4 in places and single lane so make sure those brakes are in perfect working order. The passes can be gruesome in bad weather and on busy bank holiday weekends, and they are closed in winter.

A mile south of Ravenglass is **Muncaster Castle** (☎ 01229-717614; W www.muncaster .co.uk; adult/child £5.50/3.50 gardens, owl centre & maze, £2/1.50), a grand old place with lots of classic castle clutter, dating from the 14th century and rebuilt in the 19th. Audio tours provide anecdotes on history and hauntings. The jumbled, profuse grounds are extensive and include an owl centre. Bus No 6 from Whitehaven stops at Ravenglass and terminates at Muncaster (70 minutes, at least five daily). Bus X6 travels the same route on Sunday (four daily).

Sellafield Nuclear Power Plant
Controversial **Sellafield**, a huge local employer, and its curiously popular **visitor centre** (☎ 019467-27027; W www.bnfl.com; admission free; open 10am-6pm daily Apr-Oct, 10am-4pm daily Nov-Mar) are 5 miles (8km) farther north.

Making radioactivity fun is Sparking Reaction, a huge-scale interactive exhibition created by the Science Museum. It does its PR best, focusing on opportunities for you to express your views, including an 'Immersion Cinema', where you get to choose a future means of power, see the result of your decision and sympathise with difficulties facing the poor energy supremos.

St Bees
☎ 01946 • pop 1655
The village of St Bees straggles out over gentle hills, fronted by a sweep of white sand against rusty-coloured rocks. It's the start of Alfred Wainwright's Coast-to-Coast Walk. The surrounding cliff tops are worth exploring, with St Bees Head RSPB (Royal Society for the Protection of Birds) Nature Reserve to the south.

A friendy and quiet community, with terracotta-coloured buildings dotting the central street, St Bees has a long history. The local school was founded in 1583 and the **priory church** dates from the 12th century. According to legend, an Irish girl, Bega, landed here having escaped marriage to an unappealing Viking and became a hermit in around 900. The Normans founded the priory and rebuilt her church.

Places to Stay & Eat Comfy old-fashioned rooms are available at **Stonehouse Farm** (☎ 822224; Main St; rooms per person from £20), a working farm.

Queens Hotel (☎ 822287; Main St; singles/ doubles £35/50; sandwiches from £2.35, mains from £6.50) is an ivy-covered, friendly freehouse, with excellent food, a conservatory and beer garden, and comfortable rooms.

Fairladies Barn (☎ 822718; W www.fair ladiesbarn.co.uk; Main St; singles/doubles

CUMBRIA

£20/36, with en suite £25/40), a converted 17th-century barn, offers 10 pleasant rooms.

French Connection (☎ 822600; Old Railway Station; starters £5.25, mains £11.50-13.50; open Tues-Sat dinner), in the former station waiting room and booking office, serves good food, with fresh fish daily.

Getting There & Away St Bees is on the Cumbrian Coast Line. Bus Nos 20 and X6 run regularly from Whitehaven (10 to 25 minutes, six to 10 daily Monday to Saturday, four on Sunday).

Whitehaven
☎ 01946 • pop 26,443
This small Georgian harbour town was at one time the third-largest port in England and a distasteful mover and shaker in the slave trade. Hustle and bustle is absent these days, but a facelift has spruced up the now sleepy marina, and its pastel-painted buildings fairly gleam along the front.

The **TIC** (☎ 852939, fax 852954; Market Hall, Market Place; open 9.30am-5pm daily Apr-Oct, 10am-4.30pm Mon-Sat Nov-Mar) stocks lots of information on the surrounding area.

The Beacon (☎ 592302; West Stand; adult/child £4.25/2.80; open 10am-5.30pm Tues-Sun Apr-Oct, 10am-4.30pm Nov-Mar) is a fine heritage centre overlooking the harbour. It shines a light on local mining and shipbuilding, trade and smuggling. The national meteorological obsession is given an outlet on the top floor, where you can even pretend to do a TV weather forecast (there goes another ambition fulfilled). Tickets combining admission with the Rum Story cost £7.50/5.

The Rum Story (☎ 592933; Lowther St; adult/child £4.50/2.95; open 10am-6pm daily Easter-Sept, 10am-4pm Wed-Sun Oct-Easter), housed in a former 18th-century warehouse, deals with the area's boozy connections. Intoxicating displays – complete with sounds and smells – take you through the slave trade, the Royal Navy, prohibition and the jazz age.

If you need to stay in Whitehaven try the inviting Georgian **Corkickle Guest House** (☎ 692073; 1 Corkickle; singles £22.50-30, en-suite doubles £45), 300m northeast of Corkickle train station.

Ali-Taj Tandoori Restaurant (☎ 693085; 34 Tangier St; mains £5-9) is a spacious, richly decorated place serving up good Indian food.

Henry Hornblowers (☎ 590492; Church St; starters £5, mains £13; open Wed-Sun dinner) provides modern British food in a heritage-listed building with a nautical theme.

Richardsons Tea Rooms (☎ 599860; 151 Queen St; snacks £1-2, meals £3; open Mon-Sat) is small and friendly, opening onto an attractive little courtyard.

Whitehaven is on the Cumbrian Coast Line with hourly trains in each direction.

The Lake District

I wandered lonely as a cloud
That floats on high o'er dales and hills
When all at once I saw a crowd...
William Wordsworth

If the Lake District had not existed, a Romantic poet would have had to have invented it. The surroundings are breathtaking, with ochre and green hills surrounding cobbled towns and the shapes of stark mountains bouncing back from the shimmering lakes. England's walking heartland, the area contains some of the country's finest footpaths and a huge choice of easy and challenging routes. It's a good place to feed your soul: by bike, in restaurants, on foot, in pubs, on the water, and on the literary trail.

But a hungry 14 million annual visitors pour in to sample these delights, and in summer that cloud-like feeling may seem elusive. If you can avoid the main roads and towns in mid-July to August and on bank holidays, it'll help. But the westernmost lakes are never so busy, and whatever the season, you'll always find somewhere to escape to.

The NT owns a quarter of the area, partly thanks to Beatrix Potter who sold it half of her large estate and bequeathed the rest.

Orientation
The Lake District has a rough star formation, with the highest ground at its centre, and valleys, ridges and lakes radiating out. The central area is crossed with countless footpaths, but few roads – a hikers' playground.

The main bases are Keswick in the north and Windermere and Bowness in the south. Ambleside and Coniston are less hectic alter-

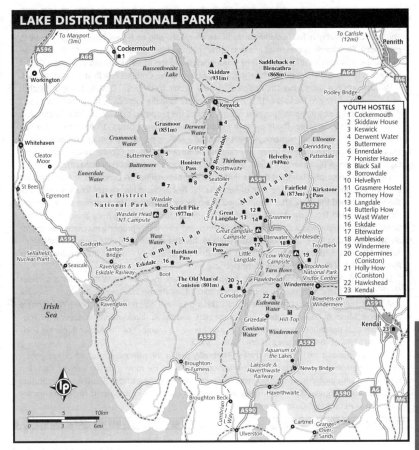

LAKE DISTRICT NATIONAL PARK

YOUTH HOSTELS
1 Cockermouth
2 Skiddaw House
3 Keswick
4 Derwent Water
5 Buttermere
6 Ennerdale
7 Honister Hause
8 Black Sail
9 Borrowdale
10 Helvellyn
11 Grasmere Hostel
12 Thorney How
13 Langdale
14 Butterlip How
15 Wast Water
16 Eskdale
17 Elterwater
18 Ambleside
19 Windermere
20 Coppermines (Coniston)
21 Holly How (Coniston)
22 Hawkshead
23 Kendal

CUMBRIA

natives. Windermere is the biggest, busiest lake. Ullswater, Coniston and Derwent Water have a speed restriction of 10mph, while there are no powerboats on Grasmere, Crummock Water or Buttermere. Wast Water feels wildest and is in the least accessible valley.

Information

The many TICs stock mountains of information. The Windermere and Keswick TICs are good places to start exploring; both have free local booking services. The national park runs nine TICs in the area, and a **visitor centre** (☎ 015394-46601; **w** www.lake-district .gov.uk) at Brockhole, on the A591 near Windermere. Another tourist board site is at **w** www.golakes.co.uk, and **w** www.lakedis trictoutdoors.co.uk covers activities.

Pathfinder produces *The Lake District Walks* books, which have useful extracts from Ordnance Survey (OS) maps, and Gordon Brown's *100 Lake District Walks* should keep you going. *A Walk Round the Lakes* by Hunter Davies will fill in some background. Alfred Wainwright's seven-volume, hand-written and drawn *Pictorial Guide to the Lakeland Fells* is a classic (but should be used with an OS map).

Many of the TICs sell cheap leaflets covering local walks of the area, which are a good alternative to lugging around a book.

Walking & Cycling

Walking or cycling are the best ways of getting around, but bear in mind that mountain weather conditions prevail and the going

A Watery Literary Trail

The Lake District scenery has hosted an array of literary greats, who each have helped shape the area's mythology. Their carefully preserved artefacts attract pilgrims from all over the world. Quite disparate, they had in common an affection for their surroundings, and the allure of this aspect of Lake-District heritage is to locate their work – perhaps getting a photo of Dove Cottage, or a Beatrix Potter box set.

Wordsworth has done more than anyone to draw people to the area. Despite being the author of *A Complete Guide to the Lakes* (1810), which he wrote to make some cash, he probably wouldn't have been best pleased. He campaigned fiercely against the proposed railway link from Oxenholme to Kendal, managing to get the line drawn against the marauding hoards at Windermere. He had moved here in 1799, and numerous others followed – Coleridge, opium-eating De Quincey, and many other illustrious writers. Today you can visit Wordsworth House (Cockermouth), Dove Cottage and his grave (Grasmere), Rydal Mount (Ambleside) and his school (Hawkshead).

The anthropomorphic books of Beatrix Potter are international hits. A Londoner, she used to visit the Lakes on family holidays. *The Tale of Peter Rabbit* first appeared in a letter to a sick child, and she self-published the work after being turned down by six publishers. Her immense success meant she could buy Hill Top Farm (Near Sawrey), which appears to have sprung from one of her illustrations. Later in life she was a passionate sheep farmer and an unlikely property magnate. Her originals are displayed at the Beatrix Potter Gallery (Hawkshead) and some early drawings at Ambleside's Armitt Museum. Serious scholars can join the **Beatrix Potter Society** – noting that it is 'not a Peter Rabbit fan club' (**W** www.beatrixpottersociety.org.uk).

Leeds-born Arthur Ransome spent his boyhood summers by Coniston Water. After a summer teaching some friends' children to sail, he was inspired to write the *Swallows & Amazons* series for and about them. A room at the Museum of Lakeland Life is dedicated to Ransome, Windermere Steamboat Museum houses Captain Flint's houseboat, and the Ruskin Museum touches on the copper mines that pervade *Pigeon Post*. You can also become a member of the **Arthur Ransome Society** (☎ 01539-722464; **W** www.arthur-ransome.org/ar).

John Ruskin was a great Victorian thinker. Frenziedly prolific, he painted, wrote and campaigned – he had a horror of the effects of industrialization on society. He moved to the calm of Coniston following health problems seemingly brought on by overwork. Apart from Brantwood, the Ruskin Museum, and his grave (Coniston), there are various of his works in the Armitt Museum (Ambleside) and in Abbott Hall Gallery (Kendal).

CUMBRIA

can be steep. A map and compass are essential. Off-road mountain biking is popular, and there are also some good touring routes. See the Activities chapter for more details on walking and for information on the Cumbrian and Sea To Sea Cycle Route.

Several outdoor shops and centres hire boots, tents and hiking equipment. Phone the **Weatherline** (☎ 017687-75757) before setting out on ambitious excursions.

Guided walks – from around the town to scrambles in the hills – are organised from June to August, many of them are free. Pick up a copy of the free *Events & Parklife* from TICs for details.

Accommodation & Food

There are almost 30 YHA hostels in the area, many of them within walking distance of each other. The YHA runs a **Lake District Accommodation service** (☎ 015394-31117) for booking less than seven days ahead, and provides an invaluable shuttle bus that links Ambleside, Butterlip How, Elterwater, Hawkshead, Holly How and Langdale YHAs with Windermere train station (June to September; phone ahead to book a seat). Call **Ambleside YHA** (☎ 015394-32304) for more information. A dedicated YHA website is at **W** www.yhalakedistrict.org.uk.

For a rustic rest, the Lake District National Park Authority administers some picturesque camping barns. A night's stay costs £4; you need to bring all the usual camping gear apart from a tent. Contact **Keswick Information Centre** (☎ 017687-72645) for full details.

The NT operates three excellent **campsites** (*adult/child/car £4/1.50/2; no caravans*):

Great Langdale (☎ 015394-37668), 8 miles (13km) from Ambleside on the B5343; **Wasdale Head** (☎ 019467-26620), on the western shore of Wast Water; and **Low Wray** (☎ 015394-32810), 3 miles (5km) south of Ambleside on the western shore of Windermere and accessed from the B5286.

Getting There & Away
There's a direct rail link from Manchester airport to Barrow-in-Furness (2½ hours) and Windermere (2¼ hours). Carlisle has several bus services to Keswick (£5; see Getting There & Away under Carlisle).

Windermere has a train station and good road links. To both Windermere and Carlisle, coaches from London take about 6½ hours, trains 3½ hours.

Getting Around
Avoid bringing a car if you can, to limit congestion and pollution. If you do, put it in a car park and use the bus network to get around. Since the distance between most points is quite small (for example, Ambleside is 5 miles (8km) from Windermere), you could even use taxis; expect to pay around £1.60 per mile, with a minimum charge of £2.30.

Bus Stagecoach has some excellent local bus services, including the No 555/556 between Lancaster and Carlisle, which stops at all the main towns; the No 505, which regularly links Kendal, Windermere, Ambleside and Coniston; and the No 517 over Kirkstone Pass.

The free booklet *Getting Around Cumbria* has details.

Train Aside from the Cumbrian Coast Line (see under Cumbrian Coast earlier) and the branch line from Oxenholme to Windermere, there are a number of steam railways, including the Ravenglass & Eskdale Railway (see Ravenglass & Around under Cumbrian Coast earlier) and the Ambleside/Bowness to Haverthwaite Steam Railway (see Windermere & Bowness, following).

Boat Windermere, Coniston Water, Ullswater and Derwent Water are all plied by ferries, often providing time-saving links for walkers. See the Windermere & Bowness, Coniston and Keswick sections later for details.

WINDERMERE & BOWNESS
☎ 015394 • pop 9198 • elevation 104m
Windermere, England's largest lake, is a shimmering 10.5 miles (17km) long. It's also the most popular lake, and bustles with all kinds of boats.

The towns of Windermere and Bowness grew on the back of the establishment of the railway in 1847, quickly becoming the Lake District's largest tourist centre. They are dominated by Victorian slate-stone houses, and you'll be hard pressed to find a business unrelated to the tourist trade. The towns, which almost merge, feel like a tasteful seaside resort, with ice creams and fish and chips galore. In summer they're hectic, with traffic, fumes and people. This bit of the track is so beaten it's almost a pit, but there's a lot to see in the area and the lake is sublime.

Orientation
It's 1½ miles (2.5km) downhill from Windermere station to Bowness Pier; a taxi will run you there for around £3. Buses and coaches all leave from outside the train station. Bowness has the nicest places to eat, and is the livelier place to be in the evening.

Information
Windermere TIC (☎ 46499; Victoria St; open 9am-6pm Apr-June & Sept-Nov, 9am-7.30pm July & Aug, 9am-5pm Nov-Mar) is excellent and provides a free accommodation-booking service for the Lake District. Internet access costs £1 for 10 minutes. **Mountain Goat** (☎ 45161; w www.mountain-goat.com; Victoria St, Windermere) is nearby.

The large **Brockhole National Park Visitor Centre** (☎ 46601; open 10am-5pm daily Apr-Oct), 3 miles (5km) north of Windermere on the A591, has hands-on exhibits and a café with sweeping views from its big terrace. The best way to reach the centre is via a cruise from Bowness or Ambleside.

The small **Bowness Bay Information Centre** (☎ 42895; Glebe Rd; open 9.30am-5.30pm daily Easter-Oct, 10am-4pm Fri-Sun Nov-Mar) has displays of information on the lake and will book accommodation.

Send mail at the **post office** (21 Crescent Rd; open 9am-5.30pm Mon-Sat).

Things to See & Do
The **Windermere Steamboat Museum** (☎ 45565; w www.steamboat.co.uk; Rayrigg

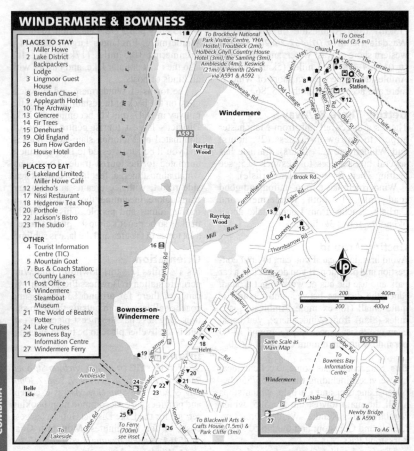

WINDERMERE & BOWNESS

PLACES TO STAY
1 Miller Howe
2 Lake District
   Backpackers
   Lodge
3 Lingmoor Guest
   House
8 Brendan Chase
9 Applegarth Hotel
10 The Archway
13 Glencree
14 Fir Trees
15 Denehurst
19 Old England
26 Burn How Garden
   House Hotel

PLACES TO EAT
6 Lakeland Limited;
   Miller Howe Café
12 Jericho's
17 Nissi Restaurant
18 Hedgerow Tea Shop
20 Porthole
22 Jackson's Bistro
23 The Studio

OTHER
4 Tourist Information
   Centre (TIC)
5 Mountain Goat
7 Bus & Coach Station;
   Country Lanes
11 Post Office
16 Windermere
   Steamboat
   Museum
21 The World of Beatrix
   Potter
24 Lake Cruises
25 Bowness Bay
   Information Centre
27 Windermere Ferry

Rd; adult/child £3.50/2; open 10am-5pm daily mid-Mar–Oct) houses a marvellous waterside collection of steam and motor boats, including the world's oldest mechanically powered vessel and *Esperance*, which Ransome imagined as Captain Flint's houseboat in *Swallows and Amazons* – you can clamber on board, where it's set up as if the captain has just popped out. The museum also offers somewhat irregular trips on a small steam launch (adult/child £5/4).

The World of Beatrix Potter *(☎ 88444; Crag Brow; adult/child £3.75/2.50; open 10am-5.30pm daily Apr-Sept, 10am-4.30pm Nov-Mar)* has lots of kid-pleasing models reconstructing bits of Potter's tales – a meandering path leads to the real focus, the shop, where you can Potterize your life.

Blackwell Arts & Crafts House *(☎ 46139; w www.blackwell.org.uk; adult/child £4.50/2.50; open 10am-5pm Apr-Oct, 10am-4pm mid-Feb–Mar, Nov & Dec)* was designed by Mackay Hugh Baillie Scott in the 19th century for a wealthy brewer. It's full of space and simplicity, particularly the White Drawing Room, which provides a bone-white frame to the blue-green views. Visit on a sunny day, when most other people will be on Bowness Pier. Its fine café (sandwiches from £3.50) has outside seating overlooking Windermere. It's 1½ miles south of Bowness, off the A5074.

At the lake's southern end is the freshwater **Aquarium of the Lakes** *(☎ 015395-30153; Lakeside, Newby Bridge; adult/senior/child £5.75/4.95/3.75; open 9am-6pm Apr-Oct,*

9am-5pm Nov-Mar). It centres on local fish and animals and the passage of the rivers from the lakes to the sea. Mischievous otters and an underwater viewing tunnel steal the show. The best way to get here is to take a cruise from Bowness or Ambleside (see Other Activities).

Walking & Cycling

Orrest Head, offering panoramic Lakeland views, is 2½ miles (4km) and a steep climb away. The path starts near the Windermere TIC. Another good viewpoint is Brant Fell, 2½ miles (4km) from the Bowness TIC, again a bit of a haul, but the panoramic views are worth the effort. Leaflets on both are available from local TICs.

Beatrix Potter's cottage at Hill Top and the picturesque village of Hawkshead are easily accessible to walkers. Catch the ferry across Windermere (see Boat under Getting There & Away later); it's a 2-mile walk to Hill Top and another 2 miles to Hawkshead (see those sections later in the chapter).

Country Lanes (☎ 44544), in the train station, rents bikes for £9/14 per half/whole day.

Other Activities

Windermere Lake Cruises (☎ 015395-31188) has a mixture of modern and old cruisers plying the lake from Bowness Pier. Regular boats run to Ambleside (adult/child £6.20/3.20), Lakeside (£6.40/3.30), Brockhole (£4.80/2.40) and Ferry House (£2.70/1.40), the latter for Hawkshead and Hill Top. A 45-minute cruise costs £4.80/2.40. A Freedom of the Lake ticket allows unlimited cruises for a 24-hour period from any pier (£11/5.50).

Combined tickets also tie in with the **Ambleside/Bowness to Haverthwaite Steam Railway** (☎ 015395-31594; railway only £4.10/2.05, from Bowness £10/5, from Ambleside £13.50/7.15; open Apr-Oct). Combined tickets for a cruise and admission to the Aquarium of the Lakes cost £10.75/6 from Bowness, £14.25/8.15 from Ambleside.

Motor-boat hire costs around £15 per hour for two adults, then £3 for each additional person. Children go free. To row around costs £3/1.50 per adult/child for an hour.

Places to Stay – Budget & Mid-Range

Park Cliffe campsite (☎ 31344; W www.park cliffe.co.uk; Birks Rd; 2-person tent £10-13.60), amid rolling, tree-peppered hills, has all mod cons, a bar and restaurant. It's midway between Windermere and Newby Bridge, off the A592 road; bus No 618 passes the turning, from where it's less than half a mile.

Lake District Backpackers Lodge (☎ 46374; W www.lakedistrictbackpackers.co.uk; High St; dorm beds £12, 2-bed rooms per person £14) has small dorms in a pint-sized slate building with a small patio.

Windermere YHA Hostel (☎ 43543; e windermere@yha.org.uk; High Cross, Bridge Lane, Troutbeck; adult £11.25; open daily mid-Feb–early Oct, Fri & Sat Nov–mid-Feb) is much larger, with fantastic valley views, but is 2 miles (3km) from the station. Leave Windermere on the A591 to Ambleside and turn right up Bridge Lane at Troutbeck Bridge. Bus Nos 555 and 559 run past Troutbeck Bridge.

Brendan Chase (☎ 45638; 1 & 3 College Rd; rooms per person from £20), an Edwardian slate-stone building, has cheery, bright rooms.

The Archway (☎ 45613; W www.commun iken.com/archway; 13 College Rd; singles/doubles from £35/40) provides pleasant rooms with slanted ceilings and some good views.

Applegarth Hotel (☎ 43206; W www.apple garthhotel.com; singles £30-35, doubles £44-76) is a Victorian mansion, ornately woody, with Pre-Raphaelite stained glass.

Denehurst (☎ 44710; W www.denehurst -guesthouse.co.uk; 40 Queens Drive; rooms per person £21-29) has been recommended by readers. It has pale, pretty rooms and is in a quiet spot.

Lingmoor Guest House (☎ 44947; 7 High St; rooms with/without en suite per person £19/17), a friendly family-run place, has seven sweet rooms.

Fir Trees (☎ 42272; W www.fir-trees.com; Lake Rd; doubles per person £26-38), heading down to Bowness, is a lovely Victorian hotel with delicately decorated rooms.

Glencree (☎ 45822; W www.glencreelakes .co.uk; en-suite rooms £25-28), across the road, is a fine house overlooking woodland and a little stream.

Places to Stay – Top End

Burn How Garden House Hotel (☎ 46226, fax 47000; W www.burnhow.co.uk; Belsfield

CUMBRIA

Rd; rooms per person £44-66) offers motel-style chalets and rooms and a restaurant in a large Victorian house with lush gardens.

Old England (☎ 42444; Church St; rooms per person £52-72, lake view extra £10-20) is an elegant lakeside Georgian country mansion, with an open-air pool.

Holbeck Ghyll Country House Hotel (☎ 32375, fax 34743; **w** www.holbeckghyll .com; Holbeck Lane; rooms per person £90-130) has grandly flounced rooms and good food in a 19th-century hunting lodge that overlooks the lake from a hillside, 3 miles (5km) north of Windermere.

Miller Howe (☎ 42536, fax 45664; **w** www .millerhowe.com; Rayrigg Rd; B&B & dinner per person £80-175) has the best lakeside views, and a sublime number of cherubs scattered about. The room decor has seen better days, but the views make up for it. There's a justly famed restaurant.

The Samling (☎ 31922, fax 30400; **w** www .thesamling.com; Dove Nest; rooms £135-295), set in 26.8 hectares, is up a steep right turn off the road to Ambleside. Its 10 luxurious rooms are desperately tasteful; staying here makes you feel like you *must* be famous.

Places to Eat

Jericho's (☎ 42522; Birch St; mains around £16) is of the food-in-little-piles-on-big-plates genre, and comes recommended.

Flower-fronted **Jackson's Bistro** (☎ 46264; St Martin's Place; starters £2.30-4.20, mains £8.40-12.90, 3-course dinner £12.95) has good food in dimly lit, intimate surroundings.

Nissi Restaurant (☎ 45055; Crag Brow; starters £3-5, mains £9-25) does Greek and Mediterranean dishes in a brash yellow and blue interior.

Porthole (☎ 42793; 2 Ash St; starters £2.50-9.90, mains £11-17; Wed-Mon evenings only) is candle lit, with white walls, wooden fittings and good Italian and modern British dishes. Book ahead.

The Studio (☎ 44065; 21 Lake Rd; mains £7.50-15.50, 2/3 courses £12.95/16.50), with splattered paintings and pointed lampshades, serves up beautifully cooked modern British with fresh ingredients.

All the top-end hotels have excellent restaurants serving first-class cuisine.

Hedgerow Teashop (☎ 45002; Crag Brow; light lunches around £4) has good light dishes in a beamed, cosy interior.

Miller Howe Café (☎ 46732; Station Precinct; cakes £2), in Windermere, has surprisingly nice cakes in the unscenic surrounds of the Lakeland Limited factory shop.

Old England (☎ 42444; Church St) is a good place for a cuppa, in a stately room or adjoining terrace, both with lake views.

Getting There & Away

Windermere is 265 miles (427km) from London, 55 miles (89km) from Blackpool, 45 miles (73km) from Carlisle and 5 miles (8km) from Ambleside.

Bus National Express runs from Preston (£9.75, 1 hour, one daily) and on to Keswick (£7.50, 50 minutes). A service from London (£26.50, 5 hours 40 minutes) also goes on to Keswick, and finishes up in Whitehaven.

Bus No 555/556 runs to Lancaster (£5.40; 45 minutes, 13 daily Monday to Saturday, three on Sunday) via Kendal, and to Keswick (£5.30, 50 minutes, 13 daily Monday to Saturday, three on Sunday) via Ambleside and Grasmere, and goes as far as Carlisle (£7) three times daily. Bus No 618 runs between Ambleside and Barrow-in-Furness via Windermere, Newby Bridge and Ulverston. Bus No 505 from Kendal (£3.15, 20 minutes) goes on to Coniston (£5.85, 40 minutes) via Ambleside (£2.25). The No 599 bus service regularly links Grasmere, Ambleside, Brockhole, Windermere, Bowness and Kendal from April to October.

Train Windermere is at the end of a spur line from Oxenholme near Kendal (see the Kendal Getting There & Around section), which connects with the main line from London Euston (£63.60, 3½ hours, eight or nine daily Monday to Saturday, four on Sunday) to Glasgow.

Boat See Other Activities earlier in this section for details on cruises. The Windermere ferry plies across the lake from Ferry Nab, Bowness to Far Sawrey (adult/car 40p/£2, every 20 minutes 7am to 10pm Monday to Saturday, from 9am on Sunday from October to March, and to 9pm between November and March).

Getting Around

Bus No 599 makes the 1½-mile journey from Bowness Pier to Windermere train station about every half-hour. You can call a taxi on ☎ 46664.

AROUND BOWNESS
Troutbeck
☎ 015394 • elevation 222m

This charming village is scattered across the hills, with flower-covered stone and whitewashed houses, crumbling barns and two great 17th-century pubs. Beatrix Potter bred sheep here, at Troutbeck Park Farm.

Townend Farmhouse *(NT; ☎ 32628; admission £3; open Tues-Fri & Sun Apr-Oct)*, a 17th-century yeoman farmer's house, stayed in the same family for centuries and provides a tantalising glimpse of domestic life 300 years ago.

The Mortal Man *(☎ 33193; w www.mortal-man-inns.co.uk/mortalman; rooms per person £35; starters £2.20-4.75, mains £9.45-15.25)* is a lovely place for a pint, either in its cosy, worn interior or outside surrounded by the fells. It's also a peaceful place to stay.

Queen's Head *(☎ 32174; w www.queens headhotel.com; rooms per person £35-45; 3-course meals £15.50)* is another low-beamed option, with fantastic food and fine rooms overlooking the hills.

Bus No 491 between Kirkby Stephen and St Bees, via Penrith, Keswick and Cockermouth, stops in Troutbeck (one daily April to September). Bus No 521 runs from Windermere (two daily on Wednesday year round, and Monday also from April to September).

AMBLESIDE
☎ 015394 • pop 2689

A small, pretty town, backed by rusty green hills, Ambleside is one of the Lake District's biggest walking and climbing bases. Its narrow cobbled streets are thick with B&Bs, teashops, hearty restaurants and rugged types bewildered at having reached this outdoor-equipment-shop heaven. It's half a mile north of the lake.

Information
For advice on where to go, head to the **TIC** *(☎ 32582; w www.amblesideonline.co.uk; cnr Market Cross & Rydal Rd; open 9am-5pm daily)*. Access the Net at the **Golden Rule** *(☎ 32257; Smithy Brow)*; 10 minutes for £1.

Compston Rd has more equipment shops than you've had hot dinners, with branches of **Rohan** *(☎ 32946)*, **Hawkshead** *(☎ 35255)*

and the **YHA Adventure Shop** *(☎ 34284)*. The **Climber's Shop** *(☎ 32297)* also hires out boots and some other equipment.

Things to See & Do
The **Armitt Museum** *(☎ 31212; w www.ar mitt.com; Rydal Rd; adult/child £2.50/1.80; open 10am-5pm daily)* fills you in on the background to the area and has some interesting stuff on Lake luminaries, including John Ruskin and Beatrix Potter (though her early botanical drawings may be for the completist fan), besides some lesser-known characters.

The TIC provides plenty of walks information. The Loughrigg circuit, which is 7 miles (11km) long, running from the Rydal Rd car park to Grasmere Lake and back, is a good combination of woods, farmland, steep hills and great views. For a shorter walk of 2 miles (3km), but still taking in the views, head for Stockghyll Force, east of Ambleside. You can either head back to Ambleside through farmland or push on to Troutbeck, returning via Jenkyn's Crag, a rocky outcrop offering superb views of Windermere – a 7-mile (11 km) circuit.

Ambleside is on the Windermere cruise route. See Boat Trips in the Windermere & Bowness section for details.

Places to Stay
Low Wray *(☎ 32810; camping per adult/child/car £4/1.50/2; open Easter-Oct; bus No 505, plus 1-mile walk)*, a NT campsite, is 3 miles (5km) south of Ambleside on the western shore of Windermere (access from the B5286). You can camp right on the lakeside.

Ambleside Backpackers *(☎/fax 32340; w www.englishlakesbackpackers.co.uk; dorm beds Apr-Oct £13.50, Nov-Mar £11)* has 72 beds in spruce, bright dorms. There's a nice wooden-floored sitting room. It has laundry and Net facilities (10 minutes for £1).

Ambleside YHA Hostel *(☎ 0870 7705672; e ambleside@yha.org.uk; Windermere Rd/A591; adult £14; open year round)*, 1 mile south of the village and perched by the lake, has 245 beds. There's Internet access (10 minutes for £1).

Church St and Compston Rd are packed with standard B&Bs.

3 Cambridge Villas *(☎ 32307; Church St; rooms per person £16-20)* has a modicum of flounce.

CUMBRIA

Melrose Hotel (☎ 32500; Church St; rooms per person from £20) is welcoming, with spacious though undistinguished rooms.

Compston House Hotel (☎ 32305; W www.compstonhouse.co.uk; Compston Rd; en-suite rooms per person £22-50) has views, comfortable rooms and American breakfasts (pancakes).

Mill Cottage (☎ 34830; Rydal Rd; rooms with/without en suite £24/23) has patterned rooms above a central teashop in a building dating from 1501.

Glenside (☎ 32635; Old Lake Rd; en-suite rooms per person £25) is tucked away and exceptional, with three beautiful, snug doubles in dark rich colours and an outside terrace.

Langdale Chase (☎ 32201, fax 32604; W www.langdalechase.co.uk; rooms per person £60-90), a grand pile, starred as a quintessential country house in Hitchcock's *The Paradine Case*.

You could swing a panther in the rooms, and terraces lead down to the lake. It's on the Windermere road.

Places to Eat & Drink

The Glass House (☎ 32137; Rydal Rd), in a swish conversion of a 16th-century watermill, serves good refined food.

Pippins (☎ 31338; 10 Lake Rd), for a solid morning start, is a long-lived café doing full English breakfasts (£4.95). It sells pizzas in the evening (from £6.25) and is BYO.

Lucy's on a Plate (☎ 31191; Church St; starters £3-6, mains £7-14; open lunch & dinner Thur-Sun), lively and charming, has wooden candle-lit tables and imaginative food. There's an adjoining deli, excellent for picnics.

Lucy 4 (☎ 34666; 2 St Mary's Lane; tapas around £4.50), nearby, has a good, cluttered atmosphere, lots of little red demons, and hearty, unusual tapas.

The Priest Hole (☎ 33332; starters £3.25, mains £6.95-14; open evenings only), in the 16th-century Kelsick Old Hall, serves international food and has outside seating.

Zeffirelli's Wholefood Pizzeria (☎ 33845; Compston Rd; pizza £5.50-7.45; open evenings only) enables you to munch pizza before adjourning to the cinema attached; the £13.95 'double feature' menu covers two courses and cinema ticket.

Golden Rule (☎ 32257; Smithy Brow), popular with walkers and a local favourite, has rambling cosy rooms away from the tourist buzz; it pours a fine pint of ale.

The Royal Oak (☎ 33382; Market Place) has central outside tables and attracts a younger crowd.

Getting There & Around

Bus No 555 (and No 599 from April to October) comes from Grasmere (20 minutes), as well as Windermere (15 minutes) and Kendal (45 minutes). From April to October, No 505 runs from Coniston (35 minutes, 13 daily Monday to Saturday, three daily on Sunday), and from Kendal (30 minutes, twice daily Monday to Saturday, once on Sunday) via Windermere.

Bike Treks (☎ 31505; Compston Rd) hires out bicycles for £10/14 per half/full day.

AROUND AMBLESIDE
Rydal Mount

Wordsworth, the only poet laureate who never wrote a line of official verse, lived at Rydal Mount from 1813 to 1850. Even then, as many as 100 fans a day would visit in the hope of catching a glimpse. Rydal Mount (☎ 33002; house & garden adult/senior/student/child £4/3.25/3/1.50, garden adult/child £1.75/1.50; open 9.30am-5pm daily Mar-Oct, 10am-4pm Wed-Mon Nov, Dec & Feb) is a 16th-century farmhouse set in a hectare of gardens (true to Wordsworth's original design). It doesn't have the pokey charm of Dove Cottage, but feels like a family home, and contains some of the original furniture as well as manuscripts and possessions. The house is owned by one of his descendants, and is located 1½ miles northwest of Ambleside, off the A591. Bus No 555 (and also No 599 from April to October), between Grasmere, Ambleside, Windermere and Kendal, stops at the end of the drive (see Getting There & Away under Windermere & Bowness earlier).

In spring it us worth diverting through the churchyard below the Mount to see **Dora's Field**, planted with daffodils in memory of Wordsworth's daughter who died of tuberculosis.

GRASMERE
☎ 015394

Grasmere village is a tidy, picturesque place to stay. The eponymous glassy, peaceful lake, surrounded by lush greenery, is undisturbed by motor boats and there are countless walks meandering off into the countryside. Although the village is ancient, it's dominated by 19th- and 20th-century buildings (mostly hotels). Wordsworth is buried in St Oswald's churchyard with his wife Mary and sister Dorothy, and Dove Cottage is nearby, ensuring a steady flow of poetry pilgrims. St Oswald's itself dates from the 13th century and has a complex raftered roof.

The **TIC** *(☎ 35245; Red Bank Rd; open 9.30am-5.30pm daily Mar-Oct, 10am-3.30pm Sat & Sun Nov-Feb)* has a flurry of information on local walks and will book accommodation. Get online next door at the **Grasmere Garden Centre** (£1 buys 10 minutes).

Things to See

Dove Cottage *(☎ 35544; w www.wordsworth .org.uk; adult/child £5.50/2.50; cottage & museum open 9.30am-5.30pm daily early Feb–early Jan)*, just off the A591 on the outskirts of Grasmere, is where Wordsworth wrote his greatest poems. Once a pub, it has uneven floors, panelled walls and fine lake views. Thomas De Quincey, author of *Confessions of an Opium Eater* lived here later. It's often busy, but entrance is managed so that it doesn't get overcrowded. The half-hour guided tours are entertaining and irreverent.

Next door, the **Wordsworth Museum** houses many interesting letters, journals and manuscripts by Wordsworth and his many impressive friends.

Places to Stay

Large and tree-shaded **Butterlip How YHA Hostel** *(☎ 0870 7705836; e grasmere@yha .org.uk; adult £11.90)* is just north of the village, off Easedale Rd.

Thorney How YHA Hostel *(contact Butterlip How; adult £10.25; open Apr-Oct)* is pretty and more remote, farther up the hill.

Grasmere Hostel *(☎ 35055; Broadrayne Farm; bus No 555; dorm beds £12.50)* is an excellent independent hostel. The bright, en-suite two- to six-bed rooms have fine views. There's even a sauna. It's about a mile north of the village along the A591. Bus No 555 will stop at the end of the road on request.

A half-mile walk from the town centre **Glenthorne Quaker Guest House** *(☎/fax 35389; w www.glenthorne.org; Easedale Rd; shared/en-suite B&B per person £26/33)* has a vague religious-convention vibe, but it's

friendly, well set up for walkers and offers dinner (around £10).

How Foot Lodge *(☎ 35366; rooms per person from £26)*, next to Dove Cottage, is a stately, huge house owned by the Wordsworth Trust. The rooms are wonderfully plain, with white curtains and linen.

Lake View Country House *(☎ 35384; w www.lakeview-grasmere.com; rooms with en suite per person £31.50)*, off the A591, has private access to the lakeside, good views and plush rooms.

Places to Eat

Dove Cottage Tea Rooms & Restaurant *(☎ 35268; lunch £4.75-7, evening starters £4.75-5, mains £9-12; tearooms open 10am-5pm daily, restaurant open evenings only Wed-Sun)* is an informal, white-tableclothed modern British enterprise.

The Travellers Rest Inn *(☎ 35604; w www .lakelandsheart.demon.co.uk; rooms per person from £34-44, mains from £7)*, a much refurbished 17th-century place, has great pub food and comfortable rooms, but suffers from the A591 running past its door. It's just north of Grasmere and bus No 555 stops outside.

Baldry's Tea Room *(☎ 35301; Red Lion Square; mains £4.95-6.75; open Fri-Wed)*, in the village, has a gentle, old-fashioned air and serves mouthwatering bread-and-butter pudding (£2.95).

Faeryland *(☎ 35060; w www.faeryland .co.uk)*, with tables on the grassy lakeside, is a small enterprise serving mighty scones and cakes. Rowing boats can be hired from here (£8 for two people). Follow Redbank Rd past the TIC, towards the lake, and it's on the left.

Sarah Nelson's Gingerbread Shop *(☎ 35428; Church Stile)* has been trading on the same spot since 1854. Follow your nose as you leave the churchyard.

Getting There & Away

Bus No 555 runs from Ambleside to Grasmere (20 minutes), stopping at Rydal church and outside Dove Cottage. The seasonal bus No 599 runs from Kendal via Bowness (one hour, four daily April to October).

LANGDALE
☎ 015394

The endless green-velvet curves of Langdale are surrounded by soaring great peaks. The area contains some of England's finest walking, encompassing the Langdale Pikes, Elterwater and Dungeon Ghyll, and is scattered with some fine traditional pubs and hotels.

The turning at Skelwith Bridge on the A593, 2½ miles (4km) west of Ambleside, leads up into Great Langdale. The valley is dwarfed by a range of five fells – the Langdale Pikes. The road passes pretty Elterwater (see following), a mile northwest of the turn-off, before continuing on to the base of the pikes. Another mile farther west from Skelwith Bridge is a second turning, this time leading to Little Langdale. At the head of the valley you can either turn right onto the connecting road to Great Langdale or continue on over Wrynose and Hardknott Passes to the coast. But be warned, it's a snaking, steep, single-track road ahead.

Elterwater

Tucked in under the fells, Elterwater – 'Elter' comes from the Norse for swan – is a small, perfectly formed lake. The nearby charming village of the same name occupies a stunning spot on the Cumbria Way, with good walks sprawling out all over the place.

There's a wonderful view from Loughrigg Terrace at the southern end of Grasmere, looking north over the lake and the village. Follow the road to Langdale YHA Hostel and continue eastwards, taking a footpath to the right off the road. It's approximately 3 miles (5km) return to Elterwater. The **Maple Tree Corner Store**, on the central green, has a list of local accommodation.

Elterwater YHA Hostel (☎ 0870 7705816; e elterwater@yha.org.uk; adult £10.25; open daily Apr-Sept, Tues-Sat Feb-Mar & Nov-Dec) is a pretty slate-stone house, nestling the other side of the bridge. Net access costs £1/10 minutes.

Langdale YHA Hostel (☎ 0870 7705816; e langdale@yha.org.uk; High Close, Loughrigg; adult £10.25; open mid-July–mid-Sept), a mile east of the village, up a windy road off the A593, is a remote Victorian mansion in extensive gardens.

The **Britannia Inn** (☎ 37210; w www .britinn.co.uk; rooms per person from £36) is a classic popular village pub, with comfy rooms, substantial food and pleasant tables spilling over the edge of the village green.

Elterwater is 3½ miles (5.5km) from Ambleside (take bus No 516; 17 minutes, five daily April to October) and 5 miles (8km) from Coniston.

Elterwater to Old Dungeon Ghyll

With wonderful fell-walking opportunities, including Harrison Stickle (724m) and Pike o' Stickle (697m), the valley rolls on for another 3½ miles (5.5km) past Elterwater to the base of the Langdale Pikes. It's beautiful, wild countryside, and accommodation possibilities are excellent – none could fail to have good views.

Sticklebarn Tavern (☎ 37356, Great Langdale) is 2½ miles (4km) on from Elterwater, and offers bunk barn accommodation in a traditional stone barn and stable for £10 per person. Meals are available at the tavern (mains £5.35 to £10.25) and you're expected to provide your own sleeping bag.

New Dungeon Ghyll Hotel (☎ 37213, fax 37666; w www.dungeon-ghyll.com; en-suite rooms per person £39-45) provides rather more comfort across the road. Its rooms are smart, with fells filling the windows on all sides.

Great Langdale Campsite (NT; ☎ 37668; adult/child/car £3.50-4/1.50/2), about a mile farther up the valley, occupies a tree-dotted, hill-backed spot.

Old Dungeon Ghyll Hotel (☎ 37272; rooms per person with/without en suite from £39.95/35.95) is located at the foot of the Langdale Pikes. A favourite of many a famous climber and not-so-famous tourist, it's a classic old hotel, with welcoming hosts and a hearty menu. Its rooms have antique furniture and the inevitable inspirational fell views.

Bus No 516 runs from Ambleside to the Old Dungeon Ghyll Hotel (30 minutes, five times daily) from April to October.

Little Langdale

Separated from Great Langdale, by Lingmoor Fell (459m) Little Langdale is a quiet village on the road running up to Wrynose Pass. There are plenty of gentle walks in the peaceful, unpeopled surrounds. At the head of the valley is the **Three Shire Stone** marking the traditional meeting point of Cumberland, Westmoreland and Lancashire.

Three Shires Inn (☎ 37215; w www.three shiresinn.co.uk; rooms from £40 per person; mains £7.50-11.25, lunch around £6) is a great, inviting, slate-stone 19th-century inn.

It's well set up for walkers and cyclists and offers a warm welcome to all, with comfortable rooms. The attractive bar, ribbed by wooden beams, serves great real ale and delicious food.

Bus No 506 from Ambleside or Coniston drops you at the junction of the A593 and the road heading to Little Langdale. From the bus stop, it's a mile walk along the marked footpath, or 2 miles (3km) along the road. The Three Shires Inn can arrange for a taxi to collect you if required.

HARDKNOTT & AROUND

The drive over the Wrynose and Hardknott Passes is breathtakingly beautiful, vertiginous and twisting, with views across green mossy mountains. Both roads are impassable in winter. The grade tips to 1 in 4 on the single-lane road – it's not uncommon to find some poor sod on the hard shoulder with a burnt-out clutch.

The Hardknott Pass takes you over to lovely Eskdale and the Cumbrian coast. On the brow before heading down into Eskdale, is **Hardknott Castle Roman Fort**, with vast valley views. Easy to zip past in a car, the 1.2-hectare site is a short walk from the road. The remains, on a projecting spur, are particularly impressive because of the haunting grandeur of the site. A nearby level area was apparently the Roman parade ground – it's an extraordinary thought among these remote jewel-green mountains. It's a good sunset spot.

Eskdale YHA Hostel (☎ 0870 7705824, fax 7705825; e eskdale@yha.org.uk; Boot; adult/youth under 18 £10.25/7, breakfast £3.40/1.90, dinner £5/2.90; open Mon-Sat Mar-Oct, Sun July & Aug), at the base of the pass and 1½ miles (2.5km) east of Dalegarth station, is friendly, has a great hillside situation and is well set up for families.

Nearby is **Boot**, a pretty, appropriately shoebox-sized village in the shadow of Scafell Pike (977m), England's highest mountain. It's the closest settlement to Dalegarth station – the other end of the Ravenglass–Eskdale line, and makes a good base for walks, or escaping the Lake District crowds.

Hollins Farm Campsite (☎ 019467-23253; w www.hollinsfarmcampsite.co.uk; adult/car £3/2; open Mar-Oct) is quiet, small and tree lined.

Brook House Inn (☎ 019467-23288, fax 23160; w www.brookhouseinn.co.uk; Boot; rooms per person from £30; mains £6.95-10.95) has comfortable though unremarkable rooms with fine views. Good evening meals are available.

Woolpack Inn (☎ 019467-23230; Boot; rooms with/without en suite per person from £29.50/25.50) is popular, with a comfortable, farmhouse feel, filling food and real ale in the bar. Bunkhouse accommodation is also on offer (B&B costs £15.50). There's 10 minutes Net access for £1.

For Ravenglass–Eskdale Railway information, fares and timetables Ravenglass & Around earlier in this chapter.

WASDALE
☎ 019467

To escape the madding crowds, head to bleak, wild Wast Water, 5 miles (8km) east of Gosforth. Hemmed in by some of the highest peaks in England (Scafell Pike and Great Gable are close at hand), it's a formidable mountain-framed lake – the deepest in England (79m) – backed by famous sharp walls of scree. It's much harder to get to than the other major lakes, reached via the twisting Hardknott Pass or from the coast. Wasdale Head – at its northern end – feels as if you've reached the end of the earth (in English terms anyway).

Wast Water YHA Hostel (☎ 0870 770 6082; e wastwater@yha.org.uk; Wasdale Hall; adult £10.25; open Thur-Mon mid-Feb–Oct, Fri & Sat Nov–mid-Feb), a friendly place with 50 beds, overlooks the southern end of the lake. It's a 19th-century Gothic mansion with many original fixtures.

Four miles (6km) northeast of the youth hostel is Wasdale Head.

Wasdale Head Campsite (NT; ☎ 26220; camping per adult/child/vehicle £3.50/1.50/ 2) huddles beneath towering mountains.

Lingmell House (☎ 26261; w www.ling mellhouse.com; per person without en suite £28) is a wonderfully solitary house, with calm, white-walled, simple rooms that set off the views outside a treat. It's popular with walkers.

Wasdale Head Inn (☎ 019467-26229, fax 26334; w www.wasdale.com; rooms per person from £45-90), nearby, is a peaceful, relaxing retreat, much beloved of hill lovers, with good food and own-brewed beer. Legendary

CUMBRIA

porkie pie purveyor Will Ritson, who inspired the annual competition at The Bridge Inn (see later), was the first landlord here.

The **Barn Door Shop** (☎ 26384) sells maps and guides, and operates a small basic campsite opposite (£2 per person). A short walk away is atmospheric, tiny St Olaf's Parish Church, the churchyard of which is dotted with memorials to mountain walkers.

The Bridge Inn (☎ 019467-26221, fax 26026; w www.santonbridgeinn.com; shared singles with/without en suite £45/40, doubles £55-60, en-suite doubles £60-65; mains £7-12) is in the small settlement of Stanton Bridge 2½ miles (4km) southwest of Wast Water. Apart from serving excellent food and providing comfy rooms it hosts the Worlds Biggest Liar Competition in September (see the boxed text 'Calling all Ugly Liars').

Public transport is rare. The **Wasdale Taxibus** (☎ 019467-25308) runs between Gosforth and Wasdale Head (£1.50 single, 20 minutes, twice daily, Thursday, Saturday and Sunday) via the YHA and campsite – ring to book a seat, or to call a taxi. You need your own transport to get to Santon Bridge.

Calling all Ugly Liars

The Bridge Inn at Stanton Bridge hosts the World's Biggest Liar Competition every November in honour of Will Ritson, first landlord of the nearby Wasdale Head Inn. Will used to regale customers with extravagant, convincing folklore, and past winners continue his mighty mendacious tradition. Members of the legal profession and politicians are barred from entering.

If your talents lie more in the aesthetic arena, you could head for the World Gurning Competition, held in mid-September in Egremont, which is near St Bees. To gurn is to pull an ugly face, and this challenge is believed to stem from the 12th century, when the lord of the manor would hand out sour crab apples to his workers. The competition is separated into junior, male and female sections, and the winner is the person who receives the most applause. Competitors stick their head through a horse's collar before pulling a face, in case there be any confusion about who's taking part. Anne Woods, a local, won the trophy *24 years running* till she was beaten in 2001.

CONISTON
☎ 015394 • pop 975

The **Old Man of Coniston** (801m) looms over beautiful, glossy Coniston Water, with its gliding steam yachts and quiet boats. The nearby village of Coniston, dwarfed by hulking hills, grew up around the area's copper mining industry.

There are just a few main streets, with two fine pubs and just a few tourist shops. It's another excellent walking base.

Information

The **TIC** (☎ 41533; e conistontic@lake-district .gov.uk; Coniston Car & Coach Park; open 9.30am-5.30pm daily Easter-Oct, 10am-3.30pm Sat & Sun Nov-Easter), on the road to Hawkshead, has lots of information on walks.

The **Village Pantry** (☎ 41155; Yewtree Rd) and **Lakeland House** (☎ 41303; Tilberthwaite Ave) both charge £2 for 30 minutes online.

Summitreks (☎ 41212; w www.summitreks .co.uk; 14 Yewdale Rd) offers a range of adventure activities and hires out walking and climbing gear as well as bikes, kayaks and canoes (£14, £15 and £20 per day).

Ruskin Museum

The Ruskin Museum (☎ 41164; adult/child £3.50/1.75; open 10am-5.30pm daily) eclectically explores Coniston's history and geology. It touches on copper mining, Arthur Ransome and the tragic story of Donald Campbell, who died on the lake in 1967 breaking the 300mph speed barrier.

It's also, of course, a good introduction to Ruskin, a great Victorian all-rounder, with various displays of his watercolours and sketchbooks illuminated by his own commentaries.

Brantwood

John Ruskin bought Brantwood (adult/ student/child £4/3/1; open 11am-5.30pm daily mid-Mar–mid-Nov, 11am-3.30pm Wed-Sun mid-Nov–mid-Mar) unseen, as he assumed that anywhere overlooking Coniston Water would be beautiful.

The house is an insight into Ruskin's relentless intellect, prolific output and eventual failing mental health. It's set among 100-hectare gardens that are worth exploring, and there's a fine café (sandwiches £4.40), with seating overlooking the lake. The best way to get there is by boat.

Boat Trips

Rescued from dereliction by the NT, the unique steam yacht **Gondola** (☎ 63850) with its luxurious saloons, was first launched on Coniston Water in 1859. The *Illustrated London News* described it as 'a perfect combination of the Venetian gondola and the English steam yacht'. It services Brantwood and Coniston Pier; the fare is £4.80/2.80 for an adult/child, and there are five services daily between April and October.

The motorised **Coniston Launch** (☎/fax 36216; **w** www.conistonlaunch.co.uk) is another option. The North Lake sailing calls at four jetties, including Brantwood, for £3.80/1.90. The South Lake cruise sails as far as Lake Bank at the southern end of the lake, and also calls at Brantwood. Tickets cost £5.80/2.90. You can break your journey, walk to the next jetty and so on.

Or you can hire a boat at the **Coniston Boating Centre** (☎ 41366; Coniston Jetty). Motor/rowing boats cost £11/5 (one hour), toppers/wayfarers (small sailing boats) will set you back £10/14 (one hour), while canoes glide out for £10 (two hours).

Walking

The popular ascent to the summit of the Old Man has ample views, and starts at St Andrew's Church in Coniston. On a clear day the top affords views of the wide sandy bays along the Cumbrian coast and across to Windermere. The walk is 7½ miles (12km) and will take four to five hours. Appropriate clothing for bad weather, plus a good map and a compass, are essential.

Another favourite walk heading north from St Andrew's Church takes in Yewdale and Tarn Hows. It's a relaxing route through picturesque woods and farmland before a steep climb next to a waterfall, to Tarn Hows, an artificial body of water surrounded by woods and backed by mountains. Allow 2½ to three hours for the 5-mile (8km) walk.

The TIC has useful leaflets on both walks.

Tarn Hows is one of the few upland tarns accessible by road. The **NT** (☎ 015394-35599) runs a free bus service on Sunday (25 minutes, five daily May to October) between Coniston and Hawkshead (connecting with bus No 505), giving you a full day to explore the area.

Places to Stay

Coniston Hall Campsite (☎ 41223; per person £3.50, 2 people & car £8.50; open Easter-Oct) has a lovely lakeside setting. To get here, turn left opposite the Catholic church. Bus 505 stops by the church.

Holly How YHA Hostel (☎ 0870 779 5770; **e** conistonhh@yha.org.uk; Far End; adult £10.25; open mid-June–Nov) is a standard hostel, among trees, off Ambleside Rd (the A593).

Coppermines YHA Hostel (☎ 0870 7705772; adult £9.50; open daily July-Aug, Tues-Sat Apr-May & Sept-Oct) was the mine manager's house. It has a spectacular mountain setting yet is only about a mile from Coniston. Be warned – the road is quite bad.

Beech Tree Vegetarian Guest House (☎ 41717; Yewtree Rd; shared rooms per person £19, with shower/en suite £21/25) is the nicest place to stay, a calm, carefully kept house.

Oaklands (☎ 41245; **w** www.geocities.com /oaklandsguesthouse/; Yewdale Rd; rooms £20-25), across the road, is friendly, with sizable, comfortable rooms and a leafy outlook.

Orchard Cottage (☎ 441373; Yewdale Rd; en-suite rooms £24) has pristine rooms with sparkling white linen.

Lakeland House (☎ 41303; Tilberthwaite Ave; singles with/without en suite £25/16, doubles per person with/without en suite £25/18) is friendly, with nine mundane rooms, good views and Internet access.

Shepherds Villa (☎ 41337; rooms per person with/without en suite £23/20) has some pink satin stuff going on, but is friendly and the rooms overlook the fells.

Coniston Lodge Hotel (☎/fax 41201; Station Rd; en-suite rooms per person from £42.50) is welcoming, highly rated and kempt, with stuffed toys and other occasional clutter in the six rooms.

Places to Eat

Black Bull (☎ 41335; Yewdale Rd; mains £7-12) is a creaky, whitewashed pub in the centre. It has good grub and brews its own Bluebird beer.

Blue Cafe (☎ 41649; Lake Rd), down by Coniston Lake, meets the boats coming in with filling jacket potatoes for £4.25.

The Sun Hotel (☎ 41248, fax 41219; **w** www.thesunconiston.com; en-suite singles

£35-50, doubles £70-80; mains around £12) is worth the effort of finding; cross the bridge on the Ulverston road and turn right up the hill. The bar has lots of photos of the Blue-bird expedition – Donald Campbell had his headquarters here during his fateful campaign. The food is great and its old-fashioned rooms have fine fell views.

Getting There & Around

From April to October, Bus No 505 runs from Windermere (50 minutes, eight daily Monday to Saturday, three on Sunday) via Brockhole and Ambleside; it also runs from Kendal (one hour 10 minutes, two daily Monday to Saturday, one on Sunday).

Summitreks (☎ 41212; w www.summitreks .co.uk; 14 Yewdale Rd) rents bicycles for £14 per day.

HAWKSHEAD

☎ 015394 • pop 570 • elevation 107m

With its quaint rose-covered, whitewashed buildings, dainty cobblestone streets and scenic countryside setting, Hawkshead is so immaculately picturesque it almost feels as if it's been constructed for the benefit of sightseers. It's home to the Beatrix Potter gallery, with all her original watercolours – a must for Potter-heads. Parking is provided on the outskirts of the village, so it's almost traffic free.

Wool has been the big money-spinner for Hawkshead from medieval times, and the Hawkshead Company is still a popular outdoor clothing maker. Wool was once a major part of the English economy. In 1678 the industry was in a mess and the government passed a law stating that coffins be wool lined and people buried wrapped in wool shrouds, just to increase its use.

The **TIC** (☎ 36525, fax 36349; open 9.30am-5.30pm daily Apr-Oct, 9.30am-6pm July & Aug, 10am-3.30pm Fri, Sat & Sun Nov-Mar), next to the main car park to the south of the town centre, has a good supply of information about the surrounding area. Hawkshead's two attractions are at either end of the town.

The **Hawkshead Grammar School** (adult/child £1/free; open 10am-12.30pm & 1.30pm-5pm Mon-Sat, 1pm-5pm Sun Apr-Sept, 1pm-4.30pm Oct), across Main St from the TIC, was founded in 1585 by the Archbishop of York. It has been unused since 1909, so is well preserved and set out as it was when its

famous pupil, William Wordsworth, attended the school (1779–87). The curator is well informed about the alarming amount of classical schooling the pupils had to undergo – probably what drove Wordsworth to carve his name so painstakingly on his desk (it's in pride of place today).

Right on Red Lion Square is the **Beatrix Potter Gallery** (NT; ☎ 36355; admission £3; open 10.30am-4.30pm Sun-Thur Apr-Oct), in the small, uneven rooms that once formed the office of her husband, William Heelis. The higgledy-piggledy gallery houses the gently lit, delicate, original watercolours from her children's books. You will be given an entry time with your ticket – usually the wait isn't too long.

Places to Stay & Eat

The TIC can arrange accommodation if required. There are a couple of camping options near to Hawkshead.

Croft Camping & Caravanning (☎ 36374; w www.hawkshead-croft.com; North Lonsdale Rd; 2-person sites & car £11-13; open mid-Mar–mid-Nov), just east of the town centre, is pleasant, grassy and close.

Hawkshead YHA Hostel (☎ 0870 770 5856; e hawkshead@yha.org.uk; adult £11.25), about a mile south on the road to Newby Bridge, has 109 beds in a fine Regency building that overlooks Esthwaite Water. It's popular with families and school groups. Net access costs 50p for 10 minutes. Bus No 505 passes here and stops in Hawkshead village.

Ann Tyson's Cottage (☎ 36405; w www .anntysons.co.uk; Wordsworth St; en-suite rooms per person £23-25) is a lovely, place with comfy rooms, if a bit haughty. It's on a little cobbled street just off the main square. **Ivy House Hotel** (☎ 36204; w www.ivy househotel.com; Main St; en-suite rooms per person from £30), around the corner, is much more welcoming, and offers B&B in a warmly decorated Georgian house.

Old School House (☎ 36403; rooms per person from £19), south of the centre, is an attractive building set back from Main St. Rooms are pleasant, a bit frilly, with fine outlooks.

Several of the pubs offer good accommodation too. Flower-fronted **Queens Head** (☎ 36271; w www.queensheadhawkshead.co .uk; Main St; singles/doubles £42/63; mains

£6-13) is flower laden, has outside tables on the main square and offers filling pub food.

Kings Arms (☎ 36372; W www.kingsarms hawkshead.co.uk; The Square; singles/doubles £35/60; mains £6-13) is pleasant and accommodating, with seating on the square.

Granny Nook (☎ 36404; Vicarage Lane; sandwiches from £2.90) is a family-run eatery in a pretty cottage around the corner from Anne Tyson's place.

Minstrels Gallery (☎ 36423; The Square), dating from the 15th century, is a beautiful place for a snack, with jacket potatoes for around £4.

Getting There & Away

Hawkshead is frequently linked with Windermere, Ambleside and Coniston by bus No 505 (April to October), and with Kendal twice daily (55 minutes, once on Sunday).

AROUND HAWKSHEAD
Grizedale Forest

Filling the space between Coniston Water and Esthwaite Water, 3 miles (5km) south of Hawkshead, is Grizedale Forest, the verdant love child of a sculpture park and an outdoor pursuits venue.

Artists have been coming here since 1977 to create things in the forest. There's a wonderful element of surprise in coming across the unlikely items, such as a large wooden xylophone or a billboard. Over 90 sculptures are scattered throughout the forest, mainly made from natural materials. Even without its eccentric furniture, Grizedale Forest is good for a bit of walking and cycling. There are single-track mountain-bike trails, and you can dabble in many other activities, such as archery.

Mountain bikes can be hired from **Grizedale Mountain Bike Hire** (☎ 01229-860369; W www.grizedalemountainbikes.co .uk; open 9am-5pm Mar-Oct, Sat & Sun Nov-Feb), at the Park Centre, for £15 for a full day or £9 a half-day, to tackle the 40 miles (65km) of marked cycle trails. You can also hire 'all terrain push chairs' (half/full day £4/8).

Grizedale Visitors Centre (☎ 01229 860010; W www.grizedale.org; open 10am-5pm Easter-Oct, 11am-4pm Nov-Easter) provides information on trails and activities. There's also a café where you can refuel (doorstop sandwiches £2.75).

Grizedale Lodge (☎ 015394-36532; W www.grizedale-lodge.com; en-suite rooms per person £35-45), half a mile north of the visitor centre on the road to Hawkshead, provides plush rooms in a comfortable building surrounded by forest.

Mountain Goat (☎ 015394-45161) Bus No 525 runs from Hawkshead via Moor Top to Grizedale (10 minutes, four daily July to September, Saturday and Sunday only March to June and November) as part of the B4 network. Buses run to Hawkshead via Hill Top from Ferry House, connecting with Windermere Cruise boats, or from Coniston, connecting with the Coniston Launch (Saturday and Sunday only March to June and November, daily July to September).

Hill Top

Beatrix Potter wrote many of her famous children's stories in this elfin 17th-century farmhouse (NT; ☎ 36269; admission £4; open 10.30am-4.30pm Sat-Wed Apr-Oct) at Near Sawrey, and you can spot the furnishings in her illustrations. Surrounded by a flower-filled garden and fronted by a vegetable patch, the house is kept as it was. Tickets are sold for set times; you may have to wait to get inside during school holidays. It's 2 miles (3km) south of Hawkshead. See Walking & Cycling under Windermere & Bowness earlier in the chapter for details of how to get there; or catch bus No 525, which connects with the ferry (10 minutes, eight daily April to October).

KESWICK
☎ 017687 • pop 4836 • elevation 195m

Ringed by fells and mountains, the old blue-slate market town of Keswick is the Lake District's busy northern centre and jostles with B&Bs, good pubs, cream-tea outlets and shops selling every type of anorak. Derwent Water lies beside the town, gigantic and comely, with thick woods around its edge and interrupted by five islands. The most convenient lake for those without their own transport, it also boasts an impressive launch service.

Keswick became a centre of the graphite-mining industry in the 16th century. Today it's an important walking base – it's on the Cumbria Way, tucked beneath the bulk of Skiddaw, and has countless trails crisscrossing the surrounding hills.

CUMBRIA

Information

The helpful **TIC** (☎ 72645, fax 75043; W www.keswick.org; Moot Hall, Market Place; open 9.30am-5.30pm daily Apr-Oct, 9.30am-4.30pm Nov-Mar) has loads of local information, and books accommodation. It's the centre to contact about camping barns.

Above the **main post office** (48 Main St) you can buy a £2.75 card that allows you an hour's Net access at **U-Compute** (☎ 75127). **George Fisher** (☎ 72178; 2 Borrowdale Rd) is an outdoor equipment shop with gear for hire. The **Keswick Launderette** (☎ 75448; Main St) is a smart place to do your washing.

Boat Trips

Derwent Water has an excellent lake transport service run by the **Keswick Launch Company** (☎ 72263; W www.keswick-launch.co.uk). From mid-March to November, a regular service calls at seven landing stages around the lake: Ashness Gate, Lodore Falls, High Brandlehow, Low Brandlehow, Hawse End, Nichol End and back to Keswick. Boats leave every half-hour, alternately clockwise and anticlockwise (adult/child £5.20/2, 50 minutes); each stage is about 10 minutes (80/40p). Discounted tickets can be bought at the TIC. The service operates six times daily December to mid-March.

The launches give access to some excellent walks and provide a restful option for those walking the Cumbria Way (the long walk from Elterwater or Dungeon Ghyll). The walk around the western side of the lake isn't particularly interesting, but Borrowdale is beautiful. Sailing boats, kayaks, canoes, windsurfers, rowboats and motorboats are available for hire from **Nichol End Marine** (☎ 73082; Nichol End).

Castlerigg Stone Circle

This mysterious loop of 48 stones, believed to be between 3000 and 4000 years old, is set on a hill top surrounded by a brooding amphitheatre of mountains that includes Skiddaw and Helvellyn. It's uncertain what the purpose of the circle was, but it seems it was a Neolithic and Bronze Age sacred meeting place – those prehistoric types certainly knew a good site when they saw one – on all sides the views stretch out to the jagged horizon.

The TIC has a good leaflet (50p) outlining a 4-mile (6km) circular walk from the centre of Keswick.

Pencil Museum

People flock to this cult attraction (☎ 73626; Southy Works; adult/child £2.50/1.25; open 9.30am-4pm daily) to pay homage to its humble, pun-prompting subject matter. It's surprisingly involving – from a mine reconstruction to the heady delights of pencil sculpture and the underwhelming bulk of the world's largest pencil. In the 16th century graphite was discovered in Borrowdale, leading to a pencil-making industry that is still making its mark – the museum is attached to the Derwent Watercolour pencil factory – though the components are now imported from as far afield as Sri Lanka.

Other Things to See & Do

The classically Victorian **Museum & Art Gallery** (☎ 73263; Station Rd; W www .allerdale.gov.uk; adult/child £1/50p; open 10am-4pm daily Apr-Oct) displays original manuscripts from Lake big guns, such as Wordsworth, Southey and Walpole, some memorable musical stones and various archaeological finds.

Choose your favourite from the **Cars of the Stars Motor Museum** (☎ 73757; W www.cars ofthestars.com; Standish St; adult/child £3.50/ 2.50). Wheeled out are Chitty Chitty Bang Bang, the full-size Lady Penelope's Rolls Royce and many more. Opening times are a little complicated: 10am to 5pm daily from the week before Easter to the end of November, as well as two weeks in mid-February and Saturday and Sunday in December.

The Puzzling Place (☎ 75102; W www.puz zlingplace.co.uk; Museum Place; adult/child £3/2.25; open 10am-6pm daily) is a great way to entertain older kids on a rainy day, with demonstrations, such as a ball rolling up a hill, and explanations for the strange effects.

Various outdoor activities, guided walks and courses – such as climbing, canoeing, abseiling and cycling – are organised by the knowledgeable, friendly **Climbing Wall & Activity Centre** (☎ 72000; W www.keswick climbingwall.co.uk; open 10am-9pm), behind the Pencil Museum.

The **Theatre by the Lake** (☎ 74411; W www .theatrebythelake.com; Lakeside), on the edge of Derwent Water, dishes out good drama.

Walking & Cycling

Many interesting walks and rides can be undertaken around the youth hostel network.

Walkers could consider climbing Skiddaw and continuing on to Skiddaw House YHA Hostel (see Hostels later) and Caldbeck along the Cumbria Way, or catching the launch to the southern end of the lake and walking up Borrowdale. (See Boat Trips earlier.)

Cyclists could make a challenging 30-mile (48km) circuit from Keswick: head south along the western bank of Derwent Water, along Borrowdale Rd (the B5289) and past Borrowdale YHA. Then climb the brutal Honister Pass, passing Black Sail YHA before freewheeling down to beautiful Buttermere and Crummock Water. From Buttermere finish the loop by returning below Knott Rigg along the Keskadale Beck past Stair. Alternatively, continue on to Cockermouth and return via the B5292.

Places to Stay

A couple of miles out of town, **Scotgate Holiday Park** (☎ 78343; **w** www.scotgate holidaypark.co.uk; bus No X5; adult/child/car £3.30/2/2) is just off the A66 on the B5292.

Keswick Camping & Caravanning Club Site (☎ 72392; Crow Park Rd; camping per person £5-6.50, per tent £4.50) has lake access and is a two-minute walk from town.

Keswick YHA Hostel (☎ 0870 770 5894, fax 770 5895; **e** Keswick@yha.org.uk; Station Rd; adult £11; open daily) is a pleasant, 91-bed place by the river.

Skiddaw House YHA Hostel (**e** skid daw@yha.org.uk; Bassenthwaite, Keswick CA12 4QZ; adult £7.75; open Apr-Oct), on the Cumbria Way, has 20 beds in an isolated former shooting lodge behind Skiddaw, 6 miles

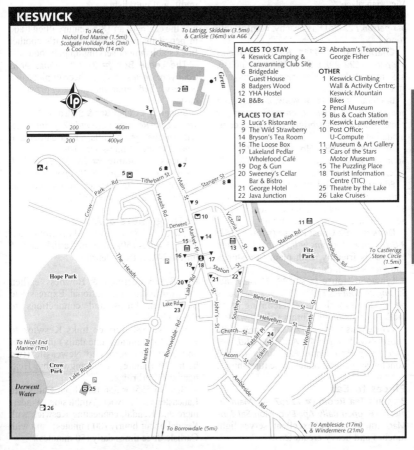

KESWICK

To A66,
Nichol End Marine (1.5mi),
Scotgate Holiday Park (2mi)
& Cockermouth (14 mi)

To Latrigg, Skiddaw (3.5mi)
& Carlisle (36mi) via A66

Crosthwaite Rd

Greta

PLACES TO STAY
4 Keswick Camping &
   Caravanning Club Site
6 Bridgedale
   Guest House
8 Badgers Wood
12 YHA Hostel
24 B&Bs

PLACES TO EAT
3 Luca's Ristorante
9 The Wild Strawberry
14 Bryson's Tea Room
16 The Loose Box
17 Lakeland Pedlar
   Wholefood Café
19 Dog & Gun
20 Sweeney's Cellar
   Bar & Bistro
21 George Hotel
22 Java Junction

23 Abraham's Tearoom;
   George Fisher

OTHER
1 Keswick Climbing
   Wall & Activity Centre;
   Keswick Mountain
   Bikes
2 Pencil Museum
5 Bus & Coach Station
7 Keswick Launderette
10 Post Office;
   U-Compute
11 Museum & Art Gallery
13 Cars of the Stars
   Motor Museum
15 The Puzzling Place
18 Tourist Information
   Centre (TIC)
25 Theatre by the Lake
26 Lake Cruises

0   200   400m
0   200   400yd

Tithebarn St

Crow Park Rd

Heads Rd

Main St

Stanger St

The Heads

Derwent Ct

Market Pl

Victoria St

Station Rd

Brundholme Rd

Fitz Park

To Castlerigg
Stone Circle
(1.5mi)

Hope Park

Station St

Penrith Rd

Lake Rd

Lake Rd

St John's St

Southey St

Blencathra St

Helvellyn St

Wordsworth St

Church St

Ratcliff Pl

Acorn St

Eskin St

Heads Rd

Borrowdale Rd

Crow Park

Lake Road

Derwent Water

To Nicol End
Marine (1mi)

Ambleside Rd

To Borrowdale (5mi)

To Ambleside (17mi)
& Windermere (21mi)

CUMBRIA

(10km) from Keswick, and can only be reached on foot (bring a torch). Contact the hostel via **Carrock Fell YHA Hostel** (☎ *0870 7705754*).

Bridgedale Guest House (☎ *73914; 101-103 Main St; rooms with/without en suite per person £23.50/18*) has good-value, floral rooms. You can leave your bags here for £2.

Badgers Wood (☎ *72621;* ☒ *www.badgers wood.co.uk; 30 Stanger St; rooms with/without en suite per person from £23/18*) is welcoming, with roomy, pleasant accommodation.

To the east of the centre along Southey, Blencathra, Helvellyn and Eskin Sts, almost every house is a B&B. Prices are competitive and standards high.

Allerdale House (☎ *73891; 1 Eskin St; rooms per person from £25*) is a popular, large Victorian place.

Tarn Hows (☎ *73217; 3-5 Eskin St; rooms per person £22-26*) has peachy, comfortable rooms.

Charnwood (☎ *74111; 6 Eskin St; rooms per person £22-29*), a listed Victorian house, has immaculately decorated rooms and stencilled hallways.

Braemar (☎ *73743;* ☒ *www.braemar-guest house.co.uk; 21 Eskin St; en-suite rooms per person from £22*) has bright, cheerful accommodation.

Avondale Guest House (☎ *72735; 20 Southey St; en-suite rooms from £23.50*) offers floral-bordered, smart rooms.

Edwardene Hotel (☎ *73586;* ☒ *www.ed wardenehotel.com; 26 Southey St; singles £28-31, doubles £52-58*) is a big, comfortable and accommodating grey-slate building.

Derwentdale Guest House (☎*/fax 74187; 8 Blencathra St; rooms with/without en suite £21/18*) is friendly, with plain furnishings and views of Skiddaw.

Lynwood House (☎ *72398; 35 Helvellyn St; singles/doubles £19/17.50, en-suite rooms per person £21*) is also welcoming, with modern prints on its vibrant yellow walls.

Whitehouse (☎ *73176;* ☒ *www.white housekeswick.co.uk; 15 Ambleside Rd; en-suite per person rooms £22*), only for the nonclumsy, has elaborately pale furnishings.

Places to Eat

Bryson's Tea Room (☎ *72257; 42 Main St; meals £6; open daily Apr-Dec, Mon-Sat Jan-Mar*), traditional and excellent, serves light lunches and heavy cream teas.

Abraham's Tearoom (☎ *72178; 2 Borrow-dale Rd; mains around £5*), tucked into the rafters of the George Fisher outdoor equipment shop, offers tasty snacks.

Lakeland Pedlar Wholefood Café (☎ *74492;* ☒ *www.lakelandpedlar.co.uk; Hendersons Yard; dishes around £5*) has picture-covered walls and wooden tables, and a great range of delicious veggie dishes.

The Wild Strawberry (☎ *74399; 54 Main St; mains £5.50*) is a sweet, twee place and a good stop for a quick bite.

Java Junction (☎ *774053; Station Rd; sandwiches around £2*) invites you to lounge around, with big red and orange sofas.

Dog & Gun (☎ *73463; 2 Lake Rd; mains around £6*), low-ceilinged and flagstone-floored, is good value and popular, with traditional pub dishes.

George Hotel (☎ *72076; 3 St John's St*) was the centre of an 18th-century illicit trade in pencil materials. Nowadays it's another fine establishment serving up pub food.

The Loose Box (☎ *772083; Kings Arms Courtyard; mains £5-6*), a cheerful place in a white-vaulted cellar, serves hearty pizza and pasta.

Sweeney's Cellar Bar & Bistro (☎ *772990; 18-20 Lake Rd; mains around £7*) is intimate, with sherbet-green walls, a beer garden and a good range of pub-style dishes.

Luca's Ristorante (☎ *74621; High Hill; starters £3-7.50, mains £8-18; open Tues-Sun*) is an upmarket Italian place, serving copious choices in an attractive dark-peach setting.

Getting There & Away

Keswick is 285 miles (459km) from London, 31 miles (50km) from Carlisle and 15 miles (24km) from Penrith.

Bus See Windermere & Bowness, earlier, for information on National Express and Stagecoach buses and connections to Keswick.

Bus No 888 service links Keswick to Penrith (35 minutes, one daily) in summer and continues across to Newcastle (two hours 20 minutes) via Langwathby, Hexham and Corbridge.

Bus No 555 or 556 runs from Carlisle to Lancaster via Keswick, Ambleside, Windermere and Kendal, connecting Keswick with Carlisle about hourly (80 minutes), and with Carlisle three times daily (50 minutes).

Getting Around

Behind the Pencil Museum, there are two places that hire out bicycles: **Keswick Mountain Bikes** (☎ 75202; 1 Daleston Court) charges from £10/13 per half/full day; **Keswick Climbing Wall & Activity Centre** (☎ 72000; w www.keswickclimbingwall.co.uk) charges £14 per day.

Taxis (☎ 72676) are also available.

BORROWDALE & BUTTERMERE VALLEYS
☎ 017687

Borrowdale and Buttermere are two of the Lake District's most beautiful valleys, where wooded, rust-and-ochre slopes meet rugged farmland and steely green-grey peaks and the changing colours glint back from the shining lakes. They're dotted with timeless villages, unspoilt despite the summer hoards.

The B5289 road running south of Keswick takes you into Borrowdale, which stretches for 6 miles (10km) from the northern end of Derwent Water to Honister Pass, south of the lake. The Buttermere valley, runs northwest from Honister Pass along the shores of Buttermere and Crummock Water towards Cockermouth. With thrilling access to some mighty peaks and some excellent low-level jaunts, they're a walker's dream.

Borrowdale & Around

Remote-feeling but accessible, Borrowdale's lovely position by Derwent Water and access to the high peaks of Scafell, Scafell Pike and Great Gable make it popular with walkers.

Derwent Water YHA Hostel (☎ 0870 770 5792; e derwentwater@yha.org.uk; Barrow House; adult £11; open daily Feb-Oct, Fri & Sat Nov-Jan), 2 miles (3km) from Keswick, is in an extraordinary setting overlooking the lake. At the back of the building is a waterfall, created by the house's original owner, descending over 30m. The 88-bed hostel is about 100m south of the turn-off to Watendlath, a small hamlet set by a small tarn.

The Borrowdale Hotel (☎ 77224, fax 77338; w www.borrowdalehotel.co.uk; B&B & dinner per person from £62) is 3 miles (5km) from Keswick along the B5289, and is welcoming, with a renowned restaurant (three-course meal £22.50). Rooms are spacious with good views – the superior rooms are regal and worth the extra cost.

Grange, a small village huddling near the southern end of Derwent Water, is a popular base for walks.

Hollows Farm (☎ 77298; camping per adult/child/tent £3/1.50/1, rooms per person £18-21) is in a lovely setting, nestled back among hills, a half-mile amble from the village. It has reasonable rooms in a big rambling farmhouse. You can camp here too.

Grange Bridge Cottage Tea Shop (☎ 77201; mains around £4-7), in a lovely rustic setting by the river, is BYO and has simple meals.

The next village south is **Rosthwaithe**, where a 1½-mile (2.5km) public bridleway winds its way to Watendlath. Accommodation possibilities are good here.

Scafell Hotel (☎ 77208; w www.scafell.co.uk/hotel; B&B per person £40, with dinner £61) has its best rooms in its older part, but they're all comfy, and you can have dinner at the hotel's **Riverside Bar** (mains around £5).

Nook Farm (☎ 77677; rooms per person from £18), a tucked-away traditional farmhouse, is owned by the National Trust.

Yew Tree Farm (☎ 77675; w www.yewtree-farm.co.uk; rooms per person from £25) is a rambling, whitewashed house, with flower-crazy rooms, one of which was once slept in by Prince Charles – don't let that put you off. Across the road the **Flock Inn Tea Room** has delicious home-baked cakes (sticky toffee pudding £2.50).

Borrowdale YHA Hostel (☎ 0870 7705706; e borrowdale@yha.org.uk; Longthwaite, Borrowdale; adult £11.25; open daily mid-Feb–Oct, Fri & Sat Nov-Feb) has 88 beds and is at the head of beautiful Borrowdale.

Seatoller, the last stop before Honister Pass, is another village offering accommodation. **Seatoller Barn Information Centre** (☎ 77294; e seatollertic@lake-district.gov.uk; open 10am-5pm daily Apr-Nov) offers organised walks and will help with finding accommodation.

Seatoller House (☎ 77218; singles/doubles £31.50/59) has appealing rooms with antique furniture and two book-lined guest lounges. A four-course evening meal is available for an extra £12.

Yew Tree Restaurant (☎ 77634; mains £5-8; open Tues-Sun lunch), next door, has low ceilings, uneven flagstones and guitars on the wall. Here you can sample the local food and get clothed in outdoor gear.

CUMBRIA

Getting There & Away Bus No 79 – the Borrowdale Rambler – provides a regular service (at least hourly) for the valley from Keswick bus station to Seatoller. From Easter to October bus No 77/77A – the Honister Rambler – makes the round trip from Keswick to Buttermere via Borrowdale and the Honister Pass every couple of hours.

On Sunday from May to October, the National Trust operates a minibus every few hours from Lakeside Information Centre in Keswick to Watendlath. The minibus stops at Ashness Bridge and Surprise View, both with impressive views of Derwent Water.

Buttermere & Around

From Seatoller, it's possible to enter the Buttermere valley over the steep Honister Pass, which can reach gradients of 1 in 4 in places. If you're in search of the middle of nowhere, there are some handy hostels in this neck of the woods.

Honister Hause YHA Hostel (☎ 0870 770580; Seatoller; adult £9.50; open Fri-Tues Apr, May, Sept & Oct; daily June-Aug) is at the summit of the pass, 4 miles (6km) from Buttermere.

A track to Great Gable starts here, and there are sweeping views from the top across the smoky, pewter-and-khaki landscape, down into Buttermere valley. Bus No 77/77A stops here May to October; it's a 1½-mile (2.5km) walk from the No 79 bus stop.

Black Sail YHA Hostel (☎ 07711-108450; Black Sail Hut, Ennerdale, Cleator; adult £9.50; open Tues-Sat Apr-May & Sept-Oct, daily June-Aug) is a bothy (mountain shelter) in a quiet wooded valley, 2½ miles (4km) west of Honister Pass and only accessible on foot.

Ennerdale YHA Hostel (☎ 0870 7705820; Cat Crag, Ennerdale, Cleator; adult £9.50; open Thur-Mon Apr-Oct) has 24 beds, 5 miles (8km) from Ennerdale Bridge and 2½ miles (4km) from Bowness Knott car park. From Black Sail it's a flat 4-mile (6km) walk to the west.

The twisting road finally reaches the bottom of the pass and skirts around the edge of **Buttermere**, which glows at the centre of a perfect crown of mountains, to reach **Buttermere village**, 4 miles (6km) from Honister and 9 miles (14km) from Keswick.

Dalegarth Guest House (☎ 70233; Buttermere; camping adult/child £4/1, rooms with/without en suite per person from £24/19) pro-vides traditional, straightforward accommodation and camping facilities.

Buttermere YHA Hostel (☎ 0870 7705736; e buttermere@yha.org.uk; adult £11.25) is a 70-bed large but squat slate house overlooking Buttermere.

Bridge Hotel (☎ 70252, fax 70215; Buttermere; rooms per person from £60, mains around £6.50), in a lovely spot, offers luxurious accommodation, with comfortable, pale-cream rooms. The cosy chintz bar serves excellent food in challengingly large portions.

From Buttermere, the B5289 cuts north along the eastern shore of picturesque **Crummock Water**.

Woodhouse Guest House (☎ 70208; w www.wdhse.co.uk; singles/doubles £43/70) is peaceful and is stunningly positioned by the lake, with tasteful, traditional rooms.

From Woodhouse, it's another 6 miles (10km) north to the junction of the B5292 road, which heads northwest to Cockermouth and east to Keswick.

Getting There & Away Bus No 77/77A services the Buttermere valley four times daily, Easter to October only, departing from Keswick Bus Station, traversing the steep Honister Pass.

ULLSWATER
☎ 017684

Ullswater stretches out, a silvery, snaking flood of a lake, with fells sinking into its surface and a shoreline encircled by trees, green and purple-brown patchwork and sturdy villages. It's the farthest northeast of them all, and despite being the second-largest lake – 7½ miles (12.5km) long – it's much less visited. In summer it can get crowded on the A592 road running along its western edge, but stick to walking along the eastern side and you'll see it in all its grandeur, undisturbed by cars. The main hamlets near the lake are Pooley Bridge to the north, among grassy banks and rounded hills, and Glenridding and Patterdale to the south, where the countryside is more rugged and dramatic. Nearby, Penrith makes a good base too.

A good way to see the lake is from the **Ullswater 'Steamers'** (☎ 82229; w www.ullswater-steamers.co.uk), which run from Pooley Bridge to Glenridding via Howtown. Steamboats started plying the lake in 1859 but the current vessels, *Lady* (in operation since 1887) and *Raven* (in operation since 1889), have now been converted to conventional power.

A return trip from either end of the lake takes two hours; boats leave every two hours from mid-April to early May and in November, hourly from mid-March to mid-April and May to September. It costs £5/2.50 for a single or £8/4 for a return.

AROUND ULLSWATER
Pooley Bridge
elevation 301m

With majestic mountains to the west, the serene village of Pooley Bridge nestles at the northern end of Ullswater, surrounded by rich green stretches of field that dip down to the water's edge. It's 5 miles (8km) southwest of Penrith.

The **National Park TIC** (*☎/fax 86530;* e *pooleybridgetic@lake-district.gov.uk; Finkle St; open 10am-5pm daily Apr-Oct)* can help with inquiries.

To steer yourself around the lake, head down to friendly **Lakeland Boat Hire** (*☎ 07773-671399; Lakeside).* Motor boats cost £15 for one to six people per hour, rowing boats cost £10 for up to seven people.

Park Foot Camping (*☎ 86309, 86041;* e *holidays@parkfootullswater.co.uk; Howtown Rd; 2-person tent sites & car £9)* has a beautiful spot at Ullswater's edge, a mile south of Pooley Bridge on the road to Howtown.

Elm House (*☎ 86334; High St; rooms per person £21),* two-minutes' walk from the lake, is flower fronted, comfortable and pleasant.

The Pooley Bridge Inn (*☎ 86215;* w *www.pooleybridgeinn.co.uk; doubles £65)* looks as if it's in the Austrian Lake District and has darkly wooden rooms with white bedspreads.

Sharrow Bay Country House Hotel (*☎ 86301;* w *www.sharrow-bay.com; doubles per person £150-190)* is sublime in its setting (to-die-for lake views), its standards (believed to be the world's first country-house hotel, it's had a lots of practice) and its snootiness (possibly less apparent if you're of a certain wealth or age). Dinner is a taste-sensation splurge (set menu £47.25).

The Sun (*☎ 486205; mains around £6)* has really excellent home-cooked pub grub, including a fine fish pie (£6), and a beer garden that overlooks fields.

Granny Dowbekin's Tea Rooms (*☎ 86453; sandwiches £2.25)* has doily tablecloths and riverside seating. Tasty home-made carrot cake goes for £1.35.

Glenridding
elevation 253m

Seven miles (11km) from Pooley Bridge to the south of the lake is Glenridding. A rust, grey and green landscape frames this one-time lead-mining village, which lies beneath the great hump of Helvellyn (949m), the second-highest peak in the Lakes. Glenridding makes a great base for walks to its summit and for sallying onto the lake; the Ullswater steamer stops here.

The **Ullswater Information Centre** (*☎/fax 82414;* e *glenriddingtic@lake-district.gov.uk; Beckside car park; open 9am-6pm daily Apr-Oct, 9.30am-3.30pm Fri-Sun Nov-Mar)* is a mine of information on walks in the area. Access the Net at **Cyber Cafe** (*open 10am-5pm),* which adjoins the lakeside Glenridding Hotel; 30 minutes for £2.

Gillside Farm Campsite (*☎ 82346;* w *www.gillsidecaravanandcampingsite.co.uk; adult/child/tent/car £4/2/1/1),* among rugged foothills, is popular with walkers.

Helvellyn YHA Hostel (*☎ 0870 770 5862;* e *helvellyn@yha.org.uk; Greenside; adult £10.25; open Mon-Sat Mar-Oct, Fri & Sat Nov-Feb)* is 1½ miles (2.5km) from Glenridding and is a good starting point for Helvellyn. It's possible to drive up to the hostel, but take care.

Fairlight (*☎ 82397, fax 82168; rooms with/without bath £22/18),* in the centre of Glenridding, has an ebullient owner and down-to-earth, rosebud-sprigged rooms.

Beech House (*☎/fax 82037;* w *www.beechhouse.com; rooms per person with/without en suite £23/20)* is a lovely, friendly bargain of a place, with great views.

Inn on the Lake (*☎ 82444, fax 82303; rooms per person with fell/lake view from £44/55),* the plushest option, provides rooms with the requisite generic smart-hotel decor, but which have remarkable fell and lake outlooks.

Traveller's Rest (*☎ 82298; sandwiches £2.75, mains £7-9)* offers excellent food in a cosy pub, popular with folk from the nearby campsite.

CUMBRIA

Patterdale

pop 409 • elevation 319m

Less than a mile south of Glenridding and 12 miles (19km) from Penrith is pretty Patterdale, a collection of wind-worn slate and white houses punctuating lush fields.

Patterdale YHA Hostel (☎ 0870 770 5990; e patterdale@yha.org.uk; adult £11; open Fri & Sat Dec-Mar, Thur-Mon Mar-Oct, Fri & Sat Nov-Feb) is a Scandinavian building. It's a 20-minute walk from Glenridding, or take bus No 108, which passes by. There's Net access for 50p for 10 minutes.

Ullswater View (☎ 82175, fax 82121; e ext@btinternet.com; rooms with/without en suite per person from £25/20), nearby, is a slate building close to the lake. It has comfortable rooms with character.

Greenbank Farm (☎ 82292; singles/doubles £25/34), on a working farm a bit south of the YHA, is all uneven angles and has creaky rooms overlooking the fields.

Getting There & Around

Bus No 108 runs from Penrith to Patterdale, calling in at Pooley Bridge and Glenridding (six daily Monday to Saturday). Bus No 517 runs from Bowness Pier to Glenridding three times daily, late July to August and weekends from end-March to late July.

East Cumbria

With all eyes drawn to the Lake District's firework display of scenery, East Cumbria can often be overlooked, but it is beautiful and well worth exploring. The lucidly green Eden Valley runs from Kirkby Stephen in the south to its largest town, redbrick Penrith, in the north. Northeast of Penrith is the town of Alston, perched high in the lovely desolation of the North Pennines – stuck in time and a good base for exploring the moors or heading northwards to Hadrian's Wall. Kirkby Lonsdale and Kirkby Stephen are close to the border of the Yorkshire Dales National Park and are attractive market towns, perfectly placed for forays east or west.

PENRITH

☎ 01768

Penrith has a distinguished, deeply rosy-bricked centre, some interesting relics of its sometime glory, and feels appealingly old fashioned, with most places firmly shut on a Sunday, and shops selling such state-of-the-art items as shooting sticks and towelling tracksuits.

It's well positioned for trips to the Eden Valley, the eastern lakes, and the North Pennines. There's a market in the central square on Tuesday, as well as a huge Saturday market just off the A66 on Saturday that shifts bric-a-brac a plenty.

Information

The brusque **TIC** (☎ 867466, fax 891754; e pen.tic@eden.gov.uk; Robinson's School, Middlegate; open 9.30am-6pm Mon-Sat, 1pm-5.45pm Sun mid-July-Aug; 9.30am-5pm Mon-Sat Sept-mid-July) has plenty of information about the Eden Valley and the Lakes and will book accommodation.

Internet access is available in the **Public Library** (☎ 242100; St Andrew's Churchyard; open Mon-Sat).

Things to See

Penrith was once Cumbria's capital, and a few indications of its former importance are scattered around the now quiet little town.

The empty, plundered ruins of **Penrith Castle** (open 7.30am-9pm daily Easter-Oct, 7.30am-4.30pm Oct-Easter) occupy a park opposite the station. The castle was built in the late 14th century by William Strickland (who climbed the career ladder to Bishop of Carlisle and later Archbishop of Canterbury) because of repeated Scottish raids, one of which razed the town in 1345. It was then passed on to its most famous tenant, the notorious future Richard III. He expanded the castle, but it fell into disrepair in the 16th century.

Red-sandstone, 18th-century **St Andrew's Church** incorporates a medieval tower. In the churchyard is an arrangement of worn, rounded stones, with two pointed menhirs at each end. Legend has it that they marked an Arthurian giant's grave, but the pillars are actually the weathered remains of Celtic crosses, while the central stones were 10th-century chieftains' gravestones.

You can take in good views from the Penrith Beacon, constructed in 1719 on Beacon Fell, a sandstone hill which provided a lot of the red bricks you see around town (Penrith means 'red fell'). The beacon – a big fire – was a handy device to warn of border raids. It can be reached from a path starting at Beacon Edge Rd.

The **Penrith Museum** (☎ 867466; same hours as the TIC), in the same building as the TIC, has displays on the town's history that could be fitted in a large cupboard.

Places to Stay & Eat

There's plenty of accommodation available, particularly on fine Portland Place, to the north of the centre, and less-fine Victoria Rd to the south.

The family-run **Glendale Guest House** (☎ 862579; w www.glendaleguesthouse.net; 4 Portland Place; rooms with/without en suite per person from £22.50/18) has comfortable, cheery rooms in a tall redbrick house.

George Hotel (☎ 862696, fax 868223; w www.georgehotelpenrith.co.uk; Devonshire St; singles/doubles from £45/74) is more up-market and central. It's a lovely 300-year-old coaching inn.

Penrith has a small, varied selection of places to eat. **George Hotel** (mains £6.30-11.75) serves international dishes in a relaxed, old-fashioned bar area.

Costas Tapas Bar & Restaurant (☎ 895550; 9 Queen St; tapas around £4.50; open Tues-Sun) has a lively and splendidly tacky atmosphere, with down-to-earth waiting staff in full flamenco flounce, and the tapas portions are huge, though not great shakes. On a Thursday night, there's a barbecue and flamenco show.

Dolce Vita (☎ 891998; Bishop Yards; pizza & pasta around £5; open dinner Mon-Sat) is set right by the church, and has filling Italian food with pizza and pasta around the £5 mark.

Villa Blanca (☎ 862221; pizza & pasta around £4.50-6.50), another Italian place, provides similar stuff served on white-clothed tables in a wood-panelled room.

Ruhm Gallery & Café (☎ 867453; 15 Victoria Rd; sandwiches £3.40-4.10) is a comfortable, soothing place to sip tea and read the papers, and has a gallery out the back.

Getting There & Away

Bus The bus station is northeast of the centre, off Sandgate. Bus No 104 frequently runs between Penrith and Carlisle (£4.30, 45 minutes, 14 daily Monday to Saturday, nine on Sunday). Bus No X4/X5 connects Penrith to the Lakes and the Cumbrian coast

hourly Monday to Saturday and six times on Sunday, calling at Keswick and Cockermouth before terminating at Workington.

Train Penrith has frequent connections to Carlisle (day return £6.10, 20 minutes, hourly) and Lancaster (£15.40, 40 minutes, hourly).

AROUND PENRITH
Rheged Discovery Centre

Housed in the largest grass-covered building in Europe, Rheged (☎ 01768-686000; w www.rheged.com; adult/child £5.50/3.90; open 10am-6pm daily year round) is cunningly disguised as a Lakeland Hill. Luckily it's well sign-posted, about two miles (3km) west of Penrith, just before the turnoff to Ullswater on the A66. It was built on a former quarry and rubbish site.

The centre houses an Imax cinema, the Helly Hansen National Mountaineering Exhibition and studio-shops producing and selling local arts and crafts.

The cinema shows a choice of three 45-minute films. *Shackleton* tells the epic story of Ernest Shackleton's adventure on the *Endeavour*, with wonderful footage of the Arctic landscape – you can almost feel the frost. The sweeping scale of the format is also well served by *Everest*, another rip-roaring piece, which tracks an assault on the mountain. Less successful is *Rheged*, exploring some of the region's myths and mysteries, using the device of a young American tracing his Cumbrian roots. The scenery shots are fantastic but the narrative fairly hums of cheese.

The fascinating mountaineering exhibition covers the history, motivations and methods of getting uphill. Its dynamic illustrations range from entertaining film footage to the poignant collection of Mallory's belongings (who died when trying to climb Everest in 1924) discovered when his body was found in 1999.

The frequent No X4/X5 bus, which runs between Penrith and Workington, stops at the centre.

Long Meg & Her Daughters

The third-largest prehistoric stone circle in England, Long Meg and Her Daughters is a remote arrangement of 59 stones. According to myth, a coven of witches were spotted by a wizard and zapped into stone. The circuit is said to be uncountable – if anyone manages twice the spell will be lifted. Other caveats are that if the stones are moved something terrible will happen to those responsible, and if Long Meg – a tall red sandstone pillar with faint spiral traces – is damaged she will bleed. The circle is 6 miles (10km) northeast of Penrith off the A686 to Alston. You'll need your own transport or to take a taxi.

ALSTON
☎ 01434 • elevation 290m

Alston is an isolated town high up in the North Pennines, at the centre of a designated Area of Outstanding Natural Beauty (AONB) and on the Pennine Way and C2C. A cluster of 17th-century buildings, with hilly cobblestone streets, alleys and a marketplace, the unspoilt setting has been used as a backdrop to film adaptations of *Oliver Twist* and *Jane Eyre*. Established around the area's mining industry, which faded in the 19th-century, it claims to be the highest market town in England, despite no longer having a market.

South of the town square is the friendly TIC (☎ 382244; e alston.tic@eden.gov.uk; Town Hall; open 10am-5.30pm Mon-Sat, 10am-4pm Sun Apr-Oct; 11am-2pm Mon & Wed-Sat Nov-Mar). Net access here costs 50p for 15 minutes, with a charge of 35p per email.

Places to Stay & Eat
Single rooms book up quickly in summer as the town gets packed with lone railway lovers.

Alston YHA Hostel (☎ 0870 770 5668; The Firs; adult £9.50; open daily mid-Apr–Aug, Fri-Tues Sept & Oct) lies just south of the town centre, by the river, and is popular with walkers on the Pennine Way and cyclists on the C2C route.

Chapel House (☎ 381112; Overburn; rooms per person from £15) has a disarming owner and is on a quiet, cobblestone street off the marketplace.

Angel Inn (☎ 381363; Front St; rooms per person £15), a 17th-century pub opposite the TIC, offers basic, simple rooms with some good views across the countryside, and filling pub grub.

Nentholme Vegetarian Guest House (☎ 381523; w www.nentholme.co.uk; The Butts; rooms per person from £20) has calmly decorated, serene rooms with iron bedsteads, and sublime views.

Blueberry's Teashop (☎ 381928; Market Place; singles/doubles £19.50/34; meals £4-6) is a great place for tea or a hefty snack such as Boozy Pie (steak and red wine; £4.65). It's snug and cosy, with touches such as colourful hand-knitted tea cosies. It also has sweet, pretty rooms with dark-red, floral walls – convenient for the delicious cakes.

Country Garden Cafe (☎ 382233; Front St) has a strangely pre-World War II ambience, with a menu to match. Its fish and chips come much recommended (£4.20 with tea or coffee).

Getting There & Away
Bus No 888 runs between Newcastle and Keswick via Alston and Penrith once daily (June to September). Bus No 680 runs from Nenthead to Carlisle via Alston twice daily, Monday to Saturday, and No 681 runs from Nenthead to Haltwhistle via Alston twice a day, Monday to Saturday. Bus No X85 connects Durham and Kendal via Alston and Nenthead once daily on Saturday, June to September.

AROUND ALSTON
The narrow-gauge **South Tynedale Railway** (☎ 381696, talking timetable ☎ 382828; w www.strps.org.uk) puffs from Alston to Kirkhaugh (adult/child return £4/2), along a route that operated from 1852–1976. It's a pretty, high-level journey, following the River Tyne northwards. There and back takes 60 minutes, but it's best to take a picnic and relax at Kirkhaugh for a while. Timetables are complicated, so you'd best phone ahead.

You can buy a joint ticket for the railway and Killhope Lead Mining Centre for £5.90/2.95 (mine trip extra; see Weardale in the Northeast chapter) or Nenthead Mines for £6.40/3.80, £8.40/5.30 with mine trip (see next section).

Nenthead
About 5 miles (8km) east of Alston on the road over the North Pennines to Durham is Nenthead, an ex-mining village formed of terraced rows of huddled small houses. It's on the C2C cycle route and is home to **Nenthead Mines** (☎ 382037; w www.npht.com; admission only adult/child £4/2.50, with mine trip

£6.50/4.50), which date back to at least the 17th century.

The mines' big attraction is a trip down the dank tunnels. There are 40 miles (64km) of them, but the one-hour guided tour takes in just a small section. It's an atmospheric experience, as the underground tour runs through the miners' hard day-to-day grind. Sturdy shoes and something warm is required; it's 10°C down there year round and you may get dirty. If claustrophobia puts the tour off-limits, you can check out the 98.4m illuminated shaft, with its drop-stone mechanism to show the depth. There are also exhibitions on zinc and lead mining and the power of water. You can buy a combined ticket for the mine and the South Tynedale Railway (see Alston earlier).

Mill Cottage Bunkhouse (☎ 382726; *bunk beds around £8, B&B £12*) is part of the mine complex – once the smelt-mill manager's home – and provides accommodation and cooking facilities.

KIRKBY LONSDALE
☎ 01524 • pop 1596
At the southeastern corner of Cumbria, and just outside the western boundary of the Yorkshire Dales National Park (covered in the Yorkshire chapter), Kirkby Lonsdale is a honey-coloured market town and a good base for exploring both areas. Centred on an oblong marketplace, it's well served by cafés and bakeries. If you walk up to St Mary's Church you can check out Ruskin's View over the river Lune (he claimed it 'one of the loveliest scenes in England', and made the logical patriotic progression '– therefore in the world') and it is indeed lovely. There are many walks into the countryside too. There's a market on Thursday.

The **TIC** (*☎/fax 271437; 24 Main St; open 9.30am-5pm Mon-Sat, 10.30am-4.30pm Sun Apr-Oct; 10.30am-4.30pm Thur-Sun Nov-Mar*) can find accommodation in the area and has lots of walking information.

Royal Hotel (*☎ 271217, fax 272228; Marketplace; en-suite singles/doubles from £38/50; lunch £4-12, dinner £7-15*) is a rambling old place, with good-value, soberly decorated rooms and fine food.

There are several decent pubs with accommodation as well.

The Snooty Fox (*☎ 71308;* **w** *www.mortal-man-inns.co.uk; Main St; singles/doubles from £36/56; mains £6.25-17*) serves inviting food in a candlelit, intimate bar decked with faded cavalry uniforms.

Kirkby Lonsdale is 17 miles (27km) from Settle and 15 miles (24km) from Windermere; the nearest railway connection is at Oxenholme (12 miles, 19km). Bus No 567 runs from Kendal several times daily.

KIRKBY STEPHEN
☎ 017683 • pop 1619 • elevation 265m
Kirkby Stephen is a long narrow market town, with Georgian houses flanking a quietly bustling High St. It's the highest town along the Eden river, and only 4 miles (6km) from the northwest corner of the Dales. A useful base and well set up for walkers, it's the central point on the **Coast-to-Coast Walk**, which runs from St Bees Head on the west coast to Robin Hood's Bay on the east.

The **TIC** (*☎ 71199, fax 72728; Market St; open 9.30am-5.30pm Mon-Sat, 10am-4pm Sun Apr-Oct; 10am-noon & 2pm-4pm Mon, 10am-noon Tues-Sat Nov-Mar*) can find accommodation.

Kirkby Stephen YHA Hostel (*☎ 0870 7705004; Market St; adult £10.25; open Thur-Mon Apr-June, daily July & Aug, Thur-Mon Sept-Oct*) is in a converted chapel in the centre of town.

Old Court House (*☎/fax 71061; High St; en-suite rooms per person from £21*), hidden behind ivy, has excellent accommodation, and has been thoroughly renovated. Guess what the building used to be?

Rattan & Rush (*☎ 72123; 39 Market St; sandwiches around £3*) is an appealing tearoom that offers Internet access (£1 for 30 minutes).

Kirkby Stephen is on the Settle–Carlisle line; the station is a 1½-mile walk (2.5km) from town along a marked footpath. Bus no 683 travels from Penrith (one hour, six daily Monday to Saturday), No 564 from Kendal (one hour, four daily Monday to Saturday) and No 574 from Barnard Castle (three daily Monday to Saturday).

CUMBRIA

Northeast England

Northeast England (also called Northumbria after the region's ancient kingdom) includes England's most remote and empty countryside: the wind-lashed wilderness of Northumberland National Park, long white-sand stretches of the Northumberland coast, the gentle heather-carpeted Cheviots, the iron-grey enormity of Kielder Water and the bleak beauty of the North Pennines.

But it's also a region packed with ancient and modern culture. There are many prehistoric sites, magnificent Hadrian's Wall, Durham's majestic cathedral and castle (a World Heritage Site) – indeed the region has more castles than any other in the country – and powerful reminders of the area's great industrial heritage. Its largest city, Newcastle, is a thriving, exciting metropolis, with infamous nightlife and sparkling new cultural developments along its riverbanks.

The area was for centuries the battleground between north and south. Before the Roman invasion, the area from the River Humber to the Firth of Forth (Northumbria) was ruled by Celtic tribes known as the Brigantes. The Romans, ever practical, came up with the simple idea of walling themselves away from the barbarians, and the incredible feat of engineering now known as Hadrian's Wall formed the Empire's northern frontier for almost 300 years.

The wild region was difficult to control because of the rugged terrain and its sheer distance from London. The local populace had to live in fortified towers to protect themselves from a wide range of enemies – Vikings, Scots, the Border Reivers (raiders and warring families) and even their neighbours. Following the Norman conquest, the south gave up and devolved power to the already mighty prince bishops of Durham, which became a separate kingdom, forming a handy buffer zone for England against tempestuous Northumberland and the Scots.

For centuries much of this was mining country, and other related industries boomed. Newcastle, Sunderland, Hartlepool and Darlington were all major industrial centres. Durham was ringed by collieries. The industrial decline of the 20th century hit northeastern cities hard. Its legacy is everywhere, overgrown, and fascinating to explore.

Highlights

- Living it up and letting your hair down in Newcastle

- Following in Roman footsteps along magnificent Hadrian's Wall

- Castle-spotting along the blustery white-sand beaches of Northumberland

- Taking a boat out to the puffin-, gannett- and seal-covered Farne islands

- Exploring Durham's spectacular World Heritage Site and wandering the leafy banks of the River Wear

- Discovering the limitless rippling expanse of remote Kielder Water

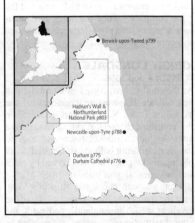

- Berwick-upon-Tweed p799
- Hadrian's Wall & Northumberland National Park p803
- Newcastle-upon-Tyne p788
- Durham p775
- Durham Cathedral p776

Despite its variety, northeast England does maintain an unlikely, loose sense of unity. There are common elements to its disparate parts: a war-torn background, proud industrial history, sense of distance from southern rule, feeling of space and passionate, independent inhabitants.

ORIENTATION & INFORMATION

The Pennine Hills are the dominant geological feature, forming a north–south spine dividing the region from Cumbria and Lancashire in the west and providing the source of major rivers such as the Tees and the Tyne.

The major transport routes are east of this spine: from Durham northwards to Newcas-

NORTHEAST ENGLAND

tle and Edinburgh. Newcastle is an important ferry port for Scandinavia. There's a northeast region website at **w** www.thenorth east.com.

ACTIVITIES

With the rugged moors of the Pennines and stunning seascape of the Northumberland coast, there's some good walking and cycling in this region. The scenery is beautiful here in a wild and untouched way – quite different from the picture-postcard landscape of areas such as Devon or the Cotswolds. If you're out in the open be prepared for wind and rain at any time of year. But when the sun shines, you can't go wrong, and this section provides a few pointers. More details on walking and cycling are given in the main Activities chapter near the start of this book, and suggestions for shorter routes are given throughout this chapter. Regional tourism websites all contain walking and cycling information, and Tourist Information Centres (TICs) all stock leaflets (free) plus maps and guides (usually £1 to £5) covering walking, cycling and other activities.

Walking

The North Pennines are billed as 'England's last wilderness', and if you like to walk in quiet and fairly remote areas, these hills – along with the Cheviots farther north – are the best in England. Long routes through this area include the famous Pennine Way, which keeps mainly to the high ground as it crosses the region between the Yorkshire Dales and the Scottish border, but also goes through sections of river valley and some tedious patches of plantation. The whole route is over 250 miles (415km), but the 70-mile (117km) section between Bowes and Hadrian's Wall would be a fine four-day taster. If you prefer to go walking just for the day, good bases for circular walks include the towns of Alston (for more details see the Cumbria chapter) and Middleton-in-Teesdale.

Elsewhere in the area, the great Roman ruin of **Hadrian's Wall** is an ideal focus for walking. There's a huge range of easy loops taking in forts and other historical highlights. A long-distance route from end-to-end is under development, with several sections already open, providing good options for anything from one to four days.

The Northumberland coast has endless miles of wide open beaches, and little in the way of resort towns (the frequently misty weather has seen to that), so walkers can often enjoy this wild, windswept shore in virtual solitude. A good base for walking is the little town of Alnmouth, and one of the finest walks is between the villages of Craster and Bamburgh via Dunstanburgh, which includes two of the area's most spectacular castles.

Cycling

A favourite for touring in this region is the Coast & Castles Cycle Route, which runs south–north along the glorious Northumberland coast between Newcastle-upon-Tyne and Berwick-upon-Tweed, before swinging inland into Scotland to finish at Edinburgh. (This route is part of the National Cycle Network – see the main Activities chapter for more details.) Of course you can also do it north–south, or just do the northeast England section. The coast is exposed though, so you should check the weather and try to time your ride so that the wind is behind you.

Another possibility is the 140-mile (230km) **Sea to Sea Cycle Route** (known as the C2C), which runs across northern England from Whitehaven or Workington on the Cumbria coast, through the northern part of the Lake District, and then over the wild hills of North Pennines to finish at Newcastle-upon-Tyne or Sunderland. This popular route is fast becoming a classic, and most people go west to east to take advantage of prevailing winds. You'll need five days to complete the whole route, but doing just the northeast England section, from Penrith (in Cumbria) to the east coast, would be a good three-day trip. If you wanted to cut the urban sections, Penrith to Consett is perfect in a weekend. The C2C is aimed at road bikes, but there are several optional off-road sections along the way.

For dedicated off-road riding, good places to aim for in northeast England include Kielder Forest in Northumberland and Hamsterley Forest in County Durham, which both have a network of sylvan tracks and options for all abilities.

GETTING THERE & AROUND
Air
Newcastle International Airport (☎ 0191-286 0966) has direct services to Aberdeen, London, Cardiff, Dublin, Belfast, Oslo, Amsterdam, Paris and Brussels.

Bus
Bus transport around the region can be difficult, particularly around the more remote parts of Northumbria in the west. Call ☎ 0870 608 2608 for information on connections, timetables and prices.

Several one-day Explorer tickets are available; always ask if one might be appropriate. The Explorer North East covers from Berwick down to Scarborough, and allows unlimited travel for one day (adult/child £5.50/4.50; available on buses), as well as numerous admission discounts.

Bus AD122 provides a useful service along Hadrian's Wall (daily June to September, Saturday and Sunday in May and October). Bus No 185 travels the route the rest of the year, less frequently (Monday to Saturday), and No 685 visits the wall-towns year round.

Train
The main lines run north to Edinburgh via Durham, Newcastle and Berwick; and west to Carlisle roughly following Hadrian's Wall. Travelling to/from the south, it may be ne-

cessary to make connections at Leeds. Phone ☎ 08457 484950 for all train inquiries.

There are numerous Rover tickets for single-day travel and longer periods, so ask if one might be worthwhile. For example, the North Country Flexi Rover allows unlimited travel throughout the north (not including Northumberland) any four days out of eight for £59/38.90.

Boat
Norway's **Fjord Line** (☎ 0191-296 1313) operates ferries to Newcastle from Stavanger and Bergen in Norway, and **DFDS Seaways** (☎ 0870 533 3000) to Newcastle from Kristiansand (Norway), Gothenburg (Sweden) and Ijmuiden, near Amsterdam (the Netherlands). See the introductory Getting There & Away chapter for details.

County Durham

County Durham has a strikingly beautiful capital and encompasses the lonely, rabbit-inhabited North Pennines, unspoilt market towns, picturesque, peaceful villages, and the plunging waterfalls and gentle ochre hills of Teesdale. Its countryside is punctuated with the relics of once-magnificent industry, slowly being reclaimed by nature, and fascinating historical sites bring its past alive.

Durham's had a turbulent history, though it pales in comparison with its troublesome northern neighbour. In the Middle Ages the south, hoping to calm the wild county and form a buffer against the bloody borderlands, allowed the local prince bishops vice-regal power. The gamble worked. Under the prince bishops the county became almost a separate kingdom, developing long before Northumberland, hence the higher population density and ordered fields. From as early as the 14th century, it was a coal-mining centre, a mighty heritage that grew to its peak in the 19th and 20th centuries. However in the mid-80s the Conservative government set about closing the surviving pits, so all that remains of this ancient tradition is some purposeless towns and an evocatively scarred landscape.

Getting Around
The Explorer North East ticket (see the earlier Getting There & Around section) is valid on many services in the county.

DURHAM

☎ 0191 • pop 38,500

Durham is a delight. It's unlike any other city in the northeast, or indeed in the country. The River Wear snakes through a woody, hilly landscape, with the neat, pretty city sitting snugly between loops in its course, dominated by the magnet of its hilltop Norman cathedral and castle. Long a centre of power, religion and learning, its wealth is evident in its buildings.

In 1832 a university was established, which today is one of the best in the country. Contemporary Durham is busy with upper-crust students – attracted to the institution's educational and rowing opportunities – and visitors drawn by the magnificent World Heritage Site and leafy, lovely surroundings.

The city was founded when the monks of Holy Island (Lindisfarne) finally came to a halt at this easily defended position in AD 995. They had been fleeing from Viking raiders with their curious, precious load: St Cuthbert's body and the illuminated Lindisfarne Gospels. From the Middle Ages, this was the capital of the county, ruled by the prince bishops who reached the pinnacle of their power in the 14th century.

Durham seems remarkably untouched by industrialisation compared with other northern cities. This is because it's restricted by the space available on the peninsula and the Wear is not navigable at this point. But mining was for centuries the region's lifeblood, and eight collieries surrounded Durham during the Victorian period, the last of

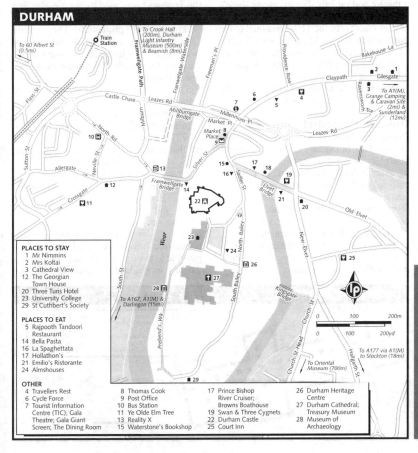

DURHAM

PLACES TO STAY
1 Mr Nimmins
2 Mrs Koltai
3 Cathedral View
12 The Georgian Town House
20 Three Tuns Hotel
23 University College
29 St Cuthbert's Society

PLACES TO EAT
5 Rajpooth Tandoori Restaurant
14 Bella Pasta
16 La Spaghettata
17 Hollathon's
21 Emilio's Ristorante
24 Almshouses

OTHER
4 Travellers Rest
6 Cycle Force
7 Tourist Information Centre (TIC); Gala Theatre; Gala Giant Screen; The Dining Room
8 Thomas Cook
9 Post Office
10 Bus Station
11 Ye Olde Elm Tree
13 Reality X
15 Waterstone's Bookshop
17 Prince Bishop River Cruiser; Browns Boathouse
19 Swan & Three Cygnets
22 Durham Castle
25 Court Inn
26 Durham Heritage Centre
27 Durham Cathedral; Treasury Museum
28 Museum of Archaeology

which closed in 1984 when the Conservatives struck the final blows to the mining industry.

Orientation

Market Place, the TIC, castle and cathedral are all on the peninsula surrounded by the River Wear. The train and bus stations are to the west on the other side of the river. Using the cathedral as your landmark, you can't really go wrong. The main sites are within easy walking distance of each other.

Information

The TIC (☎ 384 3720, fax 386 3015; e tourist info@durhamcity.gov.uk; Millennium Place; open 9.30am-5.30pm Mon-Sat, 10am-4pm Sun) is in the Gala complex, which includes a theatre and cinema. For exchange there's a Thomas Cook office (☎ 382 6600; 24-25 Market Place) near the TIC. Send mail at the post office (Silver St; open 9am-5.30pm Mon-Sat). Reality X (☎ 384 5700; 2nd floor, 1 Framwellgate Bridge) charges £3 per 30 minutes for Net access.

Waterstone's (☎ 383 1488; 69 Saddler St) has a good selection of books.

Durham Cathedral

Built as the shrine for St Cuthbert's remains, the grey bulk of Durham Cathedral's interior resembles a cave that's only partly artificial; its exterior looks like time-worn cliffs. A colossal and stunning example of 12th-century Romanesque architecture, its huge forms of weighty round arches and enormous columns are broken up by a dizzying amount of zigzagging chevron ornamentation.

It also gave a fine performance as Hogwart's classrooms in the film *Harry Potter and the Philosopher's Stone*.

Information The cathedral (☎ 386 4266; w www.durhamcathedral.co.uk; donation requested; open 9.30am-8pm daily mid-June–Sept; 9.30am-6.15pm Mon-Sat, 12.30pm-5pm Sun Oct–mid-June; private prayer only 7.30am-9.30am Mon-Sat, 7.45am-12.30pm Sun year round) has worthwhile guided tours (adult/child £3.50/free; call for times). Evensong is at 5.15pm Tuesday to Saturday (Evening Prayer on Monday) and 3.30pm on Sunday.

The tower (adult/child £2/1; open 10am-4pm Mon-Sat Mar-Nov, 10am-3pm Dec-Feb) has 325 steps leading up to spectacular views.

Inside the Cathedral You enter through the north door. The scary-haired bronze sanctuary knocker (a copy, the original is in the Treasury) was used by people escaping the rough justice of the Middle Ages and seeking church protection. They would bang the knocker to attract the attention of two watchmen who slept in a room above the door; they might then choose between a fine and exile.

The choir, transepts and nave of the cathedral (1093–1133) still survive in uncompromised Romanesque form.

Inlaid into the floor beyond the font (1670) is a narrow piece of Frosterley Marble that marked the extent that women were allowed into the medieval monastery.

Beyond, the nave is dominated by massive, powerful piers – every second one round, with an equal height and circumference of 6.6m, and carved in geometric designs. Durham was the first European cathedral to be roofed with stone-ribbed vaulting, which upheld the heavy stone roof and made it possible to build pointed transverse arches – the first in England – a great architectural

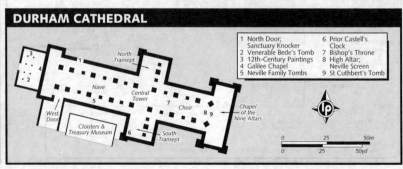

DURHAM CATHEDRAL

1 North Door; Sanctuary Knocker
2 Venerable Bede's Tomb
3 12th-Century Paintings
4 Galilee Chapel
5 Neville Family Tombs
6 Prior Castell's Clock
7 Bishop's Throne
8 High Altar; Neville Screen
9 St Cuthbert's Tomb

North Transept
Nave
Central Tower
Choir
West Door
Cloisters & Treasury Museum
South Transept
Chapel of the Nine Altars

0   25   50m
0   25   50yd

achievement. The central tower dates from 1262, but was damaged in a fire caused by lightning in 1429, and was unsatisfactorily patched up until rebuilt entirely in 1470. The western towers were added in 1217–26.

Built in 1175 and renovated 300 years later, the **Galilee Chapel** is one of the most beautiful parts. The northern side's **paintings** are rare surviving examples of 12th-century wall-painting and are thought to feature St Cuthbert and St Oswald. The chapel also contains the **Venerable Bede's tomb**. Bede was an 8th-century Northumbrian monk, a great historian and polymath whose work *The Ecclesiastical History of the English People* is still the prime source of information on the development of early Christian Britain. Among other things, he introduced the numbering of years from the birth of Jesus. He was first buried at Jarrow, but in 1022 a miscreant monk stole his remains and brought them here. Relics were like gold dust, drawing hoards of pilgrims wherever they rested.

The lords of Raby, the great Neville family, were the first lay people to be buried in the cathedral (late 14th century), but their **tombs** and a later chantry were badly damaged when the cathedral was used as a prison during the Civil War. It's hardly surprising, 4000 Scots were packed in here at the time.

The only wooden item to survive the Scots was late-15th-century **Prior Castell's Clock**, huge and much-restored. The chilly prisoners had no coal, so broke up all the woodwork they could to make fires. The clock may have been spared because of the Scots thistle towards the top of the case.

The **Bishop's Throne**, built over the tomb of Bishop Thomas Hatfield, dates from the mid-14th century. Hatfield's effigy is the only one to have survived another turbulent time: the Reformation. The **high altar** is separated from **St Cuthbert's tomb** by the beautiful stone **Neville Screen**, made around 1372–80. Until the Reformation the screen included 107 statues of saints.

The Early English Chapel of the Nine Altars (1242–80) did indeed used to have nine altars – a kind of fast food arrangement for all the crowds of priests in the monastery who needed to say Mass.

Cloisters The monastic buildings are centred on the cloisters, which were heavily rebuilt

---

An Inspirational Shepherd

St Cuthbert was originally a shepherd but he became an inspirational leader of the northern church and he was widely loved by the northern peasants. He meditated for days without food and eider ducks would get cosy in his clothing. He died on Lindisfarne in 687 and, when the Viking raids made the island untenable, the fleeing monks carried his miraculously preserved body with them. Durham cathedral was built to house his shrine and the accompanying monk community, and his reputation attracted pilgrims bearing countless offerings. All these were confiscated by the Crown during the Reformation, when the apparently still preserved body was buried under the plain marble slab where it lies today.

---

in 1828. The west door to the cloisters is famous for its 12th-century ironwork. On the western side is a **monastic dormitory** *(adult/child 80p/20p; open 10am-3.30pm Mon-Sat, 12.30pm-3.15pm Sun)*, now a library of 30,000 books and displaying Anglo-Saxon carved stones, with a vaulted undercroft that houses the Treasury Museum and restaurant.

Treasury Museum The fine Treasury Museum *(adult/child £2/50p; open 10am-4.30pm Mon-Sat, 2pm-4.30pm Sun)* includes relics of St Cuthbert from the 7th century and an interesting collection of illuminated manuscripts and cathedral paraphernalia, such as the original sanctuary knocker – he of the crazy hair.

Durham Castle

Durham Castle *(☎ 374 3800; adult/child £3/2; open for 45-min tours only, on the hour 10am-noon June-Oct, 2pm-4pm year round)* was home to Durham's prince bishops for around 750 years.

It's a mix of architectural styles, having been subjected to much alteration, partly through necessity, as it is built of soft stone on soft foundations. Each new bishop would rebuild the castle to better reflect his status, plastering new additions with his coat of arms. However, it still preserves the fundamental layout of a Norman motte-and-bailey castle. Highlights are the groaning 17th-century Black Staircase, the 16th-century chapel and the beautifully preserved Norman chapel (1080). The castle is now a university hall, and you may stay here (see Places to Stay later). Interesting tours are conducted by students.

Other Things to See

Near the cathedral, in what was the St Mary le Bow Church, you'll find the **Durham Heritage Centre** (☎ 386 8719; *St Mary le Bow, North Bailey; adult/child £1/30p; open 11am-4.30pm daily July & Aug, from 2pm daily June, Sat & Sun Apr, May & Oct)*, with crowded but interesting small-scale displays on the history and development of County Durham.

In an old fulling mill (cloth finishing mill) on the banks of the Wear, the **Museum of Archaeology** (☎ 374 3623; *adult/child £1/50p; open 11am-4pm daily Apr-Oct, 11.30am-3.30pm Fri-Mon Nov-Mar)* has a small collection illustrating the city's ancient history.

Half a mile northwest of Durham city is the **Durham Light Infantry (DLI) Museum** (☎ 384 2214; *Aykley Heads; adult/child £2.50/ 1.25; open 10am-4pm daily)*. The history of Durham's County Regiment and its part in various wars is brought to life through anecdotes and poignant artefacts; there's a small art gallery with changing exhibitions.

The **Oriental Museum** (☎ 374 7911; *Elvet Hill; adult/child £1.50/75p; open 10am-5pm Mon-Fri, noon-5pm Sat & Sun)*, a few miles south of the city centre in the university, has a good collection that ranges from fine Egyptian artefacts to a monster of a Chinese bed. Take bus No 5 or 6 heading to Bishop Auckland (Monday to Saturday).

There are superb views back to the cathedral and castle from the riverbanks; walk around the bend between Elvet and Framwellgate Bridges, or hire a boat at Elvet Bridge.

Guided walks *(adult/child £3/free; 2pm Wed, Sat & Sun May-Sept; 1½ hrs)* leave from Millennium Place – contact the TIC for details. **Ghost walks** (☎ 386 1500; *adult/child £3/1; 6.30pm Mon June-Sept, 8.30pm July & Aug; 1½ hrs)* also drift around town.

Crook Hall (☎ 384 8028; **w** *www.crookhall gardens.co.uk; Sidegate; adult/child £3.80/3; open 1pm-5pm Fri-Mon Easter, Sun May &*

Sept, Sun-Fri June-Aug) is a medieval hall with 1.6 hectares of charming small gardens, about half a mile north of the city centre.

Boating

The **Prince Bishop River Cruiser** (☎ 386 9525; *Elvet Bridge; adult/child £3.50/1.50; 2pm & 3pm June-Sept)* offers one-hour cruises.

Rowing boats can be hired for £2.50 per person per hour from **Browns Boathouse** (☎ 386 3779) below Elvet Bridge.

Places to Stay

The TIC makes local bookings free of charge, which is useful since convenient B&Bs aren't numerous; the situation is particularly pressing during graduation week in late June.

Grange Camping & Caravan Site (☎ 384 4778; *Meadow Lane; bus No 220 or 222; camping per 2 people, tent & car from £9.60)* is two miles northeast of the city centre.

Several colleges rent their rooms during the holidays (particularly July to September). Phone ☎ 374 7360 or click on **w** www .dur.ac.uk/conference_tourism/colleges.htm for information.

University College (☎ 374 3863; *B&B rooms per person £20.50)*, partly housed in Durham Castle, is the most exciting. Some rooms are available year round, such as the Bishop's suite (£75 per person) decked out with 17th-century tapestries.

St Cuthbert's Society (☎ 374 3364; *12 South Bailey; rooms per person £20)* has the cheapest accommodation in a good location.

B&Bs and hotels around town are of a good standard.

Mrs Koltai (☎ 386 2026; *10 Gilesgate; singles/doubles from £20/36)* has three reasonable, roomy options.

Mr Nimmins (☎ 384 6485; *14 Gilesgate; rooms per person from £20)* has richly decorated, spacious rooms.

Cathedral View (☎ 386 9566; **w** *www .cathedralview.co.uk; 212 Gilesgate; singles £45-50, doubles/triples £60/75)* has rooms with magnificent views. The breakfast room also has a vast vista and a small balcony. **60 Albert St** (☎ 386 0608; *singles/ doubles from £27/50)* is a friendly joint, an elegant Victorian townhouse, immaculately and stylishly restored.

The Georgian Town House (☎/fax 386 8070; *10 Crossgate; en-suite singles/doubles from £55/70)*, decorated with elaborate stencilling, is smart and comfortable; some rooms have cathedral views.

Three Tuns Hotel (☎ 386 4326; w www .swallowhotels.com; New Elvet; singles/doubles from £95/100), a former 16th-century coaching inn, is upmarket and much modernised. Ask for a room in the old part.

Places to Eat

Emilio's Ristorante (☎ 384 0096; 96 Elvet Bridge; pizza or pasta from £6; open lunch Mon-Sat, dinner daily) has a warm atmosphere and leafy riverside outlook.

Bella Pasta (☎ 386 1060; 20-21 Silver St; 2-courses meal 5pm-7pm £5.95) is a mundane chain, but has great riverside seating and an airy conservatory.

Almshouses (☎ 386 1054; Palace Green; dishes around £3; open 9am-5pm daily) serves imaginative and satisfying snacks in a 17th-century house.

Rajpooth Tandoori Restaurant (☎ 386 1496; 80 Claypath; mains from £5.95) has a good reputation for Indian food.

La Spaghettata (☎ 383 9290; 66 Saddler St; open lunch Fri-Sun, dinner Tues-Sun) is lively, with cheap-and-cheerful pizzas and pastas.

The slick **Dining Room** (☎ 332 4044; Millennium Place; mains £7.50-15) rather fancies itself, but the modern British fare is good and there's a large terrace with a great view.

Hollathon's (☎ 386 4923; 16-17 Elvet Bridge; mains around £7) has a relaxed brasserie upstairs and candle-lit cellar restaurant serving good pasta and risotto.

Entertainment

The TIC has a two-monthly *What's On* guide.

Gala Theatre (☎ 332 4041; w www.gala durham.co.uk; Millennium Place) features popular drama, music and comedy.

Travellers Rest (☎ 384 7483; 1 Marshall Terrace) is a pleasant, friendly place with a cosy bar.

Swan & Three Cygnets (☎ 384 0242; Elvet Bridge; mains around £7), a high-ceilinged riverside pub, has tables overlooking the river and good bar food.

Court Inn (☎ 384 7350; Court Lane) is a popular, tucked-away local haunt with a mix of students and professionals.

Ye Olde Elm Tree (☎ 386 4621; 12 Crossgate) is an old-fashioned real-ale pub. A popular quiz night on Wednesday hauls in the students.

Getting There & Away

Durham is 260 miles (419km) from London, 75 miles (121km) from Leeds and 15 miles (24km) from Newcastle.

Bus National Express buses run from London (£33, 6½ hours, five daily), from Edinburgh (£21, four hours, one daily) via Jedburgh and Melrose in the Scottish Borders, and from Leeds (£18.50, 2½ hours, three daily) via Newcastle (£2.75, 30 minutes). Bus No 352 links Newcastle and Blackpool via Durham, Barnard Castle, Raby Castle and Kirkby Stephen.

Train There are numerous trains to Newcastle (£3.40 single, 20 minutes), York (£22, one hour), Edinburgh (£36, two hours) and London (£79, three hours).

Getting Around

Pratt's Taxis (☎ 386 0700) charges a minimum of about £1.80.

Cycle Force (☎ 384 0319; 29 Claypath) charges £15/7.50 per whole/half day for mountain-bike hire.

AROUND DURHAM
Beamish Open-Air Museum

Beamish (☎ 0191-370 4000; w www .beamish.org.uk; admission Nov-Mar £4, adult/child Apr-Oct £12/6; open 10am-5pm daily Apr-Oct, 10am-4pm Nov-Mar) is a living, breathing, working museum and makes for a great day out. Whole slices of north-eastern life are reconstructed as they were in the 19th and 20th centuries, tellingly depicting life before and after the Industrial Revolution.

You can go underground, explore mine heads, a working farm, a school, a dentist and a pub, and marvel at how every cramped pit cottage seemed to find room for a piano. Don't miss a ride behind a replica of Stephenson's Locomotive.

Allow at least two hours to do the place justice. Many elements aren't open in the winter – call for details.

Beamish is about 8 miles (13km) northwest of Durham; it's signposted from the A1(M) – take the A691 west at junction 63. Bus Nos 709 from Newcastle (50 minutes, hourly) and 720 from Durham (30 minutes, hourly) run to the museum. You get a discount if you come by bus.

BARNARD CASTLE

☎ 01833 • pop 6000 • elevation 152m

Gentle, bustling Barnard Castle is a honey-coloured market town, with a daunting ruined castle at its edge and extraordinary French chateau on its outskirts. It's a good base for exploring Teesdale and the North Pennines.

The **TIC** (☎ 690909, 695320; e tourism@ teesdale.gov.uk; Woodleigh, Flats Rd; open 9.30am-5.30pm daily Easter-Oct, 11am-4pm Mon-Sat Nov-Mar) handles visitor inquiries.

Things to See & Do

Owned by English Heritage (EH), Barnard Castle (☎ 638212; adult £2.50; open 10am-6pm daily Easter-Sept, 10am-5pm daily Oct, 10am-1pm & 2pm-4pm Wed-Sun Nov-Mar) is huge. Partly dismantled, its burly bulk, on a cliff above the Tees, still manages to cover almost 2.4 hectares. Founded by Guy de Bailleul and rebuilt around 1150, it was important in suppressing local rebellions and repelling the Scots, and you can see why it was successful. There are wonderful views of the river.

Completely out of context, the fantastical Louvre-inspired French chateau, 1½ miles (2.5km) west of town, houses the fantastic **Bowes Museum** (☎ 690606; w www.bowes museum.org.uk; adult/child £5/free; open 11am-5pm daily). The remarkable and under-visited collection could give the V&A a run for its money, with lavish furniture, and paintings by Canaletto, El Greco and Goya. A prime exhibit is the mechanical silver swan, operated at 12.30pm and 3.30pm.

Places to Stay & Eat

Marwood House (☎ 637493; 98 Galgate; singles £22-27, doubles £42-46) has comfortable rooms.

Greta House (☎ 631193; 89 Galgate; en-suite singles £30-35, doubles £45-50), across the road, has spotless, pretty rooms and special touches such as home-made cake in your room.

Old Well (☎ 690130; w www.oldwellinn .co.uk; 21 The Bank; en suite singles £48, doubles £60-70), downhill from Market Cross, is cosy and has fine rooms with character, and excellent, filling pub food, but sometimes lacklustre service.

Hayloft off Horsemarket is nicely tucked away from the busy main street and serves light meals. It also has a wonderful, attic-like shop upstairs, and offers hat stretching 'at your own risk' (£2).

Getting There & Away

Bus No 352 runs daily between Newcastle and Blackpool via Durham, Bishop Auckland, Barnard Castle, Raby Castle and Kirkby Stephen.

AROUND BARNARD CASTLE
Egglestone Abbey

The ransacked, spectral ruins of Egglestone Abbey (open dawn-dusk), dating from the 1190s, overlook a lovely bend of the Tees. You can envisage the abbey's one-time grandeur despite the gaunt remains. They're a pleasant mile walk south of Barnard Castle.

Raby Castle

Raby Castle (☎ 660202; w www.rabycastle .com; castle only adult/child £5/2; open 1pm-5pm • grounds only adult/child £3/2; open 11am-5.30pm Wed & Sun May & Sept, Sun-Fri June-Aug) is a sprawling, romantic 14th-century castle, a stronghold of the Neville family until they did some ill-judged plotting against the Crown in 1569 (the Rising of the North). Most of the interior dates from the 18th and 19th centuries, but the exterior remains true to the original design, built around a courtyard and surrounded by a moat. There are beautiful formal gardens and a deer park. It's 7 miles (10km) northeast of Barnard Castle – follow the A688 to Staindrop. Bus Nos 8 and 352 zip between Barnard Castle and Raby (20 minutes, seven to 10 daily).

BISHOP AUCKLAND

☎ 01388 • pop 23,139 • elevation 139m

The friendly market town of Bishop Auckland, 11 miles southwest of Durham, surveys rolling countryside from a hill-top setting. It is the home of dramatic Auckland Castle, the country residence of the bishops of Durham since the 12th century. The castle is just next to the large, attractive market square, from which lead off small-town streets lined with high-street shops and a sense that anything exciting is happening elsewhere.

The **TIC** (☎ 604922, fax 604960; Market Place; open 10am-5pm Mon-Fri, 9am-4pm Sat year round; 1pm-4pm Sun Apr-Sept) is in the town hall on Market Place.

The imposing gates of **Auckland Castle** (☎ 601627; adult/child £3.50/2.50; open

2pm-5pm Sun, 12.30pm-5pm Mon & Thur Apr-Sept), just off Market Place behind the town hall, are hard to miss. Started in the 12th century, it was the favourite country residence of the prince bishops, and is now the official home of the bishop of Durham. It's palatial – each successive bishop extended the building. Underneath the spiky Restoration Gothic exterior, the buildings are mainly medieval. The outstanding attraction of the castle is the striking 17th-century chapel, which thrusts up into the sky. It has a remarkable partially 12th-century interior, converted from the former great hall.

Around the castle is a hilly and wooded 324-hectare **deer park** *(admission free; open 7am-sunset)* with an 18th-century deer shelter.

AROUND BISHOP AUCKLAND

One and a half miles (2.5km) north of Bishop Auckland is **Binchester Roman Fort** *(Vinovia; ☎ 663089; W www.durham.gov.uk/binchester; adult/child £1.60/80p; excavations open 11am-5pm daily Easter-Sept)*, or Vinovia as it was originally called. The fort, first built in wood around AD 80 and rebuilt in stone early in the 2nd century, was the largest in County Durham, covering 4 hectares. Excavations show the remains of Dere St, the main high road from York to Hadrian's Wall, and the best-preserved example of a heating system in the country – part of the commandants' private bath suite. Findings from the site are displayed at the Bowes Museum (see Barnard Castle earlier).

The stones of the abandoned Binchester Fort were often reused, and Roman inscriptions can be spotted in the walls of hauntingly beautiful **Escomb Church** *(☎ 602861; admission free; open 9am-8pm Apr-Sept, 9am-4pm Oct-Mar)*. The church dates from the 7th century – it's one of only three complete surviving Saxon churches in Britain. It's a white-washed cell, striking and moving in its simplicity, incongruously encircled by a 20th-century cul de sac. If no-one's about, collect the keys from a hook outside a nearby house. Escomb is 3 miles (5km) west of Bishop Auckland (Bus No 86, 87 or 87A; 15 per day Monday to Saturday, 10 on Sunday).

Albion Cottage Guest House *(☎ 602217; Albion Terrace; singles/doubles £18/34)*, on a quiet turning in Bishop Auckland, has plain rooms and a pretty garden.

Queens Head Hotel *(☎ 603477; 38 Market Place; singles/doubles Sun-Thur from £40/50, Fri & Sat £35/45)*, right next to the TIC, is pleasant, with big rooms. Prices drop at the weekend because a disco rages till 2am.

There are a number of tearooms in and around Market Place.

Fortune Court *(☎ 602888; 23-25 Market Place; lunch menu 11am-2pm Mon-Sat £6)* is a recommended Cantonese place, with a special three-course lunch menu. Evening mains are pricier.

Bus No 352 running from Newcastle to Blackpool passes through Bishop Auckland (daily March to November, Saturday and Sunday December to February), as does bus No X85 from Durham to Kendal (one Saturday June to September).

You need to change at Darlington for regular trains to Bishop Auckland (single £2.60, 24 minutes, every two hours).

THE DURHAM DALES

The western half of the county consists of fertile, rocky dales that run into the North Pennines. The Rivers Tees and Wear cut through the landscape, creating Teesdale to the south and Weardale to the north. Both are marked by ancient quarries and mines – industries that date back to Roman times.

Teesdale
☎ 01833

From the confluence of the Rivers Greta and Tees to Caldron Snout at the source of the Tees, Teesdale is filled with woods, scattered unspoilt villages, rivers, waterfalls and sinuous moorland. There are huge numbers of rabbits bounding about, as if competing for a role in *Watership Down*. The Pennine Way snakes along the dale.

Middleton-in-Teesdale A tranquil, pretty village of white and stone houses among soft green hills, Middleton-in-Teesdale is 10 miles (16km) northwest of Barnard Castle. It was once owned by the Quaker London Lead Company, when it probably wasn't party central, but the prosperity of that era shows in its confident, attractive buildings. It's a peaceful base from which to explore the surrounding woods and riverbanks.

There's a diffident **TIC** *(☎ 641001; e mid dletonplus@compuserve.com; open 10am-12.30pm & 2.30pm-5pm daily Apr-Oct)* with lots of information on local walks. Ring for details of winter hours.

Bluebell House (☎ 640584; ⓦ www.blue bellhouse-teesdale.co.uk; Market Place; en-suite singles £20-25, doubles £34), in the heart of the village, is accommodating and welcoming and rents bicycles for £8 per day.

Brunswick House (☎/fax 640393; ⓦ www .brunswickhouse.net; 55 Market Place; rooms per person from £24) is a Georgian house with white-and-floral rooms.

King's Head (☎ 640467; 53 Market Place; mains from £7.50), across the road from Bluebell House, has tasty food.

High Force A few miles up the valley from Middleton, **Bowlees Visitor Centre** (☎/fax 622292; wildlife display adult/child £1/50p; open 10.30am-5pm daily Apr-Oct, 10.30am-4pm Sat & Sun Nov-Feb) has lots of walking and wildlife leaflets and a small natural history display. Some gentle trails spread out from here (a leaflet with four circular walks will lighten you by 30p), taking in the nearby woods, the quaint village of Newbiggin, and the tumbling waters of Low Force – some metre-high steps along a very scenic stretch of river – and High Force, England's largest waterfall. Bus No 73 stops here and by the High Force Hotel (see following).

Thundering **High Force** waterfall (adult/child £1/50p) is 4½ miles (7km) from Middleton. Other than the roar of the water, it's a quiet place surrounded by romantic countryside, with a gentle woodland walk down to the falls. The car park costs £1.50.

The **High Force Hotel & Brewery** (☎ 622 222; ⓦ www.highforcehotel.com; Forest-in-Teesdale; rooms per person from £25), nearby, is excellent. The walls of the bar are plastered with photographs of High Force in spectacular flood, and award-winning ales are brewed on the premises. Beware the Cauldron Snout: it's got a kick like a mule. If you've had one too many the hotel serves meals and provides B&B.

Langdon Beck The B6277 leaves the River Tees at High Force and continues up to Langdon Beck, where the scenery quickly turns from green rounded hills to the lonely landscape of the North Pennines, dotted with small chapels. You can either continue on the B6277 over the Pennines to

Alston and Cumbria or turn right and take a minor road over the moors to St John's Chapel in Weardale.

Langdon Beck YHA Hostel (☎ 0870 770 5910; ⓔ langdonbeck@yha.org.uk; Forest-in-Teesdale; beds per adult £10.25; open Mon-Sat Apr-Sept, Fri & Sat Nov, Tues-Sat early Feb-Mar, Sept-Oct), a mile before Langdon Beck, is wonderfully isolated, and serves as a stopping point for walkers on the Pennine Way. It's also a good base for short walks into the dales and the Pennines, in particular to Cow Green Reservoir, the source of the Tees.

Bus No 73 connects Middleton and Langdon Beck, via Bowlees and High Force, at least once a day Tuesday, Wednesday, Friday and Saturday. Bus Nos 75 and 76 serve Middleton from Barnard Castle several times daily.

Weardale
☎ 01388

Weardale, sheltered by the Pennines, was once the hunting ground of the prince bishops. From the 13th century its history has been entwined with mining and quarrying, reaching its heyday as a lead-mining centre in the 18th to 19th centuries. The rust and olive-coloured patchwork moors are pitted with mining scars. There are splendid walks in the surrounding countryside.

Frosterley About 15 miles (24km) north-west of Bishop Auckland is the quiet, grey town of Frosterley at the start of the valley, renowned for its 'marble' (fossil-rich black limestone), which decks a lot of England's churches, including Durham Cathedral. There are some good cycle tracks in nearby **Hamsterley Forest** – over 400 hectares of woodland – but you'll need your own bike.

The **Black Bull Inn** (☎ 527784; Bridge End; en-suite singles/doubles £25/38) is in a pretty spot at the western end of Frosterley, 100m from the main road on the way to White Kirkley. It has comfy rooms, and meals are served every evening except Tuesday.

Stanhope & Ireshopburn Two miles (3km) farther up the valley is peaceful Stanhope, a honey-coloured town with a cobbled market place. It's a good base for windswept walks across the moors. Its interesting church is Norman at the base, but mostly dates from the 12th century.

The **TIC** (☎ 527650; e durham.dales.centre@ durham.gov.uk; open 10am-5pm daily Apr-Oct, 10am-4pm Mon-Fri, 11am-4pm Sat & Sun Nov-Mar) has lots of information on walks in the area, and there's a small tearoom.

Redlodge Guest House (☎ 527851; 2 Redlodge Cottages, Market Place; rooms per person with/without shower from £25/22.50) is friendly and homely. Ring ahead as there are only two rooms, and Stanhope is the last stop on the C2C route before cyclists push on to Sunderland.

Queen's Head (☎ 528160; 89 Front St; mains £4.55-8) is a friendly place offering simple, hearty pub grub.

In **Ireshopeburn**, 8 miles (13km) on from Stanhope, the **Weardale Museum** (☎ 537417; w www.weardale.co.uk; adult/child £1/30p; open 2pm-5pm Wed-Sun May-Sept, daily Aug) allows a glimpse into local history, including a spotless lead-mining family kitchen and stuff on preacher John Wesley. It's next to **High House Chapel**, a Methodist chapel built in 1760, one of Wesley's old stomping grounds.

Killhope At the top of the valley, 13 miles (21km) from Stanhope, is the **Killhope Lead Mining Centre** (☎ 537505; adult/child £3.40/ 1.70, with mine trip £5/2.50; open 10.30am-5pm daily Apr-Oct, 10.30am-4pm Sun Nov), the blackened machinery bleak and ghostly in the hills. The site is dominated by an imposing 10m-high working water wheel that drove a crushing mechanism.

'Hope' means 'side valley', but the site seems aptly named as you learn how the men who worked the mine lived. An absorbing exhibition explains what life was like: poor pay, poorer living conditions and the constant threat of illness forced many of the workers into an early grave. The most poignant records are those of the washer boys – children employed in freezing, back-breaking work. The mine closed in 1910 but you can still visit its atmospheric underground network, as it was in 1878, on an hour-long guided tour; wear warm clothes. There's also a sparkling mineral exhibition for the geologically inclined.

It's possible to buy a combined ticket for the mine and the South Tynedale Railway (see the Alston section in the Cumbria chapter). From the mining centre it's another 7 miles (11km) up over the highest main road

in England (617m) and the North Pennines and down into Alston (see the Cumbria chapter for details).

Bus No 101 makes the regular trip up the valley from Bishop Auckland to Stanhope (10 daily). If you ring ahead, it will go on to Killhope mid-morning and pick you up in the afternoon. Call **Wearhead Motor Services** (☎ 01388-528235) to arrange the service.

North Pennines

The wilds of the North Pennines only putter out just before Hadrian's Wall, and are home to the picturesque Derwent and Allen valleys, north of Weardale.

Derwent Valley Pretty Blanchland and Edmundbyers, two small, remote villages, are south of the denim expanse of the **Derwent Reservoir**, surrounded by wild moorland and forests. The 3½-mile-long reservoir has been here since 1967, and the county border separating Durham and Northumberland runs right through it. The valley's good for walking and cycling, as well as sailing, which may be arranged through **Derwent Reservoir Sailing Club** (☎ 01434-675258).

Nestling among trees, and surrounded by wild mauve and mustard moors, **Blanchland** is an unexpected surprise. It's a charming, golden-stoned, grouping of small cottages arranged around an L-shaped square, framed by a medieval gateway. The village was named after the white cassocks of local monks – there was a Premonstratensian Abbey here from the 12th century. Around 1721 the prince bishop of the time, Lord Crewe, seeing the village and abbey falling into disrepair, bequeathed the buildings to trustees on the condition that they were protected and looked after.

Lord Crewe Arms Hotel (☎ 01434-675251; w www.lordcrewehotel.com; singles/doubles £80/110; lunch £4-10, 4-course dinner £28) is in what was the abbot's lodge, a mainly 17th-century building, with a 12th-century crypt that makes a cosy bar. It's a glorious hotel, with open fires, hidden corners, tall windows and superb food.

Another inviting, quiet village, **Edmundbyers** is 4 miles (6km) east of Blanchland on the B6306 along the southern edge of Derwent Reservoir.

Edmundbyers YHA Hostel (☎ 0870 770 5810; e edmundbyers@yha.org.uk; Low House;

Flaming Allendale

Thought to be Viking or pagan in origin, the Baal Fire on New Year's Eve – a procession of flaming whiskey barrels through Allendale, has certainly been taking place for centuries. The 45 barrels are filled with tar and are carried on the heads of a team of 'guisers' with blackened or painted faces – this hot and hereditary honour gets passed from generation to generation. The mesmerising procession is accompanied by pounding music, and leads to a pile of branches, where the guisers chuck the scorching barrels to fire up an enormous pyre at midnight, doing their best not to set themselves alight.

adult £8.75; open Apr-Oct) is housed in a 17th-century former inn. The hostel helps to serve walkers in the area and cyclists on the C2C route.

It's 12 miles (19km) north of Stanhope and 10 miles (16km) south of Hexham on the B6306. Bus No 773 runs from Consett to Blanchland via Edmundbyers at least four times a day, Monday to Saturday.

Allen Valley The Allen Valley is in the heart of the North Pennines, with individual, remote villages huddled high up surrounded by bumpy hills and heather and gorse-covered moors. It's fantastic walking country, speckled with the legacy of the lead-mining industry.

Allendale Town is small, centred around a big open square. It's 7 miles (11km) from Hexham on the B6295. The quiet rural community hots up on New Year's Eve when the distinctly pagan and magical 'Tar Barrels' ceremony is performed (see the boxed text 'Flaming Allendale').

Allendale Tea Rooms (☎ 683575; Market Place; rooms per person from £20), in a little black and white fronted building, also offers B&B.

Kings Head Hotel (☎ 683681; Market Square; rooms per person from £22.50), a convivial 18th-century pub, packed with locals, has welcoming rooms and offers filling food.

Four miles (6km) farther south towards the Wear Valley is **Allenheads**, the highest village in England, nestled at the head of Allen Valley. It really just consists of a few houses

and a marvellously eccentric hotel. There's a small **Heritage Centre** (☎ 685395; adult/child £1/50p; open 9am-5pm daily Apr-Oct) with some displays on the history of the village and surrounding area and access to a blacksmith's cottage and a small nature walk.

Allenheads Inn (☎ 685200; singles/doubles £21/42) is an attraction in its own right. It's a 17th-century, low-beamed pub, packed with a bizarre collection of bric-a-brac – around 5000 assorted objects, from mounted stag heads to Queen Mum plates. It's friendly and a highly recommended, creaky place to stay, and serves up hearty, tasty food as well.

The **Hemmel Coffee Shop** (☎ 685395; open year round), in a converted barn, is part of the heritage centre and a relaxing place to grab a bite.

Bus No 688 runs up and down the Allen Valley from Hexham to Allenheads (stopping at Allendale Town; 30 minutes, five daily).

The Tees Valley

The Tees Valley – not to be confused with Teesdale farther west along the river – is largely dominated by industrial towns, once of instrumental importance to the region's economy and nowadays, following 20th-century industrial decline, somewhat forgotten. The historic opening of the Stockton and Darlington Railway in 1825 accelerated the area's industrial development as its towns thrived on the transport of coal.

The sprawling towns of Darlington and Hartlepool have interesting sights relating to their past glories (contemporary equivalents are conspicuously absent). Darlington has a fascinating railway museum, and Hartlepool an atmospheric recreated 18th-century port.

South of the river mouth lie distinctive Redcar, a typical brash English seaside resort, and Saltburn-by-the-Sea, a dramatically situated, small Victorian spa town.

DARLINGTON
☎ 01670 • pop 99,700
In 1825 the Stockton and Darlington Railway opened, and made history as the first railway in the world to carry passengers. George Stephenson's *No 1 Locomotion* chugged along at the breakneck speed of 10 to 13 miles per hour, carrying 600 people, mostly in coal trucks.

Darlington burgeoned and sprawled on the back of the railway industry that followed all the excitement. But its roots as a traditional market town can be seen at its centre, with a large market place that's still filled by stalls every Monday and Saturday. Staying more than a few hours in Darlington could make you depressed, but if you get stuck here the **TIC** (☎ *388666;* e *tic@darlington.gov.uk; 13 Horsemarket; open 9am-5pm Mon, Tues, Thur & Fri, 9.30am-5pm Wed, 10am-4pm Sat)* will help you find accommodation.

The **Railway Centre & Museum** (☎ *460 532;* w *www.drcm.org.uk; adult/child £2.10 /1.05; open 10am-5pm daily),* a mile north of the centre, is a magnet for railway lovers and those interested in industrial history. It's actually situated on the original 1825 route, in Stockton and Darlington railway buildings that date to the 1840s and 50s. Pride of place is the lovingly tended, surprisingly small *Locomotion,* but there are a number of other fine, sturdy locomotives, including the *Derwent,* the earliest surviving Darlington-built engine. It's well signposted from the town centre. The Darlington–Bishop Auckland train stops at North Road Station, built in 1842, by the museum.

St Cuthbert's Church *(Market Place)* was founded in 1183, and is a fine, quite complete example of Early English design topped by a 14th-century tower.

Bus Nos 13 and 723 run between Darlington and Durham (£4.40, 45 minutes, half-hourly Monday to Saturday, hourly on Sunday). Bus No 723 also runs half-hourly from Darlington to Newcastle (£4.40, 2 hours).

Darlington is also on the York (£15.20, 30 minutes) to Newcastle (single £5.30, 40 minutes) line so there are frequent connections to both.

AROUND DARLINGTON
Piercebridge

Piercebridge consists of an endearing array of whitewashed cottages forming a rectangle around a perfect village green. It's hard to equate it with a bustling Roman town and major highway, but the Romans pitched up here in the 1st century and a fort developed, because the main route from York to Hadrian's Wall – Dere St – crossed the River Tees at this point. The east gate and defences of a second fort, built around 270, have been

excavated east of the village green and helpful information plaques are scattered throughout the **excavations** *(admission free;* w *www .piercebridge.com)* to help you imagine what it was like. Lots of booty has been dug up at this site, it's on display at the Bowes Museum (see Barnard Castle).

Bridge House (☎ *374727; rooms per person from £21)* is pretty, with a lovely location, two comfortable rooms and an adjoining riverside garden.

Piercebridge is 5 miles (8km) west of Darlington on the A67. Bus No 75 or 76 between Darlington and Barnard Castle stop here (twice daily).

HARTLEPOOL
☎ 01429 • pop 94,400

On the northern side of Tees Bay, 19 miles (31km) from Durham, is Hartlepool. A busy port from the middle ages, it sank into decline in the 18th century, but was revitalised in the 19th as a result of the railway, becoming the fourth busiest port in England. It was also a major shipbuilding centre until economic decline hit. Nowadays, it's a disheartening, grim place, and its interesting Historic Quay and Museum only serve to emphasise the void left by the disappearance of industry. This void may also explain why the disconsolate townspeople elected a monkey as mayor in 2002 (see the boxed text 'Hartlepool Goes Bananas').

The **TIC** (☎ *869706;* w *www.thisishartle pool.com; Church Square; open 10am-5.30pm Tues-Sat, 2pm-5pm Sun)* shares the refurbished Christ Church with the **Hartlepool Art Gallery**, which features changing exhibitions.

Hartlepool Historic Quay and Museum (☎ *860006; Jackson Dock, Maritime Ave; adult/child £5.50/2.75; open 10am-5pm daily)* is an impressive complex that includes a recreated 18th-century port complete with harbour-side shops, a show about pressganging, and lots of hands-on activities and displays. The **HMS Trincomalee** (☎ *223193; adult/child £3.70/2.70; open 10.30am-3.30pm daily),* built in 1817 and Britain's oldest warship still afloat, bobs around in the harbour as well. It's a fine old ship, and the audio tour provided does a stalwart job of bringing to life what went on in each section.

The museum has extensive displays on Hartlepool's dynamic social and industrial

Hartlepool Goes Bananas

In 2002, a monkey was elected mayor of Hartlepool. Well, truth be told, he was a man dressed as the Hartlepool United mascot – H'Angus – one very surprised Stuart Drummond, who till then had been working in a call centre. But why a monkey mascot? The answer lies in a legend, which up to this point was the most notorious thing about Hartlepool.

The story goes that one December day at the beginning of the 1800s a particularly strong storm hit the northeast coast. At the time England was engaged in the Napoleonic wars with France. A French ship, the *Chasse Maree*, was spotted in trouble off the coast of Hartlepool, so local fishermen were on guard. The vessel sank, but a sole survivor was washed ashore, a monkey dressed in a military uniform. The fishermen, never having seen a Frenchman before, assumed the waterlogged fellow to be a French spy. The monkey was then questioned and, since it gave no satisfactory answers, was found guilty and hanged.

Apparently the real source of this story was a song by a popular 19th-century entertainer, and it became a popular way to poke fun at Hartlepool's citizens, who retaliated in good humour by adopting the hanging monkey as a football mascot.

So the simian saga continues. Stuart Drummond has not yet come good on his election promises, such as free bananas for all school kids. But the town's vote has a serious subtext, showing a community so disillusioned with politics as to promote H'Angus to mayor.

history, encompassing its coal, iron, steel and shipbuilding connections.

Trains leave every half-hour for Newcastle (single £5, 50 minutes).

SALTBURN-BY-THE-SEA
☎ 01287 • pop 20,000

Saltburn's prim Victorian grandeur is well conserved, and it's in a dramatic location, with tall buildings set high up on a steep incline above the beach. The wooded Valley Gardens stretch to the east of the town.

Until the arrival of the railway, Saltburn was a mere village, thriving mainly through smuggling. The railway changed all that and it was transformed into a small seaside resort.

The **TIC** (☎ 622422, fax 625074; 3 Station Buildings; open 9am-5pm Mon-Sat May-Oct, Tues-Sat Nov-Apr) can arrange accommodation if required.

One important Victorian fixture is its **Inclined Tramway** (☎ 622528; tickets 50p; open 10am-7pm daily June-Oct, 10am-1pm & 1.30pm-5pm Oct-May). Built in 1884, it's the oldest water-balanced lift in Britain, and drops 36m (120 feet) from the town to the sandy beach and pier.

The spindly, graceful pier, a simple open walkway over the sea, straddles the water like an insect. It's been washed away many times, and was last repaired in 2002.

The **Smugglers Heritage Centre** (☎ 625 252; adult/child £1.90/1.40; open 10am-6pm

daily Apr-Sept), 200m east of the pier and housed in former fishermen's cottages, delves with relish into the mysterious and popular pastime of smuggling in the late 18th century.

Brydene (☎ 622653; 23 Ruby St; singles/doubles £18/30) has simple but adequate rooms.

Spa Hotel (☎ 622544; w www.spahotels .co.uk; Saltburn Bank; singles/doubles £39.50/ 50; mains around £7) has fine views over the bay and comfortable rooms. You can also enjoy the view by dining at the **Conservatory Restaurant**.

The **Ship Inn** (☎ 622361; mains around £6), next to the Smugglers Heritage Centre, is a superb pub overlooking the sea offering good bar food, great views and a well-drawn pint.

Saltburn has frequent train connections to Darlington (£5 day return, 50 minutes) via Redcar. Bus Nos X4, 48 and 49 regularly run between Saltburn and Redcar as well.

Newcastle-upon-Tyne

☎ 0191 • pop 200,000

To a newcomer, Newcastle is an unexpected surprise. The grand 19th-century streets at its centre swoop down to the river, the focal point of the city, with its eclectic and cluttered array of bridges. There's a fierce sense of life, and the city's powerful identity is reinforced by the townspeople's strong and distinctive accent – they're not English, but Geordie (the name apparently was originally coined to disparage the townspeople, who were loyal to George I).

The largest city in the northeast (with adjoining Gateshead), it is pitching to become European City of Culture in 2008, and development has been swift and ambitious in recent years. The Millennium Bridge forms a graceful arc over to Baltic – a mammoth contemporary arts centre, and the Sage (concert venue and music centre), which sits nearby like a huge glassy insect. Developed in Gateshead to regenerate the area, they're ironically most accessible from the Newcastle side. Hardly heavenly Gateshead is also the base of the Angel of the North, a beautiful, surreal monument on an appropriately industrial scale.

Newcastle grew famous as a port for coal exportation, and in the 19th century became an important steel, shipbuilding and engineering centre. These industries went into serious decline after WWII, and the city's had a dour struggle to survive. But its on the up and full of proud, personable people; there's lots to see and the nightlife's not to be missed – Geordies let their hair down in style.

Orientation

Newcastle is north of the Tyne, Gateshead is to the south. The new developments on Gateshead's quayside are easily reached by walking over the bridges from Newcastle. The city centre is walkable, and the Metro underground system (convenient for hostels and B&Bs) is cheap, efficient and pleasant to use.

Central Station (train) is to the south of the city centre. The coach station is on Gallowgate, while local and regional buses leave from Eldon Square and Haymarket bus stations.

Information

The **main TIC office** (☎ 277 8000; w www .newcastle.gov.uk; 132 Grainger St; open 9.30am-5.30pm Mon-Wed, Fri & Sat, 9.30am-7.30pm Thur year round; 10am-4pm Sun June-Sept) is well stocked. There's also a convenient train station **TIC** (☎ 277 8000; open 9.30am-5pm Mon-Sat), and a **desk**

(☎ 214 4422; open daily) at the airport. All provide a free map, guide and accommodation list, and a booking service (☎ 277 8042). **Gateshead Quays Visitor Centre** (☎ 477 5380; St Mary's Church; open 10am-4pm Sat & Sun) has further information on Gateshead's attractions.

Send mail at the **post office** (35 Mosley St; open 9am-5.30pm Mon-Fri, 9am-12.30pm Sat) and surf the Net at **Internet Exchange** (☎ 230 1280; 26-30 Market St), which charges £1 for 30 minutes.

Thomas Cook (☎ 219 8000; 6 Northumberland St), bureau de change and travel agency, has an office here. The **Newcastle Map Centre** (☎ 261 5622; w www.newtraveller .com; 1st floor, 55 Grey St) supplies copious maps and guides.

There are two **Waterstone's** near Monument, one particularly finely housed (☎ 261 6140; 104 Grey St), or **Blackwell's Bookshop** (☎ 232 6421; 141 Percy St) has a comprehensive range of titles. If you're looking for a laundrette **Clayton Road Laundrette** (☎ 281 5055; 4 Clayton Rd) is around a mile away in Jesmond.

Newcastle General Hospital (☎ 273 8811; Westgate Rd) is a mile northwest of the city centre. For police assistance, contact the **police station** (☎ 214 6555; cnr Pilgrim & Market Sts).

Baltic – The Centre for Contemporary Art

Towering over the Tyne is a dirty yellow building, once a huge, solid 1950s grain house. Baltic (☎ 478 1810; w www.balticmill .com; admission free; open 10am-7pm Mon-Wed, Fri & Sat, 10am-10pm Thur, 10am-5pm Sun) is now a huge, solid contemporary art venue aiming to champion and inspire new work. Its glass-sided galleries are imposingly large and bright, filled with changing installations and other work by international and local names. The complex has artists-in-residence, a performance space, a cinema, a bar, a spectacular rooftop restaurant (you'll need to book) and a ground-floor restaurant with riverside tables. There's also a viewing box for a fine Tyne vista.

International Centre for Life

Life Interactive World (☎ 243 8210; w www .centre-for-life.co.uk; Scotswood Rd; adult/ child £6.95/4.50; open 10am-6pm Mon-Sat,

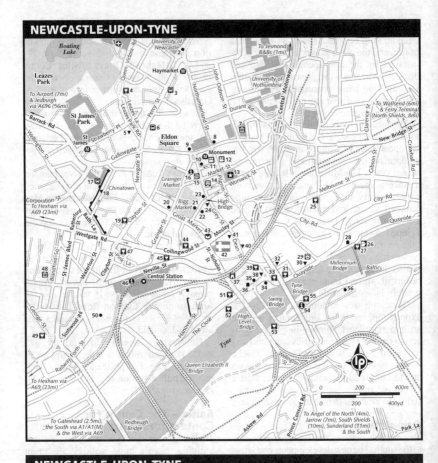

NEWCASTLE-UPON-TYNE

PLACES TO STAY & EAT
- 5 Barn Again Bistro
- 18 King Neptune
- 24 Blake's Coffee House
- 28 Malmaison Hotel & Brasserie
- 30 Heartbreak Soup
- 32 Cafe 21
- 36 Waterside Hotel
- 38 Bob Trollop; Red House
- 40 Leela's
- 41 Marco Polo

PUBS, BARS & CLUBS
- 4 Trent House Soul Bar
- 19 Playrooms
- 25 Foundation
- 27 Pitcher & Piano
- 31 Thirty 3i8ht
- 33 Chase
- 39 Crown Posada
- 44 Revolution

- 45 Head of Steam
- 47 Jazz Cafe
- 49 Powerhouse Nightclub
- 51 The Cooperage
- 52 Quayside Bar
- 53 Baja Beach Club
- 55 Tuxedo Royale

OTHER
- 1 Newcastle General Hospital
- 2 Blackwell's Bookshop
- 3 Haymarket Bus Station
- 6 Eldon Square Bus Station
- 7 Laing Art Gallery & Blue Carpet
- 8 Thomas Cook
- 9 Waterstone's
- 10 Waterstone's
- 11 Tyneside Cinema
- 12 Odeon Cinema
- 13 Police Station
- 14 Theatre Royal

- 15 Internet Exchange
- 16 Main Tourist Information Centre (TIC)
- 17 Gallowgate Coach Station
- 20 Blacks
- 21 RPM Music
- 22 Attica
- 23 Newcastle Map Centre
- 26 River Tyne Cruises
- 29 Live Theatre
- 34 Guildhall
- 35 Bessie Surtee's House
- 37 Castle Garth Keep
- 42 St Nicholas Cathedral
- 43 Main Post Office
- 46 Tourist Information Centre (TIC)
- 48 Discovery Museum
- 50 International Centre for Life
- 54 Gateshead Quays Vistor Centre
- 56 The Sage Gateshead

11am-6pm Sun) is part of the International Centre for Life, a complex comprising several institutes devoted to the study of genetic science. It's housed in a colourful, brash building designed by Terry Farrell. Almost everything is set up for a bit of hands-on fun. The attractions range from the 3-D film following a fertilised egg's development into Jack, to an exploration of the brain processes of a northeast family during breakfast, to the oddly edited how-does-this-fit-in Crazy Motion Ride. There's lots of thought-provoking arcade-style games, and if the information sometimes gets lost on the way, never mind, kids will love it.

Allow at least three hours to get round.

Castle Garth Keep

Most of the 'New' Castle that named the city was overtaken by the railway station. This square keep *(adult/child £1.50/50p; open 9.30am-5.30pm Apr-Sept, 9.30am-4.30pm Oct-Mar)* is one of the few remaining fragments. No longer so brand-spanking, it dates from 1168. It has a fine chevron-covered chapel and great views across the Tyne bridges from its rooftop.

Laing Art Gallery & Blue Carpet

The exceptional Laing *(☎ 232 7734; New Bridge St; admission free; open 10am-5pm Mon-Sat, 2pm-5pm Sun)* collection includes works by Kitaj, Frank Auerbach and Henry Moore. It's well put together and there's an imaginative children's gallery. Upstairs, *Zobop*, a zigzagging monochrome-vinyl work turns the floor into Pop Art.

The Blue Carpet *(w www.bluecarpet.co.uk)*, by Thomas Heatherwick, finished in 2002, envelops the once bleak space in front of the gallery with shimmering blue tiles, made from crushed glass and resin.

Discovery Museum

The Discovery Museum *(☎ 232 6789; w www.twmuseums.org.uk; admission free; open 10am-5pm Mon-Sat, 2pm-5pm Sun)* fills you in on Newcastle's background. It also houses the *Turbinia*, the fastest ship in the world in 1897, and there's a well-thought-out interactive science maze.

Quayside

The quayside nowadays bursts with bars and restaurants (see Places to Eat and Entertainment later). It runs along the northern side of the River Tyne, and became the natural hub of commercial Newcastle in the 16th century. The rounded **Guildhall** was built in 1658.

Bessie Surtees' House *(EH; ☎ 269 1227; admission free; open 10am-4pm Mon-Fri)* is a combination of two 16th- and 17th-century merchant houses – all dark wood and sloping angles – on Sandhill. Three rooms are open to the public. Bessie Surtees was the daughter of a wealthy banker; she, God forbid, fell in love with John Scott, a pauper. They eloped to Scotland – you can see the window through which she reputedly got away – but all ended well when he went on to become the lord chancellor of England.

Tyne Bridges & Sightseeing Cruises

The most famous view in Newcastle is the cluster of Tyne bridges, and the most famous of these is the **Tyne Bridge** (1925–8), built at about the same time as (and very reminiscent of) Australia's Sydney Harbour Bridge. The quaint little **Swing Bridge** pivots in the middle to let ships through. Nearby, **High Level Bridge**, designed by Robert Stephenson, was the world's first road and railway bridge (1849). The newest addition is the multi-award-winning **Millennium** or **Blinking Bridge** (2002), which opens like an eyelid to let ships pass.

Three-hour sightseeing cruises are run by **River Tyne Cruises** *(☎ 296 6740/1; w www .tyneleisureline.co.uk; adult £7.99-9.99, child £4.99; 2pm Sun May-early Sept)* from Quayside pier (near Millennium Bridge, opposite Baltic).

University Museums

To the north of the city centre is Newcastle University, with an array of museums and galleries.

Hancock Museum *(☎ 222 6865; Barras Bridge; adult/child £2.50/1.75; open 10am-5pm Mon-Sat, 2pm-5pm Sun)*, across Claremont Rd from the university grounds, is a traditional natural history museum, with some remarkably large spiders, iguanas, and creepy stuffed birds.

On the main university courtyard is the **Museum of Antiquities** *(☎ 222 7849; The Quadrangle; admission free; open 10am-5pm Mon-Sat)*, which has an amazing collection of Roman artefacts from Hadrian's Wall,

NORTHEAST ENGLAND

alongside other finds, such as jewellery and carvings, dating from 6000 BC to AD 1600.

Shefton Museum of Greek Art & Archaeology (☎ 222 8996; W www.ncl.ac.uk/shefton -museum; Armstrong Bldg; admission free; open 10am-4pm Mon-Fri), tiny but well stocked, has lots of fine, small ancient pieces.

Hatton Gallery (☎ 222 6057; W www.ncl .ac.uk/hatton; The Quadrangle; admission free; open 10am-5.30pm Mon-Fri, 10am-4.30pm Sat) has a permanent collection of West African art, and houses interesting temporary displays.

University Gallery (☎ 227 4424; Sandyford Rd; admission free; open 10am-5pm Mon-Thur, 10am-4pm Fri & Sat) has good changing exhibitions with 20th-century and local artists.

Markets

When it opened in 1835 **Grainger Market** (Grainger St; open Mon-Sat), in a magnificent building, was Europe's largest undercover shopping centre. It mainly sells fruit and veggies, but there are other interesting stalls, including the Marks & Spencer Original Penny Bazaar where, sadly, the original motto of 'Don't ask the price – it's a penny!' doesn't apply these days.

Quayside Market (open 9am-2.30pm Sun), a popular flea and fruit and veggie market, is held beneath the Tyne Bridge.

Jarrow

This eastern suburb is embedded in labour history for the 1936 'Jarrow Crusade', when 200 men walked from here to London to protest against the appalling conditions brought about by unemployment.

Today's visitors to this grim district might think little has changed. However, Jarrow is also famous as the home of the Venerable Bede (author of the *Ecclesiastical History of the English People*). **Bede's World** (☎ 489 2106; W www.bedesworld.co.uk; adult/child £4.50/2.50; open 10am-5.30pm Mon-Sat, noon-5.30pm Sun Apr-Oct, to 4.30pm Nov-Mar) comprises St Paul's Church, dating back to the 7th century, a museum, and many reconstructed medieval buildings. It's accessible via the Metro.

Places to Stay

Camping & Hostels In South Shields is **Lizard Lane Camping & Caravan Site** (☎ 454 4982; Marsden; camping per 1/2 people with tent & car £3.60/8.80). From the metro take bus No E1 or E3 from Market Place to Marsden Grotto or No E2 or E6 to Lizard Lane.

Newcastle YHA Hostel (☎ 0870 770 5972; e newcastle@yha.org.uk; 107 Jesmond Rd; beds per adult £11.25; open daily Feb-Nov, Fri-Sun Dec & Jan) is north of the city centre. It's a nice rambling place with small rooms. Call in advance, as it can be busy. Jesmond is the closest Metro stop.

North East YWCA (☎ 281 1233; Jesmond House, Clayton Rd; B&B per person £16) is spruce and modern and accepts men and women. Turn left onto Osborne Rd from Jesmond station and take the second right.

B&Bs & Hotels Newcastle's cheap accommodation is concentrated in the northeastern wealthy suburb of Jesmond, mainly on Osborne Rd. Catch the Metro to Jesmond or West Jesmond, or bus No 80 from near Central Station, or No 30, 30B, 31B or 36 from Westgate Rd.

Portland Guest House (☎ 232 7868; 134 Sandyford Rd; singles £18-22, doubles with/without en suite from £40/36) is cheery and simply decorated.

Hansen Guest House (☎ 281 0289; 131 Sandyford Rd; singles/doubles/triples £24/44/66), across the road from Portland Guest House, is a friendly place with lots of blowsy clutter.

Minerva Hotel (☎ 281 0190; 105 Osborne Rd; singles/doubles £23.50/36, with en suite £30/48) is a small place. The standard rooms are nothing special but those with en suite are better and the four-poster room is positively voluminous.

George Hotel (☎ 281 4442; e ghotel.book ings@btclick.com; 88 Osborne Rd; singles £35, doubles £46-50) is friendly, with clean and comfortable rooms.

Cairn Hotel (☎ 281 1358; 97-103 Osborne Rd; singles/doubles £59/79), at the top end, is large and upmarket, with the requisite canopied accommodation. Deals may be available.

Adelphi Hotel (☎ 281 3109; 63 Fern Ave; rooms per person £25), off Osborne Rd, is attractive, with floral, pleasant rooms.

Westland Hotel (☎ 281 0412; W www .westland-hotel.co.uk; 27 Osborne Ave; singles/doubles from £25/46, with en suite £32/52), off Osborne Rd on a pretty, leafy street, is friendly with 15 run-of-the-mill but cosy rooms.

Waterside Hotel *(☎ 230 0111; W www .watersidehotel.com; 48-52 Sandhill, Quayside; singles/doubles Mon-Fri from £62/88, Sat & Sun £52/62)* has snug rooms in a heritage-listed building and is close to the action.

Malmaison *(☎ 245 5000; W www.malmaison.com; Quayside; doubles Mon-Fri from £75-79, Sat & Sun from £120, suites from £150)* is affectedly stylish, with quasi-poetic publicity. But it's laid-back, and has an unbeatable location. The airy **brasserie** *(starters £3.95-7.50, mains £9.95-13.95)* serves good modern British dishes.

Places to Eat
Piazzaria Francesca *(☎ 281 6586; 134 Manor House Rd, Jesmond; mains £4-11.30)* is unpretentious, with a fake frescoed ceiling, excitable waiters and big platefuls.

Hot Box Cafe *(☎ 240 0101; Osborne Rd, Jesmond; mains around £8)* has outside seating that's ideal on a sunny day, and does tasty burgers.

Blake's Coffee House *(☎ 261 5463; 53 Grey St; sandwiches from £2)* is high-ceilinged, buzzing and great for a coffee with a background of blues.

Leela's *(☎ 230 1261; 20 Dean St; dishes around £8-13; open Mon-Sat)* is recommended; it's intimate and has excellent southern Indian dishes.

Marco Polo *(☎ 232 5533; 35 Dean St; pizza or pasta around £6; open Mon-Sat)* is straightforward Italian that'll fill you up without clearing you out.

At the bottom of The Side, **Bob Trollop**, voted best veggie pub in 2000, and the cosy **Red House**, have pub meals for £3 to £5.

Heartbreak Soup *(☎ 222 1701; 77 Quayside; open Mon-Sat; mains around £12)*, a sweet place with colourful murals, offers world-embracing dishes such as Lebanese lamb and Vietnamese monkfish.

Cafe 21 *(☎ 222 0755; 19-21 Queen St; mains £10-18; open Mon-Sat)*, all white tablecloths and smart seating, serves acclaimed food.

Barn Again Bistro *(☎ 230 3338; 21 Leazes Park Rd; mains around £12)* is a special restaurant, from the front bar, which is decorated with Norman Wisdom album covers, to the imaginative modern British cooking.

King Neptune *(☎ 261 6657; 34 Stowell St; set menus per person from £14.80)* is an upmarket Chinese restaurant, full of glitz, and specialising in seafood and Peking dishes.

If you fancy a slightly different dining experience you might want to try **The Valley Restaurant** (see Places to Stay & Eat under Corbridge later in this chapter).

Entertainment
For current listings pick up the monthly *North Guide* (£1.60) with good regional

---

Oot on the Toon

Geordies have an unrivalled passion for a night out. Like football, fun is pursued wholeheartedly, as if tomorrow might not come. It's a distraction from any other troubles, and a famously good one. It's worth being here at the weekend, when people flood in from all over the region. Just remember: wearing a coat will earn you some funny looks, even on the coldest of nights.

Club admission costs from £2 to £10.

The Toon is a guzzler's dream, a health-promoter's nightmare. There are cheap and lethal drink offers wherever you look – take the obliquely named 'Get Wrecked' where you pay to get in, then all drinks are free (Tuesday, Tuxedo Royale, if you're interested).

Along Osborne Road in Jesmond, there's a holiday vibe: many of the hotels are fronted by bars with optimistic al fresco sun-shaded seating and dotted with fairy lights. It's a good place for an early evening drink.

The most infamous area is Bigg Market, and weekends fulfil the *Viz* magazine stereotypes. Young, rowdy crowds of hardy blokes in uniform short-sleeved shirts and nearly dressed girls circulate and ogle each other, fired up on alcopops and lager, while frenetic toe-curling house blares out from the bars.

In recent years Quayside has become the place to go. It's ineffably more stylish, and attracts an older crowd. There are some superb spots near the station too. See Entertainment, get a bottle of dog and get doon.

information, and the *Crack* (free) at the TIC or bookshops.

Bars, Pubs & Clubs Jesmond's most popular haunt is **Osborne's** (☎ 281 4961; *61-69 Osborne Rd*).

Crown Posada (☎ 232 1269; *31 The Side*), an unspoilt, real-ale pub, is long, narrow and full of character.

Quayside Bar (*35-37 The Close, Quayside*) has unfortunate chain credentials, but is a well-restored cavernous warehouse with a great spot right on the river – there's some outside seating – and a quiet courtyard.

The Cooperage (☎ 232 8286; *32 The Close, Quayside*) is a popular pub with a wide-ranging clientele, and has a club upstairs. A 14th-century house modified in the 18th-century, its bulging timbers are supposedly from ships sunk in the Tyne, and it even claims a nautical ghost.

Thirty 3i8ht (☎ 261 6463; *38 The Exchange Buildings; mains £5-7.75*), winner of Design Pub of the Year 2002, features big egg-capsule seating and a room dotted with cigar-like tables dominated by a plasma screen. Suitably refined food is served and there are regular DJs.

The usually soul-sapping **Pitcher & Piano** (☎ 232 4110; *108 Quayside*) chain has an amazing setting here, with an outside terrace, huge plate-glass walls and a prime Tyneside spot.

Chase (☎ 245 0055; *13 Sandhill*) is relaxed and 70s-style, boasting fish tanks, lots of curves and neon.

Trent House Soul Bar (☎ 261 2154; *1-2 Leazes Lane*), famed for its jukebox, is the kind of place you want to take home. It has the same management as **World Headquarters** – a delectable, unpretentious club with funky, surprising music, which was on the move at the time of writing; check at the Soul Bar or magazine listings for the new venue.

The Playrooms (☎ 230 2186; *25 Low Friar St*) are pleasingly seedy, and will amuse you with hip hop, disco and funk, and some big names too. On Friday the club splits into two, so you have a bit more choice.

Tuxedo Royale (☎ 477 8899; *Hillgate Quay*), 'the boat', is a popular, cringe-inducing institution with seven different rooms and a revolving dance floor.

Baja Beach Club (☎ 477 6205; *Hillgate Quay*) has palm trees, surfing stuff, bar-maids in bikinis and top-40 toe-tappers: it's vintage cheese and a good laugh (though it probably helps to be drunk).

With dim lamps, smoky atmosphere and bearded men, **Jazz Cafe** (☎ 232 6505; *Pink Lane*) is everything a live jazz venue should be. There's salsa on Friday and Saturday.

Head of Steam (☎ 232 4379; *2 Neville St*), an unfussy, funky bar, has two floors, with great atmosphere and music on both. Expect funk, reggae and regular DJs.

Revolution (☎ 261 5774; *Collingwood Chambers*) inhabits an outrageously lavish, marble-pillared interior and specialises in vodka.

Warehouse-style **Foundation** (☎ 261 8985; *57-59 Melbourne St*) is the place to head for that heavyweight DJ thing.

Gay & Lesbian Venues Newcastle's pinkest district is around Waterloo St. The fanciest place is the 900-capacity **Powerhouse Nightclub** (☎ 261 4507; *23-23 George St*). The burly chap on the door will question you on your sexuality on the way in.

The Sage Gateshead Gateshead's once forlorn riverside now boasts the Norman Foster–designed glass-and-chrome curves of the music centre (☎ 443 4666; **w** *www.musicnorth.org*). The Sage contains a 1650-seat hall as well as a more intimate 400-seater, and promotes all types of music.

Theatre & Cinema Column-fronted **Theatre Royal** (☎ 232 2061; **w** *www.theatre-royal-newcastle.co.uk; 100 Grey St*) is full of Victorian splendour and has an excellent programme of drama. The Royal Shakespeare Company resides here in the autumn.

Live Theatre (☎ 232 1232; **w** *www.live.org.uk; 27 Broad Chare, Quayside*) is a fringe company that features lots of new drama and live music. There's a serene café.

Odeon Cinema (☎ 232 6718; *Pilgrim St*) is a four-screen 1930s classic and shows mainstream stuff, while across the road **Tyneside Cinema** (☎ 232 8289; **w** *www.tynecine.org*) will fulfil your art-house needs.

Spectator Sports

Newcastle United Football Club is followed with an unrivalled fervour. Newcastle has gone through decades of economic hardship, and football proves a welcome distraction and ideal outlet for Geordie humour and pride. **St James' Park** (☎ 201 8400; w www .nufc.co.uk (official), www.nufc.com (unofficial); Strawberry Place) is hallowed ground. Tours are available – call or check the website for details. Match tickets go on public sale about two weeks before a game (box office ☎ 261 1571), or you can try the stadium on the day (adult/child £20/5; on sale from 9am), but there's no chance for big matches, such as those against arch-rivals Sunderland.

Shopping
Shopaholics might be tempted by the enormous **MetroCentre** (Gateshead), with 360 shops. A MetroCentre shuttle bus (No 100) runs from the Odeon cinema or the train station.

Central **Eldon Square** is another modern shrine to consumerism. Needless to say, the markets, like covered **Grainger Market**, have *much* more character.

Blacks (☎ 261 8613; 81-83 Grainger St), the outdoor equipment chain, has a shop in the heart of the city.

Attica (☎ 261 4062; 2 Old George Yard) contains glittering hoards of vintage kook, both clothes and furniture.

RPM Music (☎ 221 0201; 25 High Bridge) specialises in vinyl, but also sells CDs. It has a great range of indie, hip hop, dance, rock and garage.

Getting There & Away
Newcastle is 275 miles (443km) from London (about five hours by car), 105 miles (169km) from Edinburgh, 57 miles (92km) from Carlisle, 35 miles (56km) from Alnwick and 15 miles (24km) from Durham. It's a major transport hub.

Air Seven miles (11km) north of the city is **Newcastle International Airport** (☎ 286 0966). It's linked by the Metro and is 20 minutes by car off the A696.

Bus National Express buses to/from London (£24.50, seven hours, every two hours), Edinburgh (£21, 3¼ hours, three daily), and York (£16.50, 2½ hours, three daily) go to/from the Gallowgate coach station.

Local and regional buses leave from Haymarket or Eldon Square bus stations. For local buses around the northeast, don't forget the excellent-value Explorer North

East ticket, valid on most services for £5.50. Bus Nos 505, 515 and 525 run from Berwick-upon-Tweed (£4 single, two hours, five daily) to Haymarket.

From April to September, bus No 888 links Keswick and the Gallowgate coach station (£16.50, three hours, daily).

Train Newcastle is on the main rail line between London and Edinburgh. Numerous trains serve Edinburgh (£35, 1½ hours), London's King's Cross (£79, three hours, half-hourly) and York (£19, one hour, every 20 minutes). Berwick (£14.80, 45 minutes, every two hours) and Alnmouth (£5.80, 20 minutes, four daily), for connections to Alnwick, are north on this line.

There's also the scenic Tyne Valley Line west to Carlisle. See Getting There & Around under Hadrian's Wall for details.

Boat See the Getting There & Away chapter for details of ferry links to Stavanger, Bergen and Kristiansand in Norway, and Ijmuiden in the Netherlands.

Getting Around
To/From the Airport The airport is linked to town by the Metro. There are frequent services daily, and the fare is £1.80.

To/From the Ferry Terminal Bus No 327 links the ferry (at Tyne Commission Quay), Central Station and Jesmond Rd. It leaves the train station 2½ hours and 1¼ hours before each sailing; the fare is £3.

There's a taxi rank at the terminal; it costs £12 to the city centre.

Bus, Metro & Car There's a large bus network but the best means of getting around is the excellent underground Metro, with fares from 55p. A DaySaver costs £3 (£1.50 after 9.30am) or you can get a DayRover, covering all modes of transport in the Tyne & Wear county, for £3.90. The TIC can supply you with route plans for the bus and Metro networks.

Driving around Newcastle isn't fun thanks to the web of roads, bridges and one-way systems, but there are plenty of car parks.

Taxi On weekend nights taxis can be rare; try **Noda Taxis** (☎ 222 1888), which has a kiosk outside the entrance to Central Station.

NORTHEAST ENGLAND

AROUND NEWCASTLE
Segedunum

Four miles (6km) east of Newcastle at Wallsend is Segedunum (☎ 295 5757; w www.hadrians-wall.org; adult/child £3.50/1.95; site open 10am-5pm daily Apr-Oct, 10am-3.30pm Nov-Mar), the last outpost of Hadrian's Wall. There are ongoing excavations of fort ruins. A 35m tower overlooks the whole site, and a film whips you through how the view has changed over a couple of thousand years. The conclusion is for the worse. There's a reconstructed Roman bathhouse, and interactive displays to get you into the Roman mindset. Take the Metro to Wallsend.

The Angel of the North

Aka 'the Gateshead flasher', the angel at the side of the road is a must see – it's hard to miss. Made from 200 tonnes of steel, the rust-coloured, impassive, massive Angel of the North (a human frame with wings), created by sculptor Antony Gormley, is the largest sculpture in Britain at 20m high and with a wingspan wider than a Boeing 767. It towers over the A1(M) about 5 miles (8km) south of Newcastle, and is one of the most frequently viewed works of art in the world. Bus Nos 723 and 724 from Eldon Square, or Nos 21, 21A and 21B from the Odeon cinema, will take you there.

Sunderland

☎ 0191 • pop 100,600

Bereft of the industries – shipbuilding and coal mining – that once busied the docks and employed generations, Sunderland, 11 miles (17km) southeast of Newcastle, has been battered by decades of disinterest and low employment. It may not be picturesque, but it's an interesting, friendly place, and the once industrious riverside makes for an interesting stroll. There are several worthwhile attractions in town.

The TIC (553 3000; 50 Fawcett St; open 9am-5pm Mon-Sat) is very helpful.

Museum & Winter Gardens (☎ 553 2323; w www.tyne-wear-museums.org.uk; Mowbray Gardens, Burdon Rd; open 10am-4pm Mon, 10am-5pm Tues-Sat, 2pm-5pm Sun) is worth a visit. The museum starts with a strange amalgamation of objects, from stuffed Wallace the Lion, to the first Nissan car built in the city. The rest imaginatively traces Sunderland's development, from glassmaking to coal mining. Upstairs there are evocative local works by LS Lowry.

The Winter Gardens, opened in 2002 to replace those destroyed during World War II (well, that didn't take too long!) – are a tropical hothouse in a glass building with a treetop walkway. A lovely café with a terrace overlooks adjoining Mowbray Park.

Around a half-mile walk away, on the other side of the Wear, is the National Glass Centre (☎ 515 5555; w www.nationalglasscentre.com; Liberty Way). En route, poignant sculptural works along the riverside commemorate the once-packed docks. In an appropriately translucent building, the centre comprises interactive displays on the uses of glass, glass sculptures, workshops where you can see glass-makers at work, and a fine café. Sure, it's not as famous for glass-making as Venice, but then can Venice boast a glass roof made of panels 6cm-thick that can support 4600 people standing on it at once? Walking across the roof of the centre is one powerful way to induce vertiginous paralysis.

Sunderland is best visited on a day trip from Newcastle. It takes around 30 minutes to get there on the Metro from the Newcastle city centre.

Northumberland

Northumberland is wild and beautiful. It has a magnificent, pale, sweeping coast, punctuated by dramatic wind-worn castles, with tiny, magical islands just offshore. Inland, much is national park, sparsely populated and rugged, with fortified houses and friendly villages. To the west is Kielder Water, a shockingly huge, yet secluded lake, with land on all sides enveloped by forest. The most strikingly evocative part of Hadrian's Wall slices through the south.

The county has an uncanny atmosphere, exploited in all sort of film epics, from Beckett (starring Richard Burton), Polanski's Macbeth, Hamlet (starring Mel Gibson) and Elizabeth to Harry Potter & the Philosopher's Stone. But despite all this publicity, it feels undiscovered.

Northumberland takes its name from the Anglo-Saxon kingdom of Northumbria (north of the River Humber). For centuries it served as the battleground for the struggle between north and south. After the arrival of the Normans in the 11th century, large numbers of castles and *peles* (fortified buildings), were built and hundreds of these remain. All this turmoil made life a tad unsettled till the 18th century brought calm. Today the land's ferocious history has echoes all around the sparsely populated countryside.

Getting Around

The excellent *Northumberland Public Transport Guide* (£1) is available from local TICs. Transport options are good, with a train line running along the coast from Newcastle to Berwick and on to Edinburgh.

ALNWICK

☎ 01665 • pop 7000

Charming Alnwick (pronounced annick), Northumberland's ducal town, spreads neatly out beside its colossal medieval castle. The narrow, cobbled streets, bounded by medieval gateways, lead into a serene traditional market place. It is home to perhaps the nicest bookshop in England, Barter Books.

The castle is on the northern side of town and overlooks the River Aln. The **TIC** (☎ 510665; **w** www.alnwick.gov.uk; 2 *The Shambles; open 9am-5pm Mon-Sat, 10am-4pm Sun*) is by the market place.

Access the Net for £1.50 per 15 minutes at **Barter Books** (☎ 604888; **w** www.barterbooks.co.uk; *Alnwick Station; open 9am-7pm daily*), one of the largest second-hand bookshops in Britain, housed in a Victorian railway station with coal fires, velvet ottomans and reading (once waiting) rooms.

There has been a market in Alnwick for over 800 years. Market days are Thursday and Saturday, with a Farmers' Market on the last Friday of the month.

Alnwick Castle

The outwardly imposing Alnwick Castle (☎ 510777; **w** www.alnwickcastle.com; *adult/child £6.95/free; open 11am-5pm daily Easter–end-Oct*), ancestral home of the Duke of Northumberland, has changed little since the 14th century. The interior is sumptuous and extravagant, offering an opportunity to reflect on the inequities of wealth distribution. A popular film location, it most recently appeared in *Harry Potter and the Philosopher's Stone* – the trainee wizard had broomstick lessons inside, and dazzled at quidditch outside.

The six rooms open to the public – state rooms, dining room, guard chamber and library – have an incredible display of Italian paintings, including Titian's *Ecce Homo* and many Canalettos. Magnificent carving decorates the rooms, completed by the Florentine-trained Alnwick school. The castle is set in parklands designed by Capability Brown. The woodland walk offers some great aspects of the castle. Or for a view looking up the River Aln, take the B1340 towards the coast.

The **Alnwick Garden** (☎ 510777; **w** www.alnwickgarden.com; *adult/child £4/free*) is an attempt to recreate the grandeur of the castle's 19th-century formal garden, but is very much a work in progress.

Places to Stay & Eat

Aln House (☎ 602265; **e** bill@alnhouse.worldonline.co.uk; *South Rd; en-suite singles per person £30, doubles per person £23-25*), on the A1 Newcastle road near the roundabout, is a popular Edwardian house with a pretty garden.

Bondgate Without, just outside the town's medieval gateway, has several accommodation possibilities.

Lindisfarne Guest House (☎ 603430; 6 *Bondgate Without; rooms per person from £17*) has three richly decorated rooms and is friendly.

The Teapot (☎ 604473; 8 *Bondgate Without; rooms per person with/without en suite from £19/18*) is welcoming, with sweet rooms and the largest teapot collection in town.

White Swan Hotel (☎ 602109, fax 510400; *Bondgate Within; singles/doubles from £69/108*) is a stable home for the elaborate original panelling, ceiling and stained-glass windows from the dining room of the *Olympic*, sister ship to the *Titanic*. Stop in for a look.

Wine Cellar Café Bar (☎ 605264; *Bondgate Within; sandwiches £3.95*) is popular, cheery and relaxed, with a fine selection of snacks

The several pubs present good meal options.

Market Tavern (☎ 602759; 7 *Fenkle St*), near the market square, is friendly and the food is good and generous; a giant beef stottie (bread roll) costs £4.50.

Ye Old Cross (☎ 602735; *Narrowgate*) is good for a drink and is known as 'Bottles'.

NORTHEAST ENGLAND

In the window are some dusty old bottles – they haven't been moved for 150 years as the owner collapsed and died while trying to move them and no-one's dared attempt since.

Tower Restaurant (*☎ 603888; 10 Bondgate Within; mains around £7*) is small and relaxed, with tasty food.

Getting There & Away

There are regular buses from Newcastle (Nos 501, 505 and 518; one hour, 28 per day Monday to Saturday, 18 on Sunday). Bus No 518 has 10 to 14 daily services to the attractive towns of Warkworth (25 minutes) and Alnmouth (15 minutes), which has the nearest train station. Bus Nos 505 and 525 come from Berwick (45 minutes, 13 daily Monday to Saturday). The Arriva Day Pass is good value at £3.70.

AROUND ALNWICK
Warkworth
☎ 01665 • pop 1642

Warkworth is a biscuit-coloured village that clusters around a loop in the River Cocquet, above which rises the craggy ruin of its 14th-century castle.

Warkworth Castle (*EH; ☎ 711423; adult £2.60; open 10am-6pm daily Easter-Sept, 10am-5pm Oct, 10am-1pm & 2pm-4pm Nov-Mar*) is a fine ruin on an imposing site, high above the gentle twisting river. Several scenes of Shakespeare's *Henry IV* Parts I and II are set in 'this worm-eaten hold of ragged stone' and it still looks pretty worm-eaten and ragged.

Tiny, mystical, 14th-century **Warkworth Hermitage** (*adult/child £1.70/90p; open 11am-5pm Wed & Sun Apr-Sept*), carved into the rock, is a few hundred yards upriver. Follow the signs along the path, then take possibly the world's shortest ferry ride. It's a lovely stretch of water and there is **rowing boat hire** (*adult/child per 45 min £2/1.50; Sat & Sun May-Sept*).

Bide a While (*☎ 711753; 4 Beal Croft; rooms per person from £17*) lacks character but its residents make up for it.

Sun Hotel (*☎ 711259, fax 711833; w www.rytonpark-sun.co.uk; 6 Castle Terrace; singles/doubles from £49/75; meals around £6*) is more upmarket and has views of both the castle and the river, and good pub food.

The Greenhouse (*☎ 712322; 22 Dial Place; open Mon & Wed-Sat; starters £3.25-5.75,*

mains £6.95-12.50), in the centre of the village, is spacious and friendly, with wooden tables, and makes great coffee and snacks.

Bus No 518 links Newcastle (1½ hours, hourly), Warkworth, Alnmouth and Alnwick. There's a train station on the main east-coast line, about 1½ miles (2.5km) west of town.

CRASTER

Craster is a small sheltered fishing village about 6 miles northeast of Alnwick. There's a **TIC** (*☎/fax 01665-576007; Quarry Car Park; open 9.30am-4.30pm daily Apr-Oct, to 5.30pm July & Aug, 10am-4pm Sat & Sun Nov-Mar*) by the town's car park. Famous for its kippers, in the early 20th century 25,000 were smoked here daily. They're still good, though less profuse. A great place to sample the day's catch and contemplate the fine views is the **Jolly Fisherman** (*☎ 01665-576218; sandwiches £2-4*), with a sea-facing garden.

Bus No 401 or 501 from Alnwick calls at Craster (30 minutes, around five daily). A pay-and-display car park is the only place in Craster where it's possible to park your car.

Dunstanburgh Castle

The striking, weather-beaten ruins of Dunstanburgh Castle (*EH; ☎ 01665-576231; adult £2; open 10am-6pm daily Apr-Sept, 10am-5pm daily Oct, 10am-4pm Wed-Sun Nov-Mar*), high on a basalt outcrop, make a haunting sight. The bleak, windswept ruins can be seen for miles along this exhilarating stretch of coast.

Dunstanburgh was once one of the largest border castles. Started in 1314, it was strengthened during the War of the Roses, but then left to rot. Only parts of the original wall and gatehouse keep are still standing; it was already a ruin by 1550, so it's a tribute to its builders that so much is left today.

There are no roads to the castle, but it's a dramatic one-mile walk along the coast from Craster or Embleton.

EMBLETON BAY

From Dunstanburgh, beautiful Embleton bay, a pale wide arc of sand, stretches around to the endearing, sloping village of **Embleton**. The village has the seaside **Dunstanburgh Castle Golf Club** (*☎ 01665-576562*) and a cluster of houses.

The Sportsman (*☎ 01665-576588; rooms per person £28*) is a large, relaxed place, set up from the bay. It's welcoming with a wide deck out the front and a spacious, plain wooden bar. The rooms are nothing to shout about, but the views from them are, and the bar serves good food. Bus No 401 or 501 from Alnwick calls here too (see earlier).

Embleton Bay continues past Embleton, the broad vanilla-coloured strand curving around to end at **Low-Newton-by-the-Sea**, a tiny whitewashed village with a fine pub. Behind the bay is a path leading to the **Newton Pool Nature Reserve**, an important spot for breeding and migrating birds, such as Black-Headed Gulls and Grasshopper Warblers. There are a couple of hides where you can peer out at them.

The Ship Inn (☎ 576262; mains £5.25-7.95) is set around a grassy square that meets the beach, and serves excellent food, such as Seahouses Kippers with new potatoes and salad (£6.35). You can continue walking along the headland beyond Low Newton, where you'll find Football Hole, a delightful hidden beach between headlands.

Another good place to eat is a couple of miles west of Embleton in Christon Bank.

The Blink Bonny (☎ 01665-576595; Christon Bank; mains around £6) is a friendly, cosy village pub, with excellent hearty food, welcoming owners and lots of chatty locals.

Two miles north of Christon Bank is **Preston Tower** (☎ 01655-589227; admission £1; open daylight hours), a 14th-century pele with walls 2m thick. It gives a good idea of fortified life, though two turrets are missing.

FARNE ISLANDS

The Farne Islands are almost entirely bare rock, and the site of an incredible sea bird convention. About three miles offshore from Seahouses, the islands provide a home for 18 species of nesting sea birds, including puffins, kittiwakes, Arctic terns, eider ducks, cormorants and gulls. There are few places in the world where you can get so close to nesting sea birds. It's an extraordinary experience. There are also colonies of grey seals.

The best time to go is in the breeding season (roughly May to July), when you can see chicks being fed by their parents. There are also tours in October to see the seal pups. The islands are owned and managed by the National Trust (NT), who manage the visiting hours and landing permissions to prevent environmental damage.

St Cuthbert, of Lindisfarne fame, was a hermit on the Inner Farne, and died here in 687. There's a tiny chapel (built 1370 and restored 1848) to him on the island and also a pele built around 1500. Monks lived on the island till the mid-16th century. Grace Darling lived in the lighthouse at Longstone, from where she and her father famously rescued survivors from the wreck of the Forfarshire in 1838.

There are various tours, from 1½-hour cruises to all-day specials, and they get going from 10am April to October. It's definitely worth landing on one of the islands – preferably Inner Farne. A three-hour tour and landing costs £9/7; there's an additional £4.40/2.20 fee payable to the NT (if you're not a member) if you land.

Crossings can be rough, and may be impossible in bad weather. Some of the boats have no proper cabin, so make sure you've got warm, waterproof clothing if there's a chance of rain.

Tickets are available from pierside booths in Seahouses, a couple of miles along the coast from Bamburgh. Operators include **Billy Shiel** (☎ 01665-720308; W www.farne-islands.com) and **Hanvey's** (☎ 01665-720388; W www.farneislands.com).

Seahouses is a small seaside resort, mainly a cluster of fish-and-chip shops and the launching point for the Farne. There's a **TIC** (☎ 01655-720884; open 10am-5pm daily Apr-Oct) in the Seafield Rd car park near the harbour.

If you need a place to stay, the 18th-century **Olde Ship Hotel** (☎ 01665-720200; W www.seahouses.co.uk; Main St; rooms per person £41-44; 3-course meal £17) covers all you need: fine food, good ale and cosy, cabin-like rooms.

BAMBURGH
☎ 01668 • pop 442

Dwarfed by the massive profile of an aloof, intimidating castle, tranquil Bamburgh village neatly embraces a large and pleasing green. It's just inland from long open stretches of empty white-sand beach, ideal for blustery walks.

Bamburgh Castle (☎ 214515; adult/child £4.50/1.50; open 11am-5pm daily Apr-Oct), is just how you imagine a castle should be. Impressive by day (and even more so by night), it perches high up on a basalt crag

NORTHEAST ENGLAND

rising from the sea and dominates the coast for miles. The views from the battlements swoop across the coast, the Farnes and Holy Island. The site has been occupied since prehistoric times, the keep is Norman and the castle was an important player in the border wars. It was restored in the 19th century by the great industrialist Lord Armstrong (who also turned his passion to Cragside, see Rothbury later). The great halls within are still home to the Armstrong family.

The **Grace Darling Museum** (☎ 214465; donation requested adult/child £1/50p; open 10am-5pm daily) has small displays on the lighthouse keepers, including their diminutive boat in which they rescued nine people. At the time, their heroism attracted inordinate publicity and Grace was even offered £10 a week to appear at the Adelphi Theatre in London, rowing across the stage.

Places to Stay & Eat

Glororum Caravan Park (☎ 214457; tent pitches £9-11) has a good setting, grass pitches and all the mod cons, including showers and laundrette. It's about a mile from Bamburgh on the B1341.

Greengates (☎ 214535; 34 Front St; ensuite singles/doubles per person £35/25) is on the edge of the village green and has some rooms with great castle views.

Broom (☎ 214287; 22 Ingram; singles/doubles £30/50) has pretty rooms at the back of the house, nicely furnished with extra touches, and a fine breakfast.

Blackett's of Bamburgh (☎ 214714) is recommended and does upmarket evening meals, while **The Copper Kettle** is the place to be for tea. Stock up for a picnic at **The Pantry**.

Getting There & Away

Bus No 501 runs from Newcastle (£3.90 single, 2¼ hours, two per day Monday to Saturday, one on Sunday) stopping at Alnwick and Seahouses. Bus Nos 401 and 501 from Alnwick (£3.30 single, four to six daily) take one hour.

HOLY ISLAND (LINDISFARNE)
☎ 01289 • pop 179

Holy Island (or Lindisfarne as it was once known) has an unearthly, otherworldly feel. It's two miles square and connected to the mainland at low tide, by a glinting narrow causeway. It was a medieval religious centre of great importance, and a holy atmosphere still permeates the place, despite the hoards of tourists it attracts. The north of the island is a grassy, sandy conservation area, while in the south a small fishing village clings around rich red sandstone priory ruins dating from the 11th century. A tiny story-book castle is perched half a mile from the village. The island's strange mix of magic and menace was spotted by Polanski, who filmed his black comedy *Cul-de-Sac* here, and parts of *Macbeth* as well.

In 635, St Aidan founded Lindisfarne monastery, and it became a major centre of Christianity and learning. St Cuthbert lived on the island for a while before moving to the Farne. In 793 Vikings looted the monastery, and further raids drove the monks off the island by 875. A priory was re-established in the 11th century.

Crossing to the island is an adventure in itself. The causeway crosses 3 miles (5km) of empty flats that stretch out to the horizon on all sides. Despite all the information (at TICs and noticeboards around the area) on safe crossing times, foolhardy drivers are often caught midway by the incoming tide and have to abandon their cars.

It gets mighty busy on the island at certain times – try to avoid summer weekends.

Things to See

Lindisfarne Priory (EH; ☎ 389200; adult £3; open 10am-6pm daily Apr-Oct, 10am-4pm Nov-Mar) consists of the elaborate red and grey ruins and the later 13th-century St Mary the Virgin Church. The museum next to these displays the remains of the first monastery and tells the story of the monastic community before and after dissolution.

Twenty pages of the exquisitely illustrated, luminescent *Lindisfarne Gospels* are on view electronically (completed by local monks around 698; the original is in the British Museum, London) at the **Lindisfarne Heritage Centre** (☎ 389004; Marygate; adult/child £2/free), which also has displays on the locality.

Half a mile from the village stands the tiny, story-book **Lindisfarne Castle** (NT; ☎ 389244; adult £4; open noon-3pm daily Apr-Oct), built in 1550, and extended and converted by Sir Edwin Lutyens from 1902 to 1910 for Mr Hudson, the owner of *Country Life* magazine. You can imagine some decadent parties have graced its alluring rooms. Its opening times may be extended depending on the tide. A **shuttle bus** (☎ 389236) runs here from the car park.

Places to Stay

It's possible to stay on the island, but it is best to book.

The Ship (☎ 389311; Marygate; en-suite singles/doubles from £45/58) has three comfortable rooms and serves up good local seafood in the bar.

Britannia House (☎ 01289-389218; rooms per person from £21) is a traditional B&B near the town green.

Getting There & Around

Holy Island can be reached by bus No 477 from Berwick (Wednesday and Saturday only, Monday to Saturday in July and August) and is 14 miles (23km) from Berwick train station. People taking cars across are requested to park just outside the village (£3 per day). The sea covers the causeway and cuts the island off from the mainland for about five hours each day. Tide times are listed at TICs, in local papers and each side of the crossing.

BERWICK-UPON-TWEED

☎ 01289 • pop 13,544

Berwick, England's northernmost town, feels Scottish, and reflecting geographical realities, the football team plays in the Scottish League. From the 12th to the 15th centuries, borderline Berwick changed hands between the Scots and the English an incredible 13 times. In Elizabethan times, massive ramparts were constructed that still stand almost complete, encircling the town centre.

Besides a dramatic past, the town has a dramatic location, flanking the graceful estuary of the River Tweed that's often splashed white with flotillas of swans. A prosperous port and shipbuilding centre in the middle ages, Berwick boomed in the 18th and 19th centuries when a busy fishing trade developed. Fast ships used to transport salmon to London, but the coming of the railways, coupled with fishing regulations, killed off the industry. Despite this a Salmon Queen is still chosen every July and paraded around the streets before everyone settles down to a salmon feast.

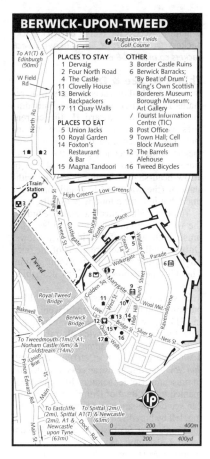

BERWICK-UPON-TWEED

PLACES TO STAY	OTHER
1 Dervaig	3 Border Castle Ruins
2 Four North Road	6 Berwick Barracks;
4 The Castle	'By Beat of Drum';
11 Clovelly House	King's Own Scottish
13 Berwick	Borderers Museum;
Backpackers	Borough Museum;
17 11 Quay Walls	Art Gallery
	7 Tourist Information
PLACES TO EAT	Centre (TIC)
5 Union Jacks	8 Post Office
10 Royal Garden	9 Town Hall; Cell
14 Foxton's	Block Museum
Restaurant	12 The Barrels
& Bar	Alehouse
15 Magna Tandoori	16 Tweed Bicycles

The grey-stone, hilly streets are interesting to explore, and the stunning circuit around its dramatic walls takes in views across the town, river and sea. The town's turbulent history is well documented in its museums, contrasting with the city's soporific calm today.

Orientation & Information

The fortified town of Berwick is on the northern side of the Tweed; the three bridges link with the suburbs of Tweedmouth, Spittal and Eastcliffe. The town centre is compact and walkable.

The **TIC** (☎ 330733, fax 330448; e tourism@ berwick-upon-tweed.gov.uk; 106 Marygate; open 10am-7pm Mon-Sat July-Sept; 10am-5pm Mon-Sat, 11am-3pm Sun Easter-June;

10am-noon & 1pm-4pm Mon-Sat Oct-Easter) is helpful. Access the Net at **Berwick Backpackers** (☎ *331481;* W *www.berwick-backpackers.co.uk; 56-58 Bridge St)*.

Things to See & Do

Berwick has had two sets of **walls**: little remains of the first, which were built during the reign of Edward II; the current ones were begun in 1558 and are still intact. They represented the most state-of-the-art military technology of the day and were designed both to house artillery (in arrow-head-shaped bastions) and to withstand it (the walls are low and massively thick, but it's still a long way to fall).

You can walk almost the entire length of the walls, a circuit of about a mile. It's a must, with wonderful, wide-open views. Only a small fragment remains of the once mighty **Border castle**, by the train station. The TIC has a brochure (25p) describing the main sights.

Designed by Hawksmoor, the oldest purpose-built barracks in Britain were begun in 1717 following pressure to stop using private local billets. **Berwick Barracks** (EH; ☎ *304493; The Parade; admission £2.80; open 10am-6pm daily Apr-Oct, 10am-4pm Wed-Sun Nov-Mar)* now house an eclectic collection of museums. Border soldiers' lives are documented in '**By Beat of Drum**' – upstairs you can see candle-smoke drawings on the ceiling, left by bored 18th-century soldiers – and the **King's Own Scottish Borderers Museum** *(open 9.30am-4pm Mon-Sat year round)*. The **Borough Museum** renders Berwick's history with bold cluttered models, and the **Art Gallery** displays assorted art pieces from European glassware to Japanese Imari pottery.

The original jail cells in the upper floor of the town hall (1750–61) have been preserved to house the **Cell Block Museum** (☎ *330900; adult/child £1.50/50p; tours 10.30am & 2pm Mon-Fri Apr-Oct)*, devoted to crime and punishment, with tours taking in the public rooms, museum, gaol and belfry.

There are recommended one-hour **guided walks** *(adult/child £3/free; 10am, 11.15am, 12.30pm & 2pm Mon-Fri Apr-Oct)* starting from the TIC.

Places to Stay

Berwick Backpackers (☎ *331481;* W *www.berwick-backpackers.co.uk; 56-58 Bridge St;*

beds per person from £9), central and excellent, has a warren of bright snug rooms including singles and twins, and provides Net access.

Dervaig (☎ *307378;* W *www.dervaig-guest house.co.uk; 1 North Rd; en-suite singles/ doubles from £40/55)* provides rooms in a spacious Victorian house.

Four North Road (☎ *306146;* W *www .fournorthroad.co.uk; 4 North Rd; singles/ doubles per person from £19)*, is another friendly, large, Victorian place.

Clovelly House (☎ *302337;* W *www .clovelly53.freeserve.co.uk; 58 West St; rooms per person £19-22)* has great breakfasts and comfy, warm rooms.

11 Quay Walls (☎ *381462; singles £20, en-suite doubles £25)* is a cheery place with a riverside setting – three rooms have river views.

The Castle *(☎/fax 307900; 103 Castlegate; rooms per person £20)* is good value and LS Lowry once bedded down here.

Places to Eat & Drink

Union Jacks (☎ *306673; 3 Wallace Green; mains £4-7; open lunch Wed-Sun, dinner Sat & Sun)* offers a variety of militarily named dishes in a Georgian house.

Magna Tandoori (☎ *302736; 39 Bridge St; mains £5-10; open lunch Mon-Sat, dinner daily)* is probably the best Indian restaurant in town.

Royal Garden (☎ *331411; 35 Marygate; 3-course lunch £4.90)*, a Chinese eatery, has a filling three-course lunch.

Foxton's Restaurant & Bar (☎ *303939; 26 Hide Hill; mains around £12)* is a great place for both a drink and a meal, with interesting dishes and dark red walls.

The Barrels Alehouse (☎ *308013;* W *www .thebarrelsalehouse.com; 56 Bridge St)* has Elvis and Mohammed Ali gracing the walls, real ale and vintage space invaders. There's regular live music in its basement bar.

Getting There & Away

Berwick is quite a transport hub; it's on the main east-coast railway line and road, and also has good links into the Scottish Borders.

There are services linking Newcastle and Berwick (Nos 505, 515 and 525; 2¼ hours, five daily) via Alnwick. Bus No 253 comes from Edinburgh (two hours, six per day Monday to Saturday, two on Sunday) via

Dunbar. Berwick is a good starting point to explore the Scottish Borders; there are buses west to Coldstream, Kelso and Galashiels.

Berwick is on the main east-coast London–Edinburgh railway line, and there are numerous trains from Newcastle (£14.80, 50 minutes) and from Edinburgh (£14.80, 50 minutes).

Berwick's centre is walkable, but if you're feeling lazy try **Berwick Taxis** (☎ 307771). **Tweed Bicycles** (☎ 331476; *17a Bridge St*) hires out mountain bikes for £15 a day.

AROUND BERWICK-UPON-TWEED
Norham Castle
Six and a half miles southwest of Berwick on a minor road off the A698 are the pinkish ruins of Norham Castle (EH; ☎ 01289-382329; *adult £1.90; open 10am-6pm daily Apr-Sept*). An imposing, battered keep (12th to 16th century) rises high on rocks above the green tiling of fields and a swerving bend in the River Tweed. It was originally built by the prince bishops of Durham in 1160 to guard a crossing on the river.

Bus No 23 regularly passes Norham Castle from Berwick train station on its way to Kelso in Scotland (seven daily Monday to Saturday).

Etal, Ford & Heatherslaw
Etal and Ford are part of a 6075-hectare working rural estate set between the coast and the Cheviots, a lush and ordered landscape that belies its ferocious, bloody history.

The pretty village of Etal perches at the estate's northern end, 12 miles (19km) south of Berwick-upon-Tweed on the B6354.

Etal Castle (EH; ☎ 01890-820332; *adult £2.80; open 10am-6pm daily Apr-Sept, 10am-5pm Oct*), a 14th-century construction on the calm rounded banks of the River Till, retains its tower house, gatehouse and a length of curtain wall. It was captured by the Scots just before the ferocious Battle of Flodden, and has a striking border warfare exhibition.

Black Bull (☎ 01890-820200) is unique as Northumberland's only thatched pub. It's a quaint, whitewashed, popular place, serving great pub food and pouring a variety of well-kept ales.

One and a half miles (2.5km) southeast of Etal, Ford is a tranquil and picturesque village.

Lady Waterford Hall (☎ 01890-820524; *adult/child £1.75/75p; open 10.30am-12.30pm & 1.30pm-5.30pm daily Apr-Oct, other times by appointment*) is an extraordinary schoolhouse. In 1860 Louisa Anne, marchioness of Waterford, commissioned the building. For the next 21 years she worked on the walls, covering them with beautiful murals depicting stories from the Bible. She used local people as models (for example, her housekeeper appears as one holy personage), and copied local flora and fauna.

Unfortunately the proud 14th-century **Ford Castle** is closed to the public.

The Old Post Office (☎ 01890-820286; *2 Old Post Office Cottages; rooms per person £22*) is flower laden and very friendly.

The Estate House (☎ 01890-820668; e *the estatehouse@supanet.com; rooms per person £23-25*), near Lady Waterford Hall, is very pretty, offers great hospitality, a guest living room and a plethora of local information.

Bus No 267 between Berwick and Wooler stops at both Etal and Ford (six daily, Monday to Saturday).

Halfway between Ford and Etal is the **Heatherslaw Corn Mill** (☎ 01890-820488; *open 10am-6pm daily Apr-Oct, 10am-5pm Mon, Fri & other days when milling Nov-Mar*) and **Heatherslaw Light Railway** (☎ 01890-820244). The restored 19th-century mill, on the banks of the River Till, is a working museum. Locally grown wheat is used to produce delicious cakes and bread that you can tuck into in its **Granary Cafe**.

Kids will love the toy-town **Light Railway** (*adult/child £4/2.50; hourly 11am-3pm Apr-Oct, to 4.30pm mid-July–Aug*), which chugs from the mill to Etal Castle. The 3½-mile (5.5km) return journey follows the river through pretty countryside.

Crookham & Around
One and a half miles (2.5km) west of Crookham on a minor road off the A697 is the site of the **Battle of Flodden**, where the English defeated the Scots in 1513. Crookham itself is 3 miles (5km) west of Ford. A monument 'to the brave of both nations' surmounting an innocuous hill overlooking the battlefield is the only memorial to the thousands used as arrow fodder. An information board next to the monument gives a brief account of how the English outflanked the Scots.

NORTHEAST ENGLAND

The Coach House (☎ 01890-820293; rooms £25-43; dinner £19.50), also in Crookham, is a quiet, pretty spot, providing accommodation and serving excellent food.

Bus No 710 between Newcastle and Kelso serves these parts (two daily Monday to Friday).

Northumberland National Park

The lonely, grand landscape of Northumberland National Park encompasses the finest sections of Hadrian's Wall, spiky moors of autumn-coloured heather and gorse, the soft swells of the Cheviot Hills, and deep colossal Kielder Water, skirted by endless acres of forest. This challenging landscape is dotted with prehistoric remains and fortified houses.

Until the relative peace of the 18th-century, people did not build their homes to last, and the only places to survive were the thick-walled *peles*. Local cattle-farming families lived in cheap turf buildings that could be quickly abandoned when push came to shove. Changes in farming practises in the 18th century kept the landscape tenantless and wild, as newly formed large estates preserved large stretches of open countryside.

If you are in search of England's open spaces, the park is an ideal place to head, with a mere 2000 inhabitants spread across its 398 sq miles.

Orientation & Information

The park runs from Hadrian's Wall in the south, takes in the Simonside Hills in the east and runs into the Cheviot Hills along the Scottish border. There are few roads.

For information, contact the **Northumberland National Park** (☎ 01434-605555; w www.nnpa.org.uk; Eastburn, South Park, Hexham, Northumberland NE46 1BS). There are visitor centres based at Wooler, Rothbury and Once Brewed (see those sections later for details), as well as **Ingram** (☎ 01665-578248; open 10am-5pm Apr, May & Sept, Sat & Sun Oct, to 6pm June-Aug). All the TICs handle accommodation bookings.

Walking & Cycling

The 81-mile (130km) **Hadrian's Wall Path** from Bowness-on-Solway in Cumbria to Wallsend in Newcastle, passes through the south of the park. This stretch is the most spectacular section (between Sewingshields and Greenhead).

There are many fine walks into the Cheviots, frequently passing by prehistoric remnants; contact the Ingram, Wooler and Rothbury TICs for information.

Though at times strenuous, cycling in the park is a pleasure; the roads are good and the traffic is light in this part of Northumberland. There's off-road cycling in Border Forest Park.

Places to Stay

There's plenty of accommodation in the south around Hadrian's Wall, but the possibilities farther north are limited. Bellingham has a YHA (see later) and there's **Byrness YHA Hostel** (☎ 01830-520425; 7 Otterburn Green; adult £7; open daily Apr-Sept), off the A68, which is on the Pennine Way.

Getting There & Around

Public transport options are limited, aside from buses on the A69. Bus No 808 operates between Otterburn and Newcastle (55 minutes, twice daily Monday to Saturday). Postbus No 815, operated by the **Royal Mail**, runs between Hexham and Bellingham (45 minutes, twice daily Monday to Saturday), as does bus No 880 (six per day Monday to Saturday, three on Sunday).

National Express has one bus daily between Newcastle and Edinburgh (No 383; £21, three hours) via Otterburn, Byrness (by request), Jedburgh, Melrose and Galashiels. See the later Hadrian's Wall section for access to the south.

BELLINGHAM
☎ 01434 • pop 1164 • elevation 144m

With grey-stone buildings clustered around a shapeless market place, Bellingham (pronounced Belling-jam) is a small, remote and friendly village. It's well placed for exploring the national park, and beautiful, deserted countryside spreads out on all sides, particularly south towards Hadrian's Wall.

The **TIC** (☎ 220616; Main St; open 9.30am-1pm & 2pm-5pm Mon-Sat, 1pm-5pm Sun Apr-Oct; 2pm-5pm Mon-Fri Nov-Mar) handles visitor inquiries.

The simple, 12th-century **St Cuthbert's Church** is unique because it retains its original stone roof. During the time of the Reivers and Border Wars, most buildings in the area were destroyed by fire. St Cuthbert's survived due to its sturdy top, and became a refuge for the local population. It's withstood some onslaughts, during 19th-century restoration, cannon balls were found lodged in the roof from a 1597 attack.

Cuddy's Well, outside the churchyard wall, supposedly consecrated by St Cuthbert, is alleged to have healing powers.

The **Hareshaw Linn Walk** passes through a wooded valley and over six bridges, leading to a 9m-high waterfall 2½ miles (4km) north of Bellingham (*linn* is an Old English name for waterfall).

Bellingham's on the Pennine Way; book ahead for accommodation in summer.

Bellingham YHA Hostel (☎ 0870 770 5694; Woodburn Rd; adult £8.10; open Tues-Sat mid-Apr–Oct, daily July & Aug) is a spartan but cosy hut.

Westfield House (☎ 220 340; en-suite rooms per person from £28) is backed by hills and up a flower-lined drive off the road towards Kielder. **Lyndale Guest House** (☎/fax 220361; beds from £20), in the village, is a home away from home.

Riverdale Hall Hotel (☎ 220254; dinner £10.95), also on the Kielder road, has a stately bar with lush views and serves good food.

ROTHBURY
☎ 01669 • pop 1805 • elevation 123m
Set amid hills, Rothbury is a traditional, restful market town on the River Coquet.

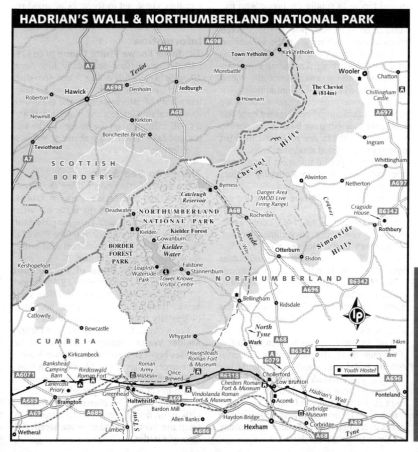

HADRIAN'S WALL & NORTHUMBERLAND NATIONAL PARK

It's a gentle place, with stony-faced Victorian buildings centred on the green, tree-lined Market Place; it makes a convenient base for the Cheviots.

There's a **TIC & visitor centre** (☎ 620887; Church St; open 10am-5pm Apr-Oct, to 6pm June-Aug).

A good reason to head here is **Cragside House, Garden and Estate** (NT; ☎ 620333; admission to all £6.90, estate & garden only £4.40; house open 1pm-5.30pm Tues-Sun Apr-Sept, to 4.30pm Oct, estate & garden open 10.30am-7pm), 1 mile north of town on the B6341. Built by the first Lord Armstrong as his countryside retreat, he hired Richard Norman Shaw, one of the top architects of the time. From 1870 to 1878 a system was developed using man-made lakes and underground piping to supply the house with hydroelectricity; it was the first house in the world to be lit by such power. The restored hydroelectric machinery can be viewed on the Power Circuit Walk. There's also a visitor centre describing Armstrong's innovations (not always so environmentally sound – he developed cutting-edge munitions).

The Victorian mansion and gardens are well worth exploring. The latter are huge and remarkably varied: from lakes and moors to one of the world's largest rock gardens. Visit in May to see myriad rhododendrons.

There is no public transport to the front gates from Rothbury; try **Rothbury Motors** (☎ 620516) for a taxi.

High St is a good place to look for accommodation.

Alexander House (☎ 621463; doubles with en suite from £40) offers cosy, cluttered rooms.

Katerina's Guest House (☎ 602334; Sun Buildings, High St; en-suite singles/doubles from £36/50) is friendly, with snug rooms.

The Haven (☎ 620577; w www.rothbury .com/roth/B&B/haven; Back Crofts; en-suite rooms per person from £25), up on a hill, has an enthusiastic owner and unfussy rooms with views.

Food options aren't copious, though a few of the pubs do meals, including the cheerful **Victoria Hotel** with standard pub grub. For takeaway you could try the **Rothbury Bakery** (High St) for pies and sandwiches or **Tully's** (High St) for fine food and flapjacks.

Bus No 416 from Morpeth (30 minutes) leaves every two hours Monday to Saturday and three times on Sunday.

KIELDER WATER

The rippling dark flood of Kielder Water is overwhelmingly huge. The largest man-made lake in northern Europe, built in 1982 to quench the thirst of the northeast, it holds 200,000 million litres and has a shoreline of 27 miles (44km). Not to be outdone on the superlative front, Kielder Forest is the largest in England, with 150 million, rather uniform, spruce and pine trees. This is England at its most secluded (you are often as much as 10 miles from the nearest village!). On all sides forests envelope the landscape, run-through with burns and the scattered remains of fortified dwellings.

Its relative inaccessibility and sparse transport means that it's a fantastic place to escape humanity (but not midges – in summer they come out in force; bring good repellent).

Information

The **Tower Knowe Visitor Centre** (☎ 01434-250312; open 10am-5pm daily June-Sept, 10am-6pm daily July & Aug, 10am-4pm daily Apr-Oct), near the southern end of the lake, has plenty of information on the area, with lots of walking leaflets and maps, a café and a small exhibition on the history of the valley and lake. There's a website at w www .kielder.org.

Things to See & Do

A few miles farther north along the lake is the **Leaplish Waterside Park** (☎ 01434-250312) where most of the water activities on the lake originate. This purpose-built complex has accommodation (see Places to Stay & Eat later), a restaurant and coffee shop, fishing, and cycle hire.

Nearby is the **Birds of Prey Centre** (☎ 01434-250400; adult/child £3.50/2; open 10.30am-5pm daily), with owls, falcons and hawks flapping about; the birds are flown twice daily from April to September.

For a closer look at the lake, the **Osprey Kielder Water Cruiser** (☎ 01434-250312) cruises between Leaplish and Tower Knowe four times a day from March to October, with evening cruises subject to demand. A return ticket costs £5/3 per adult/child.

At the lake's northern end, 6 miles (10km) on from Leaplish and 3 miles (5km) from the Scottish border, is the sleepy village of **Kielder**.

Kielder Castle (☎ 01434-250209; admission free; open 10am-5pm daily Apr-Oct, 10am-6pm Aug, 11am-4pm Sat & Sun Nov-Dec), was built in 1775 as a hunting lodge by the Duke of Northumberland. It now houses a Forestry Enterprise information centre – with countless maps and leaflets.

Cycling at Kielder and Walking at Kielder are useful leaflets available from any of the area's TICs (£2 each). They describe trails in and around the forest, their length and difficulty.

A good destination for a short walk is **Skyspace** at Cat Cairn, a small chamber with a skylight 1½ miles from Kielder Village. When observed from inside at dawn or dusk, the changing sky and an internal light system produce interesting colour effects. The route is marked from Kielder Castle car park.

Places to Stay & Eat

Leaplish Campsite (☎ 01434-250278; camping for 2 people £8; open Apr-Oct) at the waterside park charges £1 for showers.

Kielder Camping and Caravan Site (☎ 01434-250291; tent pitches from £6.80-9.50; open Apr-Sept), about two minutes' walk north of Kielder village, has a lush, green, quiet spot at the edge of the forest.

Kielder YHA Hostel (☎ 0870 770 5898; e kielder@yha.org.uk; Kielder Village; beds per adult £10.25) is well set up, with 10 bedrooms in a converted school.

The Reiver's Rest (☎ 01434-250312; dorm beds £11; open Easter-Oct), at Leaplish, has adequate facilities in dorm rooms. Separate rooms are also available.

Mrs JA Scott (☎ 01434-250254; beds per person £18) has probably the most remote B&B in England, on the eastern side of the lake at Gowanburn, accessible by a narrow road from Kielder village. The iron-grey lake spreads out before the house, the welcome is warm and the breakfast's fantastic. Mrs Scott has been doing B&B here since 1969!

Braefoot (☎ 01434-240238; Falstone; rooms per person £22.50), at the edge of a little village, is homely, relaxed and hospitable.

Falstone Tea Rooms (☎ 01434-240459; Old School House, Falstone) has filling all-day breakfasts for £3.65.

Getting There & Around

Bus No 814 goes from Otterburn to Kielder Village calling at Bellingham, Stannersburn,

Falstone, Tower Knowe Information Centre and Leaplish (two per day Monday to Friday term time, one hour) and from Bellingham to Kielder in school holidays (Tuesday and Friday). Postbus No 815 runs between Hexham train station and Kielder on a similar route along the lake and makes a detour to Gowanburn and Deadwater in the morning (two per day Monday to Friday, one on Saturday). Bus No 714 comes from Newcastle (two hours, Sunday June to October, Wednesday late July to August) in the morning and makes the journey back in the afternoon, giving you about five hours in Kielder.

Kielder Bikes (☎ 01434-250392; Castle Hill; open 10am-6pm daily, closed Fri off-peak) is opposite Kielder Castle. Bike rental costs £16/8 per adult/child. If no-one's around, there's an excellent long-distance doorbell.

WOOLER
☎ 01668 • pop 1868

Wooler, on the A697, is a small, harmonious town. Much was rebuilt in the 1860s after a disastrous fire, giving it a sense of unified design. On the edge of the Northumberland National Park 20 miles (32km) north of Rothbury and the same distance south of Berwick, it's a great base for forays into the seclusion of the Cheviots. Wooler is also the midway point for the 65-mile (105km) St Cuthbert's Way running from the picturesque Scottish town of Melrose to Holy Island on the coast.

The **TIC** (☎ 01668-282123; w www.wooler .org.uk; Cheviot Centre, Padgepool Place; open 10am-5pm daily July & Aug, 10am-5pm Mon-Sat, 10am-2pm Sun Apr-Oct, 10am-4pm Sat & Sun Nov-Mar) is a mine of information on walks in the hills. You can access the Net at the **library** (open Wed, Fri & Sat) in an alley tucked off the High St opposite the post office.

The Cheviot (814m), 6 miles (10km) southeast and the highest in the group of hills, is barren and wild; it takes around four hours to reach the top from Wooler. Check with the TIC for information before setting out.

A more sedate walk takes in Humbleton Hill (see the boxed text 'Humbleton Hill Circular Walk').

Places to Stay & Eat

Highburn House (☎ 01668-281344; Burnhouse Rd; camping for 2-people £8, child 50p) is a camp site just north of the town.

NORTHEAST ENGLAND

Humbleton Hill Circular Walk

A popular walk from Wooler bus station takes in **Humbleton Hill**. It's the site of an Iron Age hill fort and there are great views of the wild Cheviot hills to the south and plains to the north, merging into the horizon.

The hill is the site of yet another battle between the Scots and the English (1402). It's immortalised in Shakespeare's *Henry IV* and the *Ballad of Chevy Chase* (no, not *that* Chevy Chase).

The trail is 4 miles (6km), well signposted and returns to Wooler. It takes approximately two hours.

Wooler YHA Hostel (☎ 0870 770 6100; e wooler@yha.org.uk; 30 Cheviot St; adult £9.50; open Mon-Sat Apr-Jun, Tues-Sat Sept, Fri & Sat Mar) is a 46-bed hostel with all the normal amenities.

Tilldale House (☎ 01668-281450; w www .tilldalehouse.com; 34-40 High St; en-suite singles/doubles £25/40) is a pleasant house on the main drag.

Black Bull (☎ 281309; 2 High St; mains around £6) offers filling bar meals. For a lunchtime bite, the **Home Bakery** (Market Place) does a fine vegetable pastie (85p).

Getting There & Around

Wooler has good bus connections to the major towns in Northumberland. No 464 comes from Berwick (50 minutes, five per day Monday to Saturday) and No 470 (six per day Monday to Saturday) or 473 (eight per day Monday to Saturday) come from Alnwick. Bus No 710 makes the journey from Newcastle (1½ hours, Wednesday and Saturday).

Cycle hire is available at **Haugh Head Garage** (☎ 01668-281316) in Haugh Head, 1 mile south of Wooler on the A697 (from £12.50 per day).

AROUND WOOLER
Chillingham Castle

Six miles (10km) southeast of Wooler, in glorious uplifting countryside, is Chillingham Castle (☎ 01668-215359; w www.chill ingham-castle.co.uk; adult/child £4.50/2; open 1pm-5pm Sun-Fri May-Sept). The castle, first built in 1150, was fully fortified in the 14th century. It's an extraordinary, eccentric, medieval treasure, and reputedly one of the country's most haunted places, with ghostly clientele ranging from a phantom funeral to Lady Mary Berkeley in search of her errant husband.

From 1245, it belonged to the Grey family but was shut up in 1932 when the family couldn't afford the upkeep (it was used as a barracks during WWII). Sir Humphrey Wakefield, married to a Grey, bought it in 1982, and set about an energetic restoration. It's possible to visit a number of extravagant, medieval-like stately rooms (the silk, plaque and dining room) as well as gleefully gruesome torture chambers. There's also a museum with a fantastically jumbled collection of objects – it's like stepping into the attic of a compulsive and well-travelled hoarder. The wardens are charming and there are lots of carefully typed personal notes from Sir Humphrey to guide you through. Sir Jeffrey Wyatville, landscaper for Windsor Castle, designed the gardens and grounds; there's a recommended walk down to the lake.

In the 13th century the borderlands were so wild and unruly that, to protect the wild cattle that were the source of food and hunting for the castle, 148 hectares of land were enclosed by a high fence to keep out intruders. Thus, the **Chillingham Wild Cattle** (☎ 01668-215250; adult/child £3/1; park open 10am-noon & 2pm-5pm Mon & Wed-Sat, 2pm-5pm Sun Apr-Oct) were cut off from mixing with other breeds and today are the only cattle in the world to have remained pure. They were difficult to steal, as they cannot herd and apparently make good guard animals. Around 40 to 60 make up the total population of these wild white cattle (a reserve herd is kept in a remote place in Scotland, in case of emergencies).

It's possible to stay at the medieval fortress in the seven apartments designed for guests, where the likes of Henry III and Edward I once snoozed. Prices vary depending on the luxury of the apartment; the **Grey Apartment** (high season per person £49) is the most expensive – it has a dining table to seat 12, or there's the **Lookout Apartment** (per person £48), at the top of the Northwest Tower. All of the apartments are self-catering.

Bus No 470 running between Alnwick and Wooler stops at Chillingham (six daily Monday to Saturday).

Hadrian's Wall

Hadrian's Wall is an enduring testament to ambition, history and engineering, and exploring the length of this awe-inspiring feat, zigzagging through spectacular, steep landscape, brings England's ancient past alive.

With typically neat Roman practicality, Emperor Hadrian ordered the momentous structure built to delineate the border and keep out the marauding northern barbarians. An extraordinarily ambitious, yet simplistic concept, it courses 80 Roman miles (73 miles; 118km) across the narrow neck of the country, from Solway Firth in the west almost to the mouth of the Tyne in the east. The Roman era is brought into even sharper focus by the preserved remains of the excavated forts along its length, ranging from leather sandals to stunningly located latrines.

The wall was the greatest single engineering project undertaken by the Roman Empire (and they weren't shy of a bit of engineering). It involved the minor task of moving two million cubic yards of soil and took over six years (from AD 122) to build.

The section from Newcastle to the River Irthing was built of stone, and turf blocks were used on the section to Solway – roughly 3m thick and 4.5m high. A 3m-deep, 9m-wide ditch and mound were excavated immediately in front (except where there were natural defences). Every Roman mile (1.62 miles) there was a gateway guarded by a small fort (milecastle) and between each milecastle were two observation turrets. Milecastles are numbered right across the country, starting with Milecastle 0 at Wallsend and ending with Milecastle 80 at Bowness-on-Solway. The inter-mediate turrets are tagged A and B, so Milecastle 37 (a good one, see under Housesteads Roman Fort & Museum later) will be followed by Turret 37A, Turret 37B and then Milecastle 38. A second ditch (the vallum) and a military road were built between 60m and 150m to the south.

A series of forts were developed as bases some distance south (and may actually predate the wall), and 16 actually lay astride it. The prime remaining forts on the wall are Cilurnum (Chesters), Vercovicium (Housesteads) and Banna (Birdoswald). The best forts behind the wall are Corstopitum, at Corbridge, and Vindolanda, north of Bardon Mill.

History

By building the wall, Emperor Hadrian intended to establish control over a clear physical and political frontier and reduce the demand on manpower. He came to Britain in AD 122 to see it started, and the actual building was undertaken by Roman legions. The wall was mainly a means of controlling the movement of people across the frontier – it could easily have been breached by a determined attack at any single point – and of preventing low-level border raiding.

It's likely that around 409, as the Roman administration collapsed, the frontier garrisons ceased receiving Roman pay. The communities had to then rely on their own resources, gradually becoming reabsorbed into the war-band culture of the native Britons – for some generations soldiers had been recruited locally in any case.

Orientation

Hadrian's Wall crosses beautiful, varied landscape. Starting in the lowlands of the Solway coast, it crosses the lush hills east of Carlisle to the ridge of basalt rock known as Whin Sill (which is bleak and windy, still) overlooking Northumberland National Park, and ends in the urban sprawl of Newcastle. The most spectacular section lies between Brampton and Corbridge.

Carlisle, in the west, and Newcastle, in the east, are good starting points, but Brampton, Haltwhistle, Hexham and Corbridge all make good bases.

The B6318 follows the course of the wall from the outskirts of Newcastle to Birdoswald; from Birdoswald to Carlisle it pays to have a detailed map. The main A69 road and the railway line follow 3 or 4 miles (6km) to the south. This section follows the wall from east to west.

Information

Carlisle and Newcastle TICs are good places to start gathering information, but there are also TICs in Hexham, Haltwhistle, Corbridge and Brampton. The extremely helpful **Northumberland National Park Visitor Centre** (☎ 01434-344396; open 9.30am-5pm daily Mar-May, Sept & Oct, to 6pm June-Aug) is off the B6318 at Once Brewed. There's a **Hadrian's Wall information line** (☎ 01434-322002; w www.hadrians-wall.org) too. May sees a spring festival, with lots of re-creations of Roman life along the wall (contact TICs for details).

The Hadrian's Wall path along the whole length opened in 2003; see the Activities chapter for information on walking Hadrian's Wall. If you're planning to cycle along it, TICs sell the *Hadrian's Wall Country Cycle Map* (£2.50).

Getting There & Around

Bus West of Hexham the wall runs parallel to the A69, between Carlisle and Newcastle. Bus No 685 runs along the A69 hourly, passing near the youth hostels and 2 to 3 miles (5km) south of the main sites.

From June to early September, the hail-and-ride Hadrian's Wall bus (AD122) runs daily between Wallsend and Bowness on Solway via Haltwhistle train station (four daily between Hexham and Carlisle). It follows the B6318, which runs close to the wall, calling at the main sites. Bus No 185 covers the route the rest of the year (Monday to Saturday). Bus No 685 also follows the wall year round. An adult/child Day Rover ticket costs £5.50/3, or £8/4 for three days. On-board guides are provided free four times daily on Sunday and Monday (July and August). For information contact **Hexham TIC** (☎ 01434-652220), or pick up a timetable at any of the Hadrian's Wall TICs.

Train The railway line between Newcastle and Carlisle (Tyne Valley Line) has stations at Corbridge, Hexham, Haydon Bridge, Bardon Mill, Haltwhistle and Brampton. This service runs daily, but not all trains stop at all stations.

Taxi Sproul's (☎ 01434-321064) in Haltwhistle charge around £16 to Hexham.

CORBRIDGE

☎ 01434 • pop 3533

The mellow golden town of Corbridge sits above a green-banked curve in the Tyne, which is vaulted by a 17th-century bridge. The shady, cobbled streets are lined by old-fashioned shops. It's an ancient place – many buildings have stones nicked from nearby Corstopitum, and an Anglo-Saxon monastery was based here. Long-term prosperity is evident in its buildings – the busy market town thrived despite being razed to the ground three times during ferocious Border warfare.

For information, contact the **TIC** (☎ 632815; Hill St; open 10am-1pm & 2pm-6pm Mon-Sat, 1pm-5pm Sun June-Sept; 10am-1pm & 2pm-5pm Mon-Sat Mar, Apr & Oct).

St Andrew's (Market Place) is an important Anglo-Saxon church, expanded in the 13th century. In its grounds, a sturdy **fortified vicarage** brings home the danger of local 14th-century life.

Corbridge Roman Site & Museum

Corbridge (Corstopitum to the Romans) was a garrison town that became a civil settlement. It lies south of the wall on Dere St, which was once the main road from York to Scotland.

The site (EH; ☎ 632349; adult £2.70; open 10am-6pm daily Apr-Sept, 10am-5pm daily Oct, 10am-4pm Wed-Sun Nov-Mar) is half a mile west of Corbridge off Trinity Terrace (just over a mile from Corbridge train station). You get a sense of the domestic heart of the town from the visible remains, and the Clayton Museum displays Roman sculpture and carvings, including the amazing 3rd-century Corbridge Lion.

Places to Stay & Eat

Angel Inn (☎ 632119; Main St; en-suite singles/doubles from £49/74; mains around £12) is a 17th-century place with serene rooms and serves polished food in an upmarket stripped-floor restaurant.

Riverside Guest House (☎ 632942; w www .theriversideguesthouse.co.uk; Main St; en-suite singles/doubles from £38/56) has rooms filled with old wooden furniture, some with soothing river views.

Town Barns (☎ 633345; singles/doubles from £35/50), off Trinity Terrace, used to belong to romantic novelist Catherine Cookson – it's a rambling house with an appropriately sweeping staircase.

Holmlea (☎ 632486; Station Rd; rooms per person from £25), near the station, is a welcoming terraced house with comfortable, frilly rooms.

The Golden Lion (☎ 632 216; Hill St; meals £3-7) is relaxed and serves filling meals.

Corbridge Tandoori (☎ 633676; 8 Market Place; mains £5.95-10.70) overlooks the attractive central square and serves tasty Indian dishes.

The Valley Restaurant (☎ 633434; Station Rd; mains £5.50-14; open dinner Mon-Sat), in a lovely building above the station, supplies a unique service as well as delicious Indian food. A group of 10 or more diners from Newcastle can catch the train to Corbridge accompanied by a waiter, who will supply snacks and phone ahead to have the meal ready when the train arrives.

Getting There & Away

Bus No 685 between Newcastle and Carlisle comes through Corbridge, as does bus No 602 from Newcastle to Hexham (half-hourly), where you can connect with the Hadrian's Wall bus AD122. The town is also on the Newcastle–Carlisle railway line.

HEXHAM

☎ 01434 • pop 11,342

The bustling, attractive centre of Hexham is interlinked by cobbled alleyways. It's packed with high-street shops and has the most accommodation and restaurants of all the wall towns. It's famous for its handsome abbey, perched like a proud hen above a rare Saxon crypt.

The helpful TIC (☎ 652220; w www.hadri answallcountry.org; Wentworth Car Park; open 9am-6pm Mon-Sat, 10am-5pm Sun mid-May–Oct; 10am-5pm Mon-Sat Oct–mid-May) is northeast of the town centre.

Hexham Abbey (☎ 602031; open 9.30am-7pm daily May-Sept, 9.30am-5pm daily Oct-Apr), surrounded by a park, is a fine example of early English architecture. Carved misericords date from c.1425. The ancient crypt survives from St Wilfrid's Church, built in 674, and inscribed stones from Corstopitum can be seen in its walls.

The Old Gaol (☎ 652349), completed in 1333 as England's first purpose-built prison, is the setting for the Border History Museum (adult/child £2/1; open 10am-4.30pm daily Apr-Oct, Mon, Tues & Sat Oct–mid-Nov). The history of the Border Reivers is retold along with tales of the punishments handed out in the prison.

Acomb YHA Hostel (☎ 0870 770 5664; Main St; adult £7; open Fri & Sat Nov-Mar; Wed-Sun Apr, May & July-Oct; Tues-Sun June) is a basic hostel, converted from stables, on the edge of Acomb village, about 2½ miles (4km) north of Hexham and 2 miles (3km) south of the wall. Hexham can be reached by bus (Nos 745 and 880, frequently) or train.

West Close House (☎ 603307; Hextol Terrace; rooms per person from £19), off Allendale Rd (the B6305) is a bargain and has extremely comfortable rooms in leafy surroundings.

Laburnum House (☎ 601828; 23 Leazes Crescent; rooms per person from £18) is a warm, friendly, well-preserved Victorian house. Beaumont Hotel (☎ 602331, fax 606184; e beaumont.hotel@btinternet.com; Beaumont St; singles/doubles from £65/85) overlooks the abbey and offers restful, tasteful rooms. Breakfast is extra.

Langley Castle (☎ 688888; w www.langley castle.com; singles £90-140, doubles £100-200) is a 14th-century castle in 4 hectares of woodland. Its grand rooms are furnished with pointy four-posters, and the walls are 2m thick. It's off the A686 (the road for Alston), off the A69 just before Haydon Bridge.

There are several bakeries on Fore St and, if you turn left into the quaintly named Priestpopple near the bus station, you'll find some decent restaurants.

Giotto (☎ 603350; 36-38 Priestpopple; mains £5-6) offers pizza and pasta (happy hour £3.95). Next door, the Coach & Horses (☎ 601004) is a pleasant pub with a beer garden and decent bar meals.

Diwan-E-Am Tandoori (☎ 606575; 23 Priestpopple; mains £6.10-12.60), across the road from Giotto, serves all the traditional Indian dishes in a plush setting.

Dipton Mill (☎ 606577; Dipton Mill Rd; mains around £4.50-6.50) is a country pub 2 miles out on the road to Blanchland, amongst woodland and by a river. It offers sought-after ploughman's lunches and real ale.

Bus No 685 between Newcastle and Carlisle comes through Hexham hourly. The AD122 (four daily June to early September) and the less-frequent winter-service No 185 connect with other towns along the wall, and the town is on the Newcastle–Carlisle railway line (hourly).

AROUND HEXHAM
Chesters Roman Fort & Museum

The extensive and well-preserved remains of a Roman cavalry fort are found at Chesters (EH; ☎ 01434-681379; bus No 682; adult £3; open 9.30am-6pm daily Apr-Sept, 10am-5pm Oct, to 4pm Nov-Mar), set among idyllic green woods and meadows. They include part of a bridge (complex and

NORTHEAST ENGLAND

beautifully constructed) across the River North Tyne, an extraordinary bathhouse and an underfloor heating system. The museum has a large collection of Roman sculpture.

Brunton Water Mill (☎ 01434-681002; e *pesarra@bruntonmill.freeserve.co.uk; Chollerford; rooms per person £20-24)* is the other side of Chollerford bridge from Chesters, and has a pleasant conservatory.

George Hotel (☎ 01434-681611; w *www .georgehotel-chollerford.com; rooms per person £55-67.50)* is right on the river, beside the bridge and has spacious, blandly furnished rooms, but lovely watery views and a swimming pool.

Hadrian Hotel (☎ 681232; *Wall; singles/ doubles £35/40, en-suite doubles £50; mains £6-11)*, a fine, ivy-covered place in Wall, the next village along, has good views and pleasant, old-fashioned rooms. It's a popular place to eat.

The Chesters fort site has an excellent small café, **Lucullus Larder**.

Allen Banks & Staward Gorge

Allen Banks & Staward Gorge (*NT; adult £1)* is spread across 81 hectares of ancient wooded hillside, cut through by the River Allen. The area was once the pleasure grounds of private Ridley Hall and is dotted with ruined summer houses. You can climb up to a medieval peel tower in Staward Peel Wood for views across the Allen Valley. It's off the A69, near Haydon Bridge. Bus Nos 85 and 685 pass half a mile away.

HALTWHISTLE

☎ 01434 • pop 3773 • elevation 145m
Haltwhistle, just north of the A69, is subdued and attractive, centred around a straitened market place and a single main street. Haltwhistle is claimed to be the centre of Britain, and has several signs to this effect – however, it also has a rival, Dunsop Bridge, 71 miles (114km) to the south.

The **TIC** (☎ 322002; *open 9.30am-1pm & 2pm-5.30pm Mon-Sat, 1pm-5pm Sun May-Sept, 9.30am-noon & 1pm-3.30pm Thur-Tues Oct-Apr)* is in the train station.

Ashcroft (☎/fax 320213; *Lanty's Lonnen; rooms per person from £25)* is sizable, with elaborately tiled bathrooms and wonderful views from the dining room.

Manor House Hotel (☎ 322588; *Main St; singles with/without en suite £25/22,*

doubles £44) offers pastel rooms and is a friendly pub with good food.

Black Bull (*Market Place)* is an attractive one-room pub that's popular with sensible-sweatered locals and brews its own ale.

Bus No 685 comes from Newcastle (1½ hours) and Carlisle (45 minutes) 12 times daily respectively. Hadrian's Wall bus No AD122 (four daily June to early September) or No 185 (October to May) connect Haltwhistle with other places along the wall. Bus No 681 heads south to Alston (55 minutes, three daily Monday to Saturday). The town is also on the Newcastle–Carlisle railway line (hourly).

AROUND HALTWHISTLE
Vindolanda Roman Fort & Museum

Vindolanda (☎ 01434-344277; w *www.vindo landa.com; adult/child £3.90/2.80, with Roman Army Museum £5.60/4.10; open 10am-4pm late Feb & early Nov, to 5pm Mar & Oct, to 5.30pm Apr & Sept, to 6pm May & June, to 6.30pm July & Aug)* has some extraordinary relics. The time-capsule museum displays countless leather sandals, signature Roman toothbrush-flourish helmet decorations, and countless writing tablets – fragments of daily Roman life – such as a student's marked work ('sloppy'), and a parent's note with a present of socks and underpants (things haven't changed – in this climate you can never have too many).

The museum is just one part of this large, extensively excavated site, which includes impressive parts of the fort and town (excavations continue) and reconstructed turrets and temple.

It's 1½ miles (2.5km) north of Bardon Mill between the A69 and B6318 and a mile from Once Brewed.

Housesteads Roman Fort & Museum

Housesteads (*EH;* ☎ 01434-344363; *adult £2.80; 10am-6pm Apr-Sept, to 5pm Oct, to 4pm Nov-Mar)* is the wall's most dramatic site. From here, high on a ridge and covering 2 hectares, you can survey the moors of Northumberland National Park, and the snaking wall, with a sense of awe at the landscape and the aura of the Roman lookouts.

The substantial foundations bring fort life alive. The remains include an impressive hospital, granaries with a carefully worked-out ventilation system and barrack blocks. Most memorable are the spectacularly situated communal flushable latrines, which summon up Romans at their most mundane.

From here the wall nurses the cliff tops. You should walk west to Milecastle 37, taking in the rolling views north and naked Pennines to the south, and onward to Steel Rigg.

Housesteads is 2½ miles (4km) north of Bardon Mill on the B6318, and about 3 miles (5km) from Once Brewed. It's popular, so try to visit outside summer weekends, or late in the day when the site will be quiet and indescribably eerie.

Roman Army Museum
One mile northwest of Greenhead near Walltown Crags, this kid-pleasing museum (☎ 016977-47485; adult/child £3.10/2.10, with Vindolanda £5.60/4.10; open 10am-4pm Feb & Nov, to 5pm Mar & Oct, to 6pm May & June, to 6.30pm July & Aug) provides lots of colourful background detail to wall-life, such as how far soldiers had to march per day and whether they could marry. It's all done using interactives, films and Roman artefacts.

Birdoswald Roman Fort
Birdoswald (EH; ☎ 016977-47602; adult £3; open 10am-5.30pm daily Mar-Oct) is the remains of a fort on an escarpment overlooking the beautiful Irthing Gorge. A fine stretch of wall stretches from here to Harrow Scar Milecastle.

With a healthy dose of imagination, you can explore many elements of the fort system, and the exhibitions depict the day-to-day slog under harsh conditions.

About half a mile away, across the impressive river footbridge, is another good bit of wall, ending in two turrets and the meticulous structure of the **Willowford Bridge** abutment.

The fort is on a minor road off the B6318 about 3 miles (5km) west of Greenhead.

Places to Stay
Once Brewed YHA Hostel (☎ 0870 7705980; e oncebrewed@yha.org.uk; Military Rd, Bardon Mill; adult £11.25; open daily Mar-Oct, Mon-Sat Nov-Feb) is a modern and well-equipped hostel central for visiting both Housesteads Fort 3 miles (5km) and Vindolanda 1 mile (1.6km) away. Bus No 685

Hadrian's Wall Circular Walk
Starting at Once Brewed National Park Centre, this walk takes in the most complete stretch of Hadrian's Wall. The walk is 7½ miles (12km) and takes approximately 4½ hours. The wall follows the natural barrier created by steep dramatic cliffs and the views north are stunning. Some parts of the wall are so well preserved that they have featured in films. You might recognise Milecastle 39, which acted Kevin Costner off the screen in *Robin Hood – Prince of Thieves*. The trail returns to the YHA hostel across swathes of farmland. The centre has a good map.

(which you can catch at Hexham or Haltwhistle train stations) will drop you at Henshaw, 2 miles (3km) south, or you could leave the train at Bardon Mill 2½ miles (4km) southeast. Hadrian's Wall bus drops you at the door June to September.

Greenhead YHA Hostel (☎ 016977-47401; adult £9.50; open Mon-Sat Apr-June, daily July & Aug, Fri-Mon Sept & Oct) is by a trickling stream, with 40 beds in a converted Methodist chapel with a garden 3 miles (5km) west of Haltwhistle and is served by bus No AD122 or 685 (see Getting There & Around under Hadrian's Wall earlier).

Holmhead Guest House (☎ 016977-47402; w www.bandbhadrianswall.com; rooms per person from £29.50), about half a mile behind the youth hostel, offers chintzy rooms in a lovely remote old farmhouse.

Greenhead and nearby Gilsland have pubs and B&Bs.

BRAMPTON
☎ 016977 ● pop 3957
A charming market town lined with red sandstone buildings, Brampton's wide half-cobbled main street is dominated by a quirky octagonal Moot Hall. Actually in Cumbria, the town sneaked into this section because of its proximity to Hadrian's Wall. It's on the Cumbrian Cycle Way (see the Activities chapter). Its peaceable streets come alive on market day (Wednesday).

Contact the **TIC** (☎ 3433; open 10am-5pm Mon-Sat Easter-Oct) for information. The **library** offers Net access (£1 for 30 minutes; open Monday and Wednesday to Saturday).

NORTHEAST ENGLAND

The sinuous, romantic stained glass in Victorian **St Martin's Church** was designed by Edward Burne-Jones and created by William Morris.

Bankshead Camping Barn (☎ 01200-420102; **e** campbarnsyha@enterprise.net; beds £4), very close to Banks East Turret (4 miles east of Brampton, 2 miles west of Birdoswald), is on a rustic working farm in a fine setting. The barn is basic but adequate, with shower and cooking facilities and a dry space, with heating, for 10 people to sleep. Bus AD122 or 685 drops you outside.

White Lion Hotel (☎ 2338; High Cross St; en-suite singles/doubles per person £17.50/31.50; mains around £6), dating from the 17th century, is one of several creaky pubs serving good bar meals.

Oval House (☎ 2106; **w** www.ovalhouse .demon.co.uk; rooms per person £22.50) is a central Georgian house. Its attractive rooms have a musical theme.

Capon Tree Cafe (☎ 3649; 27 Front St) is snug and cosy and serves a good selection of snacks and delicious cakes.

Bus No 685 between Newcastle and Carlisle travels through Brampton (12 daily). The town is also on the Newcastle–Carlisle railway line.

Lanercost Priory

Three miles (5km) northeast of Brampton are the peaceful raspberry-coloured ruins of Lanercost Priory (EH; ☎ 016977-3030; adult £2.20; open 10am-6pm daily Apr-Sept, to 5pm Oct), originally founded in 1166 by Augustinian canons. The priory was of great temptation to the Scots, who ransacked it several times. After the dissolution, it became a private house, and a priory church was created from the Early English nave. The church contains some beautiful Pre-Raphaelite stained glass. The AD122 bus can drop you at the gate.

Glossary

abbey – a monastery of monks or nuns or the buildings they used

agister – someone paid to care for stock

aisle – passageway or open space along either side of a church's *nave*

aka – also known as

alignment – even if this doesn't conform with geography, churches are always assumed to be aligned east-west, with the altar, *chancel* and *choir* towards the east end and the nave towards the west

almshouse – accommodation offered to the aged or needy

ambulatory – processional *aisle* at the east end of a cathedral, behind the altar

apse – semicircular or rectangular area for clergy, at the east end of the church in traditional design

BABA – Book-A-Bed-Ahead scheme

bailey – outermost wall of a castle

bairn – baby

banger – old, cheap car

bangers – sausages

bap – bun (originally from northern England)

baptistry – separate area of a church used for baptisms

bar – gate (York)

barbican – an extended gateway designed to make life difficult for unwanted guests

barrel vault – semicircular arched roof

beck – stream

bent – not altogether legal

bevvied – drunk

bevvy – a drink (originally from northern England)

bevvying – drinking

bill – restaurant check

billion – the British billion, unlike the American billion (a thousand million), is a million million

biscuit – cookie

bitter – beer

black pudding – a type of sausage made from dried blood and other ingredients

blatherskite – boastful or talkative person (northern England)

bloke – man

bodge job – poor-quality repairs

boss – covering for the meeting point of the ribs in a vaulted roof (often colourfully decorated, so bring binoculars)

brass – type of memorial common in medieval churches consisting of a brass plate set into the floor or a tomb, usually with a depiction of the deceased but sometimes simply with text

bridleway – path that can be used by walkers, horse riders and cyclists

Brummie – a native of Birmingham

BTA – British Tourist Authority

bum – backside (not tramp, layabout etc)

bus – local bus; see also coach

buttress – vertical support for a wall; see *flying buttress*

by – town

BYO – bring your own

C&CC – Camping & Caravanning Club

caff – cheap café

cairn – pile of stones to mark path or junction, also peak

campanile – free-standing belfry or bell tower; Westminster Cathedral and Chester Cathedral have modern ones

canny – good, great, wise (northern England)

capital – head of column

car bonnet – hood

car boot – trunk

chancel – eastern end of the church, usually reserved for choir and clergy

chantry – *chapel* established by a donor for use in his or her name after death

chapel – small, more private shrine or area of worship off the main body of the church

chapel of ease – *chapel* built for those who lived too far away from the parish church

chapter house – building in a cathedral *close* where the dean meets with the chapter, the clergy who run the cathedral

cheers – goodbye; also thanks; also a drinking toast

chemist – pharmacist

chevet – *chapels* radiating out in a semicircular sweep, common in France but also found at Westminster and Canterbury

chine – valleylike fissure leading to the sea (southern England)

chips – deep-fried potatoes or fries

choir – area in the church where the choir is seated, usually to the east of the *transepts* and *nave*; sometimes used interchangeably with *chancel* or *presbytery*

circus – a junction of several streets, usually circular

clerestory – also clearstory; a wall of windows above the *triforium* in a church

cloister – covered walkway linking the church with adjacent monastic buildings

close – buildings grouped around a cathedral, also known as the precincts

clunch – chalk (used in connection with chalk walls in building)

coach – long-distance bus; see also bus

coaching inn – inn along a coaching route at which horses were changed

coasteering – making your way around the coastline by climbing, scrambling, jumping or swimming

cob – mixture of mud and straw for building

collegiate – church with a chapter of canons and prebendaries, but not a cathedral

corbel – stone or wooden projection from a wall supporting a beam or arch

Corbett – a mountain of between 2500ft (762m) and 2999ft (914m) in height

cot – crib

couchette – sleeping berth in a train or ferry

courgette – zucchini

courts – courtyards

crack – good conversation (originally from Ireland)

crannog – artificial island settlement

cream tea – a cup of tea and a scone with jam and thick cream

crisps – potato chips

croft – plot of land with adjoining house worked by the occupiers

crossing – intersection of the *nave* and *transepts* in a church

dear – expensive

DIY – do-it-yourself, as in handyman shop

dolmen – chartered tomb

donkey – engine

dosh/dough – money

downs – rolling upland, characterised by lack of trees

dram – whisky measure

duvet – doona

EH – English Heritage

en-suite room – a hotel room with private attached bathroom (ie, shower, basin and toilet)

Essex – derogatory adjective, as in Essex girl, meaning tarty, and identified with '80s consumerism

EU – European Union

evensong – daily evening service (Church of England)

fag – cigarette; also a boring task

fagged – exhausted

fanny – female genitals, not backside

fell race – an extreme-sports race that is a test of strength and stamina

fen – drained or marshy low-lying flat land

fiver – five-pound note

flat – apartment

flip-flops – thongs

flying buttress – supporting buttress in the form of one side of an open arch

font – basin used for baptisms, usually towards the west end of a church, often in a separate *baptistry*

footpath – sidewalk

frater – common room or dining area in a medieval monastery

gaffer – boss or foreman

gate – street (York)

ginnel – alleyway (Yorkshire)

graft – work (not corruption)

grand – one thousand

greasy spoon – cheap café

grockle – tourist

gutted – very disappointed

guv, guvner – from governor, a respectful term of address for owner or boss, can be used ironically

hammered – drunk (northern England)

hire – rent

hosepipe – garden hose

hotel – accommodation with food and bar, not always open to passing trade

Huguenots – French Protestants

inn – pub with accommodation

jam – jelly

jelly – jello

jumper – sweater

kippers – salted and smoked fish, traditionally herring

kirk – church

lady chapel – chapel, usually at the east end of a cathedral, dedicated to the Virgin Mary

lager lout – see *yob*

lancet – pointed window in Early English style

lass – young woman (northern England)

ley – clearing

lierne vault – a vault containing many tertiary ribs

lift – elevator

lock – part of a canal or river that can be closed off and the water levels changed to raise or lower boats

lolly – money; also candy on a stick (possibly frozen)

lorry – truck

love – term of address, not necessarily to someone likeable

machair – grass- and wildflower-covered sand dunes

mad – insane, not angry

manky – low quality

Martello tower – small, circular tower used for coastal defence

mate – a friend of any sex, or term of address for males

midge – a mosquito-like insect

minster – a church connected to a monastery

misericord – hinged choir seat with a bracket (often elaborately carved) that can be leant against

motorway – freeway

motte – mound on which a castle was built

naff – inferior, in poor taste

nappies – diapers

nave – main body of the church at the western end, where the congregation gather

neeps – turnips

NT – National Trust

NYMR – North Yorkshire Moors Railway

oast house – building containing a kiln for drying hops

off-license (offie) – carry-out alcoholic drinks shop

OS – Ordnance Survey

owlers – smugglers

pargeting – decorative stucco plasterwork

pee ('p') – pence

pete – fortified houses

pint – beer (not always)

piscina – basin for priests to wash their hands

pissed – drunk (not angry)

pissed off – angry

pitch – playing field

ponce – ostentatious or effeminate male; also to borrow (usually permanently)

pop – fizzy drink (northern England)

postbuses – minibuses that follow postal delivery routes, carrying mail and passengers

presbytery – eastern area of the *chancel* beyond the *choir*, where the clergy operate

priory – religious house governed by a prior, inferior to an *abbey*

provost – mayor

pub – a traditional bar or drinking place (usually with food, sometimes with accommodation)

pulpit – raised box where priest gives sermons

punter – customer

queue – line

quid – pound

quire – medieval term for *choir*

ramble – a short easy walk

rebud – a heraldic device suggesting the name of its owner

refectory – monastic dining room

reiver – warrior (northern England)

reredos – literally 'behind the back'; backdrop to an altar

return ticket – round-trip ticket

roll-up – roll-your-own cigarette

rood – archaic word for cross (in churches)

rood screen – a screen carrying a *rood* or crucifix, which separated the *nave* from the *chancel*

RSPB – Royal Society for the Protection of Birds

rubber – eraser

rubbish bin – garbage can

rugger – rugby

sacked – fired

sarnie – sandwich

sett – tartan pattern

shag – have sex

shout – to buy a group of people drinks, usually reciprocated

shut – partially covered passage

single ticket – one-way ticket

sixth-form college – further education college

Sloane Ranger – wealthy, superficial, but well-connected young person

snicket – alleyway (from York)

snogging – long, drawn-out kissing (not just a peck on the cheek)
spondulicks – money
squint – angled opening in a wall or pillar to allow a view of a church's altar
SSSI – Site of Special Scientific Interest
stone – unit of weight equivalent to 14lb or 6.35kg
subway – underpass
sweet – candy

ta – thanks
tatties – potatoes
thorpe – village
thwaite – clearing in a forest (northern England)
TICs – Tourist Information Centres
ton – one hundred (slang)
tor – Celtic word describing a hill shaped like a triangular wedge of cheese
torch – flashlight
towpath – a path running beside a river or canal
trainers – tennis shoes or sneakers
transepts – north–south projections from a church's *nave,* often added at a later date and giving the whole church a cruciform cross-shaped plan
traveller – nomadic, new-age hippy
triforium – internal wall passage above a church's arcade and below the *clerestory*; behind it is the 'blind' space above the side aisle

tron – public weighbridge
twit – a foolish (sometimes annoying) person
twitcher – obsessive birdwatcher
twitten – passage, small lane
tube – London's underground railway (subway)

undercroft – vaulted underground room or cellar
underground – London's underground railway (subway)

VAT – value-added tax, levied on most goods and services, currently 17.5%
vault – roof with arched ribs, usually in a decorative pattern
verderer – officer upholding law and order in the royal forests
vestry – robing room, where the parson keeps his robes and puts them on

wanker – a worthless/hopeless person
wide boy – ostentatious go-getter, usually on the make
wold – open, rolling country

yaya – plumby, upper-class *twit*
yob – hooligan

ziggurat – rectangular temple tower or tiered mound

Thanks

Many thanks to the travellers who used the 1st edition of this book and wrote to us with helpful hints, useful advice and interesting anecdotes. Your names follow:

Renata Alexander, Chris Allison, Odda Alyahya, Bricklen Anderson, David E. Antonsen, Chelsea Anttila, Victoria Artigliere, Heather Baker, Clive Barham, Berdina de Boer, Hervé Bonin, Jenny Branch, Samantha Briggs, Jenny Brunngard, Suzanne Buis, Melanie Buzek, Christopher Calvert, John A Castle, Ian Chivas, Tony Cooper, Graham Crews, James Davis, Caroline Despiers, Andy Dennis, Dorothy DeVoti, Jane Doran, Wally Ennis, Mary Ellen Rowe, Helen Faulkner, Carole Felce, Helen Flaherty, Tim Fosh, Emma Foulger, Jim Gardner, Matt Garwood, Jennine Gates, Anna Maria Gersd, Jackie Grace, E Griffiths, Janet Griffiths, Ronald Griffiths, Jennifer Gurbin, Karen Ha, Paula Hannon, Michael Hanratty, Ian Harrison, Karen Hart, Rowan Harvey, Caroline Heaton, Robert Hummerstone, Neil Irving, Jennifer Jameson, N E Johannie, Martin Johnson, Stephanie Johnson, Claire Jones, Evan Jones, Mrs S Jones, Billy Jonker, Matthew Kenny, Liz Kereszi, Brendan Kitchen, Noriko Kumagai, Kathryn Lamprecht, Diane Lazarus, Mike Leet, Kathryn LePage, Laszio Lieszkovsky, Anette Link, Victoria Linnett, Ian Loftus, Alex Macfie, Robert Shane McNamara, Edward Marriott, Ira Matuschke, Michael Meyer, Dani Miller, Andre Minor, Marc Nerva, Margaret Netcaffe, Mike Nixon, Carsten Olliver, J S Parkes, Sheila Phillips, Chris Picha, Kris Borring Prasada Rao, Paul Ratcliffe, Roy A Reed, Timothy Reilly, Carl & Michelle Roe, Gustavo Rubio, Howard Rundle, O M Savage, Tony Sayers, A Schneeberger, Sarah See, Oscar Sierra, Alexandra Scheidegger, Alan Sidaway, Jean D Sinclair, Simon Skerritt, Louise Smith, Bobby Stodel, Vanessa Stubbs, Diane Swift, A Taylor, Rachael Taylor, Sandrine Teodorczuk, Jillian Thomson, David Turner, Nick Tyldesly, Carola Ulander, Giorgi Usai, Chong Vee Kee, Nutthorn Vuthivongvatin, D Webster, Ken Weingart, Ola Wiejska, Andrea & Andrew Wright, C Tim Wood, Jonathan Yardley, Andrew Young

LONELY PLANET

You already know that Lonely Planet produces more than this one guidebook, but you might not be aware of the other products we have on this region. Here is a selection of titles that you may want to check out as well:

London Map
ISBN 1 86450 008 5
US$5.95 • UK£3.99

London
ISBN 1 86450 353 X
US$17.99 • UK£9.99

British Phrasebook
ISBN 0 86442 484 1
US$5.95 • UK£3.99

Western Europe
ISBN 1 74059 313 8
US$27.99 • UK£16.99

Britain
ISBN 1 74059 338 3
US$29.99 • UK£15.99

London Condensed
ISBN 1 86450 301 7
US$11.99 • UK£5.99

Ireland
ISBN 1 86450 379 3
US$19.99 • UK£12.99

Scotland
ISBN 1 86450 157 X
US$16.99 • UK£10.99

Wales
ISBN 1 86450 126 X
US$15.99 • UK£9.99

Cycling Britain
ISBN 1 86450 037 9
US$19.99 • UK£12.99

Walking in Britain
ISBN 1 86450 280 0
US$21.99 • UK£13.99

Walking in Scotland
ISBN 1 86450 350 5
US$17.99 • UK£11.99

Available wherever books are sold

Index

Text

Bold indicates maps.

Bold indicates maps.

Boxed Text

MAP LEGEND

CITY ROUTES

Motorway .... Motorway	══════ .... On/Off Ramp
Highway .... Primary Road	═ ═ ═ ═ .... Unsealed Road
Road .... Secondary Road	═ ► ═ .... One-Way Street
Street .... Street	.... Pedestrian Street
Lane .... Lane	.... Footbridge

REGIONAL ROUTES

══════ .... Tollway; Motorway
══════ .... Primary Road
.... Secondary Road
.... Tertiary Road

BOUNDARIES

▬ ▪ ▬ ▪ ▬ .... International
▬ ▪ ▪ ▬ ▪ ▪ .... Regional
─ ─ ─ ─ .... Suburb
▬▬▬ Ancient or City Wall

TRANSPORT ROUTES & STATIONS

───○── .. Railway & Station	───🚊── .... Tramway
── Ⓜ ── ... Metro & Station	⊢──🚡── Cable Car or Chairlift
⟩═ ═ ═ .... Tunnel	────── .... Walking Track

• • • • • • • • .... Walking Tour	───🚢 Ferry Route & Terminal

HYDROGRAPHY

.... Coastline	.... River, Stream
.... Lake	●─●─● .... Canal

AREA FEATURES

.... Building	.... Market	.... Beach
❀ .... Park; Gardens	.... Sports Ground	+ + + ... Cemetery
.... Forest	.... Urban Area	

MAP SYMBOLS

✪LONDON .... Capital City	🚐 .... Caravan Park	🏮 .... Lighthouse
●Bristol .. City or Large Town	🏰 .... Castle or Fort	☀ ☼ .... Lookout
●Cambridge .... Town	🏛 .. Cathedral or Church	▲ .... Monument
● Bideford .... Village	⌂ .... Cave	▲ ⌃ ⌃ .... Mountain, Range
■ .... Place to Stay	☐ ☐ ..... Cinema, Theatre	🏛 .... Museum
▼ .... Place to Eat	...... Cliff or Escarpment	🅿 .... Parking
● ...... Point of Interest	✇ .... Embassy	)(....................... Pass
✈ ♦ ...... Airport, Airfield	⚓ .... Fountain	✚ .... Police Station
⊖ .... Bank	● .... Golf Course	✉ .... Post Office
⚲ .... Bird Sanctuary	✚ .... Hospital	🍺 .... Pub or Bar
🚏 ☐ ..... Bus Stop, Station	🔲 .... Internet Cafe	💥 .... Ruins
⛺ .... Camp Site	🔲 .... Jain Temple	✿ ..... Shopping Centre
🔯 .... Sikh Temple		
⚐ .... Ski Field		
🏛 Stately Home or Palace		
🏊 .... Swimming Pool		
☎ .... Telephone		
🚻 .... Toilet		
⬛ ....Tomb		
❶ .. Tourist Information		
🚍 .... Transport		
🍇 .... Vineyard		
◍ .... Waterfall		
🦁 .... Zoo		

Note: not all symbols displayed above appear in this book

LONELY PLANET OFFICES

Australia
Locked Bag 1, Footscray, Victoria 3011
☎ 03 8379 8000 fax 03 8379 8111
email: talk2us@lonelyplanet.com.au

UK
10a Spring Place, London NW5 3BH
☎ 020 7428 4800 fax 020 7428 4828
email: go@lonelyplanet.co.uk

USA
150 Linden St, Oakland, CA 94607
☎ 510 893 8555 TOLL FREE: 800 275 8555
fax 510 893 8572
email: info@lonelyplanet.com

France
1 rue du Dahomey, 75011 Paris
☎ 01 55 25 33 00 fax 01 55 25 33 01
email: bip@lonelyplanet.fr
www.lonelyplanet.fr

World Wide Web: www.lonelyplanet.com *or* AOL keyword: lp
Lonely Planet Images: www.lonelyplanetimages.com